ARTUR WEISER

THE PSALMS

old
test
ament
lib
rary

THE OLD TESTAMENT LIBRARY

General Editors

ARTUR WEISER

THE PSALMS

A Commentary

The Westminster Press
Philadelphia

TYPESET IN GREAT BRITAIN
PRINTED IN THE UNITED STATES OF AMERICA

CONTENTS

8 CONTENTS

PREFACE TO THE THIRD EDITION

THE THIRD EDITION of this Commentary is distinguished from the two previous ones not only by the inclusion of all the psalms in the Commentary, but also by the attempt that has been made in this new edition to determine afresh the context of the composition and transmission of the psalms and to turn the conclusions derived from this enquiry to good account for the historical and theological exposition of the individual psalms. In applying this method the Commentary has to a large extent become a new book.

In recent decades the study of the psalms, especially among Scandinavian scholars, has been pursued on new lines, and the author gratefully acknowledges that his understanding of the world in which the psalms were composed and used has been greatly enriched by the results of their studies. Exegesis of the psalms has always had to face the difficulty that most of them are for us just pictures without a frame, as we are still in the dark about the details of their origin and use. The research on the psalms undertaken by scholars in the nineteenth century was stimulated by the Age of Enlightenment and by Rationalism (Herder) and, in consequence, tried to interpret the psalms as 'religious poetry', that is to say, as literary products, by examining them in the light of Israel's secular and religious history and by applying to them the categories of the psychology of the individual used nowadays for the interpretation of literature. Under the influence of the conception of history advocated by the school of Wellhausen, which long dominated the study of the Old Testament, the thesis that the psalms originated in the circles of the 'godly' during the period of post-exilic Judaism was widely accepted as an undisputed maxim of any exegesis of the psalms. It was Gunkel's research into the history of the forms and 'types' (*Gattungen*) of the psalms which first began to break down, at least in some respects, the assumption of the school of Wellhausen that the matter can be handled by *literary* methods. And he made this investigation fruitful for the exegesis of the psalms by relating the several styles of poetry, which he classified according to their different 'types' (hymns, laments, etc.), to the religious poetry of the ancient

Orient. Taking everything into consideration, however, he did not succeed in freeing himself completely from the influence which the traditional scheme of the history of literature exerted on him. For, though Gunkel had come to realize that most of the psalm types had their original *Sitz im Leben* in the cultus, he nevertheless regarded the majority of the extant psalms as late products of an individual piety dissociated from the cultus and its forms of worship.

The question of the relationship of the psalms to the cultus, to which Gunkel did not find a satisfactory answer, has in more recent times occupied the minds of Scandinavian scholars like Mowinckel, Bentzen, Widengren, and Engnell. Stimulated by the work of Grønbech, Mowinckel came to the conclusion that the festival cult is essentially 'creative drama'. Assuming that a 'Festival of the Enthronement of Yahweh' after an ancient oriental pattern was celebrated also in Israel, he then attempted to interpret a great number of psalms by means of that festival. As a result of the discoveries made at Ras Shamra there is also a tendency in Scandinavian circles at the present time to recognize a reflection of the ritual pattern of the ancient oriental royal cult, which was modelled after the rite of the dying and rising gods, in those psalms which are in the main interpreted as 'royal' psalms; in these psalms the cultic myth is said to be reflected in the drama of creation as applied to Yahweh and as 'typified' by the king in the festival cult.

Valuable as it may be by way of comparison to use the royal ritual observed in the Near East for the understanding of the nature of the cultus, including that of ancient Israel, it has, however, not been sufficiently realized and appreciated by those who have done so that the specific tradition of the Old Testament as contained in the psalms has a peculiar character of its own, and, in spite of all the similarity in details, its fundamental elements are different from those of the ancient oriental royal cult.

Those who used this comparative method obviously did not yet comprehend clearly enough the true nature of the cultus in ancient Israel, and of its tradition. The problem of the peculiar character of the pre-exilic cult of the Covenant, and of the connection of the psalms with the tradition of that cult, is discussed in the Introduction to the Commentary. In that discussion the different methods of approach peculiar to Form-Criticism, to the history of the cult, and to the history of tradition, have been combined with each other; and an attempt has been made to prove, from the stylized liturgical forms in which the psalms have found expression (forms of expression whose concrete, living significance has often been overlooked), and by adducing other evidence from the Old Testament, that the cult of the Covenant Festival of Yahweh represents the setting that is important for the determination of the cultic origin and use of the Old Testament psalms, and for the exposition of their significance in relation to the contemporary history and to theology. I am not unaware that this requires the surrender of many a prejudice which is commonly held by students of the Old Testament and which I have myself advocated in the past, and that at first many will resist the necessity of such a surrender just as I did; but I believe that the new perspective which will be achieved thereby can lead to a clearer and deeper understanding not only of the psalms themselves, but also of their relation to a large portion of the literature of the Old Testament, such as the Pentateuch and the prophets.

Since the cultic background of the psalms of the Old Testament can be demonstrated only by surveying them as a whole, that survey has been anticipated in the Introduction in order to be able, for the sake of saving space, to refer back to it in the course of the exegesis of the individual psalms. The reader will therefore be well advised to study the Introduction before making use of the Commentary itself, so that he may be able to comprehend the particular problems in the light of the whole of the tradition. For the religious character of the psalms, notwithstanding all the wealth of the individual forms in which it has found expression, is determined by the fixed framework of a common tradition of worship, to which the Psalter owes its character as the prayer-book of the Church, a character which has been preserved throughout all the ages.

ARTUR WEISER

1949

PREFACE TO THE FOURTH EDITION

A CONSIDERABLE NUMBER of publications, important at least in part, showing the keen interest taken in the study of the psalms, made it necessary to follow up the third edition, which is already out of print, by a revised edition in which the literature published since 1949 has been taken into consideration and digested. Though the character of this book as a whole and the space allotted to it made it imperative to restrict severely the references to the discussion of the literature related to the subject, the expert will not fail to observe the extent to which the relevant problems have been discussed and the book has made use of the most recent results of research. I thank my critics for various suggestions; I acted upon them whenever their wishes seemed to me to be justified and practicable within the compass of the book; thus, e.g., the superscriptions of and annotations to the psalms have been incorporated in the text and in the Commentary, and the references to the psalms' connections with Christian hymns have been augmented. Occasional criticisms of the method employed in the third edition, which made use of the traditions of the cult of the feast of Yahweh for the purpose of the theological interpretation of the psalms, have not convinced me that this method has to be altered fundamentally in any respects. I am well aware that in any such undertaking many questions still remain unanswered and new problems arise; some discussions have therefore been provided with a stronger basis or supplemented by opening up new perspectives. A further elucidation of the question of the historical differentiations and modifications of the traditions of worship in the Old Testament and of the relation of these traditions to that of the Covenant can, however, be brought about only by means of searching individual studies, and requires the unbiased collaboration of scholars doing joint research, such as has already been done on several problems. Such investigations would go beyond the limits of a condensed introduction to the Commentary on the psalms. After all, a method stands the test if, with its help, questions which have so far remained unanswered receive an answer, and vague ideas, obscure pictures, and figures of speech acquire more exact and more distinct contours and, further, if with its help the biblical character of the tradition of the Old Testament can be grasped and worked out both in its relations to and in its differences from its environment, but, above all, in respect of its peculiar theological character. To serve this main concern of biblical exegesis is the aim of the new edition as of the previous ones.

ARTUR WEISER

1955

LITERATURE

COMMENTARIES

F. Hitzig (2nd ed.), I 1863, II 1865; H. Olshausen, 1853; H. Hupfeld and W. Nowack (3rd ed.), 1888; F. Delitzsch (5th ed.), 1894; F. Baethgen (3rd ed.), 1904; W. Staerk (2nd ed.), 1920; B. Duhm (2nd ed.), 1922; R. Kittel (5th and 6th ed.), 1929; H. Gunkel, 1926; H. Schmidt, 1934; E. König, 1927; F. Wutz, 1925; C. A. and E. G. Briggs, 2 vols., 1906/7; W. E. Barnes, 1931; F. Buhl (2nd ed.), 1918; J. P. Peters, 1930; J. de Groot, 1932; M. Buttenwieser, 1938; R. Abramowski, 2 vols., 1938/9; W. O. E. Oesterley, 1939; A. Bentzen, 1939; A. Cohen, 1945; F. M. T. Böhl, I 1946, II 1947; B. Gemser, III 1949; B. D. Eerdmans (2nd ed.), 1953; Bonkamp, 1949; E. Podechard, I 1949, II 1954; Clamer, 1950; A. Bruno, 1954; W. R. Taylor, W. S. McCullough, J. R. P. Sclater, E. McNeill Poteat and F. H. Ballard, *The Interpreter's Bible* 4, 1955; H.-J. Kraus, 1958 ff.; H. Lamparter, I 1958.

OTHER BOOKS AND ARTICLES

R. Smend, 'Über das Ich der Psalmen', *ZAW* 8, 1888, pp. 49 ff.; E. Balla, *Das Ich der Psalmen*, 1912; S. Mowinckel, *Psalmenstudien* I–VI, 1921–4; G. Quell, *Das kultische Problem in den Psalmen*, 1926; H. Gunkel, 'The Religion of the Psalms' in *What Remains of the Old Testament and Other Essays*, 1928; H. Schmidt, *Das Gebet der Angeklagten im Alten Testament*, 1928; H. Gunkel, *Einleitung in die Psalmen*, ed. J. Begrich, 1933; B. H. Birkeland, *Die Feinde des Individuums in der israelitischen Psalmenliteratur*, 1933; J. Begrich, 'Das priesterliche Heilsorakel', *ZAW* 52, 1934, pp. 81 ff.; G. Widengren, *The Accadian and Hebrew Psalms of Lamentation as Religious Documents*, 1936; H. L. Jansen, *Die spätjüdische Psalmdichtung, ihr Entstehungskreis und ihr 'Sitz im Leben'*, 1938; I. Engnell, *Studies in Divine Kingship in the Ancient Near East*, 1943; J. H. Patton, *Canaanite Parallels in the Book of Psalms*, 1944; A. Bentzen, *Det sakrale Kongedömme*, 1945; Chr. Barth, *Die Errettung vom Tode in den individuellen Klage- und Dankliedern des*

14

Alten Testaments, 1947; A. Bentzen, *Messias, Moses Redivivus, Menschensohn*, 1948 (ET, *King and Messiah*, 1955); A. Weiser, 'Zur Frage nach den Beziehungen der Psalmen zum Kult', *Festschrift für Alfred Bertholet*, 1950, pp. 513 ff.; S. Mowinckel, *Offersang og Sangoffer, Salmediktning i Bibelen*, 1951 (ET, *The Psalms and Israel's Worship* I–II, 1962); idem, *Religion und Kultus*, 1953; C. Westermann, *Das Loben Gottes in den Psalmen*, 1954; idem, 'Struktur und Geschichte der Klage im Alten Testament', *ZAW* 66, 1954, pp. 44 ff.; H. Zimmern, 'Babylonische Hymnen und Gebete', *AO* VII 3, 1905, XIII 1, 1911; M. Jastrow, *Religion Babyloniens und Assyriens* I, 1905, pp. 393 ff., II, 1912, pp. 1 ff.;[1] F. Stummer, *Sumerisch-akkadische Parallelen zum Aufbau alttestamentlicher Psalmen*, 1922; R. de Langhe, *Les textes de Ras Shamra-Ugarit et leurs rapports avec le milieu biblique de l'Ancien Testament*, 1945; C. Gordon, *Ugaritic Manual*, 1955; A. Falkenstein and W. von Soden, *Sumerische und akkadische Hymnen und Gebete*, 1953; A. Johnson, *Sacral Kingship in Ancient Israel*, 1955; G. Widengren, *Sakrales Königtum im Alten Testament und im Judentum*, 1955; R. G. Boling, '"Synonymous" parallelism in the Psalms', *JSS* 5, 1960, pp. 221 ff.; Szörény, *Psalmen und Kult im Alten Testament: Zur Formgeschichte der Psalmen*, Budapest, 1961; K.-H. Bernhardt, *Das Problem der altorientalischen Königsideologie im Alten Testament* (*VT* Suppl. VIII), 1961; M. Weiss, 'Wege der neueren Dichtungswissenschaft in ihrer Anwendung auf die Psalmenforschung', *Biblica* 42, 1961, pp. 255 ff.; J. Gray, 'The Kingship of God in the Prophets and Psalms', *VT* 11, 1961, pp. 1 ff.

[1] *This is a German translation, revised and much expanded by the author, of *The Religion of Babylonia and Assyria*, 1898, chs. 17–18.

ABBREVIATIONS

ANET	J. B. Pritchard, *Ancient Near Eastern Texts*, 2nd ed., 1955
AO	*Der Alte Orient*
AOT	H. Gressmann, *Altorientalische Texte zum Alten Testament*, 2nd ed., 1926
ATD	Altes Testament Deutsch
BASOR	*Bulletin of the American Schools of Oriental Research*
BH	*Biblia Hebraica*, ed. Rudolf Kittel, 3rd ed., A. Alt and O. Eissfeldt, 1952
DOTT	D. Winton Thomas (ed.), *Documents from Old Testament Times*, 1958
ET	English translation
HUCA	*Hebrew Union College Annual*
Intr.	Introduction to the Commentary
JBL	*Journal of Biblical Literature*
JQR	*Jewish Quarterly Review*
JSS	*Journal of Semitic Studies*
lit.	literally
LXX	Greek translation of the Old Testament (Septuagint)
MT	Masoretic text
RSV	The Revised Standard Version of the Bible
S	Syriac translation of the Old Testament (Peshitta)
Symm	Greek translation of the Old Testament by Symmachus
T	Targum
TLZ	*Theologische Literaturzeitung*
TZ	*Theologische Zeitschrift*
VT	*Vetus Testamentum*
ZAW	*Zeitschrift für die alttestamentliche Wissenschaft*
ZTK	*Zeitschrift für Theologie und Kirche*
*	Translator's note (Tr. N.)

TRANSLATOR'S PREFACE

THE AUTHOR HAS based his Commentary on his own translation of the Psalter from the Hebrew, making full use of BH. In this English edition the RSV has been printed for convenience. Where it differs materially from the author's version, this latter has been used and translated, the RSV being given in a footnote.

German hymns quoted in the Commentary have been replaced by existing English translations when these were close enough to be relevant.

In the course of the translation of this book, which was originally based on the fourth edition of 1955, the fifth edition of 1959 was published. The alterations and additions, especially the new footnotes which have been added both to the Introduction and to the Commentary, have been incorporated in the present translation. My cordial thanks are due to Professor Weiser for supplying the material, and so making it possible to adapt the translation to the fifth edition without undue loss of time.

I

INTRODUCTION

THE PSALTER IS THAT book of the Old Testament which the Christian community found the easiest one to approach in a direct and personal way. The writers of Christian hymns have drawn from the inexhaustible well of the psalms at all times, and especially in the age of the Reformation, so that in this way their sentiments and ideas continue to live in the Christian community alongside the individual psalms or portions of psalms used liturgically in public worship. From the very beginning of Christianity (cf., e.g., I Cor. 14.15, 26; Eph. 5.19) right up to the present day public worship has continually created and cultivated a particularly intimate relationship of the worshipping congregation to the psalms. But this does not exhaust the significance of the Psalter for Christian use. Apart from its use in public worship it also serves as a means of individual edification, as the foundation of family worship, as a book of comfort, as a book of prayers, and as a guide to God in times of joy and affliction. It is hardly possible to grasp, and not easy to overestimate, the strength which has been derived from the psalms in this way, and the way in which they have shaped the history of individual piety. Luther's verdict as given in his second Preface to the German Psalter (1528) may here be quoted to express what many unknown people would feel:

> There you look into the hearts of all the saints as into a beautiful gay garden, indeed as into heaven; and in that garden you see spring up lovely, bright, charming flowers, flowers of all sorts of beautiful and joyous thoughts about God and his mercy. Again, where do you find words expressing sorrow more deeply and picturing its misery and wretchedness more tellingly than the words that are contained in the psalms of lament? Here you look once more into the hearts of all the saints as into death, indeed as into hell; how dark and gloomy is it there, because of the grievous spectacle of the wrath of God which has to be faced in so many ways! Again, wherever they speak of fear or hope, they use such words that no painter could portray either fear or hope with equal force and no Cicero or orator could fashion them in like manner. And the very best thing is that they speak such words about God and to God. . . .

This explains, moreover, why the Psalter is the favourite book of all the saints, and why each one of them, whatever his circumstances may be, finds in it psalms and words which are appropriate to the circumstances in which he finds himself and meet his needs as adequately as if they were composed exclusively for his sake, and in such a way that he himself could not improve on them nor could find or desire any better psalms or words. . . .

To sum up: if you want to see the holy Christian Church painted in glowing colours and in a form which is really alive, and if you want this to be done in a miniature, you must get hold of the Psalter, and there you will have in your possession a fine, clear, pure mirror which will show you what Christianity really is; yea, you will find yourself in it and the true 'gnothi seauton' ('know thyself'), and God himself and all his creatures, too.

1. THE NAME 'PSALMS'

The designation 'psalms' is derived from the New Testament (Luke 20.42; 24.44; Acts 1.20; 13.33) and has its origin in the Greek translation of the Old Testament (the Septuagint), which was a product of the Jewish Diaspora of Alexandria in the third century before Christ. In the Codex Vaticanus of the LXX the title of the Psalter is ψαλμοί and its subtitle is βίβλος ψαλμῶν, whereas the title used in the Codex Alexandrinus is ψαλτήριον (a stringed instrument); as the name of a collection of hymns this title is to be understood in a similar sense as Körner's *Leyer und Schwert* (Lyre and Sword) or Spitta's *Psalter und Harfe* (Psalter and Harp). The name ψαλμός is presumably derived from the Hebrew term *mizmōr*, which occurs before 57 psalms as an individual title and probably signifies a hymn (sung to the accompaniment of a stringed instrument). In the Hebrew Bible the Book of Psalms originally lacked a general title. The Jewish Church called the psalms *t'hillīm* = hymns: the striking use of the 'masculine' form, to which Origen, Jerome and other Church fathers also testify, is perhaps meant to denote the song-book as a whole, whereas the 'feminine' form *t'hillā*, which was normally used, is employed as the individual title of Psalm 145 as well as in the Jewish Masora. At an earlier stage in the compilation of the psalms the term *t'phillōt* = prayers appears to have been in use (Ps. 72.20). Neither of these names comprise all the types of hymns included in the Psalter, and they have probably been determined by the majority. The aforementioned terminology is restricted to the religious song, which was mostly used in public worship.

2. THE ARRANGEMENT OF THE PSALMS

The Old Testament Book of Psalms by no means comprises all the psalms which are in existence; there are a number of psalms both within and outside the Old Testament which have not been incorporated in the Psalter, e.g. Ex. 15.1–18; I Sam. 2.1–10; Isa. 38.10–20; Jonah 2.2–9 and the so-called Psalms of Solomon dating from the time of Pompey. The Old Testament Book of Psalms numbers 150 hymns; Psalm 151, which has been handed down in some MSS. of the LXX and also in the Syriac Version, is not included in the collection. In the Psalter sometimes several independent hymns have been drawn together into one psalm, e.g. in Psalms 19; 27; conversely, related material has sometimes been divided into two psalms, e.g. Psalms 9 and 10; 42 and 43. In the LXX, Psalms 9 and 10 as well as Psalms 114 and 115 are merged in one psalm, whereas Psalms 116 and 147 are split up into two separate psalms, so that the numbering of the psalms in the LXX from Ps. 9.22 to Ps. 146.11 does not correspond to that of the Hebrew text. The 150 psalms are divided into five books, probably on the analogy of the Torah; each book closes with a liturgical doxology; in the last book the whole of Psalm 150 takes the place of the closing doxology. The first book comprises Psalms 1–41; the second Psalms 42–72; the third Psalms 73–89; the fourth Psalms 90–106; and the fifth Psalms 107–150.

3. THE USE OF THE PSALMS

The Psalter has been called 'the hymn-book of the Jewish Church', and that with some justification, for it contains various features which point to the cultic use of the psalms in the worship of the Temple and especially in the synagogue service in late Judaism. The individual *superscriptions* of some of the psalms refer to the occasion for which the composition in question was appointed: thus Psalm 30 was intended for the dedication of the Temple; Psalm 100 for the thank-offerings; Psalm 92 for the Sabbath; Psalm 24 (according to the LXX) for Sunday; Psalm 48 for Monday; Psalm 94 for Wednesday; Psalm 93 for Friday; Psalm 81 (according to an early Latin and Armenian version) for Thursday. These psalms were sung at the daily morning burnt offering (*tāmīd*), and for that reason are called Tamid psalms. The Talmud, which in addition appoints Psalm 82 to be sung on Tuesday, is familiar with a ritual used in public worship according to which hymnic verses from the psalms were appointed to be sung before the offering of the prayer; again, it knows the custom, corroborated also by the New Testament (Matt. 26.30), of reciting the Hallel psalms (113–118) at the Feast of the Passover and at the other great festivals. According to the Synagogue Prayer Book, specially appointed psalms are offered by the congregation in prayer on the Sabbath, on festival days and on weekdays. Traces of the cultic use of the psalms are, moreover, to be found in the *liturgical superscriptions* which are attached to individual pieces; to this category belongs the hymnic response 'Hallelujah' appended to the so-called Hallelujah psalms: 105; 106; 111–113; 115; 117; 135; 146–149; 150, probably in order to indicate their use in public worship.[1] The *musical superscriptions* to individual psalms point in a similar direction; they, too, are later additions which have a bearing on the musical rendering of the psalms in the cultus. In this connection the term *lamᵉnaṣṣēᵃḥ*, a technical term which appears in the superscriptions of 55 psalms, is relevant; its meaning is obscure, but on the basis of II Chron. 2.2, 18 it is usually interpreted as meaning 'to the conductor' or 'for the musical performance'; Luther translates it 'to be sung to . . . ' A similar situation arises with regard to the term *selāᶜ*, which recurs 71 times in 39 psalms and perhaps was meant to denote a pause, intended to be filled by a hymnic response[2] and marked by a musical intermezzo (LXX: διάψαλμα), for the offering of prayers. Again, the term *mizmōr*, which occurs in the titles of 57 psalms and signifies 'a hymn sung to the accompaniment of a stringed instrument' (Luther: 'a psalm'), suggests that such psalms were used in public worship like chorales. The term *šīr* = song, which occurs in the superscriptions of 14 psalms, suggests that the psalm in question was sung. The significance of other designations such as *miktām*, *maśkīl*, etc., is entirely uncertain. On the other hand, such superscriptions of psalms as 'with stringed instruments', which occurs six times, and 'to the accompaniment of a flute', which appears in the titles of five psalms, probably refer to the musical rendering of these psalms in public worship. Again, statements in the titles of psalms such as 'According to "The Hind of the Dawn" ' (Ps. 22) and 'According to "The Dove of the far-off terebinths" (?)' (Ps. 56), etc., may perhaps be understood as a reference to a secular (?) song to the tune of which the psalm was meant to be sung, a phenomenon which can also be observed more

[1] Cf., however, the exegesis of these psalms in the Commentary.
[2] Cf. Snaith, *VT* 2, 1952, pp. 43 ff.

than once in the hymns of the Christian Church. Other annotations such as ʿal ʿᵃlāmōt (Ps. 46) and ʿal haśśᵉmīnīt (Pss. 6; 12) perhaps signify the key in which the psalm in question was to be sung or accompanied.[1]

4. THE CULTIC FOUNDATIONS OF PSALMODY

When the tribes of Israel entered Palestine they set foot in a land possessing an ancient culture, a culture which was the product of the intermingling of the influences and heritage of the great empires on the Euphrates and the Nile with those of the pre-Hellenic Mediterranean world and of Asia Minor. Israel's political history and history of ideas developed as she borrowed those cultural forms and then tried to come to terms with their substance and to fill the alien forms with a new content, that is, with a new meaning which had its roots in and had developed out of her own traditions. The appropriation of the achievements of the alien culture, however, did not take place, at least not in the early period of Israel's history, by means of their direct incorporation from Babylonia or Egypt, as scholars at one time assumed, but with the help of the mixed culture of Canaan, which acted as mediator and gradually became an esssential part of Israel's own life. This general viewpoint applies particularly to the religious poetry of Israel, as the discoveries made at Ras Shamra have demonstrated. Since the psalms of the Old Testament are dependent on the types of ancient oriental cultic poetry as far as their fixed forms are concerned, it will be necessary for us to refer to the latter by way of comparison; for only by making use of them as a kind of background shall we be able to perceive the true nature of Israel's own traditions and to realize the extent to which these have determined the character of the psalms, with regard to form as well as content. The form-critical approach is, however, not sufficient by itself to explore the nature of the poetry of the psalms of the Old Testament, for the reason that, as is already evident from the Song of Deborah (Judg. 5), the mixing of different types is to be found even in the earliest poetry of Israel.[2] Hence the principle advanced and

[1] More details concerning the transmission and significance of the musical annotations are to be found in Baethgen's Commentary, § 7; Mowinckel, *Psalmenstudien* IV and *The Psalms and Israel's Worship* II, pp. 207 ff.; Viana, *Indicaciones musicales en los titulos do los Salmos*, Misc. bibl. B. Ubach, Montserrat, 1953, pp. 185 ff.

[2] Cf. in this connection my essay in *ZAW* 71, 1959, pp. 67 ff.

applied by Gunkel[1] in the elucidation of the history of the Old Testament poetry, that at the beginning of that history the pure types had been in existence and that the mixing of types indicated later stages of development, does not hold good, at any rate not for the Old Testament. The history of the religious poetry of the Old Testament cannot be inferred simply from the history of the development of the types.

On the contrary, it proves necessary to bear constantly in mind, in addition to the history of the forms of the psalms, the history of the traditions manifested in them, and also the history of the Old Testament cultus as the sphere of life in which these traditions were preserved as a living force. For it can now no longer be denied that the cultus was the native soil from which the psalms sprang;[2] the only question that remains is whether it may not be possible to obtain a more distinct and accurate picture of the external and internal connections between the history of the cultus, the history of the traditions, and the history of the psalms and their forms beyond the knowledge gained so far, a knowledge founded mainly on sporadic individual studies only. In this connection we shall also use, in dealing with the religious poetry of the Old Testament, the results of the studies of Israel's history and religion, both during and before the monarchy, which have now for some time been available and are, partly at least, in process of being evaluated in the interest of a new understanding of the so-called historical literature of the Old Testament, in particular of the Pentateuch. For it is true of the psalms, as it is of some of the narrative parts of the Old Testament, that they are not only tied to definite forms, but are also tied to tradition, that is, that throughout the different types of psalms, notwithstanding all the diversity in details, there is a definite connection with and dependence on a common framework of tradition, which in its turn points back to the cultus as the setting in which the tradition was significant, not only as a reminder of what had happened in the past, but also as something which at any given time assumed the character of a present event and experience.[3] In view

---

[1] Similarly Westermann, *ZAW* 66, 1954, pp. 44 ff.

[2] This is true also of Westermann; who, in *Das Loben Gottes in den Psalmen* (1954) tries to go back to 'the fundamental process that takes place in the cult, which consists in man's turning to God in action'; in doing so, he neglects however the history of the traditions that form the background of the Old Testament cultus.

[3] With regard to the fundamental relationship between tradition and cultus, cf. now Mowinckel, *Religion und Kultus*, 1953, p. 13 and n.; also Gyllenberg, 'Kultus und Offenbarung', *Festschrift für Mowinckel*, 1955, pp. 72 ff.

of the fact that the traditions which come to light in the psalms are of an early date, it is absolutely essential finally to get rid of the prejudice which long prevailed in the school of Wellhausen, but whose fundamental validity has already been undermined at several points by Kittel, Gunkel, and Mowinckel, according to which the psalms are to be considered throughout as the product of post-exilic Judaism only. For only a comparatively small number of psalms can, in fact, be proved conclusively to have originated in the post-exilic period. The ritual laws of later Judaism are not mentioned at all in the psalms in spite of their manifold relations to the cultus. Even where individual psalms exhibit linguistic forms and modes of expression of a later period, this fact at most proves that these psalms did not reach their final form till then, but cannot in any way be used as evidence for the origin of the psalm in question and for the way in which it was used originally. This is particularly true when we take into consideration that many psalms were destined to repeated use as cultic hymns; they were therefore subject to the modifications of language and style which would take place in the course of history. On the other hand we must seriously consider whether certain linguistic forms, which are usually attributed, for instance, to the so-called Deuteronomic terminology, might not have their origin in an earlier liturgical phraseology, and whether in that case, contrary to common opinion, we shall not have to look for some stylistic dependence on the side of Deuteronomy, whose connection with the cultic tradition has latterly come to be more and more clearly recognized. It is possible to demonstrate quite generally that a great number of psalms manifest a certain constancy and uniformity as far as the fundamental characteristic features of a cultic tradition are concerned; and these features are strikingly parallel to the same basic elements which are to be found in the narrative and in the prophetic literature. In view of the variations that occur in individual features, the attempt that has often been made to explain this phenomenon as being due to literary dependence on the one side or the other is indefensible. The well-established method of literary criticism with its assumption of literary imitation, is scarcely appropriate to the nature of the psalms and has not produced any satisfactory results in this field of research.

Here the *study of the history of the traditions and of the cultus* is of greater assistance in that it takes us right back to the cultus as the common original foundation of the tradition and as the fertile soil out of which the parallel traditions of the different types of literature have grown. For instance, where the basic forms of the narrative passages of the Pentateuch (*Heilsgeschichte* and Law) are concerned, the quest for this foundation is at present rightly directed to the cultic tradition of the sacral confederacy of the Twelve Tribes which was the original bearer of the name 'Israel' and the first to make the worship of Yahweh in the cult of the Covenant its main concern.[1] If the earlier tradition of the Pentateuch is to be regarded as the literary expression of the sacral tradition of the *Heilsgeschichte*, which was recited orally at the annual celebration of the Covenant Festival of Yahweh,[2] we can right from the outset reckon with the possibility that those psalms which are externally or internally related to the fundamental elements of the tradition of that festival, the majority of which were composed in pre-exilic times, also originated in the cult of the festival as it was celebrated by the original tribal confederacy. That cult had remained the real bearer of the genuinely 'Israelite' tradition of Yahweh during the period of the monarchy, irrespective of Israel's division into the Northern and Southern Kingdoms; this is true at least of the worship that took place in the Temple at Jerusalem and in association with the sacred

---

[1] See G. von Rad, *Das formgeschichtliche Problem des Hexateuch*, 1938; A. Weiser, *Introduction to the Old Testament*, ET, 1961, § 13.

[2] The Exodus from Egypt is more than once linked in its origin with the festival of Yahweh at the Mount of God, e.g. in the Yahwistic as well as in the Elohistic stratum of the Pentateuchal tradition (Ex. 3.12; 4.23; 5.1, 3; 7.16; 8.27 f.; 9.1, 13; 10.3, 7, 8, 11, 24, 25), and in this way the narrative of the Exodus is focused on the 'divine service' at Mount Sinai as the point of orientation by means of which the revelation of Yahweh in the *Heilsgeschichte*, as it were, is legitimized as an essential part of the cult (Ex. 3.12). These facts, in addition to a series of references in the Sinai tradition itself taken from the history of the cult (Ex. chs. 19 ff.), make it clear that the cult of the feast of Yahweh, the heart of which was the revelation of God at Sinai, was the native soil on which the tradition of the *Heilsgeschichte* concerning the Exodus, the revelation at Sinai, and the conquest of the land was formed and cultivated.

The 'feast in the wilderness' (Ex. 5.1, 3) cannot be understood as referring to the Feast of Passover, as is assumed by Wellhausen, *Prolegomena*, 5th ed., 1899, p. 51 (cf. ET of 2nd ed., 1885, [reprinted 1957] pp. 87 f.), Stade, *Biblische Theologie des Alten Testaments* I, 1905, p. 174, and Procksch, *Theologie des Alten Testaments*, 1950, p. 545. This follows from the fact that according to the narrative of the Exodus this festival was not celebrated in the wilderness, at the Mount of God, but by families in their homes at the time of the Exodus.

Cf. Alt, *Berichte über die Verhandlungen der sächsischen Akademie der Wissenschaften zu Leipzig* (Philosophisch-historische Klasse, Vol. 101, No. 6), 1954, p. 24, n. 2, on the historical interpretation of the theme of the granting of leave to the Israelites to attend a sacral festival in the wilderness as indicating the way in which the tribes concerned were tied to institutions of the state of Egypt.

Ark of the Covenant as the original central shrine of the sacral confederacy (cf. I Kings 12.26 ff.; II Kings 11.17; 23.1 ff.; II Chron. 15.12 ff.; 29.10; Jer. 41.4 ff.).[1] The connection of the psalms with the Covenant Festival of Yahweh, which was celebrated at New Year in the autumn (cf. Judg. 21.19; I Sam. 1.3, 21 f., 24; I Kings 8.2; 12.32; Hos. 9.5; 12.9; Isa. 2.2 ff.; 30.29; Deut. 31.10 ff.; Ezek. 45.25), is also suggested by the fact that, though the institution of harvest festivals had been taken over from the agriculturally based religion of Canaan, the fundamental ideas of these festivals with their extensive sacrificial cult play a remarkably small part in the psalms. The reason for this is evidently that these country festivals, which were celebrated at the local shrines, in spite of their growing fusion with the religion of Yahweh, belonged to a cultic sphere which was different from the original and specifically 'Israelite' Yahweh tradition of the sacral confederacy (cf. Amos 5.25; Jer. 7.21 ff.). That difference is also important for the understanding of the background of the prophets' polemic against the sacrificial cult. Connections with the agriculturally based religion are really to be found only in Psalms 65, 67, 85, and 126, and even there only in such a form that the traditions of the Covenant religion predominate and these traditions exclusively determine the other psalms which come into question. Hence it is not possible, as far as the relation of the psalms to the cultus is concerned, to start, as Gunkel does, from the agricultural religious festivals. On the contrary, we must take as our starting-point that situation in which the Yahweh tradition, which prevails in the psalms, had its real *Sitz im Leben*, that is, the Covenant Festival as it was celebrated by the tribal confederacy of 'Israel', and also the 'cultic narratives' (*Festperikopen*) belonging to it. The literary form of these narratives has been developed in the earlier strata of the Hexateuch, especially in the traditions of the Exodus, of Sinai and of the conquest of the land (cf. the narrative of the assembly at Shechem in Josh. 24, the ἱερὸς λόγος of the celebration of the constitution of the sacral confederacy of the Twelve Tribes in Canaan).[2]

---

[1] Thus, for instance, the presence of princes of the northern tribes of Zebulun and Naphtali at the celebration of the cult in the Temple of Jerusalem is attested in Ps. 68.27. See also Noth, *Die Gesetze im Pentateuch*, 1940, pp. 22 ff.

[2] Cf. also Procksch, *Theologie des Alten Testaments*, 1950, p. 550. It is not possible to investigate here in detail the history of the various modifications which this feast underwent in the course of time (cf. the attempt made by Kraus, *Gottesdienst in Israel*, 1954, which is certainly open to criticism in many respects). It is true that the 'calendars of the festivals' (Ex. chs. 23 and 34; Deut. 16; Lev. 23), whose

Even though it is not yet possible to reconstruct the procedure of the Covenant Festival in all its details and in all the modifications which it underwent in the course of history, it is nevertheless possible to apprehend the basic elements and ideas of the cultic celebration and through them the essential character of the festival and of its traditions sufficiently to throw light on the question of the relation of the psalms to the festival tradition of the cult community of Yahweh. In accordance with the ideas on the cultus which were commonly held in antiquity[1] and which moreover to some extent are alive in Christian liturgies even today, the cult of the feast of Yahweh was in essence a *sacred action*, a 'cultic drama', in the course of which the fundamental events in the history of man's salvation were re-enacted; that is, at the performance of the sacral act, the cultic 'representation' (recitation of the cult-narrative with more or less dramatic emphasis) became a new 'event'. The congregation attending the feast experienced this as something which happened in its presence (Josh. 24), and thereby participated in the assurance and realization of salvation which was the real purpose of the festival. The theme of the Old Testament Covenant Festival is the continually renewed encounter of God with his people which has as its final aim the renewal of the

---

literary type and *Sitz im Leben* have not yet been sufficiently elucidated, show a tendency to incorporate the cattle-breeders' and agricultural festivals and rites in the cult of Yahweh. They show, however, as can be inferred from the subsequent historicizing reinterpretations (Ex. 23.15; Deut. 16.1; Lev. 23.42 f.), that a tradition peculiar to the cult of Yahweh, which in such a context naturally did not require to be mentioned in detail, is taken for granted (this point in opposition to Bückers, *Biblica* 32, 1951, p. 403).

The designation of the actual feast of Yahweh as 'Covenant Festival' has been chosen in accordance with the characteristic form into which the religion of the Old Testament is cast (cf. Eichrodt, *The Theology of the Old Testament* I [ET], 1961, pp. 36 ff.). In the different strata of tradition in the Old Testament, this autumnal feast celebrated at New Year was regarded until a very late date as the main festival even alongside other festivals, so that it was simply described as 'the feast' (Judg. 21.19; I Kings 8.2; 12.32; Ezek. 45.25; Neh. 8.14); moreover it assimilated other traditions in the course of history. And these facts still show the fundamental and supreme importance which this feast of Yahweh had for the worship of Yahweh in the Old Testament. As regards the preliminary forms of the Covenant in the ancient Orient cf. Mendenhall, 'Covenant Forms in Israelite Tradition', *The Biblical Archaeologist* XVII, 1954, no. 3. Cf. also Johnson, *Sacral Kingship in Ancient Israel*, pp. 47 ff.

[1] On the relationship of man in antiquity to the categories of causality, space and time, which is to be distinguished from our way of thinking, cf. the fundamental discussion of this subject by H. Frankfort, *The Intellectual Adventure of Ancient Man*, 1946, pp. 15 ff. (= *Before Philosophy* [Penguin Books, 1949], pp. 11 ff.)

Sinai Covenant and of the salvation it promised. This basic idea was preserved in a later period in the ancient designation of the shrine in the wilderness as '*ōhel mō'ēd*, = the Tent of Meeting (for the aetiology of this term cf. Ex. 33.7 f.).[1] Thus the cultic act falls into two parts: the primary one, which according to the general idea dominating the whole of the Old Testament is also the decisive one, is the *actio Dei*, the action of God and the Word of God; that of the congregation is therefore to be understood only as a *reactio hominum*, as something which has been determined by something else; the words offered by the congregation in prayer and in praise have the quality of a 'response' in that they somehow presuppose the *actio Dei ad salutem*. As in the narrative of the Exodus, so also at the Covenant Festival, the *theophany* as Yahweh's self-revelation in the presence of his people forms the central point of the cultic act. In the cult of the Covenant the tradition of the theophany was associated with the sacred Ark (cf. I Sam. 3.21; also the cultic aetiological narrative in Ex. 33.5 ff. in which the part of the account which refers to the making of the Ark as part of the Tabernacle furniture has been cut out in order to make way for the priestly writers' account in Ex. 25.10–22, which in its turn made use of earlier traditions). The tradition of the theophany conceived Yahweh's epiphany in the sanctuary as God's coming down to his people from Mount Sinai (Judg. 5.4 f.; Deut. 33.2), with the cloud as his chariot (cf. the pillar of cloud in the Wilderness tradition, and Ex. 16.10; Num. 16.42; Deut. 31.15; I Kings 8.10 f.; Isa. 4.5; for cultic purposes this was symbolized by the winged figures of the cherubim on the mercy seat of the Ark), accompanied by lightning, thunder, and earthquake as well as by the jubilant shouts of joy of his heavenly and earthly 'hosts', *ṣᵉbā'ōt*, and clothed in the heavenly light of glory, *kābōd* (cf. Ex. 24.10; 33.18, 22; Num. 14.10; 16.19; 20.6; Deut. 33.26; Isa. 6.3 and the pillar of fire in the wilderness period). He sits on his

---

[1] It is not possible to establish with certainty the original relation between the shrine of the Tent and the Ark of the Covenant or to pass a definite judgment on the hypothesis, advanced first by Sellin (*Alttestamentliche Studien Kittel dargebracht*, 1913, pp. 168 ff.; Eichrodt, *Theology of the Old Testament* I, pp. 109 f.) and put forward again by Kraus (*Gottesdienst in Israel*, 1953, pp. 23 ff.), which claims that a nomadic Feast of the Tent once existed with a whole range of ideas and traditions of its own. If it was really a question of independent forms of tradition, they seem already at an early date to have attracted each other and amalgamated. The passages in I Sam. 2.22 and Ps. 78.60 which call the Temple at Shiloh, in which the Ark of the Covenant was given shelter, the 'Tent' are in any case at variance with such a distinction.

throne, which is upon the Ark and towers to the clouds, but remains
hidden from the eyes of the spectators. That climax of the cultic
ceremony is preserved in the permanent designation of the God of
the Ark as *yōšēb hakk'rubīm*, 'who is enthroned on the cherubim'[1]
(I Sam. 4.4; II Sam. 6.2; Ex. 25.22: 'There I will meet with you,
and from above the mercy seat, from between the two cherubim
that are upon the ark of the testimony I will speak with you').[2] The
tradition of the theophany in its archaic mythological form has held
its own within the literature of the Old Testament with a remarkable
tenacity, which proves that it has been able to preserve in the conservative atmosphere of the cultus the importance which belongs to
it from the canonical point of view (cf. Ex. 19; Deut. 33.2; Judg.
5.4 f.; I Sam. 3.21; 4.3 ff.; I Kings 8.10 ff.; 19.11 ff.; Isa. 6.1 ff.;
Micah 1.2 ff.; Ezek. 1 f.; Hab. 3.3 f.; Nahum 1.2 ff.; and also
Weiser, *Festschrift für Alfred Bertholet*, pp. 513 ff.). The faith of the
people of Israel had a vital interest in Yahweh's personal presence,
guaranteed by the theophany, at the celebration of the cult, because
it meant that their salvation was assured; and this interest is still
reflected in the idea of the 'face of Yahweh' (Ex. 33.12 ff.; cf. Beer's
Commentary on Exodus, p. 159), which is preserved in the language
of the liturgy in various phrases: ('before the face of Yahweh'; again,
'The Lord make his face to shine upon you' and 'The Lord lift up his
countenance upon you' in the ancient benediction of Num. 6.24 f.,
etc.).

Also connected with the encounter with God in the theophany
was the proclamation of the *name of God*. The ancient law of the altar,
which was in force before Israel became a state, when the Ark of the
Covenant was not yet tied to a permanent abode (cf. II Sam. 7.5 ff.),
bears testimony to the association of the cultic theophany with the
name of God. In Ex. 20.24 it reads: 'In every place where I cause my
name to be remembered (*'azkīr 'et-š'mī*) I will come to you and bless
you.' The same association is perhaps still hinted at in the explanation of the name of Yahweh in Ex. 3.14: 'I am there as he who I am.'

[1] In Ugaritic texts Aliyan Baal, the weather god, is called 'the rider on the
clouds' (cf. Gordon, *Ugaritic Manual*, p. 324, no. 1763). From that description
alone it cannot, however, be inferred that the Old Testament idea of the cloud as
Yahweh's chariot must have been taken over directly from those texts, or that
originally Yahweh must have been a storm-god. It is not yet possible to say anything conclusive about the origin of the different aspects which the theophany of
Yahweh presents.

[2] On the 'representation' of the theophany in the cult cf. p. 488, n. 1 below, and
Weiser, *Festschrift für Bertholet*, pp. 523 f.

The original form of the revelation of Yahweh's name is that of his *self-predication* (Ex. 3.6, 14; 6.2 f.; 24.3 ff.; 33.19; 34.5 f.; cf. Ex. 20.2; Hos. 12.9; 13.4; the stereotyped formula of the law of holiness in Lev. 19.2 f., etc.). The liturgical basis of the proclamation of the name of God in a cultic act (II Sam. 6.2) is to be found in the ancient stylized formula of Num. 6.27, which still indicates the connection of the proclamation of the name of God with the theophany and with the blessing of Yahweh: 'So shall they put my name upon the people of Israel, and I will bless them'; in addition to manifesting the nature of Yahweh, it simultaneously signifies within the compass of the Covenant tradition the act of claiming and electing the people of Israel to be the 'people of Yahweh'. The content of the *revelation of the nature of Yahweh*, the original form of which was also that of his self-predication (cf. Josh. 24), consists in the *recapitulation of the Heils-geschichte* in the cult (Josh. 24.2 ff.; I Sam. 12.8 ff.), that is, of the *ṣidᶜqōt Yahweh* 'the righteous acts of the Lord' (Judg. 5.11), and of his miraculous 'mighty deeds' proving the election of the people of God. These mighty acts of God originally comprised the traditions of the Exodus, of the migration through the Wilderness and of the conquest of the land; later on they were enlarged at the beginning by the prehistory of the people of Israel and the narratives of the patriarchs and, in connection with the royal cult at the Temple of Jerusalem, by the tradition of David.[1] In the cult of the Covenant this manifestation of the nature of God was linked up with the *proclamation*

[1] We do not know exactly how the traditions of the *Heilsgeschichte* were presented at any given time or on what principle they were then selected. Though the basic factor governing the manner of presentation and the principle of selection may have remained the same on account of the conservative tendency peculiar to the liturgical tradition, we must reckon with the possibility that modifications in detail have taken place in the course of history. The objection that the feast did not allow sufficient scope for these traditions (Bückers, *Biblica* 32, 1951, p. 406) can hardly be maintained in view of the fact that it lasted several days. In any case that objection is not supported by the account of the celebration of the Feast of Tabernacles, according to which the daily reading of the Torah went on for seven days before the renewal of the Covenant took place (Neh. 8.18). It may be recalled by way of comparison that at the Attic feasts of Dionysus those attending the feast were present each day for three consecutive days at four theatrical performances lasting from the morning to the evening, and that in ancient Japan people spent up to twelve hours in the theatre (Kranz, *Kultur der Griechen*, 1943, p. 396). The fact that at the feast of Dionysus the three days during which tragedies were performed were preceded by two days devoted to a musical festival and to the performance of comedies respectively (Bickel, *Die griechische Tragödie*, 1942, pp. 69 f.) makes it evident that man in antiquity was endowed with receptivity on such a large scale that Bückers' objection (loc. cit.), that the abundance and variety of material would burst the framework of such a festival, is clearly baseless.

of his will; and that proclamation took place in the form of divine commandments (the Decalogue)[1] which were designed to regulate the relationship of the covenant people with Yahweh and to determine the rules of conduct governing the lives of the members of the Covenant in their relationship to one another. These divine commandments represented the conditions which had to be fulfilled before the *act of the renewal of the Covenant* could take place. 'History and Law' as the two foundation-pillars of the self-revelation of Yahweh determined the nature of the cult of the Covenant Festival just as it did that of the tradition of the Hexateuch, for which that cult had provided the setting in which it developed.[2]

The other series of ideas associated with the cult of the Covenant and its tradition, are grouped around these two poles. The *idea of judgment* is most closely bound up with the proclamation of Yahweh's will and with the nature of the Covenant and, according to the evidence of the Old Testament sources, is firmly rooted right from the outset in the Israelite tradition of Yahweh (Ex. 17.7; 18; 32; Num. 20.13; cf. the designation of Yahweh as 'the Judge of all the earth' in Gen. 18.25). In the cult the judgment of Yahweh signified the actual divine verdict that was passed at any given time, pronouncing blessing on those who had been faithful to him and disaster on those who had rebelled against him and had become his enemies[3] (Judg. 5.31); this seems to have found its concrete expression in ceremonial pronouncements of blessing and of curse which were a

[1] The striking formulation of the so-called apodictic commandments of the sacral Decalogue in the indicative may perhaps be accounted for by the cultic situation in which they were presented, being, as it were, the divine proclamation of the nature of the people of God, which is meant to correspond to the self-predication of Yahweh in Ex. 20.2. The indicative mood expressed the nature of the cult as *actio dei* as well as the element of 'representation' which to a large extent was associated with the Old Testament cult of Yahweh. The negative formulation of most of the 'commandments' is in keeping with the marking off of the community of Yahweh as a 'holy people' over against those who did not worship him.

[2] Cf. Josh. 24 and the introduction to the Decalogue; also Weiser, *Introduction to the Old Testament*, ET, 1961, § 13. An annually repeated sacral act of the renewal of the Covenant is attested in the Qumran *Manual of Discipline* 2.15 (Burrows' ed., 1951; see also *Oudtestamentische Studien* 3, 1950, pp. 158 ff.). The liturgy of that annual feast as preserved in the Scroll is demonstrably derived from Old Testament traditions and, in view of the survival of ancient traditions within the sect which can be observed in other respects too, it may be regarded as the result of the influence of an ancient cultic tradition which still lingered on (cf. Baumgärtel, *ZAW* 65, 1953, pp. 262 ff.).

[3] It is probable that the prophetic utterances foretelling the divine judgment also originated in the cult; cf. now Würthwein, *ZTK* 49, 1952, pp. 1 ff.

regular feature of the worship of the covenant community (Deut.
27 f.; Judg. 5.23); it was still preserved in the ritual of the feast of the
renewal of the Covenant which the sect of Qumran celebrated,
probably at New Year.[1] The ancient formula of the law of holiness in
Lev. 17.10; 20.3, 6, 'I will set my face against that man, and will cut
him off from among his people', is a reminder of the association of
the theophany of Yahweh with his judgment in connection with the
elimination of the wicked from the cult community of the Covenant
of Yahweh.[2] Hence the *profession of loyalty* to Yahweh (Ex. 19.8;
24.3, 7; Josh. 24.15 ff., 24), the *renunciation of the foreign gods* (Josh.
24.14 f., 23; Gen. 35.2 ff.; Judg. 10.16), the sanctification and self-
purification of the Yahweh community have their place within the
framework of the Covenant Festival and of its cultic tradition.[3]

It must be left undecided whether the idea of the *kingship of Yahweh*,
which received a new and exalted meaning in the New Testament,
had its origin in the cult of Yahweh, or whether and, if so, when it
penetrated the Israelite cult of the Covenant as a result of the influence exerted by the royal ritual commonly practised in the Near
East, as some indications suggest.[4] But in any case the idea of the
kingship of Yahweh occurs in the tradition of the Old Testament at
an early date (Ex. 15.18; 19.5 f.; Num. 23.21; Deut. 33.5; Judg. 8.23;
I Sam. 8.7; I Kings 22.19 ff.; Isa. 6.5).[5] The truth of this statement is
corroborated by the ancient custom of swearing by the throne of
Yahweh to wage war (Ex. 17.16) and by the association of the idea of
the throne of Yahweh with the sacred Ark of the Covenant (Jer.
3.16 f.; 14.21; 17.12); that truth may perhaps also still shine through
in the meaning of the name 'Israel' = God shows himself as sovereign.[6] In comparison with the oriental idea of the kingship of the god
and of its relation to earthly kingship the corresponding Old Testa-

[1] There is evidence that a similar rite was observed at the festival gatherings
of the Athenians (cf. Aristophanes, *Thesmophoriazousae*, 295 ff.).

[2] Cf. Zimmerli, *ZAW* 66, 1954, pp. 13 ff., on the significance ascribed to this
practice based on ritual law by the Book of Ezekiel; cf. also II Chron. 15.13.

[3] Cf. Alt, *Kleine Schriften zur Geschichte des Volkes Israel* I, 1953, pp. 79 ff.; now
also Kraus, *Gottesdienst in Israel*, 1954, pp. 58 f.

[4] Cf. Eissfeldt, 'El and Yahveh', *JSS* I, 1956, pp. 36 f.; Herbert Schmid, *ZAW*
67, 1955, pp. 168 ff., has attempted to prove that the idea of the kingship of God
has penetrated the Yahweh cult by means of the adoption of some pre-Davidic
cultic tradition of Jerusalem.

[5] Cf. Buber, *Das Königtum Gottes*, 3rd ed., 1956, pp. 3 ff.; Alt, *Kleine Schriften* I,
pp. 345 ff. The arguments put forward by Kraus (op. cit., p. 106, n. 182a) to
refute the view expressed by Alt do not get to the root of the matter.

[6] See Martin Noth, *Die israelitischen Personnamen*, 1928, pp. 208 f.

ment ideas have been developed on independent lines, that is, in the direction of a stronger differentiation between God and man—which was determined by the peculiar character of the covenant religion. Moreover, this decisively influenced the position of the kings of Israel, which differed from that of the kings of the neighbouring countries. The range of ideas associated with the notion of the kingship of Yahweh has been linked on the one hand with the proclamation of the will of Yahweh and with the idea of judgment, and on the other hand with the *idea of creation* (Ex. 19.5 f.; Gen. 18.25; Isa. 6); and these links perhaps date back to the royal ritual of the Near East.[1] The idea of creation is predominant also in the primeval history as told by the Yahwist, and is associated there with the idea of the judgment on the world and on the nations. From the point of view of the history of tradition the adoption of the idea of creation by the Old Testament must be regarded as a secondary phase in its development; and presumably it was not until the era of David and Solomon that this idea underwent a further development within the sacral tradition of the Covenant. David's religio-political action in the removal of the Ark of the Covenant to the royal city of Jerusalem (II Sam. 6), and the building of the Temple of Solomon, which thereby became both the central shrine of the confederacy of the tribes and the royal sanctuary of the kingdom, led to the amalgamation of the tradition of the Covenant with the increasingly important royal cult. And this in its turn paved the way for a development which was fraught with grave consequences for the history both of the cultus and of the tradition. In the Northern Kingdom it brought about the establishment by Jeroboam I at Bethel and Dan of new national sanctuaries, which showed a remarkable leaning towards the agriculturally-based Canaanite religion (I Kings 12.26 ff.); in the temple worship at Jerusalem, on the other hand, the position of the king was firmly established in the ritual of the Covenant Festival. The fact that the king now had a place in that ritual led to the development of new cultic traditions, namely, the election of David and of his dynasty (I Sam. 7) and the selection of Zion as the dwelling-place of Yahweh and as the place where he would reveal himself[2] (a conception which

[1] Cf. in this connection Eissfeldt, op. cit., pp. 25 ff., and John Gray, *VT* 6, 1956, pp. 268 ff.

[2] Justifiable though it is to distinguish between the Sinai Covenant and that made with David (Rost, *TLZ* 72, 1947, pp. 130 ff.), the contrasting of these two covenants involves a risk which Rost (loc. cit.) has not been able to avoid, that as a result the Sinai Covenant is pushed too much into the background, though both

was taken up again, especially by the Deuteronomic literature); and these new traditions came to be of special importance for the rise and development of the Old Testament idea of the Messiah.

5. THE PLACE OF THE PSALMS IN THE CULT OF THE COVENANT FESTIVAL (FRAGMENTS OF LITURGY)

No proper ritual of the Covenant Festival of Yahweh has been handed down to us from Old Testament times, such as has been preserved, for instance, from the Babylonian New Year Festival and the Akitu Festival at Uruk, giving instructions for the execution of the cultic acts and for the recitals of the priests. This can probably be explained by the fact that the ritual of the Covenant Festival was passed on by the priests by means of oral tradition, as is still evident from the history of the origin of the Targum. The description of the liturgy used by the sect of Qumran at the annual celebration of the feast of the renewal of the Covenant, however, enables us to draw from it valuable conclusions as to the existence of corresponding elements in the Old Testament tradition (e.g. Pss. 78; 105; 106; Deut. 32; Ezra 9.6 ff.; Neh. 9.6 ff.).[1] In the Psalter, too, are to be found individual *parts of the cultic liturgy* in considerable numbers, as well as numerous allusions to cultic procedure. It is true that they do not enable us to reconstruct the order of the feast in all its details, but they nevertheless throw into bold relief the essential fundamental elements of the cultic tradition, which our foregoing investigation has shown to belong as constituent parts to the Israelite Covenant Festival. Hence the *cult of this festival* must be assumed to be the *Sitz im Leben* for the vast majority of the individual psalms and their types.

The liturgy which we find in Psalm 50 is part of the order of the feast of the renewal of the Covenant which was celebrated at the Temple of Jerusalem. This follows incontestably from v. 5: 'Gather to me my faithful ones, who made a covenant with me by sacrifice!' and is furthermore corroborated by the references to the advent of

---

from the point of view of the history of traditions and theologically the covenant made with David is the off-shoot of the previous one. Cf. in this connection Mowinckel, *He That Cometh* (ET, 1956), pp. 98, 166, 239. There is no convincing reason for assuming the existence of a separate 'royal feast of Zion' as Kraus does in *Die Königsherrschaft Gottes im Alten Testament*, 1951, pp. 27 ff.

[1] Cf. in this connection Baumgärtel, *ZAW* 65, 1953, pp. 263 ff.

Yahweh at Mount Zion (vv. 2 f.), to the judgment that Yahweh will pronounce on 'his people' (v. 4), to the proclamation of his will and the self-predication of his name (v. 7), to the profession of the congregation that they will be faithful to the Covenant and its commandments (v. 16), and to the separation of the faithful (v. 5) from the wicked (v. 16) by executing judgment upon both (vv. 22 f.). The psalm therefore presupposes cultic events which, as has been shown in another connection, belonged to the ritual of the Covenant Festival. And when in the psalms Yahweh is said to be 'mindful' of his covenant (Pss. 105.8; 111.5, 9; cf. also Pss. 74.2; 98.3), then this figure of speech is meant to express not only the purely spiritual act of recollecting but, as is evident from Ps. 111.4 ('He has caused his wonderful works to be remembered'), the actualization of an historical tradition in a ritual act of the festival cult which was celebrated as a divine institution (cf. Ps. 97.12: 'Rejoice in Yahweh, O you righteous, and testify to his holy memory'[1]; cf. Ps. 30.4). In the liturgy of Ps. 81.3 ff. the *traditional obligation* to celebrate the feast of Yahweh regularly every year is stated even more distinctly and with historical accuracy: 'on our feast day [*sic*], for it is a statute for Israel, an ordinance of the God of Jacob. He made it a decree in Joseph, when he went out over the land of Egypt.' The tradition of the feast of Yahweh dates back to the time of the wilderness, and the tribes of Joseph were the first to give support to this tradition. That the feast mentioned in the liturgy of Ps. 81.3 ff. is that of the renewal of the Covenant is proved by the reference to the self-revelation of Yahweh, his name and his commandments in vv. 9 f., to his saving acts in vv. 6 f., and to the judgment pronounced on those who are disobedient in vv. 11 ff. Ps. 111.9, reading: 'he has commanded them to keep his covenant for ever', also refers to the tradition of the Covenant Festival at which the divine saving acts were recited (Ps. 111.6), a tradition which was meant to be permanently kept alive, and so does Ps. 78.5 ff.: 'He established a testimony in Jacob, and appointed a law in Israel, which he commanded our fathers to teach to their children . . . so that they should not forget the works of God, but keep his commandments.' For in view of the character of these psalms as a whole it cannot be denied that it is not the individual, but the community of Yahweh as a body, which is here placed under the obligation of cherishing the tradition of the Covenant. The stylized liturgical formula, 'Let Israel now say' (Pss. 124.1; 118.2 ff.; 129.1;

[1] *Ps. 97.12b reads in the RSV: 'and give thanks to his holy name.'

cf. also 107.2, 8, 15, 21 f., 31 f.) likewise points to the obligation of keeping up the tradition in the worship of the community. The place where this was done was precisely the Covenant Festival, at which the sacral confederacy of the tribes, called 'Israel', made its appearance and acted as the community of Yahweh.[1] The song of the pilgrimage to Jerusalem also has in mind the feast of Yahweh (as this was celebrated by the confederacy) and its tradition when it says in Ps. 122.4 (with reference to Jerusalem): 'to which the tribes of Yahweh went up to testify to the name of Yahweh according to the tradition ('ēdūt) that is decreed for Israel'. Again, in Psalm 47, which is a hymn in praise of the theophany and kingship of Yahweh, the same feast can still be recognized in v. 9 as the cultic background of that psalm: 'The princes of the peoples gather as the people of the God of Abraham.' Judg. 5.23 and Josh. 9 testify to the fact that non-Israelites had been admitted into membership of the Yahweh amphictyony, even before the state of Israel was established. Again, it can be assumed that that fact acquired a still greater importance as a result of the incorporation of Canaanite tribes into the kingdom of David. Hence it is by no means correct to assume that, wherever the psalms speak of 'the peoples', we have always to interpret this phrase in an eschatological-universal sense, as has so far been common practice, or to think of it as referring to the proselytes in the period between the Testaments. Consequently, it can further be assumed that the festival liturgy in Psalm 87, too, has in mind precisely that thoroughly mixed crowd of pilgrims of different extractions who had come to attend the feast of Yahweh on Mount Zion (cf. in this connection the ordinances concerning the admission of members of foreign nations to the covenant community in Deut. 23.2 ff.). In a similar way this holds good also of Ps. 102.22: 'when peoples gather together, and kingdoms, to serve Yahweh'; here, however, one might almost think of the members of the Covenant belonging to either the Northern or the Southern Kingdom, whose common tradition at the Covenant Festival is spoken of in Pss. 76.1 and 114.2 (cf. I Kings 12.26 f.; Jer. 41.4 f.). And where in the psalms, as in Judg. 5 and Deut. 33, the confederacy of the tribes or particular tribes are shown to officiate in the cult (in Pss. 80.1; 68.24 ff., 34; 108.7 ff. in connection with the theophany), or where the army of the covenant community appear and its requests are prominent (Pss. 44.9; 60.10; 108.11; 149.6 ff.)

[1] The fact that the designation 'Israel' is much more frequently used in the psalms than any other term probably points in the same direction.

—the holy wars of Yahweh had always been the specific concern of the sacral confederacy of the tribes (cf. Ps. 24.8)[1]—the Covenant Festival of Yahweh must be assumed to have been the setting in which these liturgical fragments originally had their place, all the more so as it is possible to detect in the vast majority of the psalms additional traces of fundamental elements of the festival tradition.

Thus the various allusions to the *theophany*[2] as the heart of the Covenant Festival belong to these fundamental elements. The hymns describing the theophany, which are incorporated in psalms of diverse types, have retained the archaic and mythological colours of the first theophany at Sinai, and are to be understood as reflections

[1] Cf. von Rad, *Der heilige Krieg im alten Israel*, 2nd ed., 1952.
[2] The arguments used by Westermann (*Das Loben Gottes in den Psalmen*, pp. 65 ff.) to refute the thesis that from the point of view of the history of traditions the portrayals of the theophany in the psalms are related to the original theophany at Sinai do not seem to me to be conclusive. Though he admits the cultic character of the Sinai theophany, he nevertheless denies this to the theophanies in the psalms and even to a scene such as that in Isa. 6, which quite evidently takes place in the sphere of the cultus. The distinction he makes between theophany (God's appearing for the purpose of self-revelation to convey a message to his people through a mediator) and epiphany (his appearing in order to help his people) unobtrusively substitutes for the real problem, namely, how God's presence is conceived, the secondary question of the purpose of God's presence. At the same time Westermann overlooks that it is in the cult that the presence of God, which is conceived as taking place in the theophany, includes the saving acts which he performs on behalf of the nation and the individual. The contrasting of the theophany as a cultic event with the epiphany as an historical event ignores the character of the cult as *Heilsgeschichte* and for that reason is not a method which can properly be used as conclusive evidence.
To justify his rejection of the thesis that the hymns describing the theophany which we find in the psalms are related to the Sinai theophany from the point of view of the history of traditions, Westermann compares the particular features of these theophanies in a formalistic and schematic fashion and then claims that 'the differences are greater than the things they have in common'. However, in making this comparison he overlooks the fact that such a procedure is logically bound to lead also to the denial of a connection, based on the history of traditions, between the Yahwistic and the Elohistic account of the revelation at Sinai itself and thus to the refutation of his own reasoning. Moreover, he fails to recognize the peculiar character of the hymnic portrayals of the theophany in the psalms, as reflections of cultic proceedings which have already taken place and are taken for granted, when he applies to them a standard that is appropriate only to the description of events of which there has been no knowledge so far, but which is not in keeping with the sacral character of the theophany hymns. From the language used in hymns isolated hints suffice to refer back to the cultic event which the passage in question has in mind and takes for granted, so that there is no need to give in each individual case a full description of all the particular features of that event. The theophany hymns of the Old Testament do not differ in that respect from the Christian prayers offered at the Lord's Supper (cf. also Mowinckel, *Religion und Kultus*, p. 112).

of the cultic theophany of Yahweh which took place above the cherubim of the sacred Ark, representing the cloud which was the chariot of the Deity (Pss. 18.7–15; 50.2 ff.; 68.1 ff.; 77.16 ff.; 97.3 ff.; 104.3; cf. also in this connection Weiser, *Festschrift für Alfred Bertholet*, pp. 513 ff.). The call addressed to Yahweh in the cult, 'Arise!' (Pss. 3.7; 7.6; 9.19; 10.12; 17.13; 21.13; 44.23, 26; 57.5, 11; 74.22; 82.8; 94.2; 132.8; cf. Pss. 12.5; 46.10, rendering the ancient form of Yahweh's self-predication, 'I will now arise'; cf. also Pss. 76.9; 102.13) or 'shine forth' (Pss. 80.1; 94.1; 50.2; *hōpīᵃ*' is the cultic term for the theophany that takes place in the heavenly light of glory [*kābōd*]; cf. Deut. 33.2; Ex. 24.16 f.) is likewise connected with the epiphany of Yahweh above the sacred Ark in the sanctuary of the Covenant. The ancient sayings in Num. 10.35 f. which are associated with the Ark of the Covenant (cf. also Ps. 68.1) already testify to that call and so do many psalms. It has been assumed that the cultic shout 'Awake' (Pss. 35.23; 44.23; 57.8; 59.4 f. and often) has been borrowed by the cultic poetry of the Old Testament from the rite of the dying and rising king-god, which was practised in the royal ritual of the Near East.[1] But even if that assumption should prove correct, this shout has at any rate now lost its former association with the resurrection of the god and has been applied to the encounter with God in the theophany, as is demonstrated by the parallel sayings 'be exalted' in Ps. 57.5 and 'meet me' and 'see' in Ps. 59.4 and also by the context. From Ps. 80.1 and 3 it can be proved also that the saying 'Yahweh make his face to shine', which was included in the ancient liturgical benediction of Num. 6.24 ff., is still used by the psalms in its original association with the cultic theophany (Pss. 4.6; 31.16; 67.1; 80.3, 7, 19; 118.27); for there the supplication 'Let thy face shine' is used as parallel and equivalent in meaning to 'Thou who art enthroned upon the cherubim, appear!' (*hōpīᵃ*'). These passages shed a clearer light on those formulae which speak of the '*face of Yahweh*' in order to express Yahweh's encounter with the worshipper (Ps. 95.2: 'Let us come before his face!'; cf. Ps. 69.17 f.) or his actual presence in the sanctuary (Pss. 96.13; 98.9: 'before the face of Yahweh, for he has come'; cf. Ps. 68.4 ff.) or in the sacred cultic events (Ps. 44.3: 'nor did their own arm give them victory; but thy right hand, and thy arm, and the light of thy countenance'; cf. Num. 10.35; Pss. 68.1; 80.16; 98.1 ff.; 16.11; 21.9): all these formulae have their origin in

---

[1] See e.g. Widengren, *Sakrales Königtum im Alten Testament und im Judentum*, 1955, pp. 63 ff.

the conception handed down by the cultic tradition of the theophany of Yahweh as the revelation and realization of his salvation.

To 'behold the face of Yahweh' (cf., for instance, the parallel in Ps. 17.15: 'I may satisfy myself by beholding thy form' [*t'mūnā* = form]; also Pss. 11.7; 17.15; 27.4; 63.2; 84.7 and the formula used for attending the worship of the sanctuary in Ex. 23.17; 34.23 f.; Deut. 31.11; I Sam. 1.22; Isa. 1.12; Ps. 42.2, which originally had the same wording, and also the phrase 'who seek the face of God' in Pss. 24.6; 27.8; 105.4) and to 'walk in the light of God's countenance' (Pss. 89.15; 41.12; 56.13; 102.28; 116.9; 140.13) is constantly represented in the psalms as the goal of the ardent desires of the faithful and as the attainment of salvation (the only exception being Ps. 39.13). On the other hand, God's hiding of his face (Pss. 22.24; 27.9; 44.24; 69.17; 88.14; 102.2) or the casting away from his presence (Pss. 51.11; 68.2 f.; 80.16; 104.29) is regarded in the psalms as a calamity and as the root-cause of physical and spiritual affliction. Again, in the psalms the view is adopted that when the eye of the Lord is on those who fear him, they can be assured of his grace and salvation (Pss. 13.3; 33.13 ff., 18 f.; 59.4 f.; 80.14; 84.9; 113.6 ff.; 138.6; cf. Gen. 4.4 f. and the correction of the current view by the prophet in Amos 9.4). Again, in the psalms the idea of the face of Yahweh is linked with the phenomena which accompany the theophany of Yahweh and which we find in other Old Testament traditions, phenomena such as earthquake, fire, etc. (Pss. 29.6 ff.; 114.6 f.; 68.8; 96.9; 97.3); moreover, the heavenly light of glory (*kābōd*; Ps. 63.2; cf. 24.6 f.); and 'beauty and strength' (Pss. 105.4; 96.6) and 'grace and faithfulness' (Pss. 89.14; 85.9 f., 13; cf. Ex. 34.6; Ps. 43.3) are conceived as Yahweh's acolytes who accompany him whenever he appears. All these facts—derived simply from the psalms' contents, irrespective of the 'type' to which they belong —show to what a high degree the world of ideas and language of the psalms are saturated with and determined by the tradition of the cultic theophany of Yahweh which was at the heart of the celebration of the Covenant Festival. Moreover, the *function assigned to the Ark*, the ancient central shrine of the Israel confederacy of the tribes, in connection with the epiphany of Yahweh in the sanctuary is still reflected in a number of psalms. Psalm 132 is a liturgy whose theme is the dramatic representation of an event which was epoch-making for the shaping of the feast of Yahweh at the Temple of Jerusalem, that is, of the bringing up of the Ark to Jerusalem by David; and the representation of the event was meant to be a cultic repetition of the dedication of the Temple. Psalm 132 also makes evident the fusion of the sacral tradition of the ancient confederacy of the tribes with the tradition of the family religion of the 'God of the fathers' (Ps. 132.2, 5) and of the Davidic royal ritual (as regards the theophany associated with this ceremony compare Ps. 132.8 with Num. 10.35 and I Kings 8, and also the passage in II Chron. 6.40 ff. which recalls, with every justification from the standpoint of the history of the cultus, the dedication of the Temple, quoting in this connection also Ps. 132). According to II Sam. 6.2 it is clear beyond doubt that, when Yahweh at his epiphany is described in Pss. 80.1; 99.1 (cf. Ps. 18.10) as he 'who sits enthroned upon the cherubim', this refers to the cultic theophany that takes place above the sacred Ark. The genuflexion before 'his footstool' (Pss. 99.5; 132.7; see also I Chron. 28.2; Lam. 2.1) and the conception of the throne of Yahweh, associated with this act of worship and widely used in every part of the Psalter (cf. Isa. 6.1; Jer. 3.16 f.; 14.21; 17.12; Ezek. 1 f.; 43.2 ff.), as well as the phrase 'in the shadow of thy wings' (Pss. 17.8; 36.7; 57.1; 61.4; 63.7) also point to the God who appears above the Ark which serves as his throne in the pillar of cloud towering to heaven and, hidden by the wings of the cherubim, is present at the celebration of the cult (cf. Ps. 11.4, 'The Lord is in his holy temple, the Lord, his throne is in the heavens'; Ps. 18.9 ff.; compare also Ps. 31.20, 'In the covert of thy presence thou wilt hide them' with v. 16, 'Let thy face shine on thy servant', which evidently has the theophany in mind).

Again the *proclamation of the name of God* linked with the theophany has left numerous traces in the psalms which likewise point to the same cultic connection. Here we must mention the name *Yahweh* (*'Elōhē*) *ṣᵉbā'ōt*,[1] which originally was given to the God who is present above the Ark, which still reflects the idea of the celestial court of his heavenly hosts (Pss. 29; 58.1; 82; 89.6 ff.; 103.20; cf. I Kings 22.19; Isa. 6.2 f.; Ps. 148.1 ff.; Luke 2.13 f.), which also belongs to the sphere of the theophany, but also links up with Yahweh's relationship with Israel's covenantal armies (Ex. 7.4; 12.41; Num. 10.36; I Sam. 17.45). According to II Sam. 6.2 the cultic name of Yahweh used to be 'proclaimed' over the Ark, and, as Ps. 24.10 shows, played an important rôle in connection with the advent of the Lord of the

---

[1] On the probable origin of this designation of God cf. Eissfeldt, 'Jahwe Zebaot', *Miscellanea Academica Berolinensia*, 1950, pp. 128 ff.

Ark which formed a part of the cultic liturgy. In view of the context
in which it stands it can further be assumed that in Pss. 46.7; 48.8;
59.5; 69.6; 80.4, 7, 14, 19; 84.1, 8, 12; 89.8, too, the name '*Yahweh
Sabaoth*', which is given to God in these psalms, is still related to the
God who is thought of as present over the Ark in the cultic theophany, that is, these psalms, too, have their origin in the pre-exilic
cult of the Covenant Festival. A similar connection may be presumed
to have existed with regard to the designation of Yahweh as 'the
Holy One of Israel' (Pss. 22.3; 71.22; 78.41; 89.18; cf. Isa. 6.3; 1.4;
5.19 and frequently). Moreover, the way in which the *name of Yahweh*
is mentioned in the psalms under many different aspects tells us that
it was originally associated with his self-revelation in the theophany
of the cult of the Covenant. Apart from the *self-predication* 'I am
Yahweh' (Pss. 50.7 ff.; 81.10) and 'know that I am Yahweh' (Ps.
46.10), which recalls the introduction to the Decalogue and is itself
a constituent part of the theophany (Pss. 12.5; 60.6 ff.; 68.11, 22;
75.2 ff.; cf. 35.3), other phrases which belong here include 'thy name
is near' (Ps. 75.1); 'that they may seek thy name' (Ps. 83.16, cf.
v. 18; Ps. 52.9); 'in Judah God is known, his name is great in Israel'
(Ps. 76.1); 'unapproachable and terrible is thy name' (Ps. 111.9);
'our help is in the name of the Lord' (Ps. 124.8); 'save me, O God,
by thy name' (Ps. 54.1); compare also 'the name of the God of Jacob
make you powerful' (Ps. 20.1) and 'thy name, O Lord, endures
for ever, thy memory, O Lord, from generation to generation' (Ps.
135.13), where the name of Yahweh is almost used as the equivalent
of the personal presence of God at the celebration of the cult (cf. Jer.
3.17).

The view that the psalms are rooted in the cultic tradition of the
Covenant Festival is furthermore corroborated by the fact that a
number of them also include or allude to the *manifestation of the nature
of Yahweh*[1] in the form of the representation of his *saving deeds*, that is,
the recapitulation of the *Heilsgeschichte* in the form of a cultic drama,
following the familiar pattern of the Hexateuch tradition (e.g.
Ex. 15.1 ff.; Pss. 66.5 ff.; 81.6 ff.; 89.5 ff.; 107.33 ff. and often). A
number of psalms contain variations in details from the text of the
Hexateuch, as e.g. Pss. 78; 105; 106; 135 and 136. These variations

---

[1] According to the view held in antiquity the revelation of the name of the
Godhead already implied some sort of manifestation of his nature. This can still be
inferred from the aetiological explanation of the name of God in Ex. 3.14 (cf.
Ps. 33.5 f.).

make it impossible to accept the widely held view of a literary dependence of these so-called 'historical psalms' on the Hexateuch, which after all was available in writing; they rather support the view that the adherence of these psalms to the traditional outline of the *Heilsgeschichte* is to be accounted for by the existence in priestly circles of an oral tradition which had been fostered by means of its cultic recital. Such cultic recitals of the tradition of the *Heilsgeschichte* are indicated by passages in the psalms in which the congregation testifies: 'We have heard with our ears, O God, our fathers have told us, the work thou didst perform in their days' (Pss. 44.1 ff.; 48.8, 13 f.; 62.11; 75.1; 78.3 ff.); here the cult community's duty to pass on and keep alive this tradition is explicitly confirmed (cf. Pss. 81.10; 96.3; 102.21; 105.1 f.; 111.4, 6: 'He has caused his wonderful works to be remembered; he has caused the power of his works to be made known to his people'). The *duty of passing on the tradition* even affects the cultic prayers of the individual (Pss. 71.16 ff.; 77.11 ff.; 143.5 f.) and is reflected in such solemn promises as 'that I may recount all thy praises' (Ps. 9.14; cf. 9.11; 22.22, 30 ff.; 26.7; 40.5; 73.28; 118.17, etc.). Often the saving acts of Yahweh are spoken of only in brief summaries, especially, for instance, in the abbreviated form *ḥesed weˀemet* = grace and faithfulness (cf. Ex. 34.6; Hos. 2.19 f.), which has its origin in the tradition of the first theophany: 'he has remembered his grace to Jacob and his faithfulness to the house of Israel' (Ps. 98.3; cf. Pss. 25.10; 26.3; 36.5; 57.10; 61.7; 85.10; 88.11; 89.1 f., 14, 24, 33 f.; 92.2; 100.5; 117.2; 138.2), and also in the liturgical formula 'O testify to the Lord, for he is good; for his grace endures for ever!' (Pss. 106.1; 107.1; 118.1, 4; 136.1 ff.; cf. Ex. 33.19; 34.6 which are taken from the cultic narrative read at the festival). Such references to the tradition of the *Heilsgeschichte* have in mind its cultic representation as a sacral act of actual significance for the immediate present and therefore the psalms in question are to be regarded as having their place in the cult of the Covenant. This follows from those phrases which still distinctly exhibit the character of the saving events as a cultic drama, for instance, 'Come and behold the works of the Lord!' (Pss. 46.8; 48.8; 66.5; 69.32; 90.16; 98.3; 107.42; cf. 40.3; 63.2). This assumes, however, that the members of the cult community not only experience the saving acts of the past in the rôle of witnesses as something which by means of the cult has become for them a present reality, but also have themselves a share in and are affected by the sacramental cultic activity.

God's presence in the holy place also implies that his entire redemptive work in history is simultaneously present, and through the ritual act performed in the cult exercises its influence upon the cult community: 'Today, when you hear my voice, harden not your heart, as at Meribah' (Ps. 95.7 f.); again, 'Both we and our fathers have sinned' (Ps. 106.6 f.); again, 'Sinai is in the holy place' (Ps. 68.17; cf. Ps. 50.2, where again the Sinai theophany takes place in the Temple of Jerusalem); also Ps. 114, in which the events of the Wilderness period are represented with a dramatic actuality that makes them seem immediately present. It is here in the cult that we find the origin and root of the so-called historicization and stylization of the events after the pattern of the *Heilsgeschichte*, in which also mythological themes from the world surrounding Israel were included and adapted to her cultic tradition, as, for example, the combat of the gods against the powers of chaos (Pss. 11.6; 29; 66.5 ff.; 68.2 ff.; 74.13 ff.; 89.9 f.; 46.2 ff.; 48.4 ff.; 60.6 ff.; 65.7; 76.1 ff.; 93.3 ff.; 118.10 ff., etc.). And it is here, too, that we find the root of the eschatological way of thinking peculiar to the Old Testament, which bridges the gap[1] between periods and localities, and concentrates the whole range of events in the single moment of the cultic act, so that the past, the present and the future coincide and Israel together with the whole world and all the nations are summoned to be witnesses of these events (Pss. 46.10; 47.1, 8 f.; 68.32; 93; 96; 97; 98.2 ff.; 99.1 ff.; 100.1, etc.). This cosmic and universal perspective was strengthened by the adoption of the *idea of creation*, which was linked with the range of ideas associated with the *kingship of Yahweh* within the cultic tradition.[2] That development is likewise reflected in a great number of psalms (cf. Pss. 22.28; 24.1 f.; 7 ff.; 29.10; 33.6 ff.; 59.13; 65.6 ff.; 66.7; 74.12 ff.; 84.3; 93.2 f., 95.3 ff.; Jer. 17.12 and the so-called 'Enthronement' psalms). Psalms 19 and 104 have perhaps been influenced by foreign prototypes. The *redistribution of the land* has also left traces in the psalms (Pss. 16.5 f.; 25.13; 37.9, 11; 60.6 ff.; 61.5; cf. 68.10; 105.11, 44; 135.12; 136.21 f.; 140.11 f.); according to Deut. 31.9 ff. it was carried out every seven years in the autumn within the framework of the Covenant Festival and presumably followed the tradition of the conquest and distribution of the land.

---

[1] It would be more consistent to say that the way of thinking peculiar to the cultus presupposes a notion of space and time which is different from that of the modern (historical) way of thinking.

[2] Cf. p. 33, n. 4, and p. 34, n. 1.

In the so-called 'Royal Psalms' (Pss. 2; 18; 20; 21; 72; 89; 101; 110; cf. 132.10, 17; 78.70 ff.; 144.10) it is possible to discern the enlargement of the ancient tradition of the *Heilsgeschichte* which took place in the time of the kings; this as a result of David's policy in cultic matters, led to the incorporation of the traditions of the election of David and his dynasty and of the selection of the Temple on Mount Zion as God's dwelling-place within the framework of the cult of the feast which was celebrated there; it also led to the extension of the idea of salvation to the 'grace of kingship'[1] ('the mercies of David' in Ps. 89.1, 49) within the same framework. But the intercessions for the king, which occur sporadically in other types of psalms, can also be regarded as evidence that such psalms presuppose the presence of the king at the feast of Yahweh (e.g. Pss. 28.8; 61.6 f.; 63.11; 84.9; 132.10; I Sam. 2.10). In Ps. 78.68 ff. and in Ex. 15.13, 17 *the election and the establishment of Jerusalem* as the city and sanctuary of Yahweh is embedded in the structure of the whole tradition of the *Heilsgeschichte* which begins with the Exodus. In the so-called 'Zion' psalms (Pss. 46.4 ff.; 48.1 ff.; 76.1 ff.; 84) and also in Pss. 87.1 ff.; 102.16; 132.13 ff.; 147.2 this idea constitutes the point of departure and the focal point of the individual psalms which in these hymns is more closely bound up with the place where the cult was celebrated.

The association of the revelation of Yahweh's nature with *the revelation of his will* in the tradition of the cult of the Covenant Festival has found expression in the psalms in multifarious ways. Pss. 50.7 and 81.10 have made direct use of the introduction to the Decalogue in its ancient form of self-predication. Ps. 81.9 even reproduces their apodictic style, which indicates that, in contrast to the conditional style customary in the administration of justice of the whole Near East, it originates and is used in the cult of the Covenant Festival.[2] Pss. 40.7 ff. and 149.9 refer to the written 'statutes and ordinances' which were recited in the assembly of the covenant community (compare in this connection Josh. 24.25 f.; Ps. 105.10). Again, the ultimate aim of the representation of the *Heilsgeschichte* is evidently that of exhorting the people (Pss. 105.45; 111.10; 78.7 ff.; 81.13; 106; 107.35 ff.); and the *idea of judgment*, which from the

---

1 *The German word '*Königsheil*' almost defies translation. From the context in which it is used it follows that it refers to the *charismata* connected with the office of the king.

2 Cf. Alt, *Die Ursprünge des israelitischen Rechts*, 1934.

beginning is organically connected in the Old Testament with
the ideology of the Covenant and in the tradition of the cult of the
Covenant is based on the linking up of the manifestation of the nature
of Yahweh with that of his will, continually recurs in the psalms
in the various forms in which it has found expression, and irrespective of the type to which these psalms belong. And both this
parenetic aim and the idea of judgment show that such psalms were
originally connected with the Covenant Festival (Pss. 9.16 f.; 11.4 ff.;
17.2 f., 15; 50.4; 68.1 ff.; 73.18 ff., 27 f.; 74.22; 75.2; 76.7 ff.; 94.1 f.;
95.7 ff.; 96.13; 97.2; 98.8 f.; 99.4; 132.17 f., etc.). It is difficult to
establish to what extent Near Eastern prototypes have influenced
the development of the particular ideas about judgment which are
to be found in the psalms. In view of the fact that the idea of judgment was linked to and rooted in the covenant tradition, there can
hardly be any question of the wholesale adoption from the ancient
Orient of what Mowinckel has called the 'judgment myth'; at most we
may say that some of these ideas have been included among those associated with judgment. The idea of judgment constitutes not only
ideologically, but also from the point of view of the cultus the link connecting history and law, these two focal points of the covenant tradition
around which the thought of a number of psalms revolves (e.g. Pss.
18.21 ff.; 25.9 f.; 33.4 f.; 40.5, 8 ff.; 44.1 ff., 17; 50.5 ff., 16 ff.;
75.1 ff.; 76.1 ff., 7 ff.; 78.3 ff., 7 ff.; 81.6 ff.; 106.2 f.). Its original
association with the cult of the Covenant, especially with the theophany, is still recognizable in Pss. 96.13 and 98.8 f., where the world
is said to rejoice 'before the face of Yahweh, for he has come to judge
the earth'. Presumably the prophets, too, derived the idea of judgment from the same source (cf. e.g. Amos 1.2; 9.1 ff.; Hos. 4.1 f.;
12.2 f.; Isa. 3.13 f.; 6; Micah 1.2 ff.; 6.1 ff.; Jer. 2.5 ff.; 25.30 ff.;
Mal. 3.5).[1] This is why the entire redemptive work of Yahweh as
re-enacted in the cult is frequently summed up by the psalms under
the aspect of the idea of his judgment and termed his 'righteousness'
(ṣᵉdāqā; in Judg. 5.11; I Sam. 12.7; Micah 6.5; Ps. 103.6 the saving
deeds of Yahweh are called his 'righteous acts'). It is in this treatment and characterization of Yahweh's redemptive work that the
conception of *history as judgment*, which we find again in the prophetic
literature and in the Deuteronomic presentation of history, has its
cultic root, and this is what shows what a deep and far-reaching

---

[1] For detailed evidence compare Würthwein, ZTK 49, 1952, pp. 1 ff., where he
discusses the views held by Gunkel, Begrich and Hans Schmidt.

influence the covenant cult was able to exert. Whilst the execution of Yahweh's judgment in the covenant cult signifies to the godly who are faithful to Yahweh that they will have a share in salvation, that is, in the divine grace and (covenantal) faithfulness (*ḥesed we'emet*; see above), it has the opposite effect on the 'wicked', that is, on enemies both of Yahweh and Israel and also of godly individuals; to them it signifies disaster and destruction. In these circumstances it is not surprising that the ideas associated with that notion of judgment are to be found in a great number of psalms of different types, and that in some cases they appear quite unexpectedly and cannot be derived from the train of thought of the rest of the psalm (e.g., Pss. 104.35; 139.19 ff.). This only proves that we are here dealing with a fixed tradition whose existence is taken for granted, and which probably originated within the cultic tradition. The *twofold aspect of the idea of judgment*, embracing both salvation (*Heil*) and disaster (*Unheil*) (e.g., Pss. 68.2 f.; 132.15 ff.; Judg. 5.31; I Sam. 2.6 ff.), is not to be regarded, as Gunkel assumes, as the product of the Wisdom poetry and as the result of a subsequent reflection, but is derived from the idea of the Covenant and its cultic tradition; for there in a ritual act accompanied by the revelation of Yahweh the actual verdict of salvation or disaster was executed. The element of 'crisis' is also implied in the idea of 'restoring the fortunes' (*šūb šebūt*;[1] Pss. 85.1; 126.4) which was adopted from another range of ideas associated with the cult. The fact that the thought of a great number of psalms is focused on this judgment leads to the conclusion that these psalms originated in the Covenant Festival of Yahweh. This idea of judgment is also closely related in the psalms to the ideas of blessing and curse and to that *self-purification of the Yahweh community* which takes place in the ritual separation of the 'godly' from the 'wicked'; the former may partake of the covenantal salvation, of the blessing of God's presence and of his gracious 'nearness' (see above), whereas the latter are expelled from the covenant community, excluded from any sharing in God's salvation and exposed to the curse and to destruction (cf. Deut. 27 f.; Josh. 24, and the ancient formula 'shall be cut off from God's people' in Lev. 19.8; 20.18 and frequently).

In this connection it is worth mentioning that the tradition of the *Heilsgeschichte* also includes a series of accounts of judgments of Yahweh which show a distinct tendency to inculcate the cultic and moral

[1] For the views of textual critics on this term cf. Borger, *ZAW* 66, 1954, pp. 315 f.

duties which are bound up with the Covenant of Yahweh (Ex. 32;
Num. 16; 25; Gen. 19; cf. Judg. 19 ff.). The *elimination of the wicked*
from the Yahweh community by means of a ritual judicial act (cf.
Pss. 1.4; 52.5 ff.) is related in the psalms to the presence of Yahweh,
that is, to his appearing for judgment on his people in the cult of the
Covenant (e.g. Ps. 21.9: 'you will make them as a blazing oven when
you appear'; Ps. 94.1 f.: 'Yahweh, thou God of vengeance, appear.
Rise up, O judge of the earth'; Ps. 68.1 f.: 'the wicked perish before
the face of Yahweh'; cf. Num. 10.35; Pss. 3.7; 36.12; 73.17 ff.;
80.16; 83.14 f.; Lev. 20.5 ff.); again, the judgment on the wicked is
'stylized' in Ps. 11.6 after the pattern of the Hexateuch tradition
(Gen. 19) and in Ps. 140.10 after the example of Num. 16 (cf. the
comments on Ps. 58.6 ff., pp. 431 f. below); both these facts provide
clear evidence of the connection of the psalms with the tradition of the
covenant cult. Mowinckel has already rightly disputed the view
which prevailed for a long time that the contrast between the godly
and the wicked, round which the thought of the psalms revolves
again and again, is to be accounted for only by the controversies of
the religious parties of the inter-testamental period. Moreover, it
must be stated that the separation of the godly from the wicked and
the elimination of the latter from the Yahweh community was from
the first a necessary consequence of the peculiar character of the
covenant religion and its cultus and had its assured place in it (Ex.
32.26 ff.; Judg. 5.23; Deut. 27.11 ff.; Num. 10.35; 25.1 ff.; cf. Jer.
17.12 ff. and the liturgy of the Qumran sect). To be faithful to the
God of the Covenant and to be obedient to his commandments was
regarded as the essential criterion of membership of the Yahweh
community and of participation in the salvation that went with it;
on the other hand, 'defection' (*peša'* faithlessness, a concept unknown
outside the religion of Yahweh!) and disobedience were regarded as
the specific sin which destroys the covenantal relationship with God.
The interest in the sanctification and self-purification of the covenant
community arose out of its cultic and spiritual solidarity and its
relationship with Yahweh as a 'holy nation' to him (Ex. 19.6). Hence
it had to be particularly concerned with the cutting out of anything
which, as a result of the presence of heterogeneous and rebellious
elements, threatened to interfere with or to paralyse the covenantal
salvation and the powerful blessings wherewith every part of the
festival cult was saturated (cf. Lev. 20.5 ff.; Ex. 19.5 f., 10 ff.;
22.31; Ps. 132.16). From these fundamental principles comes the

lofty moral earnestness which lifts the Old Testament Psalter high above the ethical level of the cultic practice of the ancient East. The twofold aspect of the idea of judgment, in the light of which the history of salvation is always at the same time the history of judgment (Pss. 78; 106), postulates, moreover, that strange polarity of the fear of God and of joy in God which in the psalms are the distinguishing marks of a living encounter with him in the cultic experience of his presence.

We do not know the concrete details of the procedure of the *execution of the divine judgment*, but here, too, we shall have to reckon with the possibility that particular features were modified in the course of history. Pss. 72.2, 4; 101; 122.5 lead us to presume that one of the duties of the king was to execute this judgment; Ps. 101.8 in particular suggests that the same is true of the cutting off of the wicked. Again, we may assume that the practice varied according to the nature of the case in question. Hans Schmidt holds that the 'prayer of the accused' is related to a trial by ordeal (see below). The ritual of the Covenant Festival probably also included a liturgy of blessing and cursing after the manner of Deut. 27 f. (cf. Pss. 24.5; 37.22; 118.26). It is also possible that the so-called *'entrance torah'* (Pss. 15; 24.3–6), regulating the admission to the sanctuary of pilgrims attending the festival was connected with the idea of judgment (Ps. 24.5b) and with the preservation of the purity of the community of Yahweh, in so far as admission to the festival ceremony in the Temple and to a share in the salvation and blessing associated with the presence of Yahweh depended on the priest's assurance of salvation (Pss. 15.5b; 24.5; 118.19 f.), which in its turn required the prior affirmation of those taking part in the cult that they fulfil the prescribed requirements (cf. Pss. 24.6; 40.7: 'Lo, I come, in the roll of the book I have been given instruction'). It is a striking fact that these conditions of admission to the cult are not, as might be expected, requirements of a ritual nature, which significantly enough scarcely ever occur in the psalms, but are precepts of a moral and religious nature on the lines of the covenant ethics as seen in the Decalogue. This fact cannot be accounted for, as some people have thought, by the influence of the prophets, striving to raise the moral standards of the cult. It is due to the connection of these requirements with the revelation of the will of Yahweh and with his judgment as the cardinal facts on which was based the renewal of the Covenant—the thing being celebrated in the festival cult.

Whilst the moral sublimity and purity of the idea of the righteousness and judgment of God sprang from those sources of the Israelite
covenant tradition which were peculiar to it, it may be assumed that
the *extension of the idea of judgment to all the nations* and to the whole
world, which is related, on the one hand, to the idea of the kingship
of Yahweh and, on the other hand, to the idea of creation (Pss. 82.8;
96.13; 98.8 f.; 99.2 ff.), was first stimulated by cultic traditions of the
Near East and then incorporated in the cult of the Covenant, and
adapted to its tradition. As this extension of the religious, moral and
cultic aspects is already taken for granted both in the Yahwistic and
Elohistic strata of the Hexateuch (Gen. 1–11; 18.25; Ex. 19.15) and
also in the prophets (II Kings 5.15; Amos 1.3 ff.; 9.7; Isa. 6; Micah
1.2 ff., etc.), it cannot be derived from the prophetic idea of God, as
Kittel, Stärk, Gunkel and others assume. The psalms show that it
probably dates back to an early cultic tradition of the Covenant of
Yahweh which was encouraged to develop in that direction by the
broadening of the political, cultural and intellectual horizons in the
time of David and Solomon. Again, in the context of the psalms'
cultic way of thinking, this extension is not merely to be understood
'eschatologically' in the sense that its significance is entirely restricted
to what will come to pass at the end of time, as Kittel, Gunkel and
others assume, but rather as the manifestation of the final and unlimited dominion, power and glory (*kābōd*) of God which is concentrated in the ritual cultic act *hic et nunc*, and which remained throughout the Psalter and right up to the doxology of the Lord's Prayer the
fundamental theme of the piety expressed in the prayers of the
liturgy.

The fact that by means of the presence of God at his theophany in
the festival cult the entire redemptive work of the past was represented and experienced as a present reality also involved the converse,
that is, that the particular experiences of the nation and the individual at any given time were included in the general outline of the
saving events represented in the cult, were interpreted and understood in the light of those events, and were represented in the forms
of the tradition of salvation (and of judgment) as a whole, that is,
they were 'stylized' after the pattern of the tradition of the *Heilsgeschichte* (see above); compare Ps. 59.11 ff. with Gen. 4.12; Ps. 71.20
with Gen. 6 ff.; Ps. 55.9 with Gen. 11; Pss. 11.6; 21.9; 140.10 with
Gen. 19; Pss. 55.15; 140.10 with Num. 16; Pss. 60.6 f.; 61.5 (distribution of land); also Pss. 118.10 ff.; 59.15; 83.9 ff. Hence the inter-

pretation of the psalms in a cultic sense does not by any means bar us from interpreting them in the light of contemporary history and the lives of individuals as well. But the form of presentation used by the psalms, which are tied to the tradition, and moreover are mostly couched in general terms, makes it often more difficult to apprehend the concrete historical and personal circumstances that attended the composition of individual psalms, all the more so as a number of them were composed or appointed for frequent use in public worship.

Yahweh's dealing with the *gods* occupies a special position in the psalms within the compass of the idea of judgment. The marking off of Israel as a people opposed to the worship of strange gods was right from the beginning intimately bound up with the nature of the Covenant, its ideology, and its cultic practice and was continually impressed upon the people of Israel (cf. Ex. 18.11; 20.3, 23; 23.24; 34.14 ff.; Josh. 24.14 ff., 20 ff.). Here we must mention the various *renunciations of strange gods* and of their worshippers, which occur in a number of psalms of different types as counterparts of the professions of loyalty to Yahweh. These have significance, as they help us to establish the cult of the Covenant as the place in which such psalms originated (Pss. 16.4; 25.3 ff.; 31.6; 32.10; 40.4; 73.15; 92.7 ff.; 96.5; 97.7; 115.4 ff.; 135.15 ff. and frequently). It is characteristic of the distinctive quality of the faith in God which was held by the members of the covenant of Yahweh that even the idea of *theomachy*, which was widespread in non-Israelite mythology, was transformed in Psalms 58 and 82 into the idea of *Yahweh's judgment on gods who were subordinate to him*, and further that the same idea assumed in the hymns the form of the *mocking of the gods*, which is not recorded anywhere outside the Old Testament. On the other hand, the theme of the combat of the gods against the powers of chaos, which originated in the Creation-myth, was historicized, that is, it was incorporated into the framework of the *Heilsgeschichte* as the account of the judgment which Yahweh passed on his own and his people's enemies (Pss. 74.12 ff.; 89.9 f.; 68.30; in this last psalm the cultic events are clearly actualized as a present experience; see also the exegesis of Ps. 29.3, below, pp. 262 f.).

Even though particular problems still remain to be solved, it follows from our study of the psalms, based as it is on the study of the history of the cultus and of the traditions as well as on the method of comparing the various traditions with each other, if we take everything into consideration, that compared with the knowledge gained up to now we have obtained a clearer conception of the way in which the psalms are rooted in the cultus. This is true not only in the sense that the cult of the Covenant Festival provided the external framework within which the majority of the pre-exilic psalms had their *Sitz im Leben*, but also in the sense that the cultic tradition of the festival, which had a peculiar religious character of its own, dominated the basic ideas of the Psalter and, in spite of all their diversity in details, linked these ideas to a spiritual and living unity which revolved round the revelation of Yahweh as its centre, not only from the point of view of the cult, but also from the point of view of theology. This tradition remained conscious of its individuality, resisting every foreign influence which threatened to overwhelm this, and impressed upon the elements which intruded into it from without the distinguishing marks of its own character.

6. THE 'TYPES' OF THE PSALMS

The picture that has been derived from the liturgical-cultic portions of the Psalter viewed as to the history of tradition and the cultus, is confirmed and supplemented by the picture which we obtain when, applying the method of Form-Criticism, we study the psalms according to their main types. The main types of the psalms in the Psalter are as follows: hymns, laments and thanksgivings. The last-named are akin to both the former types as regards their subject-matter and form, and frequently occur also in association with the lament.[1]

(a) HYMNS

The poetry of the hymns, the external form of which Israel borrowed from the world around her, can be traced back to the earliest period in the history of the people of Israel. The 'sea song' of Miriam (Ex. 15.21) and portions of the Song of Deborah (Judg. 5), both of them belonging to the earliest history of the tribes of Israel, show the same hymnic character as the *Trisagion* of the seraphim in the narrative of the call of Isaiah (Isa. 6.3) and as various poems of other

---

[1] It is for this reason that Westermann (*Das Loben Gottes in den Psalmen*, pp. 20 ff.), taking as his starting-point 'the two fundamental modes of man's speaking to God', wants to recognize as main types only psalms of praise and psalms of supplication (lament). However, since the effect of that simplification would be to confuse, we prefer to retain the usual classification of the psalms.

prophets. The singing of hymns accompanied the Old Testament religion from its first beginnings right up to the Magnificat and the Benedictus in the New Testament (Luke 1.46 ff.; 68 ff.). In general the following psalms are held to belong to the 'type' of hymns: 8; 19; 29; 33; 65; 67; 100; 103; 104; 105; 111; 113; 114; 135; 136; 145; 146; 147; 148; 149; 150; the 'Zion' psalms (Pss. 46; 48; 76; 84; 87; 122) and the 'Enthronement' psalms (Pss. 47; 93; 96; 97; 98; 99) also belong formally to the type of the hymn, though exhibiting peculiarities in content. The fact that portions of hymns are to be found also in other types of psalm, together with the later designation of all the psalms as *t^ehillīm* (= hymns), proves that the hymns occupied a pre-eminent place and were of supreme importance. But at the same time these facts also show that the study of the types of psalm is not by itself sufficient for a thorough investigation of the nature of the psalms.

As a rule the following pattern underlies the formal structure of the hymns: they begin with a call (sometimes addressed by the psalmist to himself) to sing the praise of Yahweh; this is followed by actual praise of God, the form of predication being used (attributes, participles, relative clauses, or sentences giving the ground of praise and beginning with the conjunction 'for'); here the nature and providential rule of God are adored or described and occasionally the worshipper's own relationship to God is also professed and defined; the conclusion often leads back to the beginning. It is characteristic of the Old Testament that in its hymns there only very rarely occurs the supplication which is customarily added in Babylonian and Egyptian hymns and there, especially in connection with conjurations, reduces the hymn to mere grasping at favours. The hymn, like most of the psalm types, has its origin in the cultus. Allusions to the sanctuary, where Yahweh's presence in the midst of the congregation is extolled (e.g. Pss. 100.2, 4; 96.8 f., 13), the mention of festive processions, dancing and music, which accompany the singing of the hymns (Pss. 33.2 f.; 68.25 f.; 98.4 ff.; 118.20, 27; 150), and direct reference to the order of the feast (Ps. 81.1 ff.) and to the prescribed custom of pilgrimage (Ps. 122.1 ff., 4), make clear beyond any doubt that, as in the religions of neighbouring nations, so also in Old Testament religion, the hymn and the festival cult belong together (compare the designation of the ancient autumn festival at Shechem as *Hillūlīm*, Judg. 9.27; cf. Lev. 19.24). In spite of all the formal affinity of the Old Testament hymns with ancient oriental prototypes (compare, e.g., the phrase 'Who is like thee, O Lord, among the gods?' in Ex. 15.11; I Sam. 2.2; Pss. 18.31; 35.10; 71.19; 77.13 and frequently, which has its parallels in Sumerian-Accadian and Babylonian hymnology), nevertheless, it cannot be shown that foreign hymns have simply been incorporated in the Old Testament (an attempt has been made to regard Psalm 19 as a hymn originally composed to the praise of the sun and Psalm 29 as a song formerly praising Hadad, the Palestinian-Syrian storm god), let alone that a whole festival ritual has been adopted by the Old Testament religion and its cultic poetry, as is suggested by Mowinckel in respect of the 'Enthronement Festival' and by the Swedish school in respect of the royal ritual of the Near East. It is not the borrowed forms which are the primary and determining factor of the Old Testament psalms, but their contents, rooted as they are in genuinely Israelite tradition, though foreign forms were also used as their vehicles. And just as little of the nature of Christian festivals can be understood from the previous contents of the forms they borrowed from pagan festivals, so the original cultic associations of the points of affinity with foreign forms which can be traced in the Psalter give as little information about the nature of the Israelite festival cult and its liturgical poetry. It is not possible to derive a true picture of the Old Testament psalms solely from their formal affinity with the cultic poetry of the Near East.

Since the tradition of the hymn in praise of Yahweh goes back to an early date in Israel's history and already at an early stage exhibited the fundamental elements characteristic of the cult of the Covenant, we have to go back to the earliest form of Israel's festival cult in order to find the place where the hymn was first used, that is, we have to turn to the Covenant Festival as it used to be celebrated by the sacral confederacy of the tribes. It was the cultic duty of the cult community 'Israel', a duty which according to tradition had been instituted by Yahweh himself (e.g. Pss. 40.7; 114.4; 105.8; 122.4; 135.13; cf. 33.1), to celebrate the 'memorial' of the establishment of the Covenant in an unbroken cultic tradition which was meant to be passed on 'from generation to generation'. This explains the psalms' continually recurring concern that the praise of God and of his saving deeds 'may last for ever', a feature which is in no way to be regarded as a poetical exaggeration (e.g. Pss. 34.1; 35.28; 44.8; 61.8; 63.4; 71.6; 75.9; 79.13; 102.12; 111.10; 115.18; 145.2). The 'everlasting hymn', the tradition of the continual singing of hymns, shows itself to be an essential ingredient of the Yahwistic festival, itself a cultic rite and part of the actualization of divine salvation at which the celebration of the feast arises. For the cult community as a whole, or one of its members, bears witness in the hymn to what they have experienced at first hand during the sacral proceedings of the cult, and in this way contribute on their part to the realization, representation and appropriation of the salvation which is continually manifested afresh in the celebration of the feast. There is a fundamental difference between the festival ritual of the Near East and Canaan on the one hand and the Old Testament hymn on the other. Whereas in the cultic drama of the former the myth performed is of the destiny of the god (typified and experienced at first hand in the royal ritual by the king as the god's representative), the heart of the Old Testament hymn is the *self-revelation* of Yahweh in his theophany.

There Yahweh's majesty (*kābōd*) is manifested; there his nature (his name and his saving deeds) and his will (precepts) are made known. There, in short, is that cultic actualization and representation of Yahweh's redemptive work which was the cause and theme of the festival tradition in the tribal confederacy. The relation of the Old Testament hymn to the cultus as 'representative' action is disclosed by the fact that in speaking of the redemptive work of Yahweh it changes the tenses in a remarkable way (albeit one for the most part too little remarked)—the perfect tense is used for an action that is already concluded; the imperfect tense for an action that is still of actual significance at the given time; there is also the evidence already mentioned that those who took part in the cult acted as eye-witnesses as well as auricular witnesses of the historical tradition (Pss. 44.1; 46.8; 48.8; 66.5; 78.3 ff.; 81.7 ff.; 95.7 ff.; 114). It is here that we find the key to the understanding of the Old Testament hymn. It is that cultic rite by means of which the congregation 'co-operates' in the divine dispensation of salvation; again, it is man's response which presupposes the *actio Dei* as a sacramental cultic event and appropriates the salvation which is offered by God in that action. The two terms most frequently used for the hymn in the Old Testament—*t*ʰ*hillā* = praise (of God) and *tōdā* = testimony—express the same thought. The hymn is a reflex, an echo; it is the Amen of the congregation following the divine self-revelation; this aspect is seen in such congregational responses as 'Amen' and 'Hallelujah' (I Chron. 16.36; the latter also in some of the psalms: Hallelujah psalms 106; 111–113; 146; 148; 150). That we have to see in the

Hallelujah the original form of the hymn (Gunkel) cannot, however, be proved and is both formally and objectively improbable. In the Old Testament cultus God's revelation and the hymn as its human correlate belong together like the two shells of a mussel. A double function devolves upon the hymn, as can still be recognized in the stylistic form used in this psalm type: in the form of prayer (invocation of Yahweh) it is a *testimony to God*, reflecting back to the divine Giver the saving energies which have been received from him (compare the familiar hymnic phrase 'blessed be Yahweh'; Pss. 18.46; 28.6; 31.21; 41.13; 66.20; 68.19, 35; 72.18 f.; 89.52; 106.48; 113.2; 124.6; 135.21), and thus serves the purpose of 'praising God more and more' (Ps. 71.14) and of activating by way of a mutually effective dialogue the abundance of his strength and saving power.[1] Secondly, in its descriptive, narrative form the hymn signifies the active collaboration of the congregation with God in spreading the knowledge of him, the *'proclamation'* of his revelation to the cult community and to the world; it has as its object the carrying on and the keeping alive of the cultic tradition of God's redemptive work. The hymn belongs to that part of the cultic act in which man has a share; it presupposes the festival ritual, the *actio Dei*, but was not intended to replace it at any point. Ps. 147.7: 'Answer Yahweh with a testimony' still conveys a clear understanding of the fact that testimony to Yahweh in the hymn has this character of a response. With this in mind we shall come to understand the form and content of the hymn, which, even when it speaks in more detail of the cultic proceedings and of the themes dealt with in the cult (of the theophany in Pss. 18.7 ff.; 97.2 ff., and of the *Heilsgeschichte* in Pss. 105; 135; 136), only refers back to what is already known and taken for granted, and for the most part only hints at it by means of brief allusions. This feature creates expository difficulties in so far as it prevents us from a clear recognition of the actual form of the festival ritual and, in consequence, makes it impossible for us to assign to the individual psalms their definite place in the order of the ceremony during the various festival days.[2] Nevertheless the portions of the Psalter which belong to the 'hymn' type contain a sufficient number of these allusions to the cultic tradition presupposed in them for us to recognize in them without difficulty the fundamental elements of the cult of the Covenant Festival; they also suggest that the place from which the hymn

---

[1] Cf. Ps. 68.34; Deut. 32.3.
[2] Cf. in this connection Mowinckel, *Religion und Kultus*, p. 112.

in praise of Yahweh has taken its rise is to be found in the feast of Yahweh's Covenant. In Ps. 50.14 hymnic testimony is clearly a legitimate ingredient of the Covenant Festival and is distinctly marked off from the sacrifice. Hence it is not possible to contend, as Gunkel does, that the hymn is the word which accompanies the sacrifice, so much the more so as nothing whatsoever can be found in the psalms which would give support to this point of view. Again, the *representations of the theophany*, which are preserved in Pss. 50.2 ff.; 68.1 ff.; 18.7–15 (cf. Ps. 29.3 ff.) in the form of a hymnic description and in Ps. 77.16 ff. in the form of prayer, point to the tradition of the cult of the Covenant Festival. That we are here dealing with a tradition which is cast into a rigid mould and whose existence is taken for granted is demonstrated by the fact that all these hymnic descriptions of the theophany have preserved with a conservative tenacity the archaic mythological forms and ideas of the Sinai theophany in which they originate (this is true even of such a psalm as Psalm 50, which attacks the attempt to reduce the idea of God to the level of man's material way of thinking!). It is further demonstrated by the fact that the reference to the theophany in Psalms 18 and 77 cannot be derived from the train of thought exhibited by the psalm itself. This tradition can be established in Psalms 50 and 97; in the other psalms it was in all probability the act of self-revelation of Yahweh in his theophany which was a constituent part of the cult of the Covenant Festival and was presupposed as having taken place there.[1]

The connection between the hymn and the theophany is also suggested by Ps. 22.3 where, in a striking image deliberately modelled on the expression 'who sits enthroned upon the cherubim' (Ps. 99.1; cf. Ps. 80.1), which is associated with the epiphany of Yahweh above the sacred Ark, 'the Holy One of Jacob' is spoken of as he 'who is enthroned on the praises of Israel'. It goes without saying that an 'eschatological' understanding of the theophany is out of the question in this context. In view of the fact that the theophany occupies a place of central importance in the cult of the feast of Yahweh it is not surprising that it has left other traces of hymnic echoes in the psalms. Fashioned after the model of Num. 10.35, the *'appearance' of Yahweh* in the *cloud* above the *Ark*, in other words his advent in the course of the cult, is in Ps. 68.1 ff., 17, 24, 33 the object of his glorification in a hymn of praise (also in Pss. 47.5, 8; 48.3; 96.13; 98.8 f.;

[1] Cf. A. Weiser, *Festschrift für Alfred Bertholet*, pp. 513 ff.

104.3 f.; 113.4 ff.); in fact *the presence of Yahweh in the sanctuary*, his
'nearness' and the revelation of his power and glory (*kābōd*) in
connection with his theophany are altogether quite generally and
frequently the occasion for a hymn and shape its content (Pss.
11.4; 16.11; 65.4; 89.15; 96.6, 13; 98.8 f.; 100.2; 105.3 f.; 113.6).
In this connection the *face of Yahweh* is spoken of in the same way
as in the liturgical portions of the Psalter (Pss. 16.1; 33.13, 18;
68.2 f.; 85.13; 96.6, 9; 97.3, 5, etc.); hence it is not possible to dispose
of the phrases in question by describing them as mere figures of
speech which had lost their former strength of meaning without
paying attention both to the concrete ideas that form their content
and to their cultic background. In a similar way this is true also of
the numerous cases in which the *name of Yahweh* is glorified in a
hymn (Pss. 8.1, 9; 22.22; 29.2; 33.21; 48.10; 66.2; 68.4; 76.1; 99.3;
100.4; 106.47; 111.9; 113.1 f.; 135.1, 3, 13; 145.1, 2, 21; 148.13, etc.).
It is evident from the context that the hymnic predication of the name
of God belongs to those brief allusions (see above) which are really
part and parcel of the language of the hymn; this is so on the analogy
of that material in the hymns which is summarized in formulas like
'grace and faithfulness', 'righteousness' and such-like (Pss. 25.10;
36.5 ff.; 40.10 f.; 48.9 f.; 57.10; 92.2; 98.2 f.; 100.5; 103.6, 17; 31.7;
59.16; 89.1, 5, 14; 7.17; 11.7; 22.31; 35.28; 71.15 f., 19, 24; 97.6;
145.7, 17, etc.). By means of these allusions the entire process of the
self-revelation of the divine nature and will, which they presuppose
and indicate, is thought of as a present event. They are *abbreviations*
of the liturgical-theological language of the cultus, embracing by
means of *one* single notion all the saving events which have previously
come to pass in the sacramental cultic act and which, in and through
that act, have become again a living reality. The same effect is
achieved when occasionally one of the fundamental *statements in the
cultic narrative of the original revelation* of Yahweh at Sinai is directly
incorporated in the hymn, as has been done in Pss. 86.15; 103.8;
111.4; 145.8: 'The Lord is gracious and merciful, slow to anger and
abounding in lovingkindness and faithfulness' (cf. Ex. 34.6). The
custom, attested for the cult of the Covenant Festival, of testifying to
the name of Yahweh (Ps. 122.4: 'for it is decreed for Israel to testify
to the name of the Lord'), of singing praises to his name (Pss. 18.49;
44.8; 52.9; 54.6; 68.4; 74.21; 89.16; 92.1; 97.12; 99.3; 103.1; 105.1;
113.2; 149.3) and of 'knowing' his name (Ps. 9.10; cf. Pss. 46.10;
67.2; 100.3; 145.12), as well as the striking part played by the name

of Yahweh precisely in the hymns—these become fully understandable only if we take into account that in the cult of the Covenant the
proclamation of the name of Yahweh not only signified the manifestation of the divine nature but also Yahweh's action of laying claim
to the people of Israel and of electing them to be the 'people of
Yahweh' (Num. 6.27; see above). Hence the praising of the name of
God in the hymnic response of the congregation signifies not simply
a hymnic reaction to the revelation of the name of Yahweh, but
symbolizes at the same time the *affirmation by the people of God of their
faithfulness* to their God, which alone is able to render possible the
renewal of the Covenant (e.g. Ps. 80.18). In contrast with Egyptian
and Babylonian hymns, where the various names of the gods are
placed together in a manner which is often wearisome, and piled up
in an arbitrary fashion which precludes the recognition of any meaningful connection between them, the momentous significance and
theological profundity of the use of the name of God, in the context
of the Old Testament cult of the Covenant and its ideology, stand out
when that name is made the object of hymnic testimony in the
psalms.

The difference between the psalms and their hymnic parallels in
the religions of the neighbouring countries becomes even more
striking when we consider the *Heilsgeschichte* which forms the subject-
matter of the psalms. The manifestation of the nature of Yahweh,
which takes place in the cultic recital of the *tradition of the Heilsgeschichte* and is reflected in the Old Testament hymns, gives them an
independent and unmistakably Israelite character (Pss. 9.14; 40.9 f.;
44.1 ff.; 47.3 f.; 48.13, cf. v. 3; 66.5 ff.; 71.16 ff.; 75.1; 76.4 ff.;
77.16 ff.; 78.3 ff.; 98.1 ff.; 99.4 ff.; 105; 106.2 ff.; 107.32 ff.; 111.6;
135; 136; 145.6). In this connection the Exodus from Egypt, the
deliverance at the Red Sea, the migration through the wilderness and
the conquest of the land are more or less distinctly and fully referred
to as the earliest principal items of the tradition of the *Heilsgeschichte*.
The history of the patriarchs is less frequently mentioned, presumably
because it was only secondarily associated with the Mosaic tradition
(e.g. in Ps. 105) and had not achieved the same importance in the
pre-exilic cult of the Covenant. Though its outline is modelled to a
large extent on the tradition of the Hexateuch (see above), the
presentation of the *Heilsgeschichte* in the psalms, as can be inferred
from particular variations from its prototype (especially in Pss.
105; 106; 135; 136), is not to be regarded as being merely a repetition

of a story recorded elsewhere (this point in opposition to Gunkel),
let alone as a written extract from the story as told by the Hexateuch.
On the contrary, even in its more detailed representations it has
preserved the character of an allusion to the oral recitation of the
Heilsgeschichte which is assumed to have previously taken place in the
cult. The 'narrating' of the mighty acts of Yahweh in the presence of
the congregation was felt to be a cultic duty and necessity, and that
not only in connection with the hymns but also with regard to the
making of vows and the singing of thanksgivings (see below). Again,
as is shown by the change of tenses (see above and especially Ps.
93.3), it follows from the fact that the *Heilsgeschichte* was experienced
as a present living reality that the same twofold significance is
attached to the hymn as has already been discussed—that it is simultaneously a *testimony borne in the presence of God and a 'proclamation' in
the presence of the congregation.*

The praise of Yahweh as the *Creator* does not occur in the hymn to
the same extent as the saving deeds of Yahweh; but occasionally it is
connected with the latter (Pss. 8; 19; 24.1 ff.; 33.6 ff.; 65.6 f.; 95.4 ff.;
102.25; 104; 135.6 ff.; 136.5 ff.; 146.6 ff.). This suggests, as has
already been established by other considerations, that the idea of
creation was borrowed from the nature religions of the Near East and
only subsequently grafted upon the tradition of the Yahweh cult. On
the strength of the Old Testament evidence it cannot be maintained,
as is done by Mowinckel, Bentzen and others, that just as in the ritual
of the religions of the neighbouring countries so also in the feast of
Yahweh the creation has become the dominating theme of the myth
enacted in the cult and has determined the fundamental character of
that feast. In fact, as an independent theme of the hymn the idea of
creation is to be found only in Psalms 19 and 104, and both of them
are hymns which seem to have modelled their subject-matter after
foreign patterns. For the rest this idea is everywhere closely bound
up with the tradition of the *Heilsgeschichte* as cultivated in the cult of
the Covenant, and it is from this tradition that it receives its special
significance in the psalms—as substantiating and emphasizing the
power of Yahweh as the Lord of history. The borrowing of particular
mythological themes from the creation-myth of the ritual of the
Near East, such as the combat of the gods against the powers of
chaos, is likewise in keeping with this method of linking up Nature
with history; the fact that in the psalms that myth has either been
'demythologized' (Pss. 29.3, 10; 46.3; 65.7; 93.3 f.; 98.7; 104.7) or

historicized and used in a metaphorical sense to depict the conquest
of the historical enemies of Yahweh and Israel (Pss. 74.12 f.; 89.9 f.;
118.10 ff.) reveals not only the anti-mythological tendency of the
Yahweh cult but also the vital power of absorption inherent in the
Yahweh religion which, starting from its own tradition of history
(*Heilsgeschichte*), mastered the foreign material and made it serve that
tradition.

It is from the viewpoint of that anti-mythological tendency, which
from the very first was an essential feature of the tradition of the
Covenant and its cult and was firmly established in them, that we
must understand, too, the peculiar form of the *dissociation from the
foreign gods* as representing an integral part of the cult and of the
hymn in which that ritual is reflected. This took the form of the
mocking of the gods and in that form occurs only in the Israelite hymn
(Pss. 96.4 f.; 115.4 ff.; 135.15 ff.). In it the differentiation between
Yahweh and the other gods assumed various forms, such as Yahweh's
judgment on the gods (Pss. 58; 82) or the reinterpretation of the
formula used in hymns 'Who is like thee amongst the gods?', which
also occurs in Babylonian hymns, giving that formula a fresh meaning
(Ex. 15.11; I Sam. 2.2; Pss. 18.31; 35.10; 71.19; 77.13; 86.8; 89.6,
8; 113.5; 135.5), or the idea of the homage paid by the other gods,
who are reduced to the rank of members of Yahweh's celestial court
and are joined, as they sing the hymn, to the glory of Yahweh, by the
whole 'host of heaven' (Isa. 6.1 ff.; Pss. 19.1; 29.1 f.; 69.34; 89.5;
96.11; 97.6; 148.1 ff.). As the *renunciation of the gods* was a constituent
part of the ritual of the covenant cult (see above), so the dissociation
from the deities and their worshippers in the hymnic testimonies is in
keeping with that repudiation of foreign gods. They are the prerequisite, and as it were the negative aspect, of the affirmation of
faithfulness to Yahweh that is made in the covenantal act of worship.
Thus they, too, are understandable in the context of the renewal of
the Covenant, just as the traditional call to the singing of a hymn
('Sing to Yahweh a new song!'—Pss. 33.3; 40.3; 96.1; 98.1; 144.9;
149.1) is probably related to the *renewal* of the Covenant (or rather,
the renewal of salvation) that comes to pass in the course of the cultic
proceedings.[1] Hence there is no need for Gunkel's assumption of a
prophetic influence to explain the opposition to the foreign gods
which is expressed in the hymns. In this connection the Yahweh
religion assimilated and absorbed foreign themes which were in-

[1] Cf. also Ps. 102.18: 'a people that has been reborn'.

corporated in the Old Testament hymn to suit its own requirements, and so gave them, in contrast to their original character, a new emphasis and significance.

This is true also of the idea of the *kingship of Yahweh* as this is represented in the festival cult and in its hymnic tradition. That idea has found its specific expression in the so-called 'Enthronement Psalms' (Pss. 47; 93; 96–99) which from the point of view of Form-Criticism do not represent a separate psalm type, but are to be classed with the hymn. The hypothesis of a separate Enthronement Festival of Yahweh, to which Mowinckel wants to assign these psalms as well as a number of others, is disproved by the fact that such a festival is nowhere mentioned in the Old Testament. We shall therefore have to modify Mowinckel's thesis in the sense that the enthronement of Yahweh did not form the subject of a separate festival but was a portion of the liturgy of the feast of the renewal of the Covenant of Yahweh; in other words, that it was, so to speak, a single scene within the whole drama of the cult.[1] It cannot claim the all-surpassing importance which Mowinckel and others attribute to it and is not influenced by the ancient oriental royal ritual and the tradition of the New Year Festival to the extent that these scholars assume. In the psalms the enthronement of Yahweh was linked up with his theophany above the Ark, part of the tradition of the Covenant Festival and, in contrast to the royal ritual outside Israel, was thereby moulded into a form of its own and acquired its own peculiar meaning; moreover, this had a determining influence on individual elements borrowed from such ritual. The fact that the idea of Yahweh's kingship is to be found also in psalms which are not related to the act of enthronement (Pss. 5.2; 8.1; 10.16; 24.8 ff.; 22.28; 44.4; 48.2; 59.13; 66.7; 68.24; 74.12; 84.3; 103.19; 114.2; 145.1; 146.10; 149.2; Ex. 15.18) likewise refutes the thesis of a separate Enthronement Festival, since the idea of the kingship of Yahweh, as can be judged from the other Old Testament evidence, seems to have taken shape at an earlier period and to have had a more far-reaching influence than did the ancient oriental royal ritual on the evolution of details in Israel's Covenant Festival. It is probable that stronger influences in the latter direction operated first in the time of David

---

[1] In the meantime Mowinckel has given to his thesis of the Feast of the Enthronement of Yahweh a restricted meaning which tends in a similar direction (*The Psalms in Israel's Worship* I, p. 115; *Religion und Kultus*, p. 76); cf., however, also Diethelm Michel's criticism, rejecting Mowinckel's thesis, in 'Studien zu den sogenannten Thronbesteigungspsalmen', *VT* 6, 1956, pp. 40–68.

and, more especially, of Solomon, when the political, economic and cultural relations with foreign countries had opened wide the gate to the world surrounding Israel and, as can still be gathered from the remaining literature, the kingship had developed in the direction of oriental despotism.

It may well be that in the course of that development the *feast of the enthronement of the earthly king*, which had been embodied in the cult of Yahweh, influenced the pattern of the Covenant Festival at the Jerusalem Temple, and did so in particular by the courtly ways it borrowed from oriental royal ritual. So, too, it firmly established and strengthéned the position of the king in the cult, partly by adopting foreign ideas such as his divine sonship (Pss. 2.7; 45.7; 89.26), the royal priesthood (Ps. 110), the election of David and of his dynasty (Pss. 78.70 ff.; 89.19 ff.), the 'grace of kingship' and the king's dominion over the nations (Pss. 2; 18; 20.9; 45.5; 72; 110; 144.10) and the intercession for the king (Pss. 72.15; 84.9; 89.50; 132.10; I Sam. 2.10). With the extension of the cultic tradition of the tribal confederacy through the embodiment of the royal tradition, there was also associated the coming into existence of the so-called *Royal Psalms* 2; 18; 20; 21; 72; 89; 101; 110; 132 and 144 (see above; as to the relation of the Royal Psalms to the cult of the Covenant compare, e.g., Ps. 72.19 with Isa. 6.3). Though the king is God's viceregent on earth, he is shown in these psalms to be pledged to constant obedience to the order of the Covenant of Yahweh and to having to give account of himself in that respect to God (Pss. 18. 20 ff.; 72.2; 101; 89.30 ff.; 45.7—even though this last is a festival song of a more profane nature, composed for the occasion of the king's marriage!). This fact, in keeping with the differentiation between God and man peculiar to the Old Testament as a whole, throws into bold relief the fundamental difference between the Royal Psalms of the Old Testament and the position held by the king in the royal ritual of the Near East. In this latter the god-king vicariously suffers and 'typifies' in a sacral act the cultic myth of the dying and rising god. The Israelite king, on the other hand, remains even in his sacral capacity a member of the community which he represents and personifies before Yahweh in the cult.[1]

---

[1] Cf. Mowinckel, *The Psalms in Israel's Worship* I, p. 46. It remains, however, an open question whether and to what extent in this connection the 'I' of certain psalms has to be interpreted in the sense of the hypothesis of Smend and others, that is, in a collective sense (Mowinckel, op. cit., pp. 42, 77 f., 225 ff.).

In the Old Testament hymns the *glorification of Yahweh as Judge* occurs more frequently than the ideas of Yahweh as Creator or King, which are occasionally associated with it (Pss. 95.5 ff.; 96.10, 13; 97.2, 8; 98.2, 8 f.; 99.4), and often appears to be the very theme of the hymn. This proves that we are here dealing with a subject whose links with the ancient covenant tradition are stronger, because they are more primitive (see above), the tradition of the Covenant having preserved its dominating superiority over the elements that intruded at a later date (Pss. 9.7 f.; 18.25 f.; 31.23; 33.5; 36.6, 12; 48.11; 65.3; 66.8 ff.; 67.4 f.; 68.2 f.; 76.8 ff.; 78; 89.14; 92.15; 96.10, 13; 97.2, 6; 98.8 f.; 103.6; 105.7; 122.5; 135.14; 145.20; 147.19; cf. 149.9). The striking fact that the judgment of Yahweh is the object of praise is explained, on the one hand, by the bond that ties the hymn to the cultic tradition of the feast of Yahweh and, on the other hand, by the ambivalent character of the Israelite notion of judgment, implying as it did the realization of their salvation for loyal covenanters in the Yahweh community but exclusion from salvation for the apostates, and destruction for the ungodly enemies of Yahweh and of Israel. The hymn in praise of the Law in Ps. 19.7 ff. and in Psalm 119, both of them being interspersed with 'lament' themes, Psalm 119 also with some from other psalm types, can similarly be traced back to its ultimate roots in the manifestation of Yahweh's will in the tradition of the cult of the Covenant (cf. Ps. 147.19 f.), even though a direct connection with the celebration of the cult cannot be proved. The votive formula at the end of Psalm 19 might nevertheless indicate, on the analogy of the laments and the thanksgivings (see below), a direct use of these hymns in the cult. That the hymns in praise of the Law can be accounted for only by the spirit that was dominant in scribal circles in the period between the Testaments is a postulate that cannot be proved.

From the point of view of their nature and subject-matter the Old Testament hymns in praise of Yahweh fit the context of the cultic tradition of the Covenant of Yahweh, so that the feast of the Covenant of Yahweh can be regarded as the original source of the tradition of the hymns in the psalms and the place where it was encouraged. Taking everything into consideration, the Old Testament hymn has, in spite of its manifold associations with ancient oriental hymnology, a character of its own formed by the religious content of the cult of the Covenant. The heart of that cult is the action of God, who manifests himself in the self-revelation of his

nature and will, who asserts himself by the execution of his judgment and the realization of his salvation, and who lays his people
under the obligation of faithfulness and obedience. This theocentric character of the covenant cult divests the hymn of its
originally independent significance according to which the power
inherent in the word brought about the strengthening of the power
of the deity and the actualization and renewal of the things which
were the object of praise. It is true that in the Old Testament, too,
the hymn serves the purpose of making God and his salvation a
present living reality in and through the cultic act. However, it
springs no longer from man's magic self-assurance in relation to the
Godhead, but is inspired by man's devoted enthusiasm and his
reverential adoration and humble worship of God—and it flows back
to the fountain which fed it. It testifies to the unbroken vitality,
dissociated from every egocentric way of thinking, of a faith ready to
profess God and entirely absorbed in him that the hymns extol in the
Psalter the 'glory' of God, his power and greatness in creation,
history and judgment, and that, in the Old Testament, supplications,
which are frequently added to the hymn in Babylonian prayers,
almost entirely recede into the background. The stereotyped forms
of hymnology have been filled with personal life and lifted to a higher
plane by that living faith in God. Psalm 103 shows what a wealth of
delicate tones profound individual piety, knowing itself to be made
a co-worker with God in his redemptive work, was able to weave into
the fabric of the hymn. The belief in Yahweh's sublimity (holiness)
far above the world, which right from the outset made it impossible
to involve God in the natural phenomena or in the course taken by
history, let alone to identify him with them, and the vital power of
absorption inherent in that belief provided scope for the extension of
the sphere of his reign in a universal and eschatological sense. This
could be done by appropriating the forms and contents of alien ideas,
but in such a way that the fundamental character of the idea of God
was unaffected thereby. The sovereignty of Yahweh and the unbridgeable distance between God and man were maintained even in
the royal cult in which the position of the earthly ruler was more
closely adapted to that of the Godhead through the taking over of
foreign patterns; and this result was achieved in the light of the idea
of the kingship of Yahweh and on the strength of the moral and
religious responsibility of the earthly ruler according to which he in
his capacity as a human being remained subject to the will of

Yahweh. The power and fame of the earthly sovereign, as the Royal
Psalms show, is therefore overshadowed by the majesty of Yahweh
who is the King of heaven.

(b) LAMENTS

The psalm type which numerically occurs most frequently in the
Psalter is that of the *lament*. For these we possess numerous parallels,
especially in Babylonian literature. Nearly a third of all the psalms
are to be classed as this type.[1] The laments within the Psalter are to
be distinguished from the dirge, which did not achieve a spiritual
relationship with the Yahweh religion in Israel and always remained
a profane type of song (cf. the two dirges of David on Saul and
Jonathan in II Sam. 1.17 ff. and on Abner in II Sam. 3.33 f.; and
with them Amos 5.1 f.). According to the person of the speaker, the
laments are classified as follows: *community laments* (Pss. 44; 74;
79; 80; 83 (90); 137; Lam. 5) and personal *laments of an individual*
(Pss. 3; 5; 7; 13; 17; 22; 25; 26; 27; 31; 35; 38; 39; 42 f.; 51; 55;
57; 59; 77; 88; 123; 140; 141; 142; 143; Lam. 3). However, themes
of the lament are also frequently found intermingled with other
psalm types (liturgies); thus themes from the lament of the community appear in Pss. 21.1 ff.; 33.20 ff.; 60.1 ff., 9 ff.; 68.28 ff.;
85.4 ff.; 89.38 ff.; 90.13 ff.; 123.3 f.; 126.4 ff.; 129.4 ff. It may be
assumed that the intercessions for the king (Pss. 20.1 ff.; 28.8 f.; 61.
6 f.; 63.11; 72; 84.8 f.; I Sam. 2.10) can likewise be classed with the
themes proper to community laments. On the other hand, the royal
lament (Ps. 144), contrary to Gunkel's view, is to be regarded as an
individual lament. The individual lament, too, is frequently mixed
with other types, especially with the thanksgiving, which is of a
kindred type as far as its subject-matter is concerned (Pss. 6; 13;
22; 28; 30; 31; 41; 54; 56; 61; 63; 64; 69; 71; 86; 94; 102; 120; 130),
with the hymn (Pss. 19.12 ff.; 104.31 ff.; 139.23 f.) and with liturgies
(Pss. 36.1 ff.; 77.1 ff.; 118.25, etc.). This indicates that here, too, a
true understanding follows only from an exegesis which simultaneously takes into account both the formal stylization and the practical
use of the psalms. Thus the *psalms of confidence*, which are an independent product of Old Testament religion and in view of the
absence of any parallel outside Israel throw a significant light on the

[1] Cf. Westermann, *ZAW* 66, 1954, pp. 44 ff., on the structure and history of the
lament.

creative power and independence of Israel's own religious poetry, are by virtue of the character of a testimony peculiar to them akin to the lament on the one hand and, on the other, to the thanksgiving, both formally and with regard to their subject-matter (Pss. 4; 11; 16; 23; 27.1–6; 62; 131). Nevertheless they are to be regarded as a 'type' which has a specific character of its own. The conjecture that the original name of the lament of an individual was *t^epillā* (thus Gunkel) which in default of 'exact conceptual thinking' was later applied to related types, is scarcely defensible; probably the term *t^epillā* has frequently, but not exclusively, been applied to individual laments in the sense of a 'supplication' or 'prayer' (cf. Ps. 72.20) because the prayer (of supplication) occupied a dominant place in them.

In their *formal structure* both community and individual laments are mostly composed of the following constituent parts: invocation; lamentation; supplication; motivation; vow. The sequence of these several items is not everywhere the same nor is it everywhere complete. In accordance with the various afflictions of a material or spiritual kind which presented the occasion for the laments and fashioned their content—be they a common calamity such as bad harvests, dearth, epidemics, wars or enemies, or disease, persecution, mockery, doubt and the burden of sin such as the individual has to suffer—it is a many-coloured picture of public and private life into which the laments provide an insight. And yet only very rarely is it possible to grasp distinctly the external historical or personal circumstances which form the background of these psalms, lacking as they do for the most part the necessary concrete details.[1] The similarity of the phrases used in these psalms, phrases which are couched in general terms and often give the impression of being stereotyped (and for that reason often have a wearisome effect in spite of all the inward life with which they are filled), can probably be traced back to the fact that the laments originated and were used in the cult, where the general predominates over the particular.

Community laments. In view of the Old Testament evidence there can be no doubt about the connection of the community lament with the worship of the sanctuary (cf. Josh. 7.6; Judg. 20.23, 26 ff.; I Sam. 7.6; I Kings 8.33 f.). Joel 1.1 ff. mentions a special service of

---

[1] The attempt made by Bonkamp to assign the psalms of individuals for the most part to the era of King Josiah fails to offer any conclusive reasons and does not carry conviction.

lamentation on the occasion of a plague of locusts and a drought
when the whole community was called upon to sing a lament in the
house of God and to observe various rites such as fasting, rending of
clothes and girding with sackcloth. Again, we may think of such a
special service of lamentation (perhaps after the catastrophe of 587
BC) in connection with Psalms 74 and 79, where the destruction and
desecration of the Temple by pagan enemies is the subject of the
people's lament. In Psalm 80, where the tribes of Joseph are mentioned
and the theophany of Yahweh above the Ark is awaited (vv. 1 f., 3,
7, 19), it is probably a question of the Covenant Festival at the
central shrine of the tribal confederacy as this was celebrated in the
time before 721 BC. Psalms 44; 83 and 106, which presuppose the
recital of the tradition of the *Heilsgeschichte* in a cultic act (Pss. 44,
1 ff.; 83.6 ff.; 106, 6 ff.; cf. the allusion in Ps. 44.23 to the theophany
which is expected to take place), are likewise to be understood in
the light of their connection with the Covenant Festival as celebrated
in pre-exilic times (this contrary to the usual late dating of these
psalms); the ideology of this festival lingers on, too, in Psalms 74 and
79. The festival where the renewal of the divine salvation was celebrated by the cultic representation and actualization of Yahweh's
saving deeds and was dependent on the testimony of the covenant
people to their God, their pledging themselves to him—this festival,
the Covenant Festival, provided in times of trouble just the setting for
community lament with its affirmation of faithfulness (Pss. 44.8, 20 f.;
80.18) and its confession of sins whose forgiveness is hoped for (Pss.
106; 79.8 f.; cf. Ps. 78). For it is from the outset probable that this
was the case, even if we disregard the special allusions to particular
features of that festival; moreover, it enables us to understand for the
first time why its fundamental ideas were still able to produce the
marked effect which we can observe in Pss. 74.2 f., 12 ff.; 79.9 f., 13.
The original democratic character of the tribal confederacy is still
preserved in the community lament—so much so that, in contrast to
Babylon, even in the royal cult of the Temple of Jerusalem the people
remained the subject of the lament and uttered it, the king being the
object of the congregation's intercessions (Pss. 89.46 ff.; 72; cf. Pss.
28.8 f.; 61.6 f.; 84.8 f.; I Sam. 2.10) unless he utters his lament
directly as an individual (Ps. 144).

Lament of an individual. This, too, had its place originally in the
cult. This conclusion is to be drawn not only from the analogy to
Babylonian psalms of lamentation but also from the occasional

mention of the sanctuary and of the votive offering (e.g. Pss. 5.3, 7; 28.2; Jer. 17.12 f.), from the fact that in most cases the vow pre-supposes the presence of the congregation (Pss. 22.22 ff.; 26.12; 28.9; 31.23 f.; 35.27; 52.9; 109.30; 140.12 f.; 142.7) and, finally, from the custom, attested in I Sam. 1–2, of bringing one's personal concerns before God on the occasion of the pilgrim festival which was celebrated in the Temple. It also follows from I Sam. 1–2 that the annual feast of Yahweh, which the confederacy of the tribes celebrated at the shrine of the Ark, presented the specific occasion when the prayer of lamentation could be offered within the cultic setting; this is true at least of the earlier period of Israel's history. The connection of the individual lament with the cult also accounts for the fact that divers individual laments close with thought of and intercession for all 'Israel' and the king (Pss. 3.8; 25.22; 28.8; 61.6 f.; 63.11; 69.35 f.; 102.28; 130.7 f.; 131.3; I Sam. 2.10); so that there is therefore no need to regard these as a later interpolation. Finally, when in a psalm of lamentation (22) Yahweh is addressed as 'the holy one of Jacob who is enthroned on the praises of Israel', then the situation peculiar to the Covenant Festival can be recognized in this allusion to the theophany that takes place above the Ark (see above).

The superscription of Psalm 102, 'A prayer of one afflicted when he is faint and pours out his complaint before the face of Yahweh', sug-gests the view that many a psalm of lamentation served as a formulary appointed for continual use, as in Babylonia. There formularies were handed down which made provision for the name of the individual worshipper in question to be inserted (cf. the exegesis of Ps. 40.13–17). This may be one of the reasons why concrete individual features occur less frequently in the laments than formulations of a more general kind, so that the specific circumstances of the worshipper often remain obscure. Another reason for this strange fact is to be found in the significance which an individual lament has also had for the cult community as a whole. For as in the hymn, so also in the lament the form of addressing God in the second person alternates with narration in the third person; that is, the lament, too, has that twofold purpose which has already been mentioned in another con-nection: it is simultaneously *prayer* and *testimony*, the former being offered to God and the latter being intended for the congregation. The attempt to explain this change of person from a psychological point of view, by saying that the relation to God has 'got lost' when the third person is used (thus Gunkel), is disproved by the fact that

in Pss. 10.1 ff.; 44.8; 68.10 f.; 94.11 f.; 123; 125.4 f. both forms
appear side by side in a manner which makes the acceptance of such
a view impossible.

The significance of the lament in the setting of the cult community becomes apparent from its *association with the thanksgiving*, to
which it is very closely related by the situation envisaged, by the
material it presents and also by its form. Thus the customary description in the thanksgiving of the affliction from which the worshipper has been delivered has frequently been replaced by the
lament which the worshipper had once uttered in his distress, so as to
bring into prominence the magnitude of the divine saving act manifested in the hearing of the lament (e.g. Pss. 6; 13; 22; 28; 30; 31;
41; 54; 55; 56; 59; 61; 63; 64; 69; 71; 86; 94; 102; 120; 130; Jer.
20.7–13). To the ancient Israelite way of thinking the individual can
enter into a relationship with Yahweh, and can participate in the
blessings of the Covenant, only in his capacity as a member of the
covenant community. It is therefore understandable that with this
in mind the individual worshipper sees himself, the answering of his
private prayer and his personal saving experience as all included in
the general realization of the covenantal salvation in history and in
the present, which has been the theme of the cult of the Covenant
Festival, and that, conversely, the members of the covenant community on their part had an active religious interest both in finding
their belief in God's presence and saving rule confirmed by such
personal testimonies to the actual granting of divine help and in
joining the individual worshipper in his praise of Yahweh. All this
is proved by a number of laments (Pss. 22.22 f.; 35.18, 27; 43.3 f.;
52.9; 71.16 ff.; 107.32; 109.30; 116.17 f.; 140.13). It is the interest
of the religion of Israel in the tradition of Yahweh's saving deeds, a
tradition that was always kept alive in the cultus, which secured also
for the individual lament and for the individual thanksgiving their
place in the cult of the Covenant; quite consistently, this interest was
also responsible for the fact that their conclusion was either the cult
community's 'everlasting hymn' in which the saving acts of God were
extolled, or an exhortatory utterance (Pss. 5.11; 22.30 f.; 30.12;
35.27 f.; 52.9; 61.8; 63.4; 64.9 f.; 86.12; 31.23; 32.10 f.; 34.11; 41.
1 ff., 13; 51.13; 69.30 ff.; 71.6). When seen in this perspective, the fact
that the lament and the thanksgiving were firmly established in the
cult of the Covenant and the position they occupied in it, can be
compared with the votive offerings and the votive stones on which

it was customary to depict the calamity of the worshipper (who appears on votive offerings in southern Arabian temples in the form of a human being assuming the posture of prayer) and the granting of his prayer (symbolized on Egyptian stones by an ear).[1] Evidence of what has been discussed so far and at the same time of the recording in writing and probably also the handing over of the individual laments to the sanctuary is provided by Ps. 102.18: 'Let this be recorded for a generation to come, so that a people that has been reborn[2] (renewal of the Covenant?) may praise the Lord.' It is this connection and not, as has been thought hitherto, the anti-cultic attitude of the prophets which accounts for the fact that in some psalms the gift takes the form of a (votive) prayer of thanksgiving and not that of a votive sacrifice (Pss. 19.14; 40.6; 50.14, 23; 51.15 f.; 61.8; 63.5; 69.30 f.; 71.16; 141.1 f.). It may be that the rejection of sacrifices was directed against the intrusion of the Canaanite peasant religion and its rites into the cult of the Covenant—a movement which had gained momentum since the amalgamation of the royal cult with the cult of the tribes (cf. the setting up of images of calves and the association of these with the Yahweh tradition in I Kings 12.28 f. and also the polemics of Hosea against the cult of Baal and the monarchy; it can be assumed that in the Davidic kingdom the granting of citizenship to the Canaanites favoured this development, though not in the same way). Thus it is doubtful whether the thesis advanced by Gunkel and others can be maintained, according to which the hymn of sacrificial thanksgiving is said to have developed into a 'spiritual hymn of thanksgiving' entirely 'divorced from the cult'.

The presence of the cult community at the recital of the lament and its participation in the prayer of thanksgiving do not, however, mean, as has been assumed (by Olshausen, Smend, Kautzsch, Bäthgen) with reference to the allegorical interpretation of the psalms in Targum and Midrash, that the cult community has been the one and only leading subject who speaks in the individual laments and that in consequence the '*I*' *of these psalms* is to be understood in a collective sense. Jeremiah's poetical laments (Jer. 11.18 ff.; 15.15 ff.; 17. 12 ff.; 18.18 ff.; 20.7 ff.) as well as a series of personal

---

[1] Cf. Heine, *Die Wallfahrt nach Kevelaer*, and now also Mowinckel, *The Psalms in Israel's Worship* II, p. 42, and Isa. 38.9 (*miktāb l^e* . . .).

[2] *The RSV renders Ps. 102.18b as: 'so that a people yet unborn may praise the Lord'.

statements in the laments within the Psalter, distinguishing the one
who speaks from other cult members (e.g. Pss. 22.22; 27.10; 69.8;
88.8, etc.), make clear beyond doubt that the 'I' which is here
used refers to an individual person (Balla, *Das Ich der Psalmen*). But on
the other hand one must not make the mistake of expounding the
Old Testament's individual laments in a sense which would identify
them too closely with the prayer of modern, individualistic piety.[1]
Their association with the conceptions and ideology of the cult of the
Covenant Festival brings them after all into closer relationship with
the piety of the cult community and with its tradition, and for that
reason the individual laments are likewise to be understood not only
from the perspective of the personal concerns of the individual worshipper but also, at the same time, in the light of the fundamental
elements of the cult of the Covenant and its traditions. The first two
chapters of I Samuel testify to the custom of reciting the lament, and
the thanksgiving, at the feast of Yahweh which was celebrated at the
covenantal shrine; the psalm of thanksgiving in I Sam. 2.1-10, which
was composed under the monarchy, but is there put into the mouth
of Samuel's mother, reaches far beyond the personal circumstances
of the worshipper uttering this prayer and clearly shows how the fate
of an individual (v. 5) is here incorporated into the larger context of
the situation of the festival cult as a whole and is woven into the
range of ideas about creation, history, judgment and the 'grace of
kingship' which are associated with it. And when in the lament those
fundamental elements of the cult of the Covenant Festival which can
be established in the hymn recur in allusions similar to those contained in the hymn, then this phenomenon can most easily be
accounted for by the fact that the laments were originally related for
the most part to the feast of the Covenant of Yahweh and had
been recited on this occasion in the presence of the covenant
community.

The prerequisite and aim of most of the laments is encounter with
God as one who is conceived to be present, an encounter which is
mediated by Yahweh's *theophany in the cult*. Of that encounter
(*mōʿēd*) Ps. 102.13 speaks explicitly; there Yahweh appears in his
glory (v. 16) to show mercy to Zion (cf. Ps. 73.17). The lamentation
is brought 'before the face of Yahweh' (Pss. 27.8; 51.11; 88.2, 13;
142.2). The fact that God 'beholds', that he 'makes his face to shine'

---

[1] Westermann (*Das Loben Gottes in den Psalmen*) does not seem to me to have
entirely escaped that danger.

is considered as evidence that he will show mercy and answer the prayer (Pss. 4.6; 13.3; 31.16; 41.12; 56.13; 59.4 f.; 63.2; 102.19 ff., cf. v. 16; 67.1; 80.1, 3, 14; 118.27; 138. 1, 6; cf. Ps. 21.9: 'in the time of thy countenance' = when you appear). Hence prayer is offered that God may not hide his face (Pss. 10.1; 22.24; 27.9; 44.24; 55.1; 69.17 f.; 88.14; 89.46; 102.2; 143.7) and, conversely, the worshipper yearns 'to behold God's face' and to be assured of his nearness and presence (Ps. 11.7, cf. v. 4; Pss. 16.11; 17.15; 27.4, 13, cf. v. 8; 42.2; 56.13; 61.7; 63.2; 116.9; 140.13; 141.8); the phrase 'to behold the face of God' (as this phrase was originally worded) was also used as a technical term to denote the visiting of the sanctuary (Ex. 23.17; 34.23 f.; Deut. 31.11; I Sam. 1.22; Isa. 1.12, etc.; parallels to the phrase are also to be found in Assyrian literature). The phrase 'to hide in the shadow of thy wings' (Pss. 17.8; 36.7; 57.1; 61.4; 63.7; 91.4; cf. Deut. 32.11 and Pss. 31.20; 27.5) likewise refers to the presence of the God who has appeared above the wings of the cherubim on the Ark of the Covenant; its derivation from Egyptian conceptions, as Gunkel assumes, cannot be proved. The call uttered in Ps. 80.1: 'Thou who art enthroned upon the cherubim, appear!' (cf. Ps. 94.1) also has a bearing upon the matter under discussion and the same is altogether true of the frequent urgent entreaty addressed to Yahweh: 'arise' or 'rise up' or 'awake', which has its origin in the idea of the theophany as that event in the drama of the cult which will determine man's destiny, be it salvation or disaster, and which, as a cultic formula used in connection with the theophany of Yahweh above the Ark of the Covenant, dates back to the early epoch of Israel's history (cf. Num. 10.35; Pss. 3.7; 7.6; 10.12; 17.13; 35.23; 44.23, 26; 57.5, 8, 11; 59.4 f.; 80.1 f.; 82.8; 94.1 f.; 102.13). The same call is preserved in greater detail in the royal lament at Ps. 144.5 ff., showing reminiscences of Ps. 18.7 ff. and being couched in the mythological language of the tradition of the epiphany: 'Bow thy heavens, O Lord, and come down! Touch the mountains that they smoke!' There can be no doubt whatsoever that this call is connected with the ancient tradition of the theophany of Yahweh in the cult, as it cannot be derived from the train of thought exhibited in the psalm itself. And when in the laments the presence of Yahweh in the sanctuary and his nearness implies assurance of an answer to prayer and of the dispensation of salvation (Pss. 3.3 f.; 5.7; 16.11; 27.4; 41.12; 56.13; 59.4; 69.18; 73.23, 28; 102.28; 141.8; cf. the Babylonian parallel in a prayer offered to the goddess Ishtar: 'Look upon me and my prayer is answered'), then according to the ancient traditional belief it is the theophany which is the cultic centre around which these thoughts revolve, and that is true even of those psalms in which this is not explicitly noted.

As in the hymn, so also in the lament, the same phraseology is used to express the *name of Yahweh*, and here as well as there Yahweh's name is related to the revelation of the name of God in the cultic act of the theophany (see above). From Ps. 142.7, 'Bring me out of prison that I may testify to thy name! The righteous will surround me, when thou wilt deal bountifully with me,' we see that the profession of the name of God has its place above all in the making of a vow, which is linked with the cult in the sanctuary; from the worshipper's point of view it is evidently out of question that he would testify to the name of God in a situation entirely divorced from the cult (cf. Pss. 106.47; 138.2). The prayer in Ps. 54.1, 'Save me, O God, by thy name!' (cf. v. 6) and the intercession for the king in Ps. 20.1 f., 'The name of the God of Jacob make you powerful! May he . . . give you support from Zion!' (cf. vv. 6 f. and Ps. 44.5, 8 and also the doxology in Ps. 72.19, which is a parallel to Isa. 6.3; cf. Ps. 75.1: 'near is thy name'[1]) likewise point to the revelation of the name of Yahweh which takes place in connection with the theophany, assuring the worshipper of the nearness of God and his salvation and so giving him cause to praise the name of Yahweh (cf. Pss. 83.16; 86.11 f.; 92.1; 140.13).

The association of the name of Yahweh with his *saving deeds* as the revelation of the divine nature in the cult of the Covenant Festival is also reflected in the laments. The 'knowing',[2] 'professing' and 'commemorating' of the mighty acts of Yahweh is at once the earnest religious concern and the pious duty of a cultic tradition that is passed on 'from generation to generation' (Pss. 9.1 f., 14; 22.22 ff., 30 f.; 26.7; 64.9; 71.16; 73.28; 102.21); and that cultic tradition in its turn refers to the representation of the *Heilsgeschichte* in the cult (Pss. 44.1 ff.; 78.3; 111.4, 6) and is recapitulated in great detail in the comprehensive general confession of Psalm 106. For the most part, however, it is referred to only by means of brief allusions ('mighty acts, wondrous deeds, righteous acts, salvation') or the

---

[1] *RSV reads: 'we call on thy name'.

[2] Cf. Botterweck, *'Gott Erkennen' im Sprachgebrauch des Alten Testaments* (Bonner Biblische Beiträge 2, 1951, pp. 23 ff.).

content of the covenantal salvation is summarized in classic formulations such as 'grace and faithfulness' and similar phrases (Pss.
25.10; 26.3; 30.9; 36.5; 40.10 ff.; 57.3, 10; 61.7; 85.10; 86.13, 15;
88.11; 89.14, 49; 92.1 f.; 138.2, etc.; cf. in this connection the basic
text for the Exodus theophany in Ex. 34.5 f.). It is precisely by means
of such abbreviations expressed in stylized formulas (cf. Pss. 106.1;
107.1; 118.1; 136) that we are referred back to things which are
already well known; again, these abbreviations presuppose that the
revelation of the saving deeds wrought by Yahweh in history has
already taken place in a cultic act. From sentences such as 'I will
tell of *all* thy wondrous deeds' and from similar sayings, which are
not merely confined to the deliverance and saving experience of an
individual worshipper (Pss. 9.1, 14; 26.7; 40.5; 73.28; 77.11 f., etc.;
cf. Ps. 106.2), it can be concluded that Yahweh's answering of a
personal prayer and his granting to an individual worshipper of the
salvation prayed for in the psalms of lamentation and experienced
in the thanksgivings are envisaged within the wider setting of the
general salvation of the covenant people and incorporated in their
Heilsgeschichte (see above), and that in consequence the personal
affirmation of faith in God's salvation includes in many psalms also
the salvation of the whole covenant community which is realized by
means of the revelation of God in the cult. The individual worshipper
experiences his own salvation in and through the general salvation of
the covenant people actualized in the cult and is thus taught to
understand it as a part of the *Heilsgeschichte* of the Yahweh community which has once more become a living present reality (Ps.
106.4); this entails that his own testimony becomes a part of the
testimony and praise of the whole cult community (see above and
especially Pss. 69.32 ff.; 107.8, 15, 21 f., 31 ff.). Thus the fact that
saving deeds of Yahweh which are not directly related to the personal
destiny of the worshipper are mentioned in the lament and in the
thanksgiving is to be accounted for by the essential character of the
festival cult and its tradition of salvation.

The important part played in the lament by the idea of *judgment* as
Yahweh's verdict on the destiny of the worshippers, or rather, of their
adversaries, can be traced back to the same root. The multifarious
and often impetuous entreaties and calls to execute judgment
(as indeed the whole ideology of the psalms of lamentation) are
based on the assumption that Yahweh appears and sits down on
his throne to execute judgment, and thus on the assumption

that the theophany and the judgment of Yahweh are linked together in the cult (Pss. 7.6 ff.; 9.4 f., 16, 20; 10.12 ff., 18; 17.2; 35.23 f.; 36.5 ff.; 54.1; 57.5, 11; 59.4 f.; 82.8; 94.1 f.; 102.13). In the divine service the 'crisis' takes place, the divine judgment is executed, pronouncing salvation or disaster. Yahweh's 'righteousness' is revealed by his presence and by his saving deeds which by means of their representation in the cultic ritual are activated and transformed into a living reality. The fact that the *ṣᵉdāqōt* (righteous acts) of Yahweh and the saving deeds which he has wrought for the benefit of the people of God can have virtually the very same meaning (Judg. 5.11; I Sam. 12.7; Micah 6.5; Ps. 103.6) and that therefore 'salvation' is synonymous with 'righteousness' (Pss. 35.28; 36.10; 40.10; 48.10; 65.5; 71.15) does not only make evident that the idea of judgment and the genuinely Israelite tradition of the Covenant Festival are inwardly connected with each other, but at the same time makes it understandable why in the laments the participation in public worship is regarded and desired as an assurance of the nearness of God and of the worshipper's partaking of his salvation (Pss. 5.7; 17.15; 27.4, 13; 23.6; 41.12: 'thou set me before thy face'; 52.8; 56.13: 'that I may walk before God'; 61.4, 7; 65.4; 68.3; 73.23; 84.4 ff.; 102.28) whereas being debarred from his presence signifies the disaster (Ps. 51.11: 'Cast me not away from thy presence!'; Ps. 31.22) which befalls the wicked and is equivalent to his destruction (Pss. 5.4 ff., 10; 52.5; 55.23; 63.9 f.; 64.7; 68.2; 69.28; 73.17 ff.; 80.16; 125.5; 129.5 ff.; 140.9 ff.; 144.5 f.).

Admission to the actual saving event which takes place in the festival cult is therefore bound up with obedience to Yahweh's will, which is a covenantal duty (Ps. 24.6). Here the *torah* regulating admission to the cult (Pss. 15; 24.3–5) as well as the *protestation of integrity* and the *affirmation of confidence*, which have their firm place in the Psalter's lament (Pss. 5.7; 7.3 f.; 13.5, 6; 16.1 f.; 17.1, 3 f.; 18.20 f.; 22.10; 25.2 f., 15, 20 f.; 26.1, 3 ff.; 31.6, 14; 40.8 ff.; 41.12; 44.8, 17 ff.; 55.23; 56.4, 11; 59.3 f.; 66.18; 69.9; 71.6; 86.5, 8 ff.; 140.6; 142.5), have this same deep cultic root. It is therefore not without good reason that the *torah* regulating admission to the cult precedes the liturgy of the theophany in Ps. 24.3 ff., and is not, as is frequently assumed, derived from a different liturgical context. The protestation of integrity occasionally takes the form of the *renunciation of the foreign gods*, which is derived from the ancient tradition of the covenant community (cf. Gen. 35.2 ff.; Josh. 24.14, 23 f.;

Judg. 10.16; I Sam. 7.3 f.), and of the worshipper's dissociation from those who follow these gods or from the wicked (Pss. 16.4; 25.1 ff.; 26.4 ff.; 31.6; 36.1 ff.; 40.4; 92.7 ff.; 101.3 ff.; 139.21 ff.; 140.2 f.), and so fits into the same situation as the corresponding tradition in the hymn. From the affirmation of confidence the *psalms of confidence* were developed as an independent psalm type (Pss. 4; 11; 16; 23; 27.1–6; 62; 131); from the viewpoint of the history of the cultus it belongs, however, to the same context as the affirmation of confidence.

Since the divine judgment presupposes the *testing* of man by God (Pss. 7.9; 9.16; 11.4 f.; 14.2; 26.2 ff.; 33.13 ff.; 35.14 ff.; 50.16 ff.; 66.10; cf. Ex. 20.20), the *confession of sins* is prominent whenever the conscience of the worshipper tells him that he will not be able to stand that test, and in most cases is a sign of a more highly developed sensitivity on the part of the worshipper. Occasionally it dominates a whole lament and in that case imparts to it the character of a *penitential psalm*, exclusively focused on the grace of Yahweh (Ex. 34.5 ff.). Among individual laments, the confession of sins is to be found in Pss. 25.7; 41.4; 69.5; 143.2; cf. Ps. 90.7 ff.; of the seven penitential psalms of the Ancient Church (Pss. 6; 32; 38; 51; 102; 130; 143), only 38, 51 and 130 are proper penitential prayers. That the confession of sins was firmly established in the festival cult is shown by the statement made in Ps. 65.2, 3 in a festal hymn of praise(!), having in view the rite observed in public worship: 'To thee all flesh bring the confession of their sins; when our transgressions prevail over us, thou wilt forgive them!' With this statement should be compared the comprehensive general confession in Ps. 106.6 ff. which follows the cultic representation of the *Heilsgeschichte* and uses this as a warning example for the congregation under the aspect of the 'judgments' of Yahweh (cf. Pss. 78; 79.8 f. as well as Ezra 9.6 ff.; Neh. 9.6 ff.; Dan. 9.4 ff.). The association of this ideology, conceiving history as judgment, with the cult of the Covenant and its theophany can be discerned in the community lament Psalm 83 and also in Pss. 66.8 ff.; 68.30; 76.3; 95.7 ff.; in a derivative form it also underlies the parallel trains of thought which were developed in the prophetic literature (e.g. Amos 4.6 ff.; Isa. 2.6 ff.; 5.1 ff.; Jer. 3.24 f.; 14.20; 31.18 f.). It accords with the twofold aspect of the Old Testament idea of judgment that the judgment of Yahweh manifests itself, as far as the godly community of his 'faithful people' is concerned, in their participation in the saving cultic events, whereas it takes effect in the form of disaster, or rather exclusion from salvation (see above), for the wicked and the enemies of the Yahweh community and its members, who are regarded in the psalms as Yahweh's enemies, too, a view which is for the most part based on the ideology of the Covenant. In the community lament (Pss. 44. 1 ff.; 83) as well as in that of an individual (e.g. Ps. 9) we find a conception which is peculiar to the cultic way of thinking, that the saving acts by means of which Yahweh aided his people in the past against their enemies are experienced at first hand as a present saving event, and so are also directed against the enemies who at the given time actually threaten the nation or an individual member of the Covenant (cf. Judg. 5.31). As a result the entire *Heilsgeschichte* is concentrated and re-enacted in the concrete individual contemporary case, which is not only viewed and understood within the context of the *Heilsgeschichte* of the past, but occasionally is also 'stylized' after its pattern (Pss. 11.6; 21.9; 34.7; 48.3 f., 8; 55.9, 15; 59.11 ff.; 66.5 ff., 12; 68.30; 71.20; 76.1 ff., 8 ff.; 83.9 ff.; 107.32 ff.; 140.10).

It is readily understandable that the *execution of judgment* also plays in the psalms of lamentation an essential part which is frequently turned into a quite concrete form, that is, the expulsion of the ungodly adversaries from the cult community or their destruction (cf., e.g., Ps. 69.28: 'let them not be enrolled among the righteous'; also Pss. 12.3; 28.3 ff.; 34.15 ff.; 40.14 ff.; 52.5 ff.; 54.5, 7; 94.1 ff., where the association of judgment with Yahweh's cultic theophany can still be recognized distinctly). In many cases an act of sacral excommunication will have to be assumed on the analogy of Judg. 5.23; Deut. 27, 28; Lev. 26 (cf. also Jer. 17.23) which took place in the cult of the Covenant and has left its mark in the psalms of cursing (83; 129; see below). In Ps. 129.5, 8 it may be a question of members of the tribal confederacy belonging to the Northern Kingdom of Israel who are excluded from the 'blessing of Yahweh' because they are opposed to the worship at the Temple of Jerusalem (for later times cf. Ps. 137). Ps. 109.6 f., 28, 30 f. suggests a lawsuit within the framework of the cult; the same is true of the 'prayers of the accused'; Hans Schmidt holds that Pss. 3; 4; 5; 7; 11; 13; 17; 26; 27; 31; 54–57; 59; 94; 140 and 142 fall into this latter category, but his view cannot be accepted as conclusive in every case; he also wants to infer from I Kings 8.30 ff.; Ex. 22; Num. 5; and Deut. 17 that an ordeal is implied in these prayers.

The *contrast between the 'godly' and the 'wicked'* was for a long time predominantly interpreted as having its origin in the controversies of the religious parties in the period between the Testaments. It is true that Mowinckel has disputed this interpretation and he was right to do so; but his own view that the enemies of an individual in the psalms of lamentation were sorcerers is as much based on a one-sided interpretation which does violence to the texts as is Birkeland's view that the enemies of the individual were the political opponents of kings and princes. The picture of the wicked which can be obtained from the psalms of lamentation shows too many shades to admit of its being pressed into such a narrow conception. The designation of the 'godly one' as *ṣaddīq* (the righteous one), who shares in the 'righteousness' (= covenantal salvation), and that of the 'wicked' as *rāšā'* (= he who is decided against) are, on the contrary, connected with the idea of judgment peculiar to the cult of the Covenant and with the exclusion of the wicked from the covenantal salvation; and it is from these conceptions that these terms have received their specific Old Testament meaning.

Special mention must be made of the so-called '*change of mood*' which can be observed at the conclusion of a number of laments where the sorrowful tones of pleading and moving lamentation are followed by expressions of confident assurance that the prayer has been heard and of strong, calm faith (e.g. Pss. 6.8 ff.; 7.10 f.; 13.5, 6; 16.10 f.; 20.6; 27.6; 28.6 ff.; 31.19 ff.; 52.8; 55.23; 56.9 ff.; 61.5; 94.22 f.; 130.7 f.; 140.12 f.; cf. Jer. 20.11). These statements differ from the usual expressions of confidence that are intermingled with the lamentation, though they are akin to them as far as content is concerned. The change of mood under discussion has been explained from the psychological point of view as indicating an inward process which is said to have taken place in the soul of the worshipper during his prayer (thus Heiler and in a certain fashion also Westermann); or it has been interpreted as the effect produced by a priestly oracle foretelling the deliverance of the worshipper (Küchler, Gunkel, Begrich and others); royal laments in Babylonia and the prophetic literature of the Old Testament provide evidence with regard to these views, which can also be presumed to prove true for some psalms (e.g. Pss. 12; 60.6 ff.; 85; 91.13; cf. Isa. 33.10 ff.), and neither view necessarily excludes the other.

However, the remarkable fact that the great majority of the laments do not refer to such an oracle refutes Gunkel's postulate that in these cases, too, we are presented with a stylistic form, cast into a

rigid mould, which at an earlier stage presupposes such an oracle.[1]
It may be assumed that, where it is a question of expressing the firm
conviction that the prayer will be answered at some future date (e.g.
Pss. 7.12 f.; 27.6), this is based simply on the sure knowledge that
results from the participation in the traditional realization of salvation in the cult; here the personal hope of salvation is based on the
actualization of the communal salvation which represents the
essential theme of the festival cult (see above). Again, it may be
assumed that in psalms in which the answering of a personal prayer is
mentioned as an event that has already taken place and is followed
by a prayer of thanksgiving (vow), it is a question of the linking
together of a lament and a thanksgiving, a procedure which has
already been discussed; here the combined lament and thanksgiving
are either presented to the Godhead in the festival cult together with
sacrificial offerings (Pss. 56.12; 66.13 f.; 107.22; 116.17; Jonah 2.9)
or are themselves regarded as a votive offering in place of the latter
(Pss. 40.6 f.; 50.14; 51.15 f.; 69.30 f.; 71.16; 141.2).

The fact that the personal experience of salvation, which was
expressed in the laments and in the thanksgivings, was incorporated
in the tradition of the salvation of the cult community as a whole,
together with the custom of offering such prayers in the festival cult
as votive offerings, gave rise to the writing down of these prayers.
This development is clearly indicated in Ps. 102.18: 'Let this be
recorded for a generation to come, so that a people that has been
reborn may praise the Lord!'[2] The preservation of the tradition of
salvation enriched by the various personal experiences of the individual worshippers was as much in their interest as in that of the cult
community as a whole and of its priesthood. Hence there is no need
to seek the authors of such psalms in circles connected with the
Temple, and, as far as Psalm 102 is concerned, it is not likely that its
author belongs to these circles. In comparison with the monotony of
the Babylonian cultic poetry, which was composed by those who
officiated at the shrines, the Old Testament psalms are much too
varied and, in spite of the general character of their forms, too
personal and lively to suggest the view that their authors belonged to
those circles. On the other hand, if the view here presented is
accepted, I cannot see at all—and I make this point in particular in
opposition to Gunkel—why hymns in which a purely personal note

[1] Cf. Wevers, VT 6, 1956, pp. 80–96.
[2] *See p. 71, n. 2.

is sounded, and that applies even to hymns which contain no direct references to the cult, and also alphabetic psalms,[1] should not right from the beginning have been intended for recitation in the festival cult. Whether Jeremiah's poems of lamentation can be quoted as evidence of a purely private 'religious lyric poetry', entirely divorced from the cultus, must be doubted in view of Jer. 17.12, where the words 'throne of glory' ($k\bar{a}b\bar{o}d$) and 'place of our sanctuary' explicitly refer to the cultic tradition of the Temple.[2] And even those hymns which, as has been proved, have been composed far away from the Temple, such as Psalms 42; 43; 137, or after the destruction of the Temple in 587 BC, such as Psalms 74 and 79, are inwardly so closely related to the sanctuary and its cultic tradition that not many hymns are left over in the Psalter of which it can be said that they are really 'dissociated from the cult' and exclusively composed for private edification. For the use of the phrase 'independent of the cult' (kultfrei), which has been coined in modern times and hardly accords with the way of thinking peculiar to antiquity, would be justified only if that phrase were used in the sense of a complete outward and inward dissociation from the cultus and its substance. All things considered we have to understand the individual lament in the Psalter, as well as other types, in the light of its association with the cult of the Covenant and its traditions.

This fact is significant in so far as in this way the cultic tradition and personal faith, the piety of the cult community and the religious experience of the individual, mutually support and enrich each other in the psalms. It may be, though we cannot be at all sure of it, that if we want to find the earliest source and the primitive foundation of the lament we must turn to the practice of exorcism, where it was meant to operate as a sort of magical counter-effect against hostile magical forces. But even if this should be the case, the few remains of magical formulas which are to be found in the Psalter have no longer the function of words producing an independent effect by virtue of their own inherent power. The decision rests solely with God, to whom the manifold afflictions of the individual worshippers, both material and spiritual, are without exception related and attributed, and who alone is able to grant deliverance from them. Hence the laments express man's submission to God, to

---

[1] *Acrostic psalms.
[2] Cf. for further details Weiser, *Jeremia* I (ATD, 1952), pp. 152 ff., and 179 f. on Jer. 20.13 (4th ed., 1960, pp. 146 ff. and 173 f.)

whom in his lament he confides his troubles and before whom he
utters his petitions in prayer. Though the miseries which individuals
have to endure on earth take many forms, they find their inward
unity and support in being orientated on God by means of a common faith nourished by a cultic tradition that continually becomes
anew a living reality. The cardinal problem of the psalms of lamentation is thereby shifted to the inner life of man, and the burden of
external threats frequently recedes into the background in face of the
heavier burden of mental or spiritual distress. The point of most of
the psalms of lamentation, more or less distinctly stated, is man's
separation from God and his yearning for the restoration of his lost
contact with God's living power, which he hopes to find again in the
evidence of God's presence and in the grace and help which God
may grant him. It is at this point that the Old Testament psalms
have risen to the highest level of spirituality and have developed their
religious power to the utmost. By relating all suffering to God and
never to a number of gods or demons, as is done in the polytheistic
religions, the Old Testament faith sees that in times of affliction the
threat to man's whole existence comes directly from God, and, conversely, realizes that man's only chance of existence consists in a life
lived in communion with that God. Starting from this premise many
a psalmist advanced to the inner certainty, reached only after his
soul had passed through most violent emotions and severe struggles,
that the indestructible relatedness of his life to God and his surrender to and devoted delight in God represent the only means in his
possession which will enable him to overcome in spirit not only every
kind of suffering but also the fear of death itself (Pss. 16.10 f.; 73.
23 ff.). In some psalms the Tammuz theme of the descent to hell,
which belongs to the world of ideas associated with the cult of the
dying and rising vegetation-gods, is used to illustrate the deadly
peril to which the psalmist is exposed (Pss. 9.13; 18.5 f., 17; 30.3;
40.2; 71.20; 103.4; 107.18; 116.3; Isa. 38.10 f.; Jonah 2.2 ff.). At
the same time, however, death and its conquest are nowhere spoken
of in the sense of an event that has actually come to pass[1]—the
majority of the passages quoted as evidence belong to thanksgivings!
This proves that the adoption of the theme under discussion can have
been only of a formal nature and that the cultic ideology of these
foreign religions has not contributed, as it might have, to the efforts

[1] Cf. Chr. Barth, *Die Errettung vom Tode in den individuellen Klage- und Dankliedern
des Alten Testaments*, 1947.

made in the psalms to find an intellectually satisfying solution to the problem of death (cf. Hos. 6.2). In the laments the most profound problems of life are tackled and ultimate decisions are contended for in prayer. The question, age-old yet ever new, of whether, and, if so, in what manner, destiny and God and guilt and destiny are related to each other recurs in many variations and is answered in different ways. These answers range from a massive belief in retribution to an ultimate fundamental knowledge of the reality both of human sin and of the divine grace which alone is able to overcome sin, a knowledge which by the power of its inwardness goes beyond the limits of every kind of stereotyped penitential formula (Ps. 51). Babylonian penitential hymns attempt to persuade the deity, by means of the accumulation of flattering predicates, to show favour to the worshipper, but in the Old Testament psalms the affirmation of trust in God is prominent and so lays the foundation on which alone petition can develop into proper and genuine prayer. And the fact that Israel's psalmody has been capable of creating out of such affirmations of trust in God a psalm type of its own—the so-called psalms of confidence—is evidence of the creative power and vitality which has been at work in this sphere of the Old Testament faith.

(c) THANKSGIVINGS

With regard to both its form and its subject-matter the so-called thanksgiving is related, on the one hand, to the hymn and, on the other, to the lament. A distinction is made between community thanksgiving and individual thanksgiving. Only a few examples of the former category are to be found in the Psalter; Gunkel classes with them Pss. 66.8–12; 67; 124; 129; however, strictly speaking, only Psalm 124 is a genuine thanksgiving in which the liturgical tradition still shines through (Ps. 124.1: 'let Israel now say'; also Ps. 129.1; cf. Pss. 107.2, 8, 15, 21 f., 31 f.; 118.2 ff.). In Psalm 129 the theme of thanksgiving is overshadowed by the arguments put forward against the adversaries. Psalms 66 and 67 (Isa. 12.3 ff.) do not differ from the usual type of hymn and contain its same fundamental elements (the cultic presentation of the *Heilsgeschichte*, the epiphany and presence of God, his reign and his judgment; cf. also Job 33. 26 ff.); thus these psalms, too, have a place in the cult of the autumn feast of the Covenant of Yahweh (Ps. 67.6) and we should not distinguish too strictly between the hymn and the thanksgiving. The linguistic usage, at any rate, does not make any fundamental distinction between the terms *t^ehillā* (praise) and *tōdā*, used with reference to the hymn. Hence it is not possible to use the word *tōdā* alone as a specialized technical term for the thanksgiving, since the lines of demarcation between the hymn and the thanksgiving are liable to change. The connection between the thanksgiving and the lament can be recognized especially in individual thanksgivings. Not only is the offering of a thanksgiving vowed in the laments, in the event that the prayer should be answered, but frequently a lament and a thanksgiving are combined in a single psalm (Pss. 6; 13; 22; 28; 30; 31; 41; 54; 55; 56; 61; 63; 64; 69; 71; 86; 94; 102; 120; 130; cf. Jer. 20.7–13). In this case the lament takes the place of the 'narration' of the affliction of the individual worshipper, which is followed by the granting of his prayer. This account of the personal fate of the worshipper forms the main part of the thanksgiving and is characteristic of it; the aim is to incorporate the witness borne to the saving experience of the individual worshipper in the representation of the corporate salvation of the cult community as a whole (e.g., Pss. 66; 107), to whom the account is mostly addressed. The terms 'the godly', 'the righteous', 'the saints', 'the needy' and similar terms used to address the cult community (Pss. 16.3; 22.23; 30.4; 32.11; 34.9; 69.33; 107.42; 118.15, etc.) make it improbable that only a small group of specially invited relatives and friends of the worshipper is referred to by these terms (this point in opposition to Gunkel and others). According to Ps. 107.32 ff. it is the cult community of the people of God who represent the forum and who themselves experience at first hand in the festival cult the cultic-dramatic representation of the general *Heilsgeschichte* (Ps. 107.42) to which their songs of praise testify. On the other hand, the form of prayer (invocation of Yahweh), which occurs beside the narrative form, does not indicate, as Gunkel thinks, that we are here merely dealing with a 'later style'. On the contrary, the linking together of the lament and the thanksgiving shows that, just as in the case of the hymn, the prayer form is to be understood in the light of the original twofold aspect of the testimony borne by the worshipper, which is simultaneously addressed to God and to the congregation— a twofold aspect which ensues from the ideology of the Covenant and its cultic tradition (see above).

From Ps. 107.2 f., 8, 15, 21 it also follows that the liturgy assigned to the recital of the prayer of thanksgivings of the different groups of worshippers, flocking to the feast from all directions, a definite place in the order of the feast. It is therefore permissible to regard the annual pilgrimage to the Covenant Festival as the occasion on which the thanksgivings (and the laments) as a rule have their fixed place in the festival context; the first two chapters of I Samuel are evidence of this as an ancient custom. The liturgy of thanksgiving in Psalm 118 (see v. 24) likewise points to the feast instituted by Yahweh; in that liturgy, too, a personal saving experience (presumably that of the king) is woven into the fabric of the feast as a whole (vv. 15 f.) and its cultic rites, such as the entry through 'the gate of righteousness' (vv. 19 f.), the blessing (v. 26), and the festal dance (v. 27). For the most part, too, the narration in a thanksgiving lacks those features which make for concreteness, and this makes it more difficult to comprehend the personal experiences of the individual worshipper. The cause of this deficiency is to be found in the influence exerted by the use of formulas and in the cultic tradition's shaping of the personal saving experience on the lines of the representation of the salvation of the cult community as a whole. On the other hand, however, the diversity of the personal traits embedded in the thanksgivings is nevertheless so clearly discernible that it is not advisable to regard the latter as mere formularies by overestimating their stereotyped character and to look for their authors among the cultic officials. Rather can we assume that the latter were trustees to whom we are indebted for the keeping and the preservation of the testimonies which had been borne in the sanctuary by individual worshippers as a kind of votive offering and which had been recorded afterwards (cf. Ps. 102.18). The association of the vow (votive offering) with the prayer of thanksgiving has to be judged on the same lines. In many cases it constitutes the link between the lament and the thanksgiving, and has found expression in the fact that votive offerings are mentioned in both types of psalms. Gunkel holds that the thanksgiving was originally part of the thank-offering. For the pre-exilic cult of the Covenant, however, it is not possible to maintain such a view directly and without qualification, since according to Deut. 23.23 the vow (votive offering) was not an absolute cultic duty. It is in the priestly laws recorded in Lev. 7.11 ff. that the general regulation of the ritual of the votive offering first seems to have been fully developed. Hence the main emphasis in the earlier cult of the Covenant lies not on the thank-offering but on the testimony. As far as the psalms are concerned, that truth is corroborated by the explicit statements which point in the same direction

(Pss. 40.6 ff.; 50.14 f.; 69.30 f.); it can also be derived from the fact that many psalms do not mention a sacrifice at all. But this latter factor by no means signifies the dissociation of these psalms from the cult. The *tōdā* is essentially not so much a prayer of thanksgiving as rather a *profession* and a testimony to the way God has acted; and this accords entirely with the theocentric character of the cult of Yahweh. It was this cult which first imparted to the *tōdā* its specific significance within the Old Testament psalms, although many a feature is borrowed from the world of ideas associated with the cultic ritual of the Near East, such as the idea of deliverance from the underworld, which was used as an image for deliverance from a deadly peril (Pss. 9.13; 18.4 f., 16; 30.3; 40.2; 71.20; 103.4; 107.18; 116.3; Isa. 38.10 f.; Jonah 2.2 ff.). The peculiar character of the ideology of the Old Testament Covenant makes itself felt also in the fact that the thanksgiving occasionally turns from personal matters to matters of common concern, in particular to exhortatory and didactic matters (Pss. 31.23 f.; 32.6, 10 f.; 34.11 ff.; 40.4; 41.1 ff.; 111.10; cf. Pss. 51.13; 58.11; 62.8 ff.; 67.1 ff.; 107.42 f.; 145.12 f.). In 'recognizing' and 'testifying to' God's nature and the reality of his being, the thanksgiving and the lament coincide with the themes of the hymn and of the Wisdom literature at the very point around which the whole cult of the feast of Yahweh revolves—the revelation of God and his presence.

(*d*) BLESSING AND CURSE

The sayings in the psalms pronouncing a blessing or a curse deserve special mention. They do not occur in the psalms as an independent 'type', but appear in different contexts and in different psalm types either in the form of an *'utterance of blessing'* (*bārūk* = blessed) or in the form of a *petition for blessing* (may Yahweh bless . . .) and less frequently as an utterance of curse and as a petition for cursing. Blessing and curse originate in the magico-dynamistic sense of being alive; originally they were conceived to be magical charms capable of producing an effect by their own inherent power and had the purpose of increasing or decreasing the vitality of human beings, that is to say, of producing 'salvation' (*Heil*) or disaster (*Unheil*) by virtue of their own power. It is characteristic of the use of formulas of blessing in the psalms that the independent magical efficacy of the utterance of blessing has disappeared. Whether the blessing is effective or not depends on the will of Yah-

weh, who alone has at his disposal the saving energies inherent in the
blessing and who is the actual dispenser of blessing (Pss. 24.5; 128.5;
134.3). The blessing is thereby raised from the magical sphere to the
religious, theistic sphere. Whether the formula 'blessed . . . in
the name of Yahweh' (Ps. 118.26) should lead us to conclude that the
miraculous power inherent in the name of Yahweh is at the disposal
of the man who uses that name for the purpose of blessing (thus
Gunkel) remains uncertain. The use of the name of Yahweh in such
a context, which was the privilege of the priest, is according to
Num. 6.27 ('you shall put my name upon the people of Israel, and I
will bless them'), and in view of the association of that saying with
the liturgical Aaronite benediction (see above), more probably to
be accounted for by the tradition of the cult of the Covenant, in
particular by the theophany and the revelation of the name of Yahweh which took place in the cult. We are led to the same conclusion
by the fact that in the psalms the blessing is almost exclusively pronounced on those who fulfil the requirements of the Covenant of
Yahweh (Pss. 2.11; 24.5; 34.8; 40.4; 84.5, 12; 91.1 f.; 106.3; 112.1;
128.1; 146.5, etc.), and in particular is imparted to the people of God
chosen by Yahweh (Pss. 33.12; 65.4; 144.15). The saying 'Yahweh bless
you from Zion' (Pss. 128.5; 134.3) likewise confirms the conclusion
reached in discussing the idea of judgment, that is, that the blessing
of Yahweh was firmly rooted in the cultic tradition of the Temple
and has more and more become the domain of the priest. The
'Beatitude',[1] on the other hand, uses the salutation 'Blessed is . . .'
('ašrē). This is not a priestly blessing only, and presumably was the
form in which the petition for blessing was uttered by the laity, too;
it was also adopted by the Wisdom literature. In the course of the
history of the religion of the Old Testament the blessing was progressively subordinated to the exclusive power of Yahweh, and this
process eventually found expression in the fact that out of the petition
for blessing the *intercession* was developed.

The *curse* as the counterpart of the blessing has its roots in the
same thought-world of magic and in the form of a ritual act was
likewise incorporated in the cult of the tribal confederacy of Israel
(Judg. 5.23; 21.5; Deut. 27, 28). In that cult it served within the

---

[1] *The German word *'Seligpreisung'* is here translated 'beatitude'—not, of
course, the technical term with a specific biblical and ecclesiastical meaning
(cf. Matt. 5.3–11). *Seligpreisung* as used in the present context simply means the
praising of someone else for the blessing he has received or is going to receive.

range of the ideas associated with the Covenant as a means of the self-purification of the Yahweh community (see above), and it is through that rite that it was preserved in the only form which relates cursing to Yahweh: 'cursed before the face of Yahweh' (Josh. 6.26; I Sam. 26.19). In a scroll of the Qumran sect also the sacral act of uttering a curse is recorded as an event that takes place within the framework of the feast of renewal of the Covenant.[1] In the psalms the curse is of lesser importance than the blessing. The utterance of a curse is attested only in Ps. 129.21; petitions for cursing occur in the exilic Psalm 137. The association of the curse with the tradition of the *Heilsgeschichte* concerning God's judgments as represented in the cult of the Covenant is to be found in Ps. 83.9 ff. and there takes the form of the sacral proscription of adversaries (cf. Pss. 37.34; 149.7 ff.). So, too, the arguments put forward against enemies and the wicked provided the basis on which the last phase in the development of the utterance of a curse into a *prayer of vengeance* was effected within the religious poetry of the Old Testament (Pss. 17.13; 28.4 f.; 54.5; 56.7; 58.6 ff.; 69.22 ff.; 79.10, 12; 109.6 ff.; cf. Jer. 11.18 ff.; 15.15; 17.12 ff.; 18.19 ff.). The connection of blessing and cursing with the cultic tradition of the Covenant of Yahweh, which is manifested also in the calling down of a curse upon those who do not comply with the demands made by the Covenant, has resulted in a parallel development of blessing and curse within the psalms. Thus the changing of the blessing into the salutation 'Blessed' is matched by the transformation of the curse into a *cry of woe* ('*ōy*) which was adopted by the prophets and the Wisdom literature.

(e) WISDOM AND DIDACTIC POEMS [2]

Lastly, another literary type needs to be mentioned which widely spread throughout the Near East, had its place in secular life, and from there found its way into the psalms, too—'Wisdom' literature. 'Wisdom', which, as we know above all from the history of Egyptian thought, was a phenomenon of epoch-making importance in the realm of rational enlightenment,[3] was especially concerned with educating people to live their everyday lives usefully. In the Old Testament its literary influence is to be found above all in collections

---

[1] See Burrows, *Manual of Discipline* 2.5, 11.

[2] See Mowinckel, 'Psalms and Wisdom', *VT* Suppl. III (1955), pp. 205 ff.

[3] Cf. H. Brunner, *Handbuch der Orientalistik* I, 1952, pp. 90 ff.

of brief maxims (*māšāl* in Hebrew) of sensible practical wisdom
which have an educational purpose, such as the book of the Proverbs
of Solomon, Ecclesiasticus and so on. Brief wisdom sayings of that
kind occur in Psalms 127 and 133. The Wisdom poem Psalm 49
deals with the subject in more detail and is explicitly described as a
'proverb', an utterance of wisdom; it also exhibits the characteristic
linguistic style of Wisdom literature. Psalms 1, 112 and 128, too, are
to be classed with the Wisdom psalms; the last-named of these
psalms exemplifies by its conclusion the fact that the Wisdom poetry
has found access also to the cult of Yahweh (cf. Pss. 34.11 ff.; 94.8 ff.).
The ideology of the idea of judgment associated with the cult of the
Covenant also forms the background of Psalm 1, so that we are
justified in assuming that Wisdom literature and the tradition of the
cult of Yahweh have mutually influenced each other. This view is
confirmed by the fact that the thanksgiving especially adopts on occasion the spirit and forms of Wisdom literature by means of warnings
of a hortatory and educational nature or by ending with a didactic
testimony (Pss. 25.12 ff.; 31.23 f.; 32.6 ff.; 34.11 ff.; 40.4; 41.1 ff.;
51.13; 62.9; 111.10, etc.; cf. Ecclus. 39.5) and that, on the other
hand, the fundamental religious ideas of the tradition of the Covenant continually prevail in these psalms in the face of the secular
tendency of Wisdom literature to concentrate upon the practical
aspects of man's temporal existence, and in this way impart to the
Wisdom poems of the Psalter a peculiar note of their own, the note of
a 'religion for everyday life'. It may be assumed that the so-called
'*didactic poem*' too, originated in an environment similar to that of the
Wisdom poem (Pss. 37; 49; cf. the thanksgiving, Ps. 73). It discusses
the religious doubts which the problem of suffering creates for belief
in God. Here, too, especially in Psalm 73, it is the living impact of
the presence and nearness of God experienced in the Yahweh cult
which fills the forms borrowed from the language of the Wisdom
literature and so brings it about that the problem of the suffering of
the godly is not theoretically solved by means of abstract discussion
but that, on the contrary, the affliction caused by suffering is overcome in a practical way by virtue of a personal decision for God,
made by faith.

If we study the psalms simultaneously in the light of Form-
Criticism, the history of traditions and the history of the cultus, we
obtain thereby a picture of the psalms which, compared with the

views held in the past, is considerably more limited in scope but
correspondingly exhibits much more clearly defined contours. Just
as the cult of the Covenant and its tradition represent only one
aspect of the history of the much more varied religious life of Israel
and of the forms in which it found expression, so also the comparatively small number of those psalms which have been preserved in
the Old Testament is to be regarded as only one aspect of the
religious poetry of Israel, which in both scope and subject-matter
occupied a much wider field. There were large areas of life in which
popular piety was expressed in one way or another, which were
originally beyond the horizon of the psalms in precisely the same
way as were the legalistic form of religion and ritual observances
developed by the priests in post-exilic Judaism. To these spheres of
life belong the religious customs observed in family and tribal cults
as well as at local shrines, religious customs which were able for a
long time to hold their own beside the Yahweh cult of the sacral
confederacy of the tribes and were only gradually (and even then
only partly) overshadowed and absorbed by the tradition of the
Covenant of Yahweh. And the same is true of the feasts with their
specific sacrificial rites which originated in the religion of the cattle-
breeders and peasants, and also of the syncretistic forms of religion
which were developed as a result of the policy of the kings, particularly in the Northern Kingdom of Israel, but also in the Southern
Kingdom. The religious songs and prayers preserved in the Psalter
are in the main traditional matter belonging to the cultic sphere of
the Covenant Festival of Yahweh celebrated by the sacral confederacy of the tribes at the Jerusalem Temple, and that traditional
matter outlasted the change of the times with remarkable constancy.
The very same streams of energy flowing from the Yahweh tradition which sustain the ideological structure of the psalms have also
compelled the forms and types of poetry borrowed from foreign
countries to serve their own purposes and have imparted to these
forms and types a significance of their own within the context of the
covenant cult. Occasionally they have even moulded them into a
form which shows an entirely independent character and which can
be fully elucidated only with the help of the covenant ideology. The
dissolution of the pure 'types' and the intermingling of their formal
elements, as well as the adoption and digestion of originally foreign
ranges of ideas, is to be understood in the light of the living creative
energies which were at work in the cult of the Covenant and its

tradition. These creative powers burst the restricting chains of the traditional fashion of stereotyped forms and by their own inner relatedness to God welded these heterogeneous elements into an entity which, compared with the prototypes of the Near East, was absolutely original in character, for its specific meaning was determined by the revelation of Yahweh and the realization of his salvation as the heart of the cult of the Covenant. The theocentric character of the cult of Yahweh and its character as *Heilsgeschichte* entail that the sacramental event of the dispensation of salvation embraces both the people of God as a whole and its individual members. In this way it constitutes the inner link between collective and individual piety, and that in such a way that the personal experience of the individual is incorporated (especially is this so in the psalms) in the great line of tradition of the cult community and is thereby transformed into a link that is necessary to the whole, that is to say, into one of the types of the experience of the cult community as a whole. It is that inner link between collective and individual piety, apparent also in the general character of the forms used in the psalms of an individual, which is responsible for the grain of truth to be found in the later reinterpretation of those psalms as psalms of the cult community. At the same time, too, that same inner link is responsible for the timeless significance of the psalms which alone has made it possible to use them in the post-exilic era and beyond, right up to the present day, as testimonies of a living tradition.

7. THE ORIGIN AND AUTHORSHIP OF THE PSALMS

The manifold connecting links between the psalms and the cult of the Covenant Festival, as this was celebrated by the tribes of Israel, justify the view that the majority of the psalms came into existence in the pre-exilic period of Israel's history. If they had been composed after the Exile, one would expect them, in view of the close relations of the psalms to the Yahweh cult, to contain allusions to the post-exilic ritual laws, but such allusions are nowhere to be found. Only a few psalms contain direct references to the conditions that prevailed during the Exile or during the post-exilic era (e.g. Pss. 74; 79; 137). In view of the chequered nature of the history of the people of Israel, it is not possible to assume that all the national catastrophes alluded to in the psalms (e.g. Pss. 44; 80; 89) refer to the downfall of the state of Judah. As regards the psalms in which the Ark or the king plays a rôle, no further proof of their pre-exilic origin is required. More recently the dating to the Maccabaean period, advocated by Olshausen, Duhm and others, has very properly declined in popularity. The fact that the psalms of the Qumran sect, which date from that period, and the somewhat later Psalms of Solomon distinctly differ from the canonical psalms as far as their form is concerned and also appeared too late to be included in the collection of the psalms makes the hypothesis of Maccabaean psalms in the Psalter appear altogether improbable.[1]

In addition, the frequently archaic character of the language of the psalms has to be taken into account.[2] It might be thought that late linguistic forms could be adduced to refute the view of the pre-exilic origin of such psalms. These forms are, however, conclusive only for the final form of the psalms in question, not for the date at which they came into existence. This is particularly true of those psalms which were appointed to be regularly used in the cult (see above). As far as parallel transmissions are concerned, literary criticism has frequently employed the method of determining the relative date of a psalm by assuming the copying of a literary prototype; but that method, too, is just as little able to keep the promise which it seems to make, since it is not outside the bounds of possibility that the presumed prototype, too, may be derived from a common cultic tradition. Hence many a theory alleging the dependence of certain psalms on Deutero-Isaiah or on the priestly writings needs to be corrected. Still more doubtful are the attempts to adduce indirect evidence for the post-exilic origin of a psalm from the universal picture provided by the course taken by the history of ideas and the history of religion. In view of the results of the research undertaken in the fields of the history of the traditions and of the history of the cultus it can hardly be denied any longer that through the mediation of the cultus the idea of creation and eschatology and also certain Messianic features had already found access to the Israelite world of ideas at an early date in Israel's history. Even the fact that the 'wisdom' movement penetrated the hymn and the thanksgiving cannot without further examination be considered as a

---

[1] Cf. W. F. Albright, 'The Old Testament and the Archaeology of Palestine', *The Old Testament and Modern Study*, 1951, p. 25; Baumgartner, *Schweizer Theologische Umschau* 24, 1954, p. 51.

[2] Cf. Tsevat, *A Study of the Language of the Biblical Psalms*, 1955, and in connection with this Mowinckel, 'Zur Sprache der biblischen Psalmen', *TLZ* 81, 1956, cols. 199 ff.

late phenomenon in the history of the psalms when we take into account the great age both of that type of literature and of the thought-world which forms its background. The view is held that when the psalms speak of the law, they must have in mind the priestly ceremonial law of Judaism. However, that view is based on the postulate of the post-exilic origin of the psalms; moreover, no conclusive evidence can be found that would justify it, and the fact that from time immemorial statutes and ordinances belonged to the fundamental constituent parts of the feast of the Covenant of Yahweh (Josh. 24.25 f.) invalidates this argument. The distinction extensively made in the psalms between 'the godly' ('righteous') and 'the wicked', which hitherto has for the most part been interpreted as referring to the religious parties which opposed each other in the period between the Testaments, is to be accounted for, as has already been pointed out, by the peculiar character of the cult of the Covenant and its ideology. The designation of the godly who are faithful to Yahweh as 'the humble', 'the needy' ('ānī; 'ānāw), which literally means those who are 'bent low'—terms which frequently occur above all in the songs of lament—likewise originated in the cult and are to be understood as expressions which are meant to typify the humble submission of the godly to the majesty of Yahweh and to his commandments, assuming an outward and an inward posture of adoration and profession. Occasionally, they are to be understood as referring to the sinfulness of the worshippers (Isa. 6.5 ff.; Ps. 65.2 f.; Jer. 20.13) and in some passages also, in the light of the history of Israel in relation to the *Heilsgeschichte*, as the oppressed nation who just as much as her individual 'suffering' members is continually in need of the help of her God. The fact that these and similar phrases are used to draw social distinctions contrasting the people so described with their rulers and oppressors (Pss. 72.4, 12 ff.; 76.9; 82.3 f.; 107.41; 113.7; 147.6) is of secondary importance in comparison with the fact that they have their origin in the ideology of the cult; and the distinction drawn between the people in question and the mighty 'violent men' (Pss. 37; 49; 52; 62; 73) is similarly derived from the ancient ethos of the Covenant which placed the poor and the needy under the special protection of Yahweh's statutes. Hence from this angle, too, no objections can be raised against the thesis of the pre-exilic origin of the majority of the psalms and of their connection with the cult of the Covenant.[1]

[1] Cf. Albright, *Archaeology and the Religion of Israel*, 3rd ed., 1953, pp. 125 ff.

Finally, the alternative 'cultic poetry or psalms entirely independent of the cult', which has been carried too far and is too subtle, has influenced the question of the origin and history of the psalms in so far as it has led to the view that the presumed dissociation of the psalms from the cultus has to be regarded as an advanced stage in the history of the psalms or even as its very climax, brought about by the influence of the prophets. This view, however, suffers from the prejudice which assumes that to be tied to the cultus is equivalent to a superficialization and objectivation of piety or to a hardening of piety into an institution in which the *opus operatum* no longer leaves any room for the manifestations of a living interior piety. Again, that view is to be accounted for by the fact that the criteria for the conception of the cultus have been taken either from the more primitive standards of the religions of Israel's neighbours and their influence or from the ritualism of post-exilic Judaism, without doing justice to the peculiar character of the Israelite cult of the Covenant and its traditions, which offered ample scope for a vital personal piety; again, it was in essence by no means as remote from the fundamental principles of the prophetic message as many people are inclined to assume. External and internal relations with the cult of the Temple and its tradition are, for instance, certain in the case of Ezekiel, and probable for Isaiah and Jeremiah and also Amos (Amos 1.2; 9.1 ff.). It must be left to the exegesis of the individual psalms to determine the date on which each came into existence, provided that such an investigation is at all possible in view of the general character of many psalms which are formulated to serve as types and are remote from the actual historical situation of their time.

We seem to be well informed about the *authors* of the psalms in view of the superscriptions which are attached to a great number of psalms. Seventy-three psalms are attributed to David, two to Solomon, Psalm 90 to Moses, 12 psalms to Asaph, 11 to the Sons of Korah, with Psalm 88 to Heman as well, and Psalm 89 to Ethan. There can be no doubt that the later tradition interpreted such titles as indications of authorship (II Chron. 29.30; II Macc. 2.13; Matt. 22.43 ff.); this is particularly true of the superscription *l^edāwīd* (= appertaining to David). Even though it is not to be assumed that that tradition is a complete figment of the imagination and though the possibility cannot be excluded that a psalm here or there dates back to the Davidic era, there can nevertheless be no question of David having been the author of all the psalms which have been attributed to him. For in a number of these psalms the Temple on Mount Zion is presupposed or a state of affairs is assumed which points to a post-Davidic date. Hence we must assume that the original purpose of superscriptions of that kind was not at all to name the author of the psalm (see below). The interpretation of the l^e in the titles of individual psalms in the aforementioned sense is, moreover, not the one immediately obvious, either from the linguistic point of view or from that of the cultic use of the psalms. Even if members of the choirs of temple singers were the authors of a number of psalms, a view which to a certain degree may probably be justified as far as liturgies, community hymns and cultic formularies are in question, the psalms of Israel have nevertheless not been without exception the cultic poetry of priests.[1] As far as laments and thanksgivings of an individual are concerned, it may be permissible to think of them as private compositions which were recited on the occasion of a feast and in this way became the property of the Temple archives, whereas Psalm 45, which was sung on the occasion of the marriage of the king, and probably also Psalm 101 and one or other of the Royal Psalms, were presumably composed by a court poet. But none of the names mentioned in the titles of psalms designates the real author; the psalms were originally anonymous and probably remained so for a long time.

8. THE COLLECTION OF THE PSALMS

It follows from Ps. 102.18 that it was not the problem of authorship but rather the question of the utilization of the psalms and of their incorporation in the cultic tradition which—understandably—primarily created the interest in the recording and preserving of the psalms. It is in this direction that we shall have to look also for the original meaning of the previously discussed superscriptions, which later on were interpreted as referring to the author of the psalm, just as indeed also most of the other annotations in the titles appear to have in view the recital of the psalm in question in public worship (see above p. 22). A comparison of Ps. 102.18 with its superscription, stating the way in which the psalm was to be used, shows that these superscriptions were attached to the psalms subsequently. The fact that such titles were prefixed to the individual psalms at different times probably presupposes an earlier stage in the collection of

[1] As against Mowinckel, *The Psalms and Israel's Worship* II, pp. 90 ff.

psalms when they were not yet grouped together in a book-roll, forming smaller or larger literary units; for in the latter case a general title or a postscript such as Ps. 72.20 would obviously have been sufficient. In place of that the psalms were kept separately in the archives of the Temple for their cultic use. The term *l⁽e⁾dāwīd* in the titles of individual psalms is therefore of an earlier date than the collection of 'Davidic Psalms' which is hinted at in Ps. 72.20 ('The prayers of David are ended'), and can probably be traced back to a custom practised already in pre-exilic times by collectors of psalms at the Temple. In its original sense it is presumably to be understood on the analogy of the terms *l⁽e⁾baˤal* and *l⁽e⁾keret*, which occur in a Ras Shamra text, and also on the analogy of the title of Psalm 102: 'A prayer of one afflicted, when he is faint and pours out his complaint before the face of Yahweh', namely as a direction to use the psalm in public worship 'for the David', that is to say, for the Davidic ruler who exercises certain functions in the cult and appears there in the rôle of the ancestor as the bearer of the promises made to David and as the recipient of the 'grace of kingship' (of the 'mercies of David'; cf. Pss. 18.50; 20.9; 21.3, 5 ff.; 89.1 ff., 24 ff., 49; Jer. 30.9, 21 and the designation of David in II Sam. 23.1 as the 'favourite of the songs of Israel'). During the earliest phase of the collection of the psalms the superscription *l⁽e⁾dāwīd* therefore probably served the purpose of marking those psalms which the king was authorized to recite in the festival cult of the Temple. The superscription of the psalm of thanksgiving in Isa. 38.9 ff., which runs as follows: 'A writing *for* Hezekiah, after he had been sick and had recovered from his sickness', is to be understood in the same sense, and this is probably true also of Hab. 3.1: 'A prayer for Habakkuk' (appointed to be recited). We do not know how many psalms and which of them once carried the title *l⁽e⁾dāwīd*. Even if one were inclined to follow the Scandinavian scholars and class with the Royal Psalms a number of those psalms which have hitherto been interpreted as private hymns, it is nevertheless not very likely that all the 73 psalms attributed to David were originally reserved for the king.

A special explanation is therefore required for the extension of titles carrying the name of David to psalms which are not Royal Psalms. The extension of the Davidic titles to these psalms seems to have taken place during the second phase in the development of the collection of the psalms, which presumably began in post-exilic times, when the royal cult had ceased to exist, so that the term *l^edāwid* also had lost the specific meaning which was originally attached to it. The priestly writings provide evidence that the destruction of the Temple did not result in the total loss of the cultic tradition of the feast of the Covenant of Yahweh. Again, from the account of the feast of the renewal of the Covenant in Nehemiah 8–9, as also from the liturgy which was used by the Qumran sect at the celebration of the feast of the renewal of the Covenant and which preserved earlier traditions, it appears that the cultic tradition of Yahweh's Covenant retained its place in the festival cult even in post-exilic times. Those who served in the worship of the Second Temple, more than anybody else, had the greatest interest in the collection, preservation and restoration to use of the ancient treasure of liturgical songs. It seems to have been incumbent especially on the guilds of temple-singers to collect and arrange the psalms, in addition to their duty of singing the Temple hymns and the *musica sacra*.[1] This is proved not only by the musical annotations to the psalms but also by the superscriptions *le'āsāph* (Pss. 50; 73–83) and *li-b^enē-qōraḥ* (Pss. 42–49; 84–88) of which at least the latter cannot originally have been meant to name the author (this point in opposition to Mowinckel), especially since Psalm 88 at the same time names Heman as author as well (cf. also the superscription of Psalm 39). According to II Chron. 20.19 the 'Sons of Korah' were a guild of temple-singers. It may be presumed that the same is true also of the families of singers who served in the Second Temple and were named Asaph, Heman, Ethan and Jeduthun after David's singers, who were regarded as their ancestors (I Chron. 6.18 ff.; 16.41 f.; 25.1 ff.; II Chron. 5.12; 35.15, etc.). The marking of individual psalms with the names of these guilds of singers by describing them in the superscription as 'belonging to the Sons of Korah . . .' at first probably served the purpose of specifying those psalms which originated in the tradition of such guilds and were appointed to be sung by them in the worship of the Temple. From this it follows that, as far as the groups of psalms are concerned which are named after the guilds of temple-singers, we are dealing with fragments of earlier collections of temple-songs. It is in this sense and context that we have presumably to understand also the marking with the title *l^edāwid*

[1] Cf., amongst others, Mowinckel, op. cit., II, pp. 94, 197. The antecedents of the guilds of temple-singers still lie in the dark. Early references to them occur in Ps. 68.25 and on the Taylor Prism; see *AOT*, pp. 352 ff.; *ANET*, pp. 287 f.; *DOTT*, pp. 66 f.

of those psalms which were not really intended to be used by the
king but originated or were thought to have originated in the pre-
exilic royal cult of the Temple; probably the term *'al y^edē dāwīd*
(= according to the directions of David; Ezra 3.10) is meant to be
understood in the same sense (cf. II Chron. 23.18). At this stage of
the collection of psalms the term *l^edāwīd* would then have been a
collective name of some sort and would have been used to specify the
psalm in question as belonging to the 'Davidic tradition' of the pre-
exilic Temple cult. It is only in this way that the striking fact can be
accounted for that the statement in Ps. 72.20 'The prayers of David
are ended' is added to a psalm which is ascribed to Solomon—unless
we are prepared to believe that the compilers of the psalms were
capable of wanton thoughtlessness.

If we are correct in assuming that the name of David once served
the purpose of specifying the psalms belonging to the cultic tradition
of the First Temple and of recommending them beside other psalms,
it was then only a small matter to proceed to the next stage of
regarding David as the ancestor of the psalms and of understanding
the term *l^edāwīd* as expressing his authorship. A contributory factor
to such an understanding of the term was probably the tendency to
legitimize the cult of the Second Temple over against the claims laid
to the tradition by the Samaritans by strengthening the authority of
David in matters concerning the cult of the Jerusalem Temple.
Efforts made in that direction took place, for instance, at the time
when the Persian régime came to an end, as can be ascertained from
the Books of Chronicles.[1] Again, it may be presumed that also in the
course of that development the biographical notes attached to 13
psalms (Pss. 3; 7; 18; 34; 51; 52; 54; 56; 57; 59; 60; 63; 142) were
drawn up in order to indicate the historical situation in which David
is said to have composed or recited the hymn in question. That these
notes with the exception of Psalm 18 were attached to laments only
betrays a certain apologetic tendency; perhaps the way in which, in
II Samuel 22, Psalm 18 was made use of in a story of David may have
served in this connection as a model. From the evidence of the
Septuagint, in which superscriptions of this kind, naming the
author, have been attached to an even greater number of psalms,
the inference can be drawn that this process continued during the
third century BC. It is commonly known that these statements
concerning the author of a psalm are of no direct historical value;

[1] Cf. Martin Noth, *Überlieferungsgeschichtliche Studien* I, 1943, § 17.

the ascribing of Psalm 90 to Moses, of Psalms 72 and 127 to Solomon, of Psalm 88 to Heman and of Psalm 89 to Ethan falls into the same category.

The Psalter in its present form is not the result of *one* single act of collecting; nor has it been compiled throughout by the same people. These facts can be inferred from the Psalter itself. For it still bears distinct traces of having grown in the course of history. The Psalter, which in its present form is divided into five books, represents the ultimate outcome of a process of collecting psalms which extended over a longer period. Thus the final compiler produced the present Psalter from various earlier collections. This follows, firstly, from the psalms which occur twice in the Psalter (Pss. 14 = 53; 40.13–17 = 70; 57.7–11 and 60.5–12 = 108), a phenomenon which would hardly have been possible if all the psalms had been grouped together all at once and by the same compiler; secondly, from the so-called 'Elohistic Psalter': in Psalms 42–83, which form a separate group, the term *'elōhīm*, which was the general designation for the deity, was substituted for God's actual name Yahweh; this is evident from a comparison of the doublets. If the whole Psalter had been assembled when this Elohistic revision was carried out, it would be incomprehensible why that action was confined to this group of psalms.

In Psalms 3–41, we have a grouping of psalms which almost without exception have the superscription *l^edāwīd*. This has evidently been done intentionally; it is, however, not possible to discover a further principle by which that arrangement may have been governed, so that the date of the collection must remain an open question. The so-called Elohistic Psalter (Pss. 42–83) seems to have been enlarged later on by adding to it Psalms 84–89 as an appendix. That Psalter is itself compiled from smaller and earlier collections: those which stand out most prominently as a separate group are the ones which are attributed to the Sons of Korah (Pss. 42–49 and, in the appendix, Pss. 84; 85; 87; 88); they are grouped together according to the specific type of song to which they belong and have their origin in the tradition of the Korahite guild of temple-singers. A similar view is to be taken of the small collection of Asaph psalms (Pss. 50; 73–83). The group of 'Davidic psalms' (Pss. 51–65; 68–70) is arranged according to the same principles which govern the grouping together of the Korah psalms; the postscript in Ps. 72.20 'The Prayers of David are ended' (see above), which concludes these Davidic psalms, marks them off from Davidic psalms occurring in later portions of the Psalter as a collection dating from an earlier period. The musical and liturgical annotations which almost without exception are attached to the individual songs prove that these groups were compiled for use in the cult. The way in which Psalms 90–150 have been collected is quite obscure. The 'Book of Pilgrim Songs' (Pss. 120–134) is a smaller collection in which each psalm carries the title 'A song of Ascents' (Luther translates: 'A song for the higher choir' *Ein Lied im höhern Chor*); but it contains, in fact, only one genuine pilgrim song (Ps. 122) beside some 'Davidic psalms' of which, to be sure, we cannot be certain that they really belong to the category of Davidic psalms (Pss. 122; 124; 131; 133). The division of the Psalter into five books is the work of the final compiler.[1] The same is true of the arrangement according to which each of these books ends with a closing doxology; this, in view of I Chron. 16.8–36, allows us to draw the conclusion that the Psalter was used in public worship. Again, it was perhaps the final compiler who assigned to Psalms 1 and 2, to which no superscription is attached, and to Psalm 150 their present position in the Psalter, intending Psalms 1 and 2 to serve as an introduction and Psalm 150 as a doxological conclusion to the whole Psalter. In all probability the process of compiling the whole Psalter must have been completed about 200 BC, in view of the fact that the Septuagint accords with the Hebrew Psalter. The Prologue of Ecclesiasticus (cf. Ps. 47.7 ff.) presupposes in the year 132 BC the existence of the tripartite Greek canon, whereas the Psalms of Solomon dating from the time of Pompey were too late to be included in the biblical Psalter.

Compared with the great age of psalmody the number of psalms that have been preserved is small. The 150 canonical psalms represent only a fraction of a much richer liturgical poetry, as is already shown by the existence of psalms outside the Psalter. This is to be accounted for not only by the fact that the hymns which were preserved in the Psalter in connection with the cult of the Covenant Festival are themselves to be regarded only as a fraction of religious and cultic activities which cover a much wider field and are more ramified, but also by the further fact that the post-exilic compilers

[1] In this connection the analogy to the division of the Torah has already been frequently pointed out. Mowinckel (op. cit. II, p. 197) holds that the division of the Psalter into five parts has no significance with regard to the history of its compilation. However, it may perhaps still imply a late indication of the original connection of the psalms with the 'Mosaic' tradition of Yahweh and of the continued existence of that tradition in public worship.

were interested only in the preservation of those psalms which could be used in the changed conditions of the cult community of the Second Temple. In the light of these facts we are able to understand how the idea of a post-exilic origin of the psalms could arise and hold its own for such a long time. This is also why a new interpretation was given to many a psalm. The loss of political independence meant that historico-political thought lost the quality of actuality resulting from its relatedness to the present and took refuge in hopes for the future; and that process entailed a transformation of eschatological ideas. It is in this way that the Royal Psalms, for instance, have come to be reinterpreted in a Messianic sense with the result that it even became possible to retain Psalm 45 in the Psalter though it is a profane wedding-song. In Ps. 51.18 f. the offence given by the psalm was mitigated by a postscript. A new meaning was given later on to Psalm 30, which is an individual thanksgiving, in that according to its superscription it was regarded as a hymn to be used at the feast of the dedication of the Temple. Thus the scope of the Psalter has indeed been still further compressed, and the splendour of its original colours has sometimes faded. However, even though the psalms preserved in the Psalter do not express the religious life of Israel in all its fullness, they have nevertheless been able, by virtue of the bond that links them to the tradition of the old Covenant regarding the revelation of God, to preserve in the prayerful devotion of the Psalter the full depth and power of a belief in God that was continually created anew as a living source of strength. Thus by its hymns, its prayers, its edifying power, the Psalter has never ceased to enrich and stimulate the religious life of the Church and of the individual believer right up to the present day.

II

COMMENTARY

1. THE TWO WAYS

1 Blessed is the man who walks not in the counsel of the wicked,
   nor stands in the way of sinners, nor sits in the seat of scoffers;
2 but his delight is in the law of the Lord,
   and on his law he meditates day and night!
3 He is like a tree planted by streams of water,
   that yields its fruit in its season, and its leaf does not wither.
   In all that he does, he prospers.
4 The wicked are not so, nay,[1]
   but are like chaff which the wind drives away.
5 Therefore the wicked will not stand in the judgment,
   nor sinners in the congregation of the righteous;
6 for the Lord cares for the way of the righteous,
   but the way of the wicked will perish.

   [1] Thus we must read the text with LXX.

The Psalter begins with a 'Beatitude'.[1] Its very first word is a word
of comfort promising happiness to the God-fearing people. The first
psalm, standing at the entrance to the Psalter as a signpost, gives clear
guidance regarding the way in which they shall conduct their lives.
Presumably the compiler of the Psalter deliberately assigned first
place to this psalm in order to call the reader to obedience to God's
will and to trust in his providential rule. The psalm, which was
probably not composed in the first instance as an introduction to the
Psalter, meets that intention of the compiler by the keynote which
determines both its form and its subject-matter, and according to
which the psalm endeavours to guide, educate and press for a
decision. If we want to understand the psalm, we shall have to start
from these established facts. It is a hymn which is full of practical and
godly wisdom. We can picture to ourselves its author as one of the
Wisdom teachers (cf. Jer. 8.9, 18.18; Eccles. 12.9 f.; Prov. 8.1 ff.) who
has set himself the task of initiating young men in 'Wisdom', that is,
of teaching them knowledge of life and the ability to live their lives

[1] * 'Invocation of blessing'—but see p. 87, n.1.

intelligently and on a moral and religious basis; he did this by passing on to them the treasures of his own experience. And to this end he uses the form of the 'Wisdom song'. The psalm serves the educational intentions of its author very well indeed by the lucidity of its structure, by its simple language using familiar figures of speech, by its imagery and by the challenging character of its exhortation. Its special significance lies in the fact that the 'practical wisdom' is based on a firm religious foundation the roots of which are firmly embedded in the tradition of public worship (see Intr. 87 f.).

The psalmist develops his thoughts in three stages: firstly, the two ways are contrasted (vv. 1–2); secondly, the author expresses in two word-pictures his views on the nature and the value of the God-fearing people and of the wicked (vv. 3–4); and thirdly, God's final verdict in his judgment is pronounced (vv. 5–6).

The two ways (vv. 1–2)

[1] In the form of a pronouncement expressing blessedness, which is reminiscent of the beatitudes in Matt. 5.3 ff., the psalmist praises the right conduct of the God-fearing people and throws that conduct into relief by characterizing it both negatively (v. 1) and positively (v. 2). The contrasting of the godly with the wicked, in fact, the psalmist's whole method of portraying this in black and white which is applied to every part of the psalm and has its origin in the Yahweh cult's claim to exclusiveness (see Intr. 48, 78 f., 93), betrays the author's educational purpose of giving expression and effect to his warnings and exhortations by means of the lucidity, terseness, simplicity and forcefulness of his words and thoughts (cf. the word-picture of the two ways and gates in Matt. 7.13 f.). It is therefore not necessary to seek the author of the psalm in the circles of the Pharisees (= those who are set apart) or of their predecessors, who as the upright turned their back on the wicked and because of their religious rigidity and presumption rejected even him who had come to deliver man from the wretchedness of sin. Presumably the psalm is of a much earlier date.

After the manner of a pedagogue the psalmist shows in detail and in phrases which are progressively intensified the various possible ways that lead to sin, and he does so by using concrete examples. The least sinful way is dealt with first, namely the way of 'walking in the counsel of the wicked', which means letting oneself be guided by the advice of the evildoers. Then there is the 'standing in the way of sinners', which means conforming to the example of the sinners.

And, finally, the worst sin is that of taking a seat in the meetings of the scoffers and actively participating in their mocking of the things which are sacred. For the root-cause of every sin and of its seductive power lies in what follows: when man begins to mock God (in accordance with Isa. 28.14 ff. we shall have to think here on similar lines), he has not only separated from God, but in his blind arrogance even tries to put himself above God; on the other hand, nothing has such an unsettling effect on young people as the mocking of the very things which ought to be their main-stay.   [2] In v. 2 God's law (instruction) that leads man in the right way is contrasted with the way of the human seducers. This betrays a tendency directed against the scoffers, who assumed a hostile attitude towards the tradition of law and judgment (v. 4 f.). To do God's will gives man true joy, and to meditate unceasingly on what he demands from man is the very thing which it is worth while to strive for in life. The psalmist does not therefore stop at the external aspect of a godliness based on the law (see below on v. 3). In contrast to the view taken of the law in the New Testament, for instance by the Apostle Paul in Rom. 3.19 ff.; 4.14 ff.; 5.12 f.; Gal. 3.2 ff., 19 ff.; I Cor. 15.56, the law is here not regarded as an irksome burden but as a source of joy (cf. Pss. 19.7 ff.; 119.92 ff.; Deut. 30.11 ff.). We can understand this delight in the law only if we think of the insecurity of man in antiquity who did not perceive a divine will which was firmly laid down and distinctly formulated and which could serve as a guide for his life. That insecurity is clearly demonstrated by the use of oracles which compelled him to explore again and again in each individual case what the Deity wanted him to do. Anyone who can speak of the law as the psalmist does regards the law as the intelligible expression of the divine will, valid once and for all, and therefore as the unerring compass, which is able to regulate his conduct, but at the same time also as a strong bond of trust in God's providential rule over his life. Hence we may assume that the meaning of the advice to meditate on the law day and night is not so much that of asking men to become versed in the law by acquiring knowledge of it in a more formal manner, as is still being done today by the orthodox Jew, but rather that of a warning challenging man to yield constantly to the will of God and let that will always pervade his whole being until it becomes his second nature and fills his whole life as the only meaning of that life. It is of the essence of the will of God as he is represented in the Bible—and this is already true of the Old Testament—that it not only manifests itself in a particular commandment which, so to speak, would enable man to cast off the burden of his responsibility by fulfilling that particular commandment, but makes itself known in the form of a constant demand by God, a laying claim to the whole man in respect of both his individual deeds and his total conduct.

It is from that total behaviour of a man who fully responds to the will of God (v. 2b; cf. I Thess. 5.17 'Pray constantly', expressing the Christian's attitude of mind concerning prayer) that the delight in the law of God springs in all its fullness (v. 2a); for that behaviour imparts to man's life the meaning and value which is ordained for it by God. This thought is now elucidated by two images in which once more the nature of the godly and that of the wicked are contrasted with each other.

Judgment on the character and value of the godly and the wicked (vv. 3–4)

[3] In a picture which was also used elsewhere in the Wisdom literature (cf. Jer. 17.8; Job 8.16; and *AOT*, ch. 4, p. 39; cf. *DOTT*, p. 178), the nature of the God-fearing man who is absorbed in doing God's will is compared with a green tree full of sap and vigour which, planted by a watercourse, bears its fruit in due season and the leaves of which do not prematurely wither in summer under the influence of heat and drought, a process which occurs considerably more frequently in the semi-tropical climate of Palestine than in the West. The image of the tree does not speak here of the reward which the God-fearing man will receive by way of the recompense to which he can look forward—it would be altogether unsuitable for conveying such a meaning—but it speaks of the meaning and the value of life which the godly man discovers by living his life in obedience to God. Just as the taking in of water, the fruit, and the sprouting leaves jointly constitute the nature and the value of a tree, because—it may be permissible to make this appropriate addition—it is in this that the tree truly fulfils the purpose for which it was created and which is willed for it by God, so the nature and the value of a godly life are to be found in the fulfilment of the divine will as the law which governs both the outward and the inward life of man. We shall therefore have to understand here the image of the tree and of its fruits as in Matt. 7.16–20, especially vv. 18 f. The conclusion of the verse 'in all that he does, he prospers' speaks of the godly man and therefore does not belong any more to the picture of the tree: if it were otherwise, it would mean an inappropriate repetition. We are here confronted with a strong faith which optimistically assumes that the God-fearing man cannot fail to be successful in all that he undertakes. Such a faith is well suited to strengthen the resolve of leading one's life in accordance with God's will, but is dangerous if it is distorted into a calculating belief in recompense and feels itself entitled to lay a counter-claim before God in order to settle accounts with him or if the idea of success becomes the sole motive of action and, consequently, the attitude of faithful obedience is abandoned. Many passages of the Old Testament show that the Jewish faith has repeatedly succumbed to these dangers. It should not, however, be said of the poet who composed this Psalm, as it often has been, that he too succumbed to these two dangers. For, what encourages the psalmist to hold that optimistic view is precisely not an attitude which disregards God or confronts him with worldly demands but the attitude of true faith in God. Because God is God it is impossible that anything can fail which man does in obedient execution of the will of God (cf. v. 6a). The true meaning and value of life is to be found not in success as such but in that joyous and unshakable trust in God which cannot be broken, and the only way which leads to that goal is precisely the obedience rendered by faith. Here the psalmist simply faces the fundamental law of the divine biology: 'A sound tree cannot bear evil fruit.'

[4] In sharp contrast to this verdict (v. 4a) the life of the wicked is characterized as being meaningless and worthless, and this is done by means of a deliberate change of the word-picture. When the harvest has been gathered in, and the sheaves have been spread out on the threshing floor, an elevated and exposed spot outside the village, they are 'threshed' by the threshing instrument, which is drawn over them, so that the grains become detached from the ears. The farmer then tosses the mixture up into the air with the winnowing shovel and the heavy grains fall to the ground, and the straw, which has been squashed and become chaff, together with the empty husks of the ears, is blown away by the wind. In the opinion of the poet the life of the wicked, a life lived apart from God, is just as empty, just as meaningless and worthless as the chaff. To anyone holding such a view God means indeed everything, and everything else which life could offer in other respects and which from the human point of view might be a matter of temptation is nothing in comparison with it. In the same way this rigid one-sidedness of the psalmist's view must be understood in the light of the faith which inspires the psalm and also

in the light of its educational purpose which presses for a decision. There is therefore no need to regard the psalmist's one-sided view as the utterance of a religious arrogance bearing the stamp of the pharisaic attitude. The words exhibit no trace of malice; here the psalmist merely draws a conclusion from the divine law that governs man's life as far as the negative aspect of that law is concerned, having dealt in v. 3 with its positive aspect.

God's verdict (vv. 5–6)

[5] If the nature and the value of the life of the upright and of the wicked can be apprehended already at the present time by anyone who ponders over them profoundly enough, how much more clearly will he be able to apprehend them by looking into the future when God himself will sit in judgment and pronounce the verdict. The previous image of the winnowing of the chaff which was frequently used as an illustration of God's judgment (Hos. 13.3; Zeph. 2.2; Isa. 29.5; Ps. 35.5; Matt. 3.12) already pointed to the prospect of God's judgment. And that prospect, as indeed the structure of the whole psalm, can be traced back to the cultic idea of blessing and curse as the act of judgment which separates and purges the cult community from the ungodly elements (v. 6; see Intr. 48, 78 f.). In the opinion of the psalmist it ensues therefrom with compelling necessity and consistency ('therefore'—a distinctive mark of the rationality of the Wisdom way of thinking) that anyone whose life at the present time is rootless and lacking any inner meaning because he is godless, will not be able to hold his own either when he sees himself arraigned before the judgment seat of God and has to face God alone. In the divine judgment the way of the wicked, that is, their conduct and their past life, is revealed in its complete futility; the way 'disappears'; it 'vergeht' (perishes) according to Luther's translation (cf. Prov. 10.28; Job 8.13). The godly, on the other hand, are approved by God in his judgment and thereafter will form the communion of the 'righteous'; the sinners are no longer entitled to belong to that cult community.

[6] The psalmist justifies this vision of the future, which is not depicted in any great detail, by adding some noteworthy reasons (v. 6). The ground of the certitude of hope is to be found in the assurance received by faith that God cares for the way of the righteous, knowing his mode of life and taking a loving interest in his future destiny; both these ideas are implied in the Hebrew. Here the

whole of life is viewed and judged from the standpoint of God: God is in everything which is being done according to his will; it is he, and not man, who secures the stability of man's life; anything, however, which is done apart from God is bound to perish.

Psalm 1 is well suited to serve as a title for the whole Psalter in view of the lucid and forceful way in which it calls to responsible obedience to God and to faithful hope of him.[1] For in an impressive manner it throws into relief what really matters—faith and obedience as the ultimate meaning of the life of the faithful cult community. It is here that the lasting fundamentals of religion are indeed to be found, and that is true not only of the fundamentals of the religion of the Old Testament. It would mean stopping at the consideration of external features (and would not even appear plausible) if we were to interpret the psalm's paraphrasing of the will of God by the use of the term 'law' as pointing to a casuistic 'legalistic religion' which has grown superficial and has hardened (Gunkel), or even if we only restricted this term to a Torah fixed in writing (Kraus) and in doing so were to single out the way in which the psalmist has expressed his mind, which after all is conditioned by contemporary history, as that which really matters in the psalm, and then would contrast this result with the Gospel. Behind the forms in which the poet has expressed his thoughts and which are conditioned by the circumstances of his time he visualizes an eternal reality. In the law he encounters the will of God in the form of an ordinance for life which is God's gift and embraces man's whole life. In that ordinance for life the divine meaning and value of life is revealed. In the last resort that ordinance for life determines man's existence or non-existence. As far as the law expresses this latter thought, it is not at variance with the Gospel, but is already a step in the direction of the Gospel. If the law is viewed in this way, it is also not impugned by the saying of Jesus, 'but I say to you'; on the contrary, when Jesus says of the law, 'I have come not to abolish the law but to fulfil it', he regards the law as the presupposition of the Gospel on which he can base his own teaching.

[1] According to Acts 13.33 the proper counting of the psalms seems to have begun with Psalm 2. (Tr. N.: The reference is to the reading in the Codex Bezae, Origen, etc.: 'in the first psalm'.)

2. GOD AND HIS 'ANOINTED'

1 Why do the nations rage, and the peoples plot in vain?
2 The kings of the earth set themselves, and the rulers take counsel together,

against the Lord and his anointed, saying,

3 'Let us burst their bonds asunder, and cast their cords from us.'

4 He who sits in the heavens laughs; the Lord has them in derision.

5 But then he speaks to them in his wrath, and terrifies them in his
   fury, saying,

6 'I have set my king on Zion, my holy hill.'

7 I will tell of the decree of the Lord:
   He said to me: 'You are my son, today I have begotten you.

8 Ask of me ' '[1], and I will make nations your heritage,
   and the world your possession.

9 You shall beat them with a rod of iron, and dash them in pieces like
   a potter's vessel.'

10 Now therefore, O kings, be wise;
   Be warned, O judges of the earth.

11 Serve the Lord with fear,
   with trembling kiss his feet,[1]

12 lest he be angry, and you perish in the way;
   for his wrath is quickly kindled.
   Blessed are all who trust in him.

[1] See BH.

When in the great empires of the ancient Orient the mighty ruler died, then all nations were in a state of extreme agitation. In the nations which had been brought into bondage the yearning for freedom was aroused, and the occasion of the change of sovereign seemed to offer to the vassals an opportunity, which more than once had proved to lead to success, to burst the chains of slavery. Thus it was often the primary and the most urgent task of a new great king on his accession to the throne to suppress the rebellion of the subjugated princes and peoples in order to consolidate and establish afresh the power of his great empire. This familiar picture, which has frequently recurred in the course of history, underlies this psalm, which seems to have been composed for the occasion of the feast of the enthronement of the king and to have been recited within the framework of the cultic ceremony. We know neither the poet nor the Israelite king into whose mouth this psalm is put as a proclamation of some sort. It is unnecessary to assign individual strophes to different speakers (the poet and the king); the whole psalm can easily be understood as having been uttered by the king alone. The psalm was composed for the occasion of the enthronement of a king of Judah at Jerusalem in the time after David. Its author, a master of words full of great poetical power and bold ideas, is probably to be thought of as belonging to the circle of the court-poets of the king.

The psalm, which was probably designed to be used again and again, confronts the rebellion of the kings of the earth (first strophe) with the transcendent grandeur of God in heaven (second strophe), and it does so with a few powerful strokes and in a manner which impressively marks the contrast. This is followed by the divine installation of the king and the promise attached to it (third strophe), to which the psalm adds a warning directed to the rulers of the earth to humble themselves before the divine Lord of the earth lest his wrath destroy them (fourth strophe).

First strophe: the kings of the earth

[1–3] The psalm opens with a question which expresses the speaker's surprise and arises out of the vivid dramatic tension of the cultic scene, and that question leads us at once right into the midst of the rebellion of the nations and their kings. In their own words the latter declare their will to cast off the foreign rule of Israel and her God. We shall look in vain for a situation in the course of the history of Israel and Judah in which an Israelite king would in reality have ruled the whole world as is implied in the psalm.[1] Nor can it be assumed that the poet would call the princes of the small neighbouring peoples, which had been temporarily subjugated by Israel, 'kings of the earth' or 'judges of the earth' (v. 10) which would have been an unjustified and extravagant exaggeration. The world-wide setting into which the psalmist projects the modest proportions of the Israelite kingship can therefore hardly be accounted for in any other way than by assuming that he copied a foreign pattern; the pattern would be that of the court etiquette of the great empires of the ancient Orient and of its royal cult where, as we have learned from Assyrian and Egyptian literary monuments, the use of such stylized types is made sufficiently understandable in the light of the aforementioned historical situation which developed on the occasion of the advent of a new king. And it is not only this universal setting which suggests that the Israelite court-poet was dependent on oriental royal traditions. There are also individual traits such as vv. 7–9 which point in the same direction, traits of which it would be difficult to assume that they had been derived from the history or from the religion of Israel. Again, in the psalm there are stylistic and material parallels to the so-called Egyptian 'Königsnovelle' (Royal

---

[1] Such a situation did not even exist in David's 'empire' (this point in opposition to Kraus).

Proclamation),[1] which likewise support this view. But, in spite of all that, must we not persist in regarding it as the presumptuous utterance of an incomprehensible and intolerable arrogance when claims implying dominion over the whole world are here voiced for which no occasion can be found at any point in the history of Israel which would justify them? This question will be answered in the affirmative only by those whose eyes remain fixed on the visible surface of history so that they do not comprehend the hidden motive forces of historical events which are controlled by God, the Lord of universal history. This explains why the psalmist recognizes even in the small fragment of history which is represented by the enthronement of a Judaic king the invisible hand and will of God who is the Lord of universal history and who, though invisible, is also present at the cultic ceremony for which the psalm was composed. The king in Zion is the anointed of God (Messiah); he is under the shadow of his heavenly Lord. Such a view, if pondered over deeply enough, is not to be characterized as the expression of an arrogant presumption but as a vision granted to the assurance that comes by faith, an assurance which comprises both humble *submission to God* and *elevation by God*, and to which has been assigned the high purpose of serving as the fundamental theme of the whole psalm. It is from that angle that the psalmist views and judges the historical events which have taken place on the surface of history. Approaching them from such a theocentric perspective, which accords with the fundamental idea of the cultic feast, he now feels justified in envisaging, too, the accession of the king to the throne within a world-wide setting. In this way the whole picture assumes a new meaning, a meaning that belongs to the *Heilsgeschichte*. At the centre of history is no longer the struggle of the great world powers for existence, but God, whose relationship with the earthly powers will determine their destiny. Viewed in this way any revolt of the world powers appears to the poet from the outset as a rebellion of man against God, the outcome of which can never be in doubt for the very reason that it is directed against God. Because the raging and plotting of the nations is rebellion against God, it is for that very reason a futile undertaking, and because the poet already apprehends here something which the pagans do not apprehend, he expresses for that very reason his surprise and enquires after

[1] Cf. Siegfried Herrmann, *Die Königsnovelle in Ägypten und Israel*, Wissenschaftliche Zeitschrift der Karl-Marx-Universität Leipzig, Gesellschafts- und sprachwissenschaftliche Reihe, 3. Jahrgang (1953/54), pp. 33 ff.

the purport of that futile effort. It is the disclosure of the contrast
evident when the power of man is confronted by the power of God
which from the outset dominates the train of thought of the whole
psalm. The exceedingly impressive antithesis of the first two strophes
is based on that contrast.

Second strophe: the Heavenly King

[4–6] The second strophe begins with an abrupt change of scene
and mood. The agitation and rebellion on earth are confronted in the
psalm with the picture of the sublime peace that reigns in heaven.
The helpless kings of the earth are contrasted with the superior might
of God who is the King of heaven. A race of pigmies is face to face
with a giant! Thus it is only by faith that men and temporal things
are seen in their right proportion in that they are related to God as
the Lord (*'adōnāy*). Again, it is only when we know the overwhelming
power of God, which surpasses all works of man, that we achieve
that inward superiority, fearlessness and serene confidence which is
so graphically expressed in the magnificent picture of God who from
his exalted throne smiles at the manikins and mocks at them. This
picture reminds us of Isaiah, who was the ideal man displaying noble
serenity at a time when everybody else was in a state of extreme
agitation as a result of political events which followed each other in
quick succession. He, too, derived his peace of mind from his faith
in God, and his unruffled assurance is nothing else than the image of
the tranquil sublimity of his God who, like the cirrus clouds which
float high above in the blue sky on a summer day, stands still and
watches the tumults that convulse the nations (Isa. 18.4). It is to this
God that the psalm bears witness, characterizing him as a God who
is present and active, who knows how to make himself respected by
those who do not want to give heed to him, and who accomplishes his
purpose even though men rebel against him. The conclusion of the
strophe sounds like the far-off rumbling of the thunder of judgment
that threatens the rebellious kings and rulers of the earth. When God
speaks to the princes of the nations, then his awesome majesty will
spread terror round about and the nations will have to realize with
trembling what it means to rebel against the king whom God himself
has 'consecrated' on Zion. Thus it is from God that the historical yet
cultic situation which arises at the enthronement of a new king
receives its impetus and the responsibility which it involves.

Third strophe: the king in Zion

[7-9] Having dealt with the divine installation of the king at Jerusalem, the poet follows up this theme with the account of the 'divine decree' (probably the legitimation by prophets and priests of the so-called 'royal protocol' which is well known from the Egyptian royal ritual, cf. II Kings 11.12) which he puts into the mouth of the king and on which the latter's reign is based. Yahweh has promised him divine sonship and the privileges of a son of God. The form of this oracle once more follows prototypes of the ancient Orient which were adopted by the royal ritual of Jerusalem, Canaan probably having acted as a mediator, as is suggested by reminiscences in vv. 4–7 of that section of the Ras Shamra texts which deals with Baal. The idea of the divine sonship points to the deification of the king in consequence of which the king was regarded as having been begotten by the deity. It is understandable that the Old Testament rejected the idea of the physical divine sonship of the king as incompatible with its spiritual notion of God.[1] In fact, the psalmist, too, excludes the idea of a physical begetting by adding the word 'today' and by using the ancient formula of adoption 'you are my son', though he leaves untouched the formula 'I have begotten you' which originated in that foreign world of ideas. He transforms that alien idea into the idea of adoption, that is to say, into the declaration of the sonship of the king that took place on the day of his enthronement. By that act special importance is attributed not to the person of the king as such but to his office as king. The Old Testament kingship thereby becomes a function and the instrument of the will of the divine Ruler.

The privileges of sonship which are conferred upon the king by God are to be understood similarly. He may ask favours,[2] and God gives him nations and the earth for his inheritance and also power to sit in judgment upon his enemies. Here, too, faith boldly soars beyond the boundaries of historical reality. As the poet did in the first strophe, so here, too, he borrowed the setting which belongs to universal history, the setting of victories over the other nations and of dominion over the whole world, from foreign prototypes. His method here is similar to that of the oracles which have been preserved about

---

[1] Cf. Ps. 89.26 f.; II Sam. 7.14; I Chron. 28.6.
[2] Cf. II Sam. 7.18 ff.; I Kings 3.5 ff. and Herrmann, op. cit., p. 55, concerning the prayer offered in connection with the 'Royal Proclamation' (*Königsnovelle*).

Assyrian and Egyptian rulers[1] where such ideas could easily be applied to the historical position of those kings. We would now be equally wrong if we wanted to dispose of this application of the afore-mentioned grand ideas to the small proportions of the affairs of Israel by stigmatizing it as the product of a bragging presumption. For in so doing we would overlook an essential feature of the biblical way of thinking. If two people say the very same thing, it is neverthe-less not the same thing. The oracles of the ancient East impart to the historical aspirations of the kings for power a greater energy by the promise of divine help; the emphasis is, however, on the internal affairs of the nation in question. In the Old Testament, on the other hand, the internal historical events—in our present context the kingship in Zion—are recognized as bearers of a divine will which transcends history and for that very reason encompasses it totally—both as regards space and time—and that divine will bursts the nar-row bounds which limit the internal historical events and, contrary to all expectations that may seem to be justified from a worldly and historical point of view, makes these events the blueprint of and the signal for that divine judgment which in terms of space is universal and in terms of time is final (eschatological). Here the emphasis is on the will of God: the eternal will is at work in the historical events, and it is only by the intervention of that will that these events receive their ultimate meaning and setting. Hence after all it makes a difference whether words which bear a likeness to each other express the human lust for power, as they do in the oracles of the ancient East, or whether they bear witness to the vision of faith, as they do in the Old Testament, where man's eyes are lifted up to the power of the divine Judge of the earth who subjects men to his will and in the midst of history reveals ultimate visions of his coming kingdom. What appears to be a colossal exaggeration, if looked at from the standpoint of the purely internal history of Israel, is, in the world of ideas associated with the Old Testament's cultic tradition, the power-ful expression of a strong faith in the miraculous might of God, which is also the main source and support of the prophetic hope of the Old Testament for the future and the consummation of all things at the end of time. That this is the true interpretation is shown by the last

---

[1] Cf. Sethe, *Die Ächtung feindlicher Fürsten, Völker und Dinge auf altägyptischen Tongefässscherben des Mittleren Reiches*, Abhandlungen der Berliner Akademie (1926), no. 5; and Spiegel, *Das Werden der altägyptischen Hochkultur* (1953), para. 811, concerning the rite of the 'smashing of the earthen vessels'.

strophe of the psalm, in which the poet draws practical conclusions
for the kings of the earth.

Fourth strophe: the warning

[10–12] The psalm reverts to its starting-point by addressing the
rulers of the earth, exhorting and warning them. For it is the aim of
the train of thought dominating the whole hymn to show that in the
face of the rebellion of the would-be lords of the world God stands
behind the king of Zion as a living reality, as the true Lord of the
earth, who reigns by the power of his imperturbable will. This is
what the kings of the earth should now realize, and from that knowledge they should draw the only conclusion which is both possible and
reasonable, the conclusion that they must humble themselves before
Almighty God and must serve him with fear and trembling. The
phrase 'kiss his feet' is applied to God in a truly human fashion and is
probably derived from the custom of kissing the feet of the king as an
act of homage, a custom which is well known to us from Babylonian
and Egyptian documents. We shall presumably have to understand
this phrase in a figurative sense too—in the sense of submission and
homage. (The literal translation 'and rejoice with trembling, kiss
with purity', or 'kiss the son', scarcely renders a satisfactory meaning
within the context which we have just discussed.) The fact that there
is no further mention of the king of Zion, not even a single word,
shows clearly enough that the emphasis is not on the historical situation as such, but on the theocentric perspective. What is ultimately at
stake in the psalm, as indeed in the whole cult, is precisely the recognition of God as the Lord of the earth. The psalm leaves no doubt
whatsoever about the seriousness of man's position in relation to God.
He who lives his life in the fear of God will keep it; anyone who does
not fear God will lose it 'in the way', for he is subject to the wrath of
God. It is possible that the poet here thinks of the conversion of the
Gentiles to the Yahweh religion which is attested elsewhere, too, as
a feature of the cult. But what is really before his mind's eye at the
conclusion of the psalm is not any single historical event but the
problem which God himself presents. The whole psalm has but one
aim—to show that God is the Lord and to make sure that he will be
recognized as such. Particular matters, even the association of the
psalm with the accession of the king to the throne, recede almost
completely into the background under the powerful impact of that
one decisive question. The awe in which the world-wide might of

God is held also dominates the final chord of the powerful hymn: the wrath of God threatens those who scorn him; but those who take refuge in him can be assured of his help. And that final chord once more marks the difference between the prototypes of the ancient East and the keynote of the Old Testament hymn: it is the unconditional awe in which the divine Lord of the world is held which imbues the psalm with its genuinely biblical character; again, it is that unconditional awe of God which in the cultic act places the historical events in a wider setting and invests them with the exalted character of things which are final and belong to the end of history. From that point of view it is understandable that the New Testament interprets the words of the psalm in a Messianic sense and regards them as referring to Jesus (Acts 13.33; Heb. 1.5; 5.5).

3. MORNING PRAYER

A Psalm. Of David, when he fled from Absalom his son[1].

1 O Lord, how many are my adversaries!
  Many are they that rise up against me.
2 Many are they who say of me,
  'There is no help for him in God.' *Selah*[2]
3 But thou, O Lord, art a shield about me,
  thou art my glory, and lift up my head.
4 I cried aloud to the Lord,
  and he answered me from his holy hill. *Selah*
5 I lay down and slept.—
  I wake again, for the Lord sustains me.
6 I am not afraid of the multitude of warriors
  who have set themselves against me round about.
7 Arise, O Lord! Help me, O my God!
  For thou hast bruised the cheeks of all my enemies,
  thou hast broken the teeth of the wicked.
8 Deliverance belongs to the Lord—
  thy blessing be upon thy people! *Selah*

[1] See Intr. p. 94–100.
[2] See Intr. p. 22.

According to the title, attached at a later date, the psalm is ascribed to David, who is said to have composed it when he fled from his rebellious son Absalom (cf. II Samuel, chs. 15–19). The content of the psalm does not enable us either to prove or disprove the truth of that statement. Only so much can be inferred from the psalm with some probability that it appears to be the prayer of a ruler (king) who is in a desperate situation as he faces a great number of enemies.[1] Presumably the psalm belongs to the royal ritual where the idea of Yahweh's warfare against enemies formed the framework of *Heilsgeschichte*, which is important for a true understanding of the specific situation in which the worshipper is placed (see the exegesis of v. 7).

[1–2] The worshipper pours out his heart to God in prayer, describing in the form of a lament the perilous situation with which he is afflicted. It is not only the great number of enemies who have risen up against him which frightens him, but his friends, too (v. 2), have turned their back on him (cf. the use of the third person in v. 2b), and have not only abandoned any hope that anyone will come to his aid but also their faith in God's help. So he is left alone to endure the trial of his faith; but he does not yield to the temptation to doubt. Forsaken by men, he clings the more firmly to his God. The knowledge that God will always be ready to listen to him, whenever he brings his afflictions before him, already means to him an easing of the state of anxiety in which he finds himself and which is such a burden.

[3] His faith is aroused to utter a defiant 'but' when his friends doubt whether God will help him. Though all appearances may be at variance with it, he pulls himself together and courageously affirms his faith in God, into whose arms he flings himself in utter abandonment. God is his protector and the shield which saves him from any kind of danger. He is aware that God himself is his honour which nobody can take away from him. It is for that reason that he is convinced that God will 'lift up his head', that God will restore his honour before men.

[4] It would, however, be wrong to assume that it was in the first instance his defiant refusal to fall into despair which induced the worshipper to express his faith in God. On the contrary, his trust in God firmly rests on his experience of a life rich in prayer. Yahweh has answered his prayer from the holy hill of Zion more than once (this is expressed by the use of the Hebrew imperfect). The poet brings back the memory of such sacred moments in his confession before God and the congregation (notice the change of style) and draws from his experience the strength of his hope which will not be confounded even in the present situation.

[1] It is less probable that the speaker is a private individual (thus Gunkel), or one who 'puts himself in his imagination in the position of a king' (thus Kraus).

[5] The psalmist thinks of the night which has just passed and finds his experience substantiated by that thought. He had lain down feeling safe with God and was able to sleep peacefully in spite of the many dangers surrounding him.[1] And does not the fact that he now sees again the light of the sun clearly prove that he is under the protection of God? [6] Of what should he be afraid, seeing that it is the mighty power of God which protects him? Having God as his ally, he can face fearlessly the innumerable multitude of enemies who threaten him on all sides. God's power outweighs the total strength of the hostile hosts. And it is this faith alone, not any reliance on his own strength (see v. 1), which gives this man courage and strength. [7] After some struggle his trust in God is now firmly established. Having reached confidence through faith, he is now able to pray to God and ask for his help. His action is not that of a beggar, who asks for help because he feels helpless, but has the character of true prayer which is born of and imbued with the conviction that the prayer will be answered. For, praying in this manner, the worshipper may rely on the tradition of the *Heilsgeschichte* as this is actualized in the cult—the tradition of Yahweh's victories over all his enemies and over the wicked—and know that his own adversaries, too, are included in that host of Yahweh's enemies. God *has* already smitten the enemies just as a man kills wild animals. The past, the present and the future intertwine at this moment; God has already helped, he has already wrought deliverance, and yet at the same time his help and his deliverance are prayed for and hoped for by man.

[8] In the concluding verse we see the scene represented in the cult of the Covenant, and the keynote of the prayer is once more briefly and impressively linked up with the theme of the cultic ceremony: deliverance belongs to the Lord and to him only; there is no one else who could help and, consequently, there is also nothing apart from God in which man could trust absolutely. The blessing of God is really all that matters. By calling for God's blessing upon his people (cf. II Sam. 6.18) the royal worshipper joins the cult community in order to share with them in the benefits which will be bestowed upon the people of God. The salvation of the God-fearing people is included in the judgment which God will pronounce on the evil-doers (see Intr. 78). The hymn ends on a note of trust and confident

[1] There is no question in the psalm of an oracle revealed to one sleeping in the Temple, as is assumed by some of the expositors.

hope. The worshipper prays for God's blessing upon the whole nation and by that prayer identifies himself with his people.

4. THE PEACE OF GOD

To the Conductor: with stringed instruments.[1] *A Psalm. Of David.*

1 When I cried, the God of my salvation answered me.[2]
   He gave me room when I was in distress;
   was gracious to me, and heard my prayer.[3]
2 O you men, how long shall my honour suffer shame?
   How long will you love vain words, and seek after lies? *Selah*
3 But know that the Lord did wondrously show his mercy to me;[4]
   the Lord hears when I call to him.
4 Tremble and sin not;
   meditate in secret[5] and be silent! *Selah*
5 Offer right sacrifices, and put your trust in the Lord!
6 There are many who say,
   'Who shows us good?'
   Lift up the light of thy countenance upon us, O Lord!
7 Thou hast put more joy in my heart
   than there is in days of a rich harvest.[6]
8 Altogether in peace I will lie down and sleep;
   for thou alone, O Lord, makest me dwell in safety.

[1] See Intr. 22.
[2] Read with LXX all verbs in verse 1 in the third person of the perfect tense.
[3] * V.1 in RSV:
   Answer me when I call, O God of my right!
   Thou hast given me room when I was in distress.
   Be gracious to me, and hear my prayer.
[4] See BH. (Tr. N.: RSV has, 'but know that the Lord has set apart the godly for himself'.)
[5] Lit.: 'meditate in your own hearts on your beds'.
[6] Lit.: 'when their grain and wine abound'. (Tr. N.: RSV has, 'than they have when their grain and wine abound'.)

[1] The psalm is a prayer of confidence which, mostly on account of v. 8, is called an 'evening hymn', and for that reason has probably been inserted after Ps. 3, a 'morning hymn'. It enables us to get an insight into the struggle of a man who, rejoicing in his faith, contends with his friends who are disheartened and discontented because they are passing through difficult times. Because any clear indication is lacking it is no longer possible to apprehend the specific circumstances to which the psalm alludes. However, the fundamental attitude inspiring the thoughts of the psalmist and the goal he is striving after can clearly be recognized.

In the present text part of the opening of the psalm is in the form of a supplication; the invocation which we would expect in such a case is, however, lacking. Moreover, v. 2 would hardly be conceivable if it were preceded by a supplication. Probably it is a question of the text having been altered at a later date in order to adapt the psalm to its future liturgical use as a prayer of supplication. In the original version of the first verse the poet stated that his prayer has been answered, and he seems to have thus brought into prominence the fundamental fact which he takes as his point of departure. He had learned that his own experience of the divine mercy was his strongest support on which he could always rely in any kind of affliction. For on many occasions when he had been in trouble he had experienced this divine mercy in that God had granted him his help and his 'righteousness' (= salvation) and had answered his prayers. This is the firm foundation on which the psalmist can take his stand and that also in face of the temptations which beset both him and his friends. The religious experience which the poet has thus gained forms the background of the psalm and provides the key for its true understanding. [2] Fortified by his firm trust in his religious experience, to him a fact of which he is absolutely certain, he derives from that trust the authority to reprove the doubts and reproaches of his opponents[1] in no uncertain terms. The caustic and peremptory manner in which the reproof is uttered finds its explanation in the faith of the poet who knows that God himself is the motive power behind his personal experiences. Therefore anyone who slanders the psalmist and tells lies about him not only impugns thereby the latter's dignity as a human being, but indirectly attacks also his God. The psalmist's glory is his faith in God. [3] If his friends would know this truth, they, too, could then not help realizing that their reproaches and doubts were unfounded. The poet wants to open their eyes that they may see that truth, and he also wants to turn their thoughts from their material afflictions to the invisible Lord in heaven who is their Helper, so that they may know him as he was privileged to know him through his experience of the miraculous way in which his life had been guided by God and his prayers had continually been answered. [4–5] He therefore offers them the following pastoral advice: 'Tremble and sin not!' If they would care to ponder quietly

---

[1] On the analogy of Egyptian and Babylonian linguistic usage the apostrophe 'O sons of a man' (in the translation 'O you men') signifies wealthy and influential people.

over these things, they would come to realize that they are men of little faith, and that it was really the smallness of their faith which caused them to express doubts and slander the poet. And then they will be terrified by the thought that they dared to distrust God, and that realization will lead them to true repentance, so that in future they will be preserved from sinning any more. The fact that the poet —perhaps a priest (v. 6)—calls upon his friends to offer fitting sacrifices (for sin) is only the outward cultic manifestation of that spirit of true repentance; a heart that is inwardly disposed to fear God and trust in him is for the poet all that really matters. It is precisely in the interaction of fear and trust, these two basic motives of true piety, that an essential feature of Old Testament religion is to be found in which these two sentiments arise out of the vivid impression produced by the sovereign power and the sublime reality of God. Again, it is precisely because God is here thought of as God, that is, as the Power with whom the final decision lies, that the God-fearing people of the Old Testament, whenever they are confronted with the reality of God, are continually overwhelmed by the feeling, a feeling which makes them tremble, of being divested of all safeguards in their relationship with God. On the other hand, absolute trust that cannot be disappointed is for the same reason possible only if the object of their trust is God, since it is he who holds in his hands both the final decision and the supreme power. The poet himself stands firm as a rock because of that trust. That his wavering friends, too, regain that goal by way of repentance and stand firm in their trust in God is the aim of his efforts.

[6] However, the poet's strong faith in God does not blind him to the fact that so many people round about him are in danger of succumbing to deep despair and to sore temptations. From the human point of view he can well understand that they are eaten up with worry by their afflictions, and in their distress feel urged to ask what God is going to do in this matter; 'Who shows us good?' And he shares in their sufferings resulting from the doubt expressed in their question. He unites therefore with the congregation in the priestly prayer which is taken from the Aaronite benediction: 'Lift up the light of thy countenance upon *us*, O Lord.' In doing so he has in mind not simply the deliverance from material afflictions; he does not pray: Grant us once more to live a happy life. The one thing that really matters to him is that *God's* nature be once more revealed, that God himself may appear (see Intr. 38 f.), to lead those who have gone astray into the

right way and to awaken in them that joy in God which the psalmist
himself has been able to keep in his heart in spite of all the adversity
that has befallen him.

[7–8] This delight in God, which is God's own gift to him,
signifies to him supreme happiness which in his eyes is of greater
value than any earthly riches. For it gives man inward freedom
from any dependence on earthly things and allows him to keep a
joyful heart even when he is deprived of all earthly possessions.
Lifting up his eyes in gratitude to God who has given him this
joyful heart as his most precious possession, the worshipper lies
down to spend the night in the peace of God. He knows that it is
only in God's arms that he is well sheltered, and that no affliction
can disturb the peace which dwells in his heart and which passes
all understanding.

The strength which emanates from this song is to be found in
the imperturbability and assuredness of a heart which knows itself
secure in the peace of God and which does not vacillate even when
it has to face the controversies of the world and the pressure of
spiritual and material afflictions, and in this way is always capable
of mastering every situation. And that imperturbability and assuredness are always superior to the restlessness and apprehension in those
who, because they have little faith, are always in doubt. But the
strength which the psalmist possesses by virtue of his innermost
treasure also enables him, as he lifts up his eyes to God together with
his friends, to lead them to a higher vision which transcends their
momentary tensions—to show them the way which through true
repentance will bring them to God's peace and to renewed joy in
him.

5. IT IS GOD WHO DECIDES

To the Conductor: to the accompaniment of flutes. A Psalm. Of David.

1 Give ear to my words, O Lord,
   give heed to my musing;
2 hearken to the sound of my cry,
   imploring thee, my King and my God!
   For to thee will I pray.
3 O Lord, in the morning thou wilt hear my voice;
   in the morning I make ready for thee[1] and watch for thee.
4 For thou art not a God who delights in wickedness;
   an evil man may not sojourn with thee.
5 The boastful may not stand before thy eyes;
   thou hatest all who do futile things.[2]

6 Thou destroyest those who speak lies;
  the Lord abhors bloodthirsty and deceitful men.
7 But I through the abundance of thy mercies
  may enter thy house,
  to worship thee toward thy holy temple in awe of thee.
8 Lead me, O Lord, according to thy righteousness,
  because of my oppressors;
  make straight my way before thee.[3]
9 For there is no truth in their[4] mouths,
  their inward part—destruction,
  their throat is an open sepulchre,
  they flatter with their tongue.
10 Hold thou them guilty, O God,
   that they fall by their own counsels;
   because of their many transgressions cast them out,
   for they have rebelled against thee!
11 But let them that trust in thee rejoice;
   they will ever shout with joy;[5]
   in thee will exult all that love thy name.[6]
12 For thou dost bless the godly,[7] O Lord;
   thou dost cover him[5] as with a shield
   and crown him with favour.

[1] * V. 3b reads in RSV as follows: 'In the morning I prepare a sacrifice for thee.'
[2] * V. 5b in RSV: 'thou hatest all evildoers.'
[3] See BH. (Tr. N.: RSV reads: 'make thy way straight before me.')
[4] See BH.
[5] The words 'thou dost cover him' are to be transferred to v. 12, where they fill an obvious gap and give the verse its true meaning.
[6] * In RSV v. 11 is rendered differently:
  But let all who take refuge in thee rejoice,
  let them ever sing for joy;
  and do thou defend them,
  that those who love thy name may exult in thee.
[7] Lit.: the righteous.

According to its form and subject-matter the psalm is to be classed with the type 'individual lament'. Its metre is that of the strophes of the lament, being three and two beats throughout. The present song still distinctly exhibits that psalm type's original association with the cult as its place of origin (see Intr. 68 f.). The psalm is to be thought of (v. 7) as having been uttered in the Temple during the offering of the morning sacrifice (v. 3; cf. II Kings 3.20; Amos 4.4); this excludes the view that it was composed by David. In vv. 4 ff. a particularly high value is attached to the cultus, but this evidence does not necessitate the conclusion that the author of the psalm must have been a priest. The psalm as a whole rather suggests that its author

belonged to the community of the 'godly' who were menaced by a
group of the 'wicked', and that the psalmist pleads with God in the
festival cult (see v. 2), entreating him to pass judgment on the machinations and intrigues of those wicked men (v. 10) and hoping for his
protection (vv. 11 f.). There are no particular clues which would
enable us to assign a definite date to the psalm.

The structure of the psalm is clear and simple: in the opening
verses 1–3 God is called upon; this is immediately followed—the
trend of thought here is one which is peculiar to the psalmist—by
a general reflection on God's relationship with the wicked who are
not admitted to the Temple, that general reflection being clothed in
the form of a confession before God (vv. 4–6); in v. 7 the psalmist
outlines his own position in relation to God in contrast to that of the
wicked and then proceeds in v. 8 to a personal prayer for right
guidance. Whilst vv. 7–8 revert to the theme of the opening verses,
the subsequent petition in vv. 9–10 for the condemnation and
destruction of the adversaries forms, in its turn, a parallel to vv. 4–6,
and by means of the linking together of these two groups of verses
even creates the vivid impression of a certain dramatic intensification
of the prayer which in the final strophe (vv. 11–12) reaches its
climax and fullest extent in the confident expectancy of the gracious
help which God will grant to the whole community of God-fearing
people.

[1–2] The psalm opens with a comprehensive introduction
(vv. 1–3). The accumulation of several invocations of God and the
association of the latter with repeated cravings for a hearing enable
us at the same time to gain an insight into the soul of the worshipper.
The intensity of his entreaties gives us an inkling of the magnitude of
the affliction which weighs heavily upon him and of the importance
he attaches to the fact that his prayer will be answered. His entreaties
are, however, at the same time the means whereby he is able to draw
near unto God, and through a clearly recognizable process of intensification they also serve the purpose of preparing the worshipper's
soul for praying in the right spirit. The worshipper is anxious that
his words and his 'cry' do not merely reach the ear of God, but that
God also gains an insight into his 'musing' and 'understands' his
thoughts. It is only when the heart is unburdened to God with
absolute candour and without any hidden mental reservations that
that atmosphere of truthfulness and trust is created in which the
communing with God serves a real purpose and the answering of

prayers becomes possible. Also, the form of addressing God with the words 'my King', which belong to the ritual of the festival cult and, having in them the true ring of a hymn, give praise and glory only to God (cf. Isa. 6.5)—this has perhaps been chosen on the ground that the poet calls for God's final decision, just as the Israelite king, too, had to judge legal cases as the final court of appeal (cf. II Sam. 14.1 ff.; 15.2 ff.).

[3] There is evidence in v. 3 which suggests that the psalm was uttered in the worship of the Temple and in connection with the offering of the morning sacrifice (cf. II Kings 3.20; 16.15; Ex. 29.39 f.). The terms which are here used, namely, 'make ready' (add, 'the sacrifice') and 'watch' (perhaps the psalmist has in mind here the theophany which will take place in the cult) are borrowed from the language of the cultus. It would nevertheless be wrong to think of the piety of the psalmist in terms of a rigid ritualism which is only concerned with external forms. The psalm still indicates sufficiently that the springs of true inwardness are not necessarily stopped thereby. The very interaction of sure knowledge that prayer will be answered, a knowledge which alone is able to impart to the petitions the character of true prayer, and of the waiting for God himself, which in spite of that sure knowledge must continually be anxious about the achieving of communion with God,—in short, the tension between possessing and waiting—this it is to which v. 3 bears witness in such a striking fashion; this is the unmistakable sign of that inspired inwardness, here hidden beneath the language of the cultus; this is of the essence of the biblical faith in God.

[4–6] In the next strophe (vv. 4–6) the worshipper expresses the thoughts which occupy his mind as he enters the house of God (see v. 1). That strophe appears to be rather out of place within the setting of a lament, and its form recalls the cultic 'entrance torah' (cf. Pss. 15 and 24.3 ff.). The poet states that the wicked will not be admitted to the sanctuary as the 'guests' of God (vv. 4 f.), whereas he himself may enjoy this privilege (v. 7). Gunkel interprets this passage as meaning that the psalmist wants to use the fact of his admission to the Temple to derive therefrom in a superficial and convenient manner his own righteousness in the sight of God and the unrighteousness of his adversaries. But that interpretation does not do justice to the psalmist. His train of thought here is just the reverse. The admission to the sanctuary and thereby to the presence of God presupposes, according to the usual tradition of the covenant cult see Intr. 47 f., 76), that the worshipper has been faithful to God and that he has kept aloof from the wicked. In fact, in vv. 4–7 it is not a question of the self-glorification of the worshipper at the expense of his opponents, but of the worshipper making an affirmation of some sort professing in a hymnic form his loyalty to God—who throughout vv. 4–6 is the subject and for that reason the central point on which the reflections of these verses are focused. Rather, what is at stake here is the nature of *God*, more particularly, his unapproachable holiness which is opposed to anything evil. The worshipper visualizes God as the Holy One, the enemy of all iniquity, and by making this affirmation he reaches the point which throws light upon his own affliction and furnishes the inward justification of his petition for the condemnation of the wicked. The general form of the tradition which is above all used here to speak of the wicked serves a useful purpose within the structure of the psalm as a whole. For vv. 4–6 contain the general presupposition behind the specific personal supplications which begin in v. 8. The worshipper is conscious of being confronted by the holiness of God and so that holiness becomes for him the starting-point of his thoughts and, in consequence, has to be regarded by us as the cardinal point on which the true understanding of the whole psalm turns. Since God for his own sake— notice the formulation 'thou art not a God who delights in wickedness'—cannot suffer any wickedness and presumption to last in his presence, but destroys the sinner, the worshipper for that very reason can confidently leave the final judgment even on his adversaries in the hands of God. Moreover, he can do so even though he feels momentarily threatened by their deceitful falsehood and their vile malice, which does not hesitate at riding roughshod over other people. Although vv. 4–6 speak of the wicked quite generally, we may assume that the picture presented in these verses has taken its colours from the experiences which the poet had undergone in his contacts with his special enemies. That he suffers from their lies and their falsehood more than from anything else (cf. the comments on v. 9), does the poet credit and makes him a champion of truth; for true life can prosper only in an atmosphere of truth.

[7] It is the encounter with the Holy God, who abhors everything evil, which in the first instance opens the worshipper's eyes so that he is able to understand his own position. He has prostrated himself before his God in the forecourt of the Temple, turning his face towards the sanctuary where God is thought to be present, and, filled

with awe, has worshipped him. It is precisely because he is fully
aware of the presence of the holy God that his affirmation of being
able to draw near to God in the sanctuary is not the outburst of a
feeling of stiff-necked self-righteousness, but, as the psalmist himself
confesses, an undeserved gift of the divine grace in which he may
partake in all humility and with gratitude in his heart. Again, it is by
no means a guarantee of his innocence, an innocence which is
naïvely self-conscious. The fear of God—that clear-sighted awareness of the essential difference between the majesty of God and
human inadequacy, which in the Old Testament excludes any kind of
gross familiarity and self-assurance in man's intercourse with God—
therefore truly expresses what the poet, too, feels in that very moment
when he partakes of the blessed certitude of having communion with
God. Even the Old Testament fear of God is after all basically not
the outcome of any human effort, but the result of the divine self-
revelation and, in consequence of that, the free gift of his grace (cf.
Ps. 130.4). **[8]** It is only at this point that the poet feels capable of
uttering his supplications. Everything which he has done so far
merely served to prepare him till he had reached the point when he
was able to utter his petitions in the right spirit; but this preparation
is an essential part of prayer itself, as is proved by what follows. It is
once more characteristic of the worshipper's sincerity that he first
asks for God's guidance so that his conduct may be acceptable to
him. He is aware of the risk involved in the partaking of the divine
grace, the risk of behaving arrogantly and unjustly towards others
for the very reason that he is conscious of being admitted to the
presence of God. Only if he himself, guided by the righteousness of
God, does not deviate from the right way, is he justified in calling for
God's judgment on his adversaries. Otherwise he only gives his
opponents who are lying in wait the welcome opportunity of bringing
him down with his own weapons. The fight for truth requires a
champion who is blameless and honest.

[9–10] That it is here indeed a question of the battle for truth is
shown by the characterization of the enemies in v. 9. With a 'smooth
tongue' they feign to be friends, but there is no 'relying' on their
words. In the innermost recesses of their heart which resembles the
gaping mouth of an open grave they scheme the ruin of the psalmist,
being urged on by a sinister greed. The poet knows that lies and
hatred can exert a most powerful and terrible influence upon men
and can destroy their lives. But he also knows that these evil powers

cannot last in the presence of God because God ultimately turns
against those who, thinking they can use these evil powers for their
own ends, are bound, in doing so, to bring upon themselves his
hidden judgment. The psalmist's opponents have reached the limit
of their wickedness. It is for this reason that he asks God to pass
judgment on them and cast out the wicked adversaries—thus not at
all simply because he himself thinks that he can endure no longer the
agony of his enemies' threats. The fact that he justifies his petition
by saying 'for they have rebelled against thee' shows clearly enough
that his action is prompted primarily by his concern for God and by
his desire that the victory of God's power over every kind of wickedness be made manifest. This is precisely what judgment means in the
cultus. It is from this perspective, too, that the merciless severity of
the psalmist's supplication has to be understood. It signifies the stern
character of a distinct Either-Or which must eventually make itself
felt in a final verdict, unless those who believe in God are prepared
to abandon their faith.

[11-12] Once that judgment has been passed, the pressure of persecution comes to an end, and the heart of the godly man is full of joy
and gratitude. But one of faith's peculiarities is that by means of a
bold stroke it anticipates that situation before the crucial event has
actually taken place, and so lives by the assurance of what it cannot yet
see but nevertheless believes will come true. What the psalm had
hitherto hinted at only slightly by its hymnic allusions, now at its
conclusion rings out in the full chord of the hymn which, having
reached the climax of its rapture, extols the blessing of putting one's
trust in God, a trust which knows itself safe under God's protection
and may be assured of God's blessing—and by God's grace wears the
invisible crown of life in spite of all afflictions. It is the delight in God
himself (v. 11) which at the end of the psalm irradiates the whole
situation depicted in the psalm with a brilliant light and transfigures
the way of the worshipper, a way which led him out of the strain and
narrowness of human conflicts and lifted him up to a higher realm
where trust in God and love for God reign in freedom, with no
reservations. It is no less significant that the poet includes *all righteous
people* in the jubilant hymn which he composed to the glory of God.
Since it is the power and the victory of God in which he is primarily
interested, the goal for which he strives is at the same time the concern of the whole religious community, too; for its sake he *vicariously*
suffered and for the attainment of it he *vicariously* prayed. The fact

that at the conclusion of the prayer the personal barriers and the barriers of space and time surrounding the individual case are broken down by looking at it from the perspective of the cult—that broad new fields of vision bordering on eschatology are opened up—this gives the psalm a significance which transcends its own scope and points the way to that truth which the Apostle Paul held out to the community of Christian believers as the law that should govern their lives (I Cor. 12.26): 'If one member suffers, all suffer together; if one member is honoured, all rejoice together.'

6. A PRAYER OF LAMENT ARISING OUT OF SIN AND SUFFERING

To the Conductor: with stringed instruments. On the Octave (?)[1] *A Psalm. Of David*

1 O Lord, rebuke me not in thy anger,
   nor chasten me in thy wrath!
2 Have mercy on me, O Lord, for I am weak;
   O Lord, heal me, for my heart is troubled.[2]
3 My soul is indeed sorely troubled.
   But thou, O Lord,—how long?
4 Turn, O Lord, save my soul;
   deliver me for the sake of thy steadfast love.
5 For in death there is no remembrance of thee;
   in the underworld who can give thee praise?
6 I am weary with my moaning;
   every night I flood my bed with tears;
   I drench my couch with my weeping.
7 My eye wastes away because of grief;
   it grows weak because of all my foes.
8 Depart from me, all you workers of evil;
   for the Lord has heard the sound of my weeping!
9 The Lord has heard my supplication,
   the Lord accepts my prayer.
10 ' '[3] All my enemies shall be greatly terrified;
   they shall be put to shame and turn back in a moment.[4]

[1] See p. 22.
[2] Lit.: my bones are troubled.
[3] See BH.
[4] * In RSV v. 10 reads:
   All my enemies shall be ashamed and sorely troubled;
   they shall turn back, and be put to shame in a moment.

Psalm 6, the biblical prototype of the hymn 'Straf mich nicht in deinem Zorn',[1] is regarded as the first of the seven penitential psalms

[1] * A hymn by Johann Georg Albinus (1624–1679), translated by Catherine Winkworth (1829–1878): 'Not in anger, mighty God.'

P.–E

of the ancient Church. The others are: Psalms 32, 38, 51, 102, 130
and 143. However, the theme of penitence is not particularly prominent in the present psalm. The recognition of the psalmist's sinfulness
indeed forms the background of the psalm and is implied in it, but
the actual confession of sin is entirely lacking. From the artistic point
of view the psalm is not distinguished by any features worth noting,
but the lack of poetical greatness is compensated for by the moving
simplicity of the representation of the subject-matter of the psalm, its
main part consisting of lamentations and petitions which alternate
in a manner which is deeply impressive. It is not possible to establish
any particulars providing precise information about the author of
the psalm and his specific circumstances. From vv. 8 ff. it can be
concluded that the psalm was recited within the setting of the cult
after the worshipper had obtained the assurance that his prayer had
been answered. But it is not even possible to make out with any
degree of certainty whether it is a serious malady from which the
worshipper wishes to be delivered or whether the words, which, in
the opinion of some expositors could be interpreted as referring to an
illness, are used by him only in figurative sense, expressing in metaphorical language the suffering that is inflicted upon him by the
attacks of malicious enemies. Perhaps we must allow for the possibility that both sickness and enemies play a part in the psalm. The
fact that it is primarily mental distress which weighs heavily upon
the poet's mind suggests that he must have had an introspective
nature. The style of the psalm is characterized by the use of traditional phrases, as can be gathered by the number of sayings which
are similar to those used in other psalms and partly even verbally
accord with them. The metrical structure of the strophes is not the
same throughout, and the ideas expressed in them do not exhibit a
strict sequence of thought. The order in which the thoughts follow
each other has been influenced by the emotional and impressionistic
feelings of the psalmist. Supplications and lamentations alternate in
the first three strophes; in the last strophe the assurance that his
prayer has been answered fills the heart of the worshipper with new
strength and hope.

First strophe

[1-3] Anyone on whom God pours out his wrath is lost. The poet
therefore prays to God: 'Rebuke me not in thy anger.' These words
imply the unspoken confession that God is justified in punishing him.

The worshipper cannot dare to make God incline favourably towards his petition for help by protesting his innocence, as is commonly done otherwise. The only way open to him is to take refuge in the grace and mercy of God. If only God would have compassion on his weakness and would deliver him from the terror with which his soul is stricken! The poet knows that he has brought upon himself the judgment of God, but he also knows that this God is the only hope which is left to him. He stretches out his arms towards God whenever he is overcome by his misery, and the unfinished question 'but thou, O Lord,—how long?'—in which hope and doubt contend with each other—sounds like the gasping of a stammerer.

Second strophe

[4-5] The second strophe opens with a renewed supplication for deliverance and help, but this time in face of death. It is not only that he feels a natural craving for survival, which makes itself more strongly felt when, as in his case, the possibility of imminent death is contemplated. In the words 'for the sake of thy steadfast love' a more profound thought is implied than that of survival. The poet has not set his heart on survival at all costs. What is vitally necessary and in the poet's view would be the very help for which he is praying is that he may experience that the grace of God becomes manifest in his own body and soul as a living reality, and further that on account of that experience his soul may be inwardly lifted up above the strain of sin and guilt. Again, what is at stake here for the worshipper is not only his life but at the same time God himself. The decisive question which the psalmist raises is whether or not the living reality of God's nature and his providential rule will in some measure be made manifest in his own destiny. His strong interest in what takes place in this world and in the things which are visible, an interest which is apparent even when his thoughts are directed to God, finds its explanation in the peculiar character of the Old Testament faith which concentrates on what happens in this world and wants to experience the God in whom it believes in the phenomena of this world and to be assured of him by these phenomena. Since there are but few passages in the Psalter where the spirit of man has been able to master even death by virtue of the religious beliefs he held (see Pss. 16; 49; 73), we must not be surprised that the psalmist believes that death completely severs every bond between God and man (v. 5). The idea that after death God cannot be praised

any more is here used in a way similar to Isa. 38.18; Pss. 30.9; 88.10 f.; 115.17 (attested also in the prayers of Mursilis II, offered on the occasion of a plague)—almost like a formula designed to justify the petition for the preservation of the worshipper's life. Some expositors think that no other significance can be found in that idea than that of a *demonstratio ad hominem*, as if the poet for the sole purpose of saving his life here wanted to remind God that the preservation of his worshippers was in his own interest. Anyone who holds that view, however, has not yet grasped the ultimate motives of the worshipper. These motives are to be found, on the one hand, in the worshipper's fear of losing the relationship with God which is vital to his life, and in the realization that he would for ever be robbed of the happiness of being able to remember God and praise him. On the other hand, he is equally interested in the spreading of the knowledge of the providential rule of God, and how could this be done unless those who are privileged to experience that divine rule are able to bear witness to it? After death all these things are no longer possible. What is at stake here is the interaction of the certainty of survival and the assurance of faith, though that interaction can as yet take place only within the scope of the Old Testament religion, limited as it is by its subjection to the phenomena of this world. There is no way here which would lead the worshipper to a faith that cannot see and yet believes.

Third strophe

[6–7] Once more the worshipper relapses into complaining about his fate. It accords with the picturesque oriental style that he speaks in partly exaggerated figurative language of the tears which he sheds and the grief which burdens his heart at night, and also of the suffering which his enemies—one might think here of the mocking of the wicked (v. 9)—inflict upon him.

Fourth strophe

[8–10] The final strophe opens by abruptly changing the train of thought as well as the tone and mood. In place of the weary and despondent lamentation we now hear the psalmist speaking like a man who has regained his composure and displays a strong will. What has happened? There is nothing in the psalm which would indicate that a special event has taken place. It is therefore improbable that in answer to the prayer a special priestly oracle has preceded announcing the future happiness of the worshipper (see Intr. 79 f.). We shall probably be nearer to the truth if we assume that the psalm was uttered after the cult community had partaken of the general assurance of salvation and that from this the worshipper had then derived the conviction that he, too, could be assured of salvation. The sure knowledge that his prayer has been answered is not something which man can work out for himself, but is a gift from God. It is only and solely God himself who has brought about what has here come to pass (cf. vv. 8b; 9a). The complete change which has taken place in the worshipper's mind proves the power of that God-given assurance of faith. Fear and despondency have given way to a new zest for life and to a vigorous determination which pulls itself together and all at once frees itself inwardly from the pressure of enemies. The assurance of faith has, however, an even wider significance. By virtue of that assurance the worshipper knows that the prayer *has been answered* by God. By virtue of that assurance he even knows that God *will* answer his prayers again and again in the future, too (v. 9b). In reaching this conviction the worshipper has now established a relationship with God on which he can take a firm stand and which enables him to look into the future with a peaceful mind. For the very thing which inspires him with a confident assurance strikes terror into the hearts of his enemies, so that they are put to shame and cease to trouble him. This is stated in v. 10 as the worshipper's simple conviction. What is expressed here is not any desire or anger, but the certain knowledge that has come by faith, the knowledge namely that what God will do with him and in him will have the described effect on his adversaries (see Intr. 46–8). That on this point the poet does not allow himself to give way to gloating, hatred and passion when he comes to think of his enemies is evidence of the moral strength inherent in a faith that is given by God, a faith which purges the heart of man and ultimately delivers him from himself.

7. PERSECUTION OF THE INNOCENT

Šiggāyōn.[1] *Of David.   Which he sang to the Lord because of Cush the Benjaminite*[2]

1 O Lord my God, in thee do I take refuge;
   save me from my persecutor[3] and deliver me,
2 lest like a lion he rend me,
   mangling me, with none to rescue.

3 O Lord my God, if I have done this,
      if there is wrong in my hands,
4 if I have injured him who (now) requites,[4]
      and have distressed[5] him who oppressed me without cause,[6]
5 then let the enemy pursue my soul and overtake it,
      and let him trample my life to the ground,
      and lay my honour in the dust! *Selah*
6 Arise, O Lord, lift up thyself in anger!
      Awake, my God,[5] at the fury of my adversaries!
      Appoint[5] a judgment![7]
7 Let the assembly of the heavenly[5] host be gathered about thee;
      and over it take thy seat[5] on high.
8 The Lord judges the peoples;
      judge me, O Lord, according to my righteousness
      and according to the integrity that is in me.
9 O let the spite[5] of the wicked come to an end,
      but establish thou the righteous!
      He who tries the hearts and reins is a righteous God.
10 My shield over me[5] is God,
      who saves the upright in heart.
11 God is a righteous judge,
      and a God who is angry with the wicked.[8]
12 If a man does not repent, but whets his sword,
      and has bent and strung his bow,
13 for himself has he prepared the deadly weapons,
      making his arrows red-hot.[9]
14 Behold, the wicked man travails with iniquity;
      he is pregnant with calamity
      and brings forth falsehood.
15 He made a pit, digging it out,
      and falls into the hole which he has made.
16 His mischief returns upon his own head,
      and on his own pate his violence descends.
17 I will testify to the Lord that he is righteous,
      and I will sing praise to the name of the Lord in the highest.[10]

---

[1] The meaning of the word is quite uncertain; some commentators presume an affinity with the Assyrian term *šegu* (= lament).
[2] It is not possible to specify the incident to which the biographical note alludes.
[3] See BH. (Tr. N.: RSV reads, 'save me from all my pursuers'.)
[4] Lit.: 'if I have inflicted (such) upon him who requites me with evil'.
[5] See BH.
[6] * In RSV v. 4 is rendered:
      if I have requited my friend with evil
      or plundered my enemy without cause,
[7] * In RSV v. 6 is:
      Arise, O Lord, in thy anger,
      lift thyself up against the fury of my enemies;
      awake, O my God; thou hast appointed a judgment.

[8] Read perhaps *bak^e silīm* instead of 'every day'.
[9] What is meant here are incendiary arrows.
(Tr. N.: Vv. 12 and 13 in RSV are:
(12) If a man does not repent, God will whet his sword;
    he has bent and strung his bow;
(13) he has prepared his deadly weapons,
    making his arrows fiery shafts.)
[10] Lit.: Of the 'Most High'. *ᶜelyōn* was originally a name of God which was used outside Israel and, being associated with the idea of a pantheon, designated the king of the gods, the creator and ruler of the world. According to Gen. 14.18 ff. it seems to have been adopted by the Yahweh cult from the pre-Davidic cultic tradition of Jerusalem, where as an epithet of Yahweh it was deprived of its polytheistic character. Cf. Herbert Schmid, *ZAW* 67, 1955, pp. 168 ff.

The literary unity of the psalm is not undisputed. In fact various problems are raised by the change of style and rhythm, the linguistic peculiarities of phrases used in the psalm, and the wide range covered by the feelings, moods and thoughts which have found expression here. It is nevertheless not outside the realm of possibility to regard the psalm as a unity and to interpret it as a lament of an individual if, apart from some textual defects, we take into account the specific circumstances of the author and his lively temperament. Tormented by his fear of an adversary who threatens to kill him, the psalmist takes refuge in God (vv. 1–2), protests his innocence by taking an oath of purgation (vv. 3–5), and then calls upon God to pass judgment (vv. 6–8). Following Hans Schmidt, we might picture to ourselves in this connection a situation such as is envisaged in I Kings 8.31 f., where a man who has been accused, though he is innocent, calls in the Temple for God's verdict—which shall vindicate him by establishing his righteousness and shall condemn the adversary, who has slandered him, by punishing him as he deserves (vv. 9–11; 11–16). In view of the fact that the idea of judgment has been formulated in a very general way (vv. 6–8), we shall have to assume that what is here described is taking place within the framework of the festival cult. Envisaging the worshipper's vindication which is anticipated with confident assurance, the psalm closes with a short vow of thanksgiving to God (v. 17). It is not possible to establish any particulars which would provide information about the author and the psalm's date of origin. Even the title, which relates the psalm to a now unknown tradition about David's life, is of no assistance in that respect.

Invocation and supplication
[1–2] The worshipper calls upon God in prayer, an act which

recurs in other psalms, too (cf. Pss. 11.1; 6.1 and often), and thereby takes refuge in God's protection, which is the only and last hope of deliverance left to him. The words he utters are those of a man shaken by mortal terror, who is left trembling and short of breath, and yet they are at the same time the words of a man upheld by the feeling that in God he will find a place of safety in which he can trust. But the comparison of the enemy in v. 2 with a ravening beast of prey (cf. Pss. 10.9; 17.12; 22.13, 21) also expresses the fact that the Bible is fully aware of that demonic and bestial purpose of destruction to which man falls and at the mercy of which man is if he lives apart from God.

The protestation of innocence

[3–5] However, what shocks the worshipper even more deeply than his dread of the cruel adversary who seeks his life is the insidious character of the latter's calumny which robs him of his honour (v. 5) and threatens to deprive him of his balance of mind. In the face of such an insidious attack he feels equally helpless, and, consequently, there is only one thing left for him to do—to take refuge in his Lord (notice that God is addressed in vv. 3 and 1 in the same manner), before whom he solemnly protests his innocence. The tumult within his deeply wounded heart still continues to echo with undiminished force in the words which he uses in making that protestation. Just as Job, misunderstood and suspected by his friends, takes the great oath of purgation in a last gigantic effort to give voice to his good conscience (Job 31.1 ff.) and submits to the judgment of God, so the psalmist, too, knows of no other alternative than that of seeking God's verdict in his judgment. The protestation of his innocence is obviously related solely to the accusations of his enemy which have previously been levelled against him ('if I have done this') and is not at all meant to be a sweeping affirmation of not having committed any sins whatsoever against God. The vague hints in vv. 3 f. no longer reveal the particular circumstances on which those libellous reproaches had been based. At any rate, the psalmist feels oppressed without cause. He has not inflicted any evil upon his adversary for which the latter could now hold him responsible. If it were otherwise, then he would have no right to complain about the fact that he is persecuted and that his life and his honour are threatened by his adversary. Nay, in that case he himself would then wish to be afflicted in this way. This 'self-imprecation' took the place of the original cursing of one's own person when men became afraid of using words by means of which a curse was uttered, words which were dangerous and full of magical power.

The demand for judgment

[6–8] This closely follows the oath of purgation, and shows the strength of the impulses released in the soul of the worshipper by the opening of his conscience to God. The worshipper is conscious of the fact that he has now reached the crucial moment of judgment, and so the boldness of his faith unites with the moral strength of his conscience in an appeal to God which by its elemental force threatens to push aside the reserve demanded from man by the reverence he owes to God, and which also gives graphic expression to the living reality and actuality of the immediate situation, and does so even in the form of style which he uses, a style that is terse and moves in a jerky fashion. We are here confronted with a picture of almost mythical creative power, a picture which still indicates the dramatic quality of the cultus as the place of its origin, when the poet calls upon God asking him that he may appear and may sit in judgment, a judgment in which the fury of men will be confronted with the wrath of God: it shows, on the one hand, the uncompromising will of God to establish 'righteousness' (see vv. 9, 11) and, on the other hand, the demonic forces of man's fury, bent as it is on destruction. Ultimate fundamental decisions are here at stake. That the poet sees his personal circumstances in such dimensions is not caused, as might perhaps be assumed, by any inability on his part to see them any longer in their true proportions, an inability which might ensue from an excessive self-confidence. Again, it is not caused by the fact that as a result of that excessive self-confidence he now thinks far too highly of himself, but it arises out of the uttermost depths of that faith in God which was a living power in the Old Testament cult of the Covenant. The conception according to which God, surrounded by his heavenly host, sits down on his throne, towering to heaven, as the King and Lord of the whole world and passes judgment on the nations, belongs to the tradition which was handed down in the festival cult (cf. Isa. ch. 6; Pss. 18.6 ff.; 82.1; see Intr. 32 f., 50, 75 f.). In that tradition reverential testimony is borne to the holiness of God, which in its sublimity transcends the world. The fact that this whole range of ideas is expressed by the psalmist proves that he does not allow his thoughts to be determined by his own little self, but rather by God; it proves further that side by side with the firm hold boldly taken by his faith there is yet alive in his heart a humble reverence which guards him against overstepping the bounds set by God when the impulse of his conscience craving for justice urges him to do so. He knows that in God's sight the struggle for his own right is at the same time the struggle for 'right' as such—which applies to 'all the nations'; and when he now submits to the judgment of God, his words are marked by an apprehension which is modified by the certainty of having God on his side and by reserves of power.

The assurance

[9–11] Contemplating the situation from the lofty viewpoint of his faith in God the psalmist comes to realize clearly and be firmly convinced that the righteousness of God signifies the end of the evil of the wicked and the 'establishment' and consolidation of righteousness in the world. The latter is equivalent to the manifestation of the truth which cannot remain hidden from the God who tries even the most secret thoughts of men, and which will now be revealed. The fact that the psalmist clothes that knowledge in the form of petition (v. 9a) and testimony (vv. 9b; 10 f.) once more exhibits that peculiar intertwining of the assurance of faith and of the simultaneous striving for that assurance which not only provides the psalm with its dramatic excitement but is the mark of any faith which is truly alive. The emotional turmoil which has raged in the psalmist's soul has, however, been hushed by the assurance of the victory of God's truth and righteousness, which he has gained by a whole-hearted effort and now steadily flows like the strong current of a large river, the strong current of a firm trust in God. The righteousness of God guarantees the worshipper protection and help (v. 10); for the wicked, however, it signifies his doom (v. 11).

The latter end of the wicked

[12–16] The statement which has just been made provides the starting-point which makes it possible to achieve for the first time a full understanding of the utterance concerning the judgment that is to be pronounced on the evil devices of the adversary. In this connection the poet emphatically advocates in a series of images the truth that the biter will be bitten. In doing so he not only makes use in an external fashion of a legal maxim which was well known in the whole of the Ancient East, the principle that the same punishment shall be inflicted upon the slanderous accuser which he had intended for the accused. Rather, he wants to show—and the didactic note sounded in the verses we are now dealing with confirms it— that it is precisely the mysterious working of God's righteousness which causes sin to pass judgement on itself. The sharp irony of the word-pictures, showing the wicked man to travail with iniquity and to bring forth falsehood, points to those correlations which appear paradoxical to those who live apart from God ('if a man does not repent'), namely, that man's oppressive power, violence (see the image of the warrior in vv. 12 f.) and cunning (see the image of hunting with a wooden trap in v. 15) recoil upon the head of those who think that they can use these forces to their own advantage and according to their own discretion and choice. The peculiar character of the truth and righteousness of God is marked by the very fact that they strike the man who is separated from him as an incomprehensible paradox, whereas the eyes of faith are able to perceive that the hidden providential rule of God is the factor which determines the deeper relationships of an order of events which is both purposeful and just. The psalmist looks forward to the realization of that truth, and the conclusion of the psalm serves the purpose of acknowledging that same truth. Here the psalmist vows that he will thankfully testify to the righteousness of God and will praise his name in a song (see Intr. 31, 74 f. concerning the cultic origin of these phrases). The sure knowledge that he has found God to be the Advocate and the Protector of truth and righteousness in his own case fills him with confidence and joy. For it shows him that even his personal affliction serves the purpose of the glorification of God, so that God's truth and righteousness may be revealed to all the world. It cannot be doubted that the psalm as such also serves in its own way the same purpose.

8. CREATOR AND CREATURE

To the Conductor. According to the Gittith tune.[1] *A Psalm. Of David*

1 O Lord, our Lord, how majestic is thy name in all the earth!
   Thou whose glory is praised[2] in the heavens.
2 By the mouth of babes and infants[3] thou hast founded a bulwark
   to defy thy adversaries,
      to still the enemy and the rebellious.[4]
3 When I look at the heaven,[5] the work of thy fingers,
   the moon and the stars which thou hast created:

4 what is man that thou art mindful of him,
   and the son of man that thou dost care for him?
5 Yet thou hast made him little less than God,
   and hast crowned him with glory and honour.
6 Thou hast given him dominion over the work of thy hands;
   thou hast put all things under his feet,
7 all sheep and oxen, and also the beast of the field,
8 the birds of the air, and the fish of the sea,
   whatever passes along the paths of the waters.[4]
9 O Lord, our Lord, how majestic is thy name
   in all the earth!

[1] The LXX associates the phrase with the term *gat* = wine-press; accordingly its meaning would be 'song of the wine-press' which perhaps might be understood as signifying a tune.

[2] Read *tānā*; in respect of *tānā* as a term to denote 'to be repeated in an antiphonal song' cf. Gordon, *Ugaritic Manual, Glossary* 2047, and Gray, *The Legacy of Canaan*, 1957, pp. 156 f. We shall have to picture to ourselves such a hymn, sung by celestial beings, on the analogy of Isa. 6.3; cf. I Kings 22.19; Job 1.6; 38.7.

[3] * In RSV 'by the mouth of babes and infants' does not start a new sentence but is part of v. 1b, which reads, 'Thou whose glory above the heavens is chanted . . .'

[4] See BH.

[5] According to LXX.

The psalm is a song of praise (hymn), glorifying God the Creator. It combines a fine sense of feeling responsive to the sublime beauty of Nature and a profound understanding of the revelation of God expressed and yet hidden in Nature. What captivates the poet more than anything else, however, is not so much the wonder which the contemplation of the starlit sky at night calls forth in his soul, an experience which he contentedly enjoys to the full. On the contrary, that contemplation leads him to a more profound insight. Behind the glorious splendour of the brilliant sky his mind's eye envisages him who has created that splendour. It is for him, for the divine Creator, that his song is intended; his first and his last thought is directed to the glory of God and to the praise of God. Just as the broad expanse of the sky encompasses the whole world, so the glory of God spreads out over the whole earth. [1] The beginning and the end of the psalm give expression to this thought (vv. 1a, 9) in a hymnic phrase which serves the purpose of providing a frame for the song and is probably to be understood as the response of the congregation ('our Lord') to the revelation of God as Creator that takes place in the festival cult when Yahweh manifests his 'name' and his nature (see Intr. 30–2, 41 f., 56–9). The hymn which is here sung by the congregation (cf. Ps. 145.4 ff.) provides the keynote for the

thoughts which the psalm develops, thoughts which in part have
been borrowed from the treasure of the tradition of the cult community and for the rest have been derived from the psalmist's
personal experience and, having been welded into a whole, now
throw into bold relief two aspects of the psalm's basic mood, namely,
awe of God ('our Lord') and *joy* in his glory (cf. Ex. 33.18 ff.; Isa. 6.3).
The melody of the whole psalm is inspired by and rings with fear of
God and joy in him. Its timbre and dynamic power flow from the
splendid blending of those two opposite fundamental religious
attitudes. It shows the boldness of his faith when an Israelite speaks
of the glory of his God in terms which make that glory encompass the
whole world. In the Old Testament a faith such as that of the psalmist was frequently compelled to fight against the reducing of the idea
of God to a national level where the boundaries of the Israelite
kingdom also signified the sphere of influence to which the God of
Israel was confined. The acceptance of that restricted idea of God
was made easier by the fact that strange gods were worshipped in the
foreign countries. The psalmist, too, is filled with wonder as he faces
that living reality of God which encompasses the whole world and
impels him to ponder over it. Wherever in the world men gaze up in
awe to the firmament, there, intentionally or unintentionally, they do
honour to God; and heaven itself eloquently bears witness to his
majesty (v. 1b). The poet is so firmly rooted in his faith in his God
that the thought that other nations might think in this connection of
other gods as the creator of the universe does not enter his mind at all
(Isa. 40.12–26 deals with this problem in a similar way). He can
conceive of the demand which God makes on him in no other way
than that it is something which is unqualified, absolute and final;
also, the glory of God, that fills the whole earth, appears to him to be
the result of the self-revelation of that same God who has made
himself known to the whole world. **[2]** The poet finds these thoughts
proved true when he contemplates little children and those under
age; by the mouth of children and infants God has erected a bulwark
which is designed to silence his adversaries. Even the adversaries
(sceptics and atheists) cannot disregard the fact that the child utterly
and completely surrenders to the impression produced by things
which are great and glorious, and does so in an unaffected and direct
manner, albeit he expresses his wonder in a childlike and halting
fashion, and gives expression to his childlike joy in the works of God's
creation by his games (*'ōlēl*) and songs (we might think of the song

'Canst thou count the stars that twinkle')[1]; in short, they cannot disregard those first stirrings of a naïve and unreflecting piety which are
after all a fact.[2] But in the mind of the poet that fact is also part of
the very revelation of God. How often are the trains of thought of
adults put to shame by the unfeigned purity of the feelings expressed
in the words of a little child, trains of thought which are twisted,
puzzled out, and have got bogged down! Yet the poet discerns an
even greater truth than the one presented by this empirical fact;
he hears the voice of the living God speaking through the harmless
utterances of children, and he feels God's power working in them
('thou hast founded a bulwark') whereby he subdues all his adversaries. A new vision is here granted to the eyes of faith: it is in small
and insignificant things that the greatness of God is revealed. The
miraculous power of God is to be found in the very fact that he
'chooses what is weak in the world to shame the strong so that no
human being might boast in the presence of God' (I Cor. 1.27, 29).
In Matt. 21.16, v. 2 of Psalm 8 is interpreted as referring to the
jubilant praise of the children at the entry of Jesus into Jerusalem.

[3] Verse 2 constitutes the bridge which spiritually connects the
thought of the name of God which encompasses the whole world with
the subsequent meditation on man. The poet himself is overwhelmed
by the impression which the illimitable expanse of the firmament
with its sparkling splendour makes upon him. Once more he is overwhelmed not so much by the noble feeling of the immense grandeur
of that spectacle in which he indulges as by the incomprehensible
greatness of God. What a mighty God must he be who created the
boundless canopy of heaven by his 'fingers', and how excellent must
be the mind of him who 'established' the moon and the innumerable
stars and determined the laws according to which they run their
course silently and steadily: 'The Lord God determines the number
of the stars' (Ps. 147.4; cf. also Isa. 40.26). [4] It is the impression
made by God's revelation which enables man in the first instance to
attain the right understanding of his own self. In the Bible the revelation of God and man's understanding of his own existence are intimately bound up with each other (cf. Ps. 144.3 ff.; Isa. 6). And this
is true also of this psalm; there is no revelation of God except it also

---

[1] * In the German original 'Weisst du, wieviel Sternlein stehen', a hymn by
Johann Wilhelm Hey (1789–1854), translated by C. S. Bere.
[2] Stamm considers the crying of children as a sign of their viability, *TZ* 13
(1957), pp. 470 ff.

throws at the same time a special light on the nature of man; and, conversely, a true understanding of man cannot be achieved if God is disregarded. This, too, is part and parcel of the faith—that we see ourselves in those proportions which are revealed when we look at ourselves from the perspective of God. In comparison with God, the Creator, man is only a creature. Again, face to face with God man becomes aware of the total insignificance of his existence. When man gazes up at the illimitable expanse of the heavens studded with stars, the difference between God and man is revealed in all its magnitude, and the wholly contradictory quality of that difference is made manifest. The finite is confronted with the infinite, the transient with the eternal, the perpetual sorrows and anxieties of man, who constantly goes astray, with the peace, steadiness and order manifested by the heavenly bodies which run their prescribed course. All these thoughts are implied in the question, 'What is man?' Quite deliberately the poet uses words which emphasize that part of man's nature which is mortal and earthbound. But he does not stop at contrasting God and man in this manner. It is only if man stands in awe of the greatness of God, which strikes terror into his heart and makes him aware of his total insignificance, that, taking that awe as a starting-point and as the basis of his thoughts, he learns to gain a full understanding of the divine miracle which is made manifest in the relationship between Creator and creature, the miracle namely that it did not seem too small a matter for this Almighty God 'to be mindful' of man and lovingly 'to care' for him.[1] As soon as man comes to realize his total insignificance in the sight of God from whom he cannot demand anything, he clearly recognizes that the innermost nature of his relationship with God is that of an *incomprehensible grace*. Polar interaction of an awe which trembles at the thought of the majesty of the Lord of the universe, and of the joy which is filled with gratitude for the loving care of that same God— this, and this alone makes v. 4 ring with the inimitable note of genuine and profound piety. That the man who just felt constrained to recognize the total insignificance of his life in the sight of God may nevertheless say 'yes' to that life and accept it with confidence, represents the most profound miracle of divine grace which man is privileged to experience. He receives, as it were, his life back from the hand of God and receives it as a new life. The peculiarity of the

---

[1] Cf. Jer. 15.15 and also Baumgartner, *Die Klagegedichte des Jeremia*, 1917, p. 35, and Weiser, *Jeremia*, p. 138, on the cultic origin of these phrases.

biblical teaching on creation is that the grandeur of the creation is
recognizable throughout the lowliness of the creature. Like the New
Testament saying, 'By the grace of God I am what I am' (I Cor.
15.10), this teaching combines humble reverence and joyful pride.
It is only in this way that it is able to avoid the risk of taking the
wrong course by declining into human arrogance. **[5–6]** Again, it is
this peculiar teaching of the Bible on creation which is the cardinal
point on which the whole question turns of how we are to understand
the verses which follow. For without the foregoing setting up of the
religious signpost of humility in the sight of God vv. 5–8 could be
understood—and this has repeatedly been done—as expressing
merely delight in culture and as singing merely the praise of man.
That delight in culture has found its classic formulation in Hellenism,
namely in a saying of Sophocles in the *Antigone* (332), 'Wonders are
many, and none is more wonderful than man.' The difference between the Greek and biblical estimates of man is demonstrated by
the very fact that in the Old Testament human dignity has no value
of its own, but has value only because it is a gift from God. In this
connection we must take notice of the fact that in vv. 5 and 6 it is
always God who is the subject, and that it is from his hand that man
receives the position of a ruler in the world. In these verses, too, the
note of wonder is sounded, the wonder which fills the heart of the
psalmist as he contemplates the miracle of the divine order of
creation. In spite of his insignificance man has been appointed by
God to have dominion over the earth. The poet pursues this thought
in great detail in order to be able to grasp to the fullest extent the
grandeur of that miracle. The Lord of the universe has entrusted
man even with the divine function of governing; man's status would
even have been equal to that of God but for the fact that God made
the status of man 'wanting', though only in a little. The King of the
universe has even gone so far as to install man as the king of the earth
and to 'crown' him with the regalia of 'majesty and glory' which
really are the attributes of God's own appearance (see Intr. 40). It is
in this sense that we can speak here of man being created 'in the
image of God and after his likeness' (Gen. 1.26–28; 2.19 f.). According to the Old Testament faith, man has not gained power over
Nature by means of a titanic rebellion against the Deity, but he
receives dominion over 'the works of his hands', as a commission
given to him by God; and it is *God's* will that all things be subject to
man, and it is by virtue of *God's* might that all things are subject to

man. It has not come about by chance that the aforementioned
Greek interpretation of culture, which made man entirely depend
on his own strength, ended in tragedy, whereas the biblical interpretation still represents even today the religious foundation on which
all truly creative culture can be built. In the New Testament vv. 5
and 6 have been understood in the sense of a prophecy; the term
'son of man'[1] (v. 4) is interpreted as referring to Jesus as the 'Son of
man', and by means of a different translation and interpretation an
allusion to the Passion and Exaltation of Jesus has been deduced from
vv. 4–6 (Heb. 2.6–8; I Cor. 15.27), relating Creation and Redemption to each other.

[7–8] The poet depicts in attractive detail the extent of man's
dominion within the order of creation by using animals as examples.
The enumeration of the animals is modelled on a probably ancient
cultic tradition, which also underlies the creation story in the first
chapter of Genesis, and is arranged according to the several elements
and according to the species which belong to each of them:
domestic and wild land animals, creatures of the air and those inhabit-
ing the sea.

[9] It is characteristic of the poet's attitude that he does not conclude his song with the contemplation of man's dominion over the
earth and of the sphere of influence which is thus granted to man, a
contemplation on which he obviously dwells with particular pleasure,
but that his thoughts once more turn back to the hymn, sung by the
congregation to the glory of God, which had been the starting-point
of his meditation. Thus the thought expressed in that hymn not only
encloses the whole psalm outwardly and elevates it to a work of art,
the unity and forcefulness of which are most impressive, but it also
makes quite clear once more that human dignity in its entirety points
to God, who has given that dignity to man: 'Let him who boasts,
boast of the Lord' (I Cor. 1.31; II Cor. 10.17). It is the awe of God
from which the poet's joy in life springs and to which it flows back
again. With this reflection the psalmist's train of thought has in v. 9
come full circle in respect both of form and conception—and that in
such a manner that it is symbolical of the psalmist's theocentric
attitude of mind. His meditation on God has enabled him to see all

---

[1] * It is impossible to render an accurate translation of the German term (in the
singular!) 'Menschenkind' (lit. child of man) which in the German original is used
both in v. 4 and here. The translation 'son of man' comes nearest to its true
meaning.

things in their true light and to establish a right relationship with the
world and with himself; and the contemplation of the world and of
his own person has once more led him back to God. The truth that
dawned upon the psalmist of the Old Testament as he looked at
creation with the eyes of faith St Paul perceived as a result of his
reflections on history and expressed in the immortal words of the
doxology (Rom. 11.36): 'from him and through him and to him are
all things. To him be glory forever. Amen.'

9 and 10. THE JUDGMENT OF GOD

To the Conductor. According to 'Die for the son'.[1] A Psalm. Of David

1 I will testify to thee,[2] O Lord, with my whole heart;
   I will tell of all thy wonderful deeds.
2 I will be glad and exult in thee,
   I will sing praise to thy name, O Most High,[2]
3 when my enemies turn back,
   stumble and perish before thee,[3]
4 that thou hast pleaded my cause and upheld my right,
   hast sat down on the throne giving righteous judgment.[3]
5 Thou hast rebuked the Gentiles, thou hast destroyed the wicked;
   thou hast blotted out their name for ever and ever.
6 The enemy have vanished in everlasting ruins;
   thou hast rooted out cities;
   the very memory of them has perished.
7 But the Lord sits enthroned for ever,
   he establishes his throne for judgment;
8 and he judges the world with righteousness,
   he judges the peoples with equity.
9 Let the Lord be a stronghold for the oppressed,
   a stronghold in times of trouble.
10 Those who know thy name put their trust in thee,
    for thou, O Lord, hast not forsaken those who
    sought thee.
11 Sing praises to the Lord, who sits enthroned in Zion!
    Tell among the peoples his deeds!
12 For he avenges blood and is mindful of them;
    he does not forget the cry of the afflicted.
13 The Lord was[4] gracious to me, he saw[4] my affliction ' '[4]
    and lifted me up from the gates of death,[5]
14 that I may recount all thy praises
    and in the gates of the daughter of Zion may rejoice in thy deliver-
        ance.
15 The Gentiles have sunk in the pit which they made;
    in the net which they laid has their own foot been caught.

16 The Lord has made himself known,
   he has executed judgment;
   the wicked is snared[4] in the work of his own hands. *Higgāyōn.*[6] *Selah*
17 The wicked shall depart to hell,
   all the nations that forgot God!
18 For the poor shall not always be forgotten,
   and the hope of the afflicted shall not perish forever.
19 Arise, O Lord! Let not man prevail;
   let the nations be judged before thee!
20 Put them in fear,[4] O Lord!
   Let the nations know that they are but men!

Psalm 10

1 Why dost thou stand afar off, O Lord?
   Why dost thou hide thyself in times of trouble?
2 The arrogance of the wicked frightens[7] the poor;
   he is caught[8] in the schemes which the other has devised.
3 For the wicked boasts of the evil[4] which his heart desires,
   he praises the gain[4] and contemns the Lord.
4 In the pride of his countenance the wicked (thinks):
   he will not punish;
   all his thoughts are, 'There is no God'.[9]
5 His ways prosper[4] at all times;
   thy judgments are on high, out of his sight;
   as for all his foes, he does not care a straw for them.[10]
6 He says in his heart, 'I shall not be moved;
   throughout all generations I shall not meet adversity.'
7 His mouth is filled with cursing and deceit and oppression;
   under his tongue are affliction and mischief.
8 He sits in ambush in the villages;
   in hiding places he murders the innocent.
   His eyes stealthily watch for the hapless,
9 he lurks in secret like a lion in the thicket;
   he lurks that he may seize the poor.
   He catches the poor and drags him away in his net.
10 He bends down[4] and crouches,
   and the hapless fall into his power.[11]
11 He says in his heart, 'God has forgotten,
   he has hidden his face, he will never see it.'
12 Arise, O Lord; O God, lift up thy hand;
   forget not the afflicted!
13 Why is the wicked allowed to scorn God
   and say in his heart, 'Thou wilt not call to account'?
14 Thou dost see; for thou dost note trouble and vexation
   and takest it into thy hands.
   The hapless and the orphan leave it to thee,
   for thou hast been their helper.[12]

15 Break thou the arm of the wicked; and the evildoer—
    punish his wickedness that he cease to exist![13]
16 The Lord is King for ever and ever;
    the nations are perished from his land.
17 O Lord, thou hast heard the desire of the meek;
    thou dost strengthen their heart, dost incline thy ear,
18 to do justice to the oppressed and the orphans,
    so that man who is of the earth may strike terror no more!

[1] The meaning is obscure; it may perhaps signify the quotation of the opening words of a song to the tune of which the psalm was to be sung or accompanied.
[2] Cf. the comments on Ps. 7.17.
[3] * Vv. 3–4 in RSV run as follows:
   (3) When my enemies turned back,
        they stumbled and perished before thee.
   (4) For thou hast maintained my just cause;
        thou hast sat on the throne giving righteous judgment.
[4] See BH.
[5] * In RSV v. 13 reads:
Be gracious to me, O Lord!
Behold what I suffer from those who hate me,
O thou who liftest me up from the gates of death.
[6] The meaning is doubtful; perhaps it signifies a pause to be made in the offering of prayer (see Intr. 22) which was marked by a musical interlude.
[7] Lit.: he is consumed with; is feverish (because of anxiety).
[8] Read the word in the singular.
[9] * Vv. 2–4 are in RSV:
   (2) In arrogance the wicked hotly pursue the poor;
        let them be caught in the schemes which they have devised.
   (3) For the wicked boasts of the desires of his heart,
        and the man greedy for gain curses and renounces the Lord.
   (4) In the pride of his countenance the wicked does not seek him;
        all his thoughts are, 'There is no God.'
[10] * RSV renders v. 5c: 'as for all his foes, he puffs at them.'
[11] * V. 10 reads in RSV:
The hapless is crushed, sinks down,
and falls by his might.
[12] * Vv. 13 and 14 in RSV:
   (13) Why does the wicked renounce God,
        and say in his heart, 'Thou wilt not call to account?'
   (14) Thou dost see; yea, thou dost note trouble and vexation,
        that thou mayest take it into thy hands;
        the hapless commits himself to thee;
        thou hast been the helper of the fatherless.
[13] * In RSV v. 15 reads:
Break thou the arm of the wicked and evildoer;
seek out his wickedness till thou find none.

Psalms 9 and 10 probably constituted a unity in their original form. In the Septuagint and in the translations dependent on it both psalms appear as a *single* psalm. Moreover, the fact that there is sometimes an identity of expression in both psalms and that there are traces of an acrostic scheme embracing both psalms (the opening words of each verse are arranged according to the order of the letters of the Hebrew alphabet; cf. Pss. 25; 34; 37; 111; 112; 119; 145) and also that no title is attached to Psalm 10 likewise suggests that the two songs originally constituted a unity. Supposing that the writer of the psalms had ever intended the alphabetic arrangement to be complete, it must be admitted that the psalms are no longer preserved in their original integrity, that the acrostic scheme has become obliterated, and that the psalms' original shape cannot be restored without interference both violent and questionable. To refute the thesis of the original unity of the two psalms it is usually pointed out that a change of thought, tone and mood is exhibited in them. But that change is partly explained by the peculiar character of the 'lament' type and by its dependence on a cultic situation in which general forms used in the liturgical tradition have their place beside utterances of thoughts and feelings of a very personal nature. The worshipper who prays in these psalms belongs to the community of the 'godly' (Ps. 9.10), who also call themselves 'the poor' (Ps. 10.2, 9) and 'the meek' (Ps. 10.17; see Intr. 93). He is oppressed by an ungodly adversary and therefore classes himself with the poor and the afflicted and the hapless (Ps. 9.9, 12, 18; Ps. 10.8 ff., 12, 14). In a prayer of lament, in which the adversary is characterized in detail, he brings his affliction before God—probably in the Temple of Jerusalem (Ps. 9.11, 14)—and prays for deliverance from his enemy (Ps. 10.1–15). Nevertheless, this personal lament is set in a wider general setting which is probably to be accounted for by the festival cult: Yahweh sits down on his throne as King (Pss. 9.4; 10.16) to pass judgment on the nations (Ps. 9.7 f., 19). Evidently, the celebration of the feast of Yahweh's Covenant was the occasion when the psalm was recited and the poet stated his own case in accordance with the fundamental ideas of the feast.[1] The alternating forms and thoughts in Psalm 9 and likewise also the closing verses of both psalms which run parallel, are to be accounted for in this way—by their connection with the range of ideas actualized by the cultic liturgy.

[1–4] Psalm 9 is usually regarded as a thanksgiving uttered in gratitude for a decisive victory, which the psalmist, who in that case

---

[1] In this connection archaic elements of the tradition of the pre-Davidic cult of Jerusalem have presumably likewise been incorporated. Cf. Herbert Schmid, *ZAW* 67, 1955, pp. 168 ff.

must have been a king or a commander-in-chief, had gained over his enemies. Quite apart from the fact that in that case the statements made about those enemies would have to be understood as referring to the event which already belonged to the past, and that this would, moreover, require that the text be altered in part, it would in that case hardly be possible to explain the supplication at the end of Psalm 9 and even more so the lamentation in Psalm 10 on the basis of that same situation and mood. A more careful consideration of the tenses suggests that it would be more accurate to interpret the two psalms as representing a prayer of supplication; by means of such an interpretation we are in a better position to overcome any difficulties. On this assumption the opening of the psalm is to be understood as a vow which as a rule is customarily made at the end of the supplication. The worshipper vows to the Lord (vv. 1–2) that he will testify to his name and tell of his wonderful deeds (see Intr. 58) if God, sitting down on his throne to pass judgment, will defend his right against his enemies (vv. 3–4). **[5–6]** He firmly trusts God that he will act in this manner, since God once destroyed his enemies, the wicked pagan nations, for ever.[1] The psalmist derives his confidence and assurance that his cause, too, will be maintained by God from the tradition of the *Heilsgeschichte*—we may perhaps think in this connection of the conquest of the Promised Land—which was recited in the cult and was experienced by the members of the congregation at first hand and in such a manner that the latter thereby saw themselves confronted with their God in a living encounter (cf. Ps. 22.3 ff.). The religious experiences of the cult community, preserved in the tradition, are here activated as a source from which the individual can draw fresh religious strength. **[7–10]** The subsequent verses are to be understood as moving in the same direction. The fundamental idea of the festival cult—that God enters upon his eternal reign over

---

[1] Junker (*Revue Biblique* LX, 1953, pp. 161 ff.), who adopts the above interpretation of vv. 1–4, also wants to interpret vv. 5–12 in the same sense as v. 4, namely as the text of the anticipated hymn. He interprets the latter as referring to the realization of the eschatological kingdom of God, an interpretation which from the grammatical point of view is possible. But our difficulty here lies in the fact that Junker understands Ps. 9.13–20 as being a prayer for the coming of that kingdom of God and Ps. 10.1–18 as serving the purpose of re-enforcing that prayer by a complaint about the delaying of its fulfilment. This interpretation seems to me to create a tension between the assurance of the hymn, which has been extended to vv. 5–12, and the fundamental mood of Ps. 10.1–15, a tension which it would be difficult to account for; it also seems to me that this interpretation neglects the personal element contained in the prayer (Ps. 9.13 f.).

the world and, judging the nations, establishes that reign on an order founded on righteousness (vv. 7-8; cf. Pss. 96.13; 98.8 f.)—serves all who are oppressed as the basis of a firm trust in God (v. 9); and that trust in God is corroborated by the personal religious experiences of God-fearing people who did not seek God in vain (v. 10). **[11-12]** How personal experience and hope are fitted into the larger framework of the saving events celebrated in the festival cult is shown by the call upon the congregation to join in the hymnic profession of the psalmist so that God may be glorified among the nations. The religious experiences of the individual, too, are woven into the texture of the growing Kingdom of God; they on their part serve the propagation of the revelation of God's saving will in the world, as they themselves draw their vital energy from that revelation of the divine redemptive work. **[13-14]** It is within this vast setting, which he has derived from the worship of God in the cult, that the psalmist now assigns a place to his supplication that God may be gracious to him and may have mercy upon him in his personal affliction. The changing over in v. 13c from the form of supplication to that of the hymn already shows how firmly he keeps in mind that sublime goal. Again, it shows that his affliction is not only a burden, which he himself has to carry, but that it, too, must serve the glory of God in that God's grace and help are manifested in his destiny and place him under the obligation of bearing witness and testifying to them in the midst of the congregation. It is only by connecting his personal supplication with his testimony to God's might and saving will that the worshipper has reached a point where his personal supplication is transformed into a prayer that is safe from becoming reduced to the level of unrestrained lamentations and entreaties; and it is in the light of this that we can understand why he does not open his psalm by uttering at once his supplication and lament, but makes the acknowledgment of God and the testimony to his deeds the first theme of the psalm.

[15-18] The worshipper once more reflects on the tradition of the past. He discerns the judgment of God in the fact that the Gentiles perished because of their own sins; he discerns this fact in that mysterious ordering of human affairs according to which evil carries within itself the germ of self-destruction. Again, he discerns that in that judgment God 'has made himself known', that he has manifested therein his nature, his will, his wisdom, and his might. The godly can derive therefrom hope and comfort in their affliction, but for the ungodly it means death. **[19–20]** Having got his breath back by dwelling on the tradition, the worshipper—probably using the words of an ancient formula associated with the rite of the theophany (cf. Ps. 10.12; see Intr. 39, 73)—calls upon God to execute judgment on the nations, which will reveal to whom power really belongs and will make the nations aware of the fact that limits are set to man's power. It is a profound truth, a truth the importance of which is not confined to the Old Testament, which is here derived from the range of ideas associated with the festival cult, the truth namely that the purpose of the judgment is to reveal the reality of God to the whole world, and that man cannot grasp the revelation of God unless he realizes his own human weakness and helplessness.

[10.1–11] It is within this vast setting of the range of conceptions and ideas presented by the cult's celebration of the kingship of Yahweh that the psalmist now introduces his personal concern—his lamentation about the suffering inflicted upon him and upon his fellow believers by wicked enemies who persecute them. In the first place the different subject-matter ensuing from the lament, but then also the fact that the poet, being no longer tied down to the more formal style and wider-ranging ideas of the solemn festival liturgy, is here in a position to give full scope to his own mood and to his personal feelings—these entail the language now becoming more lively and more concrete, and the style and tone assuming a more severe, a more urgent, character. We are therefore not compelled to attribute that change to another author or to a different situation. A similar 'change of mood' can be observed in Psalm 44. We would, however, be wrong if we were to assume that the worshipper, having safeguarded himself by following the outlines of the cult, now thinks he can give full vent to his feelings in his lament before God and can do so the more unrestrainedly. His procedure is just the opposite: because it is God himself who is his real concern, and because his view of God has been dimmed by his affliction, it is for this very reason that he tries to establish the assurance and the steadiness of his faith on the firm foundation of the cultic tradition and thus to strengthen them so as to gain inner mastery over his affliction. The first question he asks is concerned with God. The fact that God stands afar off and is hidden from his faith, which seeks to see him, first raises on his lips that tormenting question 'Why?' Everything which he has to complain of as having been done to him by the evildoer receives its distinctive mark by the question thus addressed to God. The importance which God and faith in God have for the life of the worshipper can be judged from the fact that this man feels his faith in God to be tempted by the persecution which he has to suffer from the hands of his adversaries and that he has to struggle for the preservation of that faith. Temptation occurs only in the lives of those for whom faith is really still an indispensable principle of life. This is shown by the characterization of the evildoer which represents a typical mirror-image of the godless man: he does not care for anything except for himself and for his profit; the only criterion of his actions is the desires of his heart; he rides roughshod over other people without any restraint whatsoever; oppression and lies are the means whereby he obtains his objects. What does he care for the terror and the misery which he spreads around him? Arrogantly he even glories in his wickedness. He does not care for God; he scorns him and is on the point of denying him altogether. Lulled into security by his outward successes, he unscrupulously stifles the voice of his conscience. Because he has forgotten God, he imagines that God has forgotten him. What man actually is when he lives apart from God is shown by the picture of the beast of prey lying in ambush for its victim, a picture which is worked out in greater detail: *homo homini lupus!*

[12–15] Who would want to deny that the existence of such evildoers is continually capable of causing grave crises in the lives of those who believe in God, the more so when, as in the present case, the godly man himself has to suffer in his own life from being brutally maltreated by the wicked! Again, is there any man who would want to deny that there are times when he believes himself to be separated from God and to have been forgotten by him because the incomprehensible reality of evil bars him from discerning the providential rule of God! In this inner distress the worshipper reaches out for God of whom he has become assured in the cult that he is the Judge of the nations and the Protector of the oppressed. In virtue of the experience gained in the cult he knows that God sees his affliction even though this obscures his own vision of God. And God takes into his hand what the oppressed, having full confidence in him, leaves to his care. The power of the wicked, however, will be broken to pieces when God arises to sit in judgment and brings evil to an end. [16–18] The more the worshipper directed his thoughts to God, who had met him in the encounter that took place in the festive hour of celebration through the recounting of the tradition of his saving deeds and of the

experiences of the help given by him in the past, the more he recovered to an ever-increasing degree the peace of mind and the
assurance rooted in confidence which had been shaken by his
adversity. At the end of the psalm the prayer once more soars to the
solemn heights of a hymn ringing with the praise of God and takes up
once more the themes of the festival cult. The acclamation of God as
King, which has its place in the ceremony of his enthronement (cf.
Pss. 47.7 ff.; 93.1; 97.1; 99.1; see Intr. 62), and the tradition of the
Heilsgeschichte of the conquest of the land (see Ps. 9.5 ff. and Intr.
42 f., 59 f., 74 f.) are regarded by the worshipper as a confirmation of
the fact that God has definitely entered upon his reign. So he feels
assured that his prayer will be answered and derives therefrom
confidence that his personal cause, too, will be vindicated by God's
judgment, and that no man will any longer be able to frighten him,
since God himself has 'strengthened' his heart through faith.

11. TRUST IN GOD
To the Conductor. Of David

1 In the Lord I have found refuge;
   how can you say to me,
   'Flee to your mountains, you birds'?[1]
2 'For behold the wicked, they bend the bow,
   they have fitted their arrow to the string,
   to shoot in the dark at the upright in heart!
3 If the foundations are destroyed,
   what can the righteous do?'
4 The Lord is in his holy temple,
   the Lord, his throne is in the heavens;
   his eyes behold, *his* eyelids test the children of men.
5 The Lord tests the righteous and the wicked,
   and his soul hates him that loves violence.
6 On the wicked he will rain coals of fire[2] and brimstone;
   a scorching wind shall be the portion of their cup.
7 For the Lord is righteous, he loves righteousness;
   the upright shall behold his[2] face!

[1] * RSV translates v. 1 as:
   In the Lord I take refuge;
   how can you say to me,
   'Flee like a bird to the mountains'?
[2] See BH.

The dispute between the godly and the wicked forms the background of this courageous song. Insidious and violent actions of the
wicked seem to have shaken the foundations of the life of the religious

community to such an extent and in particular to have endangered
the life of the poet, who was probably one of their leaders, that his
friends, who are apprehensive for him, do not know of any other
advice which they can give him in these circumstances than that of
flight. But the poet is not afraid, for he knows that there is another
place of refuge where he is more safely sheltered than when he would
flee from his enemies, and that place is God, in whose sanctuary he
has found refuge. It may be assumed that the psalm was uttered in
that holy place where the judgment of God on the godly and on the
wicked is waited for in the epiphany of God, which takes place in the
festival cult (vv. 4 f., 6 f.; see Intr. 32 f., 46–9). The poet scorns the
faint-heartedness of his friends by manifesting his trust in God (vv. 1–3)
and gives his reasons for facing the future in a calm spirit (vv. 4–7).

Opposing the faint-heartedness of the friends (vv. 1–3)

[1] The opening words 'In the Lord I have found refuge' sound
like a reply to the well-intentioned advice of the friends to flee:
there is only one direction in which one can flee—to God. By that
statement the poet has concisely and distinctly sketched the unshakable foundation of his life. He vigorously points to what alone is
the starting-point and guiding principle of his confidence, to that
which forms the basis of the thoughts developed throughout the
psalm. He says, in fact: Here I stand. That he has been advised to
flee from his enemies may therefore appear to him to be almost an
insult. For he has taken his stand on that foundation of which Isaiah
(28.16) says: 'He who believes will not flee.'[1] We can distinctly sense
the indignation echoing in the words he uses to scorn the expectation
of his willingness to flee. The word-picture of the flight of the birds to
the mountains, which is used in an allegorical sense, seems to be a
proverbial saying (cf. Ps. 55.6 f.). The poet also repeats in vv. 2 f.
word for word the detailed reasons which his friends gave him to
justify their advice—this shows, after all, that he can understand
their arguments from the human point of view, though he judges
their significance quite differently from his own point of view. The
danger is actually not a trivial one. [2] His friends had justified their
advice to flee by referring to the insidious machinations of the
wicked who seek the life of the upright in heart; and they had done
so by employing the frequently used picture of the hunter who lies
in wait for his victim, having made ready his arrow to shoot. [3] If

---

[1] * RSV of Isa. 28.16 is: 'He who believes will not be in haste.'

by means of such machinations the foundations break down, the foundations, that is, of life, of security, of the community, of justice, and of religion—all these values seem to be implied in that phrase the meaning of which just defies definition—what more can the righteous do in such circumstances? A situation such as this one reveals not only the peril which threatens him directly but also his helplessness, and so provides a further reason for fleeing from what, after all, is only a dismal heap of ruins. Such is the train of thought of his friends. That train of thought, however, is faulty in one respect. It does not rise above the level of judging the situation from a purely human point of view and overlooks what matters most. The second part of the psalm deals with this latter point.

Faith in God (vv. 4–7)

[4] Proceeding from v. 3 to v. 4 we are made aware by the thoughts expressed in these verses that the poet boldly throws off the depressing chain of human insecurity and peril, so that he may be able freely to contemplate the reality which grants man a vision that transcends every kind of danger and every kind of insecurity and that also transcends human hatred and human fear; and that reality is God. The poet directly confronts the aforementioned human train of thought with the image of the holy God who is conceived to be simultaneously present in heaven and, through his epiphany, in his earthly sanctuary (cf. the comments on Ps. 68.4; see Intr. 29 f., 38–41). The words which he uses in this matter ring with the note of a hymn, and there echoes in them something of the power of a faith which overcomes every kind of paralysing anguish and heavy-heartedness by the sure knowledge that is expressed in these words of a hymn-writer:

> 'What though thou rulest not?
> Yet heaven, and earth, and hell proclaim:
> God sitteth on the throne and ruleth all things well!'[1]

Boldly clinging to God as the Ruler and Judge of the world, the poet is thus provided with the right criterion by which he can judge his own critical situation. A twofold thought enables this man to enjoy the peace of mind and the assurance which are the fruit of trust, the thought namely that both *power* and *righteousness* are with God. It is not man but someone else who has the final say. The foundations of

[1] * These words are from the seventh verse of the German hymn by Paul Gerhardt (1607–1676): 'Befiehl du deine Wege' (Commit thou all thy griefs), which John Wesley translated into English.

life are safe in God's firm hands and for that very reason they will
not collapse, because *he* does not lose sight of the children of men and
tests the righteous and the wicked. **[5]** In this way God safeguards
the order of life in both directions by helping the righteous and by
destroying the wicked. Viewing man's position from that angle, it is
just as foolish to ask the sceptical question 'What can the righteous
do?' as it is to flee timidly from the plots of the brutal enemies which,
after all, are already subject to the judgment of God. With these
two thoughts the poem reaches its final section. **[6]** Here it first deals
with the judgment on the wicked; this, following the cultic tradition
of the *Heilsgeschichte*, is stylized after the pattern of the catastrophic
events that came to pass at Sodom and Gomorrah (see Intr. 50 f.,
78). The purpose is to throw into relief the terrible power of the
mighty God by contrasting it with the acts of violence perpetrated by
men (cf. Amos 4.11). The reference to the scorching wind produces
in that respect a particularly strong effect in conjunction with the
background of the peaceful image of the 'portion of their cup',
which is perhaps derived from the serving out of the drink by the
head of the family at meal-time (see, however, the comments on
Ps. 16.5). **[7]** The prospect for the righteous is very much more comforting. For him the statement concerning God's judgment has a
quite different ring. He may rightly infer from it God's care for those
who belong to him, a care which is manifested in God's 'righteous
acts' and in his willingness to take cognizance of the 'righteousness'
of man and to acknowledge it on his part. (Both these thoughts are
probably implied in the phrase which we have rendered by the term
'righteousness'.) The godly recognizes in that mutual relationship
between God and man which forms the basis of the life of mankind
the nature and the will of God, and he is taught thereby to understand also the meaning and purpose of his own life. It is this thought
which is in the mind of the poet when he confidently declares, 'The
upright shall behold his face.' The phrase 'behold the face of God' is
derived from the language of the cultus and refers to the theophany
as the climax of the rites performed in the cult when the worshipper
experiences the presence of his God with joy and trembling (see Intr.
39 f., 72 f.). In the Old Testament religion the presence of God at the
festival cult signified the realization of his salvation—which implied
for the cult community the blessing and the strength of a living communion with God. By virtue of the power of such a faith the poet
conquers both fear and temptation, and his spirit rises victoriously

above the faint-heartedness of his friends and above the oppression of his enemies. In the Bible trust in God and strength, faith and courage, always belong together.

12. THE WORDS OF MEN AND THE WORD OF GOD
To the Conductor. On the Octave.[1] *A Psalm. Of David*

1 Help, Lord; for there is no longer any that is godly;
   for the faithful have vanished from among the sons of men.
2 Everyone utters lies to his neighbour;
   with flattering lips and a double heart they speak.
3 May the Lord cut off all flattering lips,
   the tongue that makes great boasts,
4 those who say, 'With our tongue we will prevail,
   our lips are with us; who is our master?'
5 'Because the afflicted are oppressed, because the poor groan,
   I will now arise', says the Lord;
   'I will grant my[2] salvation to him who longs for it.'[3]
6 The words[4] of the Lord are words[4] that are pure,
   silver refined in a furnace ' ',[2] purified seven times.
7 Thou, O Lord, wilt keep them,
   thou wilt guard us[2] from this generation for ever,[5]
8 even though the wicked prowl on every side,
   and vileness is exalted among the sons of men.[5]

[1] See p. 22.
[2] See BH.
[3] * V. 5c reads in RSV, 'I will place him in the safety for which he longs.'
[4] * For 'words' RSV uses 'promises'.
[5]* Vv. 7 and 8 are in RSV:
   (7) Do thou, O Lord, protect us,
       guard us ever from this generation.
   (8) On every side the wicked prowl,
       as vileness is exalted among the sons of men.

This psalm served Luther as a model for the composition of his hymn 'Ah God, from heav'n look down and see'.[1] It is a prayer which originated in the circle of the community of the godly (v. 1), who also called themselves the 'faithful' (v. 1), the 'afflicted' and the 'poor' (v. 5; see Intr. 93). The theme of the moving lament (vv. 1–4) is the general decadence brought about by the lying and boasting which had become a predominant feature in the life of the influential circles and from which the godly have to suffer. The prayer is answered by a word from God which as in Isa. 33.10 promises the worshippers that they will be saved. This is followed in vv. 6–8 by

[1] * In German 'Ach Gott vom Himmel sieh darein'; the translation is by Catherine Winkworth.

the response of the cult community; this takes the form of a hymn glorifying the trustworthiness of God's words and of something founded on this—the confident expectation that the prayer will be answered (vv. 7 f.). It follows from this that the psalm is a liturgy of some sort and, like Isa. 33, is to be accounted for by its origin in the festival cult.

[1-2] The author sorrowfully meditates on the state of affairs in his own time and, before he deals with the gloomy picture thus revealed, he utters a brief cry for God's help. He fears that the godly and the faithful amongst his people are doomed to destruction as a result of a general decadence brought about by the spread of the habit of lying and boasting. It would, however, hardly be right to regard the fear which he thus expresses as the pessimistic utterance of an old man who is embittered and in vain longs for the return of the 'good old days'. On the contrary, it is the well-founded opinion of a man who has learned to apprehend what is going on in the depths of human nature, and who recognizes the root-causes of the corruption of the community to which also the discord between the godly and the wicked is to be traced back. He is not alone in holding such a 'radical' view, but is supported in that respect by the great prophets who took a similar stern view of the signs of their times (cf. Hos. 4.1 ff.; Micah 7.1 ff.; Jer. 5.1 f., etc.; Isa. 57.1 ff.; 59.14 ff.). Being mindful of man as he actually is, there is surely no cause for taking things less seriously than they really are. No improvement can be hoped for from that quarter. The lie which destroys every kind of fellowship that men might have with one another is here clearly recognized and stigmatized as original sin. When truth and reality, which ultimately belong together, come to differ from each other, then the foundations of human social life are shaken. When words no longer serve the purpose of throwing a bridge across from heart to heart, but assume the character of a partition or of a façade serving no other purpose than that of simulating one thing or veiling another thing, then such a state of affairs reaches down to the deepest strata of the metaphysical processes on which the existence of fellowship depends. For fellowship cannot exist unless it is based on truth. [3-4] However, the sin against truth and faithfulness is not only directed against man, but in arrogant delusion it also rebels against God. This explains why the psalmist prays that God may 'cut off all flattering lips'. The sin against the sacred character (*den heiligen Geist*) of language is accurately characterized: language was originally man's most personal expression of the fact

that by virtue of the principles governing the creation of the world he
is tied up with all created things and is allied to them (cf. Gen. 2.19);
it becomes, however, a dangerous instrument of power and a deadly
weapon if used by someone who dissociates himself from the obligation under which he is placed by his creatureliness and falls into the
hubris of an arrogant pride in power, caring for nothing but himself.
The change in the meaning of words which can be traced throughout the linguistic history of the nation runs strikingly parallel to the
history of the ideas of these nations and to the history of their religion;
and if man plays upon words in a rhetorical, sophistical fashion, then
such behaviour is always also an indication of man's rebellion against
God. But however much men may arrogantly glory in the power
which they are able to gain for themselves by their ability to 'master'
language, they cannot be misled by their arrogant joy into thinking
that they can disregard the ultimate truth and reality that their
arrogant joy, without their noticing it, has already come under the
judgment of God.

[5] In the psalm this fact is expressed in the Word of God which
was perhaps uttered by the priest or a cultic prophet as speakers of
the oracle foretelling future happiness (see Intr. 79 f.) and is deliberately set in opposition to the boastful words of men without any
transition whatsoever. Thus the Word spoken by God is most tellingly
contrasted with these words of men and sets a limit to their presumption. The Word spoken by God recalls Isa. 33.10, a prophetic liturgy
which had its place in the festival cult of the Temple. The result is
that the entire prophecy handed down in that passage, and including
both the threat uttered against enemies and the promise made to the
community of the godly, is experienced by the latter as a living
reality. They long for the deliverance which God already holds in
readiness for them in their affliction, whilst he is about to appear in
order to grant to them his salvation. [6] The hymn which follows,
glorifying the trustworthiness of the Word of God, is the 'Amen' of the
congregation, sung in response to the divine promise of deliverance.
In fundamental contrast to the hypocritical and impure words of
human falsehood the Word of God is praised as a word which is pure,
undefiled and true, tried in repeated tests like silver refined in a
furnace; with God truth and reality do not differ. God keeps his
word and remains faithful to it. [7] It is on this fact alone that the
confident hope of the worshipping congregation is now founded.
God executes the final verdict by protecting the godly 'from this

generation for ever'. **[8]** Taking their stand on the foundation of the truth of the Word of God, those who have faith can firmly hold their own. They can look around without fear at the illusive glamour and haughty pretence of men's boastful vileness which surrounds them. The thoughts of the psalmist are now directed to God; a new perspective thus presents itself to him which is the very opposite of the one which determined his thoughts at the opening of the psalm, exclusively focused as they were on the human situation. The illusory world in which lying and boasting are an everyday occurrence is doomed to destruction, but faithfulness and truth enjoy the abiding protection of God. According to the testimony in v. 5 the Word of God has proved true in the poet's life and in that of the community of the godly. The psalm itself represents the way which brought them out of their fear of the words of men and led them to the place where they were able to enjoy the protection and power of the Word of God. The relating of the contrast between the Word of God and the word of men to 'false' and 'pure' doctrine, which was already suggested by Luther's translation of the psalm, determined the poetic adaptation of the psalm in his hymn, 'Ah God, from heav'n look down and see'.

13. HOW LONG, O LORD?
To the Conductor. A Psalm. Of David

1 How long, O Lord? Wilt thou forget me for ever?
  How long wilt thou hide thy face from me?
2 How long must I harbour sorrow in my soul
  and grief in my heart day by day?[1]
  How long shall my enemy rise against me?[2]
3 Look upon me and answer me, O Lord my God;
  lighten my eyes, lest I sleep the sleep of death;
4 lest my enemy say, 'I have prevailed over him';
  lest my foes rejoice in case I should be shaken.[3]
5 As for me, I trust in thy grace,
  may my heart rejoice in the help thou hast sent me.[4]
  I will sing to the Lord,
  because he has dealt bountifully with me.[5]

[1] See BH.
[2] * V. 2 reads in RSV:
  How long must I bear pain in my soul,
  and have sorrow in my heart all the day?
[3] * V. 4b in RSV, 'lest my foes rejoice because I am shaken'.
[4] * V. 5 is in RSV:
  But I have trusted in thy steadfast love;
  my heart shall rejoice in thy salvation.
[5] * In RSV the last two lines of v. 5 form a separate verse (v. 6).

P.—F

This is a simple lament of a sick man. Its formal structure is lucid, the thoughts developed in the psalm are well arranged and the psalm itself is very impressive on account of the deep emotions which, welling up from the innermost recesses of the psalmist's soul, are exhibited in the feelings and moods expressed. Verses 1–2 contain the lamentation and vv. 3–4 the prayer; v. 5 concludes the psalm with an affirmation of trust and a vow of thanksgiving. On account of v. 3a we shall have to think of the prayer as having been uttered in the sanctuary where God is presumed to be present (see Intr. 72).

[1–2] The worshipper fears that he may break down under the burden of his suffering, which seems to go on for ever, and in a moving lament he gives vent to the anxiety and impatience which torments his soul. The peculiar way in which the first sentence is formulated at once reveals how his despair that God may have forgotten him 'for ever' struggles with his hope that his affliction will be brought to an end. In that struggle the worshipper pulls himself together in a last whole-hearted effort which finds vehement and almost reproachful expression in the question, repeated four times, 'How long?'—a question which is typical of the lament (to be found also in Babylonian laments).[1] His first thought is his relationship with God. The most profound problem which occupies his mind in his affliction is the fact that he believes himself to be forgotten by God and that, feeling himself far from God, he must seek him and stretch out his hands towards him who is hidden from his sight, that he may find him. From the contemplation of God his thoughts then turn to his own heart, which is filled with grief, and, lastly, to the enemy whose arrogance and gloating (v. 4) make his affliction even worse. The supplication runs parallel to his pattern of thought in the lament.

[3–4] It, too, first deals with the worshipper's relationship with God and then with the personal circumstances of the worshipper; similarly it ends with a remark about his enemy. The poet, feeling himself far from God, gradually draws near to God by praying to him most fervently and most imploringly—note the terseness and brevity of the imperatives—and expresses the desire that God may resume the mutual relationship which had been established between him and God by their living in communion with one another and

---

[1] Cf. Zimmern, *AO* VII, pp. 20–24; *AOT*, pp. 25 ff.; and on the same subject Baumann, *ZAW* 1945/48, pp. 126 ff., who emphasizes that in comparison with the Babylonian laments the psalm shows greater freedom in the choice of the forms which it uses.

which had been broken. For he knows that he is wholly dependent on it and endeavours on his part to maintain it by his prayer. He knows indeed that he can live only if God is willing to 'look upon' him and to 'answer' him. In the cultic thought of antiquity the view was widely held, as is proved by Babylonian parallels, that the presence of God, his 'beholding', signifies that the prayer of the worshipper has been answered (see Intr. 40, 73). Without the presence of God and his goodwill he is doomed. It is for this reason that his petition in spite of its forcefulness is, in fact, a supplication for God's grace. The beautiful and profound phrase 'lighten my eyes' comprises the knowledge that comes by faith in all its fullness and profundity, the knowledge that the grace of God is the source of all life, both material and spiritual, and of the strength and joy which life can impart (cf. v. 5). In the light of this utterly religious perspective the physical suffering is of little importance. Even when the worshipper speaks of his enemies, his thought is dominated by one anxiety only, the anxiety that he might waver in his faith and lose confidence in God and so might provide for his adversaries the opportunity of gaining an easy victory. In the light of other psalms the fact that this psalm does not indulge in any feelings of hatred or in vindictiveness side by side with that strongly marked sense of religious honour deserves our special attention. [5] What the poet has asked for is granted to him: his eyes have been opened. The fear which by its violent fluctuations made his impatient heart tremble has subsided, and the prayer ends on the serene note of a firm and confident assurance. Just as the lamentation and the prayer have done, so the affirmation of trust, too, starts at the cardinal point—with God. But now the worshipper is assured of the grace of God for which he had yearned and prayed, and, trusting in that grace, he has reached a firm position which enables him by God's help to disregard all his present suffering and look into a bright future. His assurance that his prayer has been answered is vouched for by his encounter with God present in the cult; the prayer has therefore been recited after it had been answered (see Intr. 80). It is on this foundation that the vow is made which in itself is already a glorification of God, rising to the full chords of the hymn, and in that vow gratitude is combined with joy in the living communion with God which has been granted anew to the worshipper.

14. THE FOOLS

To the Conductor. Of David

1 The fools say in their heart,[1] 'There is no God.'
  They are corrupt, they do abominable deeds,
    there is none that does good.
2 The Lord looks down from heaven upon the children of men,
  to see if there are any that act wisely,
    that seek after God.
3 They have all gone astray,
  they are all alike corrupt;
    there is none that does good, no, not even one.
4 Have they no understanding, all the evildoers
  who support themselves by eating up my people,[2]
    but do not call upon the Lord?
5 There they shall be in great terror one day,
  for God is with the generation of the righteous.
6 Your plan against the poor will be confounded,
  for the Lord is his refuge.[3]
7 Who then will bring deliverance for Israel out of Zion?[4]
  When the Lord restores the fortunes of his people,
    Jacob shall rejoice, Israel shall shout with joy.

[1] MT has the singular as representing a class.
   (Tr. N.: RSV reads, 'The fool says . . .')
[2] * V. 4b runs in RSV, 'who eat up my people as they eat bread'.
[3] * V. 6 in RSV:
   You would confound the plans of the poor,
   but the Lord is his refuge.
[4] * V. 7a is in RSV, 'O that deliverance for Israel would come out of Zion!'

The psalm has been transmitted in the Psalter a second time, in Psalm 53. The original text seems to have been better preserved in Psalm 14. This strange song reminds us in several respects of the manner of thinking and speaking which was peculiar to the prophets. The first part of the psalm (vv. 1–3) contains a forceful lament about the depravity of the wicked, in form a prophet's philippic. The second part (vv. 4–6) at first resumes once more the theme of rebuking the wicked and then follows it up in vv. 5 and 6 with a threat. The psalmist concludes the poem by hopefully looking forward to God's help and deliverance (v. 7). The threat is apparently directed against the leading circles of Israel who, devoid of any sense of their duty to God and of their responsibility for their fellow countrymen, impoverish the poor for the sake of their own selfish ends and thus destroy the nation. Such distressing pictures of the renunciation of God by the ruling circles have been passed on to us in the Book of Isaiah (5.8 ff.,) for example, and in the Book of Jeremiah (5.12 f.).

[1] The psalmist at once gets down to the root-cause of the evil, and he does so with a sure grasp of the human scene and with great energy: the widespread depravity against which his rebuke of the wicked is directed has its origin in the ungodliness of men's way of thinking. He is equally sure of the view he must adopt on this matter: only a fool can hit on the idea, 'There is no God.' It is characteristic of the biblical idea of God that that statement is not meant to be understood as a reflection on the existence of God and thus not as some kind of dogmatic atheism, but as a 'practical atheism' which tries to elude the demands which the reality of God makes on man's life. But it is precisely this which man cannot possibly achieve. Nobody can flee from the reality of God. Hence it is foolish to attempt to do so. Such an attempt must necessarily end in moral corruption; for it is the fruit of disobedience which results in the inability to do that which is good. Where there is no sense of duty to God, there man goes astray and experiences already by that very fact that the hand of God the Judge is upon him and he cannot escape. **[2-3]** This thought, which is of a rather general nature, is now followed by a more specific statement. God, from whose searching eyes nothing that happens on earth remains hidden, himself seeks in vain those who act wisely and care for him. Even the most lenient investigation leads to the shocking result that there is none that does good, that all of them have gone astray and are corrupt. The radical verdict on man's inability to do what is right accords with the basic earnestness with which man is confronted by God. **[4]** God's Word now turns against the particular abuses which exist among 'his people', and it does so by expressing its threat in an even more pointed and intensive form. The question, asked in utter amazement and revealing the folly of their acting without any concern whatsoever for God or for their own people, almost sounds like an appeal to the evildoers, made at the very last moment, for them to realize the utter absurdity of their conduct. The psalmist can see in the total absence of a sense of religious and social responsibility nothing but foolishness and a failure to understand the true state of the human situation; and that total absence of a sense of religious and social responsibility is demonstrated by the fact that these people support themselves by ruining their fellow countrymen without in the least caring for God. Moreover, that true state of the human situation and, above all, the reality of God can neither be removed nor evaded by shutting one's eyes to it. **[5]** It is precisely *'there'*, in the blind fool's imagining that this is possible, that God will make himself respected by him and will assert himself by passing judgment on the evildoer. The orienting word 'there' at the same time points to the tradition according to which God is present in the cult for the purpose of judgment (cf. v. 2; see Intr. 75 f.). The evildoers will then become aware of the true significance of the reality of God, but then it will be too late. Panic-stricken, they cannot help realizing that it is God who confronts them as their adversary, 'for God is with the generation of the righteous'. **[6]** Their 'clever' plans against their poor fellow countrymen, whom they intended to exploit for their own selfish ends, will be thwarted by God himself; for God is the refuge of the innocent who are oppressed. The psalmist, acting like a prophet, hurls that truth at the evildoers as a threat directly addressed to them. Human sin is revealed—and confounded—by the reality of God.

[7] In the concluding verse the poet enables us to get an insight into his own heart. In view of the depravity of the ruling classes of Jerusalem the question of the future destiny of the people of God presses heavily upon his soul and fills it with anxious sorrow. Who, after all, is to bring deliverance when the leaders fail so shamefully? But it is only for a short moment that human sorrow has its say here. Looking up to God, the psalmist's faith immediately prevails once more. God's judgment is not his last word. His grace is even greater. He will 'restore the fortunes of his people'; he will provide them with a new foundation. Probably the psalmist has in mind here the act of the divine judgment which was firmly established in the ritual of the covenant cult at Jerusalem. For the evildoer that act meant his expulsion, but for the godly community of God's people it meant the realization of their deliverance (see Intr. 47). The faith expressed in the psalm is founded on God's willingness to forgive.

Though the future may be veiled in obscurity through human guilt, the grace of God knows the way which leads out of darkness into light; God will take that way and so turn mourning into joy and exultation. Here faith is shown to have a true sense of reality, fighting with clear insight and firm resolve for God and against sin and foolishness; it points the way to judgment and grace. This makes the psalm a valuable testimony, bearing witness to a faith assured of God and, in consequence, full of vital energy. Even today it is still capable of proving its power in the lives of men.

15. WHO MAY SOJOURN IN THE HOUSE OF GOD?

A Psalm. Of David

1 'O Lord, who may sojourn in thy tent?
  Who may dwell on thy holy hill?'
2 'He who walks blamelessly, and does what is right,
  and speaks truth from his heart.
3 He does not slander with his tongue,
  and does no evil to his friend
  nor utters abuses against his neighbour;[1]
4 in his eyes a reprobate is despised,
  but he honours those who fear the Lord.
  He keeps the oath even when it hurts him.[2]
5 He does not put out his money at interest,
  and does not take a bribe against the innocent.
  He who does these things, will never flinch.'[3]

[1] * V. 3c in RSV: 'nor takes up a reproach against his neighbour'.
[2] * V. 4c in RSV: 'who swears to his own hurt and does not change'.
[3] * V. 5c in RSV: 'He who does these things shall never be moved.'

The psalm is closely related to Ps. 24.3–5 and to Isa. 33.14–16.
The explanation of this is not to be found in any direct dependence
of the psalm on these passages, but in the use of a fixed type of style
which still gives a hint of its place of origin. A song which opens with
the question of who may sojourn in the house of God and then names
the conditions governing admission to the sanctuary obviously
originated in the cultus. Questions such as the one which is asked
here, the question of the ritual fitness required for taking part in
public worship, were customary in antiquity in various forms and
have been preserved right into the Christian cultus. Once every
sanctuary probably laid down its own rules in accordance with which
admission was granted by the priest. Those rules above all included
the requirement of ritual purity. Similarly, at the shrines of Israel,
and in particular at the Jerusalem Temple of which we have to
think in this context (v. 1), such enquiries into the conditions of
admission, followed by the instructions of the priest, seem to have
been customary, as is evident from II Sam. 21.1 ff.; Zech. 7.3;
Hag. 2.11 ff., just as even in the time of Jesus it was still the duty of
the priests to decide whether or not someone was cleansed from
leprosy; they also decided the associated question, whether he was
fit to participate in the cult (Luke 17.14). The form of our psalm is
likewise to be understood in the light of that custom. The use of the

psalm for liturgical purposes is still reflected in the question and answer it contains. On the strength of Ps. 24.6 we might think in this connection of a larger choir of pilgrims attending the festival and asking the Deity what the requirements are for their admission to the sanctuary (v. 1). In that case the second part of the psalm (vv. 2–5b) would represent the answer which the priest gives in the name of God. As in Ps. 24.6, one might expect the psalm to conclude with an affirmation of the pilgrims that they fulfil the requirements of admission, to be followed by the permission of the priest to enter the holy place. In the text handed down to us both these statements are replaced by a promise formulated in very general terms which was not perhaps added until the psalm had ceased to serve its original purpose; it then rendered possible a wider interpretation of the psalm, as referring quite generally to the communion of the God-fearing people with God.

[1] The *question* 'who may sojourn in thy tent as thy guest?' which in poetical language has preserved the memory of the holy Tent of Yahweh (cf. II Sam. 7.6), shows the high regard in which the sojourn in the sanctuary was held. As they were the guests of God, those who entered the sanctuary were protected against their pursuers by the peace of God (Pss. 27.4 f.; 61.3 f.); they participated in the deliverance wrought by God and in his blessing—and these, by virtue of the communion with God, proved effective even beyond the pale of God's house. In the second half of the verse the blessed awareness of the nearness of God is depicted in the image of sharing the Deity's dwelling. That image was probably used originally to indicate the fact that the pilgrims attending the feast were accommodated in the immediate neighbourhood of the sanctuary. But, when it became dissociated from the cultus, it could be interpreted in the same sense as in Eph. 2.19, as illustrating the purely spiritual relationship with God that is brought about by faith.

[2–5b] The *answer* is remarkable in several respects. First of all, it is a striking fact that in a song designed for the cultus no mention whatsoever is made of cultic matters such as sacrifices, offerings and purity rites, but only of moral requirements. It is these which are especially emphasized here. It is part of the essence of the Old Testament cult of the Covenant that 'obedience' matters more than sacrifices. This is in keeping with the line of action taken by the prophets who in face of a wrong cultic development fought for the spiritualization of religion (Amos 5.21 ff.; Hos. 6.6; Isa. 1.11 ff.;

Micah 6.6 ff.; Jer. 7.21 ff.). The spiritual grandeur of the psalm rests on the high level of its ethics.

If we consider the psalm's positive requirements for admission to the sanctuary there are two things which are noteworthy: the first thing we notice is the endeavour to formulate the basic moral attitude required as comprehensively and as axiomatically as possible (v. 2). What strikes us next is the strong emphasis put on the social ethics to be observed by man in his behaviour towards his neighbour (vv. 3, 5a, b). It is precisely the attempt, an attempt whose roots can be traced back to the beginnings of the Old Testament religion, to grasp the nature of the basic moral attitude which shows that the Old Testament already takes great pains to reach a point beyond the casuistry of particular requirements which will enable it to find the uniform divine will from which they emanate and which gives to each particular requirement its true meaning. In exhibiting this tendency, which finds its explanation in the nature of the cult of the Covenant, the psalm continues a line of approach which can already be discerned in the Decalogue. With the latter the psalm also has in common the formulation of the 'apodictic' precepts in vv. 3 ff. in the indicative. In this way a distinction has been quite clearly recognized; it is that between the nature of the moral law as a spiritual phenomenon which concerns man's whole being and can be comprehended by man himself, and the external fulfilment of demands made upon man by a will different from his own, a fulfilment which moreover is often only an enforced one. By attributing the 'perfection' of man's conduct and the 'righteousness' of his actions to the inward truthfulness of his convictions (v. 2), the psalmist has arrived at a conception of the moral law which is not very different from the basic moral truths taught in the Sermon on the Mount. The particular precepts derive their specific impetus and significance from that fundamental conception of the moral law. Thus the particular examples which the psalm quotes also need to be understood in the light of those general principles of moral conduct; they are partly taken from the traditional statutes and ordinances which had resulted from the morality of the Covenant. The fruit of integrity in the feelings of the human heart is a behaviour towards one's neighbour which is utterly sincere both in word and deed (v. 3), and the adhering to the principle of truthfulness results in the absolute seriousness of the oath that has been sworn and of the promise that has been made and will be kept even if it proves hurtful (cf. Lev. 5.4). Righteousness prohibits (vv. 5a, b) the deriving of any personal benefits from the affliction of a fellow countryman by practising usury (cf. Ex. 22.25; Lev. 25.36 f.; Deut. 23.19) or the perverting of the justice due to the innocent for the sake of one's own profit (cf. Ex. 23.8; Deut. 16.19). The particular value which the psalm has for all generations is to be found in the realization that truth and justice are the foundation-pillars on which rest the social ethics that govern community life, the administration of justice and man's behaviour in the economic sphere. It must, however, be admitted that in one respect the psalm does not reach the full height of the biblical teaching on the moral law; this is when the psalmist demands that the godly be indeed honoured, but that those who are rejected by God be despised (v. 4). By the reprobates are meant beside notorious evildoers who have been expelled from the cult community perhaps also people whose sinfulness has been inferred from the fact that they have been 'punished' by God by some kind of heavy blow. We shall have to understand this viewpoint of the psalmist as meaning that, where God has turned against a man, it does not befit the godly to go beyond that divine decision. In the Old Testament the godly man believes that he can see the proof of the righteous providential rule of the Living God in the retribution which takes place in this world, and for his part he acknowledges that providential rule by behaving accordingly. What is ultimately at stake for him is therefore his relation to God rather than his relation to his fellow men. However much we may be able to understand the religious concern behind the application of the doctrine of retribution in this fashion, we must nevertheless not overlook the fact that it is precisely that superficial mechanical conception of the working of God's righteousness which erected a barrier strong enough to prevent the psalmist from pressing on towards love as the deepest motive power for moral action and from recognizing his neighbour in anyone who is in need of help. It is for this reason that on this point the psalm does not go beyond that barrier, which has been surmounted in the New Testament (cf. Luke 7.36 ff.; 15.2; Matt. 23.5 ff.). This shows in a highly suggestive manner how closely the idea of God and the standard of the moral law are connected with each other.

[5c] The 'promise of blessing' with which the psalm concludes is formulated in such general terms that it remains doubtful whether the phrase 'will never waver' is to be understood in the superficial

sense of being spared the divine punishment which brings about the 'downfall' of the sinner by means of an untimely ending—in view of v. 4 it might be possible to hold such a view within the compass of the cultic idea of judgment—rather than as a reference to the firm support which moral conduct is able to give to man's soul by leading him to a lasting communion with God (v. 1). To be sure, even this latter view, which would be entirely in keeping with the thoughts developed in the psalm and would once more emphasize the strength of the moral ideas expressed therein, lacks the truth of the Gospel that man is incapable of being perfectly obedient by virtue of his own strength and is therefore unable to achieve communion with God by means of his own efforts, but can reach that goal only by the grace of God, who, forgiving man his moral weakness and sins, grants him that communion by his own free will.

16. JOY IN THE PRESENCE OF GOD

Miktam.[1] *Of David*

1 Preserve me, O God, for thou hast been my refuge.
2 I said[2] to God, 'Thou art my Lord;
  my happiness depends wholly on thee'.[3]
3 The Lord deals gloriously[4] with the saints in the land;
  in them is all my delight.[5]
4 Those who flatter other (gods), multiply their sorrows;
  their libations of blood I will not pour out,
  nor may their names pass my lips.
5 The Lord is my portion and my cup;
  thou art my lot for ever.[6]
6 Property has been allotted to me in pleasant places;
  I am very pleased with my[2] heritage.[7]
7 I will praise the Lord who has given me wise counsel;
  in the night my heart exhorts me to do the same.[8]
8 I kept the Lord always before me;
  if he is at my right hand, I shall not be moved.[8]
9 Therefore my heart is glad, and my soul rejoices;
  my body also will dwell in safety.
10 For thou wilt not give me up to death,
  nor suffer thy godly one to see the Pit.
11 Thou dost show me the path of life;
  in thy presence there is fullness of joy,
  in thy hand are raptures for evermore.[9]

[1] Its meaning is uncertain; in Luther's opinion 'a golden jewel' (from *ketem*).

[2] See BH.

[3] Cf. O'Callaghan, *VT* 4, 1954, pp. 164 ff. regarding the meaning of *bāl* as a term expressing confirmation. (Tr. N.: V. 2b reads in RSV, 'I have no good apart from thee.')

[4] According to the LXX.

[5] * V. 3 in RSV:
   As for the saints in the land, they are the noble,
   in whom is all my delight.

[6] Read *tāmīd*. (Tr. N.: In RSV v. 5b reads, 'thou holdest my lot'.)

[7] * V. 6 in RSV:
   The lines have fallen for me in pleasant places;
   yea, I have a goodly heritage.

[8] * Vv. 7 and 8 in RSV:
   (7) I bless the Lord who gives me counsel;
       in the night also my heart instructs me.
   (8) I keep the Lord always before me;
       because he is at my right hand,
       I shall not be moved.

[9] Lit.: 'In thy right hand are lovely things for ever.'

The text of this very significant psalm is in places so corrupt that an accurate translation is not always possible. For the same reason neither can it be established beyond doubt how the verses were originally divided up. The psalm takes the form of an affirmation of trust; the style of prayer (invocation of God) is clearly seen only in vv. 1 f., 5, 10 f. The commentators are divided in their views on the specific circumstances of the worshipper and also, in consequence, in their views on the specific meaning of particular phrases and ideas in the psalm. Whereas the majority of scholars try to interpret the psalm in the light of the period immediately following the return of the people from the Babylonian captivity, and, in doing so, have in mind conditions such as are alluded to, for instance, in Isa. 57.3 ff.; 62.11 f.; 65.1 ff., other scholars assume that the author of the psalm belongs to the group of the *Hasidim* (the godly ones) which existed in the period between the Testaments, and endeavour to interpret the psalm in the light of the conflict of Old Testament religion with the activity of sects and mystery cults in the 'Hellenistic' age. The various allusions to features of the cult of the Covenant Festival, such as the presence of God (vv. 1, 8, 11), the glorification of God by his dealings with the community of his saints (v. 3), the renunciation of strange gods and the turning away from the worshippers of idols (v. 4), the declaration of fate and the bestowal of land (vv. 5 f.), and the assurance of salvation (vv. 8–11)—all these suggest (see Intr. 29 ff., 44, 51) that the psalm's origin is to be accounted for by the pre-exilic

cult of the Covenant Festival and that the psalm is to be interpreted
as the personal confession of a worshipper in which he sets forth what
the encounter with God in the sanctuary means to him.[1]

First strophe: affirmation of faith in God (vv. 1–4)

[1] The worshipper opens his prayer with a petition for preservation. This does not necessarily imply that he is faced by a calamity
from which he desires to be delivered. What we read in other parts of
the psalm points to quite a different basic mood, to gratitude and
joy in God and in his salvation. Here the psalmist simply prays that
God may also protect him in future as he has done in the past. This
interpretation is suggested by the way in which the worshipper
justifies his petition: 'for in thee have I found refuge'. The prayer
therefore arises out of the religious experiences of the worshipper
who knows himself to be sheltered by God on account of God's
presence in the Temple. True religious experience inevitably impels
man again and again to take refuge in the arms of God and brings
about man's dialogue with God. A constant life of prayer is the
natural way in which faith manifests itself in life. [2] The poet unfolds his thoughts before God in prayer and expresses them primarily
in the form of an affirmation of faithfulness, which is the proper
thing to do on the occasion of man's encounter with God. Moreover,
so far it had always been the foundation of the psalmist's piety
(literally, 'I said ever again'), 'Thou art my Lord'. That acknowledgment of God as the Lord implies the unqualified acknowledgment of God's claim on him as well as of God's care for him.
Developing this latter thought in the same direction, the worshipper
adds, 'There is no happiness for me apart from thee.'[2] For him God
is not only the 'supreme good' within a scale of other good things,
but the *only* good thing, the absolute 'blessing' which comprises
everything else. The relation to God dominates the whole of human
life, because God lays claim to the whole man. [3] As for the aforementioned two aspects of acknowledging God's sovereignty, in
vv. 3 and 4, the psalmist sets forth in more detail the significance
which this recognition has for the godly. If we may venture to follow
the Greek translation, which can be done without requiring any
major alteration of the Hebrew text, then the author speaks in v. 3

[1] Kraus attempts to interpret the psalm as the hymn of a priest who belonged
to the Levites.
[2] * The text of the German here differs from the author's translation of v. 2b.

above all of the way in which the divine Lord cares for his people:
God deals gloriously with the saints in the land.[1] That thought
includes not only the material welfare of the religious community,
but also, more profoundly, the *Heilsgeschichte* which ever again
'comes to pass' afresh in the festival cult. The term 'saints' derives its
meaning from its origin, from the notion of the holy people, set
apart by God, whose calling, as the Old Testament shows, is that the
glory of God may be revealed to the world both by God's dealings
with his people and through their witness. This idea of the self-
glorification of God in the midst of his people and through his people
is therefore also implied in the saying that God deals gloriously with
the saints. It is in this very fact that the poet discerns God's absolute
faithfulness to his people; in consequence, he testifies to his fellowship
with the people of God. [4] However, God's care for his people includes
his absolute claim upon man and excludes all relations to other gods
(cf. Ex. 20.2 f.). The poet clearly recognizes how everything hangs
together: if man's happiness depends on the exclusiveness of his
relationship with God, then the associating with another god can
only result in misery and sorrow. Anything which does not arise
from man's relationship with the One and Only God is sin against
that God. The commandment to keep that relationship undefiled by
anything in any way related to a strange religion grows out of the
intimacy of the communion with God which claims the whole man.
It is in this thought that the inner theological justification is to be
found of the renunciation of foreign gods which was a constituent
part of the cult of the Covenant (see Intr. 51, 76 f.). The psalmist
mentions two foreign religious customs, the libations of blood, to
which a reconciling and redeeming power was ascribed, and the use
of the names of other gods, which were considered as charms possessing magic power. The psalmist seems to avoid quite deliberately even
the mere mention of such a name; indeed, he goes so far that he even
denies to those other gods the designation 'god'. All things considered,
it is remarkable that the psalmist does not extend his aversion to that
practice to the people who behave in this way, though, making use
of an idea which is also firmly rooted in the cult of the Covenant
(cf. Ps. 15.4), he meticulously draws the line of demarcation which

---

[1] Mowinckel (*TLZ* 82, 1957, col. 649 ff.) expunges in v. 2 *'adōnāy* and reads
beliyya'al kol-qedōšīm . . . we'addīrē baššamayim bal ḥepṣī bām: 'worthless are all
the saints in the earth and the rulers in heaven; I am not pleased in them.' In that
he interprets the 'saints and rulers' as referring to strange gods, he already finds
here the idea of renunciation (see v. 4).

separates him from those of his fellow countrymen who follow strange gods; his way of thinking, which is entirely focused on God, may have prevented him from committing such a mistake.

Second strophe: the happiness of having communion with God (vv. 5–8)

[5] The poet now expresses in two ways what the communion with God, what salvation, means to him. The cup, perhaps the 'festival cup' of Yahweh, which was passed round at a cultic meal of those who participated in the feast, is simultaneously the symbol and the pledge of divine saving grace.[1] So, too, the terms 'lot' and 'portion' (of land), which are here used as parallel terms, point in the same direction (see Intr. 44). The verse is therefore meant to express the thought that the destiny of the worshipper for ever remains connected with God; it cannot be imagined that God plays no part in his life. [6] It is not merely a loose sequence of thought when the poet, having referred to the lot, now proceeds to speak about the allotting of landed property, which was probably carried out by means of a sacred ritual and decided by lot. The connection between these thoughts is more profound than that. If man turns his thoughts to the providential rule of God and envisages that providential rule with gratitude and joy, he is thus taught to discern in material benefits the visible proof of the benevolence of his God. He also derives from his faith in God the right criterion for the estimation of material values; he accepts these with joy and satisfaction as a gift from God, being his 'heritage'. To be sure, the writer of this psalm seems to have been spared the mystery of suffering and affliction which plays such an important part in earthly life and was a great shock to the author of the Book of Job. And in this respect he also differs from the poet of Psalm 73, whose attitude in other respects is in many a way similar to his own. [7] The justification of interpreting v. 6 in this way follows from v. 7. Thinking of his temporal lot, the poet instinctively reverts to his contemplation of God. The pious soul naturally and beautifully expresses its feelings by singing the praise of God. Looking back on his past life, the poet realizes with heartfelt gratitude how graciously God's wise counsel has guided him. In the silence of the night, when the bustle of the day dies down, he distinctly hears a voice speaking in his heart, exhorting him to turn to

---

[1] Cf. Ringgren, *Svensk Exegetisk Årsbok* 17, 1952, pp. 19 ff., concerning the original connection between the idea of the cup of wrath or blessing (cf. Jer. 25.15 ff.) and the ideology of the New Year Festival.

God in prayer. In his view prayer is one of the indispensable neces-
saries of life required by faith. As he feels unable to live his life in any
other way than in the sight of God, he does not regard prayer merely
as an expedient way of bringing the desires of his heart before God,
but as an opportunity offered to him in his life of being made more
perfect by God's counsel and chastisement than he is at the moment.
In submitting himself to the discipline of prayer he reminds us of the
prayer-life of such a man as Jeremiah. [8] It is simply the result of the
vivid experience of the impression made on him by God's presence
that the poet continually concentrates his thoughts on God and sees
himself confronted by God in whatever he experiences or does.
Acting in the way he does, the particular events of his life assume the
character of signposts leading him to God; the encounter with God
and the dialogue with God in prayer bring about a communion with
God which will last for life. If God stands by him, then he will not
waver: he may be assured of God's help whenever he is in danger or
afflicted, and of God's counsel and guidance in the decisions which
he has to take.

Third strophe: rejoicing in hope (vv. 9–11)

[9] Being assured of his lifelong communion with God, the
psalmist's heart is filled with gladness and he breaks forth into
rejoicing. He knows that in the future he will be safe in God's arms,
and that this is true both of his body and his soul. In this connection
attention must be drawn to the fact that he gives expression to that
optimistic conviction, based on faith, at the very moment when his
thoughts turn to the contemplation of death! [10] Indeed, it is
precisely what he feels bound to say as he faces the thought of death—
which does not frighten him, but on the contrary gives him confidence (cf. the connecting word 'for'). Opinions are divided as to
the concrete meaning of the statement made in v. 10. The great
majority of more recent expositors hold the view that what the author
has in mind is that God will protect him from a sudden, untimely, or
evil death. However, neither the wording of the verse nor the general
circumstances and attitude of the poet suggest such an interpretation;
moreover, it is precisely the decisive feature of that interpretation—
the specific kind of death—which is read into the text. There is no
reason to doubt that the poet, speaking of death in quite general
terms, has in mind death as such, that is, death in general, and that
by virtue of his faith in God he is progressing towards the conquest

of the fear of death in his heart. How he actually conceives of the particular circumstances of that process cannot be clearly deduced from his statement. If the second half of the verse is translated as an exact parallel to the first half, as has been done here, we might be able to think that the psalmist will be taken up by God into heaven (cf. Gen. 5.24; II Kings 2.1 ff.). If the word which in accordance with its usual meaning we have rendered 'pit', is derived from the Hebrew root of the word 'decay' (= rot), then it may be possible to infer from that reading that the psalmist is here thinking of the resurrection from the dead. Such an interpretation—and it is not impossible—would be in keeping with the Greek translation and with the New Testament, where the verse has been interpreted as referring to the resurrection of Jesus (Acts 2.25 ff.; 13.35). It seems to me, however, that in attempting to interpret the psalmist's statement the question of *how* he conceives of his being spared death has been given undue prominence by the very manner in which that question has been formulated; and this view is supported by the true meaning of the psalm itself. The poet, at any rate—probably deliberately—does not particularly emphasize that question. Presumably he refrains from doing so in the first place because, standing as he does in the front line of those who are opposed to the religious practices of their time, he does not want to expose himself to being accused of paganism by adopting the belief in the resurrection from the dead, which after all was encouraged in the worship of the vegetation gods (cf. the cultic myth of Baal and Mot in the Ras Shamra texts and Hos. 6.1 ff.); and secondly, and this is what matters most, because, on the basis of his faith in God, the 'that' is of greater importance to him than the 'how' (cf. also the comments on v. 11). True, the author wants to express the fact that his belief in the overcoming of death is equal to that of others. But the source from which he derives his belief is a different one. It is the same source which has become manifest throughout the psalm as the foundation of the psalmist's faithful optimism—a life lived in communion with God. Where such a life in communion with God involves the whole man, there death for all practical purposes loses that dreadful importance which it has for those people whose sense of life is rather naïve. The problem of death here gives way, not to an excessive craving for the enjoyment of life to the full in the natural sense, but to the abundance of life lived on a higher level which flows from communion with God. By reaching a deeper religious insight into the meaning of life, the worshipper, in fact, considers the problem of death as no longer the most crucial question. This is the course which the psalmist adopts to overcome death. To the life-giving power of God in which the poet is privileged to share, death and the underworld are no insurmountable obstacles which could shatter that living communion with God. Living in utter dependence on God as he does, the psalmist possesses the victorious power that is able to overcome death. In the light of this interpretation we come to understand the sense in which the verse in question has been used in the New Testament. There can be no doubt that v. 10 is not meant to be understood as a prophetic prediction of the resurrection of Jesus, but the New Testament teaching of the resurrection from the dead and the thoughts which here occupy the mind of the psalmist are based on the same fundamental conviction, namely, an unshakable belief in the life-giving power of God (which in the resurrection of Christ has definitely conquered death). [11] Verse 11 immediately follows up that thought and develops it further. The fact 'that' death has been overcome by God is the firm foundation which enables the poet to envisage death with an assurance that does not doubt, whereas the question of 'how' God will achieve that goal remains a divine mystery which is still concealed. There is one thing which he knows, however: 'Thou wilt show me the path of life.' In view of the context in which this saying stands, the phrase 'path of life' can hardly be understood in any other sense than as a life lived in communion with God which will be carried on even after death; in other words, as the consummation of salvation, the future form of which is at present still hidden from the poet. But God himself will remove the veil from that mystery, and only then will the psalmist be able to share in the perfect fullness of joy in God's presence and in the blessed communion with him (literally, 'there is satisfaction in the joy at the sight of thy face'). The raptures which God's hand holds in readiness for him last for ever. It is in such a joyful affirmation of God's life-giving might that the power of the biblical faith is to be found, a faith which far surpasses the other religions because it enables man by virtue of his faith to adopt a positive outlook on the total reality of life including death.

17. THE DIVINE VERDICT

A Prayer. Of David

1 Hear me, O Lord of my salvation;[1] attend to my cry![2]
Give ear to my prayer from lips free of deceit!

2 My vindication comes forth from thy presence,
 thy eyes see what is right![3]
3 If thou triest my heart, if thou visitest me by night
 and testest me, thou wilt find nothing.
 I thought, nothing (evil) shall slip out of my mouth.[4]
4 With regard to the works of men, by the word of thy lips
 I have avoided the ways of the violent.
5 My steps I held fast to thy paths,
 hence my feet did not slip.
6 I call upon thee,
 for thou wilt answer me, O God;
 incline thy ear to me, hear my words.
7 Wondrously show thy steadfast love,
 O saviour of those who seek refuge
 from those who rebel against thy power.[5]
8 Keep me as the apple of the eye;
 hide me in the shadow of thy wings
9 from the wicked who did violence to me,
 my enemies who greedily surround me.
10 They have closed their fat hearts to pity;
 with their mouths they speak arrogantly.
11 They track me[6] down and surround me;[6]
 they set their eyes to cast (me) to the ground.
12 He is like a lion, eager to tear,
 as a young lion lurking in ambush.
13 Arise, O Lord! Confront him, overthrow him!
 Deliver me from the wicked by thy sword,
14 from men, O Lord, by thy hand,
 from men whose portion in life may be shortlived.
 Fill their belly with what thou hast hidden
 that their children still get enough to be satiated
 and leave something over to their babes.[7]
15 As for me, I may behold thy face in my deliverance;
 when I awake, I may satisfy myself by beholding thy form.[8]

---

[1] Following the LXX read *ṣidqī*.
[2] * V. 1a in RSV reads, 'Hear a just cause, O Lord; attend to my cry!'
[3] * V. 2 in RSV:
 From thee let my vindication come!
 Let thy eyes see the right!
[4] * V. 3 in RSV:
 If thou triest my heart, if thou visitest me by night,
 if thou testest me, thou wilt find no wickedness in me,
 my mouth does not transgress.
[5] * V. 7c in RSV reads, 'from their adversaries at thy right hand'.
[6] See BH.
[7] * V. 14b–e in RSV:
 from men whose portion in life is of the world.
 May their belly be filled with what thou hast stored up for them;

may their children have more than enough;
may they leave something over to their babes.
8 * V. 15 in RSV:
As for me, I shall behold thy face in righteousness;
when I awake, I shall be satisfied with beholding thy form.

Many difficulties have to be faced in interpreting this psalm, the
language of which is unyielding and rugged. Verses 3 f. and 14 in
particular admit of diverse interpretations which in part differ
widely from each other, so that both translation and exegesis can be
offered only tentatively. The structure of the psalm is evidently as
follows: the introduction (vv. 1–2) is followed by the protestation of
innocence (vv. 3–5); the supplication begins in v. 6 and changes in
v. 9 into a description of the enemies; that description is followed in
vv. 13 and 14 by a prayer that vengeance may be taken on the
enemies; v. 15 concludes the psalm with an affirmation of hope of
deliverance, which is expected to be brought about by the encounter
with God. The author belongs to the community of the 'godly'
(vv. 3 f., 7; Duhm classes him with the Pharisees, but that view is
hardly correct). He is persecuted by wicked adversaries and is
wrongly accused by them. He therefore pleads his cause before God
in the Temple that he might be vindicated by him (v. 2) and asks for
his help (vv. 6 ff.). From vv. 7 f., 13, 15, it may be inferred that the
prayer was uttered at the celebration of the cult of the Covenant
Festival where Yahweh appears above the sacred Ark to sit in
judgment on evildoers and to reveal his salvation to the community
of the godly (see Intr. 37–40, 72 ff.).

[1–2] The idea of the worshipper's innocence, which dominates
the first part of the psalm, is already prominent in the lengthy invocation of God in prayer (see Intr. 76). Only a sincere prayer which is
frank and 'free of deceit' can hope to be answered. The worshipper
hopes to be vindicated by God, trusting in God's unprejudiced
righteousness and relying on a good conscience. (Hans Schmidt
holds, as he frequently does, but here perhaps justly so, that we have
here a reference to an ordeal which took place in the Temple.)
[3–5] The detailed protestation of innocence is not to be understood
as the expression of a naïve self-righteousness, let alone as the affirmation of the worshipper's sinlessness, but as an effort of the latter to
justify himself in the face of unwarranted accusations—hence the use
of negative formulations, fashioned in the traditional style of the
confession (cf. Pss. 15; 24.3 ff.; Deut. 26.13 ff.; Ezek. 18.5 ff.). The

primary concern of the poet is that his relationship with God should not be impaired by the slanderous attacks from which he suffers in addition to what he already has to endure in that respect. He is quite in earnest with his concern for an untroubled relationship with God, and without any hesitation he is quite prepared to have his thoughts, words and deeds subjected to a most thoroughgoing testing by God. For he has taken great care not to yield to the temptation of being rash in his speech or of being violent, as human nature is prone to do. On the contrary, God's commandments have been the guiding principle and the support of his life. **[6–9]** It is only at this point, when the worshipper feels that he is delivered from the burden of suspicion by the testimony he has made before God, that he is able to state his main concern with an easy conscience. His supplication at first takes up again the theme of v. 1, the invocation of God, but now it includes—and this is a remarkable variation—the theme of the worshipper's 'certitude that the prayer will be answered' (see Intr. 79 f.). To my mind this is the proof of the previous protestation of innocence. Confronted by the violence of his enemies, from which he had to suffer and by which he feels threatened, the worshipper seeks refuge in God. He knows that he himself is helpless and that only a miracle of divine grace can save him. But he also knows that God will help him; for what is at stake is God's own cause, since God is confronted by those 'who rebel against his power'. The writer's supplication is not to be regarded as a challenge to God to work a miracle, but, on the contrary, arises from a heartfelt trust which is upheld by tradition; this is impressively expressed in the two word-pictures of v. 8, which show the psalmist's childlike and tender affection for God. The second picture is associated with the idea of the God of the sacred Ark who appears upon the wings of the cherubim and sits enthroned there (see Intr. 39 ff., 73). **[10–12]** In contrast to the attitude of the poet the conduct of the threatening adversaries is arrogant and violent, hard-hearted and brutal, greedy and insidious; it is summarized (hence the changing over to the singular in v. 12) in the picture of the ravenous lion lying in wait for his prey (cf. Ps. 10.8 f.). **[13–14]** The contrast thus expressed in the imagery of vv. 8 and 12 as well as the contrast of the feelings underlying these images—on the one hand, feelings of being sheltered, and, on the other, of fear— already indicate the strong tension that torments the heart of the worshipper; and that tension, exploding with the primitive force of accumulated emotions, finds its relief in a prayer for vengeance

(vv. 13, 14). That the poet has lost all control over his emotions we can still sense—provided that the original text has been preserved—in the way in which the sentences follow each other precipitately and are uttered abruptly, as if the worshipper were panting for breath; we sense it, too, in the train of thought expressed in these sentences, marked as it is by unsteadiness. This makes these verses difficult to understand. At the same time, however, it warns us against any attempt to construct a train of thought which would be unobjectionable from the logical point of view by amending the text with that end in view. Enraged and embittered as he is, tortured, too, by a secret fear, the poet imagines that God must save him by overthrowing his adversaries, killing them with the sword or with the fist or, as he elaborates in v. 14 with gruesome irony, destroying them by means of a mysterious food secretly stored up by God for future retribution, whereby they as well as their children and grandchildren shall 'be satiated'. But the worshipper does not remain for ever in the depths of the abyss into which his human feelings of vindictiveness have thrown him and into which he had tried to drag his God as well. By a vigorous turn of his thoughts he once more lifts up his eyes to the sphere in which God lives, whom he is permitted to behold in his 'salvation', that is, as one who has been vindicated and saved. The worshipper hopes that his encounter with God 'when he awakes' —probably an allusion to the theophany[1] which is expected to take place in the cult the following morning (cf. v. 3)—will be the means whereby he on his part 'will be satisfied'. That encounter with God will be the pledge that he has communion with God in his heart, a communion which will help him to overcome all his afflictions, afflictions which are caused not only by his enemies, but also by his own troubled heart.

[1] Other commentators interpret the verse as expressing hope in a future life. But the terms 'face' and 'form', which are used as parallels, point rather to the presence of God in the theophany.

18. THE 'GRACE OF KINGSHIP'

To the Conductor. Of David, the servant of Yahweh, who addressed the words of this song to Yahweh on the day when Yahweh delivered him from the hand of all his enemies, and from the hand of Saul. He said:

1 I will love thee, O Lord, my strength.
2 The Lord is my rock, and my fortress, and my deliverer,
   my God, my protector, in whom I trust,
   my shield, and the horn of my salvation, my refuge.

3 I called upon the Lord, who is worthy to be praised,
  and I was saved from my enemies.
4 The waves[1] of death encompassed me,
  and the torrents of perdition frightened me;
5 the cords of hell entangled me,
  the snares of death confronted me.
6 In my distress I called upon the Lord
  and cried to my God on high:
  from his temple may he hear my voice,
  and my cry to him may reach his ears![2]
7 Then the earth reeled and rocked;
  the foundations also of the mountains trembled;
  they quaked because he was angry.
8 Smoke went up from his nostrils,
  and devouring fire from his mouth;
  glowing coals flamed forth from him.
9 He bowed the heavens, and came down;
  dark clouds were under his feet.
10 He rode on a cherub, and flew;
  he came swiftly upon the wings of the storm.
11 He made darkness his covering around him,
  his canopy the drizzle of clouds dark with water.
12 In the brightness before him clouds swept onwards
  and hailstones and coals of fire.
13 The Lord let his thunder rumble in the heavens,
  the Most High let his voice be heard ' '.[3]
14 He sent out his arrows, and scattered them;
  he flashed forth[1] lightnings and terrified them.
15 Then the channels of the sea[1] were seen,
  and the foundations of the earth were laid bare, at thy rebuke, O Lord,
  at the blast of the breath of thy wrath.
16 He reached from on high, he took me,
  he drew me out of mighty[4] waters.
17 He delivered me from my strong enemy,
  from those who hate me;
  for they are too mighty for me.
18 They came upon me in the day of my calamity;
  but the Lord was my stay.
19 He brought me forth into a broad place;
  he delivered me because he loves me.
20 The Lord rewarded me according to my righteousness;
  according to the cleanness of my hands he recompensed me.
21 For I have kept the ways of the Lord,
  and have not wickedly departed from my God.
22 For all his ordinances were before me,
  and his statutes I did not put away from me.
23 Thus I was blameless before him,
  and took good care to keep myself from guilt.

24 Therefore the Lord has recompensed me according to my righteousness, according to the cleanness of my hands in his sight.
25 With the upright thou dost show thyself upright;
with the perfect thou dost show thyself perfect;[5]
26 with the pure thou dost show thyself pure;
but with the perverted thou dost deal perversely.
27 For thou dost deliver a humble people,
but the haughty eyes thou dost bring down.
28 Yea, thou, O Lord, dost light my lamp,
my God that lightens my darkness.
29 By thee I can crush the troop;
and by my God I can leap over the wall.
30 Yea, this God—his way is perfect;
the word of the Lord is pure.[6]
He is a shield for all those who take refuge in him.
31 For who is God, but the Lord?
And who is a rock, except our God?—
32 the God who girded me with strength
and made my way blameless;[7]
33 who made my feet like hinds' feet,
and set me secure on the heights;[1]
34 who trained my hands for war
so that my arms could bend a bow of bronze.
35 Thou hast given me the shield of thy salvation,
thy right hand supported me,
and thy condescension[8] made me great.
36 Thou didst give a wide place for my steps under me,
and my ankle-bones did not give way.
37 I pursued my enemies and overtook them;
and did not turn back till they were consumed.
38 I knocked them down so that they will never be able to rise;
they fell under my feet.
39 For thou didst gird me with strength for the battle;
thou didst make my assailants sink under me.
40 Thou didst make my enemies turn their backs to me,
and those who hated me I destroyed.
41 They cried for help, but there was none to save,
they cried to the[1] Lord, but he did not answer them.
42 I beat them fine as dust before the wind;
I trampled them down[1] like the mud of the streets.
43 Thou didst deliver me from the conflicts of the people;[9]
thou didst make me the head of nations.
People whom I had not known served me;
44 as soon as they heard of me, they obeyed me;
sons of strangers came cringing to me.
45 Sons of strangers brought gifts unto me,[10]
and came trembling out of their strongholds.

46 The Lord lives; blessed be my rock.
   He rises, the God of my salvation.[11]
47 He is the God who gave me vengeance,
   who subdued the peoples under me;
48 who delivered me from the wrath of my enemies;
   yea, thou didst exalt me above my adversaries;
   thou didst deliver me from men of violence.
49 For this I will testify to thee, O Lord, among the nations,
   and sing praises to thy name,
50 who makest great the blessings of his king[12]
   and shows steadfast love to his anointed,
   to David and his descendants for ever.

[1] See BH.
[2] * V. 6b–d in RSV:
   to my God I cried for help.
   From his temple he heard my voice,
   and my cry to him reached his ears.
[3] See BH. (Tr. N.: V. 13 in RSV:
   The Lord also thundered in the heavens,
   and the Most High uttered his voice,
   hailstones and coals of fire.)
[4] * V. 16b reads in RSV, 'many waters'.
[5] * V. 25 in RSV:
   With the loyal thou dost show thyself loyal;
   with the blameless man thou dost show thyself blameless.
[6] * V. 30b runs in RSV, 'the promise of the Lord proves true'.
[7] * RSV reads in v. 32b, 'and made my way safe'.
[8] * V. 35c has in RSV 'help' instead of 'condescension'.
[9] * V. 43a in RSV: 'Thou didst deliver me from strife with the peoples.'
[10] V. 45a in RSV, 'foreigners lost heart.' See B.H. (Tr. N:.)
[11] * V 46b in RSV, 'and exalted be the God of my salvation'.
[12] * V. 50a in RSV: 'Great triumphs he gives to his king.'

The opening words of the psalm were used by Johann Scheffler as
the first line of his hymn 'Thee will I love, my strength, my tower'.[1]
In form the psalm is a king's thanksgiving, commemorating his
deliverance from a great peril and his victory over his enemies.
According to the title, which was attached to the psalm at a later
date, David is said to have composed 'the song' after he had been
delivered 'from all his enemies' and 'from the hand of Saul'. The
psalm also occurs in II Sam. 22 in a form which is somewhat later,
but which seems to go back to an earlier manuscript than the one
used for the text of Psalm 18. Though these two facts together only
prove that the psalm was ascribed to David at the time of the composition of the Books of Samuel, the psalm itself does not contain

[1] * In the German original 'Ich will dich lieben, meine Stärke', a hymn by
Johann Scheffler (1624–1677), translated by John Wesley (1703–1791).

anything which would exclude the possibility that it was composed at the time of David. Parallels in the literature of a later period (compare Micah 7.17 with v. 45; Hab. 3.19 with v. 33; Prov. 30.5 with v. 30 and also Pss. 116; 144) can be considered as quotations from the psalm or as having been derived from a common liturgical tradition in the cult. The so-called Deuteronomic style in vv. 21 ff. is confined to phrases which by are no means characteristic only of the Deuteronomic literature. The affinities in v. 31 to Deutero-Isaiah (cf. Isa. 43.11; 44.6, 8; 45.21) certainly do not compel us to assume a dependence on the part of the psalm. On the other hand, the psalm exhibits some features which make it impossible to assign a late date to it. To these features belong the description of the theophany in vv. 7 ff. which, as in the ancient traditions of Judg. 5; Ex. 15; Josh. 10.12 ff., determines the outcome of the battle, as well as the mention of the king's archaic method of fighting on foot, in which all depends on swiftness in running and pursuing (vv. 29, 33; cf. II Sam. 1.23; 2.18); and other peculiar features, such as the archaic orthography of the psalm, point in the same direction. We shall therefore have to reckon with the possibility that the psalm was composed by David or, as the stereotyped forms of the liturgical 'court-style' suggest (cf. the comments on Psalm 2), by a poet of his court. Moreover, it is doubtful whether, as the great majority of commentators assume, the psalm was composed for the special purpose of being used at the celebration of a particular victory, and has in mind only that single event, the historical particulars of which can hardly be established with any degree of certainty. The first part of the psalm deals exclusively with the deliverance of the king from a grave peril 'in the day of his calamity' (v. 18); after v. 14 the enemies are scattered, but it is not until the second part of the psalm that the victory over the enemies and the triumph are described. Hence the psalm seems to cover a larger period of time and to have in mind not just one but several events (v. 43 probably refers to conflicts amongst the psalmist's own people).

We are, however, dissuaded from dividing the psalm into two independent prayers (as Hans Schmidt and others do), since the two main themes are clearly treated as a unity in vv. 43 f. and 48, and since the same metre is used in both parts. We must, of course, reckon with the possibility that in the course of the psalm's use in the cult the text has been made the object of alterations, affecting a number of passages, so that it is not always possible to restore the original form. The extraction of a great proportion of the psalm by means of literary and historical criticism, a method which has more than once been attempted, cannot be recommended—especially when we consider that in the sphere of the cultus, the primary source of a true understanding of this psalm, too, different structural elements were welded into a single whole. The psalm, after all, does not present us with an account of the course of certain historical events, nor, and this is particularly true of vv. 7 ff., with a description of a natural phenomenon (be it a thunderstorm or the eruption of a volcano), but is itself part of the ritual used in the cult and, having arisen from the sacred tradition, was probably appointed to be used at the celebration of a particular divine service which was held at regular intervals (see the comments on v. 50). The focal point of that service was the representation of the mighty acts wrought by God to save the king, and its main purpose was to establish and safeguard the 'grace of kingship'. It is only in this context that the tremendous dimensions embracing heaven and earth can be accounted for. In the midst of these is set the destiny of the royal worshipper—in much the same way as it is incorporated in the traditions of the biblical *Heilsgeschichte* which can be glimpsed here and there and which far transcends the natural-historical scope of purely human events and conditions.

Like the two spires of a cathedral the two parts of the mighty hymn soar to heaven, a hymn of praise to the glory of God who appears to help the worshipper in his affliction (vv. 1–30) and 'rises' (v. 46) to 'make great the blessings of his king' (v. 50). The meaning and purpose of the whole psalm and of the ceremony which was its setting are crystallized in the representation of the divine redemptive work as a living reality. Though each of the psalm's two parts has a character of its own appropriate to its special subject-matter, yet it is only when they are viewed as a unity that they produce the full effect of a perfect testimony to the majestic power of the Living God and to the unimpaired trust of the royal singer, who is sure of his blessings and rejoices in them. The manner in which the psalm has been arranged is in harmony with its flexible language, which is adapted to the changing trends of the different kinds of mood. It is carefully thought out and reflects the dramatic events which are so vividly depicted in the psalm; again, it welds crescendos, climaxes, and pauses into a unity by combining them in a consistent thought-sequence.

First Part: The Deliverance (vv. 1–30)

The opening hymn (vv. 1–2)

[1–2] It is not beyond doubt whether the opening words 'I will love thee, O Lord, my strength' render the original text. However, having made this admission, it can be said that these words irradiate the whole psalm, illuminating it with the gentle light of the worshipper's surrender of his heart to God, an act which springs from the uttermost depths of his personal inner life and, as can be gathered from the psalm's conclusion (cf. vv. 50 and 19), draws its motivating power from the love which God bestows upon the worshipper. It is to this love of God that the king's 'strength' is due; his song is a testimony in which this intimate relationship with God finds topical and ejaculatory expression (cf. Judg. 5.31). Thus the psalm opens at once with a hymnic testimony which, by its lapidary style, its piling-up of predicates, paints a vivid picture of the abundance of meaning which God's support has for the king. Also depicted is the wealth of energies which the worshipper derives from his relationship with God, with whom he feels safe and in whom he trusts. Similarly the image of the 'horn of salvation' is probably to be understood as a symbol signifying 'strength'.

Affliction and supplication (vv. 3–6)

[3] In v. 3 the 'hymn' style changes into the form of a 'narration' (see Intr. 56); this continues till v. 19. The purpose of the narration is to make the events reported therein the theme of the liturgy and to actualize them; the events thus bring about the experience of God's actual presence and his redemptive work, and receive their cultic sanction. This purpose explains the striking use of different tenses, the perfect and the imperfect being used alternately. This change of tense, which cannot be rendered adequately in German, continues throughout the psalm and is designed to express the reality of what has happened in the past, a reality which is still effective in the present. The theme of the first part, the deliverance from the enemies, is briefly outlined in v. 3; **[4–5]** in vv. 4 and 5 the king describes the peril which confronted him as having been so grave that he imagined himself to have already departed to the underworld, being entangled in the cords of death. In v. 4 the realm of death is conceived as it was by the Babylonians and Greeks, namely as a river or an ocean (cf. Pss. 9.13; 30.3; 88.3, 6; Jonah 2.2 f., 5 f.), and in v. 5 as a hunter who sets snares. **[6]** It remains doubtful whether this imagery alludes to the widespread theme of the cultic myth of the descent into hell; nevertheless the pitiless severity of the sphere of death, of the mortal danger to life which encompassed him and from which, humanly speaking, no deliverance was possible—this severity stands out in order to make evident that the worshipper owes absolutely everything to the saving act of his God who rescued him. Embracing the widest possible dimensions, the prayer reflects the hard struggle in which the worshipper is involved whilst he prays, his thoughts dwelling first on the uttermost depths of hell, into which the hopeless despair of his affliction had thrown him, and then gradually rising to the heavenly sanctuary of God. And the great miracle comes to pass: God himself appears in his adversity to rescue him.

The theophany (vv. 7–15)

[7–15] The coming down of God from heaven is portrayed down to the smallest detail. By this method a powerful impression is created. In its archaic and almost mythical traits the description is related to that original theophany which took place at Sinai. Evidently it is to be classed with the basic constituents not only of the ancient literary tradition but also of the cultic tradition of the people of the Covenant (cf. Judg. 5.4 ff.; Deut. 33.2; Isa. 30.27 ff.; Hab. 3.3 ff.; Ps. 97.2, with Ex. 19 and I Kings 19.11 f.). Moreover, as far as Psalm 18 is concerned, the description of the theophany is to be understood in the light of its significance within the framework of the tradition of the cultus. We have here not, as the great majority of the commentators assume, a description in archaic poetical language of the natural phenomenon of a thunderstorm or an earthquake, nor a fragment which, having been adopted from an ancient tradition, has been interpolated in the psalm and is only loosely connected with the subject-matter of the psalm as a whole. The account of the theophany has a twofold significance as far as the recital of the psalm in the cult is concerned. Firstly, it has a ritual importance of its own on account of the fact that by means of the 're-presentation' of the theophany, itself celebrated as a cultic event (see Intr. 28 ff.) and as such taken for granted in the psalm, the whole cult community together with the worshipper experience in the traditionally fixed form of the theophany the God of Sinai as the God who is present and now appears before them so that they can see and hear him. By virtue of the spoken word, sanctified by the liturgical tradition, they feel themselves confronted by that God, with the result that that tradition in all its fullness becomes for them a living present event (cf. Ps. 50.2 ff.). This explains the striking prolixity of the description of the theopany, which is couched in solemn terms and worked out in great detail. Secondly, the particular events of which the psalm speaks —the personal rescue of the king and the realization of his 'blessings' —are made an essential part of the redemptive work of God, of fundamental importance for the cult community, in that they are related to the Sinai theophany, which is experienced as an actual present event and in which they are now incorporated. They are thus made an essential part of the *Heilsgeschichte* in which the cult community participates, the *Heilsgeschichte* which is represented within the ritual framework of the cult and is continually realized afresh within that setting. The historical events derive their import- ance only from their association with that *Heilsgeschichte*. Within the scope of the psalm they cannot claim any 'historical' importance of their own in the modern sense; it would therefore be a mistake to apply to the psalm the critical standards which are used to judge the method of representing historical events.[1]

The particular features of the magnificent portrayal of the appearance of God coming down from heaven, strange as they may seem to us on account of their archaic imagery, serve the purpose of illustrating—and of veiling—the awful majesty and might of God. Nowhere is God's form described. The nearness and the greatness of God, hidden behind the brightness of fire and behind dark clouds (cf. Ex. 24.10 and the pillars of cloud and of fire in the tradition of the Exodus), can be recognized only by means of the impression pro- duced by his appearance—which has the proportions of cosmic catastrophes; and even within these limits they can only be surmised. From the cloudy sky which bows down to the earth God descends in a storm, riding on a cherub, that mythical-poetical embodiment of the clouds which serve as his chariot (cf. Isa. 19.1; Ps. 104.3 f.). At this point we can clearly see, too, that the psalm's account of the theophany is related to the sacred ritual of the cult. For the clouds which serve as a chariot of the Deity are symbolized by the cherubim

---

[1] Westermann (*Das Loben Gottes in den Psalmen*, pp. 65 ff.) holds that it is not possible to assume here a reference to the Sinai theophany, because the psalm does not include all the particular features of the tradition of the Exodus. But that view applies a standard which may rightly be used when it is a question of investi- gating the literary dependence of a composition, but is scarcely adequate to the nature of the cultic tradition and its linguistic forms (cf. p. 38, n. 2).

on the mercy-seat of the Ark of the Covenant whose outstretched wings hid the God, who was thought to sit enthroned upon the Ark, from the eyes of the congregation (cf. II Sam. 6.2; Ex. 25.22; I Chron. 28.18; Ezek. 1 and 2; Pss. 81.7; 105.39; Num. 7.89). God intervenes in the earthly battle with thunder and lightnings, which he sends out like arrows, and strikes terror into the hearts of the enemies and puts them to flight (cf. Judg. 5.20). That the psalm is also closely bound up with the tradition of the *Heilsgeschichte* at this point is suggested by the fact that in this account the same phrase is used as in the story of the intervention of Yahweh in the battle against the Egyptians at the Red Sea (cf. Ex. 14.24); furthermore, before the psalm deals with the deliverance of the king, it is said in v. 15 that the channels of the sea became visible because of the rebuke of the Lord and because of the blast of the breath of his wrath, though that feature does not play any part in the continuation of the story. The allusion to Israel's deliverance at the Red Sea is designed to associate the deliverance of the king with that saving act of God which laid the foundations on which the Yahweh community was built; it is also meant to bear witness thereby to the truth that the same miraculous divine saving grace, to which the people of God owe their existence, is also at work in the deliverance of the king and is glorified in the cultic act.

The deliverance (vv. 16–19)

[16–19] The association, based on the *Heilsgeschichte*, which has just been explained, imparts also to the rescue of the king the character of an event which has a part to play in the sacred ritual of the cult. It is not the fact that it is the king who is rescued but that it is *God* who saves him which accounts for the far-reaching cosmic setting and the great pathos of the psalmist's account. It also explains why less prominence is given to the story of the king's rescue, explaining in concrete details how he was saved, than to the fact, a fact which is expressed in several ways, that he owes his life to the love of God and to his miraculous power. The mighty God comes to the aid of the king (cf. v. 35) whose cry for help had struggled to reach God on high from the depths of human helplessness. God reaches down from on high and draws him out of the great waters (v. 4). The expression *māšā*, which is used to describe this divine action (cf. the passage in Ex. 2.10 to which Luther long ago referred), suggests that here, too, a reference is intended to the ancient tradition of the *Heilsgeschichte*.

The righteousness of the king (vv. 20–24)

[20–24] The following section is likewise to be accounted for by
the cult of the Covenant Festival. At first sight, it is true, it gives the
impression that its purpose is to justify the deliverance of the king by
means of a 'protestation of innocence' with the result that at the
centre of such an argumentation would be the righteousness of the
worshipper, of which he seems to boast, and not the grace of God
at all. This impression, together with the spirit and language of the
so-called 'Deuteronomic' legalism which some commentators have
imagined they could trace in this section and partly, too, in the
following section, has led to doubts about the originality of these
portions. However, these doubts may not be justified after all. For
though it is a postulate of the method of literary criticism that faithfulness to the covenant ordinances and the expression of this attitude
in the terms *ḥōq* and *mišpāṭ* are to be considered as features exclusively
peculiar to the Deuteronomic language, that postulate does not do
justice to the historical facts. Ordinances and statutes given by God
belong to the constituent elements of the Covenant of Yahweh right
from its beginning and were firmly established in its cultic tradition
long before the time of Deuteronomy (cf., e.g., Josh. 24.25). The
statements made in vv. 19 ff. are related to that moral and ritual
aspect of the ordinances of the Covenant. It is understandable that
the king attaches great importance to the fact that the correctness
and legality of his attitude to the covenant ordinances cannot be
questioned, since his whole existence depends[1] on the certainty of his
bond with God, which is based on the tradition of the Covenant, and
seeing that what has happened to him once more confirms that he
stands in this mutual covenantal relationship with God. It is therefore not a question of a protestation of innocence which, prompted
by pharisaic self-righteousness, gives an account to God of the king's
own deserts, but of an affirmation of faith in the covenantal faithfulness of God, which may be experienced by those who in obedience to
God's ordinances keep their faith in him. That it is at all possible to

---

[1] The fact that the king is subject to the morality of the Covenant (cf. the
exegesis of Psalms 89 and 132), together with the reference to the Sinai theophany
(vv. 7–15), proves that the Davidic Covenant by no means pushed into the background the tradition of the Sinai Covenant and replaced it (this point in opposition
to Rost, *TLZ* 72, 1947, pp. 130 ff.; Kraus, *Gottesdienst in Israel*, pp. 88 ff.). Kraus
wants to attribute the first incorporation of the Sinai tradition in the Davidic cult
of the State to the reform of Josiah (cf. Mendenhall, 'Covenant forms in Israelite
tradition', *The Biblical Archaeologist* 17, 1954, pp. 72 ff.).

do so is not the merit of man but a gift of the grace of God who has instituted the Covenant and its ordinances for the benefit of his people. And thus, too, the 'righteousness' of the king is ultimately the gift of the divine saving grace, though, of course, within the framework (and consequently the limits) of the ancient Covenant. Just as the special 'power' of the king is held to be an ingredient of the 'grace of kingship' granted to the king by God, on which the king's real authority ultimately depends, so is his righteousness; and that truth is evidently meant to be confirmed in the cult and, since the 'grace of kingship' had been exposed to danger, to be sanctioned afresh.

Profession (vv. 25–30)

[25–27] The king once more throws into relief the universal truth of the hidden working of the covenantal faithfulness of God; and he does so by means of a hymnic profession in which the king's trust in God and at the same time the king's authority are made manifest in the presence of the community of God-fearing people. And that universal truth, which the king was privileged to experience in what had happened to him personally, is that man's behaviour determines God's action. This does not mean that God's nature and his sentiments are subject to changes and depend on man's attitude at any given time. God remains faithful to his nature, but that faithfulness operates differently according to the way in which man responds to it. The godly man can be assured of God's love for him only by loving God (this meaning underlies the root of the term used in the original language for the word 'godly'; notice the bearing on vv. 1 and 50). Again, the godly can be assured of the perfection of the faithfulness of God only by being absolutely faithful to him, and only he who is pure is admitted to the presence of God whose nature is pure. The promises of God are fulfilled in the lives of those who belong to the 'godly ones'. On the other hand, to those who are perverted, who infringe the ordinances of the Covenant, God, too, appears to be 'perverse'; they see him in this light just because, in opposition to those who are disobedient, he carries his order into effect and executes his judgment. Again, they see him in this light precisely because he leaves the sinner to the perversity of his character (cf. Isa. 31.3; Job 5.13; Rom. 1.18 ff.). What is said in vv. 25 and 26 with regard to the individual is applied in v. 27 to the people of God as a whole. The people who humbly submit to the will of God experience that God is their helper. On the other hand, the people who arrogantly exalt themselves will be 'brought low' by him. The king finds that truth confirmed in what had happened to him personally. [28–30] His heart overflows with gratitude and confidence, and he is able to confess that God 'doth light his lamp', that is, that God bestows upon him new vitality so that the darkness of his affliction gives way to a renewed joy in life and a new zest for life which, allied to God, urges him on to further deeds. God has kept faith with him and has fulfilled his promises. He had been a shield to him which protected him when he took refuge in God. All those things he is now able to confess with gratitude in his heart as something which has come true both in his own life and in the life of the whole community of the godly.

Second Part: The 'Grace of Kingship' (vv. 31–50)

The preparation (vv. 31–36)

[31] The second part of the psalm starts with a hymnic profession of the cult community of Yahweh ('our God') which takes the form of a rhetorical question. In it Yahweh is compared with the other gods who are worshipped and his superiority is glorified. The cult community's testimony constitutes the bridge between the first and second parts of the psalm, being simultaneously a response to the king's profession (vv. 2 f.) and the theme developed in the second part of the psalm. Its conception and form were later adopted by Deutero-Isaiah, but they are already used (even outside the Old Testament) in ancient cultic songs (cf. Ex. 15.11; Deut. 33.26 (29); I Sam. 2.2; cf. also the name 'Micah' = 'Who is like Yahweh?'; see Intr. 53 f.). Again, the conception and form of the cult community's testimony find their explanation, as far as the Old Testament is concerned, in the religious ideology of the Covenant of Yahweh. This consideration is sufficient to put an end to the doubts which have been raised as to whether v. 31 forms part of the original text. It is in this ideology that the exclusive obligation of faithfulness to Yahweh, which stigmatizes every other cult as 'apostasy', has its deepest religious justification. [32–36] The theme expressed in the conception of that liturgical Introit is now taken up by the king, who, using the participial style of the hymn (this changes in v. 35 to the more personal style of prayer), develops it further by describing how he had been prepared for his exalted position as a recipient of the

'grace of kingship'. The diction now runs more smoothly and is broadened; it is no longer harassed by the anxious concern for mere survival. As far as details are concerned, the account of the king's preparation uses ideas and conceptions which are borrowed from the contemporary court-style and which, at least in part, have also become familiar through ancient oriental documents and pictures: God is the teacher and protector of the royal hero; he bestows upon him irresistible strength and swiftness, so that he strides over the mountain peaks with long, confident steps like a god (cf. Deut. 33.29; Amos 4.13; Micah 1.3); God trains the king in the proper use of weapons; he gives him the protection of the divine shield and, whenever his strength wanes, supports him by the divine might of 'his right hand'. However, the 'grace of kingship' and its victorious power do not give him cause to glory in the knowledge of his human might. By making God the subject of all these verses, the literary form already testifies to the fact that it is *God*'s blessings which are bestowed upon his protégé. And the final sentence of v. 35, stating that the king owes his rise to greatness to the 'condescension' of God, a statement which is unique even in the language of the Old Testament, clearly removes the danger that the king might transgress the bounds of humility and in arrogant presumption dispute God's claim to that glory which of right is his alone.

The victory (vv. 37–42)

[37–42] The verses that follow are similarly to be understood in the light of the knowledge that any boasting can be only a boasting of God. In these verses the king speaks of the decisive battles which ended in his victory. Though he himself is now seen to act side by side with God, he yet emphasizes that it is God who led him to the height of his power (notice how in the statements made by the king about himself the style of prayer alternates with the narrative form). For in the account given by the king, besides the pride of the warrior crowned with the victor's wreath, we cannot miss the tone of awe and wonder as he once more looks humbly back upon the successes which God has lavished upon him. It follows from vv. 41 and 43 that what is here in question is not simply *one* victorious battle, as is frequently assumed, but a number of combats with external and internal adversaries. Consequently the view that the psalm is a song celebrating a particular victory is too narrow.

The dominion over other nations (vv. 43–45)

[**43–45**] The worshipper contemplates with, if possible, even greater wonder the fruits of his battles which God has laid in his lap. Surmounting dangerous conflicts amidst his own people (v. 43; cf. the comments on Ps. 132.5) he has risen to the high position of the 'head of the nations'. At the mere rumour of his victories foreign nations, whom he had not known so far, had made haste to call on him, trembling with fear, to demonstrate their subservience to his sovereign authority through the sending of flattering envoys and the paying of tribute.

Praise and thanksgiving (vv. 46–48)

[**46–48**] In the festive hour of the celebration of the divine service the king once more recapitulates in his prayer and recalls before the whole community of his people the dramatic rise of his life from the depths of utter distress to the supreme height of his dominion over the nations. Surveying that course of events, he realizes with joy and gratitude in his heart that he is assured of the blessing of God, of the 'grace of kingship'. And even more than this assurance is granted him: he stands in that moment before the living[1] God himself, who is the bearer of that saving power; 'the God of his salvation' 'rises' before him in all his majesty. That encounter with God, which not only the king but with him the whole cult community experiences in the sanctuary as a living reality, is the actual theme of the cultic ceremony and of the psalm which is sung there. We cannot picture to ourselves realistically enough the representation of God and of his salvation which is summed up in the concluding hymn. [**49–50**] At the psalm's conclusion the affirmation of faith in the God who is present, together with the vow to sing praises to his name (see Intr. 30 ff., 41 f., 58 f.) among the nations (v. 49), are once more irradiated by the hymn in v. 50; in this God's love for his anointed and the certitude of the 'grace of kingship' are no longer merely felt to be a living present reality, but are experienced as part of God's great *Heilsgeschichte* which points beyond future generations to eternity.

---

[1] In the formula 'Yahweh lives' the contrast is expressed with the corresponding phrase in the cults of the dying and rising vegetation gods, e.g. as that phrase is handed down in the Ugaritic *'Al'iyan Ba'al*; cf. Vriezen, *An Outline of Old Testament Theology*, ET, 1958, p. 171.

19. 1–6. THE HEAVENS PROCLAIM THE GLORY OF GOD

To the Conductor. A Psalm. Of David

1 The heavens are telling the glory of God;
   and the firmament proclaims his handiwork.
2 Day to day pours forth speech,
   and night to night whispers knowledge.
3 There is no language nor are there words
   in which their voice is not heard.
4 Their law is proclaimed throughout all the world,
   and their words go to the end of the earth.[1]
   He has set a tent in the sea[2] for the sun
5 which comes forth like a bridegroom leaving his chamber,
   and like a strong man runs its course with joy.
6 Its rising is from the end of heavens,
   and its circuit to[2] the end of them;
   and there is nothing hid from its heat.

[1] * In RSV vv. 3 and 4 ab are as follows:
   (3) There is no speech, nor are there words;
       their voice is not heard;
   (4) yet their voice goes out through all the earth,
       and their words to the end of the world.
[2] See BH.

Psalm 19 consists of two independent songs which in subject-matter, mood, language and metre differ from each other so much that they cannot be composed by the same author. Verses 1–6 are a Nature psalm arising from a poet's profound vision and expressed in forceful language. Verses 7–14 comprise a psalm whose theme is the Law and whose thoughts and language are characterized by a homely simplicity. Why these dissimilar poems were united in one single psalm cannot any longer be established with any degree of certainty (see, however, the comments on vv. 7 ff.).

The author of the hymn in praise of Nature (vv. 1–6) was inspired by an attitude of mind similar to the one which inspired the author of Psalm 8, to which our present song is a kind of supplement. Both these poets contemplate with awe the majesty of God revealed in creation, and the composition of their songs is the fruit of the rapture which was aroused in them by their moving experience of God in Nature. The reflective mind of the author of Psalm 8 dwells more on the reationship between Creator and creature, whereas the theme of Ps. 19.1–6 is the peculiar character of the revelation of God in

Nature.[1] The author of the latter is undoubtedly the greater artist. His insight, the result of great concentration, combines with his powerful metaphorical language to raise him to the status of a great poet who has stimulated the creative work of such eminent men as Goethe, Haydn, and Beethoven.

[1] In view of the poet's capacity to express in lyrical language the sentiments which the beauty of Nature has evoked in him it is the more remarkable that he tunes his contemplation of Nature right from the outset to a religious keynote and thereby emphasizes the main idea which he wants to be regarded as the key to the true understanding of the two parts of his hymn—the song in praise of creation (vv. 1–4b) and the hymn in praise of the sun (vv. 4c–6). The whole of Nature is in the service of a Supreme Being; its duty is to sing the praise of God and to be the vehicle of his revelation. The poet's vision vivifies the inanimate things in Nature; to him heaven, the firmament, day and night, are witnesses who have the gift of speech; by their words they testify to the divine majesty and to the grandeur of the work of creation. A master is known by his work.

[2] The mention of day and night (v. 2) makes it impossible to regard these personifications as reminiscences of the former deification of the heaven and the stars or to deduce from them the notion of the harmony of the spheres—which is not to be found in the Old Testament. Our poet holds a view on these matters which is entirely his own. The grandeur of Nature reveals to him, too, as it did to the poet of Psalm 8, the majesty of its Creator, but he realizes that the created world is at the same time the vehicle of the revelation of the divine wisdom and order ('his handiwork'), which it passes on from day to day in an unbroken tradition like a secret knowledge (v. 2). Nature itself is the record of creation, an essential part of the self-revelation of God to the whole world, and in that record God has entered by means of powerful signs the story of the genesis of the world and of its laws. Each day is for those who know how to read therein a new leaf in that record of the history of God's creation which like a living fountain flows for ever. [3–4b] The language which God speaks through Nature is not tied to the linguistic frontiers of men which hinder men from making themselves understood by each other. Mankind does not know of any language in which that silent voice of God's revelation in Nature would not make

---

[1] Jirku, 'Die Sprache der Gottheit in der Natur', *TLZ* 76, 1951, p. 631, refers to a remarkable parallel in the Ugaritic texts.

itself heard and understood. The knowledge of the world's divine ordering (literally, plumb-line or canon) penetrates into every country, because the laws of Nature can be inferred everywhere and directly from the orbits of the celestial bodies and from the change of day and night. The language of Nature is understood in every part of the world ('to the end of the earth'). The heavens are the book from which the whole world can derive its knowledge of God! This is by no means simply an idea born of a momentary religious enthu-siasm which has been roused by the contemplation of Nature. It is a most profound recognition of the nature of God and a quite compre-hensive programme for the way in which the study of Nature should be pursued at all times. Anyone who approaches Nature with awe does not regard it as an accumulation of inanimate, mute matter; he also does not regard its physical and chemical laws as lifeless formu-lae, but as the characters of a living language which everyone can understand, a language which is spoken by God and is the way he has made silent Nature bear witness to his might and wisdom. This glimpse into the interior of God's workshop can be accomplished only if understanding of real things from artistic and scientific points of view combines with religious reverence to achieve that God-given, consistent, harmonious vision of Nature which constitutes the pecu-liar greatness of our psalm.

[4c] The hymn in praise of the sun which follows is similarly to be understood in this perspective. The fundamental theme of v. 1 dominates the second part of the psalm, too. In what the poet has to say about the sun, he forcefully joins his artistic impressions to a searching knowledge of his age and welds them into a unity under the religious aspect of the creative wisdom of God. The religious thought is once more prominent: it is *God* who has set a tent for the sun in the sea. In this way the author, deliberately alluding to the ancient mythical idea of the abode which the Sun-god has built for himself, discards the pagan character of that idea without destroying its poetic beauty. [5] In like manner the comparison of the sun with the bridegroom, who comes forth from his chamber in the radiant splendour of his youthful strength and beauty, is based on the wide-spread mythological idea that the Sun-god rests during the night in the sea, lying in the arms of his beloved; and the image of the champion who delights in contests probably has its roots in mytho-logy, too. The poet faces these mythological themes with remarkable freedom and ease. His faith in the one and only Creator of the

universe guards him against any kind of pagan superstition; thus the myth is useful to him only as a poetic allegory ('like' a bridegroom). But in the same way that faith also liberates him from any sort of fearful timidity; the freedom of his faith is such that he is capable of doing justice to the myth's profound meaning. Just because he himself is a poet, he hears the voice of the poetic imagination at work in the myth; he has an ear for man's elemental response, so similar to his own, to the impressive language of Nature, a language which is understood by every sensitive human being including the Gentiles. **[6]** What has been visualized in v. 5 with artistic feeling and clothed in the colourful language of the poet, is comprehended in v. 6 by the searching mind of the thinker and expressed in the simple and lucid language peculiar to him. The observation of the circuit of the sun and the establishment of the fact that its light thus reaches every part of the earth is not the momentary product of an artistic impression, but the result of a process of scientific observation extended over a longer period. This observation provides the basis of that well-known 'cyclic way of thinking' which attempted to mould oriental science and cosmology on the results of observation of the sky—helped by the idea of the eternal recurrence of the same things. The psalmist faces this pagan science with the same freedom of thought and the same discernment which he applied in his use of the myth. After all, this science is man's attempt to decipher the mysterious writing, exhibited by Nature, which God's finger has engraved there for all to read, that his power and his wisdom may be proclaimed. The comprehensiveness of the poet's belief in God thus enables him to grasp the true meaning and significance of those phenomena to which anxious and prejudiced minds turn a blind eye. This harmonious, uniform vision, achieved by a comprehension of Nature based on faith, poetic insight and deep thought, imparts to the psalm a significance which reaches far beyond the scope of the Old Testament.

19. 7–14. GODLINESS BASED ON THE LAW

7 The law of the Lord is perfect, refreshing the soul;
the testimony of the Lord is trustworthy, making wise the fool;
8 the precepts of the Lord are upright, rejoicing the heart;
the commandment of the Lord is pure, enlightening the eyes;
9 the fear[1] of the Lord is pure, enduring for ever;
the judgments of the Lord are faithful, and righteous altogether;[2]

10 they are more precious than gold, even much fine gold;
    sweeter also than honey and drippings of the honeycomb.
11 Thy servant also is warned by them;
    he who keeps them, will be richly rewarded.
12 But who can discern his errors?
    Forgive me my hidden sins!
    Protect thy servant also from evildoers,[3]
    let them not have dominion over me!
13 Then I shall be perfect
    and innocent of grave transgression.[4]
14 Let the words of my mouth be acceptable to thee,
    and let the meditation of my heart come before thee,
    O Lord, my rock and my redeemer![5]

[1] Following the example of Ps. 119.38, this reading has been suggested: *'imrāt* (= word; see BH); this term would indeed fit more easily into the parallelism of v. 9, but to me its acceptance does not seem necessary.

[2] * RSV of v. 9b reads, 'the ordinances of the Lord are true, and righteous altogether'.

[3] * V. 13a in RSV: 'Keep back thy servant also from presumptuous sins.'

[4] * In RSV the first two lines of v. 12 form v. 12 and the last two lines of v. 12 form the first part of v. 13.

[5] * V. 14a, b reads in RSV:
    Let the words of my mouth and the meditation of my heart
    be acceptable in thy sight.

Presumably the two parts of Psalm 19 had their origin in the cultic tradition and, being hymns in praise of the creation and of the law of God, were united in one psalm for use in public worship, the idea of the divine order constituting the spiritual bond which linked the two parts together (cf. the term 'law' in v. 4).

In form and content Ps. 19.7–14 bears analogy to Psalm 119 and this is often true even of its wording. But when we compare these two psalms, Ps. 19.7–14 proves to be the earlier model, since it is clearly divided into a hymn in praise of the law (vv. 7–10) and a personal prayer of supplication (vv. 11–14); there are other factors which lead to the same conclusion.

[7–10] Following the style of the hymn, the praise of the law proceeds in sentences which exhibit the same structure. In each of these sentences (vv. 7–8) first a characteristic peculiarity of the law is described and then a specific effect produced by the law, though it is not always possible to recognize a pertinent relationship between these two statements. In respect of the predominance of form over subject-matter—caused by a playful impulse rather than by the poet's creative power—the psalm is quite surpassed by Psalm 119.

The content of the psalm allows us a valuable insight into godliness based on the law, as this is represented in the Old Testament, and teaches us to pay attention to the positive values inherent in it. That law-based godliness is by no means confined only to the perfunctory fulfilment of a definite number of fixed precepts. The various terms used in the psalm to describe the law of Yahweh can hardly be interpreted as interchangeable designations of the law in the intertestamental period. For the poet the law is the point at which an encounter takes place with the living God who reveals himself in the law, a conception which has its roots already in the pre-exilic cult of the Covenant. The characteristic peculiarities attributed to the law are true also of the God who is behind the law and from whose authority the law derives its value in the first instance. Thus in praising the law the psalm praises the God who is revealed in that law. Being the law of God it is perfect, trustworthy, upright, pure, clean, and faithful. The 'law' comprises the testimony which God bears to himself, that is the manifestation, of his will in history (cf. the term 'testimony' in v. 7, and of the two tablets of the testimony as the foundation of the covenant which God made with Israel, Ex. 25.16, 21; 31.7 and frequently). But equally it also comprises the attitude which man adopts in response to the revelation of God (the 'fear of the Lord' in v. 9). In the law the will of God is manifested to educate and to save, and for that reason it is also the basis of a firm trust in the lovingkindness of God. Every sentence of the psalm resounds with this note of joyous confidence. The author holds that in the law is the mutual relationship between God and man, and his personal experience has taught him to value the law as the source of a rich life: it imbues the soul with new vitality and gives wisdom to those who err (v. 7); it delights the heart and enlightens the eyes (v. 8); it offers sure guidance for the duration of life (cf. the exegesis of Psalm 1); it comprises the most precious good known to the godly Israelite—righteousness (v. 9). No wonder, then, that the poet ranks the law higher than all earthly values and pleasures (v. 10). To him it is the ultimate value and the supreme good. There were good reasons also from the historical point of view for the high esteem in which the law is here held, an esteem which is based on personal experience. Thus, with its high standards of moral and religious precepts, it far surpasses the standard of the corresponding demands made by the world around Israel (cf. Lev. 19.18, 32 ff.; Deut. 6.4 f.; 4.7 f.); and the loftiness of the Jewish ethics of everyday life won

Judaism the respect of the world. And not only that—those ethics were adopted by early Christianity and by the teaching of the Gospels were imbued with an even more profound meaning.

[11-14] In its second part the psalm proceeds to a personal prayer and now employs a style which is both more vivid and more natural, though here, too, the diction makes use of familiar phrases. The poet's testimony that he is conscious of his being protected by the law and that he is privileged to experience its blessings (v. 11) makes one realize that a living personal experience underlies the preceding hymn in praise of the law, in spite of the traditional rigidity of its form. Even from the Christian point of view one can hardly take exception to the manner in which the idea of reward and retribution is presented here, an idea which the teaching of the New Testament has not abandoned either (Mark 9.41; Luke 6.23, 33 ff.; Rom. 2.5 ff.; II Cor. 5.10). This would be particularly true if the text should admit of the interpretation that the poet already finds his reward, a reward which is abundantly worthwhile (lit.: there is great reward in keeping them), in the inner freedom that ensues from his obedience to the law—in the joy of being saved from wrong-doing, moreover, and also in the inward happiness which is expressed in vv. 7-10. For with such an interpretation the risks involved in the idea of reward are avoided. These risks, which the piety of the psalmists was not able to avoid, were—that the relationship with God was held to be concerned with the settling of accounts and that in consequence a reward was claimed from God, that the recompense was sought in material gifts or that the hope of reward was made the reason for obeying the law. That the psalmist's real desire was to be spiritually rewarded and to enjoy the peace of a clear conscience is shown by the fact that he beseeches God to forgive him those sins of which he was not aware (v. 12) and to protect him from being seduced by evildoers (v. 13a, b); and this petition forces from his lips the ardent wish that he may stand blameless and innocent before his God (v. 13c). He is aware of his inadequacy as a human being, slipping back into his old ways through carelessness; he is aware of the human weakness which so easily yields to temptation, but he is also conscious of the divine grace which has the power to forgive him his sins and to preserve him from sinning. He therefore prays, 'Forgive me my hidden faults' and 'lead me not into temptation'. The worshipper is not moved by pride, but by the same humility which speaks when he prays, assured by faith that his prayer will be answered, and

confidently looks forward to the time when he will be free from sin. For he knows that in his case, too, the attainment of that goal ultimately depends on God's forgiving and preserving grace. Moreover, it is only in the light of this knowledge that the significance of the concluding invocation, 'O Lord, my rock and my redeemer', can be fully appreciated.

The psalm concludes with the petition that God may hear this prayer and that it may be acceptable to him (v. 14; see Intr. 64); the petition takes the form of a solemn 'dedicatory formula', such as was also in use outside the Old Testament (cf. Pss. 104.34; 119.108). The fact that at the beginning of v. 14 the formula used is that which is employed in the priestly law for the offering of the sacrifice (Lev. 1.3 f.) proves that the prayer is offered in place of the sacrifice (cf. Ps. 141.2). However, we would not do the psalmist justice if we were to attribute to this prayer only the value of a pious act, a perfunctory fulfilment of a religious duty. How profound the spirit is in which he prays we can only grasp if we take into account his addition, 'let the meditation of my heart come before thee'. Man behaves towards God in the right spirit only if he not only fulfils the will of God in word and deed but pours out his heart to God, withholding nothing, so that God is able to gain an insight into the true sentiments of his heart. That simple candour, full of childlike confidence, which is offered to God and does not hide from him the worshipper's concern about the weakness of these sentiments, is the keynote which rings throughout the psalm, the keynote which moves our hearts too.

Of course, for all that, we must not overlook the limits which are set to this type of godliness. The piety with which we are confronted in this psalm is like a river flowing quietly between sheltering banks. The point at issue here is not the God who says to a world full of suffering, 'My thoughts are not your thoughts' (cf. Ps. 103.10); the point at issue is not the dreadful demonic power of sin, which drags man down into the darkness of the night in spite of his yearning for the light of day, so that only God, in whose presence alone the great abyss of sin is made manifest, is able to redeem him from his sin by transforming his whole being by virtue of the abundance of the free gift of his grace. The prophets and the New Testament have shed light on this situation—man without guarantees before the reality of God—as also on the consequent uncertainties of law.

20. A PRAYER FOR THE KING

To the Conductor. A Psalm. Of David

1 The Lord answer you in the day of trouble!
   The name of the God of Jacob make you powerful![1]
2 May he send you help from the sanctuary,
   and give you support from Zion!
3 May he remember all your offerings,
   and regard with favour your burnt sacrifice! *Selah*
4 May he grant you your heart's desire,
   and fulfil all your plans!
5 We will shout for joy over your blessings,[2]
   and in the name of our God set up our banners!
   May the Lord fulfil all your petitions!
6 Now I know that the Lord has helped his anointed,
   has answered him from his holy heaven
   with the mighty saving acts of his right hand.[3]
7 The others trust in chariots and horses;
   but we remember the name of our God.[4]
8 They went down on their knees and fell;
   but we rose up and stood upright.[5]
9 O Lord, do help us, O King,
   who answers us in the day we call![6]

[1] * V. 1b reads in RSV: 'The name of the God of Jacob protect you.'
[2] * V. 5a in RSV: 'May we shout for joy over your victory.'
[3] * RSV renders v. 6:
    Now I know that the Lord will help his anointed;
    he will answer him from his holy heaven
    with mighty victories by his right hand.
[4] * V. 7 in RSV:
    Some boast of chariots, and some of horses;
    but we boast of the name of the Lord our God.
[5] * RSV renders v. 8:
    They will collapse and fall;
    but we shall rise and stand upright.
[6] * V. 9 in RSV:
    Give victory to the king, O Lord;
    answer us when we call.

Most commentators hold that the psalm is a liturgy in the form of prayer designed to be used in a service of intercession on the eve of war. That interpretation is possible but not convincing. The fact that reference is made to 'trouble' and 'help' (vv. 1 and 2) and that the psalmist directs his thoughts to the enemies (vv. 7 and 8) does not necessarily lead to such a conclusion if we take into account the historical and geographical situation of Israel—a country at almost any time the coveted object of the policy of expansion of neighbouring

states both great and small. The psalm is, after all, couched in too
general terms and is also too colourless, its sentiments are developed
on lines which are too composed and too measured, to make the
situation of a mobilization plausible, quite apart from the fact that all
attempts to ascertain the concrete historical circumstances in more
detail are bound to end in failure (such as, *inter alia*, the time of
Hezekiah and the Maccabaean wars). We are probably nearer to the
truth if we assume that the psalm is an essential part of the ritual of
the feast at which Yahweh is glorified as King (v. 9), a feast which
was celebrated at Jerusalem on the New Year's day in conjunction
with the accession of the king to the throne (v. 2; cf. Jer. 26.1;
27.1; 28.1). Presumably the psalm was appointed for regular use in
the festival cult. There is no question of David being the author, since
the king is addressed in the first part (vv. 1–5), whilst in the second
part (v. 6) he is spoken of in the third person; on the other hand, it
would not be entirely impossible to assume that the psalm originated
in the time of David if we may draw the conclusion from v. 7 that
at that time Israel did not yet use war-chariots in battle (cf. II Sam.
8.4; 15.1; I Kings 10.26). That would account for the fact that there
are certain points of affinity with Psalm 18, above all the petition for
the 'grace of kingship'.

First part (vv. 1–5)

[1–4] The liturgy of the psalm begins after the king's burnt sacrifice has been offered (v. 3). It opens with an intercession which the
whole cult community makes on behalf of its king. We may be
justified in thinking that this intercession was probably spoken by the
priest. The fellowship of prayer which existed between the ruler and
his people is the spiritual bond and the sustaining power which gives
the psalm its peculiar character. The theme of this intercession is
that God may regard with favour the offerings and the sacrifice of
the king (the literal translation 'may declare the sacrifice to be fat'
betrays the ritual language of the cultus) and that he may fulfil the
desires and plans of the ruler which he had uttered in prayer (cf.
v. 5) and cherished in his heart; again, that he may answer his
prayers in times of affliction and may 'exalt' him (= bestow upon
him the royal prerogatives and make him powerful; cf. Isa. 9.11) and
may 'support' him by sending him his help. The expectation is that
the 'grace of kingship' will be sent 'from the sanctuary' on Mount
Zion, the place where God usually appears (cf. Amos 1.2) and where

he is thought to be present at the cultic ceremony (cf. Psalm 18). In the course of this the 'name' of God was uttered in order to proclaim his nature and his power over the community of his people (Ex. 3.15; 33.19; 20.2; cf. Pass. 44.5–8; 89.24; see Intr. 30 f., 41 f.). In this connection the name becomes the direct embodiment of God's presence at the cultic ceremony, being mysteriously surrounded with the primaeval belief in the reality of the efficacious power of the holy word uttered at a sacred moment. **[5]** The intercession of the priest for the king is taken up in v. 5a by the whole congregation ('we') whose members confirm by a vow that they have taken part in that intercession in their heart. They vow that they will shout for joy over the 'grace of kingship' (perhaps by passionate cries of 'Blessed . . .' [cf. I Sam. 4.5 and the Hosanna in Matt. 21.9] or else during the recital of the saving acts of God in the cult when the royal feast was celebrated; it can be assumed that this was done in connection with the recital of Psalm 18). The setting up of the banners in the name of God perhaps signifies a cultic act whereby a standard or a similar symbol of the presence of Yahweh was solemnly set up and exhibited, perhaps on the analogy of the aetiological tradition of Ex. 17.15, 16 or Num. 21.8 (cf. II Kings 18.4).

Second part (vv. 6–9)

[6] The second part of the psalm is separated from the first part by a distinct caesura. A single voice, probably that of the officiating priest or cult prophet, who in the first place would be authorized to perform this act, solemnly proclaims that God has answered the prayer of his anointed and has granted him his blessings (this is the specific meaning of *hōšī'a*). The opening words of this proclamation, 'now I know', as well as the verbal forms, presuppose that in the meantime the decisive event has taken place which was the primary object of the petition in the first part of the psalm. Most expositors assume that the assurance that the prayer has been granted was obtained by means of an oracle, such as has been handed down, for instance, in respect of the Assyrian king Asshurbanipal or the Pharaoh Rameses II, or by means of some specific evidence provided by the sacrifice, or by means of the inspiration of a prophet officiating in the cult. On account of the closing remark in v. 6, 'with the mighty saving acts of his right hand', we shall, however, be nearer to the truth if we assume that the psalm has in mind here the cultic representation of the divine saving acts in the form of the liturgical recital

of the ancient traditions of the *Heilsgeschichte*, and that this recital
followed the cultic theophany as the latter is depicted in Ps. 18.6 ff.
It may be that the epiphany of God coming down from heaven,
which by means of the cultic recitation of the ancient tradition and in
connection with the performance of certain rites of a dramatic
character was celebrated as the climax of the Covenant Festival of
Yahweh, is described in the psalm in greater detail because it
belonged to the permanent constituent parts of the festival liturgy
and is here simply taken for granted. In this way, too, is explained
the alleged inconsistency (which some commentators have thought
they should point out) arising from the fact that here the sanctuary
on Mount Zion, the place where Yahweh appears and from which
he is asked to send help (v. 2), and his heavenly sanctuary, from
which he answers the prayer of the king (v. 6), are placed side by
side; hence there is no need to have recourse to tortuous theological
speculations (see Intr. 28 ff., 37 ff.). The priest therefore announces
what the whole cult community will see confirmed by the coming of
God into their midst: God has accepted the sacrifice; he has answered
the prayers and by the representation of the 'mighty savings acts of his
right hand' has made it clear that he will not withhold his blessings
from the king who prays in fellowship with his people. The mystery
of the presence of God in public worship and of his dispensation of
salvation welds the tradition of the past, the present experience, and
the expectation of the things to come into one single event which
carries with it the immediate assurance of all these experiences;
again, this mystery first enables us to grasp the peculiar sense in
which History and *Heilsgeschichte* are understood in the Old Testament, where we continually encounter it.

[7–8] In response to the priest's proclamation of the granting of
the king's prayer and of the 'grace of kingship' the members of the
congregation testify to the firmness of their faith and affirm their
covenantal faithfulness and their exclusive bond with their God; this
latter affirmation will likewise be best understood if it is considered
in the light of the cultic scene, as the congregation's response to the
theophany and to the assurance of salvation (cf. Josh. 24.16 ff.,
21 ff.). At this point the trust of the cult community in God reaches
its climax. The thought of the dreaded horses and chariots, on which
the adversaries' power was based, may sometimes have weighed
heavily on the people like a nightmare, since they were seriously
concerned for their future; nevertheless, they have now adopted a

quite different outlook. They know that 'with our strength nothing can be done';[1] the decision does not ultimately depend on human might, but lies in the hand of God, with whom the people know themselves to be associated in a covenantal relationship. Two different worlds are here deliberately confronted with each other, the one being the world in which man does all that he can possibly do, a world which may perhaps be terrifying but which is transient, as experience has continually proved (v. 7); the other being the world in which God proves himself to be a reality, a reality with which the cult community now sees itself to be confronted whilst it reverently remembers the saving deeds of God. God has continually enabled his people to rise; he gives them at this very moment the strength of faith which holds them, as it has always done so far, upright in the face of their affliction. We find the antithesis of trust in the power of men and of trust in the power of God already in the narrative of Gideon (Judg. 7.1 ff.) and in the story of Goliath (I Sam. 17.45), and as far as the biblical faith is concerned it plays a decisive part particularly in Isa. 31.1 ff. (cf. Isa. 7.9; 30.15; Ps. 33.16, 17). But that antithesis does not mean that human resources of power are to be renounced—a utopian act. On the contrary, it represents the clear orientation and the consistent attitude which man is able to accomplish by his faith in God, since God is the 'cardinal fact' which has to be taken into account in whatever may come to pass and on which the ultimate decision depends. The psalm's thus taking quite seriously the reality of God's existence arises from the living encounter with the God of the *Heilsgeschichte* which by means of the cultic ceremony is here brought about as an event that actually takes place. It is in this connection that we also come to understand why v. 8 presents a twofold aspect that strikes us as strange in that it speaks indeed of events which belong to the past and yet gives a hint that the God who can be felt to have been behind these past events appears as the God whose power decides the present and the future and is at work in both of them. Ex. 3.15 and Pss. 30.4; 97.12 suggest that the phrase 'we remember the name of our God' may actually be regarded as the act whereby that representation of the revelation of his name and of the *Heilsgeschichte* was denoted in the tradition of the cultus. This

---

[1] * These are the opening words of the second verse of the well-known German hymn by Martin Luther: 'Ein' feste Burg ist unser Gott' ('A safe stronghold our God is still'). Thomas Carlyle's translation of the German original: 'Mit unserer Macht ist nichts getan' ('With force of arms we nothing can') does not render the full meaning of the original.

interpretation would also explain the mention of the 'name of the God of Jacob' (v. 1) and the striking emphasis which the psalm lays upon the 'name of God' (see Intr. 30 f., 41 f.).

[9] At the conclusion of the psalm the cult community, recapitulating the psalm's fundamental idea, once more prays for the salvation of their king. They turn in prayer to God, the Heavenly King, who is the real object of the feast they celebrate. In the early translations of this passage the petition of the cult community was already interpreted as meaning—and, in consequence, was so translated—'O Lord, help the king' (the Vulgate reads: '*Domine, salvum fac regem*'), and that reading became the model of the English National Anthem 'God Save the King' and has been adopted by many modern expositors. They are, however, hardly justified in doing so, as this reading obliterates the original connection between the 'grace of kingship' and the feast of Yahweh the King and probably originated at a time when that feast was no longer celebrated. The closing sentence of v. 9 'who answers us in the day we call' once more refers to the cultic experience described in v. 6. The cult community derives from that experience the assurance that its prayers will be answered—and that not only during the present celebration of the feast but also on all future occasions on which it will intercede for its king.

21. THE CORONATION OF THE KING

To the Conductor. A Psalm. Of David

1 In thy might the king rejoices, O Lord;
  and in thy blessings[1] how greatly he exults!
2 Thou hast given him his heart's desire,
  and hast not withheld the request of his lips. *Selah*
3 For thou hast[2] met him with goodly blessings;
  thou hast[2] set a crown of fine gold upon his head.
4 He asked life of thee; thou gavest it to him,
  length of days for ever and ever.
5 His glory is great through thy blessings;[3]
  sovereignty and power thou dost bestow upon him.
6 For thou dost make him a blessing[4] for ever;
  thou dost make him glad with the joy of thy presence.
7 For the king trusts in the Lord;
  and through the grace of the Most High[5] he will not waver.—
8 Your hand will find out all your enemies;
  your right hand will shatter those who hate you.
9 You will make them as a blazing oven when you appear ' '[6],
  you will consume them in your wrath[6] like fire.[7]

10 You will destroy their offspring from the earth,
   and their children from among the sons of men.
11 If they plan evil against you,
   if they devised mischief, they will not succeed.
12 For you will put them to flight;
   you will aim at their faces with your bows.
13 Arise, O Lord, in thy strength!
   We will sing and play thy mighty acts.[8]

[1] * RSV reads in v. 1b 'help' instead of 'blessings'.
[2] * In v. 3 RSV uses the present tense.
[3] * RSV reads in v. 5a 'help' instead of 'blessings'.
[4] * RSV has in v. 6a 'most blessed' instead of 'a blessing'.
[5] See the comments on Ps. 7.17.
[6] See BH.
[7] Read *kā'ēš*. (Tr. N.: V. 9b consists of two lines in RSV and reads:
   The Lord will swallow them up in his wrath;
   and fire will consume them.)
[8] * V. 13b reads in RSV: 'We will sing and praise thy power.'

The psalm bears analogy to Psalm 20 in so far as it presupposes a similar situation. Assuming that Psalm 21 is a prayer for the king on the eve of his going to war (a view which we do not feel able to share), many expositors even go so far as to regard Psalm 21 as a supplement to Psalm 20 and believe that it can be interpreted as a thanksgiving appointed to be sung in a divine service in which a victory was celebrated after the return of the king from his victorious battle. But apart from the fact that the psalm does not contain any real thanksgiving, it entirely lacks any concrete references to the prior achievement of a victory. The defeat of the enemies is mentioned only in the second part of the psalm (vv. 8 ff.) and even there it is spoken of not as an event of the past but as something which is expected to take place only in the future. In the case of the celebration of a victory one would expect the sequence to be rather the reverse. The association of the psalm with a campaign successfully concluded rests on a too narrow interpretation of the term $y^e\check{s}\bar{u}^c\bar{a}$ (= help or blessings) as this is used in vv. 1 and 5, taking it to mean 'assistance rendered in war'. As in Ps. 20.5 (Ps. 20.6, 9: $y^e\check{s}\bar{u}^c\bar{a}$ and $h\bar{o}\check{s}\bar{i}^c\bar{a}$) the term designates a set of circumstances the scope of which is much wider, and which can best be rendered by the term 'blessings' (*Heil*). It is only in the light of that 'grace of kingship' extolled in the psalm that other terms such as 'might', 'glory', 'life', 'majesty', 'sovereignty', etc., become intelligible, all of which are part of the 'grace of kingship' and represent the actual theme of the psalm. Since as in Psalm 20 these several divine favours, which are the 'grace of kingship', are referred to only

in a quite general and indefinite way, it is neither possible nor
advisable to look for a specific historical situation or for the person
of a particular king in the history of Israel for which the psalm can be
said to have been intended. More probable is the view that the psalm
is a fragment of the ritual of the coronation of the king, belonging to
the cultic tradition of the royal feast (cf. Hos. 7.5), and was not
composed for one single occasion only. Moreover, the mention of the
king's coronation in v. 3 supports this view. The psalm shares with
Psalm 20 the characteristics of part of an order of service from the
cult; the date of the psalm's composition, too, may have to be fixed
accordingly.

The cultic scene which forms the framework of the psalm can
perhaps be imagined as follows: the sacral act of the coronation of the
king has taken place in the sanctuary before the assembled community of the people (v. 3); a prayer of supplication offered by the
king (v. 2), perhaps also the intercession of the congregation (Ps.
20.1–5) and the solemn climax of the feast of Yahweh, the theophany
(cf. the comments on Ps. 20.1–4), have preceded the moment marked
by the beginning of the psalm. The king, surrounded by the members
of the royal household, dressed for the feast and adorned with the
golden crown, now stands 'in the presence of God' (v. 6) in the full
splendour of his royal dignity. In a prayer to God, who is thought to
be present (vv. 1–6), the priest gives expression to this spectacle, and
the congregation sets its seal to that prayer by making an affirmation
of faith (v. 7). The second part of the psalm (vv. 8–12) envisages the
subjugation of all the enemies and is a prayer of confidence which
again was probably spoken by the priest (other expositors interpret
these verses as a promise of future blessings made to the king; see
below). It likewise closes with a response of the congregation (v. 13),
including a supplication and a vow.

The first part of the psalm serves as the *cultic 'representation'* of the
'blessings' that have been granted the king by the act of his coronation. Its form has to that extent a certain resemblance with the
hymn in which the congregation 'represented' to itself the saving acts
of its God. The things which are here described and portrayed are to
be thought of as having been accomplished by the ritual act of the
coronation, and the prayer is intended not only to make clear but to
sanction their 'reality'. The *acts* performed in the cult and their
subsequent verbal *representation* by means of the words spoken by the
priest belong together as the two halves of a standard sacred action

accomplished in the ritual of the cult. It is not without significance
that this verbal representation takes the form of a prayer. For in
this way a considerable obstacle is right from the outset put in the
way of any attempt to go astray by indulging in boasting, as human
nature is prone to do, and by adopting an attitude of flattering subservience to the person of the king, which after all might be the
obvious thing to do. In that the verbal representation takes the form
of a prayer, the king himself and the congregation are made aware of
the fact that all the splendour of the royal pomp here displayed is
only a reflection of the power and glory of God—it is the gift of his
lovingkindness. [1] The whole first part of the psalm is dominated by
that conception. It is God who has granted the king 'might' and
'blessings'; it is he who is the real source of the joy which is expressed
in the feast in shouts of joy and now, as it were, is given back to him.
[2] God has not only answered the king's prayers (cf. Ps. 20.4, 5) but
has even fulfilled the desires of his heart. [3] The encounter with the
divine occurs at that solemn moment when the king stands face to
face with God, who has appeared and is present in his sanctuary (cf.
Ps. 18.7 ff.). It is outwardly manifested by the coronation, and
according to the symbolism of that divine-human encounter, which is
pregnant with meaning, it is at the same time the point at which the
'divine blessing' and 'the good fortune of the king' are granted, on
which the power and the authority of kingship rest; for everything
depends on God's blessing. The imperfect tenses used here indicate
that this encounter still continues to exert its influence. [4–5] After
these general statements vv. 4–6 set forth in detail all that is included
in the 'grace of kingship' and mention, first of all, the favour which
the king has asked of God, namely *life* (cf. I Kings 3.11, 14; Ps.
61.6). In our opinion it would hardly be correct to interpret the
phrase 'length of days for ever and ever' as implying the idea of
immortality, which is unknown to the Old Testament; nor must the
phrase be used, as late Judaism interpreted it, in a Messianic sense;
nor must we, as Calvin and others did, regard it in accordance with
II Sam. 7.13 ff. and Ps. 72.17 as referring to the everlasting reign of
the Davidic dynasty. It belongs to the ancient oriental court-style
and is also to be found in the Old Testament as part and parcel of the
forms of salutation employed in the court etiquette (I Kings 1.31;
Neh. 2.3; Dan. 2.4). At the root of this phrase is the religious idea
that the life of the king by virtue of his anointing possesses a super-
personal quality which makes it sacrosanct because it is ultimately a

life lived in utter dependence on God. In ancient Israel the idea of
the inviolable sanctity of the king's life had a practical significance,
the implications of which are evident from the fact that David was
restrained by the regard and the awe in which he held the king from
putting forth his hand against the Lord's anointed (I Sam. 24.11;
26.23), and further that he ordered the death of the messenger who
delivered to him the message of Saul's death because he had not
been afraid 'to put forth his hand to destroy the Lord's anointed'
(II Sam. 1.14, 16). Further manifestations of the king's 'grace of
kingship' are the 'glory' that is, the royal dignity and majesty, and
his 'sovereignty' and 'power'; all are attributes which in the first
place are applied to God in the Old Testament and thereby make
evident that it is God who enables the king by his free gift to participate in his own majesty, sovereignty, and power. These terms circum-
scribe the special position which the king occupies among the people
of the Old Testament as the viceregent of God, a position according
to which the special prerogatives not only include the external
splendour of the power and pomp displayed by the court for the
purpose of representation, but are extended so far that they even
embrace the hidden religious motives on which the king's power to
command, his dignity, and his authority to order the material and
spiritual life of the nation are ultimately based. **[6]** He is not only
the bearer of the divine blessing, but like the patriarch to whom the
fundamental promise of blessing was made (Gen. 12.2) he also
dispenses that blessing. Health and prosperity, happiness in everyday
life, including even the fertility of the fields and flocks (cf. Ps. 72.16),
successful wars and preservation in war-time, increase and expansion
of property and of political power—all these things were regarded
since ancient times as blessings resulting from the 'grace of kingship'
and woe to the king under whose reign afflictions and failures were
imagined to be an indication of the fact that God's blessings had
been withdrawn from him! Hence it is more than understandable
that the prayer, reverting to the beginning, once more emphasizes
the joy which in this festive hour unites the king with his people in
the blessed awareness of the presence of God ('with the joy of thy
presence') and in the knowledge of the assurance of his saving
will!

[7] The fact that in v. 7 the prayer-form is abandoned and that
God and the king are spoken of in the third person suggests that now
it is no longer the priest who speaks but the congregation. Uttered

by the congregation the words would have to be understood as an acclamation of some sort, whereby the people of the Covenant would give their assent to the coronation of their king (cf. I Sam. 10.24; 11.14, 15). The congregation confirms on its part the 'grace of kingship' by pointing out the exemplary religious attitude of its sovereign, affirming that he has put his trust in Yahweh and so may be assured of his grace, and that his position will remain unshakable. It is therefore not at all a question of special human merits for which the king is to be rewarded. On the contrary, the fact that the moral and religious conduct of the king is exemplary and actually marks him out as a model character (cf. Pss. 18.20 ff.; 101) forms a part of the 'grace of kingship' and is similarly a gift of the divine grace.

[8–12] The subject-matter of the second part of the psalm likewise belongs to the traditional stock of the royal feast (cf. Ps. 20.6 ff.) in view of the general character of its terms, which corresponds to that of the first part. It raises the question of the foreign policy of Israel which always weighed heavily on the minds of the people and speaks of a victory over 'all the enemies'. From this point of view 'victory' and 'blessings' are terms which have an almost identical meaning (cf. I Sam. 11.13), so that this portion of the psalm, too, fits without any difficulty into the fundamental idea of the granting of blessings to the king at his coronation. It cannot be stated for certain to whom vv. 8–12 are addressed. They are usually interpreted as a promise made to the king. However, the manner in which the victor is spoken of is more suited to the ancient idea of Yahweh as the God of war. If these words were meant to refer to the king, they would have to be regarded as a boundless exaggeration even if we took into account the hyperbolical character of court-style. Since the form of prayer has been chosen already in the first part of the psalm to represent the 'grace of kingship', it is more natural to assume that here, too, the same attitude of mind is maintained, and that the same appropriate form (see above) is observed, quite apart from the fact that v. 13 seems to sum up the prayer which precedes it under the aspect of the 'mighty acts' of Yahweh. It seems probable that the early gloss in v. 9, which explicitly names Yahweh as the one who destroys the enemies, has already interpreted the prayer in the same sense. After the acclamation of the king by the community of the people the priest once more begins to speak. He offers a prayer of confidence in order to remove any anxiety that might still linger on in the face of the serious situation in which the nation finds itself, being threatened by enemies, and therefore might cast a gloom on the 'grace of kingship' and thus spoil the people's festive joy. The presence of God vouches for the assurance that he will find out all the covenant community's enemies, who, after all, are also his 'enemies' and 'those who hate him' (cf. the relation to the ancient tradition associated with the Ark in Num. 10.35), and will destroy them. This idea of the extermination of the enemies is likewise a constituent part of the ancient tradition of the Covenant and plays an important part especially in the tradition of the conquest of the land; in promise and demand it serves there the same purpose for which it is used here in the cultic prayer, as proving the exclusive power and sovereignty of the God of the Covenant. When Yahweh 'appears' in his awful majesty as the mighty warrior (cf. Ex. 15.3) who knows how to strike a mortal blow at the adversaries, using his bow and his arrows with a strong hand so that nobody can resist him (see Hab. 3.9), then the enemies are consumed by the passion of his 'wrath' as in a 'blazing oven' (cf. Gen. 15.17; and also Mal. 3.2; 4.1, picturing the Day of Judgment). In all these highly poetical, archaic illustrations and ideas are implied allusions to the traditions of the theophany which are handed down in the cultus (cf. Pss. 18.14, 15; 97.3, 4) and to which the psalm is most closely related. These allusions here serve to demonstrate the immense power of God, who has appeared to employ that power in the interest of the ultimate realization of his blessings for the benefit of the king and his people. In these circumstances all the plans of the enemies and all their cleverly devised plots (cf. Ps. 2.3) are from the outset bound to end in failure and, in consequence, all the clouds are dispelled which threatened to darken the political horizon on the day of the king.

At the end of the psalm the thoughts of the cult community—as in Psalm 2—are now entirely focused on God. Under the spell of his miraculous power the members of the cult community now realize that they are made partakers of the great divine saving event which they celebrate and at the same time anticipate with eager expectation. Giving themselves unreservedly up to the living encounter with God they themselves take, as it were, an active part in that event by shouting 'Arise, O Lord', a rite which is likewise related to the theophany (see Intr. 39), and vow that they will glorify the 'majesty' of God by praising him with songs and stringed music.

22. MY GOD, MY GOD, WHY HAST THOU FORSAKEN ME?

To the Conductor. According to The Hind of the Dawn.[1] *A Psalm. Of David*

1 My God, my God, why hast thou forsaken me?
 I cried for help, but alas, thy help is far from me.[2]

2 ' '[3] I cry by day but thou dost not answer;
 and by night, and still I cannot keep silence.[4]

3 Yet thou art holy,
 enthroned on the praises of Israel.

4 In thee our fathers trusted;
 they trusted, and thou didst deliver them.

5 To thee they cried, and were saved;
 in thee they trusted, and were not put to shame.

6 But I am a worm, and no man any more;
 scorned by men and despised by the people.

7 All who see me mock at me,
 open wide their mouths in derision and wag their heads:

8 'He waited[3] for the Lord;
 let him deliver him,
 let him rescue him if[5] he delights in him!'

9 Yet thou art he who took me from my mother's womb;
 thou didst keep me safe upon my mother's breasts.

10 Upon thee was I cast from my mother's womb,
 and from my mother's belly thou hast been my God.

11 Be not far from me, for trouble is near,
 and there is none other to help me.

12 Mighty bulls encompassed[6] me,
 strong bulls of Bashan surrounded[6] me.

13 A lion opened wide[7] his jaws upon me,
 a lion ravening and roaring.[8]

14 I am poured out like water,
 and all my bones are out of joint;
 my heart became like wax,
 it melted within my breast.

15 My throat[9] is dried up like a potsherd,
 and my tongue cleaves to my palate;
 thus thou layest me in the dust of death.

16 Alas, dogs were round about me;
 a horde of evildoers encircled me;
 my hands and my feet hurt me.[10]

17 I can count all my bones,
 but they stare and gloat over me;

18 they divide my garments amongst them,
 and for my raiment they cast lots.

19 But thou, O Lord, be not far off!
 O thou my strength, hasten to my aid!

20 Deliver my soul from the sword,
 my only possession[11] from the power of the dogs!

21 Save me from the mouth of the lion,
    rescue[12] me from the horns of the wild oxen!
22 I will tell of thy name to my brethren;
    in the midst of the congregation I will praise thee:
23 'You who fear the Lord, praise him!
    All you sons of Jacob, glorify him,
    and stand in awe of him, all you children of Israel!'
24 'For he has not despised or abhorred the affliction of the afflicted;
    and he has not hid his face from him,
    but has heard when he fervently cried to him.'
25 From thee comes my praise in the great congregation;
    my vows I will pay before those who fear him.
26 Then the meek shall eat and be satisfied;
    those who seek him shall praise the Lord!
    May your hearts be revived[13] for ever!
27 All the ends of the earth shall remember and turn to the Lord;
    and all the families of the nations shall bow down before him.[3]
28 For dominion belongs to the Lord,
    and he rules[3] over the nations.
29 Yea, they that sleep[3] in the earth, must worship him;[3]
    before him all must bow who went down to the dust ' '.[14]
30 The offspring of those who fear him
    shall tell[3] of the Lord to the coming generation,[15]
31 and proclaim his deliverance to a people yet unborn,
    that the Lord[3] has wrought it.

[1] This probably refers to the title or the opening words of a song to the tune of which the psalm was sung or accompanied. Cf. on this Jirku, *ZAW*, 1953, p. 857, who points out that the history of religion and archaeology show an original connection between the hind and the goddess of dawn.

[2] Lit.: 'far from helping me are the words of my crying'.
    (Tr. N.: V. 1b in RSV is 'Why art thou so far from helping me, from the words of my groaning?')

[3] See BH.

[4] * RSV begins with 'O my God'; v. 2b reads 'but find no rest' instead of 'and still I cannot keep silence'.

[5] * V. 8 in RSV reads 'He committed his cause to the Lord' instead of 'He waited for the Lord' and 'for he delights in him' instead of 'if he delights in him'.

[6] * RSV uses the present tense.

[7] Following Beer, *Festschrift für K. Marti* (Beihefte der ZAW, 41, 1920, pp. 15 f.), read *yiḥēl*.

[8] * In RSV v. 13 is:
    they open wide their mouths at me,
    like a ravening and roaring lion.

[9] See BH. (Tr. N.: RSV has 'strength' for 'throat'.

[10] Read perhaps *kā'abū*. (Tr. N.: RSV has the present tense in v. 16ab and v. 16c reads, 'they have pierced my hands and feet'.)

[11] * V. 20b reads in RSV 'my life' instead of 'my only possession'.

[12] Lit.: 'give a favourable hearing'. (Tr. N.: V. 21b reads in RSV 'my afflicted soul' instead of 'rescue me'.)

[13] * V. 26c is in RSV 'may your hearts live for ever'.

[14] The words that follow, 'and he who does not renew his soul', are probably a later doctrinal addition. (Tr. N.: in RSV v. 29:
> Yea, to him shall all the proud of the earth bow down;
> before him shall bow all who go down to the dust,
> and he who cannot keep himself alive.)

[15] * V. 30 in RSV:
> Posterity shall serve him;
> men shall tell of the Lord to the coming generation,

To Christian memories this psalm is sacred, because Jesus used its opening words in his prayer on the Cross. The song first leads us down into the uttermost depths of suffering, a suffering which brought the worshipper to the brink of the grave and reduced him to utter despair. It then soars to the heights of a hymn of praise and thanksgiving, sung in response to the answering of the prayer, and of a vision which ranges over a wide field and is achieved by the power of a triumphant faith. The song thus falls into two parts which are clearly marked off from each other by their different moods, thoughts, and styles—the prayer of lamentation (vv. 1–21) and the psalm of thanksgiving (vv. 22–31). In the interval between these two parts has occurred the answering of the worshipper's prayer, and this fact sufficiently explains the dissimilarity of the psalm's two parts so that we are not compelled to assume the authorship of two different people. The psalm is to be thought of as having been uttered in its entirety in the worship of the cult community (v. 25) after the prayer has been answered (v. 24). In that setting the psalmist uses lamentation as well as the 'narration' he includes in the thanksgiving as the background and starting-point in order to throw into relief the magnitude of the deliverance which God had wrought. This method also enables him to represent and acknowledge that saving work of God before the congregation by bearing personal testimony in their midst (see Intr. 69, 74 f). In the first part of the psalm moving laments and petitions alternate. The mood of the worshipper restlessly fluctuates to and fro between trembling fear and a yearning desire to seek his refuge in God. The second part of the psalm proceeds in a more composed vein, its train of thought being more ordered, as the psalmist now contemplates the effects which the providential rule of God has produced or is going to produce upon Israel (vv. 22–26), the nations (vv. 27, 28), and past and future generations (vv. 29–31).

The poet who composed the psalm has the gift of describing his sufferings in words which deeply move our hearts and in figurative

language which grips our imagination. His lamentation is one of the
most touching portions of the Psalter. However, the stylistic quality
of the lament with its pictorial allusions involves our not being able
to recognize clearly the specific circumstances which impel the
worshipper to utter his lament echoing with the sufferings ensuing
from his affliction. His adversaries stand out more distinctly than
anything else as the cause of his affliction (vv. 6b, 7, 8, 12, 13, 16,
17b, 18). The poet speaks of them throughout only by way of
imagery. And in other respects, too, we often do not know where to
draw the line between imagery and actual fact. It is therefore open
to question whether, adopting the view held by many expositors,
we shall have to think only of physical illness—because of vv. 14, 15
and 17a. At all events it is not so much the physical suffering which
lays the lamenting worshipper so low as the anguish of mind caused
by his calamity. A full understanding of the psalm can be achieved
only if we consider the latter in the light of the religious doubts which
torment the psalmist's soul; making the most desperate efforts he
strives for an assurance from his God and for communion with him.
The fundamental theme of the psalm, the spiritual bond linking its
two parts, is really that of seeking God and of finding God. It is
precisely because the demonstration of the divine granting of salvation is at stake that the community of the godly ones, who are also
called the 'afflicted' and the 'meek' (see Intr. 93), are interested in
the personal experience of the psalmist, and it is for the same reason
that the psalm has its place in the cult of the community, the fundamental ideas of which shine through here and there. This observation must not, however, be generalized so that the ideal people of
Israel or the cult community are made the subject of the whole psalm
and are regarded as speaking throughout. The psalm contains a
number of entirely individual features which refute any attempt to
interpret it in a collective sense.

First part: lament and supplication (vv. 1–21)

[1–2] The prayer opens with a cry of despair uttered by one who
is in the very depths of affliction. What grieves the worshipper
more deeply than anything else in his fearful loneliness is the fact that
he imagines himself forsaken by God, that God seems not to answer
him as he cries out aloud to him for help. Moreover, he asks himself
the poignant question 'why' God has forsaken him and 'why' he does
not answer him, but knows no answer. He struggles to find the

bridge which will lead him out of his affliction and will bring him to
God, on whose nearness his whole existence depends, but he sees only
the abyss which separates him from God, only how far he is from
God. It would be entirely wrong to interpret his words as implying
a reproach levelled at God. On the contrary, they give expression to
the fact that the psalmist is terrified when he becomes conscious of
the agonizing mystery of the hidden God which presents itself to
him. **[3–5]** God keeps silence, and the psalmist cannot help crying
out; therein lies the immense tension from which he suffers. But, after
all, what is man with all his problems? Must he not be silenced by the
sublime nature of God whose thoughts he will, after all, never be able
to penetrate? The poet primarily senses this vast difference between
the majesty of God and his own self when he says: 'Yet thou art
holy.' But it is precisely this God, who far transcends everything
which is human and remains unapproachable whenever men
endeavour to obtrude on him, with whom the people of God have
nevertheless a special relationship. They owe him their deliverance
from Egypt and thereby their historical existence; at the same time
they may glorify him in their cultic hymns as their King and Lord
and as the God who is exalted and who helps, so that, to quote the
bold metaphorical phrase which the poet uses to describe the cultic
scene, God is present as the Lord of the cult community 'enthroned
on the praises of Israel' (cf. the affinity with the designation used of
Yahweh in connection with the sacred Ark: 'who sits enthroned
upon the cherubim'; see Intr. 29 f., 57). The trust of the fathers in that
God and their prayers offered to him have not been in vain. When
the poet comes to think of the beginnings of the *Heilsgeschichte* of
Israel, this recollection appears to him as an island of comfort in the
midst of the ocean of his suffering. His restlessly searching mind finds
peace in the contemplation of those events in the history of Israel in
respect of which the providential rule of God is not yet obscured
from him. Is he not himself a link in the same order of succession to
which his forefathers belonged, and is he not for that reason likewise justified in putting his trust in the God who once helped them?
At this point it can clearly be seen how important it was for the piety
of the individual worshipper that the Old Testament tradition of the
Heilsgeschichte was fostered in the cult of the Covenant.

[6–8] The restlessness caused by the agony of his suffering does
not, however, allow the poet to dwell too long on that comforting
story. At the very next moment his mind is once more overwhelmed

by sorrow and grief. In that the worshipper's thoughts (in a way
typical of his whole lament) restlessly wander about trying to find
the right way, being directed sometimes to God, sometimes to himself, and sometimes to his adversaries, the desperate seeking and
struggling of the psalmist speaks to us in a language which deeply
affects us by its truthfulness. He perceives how utterly miserable
his position is; he fancies himself to be a worm that has been
trampled underfoot, and not a human being. In the eyes of his
enemies—and in this he differs from his forefathers—he has been put
to shame by God. At this point he is not so much afflicted by his
physical sufferings; on the contrary, he suffers much more from the
fact that the scorn of his adversaries affects his relationship with God
and ironically confirms his own feeling which had caused him to
struggle so hard for the true answer to his problems, the feeling,
namely, that God has broken off his relationship with him and that,
in consequence, he is hoping for God in vain. The real sting of his
suffering is the strain on his faith.

[9–11] However, the attack on his faith evokes in him at the same
time new strength, too. Is his trust in God really in vain when he
considers that it was God himself who guided his first movements
which culminated in his birth, that God's hand has been upon him
since the first days of his infancy? Is there really anything he *can* do
other than trust in him on whom he was utterly dependent from his
mother's womb? Even in the face of the derision with which his
adversaries treat his faith, the worshipper finds a further comfort, a
comfort which fills his heart with peace and confidence, in the
religious teaching on creation which has taught him always to see his
whole existence as God's dealing with him. As soon as he realizes
that it is God who is the subject who directs his life, he is standing on firm ground. Now, too, he is able to do what had been
impossible for him before, namely to stretch out his hand to that God
in prayer. Whereas he had previously only perceived the unbridgeable distance which separated him from God, he now feels as if he
experiences for the first time how the hand of God takes hold of him
—the hand of God which he is now able to seize, though he can do
so only indirectly, by means of the tradition of the past. A spark of
faith kindles in him; through prayer he has gradually drawn nearer
to God. At this very moment, too, in the hour of his direst need, he
feels himself thrown upon God as the One who alone is able to help
him.

[**12–13**] And yet, the poet has still not reached the end of his struggle. Fear of enemies arouses in him once more violent emotions. The bulls, that is, the strong bulls of Bashan, the fertile pasture land east of the Jordan, well known for its strong race of breeding cattle, and the ravening and roaring lion—these images are not to be understood as opprobrious names which the psalmist uses to describe the enemies, but as reflections on the helpless fear which overcomes him at the sight of them and makes him tremble.[1]

[**14–15**] The poet uses the strongest language he can think of to describe this state of anxiety. We shall probably have to assume that the various phrases are mere figures of speech. When the psalmist says that he is poured out like water and that his bones are out of joint, that is, that his limbs fail him; again, when he says that his heart is melting like wax and that his throat is dried up like a potsherd, then we can interpret all these phenomena as manifestations of the physical reaction which takes effect in his body at the moment of extreme distress, making him shake with fear—we are not compelled to think in this connection of an illness. This interpretation also helps to preserve the connection with what has taken place beforehand and with what is going to follow. It is not surprising that this feeling of utter helplessness gives rise to the thought of death in the poet's soul! And the peril of death once more raises the problem which God presents; it is God who lays him in the dust of death. The unsolved mystery lies in the very fact that the psalmist sees the same God, by whom alone he can expect to be saved, at work also in his suffering. Thus the whole discord in the poet's soul becomes a discord in his idea of God. It is not given to the poet to reach that supreme height of faith which has the strength to acknowledge God even when he is obscured by suffering. His faith still needs to be supported by a visible proof of divine help.

[**16–18**] He is still not able to get rid of the anxious thoughts which continue to be directed to his enemies and to himself. It is part of the essence of the Old Testament piety, as this is expressed in prayer, to be true to life at all costs and therefore also not to hide from God the worshipper's conflicting emotions which cause his mood to change continually. The way which leads him to God is

---

[1] I doubt whether the metaphorical use of the names of animals in the Old Testament laments is to be understood, as Kraus assumed, on the analogy of Sumerian and Babylonian texts of incantations, as a means of designating demons.

already partly covered by the fact that he may disclose to God the
depth of his affliction so unreservedly. This time the psalmist uses a
different kind of image to describe his enemies—dogs, a horde of
evildoers, and robbers who, eager for plunder, seize upon his
garments. It is the thought of imminent death which has led the poet
to use the illustration of the dogs, which his mind's eye sees fall upon
his dead body (cf. I Kings 21.19), though he does not say so explicitly,
as the Greek, Syriac, and Latin versions of v. 16c do; the same
thought is behind the word-picture of the robbers who divide
amongst themselves the garments of their victim. Hence the facts
with which we are here presented do not suffice to justify an interpretation of these individual features whereby, contrary to v. 8, they
referred to ungodly people who act as opponents in a lawsuit against
the author. For the same reason we would not be justified in assuming
from v. 16c that the psalmist was in danger of suffering the penalty of
crucifixion. The hints which we find in these verses and which in
accordance with the style of the lament are couched in very
general terms are not sufficient to draw such conclusions. Whilst
his enemies stare at him and gloat over his misfortune, the worshipper is once more overwhelmed by the whole misery of his
affliction.

[19–21] Conscious of his own helplessness, the worshipper pulls
himself together and in a last effort of his ebbing strength clings to
God whom he entreats to save his life, 'his only possession', from the
power of his adversaries. He knows that God alone is his 'strength'
and that without God's nearness and visible help he cannot exist. At
this point he reaches the limit which is set to his piety by the Old
Testament faith. That he does not think of vengeance and that he
does not beseech God to pour out his wrath from on high on his
enemies, makes this psalm especially valuable for us in comparison
with others.

Second part: praise and thanksgiving (vv. 22–31)

[22–24] The darkness which filled the worshipper's soul has
vanished and, rejoicing with great joy, he begins to sing a song of
thanksgiving. He has become assured that his prayer has been
answered and that God has helped him. He also calls upon the
congregation to praise God—which presupposes that the congregation, too, has satisfied itself about the actual giving of the divine help.
It is therefore more likely that the worshipper's prayer has already

been granted than that he still anticipates even in the prayer itself
the future answering of his prayer and his future deliverance. This
latter view is, however, held by most expositors. The thanksgiving
therefore recalls the fact that the prayer has been granted and reflects ideas prominent in the festival cult with which the personal
experience of the worshipper is conjoined. Just as the problem
presented by God had been his ultimate concern during his suffering,
so, seeing that he is saved, his deepest need now is to proclaim the
glory of God and to have him acknowledged by men. He sees himself
united with the group of his friends among the members of the
congregation; they praise God, who has not 'abhorred' to stoop to
the affliction of the afflicted. Here the tension has been resolved:
by virtue of his grace and mercy the majestic and holy God (v. 3)
has himself bridged over the gulf which man is unable to cross
in order to reach God, and this fact makes the greatness of God
even greater (v. 24). And that realization encourages the poet to call
also upon those who had not shared in his experience and had stood
aloof from him—his adversaries, too, are probably included in 'all
you children of Israel'—to 'glorify' and to 'fear' God whose greatness
and sternness are revealed in his grace.

[25–26] Having been delivered by God the psalmist is so fully
conscious of the happiness which has been brought about by the
re-establishment of his communion with God that even the fact that
he is now able to give thanks to God is accepted by him as a gift
from God's hand. As a visible sign of his gratitude he will pay a
votive offering in the midst of the godly ones and invite the poor to a
meal so that they may share in his happiness; then 'their hearts shall
be revived for ever'; they may be confident that the God who has
come to his help will not forsake their cause either.

[27–28] However, the psalmist does not rest content with the fact
that the help of the gracious God is praised by his own God-fearing
people and that homage is paid in Israel to God's nature and his
providential rule. The whole world, all the nations, will realize the
power of Yahweh and will bow down before him as their God. This
bold flight of the poet's thought, inspired by his faith, cannot be
accounted for by saying that he merely copies a type of style well
known from Babylonian and Egyptian hymns; nor can it be accounted for, by saying that he expected the conversion of the pagan
nations to take place as an immediate result of his deliverance. The
direction of his thoughts is on the contrary determined by his

P.–H

conception of God, to whose dominion and power there are no limits. The ultimate reason for the conversion of the nations (v. 28; see Intr. 50) is to be found in the kingship of God—which is the glory of Israel, the foundation of the trust of the fathers (v. 3) and which belongs to the theme of the festival cult (cf. Ps. 66.8). The doxological nature of the psalm's conclusion is to be understood as a reflection of that cultic tradition.

[29–31] The rule of God presses on to its consummation. Even death can no longer act as a bar to that rule. The past generations, too, who sleep in the earth will submit to God. By virtue of his faith in God's omnipotence the poet is able to achieve that magnificent vision of the eschatological consummation of the Kingdom of God which embraces the past, the present and the coming generations, and thus the whole world. The knowledge of the 'saving acts' of Yahweh will be passed on from one generation to another—that knowledge which had its origin in the festival cult and with which the worshipper may also class the saving experience of his own personal deliverance. And that tradition of the divine *Heilsgeschichte* will be the means whereby the belief in God will be propagated throughout the world and throughout the ages.

In the hour when he seemed forsaken by God Jesus remained faithful by uttering the opening words of this psalm whilst he was enduring the agony of the Cross; by constant prayer he overcame the grievous hour of his trial. Guided by the psalm, he entered upon the way which led him through his most bitter Passion, but ended in the triumph of faith and in the victory of the Kingdom of God. The fact that Jesus spoke the opening words of this psalm on the Cross as an affirmation of faith in God probably induced the early Christian tradition to quote in its account of the Passion of Jesus other sayings from the psalm. This is particularly true of the way in which that account is given by Matthew. Thus Psalm 22 has been used in the New Testament in the sense of a Messianic prophecy pointing to the consummation of the rule of God in Christ.

23. THE LORD IS MY SHEPHERD

A Psalm. Of David

1 The Lord is my shepherd, I shall not want;
2 he makes me lie down in green pastures
    and rest in a camp beside the water.[1]

3 He restores my soul.
   He leads me in paths of righteousness for his name's sake.
4 Even though I walk through the valley of deep darkness,[2]
   I fear no evil, for thou art with me;
   thy rod and thy staff, they comfort me.
5 Thou preparest a table before me
   in the presence of my enemies;
   thou anointest my head with oil,
   my cup overflows.
6 Only goodness and lovingkindness will follow me
   all the days of my life;
   and I may dwell[3] in God's house
   to the end of the days.[4]

[1] * V. 2b reads in RSV, 'He leads me beside still waters.'
[2] * RSV reads in v. 4a 'through the valley of the shadow of death' instead of 'through the valley of deep darkness'.
[3] See BH.
[4] * V. 6 reads in RSV:
   Surely goodness and mercy shall follow me all the days of my life;
   and I shall dwell in the house of the Lord for ever.

This psalm has gained immortality by virtue of the sweet charm of its train of thought and its imagery, and by the intimate character of the religious sentiments expressed therein. It is marked by the tender touch of a serene soul enjoying perfect peace of mind, a peace of mind that flows from an undoubting trust in God. The sentiments of an almost childlike trust which the poet is able to express in this psalm are, however, by no means the product of a carefree unconcern characteristic of young people; on the contrary, they are the mature fruit of a heart which, having passed through many bitter experiences and having fought many battles (vv. 4, 5), had been allowed to find at the decline of life in its intimate communion with God (vv. 2, 6) the serenity of a contented spirit—peace of mind (v. 6) and, in all dangers, strength. The fact that the interpretation of the psalm is so attractive but at the same time also so difficult is to be accounted for by the wealth of oriental imagery in its language and thoughts. For this abundance makes it more difficult to state precisely, point by point, what has to be regarded as a mere figure of speech and what can be accepted as actual fact, since both of them, image and fact, often blend in the poetical, allegorical style of the psalm. The word-pictures of Yahweh as the loving Host (v. 5) and of living with God in his household (v. 6) suggest that the occasion of the psalm's composition is to be looked for in an experience the psalmist had during a divine service which brought home to him with particular urgency the happiness and the blessing of communion with God.[1]

[1] In the Old Testament the image of the shepherd, which was also used in the rest of the ancient Orient, did not originally refer to God's relationship with the individual, but to his relationship with a number of people; and elsewhere, too, the Old Testament applies that picture to those acts of God whereby he had guided the people of the Covenant in the course of the divine *Heilsgeschichte* (thus especially in Isa. 40.11; 49.9 f.; 63.14; Ezek. 34.10 ff.; Pss. 80.1; 95.7; 100.3). It follows that the poet may perhaps have been inspired by a hymn, sung by the congregation in an act of worship and praising Yahweh as the Shepherd of Israel (cf. Ps. 80.1), to interpret that picture as applying also to his personal relationship with God and, making it the starting-point of his own meditation, to develop his devout thoughts in a psalm. This is a small and yet significant indication of the way in which the faith of the individual can be kindled anew by the corporative worship of those who are united with him in a community of faith and by the tradition of that community! The picture of the shepherd evokes in the psalmist grateful memories which take shape in his mind in the confident hope: 'I shall not want.' [2] In his imagination he goes back to the sunny days of his youth when he was in the happy position of enjoying a carefree life under the protection of God, lying on green meadows like a lamb on the pasture or resting in a tent by the brook. That lovely dream of his youth has not, however, vanished; the poet has been able to retain that childlike happiness, and in the present period of his life, too, the thought of God, nay, even God himself ever again refreshes his soul and imbues him with new vitality and a new zest for life. It is a characteristic feature of the Old Testament belief in God, following on the actualization of his saving acts in the cultus, that it powerfully draws together in a single integrated reflection thoughts of the past, the present and the future (see Intr. 43 f.). Thus the faith of the psalmist joins together as in a focal point 'experience and hope', because the eternal God, before whom what men call time fuses into an eternal present, has taught him to see things in this light. The German language is not capable of express-

---

[1] The attempt of L. Köhler, *ZAW* 68, 1956, pp. 227 ff., to interpret the psalm uniformly in the light of the image of a change of grazing-place likewise proves unavailing in view of vv. 5 and 6.

ing this concentration of the different epochs as the Hebrew language does, by means of *one* single tense. A full understanding of the psalm cannot, however, be achieved without that capability.

[3] In v. 3 a further interpretation of the shepherd image is added: here God appears as the guide of the wanderer on his paths through life. Looking back on his past life the poet is now able to recognize what in the years of apprenticeship and of travel he had not perhaps always been able to apprehend with equal clarity, that God has always led him in the paths of righteousness. The author also quite briefly indicates the viewpoint which had enabled him to adopt this attitude of grateful acknowledgment—he adds: 'for his name's sake'. He has realized that what is at stake in life is the fulfilment not of the human will but of the divine will, so that God's name (see Intr. 30 f., 41 f.), his glory, and his wisdom may be extolled. This had been the meaning of his own life, too, and it shall remain so henceforth. And because he has learned to judge his own life from God's viewpoint, his life appears to him to have been guided by God 'in the paths of righteousness' (= salvation). It is part of the essence of faith that he who believes is able to say already in his lifetime:

> Could I from on high in heaven
> once my former life survey,
> Then I'd in stirring measure say,
> 'Thou hast led and blessed my way.'[1]

[4] This hope has its roots in the poet's experience and is the more firmly established as he is able to boast also of affliction. He has by no means been spared the way through many a valley of deep darkness. The blessing of his close association with God becomes particularly evident to him when he now comes to think of those times of distress and danger. At this point the poet turns to the note of prayer, addressing God by the word 'thou' as if, remembering the trials he had to endure, he wanted to cling to God even more ardently. Even during those trials God had not forsaken him, but had been merciful to him especially in times of peril and had delivered him from the fear of loneliness. God had been his guide, his refuge, and his comfort on his arduous pilgrimage, and consequently even that painful recollection is transfigured by his feelings of gratitude for that intimate intercourse with God which allows him to face the

---

[1] * I have not been able to trace the author of this German hymn.

future without fear and with confident hope, no matter what may be in store for him. [5] The psalmist then casts a glance at what is going on around him at the place in which he sojourns, and his thoughts change direction. The sacred rites have been performed, the songs have faded away; the members of the congregation, dressed in their festive attire and their heads anointed with oil (cf. Ps. 45.7; Luke 7.46), proceed to the joyful sacrificial meal in the house of God. What a blessing and joy it is to be able to take part in that meal as the guest of God (cf. Ps. 15.1). Overwhelmed by the emotions which this thought arouses in his soul, the poet casts his mind back to all the festive hours which he had already been able to spend in the house of God. How often had God already prepared a table before him and, acting as a loving Host, had honoured him! Indeed, had he not actually been the guest of God all his life, and had he not been privileged to receive from his hand blessings in abundance, meat and drink, and joy at many festivals? Even his enemies who look askance at his joy cannot spoil his delight in the goodness and presence of God. Thus the fact that he is able to enjoy God proves to be itself a means of grace whereby the bitter sorrows caused by the frictions of human social life can be overcome. The fact that the poet leaves matters as they were, as far as his enemies are concerned, and does not take that ultimate step which would lead to the overcoming of their enmity, shows the limit set to his piety, a limit which we must not overlook in view of the saying of our Saviour 'Love your enemies.' But it cannot be proved that his words express envy or gloating, though many expositors maintain that this is the case.[1] [6] The abundance of divine blessings and sunshine which the poet perceives to have poured in upon his life, draws from him the cry: 'Only goodness and lovingkindness will follow me all the days of my life', an utterance which testifies to his boundless happiness. Ever more distinctly and with growing enthusiasm he has come to realize how unfathomably rich is the blessing of God which rules over his life. Filled with bliss, he has reached the culminating point of his inward happiness. He can no longer be troubled by sad experiences, and nothing will be able to separate him from the 'goodness' and 'lovingkindness' of God till he finds his eternal rest. Now his soul is radiant with light:

[1] E. Vogt (*Biblica* 34, 1953, pp. 195 ff.) holds that the psalm was sung by an accused at a banquet after his acquittal, following a sacrificial offering. But that view, too, goes at least in part beyond what can be deduced from the psalm itself.

My heart for gladness springs,
It cannot more be sad,
For very joy it laughs and sings,
Sees nought but sunshine glad.[1]

At this very point, as his delight in God reaches its climax and throws him into raptures, the experience of the hour which he spent in the house of God in the direct presence of the Lord symbolically transcends the barriers of space and time. By virtue of the power of his faith the experience of the divine presence is transformed into the experience of the eternal future. He will 'dwell' with God 'to the end of the days' and that not only as his guest, but indeed as a member of his household, that is, in a most intimate and unbroken fellowship with God. The main emphasis of these words does not lie on the fact of his external nearness to God in the Temple, but on the spiritual aspect of his communion with God.[2] As in v. 5, image and actual fact are here more closely interwoven than anywhere else in the psalm. Hence no justice is done to the profundity of the piety of the psalmist by those expositors who on account of v. 6 think that the author of the psalm must have been a priest reflecting on his permanent dwelling in the Temple, and, in consequence, speak of a relapse of the psalm into the purely external and restricted style of cultic language. On the other hand, we must not overlook the fact that for the poet the worship in the house of God is the place where this fair fruit of the blessed knowledge that comes by faith was granted him. The hallowed atmosphere of worship is and remains a holy experience whereby the heart feels exalted and becomes more strongly conscious of the nearness of God than is possible in the noise and din of the streets.

[1] * From Catherine Winkworth's hymn, 'If God be on my side,' a translation of Paul Gerhardt's 'Ist Gott für mich, so trete gleich alles wider mich.'
[2] It is therefore entirely in accordance with the keynote of the psalm when the Reformation hymn (Augsburg, 1531) 'Der Herr ist mein getreuer Hirt' ('The Lord is my faithful shepherd'), which is based on Psalm 23, supplements at its conclusion the idea of communion on earth by the idea of communion with Christ after death.

24. LIFT UP YOUR HEADS, YE MIGHTY GATES

Of David. A Psalm

1 The earth is the Lord's and the fullness thereof;
  the world and those who dwell therein;
2 for he has founded it upon the seas,
  and established it upon the floods.

3 'Who shall ascend the hill of the Lord?
  And who shall stand in his holy place?'
4 'He who has clean hands and a pure heart,
  who does not direct his[1] thoughts to wrongdoing,[2]
  and does not swear deceitfully.
5 He will receive blessing from the Lord,
  and salvation from the God who helps him.'[3]
6 'Such is the generation of those who seek the Lord [1]
  who desire to behold thy face, O God[1] of Jacob.'[4] *Selah*
7 'Lift up your heads, O ye gates!
  and lift yourselves up, ye everlasting doors,
  that the King of glory may come in!'
8 'Who is this King of glory?'
  'The Lord, strong and mighty,
  the Lord mighty in battle.'
9 'Lift up your heads, O ye gates,
  and lift yourselves[1] up, ye everlasting doors,
  that the King of glory may come in!'
10 'Who is then the King of glory?'
  'The Lord Sabaoth,[5] he is the King of glory.' *Selah*

[1] See BH.
[2] * V. 4b reads in RSV, 'who does not lift up his soul to what is false'.
[3] * V. 5b is in RSV, 'and vindication from the God of his salvation'.
[4] * In RSV v. 6b reads, 'who seeks the face of the God of Jacob'.
[5] * RSV has in v. 10b 'the Lord of Hosts' instead of 'the Lord Sabaoth'.

The song consists of three sections each of which is clearly marked off from the others by its different style and subject-matter; and yet these three sections are probably to be interpreted as arising out of the same cultic situation. The psalm is presumably part of the liturgy of the autumn festival whose climax is the appearance of Yahweh as the King (vv. 7 ff.; see Intr. 29 f., 37 ff., 44). Verses 1 and 2 speak of God's dominion over the earth; vv. 3–6 are a liturgy which like Psalm 15 is designed to be used at the entry of those who visit the Temple, and answer the question of who can gain admission to the celebration of the cult in the Temple; vv. 7–10 are liturgical utterances accompanying the epiphany of Yahweh in the Temple.

[1–2] The opening theme of the psalm is one of great power and in conception goes far back. The psalmist declares that the whole earth and all the creatures that dwell therein belong to God as their Lord and are subject to him, because everything has been made by his hands who is the Creator of all. The manner in which in antiquity the earth was conceived to exist—floating on the currents of the ocean like an island and yet 'firmly established' by the fact that God conquered the chaotic powers of the primeval waters and put them in their place (v. 2; cf. the comments on vv. 7 ff.)—shows the feeling of amazement of those who gazed with awe at the wonder of his creation (cf. Pss. 104.5; 136.6; Job 38.4 ff.). In the Old Testament more than once an attempt has been made to argue the legitimacy of the power of God by means of a deduction from his creation (I Sam. 2.8; Pss. 74.16 f.; 89.11 f.; 95.4 f.), and that reasoning is here used as an introit which effectively precedes the rest of the psalm, so that the demands subsequently made appear against a background which places a particularly strong emphasis on them. In view of the examples quoted there is little likelihood that these verses have once existed apart as an independent hymn; on the contrary, the hymn contained in these verses refers back to a more detailed representation of the creation which took place previously in the ritual of the festival.

[3–5] The association of the 'Entrance Torah' with the idea of the dominion of God over the whole world throws into relief two important fundamentals of the Old Testament religion: (1) the strong and joyful *confidence* which is created by the fact that the faithful believer is permitted to enter into communion with such a powerful God (v. 3) so that the blessing, salvation and help of that God appear to be the supreme good that life can offer, which cannot be surpassed (v. 5); (2) the immense greatness and force of the *responsibility* which is laid upon the faithful believer in face of the demands made on him by God whose omnipotence imparts to these demands the character of absolute claims and imbues them with an ultimate and inescapable earnestness. It is precisely the interaction of a trustful yearning for God and of an unconditional obedience springing from the fear of God which constitutes the nature of Old Testament piety. Martin Luther has summed up the nature of this piety in his exposition of the Ten Commandments by saying: 'We shall fear God, and we shall love him.' The middle portion of the psalm is closely related to Psalm 15 (see above, pp. 167 ff.). The pilgrims who have come to celebrate the feast and are assembled outside the Temple gates put the question of who is worthy to enter the holy place (v. 3). The answer is given by a priest and, as in Psalm 15, gives prominence to the basic moral requirement of purity of mind and action and of freedom from vain and evil thoughts (v. 4a, b). This is followed by a single concrete command against perjury, which serves as an illustration of the inward integrity required

(v. 4c), and this was perhaps introduced in view of the fact that legal decisions had to be taken at a sacred place and within the framework of the ritual of the feast. The exclusive stress laid on the moral purity of the worshipper both in heart and hands is particularly significant in view of the fact that the performing of cultic rites of purification is otherwise a customary requirement of the cultus; for it shows us the profound inwardness which is peculiar to the Old Testament covenantal religion. Where a heart free from evil thoughts and desires[1] is made the basic condition of communion with God, there the communion with God itself is no longer founded only on an external belonging to that communion but on a spiritual bond which is deeply rooted in the heart of the worshipper. Thus we shall have to understand also the promise of 'blessing and salvation' (v. 5) not only in the sense of a material reward but as including the spiritual help which God will give to those whose privilege it is to enjoy the blessing of communion with him. Again, the psalm differs from Psalm 15 in so far as from the beginning the thought is directed to the omnipotence of God and to his exclusive right to order all things. By treating the theme in this manner the psalmist has reduced the impression that men were entitled to fashion their lives according to their own devices and were able to do so by virtue of their own strength. To make claims as well as promises and their fulfilment is something which is exclusively in the hand of the gracious and helpful God (v. 5). **[6]** This thought is followed in v. 6 by the affirmation of those who ask for admission that they fulfil the required conditions and now look forward to the revelation of God in the sanctuary in order to participate in the blessing and salvation of the divine presence (v. 5).

[7–10] The third section of the psalm refers to this theophany in the sanctuary. Expositors usually regard it as a liturgy of the procession of Yahweh, returning home from a war with the sacred Ark. But that interpretation is at variance with the account in I Kings 6.23–28 which makes it an open question whether the Ark, which belonged to the equipment of the cult and signified the presence of Yahweh in the Temple of Jerusalem, ever belonged to the sacred equipment for processions. It therefore seems to me more likely that what this section has in mind is the representation of the theophany in the Temple which was dramatized in the cult (see Intr. 28 ff., 37 ff.).

---

[1] The Hebrew term reminds us of the passage in the Decalogue (Ex. 20.7) which has in mind the things that do not fit in with man's relationship to God.

In this connection the victorious combat (v. 8) against the hostile powers of chaos, in which Yahweh as the Creator established his dominion over the world (vv. 1 f.), is presumably presupposed, as is done, for instance, in Psalm 77. That theme is a reminiscence of the ancient oriental creation-myth from which also the cultic name 'Yahweh of hosts' (v. 10) is derived (see Intr. 41 f., 60 ff.). A choir announces the advent of the 'King of honour' (= glory) by solemnly addressing the 'ancient doors'[1] (v. 7). The command to the inanimate stone to lift itself up reveals in like manner both the boldness of the poetical language and the forceful power of the conception of God which transcends all human limitations—doors built by the hands of men are not adequate to admit the mighty God (cf. the parallel in I Kings 8.27). But the gates are not open to everybody. From inside the gates the question is asked: 'Who is this King of glory?' To this the reply is given from outside the gates: it is Yahweh, the mighty warrior (v. 8). Once more request and question alternate, using almost identical phrases (v. 9). Everybody is eagerly waiting to hear the name of God, at which utterance the gates will be opened. The proclamation of that name—'Yahweh of hosts' (v. 10)—has the effect of a magic key, as we may infer from well-known accounts of that occasion: the doors are now opened wide in order that God may appear in his glory (*kābōd*) before the congregation assembled in the sanctuary (cf. Isa. 6.3 and II Sam. 6.2, where the conception of the theophany is associated with the sacred Ark 'over which is called the name of Yahweh of hosts who sits enthroned on the cherubim'). Here ends the brief cultic drama which precedes the solemn moment of the divine advent and prepares the congregation for that climax of the feast they celebrate.

The fact that according to tradition the psalm was sung at a later period every Sunday in the Jewish worship of the Temple shows how firmly the ancient tradition of the theophany was rooted in the religious life of Judaism as this was expressed in worship. In the psalm we are confronted with the characteristic ability of the Old Testament's idea of God to embrace the most diverse historical elements and to merge them into a unity. Only a monotheistic belief in God displaying such a strong capacity for expansion and absorption as

---

[1] The ancient tradition of the theophany at the door of the sanctuary is perhaps still reflected in this phrase; cf. Ex. 33.9; Ps. 68.17; Ezek. 43.4. Even if viewed from this angle, it is unnecessary to assume that the sacred Ark formed part of the procession to the Temple.

did the Old Testament one was capable of combining the tradition
of the creation, in part of alien origin, with its own cultic and moral
traditions, in such a way that the consistency and unity of the idea of
God was not destroyed, but rather gained in liveliness, strength and
force. In the Old Testament the active nature of the ever-Living God
means that creation and history are not primarily the object of man's
pious contemplation of past events (in that case he would be a mere
spectator); rather are they first and foremost the place where the
claim of the Deity, making demands on man, asserts itself once and
for all in such a way that the man who lives in the present feels those
demands to be made on himself and comes to realize that the
past represents the eternal, and yet at the same time the actual,
presence of the God who is powerful in Nature and in History, and
that that divine presence calls precisely on him and at this very
moment to make a decision. This live, dynamic character of the
knowledge of God also accounts for the fact that it is precisely in
those moments in the cult when Old Testament piety reached its
climax that God is comprehended as a Will which claims the whole
man, because the cult provided a singular opportunity to experience
all the traditions of history as the immediate presence of God. But
that vision of faith which views everything from the standpoint of
God not only embraces at the very moment of God's appearance in
the Temple what had come to pass once and what is taking place
now; the future, too, as it were, is anticipated by faith already here
and now, in this very hour in which God's presence dominates everything else. The barriers of time disappear in face of the eternal
presence of God. This accounts also for the fact that the ancient song
of the epiphany of God in the Temple of Jerusalem could become for
the God-fearing man of the Old Testament a hymn which in spite of
the great interval in time told him of the coming of God in his own
time *and of God's future coming*. And this is the same faith, joining
together the things of the past, the present and the future, which
inspires us to celebrate every year the advent of God in Jesus Christ
by singing the hymn, 'Lift up your heads, ye mighty gates!'[1]—the
faith in the God who is and who was and who is to come.

---

[1] * These are the opening words of the German hymn 'Macht hoch die Tür,
das Tor macht weit' by Georg Weissel (1590–1635), translated by Catherine
Winkworth (1829–1878).

25. MAKE ME TO KNOW THY WAYS, O LORD
Of David

1 To thee, O Lord, I lift up my soul,
2 O my God, in thee I trust,
  let me not be put to shame;
  let not my enemies exult over me.
3 Yea, none that wait for thee are put to shame;
  but only those who are wantonly treacherous.[1]
4 Make me to know thy ways, O Lord;
  teach me thy paths!
5 Let me walk in thy faithfulness, and teach me,[2]
  for thou art the God of my salvation;
  for thee I wait all the day long.
6 Be mindful of thy mercy, O Lord,
  and of thy steadfast love,
  for they have been from of old.
7 Remember not the sins of my youth, or my transgressions;
  according to thy steadfast love remember me,
  for thy goodness' sake, O Lord!
8 Good and upright is the Lord;
  therefore he instructs sinners in the way;
9 he leads the humble in what is right,
  and teaches the humble his way.
10 All the paths of the Lord are lovingkindness and faithfulness,
  for those who keep his covenant and his testimonies.
11 For thy name's sake, O Lord,
  pardon my guilt, for it is great!
12 Who, then, is the man that fears the Lord?
  Him will he instruct in the way that is best for him.[3]
13 His soul shall abide[4] in what is good,[5]
  and his seed shall inherit the land.
14 In communion with the Lord live those who fear him,
  and his covenant teaches them knowledge.[6]
15 My eyes are ever toward the Lord,
  for he will pluck my feet out of the net.
16 Turn thou to me, and be gracious to me;
  for I am lonely and afflicted!
17 Make wide the narrowness of my heart,[7]
  and[8] bring me out of my distresses!
18 Consider my wretchedness and my affliction,
  and forgive all my sins!
19 Consider how many are my foes,
  and with what wicked hatred they hate me!
20 O guard my soul, and deliver me;
  let me not be put to shame,
  for I take refuge in thee!

21 May integrity and uprightness preserve me,
      for I wait for thee, O Lord. [8]
22 Redeem Israel, O God,
      out of all his troubles!

[1] * V. 3 reads in RSV:
      Yea, let none that wait for thee be put to shame;
      let them be ashamed who are wantonly treacherous.
[2] * V. 5a is in RSV, 'Lead me in thy truth, and teach me.'
[3] * RSV has in v. 12b 'in the way that he should choose' instead of 'in the way
that is best for him'.
[4] Lit.: 'stay overnight'.
[5] * RSV has in v. 13a 'in prosperity' instead of 'in what is good'.
[6] * In RSV v. 14 runs:
      The friendship of the Lord is for those who fear him,
      and he makes known to them his covenant.
[7] * V. 17a reads in RSV, 'Relieve the troubles of my heart.'
[8] See BH.

The ancient Church borrowed from this psalm the introit, and so
the names of the Sundays *Reminiscere* (v. 6) and *Oculi* (v. 15).[1] The
psalm has also found a beautiful lyrical echo in Paul Gerhardt's
hymn 'Nach dir, mein Gott, verlanget mich'.[2] It is the prayer of
lamentation of a pensive soul earnest in its piety. According to
vv. 10, 13, 15 (22) the psalm seems to have been recited in the cult
of the Covenant Festival. Having been composed in the quiet of a
lonely life, it is by virtue of the universally applicable truths it proclaims a perpetual source of comfort for people who are lonely or
forsaken. As so often in laments, the concrete features of the author's
external circumstances are only of secondary importance in comparison with the spiritual aspect of a timeless piety which by the use of
forms belonging to the Wisdom literature (see Intr. 88 f. and Pss. 1 and
49) has acquired the character of something both typical and exemplary. The acrostic form of the psalm, observing the alphabetic order
for the beginning of each verse, is preserved apart from a few omis-
sions (cf. Pss. 9, 10 and 111); it necessitates, however, a somewhat
artificial style, joining the individual sayings in a formal and superficial manner at the expense of the poet's free creative power and of
a lucid development of his thoughts. Whereas in vv. 1–7 and from
v. 16 onwards the personal petitions prevail, general reflections are
predominant in vv. 8–14 and here take the form of Wisdom sayings.
    [1–3] In the opening verses the keynote is at once given which
dominates the whole song. Only in God is the soul able to find edifi-

[1] * *'Reminiscere'* is the second and *'Oculi'* the third Sunday in Lent.
[2] * This hymn seems not to have been translated into English.

cation and only in him can man really trust. In men's dealings with one another disappointments are always bound to occur; it is only when we trust in God that we can hope not to be 'put to shame'. The prayer of the psalmist which now begins is based on this religious truth (v. 3), which is verified by faith and springs from his personal experience. And the comforting assurance with which he can pray is founded on the fact that his experience can be identified with the truth that is valid for all God-fearing people. Only those who wantonly pay no heed to God's faithfulness and respond to it by acting treacherously will be put to shame by him; and that may be the fate of the evildoers whom the worshipper regards as his enemies (cf. v. 19). [4–6] Though the poet is firmly assured of his close relationship with God or perhaps, indeed, just because of that assurance, he is conscious of the fact that he cannot exist nor walk in God's ways without God's gracious help and without his faithfulness and mercy. Just as a body is in daily want of food, thus the soul needs to be lifted up to God day by day in order that it may obtain from him as a gift a true insight into his ways and be instructed in them—and at the same time may also be granted strength to be obedient to his will. Both these gifts are included in the supplication made in v. 4 which concisely formulates the leading idea of the psalm, and that idea displays the religious and moral earnestness which is characteristic of the whole psalm. Moral knowledge is not the product of human wisdom, and a moral conduct of life is not the accomplishment and the merit of human effort; rather it is a gift of the divine grace and mercy which 'from of old' rules the lives of men (v. 6) and continues to do so only because God remains 'faithful' (v. 5) to his true nature in his relationship with men. (Luther's translation of the word 'ʿmet by 'truth' and his interpretation of that term as meaning the 'true doctrine' is possible in the abstract, but does not do justice to the context in which the word is used.) Here, too, the worshipper envisages his own concern within the widest possible dimensions and regards it as being most profoundly related to God's saving will and his redemptive work. [7] The moral earnestness of the psalmist is matched by the earnestness and depth of his consciousness of his sinfulness. Three times he asks God to forgive him his sins, the number and weight of which he does not hide either from himself or from God (cf. vv. 11, 18). As he searches his own heart, the sins of his youth, committed under the pressure of a heedless and unrestrained passion, appear before his mind's eye just as much as the deliberate transgressions of his manhood. And only the lovingkindness of God, who *seeks the sinner* in that he disregards his sins, is able to restore the broken relationship between God and man. **[8–10]** The poet once more expresses this knowledge, which he has gained by wrestling with the problem in his soul, in the form of a universally valid religious truth; he discloses in his testimony to God's nature and rule, a testimony which has a hymn-like quality, the foundation on which his life is unshakably established by saying that God is 'good' and 'upright'. In that statement the two aspects of God's nature and rule are interwoven, that is, his inflexible will to do what is good is equally manifested in his *demands* and in his *lovingkindness*, instructing the sinner in the right way and helping him to walk in that way. In both these activities God remains faithful to his nature. And that nature is the fundamental law of the Old Covenant which has not been abolished in the New Covenant either. To this the saying of Jesus bears witness which concludes his exposition of the Ten Commandments: 'You, therefore, must be perfect, as your heavenly Father is perfect' (Matt. 5.48). The psalmist's statement 'All the paths of the Lord are lovingkindness and faithfulness for those who keep his covenant and his testimonies' embraces the whole *Heilsgeschichte* in a single vision (cf. Intr. 43, 58 f., 74 f. on the formula 'lovingkindness and faithfulness'), and expresses the utter profundity and the abundant richness of a life which is based on faith and finds its peace in God's mercy. The perspective opened by this statement embraces much more than just the moral aspect of man's relationship with God and reminds us of the triumphant comfort with which the New Testament faith is able to fill the heart of the believer, and which is expressed in the immortal saying of the Apostle Paul: 'We know that all things work together for good to them that love God' (Rom. 8.28). **[11–14]** The worshipper's thoughts once more follow the same course, beginning with a prayer for the pardoning of his guilt which presses heavily upon him, and then turning to the springs of the theology of the Old Testament Covenant. The fear of God is also for him the beginning (*principium*) of all 'wisdom' (note the question form of the epigrammatic saying in v. 12; cf. also Ps. 34.11). But contrary to all rational comprehension this fear of God is at the same time coupled with the '*friendship of God*', with a life lived by the godly man in intimate personal communion with his God; and in that life the fear of God finds its fulfilment. In this way the Old Testament idea of the Covenant is imbued with a definitely personal character and is here used by the psalmist as the starting-point of his main thought that God is the Teacher and Leader of man, instructing him in moral knowledge and guiding him in the way of moral actions (vv. 12, 14). A beautiful picture, together with the promise of inheriting the land (see Intr. 44), similarly stemming from the tradition of the Covenant, makes evident the ultimate religious depth of a moral life; the poet declares that the soul which fears God 'stays overnight in what is good', in other words, that such a soul has, as it were, its home in what is good (v. 13).

[15–21] The affirmation of trust in God in v. 15 forms a transition to the petitions which, intermingled with themes of lament (vv. 16b, 18 f.), dominate the last portion of the psalm. Oppressed by his enemies, but perhaps even more so by the weight of his own sins (v. 18), the psalmist in his loneliness (v. 16) takes refuge in the gracious God and asks for protection and deliverance (v. 20). In doing so, he reverts to the beginning of his prayer and to the fundamental moral idea expressed there; but in v. 21 he now expresses that idea in a new creative way; 'integrity' and 'uprightness' shall watch over him as if they were God's messengers, so that he will not cease to live in communion with God. [22] The psalm's concluding verse, which contains a prayer for the redemption of the people of Israel, is only loosely connected with the rest of the psalm as far as its subject-matter is concerned. Since it is also not formally included in the structure of the alphabetic sequence observed for the beginning of each verse, we shall have to regard it as a postscript added to the prayer later on in order to make it suitable for liturgical use as a corporate prayer of the congregation. The concluding verse thus indicates in a striking fashion to what a large extent the cult community lives by the fruits for which its individual members have wrestled in their prayers.

26. O LORD, I LOVE THE HABITATION OF THY HOUSE

Of David

1 Vindicate me, O Lord,
  for I have walked in my integrity,
  and I have trusted in the Lord without wavering.
2 Prove me, O Lord, and try me;
  test[1] my reins and my heart!
3 For thy steadfast love was before my eyes,
  and I have walked in thy truth.[2]

4 I did not sit with false men,
   nor did I consort with dissemblers;
5 I hate the company of evildoers,
   and I will not sit with the wicked.
6 I wash my hands in innocence,
   and go about thy altar, O Lord,
7 bearing testimony to thee with a loud voice,[3]
   and telling all thy wondrous deeds.
8 O Lord, I love the habitation of thy house,
   and the place where thy glory dwells.
9 Sweep not away my soul with sinners,
   nor my life with bloodthirsty men,
10 men whose hands are stained by misdeeds,
   and whose right hands are full of bribes.
11 But as for me, I walk in my integrity;
   redeem me, and be gracious to me!
12 My foot stands on level ground;
   in the great congregation I will praise the Lord.

[1] See BH.
[2] * The RSV reads in v. 3b 'in faithfulness to thee' instead of 'in thy truth'.
[3] * V. 7a runs in the RSV, 'singing aloud a song of thanksgiving'.

Like Psalm 7 the psalm is a psalm of innocence and is probably to be accounted for by a situation such as the one which presumably forms the background of that psalm and is presupposed in I Kings 8.31 f. (see Intr. 76 f.). In the face of an unwarranted accusation the worshipper seeks to attain his vindication by means of an ordeal in the Temple (vv. 1–3), where he submits to the ritual ceremony of purification (v. 6) after he had taken the oath of purification (vv. 3–5); he prays (v. 9 f.) for his preservation from dying 'with sinners and bloodthirsty men' (perhaps as a result of the penalty of death?). In his protestation of innocence the worshipper takes great pains, on the one hand, to dissociate himself from any intercourse with the wicked and the evildoers and from their gatherings, and, on the other hand, to emphasize his devotion to Yahweh and to the cult performed to his glory. It is therefore only natural to regard the realm of the sacral law as the sphere in which the accusations, against which he protests, were levelled at him. The violation of these ordinances (apostasy or unfaithfulness?) was punished by putting the offender to death (cf. Deut. 17.2 ff.) or by cursing him and expelling him from the covenant community (cf. Deut. 27.11 ff.; see Intr. 47). It goes without saying that in such a critical situation and in view of the limitations imposed upon the range of ideas by that situation, the worshipper does not fully express what he would be able to say about his attitude to God and to sin. Again, it goes without saying that the criticism levelled at him of boasting of his 'self-righteousness' and the comparison of the psalmist with the Pharisee in the parable of the Pharisee and the Tax-collector (Luke 18.9 ff.), which is usually quoted in this connection, is neither pertinent nor does it do him justice. It cannot be disputed that the psalm has its Old Testament limitations which are necessitated by a certain legalism in the cultic rites. However, in view of v. 11b there can certainly be no question of the psalmist lacking entirely knowledge of man's need of redemption and of the sinner's utter dependence on the grace of God. In default of any particular features which would enable us to determine their historical background it is not possible to ascertain the date of the psalm; the customary interpretation of the psalm as a creation of the spirit of later Judaism is, however, neither assured nor probable.

[1–2] The opening petition of the psalmist for his vindication by God and the brief motivation of that petition lead us at once *in medias res*. Against the accusations levelled at him he protests the 'innocence' (a term which in this connection perhaps means much the same as 'correctness') of his mode of life and of his unwavering faith in God. Having probably subjected himself to a searching examination of his own conscience (Calvin), he is looking forward to being tested by God, who searches and knows the hearts of men. For he has no need in this case to shrink from that test even if it should penetrate the innermost recesses of his heart. [3] Indeed, he himself is concerned that the truth concerning himself be known before God. The whole revelation of the divine nature and will, which the ancient tradition of the covenant community sums up in the two terms 'grace and faithfulness' (*ḥesed we'᾽met*; Ex. 34.6; see Intr. 43, 58 f., 74 f.), was actually before his mind's eye as a living reality; this he affirms for the purpose of his exoneration in a kind of oath of purification, so that there is no justification for the charge of having been unfaithful. [4–5] He emphatically denies that he has associated with the wicked and has taken part in their secret and forbidden gatherings, activities which were probably also the subject of accusations brought against him. [6–8] The oath of purification, formulated positively in v. 3 and negatively in vv. 4 f., is followed by the ritual ceremony of purification as its confirmation. The cultic rite of washing the hands, which is well known and that not merely in the whole of antiquity (cf. Deut. 21.6; Ps. 73.13; Matt. 27.24), is at the same time the condition of admission to the act of worship (cf. the meaning of Holy Water); in his critical situation it was a matter of special importance to the worshipper that he could participate in that act. The worshipper then promises to take part in the solemn procession around the altar and in the 'testimony' to God's wondrous deeds whereby he has saved his people (the usual interpretation of v. 7 as a thanksgiving for a deliverance which has already taken place or is anticipated is too narrowly conceived and does not fit in with the context). And this promised participation, too, is intended to emphasize his faithful devotion to Yahweh and to his worship just as much as the beautiful confession of his love for God's house, that is, for the place where according to ancient tradition his majesty (= glory) is thought to sit enthroned upon the sacred Ark in the heavenly light of glory (cf. I Sam. 4.21; Ex. 16.10; Ps. 78.61 and Intr. 29 f.). **[9–10]** It is only at this point, after the removal of the reproaches which overshadowed his relationship with God, that the worshipper dares to ask God that he may not be 'swept away' from the community of God's people, who are the object of his faithfulness and his love, like a criminal, with sinners and 'bloodthirsty men' whose hands are stained by misdeeds and 'filled' with bribes (cf. Deut. 27.25). **[11]** Once more he protests his innocence and humbly surrenders to the grace of God by asking him to redeem him— without boasting of living a perfect life. **[12]** His willingness to be faithful to God and his trust in God's grace provide for him faith's support, so that he is able to stand firmly 'on level ground', where he will not be ruined, and, being joyfully confident that his prayer will be answered, vows to give thanks to God by praising him in the 'great congregation' of the cult community.

27.1–6. THE COURAGE OF FAITH

Of David

1 The Lord is my light and my salvation;
   whom shall I fear?
   The Lord is the stronghold of my life;
   of whom shall I be afraid?
2 When evildoers assail me,
   to devour me,[1]
   my enemies and my oppressors,
   they shall stumble and fall.

3 Though a host encamp against me,
   my heart shall not fear;
   though war arise against me,
   even so I will be confident.
4 One thing have I asked of the Lord only,
   and that will I seek after:
   that I may dwell in the house of the Lord
   all the days of my life,
   to behold the graciousness[2] of the Lord,
   and to say prayers[3] in his temple.
5 For he will hide me in his shelter
   in the day of trouble;
   he will protect me under the cover of his tent,
   he will set me high upon a rock.
6 And now I lift up my head
   above my enemies round about me;
   and I will offer in his tent sacrifices of joy;
   I will sing and make melody to the Lord.

[1] * V. 2b reads in RSV, 'uttering slanders against me'.
[2] * RSV reads in v. 4e 'the beauty of the Lord' instead of 'the graciousness of the Lord'.
[3] We cannot be certain whether this translation is correct. The Hebrew term presumably means 'ponder over, consider, contemplate'. (Tr. N.: The RSV reads in v. 4f 'to enquire' instead of 'to say prayers' [in the German original: 'zur Andacht'].)

The twenty-seventh psalm consists of two parts which differ from each other in mood and subject-matter. They cannot have been written in the same circumstances, and also they can hardly have been composed by the same author. Ps. 27.1–6 is a powerful song which expresses unshakable trust in God and, being complete in itself, exhibits a distinct character of its own. Ps. 27.7–14, on the other hand, which is likewise self-contained, represents the prayer of lamentation of a man who is in need of help in his great distress; it follows the traditional style of the 'lament'. It is therefore a question of two originally independent poems. It may be that the similarity of the phrases used in vv. 4 and 13 (to behold the 'graciousness' and the 'goodness' of the Lord respectively), which presupposes an analogous cultic situation, has resulted in the joining together of the two hetero-geneous poems.

The form and the content of Ps. 27.1–6 are similar to those of Psalm 23. The song clearly exhibits the marks of a testimony. As regards the form, this is shown by the fact that Yahweh is spoken of in the third person. In pithy words the poet expresses fearless trust in God which enables him to face the future calmly and undauntedly in spite of many perils. These words are the upshot of many a hard struggle and of many a grievous affliction which he has experienced during his life, but they also flow from the experience of the help which he has received from God and of the victories which he has been able to achieve by faith. We are here confronted not with the exuberant strength of a courage characteristic of an untroubled and lighthearted young man, who treats with indifference the seriousness of a dangerous situation, but with the strength of a mature man which is grounded in faith and has been acquired in the course of many conflicts and has been tested in many battles; such a man reckons with the grim facts of life, but on that account does not only not lose courage but on the contrary 'lifts up his head' the more confidently, being inwardly strengthened and fortified by the power of a faith that rejoices in hope. It is in this attitude and spirit that the song has been written as a striking testimony to the fact that the faith of a man cannot at all be equated with cowardly subservience to the facts of life, but steels man's heart in the struggle for existence and lifts him up to the higher level of heroic greatness. It is not possible to establish any facts which would help us to determine the date of the psalm's composition. In any case it would be a mistake to rob the poet's high-spirited figurative language of its attractiveness by attempting to interpret the phrases concerning the host of enemies and war, which are here used only in a hypothetical sense, as referring to a strategic situation the historical background of which could be determined. The construction of this psalm is simple: vv. 1–3 contain the intrepid affirmation of faith in God, and vv. 4–6 express the psalmist's desire to live in perpetual communion with God and enjoy his protection, a desire which culminates in the vow of confident joy in God.

Courage and trust in God (vv. 1–3)

[1] The form and the thoughts of the opening words are similar to those of Psalm 23. With firm steps the poet takes his stand on the ground of his religious experience. God is his light and his salvation; he is the safe stronghold of his life. It is in these words, full of power and joy, that he sums up what according to his personal experience has stood the test in his struggle for existence as the mainstay and meaning of his life, and what now enables him to face new dangers with confident assurance and with a courage that springs from faith and is unshakable. If God is for him, of whom should he be afraid?

> If Jesus be my friend,
>   If God doth love me well,
> What matters all my foes intend
>   Though strong they be and fell.[1]

Only he can speak thus who has given up all dependence on his fellow men and above all on himself in exchange for an exclusive dependence on God which is unconditional and accepted without any reservation whatsoever. That inward independence of anything which is human makes a man truly free from any kind of fear, but is only granted to him to whom God means everything and for whom God is the ultimate goal in the actual practical circumstances of his life. The great prophetic figures of the Old Testament emphatically demonstrate that it is here that we find the deepest roots of a heroic attitude to life. **[2–3]** The certitude resulting from such a faith enables the poet to face his enemies and oppressors with equanimity even if they want to assail him and devour him like beasts of prey. Though they may encamp against him in countless numbers like a host, as the psalm says, intensifying the actual situation by hyperbole, indeed even though a war may break out against him, all these perils are not able to shake the inward calm and assurance of the intrepid man. No prayer for help, let alone the slightest hint of a lament, passes his lips. On the contrary, his faith in God assures him that the evil which the adversaries devise will fall upon them. He knows that the righteous God has so firmly in his hand whatever may come to pass that not even for one moment does he doubt what the ultimate fate of the evildoers will be. The words of the psalmist, who faces his own self and his fellow men with equanimity, reflect an enviable peace of mind. What makes him so confident is the power of a valiant faith which conquers every emotion. God is *the* one and only Power and possesses all power; and in consequence, the focus is no longer on the poet's own affairs but on God himself, whom nobody can resist. In that the psalmist is set free from every anxious concern for himself and concentrates his thoughts exclusively on God, his faith gains that inner balance and that confident and stable strength which enables him to make the right decision: he who believes will not run away (Isa. 28.16).

The one and only desire (vv. 4–6)

Whereas the first part of the poem exhibits the consistent firmness

---

[1] * See p. 231 n. 1.

and valour of a faith which goes forward in its own way, unmoved
by the apprehensions of the ego and untroubled by any attacks from
without, the second part allows us an insight in that aspect of the
same faith which is turned towards God and opens itself up to him;
and it guides us to where the source of faith's courage and strength
is to be found. The valiant and resolute tone of the psalm here gives
way to moods and emotions which are animated by a spirit of warm
and heartfelt affection. The peculiar charm and the lifelike character
of the psalmist's testimony of faith are to be found in the very way in
which his manly sternness is supplemented by an almost gentle
inwardness. As a hero of faith who at the same time displays a piety
that is both childlike and tender the poet ranks with the greatest
figures in the history of religion. That harmonious unity of apparent
contrasts indicates not a weakness but the maturity and greatness of
his faith. **[4]** There is only *one* desire and only *one* aspiration which
fills the poet's heart and in which all his other wishes converge and
find their fulfilment—that he may live in perpetual communion with
God. If he can have that, then he has everything. The form in which
the poet clothes this desire, his only and supreme concern, is borrowed from the language of the cultus. In a way very similar to
Ps. 23.6, the concrete experience of the nearness of God in the Temple
is expanded and deepened by the psalmist in that it becomes for him
a picture which symbolically typifies man's relation to God in
general, without restricting the communion with God in any way
by tying it locally and physically to the sphere of the divine service.
The poet desires 'to dwell in the house of the Lord all the days of his
life', that is, to become a member of the household of God. The
reason for this, however, is not at all that he is a priest who permanently lives in the Temple, but that the nearness of God, of which
he has continually been made aware afresh in the sanctuary, has
become the spiritual purpose of his life outside the walls of the
Temple, too. And the 'beholding of the graciousness of the Lord', a
phrase which has its origin in the theophany as the climax of the
celebration of the cult (see Intr. 38 ff., 72 ff.), also means, as the last
phrase in v. 4 seems to indicate, that the psalmist becomes assured of
the love and grace of God and that he comprehends the divine
reality more and more deeply by means of the 'saying of prayers' and
by his meditation on the encounter between God and man which he
has experienced in the theophany of the festival cult. Here the divine
service (*Gottesdienst*) is really a 'service rendered by God' (*Dienst*

Gottes); it is the means whereby God himself delivers man from the profane attitude of his mind and enables him to adopt a different attitude, an attitude determined by the experience and assurance of the nearness and reality of the Living God. In presenting this view the psalm advocates a theocentric conception of worship the purport of which is to be found in the glorification of God who accomplishes his will to save. **[5]** This interpretation is confirmed by v. 5, where words such as 'shelter', 'tent' and 'rock' are employed metaphorically to express the refuge and security which communion with God offers to man. Just as the stranger finds protection from menacing dangers in the hospitable hut or tent of a friendly host, so the faithful man knows that God will hide him in his shelter in the day of trouble. In God he can trust completely. If God is the real purpose of his life, then he knows for certain that he who himself transcends all earthly things will deliver him in faith from the misery of his earthly afflictions and will set him, as it were, high upon a rock where the surge of earthly perils cannot reach him. The springs of the poet's own true life flow within the compass of his communion with God who, though the psalmist is in the midst of his struggle for existence, yet lifts his soul above that struggle. From these springs the psalmist draws confidence and faith, courage and strength, so that he is immune from human fear and from trembling faint-heartedness. **[6]** Since his heart is assured of victory by faith, he joyfully and proudly lifts up his head, though he may see himself surrounded on all sides by enemies who threaten him. Strengthened by drinking from the well of his communion with God the poet reverts to the courageous testimony which he has borne at the beginning of his song. Anticipating his joy in the victory of faith, he at once turns again to God, the ultimate cause and the goal of his strength and joy. Using the form of a vow, he promises to offer the 'sacrifice of joy' and thanksgiving; he promises that he will joyously testify to his Lord and will sing praises to the name of him to whom alone he owes everything. At this point, too, the psalm goes beyond the external scope of the cult's convention. The vow implies more than merely the performance of a cultic observance. By means of the 'sacrifice of joy' and the thanksgiving the poet surrenders his whole being to God, who is the sole object of his happiness. We are here confronted with a truly living communion with God, with a mutual receiving and giving. Here the strength and joy issuing from faith are an ever-flowing fountain. Thus side by side with the great figures of the prophets, this psalm is a precious testimony to the things which can be achieved by faith, an Old Testament illustration of the word of the Apostle Paul: 'If God is for us who is against us?'[1] Again, the psalm is particularly valuable and relevant inasmuch as it makes it evident that the things which are regarded as heroic in life are not accomplished on the unsteady ground of man's own self, but by the conquering of the human ego through faith in God as the only firm foundation of man's existence.

[1] * Rom. 8.31.

27.7–14. THE WAY THAT LEADS TO GOD

7 Hear, O Lord, for I cry aloud,
  have mercy upon me and answer me!
8 I say in my heart, 'Thou wilt that we seek thy face;[1]
  thy face, O Lord, do I seek.'
9 Hide not thy face from me;
  turn not thy servant away in anger,
  for thou art my help![2]
  Cast me not off, and forsake me not, O God of my salvation.
10 Though my father and my mother forsake me,[3]
  the Lord will take me up.
11 Teach me thy way, O Lord;
  and lead me in what is right[4]
  because of my enemies.
12 Give me not up to the greed[5] of my oppressors;
  for false witnesses have risen against me,
  and they breathe out[6] violence against me.[6]
13 I know that I shall see the goodness of the Lord
  in the land of the living!
14 ' '[6] Be brave, and let your heart be strong;
  and wait for the Lord![7]

[1] The meaning of v. 8a is not entirely clear; the translation is only an expedient. (Tr. N.: in RSV v. 8 reads:
  'Thou hast said, "Seek ye my face."
  My heart says to thee,
  "Thy face, Lord, do I seek." ')
[2] * V. 9c reads in RSV, 'thou who hast been my help'.
[3] * V. 10 is in RSV:
  For my father and my mother have forsaken me,
  but the Lord will take me up.
[4] * RSV reads in v. 11b 'on a level path' instead of 'in what is right'.
[5] * RSV reads in v. 12a 'to the will' instead of 'to the greed'.
[6] See BH.
[7] * V. 14 reads in RSV:
  Wait for the Lord;
  be strong, and let your heart take courage;
  yea, wait for the Lord!

The vow in v. 6 is an appropriate conclusion to the first part of Psalm 27. A fresh start is made in v. 7, and what follows is another psalm which differs fundamentally from the poem in vv. 1–6. The dissimilarity of the two parts of Psalm 27 in prevailing tone and mood as well as in the external circumstances and the poet's inward attitude can hardly be accounted for in any other way than by assuming that we are now dealing with an independent psalm by another author.[1] The poet who composed this latter psalm clings in prayer to God who is his only helper; he is oppressed by enemies, forsaken by his next of kin and suffers from a feeling of guilt which presses heavily upon his heart. The simple and sincere honesty expressed in his prayer makes this man worthy of our love. And the way in which he prays with a contrite heart whilst afflicted by enemies and, in so doing, gradually gains the strong assurance which comes by faith, makes his prayer the very model of prayer's true piety. Though the psalm follows closely the traditional stylistic form of the lament, yet because of the personal attitude of the worshipper it has a thoroughly distinct character of its own.

The psalm is entirely lacking in any specific clues which would enable us to fix the date of its composition. It opens (vv. 7–8) with an invocation of God to which a noteworthy motivation is added. In the first part of the psalm (vv. 9–10) the poet, overwhelmed by his feeling of guilt, prays God not to turn away and forsake him. And he concludes the psalm by uttering words which are full of hope, expressing the assurance that his prayer will be granted and calling upon himself to be brave and patient.

The invocation (vv. 7–8)

[7] The psalmist opens the prayer with the customary petition for a hearing. The fact that he at the same time also invokes God's mercy indicates that he himself feels guilty, a feeling which stops him from seeking to deal with his adversaries too hastily and too superficially, and compels him to engage in a searching self-criticism and to surrender to the grace of God. [8] On this premise, too, are based the poet's reflections which encourage him to pray to God in spite of the sin that separates him from communion with God. Whilst he is tormented by the thought of the affliction which he has brought upon

---

[1] The attempt made by H. Schmidt and accepted by Kraus to adhere to the view of the psalm being a literary unit is based on imaginative additions derived from the situation of an accused man, which, however, have no basis in the text itself.

himself by his sin, a recollection flashes across his mind like a light in the darkness; he recalls his traditional covenantal obligation and a word of God which at one and the same time expresses both a command and a promise—'Seek ye my face'. We are reminded of such passages as Ex. 23.17; 34.23; Amos 5.4; Deut. 4.29; Jer. 29.12 ff.; Zech. 13.9; Ps. 50.15. The poet certainly discerns God's command in this word of God and is willing to act in obedience to it; but even more distinctly he can perceive the promise it contains, the invitation of the divine love as well as God's readiness to be gracious to him, as he offers of his own free will to restore the relationship which had been broken through human guilt. 'When you seek me with all your heart, I will be found by you.'[1] This is why the poet dares to ask a favour from God; for he has been told by God himself that he will be willing to listen to him. Trusting in God's promise he will acknowledge God as his Lord and will stretch out his hands towards him, and that even though he is now confronted with the hidden God because of his guilt. Here true faith is at work—living from the promise of God in which it seeks to find its ultimate and exclusive support.

Striving for communion with God (vv. 9–10)

[9] The crucial situation for the worshipper's faith is revealed by the urgency of his repeated entreaties that God may nevertheless not forsake him just now—and by the intense feeling of guilt by which those entreaties are marked. He cannot help owning that God would be right if he did 'hide his face from him' and did 'turn him away in anger'. In this we can gather how vividly the psalmist experiences the pressure brought to bear upon him by the power of God and by his own conscience. He is not facing the whim of a divine despot from which he might be able to extricate himself, but the righteousness of God to which in honesty his conscience feels constrained to submit. And yet he knows—and the crisis consists in this very knowledge—that without God there can be no help for him and no salvation. Thus he flings himself into the arms of God::

> So doth the shipwrecked mariner at last
> Cling to the rock, whereon his vessel struck.[2]

The worshipper's wrestling in prayer makes evident how closely God's judgment and grace are related to each other, and that it is precisely

---

[1] * Jer. 29.13, 14. [2] * Goethe, *Torquato Tasso* 5.

the blending of divine judgment and divine grace which constitutes the peculiar tension so characteristic of the experience
of faith. [10] Whilst he prays, the poet feels comforted and lifted
up by the grace of God. Though his friends have turned their backs
upon him, because they regarded him in his adversity as having
been chastised by God, and though he has been forsaken by his
father and his mother for the same reason, there is a light which
cheers him in his loneliness: 'the Lord will take me up'. For him God
is like a father who sides with his child by accepting him, that is, by
declaring him to be his own child. The love of God transcends every
human standard; it is greater than the love of father or mother.
Forsaken by men the poet finds in the divine character of that love
the assurance of ultimate support. Thus the first part of his prayer
ends on a note of confident hope, the confident hope of a faith which
knows itself to be safe in the communion with God which has been
granted to the worshipper by the grace of God.

A prayer for guidance and protection (vv. 11–14)

[11] The author knows from his own personal experience the
weakness of human nature which is in continual danger of relapsing
into errors and sins and is unable by its own strength to find or
traverse the way which leads to a righteous life. Being in earnest with
his will for repentance and being determined to mend his ways, he
therefore asks God to teach him the way which he wants him to go
and to lead him 'in what is right'. The poet also utters this petition
on account of his enemies. The additional clause 'because of my
enemies' can in the context in which it stands have hardly any other
meaning than that the poet, feeling that the accusations of his
adversaries are justified at least in part, endeavours to give them no
further offence by his conduct, and in this way to remove the basis
for any further accusations so that his enemies may be silenced.
[12] It is only at this point, that is to say, after he has begun—being
firmly determined to put his relationship with God in order—to
apply to his own person and take quite seriously the knowledge that
God is not only gracious but makes demands upon men, I repeat it is
only at this point that the psalmist has attained the inner freedom to
ask God for his protection against the violence and lies of his oppressors. Faith works from within towards that which is without and not
vice versa. Only those who have surrendered their hearts to the will
of God in humility and are ready to act according to that will avoid

the risk of seeking to make God the servant of their own desires in asking for external help. Thus the psalmist's entreaties do not take the form of begging, but become a true prayer. And because the poet has first directed his criticism against his own person and has manifested his will to mend his ways, he is now justified in speaking of the greed, the violence and the lies of his enemies without falling into self-righteous arrogance. If the term 'false witnesses' is to be taken literally, we would have to think of the author as a defendant in a court of justice (see Intr. 78), and his supplication would in that case have to be understood as a prayer for God's help, asking God to act as his counsel in that concrete situation. It is, however, equally possible to interpret the term 'false witnesses' in a more general sense as depicting slander in general, by means of which the powerful adversaries seek to secure for themselves the semblance of being in the right in relation to the poet. However earnest the sincerity of his efforts may be, it does not avail in the face of slander; the psalmist feels he cannot defend himself against that slander. He therefore prays God not to give him up to the plots of his enemies. **[13]** The psalmist has now freed himself from his outward and inward afflictions by means of his prayer and has thus regained the strength which is the fruit of faith. The certitude of having communion with God, of which he had already become conscious as a comforting possibility at the end of the first part of his prayer, though at that time it was intimated to him only in mere outline, is now made manifest in the full clarity and firmness of his faith. The real content of that faith and its goal is to 'see the goodness of the Lord in the land of the living', that is to say, the encounter with God as evidence of his grace and as guarantee of the psalmist's life (see Intr. 72 f.). In this way the poet has drawn near to God in prayer and so has come to believe that through his communion with God he will be delivered from all afflictions and obtain the fulfilment of his ultimate desires. **[14]** God has become to him his only support and his only good. The last verse bears testimony to the strength of that attitude of faith. In that verse the poet, as it were, confronts his own self and arouses himself to courageous hope in God.[1] Here faith is the power which enables the faithful to endure the tension between his present afflictions and his future deliverance from those afflictions. The faith which has been granted the poet by God in prayer is a faith which

---

[1] Kraus regards v. 14 as a priestly oracle foretelling future happiness which is said to have been 'attached' to the psalm.

does not see and yet lives in confident assurance. In the phrase 'and yet' the courage and the new strength are expressed whereby the tension[1] is overcome. 'They who wait for the Lord shall renew their strength.' In prayer and through repentance and faith the poet accomplishes the overcoming of his inward and outward afflictions in a truly remarkable fashion, and the way in which he does it gives this psalm its lasting significance as an example that should be followed by everyone. For it is the way upon which the blessing of God's promise rests.

[1] The moment of 'tension' is contained in the root of the word *qāwā*.

28. THE SILENCE OF GOD

Of David

1 To thee, O Lord, I call, my rock;
  do not turn away from me in silence,
  lest through thy silence I become like those
  who went down to the Pit.[1]
2 Hear the voice of my supplication,
  as I cry to thee for help,
  as I lift up my hands
  towards thy most holy sanctuary.
3 Sweep me not away with the wicked,
  with those who are workers of evil,
  who speak peace with their neighbours,
  while mischief is in their hearts.
4 Requite them according to their work,
  and according to the evil of their deeds;
  requite them according to the work of their hands;
  render them their due reward!
5 For they do not regard the deeds of the Lord,
  nor the work of his hands;
  he will break them down and build them up no more.
6 Blessed be the Lord!
  For he has heard the voice of my supplications.
7 The Lord is my strength and my shield;
  in him my heart trusts;
  I am helped, and my heart exults;
  with my song I will praise him.[2]
8 The Lord is the strength of his people,[3]
  the protection and salvation of his anointed.[4]
9 O save thy people and bless thy heritage;
  be thou their shepherd, and carry them for ever!

[1] * V. 1 in RSV:
  To thee, O Lord, I call;

my rock, be not deaf to me,
lest, if thou be silent to me,
I become like those who go down to the Pit.

  2 * V. 7d reads in RSV 'and with my song I give thanks to him' instead of
'with my song I will praise him'.

  3 See B.H.

  4 * In RSV v. 8b reads 'he is the saving refuge of his anointed' instead of 'the
protection and salvation of his anointed'.

The psalm belongs to the section of laments and thanksgivings
(see Intr. 70 f., 83 f.). On account of its mood and its range of ideas it
falls into two parts which are sharply marked off from each other.
Whereas vv. 1–5 contain a fervent supplication for deliverance from
death and for requital of the wicked, vv. 6–9 comprise a jubilant
hymn of praise sung in gratitude for the answering of the worshipper's
prayer and conclude with an intercession for the people of God. It
can be assumed that the prayer was recited in the Temple (v. 2),
probably in the presence of the covenant community and of the king
(vv. 8 f.) and, consequently, that the psalm may originate in the pre-
exilic cult of the Covenant Festival. It is not possible to ascertain with
any degree of certainty the particular circumstances of the worshipper. In view of God's silence (v. 1) he lives in fear of being swept
away with the wicked (v. 3), but we do not know for certain whether
in this he envisages a general catastrophe threatening everybody as
a punishment to be meted out by God and afflicting the innocent
together with the wicked, or whether he has in mind the divine
judgment which takes place within the context of the festival cult
celebrated at the sanctuary. The similarity of the psalm to Psalm 26,
observable also in other respects, makes the latter interpretation the
more probable (cf. Ps. 26.7, 9). It would then be a question of the
divine judgment, the representation of which enabled the members
of the covenant community to assure themselves again of the salvation and blessing of their God (vv. 8 f.) and probably also to effect,
by means of the blessing and curse, their separation from the un-
worthy elements in their midst (cf. Deut. 27.11 ff.; see Intr. 78). In
this case the 'answering' of the worshipper's prayer is to be found in
the general assurance of salvation which, as in the case of Pss. 18;
20; 21, would have to be thought of as taking place in connection
with the tradition of the theophany. That 'answering' of the prayer
would, moreover, make understandable the worshipper's change of
mood (vv. 6 ff.; see Intr. 79, 84) and at the same time also the hymn
in praise of the salvation granted to the king and the people (v. 8),

showing that these two events arise out of one and the same situation.

[1–2] The worshipper lifts up his hands in the Temple of Jerusalem —originally probably the gesture of one who implores someone else for protection, later on the common attitude of prayer (cf. Pss. 63.4; 134.2; 141.2; I Tim. 2.8)—and he does so towards the 'innermost' place, the Holy of Holies, where Yahweh would appear above the cherubim of the sacred Ark at the time of prayer (cf. I Kings 6.16; 8.6 ff., 30, and Intr. 29 f.). The invocation with which the psalm opens betrays the worshipper's profound inner distress and feeling of insecurity; he does not know whether God will manifest himself to him or, remaining silent, will abandon him to his fate, which for him would be equivalent to death. This demonstrates in an impressive fashion how strongly the godly man is aware that his whole existence depends on a living mutual relationship with God; it demonstrates the great significance which the continual renewal of the assurance of salvation has for the faith of the godly man in the matter of the preservation of that relationship. In this light we must also see and judge the considerable influence which the regular celebration of a cultic feast had in the Old Testament, an influence which should not be underrated. **[3–5]** The psalmist, first of all, prays for himself that he may not be 'swept away' by God with the wicked and evildoers (v. 3; cf. Ps. 26.9); presumably he does so because he not only wishes to have nothing in common with them, but, as is hinted at in his words, suffers himself as much from their hypocritical friendliness as from the malice concealed behind it. The fact that he is disappointed at the abuse of trust and candour in men's intercourse with one another eloquently testifies to the worshipper's disposition of truthfulness. The second part of his supplication deals with the well-deserved requital of the wicked (v. 4). The reason for this (form cf. Ps. 26.10) for 'They do not regard the deeds of the Lord nor the work of his hands,' is usually understood in the light of the warning examples of the judgments which God had passed on the workers of iniquity, reference being made in this connection to Isa. 5.12, 19; 28.21; Hab. 1.5. This interpretation is, however, hardly correct; for in Isa. 28.21 and Hab. 1.5 that meaning is indicated by explicit references; but in Isa. ch. 5 and in the psalm here under discussion we shall have to understand the deeds of Yahweh quite generally in the sense of the saving acts performed by Yahweh for the sake of his people, the saving acts, that is, which were the theme of the cultic tradition (see Intr. 42 ff.). The reproach levelled at the wicked purports that they face the reality of God without being impressed by it, and that they do not take seriously the fact that he is their God. It is in this ultimate religious depth that the cause of their hypocritical and evil actions is to be found. When man no longer directs his thoughts to God, he gets lost, indulging in his own selfish thoughts and passions. The worshipper perceives by virtue of his faith that this negligence of God by men who are entirely given up to their own devices leads to God's judgment, which they so richly deserve, and the announcement of that judgment in v. 5b looks as if it was inspired by thoughts of the prophet Jeremiah (Jer. 1.10; 18.7, 9; 24.6).

The second part of the psalm presupposes that the granting of the worshipper's prayer has actually taken place. The feeling of insecurity and the uncertainty have given way to the joyful assurance of salvation. The simplest way of accounting for this fact is that God's assurance of salvation has been given to the congregation (perhaps in connection with the theophany; cf. the exposition of Pss. 20; 21), and that the lament and the thanksgiving were recited together at the festival cult (cf. Pss. 22; 41, and Intr. 83 f.). **[6–7]** In a hymn ringing with joyful exultation the poet glorifies the God who has granted his prayer and, in doing so, as it were, records the experience of his encounter with God, an experience which has delivered him from the nightmare of his uncertainty and has become for him the source of strong confidence and firm trust in God. **[8–9]** He concludes his personal affirmation of faith in God by vowing that he will praise him with a thanksgiving. What he has experienced does not, however, belong exclusively to him as his personal possession. Being a member of the community of the people of God, he lives as such *in* the fellowship of faith and *from* that fellowship, which is here manifested in the cult; just as, on the other hand, the fellowship of faith feeds on the strength and experience of faith of its individual members. The psalm is a significant testimony to both these facts. The inclusion of the king and the people of God in the hymn and the supplication is therefore closely connected with the personal portion of the psalm with regard to both its subject-matter and its cultic form (cf. Pss. 3.8; 22.3 ff., 23; 73.15; 84.8 f.; I Sam. 2.10; see Intr. 45); in consequence, that inclusion must not result in a separation of the two concluding verses from the rest of the psalm by applying the method of literary criticism and by regarding them as later additions, since such a procedure would mean carrying too far the modern fashion of contrasting the individual and the community. The blessing and the salvation of God, as these are represented and celebrated in the cult of the Covenant as a present reality, are the same source from which the worshipper's certitude of salvation flows, and, because his own assurance of salvation is embedded in the revelation of the salvation granted to the whole people of God, the personal hymn naturally ends in a glorification of God's significance for the king and the people (on the 'grace of kingship', cf. Ps. 18.50; see Intr. 45). God's revelation to his people, which at the climax of the cult's celebration is experienced by the congregation as an encounter with God, has now brought God's silence to an end and has pierced the veil of anxious uncertainty which had lain over the opening words of the psalm as a heavy burden. Like every certitude of faith which is truly alive the assurance of salvation here, too, points beyond itself and the present; it is at once something which the worshipper possesses and for which he prays. For in a living fashion it is embedded in the great work of salvation that binds the past, the present and the future to God's eternal presence (see Intr. 42 ff.). The closing petition asking God to save and bless his people, the 'heritage' of God, is focused on that invisible central point of the whole *Heilsgeschichte*. Intimating man's trust and the safety guaranteed him, the psalm ends in the lovely picture of God as the Good Shepherd (cf. Ps. 23.1–4; Isa. 40.11) and from the viewpoint of the Bible as a whole carries on the continuity of the *Heilsgeschichte* until the One is reached who as the final revelation of the love of God had the right and the authority to apply that picture to himself.

29. THE MIGHT AND GLORY OF GOD
A Psalm. Of David

1 Ascribe to the Lord glory, ye sons of gods,
   ascribe to the Lord glory and might![1]
2 Ascribe to the Lord the glory of his name;
   worship the Lord when he appears[2] in his sanctuary!
3 The voice of the Lord resounds over the waters;
   the God of glory thunders,
   the Lord upon the mighty ocean.[3]
4 The voice of the Lord is powerful,
   the voice of the Lord is full of splendour!
5 The voice of the Lord crushes cedars,
   the Lord crushes the cedars of Lebanon.
6 He makes Lebanon to skip[4] like a calf,
   and Sirion like a young wild ox.

7 The voice of the Lord flashes forth
   licking flames of fire.
8 The voice of the Lord shakes the wilderness,
   the Lord shakes the wilderness of Kadesh.
9 The voice of the Lord makes the hind to calve;[5]
   it strips the forests bare;
   yet in his palace all cry, 'Glory!'[6]
10 As the Lord sat enthroned over the flood,
   thus the Lord sits enthroned as King for ever.[7]
11 May the Lord give strength to his people!
   May the Lord bless his people with salvation![8]

[1] * V. 1 in RSV:
   Ascribe to the Lord, O heavenly beings,
   ascribe to the Lord glory and strength.
[2] On this meaning of *hadrat* cf. Gordon, *Ugaritic Manual*, 1955, pp. 258-544.
(Tr. N.: RSV renders v. 2b, 'worship the Lord in holy array.')
[3] * RSV reads in v. 3c 'upon many waters' instead of 'upon the mighty ocean'.
[4] Cf. Gordon, op. cit., pp. 286/1047.
[5] * RSV reads in v. 9a 'makes the oaks to whirl' instead of 'makes the hind to calve'.
[6] * V. 9c in RSV, 'and in his temple all cry, "Glory!" '
[7] * V. 10 is in RSV:
   The Lord sits enthroned over the flood;
   the Lord sits enthroned as king for ever.
[8] * RSV reads in v. 11b 'with peace' instead of 'with salvation'; cf. however the author's exegesis of the latter phrase at the end of the commentary.

This psalm is a hymn in praise of the theophany of Yahweh and is distinguished by its exquisite poetical beauty and its vigorous power. The tremendous force of the terse and plastically moulded sentences, which in their dull monotone rumble along like the voice of thunder of which the main portion of the hymn speaks, helps, as far as the form of the psalm is concerned, to reinforce the religious impression which has given rise to the composition of the hymn. This seeks to reproduce and pass on that religious impression, that is the awe of the overwhelming majesty of God, filling man's heart with fear and trembling. The poet sketches the earthly picture within the lofty setting of a scene in heaven (vv. 1–2 and 10), a composition which from the point of view of its structure, its colours, and its sentiments combines the strongest contrasts and yet embodies a consistent basis in religious thought. In this song the polarity and tension of faith, welding into a unity man's fear and trembling as well as his exultation and rapture at the presence of God, is expressed in a manner which from the artistic point of view is just as original as it is appropriate to its subject. But however strong the artistic power of the psalm may be, that artistic power is not what matters most. The most important aspect of the psalm is the religious one. The fact that everywhere in the main portion of the song either Yahweh himself or his voice is the subject of the statements made there makes sufficiently clear that what matters most is not the way in which the poet has been capable of grasping and depicting the tremendous natural phenomenon of a thunderstorm but the God who appears in the tumult of the elements and manifests his awesome glory. If the psalm has its origin in an ancient Phoenician hymn praising Baal-Hadad, the weather god,[1] as it is possible to assume on the strength of the Ras Shamra texts, then the fact that so much prominence and emphasis is given to the name of Yahweh simultaneously implies a rejection of the pagan character of the prototype by way of an apologetic statement and further proves the vigorous power of absorption, peculiar to the biblical belief in God, which is able to incorporate alien matter without forfeiting its own fundamental character.

The psalm is a theophany psalm or, to put it more accurately, it is the hymnic response to the appearance and revelation of God at the climax of the festival cult (see Intr. 28 ff., 38 ff., 54 ff.).[2] The opening verses 1 and 2, following the stylistic form of the hymn, contain the poet's solemn calling on the celestial companions of God to ascribe glory to Yahweh and worship him (cf. Isa. 6.3). The main portion of the psalm (vv. 3–9) depicts the power of God, which is at once majestic in its splendour and awe-inspiring, and does so in the form of presenting the effects produced by the 'voice of Yahweh' at the latter's epiphany (cf. Ex. 19.5, 16 ff.). Verse 10, reverting to the beginning of the psalm, praises the King and Lord of heaven, sitting for ever enthroned in sublime imperturbability, and thus effectively contrasts God's attitude with the picture of the raging elements. Verse 11 concludes the hymn by asking God's blessing upon his people assembled to receive from God's hand the realization of their salvation and the renewal of their strength. The rough force and the dogmatic *naïveté* of the idea of God suggest that the psalm dates back to a relatively early period.

---

[1] Cf. Frank M. Cross, *BASOR* 117, 1949, pp. 19 ff., and T. H. Gaster, 'Psalm 29', *JQR* 37, 1946, pp. 54 ff. In spite of the formal Ugaritic parallels we must not simplify matters by classifying the song as a 'Canaanite Psalm'. For v. 8 points to a link with the Israelite Sinai tradition which cannot be disregarded (see below).

[2] If the annotation of the Septuagint ἐξοδίου σκηνῆς, is based on ancient tradition, the psalm was sung on the last day of the Feast of Tabernacles. The Talmud assigns it to the Feast of Weeks.

Introduction: 'Gloria in excelsis' (vv. 1–2)

[1–2] The poet has composed a powerful overture for his hymn. Whereas in the opening verses of other psalms the worshipping congregation, the choir or even the poet himself (Pss. 103.1; 104.1) might be called upon to sing the praise of God, the horizon is here extended to the celestial sanctuary and provides the whole psalm with a setting which alone appears to be adequate to the sublime sovereignty of God. The tongues of men do not suffice to ascribe to God the glory which belongs to him of right. The psalmist therefore calls on the 'sons of gods' to glorify Yahweh. In doing so he may have in mind a scene similar to that which Isaiah (ch. 6) visualized when he was called by God. It is true that here the original polytheistic source of the idea of the celestial companions of God even more clearly visible than in the book of the prophet Isaiah, who only mentions the seraphim as God's servants (see Intr. 41, 61). In speaking only of '*sons* of gods' the poet has however deliberately divested these celestial beings of their quality of being equal to God and has reduced them to the status of servants and acolytes of God in order to throw into relief the monotheistic uniqueness of God so much the more distinctly. The comparison based on the history of religion helps us to realize the strength of the biblical belief in God and the manner in which this was able to overcome the polytheistic phase of religion. What had been the assembly of the several gods in the ancient Orient became for the Old Testament faith Yahweh's celestial court, the members of which simply and solely existed to pay homage to God, do honour to him by their worship, serve him and praise his 'name'. Just as in Job 38.7 the morning stars hail the Creator as witnesses of his creation, so here God's 'glory' and 'might' are to be reflected in the impression which he made on his companions.

The revelation of God's might and glory (vv. 3–9)

[3] The thoughts of the main portion of the psalm move in the same direction, but they contrast most strongly, and therefore exceedingly effectively, with the solemn scene in heaven, being a hymn glorifying God's power and majesty as he is manifested in the devastating and unrestrained raging of the natural elements on earth: 'whilst the songs of the celestial choirs resound in the highest, the terror of God rages over the earth.' The hymn in praise of Yahweh's voice of thunder (in Hebrew *qōl Yahweh*; it recurs seven times in the psalm, imitating by onomatopoeia the awful rumbling of the thunder-claps) begins at the moment when a thunderstorm is gathering over the vast ocean. Since the poet simultaneously speaks of the effects which the storm of God has on the range of high mountains and in the wilderness, it is thereby made clear that what is here recorded is not an impression directly experienced in a thunderstorm. The subject of the psalmist's representation is not a natural phenomenon but the appearance of God. Verse 10 suggests that perhaps the tradition of the taming of the primeval flood lies behind his description (cf. Ps. 77.16 ff. and Intr. 60 f.). This is why the psalmist also refrains from describing in detail the tumult of the raging elements, the roaring storm, for instance, which sweeps before it the waves covered with white crests, though he would have been quite capable of doing so. [4] The psalmist's sole concern is the revelation of the might and glory of God which with lapidary force and terseness he sketches in v. 4, as the theme, so to speak, of the main portion of the psalm. Here terror trembling with fear and rapture shouting with joy are blended with each other and reflect an essential feature of the biblical belief in God, that paradoxical tension between the fear of God and the joy in God, taking the God of the catastrophes just as seriously as the God who stoops down to man to bestow upon him his blessing. It is this tension which accounts for the religious as well as the artistic uniqueness of the whole song. [5] Verse 5 illustrates the awesome majesty of God's appearance by demonstrating the effects it has in the mountains. The strong, colossal trees in the Lebanon, the cedars towering to heaven, are crushed and laid low when Yahweh makes his voice reverberate in the thunderstorm. What does the superb splendour of the far-famed cedars of Lebanon matter in comparison with such dreadful power of the glorious God! Following an old-world conception, the effect of the lightning is here attributed to the thunder. For it is the very effect produced by the roaring thunder which impresses itself upon man's mind most persistently, as we can infer from the reaction of children on such an occasion; so, too, the Teutons named their storm god *Donar* after the thunder (German: '*Donner*'). [6] In v. 6 the poet's intention to give an inkling of the whole magnitude of the absolute power of God over all earthly things stands out even more clearly because it is stressed by the use of an extravagant comparison that is almost grotesque. Though the everlasting gigantic mountains of Lebanon and Sirion (the Phoenician name for Hermon) with their snow-capped summits are firmly established in the depths of the

earth since primitive times, their foundations shake at the appearance
of God so that they skip like a calf or a young wild ox which romps
on the pasture and leaps clumsily. In this comparison the psalmist's
sense of humour is perhaps directed against an ancient tradition
according to which these mountains were regarded as the abodes of
the gods (cf. Ps. 68.15 f.); he thus reveals the inward superiority of his
joy in God's might, which he contemplates with admiration, over the
fear which is aroused in him by God's destructive power—and he
does so without lessening in the least the dreadful impression which
the reality of God produces upon man's mind. **[7]** This is proved by
the next verse which, exhibiting the strong impact of mythological
and anthropomorphic ideas, describes the lightnings as licking flames
of fire which the mouth of God flashes down upon the earth. In this
image of God's fiery breath the personal character of the onslaught of
the might of God has found a graphic form of expression which grips
the imagination. **[8]** Those features probably originate in God's
revelation on Mount Sinai where the voice of God made itself heard
by the people in thunder accompanied by smoke, fire and earthquake
(Ex. ch. 19). The poet follows up the image of the fiery breath of God
by speaking of the earthquake in the wilderness of Kadesh, which lies
on the way from Egypt to Palestine and in the Old Testament tradition is associated with the Sinai tradition. This fact likewise points
to an inner connection of his representation with the Sinai tradition
as archetype. The silent solitude of the wilderness, which as a rule
lies in infinite stillness, is shaken when God makes his awe-inspiring,
majestic voice to resound there. This further magnificent picture
throws into relief, against the background of contrast, the manifestation of the power of the Living God whose energy has the quality of
an earthquake. **[9]** Even the animal kingdom pays tribute to God.
Frightened by the hearing of God's voice, the scared hind comes to
be in labour, and the forest stripped of its leaves by storm and hail
bears witness to the God who causes such a destruction on earth. The
same power, however, which on earth makes man quake with fear
and causes terror and trembling, is regarded in heaven as God's
'glory' (*kabod*; see Intr. 29*, 40). In the celestial palace the choir, the
companions of God, rejoice, shouting with joy one word only—
'glory'—and intend it as a hymn in praise of the august majesty of
God. This sounds like the fulfilment of the request which the poet had
made to the celestial beings at the beginning of the psalm; at the
same time it shows with whom the poet himself sides. The knowledge

that God is the Lord of all things in heaven and on earth drowns the
fear of God's awesome appearance. The psalmist, enchanted by the
august Lord of heaven, can do nothing but gaze at him. Man is lifted
above himself and above his fear by discerning even in the God of the
catastrophes the splendour of his glory; he cannot help worshipping
him by adoring him. [10] This heavenly glory of God remains untouched by the everchanging events that take place on earth. Just as
he did in the days when the great flood of waters came upon the
earth and all men died, so today, too, the Lord still sits enthroned in
sublime imperturbability as the victor over the powers of chaos—
and as the King he will continue to do so in all eternity (see Intr. 33 f.,
44). In the face of the dreadful events and the fearful passing away
which are a continual threat to all earthly things man's faith finds
comfort in God, the eternal King of heaven. Something of the holy
tranquillity of God penetrates the very heart of the tumult on earth—
a heavenly comfort imparting fresh courage to man. It is entirely in
line with this thought and with the ceremony of the cult, the centre
of which is the theophany, that the poet concludes his hymn with an
intercession for his people, asking God to bestow upon them his
strength, blessing and salvation. The vital energy of the Old Testament belief in God springs from the very fact that the people know
what it means to encounter such a mighty God and enjoy the privilege of continually receiving from his hand in a time of festival his
strength, blessing and salvation. It is terrible to fall under the hand
of the Living God, and yet it is this very hand alone which is able to
sustain man and grant him salvation. The stern character of the Old
Testament religion has its roots in this lofty idea of God. The promise
made by such a God holds good; nobody is able to evade his demands; man can put his trust in such a God even if the world should
perish and the mountains should go down into the depths of the
ocean. And the very hope for 'peace on earth', which is expressed in
the last verse of the psalm, relies on the mighty God before whose
glory, the glory that shakes the earth and terrifies man, the poet bows
down in adoration.

30. THANKSGIVING FOR DELIVERANCE FROM THE PERIL OF DEATH

A Psalm. A Song at the Dedication of the House (of God). Of David

1 I will extol thee, O Lord, for thou hast drawn me up,
    and hast not let my foes rejoice over me.

2 O Lord my God, I cried to thee for help,
　and thou hast healed me.
3 O Lord, thou hast snatched away my soul from hell,
　restored me to life and delivered me from death.[1]
4 Sing praises to the Lord, O you his godly ones,
　and testify to his holy memory![2]
5 For his anger is but for a moment,
　and his favour is for a lifetime.
　Weeping may tarry for the night,
　but joy comes with the morning.
6 And yet I was self-confident, saying to myself,[3]
　'I shall never be moved'.
7 Alas, O Lord, by thy grace
　thou gavest me strength and stability;[4]
　thou didst hide thy face,
　and I was dismayed.
8 To thee, O Lord, I cried;
　and to the Lord I made supplication:
9 'What is the good of my death to thee,[5]
　if I go down to the Pit?
　Can the dust praise thee?
　Will it tell of thy faithfulness?
10 Hear, O Lord, and have mercy on me;
　O Lord, be thou my helper!'
11 Thou hast turned for me my mourning into dancing;
　thou hast loosed my sackcloth
　and girded me with gladness,
12 that my soul[6] may praise thee and never be silent.
　O Lord my God, I will testify[7] to thee for ever!

[1] Lit.: 'hast revived me so that I did not belong to those who go down to the Pit'. (Tr. N.: V. 3 reads in RSV:
　O Lord, thou hast brought up my soul from Sheol,
　restored me to life from amongst those gone down to the Pit.)

[2] * In RSV v. 4b is 'and give thanks to his holy name'.

[3] * V. 6a reads in RSV: 'As for me, I said in my prosperity.'

[4] A free translation based on the LXX. (Tr. N.: In RSV v. 7a reads: 'By thy favour, O Lord, thou hast established me as a strong mountain.')

[5] * In RSV v. 9a is 'What profit is there in my death, if I go down to the Pit.'

[6] See BH (it is, however, also possible to translate, though this would sound rather clumsy: 'I will praise thee—thy glory—and not be silent').

[7] * RSV reads in v. 12b 'I will give thanks to thee' instead of 'I will testify to thee'.

According to its superscription the psalm was used at the Feast of the Dedication of the Temple; the superscription, however, contains some features which clearly indicate that it has been added at a later date. This Feast of Dedication (*Hanukkāh*), which was celebrated annually, served to commemorate the restoration of the Temple worship after the Temple had been desecrated by Antiochus Epiphanes. From 165 BC onwards it was at the same time celebrated in memory of the miraculous deliverance of the people from the Syrian overlordship (I Macc. 4.52 ff.; John 10.22). It is precisely this latter fact which was probably the reason why the psalm, which praises the merciful deliverance of its author from grievous affliction and the speedy change of the worshipper's circumstances through God's help (v. 5), could be made serviceable for use at the Feast of the Dedication of the Temple by re-interpreting the experiences of an individual as referring to those of the community. Originally, however, the psalm was not composed for this purpose. On the contrary, it is the thanksgiving of an individual which was uttered in the course of the corporate worship of the cult community in the Temple (v. 4) and presumably on the occasion of a festival pilgrimage. Because the psalm is couched in entirely personal terms, it does not contain any definite clues which would enable us to determine the date of its composition.

Through sickness which brought him to the brink of the grave the poet has been led to reflect seriously on his relationship with God and on his attitude to life. The sudden break in his leisurely existence when 'God hid his face from him' (see Intr. 73) makes him realize that he had built the security of his life on a false foundation. What he was able to call his own in respect of 'strength and stability', did not justify his feeling of pride and security but gave him cause for humility and gratitude; for it was God's grace, as he has now come to realize, to which alone he owes all these things. Thus he experiences also his deliverance from the affliction of suffering as a miracle of divine grace which, as it were, has bestowed upon him new life (v. 3). His heart is full of fervent gratitude, and so he begins his song to which he gives the form of a prayer of thanksgiving characterized by an intense and sometimes dramatic liveliness. Not only the way in which the poet is capable of giving striking and graphic expression to his varied emotions and of making others partners of his own experience, but also the fine construction of his poem, suggest that he is an artist to whom it is given to speak impressively of the things which move his heart. The psalm has been made the object of a poetical adaption in Paul Gerhardt's hymn 'Ich preise dich und singe'.[1]

The prayer opens with a brief hymnic call of the psalmist on himself to give thanks for his deliverance from the peril of death. In vv. 1–3 that deliverance is set forth in an account which is in effect

[1] * This hymn seems not to have been translated into English.

a summary and an anticipation. The poet's call on himself is paralleled in vv. 4 and 5 by his call to the congregation of the godly ones to join in the praise of God; and that call is accompanied by a motivation which accords with the purpose of the call and links together the religious life of the individual and the corporate religious life of the community. In vv. 6–10 the poet once more reverts to a detailed and gripping description of his affliction and of his wrestling in prayer and then concludes the psalm with the statement that his prayer has been answered and with the vowing of everlasting gratitude.

[1] The psalm has arisen out of the worshipper's feeling of gratitude and his need to envisage once more and to portray in all its magnitude the work which God had accomplished in respect of his person. These sentiments impart to the psalm's opening verses the character of a hymn and illustrate the meaning of the poet's introductory call on himself 'I will extol thee, O Lord'. The song is meant to bring once more to the poet's mind and also to reveal to others the 'majesty' of God as this had come to be understood by the poet when God delivered him from the peril of death. Just as a bucket is pulled up from a cistern or as a prisoner is lifted out of a dungeon (cf. Jer. 38.10), so God has snatched him away from the peril of death. To grasp the significance of that act of God the psalmist turns his thoughts to his enemies. How much harder would his suffering and dying have been made by the thought of the scorn and triumph of his adversaries! For besides the grief which he would have felt from the purely human point of view that he had to perish helplessly in shame and disgrace, there was something else at stake for the poet, something which was even more important: the triumph of his enemies would have meant their triumph over his faith as well. Hence what is simultaneously at stake is the poet's faith in the victory of God's cause, of which the godly man regards himself as the advocate and which seems to be imperilled if he should be defeated. Consequently, it is by no means a matter of one party laying claim to God as an ally in human controversies and seeking to make him serve the party's own interests; on the contrary, the concrete situation in which the psalmist finds himself in relation to his enemies makes him to realize how closely his own life is bound up with God's cause. [2] Thus God has secured the victory of his cause in the present case by saving the godly man from destruction and by 'healing' him, though, as we are told later on, he had gone astray. [3] No wonder that in view of this act the worshipper now holds his life in his hands

as something which has been granted to him afresh by God. He had already visualized his soul as ensnared by the underworld, where according to popular belief every relationship with God is cut off. He had already reckoned himself amongst those who go down to the Pit; this shows how grievous had been his suffering and how profound his abandonment by God which, as he had come to realize, was the result of his leading a wrong life and was the punishment for such a life. Because he is delivered from his physical affliction and even more from spiritual distress and has gained a right relationship with his God and a right attitude to life, this life in a deeper sense has now really become for him a new life which he gratefully accepts from God's hand.

[4] Just as he had called on himself to praise the majesty of God, so the poet now calls on the congregation to sing the praise of God. There is no need to explain the psalmist's turning to the cult community by saying that he was probably the leader of the community which he now addresses. For it is entirely in harmony with the nature of the Old Testament Covenant that the personal experience of God gained by an individual does not exclusively belong to that individual but is at the same time the concern of the cult community. Whatever the individual experiences at the hand of God the others share with him. He who behaves in an egotistic, individualistic manner, keeping for himself what has been granted him by God and persisting in the personal enjoyment of things, does not display true faith. For what is ultimately at stake for faith is always the cause of God and not that of man. It is therefore in the direct interest of faith itself that God's nature and rule do not remain hidden but are made manifest also to others. It is the responsibility of every God-fearing man to be a witness to God (see Intr. 86). It is in this light that the call to the godly, 'testify to his holy memory', is to be understood; and the same applies to the fact that the poet finds it possible to express (v. 5) as a universal truth what has first come to him as an entirely personal experience. It is a question of the preservation of the sacred tradition in the cult and of bearing testimony to that tradition as the means whereby God's relationship with his people is characterized in general; and it is this testimony of which the psalmist's personal experience of God is made a part as well (see Intr. 36). [5] The statement 'for his anger is but for a moment, and his favour is for a lifetime' is by no means made in a frivolous spirit; the psalmist does not mean to say that we should not take the wrath of God too

seriously, since it would, after all, blow over soon. On the contrary, since it is the wrath of God, we should take it very seriously. But just because it is the wrath of *God*, it springs from a reality which is different from that from which the anger of man springs. It is not something which is ultimate and final; the purpose of God's anger is not to destroy but to educate. The worshipper has come to know this truth by his own personal experience. The true motive of God's wrath is his *grace* which seeks to assist man in giving up his wrong ways so that he may walk in the way of righteousness. The divine character of God, his 'holy' name, is shown by the very fact that the manifestation of his anger is so entirely different from that of man (cf. Hos. 11.8 f.). The poet is inspired by this blessed and comforting knowledge of God's nature when in a beautiful saying, radiant with the sunshine of the divine grace, he expresses his experience in these words: 'Weeping may tarry for the night, but joy comes with the morning.' His life is established afresh on this miracle of the grace of God; and he wants the congregation to join him in praising that miracle of grace.

This experience of God, which at the same time brought about a change of heart on the worshipper's part, had become so important and so vital to the psalmist that he speaks about it once more in detail, in the form of a confession before God. Such a form implies that what comes into prominence is not a complete biographical, chronological account of all the relevant events, but the decisive religious points such as the realization of man's sin and of God's grace and also prayer. **[6]** The worshipper's past attitude was very different from his present one ('and yet'); he had spent his life in lighthearted self-confidence. It may be assumed that he had not slipped back into a rebellious ungodliness, but that it was rather a question of a piety which had taken a wrong course, seeing only itself, relying only on its own achievements and finding it possible to believe that it offered a firm basis for the worshipper's life. Again, it was a question of a piety which was not aware of the fact that all the pious thoughts of the worshipper, no matter how much they may have occupied themselves with God, had ultimately been focused on the worshipper's own self and on his own security or, at any rate, on a God such as man would like him to be and like to use for his own ends, and not at all on God as he really is—in short, a piety which seeks itself and not God. **[7]** The worshipper is now conscious of the fact that his strength and stability, on which he imagined he could pride himself, had been

nothing but the gift of the grace of God—in respect of which there is
no justification for either pride or self-assurance, but which demands
from man modesty, humility and gratitude; for man's life is wholly
dependent on God and has no protection against him. The poet did
not become conscious of this truth until 'God hid his face from him',
until, lying on the bed of sickness, he was facing the threat of imminent death and the breaking down of all human safeguards. Terrified
by that realization he came to know God as he really is when God
withdrew his aid from him. As so often happens in life, the bed of
suffering also brought this man to his senses and compelled him to
search his own soul. In his adversity he senses the hand of God, who
clearly commands him to desist from the kind of life he had led until
then. He discovers that his sickness is a sign of the wrath of God, who
punishes him for his past life, and he also realizes what the sin is
which he has committed and for which, forsaken by God, he must
now suffer—that self-assurance, which is now taken away from him.
Under the terrifying impression which the experience of his external
and internal affliction had made upon him his eyes are opened to the
tremendous sternness of God's grace, to which he was subjected and
which he came to know when he felt his anger; and it is precisely in
this latter experience that the guidance of the hidden God is at work,
who in his very wrath seeks to lead men to a true understanding of
his grace (see the comments on v. 5). The salient point in the poet's
experience of God appears to me to be the fact that the recognition
of his sin and the perception of the grace of God, without which he
cannot live, begin to dawn upon him at one and the same time—at
the very point at which he was in danger of losing that grace. In this
way the point in question represents the 'crisis' not only of his
external life but to a much higher degree also of his inner life, that is,
of his faith. **[8]** In the light of that truth we can for the first time
fully understand the ardour with which he prays for God's grace and
mercy (the tenses used there point to repeated prayers). **[9]** He
prays by staking his whole existence as a faithful believer on his
prayer. Shall his life come to an end at the very moment when he has
just begun to comprehend that he should have given thanks to God,
to whose grace he owes that life, or would it not rather be his most
urgent duty, a duty demanded by his faith, to proclaim aloud the
grace and faithfulness of God? The will for survival and the duty of
the faithful to stand up for the cause of God here point in the same
direction, and we must not divest the naïve religious motivation of

the worshipper's supplication, arguing that in his case God's cause itself would suffer from his death, since the dead could no longer praise God's faithfulness (cf. the comments on Ps. 6.5)—I say we must not divest that motivation of its serious character by interpreting it as being merely a naïve, impudent, though clever, device of man, a device designed to appeal to God's own interest in the worshipper's survival, though in fact it is only meant to save the latter's life. The question directed to God expresses not so much the worshipper's high esteem for his own self, which at the first glance might be inferred, but rather his later realization of the obligation of faith to bear witness to the grace of God as he has now come to know it. **[10]** That interpretation is in accordance with the humble spirit expressed in the petition for a hearing, for mercy and help. It is in this very prayer that the change of heart on the part of the worshipper is indicated which began to take place during his suffering. Recognizing his sin, he commits himself wholly to the mercy and grace of God which had been revealed to him in his affliction as the foundation that sustains his life.

[11] His prayer has now been answered; the change that has taken place in his heart is followed by a turn in his external fortune. The grace of God has once more visibly intervened in the worshipper's life. Overwhelmed by exuberant joy and fervent gratitude the poet praises the miracle of God's grace which has transformed him from a mournful human being into a joyful one. He has changed the garment of penitence, worn round the body like sackcloth with a rope girdle, and been given a festive dress, in order to take part in a merry festal dance (cf. Pss. 118.27; 149.3); and this change of dress is the outward manifestation of the change that took place in the poet's soul when his prayer was granted, the change from penitence and mourning to gratitude and joy. **[12]** The song concludes with a bright prospect. The gratitude which the worshipper owes to God shall never become silent; he joins the 'everlasting praise' of God to whom he is indebted for his life and for his faith. This action once more throws light on the nature of that faith. His life has been granted to him afresh 'in order that' he may testify to God and never become silent. He takes seriously the obligation which his faith lays upon him to bear witness to God's providential rule by extolling him and singing his praise. He has been taught by his suffering to discard his proud self-satisfaction and to put in its place his joy in God. Thus his song becomes a signpost for all those—and their number is far from being a small one—who have to pass through the same experiences in the course of their life until they have conquered their self-centredness and, delivered from themselves, perceive the grace of God in which they stand and on which alone they can rely.

31. INTO THY HAND I COMMIT MY SPIRIT

To the Conductor. A Psalm. Of David

1 In thee, O Lord, did[1] I seek refuge;
  let me never again be put to shame;
  in thy righteousness deliver me!
2 Incline thy ear to me,
  rescue me speedily!
  Be thou a rock of refuge for me,
  a strong fortress to save me!
3 For thou art my rock and my fortress;
  for thy name's sake thou wilt[2] lead me and guide me.
4 Thou takest[2] me out of the net which is hidden for me,
  for thou art my refuge.
5 Into thy hand I commit my spirit;
  thou hast redeemed me ' ',[3] thou faithful God.
6 I hate[4] those who pay regard to vain idols;
  but I trust in the Lord.
7 I will rejoice and be glad for thy favour[5]
  because thou hast seen my affliction,
  thou hast taken heed of my soul's distress,[6]
8 and hast not delivered me into the hands of the enemy;
  thou hast set my feet in a broad place.
9 Have mercy upon me, O Lord,
  for I am in distress;
  my eye is wasted from grief ' '.[7]
10 Yea, my life is spent with sorrow,
  and my years with sighing;
  my strength fails because of my iniquity,[8]
  and my bones waste away.
11 I have become a disgrace to all my enemies,
  my neighbours wag their heads.[9]
  I am an object of dread to my acquaintances;
  those who see me in the street flee from me.
12 I am forgotten, passed out of mind as one dead;[10]
  I have become like a broken vessel.
13 I heard the evil gossip of many, 'terror on every side!'[11]
  As they took counsel together against me,
  they plotted to take my life.[12]
14 But I have put my trust in thee ' ',[3]
  I said aloud, 'Thou art my God.'

15 My times are in thy hands;
   deliver me from the hand of my enemies and persecutors!
16 Let thy face shine on thy servant;
   save me by thy grace!
17 Let me not be put to shame, O Lord,
   when I call on thee.
   The wicked shall be put to shame,
   let them go dumbfounded to the underworld.
18 Let the lying lips be dumb,
   which speak insolently against the righteous
   in pride and contempt.
19 O how abundant is thy goodness,
   which thou didst hide from thy godly ones,[13]
   which thou hast wrought in the sight of the sons of men,
   in the sight of those who trust thee!
20 In the covert of thy presence thou wilt hide them
   from the hordes[14] of men;
   thou wilt hold them safe in thy shelter[3]
   from the strife of (evil) tongues.
21 Blessed be the Lord,
   for he has been wondrously gracious to me
   in the time of my distress.[15]
22 I had said to myself in my alarm,
   'I am driven far from thy sight.'
   But thou didst hear my supplications,
   when I cried to thee for help.
23 Love the Lord, all you his godly ones!
   The Lord preserves the faithful,
   but abundantly requites him
   who acts haughtily.
24 Be of good cheer and let your heart stand firm,[16]
   all you who wait for the Lord!

[1] * RSV uses the present tense in v. 1a.
[2] * RSV in v. 3b and v. 4a has the imperative.
[3] See BH.
[4] * RSV reads in v. 6a 'Thou hatest' instead of 'I hate'.
[5] * RSV reads 'steadfast love' instead of 'favour'.
[6] * RSV has 'my adversities'.
[7] See BH. (Tr. N.: In RSV v. 9b reads:
   my eye is wasted from grief,
   my soul and my body also.)
[8] * RSV reads 'because of my misery'.
[9] * In RSV v. 11a reads: 'I am the scorn of all my adversaries, a horror to my neighbours.'
[10] * V. 12a is in RSV: 'I have passed out of my mind like one who is dead.'
[11] Probably a proverbial saying (note the alliteration); cf. Jer. 6.25; 20.3, 10; 46.5; 49.29.
[12] * V. 13 is in RSV:
   Yea, I hear the whispering of many—

terror on every side!—
as they scheme together against me,
as they plot to take my life.
¹³ * RSV reads v. 19:
O how abundant is thy goodness,
which thou hast laid up for those who fear thee,
and wrought for those who take refuge in thee,
in the sight of the sons of men!
¹⁴ The meaning is doubtful. (Tr. N.: RSV reads 'from the plots of men'.)
¹⁵ See BH. (Tr. N.: RSV reads in v. 21 'when I was beset as in a besieged city'
instead of 'in the time of my distress'.)
¹⁶ * V. 24a in RSV: 'Be strong, and let your heart take courage.'

The psalm is the simple prayer of lamentation and thanksgiving
of a man who, suffering from illness for many years (vv. 9 f.), calum-
niated and persecuted by haughty adversaries (vv. 4, 18, 20),
shunned by his friends (v. 11), seeks refuge in God in the face of the
threat of a violent death (vv. 13, 5). As in Pss. 22; 28; 30; 41, etc.,
we have to think of the prayer as having been recited in the public
worship of the cult community, after it had been answered (v. 21;
see Intr. 70, 75 f.). The fact that the psalm originated and was used in
the cult entails that its dependence on thoughts in common use, familiar from other psalms and the Lamentations of Jeremiah. Again, when
we consider—and on this point Christ himself in his hour of death is
the immortal example—that the man whose vital energies decline
clings to words which come readily to him from the traditional
treasure of prayer, we shall reject Duhm's view that the psalm is a
compilation of phrases by an author who is well read in the psalms;
equally we reject Kittel's interpretation of the psalm as a literary
scheme without any content of intrinsic personal value. The psalm
does not exhibit a logically constructed thought-sequence; on the
contrary, the development of its thoughts is determined by the psychology and logic of the life of prayer and, in a manner that is true
to life, reflects the vivid movement of the emotions, moods and
thoughts of a soul which in its distress seeks and finds its support in
God. Here we gain an insight into the extent of God's love—by the
fact that the worshipper in spite of all the stereotyped forms to which
he is tied can plainly and frankly confess the spontaneous emotions
that stir his heart in his distress, the constant change of his fluctuating
feelings; by the fact that the worshipper is allowed to come into the
presence of God without hiding anything from him, and, guided in
his prayer by an invisible hand, may gradually proceed from fear and
trembling, as reflected in his urgent petitions, to comfort and

strength, which are granted him in abundance as a result of his surrender to God's hidden goodness. It is in this God that the worshipper confides with the result that he himself becomes the guide and comforter of others who like him have to lead a life of suffering and are in need of comfort. The psalm has been incorporated in the treasury of Christian hymns through Reusner's hymn.[1]

Flight from affliction and refuge in God (vv. 1–8)

[1–4] Like a hunted animal for which the hunter's net, hidden in an ambush, already lies in wait, the worshipper has taken refuge from his persecutors in the sanctuary in order that he might find refuge in his God. But it is not only in an external sense that he takes to flight from his affliction; his supplications, uttered hurriedly and abruptly, are dominated by one thought only—to 'escape' from his affliction before it is too late. His fleeing from adversity is not, however, to be understood in the sense of the irresolute struggling of a man who is in a state of panic and uprooted at heart; for it has a definite objective and, in consequence, becomes the act of seeking refuge in God. In addition to making supplications couched in urgent terms, the worshipper repeatedly expresses his trust in God with equal emphasis, God who grants him support and protection, so that he is like a warrior who can retreat to a stronghold built on a rock or to a fortress. [5] What that support means to him he expresses in v. 5 in a saying which as the last utterance of the dying Saviour is particularly sacred to every Christian, and as such has been, according to tradition, a great help and support for such men—amongst others—as Polycarp and Luther in their hour of death. This simple and strong proof of his trust, by virtue of which the psalmist commits his life wholly into the hand of God, sounds like the utterance of a man who breathes a sigh of relief as he reaches the protection of the walls of the fortress after a hard battle and is conscious of being now out of danger. The submission to God's will cannot in any sense be identified either here or in v. 15 with an 'acquiescent fatalism' (this point in opposition to Duhm); the poet knows in whom he confides: God's 'faithfulness' is his firm support. He is not only safe in that faithfulness but 'redeemed' and delivered from everything which depresses him. He had been privileged to experience the faithfulness of God in his life, and that experience also gives him now the confident hope that he will be delivered from his present affliction. [6] For his trust in God,

[1] * 'In dich hab ich gehoffet, Herr'; Adam Reusner (1496–1575).

which he affirms in connection with the traditional renunciation of idols and their worshippers (see Intr. 76 f.), rests on a firm foundation and cannot come to naught, as is the case with those who rely on 'vain idols'. **[7–8]** As his thoughts turn to God, the fear which tortured his mind vanishes; his vision is now clearer and calmer and, anticipating that God will accord him his help in his affliction, he vows that he will offer him his joyful gratitude for leading him out of the narrow path of his distress into the broad place of freedom. The fact that he speaks of that prospect as if it had already materialized proves the certitude of his trust in God's presence, a certitude which is supported by the tradition of the cult.

The life of suffering (vv. 9–13)

[9–13] It is only at this point, as he has found his support in God in whom he has taken refuge in prayer, that the psalmist utters his lamentation; and he does so not only in order to arouse God's compassion. Rather does his lament spring from the primitive need of all afflicted human beings to alleviate their sufferings by unburdening their hearts to someone who understands them, so that they might be delivered from the agonizing loneliness of their pain. The fact that he may obtain a sympathetic hearing from God, to whom he may disclose everything which distresses him when shunned and forsaken by his earthly friends, is also regarded by the psalmist as a gift of the surpassing grace of God. Thus his lamentation before God becomes for him a recapitulation of his life of suffering, but now he is able to relive that life in the sight of God and under his guidance. Now his soul is no longer seeking to flee from his affliction, but holds out against it and, whilst he once more envisages that affliction, he achieves at the same time a detached view of it. He learns to see it as God sees it, and under God's guidance he is able to conquer it. Every suffering that is brought before God already goes some way towards the overcoming of that suffering. The brief account of the psalmist's suffering, which we cannot read without being moved, is typical not only of what this sufferer had to endure, but also of the conduct of those who brought that affliction upon him and aggravated his suffering. After the description of the physical agony caused by his sickness, by his grief already lasting for years and by the decline of his strength, an agony which has now reached a critical stage because his life is directly menaced by his enemies, his thoughts turn to the disgrace and dismay he encounters in his contacts with his enemies and friends and also to the spiritual distress he experiences because he is lonely, shunned and forgotten already during his lifetime as if he were dead. Hence he asks himself the tormenting question whether his life has still any meaning or value. Arrogance and brutality, lies (cf. vv. 18 f.) and insidious calumny on the part of his persecutors, as well as fear and indifference on the part of his friends, have caused him to lose confidence in his fellow men. And the knowledge that his adversity is closely bound up with his own guilt (v. 10) presses heavily upon his soul. But the very fact that, as the worshipper comes clearly to perceive in the presence of God, from the human point of view there is no remedy for the situation in which he finds himself, makes him understand that he is utterly dependent upon God; thus his suffering drives him directly into the arms of God.

The way to God (vv. 14–18)

[14–16] Turning his thoughts from his affliction to God and taking up again his supplications, the poet thus holds on to the invisible hand which is stretched out towards him from amidst his suffering. He who had become lonely has recovered in God the 'Thou' that means to him not only that he has found refuge in God but also a living communion with God which will compensate him for everything he has lost in respect of his communion with his fellow men. In so far as this latter affliction is concerned, he realizes that in this, too, he is thrown back upon God, in whom he had put his trust already in the past. So, too, now he throws himself into the arms of God by confessing him: 'Thou art my God!'; and not for the first time he sums up in this confession his entire distress and hope. He is conscious of the fact that he is utterly dependent upon God as a slave is on his master. For that reason he gives himself up to God with confidence and humbly commits his destiny into his hand. For it is indeed the gracious God to whom he surrenders, even though his heart is stricken with guilt, and whose help and blessing he invokes. [17–18] At the root of his supplications is the concern that his prayer may not be put to shame, that is, that his trust in God's grace may not be disappointed (cf. v. 22). His trust in God's presence (v. 16 points to the theophany; see Intr. 72 f.) implies, too, as far as he himself is concerned, his certitude of God's judgment, the certitude that God will make an end of the mischief and lies from which he and the other 'righteous ones' have to suffer (see Intr. 29 f., 45 ff., 75 f. on the association of the theophany with the judgment which has its roots in the tradition of the cult of the Covenant Festival).

The life that overcomes suffering (vv. 19–22)

[**19–21**] The way to God does not lead the poet away from suffering, but through the midst of suffering and at the same time beyond it. It is the way from supplication to hope, from trust to certitude, from believing to seeing. With this accords the hymnic frame (vv. 19–21) in which the affirmation of hope is embedded: God stands before the worshipper in the full glory of his divinity (v. 19), and the worshipper stands before God adoring the miracle of grace (v. 21) whereby God lets his face shine upon the worshipper in the midst of the latter's adversity (cf. vv. 16, 20). From the worshipper's experience of his encounter with God in the sanctuary during the theophany springs the certitude that his prayer will be answered (see Intr. 72 ff., 79 f.). God grants him even more than that for which he had been asked. The worshipper may not only be assured of the protection against his persecutors for which he had prayed (v. 20), but at the same time he is granted an insight into his affliction which involves his no longer seeing himself condemned to live a lonely life that has neither meaning nor value; for he learns, as it were, to see his life as God sees it. By virtue of his suffering he has joined the great company of the godly ones whose sufferings are destined to serve as manifestations to men of God's way of dealing with his godly ones (cf. John 9.3; 11.4). And on the basis of his experience (v. 19b) he is now able to gain an insight into the heart of God: the darkness of his adversity is, in fact, nothing but God's hidden goodness which he has in store for those who trust in him. No wonder that this blessed discovery inspires the worshipper to sing the praise of God, shouting with joy. But this is not the whole story. [**22**] The insight he has gained into God's heart broadens into insight into his own heart. This, too, is part of the hidden effect of God's goodness—that the poet now realizes that what constituted his guilt was the weakness of his faith, and that he repents of that weakness which had made him afraid of having been rejected by God. Again, it belongs to the hidden effect of God's goodness that the poet realizes that notwithstanding this weakness of faith he may be assured that God will grant his prayer. Now even the last shadow of his affliction has vanished. There is no longer anything which separates him from his God, not even his suffering. For this has become for him a bond which only binds him to God more closely and more firmly.

The blessing of adversity (vv. 23–24)

[23–24] The conclusion of the psalm corroborates the genuineness
and strength of the knowledge of faith that has been granted to the
poet. As his suffering is made manifest in the presence of the congregation within the larger setting of the revelation of God's 'goodness
and faithfulness' (see Intr. 58 f., 74 f.), with the result that he is no
longer the only one who is burdened with it, the certitude of his
future deliverance and his communion with God, which have sprung
from that suffering, cease to be his exclusive personal possession,
which he may enjoy privately; they lay upon him the obligation to
bear witness to them in the midst of the congregation. As he testifies
to God's faithfulness and exhorts the godly ones to stand firm in the
hope of God, the worshipper himself now joins the great company of
witnesses whom God employs in his service that he may be made
manifest to the world. God has granted a new and much deeper
meaning and value to the worshipper's life and that at the very
moment when he had imagined that his life had lost all meaning.
Again, the worshipper's affliction is blessed by God also in so far as
the loneliness from which he had suffered has become for him the
way that led him to a new fellowship, the great company, that is, of
all the sufferers whom he is able to console with the comfort with
which he has been comforted by God.

32. THE FORGIVENESS OF SINS

A Maskil.[1] *Of David*

1 Blessed is he whose sins are forgiven,
    whose transgression is covered.
2 Blessed is the man to whom the Lord imputes no iniquity,
    and in whose heart there is no deceit.
3 When I declared not my sin, my bones wasted away
    through my groaning all day long.
4 For day and night thy hand was heavy upon me;
    my tongue[2] was dried up[3] as[2] by the heat of summer. *Selah*
5 Thus I acknowledge my sin to thee,
    and I have not hidden my iniquity;
    I said, 'I will confess[2] my sins to the Lord';
    then thou didst forgive the guilt of my sin.
6 Therefore let every one who is godly offer prayer to thee
    at a time when he will find (thee).[4]
    When great waters shall flood the earth,
    they shall not reach him.[5]
7 Thou art a hiding place for me,

thou preservest me from trouble;
thou wilt encompass me with shouts of deliverance.[6]

8 I will instruct you and teach you
the way you should go;
I will counsel you with my eye upon you:

9 Be[2] not like a horse or a mule, without understanding,
which must be curbed with bit and bridle,
else it will not come near to you.[7]

10 Many are the pangs of the wicked;
but grace[8] surrounds him who trusts in the Lord.

11 Be glad in the Lord and rejoice, O you righteous,
and shout for joy, all you upright in heart!

[1] Probably the designation of a specific type of hymn. Its meaning is doubtful (Luther translates it 'instruction' in accordance with the Hebrew term *hiskīl*, that which can be grasped). The translation 'didactic poem', however, hardly corresponds with the content of the thirteen different psalms which have the term *maśkīl* in their titles.

[2] See BH.

[3] Lit.: 'changed'.

[4] Lit.: 'at the time of finding'.

[5] * V. 6 reads in RSV:
Therefore let every one who is godly offer prayer to thee;
at a time of distress, in the rush of great waters,
they shall not reach him.

[6] * RSV adds 'Selah' at the end of v. 7c; and reads 'thou dost encompass me with deliverance'.

[7] * RSV has 'else it will not keep with you' instead of 'else it will not come near to you'.

[8] * In RSV the words 'steadfast love' are used in place of 'grace'.

This favourite psalm of Augustine, which Luther has called one of the Pauline psalms (the others are Pss. 51, 130 and 143), is the second of the seven penitential psalms (Pss. 6; 32; 38; 51; 102; 130; 143) of the Ancient Church. It is, however, not a proper penitential prayer such as, for instance, Psalm 51, a penitential prayer that is uttered whilst the worshipper is still under the direct influence of the affliction of sin. It is rather a psalm of thanksgiving which looks back upon the psalmist's penitence and upon the forgiveness of sin he has obtained and derives from the psalmist's personal experience the lesson that should be learned by every God-fearing man. The juxtaposition of the two motives of thanksgiving and instruction causes a mixed style, so that the prayer of thanksgiving is interspersed with fragments which are closely connected with the 'Wisdom Literature' (see Intr. 88). The poet had tried to hide his sin from God. The result was that his heart was afflicted by very severe qualms

of conscience, and the agony thus inflicted upon him was not taken
from him till he brought himself to make a sincere confession before
God. The happy feeling of deliverance engendered thereby and the
certitude of having obtained the forgiveness of his sins constrain him
to warn others against the wrong course he had taken in the past and
to guide them into the true way; the way is that they should not refuse out of sheer obstinacy to have anything to do with the grace of
God, but should yield to it by showing candour and trust. This
reaction is entirely understandable from the psychological point of
view and accords with the style of thanksgivings (cf. Pss. 34.11 ff.;
40.4). Hence it is not necessary to adopt the view that we are dealing
here with different speakers in order to comprehend the inner dynamic of the song. Though the psalm is not of the style of the front rank
of works of art, it is nevertheless, on account of the directness of the
experience expressed therein, one of the Psalter's most powerful testimonies to the struggles and qualms of conscience in which a man
is involved who cannot run away from his God. The peculiar quality
and permanent value of the psalm are to be found in the realism of
its presentation, which makes us sensitive to the true significance of
conscience.

Like other psalms, this song, too, is couched in terms so entirely
personal that the external circumstances of the life of its poet can be
established with just as little certainty as the conditions at the time
of its composition. According to v. 11 the song was recited during the
worship of the cult community. The structure of the poem exhibits a
certain uniformity; each pair of verses are co-ordinated, and v. 5,
which stands by itself, also fits into this pattern. The psalm opens with a
'Beatitude' (vv. 1–2) which puts at the head of the psalm in a general
form and, as it were, as the psalm's theme the poet's personal experience of the blessing of the forgiveness of sins. Verses 3–7 describe in
the form of a confession before God the worshipper's arduous way
that has led him through the midst of qualms and strivings of conscience to the confessing of his sins before God and to their remission,
and has made him realize the significance which his personal
experience has for the God-fearing as a whole. The first part of
the psalm concludes with a personal note, expressing the psalmist's
trust in God and his hopeful outlook into the future. In the second
part (vv. 8–11), the psalmist draws some instructive conclusions from
his own experience by uttering a general warning against hardness of
heart and by exhorting his fellow men to put their trust in God's

grace. In accordance with the individual outlook in the first part
(v. 7) the general second part concludes with a call to all the godly
ones to rejoice and be glad in the Lord, a call which at once looks
back into the past and forward into the future.

[1–2] The poet wrote the two 'Beatitudes' with which the psalm
opens with his heart's blood. The blessed knowledge of the religious
truth they express has been gained by this man in the course of an
agonizing battle which he fought out in his soul against self that
he might attain the truth that holds good before God. Like the azure
which arises behind the storm-cloud, that knowledge appears before
the mind's eye of the poet as the victor's wreath which God presents
to him after he has mastered his own self and has surrendered to
God. It is a matter here of a knowledge which the psalmist has
gained by staking without reservation his own existence on it, the
knowledge, that is, which comes by faith in the deepest and widest
sense of that term. In speaking quite generally of the blessing implied
in the fact that God 'takes away' a man's 'sin', 'covers his transgression' and 'imputes no iniquity to him', the psalmist thereby
expresses his own blessedness, which these statements reflect. The
fact that the phrases in question, probably used in the psalm as
synonymous, are repeated three times indicates the fundamental
significance which the forgiveness of sins has for the life of this man.
The phrases he uses make evident that in speaking of the forgiveness
of sin he has in mind not the obliteration of sin or the blotting out of
the sinful deed and of its effects, which extend beyond the sinner's
person, so that what had been done would be undone; on the contrary, the forgiveness of sin is God's doing, who takes away the
burden of guilt which the sinner carries, delivers him from the
torment of self-recrimination, though this is justified when he looks
back on his sin, and who restores his relationship with God, broken
by his sin. On the part of man, that relationship with God is possible
only on the basis of complete truthfulness. Only those who are pure
in heart shall see God; this is why the poet, looking back once more
on his own experience, where only his sincere candour in the sight of
God paved for him the way to the forgiveness of his sins, adds the
following condition which man has to fulfil: 'in whose heart there is
no deceit'. He does not mean by this that we must be sinless, but that
we must be absolutely truthful in our relationship with God and with
ourselves; for man's absolute truthfulness in his relationship with
God and with his own self form, together with God's grace, the two

foundation-pillars not only of penitence but of man's whole relationship with God.

[3-4] The subsequent account of the inner struggle, through which
the poet had to go until he obtained the remission of his sins, is a
deeply moving example of such sincere conduct. The fact that he
feels constrained to let God once more gain an insight into the
uttermost depths of his conscience's strivings, of which he himself is
deeply ashamed when he recalls them (notice the form of prayer in
vv. 4-7 in which God himself is addressed!), proves more clearly
than anything else that to display the utmost candour in the presence
of God, no matter what the cost will be, still remains for the psalmist
the foundation of his relationship with God after he has obtained the
forgiveness of his sins. Since he gives his account the form of a confession before God, the poet proves by his very action the truth of
what he stated in v. 2. The way in which he speaks of his inner
struggle without sparing himself in any way shows the courage he
displays and the self-conquest he has achieved; it also shows that
courage and self-conquest were required from him that he might be
able to confess this truth before his own self and before God. He had
been on the point of fleeing from God and of evading his obligation
to give an account of himself to God by hiding his sins from him. Yet
there is no escape from God. Though the psalmist kept silence, there
was no peace in his heart. His soul is eaten up with worry and consumed by a burning heat. The voice of his bad conscience does not
allow him that peace of mind which he seeks to enforce by holding
his tongue; he cannot help crying out aloud as he is daily tormented
by fear in which he discerns the hand of God that presses heavily
upon him, the hand of God from which he would rather flee. Sudden
terror causing his 'tongue to dry up', and hot flushes as if he were
feverish, a depression that paralyses him and robs him of his vitality
and of the power of making decisions, so that he believes himself to
be withering away—these are the physical effects of the inner battle
which the man who refuses to acknowledge his sin fights against God,
because the self-assurance that spurs him on to bold defiance leads
him to imagine that he is not answerable for his conduct to anyone!
With striking realism the psalmist has stated what, in fact, remains of
that seeming audacity: a wretched creature who is consumed with
fear and anguish because the hand of God is upon him and holds him
down, that hand which no human being can shake off. It is only in
the presence of the ultimate reality of God that the reality of man, as

it actually is, is fully revealed. And there is no other way of appearing before God than the one which at its starting-point is characterized by the word of the prophet Isaiah which he used when he spoke about his encounter with God (Isa. 6.5): 'Woe is me! For I am lost.'

[5] Man really stands before God and so at the same time is subject to him only if he is entirely honest with himself, that is to say, only if he realizes that his own nature, when compared with that of God, is different and inadequate or, to use religious language, is sinful. Just as Isaiah did in the hour of his calling, so the psalmist, too, stood before the holy God, and this is the only way which enables him to live a life that is worth living. Thus he has obeyed the voice of God which spoke to him through his conscience. God and truth have won the victory in his soul. Conquered by God, he has conquered himself and has confessed the guilt caused by his sin without hiding anything. His confession of sin implied his repentance; for the fact that he speaks with candour of his sin as sin and confesses his guilt as such makes sense only on the assumption that he truly repents of his sins and longs for a clean heart (see v. 2). Now he feels that he is relieved of the burden which pressed heavily upon him and tormented him; now peace has entered his soul, and he can again freely lift up his eyes to his God. Turning his thoughts to God and experiencing the deliverance wrought in his heart, he discovers that God has forgiven him the guilt of his sins. The peace that fills his religious consciousness vouches for the remission of his sin. Because of the profoundly spiritual quality of his nature, the psalmist has no need of the material execution of a propitiatory sacrifice in order to be assured of his reconciliation with God. For him there is indeed nothing which man can do to obtain the forgiveness of his sins except that he be truthful, truthfulness being man's willingness to turn to God altogether. For even behind the violent emotions which deeply affected his soul during the strivings in his conscience he sees the hand of God, which guides him to that stage at which God can bestow upon him the grace of his forgiveness. For this worshipper, too, it is in the last resort the goodness of God which guides man to penitence, though he has to pass through bitter experiences.

[6] This background of God's grace teaches the poet to grasp the significance which his own experience has for all God-fearing people. God is willing 'to let himself be found'. Speaking of the moment

of finding God', the psalmist has in mind, first of all, the moment of God's appearance at the festival cult when the worshipper found his gracious God. It depends, however, on the individual man whether or not he finds God. It comes to pass only if the godly man readily and candidly pours out his soul before God in prayer for his grace and does not defiantly turn away from God in the hardness of his heart. Then prayer becomes for the man to whom God is gracious a strong protection, so that life's temptations and afflictions cannot affect him. It accords with the whole tenor of the psalm that the picture of the great floods of water which do not reach the worshipper is not only meant in the sense of the worshipper's preservation from outward disaster but even more in the sense of his remaining inwardly un-assailable by affliction and danger. [7] The worshipper feels that he is safe in God's grace from any kind of trouble. His delight in God's presence encompasses him like a bulwark. When he comes to think of his deliverance from the agony of sin he rejoices in his heart and is no longer afraid, no matter what the future may hold in store for him. Thus the end of the first part of the psalm resounds with the utter happiness of a man whose sins are forgiven.

[8–10] The words of the second part of the psalm are addressed to someone else. Using the form of a didactic exhortation and speak-ing in a much more restrained fashion, the poet now turns to the community of the godly ones whom he wants to spare the bitter experience of his own struggle. It accords with the style of the epi-grammatic sayings of the Wisdom writers that the psalmist uses the word 'you' in addressing them, as indeed his attempt to make the truth of his experience clear to them by using parables (v. 9) and proverbs (v. 10) throws into relief, in sharp contrast to the direct character of the first part of the psalm, the didactic element inherent in the maxims of the Wisdom writers. The detailed introduction of the second part of the psalm, which comprises the whole of v. 8, is probably in part caused by the change of subject that takes place in the second part.[1] If the first part did not precede, we would hardly be able to guess from what we read in the second part only how much personal effort is involved in the sense of duty which is evident from the warnings of the poet. With the help of a parable he tries in v. 9 to keep his fellow believers from the bitter struggles through which he has passed, warning them against behaving like a horse or a foolish

---

[1] Kraus's interpretation of v. 8 as a divine promise of salvation is at variance with the style used here, a style typical of the Wisdom literature.

mule which can be compelled to follow man only by the use of force. The point of comparison is to be found not only in man's obstinate perseverance in self-will, but also in the necessity of applying force. In the poet's view it is foolish to persist in self-will and in hardness of heart in relation to God, since God in such a case overcomes man's obstinacy by force. The poet has testified to this fact impressively enough by pointing to his own experience. There are only two possible ways of acting which the psalmist, using the form of a proverb, leaves open in v. 10 to the choice of man, a choice which should not be difficult for any sensible human being: one way, which leads to many torments, is to persist in sinning and, in hardness of heart, to care no longer for God, as the wicked do; the other way, which leads to blessedness, is to trust in God, to pour out one's heart to God candidly and truthfully, and to acknowledge him as the Lord, so as to partake of his grace in virtue of such 'faith'. The poet walked both ways and, passing through an agonizing struggle in his conscience, has thus come to realize that the first way is the wrong one. This is why he points so forcibly to the second way. [11] In conclusion the poet calls upon all the 'righteous' and 'upright in heart' (see Intr. 84) to be glad in the Lord and to join in the exultation which fills his soul. In doing so it is as if he wanted to anticipate the resolve of the godly ones to walk the way of grace and truth; at the same time he makes this call upon the godly ones resound with his own delight in God's forgiveness. Through faith his own experience becomes a testimony to God's grace and a responsibility towards his brethren.

The beginning of the psalm and the end of its first part are harmonized at the conclusion of the whole psalm in a mighty symphony of man's delight in God. It is this delight of man in God and not man's material prosperity which is the true goal of the God-fearing man. And the grace of God made manifest in the forgiveness of sins prepares the way to that lofty goal for anyone for whom truth in the sight of God is at stake. Thus the psalm is one of the most impressive Old Testament testimonies to the truth which the New Testament expresses in I John 1.8 f. as follows: 'If we say we have no sin we deceive ourselves, and the truth is not in us. If we confess our sins, he is faithful and just, and will forgive our sins and cleanse us from all our unrighteousness.'

33. IN PRAISE OF GOD

1 Rejoice in the Lord, O you righteous!
  Praise befits the upright.
2 Praise the Lord with the cither,
  make melody to him with the harp of ten strings!
3 Sing to him a new song,
  play skilfully on the strings at the shouts of joy.[1]
4 For the word of the Lord is upright;
  and all his work is done in faithfulness.
5 He loves righteousness and justice;
  the earth is full of his grace.[2]
6 By the word of the Lord the heaven[3] was made,
  and all its host by the breath of his mouth.
7 He gathered the waters of the sea as in a bottle;[2]
  he put the deeps in storehouses.
8 Let all the earth fear the Lord,
  let all the inhabitants of the world
  stand in awe of him!
9 For he but spoke, and it was done;
  and as he commanded, so it stood forth.
10 The Lord brought[4] to naught the counsel of the peoples;
  he frustrated[4] the plans of the nations.
11 The counsel of the Lord stands for ever,
  the thoughts of his heart from generation to generation.
12 Blessed is the nation whose God is the Lord,
  the people whom he has chosen as his heritage!
13 The Lord looks down from heaven,
  he sees all the sons of men;
14 from where he sits enthroned he looks forth
  on all the inhabitants of the earth,
15 he who fashioned[4] the hearts of them all,
  and observes all their deeds.
16 In his sight no king is saved by his great army;
  no warrior delivered by his tremendous strength.[5]
17 The war horse is a vain hope for victory,
  there is none who can be saved by its strength.[6]
18 The eye of the Lord is on those who fear him,
  on those who wait for his lovingkindness,[7]
19 that he may deliver their soul from death,
  and keep them alive in famine.
20 Our soul waits for the Lord;
  he is our help and shield.
21 For our heart is glad in him,
  because we trust in his holy name.
22 Let thy grace, O Lord, be upon us,
  even as we wait for thee.[8]

[1] * RSV reads 'with loud shouts' instead of 'at the shouts of joy'.
[2] See BH.
[3] In the Hebrew text the plural is used. (Tr. N.: This is true also of RSV.)
[4] * In RSV the present tense is used.
[5] * V. 16 in RSV:
 A king is not saved by his great army;
 a warrior is not delivered by his great strength.
[6] * V. 17b is in RSV 'and by its great might it cannot save'.
[7] * In RSV v. 18b reads 'on those who hope in his steadfast love'.
[8] * V. 22 in RSV:
 Let thy steadfast love, O Lord, be upon us,
 even as we hope in thee.

From the opening words of the psalm we can conclude that the psalm is a festival hymn, appointed to be recited in the worship of the cult community (the 'righteous', 'upright', v. 1; see Intr. 79, 84) to the accompaniment of cither, harp and loud 'shouts of joy'. It can hardly be assumed that the psalm served to commemorate a great act of deliverance whereby Yahweh saved the nation from the threat of some peril, such as the miraculous deliverance of Jerusalem from the siege of Sennacherib (701 BC); the hymn is couched in too general terms to suit such a purpose. Again, a purely eschatological interpretation of the psalm is not really plausible either, since the colours used in the psalm's imagery are much too soft to accord with such an interpretation. The general character of the hymn and the fact that it makes use of traditional forms and thoughts much more readily lend themselves to the view that it was composed for the Covenant Festival which was celebrated at New Year. For in that feast the traditions of the Creation (vv. 6 ff.) and of the *Heilsgeschichte* (vv. 10 ff.), which are taken for granted in the psalm, had their place; and it is in that feast, too, that the congregation experienced the presence of their divine Lord (vv. 13 ff.) and their election by him (v. 12) as well as his grace (vv. 18 ff.). Just as in our public worship on the eve of the Old Year's passing and the coming of the New, when praise and thanksgiving combine in a backward and a forward glance with supplications full of confidence, and the congregation begins the hymn 'Now thank we all our God'[1]—so in a quite similar vein the psalm praises the providential rule of the great God 'as it was in the beginning'[2] and derives therefrom strength to look hopefully into the future. The way in which the psalm's thoughts are focused on God

[1] * This is the English translation by Catherine Winkworth of the German hymn 'Nun danket alle Gott' by Martin Rinkart (1586–1649).
[2] * This is from the third verse of 'Nun danket' (literally translated).

imparts to the simple hymn forcefulness and conciseness and shows how powerful were the religious energies aroused and kept alive in the Old Testament festival cult.

The structure of the psalm does not enable us to establish a definite order of its verses; on the other hand, the following thought-sequence can be observed: the introduction (vv. 1–5), which contains a generally motivated call to sing a hymn, is followed by the hymn itself which first testifies in vv. 6–9 to the power of the 'word of the Lord' at the creation of the world and then in vv. 10–12 to his 'counsel' in history. The subsequent sections speak of the presence of God, who tries the hearts of men; they speak of his omniscience, which is the basis for man's responsibility (vv. 13–15) and trust (vv. 16–19). The psalm concludes with the congregation's affirmation of faith in God as their Helper and Protector and, as the congregation turns its thoughts to the future, with a petition for his grace.

[1–3] The call, three times repeated, to sing a song of rejoicing and to bear 'testimony' to God by means of a hymn to be recited to the accompaniment of cither and harp, indicates the cultic, liturgical occasion for which the psalm is designed. The members of the covenant community are addressed by the honorific title 'the righteous' and 'the upright'. In this fact as well as in the statement 'praise befits the upright' is to be found God's claim which is part of the liturgical tradition (see Intr. 36), a claim to which the congregation is willing to submit. The psalm is a 'new song' which was composed to be used on the festal occasion of the 'renewal' of the Covenant (see Intr. 61 f.). We do not know the manner in which this song was recited, in particular whether it was recited by the poet or by the precentor or by several choirs. It speaks in a new way of the ancient truths transmitted in the festival cult. [4–5] First, prominence is given to four statements of faith intended to form the basis of the whole psalm. This procedure looks as if these statements are meant to offer a general thematic summary of what is to be set forth later on in more detail in the various sections of the hymn. Were these verses perhaps sung by the choir, as with psalms containing refrains? At any rate, they show the facts on which the Old Testament faith is based. The hymnic predications are meant to be understood not as dogmatic propositions but as the fruit of man's experience in his everyday life, the truth of which had continually been rediscovered afresh and had been found to hold good throughout many generations; we are therefore justified in regarding them as testimonies of a living faith. Faith has its very foundation in the truth of God's Word, in the faithfulness of his actions. God is not, as so many gods of the ancient oriental world around Israel were, a Being to whose incalculable moods the godly one is exposed; nay, the promise he makes he will surely keep. His actions are not the effect of an impenetrable despotism, but are carried out with a reliability and in an order which are perpetually the same. And his 'faithfulness' lies in the fact that man can absolutely trust this God, no matter what he may do. 'Righteousness and justice' are the ordinance of the Covenant which God himself observes and which is therefore binding also on the life of the God-fearing man; it is the ordinance which alone makes it possible for a community to remain in being. The people of Israel had to experience the reality of that ordinance of God in their very own lives and through their history had to testify to the truth of the saying: 'Righteousness exalts a nation, but sin is a reproach to any people' (Prov. 14.34). And yet, 'righteousness' is not the last word that can be said about God. For behind all things, even behind the divine order of law, there is his grace. That the God who has proved himself to be the Lord of the earth and of the nations pays heed to man at all and takes care of him, though man on his part is not in the least entitled to lay claim to such an action by God, and indeed has on the contrary very frequently turned his back on him, is the greatest miracle in the eyes of faith, a miracle from which the faithful believer continually draws new vital energy. It is only to such a profound insight of faith that the fullness of the riches of God's acts of grace is disclosed so that the psalmist is able to say, 'The earth is full of his grace', words which are reminiscent of the cultic hymn in Isa. 6.3.

God's Word in creation (vv. 6–9)

[6–9] The psalm goes far back to produce a vivid impression of the truth and efficacy of the Word of God. It borrows from the tradition of creation (see Intr. 34, 60 f.) the feature that the Word of God, and indeed even the breath of his mouth, suffices to create the immeasurable heaven and the innumerable host of stars. What a God must it be who 'gathers' the huge masses of water that fill the ocean, as the farmer pours water into a bottle made from goatskin or fills his granary with corn! Though the Babylonians might tell of the mighty battle which their god fought against the monster of the primeval sea until he was able to tame it, the Bible conceives God as one whose majesty and power are infinitely more sublime. To the man who sees himself confronted with these interrelated phenomena, nothing is left but to take God absolutely seriously as the One who really is and by whom all things are made—and, in consequence, to adopt that attitude of mind which the Bible calls the fear of God. This is why God's Word is so entirely different from the word of man; 'he but spoke and it was done.' The truth of the Word of God here comprises not only what we understand by the ordinary sense of the term but includes God's effective power of bringing things into being; in other words, his power of creating reality. The prophets understood it in this deeper sense and acted upon it with equal seriousness when they knew themselves to be called to proclaim the Word of God as a word that works judgment and salvation. The dynamic power of their faith and their preaching is due to the fact that that Word possesses great effective power. According to the Bible to be subject to the Word of God means to be subject to the reality of God. It is from this perspective that the psalm envisages and praises God as the Creator.[1]

God's 'counsel' in history (vv. 10–12)

[**10–12**] The contemplation of history to which the poet now turns throws the majestic power of God no less into relief than the reflection on the creation effected in Nature. Here, too, the psalmist refers to the cultic tradition. The eyes of faith perceive behind the disorder of national conflicts the invisible hand of God, who shapes the history of the world according to his eternal purpose. Though the great nations that dominated the world may devise clever and effective plans, they have been brought to naught whenever they were at variance with the decree of God. The people of Israel, whose own destiny was so tragically bound up with the policy of the great empires in antiquity, had experienced in their own history the coming and going of these kingdoms and had learned from their own fate, subject to so many changes, this one lesson: there is only one plan which endures for ever, and that is God's plan. From this nation emerged that great vision of history which for the first time in the history of the world grasped and expressed the fact that the divine purpose inherent in everything which happens in the world is the

[1] In this connection the biblical significance of the Word of God differs from the view of the divine word as a creative power, known to have been held in Egypt and Mesopotamia; according to this the creative power did not go beyond an involvement of the divine word in Nature, an involvement which for the most part was tied to magic.

meaning of history as a whole. According to the Bible, to understand history means to understand it from the perspective of God. As believers, therefore, that they are the chosen people of God, the people of Israel also understood their own history as the realization of the divine decree of their salvation. We are here confronted with nothing less than the knowledge that comes by faith, a faith which discerns the saving will of God in the tortuous paths of the people's history, in Israel's afflictions and perils, in her rise and decline, and in the help and deliverance which was granted her. And that saving will of God imparted to these events their ultimate meaning and determined their divine purpose and object. It is in this sense that we understand the psalmist's joyful testimony to the God who revealed himself to his people as their Lord.

Under the eyes of God (vv. 13–19)

[**13–15**] It is entirely in keeping with the belief in God attested in the Old Testament tradition of the Covenant that the psalm follows up the traditions of creation and of history by speaking of the responsibility laid upon man in his relationship with God. For in the Old Testament the interpretation of creation as well as of history, an interpretation that is based on faith, is always related to the present; and this fact is closely bound up with the 'representation' of the *Heilsgeschichte* in the festival cult as a living reality (see Intr. 28 ff., 42 ff., 58 ff.). The recognition of God as the Lord of Nature and of History implies that at the same time a decision is made about the believer's own existence; by this he submits his own person and his whole life to the claim of the God who reigns over the whole world. Consequently the belief in God as the Lord of Nature and of History comprises the sphere of man's intellect as well as that of his will; indeed, according to the Bible, that belief is primarily a matter of man's thinking and behaving in his everyday life. It is in this sense that we have to understand the poet when he looks up to the Lord and King of heaven whose searching eyes he sees turned towards all the sons of men in the hallowed hour. Nothing remains of the divine presence hidden from him who created the heart of man, not even the most secret thoughts in the innermost recesses of man's heart. Whatever man may do is done in the sight of the omniscient God; and this accounts for the ultimate seriousness of man's responsibility. [**16–19**] Man is aware of the fact that he is watched by God, and that awareness, which in vv. 13–15 is presented as the motive for his obedience, becomes in the next section the motive for his confidence. The God who makes demands upon man grants his presence to those who fear and trust him, because he is at the same time the God of grace. The psalm's second main portion is entirely parallel to its first in so far as in either case faith in all its fullness is portrayed as arising out of a mixture of fear and trust. The poet confronts the wrong kind of trust with the right kind of trust and so achieves a striking contrast. What the prophets continually tell their people when they boast of their own strength or look out for powerful allies who would support their policy, the psalmist, too, condemns as manifestations of a wrong trust: neither powerful armies nor armaments nor human strength, be it ever so strong, can be relied on in any way.

> 'With force of arms we nothing can,
> Full soon were we down-ridden.'[1]

'Deliverance' and 'salvation' only God can grant. He can deliver man even from death; man's life is in God's hand, and he can preserve it even in a calamity which cannot be overcome by man, no matter what kind of help he may be able to give (in a way similar to the prophets who spoke of 'hunger and sword', death and hunger seem here to have been singled out as typical examples of all sorts of afflictions). The godly one knows who alone is to be feared and in whom alone he can trust, and because he sees that the eyes of the gracious God are towards him, he also knows himself safe in God's lovingkindness; trusting in him he can look forward to the future without fear and can even face its dangers without being perturbed. This is the right kind of trust, and from it flows a strength which is greater than any strength which man would ever be capable of mustering by his own efforts.

[20–22] In the song's last portion the theme of trust appears in the form of a testimony and supplication of the congregation, and is closely linked up with the statements made in vv. 18 and 19 in the form of a hymn. The psalmist's thoughts are now turned from the past and the present to the future. The joy, the trust, and the hope of the godly depend on the God who has once more manifested in the midst of the congregation his holy name, the majestic quality of his nature, his will and his providential rule (see Intr. 29 ff., 38 ff.). Man's hope is founded on his experience; those who cannot grasp God's

---

[1] * The first two lines of the second verse of Martin Luther's hymn, translated by Thomas Carlyle as 'A safe stronghold our God is still.'

providential rule in the past cannot hope either. The greatness of the Old Testament faith consists in the fact that it can draw the strength which hope imparts from the past, from God's creation and history. The guarantee for whatever the future may hold in store lies in nothing less than in the God who has continually proved himself to be man's 'help and shield'. The psalm closes with the prayer that God's grace may descend upon those who, waiting for him, reach out towards him—a beautiful picture of the way in which God's grace and man's faith mutually respond to each other. It is a powerful confession of faith in God, in which possession and hope are equally strong.

34. O TASTE AND SEE THAT THE LORD IS GOOD

Of David, when he feigned madness before Abimelech, so that he drove him out, and he went away.[1]

1 I will bless the Lord at all times;
    his praise shall continually be in my mouth.
2 My soul shall glory[2] in the Lord;
    let the humble[3] hear and be glad.
3 O magnify the Lord with me,
    and let us exalt his name together!
4 I sought the Lord, and he answered me,
    and delivered me from all my fears.
5 They looked on him, having flocked to him;
    their faces had no need to be ashamed.[4]
6 Here is a humble man;
    he cried and the Lord heard,[5]
    and saved him out of all his troubles.
7 The angel of the Lord encamps around those who fear him,
    and has delivered them.
8 O taste and see that the Lord is good!
    Blessed is the man who takes refuge in him!
9 O fear the Lord, you his saints,
    for those who fear him have no want!
10 Lions suffer want and hunger;
    but those who seek the Lord lack no good thing.
11 Come, O sons, and listen to me,
    I will teach you the fear of the Lord.
12 What man is there who desires life,
    and covets many days, that he may enjoy good?
13 Keep your tongue from evil,
    and your lips from falsehood and deceit!
14 Flee from evil, and do good!
    Seek peace, and pursue it!

15 [6] The eyes of the Lord are toward the righteous,
   and his ears hear their cry.
16 The face of the Lord is against the sinners,
   to cut off the remembrance of them from the earth.
17 When they cried for help, the Lord heard them,
   and delivered them out of all their troubles.[7]
18 The Lord is near to the brokenhearted,
   and saves the crushed in spirit.
19 Many are the afflictions of the righteous;
   but the Lord delivers him out of them all,
20 who watches over his bones,
   that none of them will be broken.[8]
21 Adversity slays the wicked;
   they who hate the righteous must suffer for it.[9]
22 The Lord redeems the soul of his servants,
   and none of those who trust in him will fall into guilt.[10]

[1] Cf. I Sam. 21.13–15 and Intr. 98. In place of the Philistine king Achish of Gath, mentioned in I Sam. ch. 21, Abimelech is here referred to, probably on account of Gen. chs. 20 f.; 26.
[2] * RSV has the present tense ('makes its boast').
[3] * In RSV the reading is 'the afflicted' instead of 'the humble'.
[4] * V. 5 reads in RSV:
   Look to him, and be radiant;
   so your faces shall never be ashamed.
[5] * V. 6a is in RSV: 'This poor man cried, and the Lord heard him!'
[6] See BH.
[7] * V. 17 in RSV:
   When the righteous cry for help, the Lord hears,
   and delivers them out of all their troubles.
[8] * RSV reads:
   He keeps all his bones;
   not one of them is broken.
[9] * V. 21 in RSV:
   Evil shall slay the wicked;
   and those who hate the righteous will be condemned.
[10] * RSV reads in v. 22b 'none of those who take refuge in him will be condemned'.

The psalm, which on account of v. 8 was used in the liturgy of the ancient Church at the celebration of Holy Communion, is a thanksgiving. It was recited in the festival services of the community of the godly, who are also called 'the humble, the saints, the righteous' (vv. 2b, 3, 6, 8 f., 15, 19; see Intr. 84, 93). Like the author of Psalm 25, the psalmist has the tendency to recast his personal experiences into generally valid truths, modelled on the style employed by the Wisdom writers for their maxims, a style which dominates the poem from v. 11 onwards (see Intr. 86). This fact and the further fact that a prayer of supplication is presupposed in vv. 4 and 6 does not, however, suffice to attribute Psalms 25 and 34 to the same author and to the same situation. As in most laments and thanksgivings the concrete individual features are lacking which otherwise might justify such a view. Each verse begins with a letter of the Hebrew alphabet, in order (cf. the exposition of Pss. 111; 9; 10), and this arrangement entails that the thoughts are somewhat loosely connected and that repetitions occur; however, the psalm does not lack a clear structure. The hymnic introduction (vv. 1–3) is followed by a 'representation' of the answering of the prayer which takes the form of a testimony by the worshipper in the presence of the cult community (vv. 4–10). In the second part of the psalm (vv. 11–22) these personal experiences are given a wider application by presenting them in the form of perceptions and warnings of universal significance; this shows that the Old Testament epigrammatic sayings of the Wisdom writers, too—at least occasionally—were closely associated with the cultus and that the didactic exhortation was regarded as a religious duty.

[1–3] The hymnic announcement at the opening of the psalm of the singing of a thanksgiving already expresses the profound perception that the whole life of the God-fearing man is intended to serve the praise of God; the meaning of the life of the godly one and his glory is his calling to bear witness to the glory of God. That calling is, however, at the same time a service to be rendered to the members of the cult community who hear this witness and, sharing the worshipper's joy, join him in 'magnifying' God whenever one of their fellow members is 'magnified'. Envisaging in this manner the majesty of God in their corporate praise, the members of the cult community organically grow together and become the *corpus piorum* continually apostrophized by the poet with diverse designations such as 'the humble' (vv. 2, 6), 'those who fear the Lord' (vv. 7, 9), 'the saints' (v. 9), 'the righteous' (vv. 15, 19, 21) and 'the servants of God' (v. 22). [4–7] The consciousness of being a member of the community of the godly and of being united with the other members in fellowship also determines the manner in which the worshipper presents the answering of his prayer and his deliverance, in that his thoughts pass on from his own experience (vv. 4, 6) to the general experience of those who fear God (vv. 5, 7 ff.). In v. 4 f. he speaks, first of all, of the festive hour in which he 'sought' the Lord in his sanctuary and experienced the granting of his prayer and his deliverance in the presence of the community of the godly; the latter had flocked to the sanctuary in large numbers (v. 9) and were able to witness the presence of the God who is always ready to help ('they looked on him'; cf. Ex. 24.9 f.; Zech. 12.10; see Intr. 40, 73) and did not allow their faith to be put to shame (v. 5). Now the worshipper himself stands in their midst as a living testimony to the truth that God protects his people, as he did in the time of their forefathers, and does so through his messenger who encamps around the worshipper like a mighty host (cf. Josh. 5.14; see Intr. 78). [8–10] The psalmist is sensitive to the reality of God's goodness and to his living presence to such a high degree that they actually become for him objects which he is able to perceive with his senses, since they are so near to him ('taste and see'), and inspire him to sing with joy the praise of the blessedness of those who find their refuge in God. The extravagant contrast between these people and the lions, which suffer want and hunger, similarly arises from the happiness felt by a human heart brimming over with joy in the goodness of God; the comparison of the position of the godly ones with the affliction of a creature that is left to its own resources reveals a profound appreciation of the magnitude of the gift which man, compared with such a creature, receives through his communion with God.

The knowledge gained by a most intimate experience is now also the theme that provides the spiritual link between the somewhat loosely connected exhortations and instructions of the second part of the psalm. [11–12] This part begins with an apostrophe which was regularly used in the Wisdom literature for the addressing of 'pupils' —'O sons'—and we have to think of the sons as having been present at the cultic feast. The theme of the address is 'the fear of the Lord'. The question asked in v. 12[1] (cf. Ps. 25.12) is skilfully formulated from the didactic point of view, whereas it has become obscure in I Peter 3.10 f. It starts with the joy in life and the expectation of future happiness, which, after all, can be assumed to be primarily shared by young people in general, but of which the middle-aged man is not unaware either. For every human being is on the look-out for happiness, and is there anyone who would not desire it? The psalmist here shows that his contact with the reality and wholeness of life is closer than that of some of the expositors of this psalm who imagine that they have been able to discover in it a doctrine of the

---

[1] A verbal parallel to this question, dating from the time of Tutankhamun, has been discovered in Egypt; cf. Couroyer, 'Idéal sapiental en Égypte et en Israël', *Revue Biblique* 57, 1950, pp. 174 ff.

supreme good and, reading into the psalm a clear philosophical distinction between the materialistic and the idealistic ways of thinking, a distinction which in that form is unknown to the Old Testament, hold that the psalmist must be reduced to the status of a representative of a lower level of morality. **[13–14]** The advice which the psalmist gives for the achieving of a happy life is not at all bad and, if taken seriously, it goes deep and far enough, when formulated as a principle, for nobody ever to be able to do full justice to it. Consequently it will always remain true as an ideal: the warning against doing evil, no matter whether it is done in word or deed, and the exhortation to strive after what is good, after truth and peace among men.

[15–17] The Old Testament always sees behind every moral demand made upon man the will of God, who in the eyes of the sinners is their enemy, but in the eyes of the righteous is their friend and helper in adversity (vv. 15 and 17 belong together).[1] **[18–22]** With this last thought the worshipper once more reverts to his own experience and in his statement concerning the suffering of the righteous throws out a hint that he by no means advocates a 'naïve superficial belief in retribution' nor conceives of happiness in life as consisting in an 'easy life' for the godly in the customary sense. The true happiness of a godly life consists in the *nearness of God* and in the living experience of *his* help and not in being spared suffering and affliction. On the contrary, suffering is an essential part of the life of the righteous, and only he who is brokenhearted and crushed in spirit will experience what the nearness of God and his help can really come to mean. The fact that God does not forsake the godly for ever but preserves him from utter despair and from the complete destruction of his existence (v. 20), is the blessed experience of the presence of God and of communion with him, a communion which is granted to the God-fearing man at the very time of his suffering, whereas the godless, left to his own devices, breaks down in his adversity and perishes. The impression made upon the psalmist by God's help, which he himself was privileged to experience, causes him to stop at the contemplation of life in this world. But his thoughts move in the same direction as do those of Psalm 73, and he at least sets out for the way which the worshipper in Psalm 73 has walked

---

[1] The original order was perhaps: vv. 16, 15, 17, following the order of the Hebrew alphabet, which is also attested in Lam. chs. 2–4, and was subsequently altered to the customary order (cf. Weiser, *Introduction to the OT*, pp. 305 f.).

right to the end. The psalm ends in praise of God, who 'redeems the soul of his servants' and does not let anyone fall into guilt who trusts in him. Thus the psalm at its conclusion once more reverts to the hymnic note on which it began.

35. LAMENT OF ONE OF THE 'QUIET IN THE LAND'
Of David

1 Contend, O Lord, with those who contend with me;
  fight against those who fight against me!
2 Take hold of shield buckler,
  and rise for my help!
3 Draw the spear and protect me[1] against my pursuers!
  Say to my soul, 'I am your deliverance!'
4 Let them be put to shame and dishonour
  who seek after my life!
  Let them be turned back and confounded
  who devised evil against me!
5 Let them be like chaff before the wind,
  let the angel of the Lord drive (them) on.
6 Let their way be dark and slippery,
  let the angel of the Lord pursue them.
7 For without cause they hid ' '[2] their net for me;
  and dug a pit[2] for me.[3]
8 The ruin comes upon him[4] unawares;
  let the net which he hid ensnare him;
  let him fall therein to ruin!
9 But as for me, I shall rejoice in the Lord,
  exulting in his deliverance.
10 All my bones shall say, 'O Lord who is like thee,
  thou who deliverest the lowly
  from him who is too strong for him ' '[2],
  and the poor from him who despoils him?'[5]
11 Malicious witnesses rise up;
  they ask me of things that I know not.
12 They requite me evil for good;
  they make my soul forlorn.[6]
13 But I, when they were sick—
  I wore sackcloth,
  I afflicted myself with fasting,
  my prayer turned back against my own bosom.[7]
14 As though I grieved for my friend or my brother,
  I went about bowed down;
  I went as one who laments his mother.[7]
15 But they in a body rejoice in my adversity;
  they gather together against me,

ready to strike without my knowing it;
   they slander and are not silent.[8]

16 In the midst of the impious. . . .[9]
   they gnash at me with their teeth.[10]

17 How long, O Lord, wilt thou look on?
   Rescue my soul from them that roar,[2]
   my only good from the young lions.[11]

18 I will testify to thee[12] in the great congregation;
   in the mighty throng I will praise thee.

19 Let not those rejoice over me
   who are my foes and deceive me,
   who hate me without cause and wink with their eyes.[13]

20 For they do not speak peace;
   but against those who are quiet in the land
   they conceive words of deceit.

21 They opened wide their mouths against me
   and said, 'Aha, Aha! Our eyes have seen it!'

22 Thou hast seen it, O Lord; be not silent ' '[2],
   and be not far from me!

23 Bestir thyself, and awake for my right,
   for my cause, O my god ' '[2]!

24 Judge me, O Lord, ' '[2] according to thy righteousness,
   that they do not rejoice over me![14]

25 Let them not say to themselves,
   'Aha, we have our heart's desire!'
   Let them not say, 'We have swallowed him up.'

26 Let them blush with shame altogether
   who rejoice at my calamity!
   Let them be clothed with shame and dishonour
   who magnify themselves against me!

27 Let those who desire my vindication
   shout for joy and be glad;
   let them say evermore,
   'Great is the Lord who delights in the salvation of his servant!'

28 My tongue shall tell of thy righteousness
   and of thy praise all the day long!

[1] * RSV reads, 'draw the spear and javelin against my pursuers'.

[2] See BH.

[3] * V. 7b reads in RSV, 'without cause they dug a pit for my life'.

[4] The transition to the singular makes hard reading; it is, however, also attested in a fragment from Qumran which varies a little from the MT; see J. T. Milik, *Biblica* 38, 1957, pp. 245 ff.

[5] * In v. 10 of RSV the 'weak' and 'the weak and needy' respectively are spoken of instead of 'the lowly' and 'the poor'.

[6] * RSV reads in v. 12b, 'my soul is forlorn!'

[7] * In RSV the last line of v. 13 and the first line of v. 14 form a separate sentence, reading: 'I prayed with head bowed on my bosom, as though I grieved for my friend or my brother'; v. 14 continues: 'I went about as one who laments his mother, bowed down and in mourning.'

8 * V. 15 in RSV:
    But at my stumbling they gathered in glee,
    they gathered together against me;
    cripples whom I knew not
    slandered me without ceasing;
9 The text is corrupt and defies reconstruction.
    Lit.: 'like mockers of a cake'.
10 * The RSV reading is 'they impiously mocked more and more,
    gnashing at me with their teeth'.
11 * V. 17b reads in RSV, 'Rescue me from their ravages, my life from the lions'.
12 * RSV has 'Then I will thank thee' instead of 'I will testify to thee'.
13 * V. 19 reads in RSV:
    Let not those rejoice over me
    who are wrongfully my foes,
    and let not those wink the eye
    who hate me without cause.
14 * V. 24b reads in RSV, 'and let them not rejoice over me'.

This psalm is the lament of a man who is persecuted. Besides numerous affinities with other laments (cf., e.g., Pss. 22 and 69) it contains
some features of a more personal character, not however sufficient to
establish the personal circumstances of the worshipper with accuracy.
His former friends have disappointed him and attack him. And thus he
appeals to God—probably in the sanctuary—to vindicate him against
their false accusations and deliver him from those who threaten to take
his life. Three times (vv. 1, 11, 19) the psalmist launches forth into
lamentation and prayer. This fact reflects his inward restlessness
which impels him to continually tread the road that leads him from
the depth of his human feelings of grief, from the exasperation that
fills his heart, to trust in God (vv. 9, 18, 27 f.); and his conduct gives
us an inkling of how hard he finds it to tread that road. [1–3] In his
petition for God's assistance in his suit, with which the psalm opens
(cf. vv. 11, 23, 27 f.), the worshipper uses the metaphorical language
of war which is probably borrowed from an ancient tradition (cf.
Ex. 15.3; Ps. 24.8; see Intr. 37 f.). God will stand by him and help
him, using his weapons and encouraging him; God's promise is for
him at once an inward help and a comfort. [4–6] The subsequent
imprecations which he hurls at his enemies express the cruel rage of
a heart that has abandoned itself to its powerlessness and mortal
terror. The poet here speaks of the angel of God (cf. Ex. 14.19 f.)
who shall execute the terrible judgment on them, as if he did not want
to drag God himself down to the low level of his passionate curses.
[7–8] The lamentation in v. 7, using as an illustration the image of
the hunter capturing game with a net hidden in a pit (cf. Pss. 7.15;

9.15), mentions the cause of his imprecations, and so we learn that the psalmist thinks that he is persecuted without cause. Once more he reverts to uttering imprecations against his enemies, but, associating with them the thought that evil entails its own punishment (cf. Pss. 7.15; 9.15; 57.6), a thought which arises out of a realization of the hidden righteousness of God (v. 28), he enters a realm in which the chains into which his passion had put him are gradually loosened. **[9–10]** Anticipating the future help of God, his soul rises to a vow of thanksgiving and, in doing so, he envisages himself to be entirely ('all my bones') taken hold of by the incomparable majesty of God, and this move in itself is already imbued with the pure and lofty spirit of God's world which leaves the lowland of dark passions far below.

The worshipper's grief is, however, too deep-rooted to enable him at once to take firm hold of God's hand, which he tried to grasp, and to cast off all his suffering, leaving it far behind. **[11–14]** Thus his prayer at the beginning of the second part of the psalm relapses into the plaintive tone of the lament. Yet the fervent ardour of a powerless and unbridled passion has now given way to the more restrained melancholy of a heart that has been deeply hurt. It is not a question of being only just able to understand that melancholy from the human point of view; rather are we incapable of steeling our heart against it when we hear how the worshipper's sensitive heart suffers as much from the mendacity of false witnesses, who want to implicate him in a matter with which he had nothing whatsoever to do, as from the loneliness of his present affliction. In that loneliness he had come to see the ingratitude of those for whom he himself had evinced the deepest sympathy and whose guilt had been on his mind as if it were his own guilt, so that he had offered a prayer of intercession for them (v. 13). **[15–17]** His bitterly disappointed love, which is so impressively manifested in his melancholy words, justifies us in ranking him with such men as Hosea and Jeremiah and makes us understand why the ruthless gloating and venomous scorn of his former friends affects him so deeply. We can now understand that they seem to him to behave like wild beasts of prey from whom he flees to his God in his anguish that, driven by the impatience of his anxious heart (cf. Ps. 13), he might persuade God to save the only possession still left to him, his life. **[18]** Like the first part of the lament the second part, too, closes with a vow of thanksgiving, indicating the purpose which the psalmist's severe suffering, like that

of many other people, is intended to serve—the praise of God in the
great congregation.

[**19–21**] The psalmist has once more drawn nearer to God in
prayer; and since his thoughts are now more firmly focused on him,
he develops a clearer vision and a calmer, more composed and more
confident attitude. In v. 19 he once more launches forth into prayer
and lamentation, but they now carry with them the certitude that
the deceitful and malicious actions of the enemies, who disturb the
peace of those who are the 'quiet in the land', cannot secure for them
a triumph which will make them gloat over his misfortune. [**22–26**]
The worshipper knows himself at one with the 'quiet in the land', as
he is no longer to the same extent exposed to the desolate feeling of
isolation. [**27–28**] For he can call on God himself to bear witness
against the shameless lies which his enemies utter to throw doubt on
his protestation of innocence. He can ask God to appear in judgment
and to ensure by his verdict the triumph of the worshipper's just
cause (see Intr. 75 ff.). The victory of God's truth and righteousness,
which thwarts all the boastful hopes of the adversaries, who already
imagined they had reached the goal of their desires (v. 25), is more
and more clearly visualized by the worshipper whilst he prays, until
the confident and joyous certitude after much struggle finds its
definite expression in a final vow of thanksgiving and unites the
worshipper with the friends of justice and truth in the communion
of those who gratefully recognize that they are called to sing all the
day long the praise of the majesty and righteousness of God (see
Intr. 64, 75 ff.).

36. WITH THEE IS THE FOUNTAIN OF LIFE
To the Conductor. Of David, the servant of Yahweh

1 The wicked heeds the voice of sin in his heart;[1]
  he thinks, there is no fear of God.[2]
2 For (sin) has so altered his outlook[3]
  that guilt and hate are his lot.[4]
3 The words of his mouth are mischief and deceit;
  he has ceased to act wisely and do good.
4 He plots mischief while on his bed;
  he sets himself in a way that is not good;
  he spurns not evil.
5 Thy grace, O Lord, extends to the heavens,
  and thy truth to the clouds.[5]

6 Thy righteousness is like the mountains of God,
   thy judgments are like the great deep;
   thou comest to the help of man and beast.[6]
7 How precious is thy grace, O Lord![7]
   The children of men come to thee[7]
   to take refuge in the shadow of thy wings.
8 They feast on the fat of thy house,
   and thou givest them drink from the river of thy delights.
9 For with thee is the fountain of life,
   in thy light do we see light.
10 O continue thy lovingkindness to those who know thee,
   and thy righteousness to the upright of heart.[8]
11 Let not the foot of arrogance tread upon me,
   nor the hand of the wicked drive me away.
12 Then the evildoers lie prostrate,
   they are thrust down, and will never rise again.

[1] Lit.: 'Sin whispers to the wicked in his (BH) heart.'
[2] * V. 1 reads in RSV:
   Transgression speaks to the wicked
   deep in his heart;
   there is no fear of God before his eyes.
[3] The reading is perhaps *heḥelîp* . . . *ʿênâw*.
[4] * Here not only the text of RSV but also the meaning are entirely different:
   For he flatters himself in his own eyes
   that his iniquity cannot be found out
   and hated.
[5] * RSV has 'steadfast love' instead of 'grace' and 'faithfulness' instead of 'truth'.
[6] * V. 6c reads in RSV, 'man and beast thou savest, O Lord'.
[7] See BH.
[8] * RSV has 'steadfast love' instead of 'lovingkindness' and 'salvation' instead of 'righteousness'.

In mood and subject-matter the psalm is divided into two parts distinctly differing from each other. After the fashion of the Wisdom literature, vv. 1–4 contain a stern characterization of the man who is under the sway of sin. The second part (vv. 5–9) is tuned to the psalmist's feeling of joy as he glorifies in the form of a hymn the grace and righteousness of God and the blessed happiness of a man whose life is grounded in the grace of God. This contrast between the two main parts of the psalm does not, however, justify us in splitting it up into two independent poems not originally related to each other in any way. For the fact that the poet after the closing prayer for the continuation of God's grace once more comes to speak of the end of the wicked clearly shows that the reflection on sin is put at the beginning of the psalm because it serves in the cultic situation presupposed by the psalm as the dark background against which the radiant picture of the divine lovingkindness is set off so much the more impressively. The reference to the tradition of the Covenant Festival, which was associated with the cult of the sacred Ark at the Temple (vv. 5 ff.), and the allusion to the judgment, which was executed 'there' on the evildoers (v. 12), suggest the view that the cult of the Covenant Festival was the occasion for the psalm's composition as well as the setting in which it was recited in the presence of the congregation (v. 9; see Intr. 40 f., 64). The psalm can be fully understood only if we take into account that it has arisen out of the serious problem which the existence of sin presented for belief in God. The solution of the difficult question of how the reality of sin can be reconciled with the belief in God's righteousness is not to be found with the help of the conceptual harmonization of these two categories of thought; it lies in an act of volition based on faith, man deciding in favour of God and making a strong and joyful affirmation of faith in him. The triumphant utterance of faith expressed in the one word 'nevertheless', which resolutely dissociates itself from sin and the sinners (see Intr. 47 ff.), is clearly shown doing this in the very confrontation of the two contrasting parts of the psalm. The psalm is a beautiful and living testimony to what faith is capable of attaining when notwithstanding everything it takes the risk of siding with God. Thus this song of affirmation is a testimony to the intimate communion with God of a man who knows from his own experience and therefore is able to say what the blessed experience of godliness really means. The song provides no clues about any other personal circumstances of the author or about the period in which it was written.

The arrangement of the thoughts which the psalm develops is as plain and simple as its language. The stern description of the man who is under the sway of sin (vv. 1–4) is confronted in vv. 5–9 with the praise of the lovingkindness of God and with the happiness of the man who partakes of the grace of God. In conclusion (vv. 10–11) follows a prayer for the continuation of that grace. Verse 12, reverting to the beginning of the psalm and touching on the problem that forms its background, speaks of the fate which the wicked will suffer in judgment.

Man under the sway of sin (vv. 1–4)

[1] The poet describes the effect which sin has on man by means of a quaint phrase which elsewhere in the Old Testament is mostly

used of the Word which God in a mysterious way 'whispers' to his prophets. It is obvious what the psalmist wishes to say by using that phrase: the voice of sin which man hears speaking in his heart has for the wicked the same authority and power as the voice of God has for the prophets. Irony and profound insight are at once implied in this statement. The man who is persuaded of possessing freedom, a freedom which, in fact, is only an imaginary one, boasts of the fact that, as far as he is concerned, there is 'no fear of God' and believes that he can thus evade God's rule over his life. But in doing so he is, perhaps without even noticing it, subject to a much worse power. For he has an entirely different 'god' to whom he is enslaved, and that god is his sin. When God is not accepted as Master, sin holds its sway; and, conversely, the lack of the fear of God is the root-cause of sin. This is what the seeming freedom of a man looks like who believes that he can free himself from God. Without God he is exposed to the insinuations of satanic powers and because of his delusion and self-deception is subject to them. [2] It is probably the purpose of v. 2 to explain this incomprehensible bondage to sin and this self-deception. The text is difficult. If the emendation is correct, the poet wishes to point out that sin deprives man of any criterion by which he could judge the real nature of things (*'die Wirklichkeit'*); to point out that sin alters man's outlook and deludes him to such an extent that he who believed he could gain his freedom falls into guilt and hate before God. The traditional text, 'it flatters him before his eyes that he might incur guilt and yield to hate', would similarly point in the same direction. In this rendering it is precisely the satanic element inherent in sin which is accurately observed—that sin deludes the man who succumbs to it about the real nature of things so that he overlooks it; it then lets him end up in a situation entirely different from the one which it had misled him to expect and which he himself had hoped for in his self-deception. [3-4] No wonder that as a result of such a perversity in the sinner's basic attitude his words, deeds and thoughts are diametrically opposed to what a sensible and righteous man would do. Instead of speaking the truth, his words are full of mischief and deceit. He ceases to do good and act wisely; even at night, while he is 'on his bed', he plots mischief; and during the day he walks openly and unhesitatingly in the way of evil. Such is man without God. Without noticing it, he is entirely subject to the power of sin, being utterly incapable of any clear judgment, because sin has led him astray, so that he overlooks the real nature of things.

Man under the grace of God (vv. 5–9)

In the hymn that follows the poet speaks in a language which we cannot ignore of what the 'Reality' which he sees and in the sphere of which he himself lives actually is. And that ultimate Reality, without which life is not possible at all, is God. It is characteristic of the poet that he does not contrast his description of sin and the sinner with the ideal of a godly man by using a didactic form, as one might perhaps be inclined to assume, but speaks of God and of what he means to man in the form of a hymn of praise. In this he follows the fundamental ideas of the tradition of the Covenant. The method which the psalmist here uses shows primarily the essential difference in the way of thinking characteristic of these two distinct attitudes of mind. In the one case it is a question of the anthropocentric way of thinking which makes man the centre of all things; in the other case we are dealing with the theocentric way of thinking which is wholly determined by God as its point of departure. Sin and faith are always from the outset separated from each other by this chasm which yawns between these two ways of thinking. It is, however, not only the difference between two basically different mental attitudes to the real nature of things which here emerges and is to be portrayed. The hymnic affirmation of faith in God that springs from the psalmist's humility and trust in God is in the present case a *deed*, a cultic *act* of faith by means of which the poet at once tackles and solves that serious problem with which he is presented by the coexistence of the reality of sin and the reality of God. The solution of the mystery underlying the psalm and requiring an answer can be reached only by means of a *decision* in favour of God, a decision which is made by faith and must be judged as a *deed*, and not by means of any intellectual discussion. The 'nevertheless' of faith, which implies a joyful acknowledgment of God, constitutes the spiritual link between the psalm's two parts, which outwardly seem to differ so widely from each other and yet are held together by the ideology of the cult of the Covenant. It is at the same time the religious key which enables us to understand the psalm as a whole in the light of the external and internal circumstances of the poet. It is in and through the act of the renunciation of sinners and the affirmation of faith in God's grace (see Intr. 76 f.) that the psalmist overcomes the strain from which his soul suffers and also the temptation to which he is exposed; further, it presents a solution of the problem in question in that by that act he not only points to the reality of God, which the sinner tries to by-pass, but submits himself to it as that reality in which every life has its origin and existence.

[5–6] The poet makes an attempt, which indeed is always bound to remain only an attempt, to define and praise the immeasurable greatness of the lovingkindness, faithfulness and righteousness of God, and their comprehensive range; in this he uses words which form a hymn and are inspired by wonder and awe, joyful gratitude and humble trust, and by that very quality reveal the genuineness of his faith. The whole world is full of God's 'grace and faithfulness', reaching up to the uttermost parts of the infinite heaven and its inaccessible cloud layers (cf. in this connection Ex. 34.6, the key-text of the tradition of the Sinai theophany which is here alluded to, and Intr. 58). God's righteousness is like the mountains which, having been created by him, are firmly established from time immemorial, and his ordinances are perpetually in force like the sea which is and remains always the same since it was created by him. God's reality embraces all space and time; it is the everlasting and firm foundation of the world and of every kind of life in the world. Nobody, neither man nor beast, can dispense with God's help; everything in the world lives by gifts received from his loving hand. This is the truth which the poet throws into relief as the certitude of that salvation which he envisages in his encounter with God.

[7] What the poet has stated so far by focusing his thoughts entirely on God alone, he now emphasizes in what follows and confirms it by referring to man's experience. The subsequent verses are saturated with the warm affection of a heart that rejoices in its own blessed experience of God. Is it not man's supreme and ultimate happiness that that grace of God which embraces the whole world stoops down to him, and that men on their part may come into the presence of that majestic God in order to be able to take refuge in him, just as the little chicks do under the wings of their mother? The image which the poet here uses is based on the epiphany of Yahweh above the wings of the cherubim on the sacred Ark at the Covenant Festival, implying for the covenant community the realization of their salvation (see Intr. 41). The words here imply a missionary tendency—which fits the comprehensiveness of the psalm's idea of God—when the psalmist speaks not only of the godly Israelites but quite generally of the 'children of men' to whom the divine grace offers protection and refuge. **[8]** However, the song is distinguished not only by the comprehensiveness of its religious reflections but also by their

profundity. This can be clearly seen in v. 8, where the poet begins to
speak of the other benefits of the cultus. Using metaphorical language
coloured in a typically oriental fashion he says: 'They feast on the fat
of thy house.' This can hardly mean anything other than participation in the sacrificial meal at the Temple. The material sensual
pleasures, which the public worship offers, are, however, not in the
centre of the psalmist's thoughts; to him they are at the same time a
symbol of something more profound and spiritual. The sacrificial
meal in the house of God becomes for him the symbol and an indication of man's communion with God; the sacrificial offering becomes
for him the symbol of *God's* grace and presence which he allows man
to share. The material act performed in the divine service is the
symbol of a more sublime process of a spiritual nature; indeed, it
stands for something even more important: in the act of partaking of
the sacrifice, which God, as it were, offers to those who visit his house
as a hospitable gift, the lovingkindness of God himself is at work, in
that he himself is the Giver; and in this effective sign his grace is
really experienced. The divine service is the bridge between God and
man where in a world depending on man's sense-perceptions God
makes his grace perceptible to man, and man, on the other hand,
becomes assured of the spiritual reality of God by means of the
symbol that affects his senses. In the cultus, too, it is a matter of God
himself; this is shown by the second half-line 'thou givest them drink
from the river of thy delights'. For the psalmist the meaning and
blessedness of the hallowed hours which man is privileged to spend
in the house of God consists in the partaking of the delights of God
and not in the sharing of the material enjoyment of earthly gifts. It
consists in the joy in God which God himself bestows upon those
whose souls pant for him. [9] Proceeding from this profound interpretation of the cultus as the place of man's encounter with the
gracious God, the psalmist turns to the contemplation of a much
wider vista. He now envisages a truly great perspective and a comprehensive truth which is expressed in the congregation's immortal
testimony: 'With thee is the fountain of life, and in thy light do we see
light.' This statement not only includes the perception, which in
another context is set forth by the teaching on creation, that God is
the root-cause and fountain-head of all being, but it also expresses
another truth which is still more closely linked to life, the truth that
the true life, which really deserves to be described by that name, is
one which is lived in communion with God. The comprehensiveness

of the psalmist's idea of God here postulates a conception of life as man's living communion with God, originating in God and being sustained by God, which is so profound that it can be ranked with the best which the Bible has to say in this respect. Without God man would be what the earth would be without the sun. Just as everything subsists on the sun's life and heat, and just as the flower opens and blossoms in response to the sunbeams, so it is the 'light' of God, the heavenly light of the glory (*kābōd*) of his presence, which causes the life of man to grow and prosper joyously, and which gives it its meaning and transparency, its strength and stabliity. Without God man's life is exposed to meaninglessness, darkness and destruction. In him and through him we live and move and have our being.

The prayer (vv. 10–11)

[10] It is only natural that the profound insight that man can live only by the grace of God is followed up by the prayer that God may continue to grant that grace also in future to those who 'know' him and 'his righteousness to the upright of heart'. This prayer springs from the simple and natural requirements of the life of a faithful man for whom the love for God (the Hebrew word for 'know' also expresses this aspect) and the will to order his life in accordance with the ordinances of God's Covenant are an indispensable function of life. [11] And the same tendency which governs these thoughts of the psalmist can also be observed in his specific concrete petition that follows, asking for protection against the violence of sinners. It accords with the poet's whole outlook that the immediate objects of his desires are likewise not particular material, earthly possessions, but the grace and righteousness of God, and in general the preservation of the purity of his communion with God. The supplications of the psalmist express no such thing as an unstable and for that reason impatient request, but rather a calm and firm trust which is sure of its own ground. [12] The concluding verse reverts to the beginning. The peculiar form of its wording seems to point to the judgment on the sinner, executed by means of a ritual act in the cult of the Covenant (see Intr. 47 f., 75 f., 78), and consequently this verse constitutes the point of departure of the whole psalm and the problem which it poses. It is in this perspective that the terrible seriousness of sin first acquires its actuality and that the danger involved in sin, which usually remains hidden from the sinner himself, can be clearly seen. It is, however, in this same perspective that the blessedness of

being sustained by God's grace first becomes actual, too, and can be clearly seen—the grace of God, that is, which is bestowed upon man by the triumphant certitude of his faith. The indestructible strength of the psalm lies in two features—in the way in which the nature of sin is here grasped through faith in God and forms the point of departure for the psalmist's reflections; further, in the way in which the blessedness of man's communion with God is attained and the riddle of life solved through an act of faith that bears witness to the truth.

37. COMMIT YOUR WAYS TO THE LORD

Of David

1 Fret not yourself because of the wicked,
   do not lose your temper because of sinners;[1]
2 for they will speedily fade like the grass,
   and wither like the green herb!
3 Trust in the Lord, and do good;
   dwell in the land and keep upright in heart;[2]
4 and take delight in the Lord,
   for he gives you[3] the desires of your heart.
5 Commit your way to the Lord
   and trust in him; he will do it well:[4]
6 he will bring forth your salvation[5] as the light
   and your right as the brightness at noonday.
7 Be still before the Lord, and wait patiently for him;
   fret not yourself over him who prospers in his way,
   over the man who carries out evil devices!
8 Refrain from anger, and forsake wrath;
   fret not yourself; it tends only to evil!
9 For the wicked shall be destroyed;
   but those who wait for the Lord, they shall inherit the land.
10 Yet a little while, and the wicked will be no more;
   when you look at his place, he will not be there any more.
11 But the humiliated shall inherit the land
   and delight themselves in abundant salvation.[6]
12 The wicked plots against the godly one,
   and gnashes his teeth at him;
13 but the Lord laughs at the wicked,
   for he sees that his day is coming.
14 The wicked draw the sword and bend their bows,
   to bring down the afflicted,
   and to slay the poor who walk uprightly.[7]
15 Their sword shall enter their own heart,
   and their bows shall be broken.

16 Better is a little that the righteous have
   than the piled up[8] riches of the sinners.[9]

17 For the arms of the wicked shall be broken;
   but the Lord upholds the righteous.

18 The Lord knows the days of the godly ones,
   and their heritage will abide for ever;

19 they are not put to shame in evil times,
   in the days of famine they shall be sated.

20 Yea, the sinners perish like the glory of the pastures,[10]
   the enemies of the Lord vanish like smoke.[11]

21 The wicked borrows, and does not pay back,
   but the godly one is generous and gives.

22 Those blessed by the Lord shall inherit the land,
   but those cursed by him shall be destroyed.

23 The Lord directs the steps of a man;
   he establishes him in whose way he delights;

24 though he fall, he shall not be cast down for ever,
   for the Lord is the stay of his hand.

25 I have been young, and now am old;
   yet I have not seen the godly one forsaken
   or his children begging bread.

26 He is ever giving liberally and lending,
   and his seed becomes a blessing.

27 Depart from evil, and do good;
   so shall you abide in peace![12]

28 For the Lord is a lover of justice;
   he will not forsake his saints.
   The wicked shall perish,[8]
   and the seed of the sinners shall be destroyed.[13]

29 The righteous inherit the land,
   and may dwell therein for ever.

30 The mouth of the righteous utters wisdom,
   and his tongue speaks justice.

31 The law of his God is in his heart;
   his footsteps shall not slip.

32 The sinner spies upon the godly one,
   and seeks to slay him.

33 The Lord will not abandon him to his power,
   or let him be condemned when he is brought to trial.

34 Wait for the Lord, and keep to his way,
   he will exalt you to possess the land;
   you will look on the destruction of the wicked.

35 I have seen a wicked man boasting,
   raising himself up defiantly like a cedar of Lebanon;[8]

36 but he faded away,[14] and, lo, he was no more;
   though I sought him, he could not be found.

37 Keep your godliness and foster uprightness;[8]
   for there is hope for the man of peace.[15]

38 The wicked perish altogether;
   the future of the sinners is doomed to destruction.[16]

39 The salvation of the godly is from the Lord,
   he is their refuge in the time of trouble.

40 The Lord helps them and delivers them;
   ' '[17] he will save them when they trust in him.[18]

[1] * RSV reads in v. 1b 'be not envious of wrongdoers'.

[2] Lit.: tend faithfulness. (Tr. N.: RSV has in v. 3b 'so you will dwell in the land, and enjoy security'.)

[3] * RSV reads 'and he will give you' instead of 'for he gives you'.

[4] * V. 5b reads in RSV, 'trust in him, and he will act'.

[5] * In RSV the rendering is 'vindication' instead of 'salvation'.

[6] * RSV has 'meek' instead of 'humiliated' and 'prosperity' instead of 'salvation'.

[7] * The second and the third lines are in RSV:
   to bring down the poor and needy,
   to slay those who walk uprightly;

[8] See BH.

[9] * V. 16b reads in RSV, 'than the abundance of many wicked'.

[10] This reading concurs with that of Staerk (see above under 'Literature', p. 14).

[11] * The rendering in RSV differs considerably:
   But the wicked perish;
   the enemies of the Lord are like the glory of the pastures,
   they vanish—like smoke they vanish away.

[12] Lit.: for ever. (Tr. N.: This is also the rendering of RSV.)

[13] * The third and the fourth lines of v. 28 read in RSV:
   The righteous shall be preserved for ever,
   but the children of the wicked shall be cut off.

[14] * V. 36a reads in RSV, 'Again I passed by, and, lo, he was no more.'

[15] * V. 37 in RSV:
   Mark the blameless man, and behold the upright,
   for there is posterity for the man of peace.

[16] * RSV renders v. 38:
   But transgressors shall be altogether destroyed;
   the posterity of the wicked shall be cut off.

[17] The sentence 'he saves them from the wicked' seems to be a later addition.

[18] * The reading of RSV after the first line is:
   he delivers them from the wicked, and saves them,
   because they take refuge in him.

The psalm stimulated Paul Gerhardt to compose his well-known song of confidence 'Commit thou all thy griefs'.[1] Trust in God and in his providential rule is indeed the fundamental theme of the psalm which, ringing through every part, binds together the individual sections and verses in such a way that they form a unity, though they are frequently only loosely connected. As far as type is concerned, the

[1] * In the German original: 'Befiehl du deine Wege', translated into English by John Wesley.

whole poem is not so much a psalm as a collection of proverbs such as those collected in the Book of the Proverbs of Solomon, and which, at least in part, belong to the treasure of the popular maxims of the Wisdom writers. This fact as well as the use of the purely outward form of an acrostic psalm, in which the opening letters of alternate verses are arranged according to the sequence of the Hebrew alphabet, entails that the individual sections are only loosely connected with each other and that the psalm is lacking in a consistent thought-sequence. Although, generally speaking, we cannot fail to recognize that the individual proverbs are joined to each other in a natural fashion, the repetitions occurring more than once in the psalm still indicate clearly that the poem's structure is that of some kind of collection of proverbs.

The author, according to his own statement (v. 25), is a man with the mature experience of old age, who speaks, as the Wisdom teacher does, to younger pupils. He has compiled the psalm partly from the treasure of proverbs already in existence, partly from sayings which he himself has composed. Again, he has fashioned the whole psalm to serve a definitely practical purpose. The aim he pursues is to exhort the godly to cling to their trust in God and to their obedience to God in the face of the manifold temptations in which they get involved through the existence and the behaviour of the wicked, be it anger or envy, poverty or affliction, fear of men, doubts about God's actions and his righteousness, or getting weary of obeying the moral laws. In all these respects the author wants to guide the godly into the way of true confidence in God which will never be confounded. The psalm does not therefore engage in a critical examination of the theoretical, theological problem of the theodicy or of the problematic nature of the doctrine of retribution; the psalm is not concerned with the vindication of God. Rather is it a question of the vindication of the practice of religion in man's every-day life, and that vindication takes the form of giving pastoral counsel of a didactic nature.

The peculiar way in which the psalm is composed of concise sayings which give us a valuable and instructive insight into the pious wisdom of the people entails that what is here expounded is not the ultimate depths of the problematic nature of life, but much rather the strong and sustained influence which the power of faith is capable of exerting in the actual struggle for existence—though we are not always able to see clearly and state accurately what the ultimate conceptions, reasons and thoughts are that have given rise to the particular exhortations, warnings and promises. This is why we must advise against any attempt to compare the psalm with the thoughts developed in Psalms 49 and 73, however similar the incident may be in all the three psalms which provided their starting-point. Psalm 37 moves on a different plane: at any rate, the basic mood of the psalm is not merely one of a 'naïve religious optimism'; rather does it express the calm serenity and assuredness of a firm faith which has been attained and tested in the course of many struggles and experiences, and the strength of which resides in its simplicity and transparency.

It is not possible to establish the date of the psalm's composition. We can by no means be certain that some affinities with the other Old Testament epigrammatic sayings of the Wisdom writers and with the Book of Job point to the later post-exilic era. The various references to elements of the tradition of the cult of the Covenant (references to blessing and curse in v. 22; to the distribution of land in vv. 9, 11, 18, 22, 29, 34; to judgment and salvation in vv. 10 f., 34, 37 f.) make it possible to hold the view that the psalm was composed and used in pre-exilic times.

[1–2] The two first sayings in vv. 1 and 2 and vv. 3 and 4 already exhibit clearly the motive of the psalm and the concern of the psalmist. The first saying, which in its opening words accords with Prov. 24.19 and so is probably a popular proverb, envisages, first of all, the negative aspect when it utters the *warning* that the godly man shall not lose his temper because of the sinners. This warning by no means intends to deny that the existence of the wicked gives offence to the godly (to whom all the sayings of the psalm are addressed) and causes them anxiety. The author's aim is to keep the godly from succumbing to the danger of allowing their *inward* attitude to be influenced by taking offence at the sins of others and of letting their own faith be undermined, since the result of such behaviour would be that the critic puts himself in the wrong. The poet is firmly convinced that the sinner, because he rebels against God, *cannot* last. That conviction is but the fundamental postulate of the belief in God which sees and judges all things from the standpoint of eternity and, in consequence, must not stop at the things which are transient like the grass that speedily fades away. It would, in fact, be only a sign of faint-heartedness and lack of trust if the godly were to anticipate hastily the decision which belongs to God alone.

[3-4] Guided by this reflection, the psalmist lays vigorous stress in the second saying on the positive attitude which alone will enable the godly man to overcome such human temptations—he demands joyful confidence in God and obedience to his moral laws. True confidence consists in leaving the things which are not under the control of man confidently and patiently to him who has all things in his hand; man, on the other hand, has only to take due care that he faithfully fulfils the task which is allotted to *him* and does so in the place which is assigned to him (the saying 'dwell in the land' may perhaps include this meaning). This is the true meaning of the life of the godly one, who in his reflections turns away from men to the contemplation of God; the godly man, who lets everything be irradiated by his delight in God, can, as his heart is filled with that joy, look forward to the fulfilment of the deepest desires of his heart.

[5-6] This saying, which has become immortal through Paul Gerhardt's hymn, leads us into that bright sphere where man's confidence in God prevails. Here speaks a man who knows what it means that his cause is in the hand of God. He knows that in the practice of prayer he may commit his whole life (= 'your way') to God, that he will be entirely in the faithful hands of God; he may cast all his cares upon him and, whenever the uncertainties of life overwhelm him, he may give himself up to God's guidance, saying to himself:

> 'What though thou rulest not?
> Yet heaven, and earth, and hell proclaim:
> God sitteth on the throne and ruleth all things well!'[1]

This knowledge gives him that confident joy of having peace of mind and refuge in God which fills the life of the godly man with sunshine. For his life is sustained by the hope that God's salvation will rise over him like the sun, and that his just cause, which, after all, is nothing other than the cause of God, will triumph. The darkness of night can in no way frighten a man who is assured of the coming of the day; the temptation is overcome by the hope that springs from faith.

[7] The exhortation to be still and wait for God thus naturally follows the truth which has just been stated. Reverting to v. 1, it concludes the present train of thought with the warning that the godly shall not fret themselves over the way in which the wicked

---

[1] * This is a quotation from the seventh verse of Paul Gerhardt's hymn 'Commit thou all thy griefs'; in John Wesley's translation of that hymn this quotation occurs in the eleventh verse.

prosper and carry out evil devices. The Old Testament is aware of
the fact (cf. Isa. 7.4; 30.15) that to be still and wait for God is not
something which falls into the lap of man, but is the reward for the
victory which man has gained in the struggle of his soul against his
own assertive human self; it is aware of the fact that this keeping
silence and waiting for God consists in the bearing and enduring of
that tension into which man is continually thrown whenever he
would like to see what, in fact, cannot be seen and yet must be
believed. It is only by the displaying of a faith which is capable of
waiting patiently and of neutralizing all selfish human curiosity that
patience and self-possession grow as the most precious fruit of faith
itself. Faith in the biblical sense requires the utmost exertion of
strength and the highest degree of activity. The man who has
learned to conquer his own self by waiting faithfully for God and by
being still before him can no longer be harmed in any way, not
even by the prosperity of his adversaries who hatch plots against
him.

[8–9] The psalmist now seeks to throw light on the subject in
question from another angle. He points to the moral danger which is
involved in fretting oneself because of the wicked and in allowing
oneself to be carried away by anger and wrath; for such behaviour
tends to evil. In his seemingly righteous indignation at the sinners the
godly man by that conduct unwittingly puts himself in the same attitude of mind which the sinners have adopted, that is, he opposes God
and is disobedient to him. The renewed warning is meant to draw the
attention of the godly to this danger. Moreover, why that anger, since
those who have faith are aware that in reality the destinies of the godly
and of the wicked have already been clearly decreed? Sin and sinners
do not last; only to the godly is God's promise given that they will possess the land. The author, who on judgment on the wicked (see also vv.
10 f., 22) as on salvation for the godly takes his stand upon the ground
of the tradition preserved in the cult of the Covenant, probably has
in mind here the promises of land which God made to the godly
Abraham and his seed; and he interprets them as a Word of God to
the faithful in his own time; and because they are God's Word, they
have for him the value of a certitude which is not to be doubted and
on which one can rely. It cannot readily be inferred from the test that
the psalmist, in making this statement, advocates the ideal of the poor
farmer.

[10–11] The certitude based on the tradition of the Covenant is present in the mind of the poet to such a degree that he envisages the end of the wicked as taking place in the near future. What they possess is only a brief lifetime at the end of which they are threatened by destruction; on the other hand, what the godly may expect is the fulfilment of promises and joy in the consummation of their salvation. It is true that at present they are still the humiliated and oppressed (see Intr. 92 f.), but because of their hope, assured by their faith, they are more blessed than those who are without hope.

[12–13] The psalm counters the objection that the godly man is threatened by the deceitfulness and the hatred of the wicked by pointing to God who can but laugh at the wicked (cf. Ps. 2.4, a passage from the festival cult), knowing that they cannot escape the fate that the future holds in store for them. Why should he who has faith take a tragic view of something which God thinks worth only laughing at? True faith does not require any other guarantee and assurance than the one which comes from God. To him who believes God grants the courage and the far-sightedness which enable him to attach no greater importance to temporal affairs than they have in the eyes of God himself.

[14–15] The subsequent saying explains why the psalmist is able to speak with such an assurance of the imminent end of the wicked. The true meaning of the second part of this saying can be fully understood only if we take into account the metaphorical character of the individual phrases used in v. 14. The psalmist is firmly convinced—and his conviction is well understandable from the standpoint of faith—that every sinful plot against the godly carries with it the germ of destruction, that it is doomed to perish by its own evil machinations. Sin *is* already in itself judgment: the weapon of sin turns against the sinner himself and breaks in pieces in his own hand. Though the psalmist does not say so explicitly, it is possible that behind his brief statement there is the religious truth which in a different context is perceived and proclaimed in Hos. 5.12; Jer. 2.19; 5.25; 6.21, 30; 13.23; 18.17—that the hand of the God who sits in judgment is at work in the decay which is brought about by sin.

[16–17] Using language reminiscent of a proverb preserved in a similar form in Prov. 15.16; 16.8, the author now comes to speak of that temptation which the godly man who is not favoured with many earthly possessions, has to face the temptation, that is, of begrudging the sinners their wealth. Here, too, everything depends on seeing things in their right proportions and on applying to them the right

standard. Whosoever has learned to look at things with the eyes of
faith sets more value on the little he possesses and enjoys contentedly
and gratefully than on the wealth acquired by sin and spent in sin.
Ill-gotten gain never thrives; it lacks the blessing from above. It does
not allow its owner to enjoy peace of mind and contentment. What
man possesses is bound to dwindle away; how can one hope to be
able to rely on it when this 'arm of the wicked will be broken'? It is
just the reverse with the godly man; his wealth does not consist in the
treasures of this world which are only temporal, but in his possession
of God, who upholds him and helps him to achieve true and genuine
happiness.

[18–19] It is precisely with a view to the affliction of the godly
that the next saying speaks in more detail of God's care for those
who fear him. God takes loving care of the life of the godly (this
meaning is expressed in the Hebrew word). The guarantee for
the stability of 'their heritage' is to be found solely in the fact that
it is God who gives them this heritage. It is for the same reason that
they are not put to shame in times of trouble because they are under
the care of a higher Being. The affliction, it is true, does not pass them
by without leaving its mark, but they are not shattered thereby. He
who believes does not face adversity with fear and trembling but with
a childlike and yet firm trust in his Heavenly Father, who will
provide for his people as he feeds the birds of the air. [20] Just as
faith infers from God's love and care the preservation of those who
fear him, so by the same logic faith infers from the enmity of the
wicked towards God their downfall. [21–22] Verse 21 reverts to the
thoughts developed in vv. 16 f. and shows how the blessing of God
inspires the godly man to acts of generosity and helpfulness, expressed
in joyful giving, and how, on the other hand, the dishonesty of the
wicked in money matters makes manifest the curse of God. The
former creates new bonds of fellowship and values of a spiritual and
moral nature, the latter destroys them. The demonstration of the
consequences of the divine blessing and curse provided by the present
justifies the faithful so much the more in holding fast to God's
promises of blessing which he makes to the godly (cf. vv. 8 f.) and
taking seriously the threat of the curse which God utters against
the wicked; these trains of thought likewise date back to the tradition
of the cult of the Covenant.

[23–24] In the saying that follows (cf. Prov. 20.24) the author
counters the objection that experience, after all, proves how even the

godly man, who is under God's guidance, is not always spared adversity. In doing so, he raises the problem of suffering with which the great minds of the Old Testament have continually wrestled. Though he does not investigate it to its ultimate depths, as, for instance, Isa. 53 and Psalm 73 have done, he is not wrong in saying that the godly man, though he may fall, is nevertheless not cast down for ever, because God even then still upholds him. Adversity befalling the godly man never has for him the significance of a complete breakdown, as it has for the wicked. For God is at work in adversity, too, and his children are not forsaken by him even then; they may take hold of God's hand stretched out towards them in their affliction. If they were forsaken by God in adversity, then and only then could one indeed speak of their complete breakdown. That breakdown threatens the godless, but not the man who relies on God. **[25–26]** The author finds this truth to be confirmed by his own personal experience gained in the course of a long life: never in his life has he seen that a godly man had been forsaken by God and reduced to the level of a beggar. Nay, there is a hidden blessing even in affliction which is passed on by godly people from generation to generation—the kindheartedness of the man on whom affliction has left its mark and who is sustained by God.

[27–28a] In consistently pursuing this view of the godly man the author draws from it a practical conclusion by adding the exhortation—probably in proverb form—to depart from evil and to do good. This is the only conduct which behoves the godly man. The promise that he shall 'abide in the promised land for ever' depends on that conduct. The motivation added to the exhortation is noteworthy. Man shall devote himself to a moral life because God loves justice; in other words, he shall live a moral life to please God and not at all to secure thereby a tranquil life. The ethical character of the Covenant is thoroughly founded on religion; it is obedience springing from faith and not a morality motivated by utilitarian, eudemonistic considerations. Where life is lived in such a community, God will play his part and will not leave the godly man in the lurch. **[28b–29]** Once more the psalmist compares, as he has done in vv. 9, 17, 22, the future destiny of the wicked, who are subject to the curse of God, with that of the godly, to whom God has given the promise, and he does so, as it were, in order to erect a clear signpost for the people of God. **[30–31]** In the life of the godly man his communion with God is also expressed in the fact that he 'speaks justice'. When

he hears the will of God in his heart, when his thoughts are determined by God's thoughts, then the words he utters are truly 'wisdom'.
Again, when his soul is guided by God, when he is responsive and
obedient in his life to the divine will, the godly man will not be
irresolute in matters in which others, using only their own resources,
are soon at their wits' end.

[32–33] Verse 32 once more takes up the theme of vv. 12–15 and
speaks of the pursuit of the godly by the sinners. The faithful, however, is not afraid of it. He knows that God stands by him and does
not abandon him to the violence of the evildoer. Though the latter
may arraign him before a court of justice, using either force or guile,
the God-fearing man will come into his own, since God protects him
and sees to it that he will not be condemned. [34] Here speaks the
conscience of a godly man who rests in God and whose conscience
for that reason is easy; for he does not allow his faith to be shaken by
the fear of men, knowing that God ensures the victory of the upright
in heart. It is entirely appropriate that this thought is followed by
the exhortation to wait patiently for the Lord and walk in his ways
and by the promise of the future exaltation of the godly (that is:
deliverance from affliction and peril) and of the future possession of
land as in vv. 9, 11, 18, 22, 29. Once more the psalmist reverts to the
ideas associated with the tradition of the Covenant, that is to say, to
the promise of the land, to judgment and salvation, and to
blessing and curse. The assurance which he draws thence by virtue
of his faith is so vividly present in his mind that he adds, as if he
wanted to comfort the godly, that the persecuted will look on the
destruction of the wicked. This statement is not to be interpreted as
being dictated by a feeling of vindictiveness; on the contrary, something quite different is here at stake—the providential rule of God,
which was obscured by the affliction of the godly, is once more made
manifest to them. It is not a matter of retribution but of the *validity*
of God's promise and curse which is corroborated by their fulfilment.

[35–36] The question hinges on the problem of faith whether
God's Word proves to be trustworthy. To answer this question,
which for the psalmist himself does not pose any problem, he once
more draws on the treasure of his rich experience and tells of a
wicked man who in his arrogance and defiance raised himself up like
a cedar of Lebanon and yet faded away and all his haughty pride
with him.

[37–40] The psalmist justifies his final emphatic exhortation to

live a truly godly and righteous life with the *hope* of which only the
'man of peace' (= man of salvation) can be assured. This man differs
from the sinner in so far as the sinner is without hope, since there is
no other future for him than destruction. A life without hope is not
worth living. But the hope of the godly is God. It is on God that the
conclusion of the psalm focuses its thoughts, and the psalmist once
more sums up what was either explicitly or implicitly behind the
individual sayings of the poem in the statement that whosoever trusts
in God has in him everything he needs. It is *he* who is the Helper and
Saviour in affliction and peril. A life lived with God is full of hope
and strength; without God it is doomed to destruction. This is the
simple and clear logic of faith which persists throughout the psalm.
This simplicity and transparency has been born of a courageous
resolve to believe in the face of all the deceptive appearances to the
contrary, and for this reason still carries with it even today that
unshakable strength which provides guidance and comfort for the
godly.

38. SUFFERING AND GUILT

A Psalm. Of David. For the purpose of making a confession(?)[1]

1 O Lord, rebuke me not in thy anger,
    nor chasten me in thy wrath!
2 For thy arrows have sunk into me,
    and thy hand lies heavily[2] upon me.[3]
3 There is no soundness in my flesh because of thy indignation;
    there is no health in my bones because of my sin.
4 For my iniquities have gone over my head;
    they are like a heavy burden, too heavy for me.
5 My wounds grow foul and fester
    because of my foolishness,
6 I am utterly bowed down and prostrate;
    all the day I go about mourning.
7 My loins are filled with burning,
    and there is no health in my flesh any more.
8 I am utterly spent and greatly bruised;
    I cry out for the groaning of my heart.[4]
9 Lord, all my longing is known to thee,
    my sighing is not hidden from thee.
10 My heart throbs violently,
    my strength fails me;
    and the light of my eyes—
    it also has gone from me.
11 My loved ones and friends stand aloof from me ' '[2]
    and my kinsmen stand afar off.

12 Those who seek my life laid their snares,
   those who seek my hurt speak of ruin,
   and meditate treachery all the day long.

13 But I am like a deaf man, I do not hear,
   like a dumb man who does not open his mouth.

14 Yea, I became like a man who does not hear,
   and in whose mouth are no rebukes.

15 For it is for thee, O Lord, that I wait;
   it is thou, O Lord my God, who wilt answer.

16 For I thought that they should not rejoice over me,
   who boast against me when my foot slips.[5]

17 For I am on the verge of falling,
   and my pain is ever with me.

18 For I confess my guilt,
   I am grieved at my sin.

19 Those who are my foes without cause[2] are mighty,
   and many are those who hate me wrongfully.

20 Those who render me evil for good
   are my adversaries because I follow after good.

21 Do not forsake me, O Lord!
   O my God, be not far from me!

22 Make haste to help me, O my Lord,
   thou art my salvation!

[1] Cf. the title of Ps. 70. Luther translates: for a memorial (*l hāzkīr*). Others relate the term to the' *azkārā*, the offering of incense, which was part of the 'meal offering' (*minḥā*) and in the course of which the worship of late Judaism is said to have used the psalm as a prayer.
[2] See BH.
[3] * RSV renders v. 2b 'and thy hand has come down on me'.
[4] * V. 8b reads in RSV, 'I groan because of the tumult of my heart.'
[5] * In RSV v. 16 is:
   For I pray, 'Only let them not rejoice over me,
   who boast against me when my foot slips!'

This is a lament which the ancient Church rightly numbered amongst the seven penitential psalms (cf. the commentary on Ps. 6). Its opening words are almost identical with those of Psalm 6, but lamentation and the consciousness of having sinned stand out here more clearly—though at the expense of the conciseness and forcefulness of the diction and thought-sequence. The worshipper is afflicted by a grievous sickness (perhaps leprosy, vv. 5, 7) which, according to the conviction generally shared at that time, not only the worshipper himself but also his friends, who on that account turn from him (v. 11), interpret as a punishment inflicted upon him by God. He suffers above all from his feeling of guilt which he candidly confesses before God (vv. 4, 18). Moreover, he is exposed to the persecution of

malicious deadly enemies (vv. 12, 19) whose accusations, which are
without cause, he submits to in silence (vv. 13 f.), trusting that God
will have mercy upon him. The psalm unfolds before our eyes a
deeply affecting picture of the affliction caused by most grievous
human suffering and at the same time in a touching manner bears
witness to the strong power of a sincere and patient trust in God
springing from true repentance; and because of its simple truthfulness
this testimony is able to give comfort and help to those who suffer.
The psalm has been freely used in the hymn 'Grosser Gott, du liebst
Erbarmen'.[1]

[1–2] The psalmist appeals to God's mercy in a prayer which
obviously makes use of a fixed pattern (cf. Ps. 6.1). He feels that
God's hand, which has punished him, presses heavily upon him.
Moreover, he has been pierced by the 'arrows' of illness (cf. the
comments on Ps. 91.5). Thus he turns to God in the only hope that is
still left to him that the hand which has inflicted the wound on him
will also alone be able to heal it again. [3–4] He has clearly recognized that he faces a situation for which there is no remedy, as he is
confronted with the wrath of God on the one hand, and, on the other,
with the burden of his sin; thus he regards his sickness as a well-
deserved punishment. The situation which he faces derives its
exceedingly grave character from the fact that he believes himself to
be like a man who is in danger of being drowned in the ocean of his
guilt or of breaking down under the heavy burden of his sin (cf.
Gen. 4.13). [5–8] But it is precisely the utter hopelessness of his
physical and mental breakdown which leads him into the only way
which is still left open to him, the way, that is, of making a frank
confession before God. Without in the least trying to gloss over his
sins (cf. v. 5b) he lets God look into his pitiable physical and mental
misery, his body being utterly bowed down by pain and failing to
render any service to him, and the distress of his heart making him
howl like a wounded animal; and he acts in this manner not only in
order to arouse God's compassion but even more so because he is
driven to this action by the elementary need of a God-fearing man to
pour out his heart to his God—such a frank confession before God is
felt to be already in itself a relief, and moreover is meant to restore
the lost contact with God. [9] The way the psalmist interrupts his
lamentation for a brief moment in v. 9 and lifts up his eyes to God
makes clear beyond any doubt that these are his true motives. It

[1] * By Matthias Jorissen (1739–1823).

creates in us the impression of a man whose grieved heart draws breath, a heart which in trusting humility wholly surrenders to the omniscient God who sees into the hearts of men. God knows the worshipper's every longing; he has therefore no need to ask God for the fulfilment of his desires; what he has at heart more than anything else is that the agony of his spirit does not remain hidden from God. **[10–12]** Once more he is overwhelmed by the magnitude of his misery. This time it is above all his mental suffering which he laments and confesses before God with an anxiously throbbing heart, being on the verge of fainting (v. 10). To the loneliness of a man shunned by his loved ones and friends, though his greatest need at this moment is to be encouraged by a friendly look and to be helped, be it only in a small way, there is added the further affliction that he is attacked without cause and in a deceitful manner by a great number of enemies, who not only desire his ruin but even seek to take his life (vv. 12, 19). **[13–20]** He quite candidly confesses before God in vv. 11–18 that he has patiently and without any opposition submitted to these afflictions, too, willing to endure his suffering submissively, because he is conscious of having sinned against God and of being powerless. For he entrusts his cause entirely to his God, who is the only stay and hope left to him. He trusts that God, who knows that he was striving after that which is good, will triumph and not the boastful enemies who rendered him evil for good (vv. 16, 20). Thus the worshipper stands before his heavenly Lord in genuine contrition and without any complacency or vindictiveness, confessing his guilt, sincerely repenting of his sins (v. 18), earnestly resolved to do what is good (v. 20) and 'despairing of himself, but not of God'. Having relieved his heart of its burden through prayer and having entrusted his affliction to the grace of God, he can now dare to ask God for his help and can hope to find his salvation wholly in his communion with him.

39. AND NOW, O LORD, WHERE SHALL I FIND COMFORT? MY HOPE IS IN THEE

To the Conductor. For Jeduthun.[1] *A Psalm. Of David*

1 I thought, I will guard my ways,
    that I may not sin with my tongue;
  I will bridle my mouth,
    so long as a wicked man is in my presence.

2 I have become dumb and silent,
 I held my peace, there was no happiness;
 but my suffering was intense,[2]
3 my heart became hot within me.
 As I mused, it burned (like) fire;[3]
 then I spoke with my tongue:
4 'Lord, let me know my end,
 and what is the measure of my days;
 that I may see[4] how fleeting my life is!
5 Behold, thou hast made my days a few handbreadths,
 and my lifetime is as nothing in thy sight.
 A mere[5] breath is every man who stands (self-assured).[6] *Selah*
6 Man goes about as a mere shadow.
 Surely for naught are they in turmoil;
 man heaps up, and knows not who will gather.
7 And now, O Lord, for what shall I wait?
 In thee (alone) my hope is set.
8 Deliver me from all my transgressions.
 O, make me not the scorn of the fool!
9 I held my tongue,[7] I do not open my mouth;
 for it is thou who hast done it.
10 Remove thy plague from me;
 I am sure to perish through the force[5] of thy hand.[8]
11 When thou dost chasten man with rebukes for sin,
 thou dost destroy like a moth what is most precious to him. *Selah*
 Surely every man is a mere breath!
12 Hear my prayer, O Lord, and give ear to my cry;
 hold not thy peace at my tears!
 For I dwell only as a guest with thee,
 and am a sojourner like all my fathers.[9]
13 Look away[5] from me, that I may know gladness,
 before I depart and be no more!'

[1] According to I Chron. 16.41 the name of the ancestor of one of the guilds of Temple-singers (besides Heman) at the time of David. See p. 97.
  [2] * V. 2 in RSV:
   I was dumb and silent,
   I held my peace to no avail;
   my distress grew worse.
  [3] * RSV reads in the second line, 'As I mused, the fire burned.'
  [4] * RSV is 'let me know how fleeting my life is!'
  [5] See BH.
  [6] * The third line reads in RSV, 'Surely every man stands as a mere breath!'
  [7] * In RSV v. 9 opens with 'I am dumb' instead of 'I held my tongue'.
  [8] * V. 10 reads in RSV:
   Remove thy stroke from me;
   I am spent by the blows of thy hand.
  [9] * The last two lines read in RSV:
   For I am thy passing guest,
   a sojourner, like all my fathers.

The psalm cannot be classed with any of the familiar psalm types. Though it exhibits themes of the lament, it cannot for all that be regarded as a proper lament. Its author is of such an independent disposition and the problem which agitates his mind is so closely related to his entirely personal circumstances that he throws over the restrictions which are imposed upon him by the traditional forms and in his strange dialogue with God provides us with a deep insight into the struggles of his soul in a way almost unique in the Psalter. The psalm follows its own course also with regard to the problems dealt with in Psalm 73 and in the Book of Job or in Psalm 90; and some expositors would like to relate this psalm too to those problems. Though the psalm does not achieve either the profound insight of these other compositions or their liberating breadth of vision, it does not fall short of the testimony which they bear to the struggles in which faith is engaged—in the earnestness and the truthfulness at all costs with which the psalmist tackles, on the basis of his own grievous experiences, the two fundamental problems of life, the problems of 'God and man' and 'God and sin'.

[1–3] Without any special introduction the psalm begins with the psalmist's reflection on his own self, which in this context can best be understood as a kind of confession before God. This confession is intended to expose before God quite frankly the struggles which rage in the worshipper's soul as well as the fact that his accomplishments continually fall short of his intentions (cf. Rom. 7.15, 18 f.). This is the only way that is left to a man whose heart is filled with terror when he glimpses the abyss of human nature and who is frightened and feels helpless at the hopelessness of his own sin and weakness. The psalmist, who had been sorely tried (vv. 10, 12 f.), had resolved to endure the suffering inflicted on him by God (v. 9) in silent submission, and he had done so for the sole reason that he did not want to offer the wicked a welcome spectacle by lamenting his misery and by sinfully remonstrating with God. But the strength of his dutiful self-control did not hold out against the burning agony caused by brooding over his thoughts and by unbearable pains; thus he felt compelled in the end to be disloyal to his own resolution. He now appears before God to confess that he fell into sin, and fully discloses to him the distress of his soul. [4–5] The prayer which follows shows how seriously he takes this failure. It is not really feasible to hold the view that in these words, let alone in the whole psalm from v. 4 onwards, are to be found the words which the poet had no longer been able to hold back under the pressure of his affliction, and so to interpret vv. 1–3 as presenting a kind of biographical introduction in the story of the psalm's composition. For vv. 4 ff., imbued as they are with a calm and self-composed resignation, betray nothing of the agitation or sinful rebellion which one would have to expect in that case in view of the statements made in vv. 1–3. It would rather seem that the breaking of the silence which the psalmist had imposed upon himself preceded the psalm, and in that case the psalm as such presents itself as the earnest attempt of a sensitive man to recover once more, by means of his dialogue with God, his right mind in the midst of his physical and mental suffering. It is in this connection that the knowledge of the transient nature and futility of every human life and of all human effort in the sight of God is first fully brought to light. It is by no means unimportant that the poet asks God for this knowledge, which forms the main theme of the first part of the psalm; for it is only in that perspective which sees everything as God sees it that the only trustworthy criterion and compass for *the true nature of man* can be found; man continually needs that criterion and compass if he does not want to fall a victim to his own prejudices or to those of others. The most common prejudice, from which the psalmist himself did not escape, is the general tendency to overestimate one's own importance. [6] Man sees his relation to the reality of God in its right proportions only if that prejudice is radically eliminated—if man *sub specie aeternitatis Dei*, which he grasps in the light of his end and of the transient nature and brevity of his life, comes to realize that his life and work are 'much ado about nothing', and has lost his rebellious self-assurance. The fact that the worshipper is so serious-minded and so courageous that he is even prepared to accept the radical result of that perspective, which ruthlessly puts an end to any attempt at trying to hold on to what is only ephemeral—this is not to be regarded as the manifestation of a dejected pessimism but as the expression of a sober realism, which is no longer glossed over by any kind of illusion. [7] This is proved by the question and answer which provide the first part of the psalm with some sort of a conclusion. It is only the man who has grasped the transient character, the futility, of all human nature in the sight of God who comes to understand *the true nature of God* and realizes that it is in God alone that he is able to find comfort and support when every human support has proved unreliable. Having gained his freedom from his bonds (*Bindungen*) to this world, the worshipper, making a bold decision of faith, casts

all his sorrows and hopes on God, to whom alone he now knows
himself to be tied (*gebunden*) and with whom alone he knows himself
to be united (*verbunden*).

[8] But it is precisely this knowledge which also opens his eyes to
his *sin*, separating him from God, and to the responsibility laid upon
him by his relationship with God. And his hope in God, which he
now expresses in the form of a prayer, consists in his expectation that
God will save him from his sins and will prevent him from becoming
anew the cause of the scorn and blasphemy of 'the fools'. He is in real
earnest with that heavy responsibility which true faith in God carries
with it and with which he had wrestled, but which he had already
once failed to fulfil (vv. 1 f.)—the responsibility that the life of the
godly one shall point to the reality of God and bear witness to it
(cf. Matt. 5.16; I Peter 2.11 f.). [9] This is why he once more reverts
to his previous resolve to demonstrate by his submission and patient
silence that he regards his life as being decreed by God (cf. Ps. 38.15
f.), so that his testimony to God will not once more be turned into
a denial of God either by himself or by somebody else. He has now
come to understand the nature of man and his own powerlessness too
well not to know that he is incapable of achieving that goal without
God's help. Thus he prays that God may relieve him from the force
of his hand which punished him and presses heavily upon him.
[10–11] For it is only when the knowledge of the transient nature of
man is considered under the aspect of God's punishment of human
guilt (cf. the comments on Ps. 90.7 ff.) that it leads to the realization
of that metaphysical contrast between God and man which imparts
to the fact of death the character of an inescapable fate, of God's
judgment on sin namely. Something of the truth of the Pauline
saying, 'The sting of death is sin' (I Cor. 15.56), is also woven into the
picture of the moth, illustrating the 'destructive' effect of God's
judgment passed on those who are guilty. [12] Without God's grace
man is lost. The worshipper is aware of this truth when he dares
to ask God to grant his prayer. He is not entitled to demand from
him protection and deliverance; like a guest and sojourner he has to
rely on the kindness and mercy of him to whose protection he has
entrusted himself. In spite of all his humility and cautious reserve,
which is expressed in the motivation of his petition, he clings to his
bond and communion with God ('*immāk* = 'with thee'; cf. Ps. 73.23)
which is the prerequisite without which his whole prayer would not
be possible at all. And yet fear of God and trust in God contend with

each other in his soul—which proves that his faith is genuine and that his prayer is truthful. [13] The terrifying impression which God's grave view of his sin has made upon him is so strong that he will already rest content if God will no longer look upon him in anger, but will look away from him (cf. Job 7.19; 14.6), and if he can once more breathe a sigh of relief before he enters upon the way that leads through the dark gate of death. At the conclusion of the psalm once more full force and weight is given to the spirit of profound earnestness with which the whole is imbued and from which the confession of the psalmist receives the stamp of an inescapable truth. The melancholy impression, which in spite of v. 7 this valuable testimony to the struggles of a faithful soul produces, has its origin in the limits which, with few exceptions, the fact of death sets to the Old Testament, and beyond which the psalmist does not dare to go in his reflections; in this he differs from the poet of Psalm 73. His attitude is a silent and yet eloquent indication of the necessity for mankind's salvation of Christ's death and resurrection, by which it has first been granted deliverance from the power of sin and death.

40. THANKSGIVING AND SUPPLICATION
To the Conductor. Of David. A Psalm

1 I waited for the Lord, yearning for him;[1]
   he inclined to me and heard my cry.
2 He drew me up from the gruesome pit,
   out of the miry bog,
   and set my feet upon a rock,
   making my steps secure.
3 He put a new song in my mouth,
   a song of praise to our God.
   Many see it and tremble,[2]
   and put their trust in the Lord.
4 Blessed is the man who makes the Lord his trust,
   who does not turn to the proud and to liars
   who go astray after false gods![3]
5 Much hast thou done for us,[4] O Lord my God,
   thy wondrous deeds and thy saving thoughts towards us;[5]
   none can compare with thee!
   Were I to proclaim and tell of them,
   they would be more than can be numbered.
6 Sacrifice and offering do not please thee;
   but ears thou hast dug for me![6]
   Burnt offering and sin offering thou dost not require.

7 Then I said, 'Lo, I come;
    in the roll of the book I have been given instruction.'[7]
8 I delight to do thy will, O my God;
    and thy law is within my heart.
9 I have told the glad news of deliverance
    in the great congregation;
    I have not restrained my lips,
    as thou knowest, O Lord.
10 I have not hid thy righteousness within my heart,
    I openly declared thy faithfulness and thy saving help;
    I have not concealed thy grace and truth
    from the great congregation.[8]
11 Therefore, O Lord, thou wilt not withhold
    thy mercy from me;[9]
    let thy grace and thy faithfulness
    ever preserve me!
12 Alas! Afflictions have encompassed me
    which cannot be numbered;
    my iniquities have overtaken me,
    and I cannot take them in at a glance;[10]
    they are more than the hairs of my head;
    my heart fails me!
13 Be pleased, O Lord, to deliver me!
    O Lord, make haste to help me!
14 Let them be confounded and blush with shame
    who seek to snatch away my life ' ';[4]
    let them be turned back and brought to dishonour
    who desire my hurt!
15 Let them be appalled because of their shame
    who say to each other of me,[11] 'Aha, Aha!'
16 But may all who seek thee
    rejoice and be glad in thee!
    May those who love thy salvation
    say continually, 'Great is the Lord!'
17 And though I am wretched and poor—
    the Lord takes thought for me.
    Thou art my help[4] and my deliverer;
    do not tarry, O my God!

1 * RSV reads, 'I waited patiently for the Lord!'
2 * RSV has the future tense in the third line.
3 * The words 'and to liars' are replaced in RSV by 'to those'.
4 See BH.
5 * V. 5 begins in RSV:
    Thou hast multiplied, O Lord my God,
    thy wondrous deeds and thy thoughts towards us;
6 * The first two lines of v. 6 in RSV:
    Sacrifice and offering thou dost not desire;
    but thou hast given me an open ear.

7 * The second line of v. 7 is in RSV 'in the roll of the book it is written of me'.
8 * V. 10 reads in RSV:
    I have not hid thy saving help within my heart,
    I have spoken of thy faithfulness and thy salvation;
    I have not concealed thy steadfast love and thy faithfulness from the great
       congregation.
9 * V. 11 opens in RSV:
    Do not thou, O Lord, withhold
    thy mercy from me,
10 * RSV has in the fourth line of v. 12 'till I cannot see' instead of 'and I
cannot take them in at a glance'.
11 * In RSV we read 'who say to me' instead of 'who say to each other of me'.

The great majority of recent expositors regard the psalm as an
artificial creation, the product of liturgical efforts, being compiled
from different themes which are not related to each other. This view
is based on the observation that a tension exists between the gratitude
expressed in vv. 1–10 for the deliverance, which the worshipper has
come to know, and the prayer offered in vv. 11–17 in the midst of an
overwhelming affliction, a tension, I say, which is held to make it
impossible to conceive of these two actions as having arisen out of
one and the same situation of the worshipper. Those who hold this
view deem themselves to be so much the more justified in dividing up
the psalm into various heterogeneous portions as vv. 13–17 are
preserved again in Psalm 70 with only small variations and as several
phrases and thoughts in vv. 14 ff. recur in Ps. 35.4, 21, 26 f. But
on this assumption it would be just as little possible to give a satisfactory answer to the question of the meaning and purpose of such a
liturgical compilation, which in the view of these expositors must be
regarded as being entirely untrue to life from a psychological point
of view. Moreover, quite apart from this reflection, we have good
reason for pondering over the question whether it is not possible to
understand the psalm in the light of a specific situation from which it
has sprung in its entirety, a situation, that is, which explains why,
in contrast to the lament pattern according to which one has sought
to interpret the psalm, the thanksgiving for the help given precedes
the prayer for deliverance from a calamity, and how we have to
understand the psalm's being to a certain extent identical with
Psalms 70 and 35. For the view that the sequence of prayer and
thanksgiving (in this order) can alone claim to be in harmony with
the truth, as psychology sees it, can be accepted as correct only on the
presupposition that the prayer and the thanksgiving are related to
the same facts.

This is, however, by no means the case as far as Psalm 40 is concerned. If the first part of the psalm is understood as the foundation on which the worshipper's religious experiences are based, which he has gained in the past and to which he now clings in the face of a new calamity, as the worshipper does in Psalm 22 (vv. 4–10), then neither psychological nor religious doubts arise about the unity of the psalm as a whole and about the consistency of its order. It is precisely the experiences which he has gained when the divine salvation was dispensed in connection with the general tradition of the festival cult of the cult community (cf. 'many' and 'toward us' in vv. 3–5; 'great congregation' in vv. 9 f.), and to which he clings at the very time when he has lost his self-confidence and all his courage (v. 12), which provide the inner sanction for his action and also the guarantee for his assurance which alone is able to transform his petition into a genuine prayer. And it is a manifestation of humble obedience, which can only flow from genuine piety, that he at first represses his egotistic desire, urging him to seek deliverance from his affliction, and focuses his eyes and thoughts on God, dwelling on the time during which his relationship with God was unimpaired. The tension between the possessing of the assurance of faith and the striving for it, which dominates the whole psalm right to the closing verse, must not be treated as non-existent by dividing up the psalm into several portions, which are then attributed to different authors and situations. On the contrary, that tension is of the essence of faith and is the mark of the genuine and active piety of a biblical worshipper, who is led over the heights and through the depths of a life lived by faith and progresses from experience to hope. This is the spiritual situation in the light of which the psalm is to be understood as a unity and as being true to life.

Several intimations in vv. 3–5 and 9 f. suggest that the psalm was recited within the setting of the community's public worship. The poet's attitude to the sacrificial cult (vv. 6 ff.) and the sacred tradition is to be accounted for by the peculiar character of the ancient Israelite cult of the Covenant in which the sacrificial system did not occupy the same central position which it held in the worship of the Second Temple (see Intr. 25 ff., 71). The psalm does not enable us to establish a symmetric construction of its verses. On the other hand, it can be easily divided up into the following sections, as far as subject-matter is concerned: vv. 1–3a speak of God's help which the worshipper has experienced in an earlier period of his life; vv. 3b–5

speak of the effect which the revelation of the divine salvation has on
the community of the faithful; vv. 6–10 deal with the true way of
giving thanks; this is followed in vv. 11 and 12 by the worshipper's
prayer for preservation in a new calamity which has overtaken him at
the present time and by a confession of his sins. In vv. 13–17 he
follows up this prayer, for which he uses his own words, by another
prayer, which he has not formulated himself but which seems to him
to be appropriate to his personal circumstances; as we can establish
by comparing it with the identical text of Psalm 70, he alters the
wording of the closing verse in such a way that the prayer ends with
a phrase which fits in with his personal situation and attitude.

The experience of divine help (vv. 1–3a)

[1] Choosing the narrative form, the psalmist recalls the hours
when as in his present circumstances he had looked out for God's
help in prayer and with yearning and anxiety (this sentiment is
already contained in the basic meaning of the verb). [2] At that time
his prayer had been granted, and he had been rescued. God had
delivered him from his affliction; this is what the poet means when,
using the picturesque language shaped by tradition, he speaks of
having been drawn up from the 'pit of tumult', out of 'the miry bog'
(cf. Ps. 69.2, 14; see Intr. 82). Since these images had probably originally been used of the underworld, we would not be justified in thinking,
with reference to Jer. 38.6, that the poet was imprisoned. In a
similar fashion the next saying concerning the rock and the steps
made secure is likewise to be understood as a word-picture illustrating
the assurance which (as in Ps. 18.32 f.) God's help had restored to
him. It is not the details of his personal experience which are prominent in the poet's recollection and presentation but the general fact
of God's help. At the centre of the poet's review of the past is thus not
what is of psychological and human interest but the theological,
divine aspect. [3a] This goes so far that the poet regards as God's
gift not only his experience of divine salvation but also the song of
praise to the glory of God which he had begun to sing as an expression
of gratitude for his deliverance. The genuine humility of faith is
shown by the fact that man accepts everything that he is and has as
a gift from God's hand. The psalmist speaks of a 'new song' which, he
says, God has put in his mouth (cf. Pss. 33.3; 40.3; 144.9; 149.1 and
Intr. 61). The renewal of salvation brought about by God's manifestation of himself in the cult found its corresponding expression in

a 'new song', in which the psalmist places his own experience of
salvation within the larger framework of the hymnic praise of God's
saving deeds which he has wrought for the benefit of the whole cult
community; for what the worshipper was privileged to experience
when his prayer was granted was by no means given to him as his
exclusive possession. The individual personal life lived by faith is of
significance also for everybody else (cf. Pss. 22.22 ff.; 64.9; 142.7,
etc.; see Intr. 81, 86). The fact that the psalmist speaks of 'our God'
at the conclusion of the present train of thought points to the public
worship of the cult community as the situation in which the thanksgiving had its origin; and this shows how faith proceeds to think in
terms of the community, a way of thinking which forms the subject of
v. 3b.

Of the community of faith (vv. 3b–5)

[3b] The next section enables us to get an insight into the community of faith which characterizes the covenant community. What
is done to the individual member is done to the community. We are
reminded of the New Testament saying, 'If one member suffers, all
suffer together; and if one member is honoured, all rejoice together'
(I Cor. 12.26). The genuineness and truth of the experience of the
presence of God is demonstrated precisely by this strange combination of fear and trust. Complete trust is possible only when God's
action is comprehended in such a way that the direct impression of
his power makes man tremble because he perceives that that
power is unsurpassably and superhumanly great. It would never
be possible to put absolute trust in a God to whose power a limit was
set somewhere. [4] The poet uses the form of a 'Beatitude', to which
he gives the touch of an exhortation, to depict in all its fullness the
humble and yet proud happiness of a trust in God which is enjoyed
in the fellowship of the godly, and contrasts it in a striking fashion
with the arrogant self-assurance of the wicked, who deceive themselves and others to such an extent that they overlook the true state
of affairs and in their sacrilegious rebellion against God become
thereby 'liars who go astray after false gods'. [5] True faith also
opens the eyes to the realization of the nature and ultimate motives
of disbelief. Having cast a side-glance at the adversaries, which at the
same time contains their repudiation (see Intr. 51, 76 f.), the poet
takes up again the theme of the praise of God, the purpose of which
had also been served, though indirectly, by the 'Beatitude' in v. 4,

a kind of affirmation of faithfulness. In the form of a hymnic prayer he praises the abundance of the wondrous deeds of God by which his gracious saving will was made manifest. As he fulfils this pious duty, the poet unites with his whole people, and with the tradition of the *Heilsgeschichte* recited at the cultic feast and experienced as a present event (see Intr. 44, 59 f.). The incomparable majesty of God is revealed in the divine saving will—in other words, in his grace (cf. v. 16). The impression it produces upon man makes him realize for the first time his own inability to grasp God's lovingkindness in all its fullness and give expression to it. Measured against God's greatness he becomes small, and even the most fervent thanksgiving and the most eloquent witness to that greatness of God in the hymnic praise of the congregation are not able to do justice to the majesty of the divine reality.

The true way of giving thanks (vv. 6–10)

How, then, should it be possible for grateful man to offer anything to such a God that would be appropriate and worthy of him, be it even all kinds of sacrifices? An attitude whereby man, facing the Deity at the sacrifice, puts himself, as it were, on the same footing as God and produces a 'gift' also on his part, would not accord with what is in keeping with the grace and majesty of God. It is God and his revelation and not man who in this is at the centre of the cult; and for that very reason man can only listen and obey. There is but *one* attitude of man which renders to this God what belongs to him of right, and that is the attitude of humbly receiving the grace of God and of bearing witness to it; it is the attitude of obedience and of submission to his will. It is in the direction of this train of thought that we probably have to look in order to discover the connection between v. 5 and the next section. It is the same perception which accords with the original fundamental character of the Covenant of Yahweh and is also advocated by the prophets, the perception namely that the only possible attitude which is adequate to the surpassing reality of God is expressed not by sacrifices and gift-offerings but by the subjection of man's whole personality to God's claim. This knowledge equally accounts for the view expressed in the psalm and for those prophetic passages (such as I Sam. 15.22; Amos 5.21 ff.; Hos. 6.6; 8.11 ff.; Isa. 1.10 ff.; Micah 6.6 ff.; Jer. 7.21 ff.; Isa. 40.16; 66.1 ff.) which contrast the sacrificial cult with God's all-absorbing claim upon the whole man. [6–7] At the point at which otherwise it was

customary in a thanksgiving to promise the Deity sacrifices and gift-offerings as an expression of gratitude for the help he had given (cf. Ps. 22.25 ff.), the poet who composed this psalm similarly speaks of a sacrifice—but he does so by giving the word a different and more profound meaning. He categorically pushes aside the whole sacrificial cult. This can be inferred from the fact that he also mentions burnt-offerings and sin-offerings, though they are in no wise related to the thank-offering, besides the sacrifices and gift-offerings customarily used for the thank-offering (cf. Lev. 7.12 ff.). This axiomatic repudiation of the whole sacrificial cult is to be accounted for, as in the case of the prophets, by the perception, indicated before-hand, of the wrong basic attitude to God which is expressed in the sacrificial cult and which in origin and nature was borrowed from the sphere of a different cultus. Man cannot put himself on the same footing as God by virtue of his offering of sacrifices, nor can he 'put' his relationship with God 'in order' by his own efforts. He always remains subject to God, who is the One who gives everything. And the attitude of man which alone accords with these facts is that of listening to God's voice and of obeying his will ('ears thou hast dug for me' and 'in the roll of the book I have been given instruction'). Inspired by a truly biblical understanding of the Holy Scriptures, the poet refers this traditional covenant saying to his own person and expresses his willingness to surrender his mind and soul completely to God by saying 'Lo, I have come' (add 'to the Temple'). He does not take his stand face to face with God; rather does he place himself at God's disposal. What the prophets had demanded as the true attitude of faith is here made manifest in the divine service.
[8] If the surrender to God is truly the complete giving up of man's whole personality to God, then God's claim is no longer felt to be an alien and heavy yoke, but is accepted as a call to a joyous, active life arising out of the sentiments of a heart that knows itself to be at one with the will (law) of God.

[9–10] It is of the essence of faith and of its tradition of worship that it constrains the godly man to bear witness to his faith in the midst of the congregation. The missionary task of pastoral responsi-bility to God for one's neighbour and that inward constraint of having to bear witness to what God has done cannot be separated from the experience of God which is granted to the individual. Thus the testimony to God's gift of deliverance to the individual becomes the instrument of God's providential rule, God doing his work through human beings who place themselves at his service and spread his revelation abroad. The psalmist is aware of the obligatory character of his encounter with God and of his responsibility for his neighbour. This is why he emphatically affirms before his God that he kept nothing whatsoever to himself of God's salvation, egotistically enjoying it for the benefit of his own piety; nay, he proclaimed God's 'grace and faithfulness', his saving help and righteousness (see Intr. 58) in the midst of the great congregation of the pilgrims attending the feast. All these terms are not at all to be understood in the sense of a description of God's 'qualities'; rather are they meant to express the nature of God as the One who is a living reality and is at work; they are meant to express the divine dynamic quality of the realization of his salvation in the festival cult. Thus, for instance, God's 'righteousness' is not used here in the legal sense, but as signifying God's activity, which includes his saving will, his grace and truthfulness and also the constancy of his actions. It is by such a testimony to the 'Living' God that the believer expresses his gratitude in the right way, and the proof and happiness of a living relationship with God lie in the fact that the faithful may receive the experience of God's salvation as well as pass it on to others.

[11–12] However, the saving experience of such a communion with God now forms also the basis of the poet's hope, the way which gives him access to God at the time of his separation from God and in the calamity which has overtaken him. He draws from that experience the strength and infers from it his right to pray for God's mercy and grace at a time when his heart fails him in view of his sins and sufferings. Thus he does not utter his supplications at random, nor does he beg without having a firm foundation, but offers a genuine prayer which arises out of the assurance of faith. To pray without having such a basis of faith would be to tempt God. It is the very use of the same words as in vv. 9 and 10 which throws into bold relief the same foundation of faith on which the poet takes his stand both in his thanksgiving and in his supplications. Without that experience the psalmist would not be able to pray that God may for ever preserve him by his 'grace and faithfulness'. But he now also becomes conscious of the full extent of his guilt when he sees it against the background of God's grace. He senses the sinister power of sin which has 'overtaken' him like a demonic fate. No wonder his heart fails him and he loses all his self-confidence and entirely relies on God and not on his own self. It is this 'giving up of oneself' and throwing

oneself entirely upon God' that is the factor which determines the
religious and psychological trend of the whole psalm, including its
order; in its light the whole psalm is to be understood. It is just
because he is no longer able to find support in his own strength in the
midst of his present affliction and is in danger of perishing on account
of his separation from God, brought about by his sin, that the worshipper so firmly clings to the recollection of that ceremony at which
the thanksgiving for God's help and for a life lived in obedience to
his will imparted to him the blessed assurance of his communion with
God. That recollection is the only support towards which a sinking
man stretches out his hand.

The fact that the worshipper is completely cast down and incapable of seeing things clearly on account of his sins may also explain
why he makes use in vv. 13–17 of a current liturgical text which
appeared to him appropriate to his personal circumstances and
suitable for the purpose of working out his supplication in more
detail. The incorporation of Psalm 70 here as well as the alteration of
its text, which though small is nevertheless not insignificant, and the
points of contact with Psalm 35 can in this way most easily be
accounted for, following as they do the prayer clothed in the worshipper's own words and the despair expressed in v. 12. **[13]** Thus
the psalmist repeats his urgent petition for deliverance. This depends
entirely on God's grace and is a matter for his free decision. **[14–15]**
In vv. 14 ff. the psalmist turns his thoughts to his adversaries, whom
we may presume were not only personal opponents of the psalmist
but representatives of a specific group from which the whole cult
community had dissociated itself (cf. v. 4). If this interpretation is
correct, we can then also understand why these adversaries are
contrasted in v. 16 with the godly. The thoughts expressed in these
verses do not exclusively arise out of the lower sphere of a far-too-
human hatred. In view of the fact that the Old Testament covenantal religion is characterized by its limitation to this world, the
existence of the wicked always presents at the same time a difficult
religious problem, so that the God-fearing man discerns the reviling of
God which is implied in the derision of the adversary and believes
that he does not possess the proof of the real existence of God till the
wicked are eliminated from the covenant community (see Intr.
47 ff., 76 f.). All the same, it is noteworthy that the psalmist does not
pray here for the destruction of the wicked, as is frequently done elsewhere, but asks that they may be confounded. This implies, though

he does not say so explicitly, the possibility of their ultimate conversion to God (cf. Isa. 53.1 ff.). [16] In contrast to that prayer, a contrast which is both outward and inward, the psalmist then utters a prayer of intercession for the God-fearing people who love God's salvation. Though the wicked may be terrified by God and may be confounded by him when he comes to the help of the godly, the latter will shout with joy and rejoice in the majesty of God which is experienced in his grace. The ultimate purpose of his saving grace is not an egotistically conceived deliverance of the godly as such, but the recognition on the part of the whole community of the godly of the majesty of God and of the greatness of his salvation; what is here at stake is the recognition of God's cause. [17] In the concluding verse the psalmist reverts in prayer to his personal concerns. A comparison with Psalm 70 shows that the worshipper has made an addition to the text of his prototype which, though it is only a small one, is yet full of significance. The theme of confidence, 'the Lord takes thought for me', has been added. The tenor of the whole has thus become different. The element of the comforting assurance of the psalmist's trust in God, with which the first part of the psalm is saturated, is thus brought into the note of urgency and anxiety sounded in his petitions. Thus the prayer which he adopted likewise received a personal stamp. The tension between the possessing (of something) and the waiting (for something), which imparts to the position as a whole a character of its own, is once more clearly expressed even in the last verse of the psalm in that the statement 'the Lord takes thought for me' is here confronted with the saying 'do not tarry, O my God'. At this the conclusion of the psalm reverts to its beginning. And what some expositors wanted to regard as an incongruity in the psalm and as justifying its division into heterogeneous portions shows itself to be the tension which is inherent in faith itself and present wherever a genuine faith is in action. In the realization of this truth lies the realism of the psalm and its trueness to life, things one should not seek to dispute.

41. CURED FROM AN ILLNESS—PRESERVED FROM ENEMIES

To the Conductor. A Psalm. Of David

1 Blessed is he who pays attention to the lowly!
   The Lord delivers him in the day of trouble.

2 The Lord protects him and keeps him alive;
    he is called blessed in the land.
    He does not give[1] him up to the greed of his enemies.[2]
3 The Lord refreshes him on his sick-bed;
    thou hast cured him from his illness.[3]
4 As for me, I said, 'O Lord, be gracious to me;
    heal me, for I have sinned against thee!'
5 My enemies speak evil concerning me,[4]
    'When will he die, and his name perish?'
6 And when one comes to see me,
    his heart speaks falsehood.
    He gathers mischief, goes out into the street
    and tells it abroad.[5]
7 All who hate me whisper together about me;
    they devise against me what is evil for me;[6]
8 they say, 'A base thing has fastened upon him;
    he will not rise again who is now ill in bed.'[7]
9 Even my bosom friend in whom I trusted,
    who ate of my bread, has magnified himself against me ' '.[8]
10 But do thou, O Lord, be gracious to me,
    and raise me up, that I may requite them!
11 By this I know that thou art well disposed towards me,
    in that my enemy has not triumphed over me.
12 But as for me, thou hast upheld me because of my integrity,
    and set me before thy face for ever.
13 Blessed be the Lord, the God of Israel,
    from everlasting to everlasting!
    Amen and Amen.

[1] See BH.
[2] * RSV reads, 'thou dost not give him up to the will of his enemies'.
[3] * V. 3b is in RSV, 'in his illness thou healest all his infirmities'.
[4] * V. 5a reads in RSV, 'My enemies say of me in malice.'
[5] * RSV renders v. 6:
    And when one comes to see me,
    he utters empty words,
    while his heart gathers mischief;
    when he goes out, he tells it abroad.
[6] * In RSV v. 7b reads, 'they imagine the worst for me'.
[7] * V. 8b reads in RSV, 'he will not rise again from where he lies'.
[8] See BH. (Tr. N.: RSV has 'has lifted his heel against me' instead of 'has magnified himself against me'.)

The middle portion of the psalm (vv. 4–10) is a lament. The conclusion (vv. 11 f.) contains an expression of joyful gratitude which was probably uttered in the Temple (v. 12) after the prayer had been granted. It is more difficult to establish the relation of the introduction (vv. 1–3) to the psalm as a whole. The formulation of the 'Beatitude' and the general statements is characterized by a certain didactic tendency; their subject-matter, however, is closely related to the lamentation, so that the worshipper's personal experiences, probably his recovery from illness (vv. 2 f.; cf. vv. 4, 8) and deliverance from his enemies (v. 2c; cf. vv. 6–9, 11 f.), seem to underlie these generalities. It also follows from this that the psalm as a whole is to be interpreted as a thanksgiving uttered after the psalmist's prayer had been answered (see Intr. pp. 69 ff., 83 f.). The hortative, didactic trend of the opening verses is to be accounted for as in Ps. 34.6 ff., that is to say, as arising out of the purpose of the thanksgiving to let the congregation partake of the experiences of the individual worshipper thus expressing his gratitude, and also of his praise of God. In place of the otherwise customary 'narration', dealing with his affliction and deliverance, the poet recites the lament (vv. 4–10) which had once been the subject of his prayer (cf. Pss. 116.11; 31.22; Isa. 38.10; Jonah 2.5), and concludes it by expressing his gratitude for the answering of his prayer (vv. 11–12).

[1–3] The opening 'Beatitude', in which the psalmist praises the blessedness of the man who 'pays attention' to the lowly, is addressed to the congregation gathered for the celebration of a festival service, and is designed to arouse their sympathy and to draw their attention to the fate of the psalmist, who classes himself with the lowly, probably on account of the calamity which he has survived (but see also Intr. 93). The great majority of scholars translate and interpret this passage as if it carried the same meaning as that of Matt. 5.7, regarding it as a call to show mercy to people in humble circumstances; they interpret the subsequent statements as a promise to the merciful which is meant to justify that call and moreover is said to have come true in the poet's own life. But that translation and interpretation is disproved, firstly, by the neutral meaning of *hiskīl* ('to pay attention to'; cf. Neh. 8.13; Prov. 16.20; 21.11 f.; Ps. 101.2) and, secondly, by the fact that, if that translation and interpretation were correct, the 'Beatitude' would in no wise be related to the rest of the psalm, quite apart from the further fact that it would appear strange to use a 'Beatitude' in a situation where it is said to reflect the poet's own experience, so that he who utters the praise would include himself in that praise. Consequently, the psalmist praises the blessedness of those who will 'pay attention' to him and to what he is now going to say to them—because by doing so they will share his joyful gratitude for God's help, which he is about to praise and which will

reveal to them also the grace of their Lord. He who owes to God his
deliverance from the affliction of an illness and from the pursuits of
his enemies, is himself the man who is 'considered' to be 'lucky' (*den
man 'glücklich preist'*), because his bed of suffering 'has been transformed' into joy (Calvin); he is a living witness to God's gracious
protection and help, and in his fate are implied a warning and a
promise for the whole community of the godly. If we see the opening
verses in this light, then they fit quite smoothly into the context of
the whole psalm.

[4–10] As though he wanted to justify his general testimony and
its hortative character the psalmist, instead of narrating his deliverance, now quotes the lament which he had addressed to God during
his illness; already at the end of v. 3 he had proceeded to use the
prayer form and address God directly. This prayer begins and ends
with a petition for God's grace (vv. 4, 10), since the worshipper
evidently regards his illness as a punishment for his sin (v. 4b). The
fact that the theme of his illness and his sin gives way afterwards to
lamentation over the bitter disappointment and distress inflicted
upon him by his enemies, and that the psalmist feels vindicated from
their wrongful accusations by the cure that has been achieved, does
not justify us in regarding the confession of sin and the supplication
for God's grace as being merely a conventional form that does not
contain any substance of truth (this point in opposition to Staerk);
sincere knowledge of having sinned against God does not exclude
the conviction of being innocent as far as particular accusations of
human adversaries are concerned. Indeed, it is precisely the juxtaposition of these two attitudes of mind which is a feature of the
psalm and that is both realistic and true to life; moreover, that
feature supports rather than refutes the view that the author is in
real earnest and is sincere in making these statements: *simul justus et
peccator*. The real sting in his suffering—in this respect he resembles
Job—is that he sees himself helplessly exposed to the gloating, the
hatred and the calumny of his enemies and even to the arrogance of
his friend, instead of enjoying their sincere sympathy and being
comforted by them. Here more clearly than usual, though not quite
pellucid in detail, a picture is drawn of the incomprehensible and yet
so very common hard-hearted unkindness of man, who cruelly assails
the helpless and thinks that by hypocrisy and lies and the levelling of
malicious accusations against him he can gain something for himself
at the other's expense, and whose actions become so much the more

dangerous and repulsive when in support of them he makes use of religious and moral arguments. From that perspective it becomes understandable why the Old Testament laments speak so frequently of such enemies, and also why Jesus so emphatically warned against the 'judging' of others (Matt. 7.1 ff.). **[8]** The picture requires no comment; it speaks clearly enough—against itself. Only in respect of v. 8 it is possible to be in doubt whether as in Ps. 31.13 the accusation 'a base thing has fastened upon him' alludes to a specific sin of the worshipper because of the dismal impression which a sick man makes on those around him as one chastened by God, or whether this statement has in mind a curse (*dābār*), which was pronounced on the worshipper (literally, 'poured out' over him) and now like a deadly poison operates as an evil charm; the text admits of both these interpretations. **[9]** Verse 9 is interpreted in John 13.18 as referring to the traitor Judas, and this has given rise to the interpretation of the psalm in a Messianic sense. **[10]** The psalmist's hope of being able to requite his adversaries for what they have done to him is indeed understandable, arising, as it does, out of his indignation and disappointment, but clearly shows that in this passage, under the judgment of the New Testament, Old Testament thought is restricted by emotions which are far too human.

[11–12] This hope of the psalmist once more recedes into the background in his closing profession of gratitude to God; the fact that the enemies cannot triumph over him, and that as one who has been saved he can again appear 'before God's face', i.e. that he may again enjoy the presence of God in the Temple, is regarded by the worshipper as evidence of the gracious goodwill of his God towards him and of his vindication from the wrong accusations from which he had suffered so severely. The happiness of his communion with God, which he has been able to recover, now outshines all his past suffering, after his prayer has been granted, and enables him to turn his thoughts to the contemplation of eternity. **[13]** The psalm, and at the same time the First Book of the Psalter, ends with a doxology of the whole congregation (see Intr. 21, 100). It is an open question whether the doxology was attached to the psalm only when the compilation of the whole Psalter, or at least of the Davidic Psalter (see Intr. 99), had been completed or whether it belonged to the original text of the psalm. In the latter case the psalm would probably have been placed at the end of the collection in view of its doxological conclusion.

42 and 43. YEARNING FOR GOD

To the Conductor. Maskil.[1] *To the Sons of Korah*[2]

1 As the hind pants for water-brooks,
  so pants my soul for thee, O God.[3]
2 My soul thirsts for God, for the living God.
  When may I come and appear before the face of God?[4]
3 My tears have been my food day and night,
  because men ask me continually, 'Where is your God?'
4 These things I will remember and pour out my soul upon me:
  how I went in procession to the house of God in the company of the
    exalted,[5]
  shouting with joy and giving thanks in the multitude keeping
    festival.[6]
5 *Why are you cast down, O my soul, and groanest within me?*
  Wait for God; for I shall testify to him,
  that he is the help of my countenance and my God![7]
6 My soul is cast down within me, as I think of thee,[8]
  from the land of Jordan and of Hermon,[5] from Mount Mizar.[9]
7 Deep calls to deep at the thunder of their[10] cataracts;
  all thy waves and thy billows have gone over me.
8 By day I pray to the God of my life,[11]
  and at night I sing to his praise.[12]
9 I say to God, 'My rock, why hast thou forgotten me?
  Why must I go mourning, oppressed by the enemy?'[13]
10 It cuts me to the heart,[14] when the enemies revile me
  and continually ask me, 'Where is your God?'[15]
11 *Why are you cast down, O my soul, and groanest within me?*
  Wait for God; for I shall yet testify to him,
  that he is the help of my countenance and my God![7]

Psalm 43

1 Vindicate me and defend my cause against ungodly people;[16]
  from deceitful and wicked men deliver me, O God![5]
2 For thou art the God who protects me;[17]
  why hast thou cast me off?
  Why must I go mourning, oppressed by the enemy?
3 O send out thy light and thy faithfulness;
  let them lead me and bring me to thy holy hill
  and to thy dwelling-place,
4 that I may come to the altar of God, to the God of my joy,[5]
  and may rejoice[5] and praise thee with the cither,
  O God, my God.[18]
5 *Why are you cast down, O my soul, and groanest within me?*
  Wait for God; for I shall yet testify to him,
  that he is the help of my countenance and my God![7]

---

[1] See Ps. 32.

[2] See p. 97.

[3] * RSV renders v. 1:
As a hart longs for flowing streams,
so longs my soul for thee, O God.

[4] Originally the text read, perhaps, 'and behold the face of God'; see BH.
(Tr. N.: V. 2b reads in RSV, 'when shall I come and behold the face of God?')

[5] See BH.

[6] * V. 4 reads in RSV:
These things I remember, as I pour out my soul:
how I went with the throng, and led them in procession to the house of God,
with glad shouts and songs of thanksgiving,
a multitude keeping festival.

[7] See BH. The rendering of the MT is also possible, 'I shall yet testify to him
that he helps me with his countenance'; see BH on v. 16 and Ps. 43.5. (Tr. N.:
RSV has the following, which differs in parts:
Why are you cast down, O my soul,
and why are you disquieted within me?
Hope in God; for I shall again praise him,
my help and my God.)

[8] * RSV has 'therefore I remember thee' instead of 'as I think of thee'.

[9] * Hebrew *Miṣʿār*.

[10] 'Thy' in the MT is adapted to the subsequent suffixes. (Tr. N.: RSV also
renders 'thy' instead of 'their'.)

[11] Read in the MT the last four words of v. 8 as if they followed the first
word. The phrase 'Yahweh commands his lovingkindness' seems to be a later
addition.

[12] * V. 8 reads in RSV:
By day the Lord commands his steadfast love;
and at night his song is with me,
a prayer to the God of my life.

[13] * RSV renders v. 9:
I say to God, my rock,
'Why hast thou forgotten me?
Why go I mourning because of the oppression of the enemy?'

[14] Lit. perhaps 'like murder in my bones'; see BH.

[15] * V. 10 is in RSV:
As with a deadly wound in my body,
my adversaries taunt me,
while they say to me continually,
'Where is your God?'

[16] * RSV has 'an ungodly people' instead of 'ungodly people'.

[17] * RSV reads 'in whom I take refuge' instead of 'who protects me'.

[18] * RSV has:
Then I will go to the altar of God,
to God my exceeding joy;
and I will praise thee with the lyre,
O God, my God.

These two psalms together form *one* song. Its strophes are marked
off from each other by the identical refrain 42.5, 11; 43.5. Psalm 43
is the third of these strophes and its subject-matter and the absence of

a separate title equally prove that it is merely a continuation of Psalm 42. The psalm was composed by a man whose talent enables him to express in deeply moving words the suffering he had to endure. The paraphrase of the psalm composed by Lobwasser, the well-known translator of the French Psalter, 'Wie nach einer Wasserquelle', falls short of the direct poetical effect of the original. The psalmist, probably living in exile, is compelled to sojourn far away from Jerusalem and its Temple, at which he had perhaps held a high office (Ps. 42.4); he lives in the district of the place which later on was named Caesarea Philippi, a place where the springs of the River Jordan rush down into the valley in roaring cataracts from the southern slopes of the mountains of Hermon (Ps. 42.6 f.). He pines away in longing for the time he had once been privileged to spend in the house of God, when he would give himself up to the happiness of a most intimate communion with God, a happiness of which he is now deprived. The oppression and scorn of his enemies which he has to endure make him aware of the utter misery of his separation from God and of the grief which has come over him because of his yearning for God. In all sincerity he pours out his mortally wounded soul in deeply moving lamentation; with ruthless veracity he contends for the God whom he fears to lose.

First Strophe: Yearning for God and a sad recollection (vv. 1-5)

[1] The poet expresses the grief, which has come over him because of his yearning for God, in all its fullness in a magnificent picture of incomparable beauty: his soul, which, thirsting for the Living God, stretches itself far out in prayer towards God, without whom it is bound to pine away, is like the hind which, in the blazing heat of the summer, stretching its neck forward as far as it possibly can, searches in vain for water in the dried-up bed of the brook to quench its burning thirst. For the man who is able to express his relationship with God in such a fashion, faith is the most elementary function of his life; [2] for him God is really a 'Living God', and what he longs for is only and solely that he may be permitted to appear before God's 'face' and, coming into close contact with him, may have the most intimate communion with him (v. 2); it is a longing which is bound to affect him the more grievously as he lives in a pagan land. [3] And his grief has been aggravated, till it has become an almost intolerable torment, by the fact that the scornful question of his pagan adversaries 'Where is your God?' threatens to tear to

pieces the bond which so intimately unites the worshipper's soul to God, a relationship the existence of which is very much alive in his soul notwithstanding his longing, and indeed is a living power in his soul for the very reason of his longing for God. This man has no need to be ashamed of the tears he sheds because of this (on this phrase cf. Pss. 80.5; 102.9; Job 3.24), as they are an indication of what is here at stake for him, namely, to be and to remain assured of his God and that not only by thinking of him with yearning but as One who is really present. [4] Overwhelmed by the exceedingly great distress caused by his longing for God and by the doubts arising in his soul and filling it with fear, the singer takes refuge in his memory; by dwelling on his recollection he is able to pour out his soul, to give full scope to his thoughts. For a brief moment the bitter present ceases to exist for him. He visualizes himself as he ascends to the Temple of God in a festive procession, surrounded by noble friends, when he was able to join in the shouts of joy and in the testimony of the multitude keeping festival and was assured of the nearness of his God, filling his soul with rapture. [5] As he recalls those hallowed hours, his soul takes hold of his communion with God which now threatens to become obscure to him. He reaches the point, though at first only for a brief moment, at which a way is opened to him which will lead him beyond suffering and distress: in a touching dialogue with his own soul he comes to realize that we are not at all helped by weeping and grieving, but only make our cross and our suffering worse by our sadness.[1] His self-communing 'Why are you cast down, O my soul, and groanest within me?' sounds almost like a self-rebuke by which the poet tries to arouse his soul. The way that will lead him out of darkness into light is expressed in these words: 'Wait for God!' This means nothing but his bearing the whole tension of his life in the strength of a faith which does not see and yet knows that deliverance will not be denied him, that the hour will come when God will be near him in virtue of his presence in the Temple and by means of the deliverance he will grant him there, and when the worshipper will be able to 'testify' to him as his salvation (see Intr. 56, 86).

Second Strophe: Separation from God and scorn of the enemies (vv. 6–11)

    [6] The comforting word which the poet speaks to his soul is not,

---

[1] * Cf. the second verse of the German hymn 'Wer nur den lieben Gott lässt walten' by Georg Neumark (1621–1681), translated by Catherine Winkworth: 'Leave God to order all thy ways.'

however, able to banish all at once the gloom which fills it. It is evidence of the psychological truth expressed in the poet's thoughts and of their intrinsic truthfulness that in spite of the psalmist's endeavour to wait faithfully for God they once more relapse into the grief which they had just sought to overcome, and that the psalmist quite frankly speaks of this relapse in the words of the first line of the refrain. His homesickness which had led to such heart-pangs recurs with renewed force. The more severely he suffers in the mountains of Hermon from being separated from his homeland, the more intensely does he feel his need for having close contact with God. **[7]** But the thought of God causes new anxiety in him. He does not respond to the powerful beauty of the vast scenery which spreads before his eyes —to the springs of the River Jordan whose waters rush down from rock to rock with ferocious force—but stands still and looks fixedly only at his own calamity so that even the thunder of the torrents becomes to him a symbol of his own adversity, a symbol in which he cannot help seeing a punishment which the hand of God has inflicted upon him (cf. with regard to this picture Pss. 18.16; 32.6; Jonah 2.3). **[8]** And yet he tries to take hold of the hand that chastens him, which is another trait revealing the psalmist's deeply moving candour and proving that he is speaking the truth. Praying to God by day and singing his praise at night he clings to the God who he imagines has forsaken him and chastises him. **[9]** He is convinced that no one else can deliver him but God, the 'rock', on which he is in danger of foundering in the conflicting emotions that rage in his soul like the surge of the waves. Who could give him an answer to his pondering on the mysterious purpose of his life if not the very God by whom he imagines himself to be forgotten, because he is powerlessly delivered up to the oppression of his adversaries? **[10]** No wonder his heart is on the verge of breaking when, being faced on the one hand by his own doubts about God and, on the other hand, by his longing for God and not knowing where to turn, he has to listen to the scornful question of his enemies 'Where is your God?' which like an ally seems to reinforce his own doubts. **[11]** Against the background of this desperate struggle for assurance of the reality of God the words of the refrain sound at this point like a last super-human effort of the psalmist's soul: 'I will not let you go, unless you bless me.'[1]

---

[1] * Gen. 32.26.

Third Strophe: Supplication and hope (Ps. 43.1–5)

[**43.1**] The struggle of his soul against the doubts by which he had been seized has enabled the worshipper to reach the stage where he is able to pass victoriously through the darkness of his suffering until he has risen to the sure knowledge that his prayer has been granted. It is significant that the psalmist in pursuing his thoughts no longer makes use of those words of the refrain which speak of his soul being cast down, as he had done in the second strophe, but directs his thoughts to the prospect of hope in God's help. Now the worshipper holds on firmly to the assurance of the reality of God for which he had striven with his heart's blood; he does not even allow the mockery of his adversaries to deprive him of that assurance, so much the more as he knows that he is in the right. Thus he prays in the customary fashion (cf. Pss. 7.8; 26.1; 35.1) that God may take up his just cause and may vindicate him by delivering him from the hand of the ungodly and deceitful evildoers. [**2**] The motivation of his supplication shows that this is not to be regarded as the defiant assertion of a legal claim on God, but arises out of the worshipper's ardent desire, springing from his faith, that the righteousness of God may be revealed in his case and may free him from his last doubts. It is not revenge on his enemies but faith in the reality of the righteous God that is here at stake for the poet. It is true that this faith is a bold one; and yet it is not so bold and so strong that, without any tangible guarantee of the reality of God, he is capable of overcoming the temptation which besets him by the thought that the righteousness of God, just because it is *God*'s righteousness, is not bound to accord with what the finite mind of man may conceive it to be. [**3–4**] Here the limits set to the thought of the psalmist are made manifest. Part of these material guarantees which the worshipper needs in support of his faith is that he may return to the Temple in order to be able to experience there the joyous assurance of the nearness of God. And he clothes his petition for this favour in beautiful and heartfelt phrases. May God send out his 'light' and his 'faithfulness' like friendly messengers that they may lead him home into the house of God at Jerusalem, where he will rejoice in his God with thanksgiving (see Intr. 37 ff.). [**5**] Now the struggle that raged in his soul has calmed down. Just as the struggle of a sick man who tried to resist the onslaught of his malady is followed by a gentle dream whilst he peacefully slumbers, so the pleasure of anticipating his future encounter with God at a sacred ceremony appears to the poet to be a shining and happy symbol of future joy; here the past and the future join hands. What had once been a melancholy recollection (42.4) becomes for him a joyful hope; now he has brought the struggle in his soul to a successful conclusion. It is only against this background that the sentiments of the refrain expressing confidence and hope come fully into play. Lamentation and supplication are transformed into a lofty faith which overcomes present adversity by experience of God in the past and hopefully goes forward to meet the future.

What touches our hearts here is not only the high artistic quality of the psalm inherent in the lifelike and deeply felt portrayal of the struggle which took place in the psalmist's soul; the way in which here man's longing for God is shown to be a power which sustains him through fear and torment, doubt and temptation, till he overcomes them by faith and by his waiting for God, is even today still able to bring comfort and help to troubled souls in spite of the limitations resulting from the historical conditions at the time of the psalm's composition. And the religious value of the psalm is to be found in the fact that that longing for God which it depicts does not care about what it will get *out* of God but about what it will have *in* him, in other words, that it desires God for his own sake; and this is the secret of the power of man's longing for God. This realization should restrain us from dispensing too quickly with the high esteem in which the festival cult is held in the psalm by regarding it as a peculiarity of ancient formalistic piety; for the hours which the psalmist had spent in the house of God have, after all, brought about his saving encounter with God (see the refrain) and have thus become for him the well from which he draws the power of faith which sustains him in times of struggle and adversity. No religion will ever be able to dispense with the cultus as the place from which man continually derives new strength for his struggle for existence through his communion with God and fellowship with the faithful.

44. CAST OFF BY GOD?

To the Conductor. To the Sons of Korah.[1] *Maskil*[2]

1 We have heard with our ears, O God,
  our fathers have told us,
  the work thou didst perform in their days;
2 in the days of old[3] thy hand has accomplished it;[4]
  peoples thou didst drive out,
  but them thou didst plant;

thou didst smash the nations,
but them thou didst expand;[5]

3 for not by their own sword did they win the land,
nor did their own arm give them victory;
but thy right hand, and thy arm,
and the light of thy countenance;
for thou didst love them.

4 It is thou, my King, who does it;
O God, ordain salvation for Jacob.[6]

5 Through thee we push down our foes;
through thy name we tread down our assailants.

6 For not in my bow do I trust,
nor can my sword save me.

7 But thou hast saved us from our foes,
and hast put to confusion those who hate us.

8 In God we have boasted continually,
and to thy name we testify[7] for ever.[8]

9 Yet thou hast cast us off and abased us;
thou dost not go out with our armies any more.[9]

10 Thou makest us turn back from the foe;
and those who hate us took spoil for themselves.[10]

11 Thou hast handed us over like sheep for slaughter,
and hast scattered us among the nations.

12 Thou hast sold thy people for naught,
and hast made no profit by their proceeds.[11]

13 Thou hast made us a disgrace[12] to our neighbours,
the derision and scorn of those about us.

14 Thou hast made us a byword among the peoples;
the nations wag their heads at us.[13]

15 Continually my disgrace is before me,
and shame has covered my face,

16 at the slanderous words of the revilers,
at the sight of the enemy looking at me revengefully.[14]

17 All this has come upon us,
but we did not forget thee,
neither did we become unfaithful to thy covenant.[15]

18 Our heart has not turned away from thee,[16]
nor have our steps departed from thy way,

19 that thou shouldst have broken us in the place where jackals live,
and covered us with the shadows of death.[17]

20 If we had forgotten the name of our God,
or spread forth our hands to a strange god,

21 would not God have searched out this?
For he knows the secrets of the heart.

22 Nay, for thy sake we were[18] slain all the day long,
and accounted as sheep for the slaughter.

23 Rouse thyself! Why sleepest thou, O Lord?
Awake! Do not cast us off for ever!

24 Why dost thou hide thy face?
Why dost thou forget us in our affliction and oppression?
25 Our soul is bowed down to the dust;
our body cleaves to the ground.
26 Rise up, come to our help!
Deliver us for the sake of thy steadfast love!

[1] See p. 97.
[2] See Ps. 32.
[3] * In RSV the words 'in the days of old' are included in v. 1, where they form the conclusion of that verse.
[4] See BH.
[5] * V. 2 reads in RSV:
thou with thy own hand didst drive out the nations,
but them thou didst plant;
thou didst afflict the peoples,
but them thou didst set free.
[6] * RSV reads, 'Thou art my King and my God, who ordainest victories for Jacob.'
[7] * V. 8b reads in RSV, 'and we will give thanks to thy name for ever'.
[8] * RSV adds 'Selah' at the end of v. 8.
[9] * V. 9b reads in RSV, 'and hast not gone out with our armies'.
[10] * RSV renders v. 10b 'and our enemies have gotten spoil'.
[11] * V. 12 is different in RSV:
Thou hast sold thy people for a trifle,
demanding no high price for them.
[12] * RSV has 'the taunt of our neighbours' instead of 'a disgrace to our neighbours'.
[13] * In RSV '...a byword among the nations, a laughingstock among the peoples'.
[14] * In RSV v. 16 is:
at the words of the taunters and revilers,
at the sight of the enemy and the avenger.
[15] * In RSV a somewhat different thought is expressed:
All this has come upon us,
though we have not forgotten thee,
or been false to thy covenant.
[16] * RSV has 'turned back' instead of 'turned away from thee'.
[17] * In RSV the rendering is, 'with deep darkness'.
[18] * In RSV the present tense is used.

The early church fathers of the Antioch school slready held that the psalm was composed at the time of the Maccabaean wars during the second century BC, and have been followed by Calvin and the great majority of recent commentators. Such a dating is possible, but not cogent. A tradition such as II Chron. 20.7 ff. should warn us against making any statement to the effect that a pre-exilic date for the psalm is impossible, since that text presupposes a similar service of supplication held on the occasion of a defeat. It cannot be proved that v. 22 refers to the religious persecution of the Jews by Antiochus IV, since the psalm nowhere speaks of religious persecution. An affirmation of faithfulness in refusing to desert to strange gods (vv. 17 ff.) already had a place in the pre-exilic cult of the Covenant (see Intr. 33). The remaining features of this community lament (see Intr. 66 ff.) likewise point to the cult of the Covenant Festival as the psalm's original setting. It is, however, true that our lack of knowledge regarding the details of its historical background does not allow us to fix the exact date of the psalm.

The nation has been defeated by an enemy in battle (v. 10); the prisoners have been deported to a foreign country (v. 11; cf. Amos 1.6, 9); Israel suffers from the scorn of her neighbours (vv. 14 f.); jackals have made the ruins of destroyed cities their abode (v. 19; cf. Jer. 9.11; 10.22; 49.33; Isa. 13.22; 34.13); Yahweh, the Lord of hosts and God of wars, who once had gone out to war at the head of the Israelite armies (I Sam. 4.3 ff.; II Sam. 5.24), has refused his help (vv. 4, 9); now the people prostrate themselves before God— probably in the sanctuary—(v. 25) and complain to him of their material and spiritual afflictions in order to beg for his help and for their deliverance. Besides the prayer offered on behalf of the whole people the voice of an individual speaks in vv. 4 ff., 15; judging from what he says, it is perhaps the king or the leader of the army whose words are recorded here. The first two parts of the community lament, namely vv. 1–3 (the retrospect on the saving deeds of God which opens the psalm) and vv. 4–8 (testimony and hope for victory) exhibit features of the hymn and its testimony; vv. 9–16 depict the material afflictions in the traditional manner of the lament; vv. 17– 22 describe the spiritual, religious afflictions and end in a prayer for help (vv. 23–26), in which the two themes of lamentation briefly reappear once more.

[1–3] The psalm opens with the statement that the members of the worshipping congregation have heard with their own ears the tradition of the divine saving deeds handed down to them by their fathers. From this statement it is possible to draw the conclusion, a conclusion which suggests itself most readily, that the action which the psalm immediately followed was the oral proclamation of the *Heilsgeschichte* as an integral part of the covenant cult (cf. v. 17).[1] Consequently,

---

[1] Kraus contests this view by saying that what is here alluded to is not that tradition which was recited in the cult as the most important one, but 'the family tradition and the tradition of the tribes'. But the view adopted above is supported by the fact that here the fathers are described as contemporaries of the 'days of old' and as those who handed down the saving deeds of Yahweh wrought by him during that period, and further by the form of the congregation's hymn which follows.

the hymnic testimony at the beginning of the psalm is the congregation's response to their encounter with God and his salvation which
they had experienced during that recital. In the form of a hymn the
congregation makes the content of the *Heilsgeschichte*—in the present
context the tradition of the conquest and distribution of the Promised
Land—its own by making it the subject of their testimony, praising
the miraculous power of God which is the foundation of their whole
existence. History assumes a different aspect when seen by faith; it is
not the victories achieved by force of arms or the heroic deeds of
warriors crowned with glory, such as the heroic epic would extol,
which form the subject-matter of the hymn in public worship; they
are completely overshadowed by the acts of God who, emerging
from the background of history, makes himself known to the eyes of
faith as the One who really shapes the course of events and lets the
congregation share in them. This is why the tradition of the *Heilsgeschichte* is celebrated by the cult community as a living encounter with
the God of History; the cult community behaves thus under the
impression of the divine presence which overcomes the extent of time
involved in history and transforms the past into a directly experienced present. This deeper meaning of the representation of the
divine acts in the cultic hymn is also the key to the religious understanding of the whole psalm (see Intr. 28 ff., 53 ff.). In that the saving
facts of the early history of Israel are represented, which form the
constant theme of the tradition of the conquest of the land—how
God has scattered the peoples of Canaan to provide a home for
Israel—the members of the Yahweh community know themselves
sustained by the marvellous power of their God, at the root of which
is the incomprehensible miracle of his love (see the last line of v. 3).
The whole problem of the psalm hinges on that sure knowledge.

[4–8] This sure knowledge is, first of all, the basis for the hope of
victory which has found expression in the hymnic testimonies of the
leader of the army (vv. 4, 6) and the cult community (vv. 5, 7 f.)
respectively. In this connection we can clearly see the hidden energies
of faith which that living cultic tradition was able to activate. The
very first words 'it is thou, my King' (lit. 'thou art he') still carry with
them the fresh touch of the cultic drama; they sound like a spontaneous reaction to the theophany of Yahweh as King which has just
been experienced (see Intr. 33 f., 62 f.) and by virtue of which the tradition of the past becomes transformed into the present reality of the
encounter with God—which in its turn kindles a powerful hope in

the future realization of salvation. The strength of that hope lies in
the humble and yet proud awe which ascribes power and glory
exclusively to God. He only needs to command, and help and salvation are at hand and Israel's armies advance to gain a victory. In
that the biblical view of history deliberately renounces any trust in
human power and human resources it fundamentally differs, for
instance, from the inscriptions and images of Assyrian kings, where
the intention is to express and emphasize the power belonging to the
rulers themselves. The conviction expressed in the thought 'God
alone', which dominates the backward glance at the *Heilsgeschichte* in
vv. 1–3, also remains the basic theme of the forward look into the
future (vv. 6 f.; cf. v. 3). The faith portrayed here lives on the experiences of the past which are preserved by their transmission in
public worship and are continually reactivated afresh and made
fruitful in the hymnic praise of the divine saving deeds (v. 8).

[9–16] It is not without good reason that this attitude of the cult
community, which ascribes honour and glory only to God, is so
strongly emphasized. For the real problem of the psalm arises at this
very point. On the other hand, it is also at this point that the way
begins which alone can lead to its solution. In glaring contradiction
to the hymnic affirmation of confidence in God, vv. 9–16 resound
with lamentation over the defeat of the nation. Measured against the
love of God and his saving rule portrayed by the tradition, the
present experience of the people implies not only a threat to their
material existence but also a danger to the spiritual support which
they derive from their faith in God. It is precisely because God alone
directs the history of the nation that the affliction brought about by
the enemy and all the suffering and all the burdens resulting therefrom induce them to question God—and thus become a trial of their
faith. In the face of the defeat, the enemies' looting, the ruin of the
cities, the scattering of the prisoners among foreign countries and the
scorn and derision of neighbours and adversaries, the link between
God and his people is in danger of being lost, because those who
believe in God are no longer able to understand the way God acts
when they look at it presupposing the tradition.

The lamentation receives a stamp of its own from the fact that
the material and spiritual afflictions are here inextricably intertwined; in this way it becomes, as it were, the counterpart of the
hymnic testimony to the saving deeds of God and contributes on its
part to the representation of God as a living reality and to an

encounter with him (the statements on God's activities in vv. 9–14 are made throughout in the second person). If we interpret the psalm's lamentation only in the light of the reproaches which the people feel bound to level at their God from a certain standpoint that seems to justify their self-assurance, we do just as little justice to its true meaning as we do if we regard it only as the members of the worshipping congregation simply seeking to pour out and relieve their hearts before God in lamentation. In this psalm, too, it is surely a proof of genuine piety expressed in prayer that the affliction is brought before God with a candour that has a liberating effect; but the affliction is not limited here to external and human problems only, but issues in the problem which God himself presents and which unseen is at the root of all the statements made in the lamentation and can be most clearly grasped in v. 12: the question of what profit God derives from abandoning his people remains unanswered. If God at least would thereby gain something, just as does a man who sells his property for a reasonable price! It is the enquiry into the divine purpose of suffering, the meaning of which is not understood, which causes the affliction of the people to turn into a crisis of faith.

[**17–22**] The faith of the people would not have been exposed to trial if they had had to regard the adversity that has overtaken them as God's punishment for their unfaithfulness and disobedience; for in that case their affliction would indeed have been nothing but the manifestation of God's righteousness, on which their covenantal duties are based. The people's conscience, however, refuses to accept such an interpretation. We are here just as little justified as we are in the case of Job in doubting the genuineness, earnestness and depth of the assertion of their integrity; on the contrary, the words used in this statement give the impression that they have conscientiously examined their own hearts and are unable to establish any infringement of the Covenant, either in thought or deed, which would justify such a punishment. It is not the suffering in itself which in the first place causes such anxiety to the people's faith and makes it a real temptation for them, but the fact that in their case it cannot be understood as a punishment. The tempting thought to renounce their loyalty to God (cf. Ps. 73.15) is, however, rejected, and this rejection is treated as a foregone conclusion which proves that the cult community are resolved even in the midst of their temptation not to depart from the way they chose in the past, the way of covenantal faithfulness and obedience to God. The widely-held view that these verses are to be interpreted as showing the people's defiant boasting of their integrity, intended to remind God of his covenantal duties by sounding a reproachful note, does justice neither to the particulars of the text nor to the tenor of the psalm as a whole. It overlooks the fact that the cult community's protestation of their loyalty to God not only reviews the past but holds good also in the present calamity and will remain true also in future. At the root of this attitude of faithfulness to God 'notwithstanding everything' there is something of that strength of a valiant faith which in the Psalter has found its most beautiful expression in the 'nevertheless' of Ps. 73.23. Though our psalm does not penetrate those ultimate depths revealed to the worshipper in Psalm 73, it is nevertheless true to say that here, too, suffering is recognized as a cross which is laid upon man by God and on that account must be endured even if the tormenting question of the reason and purpose of that suffering remains unanswered. I think that this is the line we should take in interpreting v. 22. In the last analysis it is the same line which St Paul has taken in Rom. 8.35 ff., where he expresses the thought that nothing can separate a Christian from the love of God. **[23–26]** But because the reason for man's suffering and its purpose are hidden in God (v. 22: 'for thy sake'), he is for that very reason also the only one who in that situation is able to help man to endure. In prayer and by means of their lamentation and affirmation of faithfulness the members of the cult community have now gradually drawn near even to the God who hides his face so that it looks as if he is asleep or has forgotten his people. And having done so, they have now reached the stage at which the temptation is no longer able to interfere with their communion with their God; the way is open for them to ask God for their deliverance. That supplication now flows with irresistible force and with unrestrained directness from the lips of the members of the congregation who, with grief in their hearts, lie prostrate before their God. The various themes of which the psalm is composed are once more alluded to and intermingle in an impressive chord: the lamenting in the sanctuary (v. 25), the tormenting question of the reason for the trial of their faith (vv. 23 ff.), and all this in the setting of a prayer that God may 'rise up' and appear as their deliverer (see Intr. 73). At its conclusion the prayer appeals to the steadfast love of God and thus deliberately reverts once more to the beginning of the psalm, where the love of God is likewise praised as the ultimate motive of his redemptive work (v. 3). That love of God is the hidden pivot of the whole psalm round which the hymn and the lamentation, the divine redemptive work in history as well as man's present temptation, revolve. It is true that in the psalm the love of God appeared to the eyes of the people at that time to be obscured by a veil because of the mystery of suffering for which the Old Covenant was not able to find an entirely satisfactory solution; it is only through the suffering of Christ that the last veil drops from the face of God and his hidden love is made manifest; it is only in the New Testament that the discords of the psalm are dissolved in the harmonious melody of the hymn of those who have overcome their temptations so that nothing in the world can separate them from the love of God which is in Christ Jesus (Rom. 8.37 ff.).

45. THE ROYAL WEDDING SONG

To the Conductor. According to 'Lilies'.[1] *To the Sons of Korah; Maskil.*[2]

A love song

1 My heart overflows with a goodly theme;
   I will sing my[3] song for the king;[4]
   my tongue is like the style of a ready scribe.

2 You are fair, very fair indeed,[3] above all men;
   grace is poured upon your lips;
   for God has blessed you for ever.[5]

3 Gird your sword upon your thigh, O mighty one,
   in your glory and majesty!

4 ' '[3] Good luck! Ride on for the cause of truth,
   for the sake of clemency and justice;[6]
   let your right hand teach you dread deeds!

5 Your arrows are sharp—
   in the heart of the king's enemies;
   the peoples throw themselves at your feet.[7]

6 Your throne, O divine king, endures for ever and ever;
   a sceptre of equity is the rod of your rule.[8]

7 You loved righteousness and hated wickedness;
   therefore the Lord, your God, has anointed you
   with the oil of gladness above your fellows.

8 Your robes are all made of myrrh
   and aloes and cassia.[9]
   From the ivory palace harps[3] make you glad.

9 Daughters of kings are your precious possessions;
   the queen, adorned with gold from Ophir,
   takes her place at your right hand.[10]

10 Hear, O daughter, consider, and incline your ear:
   forget your people and your father's house!

11 Let the king desire your beauty,

for he is your lord, and fall at his feet![11]

12 The wealthy among the people, O daughter of Tyre,
   pay homage to thee with gifts.[12]

13 The daughter of the king enters in procession,
   surrounded by splendour and clothed in gold-woven robes.[12]

14 In many-coloured garments she is led to the king,
   followed by the virgins who had been brought to you.[12]

15 With gladness and shouts of joy they are led along
   as they enter the palace of the king.

16 Instead of your fathers shall be your sons;
   you will make them princes in every part of the realm.[13]

17 I will cause your name to be celebrated in all generations;
   therefore the peoples will praise you for ever and ever.

[1] Perhaps title or opening words of a song to the tune of which the psalm was sung or accompanied.

[2] See Ps. 32.

[3] See BH.

[4] * V. 1b is in RSV, 'I address my verses to the king.'

[5] * V. 2a reads in RSV, 'You are the fairest of the sons of men'; in v. 2c RSV has 'therefore' instead of 'for'.

[6] * RSV's first two lines of v. 4:
   In your majesty ride forth victoriously
   for the cause of truth and to defend the right;

[7] * The last line reads in RSV, 'the peoples fall under you'.

[8] * RSV has 'your divine throne' instead of 'your throne, O divine king', and in v. 6b reads 'your royal sceptre is a sceptre of equity'.

[9] * V. 8a reads in RSV, 'your robes are all fragrant with myrrh and aloes and cassia'.

[10] * RSV renders v. 9:
   daughters of kings are among your ladies of honour;
   at your right hand stands the queen in gold of Ophir.

[11] * V. 11 reads in RSV:
   and the king will desire your beauty.
   Since he is your lord, bow to him.

[12] * Vv. 12–14 as rendered in RSV, differ considerably:
   (12) the people of Tyre will sue your favour with gifts,
       the richest of the people (13) with all kinds of wealth.
   The princess is decked in her chamber with gold-woven robes;
   (14) In many-coloured robes she is led to the king,
       with her virgin companions, her escort, in her train.

[13] * RSV has 'in all the earth' instead of 'in every part of the realm'.

The psalm is the only example of a profane lyric in the Psalter.[1]

[1] Bentzen, *Introduction to the Old Testament* I, 1952, p. 129, wants to relate the psalm to the cultic-mystical *hieros gamos* of the divine kings. Gaster, *JBL* 74, 1955, pp. 239 ff., regards as the occasion of the psalm an ordinary wedding celebration at which the bride and the bridegroom were treated as a royal couple. The wording of the psalm, however, points to the wedding of a king as the more obvious interpretation. The term 'profane' which has been used above is not meant to be understood in the modern sense, but is to express the contrast to the interpretation of the psalm in a sacral sense.

It is a song of praise in honour of a young king and his consort, a princess of Tyre (v. 12), which was composed and recited by a court-poet on the occasion of the ruler's wedding. Presumably the song was dedicated to a king of the northern kingdom; this view is perhaps also suggested by some phrases in the psalm which are peculiar from the linguistic point of view.[1] It is no longer possible to ascertain who the king in question was; the names of Ahab, Jehu, and Jeroboam II have been suggested as well as those of Solomon, Jehoram, king of Judah, and even Aristobulus I or one of the Ptolemys. This artistic song has sprung from the high spirits that are engendered by festive joy and is designed to enhance the splendour of the cere-mony; it shows distinctly the marks of an exuberant court-style and in that respect resembles the magnificent songs by which the kings of the Ancient Orient sought to have their fame immortalized by the hand of an artist (cf. v. 17). It is therefore not advisable to regard the poem, which ties together in a single bunch of many-coloured flowers a variety of essential motives and thoughts associated with the feast, as some kind of account of the course of events that took place at the celebration of the wedding; it is even less advisable to attempt to deduce from it exactly where and when the recital of the psalm took place within the framework of the feast.

[1] The opening verse skilfully combines the subject and the object of the song, the overflowing enthusiasm of the singer and the theme of the poem whereby he pays homage. He proudly compares his 'work' (*poiema*) with the activity of the skilful 'scribe' (chancellor), one of the most influential personages at the royal courts of the Ancient Orient. [2] The first part of his song (vv. 2–9) is concerned with the praise of the king. The blessing of God, which is to remain with the ruler for ever, can be clearly recognized by the impressive beauty of the king's appearance (cf. Judg. 8.18; I Sam. 9.2; 10.23 f.; 16.12) and by his kind and gracious disposition (as regards v. 2b one could also think of the gift of fluent speech and of writing poetry such as David and Solomon are praised for). [3–5] That blessing will express itself even more powerfully in the victories he will gain in battle, and the singer encourages his royal master to engage in such enterprises and wishes him every success in them; and he does so in choice words in which his devotion to the young 'majesty' is ably

---

[1] It cannot be proved that, as Kraus assumes, vv. 2, 6, 16 presuppose a fixed succession and that for this reason the psalm is to be related to the ritual of the 'royal feast of Zion'.

combined with his own manly and energetic endeavour to exercise influence on the decisions of the ruler. But the purpose of the striking encouragement to heroic deeds is not to kindle the flame of a blind enthusiasm for war; the warlike passions are at once curbed by the moral responsibility which sets limits to every war policy. According to the Old Testament view the cause of truth, clemency and justice (the latter in its turn is a noteworthy mutual self-restriction!) simultaneously constitutes the goal of the war and sets limits to it.

[6–7] The picture of the prince of peace is placed side by side with that of the great royal warrior. It is probably not by accident that in this very context the king is called 'God'. By referring to Pss. 2.7; 110.2 f.; II Sam. 7.13 ff. it is possible to think in this connection of the influence of the court-style of the Ancient Orient; it cannot, however, be proved from any Old Testament passage that a deification of the king took place such as was practised by the Egyptians and the Babylonians. The insurmountable distinction between Yahweh and the king, between God and man is everywhere maintained and is explicitly expressed also in v. 7 ('Yahweh, your God'; see Intr. 62 f. The designation 'divine king' (*Göttlicher*) signifies in the Old Testament the function of the king as the *righteous* ruler rather than a specific quality. It is in this sense that he becomes the representative of God in the midst of his people through his anointment as king. This accounts also for the 'perpetuity' of his reign which is symbolized by his throne and sceptre.[1] In that righteousness is emphasized as the foundation of the king's rule, an obstacle is put in the way of any kind of despotic arbitrariness; that bar, as the example of Ahab and Jezebel (cf. I Kings ch. 21) shows, was no utopian ideal, but a religious principle of real power whereby history was shaped. At this point in the psalm, too, we cannot fail to recognize that the singer's homage must by no means be regarded as the expression of a servile submissiveness to the ruler, but shows a skilful combination of lyric praise with a serious sense of responsibility for the more exalted duties of the king.

[8–9] The poet briefly sketches the overwhelming impression which the splendour surrounding the king makes on the senses. His magnificent robes are, as it were, woven of the most exquisite aromas of balsam; from the palace, the walls of which are adorned with ivory (cf. I Kings 22.39), the sound of harps can be heard like the

[1] As regards the symbolic significance of rod and sceptre, cf. F. Focke, 'Szepter und Krummstab', in *Festgabe für Alois Fuchs*, 1950, pp. 337 ff.

rush of a mighty wind; royal princesses are the inmates of the harem, the 'most precious' possession and the criterion of the might displayed by the king. All this splendour, however, reaches its climax in the king's bride, who, adorned with choice jewellery of gold, today occupies the place of honour at the right hand of the ruler. The manner in which the singer, without making any direct statement to that effect, arrives at this culminating point of his homage reveals that his masterly command of the stylistic form is distinguished by a truly charming elegance. **[10–11]** The experienced poet paternally admonishes the king's bride to forget her people and her father's house, so that she will be able to belong from now on wholly to her husband and master, to whom she, too, has to do homage, since he is the king. In this solemn exhortation once more duty (cf. Ruth 1.16) is placed above the personal feelings and desires which might be evoked by homesickness; and the justification of this exhortation can be fully understood only if we picture to ourselves the disastrous part which, for instance, Solomon's foreign wives or Jezebel, the daughter of the king of Tyre, had played by enticing the people to adopt foreign habits and customs until they were overwhelmed with foreign influence, and that even in the very sphere of their religious life. **[12–15]** The painful admonition is, however, at once followed by a soothing comfort (v. 12): though the daughter of Tyre must give up her homeland, where she has spent her youth, she will be rewarded for her sacrifice by being surrounded by the loyalty of her new subjects, who will pay homage to her with an abundance of gifts. Moreover, the link with her past life in the house of her parents is not completely broken. The solemn moment of her entry into the palace of the king, which the poet has recorded in vv. 13–15, is designed to remind her of that fact. She has entered the house, which is now to become her new home, in the company of the playmates of her youth, whose shouts of joy encircle her like the surge of the waves. **[16–17]** The singer clothes the promise of the blessing of children, which according to ancient custom was pronounced when the bride was on the point of departing for her new life (Gen. 24.60; Ruth 4.11 f.), in the form of a benediction addressed to the king; in this way he unites the young couple in their joint task and in the purpose of their matrimony, so that the queen will feel herself tied to her new homeland in her sons and by the strong bonds of her own blood, and the king and with him the whole nation will be proud of such a strengthening and safeguarding of his rule. That the singer is able to handle this theme in this manner betrays just as much the poet's delicate tact as his admirable skill in interweaving in choice words personal sentiments and objective concerns and necessities. He seems to be conscious of his own importance when in conclusion he regards it as his duty—and he has actually fulfilled it by his song—to proclaim and immortalize the fame ('name') of the king. This would, to be sure, not have happened but for the fact that the psalm was reinterpreted already at an early date as referring to the Messiah and, understood in this sense, was incorporated in the Psalter. Following the Messianic conception of late Judaism the New Testament, too, has applied the psalm's statements to Christ (Heb. 1.8 f.), and the ancient Church considered the relationship between Christ and the Church to be reflected in the relations between the bridegroom and the bride as they are depicted here. All the same, even that allegorical interpretation would not have been possible without the noble spirit, the earnest sense of moral and religious duty, which already in the psalm itself continually shines through the outer garment of the court-style and lifts up the realm of earthly and profane things to the higher regions of the things which are religious.

46. A SAFE STRONGHOLD OUR GOD IS STILL

To the Conductor. To the Sons of Korah. According to (the voices of) young women.[1]   *A song*

1 God is our refuge and strength,
    a well-tried help in trouble.[2]
2 Therefore we fear nothing though the earth should dissolve,
    and the mountains should be cast into the midst of the sea.[3]
3 The waters of the sea roar and foam,
    the mountains tremble at its violence; *Selah*[4]
    the Lord Sabaoth is with us;
    the God of Jacob is our refuge![5]
4 There is a river whose streams make glad the city of God,
    [6] the Most High has sanctified his habitation.[5]
5 God is in the midst of her,
    she shall never be moved;
    God will help her at the dawn of the morning.
6 The nations raged, the kingdoms tottered;
    he uttered his voice, and the earth melted.[7]
7 The Lord Sabaoth is with us;
    the God of Jacob is our refuge! *Selah*
8 Come and behold the works of the Lord,
    who has wrought desolations in the earth;

9 who makes wars cease to the end of the earth,
   who breaks the bow, and shatters the spear,
   and burns the shields[5] with fire.[8]
10 'Leave off[9] and know that I am God.
   I am exalted among the nations,
   I am exalted in the earth!'
11 The Lord Sabaoth is with us;
   the God of Jacob is our refuge! *Selah*

[1] This is perhaps a statement on the key in which the song was sung (soprano?) or accompanied; cf. I Chron. 15.20 (see p. 23). (Tr. N.: RSV reads, 'according to Alamoth'.)

[2] * RSV has 'very present' instead of 'well-tried'.

[3] * V. 2 reads in RSV:
   Therefore we will not fear though the earth should change,
      though the mountains shake in the heart of the sea;

[4] * RSV omits the last two lines of v. 3 and reads:
   though its waters roar and foam,
      though the mountains tremble with its tumult. *Selah*

[5] See BH.

[6] * V. 4b reads in RSV, 'the holy habitation of the Most High'.

[7] * RSV uses the present tense throughout this verse.

[8] * RSV has 'chariots' instead of 'shields'.

[9] * In RSV 'be still' instead of 'leave off'.

The psalm has found its most worthy Christian echo in Luther's battle-song 'A safe stronghold our God is still'.[1] It is similarly one of the most powerful testimonies of the Old Testament's poetry as well as of its faith. All the religious strength and hopes which the greatest characters of the Old Testament were able to achieve have found a worthy setting in the powerful language of the verses, which 'flow in long cadences', and in the vivid dramatic representation of the symmetrically constructed strophes of the psalm, and have been given immortal expression in its gripping imagery. The form of the psalm combines the tone of a hymn (vv. 1, 8 and in the refrain) with stylistic forms and images belonging to the prophetic literature; the latter have their root partly in the myth and like the psalm as a whole seem to date back to a common cultic tradition. The forceful dramatic quality of the song becomes understandable against the background of the theophany and the dramatic representation of the *Heilsgeschichte* in the festival cult which are referred to in the individual strophes (see Intr. 28 ff.). In each of the three well-proportioned strophes a different word-picture of great power is brought to a conclusion by an identical hymnic testimony to God, so that the

[1] * In the German original 'Ein' feste Burg ist unser Gott', translated into English by Thomas Carlyle (1795–1881).

refrain, which was probably sung by the congregation or the choir as an antiphon in the course of the psalm's liturgical recital, receives each time its specific colouring from the particular word-picture in question. The keynote of the psalm, which is sounded in every strophe, is the intrepid confession of faith in God. That confession triumphantly rises in the first strophe (vv. 1–3) above the raging of *Nature* at the formation and dissolution of the world, and in the second strophe (vv. 4–7) above the image of the *history* of the assaults of the nations who storm at the walls of Jerusalem like the surge of the waves; and it ends in the last strophe (vv. 8–11) in an enthusiastic testimony to God, who rises above the battlefield covered with corpses and ruins to establish his eternal Kingdom of peace on earth.

Within the framework of the cultic representation this triad of 'creation—history—eschatology' imparts to the particular events that quality of cosmic breadth, timeless surpassing worth and metaphysical importance which is of the essence of the continually recurring realization of the divine salvation (see Intr. 44). It also imparts to the psalm that never-failing strength which it shares with Luther's hymn. The irresistible power which continually flows from Luther's hymn ultimately rests, too, on an attitude of mind devoted to what is timeless and eternal; and this shows that Luther has grasped the essential nature of the psalm in all its profundity and, in spite of the liberty he took in relating his hymn to Christ, has been inspired by the same profound faith as the composer of the psalm.

First Strophe: The formation and dissolution of the world (vv. 1–3)

[1] The hymnic testimony to God, which by its compact force at the very beginning of the psalm reflects the impression made by God's epiphany in the festival cult, comprises the strength, courage and joy that spring from trust in God and thus sketches as the theme of the psalm the attitude of faith by which the whole song is characterized and sustained. The God for whom the jubilant testimony is intended because as the One who is present he is very near, is the same God who has helped in the past in thousands of adversities and whose help therefore has for the congregation professing him the significance of an imperishable memorial of his might and love. Having heard the testimony of God's deeds and providential rule, as transmitted in the books of the *Heilsgeschichte*, its members responded with a joyful affirmation of their God and drew new strength for the present and the future. The psalm's thoughts are entirely focused on

the God who was and is and is to come. This is why it embraces in a
tremendous unifying vision the whole process of the formation and
the end of the world as the sphere of God's activity and envisages the
most extensive regions and the most remote eras as drawn together in
the decisive moment when God revealed his presence (see Intr. 44,
50 f.). **[2]** Being united to their God in this faith, the members of the
cult community recognize their own place within the context of the
divine process of creation, which is made apparent in the formation
and dissolution of the world; they are confronted with the whole
world and its destiny and face its end without trepidation. Even
though the world perishes and 'changes' (this is the literal translation)
its shape, whilst the last days (*Endzeit*) emerge with terrible labour-
pains; even though the everlasting mountains sink in the waves of
the sea—this total collapse of what is only finite cannot frighten the
faithful; for his faith is grounded in eternity. After all, what harm shall
the roaring and foaming waves of the great flood, that comes surging
along at the end· of the days, be able to inflict upon a faith which
sees God at work even in such a world-catastrophe! **[3]** We may
well imagine that we can hear these verses ringing with the sound of
the unconcealed joy with which the cult community watches the
cracking of the world; for it is the triumph of the power of God to
which they are able to testify with great joy, and, in consequence,
also a triumph of their own faith. Thus the members of the cult
community already witness now by faith the victory that outlives the
destruction of the world as the victory of their God, and they await
that victory without fear and with confidence. The colours which are
here used to paint the picture of the world-catastrophe are borrowed
from the primeval myth of creation which is now also known to us
—through the discoveries made at Ras Shamra—in its Canaanite
form of the myth of the combat against the dragon. The roaring
waves of the primeval flood which in their vehemence stormed at the
Creator-God and were mastered by him will once more rise and
threaten to swallow up the world which he created. The Old
Testament adopted these magnificent pictures, but by the strength of
its monotheistic conception of God divested them of their mythological, polytheistic character; they form the background of the psalm
against which the power and the presence of God are set off so much
the more effectively. This fact would be made particularly clear here
if at this point, as is almost generally assumed, the refrain had concluded the first strophe in exactly the same way as it does in the two

other strophes. It has probably been omitted through the oversight
of a copyist.[1] For a testimony to God as the safe stronghold, a testimony that is confident of his victory, is meaningful in this context
only if God's power rises above the cataclysm of the end of the world
like an unshakable rock. This thought is perhaps still reflected in
the ancient sacred designation of God as Yahweh Sabaoth which
gives expression to God's dominion over the powers of Nature. The
testimony to God's presence 'The Lord Sabaoth is with us' reminds
us of the protective name Immanuel ('God is with us') which is used
in Isa. 7.14; and the thought which, though not explicitly expressed,
yet underlies this refrain—that God as the One who alone is exalted
triumphs over the twilight of the world—reminds us of that powerful
and magnificent utterance of Isaiah concerning the Day of Judgment
in which he speaks of the Day of Yahweh and concludes each strophe
with the refrain 'The Lord alone will be exalted in that day' (Isa.
2.11, 17). It gives us an inkling of the depth and comprehensiveness
of this faith that here a testimony is borne to God in the jubilant tones
of a hymn, though it is related to an event of which man can think
only with terror in his heart. Only the man who, having been wholly
taken hold of by God, has completely subjected his own person to
God, is so dominated by the thought of God that beside it there is no
room for anything else, not even for any kind of fear. And only the
man to whom even outside in the world God means everything and
is the ultimate goal, is able to face the total collapse of the things
which are transient with an untroubled mind and with great hope,
because he visualizes behind them something which is of greater
significance.

Second Strophe: The raging of the nations (vv. 4–7)

[4] The scene and the mood change in the next strophe. The
peaceful picture of the river in Jerusalem, on whose banks gladness has its dwelling-place, constitutes a magnificent contrast to
the picture of the waves of the seas that rush along. The waters which
generate blessing are probably deliberately contrasted with the
waters which generate desolation (it is an open question whether this
has been done in connection with the fertility-rites of the autumn
feast). Luther has once more grasped this intention of the psalm in
that he transfers this idyll into a medieval German town by rendering

---

[1] In that case it must obviously be assumed that the word Selah had its place
at the end of the refrain (see vv. 7, 11).

the verse—in a translation which admittedly deviates from the original text—as follows: 'nevertheless shall the city of God remain pleasant and gay with its little fountains'.[1] Since Jerusalem has no river, it must here be a matter of a word-picture borrowed from some other source. It seems to originate in the mythological idea of Paradise which was applied to Jerusalem and incorporated in the tradition of the cult of Yahweh (cf. the four rivers of the Paradise in Gen. 2.10–14 which water and fertilize the whole world). Old Testament prophecy is likewise familiar with the thought that Jerusalem, as once the Garden of Eden, will be established on the highest mountain (Isa. 2.2; Ezek. 40.2) and that a miraculous river flows out from the city of God for the benefit of the whole world (Ezek. 47.1; Joel 3.18; Zech. 14.8; Rev. 22.1 f.). It is probably in contrast to the scanty 'waters of Shiloah' which, 'flowing quietly and gently', were a perennial problem for the city in the event of a siege (cf. Isa. 7.1 ff.) and were referred to by Isaiah as a symbol of the invisible guidance of Yahweh (Isa. 8.5 f.) that the poet here uses the picture of the beneficial *broad river* flowing from Paradise in order to illustrate the blessing and the protection resulting from the nearness of God, the actual source of joy for Jerusalem, God's city. The river and its tributaries serve in the psalm to express in figurative language the abundant wealth of the powerful blessings that flow from God and his presence, which at the same time also preserves the city whenever it faces the threat of danger (cf. Isa. 33.21). This thought of the gracious preservation of Jerusalem, which also occurs in the book of the prophet Isaiah and probably dates back to a common cultic tradition (cf. Isa. 10.24 ff., 27 ff.; 28.16; 29.1 ff.; 31.4 f.), has been clothed by the poet in an archaic biblical form, if the version of the Greek translation, which fits more readily into the thought-sequence, accords with the original text:[2] in the passage 'the Most High has sanctified his habitation' the term 'sanctify' to a certain degree still implies its original sense, meaning 'set apart' or 'set off' against the common relationships'. Hence, what is here reflected is the ancient conception of the inaccessibility of the God of Sinai (cf. Ex. 19.12, 23), who makes his habitation unapproachable by

---

[1] * In the German original 'dennoch soll die Stadt Gottes fein lustig bleiben mit ihren Brünnlein'.

[2] Herbert Schmid's suggestion (*ZAW* 67, 1955, pp. 182 f.) *qadoš miškanī ʿelyōn* = 'holy is the habitation of the Most High' would render the same meaning. Cf. the comments on Ps. 7.17 as regards the designation of God as 'the Most High' and its presumable connection with the cultic tradition of Jerusalem.

strangers seeking to obtrude upon him. **[5]** The trusty shield and
weapon on which one can absolutely rely are not confidence in
Jerusalem's strong walls or in its secure position protected by Nature
itself, but trust in the holy and inaccessible presence of God as the
'Most High'; it is the same faith which Isaiah demanded from his
king and people in times of their affliction by enemies (cf. Isa. 7.7 ff.;
28.16; 30.11 ff.; 31.1 ff., 8 f.). God alone is the immovable centre
round which the fleeting manifestations of the world revolve, and for
that reason it is only and solely his presence which guarantees that
the city will stand firmly. The events leading to the final decision are
even more closely condensed: God intervenes and helps during the
last vigil when the peril has reached its climax; what he does comes
to pass under the cover of night, in the darkness which is full of
mystery—here the psalm speaks with reverent awe—but the dawn
of the next morning will reveal his mighty work. **[6]** It is only at this
point in the psalm—a symptom of supreme dramatic tension—that
we are told what the affliction is from which deliverance is wrought
by God. Employing the same words which he had used in v. 3 to
describe the surging waters of the ocean and the destruction of the
earth, the poet now portrays the onslaught of the nations who assault
the city like the surge of the waves, but collapse before the gates of
Jerusalem. Here, too, it is Yahweh who himself brings about this
turn of events. He only needs to let his voice be heard (cf. Isa. 17.12
ff.; Amos 1.2; Joel 3.16; Ps. 29) and 'the earth melts'. Here the
historical events have been given a cosmic significance; here natural
and historical catastrophes have been blended into each other. This
is to be accounted for, on the one hand, by the fact that originally
these themes had their roots in the natural mythology of the combat
of the gods against the powers of chaos (cf. Jer. 47.2; Pss. 104.6 ff.;
89.9 f.; Job 38.10 f.), but were 'historicized' within the framework of
the cult of the Covenant, that is, they were used to describe events
that had taken place in the sphere of history (see Intr. 51). On the
other hand, our passage makes particularly clear that the ultimate
reason for the fact that in the Old Testament the larger significance
of cosmic events is ascribed to historical events is to be found in the
specific character of the Old Testament's very idea of God. The
intensive definition of man's dependence on God (see above on
v. 3) is matched by an extensive definition of the conception of God
which at every moment simultaneously embraces all space and
every age. Because God as the exalted Lord of the world is at work

in history, the thinking of the faithful, which is focused on God's presence, envisages the concrete historical events as closely related to the things which are timeless and eternal, eschatological and final; because for the faithful it is the end which is at stake, the current events in history receive this all-embracing significance from God. [7] In the scene of the onslaught of the nations the refrain now sounds like the flourish of trumpets in the tumult of a battle, proclaiming God's victory. In the present context the name Yahweh Sabaoth may re-echo the ancient warlike tone which was associated with it as a designation of the God of the sacred Ark who fought Israel's battles; and the phrase about the 'safe stronghold' receives its specific colouring from the prospect of the deliverance of the city of God— the holy city, the visible pledge of divine protection!

Third Strophe: The Divine Kingdom of Peace (vv. 8–11)

[8] What so far has been hinted at in general outlines only quite deliberately so that the tension may be maintained, is now made quite clear with the aid of visible events and with all the liveliness peculiar to the drama of cultic representation. The members of the cult communtiy are invited to see with their own eyes what has come to pass (cf. Pss. 48.8; 66.5; see Intr. 42 ff.); God's great work of deliverance has been accomplished. In place of the enemy, whose army, confident of victory, assaulted the city, a desolate expanse of ruins appears, covered with corpses and broken weapons. At first glance the impression of dreadful horror prevails. In a most powerful manner it bears witness to what it means to oppose the living God. However, this picture of the collapse of the power of man under the mighty fist of God is not the only thing, and also not the final thing, which the eyes of faith are able to see here. [9] The destruction serves a higher purpose. It is true that broken bows, shattered spears and burned shields lie about at the end of the road which man must walk if he relies on his own power, but at the same time they are also present at the beginning of the way which mankind is to enter upon according to God's purpose. They testify to God's will for peace, who wants to make all wars in the world to cease for ever. In that the faithful dares in the face of frightful destruction to hope with exultation in his heart for God's kingdom of peace in spite of all appearances to the contrary, his faith reaches its ultimate height. It is only because he is wholly dependent on God and lets his thinking and his vision be directed by God that he is able to arrive at such a bold conception—

which like a flock of birds passes over every aspect of the reality of the events taking place on earth. It is characteristic that once more eschatological significance is here ascribed to historical events in pursuance of the idea of the kingdom of everlasting peace at the end of time; and that idea has taken shape also in the hope for the future of the prophets (cf. Isa. 2.2 ff.; 11.6 ff.) who presented this idea by making use of the picturesque language of mythology. The psalm now reaches its climax. [10] God himself appears and speaks his Word to the nations. That Word is a command; it is even something more: as the Word of God it carries with it the power and the guarantee of its fulfilment. 'Leave off (from waging war) and know that I am God'; it is the aim of the kingdom of peace that the world may know God and submit to him.[1] As the Lord of the world God 'rises' above the nations and the earth in order that he may be the One who alone is exalted above the whole world. The theophany ('ārūm), which is experienced by the festival congregation as the revelation of God when the celebration has reached its climax, signifies at the same time the culminating point and ultimate goal of his redemptive work for the whole world. What we are here presented with is not the blissful dream of eternal peace, dreamt by human beings belonging to an age that has got tired of wars and hoping for earthly happiness or yearning for rest and peace, but the strong faith which has made God's cause wholly its own and, because it has experienced the divine love, knows that the world will find its consummation in the peace of God. The ultimate goal of everything which comes to pass is not the fulfilment of human desires but the revelation and self-glorification of God. That *his* kingdom come and that *his* will be done is at once the motive and the goal of the faith pictured in this psalm. [11] At this point the refrain presents itself as the exultant and enthusiastic response of the members of the congregation to the self-revelation of God. It now expresses their happiness that they may have communion with that mighty God and may know themselves to be sheltered under his wings. And at the root of the refrain is the saving knowledge of having a share in God's kingdom of peace, and also the hope of being able to live in the expectation of the future fulfilment of these great promises. This

[1] Kraus, who in this follows Rohland, *Die Bedeutung der Erwählungstraditionen Israels für die Eschatologie der alttestamentlichen Propheten* (Dissertation, Heidelberg, 1956, pp. 123 ff.), interprets the verse as being an 'oracle in answer to a prayer'; but that view is suggested neither by the form of the verse nor by its content.

inward assurance that flows from man's total surrender to God confers on the psalm the distinction of a song of songs of that faith which confidently faces every kind of danger because it carries with it the unshakable certitude of the victory that overcomes the world.

47. THE ENTHRONEMENT OF YAHWEH

To the Conductor. To the Sons of Korah. A Psalm

1 Clap your hands, all ye nations!
   Shout to God with loud songs of joy!
2 For the Lord, the Most High,[1] is terrible,
   a king, mighty over all the earth.
3 He subdues peoples under us,
   and nations under our feet.
4 He chose our hereditary land for us,
   the pride of Jacob whom he loves. *Selah*
5 God has gone up amidst shouts of joy,
   the Lord at the sound of a trumpet.
6 Sing praises to our God,[2] sing praises!
   Sing praises to our King, sing praises!
7 For God is the king of all the earth;
   sing praises with a song![3]
8 God is become king over the nations;
   ' '[2] he sat down on his holy throne.[4]
9 The princes of the peoples are gathered
   as the people of the God of Abraham.
   For the shields of the earth belong to God;
   he is highly exalted!

[1] Cf. the comments on Ps. 7.17.
[2] See BH.
[3] The meaning is doubtful; see Ps. 32.
[4] * V. 8 reads in RSV:
   God reigns over the nations;
   God sits on his holy throne.

In later Judaism the psalm was regarded as the special psalm for the New Year Festival. Using the style of a hymn, it praises with an almost passionate enthusiasm Yahweh's kingship over the nations and in this is to be classified with Psalms 93 and 96–99. The psalm has been variously interpreted and, as in the case of many other psalms, three different methods of exegesis oppose each other at present: the 'historical', the 'eschatological' and the 'cultic' interpretation. The historical interpretation seeks to understand the psalm in the light of a quite specific historical situation, be it a successfully concluded war or the completion of the restoration of the Temple after the Exile.

The eschatological interpretation takes into account the general and universal character of the psalm and does so to a higher degree than the historical interpretation, for which that feature raises certain difficulties; it regards as the psalm's object the poetical glorification of the consummation of the Kingdom of God at the end of time. The cultic method of interpretation, on the other hand, assumes that the psalm is a portion of the liturgy of the Enthronement of Yahweh. All three interpretations contain some elements of truth which, if rightly related to each other, are able to promote our understanding of the psalm.[1] The verses 1, 6 and 9 provide evidence that the psalm was used in the cultus. The scene of the festival envisaged in the psalm, for the celebration of which the 'peoples' and their 'princes' are gathered in the sanctuary as 'the people of God' (v. 9), is concerned with the Enthronement of Yahweh (v. 8), who has 'gone up', amidst the congregation's festal shouts of joy and at the sound of the trumpet (vv. 5, 9), and enters upon his reign over the whole world (v. 7), after he has 'subdued nations' (v. 3) and 'chosen' the 'hereditary land' for his people (v. 4). This is obviously an allusion to the consummation of the *Heilsgeschichte*, which itself was a theme of the cultic tradition and was celebrated and experienced at the feast of Yahweh as a sacred event.

In this manner history and eschatology become in the cultic ceremony a present reality of actual significance in which the festival congregation shares. Particular festival rites, which also occur at the enthronement of the earthly king, such as the proclamation of the king's accession to the throne in v. 8 (cf. II Sam. 15.10; II Kings 9.13), the clapping of hands and the blowing of the trumpet in vv. 1, 5 (cf. II Kings 11.12), probably date back to the Babylonian feast of the enthronement of the god Marduk which was celebrated on New Year's Day, from which they were borrowed through the agency of the corresponding Canaanite rites. On Israelite soil the enthronement of Yahweh seems to have formed an integral part of the Covenant Festival that was annually celebrated in the autumn at the beginning of the New Year, and within this setting was given a stamp of its own which accorded with the Old Testament tradition of the cult of the Covenant (see Intr. 61 f.). The Babylonian epic poem on the

---

[1] Westermann's view (*Das Loben Gottes in den Psalmen*, p. 108) that the historical-eschatological and the cultic interpretations of the enthronement of Yahweh exclude each other is based on a lack of appreciation of the relationship between cultus and *Heilsgeschichte* and makes evident the limitations of his formalistic method of dealing with the subject.

order of the universe may have praised the yearly enthronement of
Marduk, but in the Old Testament the power of the monotheistic
idea of God gave rise to the conception of the final and eternal
dominion of God as the necessary consequence of the belief in the
God of history; it also led to the realization that the Kingdom of God,
which at the end of time will embrace the whole world, is the meaning
and the goal of all history. The psalm enthusiastically testifies to the
power of this thoroughly biblical faith.

[1–2] In the opening verses, which are clothed in the stylistic
form of a hymn, the pilgrims who from 'all the nations' have gathered
together for the feast (see Intr. 37) are called upon to pay homage to
God as the terrible and mighty King of the whole world. Thus the
scope and the theme of the psalm are outlined simultaneously. Both
of them are grand enough to rouse the congregation attending the
feast to great heights of enthusiasm. Just as the shouts of joy acclaim-
ing the earthly king surround him at his enthronement, so the
sanctuary shall resound with the rejoicing of the whole world to
greet God, who has appeared to reveal his reign over the whole
world (see Intr. 33 f.). The nations accompany their exultant hymns
with the rhythmic clapping of their hands, a thunderous echo of the
divine might. The motivation of their reaction is strange but entirely
in accordance with the essential nature of the Old Testament idea of
God: Yahweh shall be received with shouts of joy just because he is a
terrible God. For man perceives God's glory and encounters him as
Lord in the very things which cause him to tremble; he perceives
God's glory and encounters him as Lord in the things which make
him realize that the power of God is something quite different,
something which is absolutely superior and causes him to be frightened of it and to feel very humble in his presence. This is why the
fear of God is prominent in almost every aspect of the Old Testament
faith. This tremendous religious conception has not arisen out of any
desire for the establishment of Israel's dominion over the whole
world, a desire prompted by the pursuance of power politics. On the
contrary, the root of the belief in God's dominion over the world is
to be found exclusively in the religious sphere, since it is the ultimate
consequence of the Old Testament idea of God. Selfless and absolute
devotion to God's cause draws from the congregation the pure tones
of noble enthusiasm. [3–4] The same spirit animates the proud
words which the psalm uses of the tradition of the *Heilsgeschichte*, to
which it now turns. Since the earliest days of their history this people

had already learned to understand that history as something which God had done, something which revealed equally the greatness of God's might and the greatness of his love. The fact that this small nation was able to hold its own during wars against numerous peoples and had found a home in Canaan, the 'pride of Jacob', which in the eyes of the sons of the wilderness was a 'magnificent' country, had all along been interpreted by the Old Testament tradition as a mighty act of divine grace. This interpretation was based on the religious belief in the election of the people of Israel and was perpetuated in the cult of the Covenant, where that act of divine grace was celebrated as a present experience. The attitude of man which has found its dogmatic expression in the doctrine of election is not that of man's boasting of his own achievements or of his superiority over other nations, but is characterized by his amazement at the greatness of the miraculous grace of God which he humbly acknowledges with gratitude and joy. In the context of the psalm the reference to the mighty acts which God has wrought for the sake of Israel can only be meant to express that attitude of mind which is exclusively focused on God; and for this reason, too, cannot be understood as referring to the future dominion of Israel over the Gentiles. Israel must not, however, keep her history to herself, but is meant—this truth has been grasped by all the great figures of the Old Testament—to use it in the service of the realization of the divine salvation, and therefore for the purpose of her mission amongst all the nations. Israel is the 'servant of God' and her history, which takes place in the light of the revelation of God, is a history of salvation also for the other nations, so that they may recognize in that history the nature and providential rule of God and may bow down before him. A view of history such as we meet here in the psalm visualizes God as being alone at the heart of history as he is at its beginning and at its end. It is by no means a matter of indifference to the rest of the world how this nation conceives of its history.

[5–7] Seen in this perspective the whole history has a comprehensive goal towards which it moves; the course which it takes is that which leads to the final Kingdom of God that embraces the whole world. By this very thought the psalm links together the beginning and the end of history in that it follows up the backward glance at the beginnings of the *Heilsgeschichte* in Israel by the forward look to the consummation of the *Heilsgeschichte* in Yahweh's enthronement as King of the whole world. It is true that to the faithful God was

already in the past always the Lord of the earth who with a definite
purpose in view holds the destiny of the nations in his strong hands.
But in the festival cult their religious life experienced a great uplift
under the overwhelming impression of the presence of God. Time
sinks into insignificance before God: to the eyes of faith the God who
was is present also as the God who is to come. It is at this point that
the faithful experience the intersection of history and eschatology;
and this is why the psalm praises God's advent to kingship over the
world as a recently accomplished event and calls upon the
congregation to acclaim the King with enthusiastic shouts of
joy.

[8–9] In the psalm the cultic ceremony's main theme of God's
kingship over the nations is made to echo twice in succession (vv.
7, 8). The psalm pictures the King-God as he ascends his heavenly
throne and sits down in his holy majesty to signify that he has
entered upon his reign as King in the sight of the whole world.[1] The
scene on earth is placed side by side with the scene depicted in
heaven. The princes of the nations—the psalm here deliberately
refrains from giving them the title 'king' which befits only God—
have gathered together by their own free will to pay homage to their
common divine King. They have become *one* great 'people of God',
the people of the God of Abraham, the ancestor of man's faith in
God who had once received the promise that in him all the nations
of the earth shall be blessed (Gen. 12.3). Now the blessing of Abraham has found its fulfilment. The faith in which he confronted God
is now the spirit in which the whole world will stand before God.
Thus the history of the divine salvation is consummated within the
psalm's field of vision. What the prophets proclaim in their prophecies of salvation, namely that the Gentiles will one day join the people
of God (Isa. 49.14 ff.; 56.6 ff.; 60.3 ff.; Zech. 8.22 f.), is here even
surpassed; the nations become themselves the 'people of the God of
Abraham'. The psalm is in harmony with the eschatological teaching
of the New Testament in so far as both hold the view that there will
be *one* flock and *one* Shepherd. It is evidence of the theocentric
perspective of the psalm, which is entirely absorbed in its enthusiasm
for the majesty of God, that it regards all distinctions to be annulled
in the sight of God and ungrudgingly classes the converted Gentiles

---

[1] The comparison of v. 8 with vv. 2 and 7 shows that the ceremony has in mind
the Yahweh who is already the King, whose kingship, however, gains by his cultic
enthronement a renewed actual significance for the present and for the future.

with the people of the God of Abraham. The same basic view is also expressed in the summary hymnic motivation with which the psalm concludes: 'the shields of the earth belong to God'; he alone is the Lord who has at his disposal all the forces of war; no human power will arise any more. The idea of God's everlasting Kingdom of peace seems to be reflected in this statement; presumably it seeks to give expression to a thought similar to the one the prophets have in mind when they say that Yahweh makes wars cease in the world (Isa. 2.4; 9.5; Zech. 9.10; Ps. 46.9). At the end of the psalm the thoughts are exclusively focused on God who as the only One who is highly exalted sits enthroned for ever as the Lord of the whole world. This exclusive joy in God, which is completely self-forgetful and makes us ashamed when we compare it with our belief in God, so often undermined by doubt and sorrow, has made the psalm a powerful and comforting testimony of biblical faith to the God who is always the One who is to come.

48. THE CITY OF GOD

A Song. A Psalm. To the Sons of Korah

1 Great is the Lord and highly praised
   in the city of our God on his holy mountain.[1]
2 Beautiful in elevation is the joy of the land,
   'the extreme north', Mount Zion, the city of the great King.[2]
3 Within her palaces God made himself known
   as a towering stronghold.[3]
4 For lo, the kings assembled,
   they came on together.
5 As soon as they saw it, they were speechless,
   (and) in panic took to flight.[4]
6 Trembling took hold of them there,
   anguish as of a woman in travail.
7 As[5] the east wind shatters the ships of Tarshish.[6]
8 As we have heard, so did we see it ' '[5] in the city of our God;
   the Lord Sabaoth[5] preserves her for ever.[7] *Selah*
9 We have thought on thy grace, O God,
   in the midst of thy temple.
10 As thy name, O God,
   so thy praise reaches to[5] the ends of the earth.
   Thy right hand is filled with salvation.[8]
11 Mount Zion is glad;
   the daughters of Judah rejoice because of thy judgments.[9]
12 Walk about Zion, go round about her,
   and number her towers,
13 consider well her ramparts,

go through her palaces;[10]
that you may tell the next generation
14 that this is God,
    our God for ever and ever.
    He will be our guide beyond death.[11]

[1] * RSV, omitting the words 'on his holy mountain' at the end of v. 1, opens the second verse with the words 'His holy mountain'.

[2] * V. 2 reads in RSV:
His holy mountain, beautiful in elevation,
is the joy of all the earth,
Mount Zion in the far north,
the city of the great King.

[3] * RSV reads, 'Within her citadels God has shown himself a sure defence.'

[4] * RSV has 'astounded' instead of 'speechless' and its second line reads, 'they were in panic, they took to flight'.

[5] See BH.

[6] Tarshish is probably the Phoenician colony of Tartessus in Spain. The ships of Tarshish are ocean-going ships. (Tr. N.: RSV reads, 'by the east wind thou didst shatter the ships of Tarshish'.)

[7] * V. 8 reads in RSV:
As we have heard, so have we seen
in the city of the Lord of hosts,
in the city of our God,
which God establishes for ever. *Selah*

[8] * RSV has 'filled with victory'.

[9] * The exhortatory form ('let . . . be glad' and 'let . . . rejoice') is used in RSV.

[10] * RSV has 'citadels' instead of 'palaces'.

[11] * In RSV 'for ever' instead of 'beyond death'.

The psalm is usually described as a hymn in praise of Zion or as a song to be sung during a procession; it is only with some reservations that these interpretations can be accepted as correct. Only vv. 12 f. speak of a procession; and the part which Zion plays in the psalm cannot be separated from the glorification of God which is the psalm's primary object. Consequently the psalm is to be regarded as a hymn to the glory of Yahweh and is to be understood in the light of this interpretation. In a similar way as in Psalms 46, 47, 97 and others, with which the psalm has an affinity in subject-matter, the key to its understanding is to be found in the cult of the feast of Yahweh, which was celebrated in the Temple of Jerusalem (vv. 2, 9). Verse 3 as well as vv. 8 and 9 point to an event that has taken place in the cult and finds its hymnic response in the testimony to the greatness of God borne by those who attend the feast (vv. 1–11); meanwhile, the call made upon them by a priest to walk in procession round the holy city is to be understood in connection with the cultic ceremony. The exclusive interpretation of the psalm in the light of

contemporary history, relating it mostly to the deliverance of Jerusalem from the Assyrians in 701 BC, is disproved by the lack of any
specific allusions to a thanksgiving service; and an exclusively
eschatological interpretation can be justified only if the tenses are
disregarded which point to events that have immediately preceded
the psalm. The historical as well as the eschatological features of the
psalm are rather to be accounted for by the fact that they have their
place in the festival cult. There are no cogent reasons which would
exclude the view that the psalm was composed and used in pre-
exilic times.

[1–3] At the very beginning of the psalm, the keynote, to which
the whole song is tuned, is sounded by the festive and majestic tones
of the hymn—which reflects the enthusiasm of the congregation
('our God') with which they were filled during the hallowed hour in
the house of God—the keynote, that is, of the greatness and the glory
of God. The hymn glorifying Mount Zion is woven into the praise of
God, thus blending in a harmonious chord religious emotions with
aesthetic sensual pleasure.

It is probably in opposition to pagan ideas that Mount Zion is
described as 'the extreme north' where people looked for the
'mountain of the gods' (cf. Isa. 14.13 f.; Ezek. 28.14, 16; Pss. 68.15
f.; 89.12; Job 26.7; 37.22; perhaps the term *ṣāpōn* [= north] dates
back to the name of the holy mountain of Ugarit in Phoenicia which
is attested in the Ras Shamra texts). As in the prophetic teaching on
eschatology (Isa. 2.2; Ezek. 40.2; Ps. 46.4), so here, too, the idea of
the mountain of the gods and the Paradise connected with it is
applied to the mountain on which the Temple stood and thus indicates the scope of the psalm—by its cosmic, universal range it intends
to throw into relief the greatness of God, as well as the designation of
Yahweh as the 'great king', the Lord of the whole world. It is against
this background that v. 3 is to be understood: it forms the transition
to the revelation of God in the city of the Temple (vv. 4 ff.) by means
of which Yahweh has shown himself to be a 'towering stronghold'
(Ps. 46.7, 11).

[4–7] The next scene (vv. 4–7), which is laid in Jerusalem ('there'),
cannot be understood as an account of an historical event in the
modern sense, as, for instance, of the campaign of Sennacherib
(701 BC); for quite apart from the fact that in essentials it is at variance with the historical sources and according to our knowledge of
the relevant history a banding together of kings against Jerusalem

never took place, those who are taking part in the cult are according to vv. 8 f. deeply affected by the direct impression which the things they themselves have 'heard and seen' in the city of God have made upon them; and in the context of vv. 3, 4 ('for') and vv. 8 f. this trait can only refer to a cultic act in the sanctuary, the witnesses of which now declare what they have heard with their ears and seen with their eyes. To put it differently, the scene described in vv. 4–7 has its origin in the representation of the saving deeds of God by means of which he has revealed to the cult community his power to protect and deliver. Though the events of the historical tradition took place at long intervals, they are condensed in this cultic representation as in a focal point, and this is done through speech and acts of a symbolically suggestive and effective character which accord with the oriental temperament as well as with the essential nature of cultic proceedings. And these events are experienced and celebrated by the cult community as an encounter with their God which forms an integral part of the *Heilsgeschichte* (cf. the commentary on Ps. 18; see Intr. 42 ff., 50). This accounts for the 'banding together of the kings' and also the fact that the psalm makes the theological, metaphysical and miraculous aspect of God's acting the centre of its presentation, and not a single historical event which happens but once nor individual human features; hence the panicky flight of the kings who came, saw and—fled (it was Calvin who quoted the familiar saying of Caesar concerning the battle of Zela in order to draw a comparison by way of contrast) serves to present the tremendous effect of God's epiphany in its true proportions. The mystery of the theophany experienced at the climax of the cultic proceedings is hinted at only as a mystery and with reverent awe, and this entirely accords with the sentiments of those who take part in the feast; like the picture of the ocean-going fleet that is wrecked in a storm at sea, it only helps to intensify the impression of God's greatness which is reflected throughout the psalm. This portrayal is analogous to similar testimonies to the miraculous effect of the appearance of God, such as Ex. 14.24; 15.14 ff.; Pss. 18.7 ff.; 20.7 f.; 21.9; 46.6 ff.; Isa. 33.10 ff., and that not only as regards its outward form but also in its association with the cultic tradition.

[8–11] The same phenomenon which portends for the enemies the paralysing terror of God and disaster, is for the members of the community of God the symbol of his protection and salvation. Full of joy they rejoicingly (v. 11) bear witness (cf. Ps. 97.8) to what they

have been able to experience at first hand in a solemn act of 'devotion' as the gracious deed of their God, that is, his judgment and his
salvation. In this way they themselves contribute to God's glory,
which extends as far as the revelation of his 'name' (see Intr. 30 f., 41 f.);
to his power neither spatial nor temporal limits are set (vv. 8, 10).
Here, too, one can clearly see that the eschatological comprehensiveness and universality of the Old Testament idea of judgment and
salvation did not originate in an expansion of man's dreams of
gaining increased power for himself, but in the greatness and comprehensiveness of the revelation of God's true nature and reality of
which the cult community was continually able to assure itself by
means of the cultic tradition.

[12–14] However, the sacred tradition does not remain tied to its
cultic matrix; the cult community is not only the recipient and the
bearer of salvation, but like a messenger passes on the good news of
it to the next generation. The procession round the city of the
Temple, which the pilgrims attending the feast are called upon to
form, is explained by saying that they shall impress the picture of the
holy city upon their memory as deeply as possible, so that they will
be able to tell the young people at home, not yet old enough to take
part in the pilgrimage, about the great saving experience which is for
them associated with that place. In comparison with the earlier,
more massive meaning which we may presume to have been at the
root of such a procession (that those walking in procession shall carry
the 'blessing' they received in the sanctuary to those outside), this
motivation signifies a spiritualization of the ancient cultic rite—but
one which does not annul its profound basic idea. In the psalm, too,
what is at stake is the concern that the knowledge of the revelation
of God's greatness and majesty be passed on from generation to
generation in an unbroken 'tradition' of God's redemptive work (see
Intr. 36, 54 f.), and that the bond between God and his community is
maintained 'for ever and ever' as the constant source of fresh hope
which will not be shaken even by the vision of death. It is doubtful
whether the psalm's last words, 'beyond death', belonged to the
original text.[1] However, in form and subject-matter they fit in with

---

[1] Others assign this phrase to Ps. 49 and, on the analogy of Pss. 22; 45 (see
p. 23), regard it as an annotation to that psalm, giving the tune to which (ʿal) it
is to be sung. Johnson, Sacral Kingship in Ancient Israel, p. 81, in order to make a
comparison, refers to the myth of the combat of Baal against Mot, which is well
known from the Ras Shamra texts; this combat is said by him to have been trans-
muted into Yahweh's triumph over the hostile kings, representing the 'arch-enemy'.

the rest of the psalm without any difficulty and provide a significant conclusion for it: the biblical hope in eternal life flows from the reality of God which knows no limits.

49. A RIDDLE OF LIFE

To the Conductor.   To the Sons of Korah.   A Psalm

1 Hear this, all ye peoples!
  Give ear, all ye inhabitants of the world,
2 children of the common people and those who are high-born,
  rich and poor altogether!
3 My mouth shall speak wisdom;
  my heart schemes to create understanding.[1]
4 I will incline my ear to a proverb,
  and solve my riddle to the music of the cither.[2]
5 Why should I fear in times of trouble,
  when the iniquity of my enemies surrounds me,
6 men who trust in their wealth
  and boast of the abundance of their riches?
7 Truly[3] no man can buy himself[3] off,
  nor can he pay a ransom to God.[4]
8 For the price of his[3] soul is too high,
  and can never suffice,[5]
9 that he should continue to live on for ever,
  and never see the Pit.
10 Nay, he sees that even the wise must die,
  the fool and the jester, they all perish
  and leave their wealth to others.[6]
11 Graves[3] are their homes for ever,
  their dwelling places for ever and ever,[7]
  though they named lands their own.
12 *Yea, man cannot abide in his pomp,*
  he is like the beasts that are killed.[8]
13 This is the fate of those who are self-confident;
  thus end[3] those who are pleased with their own talk.[9] *Selah*
14 Like a flock they are appointed for hell;
  death will now tend them.
  . . . .[10]
15 But God will ransom my soul
  from the power of Sheol;
  yea,[11] he will receive me. *Selah*
16 Be not afraid when one becomes rich,
  when he increases the wealth[12] of his house.
17 For when he dies, he will carry nothing away;
  his wealth[12] will not go down after him.
18 Though, while he lives, he may count himself happy,

and men may praise him[13]
because he did well for himself,[13]
19 he will yet go[3] to the generation of his fathers,
who will never more see the light.
20 *Man in his pomp is without understanding,*
he is like the beasts that are killed.[14]

[1] * The second line reads in RSV, 'the meditation of my heart shall be understanding'.
[2] * In RSV 'lyre' is used instead of 'cither'.
[3] See BH.
[4] * V. 7 in RSV:
Truly no man can ransom himself,
or give to God the price of his life.
[5] * RSV renders v. 8a, 'for the ransom of his life is costly'.
[6] * The first two lines in RSV:
Yea, he shall see that even the wise die,
the fool and the stupid alike must perish.
[7] * RSV has in the second line 'to all generations' instead of 'for ever and ever'.
[8] * In RSV we read 'that perish' instead of 'that are killed'.
[9] * V. 13b reads in RSV, 'the end of those who are pleased with their portion'.
[10] The restoration of the seriously corrupt text is hopeless. (Tr. N.: RSV renders
v. 14:
Like sheep they are appointed for Sheol;
death shall be their shepherd;
straight to the grave they descend,
and their form shall waste away;
Sheol shall be their home.)
[11] * RSV has in the second line 'for' instead of 'yea'.
[12] * RSV has 'glory' instead of 'wealth'.
[13] Following Staerk and Kittel (see the section on Commentaries, above, p. 14).
(Tr. N.: V. 18b reads in RSV, 'and though a man gets praise when he does well
for himself'.)
[14] * V. 20 reads in RSV:
Man cannot abide in his pomp,
he is like the beasts that perish.

Recited by the poet to the accompaniment of a cither (v. 4), this
composition is, on its own testimony, a *māšāl*, that is, a Wisdom song
(see Intr. 88 f.). Its purpose is to give an answer to one of the very old,
recurring riddles of life; the riddle has arisen from the poet's own
personal circumstances and has been pondered over and solved. The
author, a man of humble descent and oppressed by wealthy rulers,
has conquered the fear and the envy with which his own soul was
filled in the face of the power of his influential opponents; he now
discloses the thoughts which have enabled him to achieve a balanced
state of mind and equanimity. Thus at the root of the psalm in a way
is the social problem and question of how earthly possessions are to
be valued from the moral and religious point of view, and what man's

attitude to them should be in his everyday life. The poet searches for
an attitude of mind which will grant him the inner freedom from
being subject to human beings and to earthly things and will open
his eyes to the things which alone are to be feared and which alone
are trustworthy. And he finds that attitude of mind in the vision of
eternity and of the God who has ordained man's death. In this
respect the psalm bears analogy to Psalms 37 and 73.

Formally it is still possible to trace in the psalm, the text of which
has in places suffered serious corruption, a structure of strophes of
some sort. A refrain (vv. 12, 20) divides the main part of the psalm in
two sub-sections. The psalm opens (vv. 1–4) with a large introductory section which contains a call upon the peoples to hear and the
announcement of a discourse. The main part presents in vv. 5–6 as
the theme of the psalm the problem which the poet has to face
because of his personal circumstances. Its solution is first tackled from
a negative angle by pursuing these two thoughts: nobody can buy
himself out of the power of death with the help of his wealth (vv.
7–9), and all distinctions are levelled by death which is destined for
all men (vv. 10–12). In vv. 13–15 the poet contrasts the self-
confidence of the wicked and their bleak fate with something positive
—his trust in God and his hope beyond death which is based on that
trust. In vv. 16–20 he follows up this thought by exhorting his fellow
men to display fearless equanimity, and he justifies the exhortation by
reflections similar to those in the first part of the psalm.

Introduction
[1–4] The opening of the song is characterized by verbosity and
pretentiousness, the distinguishing marks of a didactic poem. The
poet craves a hearing from all the peoples and from all the inhabitants of the earth, rich as well as poor. This is understandable, as it is,
after all, one of the universal problems of mankind which he prepares
himself to answer for all men. It is not without reason that he calls
special attention to people in humble circumstances and to people of
rank, to the poor and to the rich; for these classes are at the heart of
his problem, and he has something to say to both of them. What he
has to say he announces as 'wisdom' and 'understanding', as the
result of the meditations of his heart. In making this statement he
provides an insight into what the wrestling and brooding of his inner
struggle cost him till he had clearly and firmly reached that viewpoint from which the solution of the riddle presented itself to him.

At first sight it might look as if as a result of the knowledge which he has gained a kind of proud self-assurance has taken possession of him; the solemn statement 'I will incline my ear to a proverb', however, shows that the poet receives the word he has to declare in a way similar to the prophets—as revelation. For his wisdom is, after all, not human wisdom. And in contrast to v. 13, where he reproaches his opponents for being pleased with their own discourses, he emphasizes at this point that he has learned first to hear before he teaches. The music of the cither, to the accompaniment of which he recites his song, is likewise a reminder of the fact that Elisha once made use of the string music of a minstrel that the Spirit of God might come upon him (II Kings 3.15). The psalm does not, however, enable us to establish beyond doubt that this significance of the music still figured prominently in the author's mind.

The problem

[5–6] The way in which the poet deals with the question that agitates his mind makes evident that for him it is not a problem which can be solved in the sphere of theoretical thinking. The problem has arisen from the practical experiences of his everyday life (it is there-fore also not concerned, as has frequently been believed, with the dogmatic question of theodicy or retribution), and the answer which he gives is exclusively designed to give guidance in the practical conduct of life. It is meant to lead to that attitude of faith which the poet himself has achieved in his struggle against the temptations of life, the attitude of faith, that is, which ensures tranquillity and equanimity. The subject-matter of the psalm is directly taken from life, as it actually is, and the psalm is designed to serve life. In the apparently carefree question, 'Why should I fear in times of trouble, when the iniquity of my enemies surrounds me, men who trust in their wealth and boast of the abundance of their riches?' the emotions are still reflected which the poet has subdued in his soul in the face of the many vexatious situations into which he was led by his wealthy opponents, the sentiments, that is, of fear and envy. It is the fear with which the oppressed is filled when confronted with the power and violence of man, and it is the envy of the poor who as a result of the wealth of other people is made to feel his own privations grievously. Both these sentiments are so very common as to ensure that the question which the psalm raises will receive the widest possible hearing. How, then, has the poet been able to overcome these sentiments? Certainly not by indulging in them and by yielding to them. On the contrary, he faces them, examines whether or not they are justified, and thereafter cannot help admitting to himself that, seen in the light of man's end, it is foolish to submit to such feelings. How did he come to draw that conclusion? Simply by contemplating the matter *sub specie aeternitatis*, by bringing the light of eternity to bear upon it and by trying with the help of that criterion to ascertain its true value. At the root of the fear and envy is, in fact, regard for the value and importance of the things feared or envied. But what is, after all, the value and the importance of men's power and wealth when one considers them from the standpoint of that which indeed determines the meaning and value of life—death? Here the judgment is all at once changed which to the unbroken, naïve sense of being alive may appear to be well justified, but does not hold its own when man is on the point of dying. The poet has been taught by his contemplation of death and of him who has ordained man's death to ascribe a different value to these matters.

[7–9] Death sets man bounds which he is not able to overstep by his own efforts. Neither human power nor human possessions are sufficient to buy him out of death. For in death man inevitably encounters the power of God, no matter how often he may have tried in other respects to evade that power and rely exclusively on his own strength. And because it is the power of God, all human power that is opposed to it is on that account bound to prove unavailing. God's power and man's power lie on two quite different planes; they differ not quantitatively but qualitatively. Thus the price is 'too high' to ransom man's soul from death. It is the criterion of all human aspirations which are exclusively directed towards earthly ends that they are bound to experience God as the One who sets them limits, as a hostile power—as the 'No' to their own course. All earthly pleasures are imbued with the desire to last for ever, but God has set bounds to that tendency by man's death. Here is the point at which are revealed the foolishness and the powerlessness of that type of man who is conscious only of himself. And this is why the poet, contemplating the matter from this standpoint, comes to realize that he has no cause to fear or envy his influential enemies, when he judges their importance against death.

[10–12] But death is also the poet's teacher in another direction. Death is, first and foremost, the great equalizer. In death all distinctions, which outwardly may carry some weight in this world, lose their significance. Both the wise men and the fools must die and, when they die, they leave to others the treasures which they have accumulated during their lifetime. Just like the life of all other men, so ends also the life of those who as proprietors or rulers named vast lands their own—between the narrow confines of the grave. This shows what the end of man's glory really looks like. What, after all, is man in his pomp when he must be as certain of death as the fat stock that lives in order to be killed. Nay, considering this ending there is really no reason for being afraid of the power of men and for grudging them their wealth.

[13–15] At the beginning of the second strophe the poet in retrospect recapitulates what he said earlier. But in doing so he adds the inner reason why the destiny of death signifies a complete failure for such people. The factors which contribute to that dreadful ending are their self-assurance, their confidence in their own person and power, and their self-centredness which makes their thoughts revolve only round themselves and entails that they are merely 'pleased with their own talk'. For all those things on which the lives of these self-assured people are built collapse when they die. This is why they present themselves to the underworld like a flock, having no will of their own and being deprived of all hope; and then, as the poet goes on to say, using a magnificent picture, death will tend them and will be their master. With such a life, in which death has the final say, the poet contrasts his own, in which God has the final say. Here man's trust rests on a different foundation, and its essential quality is different from that of man's trust in his own self. It is founded on him who has power over life and death. And because in the poet's view it is not perishable earthly possessions which determine the importance of man's life but the fact that he lives his life in communion with God, the death which he will have to suffer eventually does not have for him the dreadful significance of a breaking down of everything which is valuable in life; for death is transcended by the power of his God, who is able to redeem him from the power of death. And it is this relationship to God which in his view represents man's true life. This is why he may cherish the hope that God will indeed redeem him from death and, by 'receiving' him, will hereafter establish a living communion between himself and the poet which will be even more intimate than the one which already exists at present. This is the hope of faith that reaches beyond death and in doing so overcomes death spiritually. Here the

poet has reached the point where he is able to find the solution of the
riddle of life—in the victory of faith's hope over the power of death.
How this will come to pass the author does not explain. This is
something which remains hidden from the eyes of mortal man; but
faith is not vitally interested in that point. To the eyes of faith it
suffices to have the assurance that God will take care of man after his
death and does not abandon him to the power of the underworld.
Hence it is a futile effort of expositors—and an effort which hardly
accords with the text and the subject-matter dealt with here, and
does no justice to the poet's real intentions—to seek to make the
question of how the psalmist conceives man's redemption from death
the centre of their interest, though the poet himself does not do so. On
the basis of the text alone it is not possible to give a definite answer to
the question of whether what is at the back of the poet's mind is the
idea of being taken away before his death, as in Gen. 5.24 and II
Kings 2.9 ff., or a deliverance from Sheol (the underworld), perhaps through his resurrection as in Isa. 26.19 or Dan. 12.2. For the
poet, at any rate, his trust in the God who alone has the power over
death and his hope of eternal life founded on that trust is at the
centre not only of his thinking but of his life as well. The religious
certitude of which he speaks is for him not so much a knowing what
is going to happen but rather a power which sustains him and
enables him to proceed steadily even when he cannot see clearly the
course which his life is going to take. The certitude that at his death
some other Being than man and his power will decide on his life is his
comfort and help—at the very time when the man who sees and
knows nothing but himself will experience his complete failure before
the eternal death he is about to suffer.

[16–20] The standpoint from which the poet is able to face death
with a tranquil mind constitutes the point of departure for the
exhortation that now follows. What he has previously stated with
regard to his own person he now uses as guidance for others. This
accounts for the similarity of the thoughts, which makes itself felt
even to the extent of his using the same phrases. But the poet's
hearers, too, are now able to recognize that these phrases are based
on the hope expressed in v. 15, and it is for this reason that they
exert a stronger influence on them and are more intelligible, conveying as they do now the poet's exhortation (v. 18): be not afraid
of influential people nor envy them! The splendour of their earthly
glory is doomed to destruction. They face not the light but an endless

night; for the future holds no hope for them beyond death. And a
life without hope is no longer a life worth living. The refrain with
which the poet concludes the psalm points to this train of thought
with the help of a modification which, though small, is not insignificant. If man lacks understanding (which in this context can mean
nothing but that knowledge which comes by faith—that his life and
his death are in God's hands), he is like the beast that is killed. The
man who imagines that he can heedlessly pass over the ultimately
decisive reality, that is, over God, bases his life on a delusion in that
he deceives himself about the true circumstances of his existence, no
matter how much other people may count him to be a lucky man;
and it is precisely this truth which can be grasped only by the man
who takes the reality of God quite seriously. Considering its end, such
a life remains for all that hollow and purposeless. Thus the psalm is
stern warning against the identification of happiness with cultural
activities, wherein man knows only himself and deceives himself by
disregarding the fact that it is not man but God who stands at the
centre and at the end of life.

50. TRUE WORSHIP

A Psalm. To Asaph[1]

1 The Lord[2] is God.
   The Lord has spoken
   and summoned the earth
   from the rising of the sun
   unto the going down thereof.[3]
2 Out of Zion, the crown of beauty,
   the Lord shines forth!
3 Our God comes, he cannot keep silence;
   before him is a devouring fire,
   round about him a mighty tempest.
4 He calls to the heavens above
   and to the earth, that he may judge his people:
5 'Gather to me my godly ones,
   who made a covenant with me by sacrifice!'
6 That[4] the heavens declare[4] his righteousness,
   for he is a God who judges.[5] *Selah*
7 'Hear, O my people, and I will speak,
   O Israel, I will testify against you!
   I am the Lord, your God!
8 I do not reprove you for your sacrifices;
   your burnt-offerings are continually before me.

9   I need[6] no bull from your stall,
    nor he-goats from your folds.
10   For every beast of the forest is mine,
    the cattle on the mountains in thousands.[7]
11   I know all the birds of the air,[4]
    and all that moves in the field is mine.
12   If I were hungry, I would not tell you;
    for the earth and all that is in it is mine.
13   Do I eat the flesh of bulls,
    or drink the blood of goats?
14   Offer to the Lord a sacrifice of praise,[8]
    and pay your vows to the Most High;[9]
15   and call upon me in the day of trouble;
    I will deliver you, and you shall glorify me.'
16   But to the wicked the Lord said:
    'Why do you recite my statutes
    and take my covenant on your lips,[10]
17   though you hate discipline
    and cast my words behind you?[10]
18   If you see a thief, you are a friend of his;
    and you keep company with adulterers.
19   You give your mouth free rein for evil,
    and your tongue frames deceit.
20   You speak lies[4] against your brother,[11]
    you slander your own mother's son.
21   These things you have done, but I was silent;
    and now you think that I am one like yourself.[12]
    But I rebuke you and lay the charge before you.[4]
22   Mark this, then, you who forget God,
    lest I rend, and there be none who will deliver:[13]
23   he who offers praises as his sacrifice, honours me;
    and to him who walks uprightly[4]
    I will show the salvation of God.'[14]

[1] See p. 97.
[2] I interpret the first two words as representing the testimony of the cult community (cf. 'our God' in v. 3); the original term *Yahweh* seems to have been altered to *'El* by the elohistic redactor (see p.99) because of the subsequent designations of God (cf. v. 7).
[3] * RSV reads:
    The Mighty One, God the Lord,
    speaks and summons the earth
    from the rising of the sun to its setting.
[4] See BH.
[5] * RSV reads:
    The heavens declare his righteousness,
    for God himself is judge!
[6] * RSV has 'I will accept' instead of 'I need'.
[7] * V. 10b reads in RSV, 'the cattle on a thousand hills'.

8 * RSV has 'a sacrifice of thanksgiving' instead of 'a sacrifice of praise'.
9 Cf. the comments on Ps. 7.17.
10 * In RSV vv. 16bc–17 read:
'What right have you to recite my statutes,
or take my covenant on your lips?
(17) For you hate discipline,
and you cast my words behind you.'
11 * V. 20a reads in RSV, 'You sit and speak against your brother.'
12 * RSV reads:
These things you have done and I have been silent;
you thought that I was one like yourself.
But now I rebuke you, and lay the charge before you.
13 * RSV has 'and there be none to deliver'.
14 * RSV has 'brings thanksgivings' instead of 'offers praises' and 'orders his way aright' instead of 'walks uprightly'.

The psalm has the character of a liturgy. Its main part consists of a divine utterance of judgment delivered in the style of a prophetic rebuke. God himself appears to sit in judgment on the overestimation of sacrifices in the cult. In view of the dramatic description of the theophany on Mount Zion (vv. 1, 6, 7), which opens the psalm, and of the mention of the making of a covenant (v. 5), the place of the psalm in the cult of the Covenant Festival can be more closely defined as the moment when Yahweh appears before his people (v. 4) to sit in judgment on them and reveal his salvation (v. 23) to them (see Intr. 38 ff.). The essence of that cult does not consist, as the psalmist explicitly emphasizes, of the external offering of sacrifices and the observance in man's intercourse with God of a ritualism borrowed from the Canaanite environment; rather it consists of the humble testimony which is borne by the cult community in praise of God (vv. 14, 23), and of man's obedience to God's commandments (vv. 16 ff.), and so of a piety which is in real earnest about the manifestation of God's nature and will that took place in the cult (vv. 7, 17 ff.), and which acts accordingly. The same conception which is here expressed in the cult of the Covenant is advocated also by the prophets, who take their stand on the ancient tradition of the Covenant, the heart of which was not sacrifice but God's revelation. Psalms 40, 51 and 69, too, show a similar outlook.

The psalm is by no means, as some expositors have thought, merely a weak imitation of prophetic oratory, showing that the author's abilities do not match his model. Its structure as a whole exhibits a clear construction: the first part (vv. 1–6) is an introductory hymn describing the appearance of God, and already contains the main religious idea of the psalm, though keeping it still in the background. The second part (vv. 7–21) presents the actual rebuke uttered by God. This denounces in two sections the dishonouring of God as expressed in the sacrificial cult (vv. 7–15) and in the moral life of the wicked (vv. 16–21). The conclusion (vv. 22–23) contains a warning and a threat, and then a summary in the form of an exhortation and a promise of salvation.

The appearance of God (vv. 1–6)

The congregation's testimony, borne in response to Yahweh's theophany in the Temple, rises at the beginning of the psalm like a monumental gate. The impression of a miraculous and quite tremendous experience—of the kind in which Moses (Ex. 3; 19), Elijah (I Kings 19), Isaiah (Isa. 6), and Ezekiel (Ezek. 1) experienced their God—still re-echoes in these verses, which are to be understood as reflecting the events of the cultic drama that preceded the psalm. What they assert of God is not so much a portrayal of what God is like as an account of what he *does*: [1] God has come to sit in judgment; he has already summoned the whole earth from the east to the west (cf. Isa. 1.2 ff.; 6.1 ff.; 6.1 ff.; and p. 45 ff.). What a God must he be whom the whole world obeys and who uses the whole world as the background of his actions! The psalmist deliberately throws into relief those features of the tradition of the theophany which emphasize the powerful impression produced by God's might. These features are not at all, as Duhm assumes, merely a 'display of artistic devices', creating a strange 'incongruity' between the powerful impression produced by the appearance of God and the 'unassuming tenor of the utterance that follows'. For they are organically connected with the living encounter with God in the cultic ceremony and with the main theological attitude of the whole psalm: the particular conduct reproved in the rebuke has its origin in the failure of the people to let themselves be spiritually affected by God's appearance before them, a failure which Amos had already recognized as the root-cause of the corruption of the people in every sphere of life. And just as Amos (4.12) prophesies for the unsuspecting people encounter with God's dreadful power as revealed in catastrophes, so the power of the appearance of God provides here in the psalm the criterion by which everything which follows is to be judged. The point of the whole psalm is the powerful experience of man's encounter with God and the conclusions which are to be drawn therefrom. [2] Thus the cult community's testimony, which the prophetic speaker here makes his own (cf. v. 16), becomes the point of departure and the pivot of the divine rebuke which he feels bound to proclaim (vv. 7 ff.). The manner in which the appearance of God is depicted in the psalm shows how the ancient traditional representation of the Sinai theophany has been able to preserve its original traits in the cultic tradition. The majestic God is surrounded by a radiant light so that no human eye is able to see him (cf. Deut. 33.2; Ps. 18.7 ff.; Ex. 34.29–35), and the reflected splendour of that divine glory shines upon Jerusalem itself which the psalm calls 'the crown of beauty'. This shows how closely religious enthusiasm and aesthetic value judgments are here associated with each other. **[3]** A devouring fire and the roar of a tempest, which at the Sinai theophany are the attendants and servants of God when he appears (cf. Ex. 19.16 ff.; I Kings 19.11 ff.), are also regarded by the psalmist as the visible sign of the terrible divine power which makes the people tremble violently when God, having looked on for a long time, now breaks the uncanny silence. **[4–6]** It is only at this point that what so far was only hinted at in v. 1 is fully disclosed. God calls upon heaven and earth to summon the people that he may judge them (v. 5), and to appear as his witnesses that they may testify to the righteousness of his judgment (v. 6). For the theophany as well as for the prophets (cf. Isa. 1.2; Deut. 32.1; Micah 1.2 ff.; 6.1 f.) this tremendous forum, which was worthy of the divine judgment, served the purpose of manifesting the might and moral significance of the acts of God. The cosmic setting gives everything a universal and eschatological emphasis. Man's justification before an ultimate Authority is at stake. It is precisely his own people whom God has the right to call to account because they are under a special obligation to him as a result of the covenant which they solemnly made with him by sacrifice (Ex. 24.4 ff.). The phrase 'my godly ones' is also to be understood as pointing in the same direction, since it addresses the members of the people of God not on account of their special virtues but on the strength of their responsibility, which follows from their relationship with God.

Opposing the sacrificial cult (vv. 7–15)

The tremendous background of the theophany produced such an impression of God's power and superiority that the people's fundamental mistake in their behaviour at the sacrificial cult and in their moral conduct first becomes clear and can now be comprehended as a denial to the sovereign God of his due. Here lies the inner link which firmly joins together the several parts of the psalm. **[7]** The opening words of the rebuke also point in the same direction; at a prominent place in the psalm they once more strikingly throw into relief its basic religious idea by their call upon the people to hear and, above all, by their recourse to the theophany formula of the Ten Commandments from the cult of the Covenant. It is simply a matter here of the recognition of the rule of the Living God from which the people, as is shown by what follows, had departed in spite of their religious activities. The meaning of the saying to which in this context a special emphasis has been given—'The Lord, your God, am I' (notice the different word order in Ex. 20.2; Deut. 5.6)—is that God as God wants to be taken absolutely seriously. The purpose of the psalm is to impress on the minds of the people that their cardinal mistake is, in spite of all their religious zeal, a lack of respect for God. This is why the psalmist dwells in rather full detail on his efforts to gain an insight into the real facts of the case. In this way the psalm acquires a didactic, theological character and makes clear that the 'testimony' (ʿēdūt) to the divine statutes and their practical interpretation and application (see below) in the hortatory utterances of the prophets had their place in the cult of the Covenant itself (cf. Pss. 60; 75.5 ff.; Isa. 8.16; Micah 1.2).[1] **[8–11]** It is not the sacrifices as such, nor the manner in which they are performed, nor their number, nor the zeal that they bring to light, which is the cause of God's reproof. On the contrary, the number of sacrifices is so great that God has them 'continually before his eyes'. The cause of his censure is to be found in something quite different—in the wrong spiritual attitude which the people adopt in their relationship with him and which has found expression in their sacrifices. The people think that God is in need of their sacrifices. God is therefore conceived as being dependent on man and his gifts; it is this fact which reveals the abyss of an inward insincerity in consequence of which man makes himself independent of God, sets himself up in opposition to God and by virtue of his gifts tries to make God amenable to his own human will and to extort salvation from him. The true position is, however, exactly the reverse. God is God and not man, and therefore he is not

---

[1] This interpretation throws light also upon the exhortations and warnings which belong to the same class, and imparts a special significance to them. This applies in particular to those exhortations and warnings which we meet in the Book of Jeremiah.

dependent on the help of men. It is he and not man who is the Lord and Owner of the animals. How then could man want to exert an influence on God by his presumed gifts, seeing that he, after all, owns everything? Thus the whole folly and insincerity of man's attitude is revealed; in his bold arrogance he wants to put himself on the same footing as God. He lacks the respect which he owes to God —the Lord of the whole world and so also the Lord of man himself. The diminution of God's dignity and the sacrilegious presumption of man are closely related to each other. [12–13] Even if we were to assume that God feels hungry like a human being, he, the Lord of the world, would in that case not need to turn to man for help. In that hypothetical assumption, of course, lies already hidden that thoroughly preposterous idea which the psalm repudiates—the anthropomorphization of God as if he were someone who feeds on the flesh of bulls and the blood of goats. God's honour makes his reduction to the material sphere of man's existence intolerable.

[14] Accordingly, the psalmist's positive demand is to offer God 'a sacrifice of praise'. The cultic terms 'to offer a sacrifice' and 'to pay vows' are retained, but are now used only in a metaphorical sense, with the result that the materialistic, cultic significance of the whole is abolished (cf. Ps. 51.17). Instead there is here required of the inward man an attitude which wholly subordinates him to God by offering God man's praise, that is, by bearing testimony to him, acknowledging him as the 'Most High'. This is the true purpose of the cult of the Covenant. It involves a complete reversal of that attitude of the people which has incurred reproof. [15] The people are to realize to what a large extent they depend *on God* in everything; they are to give expression to their recognition of his supreme power and saving will (which is in no need of first being persuaded by sacrifices) by adopting the attitude which alone befits man in his relationship with God—that of prayer. It is on this level that true worship takes place: the people are to show that honour to God which belongs to him of right as God; this is the meaning of the saying 'Call upon me in the day of trouble and I will deliver you and you shall glorify me', which in its turn refers back to the fundamental theme 'I am the Lord, your God' (v. 7; on the whole section see Intr. 42) and in fact should have been inferred from the cult community's testimony to God (v. 1). The way from sacrifices to testimony and prayer, from external ritual acts to a continuous spiritual

attitude of mind, brings us very close to the New Testament saying of worshipping God in spirit and in truth.

Commandment and morality (vv. 16–21)

[**16–17**] The rebuke which follows is addressed to the wicked, that is, to those members of the covenant community who do not put God's commandments into practice in their everyday life. The separation of the wicked from the godly, that self-purgation of the cult community which is continually enjoined on it by the Old Testament tradition as a duty, has been of old an integral part of the cult of the Covenant, taking the form of a divine act of judgment and being as such presupposed in the psalm, too (see Intr. 45 ff.). There is an inward connection between what is here said to denounce disregard of God's statutes, also made known in the cult of the Covenant, and the attitude demanded in the psalm's statement on sacrifices. In addition to the intensification of the sacrificial cult the superficial appropriation of the commandments, learning them by heart, reciting them and boasting of knowing and keeping them (cf. Jer. 8.8), has been a symptom of the fact that the religious life of the people of Israel has become superficial. Isaiah (29.13) called this type of piety 'a commandment of men learned by rote', with the heart keeping away from God. The psalm sounds an even sterner note in castigating that sort of legalistic spirit (vv. 16 f.) in phrases which are couched in general terms based on principle. Here, too, as in the first part of the psalm it is spiritual insincerity which the psalmist seeks to denounce as he contrasts recital of the commandments and boasting of the Covenant with hatred of God's discipline and disdain for his precepts, as if one could possibly do away with the Word of God or elude its claim when one is prepared to be in real earnest about God. But it is precisely this attitude of mind which is lacking. In the statement 'I am the Lord your God' a special claim is made on man's moral life, but that claim seems to carry no more weight than it does upon the 'righteousness of the Pharisees and scribes' of which Jesus speaks (Matt. 5.20). They 'dispose' of God's statutes; they transform the will of God into a human affair which is open to discussion instead of submitting to it unconditionally. [**18–20**] When they interpret the law of God, they put themselves *over and above* the law instead of subordinating themselves to it. By referring to their keeping company with thieves and adulterers and to their spreading of deceit, lies and slander even against their own flesh and blood, the psalm demonstrates what the earnestness of their testimony to Yahweh and their obedience to God's statutes actually amount to. [21] But the psalmist also leads us down to the level on which such an insincerity, without noticing it, is able to clothe itself with the garment of an imaginary piety. It is once more the hypocritical conception of God which makes such behaviour possible. It is an anthropomorphizing of God to think that the absence of an immediate retribution, which they conceive in human terms, and God's silence justify their equating their own will with the will of God and holding that God is one like themselves. This is their actual 'sin'. For they always see God only in that light in which he appears to be useful to them and not as he really is, as the One whose claim and command are *unconditionally* valid. [22] What the psalm in the last analysis is really concerned with is to confront the hearers with God as he really is and with the demands which he makes upon them, to open their eyes so that they may realize their true position. Because they have turned the cultus and ethics into a human affair and have set *their* idea of God in the place of the true God, and because they have 'forgotten' this God, the threat speaks for that very reason of the terrible gravity of God who sits in judgment and asserts his authority wherever he is disdained. [23] When God now appears to sit in judgment, like a lion which tears his prey to pieces, then man will clearly see who God really is from whose hand no human help can deliver. Under the dreadfully serious impression produced by the reality of God the concluding verse once more recapitulates the positive themes of the prophetic psalm by summing them up in an exhortation that implies a promise: the promise of salvation, which the God-fearing members of the cult community may hope for from God, is only intended for those who honour God in their way of thinking and in their deeds and who through prayer, submission and obedience make manifest that they are in real earnest about the fact that God is their Lord.

51. CREATE IN ME A CLEAN HEART, O GOD!

To the Conductor. A Psalm. Of David, when Nathan the prophet came to him, after he had gone in to Bathsheba

1 Have mercy on me, O God, according to thy lovingkindness;
   according to thy abundant mercy blot out my transgressions.
2 Wash me throughly from my iniquity,
   and cleanse me from my sin!

3 For I know my misdeed,[1]
  and my sin is ever before me.[2]

4 Against thee, thee only, have I sinned,
  and done that which is evil in thy sight,
  so that thou mightest be justified in thy word[1]
  and remain blameless in thy judgment.[3]

5 Behold, I was brought forth in iniquity,
  and in sin did my mother conceive me.

6 Behold, thou desirest truth in the inward being,
  and teachest me[4] wisdom in secret.

7 Purge me with hyssop that I may be clean;
  wash me that I shall be whiter than snow![5]

8 Fill me with joy and gladness,
  that the bones which thou hast broken may rejoice.[6]

9 Hide thy face from my sins,
  and blot out all my iniquities.

10 Create in me a clean heart, O God,
   and put a new and steadfast[7] spirit within me.

11 Cast me not away from thy presence,
   and take not thy holy Spirit from me.

12 Restore to me the joy of thy help,
   and endow me with a willing spirit.[8]

13 I will teach the sinners thy ways,
   that transgressors may return to thee.

14 Deliver me from bloodguiltiness ' ',[9]
   O God of my salvation,
   that my tongue may praise thy righteousness.[10]

15 O Lord, open thou my lips,
   that my mouth may show forth thy praise.

16 For thou hast no delight in sacrifices;
   were I to give[1] burnt-offerings,
   thou wouldst not be pleased.

17 The sacrifice acceptable to God is a broken spirit;
   a broken and contrite heart, O God,
   thou wilt not despise.

18 Do good to Zion in thy grace;
   rebuild the walls of Jerusalem!

19 Then wilt thou delight in right sacrifices ' ';[1]
   then young bulls will be offered on thy altar.[11]

---

[1] See BH.
[2] * RSV has 'transgressions' instead of 'misdeed'.
[3] * In RSV the third and fourth lines are:
    so that thou art justified in thy sentence
    and blameless in thy judgment.
[4] * V. 6b reads in RSV, 'therefore teach me wisdom in my secret heart'.
[5] * RSV has 'and I shall be' instead of 'that I may be'.
[6] * V. 8b reads in RSV, 'let the bones which thou hast broken, rejoice'.

7 * RSV reads 'right spirit' instead of 'steadfast spirit'.
8 * RSV has 'salvation' instead of 'help' and 'uphold' instead of 'endow'.
9 Delete *'elōhīm*.
10 * RSV reads:
   Deliver me from bloodguiltiness, O God,
   thou God of my salvation,
   and my tongue will sing aloud of thy deliverance.
11 * RSV reads:
   then wilt thou delight in right sacrifices,
   in burnt offerings and whole burnt offerings;
   then bulls will be offered on thy altar.

Of the seven penitential psalms Psalm 51 is the most important one. It demonstrates the essence of true penitence. Here with inflexible earnestness the uttermost depth of sin is grasped and the way is shown that leads to forgiveness and true communion with God. The unflinching candour with which the worshipper carries his thoughts and emotions before God enables us to gain most valuable insights into the struggles of a human heart as it strives upwards until it has reached the heights of prophetic experience and thus prepares the way for a piety which brings us right up to the New Testament. Last but not least this peculiarity of the psalm is caused by the fact that the otherwise common description of material sufferings here recedes into the background and so the worshipper's spiritual affliction is made to occupy the very centre of the psalm. Automatically a deepening of the specifically religious ideas is thus achieved.

The directness of the life of prayer out of which the psalm has arisen has also moulded its outward form. There is no evidence of a homogeneous construction of the strophes; it would hardly accord with the tremendous spiritual tension with which the prayer is imbued. On the other hand, it is possible to trace a consistent thought-sequence which imparts to the whole a transparent and cogent structure. The invocation, which at once raises the theme of the forgiveness of sins (vv. 1–3), is followed by a confession of sin and a profound realization of its nature (vv. 4–6); this is followed by the worshipper's actual prayer for the forgiveness of his sins (vv. 7–9) and the renewal of the inner man (vv. 10–13) and ends in praise and thanksgiving (vv. 14–17). Verses 18 and 19 are a later addition which contains a subsequent reinterpretation of the last words of the psalm.

According to its superscription the psalm is said to have been composed by David when the prophet Nathan called him to account after his adultery with Bathsheba and the murder of Uriah. The psalm itself, however, does not contain any clues which conclusively

point to that situation; on the contrary, a series of passages directly
exclude such a dating and are at variance with II Sam. 12. Hence
we would not be justified in attributing any historical value to this
later ascription of the psalm to David. Since the appendix (vv. 18 f.)
envisages the future rebuilding of Jerusalem (and its Temple), the
reconstruction of the Temple directly after the Exile would supply
the earliest possible date for the psalm in its present form; in its
original form it dates back to pre-exilic times.

Invocation of God asking for the forgiveness of sins (vv. 1–3)
   [1–2] In the very midst of the distress caused by his sin the worshipper stretches out his hands towards God and implores him to have
mercy on him. If he were not conscious of the abundance of the
divine mercy, he would surely have broken down under the weight of
his guilt. How greatly he suffers from his sin is eloquently attested by
the reiteration of the same petitions and by the urgency of his entreaties, but also by the remarkable fact that it does not occur to him
at all to recall his previous integrity or his past good deeds in order to
lessen the weight of his present guilt, a thought which in such a
situation was otherwise quite familiar. This shows how completely
sin dominates his mind. Whence does this tremendous earnestness
in his sense of sin arise? Since there is no reference in the psalm to a
particularly grave offence nor to unbearable material sufferings as a
punishment for sin, it can only be the weight of the spiritual affliction
caused by sin which depresses this man. And that weight in the last
analysis can be understood only in the light of his relationship to God.
Because the worshipper is quite serious about God, for that reason
he takes his sin quite seriously too. It means to him nothing less than
failure in the sight of God caused by his own guilt. The significance
which such a failure has for the poet can be properly judged only if
we take into account, what can be observed throughout the psalm,
that he realizes that he is wholly dependent on God in everything.
This is why the forgiveness of sins is equivalent to the restoration of
the broken relationship with God which forms an essential part of his
life. It is true that the poet in speaking of the forgiveness of sins uses
phrases which are borrowed from the range of ideas associated with
the cult, phrases such as 'blot out' (add: 'from the book of guilt';
cf. Ex. 32.32; Ps. 69.28), 'wash' and 'cleanse'; but he envisages
behind these phrases the spiritual deliverance from his sins which he
asks for from God.

[3] The first step to true penitence is a clear recognition of one's own sin. The worshipper's confession 'I know my misdeed, and my sin is ever before me' expresses the sincerity of his consciousness of sinfulness which never leaves him and the firm resolve to be truthful to himself and candid in his intercourse with God. This is not the fleeting mood of a depressed conscience, but the clear knowledge of a man who, shocked by that knowledge, has become conscious of his responsibility; it is a knowledge which excludes every kind of self-deception, however welcome it might be, and sees things as they really are. In the courage to deal impartially with himself and in the objectivity of the knowledge of his own limitations there is already inherent a strength which causes man to disavow his sin in his heart and to pass judgment on himself. This strength is given to the poet by his experience of being confronted in prayer with the inescapable reality of God—which condemns him and towards which he nevertheless feels drawn as with invisible cords.

The confession (vv. 4–6)

[4] However, the true extent of grace is experienced only where the true depth of sin is grasped. This comes about only when man's sin is seen in the light of its relationship to something which is final, that is, in its relationship to God. In the presence of the God whose mercy alone is able to save the worshipper he has to confess: 'Against thee, thee alone, have I sinned.' These words by no means imply a limitation of his sins, as if sins committed against his fellow men were excluded; on the contrary, sin is here conceived in the much wider setting of its relation to God, no matter against whom it has been directed. In the last analysis every sin is directed against God, for it reflects the basic tendency of the human will which accomplishes 'what is evil in God's sight' and thereby destroys the living contact with God. So strong now is the impression which God produces on the speaker that he envisages only this aspect of his sin—its relation to God: sin is ultimately a religious concept rather than an ethical one. But it is precisely in regard to God that man is able to discern his state of sin with particular clarity: it loses its character as a particular offence and presents itself as the basic perverse tendency of the human will which rebels against God (cf. the comments on v. 5). How greatly the poet's reflections are influenced by his thought of God is evident from the strange passage that follows: 'so that thou mightest be justified in thy word and remain blameless

in thy judgment'. In the worshipper's view the ultimate purpose of
the recognition of sin is to be sought in the first place not in his own
person but in God. The purpose which the recognition of sin must
serve is that God is known to be God, and that he is acknowledged as
such—and that means that God's right to make demands and call
to account, and also his word of promise and of threat, whereby he
binds man's existence to the fulfilment of his will, are proved to be
incontestable and are vindicated. But the recognition of sin implies
even more than that. Like a flash of lightning an ultimate mysterious
relationship becomes apparent: the poet discerns in the very midst of
the affliction caused by his sin that this affliction has, too, a deeper
significance for himself. The grievous shock which the recognition of
his sin was to him served not to depress him and leave him helpless;
on the contrary, he senses the divine plan ('so that') to arouse him
precisely by means of the distress inflicted upon him by his sin and
make him conscious of the majesty of God and of the absolute
seriousness of his will. Thus the very facts which thrust him down into
the abyss of the realization of his own wretchedness point him to the
God who in his exalted majesty is at work far beyond the level of sin,
even using man's sin in pursuance of his lofty aims. The recognition
of his sin becomes for the psalmist the means whereby he is able to
know God—the absolute seriousness of his judgment and the abundance of his grace. This latter experience would be made particularly
clear if it should be permissible to interpret the first half of the half-
line in question in the sense of Ex. 34.6 f.; Jer. 29.13 f.; 31.34; 33.8;
but even apart from that interpretation, both these experiences are
implied in the personal circumstances of the worshipper: being fully
conscious of the seriousness of his sin, he comes to know the serious
character of the divine judgment in all its severity; and he senses the
gracious hand of God, which will not leave him alone in his state of
sinfulness, in the fact that by means of the recognition of his sin his
eyes are opened to the reality of God in a new way. Thus the
worshipper's reflection on the abyss of his sin becomes at the same
time a lifting up of his eyes to the inscrutable God whose grace is
revealed in his judgment on sin (cf. also v. 8). The divine miracle
which is disclosed to this man, as he wrestles in his soul with the
riddle of his life, has been glorified by the Apostle Paul in an immortal hymn on God's plan for the salvation of the world (Rom. 11.32
ff.): 'God has consigned all men to disobedience, that he may have
mercy upon all. O the depth of the riches of both the wisdom and the

knowledge of God! How unsearchable are his judgments and how inscrutable his ways! For from him and through him and to him are all things. To him be glory for ever. Amen.' The continuation of the confession in v. 5 shows that these thoughts on God's ultimate purpose being made manifest by sin are not felt to imply a lightening of man's responsibility and a weakening of the seriousness of sin (cf. Rom. 6.15).

[5] Whereas the insight into the depth of sin has led to the understanding of the nature of God, here, conversely, the ultimate realization of the nature of man is derived from the understanding of the innermost being of God. Before the absolute seriousness and inviolability of the divine will as expressed in judgment and in grace the worshipper now sees that his whole life is dominated by sin. And when he now declares, speaking ('behold') as if he had made a new discovery, 'Behold, I was brought forth in iniquity', then this is, to be sure, by no means intended to serve as an excuse, but is regarded by him as a truth which is even more dreadful and more serious. Common sense and natural instinct as well as reverence for man's destiny as determined by creation (a reverence which the Old Testament has never given up) forbid us to conclude that matrimony as such is here thought to be sinful. The poet's thought here ranges over a much wider field. It is the tragedy of man that he is born into a world full of sin. The environment in which a child grows up is already saturated with sin and temptation; and when the child learns to distinguish between good and evil he discovers already in himself a natural tendency of his will that is at variance with the will of God. The poet's experience is here similar to that of the prophet Isaiah who, being confronted with God in the hour of his call, becomes fully aware of the utter contrast between the exalted, holy and pure God and his own impurity and that of his people. In the light of the divine perspective, which embraces everything, the poet's thoughts penetrate to the ultimate cause of every sin. No longer does he see only particular transgressions; rather, all particular sins point back to that demoniac disposition of self-willed humanity addicted to self-glorification which is naturally ingrained in its own nature and threatens to lead it at any time into temptation. The poet realizes that these profound relations between sin and human nature operate in his own life.

[6] The poet does not even shirk this last deeply moving truth. He who wants to walk in God's ways must not shrink from the truth

which penetrates the innermost recesses of the human heart and ruthlessly exposes life's most secret relations and contacts. Indeed, it is precisely the deeply humiliating realization of the nature of his sin which is regarded by the worshipper as proving that in this first step of doing penance the will of God is taking effect in him. In this context the second sentence, 'teachest me wisdom in secret', seems to describe the manner in which the author arrives at that profound knowledge of God's nature and of the peculiar character of his sin. His earnest meditation before God in his heart (in secret) is the place where God himself reveals to the worshipper how everything ulti- mately hangs together (the poet like Paul in Rom. 11.33 calls it 'wisdom'). As for many other people—in this connection one might think above all of Jeremiah—so also for the psalmist prayer is that point in his life where his religious knowledge is advanced; this, however, is not brought about by his own clever thoughts but by the insight into ultimate truths which is granted to him by God.

Prayer for forgiveness (vv. 7-9)

[7] That divine gift of spiritual perception gives the worshipper so much confidence that he feels able to ask once more for forgiveness. Here, too, he uses phrases borrowed from the ritual language of the cult to illustrate a spiritual process. At the rites of purification those who had been healed of leprosy (Lev. 14.4 ff.) or had been defiled by coming into contact with corpses (Num. 19.18) were sprinkled with a bunch of hyssop; the second picture is similar to that in Isa. 1.18. [8] The petition that God may make him to hear joy and gladness probably refers to the word of forgiveness and to the promise of salvation which he hopes for from God. Then the bones (this phrase denotes here the whole human being) which God has smitten shall rejoice. This saying does not necessarily imply an allusion to a physical malady; in the present context it can just as well refer to the depression of the poet's soul brought about by the recognition of his sin, which he attributes to God exactly as he does the grace of for- giveness for which he hopes. It is in this very interaction of judgment and grace that he first experiences God in all his fullness. [9] This is why he once more asks that God may disregard his sin and blot it out.

Prayer for renewal (vv. 10-13)

[10] The forgiveness and cancellation of sin do not, however, mean that the way of true penitence has thus already come to an end. The

mere fact that the question of a new attitude to life, giving it a positive meaning, agitates the mind of the poet at all manifests the
earnestness and sincerity of his feeling of penitence. But the familiar
saying 'Create in me a clean heart, O God, and a steadfast spirit,
renew them within me' (this is how the text reads literally) signifie,
a further truth. At the root of it is the bitter realization that man is
not *able* by virtue of his own efforts alone to do that which is goods
because it would mean nothing less than complete self-conquest. The
petition for a new heart accords with and springs from the profound
realization of the nature of man (see v. 5): when sin is an intrinsic
part of man's 'nature', its overcoming is possible only if God creates
a new nature which accords with his purpose; and when man is to
overcome his own self, he cannot do so by virtue of his own efforts,
but only with the help of a steadfast spirit given to him by God. What
the prophets have proclaimed as a certitude to be realized in the
future history of their people—that it will be God who will bring
about the change of men's hearts (Jer. 31.31 ff.; Ezek. 11.17 ff.;
36.25 ff.)—is here grasped and believed as the result of a personal
experience. The moral life, too, is in the last analysis not an achievement of man, but the gracious gift of God. This is the Old Testament
root of the New Testament idea of man's rebirth (cf. Titus 3.5).
[11] In fact, the poet conceives of the help which God gives towards
a new life not in the ancient, mechanical form of man's endowment
with a new spirit, which will happen but once, but as being a kind of
organic relationship which will permanently link man's life to God.
It is only when we interpret the petition in v. 11 in this sense that we
shall be able to understand it without its being at variance with
vv. 10 and 12. The worshipper's true desire is that he may not be
cast away from God's presence; that is to say, that he may always be
allowed to enjoy the presence of God and through continuous contact
may be able to partake of his Spirit so as to receive power for 'sanctification'. For the worshipper judges his own human nature so soberly
and so realistically that he is fully aware of the fact that a new life is
impossible for him unless he lives continually in a living communion
with God. [12] Similarly the petition for joy through God's help has
more in mind than the particular forgiveness for which the worshipper hopes; for, as the connection with the second half-line shows, the
joy in the helpful nearness of God is the actual motive-power of the
new way of life which the poet here envisages. Man is not able joyously to affirm in his own strength that he will do the will of God;

or, to put it differently, he is not able to create the spirit of 'willingness' by his own efforts. Where the soul is not nourished by the power
of God, there man cannot rise above a servile obedience nourished by
fear. It is the joy in God as the motivating force of man's actions
which alone is able to transform ethical obedience into an obedience
based on faith. The poet is conscious of this fact when he prays to his
God for joy and for help with the new life which he wants to lead.

[13] It is of the essence of the new life lived by faith that it does not
remain confined to itself, exhibiting the character of an egotistic
piety that enjoys itself and finds its satisfaction in its own joy in God.
And the genuineness of the worshipper's experience of God can be
judged by the very fact that he feels urged on by an inward compul-
sion to turn to the sinners that he may bear witness to the way which
God has taught him to walk. The action which he thus plans is more
than merely an expression of gratitude for the forgiveness he has
obtained; it is the necessary manifestation of a life lived by faith:
'we cannot but speak of what we have seen and heard' (Acts 4.20).
Where God is at work, there the matter does not end with the experience of an individual; he becomes a messenger of God who cannot help
leading others in the way which he himself was privileged to walk.
The poet realizes that the concrete task of his new life is to convert
the sinners to God. The fact that he is chosen as God's instrument to
serve in this capacity, so that by his service God may be acknowledged and glorified in the world, fills him with a confidence based
on faith and desiring to do great things.

The vow (vv. 14–17)

[14] At first sight the petition 'Deliver me from bloodguiltiness'
appears to interrupt the train of thought. This would unquestioningly
be the case if the petition had in mind crimes which the poet himself
might commit. Such an interpretation has, however, no basis in any
part of the psalm. On the other hand, the verse becomes understandable within the context in which it stands if it is a question of
the poet's deliverance from a peril which threatens his life. If he were
to die, then he would indeed for ever be deprived of the opportunity
(cf. the comments on Ps. 6.5) of performing any acts of faith and
praising God's righteousness (this term embraces the whole salvation
which God dispenses). It is therefore understandable that the poet
thinks of the preservation of his own life at the very moment
when his whole being is deeply affected by the awareness of the new

life granted him by God, and of his new task. **[15]** How completely
the worshipper considers himself dependent on God in everything is
evident from the fact that even the praise of God in the midst of the
congregation becomes for him a gift from God for which he now asks;
God shall open his lips that his mouth may show forth his praise—
all things are from him and to him! **[16]** The psalmist, too, is familiar
with the custom of rendering God thanks by means of sacrifices and
offerings (cf. Ps. 22.25 f.). But whereas others on such an occasion
habitually spoke of paying vows and offering sacrifices, he boldly
dares to say that God has no delight in sacrifices and in burnt-
offerings; and in doing so he draws the ultimate conclusion from the
wholly spiritual quality of his conception of man's relationship with
God, a spiritual quality which permeates the whole psalm and dates
back to the original, fundamental character of the Old Testament
covenantal religion—it is also apparent in the preaching of the
prophets, rejecting the sacrificial cult and its underlying motives (cf.
Amos 5.21 ff.; Hos. 6.6; Isa. 1.11 ff.; Micah 6.6 ff.; Jer. 7.21 ff.; see
Intr. 25 ff., 85 f.). The man who has been made to see the hidden relations of his life to God as clearly as the worshipper, cannot possibly want
to obtain God's favour by means of material gifts and outward acts.
The poet walks in the way at the end of which the word is written:
'God is spirit, and those who worship him must worship in spirit and
truth' (John 4.23 f.). **[17]** This thought is no restriction and curtail-
ment of piety; on the contrary, it means a final widening and deepening of that piety. God desires not only material gifts and outward
acts, but claims the whole man. God has delight in a broken spirit
and in a contrite heart; that is to say, he has delight in human beings
who do not seek by the use of material means to exert an influence on
him, be it ever so refined, but who take the reverse course in that they
give up all claims to him and face him with a broken spirit—
entirely depending on his grace, completely giving themselves up to
him and whole-heartedly submitting to him. God is gracious to those
who are humble in heart. We would be mistaken if we were to
interpret the phrase of a contrite heart as reflecting only the poet's
momentary state of mind, caused by his expectation of the forgiveness
of sins in his particular case; for these words are spoken with a view
to the thanksgiving that will *follow* the forgiveness of sins and therefore characterize the basic attitude which man is to observe in all
circumstances. Penitence has here become a daily attitude of
penitence and, without saying so explicitly, the poet, in fact, also

accomplishes a far-reaching transformation of the notion of sacrifice. The sacrifice that God demands is a sacrifice of man's self-will and self-importance; in other words, it is the surrender of man's own self to God. This elevation of the idea of sacrifice to the height of an ethical and religious spirituality is one of the most mature fruits on the Bible's tree of religious knowledge.

Appendix (vv. 18 f.)

[**18–19**] It is understandable that this lofty religious conception, with which the whole psalm grapples, and especially its closing thought, could not be fully grasped and borne by the piety of a later period deeply rooted in cultic ritualism; for this would have meant nothing less than the disruption of the whole mode of religious life. It is in this light that we have to understand the restriction subsequently added to the psalm regarding the sacrificial cult. That addition, to be sure, was possible only as the result of a reinterpretation of the psalm which cannot be judged to be anything else but a misunderstanding of its very substance. The author of the appendix wants the psalm to be interpreted in the light of the absence of cultic observances during the Exile, when it was not possible to carry on public worship in the proper way. But he expresses the hope and utters the petition that God will again delight also in 'right' sacrifices after rebuilding the walls of Jerusalem (and of his Temple). The explicit mention of 'burnt offerings and whole burnt offerings' is an unnecessary addition which overloads the verse. The appendix (vv. 18 f.) is most easily accounted for by regarding it as originating in the period that preceded the reconstruction of the Temple; its author has presumably been a contemporary of Haggai and Zechariah. It does credit to the guardians of the Old Testament tradition that in spite of the doubts expressed in the appendix they have cherished this precious treasure of a profoundly spiritual piety and have preserved it for posterity as a document testifying to the struggles through which faith had to go, a testimony which is not even surpassed by what the New Testament has to say of penitence.

52. THE END OF THE MAN WHO LOVES VIOLENCE

To the Conductor. Maskil.[1] *Of David when Doeg, the Edomite, came and reported to Saul and said, 'David has gone into the house of Abimelech'*

1 Why do you boast of your malice, O mighty man?
The grace of God endures for ever.[2]

2 You are plotting destruction;
   your tongue is like a sharp razor,
   you worker of treachery.[2]
3 You love evil more than good,
   and lying more than speaking the truth. *Selah*
4 You loved[3] all words that devour,
   O deceitful tongue.
5 Therefore[4] God will destroy you for ever;
   he will snatch and tear you from your tent;
   he will uproot you from the land of the living.[5]
6 The righteous shall see it and fear,
   but at him they will laugh, saying,[6]
7 'See the man who would not make God his refuge,
   but trusted in the abundance of his riches,
   and boasted of his malice!'[7]
8 But I am like a green olive tree in the house of God;
   I trusted in the grace of God for ever and ever.
9 I will testify to thee[8] for ever, because thou hast done it.
   I will proclaim[9] thy name, for it is good,
   in the presence of the godly.

[1] See Ps. 32.
[2] * Vv. 1 and 2 in RSV, and the verse-division, are different:
   (1) Why do you boast, O mighty man,
      of mischief done against the godly?
      All the day you are plotting destruction.
   (2) Your tongue is like a sharp razor,
      you worker of treachery.
[3] * RSV uses the present tense.
[4] * In RSV v. 5 opens with 'but' instead of 'therefore'.
[5] * RSV has 'Selah' at the end of v. 5.
[6] * V. 6b runs in RSV, 'and shall laugh at him, saying'.
[7] * The last line of v. 7 reads in RSV, 'and sought refuge in his wealth'.
[8] * V. 9a reads in RSV, 'I will thank thee for ever, because thou hast done it.'
[9] See BH.

[1-4] The psalm, which has undergone a poetic adaptation in a hymn by Paul Gerhardt,[1] exhibits a mixture of different stylistic forms. Verses 1-4 are formed after the fashion of the rebuke which the prophets used to utter; this is followed in v. 5 by the threat of future punishment; vv. 6 and 7 depict the impression produced by this punishment on the 'righteous'; the concluding verses 8 and 9 contain an affirmation of trust and a vow of thanksgiving and so take up themes of the lament. The psalmist speaks with such determination and authority that we can assume that he occupied a position of great importance within the community of the godly (a priest?—cf. v. 8).

[1] 'Was trotzest du, stolzer Tyrann'.

His spirited reproaches are directed against the deceitful and destructive machinations of a man who exerted great influence through his wealth and his haughty behaviour, and the cult community and the psalmist himself probably had much to suffer from him. Isaiah's threat against the Judaean court official Shebna (Isa. 22.15 ff.) has been referred to as a parallel, and not without justification. The statement in the superscription, added at a later date, that the psalm was composed by David to denounce the betrayal of Doeg (I Sam. 22.9 ff.) is historically indefensible; for the mention of the Temple as well as the reproaches require a different situation. On the other hand, as in Psalms 26 and 28, one might think here, too, of an act of the covenant community based on ritual law (vv. 6 f.), the purpose of which was the cursing of the evildoer and his expulsion from the community. The wording of the accusation in v. 3, with its stereotyped formulation, and the reference of the congregation to the fact that the opponent 'had not made Yahweh his refuge' seem to point in the same direction (see Intr. 47). In this case the terms 'the righteous' and 'the godly' would have to be understood as referring, as in many other psalms, not to the religious parties of late Judaism but to the community of the Covenant of Yahweh, probably as it existed before the Exile.

Using a method not infrequent in the psalms, the opening verse sketches the theme of the whole psalm in a twofold way, though it leads us at once into the very midst of a situation which is filled with dramatic action. The sarcastic and acrimonious accusation, levelled with indignation at the lamentable hero who grandiosely boasts even of his malice, is followed by the statement—the point of departure and stay of the verdict expressed in the psalm—that the grace of God cannot be shaken and will last for ever. Presumably trust in God had been called in question by words or actions of the person indicted (cf. v. 7). From that fundamental religious truth the psalmist derives the right to his severe impeachment and the criterion which determines it; and by means of that impeachment he fearlessly unmasks his adversary. In doing so he exposes the utter perversity of the godless man who loves evil instead of good. His verdict expresses the profound knowledge of the nature of sin which is characteristic of the Old Testament, and it is no accident that the story of the Fall regards untruthfulness as the sign of man's broken relationship with God. [5] Thus as a logical necessity punishment ensues from sin, and threat from rebuke; and the threat, like the curse, is to be understood as a word that produces an effect. The sinner is threatened with everlasting destruction. We cannot be quite certain whether the other terms are to be interpreted as word-pictures which are merely variations on the subject of death as such, not based on any concrete facts. Since the term 'tent' is used without being defined in more detail, it can be interpreted as referring equally well to the sinner's dwelling-place and to the Temple as Yahweh's abode (cf. Ezek. 41.1; Ps. 78.60); in the latter case one might think of the expulsion from the sacred confederacy of the covenant community which would precede the uprooting from the 'land of the living', that is to say, the punishment by death. **[6–7]** That the psalmist had such an action in mind is also suggested by vv. 6 f. The righteous, here the community of those faithful to Yahweh, are witnesses of these practices in which God decisively intervenes; this accounts on the one hand for their fear of the God who appears to sit in judgment (cf. Ps. 9.4, 19) and, on the other, for their joy in the victory of righteousness. The original participation of the cult community in that legalistic rite whereby they sanctioned the curse may still be visible in the mocking of the condemned, which once more summarily recapitulates the main points of the accusation and, to judge from its wording (*hinnē*), may have taken place whilst those on whom judgment was passed were still present (cf. Deut. 27.11 ff.). What had only been hinted at at the beginning of the psalm is now made quite clear. Without trust in God man falls a prey to the power of evil; he cannot help trusting in something and, if it is not God whom he trusts, then it is his own self or his wealth which he makes his idol, and even his malice appears to him to be a sign of strength of which he can boast.

[8–9] The psalmist observes that in contrast to the completely perverted behaviour of the man uprooted and alienated from God, and for that reason doomed to destruction, he himself is in possession of that wholesome saving strength and vitality which issues from his relationship with God, a relationship that is based on trust and is an imperishable gift of his grace. In striking contrast to his adversary, who is doomed to death, he compares himself with an olive tree in the house of God which is in full sap (cf. Ps. 1.3). Even if this last statement should formally be a part of his metaphorical language, it nevertheless belongs to the subject-matter itself in that it points to the important part which the house of God and its cult played in the psalmist's life in contrast to the man who has lost his membership of

the cult community. It is quite another world which is here revealed
in the psalmist's profession that his ultimate refuge is in God and
within the bosom of the community of the godly: here is the true life,
a life full of happiness, in contrast to the deceptive illusion of the
power of the arrogant. However, that joy in life which the poet experiences in contrast to the fate of his adversaries does not induce him
to be proud of himself; on the contrary, it makes him feel humble and
grateful. He vows to the God who has preserved him from the persecution of the violent that he will testify to him in the midst of the
community of the godly, a testimony that will never come to an end.
His greatest desire and his urgent prayer is that he may serve in and
with the cult community the glory of the 'name' of God whose
goodness he had been privileged to experience (cf. Ps. 22.22, 25 and
frequently; see Intr. 41 f., 58 f.).

53. See Psalm 14

54. THREATENED BY ENEMIES

To the Conductor. With stringed instruments. Maskil.[1] *Of David when the
Ziphites came and told Saul, 'David is in hiding among us'*[2]

1 Save me, O God, by thy name,
  and vindicate me by thy might!
2 Hear my prayer, O God;
  give ear to the words of my mouth!
3 For strangers[3] have risen against me,
  ruthless men seek my life;
  they do not set God before them. *Selah*
4 Behold, God is here; he is my helper;[4]
  the Lord is the upholder of my life.
5 May he requite[5] my enemies with evil;
  in thy faithfulness put an end to them.
6 With a free-will offering I will sacrifice to thee;
  I will praise thy name, O Lord,[6]
  for it is good.
7 For it has delivered me from every trouble,
  that my eye looks in triumph on my enemies.'[7]

[1] See Ps. 32.
[2] Cf. I Sam. 23.19 and Intr. 98.
[3] * RSV has 'insolent men' instead of 'strangers'.
[4] * V. 4a is in RSV, 'Behold, God is my helper.'
[5] See BH. (Tr. N.: RSV has 'He will requite' instead of 'May he requite'.)
[6] * V. 6b is in RSV, 'I will give thanks to thy name, O Lord, for it is good.'
[7] * V. 7 reads in RSV:
  For thou hast delivered me from every trouble,
  and my eye has looked in triumph on my enemies.

According to its title added later, the psalm is ascribed to David; he is said to have composed it when he was fleeing from Saul and the Ziphites had betrayed his hiding-place to Saul. This dating, which is not supported by the subject-matter of the psalm itself, is derived from I Sam. 23.19 (cf. I Sam. 26.1), perhaps because of a vague similarity between v. 3 and I Sam. 23.15; the Syriac version relates the psalm to another situation in the life of David. The psalmist is a man who was persecuted and threatened with death by violent and overbearing enemies; and after his deliverance (v. 7) he utters his previous lament before God on the occasion of his thanksgiving (see Intr. 69 f., 83 f.). If the worshipper's petition that God may vindicate him (v. 1) can be interpreted literally, then we might think of proceedings before a court of justice, in which the poet is involved, and first his hope and then his actual experience of vindication and acquittal by virtue of the judgment of the God who has appeared in the sanctuary (v. 4; see Intr. 78). The psalm proceeds in the usual style of the lament and shows a simple and lucid structure: it opens in vv. 1 and 2 with a general petition, in which the psalmist asks for help and craves a hearing; v. 3 contains lamentation describing the cause of the psalmist's affliction; in vv. 4 and 5 the psalmist expresses his trust in God and asks for the destruction of his adversaries; and the psalm ends in vv. 6 and 7 with a vow and a thanksgiving.

[1] The worshipper immediately begins with a cry for help addressed to God. The striking formulation of that prayer, namely that God shall save 'by his name', presupposes, as the parallelism shows, that the divine name possesses a special miraculous power, a conception whose roots reach down to ideas about magic. The name is, however, used here to represent the nature of the Godhead—his character—and has its origin in the revelation of God's name and nature which are proclaimed together in the cult of the Covenant (see Intr. 30 f., 41 ff., 74). The worshipper confides in the superior power of God at a time when he has nothing to expect from the power of man. He asks God, with whom the final decision lies, to see that justice is done to him, that is, probably, to acquit him by means of the divine judgment passed in God's name. [2] The subsequent petition for a hearing is intended to draw God's attention to the lament that follows and to the affliction of the worshipper.

[3] Ruthless enemies have risen against the hapless man and seek his life. He calls his adversaries 'strangers'. It is, however, evident from v. 3 that they, too, belong to the Yahweh community. What

separates this worshipper from his opponents and deepens the gulf
between them is their ungodliness which calls into question their
membership of the Yahweh community. From their behaviour the
psalmist derives spiritual justification to ask God to come and help
him in his struggle against them, and also the assurance that God himself will stand by him at his trial.

[4] The third strophe opens with a new theme, the theme of trust
in God. Verse 4 alludes to the cultic theophany which is the cause of
the worshipper's trust in God and of his assurance that his prayer will
be answered; God stands before him as his helper and as the stay of
his life. [5] Since the petition is based in v. 5 on the 'faithfulness' of
Yahweh, the psalmist also seems to recall examples of divine help in
the past and so incorporates his personal cause in the larger framework of the general revelation of divine salvation. His thoughts are
determined by the familiar conception that the punishment which
his opponents had intended to inflict on him shall come upon them
by reversion; thus he asks for the destruction of his enemies who in
their turn seek his life. The divine judgment shall become for them
the verdict of their destruction, but for him an act of deliverance.

[6–7] In the concluding verses the worshipper vows to sacrifice
free-will offerings, which probably means first that he vows to offer
sacrifices which exceed the usual thank-offerings (cf. Lev. 7.11 ff.;
22.17 ff.). The special emphasis laid on the voluntary character of
these sacrifices does not lack a certain anthropomorphic intention to
make a favourable impression on God. The psalm concludes with a
hymnic testimony to the 'name' of God which is intended to express
the worshipper's gratitude; it looks back to the beginning of the
psalm and has in mind the cultic situation in which the worshipper
experienced his deliverance and his adversaries suffered the divine
judgment.

The psalm shows its limitations clearly. We have no right to doubt
the subjective sincerity of its author; his trust in the divine faithfulness and help, which like the whole psalm can be properly understood
only in the light of its connection with the cultic tradition, does not
lack power. The worshipper is, however, neither able nor ready to
give himself up wholly to God, trusting him absolutely, and accept
his suffering from his hand, enduring it patiently. Human self-will
and man's low instincts of vindictiveness and gloating retain their
power over his thoughts and affect also his idea of God and his
relationship to him. In spite of his hope in God the worshipper

thinks of God in a rather human fashion and wants to make use of God's might in the service of his human sentiments. Thus the hope in God's power, too, is overshadowed in this psalm by this way of thinking, which is only too common, deeply rooted as it is in human nature. This is why the worshipper's prayer is also unable to exercise a liberating influence; for it does not lead on to the uttermost depths of ultimate truth. In this respect the prayer is subject to the judgment of the New Testament.

55. OPPRESSED BY ENEMIES, BETRAYED BY A FRIEND

To the Conductor. With stringed instruments. Maskil.[1] *Of David*

1 Give ear to my prayer, O God;
   and hide not thyself from my supplication.
2 Attend to me, and answer me;
   restless am I with anxious thought, I groan[2]
3 because of the utterances of the enemy,
   in face of the noise[3] of the wicked;
   for they turn[3] evil upon me,
   and in anger they bitterly assail me.[2]
4 My heart doth writhe within me,[4]
   the terrors of death have fallen upon me.
5 Fear and trembling come upon me
   and horror overwhelms me.
6 I said, 'Who gives me wings like a dove?
   I would fly away and settle down;[5]
7 yea, I would wander afar,
   I would stay overnight in the wilderness. *Selah*
8 I would haste to find me a shelter
   from the raging wind and tempest.'
9 Confuse, O Lord, divide their speech;[6]
   for I saw wickedness and strife in the city.
10 Day and night they go around it on its walls;
   and trouble and deceit are within it,
11 ruin is in its midst;
   oppression and fraud do not depart
   from its market-place.
12 For it is not an enemy who taunts me—
   then I could bear it;
   he who hates me did not deal insolently with me—[7]
   then I could hide from him.
13 But it is you, a man my equal,
   my companion and intimate friend.
14 We used to hold sweet converse together;
   within God's house we walked in the midst of the throng.[8]

15 Let death come upon them;
    they must go down to hell alive;
    for wherever they are, evil is in their heart. [9]

16 But I call upon God;
    and the Lord will save me.

17 Evening and morning and at noon
    will I meditate and moan,
    that *he* may hear[3] my voice,[10]

18 and deliver my soul in peace[11]
    from the battle that I wage;
    for many are arrayed against me.

19 God will give ear and humble[12] them,
    he who is enthroned from of old;
    because they do not change nor fear God.[13] *Selah*

20 He[14] stretched out his hand against his friends,
    he violated his covenant.

21 His speech was smoother than butter,
    yet war was in his heart;
    his words were softer than oil,
    but actually they were sharp swords.[15]

22 Cast your burden on the Lord,
    and he will sustain you;
    he will never permit the righteous to be moved.

23 Thou, O God, wilt cast them down into the lowest pit;
    the men full of murder and treachery
    shall not live out half their days.
    But I will trust in thee.

---

[1] See Ps. 32.

[2] * Vv. 2b and 3 in the RSV read:
    (2b) I am overcome by my trouble.
    (3)   I am distraught by the noise of the enemy,
        because of the oppression of the wicked.
        For they bring trouble upon me,
        and in anger they cherish enmity against me.

[3] See BH.

[4] * V. 4a is in RSV, 'My heart is in anguish within me.'

[5] * RSV is:
    And I say, 'O that I had wings like a dove!
    I would fly away and be at rest . . .'

[6] * V. 9a is in RSV, 'Destroy their plans, O Lord, confuse their tongues.'

[7] * RSV has 'it is not an adversary who deals insolently with me'.

[8] * RSV has 'we walked in fellowship' instead of 'we walked in the midst of the throng'.

[9] * V. 15bc is in RSV:
    let them go down to Sheol alive;
    let them go away in terror into their graves.

[10] * RSV has:
    Evening and morning and at noon

I utter my complaint and moan,
and he will hear my voice.
[11] * RSV starts v. 18 with a new sentence, beginning 'He will deliver my soul in safety.'
[12] Read *Picēl*.
[13] The translation is doubtful. (Tr. N.: V. 19b is in RSV, 'because they keep no law, and do not fear God'.)
[14] * RSV has 'My companion' for 'he'.
[15] * RSV has 'yet they were drawn swords'.

The translation and interpretation of this psalm of lament is impeded by difficulties arising from its text and its content which thwart any attempt to arrive at a clear picture of the external circumstances of its author and only admit of hypothetical suppositions. More than once an attempt has been made to divide up the lament into two originally independent psalms, but these endeavours, too, are no real help. I venture to think that the swift and disconnected change of thoughts and moods and the consequent lack of a steady train of thought should not be eliminated by means of the drastic alterations of literary criticism, but should be accounted for by the personal circumstances of the psalmist. He is of a gentle disposition and is made exceedingly restless by emotions and passions aroused in him by the enmity of violent opponents and above all by the treachery of a friend. That he may appear before his God just as he is and may lay bare to him the uttermost recesses of his soul is part of the peculiar character of the Old Testament psalm of lamentation, and also indicates tacitly and yet emphatically the largeness of God's heart, which is particularly stressed in the Old Testament in view of the fact that as a rule the disparity between God and man is emphasized there, and which should not be obliterated by the shadows cast beside it in such psalms by weaknesses and imperfections which are far too human.

[1-5] The affecting lamentation, which begins in vv. 1-2a with the craving for a hearing, presents in a deeply moving way the great distress of a sensitive soul which breaks down under the weight of its agony. [6-8] No wonder that this man, who reacts so susceptibly to the disturbing influences that threaten to upset the balance of his mind, has only one desire—to flee like Jeremiah (cf. Jer. 9.1 ff.) from the bustle of the city and to wander afar or to seek desert loneliness so as to get away from the repugnant impressions which assail him there like a 'raging tempest'. [9-11] Disgusted by the oppression and fraud which have taken control of the market-places quite openly, he

prays that that place of vice may be overtaken by a divine judgment similar to the one which is reported in the tradition of the confusion of tongues at the building of the tower of Babel. Some commentators want to interpret the statement at the beginning of v. 10, 'Day and night they go around it on its walls', as referring to a siege and so infer that the psalm dates from the time of Jeremiah or the Maccabees. However, nowhere else in the psalm can an allusion be found to such a situation; moreover, the corruption that prevails in the city seems to be connected with the 'going around' it. Hence the statement is presumably to be interpreted figuratively, as signifying a symbolic procession of magical efficacy round the city-walls (cf. Josh. 6.1 ff.) which had the effect of infecting the whole city with the vice in question; in this way the statement is intended to express, as it were, the contagious influence which the evildoers incessantly exercise upon the city. Thus it becomes even more intelligible that the poet no longer knows which way to turn and follows the only possible and right course by unfolding his calamity in all its magnitude to God. [12–14] For all that, what grieves him most and intensifies his suffering until he can bear it no longer is not the behaviour of his enemies, whose arrogant abuses he would, after all, be able to deal with, but the disappointment caused by the breach of confidence of a friend whom he now sees siding with his opponents. Understandably agitated, he reminds his friend of the many hours which they had spent together in intimate fellowship and which are now but a sad and bitter memory. [15] His soul is so deeply hurt that, flying into a helpless rage, he wishes that his adversaries may suddenly be swallowed up alive by the underworld, as once happened to the company of Korah (Num. 16.30 ff.; see Intr. 51, 77 f.). [16–18] Thereafter the psalm relapses into lamentation; but the thoughts of the worshipper no longer dwell only on the grief that depresses him—he lifts up his eyes to God, trusting that he who is enthroned from of old as the Judge of the world (cf. Ps. 9.4 ff.; see Intr. 32 f., 45 f.) will answer the prayers of the community of the godly, but will humble the wicked who persist in their alienation from God. [19–21] The worshipper is, however, once more overcome by his indignation and disappointment at the disloyalty of his friend; he complains bitterly of his hypocritical falsehood which deprives him of the last shreds of his confidence in man. And as if he himself felt that he was in danger of having the ground cut from under his feet and was in need of support, he clutches at a saying (cf. Ps. 37.5) with the aid of which his better self, as it were, once more admonishes him to trust in God. We are here presented with an insight into the very heart of a man's earnest and sincere battle with himself for confidence in God, and that struggle creates a close human bond between him and us, even though at the conclusion of his prayer he is once more dominated by sentiments of vindictiveness and retaliation which contend for victory with his profession of trust in God. Thus the psalm ends in an open question; and the struggle against human failure and for faith in God does not reach a satisfactory solution in the psalm. This twofold struggle is for us a signpost which points to the answer and deliverance given to the faithful in Christ.

56. WHEN I AM AFRAID, I PUT MY TRUST IN THEE

To the Conductor. According to The Dove of the Far-off Terebinths.[1] Of David. Miktam,[2] when the Philistines seized him in Gath[3]

1 Be gracious to me, O God,
   for men lie in wait for me;
   all day long warriors oppress me.[4]
2 They are greedy for me all day long,
   who lie in wait for me;
   for there are many who fight proudly[5] against me.[6]
3 When I am afraid,[5]
   I put my trust[5] in thee.
4 As for God, it is his word I praise.
   In God do I trust and am not afraid.
   What can men[7] do to me?
5 All day long they speak and take counsel[8] against me;
   all their thoughts are against me for evil.[9]
6 They lurk[5] and spy on me, they watch my steps,
   as they wait for my life.[10]
7 Should there be deliverance for them in spite of their deceit?[5]
   In wrath cast down the violent,[11] O God![10]
8 Thou hast kept count of my misery;[5]
   collect then[12] my tears in thy bottle! ' '[13]
9 Then my enemies will be turned back
   in the day when I call.
   This I know, that God is for me.
10 As for God, it is his word I praise,
   I praise the word of the Lord.[14]
11 In God do I trust, and am not afraid.
   What can men do to me?
12 My vows to thee, I know, are upon me;[15]
   I will render thank-offerings to thee.
13 For thou hast delivered my soul from death,

yea, my feet from falling,
that I may walk before God in the light of life.

[1] See BH and Intr. 22 f.
[2] See Ps. 16.
[3] Cf. I Sam. 21.12 ff. and Intr. 98.
[4] * RSV has 'trample upon me' instead of 'lie in wait for me' and 'foemen' instead of 'warriors'.
[5] The translation is doubtful.
[6] * V. 2 reads in RSV:
  my enemies trample upon me all day long,
  for many fight against me proudly.
[7] Lit.: 'flesh'. (Tr. N.: RSV of v. 4 is:
  In God, whose word I praise,
  in God I trust without a fear.
  What can flesh do to me?)
[8] See BH.
[9] * V. 5a is in RSV, 'All day long they seek to injure my cause.'
[10] * RSV of vv. 6 and 7 differs:
  (6) They band themselves together, they lurk,
    they watch my steps.
    As they have waited for my life
  (7) so recompense them for their crime;
    in wrath cast down the peoples, O God!
[11] Read ʿazzīm (Duhm and others).
[12] Or 'my tears are collected'.
[13] See BH. (Tr. N.: V. 8 is in RSV:
  Thou hast kept count of my tossings;
  put thou my tears in thy bottle!
  Are they not in thy book?)
[14] * RSV of vv. 10–11a reads:
  In God, whose words I praise,
  in the Lord, whose words I praise,
  in God I trust, without a fear.
[15] * V. 12a is in RSV, 'My vows to thee I must perform, O God.'

The text of this lament is unfortunately transmitted in such a corrupt state that it is frequently impossible to arrive at sure interpretation. The author is persecuted by numerous enemies who lie in wait for him and seek his life (vv. 1, 5 f.). The fact that the poet conquers grief and anguish by his trust in God gives to the psalm a hopeful note of its own. The conclusion of the psalm (vv. 9b–13) and the echo of v. 4 in vv. 10 f., firmly linking together the lament and the thanksgiving, give rise to the impression that the psalm as a whole was recited in public worship after the prayer had been answered and before the thank-offering (v. 12)—and further that the lament and the petition, which of course had originally been uttered before that point in time, here take the place of the 'narrative' exactly as in Psalm 41 and many others (see Intr. 69 f., 83 f.).

[1-2] The psalm opens with a brief cry for help, followed by the lament and the reasons for it. As in Psalm 35 the enemies who incessantly threaten the worshipper are described by the warrior metaphor. [3-4] Though their large numbers, their greed and their self-assurance, which make them treat him 'with condescension', more than justify his being afraid of them, the worshipper does not succumb to his fear. He resolutely sets his trust in God over against his fear of men and thus gains a firm footing whilst everything else is in danger of tottering. But this does not mean that he is thereby already relieved of all his fear. The poet is sufficiently earnest and truthful to face the danger and his own human weakness soberly, and thus he knows that he is continually overcome with fear. But he is also courageous enough, a courage which is of the essence of true faith, to throw himself into the arms of God at the very moment when he is in danger of succumbing to his fear. The nature of faith as a bold venture has found truly classical expression in v. 3. Trust in God robs fear of its quality of terror; the fear of men is mastered by the fear of God. However, this fact by no means justifies any feeling of pride in the strength of one's own courage based on faith. On the contrary, the bold venture of faith consists in the very renunciation of every kind of self-assurance, be it ever so devout. It is the exclusive recognition of the power and authority of God, the surrender of man's whole being to God which knows but *one* 'glory'—the humble praising of the Word of God in which alone promise and fulfilment, truth and reality form an inseparable unity. For the psalmist the Word of God is the only warrant of his confidence; it is from that source that he receives strength and hope and at the same time the criterion by which he is able to see the values of life in their true proportions; for man, if left to himself, is always only capable of judging these values from the viewpoint of his own prejudices and distorted feelings. In the light of the perspective of faith, however, a faith which learns to judge all things from the standpoint of God, everything which is human is only 'flesh' (cf. Isa. 31.3), a helpless creature in the hand of his Creator and on that account in the last analysis not a threat to him who knows that he is at one with God. [5-7] That the worshipper in spite of that knowledge again relapses into the lament proves that the knowledge of faith must continually be achieved afresh in an ardent struggle with oneself, a struggle which even the godly man is not spared. But it is not an aimless battle. The worshipper's faith in God's righteousness, which was

questioned by him only for a brief moment (v. 7), finally wins
through in the petition that the 'wrath' of God may cast down the
deceitful adversaries. **[8–9a]** But neither will God disregard the
suffering of the godly. Sleepless nights and many hours spent in
torment and weeping are not endured in vain as far as God is concerned. Suffering, as it were, is capital invested with God, booked by
him (cf. Mal. 3.16; Job 19.23) and collected by him. (On the picture
of the tears collected in a bottle compare, for instance, Paul Gerhardt's hymn, 'Ich singe dir mit Herz und Mund', v. 11 of which,
literally translated, reads:

> Thou count'st how oft'n a Christian weeps,
> And where his grief may lie;
> No silent tear can be too small,
> Thou tak'st and lay'st it by.[1])

The worshipper's hope that his prayer will be answered is based on
this trust which flows from an intimate personal relationship with
God. **[9b–11]** V. 9b speaks of the granting of the prayer (cf. Ps.
20.6); the experience which has given rise to the worshipper's
assurance that his petition has been granted is not explicitly mentioned, but only alluded to; presumably it was the promise of the
divine grace, pronounced in public worship only a short while before,
which had assured him of his communion with God. Since God's
promise has found its fulfilment in him, he now reaches back to the
saying by which he had professed his trust in God's promise (v. 4); in
this he corroborates the truth of the Word of God which has again
proved true in his own life and justifies his confidence. **[12–13]** In
honouring God he does not forget the gratitude which he owes him.
He will now present the thank-offerings, which he had promised in
his plight, for his deliverance from death and for the grace bestowed
upon him, so that unshaken he may take his stand on the firm foundation
of his trust in God and in communion with God may walk in his sight
out of the darkness of suffering into the 'light of life'. The two
phrases 'walk before God' and 'light of life' probably have their
origin in the presence of God experienced in the festival cult; though
elsewhere they have occasionally become detached from their cultic
place of origin, it is, however, not improbable that this is still
detectable in this psalm.

---

[1] * In German: 'Du zählst wie oft ein Christe wein'
                    und was sein Kummer sei;
                    kein stilles Tränlein ist so klein
                    du hebst und legst es bei.'

57. THY STEADFAST LOVE IS GREAT TO THE HEAVENS

To the Conductor. 'Let not be destroyed.'[1] *Of David. Miktam,*[2] *when he fled before Saul into the cave*[3]

1 Be merciful to me, O God,
 be merciful to me,
 for in thee my soul takes refuge;
 in the shadow of thy wings I will take refuge,
 till the affliction[4] passes by.
2 I cry to God, the Most High,[5]
 to God who will let it pass by for my sake.[6]
3 May he send from heaven and save me
 whom he who lies in wait for me has slandered.[7] *Selah*
 May he send forth his grace and his faithfulness from heaven.[8]
4 In the midst of lions I have to lie
 that thirst[7] for the blood of men;[9]
 their teeth are spears and arrows,
 and their tongue a sharp sword.
5 Be exalted, O God, above the heavens!
 Let thy glory be over all the earth!
6 A net have they spread for my feet;
 my soul is bowed down.[7]
 They dug a pit in my way,
 (but) they have fallen into it themselves. *Selah*
7 My heart is steadfast, O God,
 my heart is steadfast!
 I will sing and make melody,
8 thou[10] art my glory,
 Awake, O harp and cither![11]
 I will awake the dawn.
9 I will praise thee, O Lord, among the peoples;
 I will make melody to thee among the nations.[12]
10 For thy steadfast love is great to the heavens,
 and thy faithfulness to the clouds.
11 Be exalted, O God, above the heavens!
 Let thy glory be over all the earth!

---

[1] This is probably the opening of a song to the tune of which the psalm was to be sung or accompanied; see Intr. 22 f.
[2] See Ps. 16.
[3] Cf. I Sam. 24.4 ff. and Intr. 98.
[4] * RSV has 'the storms of destruction' instead of 'affliction'.
[5] See the comments on Ps. 7.17.
[6] * V. 2b is in RSV, 'to God who fulfils his purpose for me'.
[7] The translation is doubtful.

8 * RSV has:
    He will send from heaven and save me,   ˢ
    he will put to shame those who trample upon me. *Selah*
    God will send forth his steadfast love and his faithfulness!
9 * RSV has for this line, 'that greedily devour the sons of men'.
10 See BH. (Tr. N.: V. 8a reads in RSV, 'Awake, my soul!')
11 * RSV has 'lyre' instead of 'cither'.
12 * V. 9 is in RSV:
    I will give thanks to thee, O Lord,
    among the peoples;
    I will sing praises to thee
    among the nations.

In this psalm a lament (vv. 1–6) and a thanksgiving (vv. 7–11) are combined. Since both parts are linked together by a refrain (vv. 5 and 11), there is no reason to doubt that they belong together, even though vv. 7–11 reappear in Psalm 108 with slight variations. The subject-matter of the psalm, too, does not necessitate the view that the psalm is composed by different authors and is related to different situations. The fact that the lament and the thanksgiving are placed side by side, as in Psalms 22; 41; 56, etc. (see Intr. 69 f., 83 f.), and the embodiment of the same thought in both parts of the psalm by means of the refrain (cf. Ps. 56.4, 10 f.), is probably to be accounted for by the fact that the psalm was recited at a thanksgiving service where the lamentation and petition took the place of the otherwise customary 'narrative' of the deliverance of the worshipper. Apart from several cultic allusions the striking narrative form used for the prayer in v. 2 likewise points to this view; so, too, the fact that vv. 6b, 7 ff. recall the deliverance that has already come to pass. The external personal circumstances of the worshipper are hidden behind traditional phrases and images of a general character. Against the machinations of his enemies, from whose defamations he had to suffer, he has sought and found protection and help from God in his sanctuary. The firm note of confidence is sounded throughout his prayer, and the impression of a controlled restraint is strongly underlined by his refraining from aggressive emotional outbursts against his enemies.

[1] The cry for help with which the psalm opens is very similar to Ps. 56.1; it differs, however, substantially in so far as it is not explained as in Ps. 56.1, by a reference to the worshipper's affliction, but is based on his trust in God. The grace of God is revealed only to the man who trusts in God, and the feeling of being out of danger in the house of God, where Yahweh sits enthroned upon the wings of the cherubim, under the 'shadow' of which the worshipper has taken

refuge (see Intr. 40 f., 72 f.), is already a gift of the divine grace which the poet invokes. As he seeks refuge in the Temple of God 'till the destruction passes by', the view most easily suggested by this is that he expected his prayer to be answered in that very place. **[2]** Trust in the power and steadfast love of God is again reflected in the account given in the prayer (v. 2); the poet knows that God will take good care of his cause; **[3]** this is why he rests satisfied with the general petition for help, asking that God may send his grace and his faithfulness, as it were, as his messengers (cf. Ps. 43.3); they are the fundamental attributes of God which, with his holy majesty, are made manifest in the covenant theophany (cf. Ex. 34.6; see Intr. 43, 75). **[4]** The actual complaint about the persecutors, who are portrayed by the familiar pictures of lions and warriors (cf. Pss. 9.3 ff.; 10.9; 17.12; 35.1 ff.; 56.1, etc.) does not begin till v. 4. Significantly, it is the offensive *word* which is continually stigmatized in the Psalms as the most dangerous weapon in human conflict (cf. Pss. 12.2; 52.2; 55.3; 59.7; 64.3 and the comments on Ps. 12). **[5]** The petition expressed in the refrain also reaches far beyond the compass of the personal circumstances of the worshipper which caused his distress. It calls upon God to appear above the (clouds of) heaven and reveal his glory over all the earth. That petition we shall probably have to interpret as referring to the theophany (cf. Isa. 6.3; Hab. 3.3) through which the members of the cult community and with them the worshipper became assured of the presence of God and of the revelation of his grace and protection (see Intr. 28 ff., 72 f.). Hence it is not that the worshipper regards himself as so important that in the exuberance of his self-importance he wants to set God and the world in motion for the sake of his personal cause; rather, he does the opposite—he incorporates his personal affliction in the larger context of the general dispensation of salvation in the hope that the assurance of his personal salvation and of the granting of his petition will be given to him in the liturgical enactment of salvation at the festival, in which he himself will participate. **[6]** Verse 6 forms the link between the lament and the thanksgiving. It opens by taking up once more the lamentation about the wiles of the adversaries, using this time the traditional picture of hunting with net and pit (cf. Pss. 7.15; 9.15 f.); the verse concludes, on the other hand, by recalling the granting of the prayer which has already taken place, and it does so by applying the familiar idea of the judgment which the sinner brings upon himself. From the religious viewpoint of God's saving

action the two temporally separate acts of the uttering of the petition
and of its fulfilment draw together and become one coherent event.
[7] In a hymnic testimony the poet first gives expression to the spirit
which has now taken possession of his soul; he opens his heart to God
and, his confidence being fortified, he is now quite sure of his God
and in a mood of joyful thanksgiving. [8] The worshipper's whole being
is filled with the thought of God; and this state of mind is his 'glory'
which is spread over him like a reflection of the resplendent majesty
of God. As God has taken complete hold of him, so he feels greatly
inspired and wants to hail the dawn of another day (on the poetic
expression compare the *evocat auroram* in Ovid's *Metamorphoses*
11.597) with a profession of thanks, uttered to the glory of God; and
he wants to recite it in the sanctuary to the accompaniment of the
Temple music ('psaltery and harp, awake')[1] [9] and in the presence
of the great congregation, which has flocked to the feast from many
different nations. (The interpretation of the term 'peoples' as referring
to the Gentiles, amongst whom the poet is said to sojourn in the
Diaspora, is made impossible by the thanksgiving's association with
the Yahweh cult; see Intr. 38 f.). [10] The worshipper borrows the
profession from the cultic tradition (cf. Ps. 36.5); it praises the
immeasurable greatness and the inexhaustible riches of the divine
'steadfast love and faithfulness' which is bestowed upon the cult
community by means of the revelation of their God (cf. Ex. 34.6; see
Intr. 58, 74 f.) and which they continually experience in the cult. That
the worshipper may partake of it is interpreted by him as a pledge of
the granting of his petition (cf. v. 3) and makes him rejoice in his
God. [11] And just as he had yearned in his plight for the solemn
moment of God's epiphany that he might be assured of his help
(vv. 3, 5), so now he stands before him as *one who simultaneously
possesses and yet expects*. Because everything here revolves round God
himself, the heart and the climax of the cultic experience becomes at
the same time the final goal of a hope that reaches beyond the
momentary historical event and looks forward to the constantly
recurring appearance and revelation of God; it becomes a homogeneous act of salvation in which past and future are simultaneously efficacious by virtue of the eternal presence of God.

---

[1] * This is a quotation from the first verse of the German hymn, 'Lobe den
Herren, den mächtigen König der Ehren' by Joachim Neander (1650–1680),
translated by Catherine Winkworth and others: 'Praise to the Lord, the Almighty,
the King of creation'. The English has no equivalent to this line.

58. UNJUST JUDGES

To the Conductor. 'Let not be destroyed.'[1] *Of David. Miktam*[2]

1 Do you indeed decree what is right, you gods?[3]
  Do you judge the sons of men uprightly?

2 Nay, you work in the land with a wicked heart;
  you weigh out the violence done by your hands.[4]

3 The wicked are rebellious from the womb,
  they err from their birth who speak lies.[5]

4 They have venom like the venom of a serpent,
  like the deaf adder that stops its ear,

5 that does not heed the word of the charmer,
  of the skilled weaver of spells.[6]

6 O God, break the teeth in their mouths;
  crush[7] the fangs of the lions, O Lord!

7 Let them vanish like water that runs away;
  let them wither[8] like the grass on the path,[9]

8 like the snail that is dissolved whilst it creeps,[10]
  like the untimely birth that has never seen[3] the sun.

9 Sooner than your pots can feel the briar,[11]
  whether green or ablaze, the high wind sweeps it away.[12]

10 The righteous will rejoice when he sees the vengeance;
   he will bathe his feet in the blood of the wicked.

11 Then men will say, 'Surely, the righteous has fruit;
   yea, there is still a God who sees that justice is done[3] on earth!'[13]

[1] See Ps. 57.
[2] See Ps. 16.
[3] See BH.
[4] * V. 2 reads in RSV:
  Nay, in your hearts you devise wrongs;
  your hands deal out violence on earth.
[5] * RSV has 'go astray' instead of 'are rebellious' and 'speaking lies' instead of 'who speak lies'.
[6] * In RSV v. 5 reads:
  so that it does not hear the voice of charmers
  or of the cunning enchanter.
[7] * RSV has 'tear out' instead of 'crush'.
[8] The translation is doubtful.
[9] See BH. (Tr. N.: V. 7b is in RSV, 'like grass let them be trodden down and wither'.)
[10] * RSV has, 'Let them be like the snail which dissolves into slime.'
[11] The briar was used for kindling.
[12] * V.9 reads in RSV: The translation is doubtful. (Tr. N.:
  Sooner than your pots can feel the heat of thorns,
  whether green or ablaze, may he sweep them away!)
[13] * In RSV v. 11 is:
  Men will say, 'Surely there is a reward for the righteous;
  surely there is a God who judges on earth.'

Full of dramatic power, this psalm is characterized by a graphic,

poetic quality of its own which is manifested above all in the swift
change of the numerous word-pictures and comparisons. In its
fundamental idea of how belief in God can be reconciled with the
existence in the world of ungodliness and sin, as in the mythological
conception of the judgment of the gods, the psalm is most closely
related to Psalm 82, which should be drawn on for the purpose of
exegesis. Here, too, the widespread depravity on earth caused by sin
seems to be attributed—in Psalm 82 this thought is expressed even
more clearly—to dereliction of duty by the 'gods' who constitute the
celestial court of Yahweh and are to dispense justice on earth as his
servants and functionaries. They are now themselves called to
account by God for that dereliction of duty. It is a matter of the
process, which finds its explanation in the history of religion, whereby
the Yahweh religion absorbed and reduced to a lower rank the gods
associated with the worship at the Canaanite shrines; in the course
of this process, the Old Testament monotheistic idea of God made
use of the foreign polytheistic religious elements to suit its own
purposes and brought its own moral superiority to bear on them.
Thus the tendency to a dualistic explanation of the origin of evil,
which would produce a basic tension between itself and the Old
Testament idea of the One and Only God, has likewise been banished right from the outset (see the exposition of Psalm 82); for at the
conclusion of Psalm 58, too, the One and Only God is professed who
by virtue of his judgment also holds in his safe hands the moral order
of life on earth. It seems that this process, whereby Yahwism came to
terms with local shrine-gods by means of the idea of the divine
judgment, took place within the sphere of the Old Testament cult
of the Covenant, also the home of the idea of God's judgment on the
wicked (see Intr. 47 ff.). In this context we shall have to understand
the term 'the righteous' as referring not to a religious party but
to the God-fearing members of the Yahweh cult community.

[1–2] The opening verses of the psalm take us at once into the very
midst of the heavenly court-scene. God, who executes judgment in
heaven and on earth, addresses the 'gods', who constitute his
celestial entourage, by asking them a question implying a rebuke.
(It is only on his lips that the judge's words are meaningful; cf. Ps.
82.1 f.) He reminds them of their duty to judge righteously and
follows this up by passing upon them the verdict that instead of
'weighing out' righteousness on earth they let violence take its
course instead of justice. [3–5] According to the ancient oriental

way of thinking, things done in heaven serve as archetypes, that is to say, they have a direct effect on what is done on earth. Thus the psalm turns from the heavenly scene to the conditions on earth, which are considered to be the result of the failure of the gods, so that the verdict which God has just passed on them will not fail to produce results on earth too. It is in such a context that one is to understand the judgment which is passed on the wicked in vv. 3–5, a judgment which, after all, is probably also to be regarded as forming an essential part of the Word uttered by God. Their guilt, characterized as a going astray from the womb, consists in rebellion, lies and hardness of heart, which is just as little susceptible to admonition as a deaf adder is to the incantations of the skilled snake-charmer who tries to cast a spell over it. In this verdict a profound knowledge of the nature of sin is implied: in its demoralizing and even fatal effect it is compared with the venom of the serpent; its root-cause is that mysterious alienation of human nature from God which can be traced back to the very first beginnings of mankind and casts its shadows already in the story of the Fall of the first human beings; one might even imagine one could discern that story colouring the passage under discussion (cf. also Gen. 8.21; see Intr. 47). In some way or other sin is always coupled with untruthfulness and for that reason also issues in that incomprehensible delusion which makes man either carelessly or defiantly disregard even the most well-intentioned advice and warnings. And there is another factor which also deserves consideration, namely the fact that the seriousness of man's own responsibility for his sin—in this, too, there is an analogy to the story of the Fall—is not at all attenuated by the fact that the origin of evil is looked for beyond man, even in 'higher' beings: everyone has to answer and pay for his own sin.

[6–9] The psalm gives expression to this thought in the psalmist's address to God on behalf of the members of the cult community who are faithful to Yahweh (= righteous, v. 11), asking God to execute judgment by destroying the evildoers. The comparisons, gradually intensified, still distinctly show traces of potent curses which are meant to operate after the manner of the analogous spells; the members of the cult community probably used to utter such curses when they eliminated the sinners from their midst by means of a legalistic rite (cf. Deut. 27.11 ff.). In this connection we must not, however, overlook the fact that under the influence of the Old Testament idea of God the imprecations are here not thought of as

being effective solely by means of their magical power, but are cast
in the form of a 'prayer for vengeance' (see Intr. 78, 88), so that
punishment is wrested from the hands of man and is entirely entrusted to God, to whom it is left to exterminate the wicked completely. [10–11] Though ultimately the cause of God is at stake in
that judgment, the psalm's conclusion, speaking of the effect of the
judgment on the righteous, shows on the other hand the undisguised
gloating and the cruel vindictiveness of an intolerant religious
fanaticism (cf. Ps. 68.23); it is one of those dangerous poisonous
blossoms which are liable to grow even on the tree of religious
knowledge and clearly show the limits set to the Old Testament
religion. All the same, in expressing this view we must not forget that
as the study of Ps. 139.19 ff. shows, it is already in the Old Testament
itself that the very idea of God attacks its being entangled with
error in very human lapses. The problem underlying the whole
psalm is now clearly stated at its conclusion in the testimony that
distinctly recalls the beginning of the psalm: the judgment on earth
is in the hands of the true God and not in those of the false gods, and
for that reason the faith of the community of the godly is not without
'fruit'; God will see to it that justice will be done to them.

59. DELIVERANCE FROM ENEMIES

To the Conductor. 'Let not be destroyed.'[1] *Of David. Miktam,*[2] *when Saul
had sent (messengers), and they watched the house in order to kill him*[3]

1 Deliver me from my enemies, O God,
   protect me from those who rise up against me!
2 Deliver me from those who work evil,
   and save me from bloodthirsty men!
3 For, lo, they lie in wait for my life;
   mighty men assail me.
   I am without guilt or sin, O Lord.[4]
4 For no fault of mine,[5] they run up and make ready.
   Rouse thyself, and meet me, and see![6]
5 Thou, Lord ' '[5] of hosts, God of Israel,
   awake and punish all the nations;
   spare none of those who treacherously plot evil.[7] *Selah*
6 Each evening they come back,
   howling like dogs and prowling about the city.
7 Behold, they slaver with their mouths,
   a sword is in their lips:
   'for who (they say) should hear it?'[8]
8 But thou, O Lord, wilt laugh at them;
   thou wilt hold all the nations in derision.[9]

9 O my Strength,[5] I will watch for thee,
   for God is my fortress.[10]
10 My[5] God meets me and is gracious to me;
   let me look in triumph on my enemies, O God![11]
11 Show no mercy upon them,[12]
   lest my people forget;
   make them spin round by thy host,
   O Lord, our shield![13]
12 The sin of their mouths is the word of their lips;
   they will be trapped in their pride,
   for the cursing and lies which they utter.[14]
13 Consume them in wrath,
   consume them till they are no more,
   that men may know that God rules over Jacob
   to the ends of the earth! *Selah*
14 Each evening they come back,
   howling like dogs and prowling about the city.
15 They wander about[5] looking for food
   and murmur[5] if they are not sated.[15]
16 But I will sing of thy might;
   I will exult at thy grace in the morning,
   that thou hast been to me a fortress
   and a refuge in the days of my distress.[16]
17 O my Strength, I will sing praises to thee,
   for God is my fortress,
   the God who is gracious to me.[17]

[1] See Ps. 57.
[2] See Ps. 16.
[3] Cf. I Sam. 19.11 and Intr. 98.
[4] * Vv. 3bc–4a read in RSV:
   fierce men band themselves against me.
   For no transgression or sin of mine, O Lord,
   for no fault of mine, they run and make ready.
[5] See BH.
[6] * RSV has 'come to my help' instead of 'and meet me'.
[7] * The first line of v. 5 is in RSV, 'Thou, Lord God of hosts, art God of Israel.'
[8] * V. 7 reads in RSV:
   There they are, bellowing with their mouths,
   and snarling with their lips—
   for 'Who', they think, 'will hear us?'
[9] * RSV uses the present tense.
[10] * V. 9 is in RSV:
   O my Strength, I will sing praises to thee;
   for thou, O God, art my fortress.
[11] * RSV has:
   My God in his steadfast love will meet me;
   my God will let me look in triumph on my enemies.

¹² The reading of the MT, 'slay them not', is at variance with v. 13 and is probably due to a copyist's mistake.

¹³ * RSV has 'slay them not' instead of 'show no mercy upon them' and in the
third line 'make them totter by thy power, and bring them down'.

¹⁴ * RSV has:
    (12) For the sin of their mouths, the words of their lips,
          let them be trapped in their pride.
          For the cursing and lies which they utter,
    (13) consume them in wrath,
          consume them till they are no more, . . .

¹⁵ * V. 15 is in RSV:
    They roam about for food,
    and growl if they do not get their fill.

¹⁶ * RSV begins the third line with 'for' instead of 'that'.

¹⁷ * In RSV the second and third lines are:
    for thou, O God, art my fortress,
    the God who shows me steadfast love.

A man who sees himself as innocently persecuted by mighty
adversaries, whom he calls bloodthirsty men and rebellious workers
of iniquity (therefore probably enemies within his own nation),
seeks God's protection and takes refuge in him in his lament. The
personal circumstances of the worshipper cannot be established in
detail in spite of some concrete allusions. In view of the otherwise
personal character of the prayer it is not possible to draw from the
designation of Yahweh as 'our shield' and from the reference to the
people of Israel in vv. 11, 13 and 5 the conclusion that the psalm is a
community lament. On the other hand, it is possible to deduce from
this that the psalm was recited in the Temple in the presence of the
congregation and is to be understood in the light of the cult of the
Yahweh community. The author awaits an encounter with God
(vv. 4, 10) whom he invokes by addressing him with the cultic name
of the God of the sacred Ark (v. 5), and whose epiphany he hopes
will, in connection with the judgment on all the nations (v. 5), result
in a verdict on his own cause, too (vv. 5, 9–11). In this psalm also the
personal request of the worshipper is incorporated in the larger
context of the cult of the community in which expression is given to
the 'rule of Yahweh over Jacob', to his power and his judgment on
the rebellious evildoers as well as to the grace which he bestows upon
his faithful followers. A series of otherwise obscure features find their
explanation in the fact that they are tied to the cultic tradition, a
bond which automatically ensues from such a situation. The references to the God of the Ark (v. 5) and to his rule over Jacob (v. 13)
cause us to think of the celebration of the kingship of God at the

Covenant Festival in the pre-exilic worship of the Temple (see Intr. 62). The psalm is artistically constructed and the thoughts are closely interwoven, making use of the familiar elements of the lament and the thanksgiving. Its two parts are marked off from each other by means of a refrain (vv. 9, 17), and each is once more subdivided by a further refrain (vv. 6, 14).

The first strophe (vv. 1–5) first presents in very general terms a cry for help with its explanation and a call upon God to appear and sit in judgment; to indicate the theme by way of introduction it already contains the main fundamental ideas of the prayer. **[1–2]** The brief petition for help, varied four times, is justified **[3–4a]** by pointing out both the dangerous threat which the worshipper has to face from mighty and treacherous enemies, and his own integrity. **[4b–5]** The opening strophe ends in the poet's call upon the God of the sacred Ark (Yahweh Sabaoth) to 'rouse himself' (see Intr. 73) and appear to sit in judgment on the nations; by that call he expresses his expectation of the theophany in the Temple which will imply for him his saving encounter with God, but for the rebellious evildoers their conviction (as to the traditional stylistic form cf. Pss. 35.23 f.; 44.23, 26; also Pss. 7.6; 9.19; 10.12; 17.13). **[6–7]** The general introduction is followed by a more specific accusation against the enemies which continues the thought of v. 4 and is closely connected with the first strophe. Unfortunately we can no longer grasp clearly the significance of the comparison of the enemies with the half-wild dogs which prowl about the streets of the city in their search for food (v. 15); we are hardly justified in thinking of a siege by enemies; the comparison seems rather to be designed to mark the savagery and greed inherent in the attacks of the poet's adversaries to which he is exposed afresh day by day. He is obviously afraid that he will fall a victim to their biting words and their venomous calumnies and curses (cf. v. 12) unless God intervenes and puts an end to their presumption, their imagining that they will remain unnoticed by God. **[8]** However, the worshipper conquers this fear by his hope in God, who will set his own 'derision' over against the blasphemous mockery of the wicked and will be the one who will 'laugh' last. The fact that the psalmist gives expression to this hope in a stylized form (cf. Ps. 2.4) both proves the psalm's connection with the general tradition of the feast of Yahweh in which his kingship was celebrated and at the same time shows the wealth of the springs of personal individual piety which flow in that cult. **[9]** In view of the imminent appearance of God, which will make manifest his supremacy over the nations, the refrain which is now uttered arises out of the mood of eager expectation ('I will watch for thee') and confident hope.

The epiphany of God before the congregation (cf. 'O Lord, *our* shield' in v. 11) is also intended to bring about **[10]** an encounter of the poet with God (cf. Ps. 21.3) whereby he will partake of the divine grace and may experience how God's judgment is executed on the enemies. This last thought is not quite free of a certain gloating (cf. Pss. 54.7; 112.8; 118.7); v. 13, however, shows that joy in the manifestation of the power of *God* prevails over that human weakness. The twofold aspect of the divine judgment is the dominating keynote of the whole second part of the psalm (see Intr. 47). **[11–13]** The subject of the third strophe is God's judgment on the enemies. They cannot hope for God's grace like the community of the godly who know themselves to be safe under God's protection; as a warning example that God does not allow himself to be mocked their fate will become apparent to the people of God in an impressive fashion; hunted by the heavenly host of God (cf. the exposition of Pss. 58; 82)—we are here reminded of the Greek Furies—and cast off by God like Cain they are forced to wander about restlessly like a fugitive (Gen. 4.12; see Intr. 50 f.) and their blasphemous utterances (cf. v. 7) and perjured curses redound upon themselves. Their downfall and their end make manifest not only to the Yahweh community (v. 11) but to the whole world (v. 13) that God is the ruler over Jacob. God reveals himself as the Lord in his judgment on the nations (see Intr. 50); this accounts for the strong religious interest which the psalmist and with him the whole congregation take in the fate of the wicked, as well as for the inward and outward connection of the idea of judgment in the laments with the revelation of God's nature and will in the worship of the people of God. **[14–17]** In the last strophe the poet's thoughts turn from his enemies to his own relationship with God. The refrain (v. 14; cf. v. 6) and the amplification of the picture of the roving dogs in v. 15 serve as a background which throws into relief the two contradictory attitudes: insatiable greediness on the part of the adversaries leads to their rebellion against God (notice here the probably deliberate use of the phrase which in the tradition of the *Heilsgeschichte* denotes the rebellion of the people against God in the wilderness period; cf. Ex. 16.2, 7, 8; Num. 14.27, 29; see Intr. 50 f.); this view implies the profound knowledge that every rebellion against God has its ultimate roots in the dull realms of animal sensuality, a knowledge which can be traced back to the story of the primeval Fall of man (Gen. ch. 3). The worshipper, on the other hand ('but I'), lives in quite a different world: whereas those men are impelled by their consuming greediness to rush around, he is wholly filled with confidence in God whose power is the mainstay of his life and determines its purpose, so that, resting content with his God and rejoicing in him, he begins to sing a thanksgiving. The slight but not unimportant difference in the wording of the refrain (v. 17: 'I will sing praises to thee'; cf. v. 9: 'I will watch for thee'), which should not be obliterated by a mechanical equalization of these two verses, delicately indicates the inward freedom which the poet has gained for himself, and which makes his soul, like a lark, soar upwards to his God with shouts of joy.

60. WITH GOD WE SHALL DO VALIANTLY

To the Conductor. According to 'Lily'.[1] A Testimony.[2] Miktam.[3]
Of David. For instruction,[2] when he fought with Aram of the land
of the two streams and Aram of Zobah, and when Joab returned and
smote twelve thousand men of Edom in the Valley of Salt[4]

1 O God thou hast rejected us, torn us to pieces;
   thou hast been angry and drivest us back.[5]
2 Thou hast made the land to quake,
   thou hast rent it open;
   repair its breaches, for it totters.
3 Thou hast made thy people suffer hard things;
   thou hast given us wine to drink
   that made us reel.
4 Thou hast set up a banner for those who fear thee,
   to rally to it from the bows.[6] *Selah*
5 That thy beloved may be delivered,
   save with thy right hand[7] and answer us!
6 God has spoken in his sanctuary,
   'I will exult; I will divide up Shechem
   and portion out the Vale of Succoth.
7 Gilead is mine and Manasseh is mine;
   Ephraim is the bulwark of my head[8] and Judah my sceptre.
8 Moab is my washbasin;
   upon Edom I cast my shoe;
   acclaim me with shouts of joy, Philistia!'[9]
9 Who will bring me to the fortified city?
   Who will lead[6] me to Edom?
10 Wilt thou not do it, O God,
   who hast rejected us
   and didst not go to war ' '[6] with our armies?[10]

11 O grant us help against the oppressor,
   for vain is the help of man!
12 With God we shall do valiantly;
   it is he who will tread down our foes.

[1] This is probably the opening of a hymn to the tune of which the psalm was to be sung or accompanied (see Ps. 45).

[2] See the comments on vv. 6–8.

[3] See Ps. 16.

[4] Cf. II Sam. 8 and Intr. 98.

[5] * RSV has 'broken our defences' instead of 'torn us to pieces' and 'oh, restore us' instead of 'and drivest us back'.

[6] See BH.

[7] * RSV has 'give victory by thy right hand' instead of 'save with thy right hand'.

[8] * In RSV 'Ephraim is the bulwark of my head' is 'Ephraim is my helmet'.

[9] * V. 8c is in RSV, 'over Philistia I shout in triumph'.

[10] * V. 10 is in RSV:
   Hast thou not rejected us, O God?
   Thou dost not go forth, O God, with our armies.

The psalm presupposes a situation similar to that in Psalm 44 and, as far as subject-matter is concerned, the psalms are closely related. It is a fragment of liturgy, part of a service of supplication in the course of which the people, who are in a mood of deep depression after a heavy defeat, bring their lamentation and petitions before God (vv. 1–5, 9–11; the single voice in v. 9 is probably that of the king speaking as the leader of the armies). The central portion (vv. 6–8) contains a divine utterance—probably spoken by a prophet as the mouthpiece of God—which is intended to be an answer to the lamentation, an answer that is full of comfort and promises victory. But since the scope of the divine utterance is much wider than that of the lament it may be assumed that the former (vv. 6–8) stemmed from an earlier, pre-existent cultic tradition (v. 6: 'in his sanctuary'), in which it was originally used in a different context from the present one in the psalm (see below). The entirely different moods prevailing in the lament and the divine answer again point in the same direction. In that case, however, it is not possible to make use of vv. 6–8 for the reconstruction of the historical situation in which the psalm had its origin. In consequence of the ambiguity of various passages, which already makes itself felt in the early translations, this situation remains obscure so that the evaluation of the historical allusions produces no accurate results which could be used to date the psalm. Presumably it is a question of a campaign against the territory of Edom (v. 9). The mention of the Israelite armies under the command of Yahweh as well as the parallel to Psalm 44 (see ad loc.) seem to point to the pre-exilic era rather than to the wars of the Maccabees, in the light of which commentators have frequently sought to interpret this psalm. Verses 6–8 date back to an even earlier tradition which seems to reflect the conditions of the Davidic era (cf. v. 8 with Num. 24.17). The historical note in the psalm's later superscription relates the psalm to David's victories over Edom, Moab and the Philistines (II Sam. 8; I Chron. 18.3 ff.), presumably on account of vv. 6–8 (see the comments on these verses); the rest of the psalm, however, is concerned with a defeat.

[1–5] The lament for the defeat does not merely dwell on its external aspects, though it is true to say that it gives full expression to the plight of a defeated nation whose lines of battle when broken recede like a flood (II Sam. 5.20), and whose land is convulsed and fissured as if by an earthquake. The people themselves are intoxicated, as if by a poisoned drink, and in the frenzy of their confusion they feel the ground shake beneath their feet. But at the same time they are able to see beyond the immediate events and are startled to perceive behind them the figure of God, who has done all these things and, emerging from the background of the events, now confronts them in a manner utterly different from the one they had expected from him —namely as author of the whole disaster. The actual affliction, about which they here complain, is the spiritual affliction of a nation who know themselves to be rejected by God in his anger and yet are neither able nor willing to let him go. However, the fact that this shock to their faith does not lead to doubt about God or to rebellion against him, but is expressed in prayer to him, shows how deep-rooted that faith in God is and how serious is the people's attitude to God as they pray. It is only when spiritual affliction reaches these uttermost depths that it is capable of becoming the only means of overcoming *every* adversity. The lament, it is true, by no means conceals the people's disappointment at their misfortune, but for all that they do not renounce God (cf. Ps. 44.17). The fact that the cult community may nevertheless believe themselves to be the people of God (v. 4: 'those who fear thee'; v. 5: 'thy beloved') and may confide their affliction even to the God who is angry with them, remains their ultimate and only stay. After all, God himself has set up a banner to rally again the army's scattered ranks in the face of the threat from the enemy (v. 4). It can be assumed that the psalm was recited in the military assembly now rallied round the banner (a standard?) of Yahweh (cf. Ex. 17.15; Ps. 20.5). (Other commentators understand

v. 4 as a bitter irony, implying that Yahweh set up the banner as a
sign for the mobilization of the people in order to lead them not to
victory but to defeat and flight; the text and the context, however,
refute such an interpretation.) **[6–8]** The petition for deliverance
and for the prayer to be heard is followed by the proclamation of the
divine answer. This takes the form of a divine utterance borrowed
from the sacred tradition of the distribution of the land; this, according to Deut. 31.10, was settled afresh every seven years at the autumnal feast in connection with the renewal of the Covenant, and has
found its literary record mainly in the accounts transmitted in the
Book of Joshua (see Intr. 44, 50). The fundamental idea of the
prophetic oracle, in which perhaps is reflected the extent of conquests
at the time of David, is Yahweh's ownership of the land of Canaan,
the 'Promised Land'; this is meant to serve as a manifestation of his
royal power, just as the people of the Covenant, to whom this land is
promised and awarded, are meant to serve the same purpose. The
two cities of Shechem and Succoth are perhaps mentioned with a
view to the Jacob tradition in Gen. 33.17 f. in order to substantiate
claims to ownership in the west and east of Jordan from an early
epoch. It is probably for the same reason that mention is made of the
region of Gilead east of Jordan, which belonged to that territory in
the east in which the people of Israel had first settled, and also of the
tribe of Manasseh who at an early date had gained a footing in the
central part of the land west of Jordan. The two most prominent
tribes of the people of the Covenant, Ephraim in the north and Judah
in the south, are described in archaic language and in a bold poetical
picture as the helmet and the sceptre (cf. Gen. 49.10) of Yahweh, the
Warrior God of the Covenant, who also extends his claim to sovereign
authority to the neighbouring countries of Moab in the south-east
and Edom in the south. The pictures of the washbasin and the casting
of the shoe are meant to convey this truth and to emphasize God's
august majesty and power; the same purpose is to be served by the
Philistines' reception with their 'acclamation as King' (cf. Num.
23.21); reverting to the beginning of the divine oracle, it is emphasized that the kingship of Yahweh is one of the feast's fundamental elements. The opening words of the divine utterance 'I will
exult', usually understood as shouts of joy on the occasion of a victory
and so interpreted as referring to the distribution of the spoil at a
victory celebration, cannot be adduced against the derivation of the
God-given oracle from the cultic tradition of the distribution of the

land which took place at this feast. For a victory celebration is nowhere mentioned in the psalm and, as far as we know, there has never been an historical situation in the history of Israel—a necessary reconstruction in this context—in which the aforementioned territories had been at one and the same time conquered and distributed. Rather is the exultation of God to be understood as Yahweh's self-predication at his theophany in the cult, for which the tradition of Ex. 34.6 is the standard basis (see Intr. 30 f., 40 ff.). In Ps. 108, too, a memory of that connection of the divine oracle with the cultic epiphany is still preserved in that there Ps. 60.5–12 (=Ps. 108.6–13) are preceded by the words used in Ps. 57.7–11 (= Ps. 108.1–5), which in their turn refer to the appearance of Yahweh during the liturgical celebration (see the exposition of Ps. 57). The lament (vv. 1–5) has already revealed how their faith in God preserved the people of the Covenant from losing heart in their desperate situation; now it is fully revealed what hidden energies they are able to draw from the revelation of God, before whom they can appear again and again in the cult to hear the Word of God, transmitted in the tradition of the *Heilsgeschichte*, as a living word of promise which in every given situation will ever again prove to be true. The two phrases *ʿedūt* and *lᵉhaskil* in the superscription of the psalm presumably have a bearing on these associations, for they point to the 'testimony' borne to the God-given oracle that originates from the pre-existent tradition, and to the 'didactic' purpose of its interpretation and application to the situation under discussion (see also the comments on Ps. 50.7).

[9] Admittedly, the fog has not all disappeared immediately; the commander-in-chief, who is responsible for the outcome of the campaign, cannot entirely suppress the doubts which are stirred up in him by contemplation of the actual political eventualities that might arise from his completely insecure position. In his question the doubts which so easily beset man's thoughts still struggle with his readiness to trust in God's Word. [10] But faith in God's promise wins through, not only overcoming the doubts of man but also asserting itself in the face of the angry God himself who denied his help to the nation (cf. Ps. 44.9)—no matter whether the statements made in v. 10 are expressed in a relative clause, as above, or whether one translates, 'Hast thou not rejected us?'. [11] For the petition for God's help and the striking reason for it, that all human help is vain, is, in fact, nothing else than the *bold venture* of a genuine faith: it

renounces every kind of effort that man might be able to make and casts away all doubts in the sure knowledge that no human deed can be accomplished without God's grace; it also knows for certain that God's promise carries with it the guarantee of its fulfilment, even though man is aware of the fact that he is supported by no other power than that of God alone. [12] This strong faith is granted to the members of the cult community as they pray; in prayer they are able to overcome their doubts and their helpless depression. In that they decide to turn to God their faith is supplied with fresh invincible energy so that they rise to a daring hope and to a strong courage which inspires them to do great things, with God as their ally.

61. O THAT I MIGHT DWELL IN THY TENT FOR EVER

To the Conductor. With stringed instruments.[1] *Of David*

1 Hear my cry, O God.
 Listen to my prayer!
2 From the end of the earth I call to thee,
 for my heart faints.
 Lead me up to the rock that is too high for me![2]
3 Yea, thou hast become my refuge,[3]
 a strong tower against the enemy.
4 O that I might dwell in thy tent for ever,
 and hide me under the shelter of thy wings![4] *Selah*
5 For thou, O God, hast heard my vows,
 thou hast given me the heritage of those who fear thy name.
6 Mayest thou add days to the days of the king;
 may his years endure like the days[5] from generation to generation![6]
7 May he be enthroned for ever before the face of God;
 grace and faithfulness apportion to him that they may watch over him![7]
8 So will I ever sing praises to thy name,
 as I pay my vows day after day.

[1] The MT reads, 'according to David's string music'. Following the early translations, we shall probably have to read the plural (*binᵉgīnōt*).
[2] * V. 2bc reads in RSV:
 . . . when my heart is faint.
 Lead thou me to the rock that is higher than I.
[3] * RSV has 'for thou art my refuge'.
[4] * V. 4 reads in RSV:
 Let me dwell in thy tent for ever!
 Oh to be safe under the shelter of thy wings!
[5] See BH.
[6] * RSV reads:
 Prolong the life of the king;
 may his years endure to all generations!
[7] * V. 7b reads in RSV, 'bid steadfast love and faithfulness watch over him'.

The psalm combines such themes as lament, petition, thanksgiving and vow; to them is added in vv. 6 f. an intercession for the king. Since the spirit of thanksgiving prevails already from v. 3 onwards over the tone of lament and depression (vv. 1 f.), the song is to be regarded as a thanksgiving and, like Psalms 41, 56 and others (see Intr. 83 f.), is to be interpreted as a recital by the author, at the time of the cultic festival, of the petition for the fulfilment of which he is now able to give thanks. Everything which he has gone through and expressed in his prayers from the time when he first uttered his lament until its answer is compressed into a single act of salvation, so that his prayer now unites in itself the two poles between which his mood had oscillated all along, and thereby indicates the way he was led from the stage of pining away in separation from God to the blessedness of God's nearness. The customary view that the poet, like the author of Psalms 42 and 43, sojourned in the Diaspora as an exile, is based on an interpretation of the phrase 'from the end of the earth' in v. 2 which is by no means certain; we are also dissuaded from holding it by the character of the psalm, which is completely different from that of Psalms 42 and 43 in mood and subject-matter. On the contrary, vv. 3 ff. presuppose the presence of the worshipper in the Temple.

[1–2] The invocation and the petition betray, though they indicate it only in quite general terms, the profound distress of a man whose soul is suffering from being separated from God and who is probably threatened by enemies (cf. v. 3); he has lost courage, so that God and the help he can give rise up before his eyes like a towering rock which he cannot scale. It is in such a mood of feeling himself separated from God by an unbridgeable gulf that in the helplessness and misery this causes he pictures himself at the other 'end of the earth', and from its depths (cf. Pss. 130.1; 135.6 f.) he calls to the God who is enthroned in the distant heights. The phrases of v. 2 are used in a metaphorical sense; hence it is not necessary to assume that the worshipper imagines himself transferred into the underworld.

[3–4] However, his separation from God is now overcome. The poet has found his refuge in God and has gained his protection; he knows that in the house of God he is sheltered from the enemy just as well as if he were in the strong towers of a fortress, and therefore desires that he may be able to dwell in it for ever as the guest of God (cf. Ps. 23.5 f.) and may be protected by him who sits enthroned upon the wings of the cherubim of the sacred Ark (cf. Pss. 17.8; 36.7; 57.1,

etc.; see Intr. 40 f.). The emphasis in v. 4 is on the words 'for ever'; in
its context the verse cannot mean that the worshipper, sojourning
abroad, grievously misses the nearness of God in the sanctuary, but
that he desires never again to lose the communion with God which
he now enjoys in God's house. **[5]** Only if we interpret v. 4 in this
sense can a connection be established between this verse and what
follows; v. 5, too, does not say that the worshipper is longing for
something, but speaks of the fulfilment of his petition. God has
answered the prayers of the poet and has granted the vows associated
with them; he has given him the land which is due to those 'who fear
his name'. Here we can discern the special occasion on which the
psalm seems to have been recited. It is that ceremony of the covenant
community of Yahweh at which the 'lots' of land, into which the
Promised Land was divided, were distributed amongst the members
of the Covenant, that is to say, among 'those who fear thy name' (see
Intr. 44, 75). It is in connection with this sacred act that the poet
brings his personal cause before God, inferring from the actual
apportioning of his lot of land (cf. Ps. 16.5 f.) confirmation that his
lament has been answered, or obtaining that assurance at a different
point in the divine service which he had witnessed, and he now links
these two gifts together as he gives thanks for them both in his prayer.
We can clearly see at this point to what a high degree the cultic
sphere extended into the private regions of the personal individual
life and how it tied the whole existence of the individual to the
community of the people of the Covenant and to its concerns. **[6–7]**
The intercession for the king also finds its explanation in such a
sacred link with the covenantal ceremony (see Intr. 45) without
necessitating a solution of the awkwardness by literary criticism's
elimination of vv. 6–7 as a later interpolation. The king is the
guarantor of the observance and execution of the order based on
sacral law; the long duration of his righteous government, for which
the psalmist prays, is not only in the material interests of the people
of God. If the king partakes of the divine saving grace and faithfulness, then the whole nation with him stands under God's protection
and benefits from his salvation. In this way the idea of the apportioning of the divine saving blessings to the king—'grace and faithfulness' form an essential part of the revelation of the nature of the
God of the Covenant (cf. Ex. 34.6; see Intr. 58, 75)—also relates the
intercession for the king very closely to the apportioning of the land
mentioned in v. 5 as the 'heritage of Yahweh', which was distributed

to the covenant community in a sacred cultic act; and the petition
that the king's rule in God's name may last for ever (v. 7a) also fits
in with the scope of the 'grace of kingship' which includes the welfare
of the whole nation (cf. in this connection Pss. 21.4; 28.8 f.; 72.17).
[8] The blessing flowing from the celebration of the divine service
penetrates the innermost recesses of the human heart and embraces
the life of the people of God in all its aspects; by their communion
with God it welds the members together into a true Church in which
they are united with one another in faith and life, and it reminds the
worshipper of his duty to give thanks, a duty which ensues from the
happiness of having God always present with him. By praising God
day by day he not only fulfils his vow but also realizes the purpose of
his life as a member of the Church. The communion with God in
prayer, which is vitally necessary for the achievement of true faith,
becomes in the Church an unbroken tradition of testifying to his
name and professing it, and thus serves the eternal self-glorification
of God as the ultimate purpose both of the cultus and of life in
general.

62. MY SOUL IS STILL UNTO GOD

To the Conductor. According to Jeduthun.[1] *A Psalm. Of David*

1 *Yea, my soul is still*[2] *unto God,*[3]
   from him comes my salvation!
2 *Yea, he is my rock and my help,*
   my fortress, that I do not waver! ' '[4]
3 How long will you assail *one* man,
   all of you, that you might slay him,
   like a leaning wall, a fence that is in danger of collapsing?[5]
4 Yea, they plan to thrust him down from his eminence;
   they take pleasure in falsehood;
   they bless with their[2] mouths,
   but inwardly they curse. *Selah*
5 *Yea, my soul is still*[2] *unto God,*[3]
   for my hope is from him!
6 *Yea, he is my rock and my help,*
   my fortress, that I do not waver![6]
7 On God rests my salvation and my honour;
   my rock that shelters me, my refuge is God!*[7]
8 Trust in him, all of you in the congregation;[8]
   pour out your heart before him!
   God is a refuge for us. *Selah*
9 The children of men are but a breath;
   the sons of men are a delusion;

when they are weighed, they are found too light,[9]
they are together lighter than a breath.
10 Put no confidence in power,[10]
set no vain hopes on robbery!
Set not your heart on this that riches may increase!
11 It is one thing which God has spoken;
there are two things which I have heard:[11]
that power belongs to God,
12 and that to thee, O Lord, belongs grace.
For thou dost (requite) every man according to his work.

[1] Another reading is 'for Jeduthun'; see Ps. 39; both these versions (see the early translations) seem to denote that this psalm was recited by the guild of Temple singers named after their ancestor Jeduthun (see above p. 97).
[2] See BH.
[3] * RSV has 'For God alone my soul waits in silence.'
[4] See BH. (Tr. N.: RSV has:
He only is my rock and my salvation,
my fortress; I shall not be greatly moved.)
[5] * RSV has:
How long will you set upon a man
to shatter him, all of you,
like a leaning wall, a tottering fence?
[6] * RSV has 'I shall not be shaken' instead of 'that I do not waver'.
[7] * RSV has 'my mighty rock' instead of 'my rock that shelters me'.
[8] See BH. (Tr. N.: RSV has 'Trust in him at all times, O people.')
[9] Lit.: 'On the scales they are (destined) to rise suddenly.'
(Tr. N.: The first three lines are in RSV:
Men of low estate are but a breath,
men of high estate are a delusion;
in the balances they go up; . . .)
[10] * RSV has 'extortion' instead of 'power'.
[11] * The first two lines are in RSV:
Once God has spoken;
twice have I heard this . . .

The poet of this psalm is facing a difficult situation. He has been forsaken and is now persecuted by his former friends, and so he believes himself and seems to them to be like a leaning wall and like a 'fence that is in danger of collapsing'. The attacks of his adversaries, who outwardly, indeed, behave as friends but are inwardly full of lies and hatred and seek his life, have worn him down to such a degree that he is in danger of succumbing to their pressure. His confession, 'My soul is still only if turned to God', arises out of the very midst of that affliction the gravity of which the poet by no means conceals from himself. This confession, which is the fruit of the wrestling of his soul in prayer, is in itself one of the finest testimonies in the Psalms to the true spirit of prayer. The thoughts of the worshipper have turned away from the contemplation of his human sorrows and afflictions and are wholly focused on God; he no longer sees anything but God who is his helper, his rock and his fortress. There is now stillness in his soul.

He is lifted out of the fluctuating situation, the sense of not knowing where to turn in his anxiety and anguish, and has again gained a firm footing, so that he no longer wavers. As in Psalms 42 and 43, this hymn, too, is filled with conflicting emotions because of the struggle going on between despair and trust in God, only here the trust in God is more markedly the dominant central position in the psalm, and by it the poet is able in spirit to master his affliction. He attains not only peace of mind, but the right standard and sound judgment on which alone one can rely in life, so that he is also enabled to become the leader of the other members of the community, one who can, out of his own experience, give them advice and help. The song presupposes the psalmist's personal experience of the self-revelation of God (vv. 11 f.), for which we have to turn to the cult of the Covenant (see Intr. 28 ff., 42 f.); it can be assumed that the psalm, too, had its place in that cult (v.8).

The intensity of the author's struggle and the spiritual force latent in the situation have found expression even in the form of the psalm. Here formal features from various types of song illustrate in a quite clearly discernible fashion that it is not the form which dominates the subject-matter, but that the living substance chooses and creates its specific forms. Thus in vv. 1–8 the note of trust predominates, whereas the song's second part changes over to the patterns of exhortation and Wisdom poetry. The directness of the emotions expressed is also the reason for the poem's lack of a well-proportioned structure. It is only towards the end of the psalm that the calm note which is sounded can be accounted for by the strength which the psalmist has acquired by his peace of mind and by his self-control based on trust in God, and which is also manifested in the sound judgment he is able to pass on the situation. The psalm does not provide any particular clues which would make it possible to date it.

[1–2] The confession with which the poet opens his song still gives an inkling of the struggle that had previously taken place in his soul, before he found in turning to God that stillness from which he is able to draw the inner strength he needed to overcome his affliction. Calling to mind the inward struggle that has preceded it, it states the fundamental truth that man's spiritual torment cannot come to rest and be stilled until he turns to God. If v. 1a is translated as has been done here, then the subjective aspect of the new religious truth stands out more distinctly; it is, however, also possible to render this line, 'my soul is still if focused on God alone', in which case the objective aspect of the truth in question would acquire greater importance, showing what the presence of God means to the worshipper. As often in the Psalms, so here, too, the main fundamental idea of the whole hymn is stated at the beginning, thereby laying down right from the outset the main trend of the thoughts to be developed in the psalm. The poet has concentrated his thoughts on God by exerting his mental faculties to the utmost and, having opened up his heart to God in prayer, has turned his whole inner being to God. He has abandoned his search for human help and has completely entrusted himself to his God. Now he becomes still, whereas previously he had been tormented by thoughts and doubts which had made him restless. He now clearly sees from whom alone his salvation comes. However, this is not the whole story: not only has he ceased to look anxiously around for help, but he has now a firm footing: God is his unshakable rock, his fortress. The anxiety which made him waver has given way to a confident assurance and to a sure and firm faith; and this has been brought about by the knowledge that his seeing and his thinking and indeed his whole life are turned in a different direction, are transferred to a different dimension, and determine his existence in all its aspects exclusively from the standpoint of God, providing him with a new focal point and, consequently, with a different horizon. [3] The poet's mental distress and bitter disappointment, caused by the hostility of his former friends, are disclosed to us in all their magnitude by the words he uses in turning against his persecutors. The note of reproach sounded in this betrays, however, that he inwardly feels superior to the situation that threatens him; but he does not indulge in even the slightest illusion which might delude him into overlooking the fragile nature of his position. From a purely human point of view he is fully conscious of the hopelessness of his calamitous situation, seeing, as he does, that all his former friends assail him, a single man, as if he were a leaning wall, a cracked fence which might collapse at any moment. And though he knows that they seek his life, urged on by that deplorable ruthlessness against the weak which imbues even the coward with a dismal courage, he is indeed humble but nevertheless not broken, mortally wounded and yet not defeated.

[4] The poet characterizes the behaviour of his adversaries, which he now sees quite clearly, with a certain inward detachment (cf. his description in the third person). They can no longer deceive him by the friendliness of the good wishes which are always on their lips when they talk to him. He has both recognized their true intention to ruin him and has seen through their hypocritical behaviour. That their opposition is to be accounted for by party struggles between 'the wicked and the godly' does not follow from the psalmist's statements themselves; the manner in which the persecution is carried out is so very much in accordance with human nature in general that there is hardly any need to surmise that these hostile activities are the result of the formation of special groups or parties. Moreover, it is not very likely that the victim of the persecution was a man who occupied a position of importance; the esteem in which he was held does not go beyond the respect which is usually accorded to a truly God-fearing man within the circle of his acquaintances. As so often in the psalms, so here the external circumstances of the poet remain in the dark (and the repeatedly expressed view that it is a question of a man who is seriously ill is no more than a guess); it is therefore so much the more valuable that we are allowed to gain an insight into the soul of the psalmist. We can sympathize with him in the indignation and legitimate anger which bitter disappointment at the hypocritical and treacherous insincerity of his former friends evokes in him. **[5–6]** And yet he does not allow these sentiments to become his master. This is the result of the fact that he has reached a position enabling him to ignore every kind of trouble which man may try to bring upon him and every kind of human untrustworthiness, the position of having peace of mind and of feeling secure, gifts granted him as he focused his thoughts on God in faith. Though he may appear in his own eyes and in the eyes of his opponents to be like a leaning wall, he has found in that position a support which holds him upright. A new ray of hope flashes forth from God; his situation is penetrated with a new light in which the turbulent emotions aroused by his indignation die down, and there is now stillness in his soul. Against his agitation the poet now sets the confident assurance of his trust in God; the angry words he had uttered about his adversaries are now followed—taking up once more the outward and inward starting-point of the psalm—by his firm profession that his soul is still in God, a profession from which alone he draws his strength. The contrast presented by the statements in the psalm indicates

P.–P

outwardly the inward tension which the poet has mastered by lifting his eyes up to God. Now his life is based on a new and firm foundation. [7] His salvation and his honour are not at the disposal of men but rest on God, in whom he has found his refuge and on whom his existence is built as on a firm rock. The sentiments which henceforth dominate his life are no longer those of anxious sorrows, human fears and disappointments. If God is the foundation and the goal of man's life, then man's existence is built on confidence and hope, safety and trust, assurance and strength. His stillness before God has become for him the source of new strength. [8] In v. 8 that truth is made evident in a special direction. The poet's heart is so engrossed by the thoughts which move him deeply that he does not keep them to himself, but turns to his fellow men, calling upon them and exhorting them to trust in God (see above p. 86). Trust in God is not a place of refuge to which the believer can retreat from the turmoil and the disappointments of the world in order to find there his satisfaction and rest. Trust in God is a cell of organic life, a power-centre which does not remain in isolation, but cannot help bearing fruit because it feels inwardly constrained to prove its living reality through acts of faith. Hence what has been imparted to the poet by his encounter with and reflection on God has for him not merely the significance of an opinion, but has become for him a new source of strength; again, it has for him not merely the meaning of a certain view or of a certain interpretation, but is a present reality. And that present reality is bound to have its effects. As far as the psalmist is concerned, this comes about in such a way that he calls upon his fellow believers to display, when they commune with God in prayer, the same unrestrained candour and resultant trust in God which for himself represents the elemental force of his new life: 'Pour out your heart before him!' In doing so the psalmist unites with the cult community, forming a fellowship of those who have their refuge in God, and so throws into bold relief not only for himself but for them all the keynote of trust which sustains his whole song.

In v. 8 the poet has already given expression to the responsibility he feels for his brethren by exhorting them to trust in God; he has already begun to turn to the cult community. In the second part of the psalm he pursues the same course by sounding a more didactic note and, in consequence, proceeds to a more composed and sober contemplation of the situation, reflecting on it in the light of his own experience of God and through the energies which have been aroused in him as a result of this. **[9]** Here the connection between cultic experience and hortatory 'wisdom' can be seen particularly clearly (see Intr. 88 f.). In the presence of God the things which are emphasized and the standards which are employed are entirely different from those which usually carry weight in ordinary life. In the face of the majesty of God the glory of man shrinks into an ephemeral nothingness; before God man is but a breath which cannot be relied on. And there is a further truth which is disclosed to the poet as he focuses his thoughts on God and as his eyes are opened by the demands which God makes on him—the truth that man cannot be trusted because truthfulness is not a part of his nature. At the root of that knowledge is his observation, which greatly shocks him, that man's utterances and actions are not capable of standing the test when they are seriously examined; if they are weighed with a view to the things which alone ultimately matter, they turn out to be too light. The poet is aware of the contradictory character of human nature; he is aware of that ultimate lie which deprives man of any trustworthiness. And when he extends his grave indictment to all men, there is no reason to assume that in passing this pessimistic judgment on man he has in view only the behaviour of his adversaries but wants to exempt himself from it. The profundity of the religious truth expressed in this psalm consists in the very fact that the psalmist knows that to see through the eyes of God means to get to the root of all things, of men and, last but not least, of one's own self, and to see life without any camouflage or self-deception as it actually is in its unadorned truth. It is by no means a question of the pessimistic lament of a man who, having become disgusted with his fellow men, unburdens himself and finds his satisfaction in his tacit joy that he himself is not one of them. On the contrary, it is an absolutely realistic and sincere judgment on the true nature of man, from which he cannot exempt himself as he stands before the Living God. **[10]** The psalmist now draws the practical conclusion from the realization of the ultimate basis for human behaviour, and warns against placing one's trust in the might and power of man. No matter how impressive all these may outwardly appear to be at first sight, in the last analysis they are, after all, but a 'vain and futile hope'. The poet also endeavours to turn men's eyes away from the power which wealth confers upon man; for it is the wrong way of looking at life when man allows himself to be deceived by outward appearances and runs after the merely spectacular; the psalmist knows from his own experience that such an outlook is bound to end in disappointment because it disregards the relatedness of life. **[11-12]** In contrast, the closing portion of the psalm once more states the true viewpoint and the standard which alone is valid because it derives its rules from God. This knowledge has been granted to the poet in the form of the revelation of the divine nature, and he passes it on to the cult community as a Word spoken by God. He clothes his thoughts in the form of the so-called 'numerical proverb', which was frequently used in the Wisdom literature (cf. Prov. 6.16 ff.; 30.15 ff.; Job 5.19; 33.14; Ecclus. 23.16 ff.; 25.1 ff.); it is meant to record by means of a maxim what the worshipper has continually 'heard' at the recital of the cultic tradition. The whole content of the revelation of God in the cult of the Covenant is contained in the two statements in which that knowledge is expressed: power belongs to God, and it is he who bestows grace upon man. It is in the *union* of power and grace that the essential nature of the Old Testament belief in God is truly expressed; for power without grace does not admit of any trust, and grace without power is deprived of its ultimate seriousness. The miracle, however, lies in the very fact that, though man shrinks into nothingness before God's majesty (cf. vv. 9 f.), he may nevertheless base his trust on God's grace, knowing that this mighty God will not reject and forsake him if in faith he submits to both the power and grace of God. The transition from the maxim to the style of a prayer addressed to God, which is not to be removed by altering the text, implies a delicate hint that these ultimate fundamental truths hold good only in the life of a man who keeps his soul turned to God and continually opens up his heart to him. The psalm closes with a general statement on God's 'righteousness', so stressing the obligatory character of man's faith, which the Old Testament seldom omits to point out. In such a context the statement that God requites everyone according to his work will have to be understood in accordance with the covenant principle by which the God-fearing man may expect from God's righteousness a reward for his deeds as long as he seriously endeavours to live a righteous life. Thus the conclusion of the psalm is built on the same firm foundation of faith which forms the basis of its beginning and to which it continually looks back in order to draw thence new strength of comfort and trust from the soul's stillness before God. This song has become a source of comfort for struggling souls far beyond the limits of the Old Testament. Its echo in hymns of the Christian Church, especially, for instance, some of Paul Gerhardt's,[1] testifies to its appeal.

[1] * For example, 'Meine Seele ist in der Stille', 'Zu Gott sei deine Seele still';
and perhaps also 'Harre meine Seele, harre des Herrn', a hymnal prayer by
Friedrich Räder (1815–1872).

63. THY GRACE IS BETTER THAN LIFE

A Psalm. Of David when he was in the Wilderness of Judah[1]

1 O God, thou art my God whom I seek,
   my soul thirsts for thee;
   my flesh longs for thee,
   fainting in a dry land where no water is.[2]
2 So I have looked upon thee in the sanctuary.
   to behold thy power and glory.
3 For thy grace is better than life.
   My lips shall praise thee.[3]
4 So I will praise thee as long as I live;
   in thy name will I lift up my hands.[4]
5 My soul is satiated as with marrow and fat,
   and my mouth praises thee with joyful lips.[5]
6 When I think of thee upon my bed,
   I meditate on thee in the watches of the night.[5]
7 For thou hast become my helper,[6]
   in the shadow of thy wings I sing for joy.
8 My soul clung to thee;
   thy right hand has upheld me.[7]
9 But they that seek my life at the cost of their own ruin[8]
   shall go down into the depth of the earth.
10 They shall be given over[9] to the sword,
    they shall be prey for jackals.
11 But the king shall rejoice in God;
    all who swear by him shall glory,
    that[10] the mouths of the liars will be stopped.

[1] Cf. I Sam. 24.1 ff.
[2] * The last two lines are in RSV:
   my flesh faints for thee,
   as in a dry and weary land where no water is.
[3] * RSV has:
   Because thy steadfast love is better than life,
   my lips will praise thee.
[4] * In RSV v. 4b is, 'I will lift up my hands and call on thy name.'
[5] * Vv. 5 and 6 form one sentence in RSV:
   (5) My soul is feasted as with marrow and fat,
       and my mouth praises thee with joyful lips,
   (6) when I think of thee upon my bed,
       and meditate on thee in the watches of the night;

⁶ * RSV has, 'for thou hast been my help'.
⁷ * RSV uses the present tense.
⁸ * In the RSV v. 9a is, 'But those who seek to destroy my life.'
⁹ See BH.
¹⁰ * RSV has 'for' instead of 'that'.

The profoundly intimate communion with God and the elemental
yearning of a faithful heart to which the psalm bears witness in
continually changing phrases places this hymn, which is also remarkable from the poetic point of view, side by side with the finest testimonies to the piety of the Psalms. The poet is probably in the sanctuary, where he had been allowed to behold the revelation of the
majesty of God and experience his gracious help, and now knows
himself to be safe, being under the protection of God (vv. 2, 6; see
Intr. 72 f.). In that experience is found the fulfilment of the longing
prayer which he had previously addressed to God and with which he
now begins his thanksgiving (cf. Pss. 41; 56; 57; 61; see Intr. 70,
83 f.); and he has thereby come to be quite sure that his adversaries,
who seek his life, will be overtaken by the divine judgment (vv. 9 ff.).
The mention of the king in this connection (v. 11) allows the conclusion that we are here dealing with the pre-exilic festival of the
Yahweh cult which was celebrated at the sacred Ark (v. 7; see
Intr. 40 f., 45 f.) in the royal Temple—and that the worshipper recited
his psalm there. The decision about the fate of the enemies was
probably also taken within that festival's framework of the ritual
performed in the presence of the king and the cult community (see
Intr. 44). In this way the psalm is to be understood as forming a
unity, so that the many different suggestions, based on literary
criticism, which aim at the transposition or elimination of certain
passages, are superfluous.

[1] It is only against the background of the worshipper's ardent
yearning for the presence of God that the experience which fills his
heart with joy and gratitude to God is clearly set off in all its magnitude. In the time of his affliction and persecution that yearning for
God had once consumed his soul and body like the burning thirst
(cf. Ps. 42.1 f.) of an exhausted wanderer who is exposed to the
blaze of the sun in the dried-up wilderness, where no water is.
[2–3] That 'dry land' is to be understood in the sense of a comparison
and not as a reference to the place where the poet was staying,
follows from the opening of v. 2: the word 'so' means that as his soul
thus thirsted for God and longed for him, he was allowed to behold

him (cf. Isa. 6.1 ff.); and the hallowed hour he spent in the sanctuary, when God revealed his 'power and glory' to the congregation in the theophany (see Intr. 40), gave him the fulfilment of his longing in the certainty that he, too, would partake of God's grace. The grace of God (*ḥesed*), which is that element in the divine majesty (*kābōd*) which characterizes God's turning to man, has for the psalmist the significance of the supreme good, outweighing all the other earthly possessions that are worthy of man's aspirations, including even life itself (cf. Pss. 36.7 ff.; 73.25); so completely does it take hold of his heart that his lips cannot help praising God, bearing witness to the things with which his heart is full. **[4]** Thus he can no longer conceive of the purpose of his life in any other way than that his soul, being filled to the utmost with the thought of God, should be a living echo of God and his life a continuous prayer, a testifying to God by singing his praise (see Intr. 55 f., 69 f.). **[5–7]** This communion with God has become for him such a basic and immediate necessity of life that it 'satiates' him as if it were the richest food, incessantly occupying his mind, even at night, with meditation on God, and continually leading him during that meditation to the blessed realization of all that the helpful grace and protection of God, which he is now able to enjoy, mean to him. What the worshipper has come to realize in the house of God does not therefore remain confined to the place of that cultic encounter, but accompanies him right into every sphere of his daily life; for its roots reach down to the uttermost depths of a person's religious life in and with God, the far-reaching consequences of which cannot easily be judged or overestimated when we ponder over the things to which he never tires of bearing testimony in continually changing words and images. **[8]** With all the strength of his will he clings to God, to whom he owes his outward and inward support. **[9–10]** But there is still *one* thought which casts a shadow over the happiness of his soul, which is otherwise so wholly absorbed in God—the thought of his enemies. But even that thought gives way to the sure knowledge that those who seek his life shall not escape God's judgment. Their conviction and execution, and the later abandoning of their corpses as prey for jackals (v. 10; cf. Jer. 7.33), is obviously still in store for them and will take place as a sacred act based on ritual law, in the cultic sphere to which the psalm owes its origin (see Intr. 32 f., 78 f.). The assumption of such a link with the cult of the Yahweh community is suggested not only by the allusion to the presence of God upon the sacred Ark (v. 7), but also

[11] by the mention of the king and of all who 'swear by Yahweh' (cf. Deut. 6.13; 10.20) in the worshipper's closing testimony, in which he links his own concern with that of the whole cult community. In connection with the statement that the mouths of 'liars' will be stopped, the explicit emphasis on the affirmation of faithfulness to Yahweh (see Intr. 32 f., 59) and on the joy in him experienced by both king and people suggests that it is not so much a question of mendacious calumnies on the part of personal enemies, but rather of the enemies' denial of fundamental religious truths or even of their refusal to recognize Yahweh as their Lord (cf. 'lying idols' in Amos 2.4). So the strong religious interest which the poet takes in the enemies' fate is accounted for: it links him with the faithful members of the Yahweh community and their king. For it is, after all, the preservation of the cult community's purity and of the integrity of their faith which is at stake; and for this the whole cult community as well as its individual members are responsible to God (see Intr. 48 f.).

64. GOD'S RECOMPENSE
To the Conductor. A Psalm. Of David

1 Hear my voice, O God, in my trouble;[1]
  preserve my life from dread of the enemy!
2 Hide me from the secret plots of the wicked,
  from the scheming of the evildoers,
3 who whet their tongues like swords,
  who sharpen[2] bitter words like[2] arrows,[3]
4 to shoot from ambush at the godly;
  suddenly and without fear they shot at him.[4]
5 They hold fast to their evil purpose;
  they talk to conceal their traps,
  thinking, 'Who will notice them?'[5]
6 They devise crimes, keep secret[2] their plot;
  for a man's bosom and heart are deep.[6]
7 Then God shot his arrow at them;
  suddenly they are hit.[7]
8 Their own tongue brought them to ruin;
  all who see them, wag their heads.[8]
9 All men were frightened,
  and they told what God had done
  and pondered over his work.
10 The righteous rejoices in the Lord
  and finds refuge in him;
  and all the upright in heart shall glory.[9]

[1] * RSV has 'complaint' instead of 'trouble'.
[2] See BH.

³ * RSV has 'aim' for 'sharpen'.
⁴ * RSV has:
shooting from ambush at the blameless,
shooting at him suddenly and without fear.
⁵ * In RSV v. 5bc is:
they talk of laying snares secretly,
thinking, 'Who can see us?'
⁶ * In RSV v. 6ab continues the direct speech begun in v. 5c:
'Who can search out our crimes?
We have thought out a cunningly conceived plot.'
V. 6c reads, 'For the inward mind and heart of a man are deep!'
⁷ Lit.: 'their blows have become a sudden arrow'. (Tr. N.: RSV has:
But God will shoot his arrow at them;
they will be wounded suddenly.)
⁸ * RSV has 'Because of their tongue he will bring them to **ruin**', and uses the
future tense throughout vv. 8 f.
⁹ * RSV uses 'let . . .' throughout v. 10.

Though the text of the psalm has been handed down in a corrupt state, it is nevertheless possible to distinguish clearly its consistent structure and its main fundamental idea. The first part (vv. 1–6) contains after the introduction with its invocation and petition (vv. 1–2) the account of the machinations of the evildoers, cast in the style of a lament; the second part reports the retribution they suffered in the divine judgment (vv. 7–8) and the effect which that divine action had on the 'righteous' in particular (vv. 9 f.). From the general terms of these statements it is not possible to derive any specific clues as to the historical background of the psalm and the date of its composition; nor is it possible to prove the accuracy of the hypothesis that behind the psalm are controversies of the religious parties of post-exilic Judaism. The historical and personal biographical questions, which modern man would like to see answered, are regarded by the psalmists as insignificant in comparison with what God has done (v. 9); and in this psalm, too, the personal cause with which the prayer opens is incorporated in that theological concern of the whole cult community in which the psalm issues. If we want to achieve a true understanding of the 'situation' with which the psalm is concerned, we must therefore view it from the standpoint of the Yahweh community—for it is their members who are meant by the terms 'godly' (v. 4) and 'righteous' (v. 10). Within the bosom of that community, that is to say, in its cultus, the 'proclamation of what God has done' and the 'meditation on his work' (v. 9) takes place, and the psalm itself is nothing but a part of that proclamation of, and meditation on, the action whereby God has proved himself to be the Judge of the wicked and the Helper and refuge of the 'righteous' (see Intr. 74 ff.). The psalm is therefore a testimony to and an acknowledgment of God's retaliatory judgment, based on the worshipper's personal experience; he recited it in the presence of the congregation after his petition had been granted, and, as in Psalms 41, 56, 57 and often, the psalm opens with the petition that preceded the answering of the prayer (see Intr. 69 f., 83 f.).

[1–2] Because of its liturgical context in the cult, the petition is couched in such general terms that it provides no clear picture of the enemies and their machinations; this much, however, is clear, that from the purely human point of view the psalmist would have plenty of reason to be consumed with anxieties and dread, but for the fact that he finds his refuge and support in God. Knowing to what a high degree fear is able to deprive man of all clear thought and sound judgment, he first of all asks God to deliver him from the terror which his enemies strike into his heart. [3–8] The way the poet speaks in what follows of the machinations of the evildoers shows that he has found in God that support for which he had prayed, and that he has overcome his anxieties and fears. The characterizing of the enemies by description of particular traits of their behaviour cannot be separated from the account of the divine judgment (vv. 7 ff.; see Intr. 78 f.), as the latter refers back to the former. The account of the misdeeds and of their punishment, which occupies the central portion of the psalm and spiritually relates these acts to each other, serves the fundamental idea of the psalm by making clear on the particular points emphasized the just retribution which God executes in judgment. The enemies have sharpened their bitter words like arrows (v. 3); in return God has shot 'his arrow' at them. 'Suddenly they shot at the godly' (v. 4); equally 'suddenly' God's judgment overtook them (v. 7). They have 'laid traps' (v. 5); now their own tongue has trapped them (v. 8). They imagined that their secret plans could remain unnoticed (vv. 4 f.), but God's judgment has brought to light and made public every hidden plot (v. 8b). With no fear, not even of God (vv. 4b, 5b; cf. Ps. 55.19), they unscrupulously set to work to further their sinister plans, but God has shown by 'his work' that he is to be feared by all men (v. 9). The cunning secrecy of human behaviour and the incalculable irrationality of evil is summed up at the conclusion in the verdict which, though it conveys only a hint, is yet highly suggestive: 'a man's heart is deep'. And that secrecy and irrationality are now contrasted with the *ratio* of God's actions whose righteousness, power and wisdom triumph in judgment over human malice, pride and craftiness. In the eyes of the psalmist the retribution, which even entered into particulars, is evidence of that divine *ratio*; and the wisdom and power of God are revealed in the fact that the evildoers are ruined by their own sin and by their very downfall are compelled against their own will to bear witness to the nature and reality of God (cf. Amos 3.13 ff.).

[9–10] The statement on God's judgment is commonly interpreted—and this also applies to Luther's translation—in the sense of a wish whose fulfilment still lies in the future. The fact, however, that the early translations render v. 7 in the future tense cannot be considered as a sufficient support of that interpretation to justify our altering, contrary to the Hebrew text, the narrative tenses in all the passages concerned, especially as the original text produces a satisfactory meaning. Verse 9, too, recalls the divine judgment as an event that has already taken place. It describes the effect of 'what God has done' on the members of the cult community. Their first impression is that of fear of the mighty God who has appeared to sit in judgment (cf. Pss. 50; 55.19; 59,13, etc.; see Intr. 75 f.). This fear of God implies the recognition of his Lordship and affirmation of faith in him which finds its expression in the fact that the cult community makes God's actions the object of its 'proclamation' and 'meditation'; and this is done by means of the cultic representation of the divine deeds, to the glory of God (v. 10b) and for their own edification (v. 9c; cf. Ps. 106. 7 ff.). Here lies the key to the true understanding of the psalm. The psalm itself belongs to the proclamation of, and meditation on, the way of God, which for the poet begins with the lament about his affliction and ends in the manifestation of God's righteousness in the judgment before the whole cult community. Thus the psalm is the joint product of a personal experience and of the cultic tradition; they have grown together into a confession testifying to faith in God which is appointed to be recited in the worship of the cult community, and in this way have become themselves in their turn a living cultic tradition and a source of common joy in God and of a confident faith in him, a faith which is continually strengthened afresh (v. 10).

65. THOU CROWNEST THE YEAR WITH THY BOUNTY

To the Conductor. A Psalm. Of David. A Song

1 Praise is due[1] to be sung[1] to thee, O God in Zion;[2]
and to thee shall vows be fulfilled.[3]

2 O thou, who hearest prayers!
To thee all flesh bring[1]

3 the confession of their sins;
when our transgressions prevail over us,[1]
thou wilt forgive them.[4]

4 Blessed is he whom thou dost permit to be near to thee,
to dwell in thy courts and satisfy his hunger
with the goodness of thy house, thy holy temple![5]

5 Thou art terrible[1] when thou dost answer us to save us,
O God of our deliverance,
who art the refuge of all the ends of the earth,
and of the farthest shores;[6]

6 who by thy strength hast established the mountains,
being girded with might;

7 who hast stilled the roaring of the seas ' '[1]
and the tumult of the nations;[7]

8 then they were afraid at thy signs
who dwell at earth's farthest bounds;
thou hast made the[1] outgoing of morning
and evening to shout for joy.[8]

9 Thou didst bless the land and water[1] it,
thou hast greatly enriched it;
a river of God, full of water ' ',[9]
so dost thou prepare it.[10]

10 Thou waterest its furrows, levelling its ridges,
softening it with showers and blessing its growth.

11 Thou hast crowned the year with thy bounty;
thy tracks drip with fatness.[11]

12 The pastures of the wilderness drip,
the hills gird themselves with joy,

13 the meadows clothe themselves with flocks,
the valleys deck themselves with grain,
they shout and sing together for joy.

[1] See BH.
[2] * RSV omits 'to be sung' (in German *erklingen*, lit. 'to ring out').
[3] * RSV has 'performed' instead of 'fulfilled'.
[4] * Vv. 2b, 3a read in RSV:
To thee shall all flesh come
on account of sins.
[5] * In RSV v. 4 is:
Blessed is he whom thou dost choose
and bring near, to dwell in thy courts!

We shall be satisfied with the goodness
of thy house, thy holy temple!
⁶ See BH. (Tr. N.: RSV has in v. 5a:
By dread deeds thou dost answer us with deliverance,
O God of our salvation
and in v. 5b 'hope' instead of 'refuge' and 'seas' instead of 'shores'.)
⁷ * RSV has:
who dost still the roaring of the seas,
the roaring of their waves,
the tumult of the peoples . . .
⁸ * In v. 8 RSV continues v. 7:
so that those who dwell at earth's farthest bounds
are afraid at thy signs;
thou makest the outgoings of the morning and the evening
to shout for joy.
⁹ Thus in accordance with Staerk (see above under 'Commentaries', p. 14).
¹⁰ * RSV has:
Thou visitest the earth and waterest it,
thou greatly enrichest it;
the river of God is full of water;
thou providest their grain,
for so thou hast prepared it.
¹¹ * RSV has 'the tracks of thy chariot drip with fatness'.

It is still possible to infer from the song with a certain degree of probability the specific occasion which gave rise to the composition of this hymn. A time of drought had filled the country with great concern for the growth of the seed and had brought on the spectre of a year of famine. But now the prayers have been answered. The barren steppes have been transformed into green pastures and sprouting fields. The cult community has gathered in the Temple to fulfil the vows they had promised to the God of Zion when they prayed in their distress. In this way the cultic features of the song as well as its communal nature are accounted for. The value of the psalm lies not only in its fine poetic sense and language, but also in the fact that it demonstrates how within the framework of the cultus a very narrowly circumscribed section of what happens on earth can lead to the Old Testament belief in God being displayed in all its profundity and comprehensiveness, its inner harmony and wholeness —the concrete and the general, the visible and the invisible, the external and the internal, the temporal and the eternal, the things of the past, the present and the future being seen and experienced at one and the same time. To have God at *one* point means to have him in all his fullness. The poet envisages the entirely concrete particular event that provokes his thanksgiving in the widest possible context of the redemptive work of God; and it is really only by reflecting on the particular in the light of the whole that he is able to grasp its weight and significance. In this psalm, too, God is the focal point of the psalmist's thoughts, and the delight in the blessings of earthly life which the poet makes his starting-point is ultimately nothing but joy in God and in man's communion with him. And all this shows particularly clearly how the Old Testament faith conceives the whole reality of man's practical earthly life to be embedded in his comprehensive relation to the reality of God.

The poem consists of three sections which are not quite symmetrically constructed. In vv. 1–4 the gifts of grace of the house of God are praised; vv. 5–8 are a hymn to the God of the world and his salvation in creation and history; the concluding section depicts with lyrical delicacy the blessing of fertility with which God crowns the year. It is not possible to establish the psalm's date accurately, in view of its general character and the fact that its theme lies off the beaten track of history. Although various motifs point to the tradition of the New Year Festival (vv. 4, 5–8, 11), which in earlier times was celebrated in the autumn (cf. Ps. 118), the description of the blessing of fertility (vv. 9 ff.) envisages the Palestinian landscape clothed in the garment of spring; one is therefore led to think of a ceremony which took place in spring within the setting of the New Year Festival, as was the case from the reign of King Josiah, when the New Year was postponed to the spring; this perhaps brings us to the latter part of the pre-exilic era as the date of the psalm's composition.

The gifts of grace of the house of God (vv. 1–4)

[1] The usual hymnic introduction, which otherwise usually contains a call to sing God's praise, is here modified. The psalm opens with the more general statement 'Praise is due to be sung to thee', which strongly emphasizes the theocentric trend of the psalmist's thoughts and at the same time outlines the cultic tradition in which the song was recited: to the God who 'hears the prayers' are due thankful praise and the fulfilment of the vows made to him; the psalm itself is the song of praise which was sung in the Temple at the annual feast at which the vows used to be paid. [2–3] It is characteristic of the deep-rooted earnestness of Old Testament piety that the first thought which comes into the psalmist's mind under the impression of the blessed goodness of God and which points to a firmly established tradition is that of man's sinfulness. The New Testament truth that it is God's goodness which brings man to

repentance largely holds good also of the faith of the Old Testament. The greatness of the divine goodness arouses in man's soul shame and remorse at his own guilt and a yearning for the untroubled communion with God which can be fulfilled only by the forgiveness of sins. The poet indeed senses—and, to be sure, he expresses this feeling not only on his own behalf and on behalf of his fellow believers, but quite generally on behalf of 'all flesh', since it is a matter of a truth which concerns every human being—I repeat, he senses that man is incapable of getting rid of his sin by virtue of his own strength when sin 'prevails over him'; he knows that he would be bound to break down under the burden of sin but for the fact that he may appeal to the grace of God by confidently confessing his transgressions in the firm conviction that in it he will receive forgiveness. Thus the psalmist pictures himself as belonging to the large community of those who, united in the confession of their sins and in their prayers for God's forgiveness, may partake of the whole wealth of the divine goodness. It is not without good reason that the thought of the forgiveness of sins occupies first place in the psalm. Just as in the New Testament, so here, too, the forgiveness of sins is the prerequisite of a true relationship with God. In it all the other blessings of salvation are included as well. For it is only when God breaks down the wall of sin which man has erected between himself and God, and which separates him from God, that the way is opened for man's living intercourse with God. And it is only when man is terrified at the seriousness of the reality of God, as he comes to grasp his state of sinfulness and, in consequence, wholly gives himself up to God's grace, that his eyes are opened to the realization of the *true* nature of God. Thus he avoids the danger of forming a picture of God based on his own ideas and of pursuing that phantom of his desires. **[4]** To start from this assumption of the forgiving grace of God throws the fullest possible light on the blessing of God's presence and nearness which the poet, together with the community of the faithful, experiences in the hallowed hour he is permitted to spend in the Temple. It is not only the fact of the poet's physical presence in the house of God and the material aspect of the cultic piety which creates the happiness of that hour, but even more the inward spiritual communion with God whose willingness to act graciously has become a certainty in the act of the forgiveness of sins. 'To satisfy his hunger with the goodness of the holy temple' means much more than merely being able to share in the delights of the sacrificial banquet; it means

above all that the holy God, unapproachable in his sternness, favours
wretched man with the nearness of his presence, that the hour which
the psalmist spends in the house of God will become for him the
material and spatial pledge of being near to God in spirit. The cultic
apparatus and setting is here not an end in itself but a means to an
end and the way to a communion with God which is inwardly alive;
it is a means of the divine grace whereby God gives himself to man,
and with his Person the abundance of his salvation.

The God of the world and his salvation (vv. 5–8)

The great preoccupation with God, whose revelation is at the
heart of the festival cult, also accounts for the fact that the song which
the psalmist sings in praise of and in gratitude for the answering of
his particular prayers is preceded by a hymn to the God who makes
his salvation come true in creation, in history and at the end of time.
This hymn is the response of the festival congregation in which they
recapitulate the main items of the tradition of the *Heilsgeschichte* that
was cherished and recited in the covenant cult, and so testify to the
God who reveals his power and accomplishes his salvation in creation
and in history (see Intr. 57 ff.). As the members of the congregation
thus praise God, they discern in these very same facts at the same
time the granting ('answering') of their prayers. Here, too, it is the
wide range of the psalmist's God-centred outlook which causes the
individual particular event to be incorporated in the most comprehensive and ultimate relationships and seeks to understand its wider
significance from that angle. [5] Starting from the answer to prayer,
which has just been experienced, the testimony to the God of the
world in whom the uttermost 'ends of the earth' and the 'farthest
isles' take their refuge begins with a hymnic predication of God which
pithily expresses the essence of the whole Old Testament faith: 'Thou
art terrible when thou dost answer us to save us.' Active intercourse
with God rests on a twofold basis which actually represents a unity
full of tension. The believer takes God equally seriously as the One
who is to be feared because of his power, which makes man tremble,
and as the One whom he cannot help loving because of his incomprehensible grace. Trust, if placed in God, is not a gross familiarity
but the simultaneous manifestation of fear and love. Indeed, it is
precisely because God is to be feared in all earnestness that man can
absolutely trust in him. Again, it is precisely because God proves
himself by the ultimate seriousness of the unity of his judgment and

grace (cf. vv. 3 and 5) and of his power and salvation to be truly *God*, that he is also the only true 'refuge' of the whole world. **[6–7]** As the believer thus focuses his thoughts on God as the Lord of the whole world, he comes to see that everything which has come to pass in creation and in history is the work of God whereby he has manifested his power and majesty before the whole world. The mountains which, firmly established on foundations that cannot be shaken, survive for thousands of years, bear witness to the creative power of God, and so does the sea, the violence of which has been tamed by the Creator and restricted within its shores (for the mythological background of this thought see Intr. 51, 60 f.). The history of the nations, too, testifies to the same power of God who has set a limit to their 'tumult'. **[8]** 'God is the Alpha and the Omega of everything that comes to pass in the world'; and that which takes place is itself an act of God which has an ultimate purpose and goal. Everywhere are the visible 'signs' of God which point to him who is at work in everything until the whole world is terrified at his effective power, seeing that he is God who, 'terrible when he saves,' causes men to draw nigh unto him from the remotest east and west—until they pay homage to him as the One who accomplishes the salvation of the world. Here, like a bird mightily spreading its wings, belief in God embraces the beginning, the middle and the end of all earthly happenings and interprets them in the light of their divine purpose as God's dealing with mankind by way of the *Heilsgeschichte*, the aim of which is God's rule over the world; and the festival congregation experience this *Heilsgeschichte* as the present reality of God which they now worship and extol in their hymn.

Thanksgiving for the blessing of fertility during the past year (vv. 9–13)

It is only at this point, after a foundation has been laid which is both deep (vv. 3 f.) and vast (vv. 5 f., 8), that the thanksgiving arises for the blessing of fruitful growth which constitutes the external motive of the psalm's composition. It is by no means a matter of indifference from which viewpoint the thanksgiving for the divine help is here framed. The psalmist regards even help in human affairs as being only a particular case of the universal divine salvation; he understands this particular case and wants it to be understood in the light of the wider setting of God's whole saving purpose for mankind. **[9–11]** It is only now that the poet concentrates all his thoughts on depicting the blessing which the congregation prepares itself to praise in the Temple in a song. The deeply felt lyrical portrayal of the divine blessing which spreads over fields and meadows expresses the poet's abandonment to a feeling of warm gratitude to and jubilant joy in God, who has given a fresh sign of his grace by the growth in the sprouting fields. Unrestrainedly the psalmist describes in great detail how by precious showers God has 'prepared the land' for the future harvest. The parched land was watered by the 'river of God' dispensing an abundance of plentiful rain; the hard clods, softened by the water, have sunk so that the soil has again become even. The new seed, sown just before the rain started, begins to sprout from that soil, a distinct sign of the divine blessing. Inspired by joy and gratitude the poet's vivid imagination animates Nature by personifying it. He pictures to himself the year that had thus been blessed by God as a queen, 'crowned' by God himself with divine jewels and bounty. Wherever one follows God's 'tracks', there fruitful growth bears witness to the course which his blessing has taken; at the back of the poet's mind seems to be here the common idea that God drives over the earth in a chariot of clouds. [12-13] This thought is expressed in a graphic picture characteristic of the oriental way of thinking: God's tracks drip with fatness. In his concluding account of the abundance of blessings and of man's joy in living the psalmist is able to find the most exquisite tones, showing the poet's gift of sympathetic understanding and effective representation. The barren steppe has been transformed into green pastures; the bare hills are pictured by the poet as living creatures who 'gird themselves with joy'; the flocks on the green pastures seem to him to be like a festive garment adorning the meadows. The valleys with their rolling cornfields are wrapped in a fresh green garb. Nature awakened to new life is filled with ringing and singing. The poet's ear hears the hidden tones of the spring symphony woven from the delight in spring and joy in living, a song of praise which has a quality of its own, praising the divine Creator and Lord. For the poet this praise of the divine Lord likewise becomes a part of the praise of the grace of God to which his song is dedicated. The same goodness of God is in question whether he confers earthly blessings or forgives human sin, whether he favours the godly with the communion of his presence in the house of God or makes the nations to testify to his glory. The psalm's strong and beautiful harmony has its source in that inward union with God which is the most precious fruit of the liturgical celebration.

66. SHOUT FOR JOY UNTO GOD, ALL THE EARTH!

To the Conductor. A Song. A Psalm[1]

1 Shout for joy unto God, all the earth!
2 Sing praises to the glory of his name;
   give to him glorious praise!
3 Say to God, 'How wonderful[2] are thy deeds!
   So great is thy power that even thy enemies
   must pay homage to thee.[3]
4 Let all the earth worship thee;
   they shall[4] sing praises to thee,
   sing praises to thy name.' *Selah*
5 Come and see what God has done:
   he is terrible in his deeds among men,
6 who[5] turned[5] the sea into dry land,
   that men passed through the river on foot;
   there we will rejoice in him.[6]
7 He who rules by his might for ever,
   his eyes keep watch on the nations.
   The rebellious cannot rise against him.[6] *Selah*
8 Bless our God, O ye peoples,
   let the sound of his praise be heard,
9 who has given a place to our soul in life,
   and has not let our feet slip.
10 For thou, O God, hast tested us;
    thou hast tried us as silver is tried.
11 Thou didst bring us into prison[5]
    and didst lay oppression[7] on our loins.[8]
12 Thou didst let men ride over our heads;
    through fire and through water had we to go;
    yet thou hast brought us forth to freedom.[9]
13 I will come into thy house with offerings;
    I will pay thee my vows,
14 that which my lips uttered
    and my mouth promised when I was in trouble.
15 I will offer to thee burnt offerings of fatlings,
    with the incense of the sacrifice of rams;
    I will make an offering of bulls and goats. *Selah*
16 Come and hear, all you who fear God,
    and I will tell what he has done for my soul.[10]
17 I cried aloud to him with my mouth,
    and high praise was under my tongue.[11]
18 If I had cherished iniquity in my heart,
    the Lord would not have listened.
19 But truly God has listened;
    he has given heed to the voice of my prayer.
20 Blessed be God because he has not rejected my prayer
    or removed his grace[12] from me!

[1] It is beyond our knowledge what musical distinction was implied in the terms 'song' and 'psalm' used here.

[2] Lit.: terrible. (Tr. N.: so RSV.)

[3] * RSV has 'that thy enemies cringe before thee'.

[4] * RSV uses the present tense.

[5] See BH.

[6] * RSV has 'There did we rejoice in him', and continues:
who rules by his might for ever,
whose eyes keep watch on the nations—
let not the rebellious exalt themselves.

[7] The meaning is doubtful.

[8] * RSV has:
Thou didst bring us into the net;
thou didst lay affliction on our loins;

[9] See BH. (Tr. N.: RSV has 'to a spacious place' instead of 'to freedom'.)

[10] * RSV has 'for me' instead of 'for my soul'.

[11] * V. 17b is in RSV, 'and he was extolled with my tongue'.

[12] * RSV has 'steadfast love' instead of 'grace'.

The psalm, on which the hymn 'Jauchzt, alle Lande, Gott zu Ehren'[1] is based, consists of two parts: in vv. 1–12 we are presented with a festal liturgy of the congregation who in hymnic style extol the majesty (*kābōd*) of God which has been manifested in his 'everlasting rule' (v. 7) and miraculous saving deeds (vv. 3, 8–12); vv. 13–20, on the other hand, contain the thanksgiving of an individual who desires to offer in the Temple the promised votive offerings (vv. 13–15) and 'tells' the congregation how his prayer was answered (vv. 16 ff.). These two parts must not be separated from each other (this point in opposition to Briggs, Duhm and others); otherwise the first part would be left without any conclusion and the second without any introduction. They belong together not only from a literary point of view but also as to the occasion on which they came to be recited. The vast majority of the more recent expositors hold the view that the author has prefaced his private thanksgiving with an earlier choral liturgy and has done so for the exclusive purpose of providing a 'splendid' introduction, so that he might be able to give adequate expression to his exuberant feelings. However, that view cannot be regarded as satisfactory. Rather, the exposition of the psalm must begin with the cult of the common annual festival of Yahweh, from whose liturgy the first part of the psalm is borrowed and which forms the framework within which the worshippers' votive offerings (cf. I Sam. 1.21; 2.1 ff.) were offered and the personal thanksgivings

[1] * By Matthias Jorissen (1739–1823).

were recited. But the essential connection of the two parts of the psalm lies not only in the fact that they are ingredients of one and the same cultic ceremony, but in the further fact that the individual worshipper lets his individual cause, for which he owes personal thanks to God, be enlightened by the universal thoughts on salvation which form the heart of the common cultic feast. The voice of the individual worshipper thus joins the great chorus of the cult community assembled for the celebration: what the worshipper has experienced (vv. 13–20) is nothing but a piece of that *Heilsgeschichte*, wrought by God on behalf of his people, the realization of which the cult community continually experiences during the regular performance of the ritual of the festival cult and to which it bears witness in its hymnic testimony to God's 'glory' (vv. 1–12). Only this theological focus in communal worship can account for the outward and inward unity of the psalm's two parts, which at first sight seem quite dissimilar (see Intr. 83 f.).

[1–4] The whole first part of the psalm is a reflection on what the congregation has experienced in the festival cult. Thunderous shouts of joy and enthusiastic songs of praise are to be offered to God, thus giving him back again the 'glory' and the 'praise' (both these thoughts are implied in the twice-mentioned *kābōd*) with which, in his appearance before the congregation, he fills the whole earth (cf. the account of the theophany in Isa. 6.3; Hab. 3.3). The whole world worships God, trembling at his august presence (v. 4),[1] and even his enemies cannot help admitting, against their own will, the abundance of his power. There is nothing that can escape the reach of God's activity. [5–7] In the eyes of his people, however, God is not an impenetrable and ineffable mystery before which they bow down to the dust, overwhelmed by mystical emotions; for he has proclaimed his name before them and has revealed himself to them by his 'terrible deeds', that is to say, by his miraculous redemptive work which they are allowed to 'see' with their own eyes, so that being witnesses of 'what God has done among men' (v. 5), they can testify on their part to the 'everlasting rule of his might' (vv. 3, 7). The phrase 'see' indicates in the context in which it is used the dramatic character of the cultic representation of the *Heilsgeschichte* (cf. Pss. 46.8; 48.8; see Intr. 42 f.). The witness which the members of the cult community are able to bear is based on the fact that they experience

---

[1] Notice the transition from the hymnic call (vv. 1–3a) to the invocation of God in the form of prayer (vv. 3b–4).

God's redemptive work at first hand, that is to say, in their own person and as an immediately present event, by means of the cultic representation of the *Heilsgeschichte*. In v. 6 the miracles of the deliverance of the people of Israel at the Red Sea (Ex. 14.21; 15.19) and of the passing over the River Jordan (cf. Josh. ch. 3), which form an essential part of the *Heilsgeschichte*, are once more particularly emphasized as the foundation-pillars of the traditions of the Exodus and the Conquest. The psalm therefore presents itself as the response of the cult community to the recital of the *Heilsgeschichte* tradition which has taken place in a previous cultic act; this act was understood as a present action of God directed towards the members of the cult community themselves and causing all historical differences of space and time to disappear in face of the reality of God, so that participants in the cult, in facing God, faced the same situation in which the people of God had once found themselves at the time of the Exodus and their entry into the Promised Land. In this way the biddings in vv. 3 and 5 are easily accounted for, and so, above all, is the wording of v. 6c: '*there* we will rejoice in him'. In the cultic representation the 'there' and the 'once' of history becomes the 'now' and the 'here' of the *Heilsgeschichte*; it becomes the eternal presence of the rule of God which is the true object of the cultic ceremony and of the hymnic praise of the tribes of the covenant people (see Intr. 42 ff.). **[8]** Whereas v. 7 speaks of God's power over the non-Israelite nations (*gōyīm*), v. 8 takes its stand on the basis of the covenant community, composed of the individual tribes (*'ammīm*), and forms the transition to a serious reflection on the *Heilsgeschichte* which God has wrought in the midst of his people **[9–12]**; this meditation is so much the more important since, with its hymnic form, it serves the praise of God. The way to salvation, along which God leads his people to freedom (v. 12), is by no means the *via triumphalis* of a man who, sustained by the happiness he enjoys on earth and by the applause of his fellow men, proudly takes comfort in his own successes; it is, on the contrary, the *via crucis* that leads man through temptations, through prison and oppression, through humiliations and defeats, through all sorts of mortal dangers ('fire and water' in v. 12 are probably to be understood in this general sense; cf. Isa. 43.2) and through human failure and despair. This is what the 'life' really looks like in which God 'has given a place' to his people (v. 9). It is the same viewpoint as the one which determined the compilation of the ancient historical traditions of the Pentateuch:

the history of God's dealing with his people is at the same time the history of his judgments (see Intr. 46 ff., 75 ff.); these bring to light human sin so that the bearers of the promise might be delivered and purged from it (v. 10) and that the reality of God's exclusive power and the seriousness of his demands upon man and of his promised grace might thus be made manifest in them. It is precisely because the history of suffering is the history of God's hidden grace which leads to salvation that this deadly serious meditation on the way of the cross of the people of God is fully justified in its prominent place in the jubilant praise of God.

[13–20] Seen in the light of this train of thought the individual's prayer of thanksgiving (vv. 13–20) readily fits in with the vast scene which has been laid by the festival liturgy of the cult community. The personal fate of the worshipper, which he now recalls with gratitude, has also been such a way of the cross by which God had disciplined him (v. 18) and led him out of his trouble (v. 14) to freedom—so that he is able to offer at the feast the promised votive thank-offerings (vv. 13–15) and to join in the chorus of the festival congregation by singing his own hymn (v. 20), which he had once vowed as he passed through evil days (v. 17). And when he bids his fellow believers (= 'you who fear God'; see v. 16) hear what God has done for him, then this 'narration' (see Intr. 83 f.) is likewise meant to form a part of the glorification of God's saving deeds in the presence of the congregation, which forms the purpose and theme of the cultic ceremony. The individual, too, has a divine *Heilsgeschichte* of his own; and the conclusions which the worshipper draws from the experience of his own heart and to which he bears witness—it is characteristic that the emphasis is on the decisive *act of God* and not on the details of the human 'experience' which might satisfy a biographical or psychological interest!—become in this way a living source from which the faith of the cult community derives new strength and joy. In his account of the way in which his prayer has been answered the worshipper stresses the sincerity of his heart (v. 18) and his firm trust in the grace of God which had sustained his petitions in time of trouble and had put in his mouth even then praise for the assurance given him that his prayer would be granted (v. 17b). That attitude of mind, however, must not be interpreted as a boasting of the merit of his prayers; on the contrary, within the context of the whole psalm it is to be judged as an affirmation of faithfulness and as a grateful reference to the way of discipline and

purification along which God led him (cf. v. 10), so that his prayer
was preserved from wicked doubts and secondary aims which would
have precluded its having any hearing. The ability to pray with a
pure heart, that can wholly rely on God, is itself a gift of his grace
and carries with it the promise that the prayer will be answered.

67. THE BLESSINGS IMPARTED BY GOD

To the Conductor. With stringed instruments. A Psalm. A Song[1]

1 May God be gracious to us and bless us
   and make his face to shine upon us, *Selah*
2 that thy way may be known upon earth,
   thy saving power among all nations!
3 *Let the peoples praise thee, O God;*
   let all the peoples praise thee!
4 Let the nations be glad and sing for joy,
   for thou dost judge the peoples with equity,
   and it is thou who guidest the nations upon earth! *Selah*
5 *Let the peoples praise thee, O God;*
   let all the peoples praise thee!
6 The earth has yielded its increase;
   God, our God, has blessed us.
7 May God bless us![2]
   Let all the ends of the earth fear him!

[1] See Ps. 66, note 1.
[2] * RSV has 'God has blessed us'.

Verse 6 indicates the specific occasion to which this psalm (which
has found an echo in a hymn of Luther's)[1] owes its existence: the
earth has yielded its increase; the harvest has been gathered. It
therefore seems to have been sung at the harvest-thanksgiving
festival. Judging from its form it is a community thanksgiving, a piece
of the festival liturgy recited during the autumn festival and perhaps
sung antiphonally by choirs. This view is also suggested by the link
with the liturgical Aaronite blessing (Num. 6.24 ff.) with which the
psalm opens; it is connected with the Sinai theophany to which the
Aaronite blessing in its turn refers back and which also had its place
in the cultic tradition of the Yahweh festival. For the psalm also
presupposes such a coming of God to his people (v. 1), and its train
of thought is to be understood in the light of that background of the
theology of the cult (see Intr. 28 f., 38 ff., 83 f.). Consequently the
psalm is to be classed with Psalm 65, with which it shows a certain

[1] * 'Es wolle Gott uns gnädig sein und seinen Segen geben'.

affinity, not only with regard to origins. Though we have every reason to assume that in view of the rural way of life of Palestine the harvest festivals played an important part also in the religious life of the people of Israel, it is nevertheless a striking fact that so little evidence of cultic piety linked to Nature has been handed down in the Psalter. The cause of this remarkable phenomenon, which has impressed its specific character on the present psalm, too, is to be found in the fact that the peculiarity of Old Testament belief in God, also discernible in the cultic tradition of the psalms, is derived from the idea that God is he who directs and shapes *history*; in consequence, the aspect of Nature which had been borrowed from the sphere of the Canaanite religion of agriculture, originally alien to the cult of the Covenant, was not allowed to make itself fully felt (see Intr. 25 ff.). For, strange to say, the widely ranging aspirations of the psalm do not take as their point of departure, as might be expected, the thanksgiving for the blessing of the harvest, but the blessing which ensues from God's presence in the midst of his people; at once they proceed to the fundamental idea of the psalm, that is, the revelation and recognition of the divine salvation granted to all the nations. In that thought-sequence the harvest-thanksgiving is entirely over-shadowed by this bold cultic, eschatological vision. The refrain, too (vv. 3, 5), which was probably sung by the congregation or by the choir, lays particular stress upon that fundamental idea.

What here leaps to the eye is the peculiarity of the biblical way of thinking which is at variance with the natural religion of the land of Canaan (which, as the polemics of the prophets show, had also penetrated the sphere of Israelite worship): the point of departure and the goal of the cultic ceremony is not the safeguarding of the natural means of existence required for the preservation of human life, but the revelation of God. It is true that the Old Testament cult community also gives thanks to its Creator and Preserver for the blessings of the fruits of the earth and knows how to express its appreciation of the value of the promise which God has attached to the ordinances governing natural life (Gen. 8.22); but the Old Testament relation between God and man does not merely consist in these blessings. In the Pentateuch tradition the reorganization of Nature in the covenant made by God with mankind after the Flood is set forth *before* the special history of God's redemptive work which begins with the Patriarchs is dealt with; similarly the realm of the ordinances governing natural life is the presupposition of God's

Heilsgeschichte, its basis from which it presses on to its own specific goal. It is not man and the satisfaction of the necessities of life which is at the vanishing-point of this *Heilsgeschichte*, but God and the recognition of the course he takes through history, accomplishing his redemptive work with gracious guidance and righteous judgments (vv. 2, 4). The Copernican perception with which the Old Testament opposes every kind of natural religion and every attempt to look at life from the anthropocentric point of view is the inexhaustible truth that God and not man is at the heart and is the goal of everything that comes to pass—and the theocentric conclusion to be drawn therefrom, that the purpose of all public worship is the manifestation and realization of God's will to save. In such a context the blessing of the harvest from the earth is no longer a cultic end in itself, as it is in the fertility-rites of the natural religion; it is no longer a kind of divine echo of human desires, but it is just the opposite— it is the guarantee of the grace of God and of the free testimony of the Lord of the harvest to his own Person which in virtue of the parabolic character of all earthly things points to the final harvest that will take place at the consummation of the Kingdom of God (Matt. 9.37; John 4.35 ff.) when all the ends of the earth will fear God and all the nations will praise him in response to the revelation of *his* salvation (vv. 7, 3). The high flight of the psalmist's thoughts and their spiritualized profundity have found a worthy Christian echo in Luther's hymn already mentioned.

[1] The linking up of the opening verse of the psalm with the Aaronite blessing makes the thought of the material blessing of the gifts of Nature appear insignificant in comparison with the desire to become assured of God himself, of his grace and lovingkindness. And as regards the earthly blessings it is ultimately a matter of the living relationship with God himself as the true and supreme good with which man is supplied in and through the gifts for his bodily needs. In the first place this encounter with the living God, with the assurance it gives of his grace and lovingkindness towards men, transforms earthly good fortune into a blessing that in gratitude to God and joy in him is of inner and spiritual value. [2] That this interpretation is correct is confirmed by what follows. Here the purpose of the divine blessing is seen to be not so much the preservation of material human existence by the gratification of the bodily necessities of life, but rather the knowledge of God, of the course he takes in the history of the nations and of his plan of salvation for the

whole world. Throughout this section thoughts are turned away from
the gift and directed to the Giver; to God himself who bestows the
blessing, and this is done by means of a striking change of style to an
address in the form of prayer, itself to be regarded as an indication
of the psalmist's direct turning to God who is thought to be present.
And the tones of a hymn, which the psalmist employs, are an expression of the deep emotion which this point of view, directed to God
himself, is able to arouse. In this way not only are the chains burst
which fetter a way of thinking that is primitive and sensual and
dependent on material things, but the national barriers set up by
religion are lifted so that the faithful are set free to take fresh thought
and perceive in the light of their common bond with the Creator of
the world and the Lord of their history the universal purpose of God
to save all nations, and through their joint praises and thanksgiving
to unite in a great congregation of those who are blessed by God.
The psalm is an impressive example of how the great religious ideas
about God are rooted in the cultus, and of how they have made the
cultus the centre of a religion provided with a new horizon that
embraces the whole world, and moreover have led to a deepening
and spiritualization of piety. And, to be sure, what is here implied is
not only the idea that the blessing bestowed upon the people of
Israel shall become an indication to the other nations of the goodness
and grace of God (cf. in this connection Isa. 45.23; 55.8). God's way
'upon earth' also embraces the destinies of the foreign nations
themselves in and through which God's providential rule is made
manifest, the final goal cf which is the salvation of the whole world
(see also the comments on v. 4). Particular happenings, whether
natural blessings or divine guidance granted in the events of history,
are the footprints of God on his way through the world; they are the
guarantee of the materialization of his plan of salvation that comprises the whole wide world of nations (see Intr. 37, 50). [3] Inspired
by such immensity of the divine salvation the psalmist bids the whole
world of nations testify to God by singing his praise and, in doing so,
he links together in a common bond the cult community of Israel
and the nations beyond her frontiers. To come before God and really
to encounter him means to praise him with thanksgiving; for God is
the one who is always the first to give, who gives his own self in his
goodness and therefore lays men under an obligation to himself.
And, on the other hand, in giving thanks to God all men meet in
a great congregation united by their common obligation to God as

the Giver. Here lies the decisive point of the psalm, as is already
shown by the fact that this thought is repeated in v. 5 in the form of
a refrain. That God is given the praise which is due to him as God is
the true purpose which unites the assembly in Israel celebrating the
feast with the nations of the world in a single worshipping congregation. [4] The thanksgiving leads to joy in God. And the nations are
to give outward expression to it by shouting for joy in a hymn. They
are to rejoice in God's righteous judgments and in his guidance
which they have been privileged to experience in their own lives.
The verse makes clear that we usually interpret the idea of God's
judgment in too narrow a sense. *Joy* in God's judgment is possible
only if the ultimate and decisive factor in that joy is not the fear of
whether we ourselves shall be able to stand the test in the sight of the
righteous God—that is, not an egocentric motive—but the theocentric idea that in God's judgment *his* 'righteousness' will be made
manifest as the law and order which he has ordained for the world;
that in that judgment his 'righteousness' will be shown to be the
divine fulfilment of the purpose of history, the final goal of which is
the salvation of the world. The judgment of God as here understood
is the divine order of salvation on which one can build and in which
one can trust. This is why it is the source of genuine joy in God.

[5-6] At the beginning of the second main section of the psalm
another call to praise God rings out in the form of a refrain, echoing
far and wide. The verse here serves as a transition to the subsequent
reference to the blessing of the harvest, and, in this context, acts at
the same time as a mighty protective dike intended to preserve man,
by its exhortation to thank God, from the danger that lies dormant
in all earthly good fortune, the danger that man is prone to be
absorbed in the enjoyment of earthly pleasures and, in doing so, to
neglect the blessing which God has attached to the good things of the
earth. For these do not become a blessing unless to joy is added
humility, to enjoyment thanksgiving, to the earthly blessing the
personal, spiritual and religious value which in praise of God
establishes a living link with him. It is only by turning to God in
gratitude that man is preserved from getting stuck in earthly things,
because he thus comes to realize that God desires to give greater
things in and by means of the temporal blessings, means to give his
blessing conferred in his salvation. Thus the psalm visualizes the
harvest-thanksgiving in such a way that it looks beyond the increase
of the earth to the greater blessing which God grants in the execution

and consummation of his redemptive work. The temporal things become the promise of the things that are eternal. [7] And the thanksgiving issues in the hope of salvation. It is therefore quite natural that the psalm at its conclusion reverts to the thought expressed at its beginning and ends in a prayer that God may grant his blessing in the future. The blessing of God works gratitude, but it also works fear of God. It is characteristic of the Old Testament idea of the grace and lovingkindness of God that the psalmist is able to establish such a close connection of thought between the petition for God's blessing and the call upon the ends of the earth to fear God. In the lovingkindness of God the majesty and the sovereignty of God are revealed in all their fullness; his grace and his blessing are something which in the eyes of man are incomprehensibly sublime and inconceivably powerful so that he is forced to his knees to worship with fear and trembling (cf. in this connection Ps. 130.4). In the Old Testament the grace of God, and so also man's gratitude to God and his joy in him, are regarded as a thoroughly serious matter and have nothing whatsoever in common with the reducing and softening which these notions have suffered in the sultry atmosphere of the mysticism of later times. And this very psalm is a typical example of how the austere feature of the Old Testament belief in the majesty of the holy God draws piety out of the temporal, the sensual and the materialistic, and thus out of the narrowness of earthly limitations, and lifts it up to the higher level of the eternal, the spiritual and the religious, to a vision of universal range and great power which, looking at all things and all events with the eyes of God, sees them as a unity; it places man's piety in the light of the inscrutable greatness of the consummation of the divine salvation.

68. THE ADVENT OF GOD

To the Conductor. Of David. A Psalm. A Song[1]

1 God arises; his enemies are scattered;
  those who hate him, flee before him.[2]
2 As the smoke drifts away,[3] so thou drivest (them) away;
  as wax melts before fire,
  so the wicked perish before the face of God.
3 But the righteous are joyful;
  they exult before God and are jubilant with joy.
4 Sing to God; make melody to his name;
  praise[4] him who rides upon the clouds!
  Yah is his name; exult before him![5]

5 Father of the fatherless and protector of widows
is God in his holy habitation.
6 God leads[3] the lonely home;
he leads out the prisoners to prosperity;[6]
but the rebellious were left in the wilderness.[7]
7 O God, when thou didst go forth before thy people,
when thou didst march through the wilderness, *Selah*
8 the earth quaked, the heavens poured down rain,
at the presence of God, the Lord of Sinai,
at the presence of God, the God of Israel.[8]
9 Rain in abundance, O God, thou dost shed upon thy heritage,
and, what had languished, that hast restored.[9]
10 Thy flock found a dwelling in it,
in thy goodness, O God, thou dost prepare it for the afflicted.[10]
11 The Lord gives utterance with a loud voice;
great is the host of the maidens who bring glad tidings.[11]
12 The kings of the armies flee, they flee,
and the women at home divide the spoil.[12]
13 Do you want to camp among the sheepfolds?
The wings of a dove covered with silver
and its pinions with green gold,[13]
14 when the Almighty scattered kings therein,
thou causest snow to fall on Zalmon.[14]
15 A mountain of God is the mountain of Bashan;
the mountain-range of Bashan is full of peaks.[15]
16 Why look you with envy, O you many-peaked mountains,
at the mount which God desired for his abode?
Yea, the Lord will dwell there for ever.[16]
17 The chariot of the Lord are the ten thousands,
the roaring voices[17] of the thousands upon thousands;
the Lord is with them, Sinai is in the holy place.[18]
18 Thou art gone up on high,
hast made prisoners and received gifts from men,
even from the rebellious, to be enthroned as Yah God.[19]
19 Blessed be the Lord day by day
who bears us up;[20] God is our salvation. *Selah*
20 Our God is a God who helps us;
Yahweh, the Lord, can also save from death.[21]
21 Verily, God will shatter the heads of his enemies,
the hairy crown of him who walks in his sins.
22 The Lord said, 'I return[22] from Bashan,
I return[22] from the depths of the sea[23]
23 that you may bathe[3] your feet in blood,
that the tongues of the dogs may have their
portion from the foe.'
24 They saw thee enter in procession, O God,
the advent of my King and God at the temple.
25 The singers walked in front, the players of stringed music followed,

surrounded by maidens beating the timbrels.[24]

26 To God, the Lord, give praise with your choirs,
O you who are of Israel's congregation,
attending the feast.[25]

27 There is Benjamin, the youngest[26] of them, in the lead,[3]
the princes of Judah in their throng,
the princes of Zebulun, the princes of Naphtali.

28 Summon thy might, O God;[3]
the might of God[27] which thou hast prepared for us,[28]

29 from thy temple above Jerusalem![29]

30 Rebuke the beast that dwells among the reeds,
the assembly of the mighty, the rulers[3] of the nations. . . .[30]
Scatter the peoples who delight in war!

29b Kings bear gifts to thee.[31]

31 The noblemen come to thee from out of Egypt;
Kush hastens to come before God with hands full of gifts.[32]

32 Sing praises to God, O you kingdoms of the earth,
strike up music[33] to the Lord, *Selah*

33 to him who rides in the heavens,[3] the ancient heavens!
Lo, he sends forth his voice, his mighty voice.

34 Ascribe power to God, whose majesty is over Israel,
and his power is in the clouds.

35 Terrible is God as he reigns from his[3] sanctuary,[34]
the God of Israel, he gives power and strength to his people.
Blessed be God!

[1] See Ps. 66, note 1.
[2] * RSV uses the imperative throughout vv. 1–3.
[3] See BH.
[4] In accordance with T and S.
[5] * V. 4 reads in RSV:
Sing to God, sing praises to his name;
lift up a song to him who rides upon the clouds;
his name is the Lord, exult before him!
[6] The translation of this passage is doubtful; after the example of the Ugaritic *kṯrt*, v. 6 is perhaps to be translated 'accompanied by songs of rejoicing'; cf. Gordon, *Ugaritic Manual* 20/989.
[7] * RSV begins v. 6 with 'God gives the desolate a home to dwell in' and ends 'but the rebellious dwell in a parched land'.
[8] * V. 8bc reads in RSV:
at the presence of God;
yon Sinai quaked at the presence of God,
the God of Israel.
[9] * RSV has:
Rain in abundance, O God, thou didst shed abroad;
thou didst restore thy heritage as it languished . . .
[10] * RSV has 'thou didst provide for the needy' instead of 'thou dost prepare it for the afflicted'.
[11] * V. 11 is in RSV:
The Lord gives the command;
great is the host of those who bore the tidings:

12 * RSV puts v. 12a in quotation marks as being the 'tidings' of v. 11.

13 * RSV treats v. 13a as a continuation of v. 12b, 'though they stay among the sheepfolds', and v. 13b is in apposition to the spoil which the women divide.

14 Translation doubtful. (Tr. N.: In RSV v. 14 is treated as a new sentence, 'When the Almighty scattered kings there, snow fell on Zalmon.')

15 * In RSV v. 15 is an invocation, preceding the question of v. 16:
O mighty mountain, mountain of Bashan;
O many-peaked mountain,
mountain of Bashan!

16 * In RSV the last line continues the question of the first two lines: 'yea, where the Lord will dwell for ever?'

17 Read šā'ōn; the term šimyan = 'duplication' in the sense of 'thousands and thousands' is also to be considered (Mowinckel). (Tr. N.: The German original reads die Tausendschaften des Brausens: lit. the thousands upon thousands who are roaring.)

18 * RSV has:
With mighty chariotry, twice ten thousand,
thousands upon thousands,
the Lord came from Sinai into the holy place.

19 * RSV has:
Thou didst ascend the high mount,
leading captives in thy train,
and receiving gifts among men,
even among the rebellious, that the Lord God may dwell there.

20 Lit.: who bears a burden in our stead. (Tr. N.: RSV has 'Blessed be the Lord, who daily bears us up'.)

21 * RSV has:
Our God is a God of salvation;
and to God, the Lord, belongs escape from death.

22 Read 'āšūb.

23 * RSV has:
The Lord said, 'I will bring them back from Bashan,
I will bring them back from the depths of the sea,

24 * RSV gives vv. 24 f. as:
Thy solemn processions are seen, O God,
the processions of my God, my King,
into the sanctuary—
the singers in front, the minstrels last,
between them maidens playing timbrels:

25 See BH. (Tr. N.: RSV gives v. 26 as:
'Bless God in the great congregation,
the Lord, O you who are of Israel's fountain!')

26 * RSV has 'least' for 'youngest'.

27 Read ʿoz hā' ᵉlohīm.

28 * V. 28b in RSV is 'show thy strength, O God, thou who hast wrought for us'.

29 * In RSV v. 29, here divided, forms a complete sentence:
Because of thy temple at Jerusalem,
kings bear gifts to thee.

30 The text is corrupt; perhaps, 'that they submit, offering pieces of silver'. (Tr. N.: In RSV v. 30bc reads:
the herd of bulls with the calves of the people.
Trample underfoot those who lust after tribute;

scatter the peoples who delight in war.)
[31] According to its subject-matter the half-verse belongs to v. 31.
[32] * RSV of v. 31 is:
Let bronze be brought from Egypt;
let Ethiopia hasten to stretch out her hands to God.
[33] * RSV has 'sing praises' instead of 'strike up music'.
[34] * RSV has 'in his sanctuary' for 'as he reigns from his sanctuary'.

In no other psalm are the various attempts at interpretation so
diverse as in Psalm 68. It is not only that the severely corrupted text
and the wilful and often disconnected style offer great difficulties to
the exposition of the psalm. The style in particular moves to and
fro, alternating between the forms of speech and those of narration,
between description, prayer and hymnic portions, and between the
various verbal tenses. It has therefore been possible to advocate and
dispute with equal emphasis both the 'historical' interpretation of
the psalm as a song of victory and the 'eschatological' interpretation
which seeks to understand the whole psalm as a document expressing
man's hopes for the future when the end of time will have come.
These difficulties are moreover increased by the lack of a coherent
and progressive train of thought and by a series of brief allusions,
mostly couched in general terms, to incidents which evade any
attempt on our part to relate them accurately to historical facts
known to us, and finally by reminiscences of other Old Testament
traditions (above all Num. 10.35 f.; Judg. 5; Deut. 33; Hab. 3).
Hence some commentators are inclined to regard the psalm as an
anthology of quotations or as a collection of particular songs (or,
more precisely, of the opening lines).[1] However, it is hardly possible
to approach the fundamental problem of the psalm by assuming the
psalmist's purely literary dependence on the literature which he is
alleged to have quoted in the interest of educated readers so as to
provide them with some sort of 'learned' adornment of his poem; for
such a way of thinking is more familiar to the world of modern
scholarship than to that of the psalms. Though with regard to many
details the exposition will not be able to go beyond tentative and
questionable attempts, a firm point of departure can nevertheless be
established which throws a clarifying light on the situation as a

[1] Thus H. Schmidt and Albright, *HUCA* 23, 1950/51, pp. 1 ff.; this thesis is,
however, opposed by Mowinckel, *Der achtundsechzigste Psalm, Avhandlinger utgitt av
det Norske Videnskaps-Akademi i Oslo, II. Hist.-Filos. Klasse* (1953) No. 1, and Johnson,
Sacred Kingship in Ancient Israel, pp. 68 ff.

P.–Q

whole, within the scope of which the seemingly *disjecta membra* of
the psalm have their common focal point and their coherence. The
repeated mention of the sanctuary of Jerusalem (especially in vv. 16,
29), the emphasis laid on particular tribes of the people of the
Covenant (v. 27), the mention of the choral singers and of the
players of stringed music (vv. 25 f.), the continually recurring
prayer style and the call upon the gathered cult community to sing
praises to Yahweh (v. 26) leave no doubt whatsoever that the psalm
presupposes a communal act of worship in the course of which it was
recited.[1] On the strength of vv. 24 and 9 we might think of the
Covenant Festival of Yahweh which was celebrated at the central
sanctuary in autumn as the main festival of the whole covenant
community. At the heart of that festival is the revelation of God who
according to ancient thought comes to his sanctuary from Mount
Sinai and by his presence 'actualizes' his redemptive work, that is to
say, he makes all the saving deeds to which the covenant people owe
their existence to become a present reality (see Intr. 28 f.).[2] The cult
community commemorates these saving deeds at the celebration in
such a way that the tradition of the *Heilsgeschichte* of the past becomes
for them a present saving action of God directly aimed at themselves; deeply moved and enraptured by the fact of God's nearness,
they experience the divine action and testify to it, praying that its
blessing may continue in the future. The striking change of the
tenses (something to which far too little attention is usually given) is
thus accounted for. In the psalm, too, the theophany of Yahweh in
the midst of his people presents the focal point which from beginning
to end holds together the different sections like a centripetal force
even where their mutual connection is not immediately apparent.
The reminiscences, already mentioned, of other sections of the Old
Testament tradition are therefore not to be accounted for as the
result of a literary dependence on the part of the psalmist, which in
the opinion of those who hold that view would justify the dating of
the psalm as late as the post-exilic era. They are on the contrary to
be regarded as having their origin in a common cultic tradition in
connection with which it is no longer possible to raise the question of

[1] The hymn 'Erhebet er sich, unser Gott' (by Matthias Jorissen, 1739–1823),
though using the psalm only selectively, seeks to imitate this aspect of its model.

[2] Mowinckel (op. cit.) also has in mind the cultic epiphany at the autumn
festival. Following H. Schmidt, he relates the theophany to a procession in which
the Ark was carried along. The psalm, however, does not contain any concrete
allusions to that effect.

dependence or priority in the way hitherto customary. This cultic
tradition is, at any rate, a very ancient one, and the way in which
it has been used in the psalm also supports the view that the psalm
dates from a very early period. And with this viewpoint there is an
explanation for the strange allusions, like sketches from pre-existing
models, to various incidents and traditions which form the background of the psalm and are taken for granted, but are frequently
quite obscure to us. This background, out of sight for us, is the sacral
act of salvation which in the presence of the festival congregation is
executed in a stylized pattern of sacred phrases and rites cast in a
fixed form by tradition; and the psalm refers to this, though mostly
only in brief hints (see Intr. 43). The psalm itself is therefore only a
reflex of the cultic drama of salvation of which it forms an intrinsic
part and without which it would remain a torso; and it is just as
little possible for us to achieve a full understanding of the psalm as
of the choruses of the ancient tragedies which, detached from their
original context, were recited in the time of the Roman emperors.

The difficulty which the exposition of the psalm has to face lies in
the fact that we do not know the whole liturgy of the festival cult and
are only able to establish some fragments of it with the aid of in-
ferences from this partial liturgical score—this may be the proper
way of classifying this psalm. At any rate, it is at least possible to
maintain that the psalm is the response of the cult community to the
revelation of God who during the cultic ceremony has drawn near
to them with his salvation. The advent of God in the light of the
history of his redemptive work as concentrated in the cultic act is
the proper theme of the psalm and sets the limits for its true understanding.

[1–3] At its very beginning the psalm speaks of the appearance of
God in the midst of his people and does so in the form of the ancient
cultic liturgy which has also been preserved in the so-called 'Lade-
sprüchen' (sayings associated with the sacred Ark; see Num. 10.35 f.),
although there admittedly in a context which is secondary and
also historicized. Originally it was probably here, as there, a matter
of God's epiphany as he comes to his sanctuary from Mount Sinai
and sits down upon the sacred Ark in the midst of his people in
order that he may take their future destiny into his own hands by
means of an act that will bring about their salvation. The statements
made here are not a promise (this point in opposition to Gunkel) but
a testimony to past events which are re-enacted in the cult and

experienced there as a present reality; for the presence of God is
assumed in the form of prayer to which the psalm turns in vv. 2, 4
and also in v. 5. The images employed in v. 2—Micah 1.4 proves
that the second one originates in the tradition of the theophany—
throw into bold relief the irresistible superiority of God, who controls
history. Where he appears, there men face selection and separation;
there they are confronted with a decision. In the presence of God
('before the face of God'), there is only an Either-Or between those
who are 'wicked' and those who are 'righteous'. For the former God's
presence means judgment and destruction; for the community of the
godly it means joy and salvation (cf. Judg. 5.31; see Intr. 31 ff., 64 f.).
In this twofold verdict prominence is given right at the beginning of
the psalm to its theme, God's activity in his redemptive work. And
in the middle portion of the psalm that divine saving activity is once
more the subject of the testimony of the whole cult community (vv.
19 ff.).

[4–6] The subsequent hymn is also linked to the tradition of the
theophany. The praise which the cult community is called upon to
sing (v. 4) is intended for the God who has appeared riding upon the
clouds[1] (cf. v. 34; Ex. 19.9 ff.; Ps. 18.9 ff.; Deut. 33.26; Isa. 19.1;
Ps. 104.3) and is thought to be present in the sanctuary, enthroned
upon the wings of the cherubim of the sacred Ark (v. 5). In Pss.
18.10; 99.1, too, the cherubim are associated with the theophany,
symbolizing the divine chariot of clouds. This cultic symbolism at
the same time accounts for the fact that the epiphany of God in the
heavens is frequently not distinguished from his appearance in the
sanctuary (cf. in this connection Ps. 11.4; Isa. 6; Deut. 26.15; Jer.
25.30 with vv. 5, 18, 33 ff.). In the cultic act the celestial world and
the terrestrial meet each other. The barriers of space and time are
insignificant in comparison with the presence of God to which every
cultic action is related (see Intr. 42 f.). In the ancient sacral traditions
of the *Heilsgeschichte* the appearance of God is associated with the
revelation of his name and his nature (cf. Ex. 3.14 f.; 33.19; 34.5 f.;
see Intr. 30 f.). That revelation is reflected in the hymn which in v. 4
employs the ancient liturgical form of God's name which is Yah
(cf. Ex. 15.3 and the term 'Hallelujah') and in vv. 5 f. stresses the

---

[1] The rendering of the MT 'through the wilderness' seems to have been influenced by v. 7 (cf. Isa. 40.3; 50.2). However, the MT does not need to be
corrected, since according to the Ras Shamra texts the same phrase is used of
Baal as 'he who rides upon the clouds'. Cf. Gordon, *Ugaritic Manual* 20/1451.

mercy shown by God to the afflicted as the main characteristic of the divine nature. It is not quite clear whether the statements made here, probably deliberately couched in general terms, have in mind the way in which God has led his people at the Exodus from Egypt and during their wilderness wanderings—v. 6b seems to refer to the death in the wilderness of the rebellious generation to whom, as to their leader Moses, entry into the Promised Land was denied. However, v. 5 leaves no doubt whatsoever that this tradition of the *Heilsgeschichte* had for the cult community assembled in the Temple the significance of an actual and present experience (see Intr. 36, 41 ff.). The wide scope of the Old Testament idea of God is shown by the fact that the mighty God, before whom his adversaries perish (vv. 1 f., 6b), is the merciful father of the helpless (cf. Hos. 11.1 ff.) and the compassionate helper of the oppressed. Here, too, as in the first section, history penetrates the present in simultaneous consolation and warning.

[7–10] The second section (vv. 7–10), which is entirely fashioned in the prayer style, also proceeds from the tradition of the theophany, as handed down in the opening lines of the Song of Deborah (cf., however, also Ex. 19.4, 18; Ps. 18.6 ff.; Deut. 33.2; Micah 1.2 ff.; Hab. 3.6 ff.; see Intr. 37 ff.), admittedly with striking modifications; whereas the parallel passage, Judg. 5.4 f., speaks of the God of Sinai who comes to his people as proceeding from Seir and Edom to Canaan, God is here said to go forth 'before his people', marching through the wilderness, and this statement is followed by an allusion to the conquest of the land. The common point of departure is the theophany, the liturgical form of which is firmly established and which in both cases indicates cultic origins. And the fact that its relationship to historical events is subject to modifications shows that we have here not the representation of historical incidents according to historical methods, but an attempt to grasp the divine background of history in the light of the *Heilsgeschichte*; it shows, too, that the transmission of the *Heilsgeschichte* has itself had its place in the cultus. In contradistinction to the discursive structure of the historical way of thinking, history as a whole is, from the perspective of the *Heilsgeschichte*, focused on the presence of God as experienced in the cultic act and is summarized in the 'here' and 'now' of a comprehensive event whose reality is of decisive significance. The adequate outward expression of this peculiar way of thinking in terms of the *Heilsgeschichte* is the form of prayer—together with the characteristic change of tense used here in this so-called historical retrospect for acts already completed and for acts still operative in the present, a retrospect which, after all, is in fact not a 'historical' retrospect but the hymnic response of the congregation to something they have directly experienced as a present reality (see Intr. 28 f., 44). Thus the rain, which once accompanied the coming of God in the clouds, is simultaneously the winter rain for which the congregation prays at the autumn festival, that it may fall upon the land of Canaan, the heritage of Yahweh; and the various ways in which God helped his people in their difficulties as they took possession of the land and settled in it are at the same time a demonstration of the goodness of God which prepares here and now a home for the present generation.

[11–13a] That Yahweh speaks with a loud voice is also a permanent feature of the tradition of the theophany (Ex. 19.16 ff.; Amos 1.2; Hos. 11.10 f.; Jer. 25.30; Joel 3.16; Ps. 18.13), so that the brief allusion of v. 11 is to be understood as reflecting the cultic epiphany. The 'Word of Yahweh', which he gives with a loud voice, is not contained in v. 12, interpreted by others as a 'song of victory'—this verse is not a song of victory nor would it be fitting to attribute such a song to Yahweh—but is the self-manifestation of God at his appearance. In this connection it is possible to assume that what the psalmist has in mind is God's voice sounding like thunder (Ps. 29.3), perhaps also the manifestation of his name Yah(u) (Ex. 33.19; 34.5 f.), which finds a joyous response in the jubilant acclamations of the heavenly hosts attendant on him (cf. Isa. 6.2 ff.). The phrases used in v. 11, deliberately confined to dark hints, seem to have been modelled on a cultic incident resembling the one which took place at Isaiah's vision (Isa. 6) at his call in the Temple of Jerusalem (see Intr. 41). Whereas the heavenly 'host', and with them the worshipping congregation, rejoice and welcome the advent of God with shouts of joy (cf. v. 4), the kings of the earthly 'armies' (note the striking antithesis) scatter, fleeing headlong from the terrifying majesty of the divine advent (cf. vv. 33 ff.).[1] As in Judg. 5, the psalm contains two pictures borrowed from the cultic tradition of the 'wars of Yahweh'; they present the beginning and the end of the collision of God's power with the earthly powers, namely the flight of the enemy and the dividing of the spoil after the homecoming of the

---

[1] It is also possible that v. 11b is to be connected with v. 12; in that case v. 12 would have to be understood as rendering the content of the 'glad tidings' (Mowinckel).

warriors. In these pictures history is condensed in the dramatically experienced present action which is still reflected in the reproachful question with its distinct admonition to all who are indifferent (v. 13a; cf. Judg. 5.16): when Yahweh appears and takes history into his hands, who could stand aloof and keep silent! **[13b–16]** It may perhaps also be possible to extract an understanding of the obscure verses 13b and 14 if we interpret them in the light of the theophany. Verse 14 obviously refers to a particular tradition, localized at Mount Zalmon, of a victory over native kings.[1] Judging from its context, one might think of the kings of the Amorites, Sihon of Heshbon and Og of Bashan (cf. Num. 21.21 ff., 32 ff.), who are more than once mentioned as typical examples in connection with the cultic tradition of the *Heilsgeschichte* (Pss. 135.11 f.; 136.17 ff.; cf. Deut. 2.24 ff.; 3.1 ff.). Their defeat is attributed to the God who caused snow to fall in the high mountains. In this connection the image of the wings of a dove covered with gleaming silver and gold could be a simile alluding to the cloud in which (*bāh*; see v. 14) Yahweh appeared on the battlefield and which lay on the mountain as the symbol of the divine presence—like a snowdrift glistening in the sunlight after a snowstorm. The possibility of such an interpretation from the theophany tradition may be suggested by the analogy to the Sinai theophany (Ex. 19.16) and the parallel to the golden wings of the cherubim upon the Ark, symbolizing the chariot of clouds in which God appears (Ex. 25.18, 22; Ezek. 1.4 ff.). Again, it may be that the name 'Shaddai',[2] used for God, conceals the name of the god whose abode is the 'mountain of the gods', and that this name, together with the local tradition, was only secondarily ascribed to Yahweh of Mount Zion who was worshipped in Jerusalem (cf. the comments on Ps. 48.2). It seems that this transaction, which belongs to the history of religion, lies behind vv. 15 f. and involved the taking over and adoption of an originally alien cultic tradition by the Yahweh cult, thus making evident the superiority and the power of absorption of Old Testament religion. In these verses the claims of the rival sanctuary in the north are disposed of with an almost mythological dramatic force in favour of those of Mount Zion and its Temple which God himself had chosen as his eternal dwelling-place. Here in the holy place, that is, where Yahweh

---

[1] In the context of this passage the site and name of the mountain are doubtful.

[2] The rendering of this name by 'the Almighty' dates back to the Septuagint, which itself was no longer acquainted with the original meaning of the name.

dwelt among his people and where the cult community is continually assured of his presence and rejoices in it, all the threads of God's *Heilsgeschichte* converge.

[**17–18**] This is immediately followed in vv. 17 f. by a testimony to God present in the sanctuary, who, surrounded by myriads of his heavenly hosts (cf. II Kings 6.16; see Intr. 29, 41 f.), has appeared in the Temple, rising in the sky (v. 18) in his chariot of cloud and accompanied by a jubilant roar from thousands of voices. Here, too, before the presence of God (see vv. 4 ff., 14) the barriers of space and time have disappeared so that even the very mountain of God is thought to be present in the Temple with the God of Sinai.

Hence, the brief allusions of the account given in v. 17 in the form of a hymn refer back once more to the traditional act of the theophany which preceded this testimony in the cultic ceremony (cf. Num. 10.35 f.; Ps. 18.10–14; Jer. 25.30 f.; Hab. 3.8–15).[1] Changing to the style of prayer, v. 18 alludes to the homage before God when, returning from a war, he has occupied his throne to receive the voluntary or enforced gifts of homage rendered to him.[2] [**19–23**] Without any awkwardness, this homage is followed in vv. 19 ff. by a hymn sung by the members of the congregation ('us') who regard God as their salvation, as the one who helps them in their struggle against death, enemies and sinners (cf. vv. 1 ff.). A divine utterance, which probably alludes to the cultic tradition of Yahweh's saving deeds at Bashan (see the comments on vv. 13 f.) and at the Red Sea (cf. Hab. 3.15),[3] and which with a bold stroke encompasses

---

[1] From Lev. 16.12 f. (cloud of smoke; cf. Isa. 6.4) and Ex. 19.16, 19; Isa. 30.29 ff.; Pss. 47.5; 98.6 (sound of trumpets) one can infer how concretely one must visualize the primitive drama, only hinted at, of that cultic act by which God's epiphany in the cloud was celebrated in the Temple to the accompaniment of a terrific din. Here one should remember that for man in antiquity very scanty intimations sufficed to call to his mind the whole familiar background of the cultic dramatic scene.

[2] The link with vv. 14 ff. would be shown as even clearer and closer if v. 18 could be read: *yāšabtā šadday lākaḥat* (instead of *šābītā šebī lākaḥtā*)—'thou didst occupy the seat on the throne, Sqaddai . . . to dwell there as Yah Elohim'.

[3] Gaster (*Thespis, Ritual, Myth and Drama in the Near East*, 1950, pp. 415 ff.) takes Ps. 68 to be the libretto of the pantomime performed at the Canaanite New Year Festival, which in his opinion was worked over for liturgical use in the Yahweh cult; he considers *basan* to be the designation of the dragon at the time of the chaos, corresponding to the Ugaritic *btn*, a designation which would fit in very well with the phrase 'the depths of the sea' in v. 22. The interpretation from Israelite tradition is, however, the more natural one in view of the whole tenor of the psalm. In *Thespis* (rev. ed., 1961), the text has been curtailed, and only brief reference is made to Ps. 68 on p. 451.

the whole tradition of the Exodus and the entry into Canaan by referring to the cruel custom of putting enemies to the ban, confirms God's 'homecoming' (cf. Num. 10.36) to his people and fortifies them in their assurance that God is in their midst.

[24–27] In vv. 24 ff. the cultic background of the psalm stands out quite clearly and unequivocally. Here those people are named who were privileged to be eyewitnesses of the divine advent and its manifestation of salvation in the sanctuary (cf. Hab. 3.6; Ps. 77.13). In a solemn procession, led by the choir of Temple singers and the band of musicians and accompanied by dancing maidens (cf. Ex. 15.20; II Sam. 6.14 ff.), they now appear before the festival congregation expectantly assembled in the forecourt of the Temple; the congregation is called upon to join with shouts of joy in the praise of God. We do not know why amongst the community of the confederacy of the Twelve Tribes only Benjamin and the princes of Judah, Zebulun and Naphtali, are specially singled out; it may be that they had been deemed worthy of receiving a special blessing at this feast (cf. in this connection Deut. 33),[1] or it is a question of the participation of particular tribes, resembling that of the Greek *phylae* to whom was assigned the duty of taking part with 'cyclical choruses' in the performance of dithyrambs at the great festivals.[2]

It is also possible that this singling out of particular tribes is connected with the incorporation of the cultic tradition of the northern tribes in the tradition of the Jerusalem sanctuary (see the comments on vv. 13b–16).[3] [28–31] Being assured of the presence of God and of his salvation, the cult community now turn their thoughts to the future and pray that God may summon his 'might', made manifest before them in the divine service by the tradition of the *Heilsgeschichte*, and may use it against the nations who, lusting after war, threaten the people of God; they pray that in the days to come,

---

[1] That such sayings about particular tribes, long known to have belonged to different periods, have had their place in a cultic ceremony similar to that assumed in the psalm, follows from the beginning of Deut. 33, which is a hymn in praise of God's epiphany in the cult of the tribal confederacy.

[2] See Kranz, *Kultur der Griechen*, 1943, p. 394.

[3] In that case the mention of Zebulun and Naphtali (cf. Judg. 4.6, 10; 5.18), as well as the affinities in the psalm with the Song of Deborah, could be interpreted as after-effects of the tradition of the *Heilsgeschichte* of Israel's pre-state period; it could then also be assumed that these after-effects took place within the framework of the cultic tradition. As regards the exposition of the Song of Deborah from the point of view of the cultus I refer to my treatment of this subject in *ZAW* 71, 1959, pp. 67 ff.

too, the subjugation of the nations and their homage, which had just been the theme of the liturgical celebration, may be repeated. The hope thus expressed for the future is coloured by the Exodus tradition which forms part of the *Heilsgeschichte*; the 'beast that dwells amongst the reeds' recalls the threat by the Egyptians at the Red Sea (cf. Isa. 27.1; Ezek. 29.3). That things to come are uniformly stylized after the pattern of things already accomplished bears witness to the unity of the saving acts of God—which results from the fact that God is present both in the past and in the future, and accords with the nature of the cultic experience (see Intr. 28 f., 42 f.).

[32–35] Not till its conclusion does the psalm display its full universal scope by bidding the 'kingdoms of the earth' to pay homage to God and sing his praise. And at its end it once more reverts to the cultic pivot round which the whole revolves and which now also forms the subject of the hymn which the whole world sings: the advent of God who, riding upon the clouds in the primeval heavens, appears in his sanctuary and in the thunder-clap of his Word reveals to the people of God, trembling with fear and joy, his majesty and power (cf. Deut. 33.26 f.; Hab. 3.6). The appearance of God, which has featured throughout the psalm, now comes into full and sole prominence. And the congregation's praise, 'ascribe power to God', like the whole psalm, is nothing but the reflection of that revelation, the throwing back again on God of the light that proceeds from him.

69. THE ZEAL FOR THY HOUSE HAS CONSUMED ME

To the Conductor. According to 'Lilies'.[1] *Of David*

1 Save me, O God,
   for the waters have come up to my neck!
2 I am sunk in deep mire
   where there is no foothold;
   I have come into deep waters,
   and the flood washes me away.[2]
3 I am weary with my crying;
   my throat is parched.
   My eyes have grown dim with waiting[3] for my God.[4]
4 More in number than the hairs of my head
   are those who hate me without cause;
   mighty are those who would destroy me,
   those who attack me with lies:
   what I did not steal, I am now to restore.[5]

5 O God, thou knowest my folly;
   the wrongs I have done are not hidden from thee.
6 May not those who hope in thee ' '[3]
   be disappointed in me, O Lord Sabaoth!
   May not those who seek thee
   be put to shame through me, O God of Israel.[6]
7 For it is for thy sake that I have suffered humiliation,[7]
   that shame has covered my face.
8 I have become a stranger to my brethren,
   an alien to my mother's sons.
9 For the zeal for thy house has consumed me,
   and the insults of those who insult thee
   have fallen on me.
10 When I fasted and wept,[8]
   it became my reproach.
11 When I made sackcloth my clothing,
   I became a mockery to them.[9]
12 I am the talk of those who sit in the gate,
   and those who drink wine make songs about me.[10]
13 But as for me, my prayer may come before thee, O Lord,
   at a time that is acceptable to thee.
   Answer me, O God, in the abundance of thy grace,
   with thy faithful help![11]
14 Draw me out of the mire that I do not sink ' ';[3]
   rescue[3] me from the deep waters![12]
15 The water-floods shall not wash me away,
   and the whirlpool shall not swallow me up,
   the well shall not close its mouth over me.[13]
16 Answer me, O Lord, according[3] to thy lovingkindness and grace;[14]
   turn to me according to thy abundant mercy!
17 Hide not thy face from thy servant;
   for I am afraid;[15] make haste to answer me!
18 Draw near to my soul; redeem it;
   set me free because[16] of my enemies!
19 Thou knowest my reproach,
   and my shame and my dishonour;
   my oppressors are all known to thee.
20 Insults have broken my heart,
   so that I trembled;[17]
   I looked for pity, but there was none;
   and for comforters but I found none.
21 They gave me poison for food,
   and for my thirst they gave me vinegar to drink.
22 Let their own table before them become a snare;
   let their sacrificial feasts[3] be a trap!
23 Let their eyes be darkened so that they cannot see;
   and make their loins tremble continually!
24 Pour out thy indignation upon them,

and let thy burning anger overtake them.
25 May their bed[18] be a desolation,
   let no one dwell in their tents.
26 For they persecute him whom thou hast smitten,
   and they aggravate[3] the pain of him whom thou hast wounded.[19]
27 Add guilt to their guilt;
   they shall not come to thy salvation.[20]
28 Let them be blotted out of the book of the living;[21]
   let them not be enrolled among the righteous.
29 But I am afflicted and weighed down through pain;
   may thy help, O God, lift me up.[22]
30 I will praise the name of God with a song;
   I will magnify him in my testimony.[23]
31 This will please the Lord more than an ox
   or a bull with horns and hoofs.[24]
32 Behold[3] this, you who are humble, and be glad;[25]
   you who seek God, let your hearts revive!
33 For the Lord has heard the needy,
   and he does not despise his own that are in bonds.
34 Let heaven and earth praise him,
   the seas and everything that moves therein.
35 For God will save Zion
   and rebuild the cities of Judah ' ';[26]
36 the seed of his servants will inherit it,
   and those who love his name, dwell in it.[27]

[1] Cf. Ps. 45, note 1.
[2] * RSV has 'sweeps over me' instead of 'washes me away'.
[3] See BH.
[4] * RSV uses the present tense.
[5] * RSV has 'What I did not steal must I now restore?'
[6] * In RSV v. 6 is:
Let not those who hope in thee be put to shame through me,
O Lord God of hosts;
let not those who seek thee be brought to dishonour through me,
O God of Israel.
[7] * RSV has 'borne reproach' instead of 'suffered humiliation'.
[8] * RSV has 'When I humbled my soul with fasting'.
[9] * RSV has 'byword' instead of 'mockery'.
[10] * RSV has 'and the drunkards make songs about me'.
[11] * In RSV the last line of v. 13 is taken with v. 14.
[12] * V. 14 is in RSV:
With thy faithful help rescue me
from sinking in the mire;
let me be delivered from my enemies
and from the deep waters.
[13] * In RSV v. 15 reads:
Let not the flood sweep over me,
or the deep swallow me up,
or the pit close its mouth over me.
[14] * V. 16a is in RSV, 'Answer me, O Lord, for thy steadfast love is good'.

[15] * RSV has 'in distress' instead of 'afraid'.
[16] So that they do not triumph.
[17] The meaning is uncertain. (Tr. N.: RSV has 'so that I am in despair' instead of 'so that I trembled'.)
[18] * RSV has 'camp' instead of 'bed'.
[19] * RSV has 'and him whom thou hast wounded, they afflict still more'.
[20] * In RSV v. 27 is:
Add to them punishment upon punishment;
may they have no acquittal from thee.
[21] See the comments on Ps. 139.16; cf. Ex. 32.32 f.; Dan. 12.1.
[22] * RSV has 'let thy salvation, O God, set me on high!'
[23] * The RSV has 'with thanksgiving' instead of 'in my testimony'.
[24] The marks of the full-grown and pure sacrificial animal (cf. I Sam. 1.24; Lev. 11.3 f.).
[25] See BH. (Tr. N.: RSV has 'Let the oppressed see it and be glad'.)
[26] See BH. (Tr. N.: RSV adds, 'and his servants shall dwell there and possess it'.)
[27] * RSV has 'children' instead of 'seed', 'shall inherit' instead of 'will inherit' and 'shall dwell' instead of 'dwell'.

After Psalm 22, Psalm 69 is the psalm most frequently quoted in the New Testament and so was interpreted in a Messianic sense as referring to Christ. Though originally the individual statements in the psalm were not meant to be understood as prophecies pointing to Jesus, this deeply moving testimony to human suffering nevertheless exhibits features which are so characteristic of suffering in general that their relation to him who has borne the suffering of the whole world automatically forces itself upon any serious consideration of the psalm. The psalm is an individual lament which in v. 30 changes into a thanksgiving and was probably recited (see Intr. 69 f., 83 f.) in public worship in the presence of the congregation (alluded to in the phrases used in v. 32, 'the humble' and 'you who seek God'). It is true that the lamentation of the poet, consumed as he is by his 'zeal for God's house' (v. 9; cf. John 2.17) and suffering for God's sake (vv. 7, 9; cf. Rom. 15.3), with its breadth of treatment, abounds in allusions to those manifold and severe trials through which he had to pass on his way of suffering; but for all that it is not concrete enough for us to grasp clearly the worshipper's historical situation and personal circumstances. Some expositors have thought of the martyrdom of the prophet Jeremiah, others of the religious persecution at the time of the Maccabees; the controversies that preceded the time of Ezra in the fifth century BC have also been brought in to explain the contemporary background of the psalm. We refrain from assigning a precise date to the psalm; only so much can be presumed: that religious controversies—perhaps about questions arising out of the sacrificial cult at the Temple (vv. 22, 31; cf. in this connection Pss. 40.6 ff.; 50.14 f., 23, where, too, hymnic testimony is preferred to sacrifices; see Intr. 71)—form the background of the psalm, and these exposed the poet amongst other things to unfounded accusations from his numerous adversaries (v. 4; cf. John 15.25) and possibly even brought about his imprisonment (v. 33).

[1–4] The lamentation with which the psalmist justifies his cry to God for help (vv. 1–2) expresses the fearful anxiety of a man no longer able to see beyond his adversity, who is afraid of being swallowed up by it like a drowning man, with the ground cut from under his feet and his hold lost against the floods of water that sweep over him (cf. vv. 14 f.; Pss. 18.16; 40.2; Jonah 2.3 ff.). However, his real affliction is not merely the anguish caused by suffering (cf. v. 17), nor the anxiety caused by the great number and might of his malicious adversaries, who seek to destroy him in his helplessness and have wrongly accused him (v. 4), but the distress of his soul in prayer, as he waits for God—apparently in vain—till his physical strength fails him. In this affliction there is already a hint of the fundamental idea which pervades the whole psalm, that all suffering of the godly is ultimately suffering for God's sake. [5] The poet is well aware that he does not suffer unjustly, and that he is 'smitten' by God (vv. 10 f., 26) because of 'follies' and 'wrongs' which he neither can nor will hide from God's omniscience. His prayer would not be genuine if he were not willing to confess his sins frankly before God; for it is his sincere acceptance of God's judgment on the sins he had confessed which first makes it possible for him to pray for God's grace and help (v. 13). [6] His only concern is that his trust in a God who is gracious to the contrite sinner (v. 10), and to whom not only he himself but the whole community of the godly look, will not be disappointed. [7–12] Thus he is able to say that he suffers for God's sake, and that the derision and abuse which he has incurred in his consuming zeal for God's house and in the earnestness of his penance are actually aimed at God, for whose sake he has even taken upon himself estrangement from his own brothers and public disgrace (v. 12).

[13–21] In the first instance this conduct of the psalmist provides the inner foundation and justification for his urgent petition which once more takes up lamentation and asks for a hearing and for God's gracious help. Now, 'at the acceptable time', that is, at the granting of his prayer (cf. Isa. 49.8; 55.6; Ps. 32.6; see above), he is

allowed to confess once more to his God before the congregation all
the things he had been moved to feel and say when he strove in
prayer for communion with him, for his nearness in calamity
(vv. 17 f.). **[22–28]** What God's grace and mercy truly mean can
clearly be seen only when they are set against the dark background
of the suffering and lamentation of a man whose hope in human compassion and comfort were disappointed every time (v. 20) and who was
spared no disillusionment (v. 21; cf. Matt. 27.34), till his heart broke
and he was overwhelmed by the blind fury of cruel feelings of vindictiveness to which he gave vent by hurling horrible curses at his enemies
so that, **[29]** exhausted by the violent outburst of his passion, he could
only sigh for help (v. 29); for it is the grace and mercy of God which
'lifts him up' from those depths and 'redeems' and 'sets free' his 'soul'
(v. 18). **[30–36]** The psalmist, whose mouth had uttered desperate
laments and the most terrible curses, is now able to join the congregation in grateful praise of God (vv. 30–33) and with them is able to be
revived once more (cf. Ps. 22.26); this fact shows the full extent of the
path along which this sufferer had been led by God till he could join the
host of witnesses of God's salvation—it is precisely 'the humble', 'the
needy', and 'the prisoners' whom God without justification has chosen
as these witnesses. The whole creation's song of praise is due to God
for this divine salvation in which everything created finds its goal
(v. 34). And even the cult community's concern for the future of its
native country, whose cities lie in ruins, is transformed in the light
of such an experience into confident hope in God.

70: *See Psalm 40.13–17*

71. I WILL PRAISE THEE YET MORE AND MORE

1 Thou, O Lord, art my refuge;[1]
  let me never be put to shame!
2 In thy righteousness deliver me and rescue me;
  incline thy ear to me, and help me!
3 Be thou to me a rock of refuge,
  a citadel,[2] to save me,
  for thou art my rock and my fortress.
4 Rescue me, O my God, from the hand of the wicked,
  from the grasp of the violent evildoer.[3]
5 For thou, O Lord, art my hope,
  my trust, O Lord, from my childhood.

6 Upon thee I have leaned from my birth;
thou art he who took[4] me from my mother's womb.
My praise is continually of thee.

7 I have been as a portent to many;
thou art my strong refuge.[5]

8 My mouth is filled with thy praise
to glorify thee at all times.[6]

9 Do not cast me off in the time of old age;
forsake me not when my strength is spent.

10 For my enemies speak concerning me,
those who watch for my life consult together,

11 and say, 'God has forsaken him;
pursue and seize him,
for there is none to deliver him!'

12 O God, be not far from me;
O my God, make haste[2] to help me!

13 May those who show enmity to me die in shame;[7]
with scorn and disgrace may they be covered who seek my hurt.

14 But I will wait for thee continually,[8]
and will praise thee yet more and more.

15 My mouth shall tell of thy righteousness,
of thy deeds of salvation all the day,
for their number is past my knowledge.

16 With the mighty deeds of the Lord ' '[9] I will come,
I will remember thy righteousness alone.[10]

17 Thou, O God, hast taught me this from my youth,
and I still proclaim thy wondrous deeds,[11]

18 yea, even to old age.[12] Do not forsake me, O God,
till I proclaim the might of thy arm
to the generation that is to come,[2]

19 thy power and thy righteousness, O God,
that reach to the high heavens;[13]
thou who hast done great things,
O God, who is like thee?

20 Thou who hast made us see many troubles and adversities revivest
us again;
from the floods upon the earth thou bringest me up again.[14]

21 Thou liftest me up higher and higher,[15]
and turnest to me to comfort me.[16]

22 I will also praise thee with the harp,
I will praise thy faithfulness, O my God;
I will make melody to thee with the cither,
O thou Holy One of Israel.[17]

23 My lips shall shout for joy, when I play to thee;
my soul also which thou hast redeemed.[18]

24 My tongue also shall talk of thy righteousness all the day long,[19]
for they have been put to shame and disgraced
who sought to do me hurt.

[1] * RSV has 'In thee, O Lord, do I take refuge.'

[2] See BH.

[3] * RSV has 'the unjust and cruel man' instead of 'the violent evildoer'.

[4] The meaning is uncertain.

[5] * RSV begins v. 7b with 'but'.

[6] * V. 8b reads in RSV, 'and with thy glory all the day'.

[7] * RSV has 'May my accusers be put to shame and consumed.'

[8] * V. 14a reads in RSV, 'But I will hope continually.'

[9] Delete '^{a}dōnāy.

[10] * In RSV v. 16 reads:
With the mighty deeds of the Lord God I will come,
I will praise thy righteousness, thine alone.

[11] * V. 17a reads in the RSV, 'O God, from my youth thou hast taught me.'

[12] RSV takes this clause with the next sentence, reading:
So even to old age and grey hairs,
O God, do not forsake me,
till I proclaim thy might
to all the generations to come.

[13] * RSV treats v. 19ab as a separate sentence, omitting 'that'.

[14] * RSV has 'me' instead of 'us' in v. 20a and 'depths of the earth' instead of 'floods upon the earth' in v. 20b.

[15] Lit.: thou increasest my greatness.

[16] * In RSV v. 21 is:
Thou wilt increase my honour,
and comfort me again.

[17] * In RSV v. 22 is:
I will also praise thee with the harp
for thy faithfulness, O my God;
I will sing praises to thee with the lyre,
O Holy One of Israel.

[18] * RSV has 'sing praises' instead of 'play' and 'rescued' instead of 'redeemed'.

[19] * In RSV v. 24a is 'And my tongue will talk of thy righteous help all the day long.'

The author of the psalm, which inspired a hymn by Paul Ger-hardt,[1] is not safe from persecution by malicious enemies, despite his old age. But it is part of the grace of old age that it can look back on a wealth of experience and can draw new hope from it. Thus a firm note of confidence runs through this lament, sustained as it is by a faith whose self-control permits no outbursts of passion. The fact that the psalm is slightly akin to various other psalms of lament is hardly due to a shortcoming in the psalmist's own abilities which had to be made up for by borrowing from other literary sources; rather it is the result of the common tie that binds compositions of this kind to the liturgical language of the cultus, with which, as is

[1] 'Herr, dir traue ich alle Tage'.

shown by the psalm itself, the poet must have been familiar. The
prayer was recited in the public worship of the cult community after
the petition had been granted (cf. vv. 23b, 24b), and in order that it
may serve this purpose, lamentation, petition and the prayer of thanksgiving are combined (as in Psalm 41 and often) in a uniform testimony
to the saving deeds of God (cf. vv. 14 ff.), a testimony that is intended
to be incorporated in the salvation tradition of the whole cult
community (v. 20; see Intr. 69 ff., 83 ff.).

[1–4] The prayer opens with a note of trust which, like the sign
before a bracket, determines the nature of the subsequent supplications; these are handed down in an almost identical form in Ps.
31.1–3. The worshipper has sought and found refuge with God in his
sanctuary and has thus reached a position which fills him with
confident trust and enables him to pray that God may hear and
rescue him, that he may deliver him from the persecution of his
ungodly and violent adversaries. In doing so his prayer, based on
faith and exclusively focused on God, is phrased in a characteristic
fashion which at first sight appears to be paradoxical: 'Be thou to
me a rock of refuge . . . *for* thou art my rock', a figure of speech
which accords with the New Testament saying, 'Lord, I believe,
help thou my unbelief'. [5–8] Before he utters his second supplication,
the worshipper once more reverts to the position of trust from which
he started, going far back to his early youth like his fellow sufferer in
Psalm 22 (cf. Ps. 22.9 f.). The Old Testament teaching on creation
according to which the psalmist knows himself to be wholly thrown
upon God from his mother's womb becomes also for him both a
source of trust and hope and also a means of orientation which
enables him to see the ultimate meaning of his life and how it all
hangs together: he is the sign or portent which in a visible way makes
manifest 'to many' God's providential rule, his power and his help.
To be God's witness gives a child of God his sanctity and dignity,
and these supply him with the inward support he needs so that he
does not let himself fall; but at the same time they also lay him under
the obligation to recognize the continuous praise of God as the true
purpose of his life, so that God may be glorified in him and through
him. [9–13] The supplication in vv. 9–13, which once more arises
out of the psalmist's trust in God, is also closely connected with these
personal considerations which are the object of the psalmist's
reflections in prayer and are wholly focused on God. What ultimately
matters to the worshipper is not so much his deliverance from the

enemies' threat to his life, but rather the anxiety troubling his soul
that God may forsake him and cast him off now he is old; this
thought is twice expressed in his supplication (vv. 9 and 18). And the
lamentation about the behaviour of his adversaries is also concerned
with the same question, of decisive importance for the psalmist,
whether his adversaries' view that God has forsaken him (v. 11) will
in the end be vindicated or whether they will be 'disappointed' in
that respect (v. 13). Consequently, the lamentation and supplication
point in the same direction as does the thought of the preceding
hymn: that the relationship with God which is based on trust and on
which the worshipper's life of faith is built may not be impaired but
may stand the test afresh in his present calamity—this is the salient
point made here; it is the foundation of the psalmist's belief in God
which is here at stake. The psalmist's self-control and restrained
reserve towards his enemies is in striking contrast with Psalm 69.
Should that attitude of mind really be only a sign of the weariness of
old age, as some expositors maintain?

Though the poet has occasionally turned his thoughts to the
praise of God already in his lamentation and supplication (vv. 3b,
6, 8), the whole second part of the psalm—in contrast to other
psalms of the same type—is now devoted to the glorification of God
in a hymn of praise; this proves that vv. 5–8 are not merely 'pious
phrases' borrowed from other sources, but that the deepest meaning
of the poet's life finds its true fulfilment in the praise of God. [14–19]
Just as others come with their sacrifices and offerings, so he comes
into the house of God 'with the mighty deeds of God' (cf. Pss. 66.13;
40.5) to proclaim in the midst of the congregation the righteous acts
of God and his saving deeds. He will remember the tradition of
God's *Heilsgeschichte* with which he had become acquainted in public
worship from his youth (v. 17), and will praise God more and more
by means of his hymn and thanksgiving (v. 14) which signify—and
certainly not to him alone—the main purpose of the cultic ceremony
(v. 16; see Intr. 55 f., 74 f.). He regards this preservation of the tradition
of God's saving deeds and its transmission to the coming generation as
a holy legacy; and his witness to the innumerable wondrous deeds of
God, which demonstrate his incomparable greatness 'to the high
heavens' (vv. 15, 17, 19), seems such an important duty that, in order
to be able to accomplish it, he once more entreats God's help (v. 18).
[20] In his meditation on the *Heilsgeschichte*, in which he unites with
the congregation (see v. 20: 'us'), the poet in the very midst of his

inspired praise is also mindful of the many afflictions and various calamities through which God had led his people on their path to salvation; and this fact proves, as it does in Ps. 66.10 ff. (see the comments on this passage), that even the optimism that arises out of an enthusiastic faith need not be blind to the dark aspects of life; indeed, it proves that it is the history of human suffering which alone makes God's way to salvation appear in full light and reveals its full grandeur. The poet knows that all salvation is the fruit of suffering; and because of this knowledge he also incorporates in the large framework of God's *Heilsgeschichte* in relation to his people (see Intr. 77 f.) the way which he has just been compelled to walk, a way which led him through persecution and fear and now appears to him like the miraculous deliverance from the Flood. It is not the faith of the psalmist which has been disappointed, but on the contrary the belief of his adversaries; God has not abandoned the worshipper, but has remained faithful to him and has turned to him in consolation. This is both the reason for the worshipper's thanksgiving and also its theme.

72. PRAYER FOR THE KING

Of Solomon

1 Give the king thy statutes,[1] O God,
  and thy righteousness to the royal son!
2 May he judge thy people with righteousness,
  and thy afflicted[2] with justice!
3 May the mountains bring peace to the people,
  and the hills righteousness.[3]
4 May he defend the cause of the needy of the people,
  give prosperity to the sons of the poor,[4]
  and crush the oppressor,
5 as long as[5] the sun shines and the moon,
  from generation to generation![6]
6 May he descend like rain on the meadows,
  like showers that water[5] the land![7]
7 In his days may salvation[8] flourish,
  and peace abound, till the moon be no more!
8 May he have dominion from sea to sea,
  and from the River[9] to the ends of the earth!
9 His foes[5] shall kneel before him,
  and his adversaries lick the dust!
10 The kings of Tarshish[10] and of the isles,
  they shall bring gifts,
  the kings of Sheba[11] and Seba[12]
  shall render their tribute!

11 All kings shall pay homage to him,
   all nations serve him![13]
12 For he delivers the poor when he calls,
   and the needy who has no helper.[14]
13 He has pity on the weak and the poor,
   and helps the souls of the needy.[15]
14 From oppression and violence he redeems their life;
   and precious is their blood in his sight,
15 that he[16] may live and gold of Sheba be given to him,
   and that he may pray for him continually
   and may bless him at all times.[17]
16 May there be abundance of grain in the land
   on the tops of the mountains;
   may its fruit rustle like Lebanon
   and may they blossom forth from the cities
   like the grass of the field![18]
17 May his name endure for ever,
   his fame continue as long as the sun;
   all nations shall bless themselves by him,
   and shall call him blessed.[19]
18 Blessed be God, the Lord, the God of Israel,
   who alone does wondrous things.
19 Blessed be his glorious name for ever;
   may his glory fill[5] the whole earth!
   Amen and Amen.
20 The prayers of David, the son of Jesse, are ended.[20]

[1] * RSV has 'thy justice' instead of 'thy statutes'.
[2] * RSV has 'poor' for 'afflicted'.
[3] See BH. (Tr. N.: RSV renders v. 3:
   Let the mountains bear prosperity for the people,
   and the hills, in righteousness!)
[4] RSV has 'the cause of the poor' instead of 'the cause of the needy', and
'deliverance to the needy' instead of 'prosperity to the sons of the poor'.
[5] * See BH.
[6] * RSV makes v. 5 a separate sentence:
   May he live while the sun endures,
   and as long as the moon,
   throughout all generations!
[7] * RSV renders v. 6 as follows:
   May he be like rain that falls on the mown grass,
   like showers that water the earth!
[8] See BH. (Tr. N.: RSV has 'righteousness' instead of 'salvation'.)
[9] Euphrates.
[10] Probably Tartessus in Spain.
[11] In Arabia.
[12] In Ethiopia.
[13] * RSV has 'fall down before him' instead of 'pay homage to him'.
[14] * RSV reads 'the needy' instead of 'the poor' in v. 12a and renders v. 12b as
'the poor and him who has no helper'.

15 * V. 13 reads in RSV:
  He has pity on the weak and the needy,
  and saves the lives of the needy.
16 That is, the poor.
17 * RSV makes v. 15 a separate sentence, referring to the king (see the preceding note):
  Long may he live,
  may gold of Sheba be given to him!
  May prayer be made for him continually
  and blessings invoked for him all the day!
18 * RSV has:
  May there be abundance of grain in the land;
  on the tops of the mountains may it wave;
  may its fruit be like Lebanon;
  and may men blossom forth from the cities
  like the grass of the field!
19 * In RSV v. 17cd is:
  May men bless themselves by him,
  all nations call him blessed!
20 See above, p. 98.

According to the superscription the psalm was composed by Solomon; it is, however, an intercession for the king which cannot originate with the king himself. This is why the Septuagint, probably on account of vv. 1 f., 10, has interpreted the psalm as referring to Solomon, whereas the Targum has interpreted it as referring to the Messiah; in the ancient Church the psalm was regarded as the main psalm of the epiphany. The king is not mentioned by name and the thoughts expressed in the intercession made on his behalf are of a general character, since they occur above all also in prophetic visions of the future; it is therefore useless to ask who the historical royal personage is for whom the psalm was intended. Rather is the psalm to be regarded, like Psalms 20 and 21, as a portion of the liturgy for the festival of the king's enthronement, the rite for which was determined by traditional forms not designed for a specific king, but intended for an ideal type of king and appointed to be used continually (cf. Psalm 101). The psalm's affinity with prophetic eschatology, which seems to have encouraged the Messianic interpretation, probably originates in a common tradition of God's reign as King which was incorporated in the cultic tradition of the Covenant of Yahweh at an early date.

The form of the prayer of intercession as well as its subject-matter, which often far transcends the limits set by the actual conditions prevailing on earth, are accounted for by this connection between the celebration of the king's accession to the throne and the festival of the kingship of God (cf. the comments on vv. 18 ff.; see Intr. 33 f., 62 f.). This is true even if certain ideas and phrases should have been borrowed from ancient oriental 'court-style'. That these ideas and phrases could be used meaningfully within the much more restricted scope of the Old Testament kingship is due to the very fact that this kingship was moulded in its own peculiar way through its association with the idea of the kingship of God. [1–7] In direct contrast to the autocracy of oriental despotism the Old Testament kingship is *subject* to the statutes of God for the execution of which the king is responsible to his divine Lord. The prayer was perhaps offered on the occasion of the handing over of these divine statutes (v. 1) to the king and his pledging himself to keep them (cf. I Sam. 10.25, where a cultic custom seems to be alluded to). This is why pre-eminence has been given in the psalm to the idea of the righteousness of the king's reign, a pre-eminence which imparts to the prayer a special note of its own. It is not by chance that the psalm speaks first of righteousness (vv. 1–7) and only afterwards of the king's power (vv. 8–10), and then reverts again to its point of departure (vv. 12–15), and further that the blessings of peace (v. 3) and salvation (vv. 4, 6 f., 16) and even the display of the power of the king's reign (v. 12) are derived from righteousness. Righteousness is ultimately not a relative human requirement of 'humanitarianism', but a divine, and for that reason absolute, requirement of a religiously binding character. For behind the reign of the earthly king is God's rule as King; the righteousness of the king is a function and the mirror-image of the righteousness of God which he has promised to his people in their need for protection ('thy needy' in v. 2) and to those individual members who depend on his assistance, and which does not allow the weak to become the prey of the mighty. The significance of the king's duties and of the far-reaching hopes which the people cherish for their ruler is to be judged by that eternal divine order of salvation which arises on the foundation of God's eternal order of Nature and cannot be separated from it (vv. 5, 7; cf. Gen. 8.22). It is not the immortalizing of human nature but the participation of human nature in the eternal character of the divine order of salvation which imparts to the king and his office their special importance and to the prayer of the cult community the tones peculiar to that divine order of salvation.

[8–11] The wishes expressed for the extension of the power of the king's dominion no more arise from a political megalomania

which could only be characterized as grotesque than do their
parallels in the prophetic eschatology (cf. Micah 7.12; Zech. 9.10);
they come rather from this linking of the earthly kingship to the
idea of the Kingdom of God as embodied in the dominion of the
king and aiming at the subjection of all the nations to God. **[12–15]**
For the expansion of the king's power is motivated in vv. 12–15
by righteousness and compassion for the weak whom he shall
deliver from the pressure of violence. The extension of power
cannot therefore be regarded, as has frequently been assumed, as a
reward for the righteousness of the king—such a thought is neither
proper in an intercession nor appropriate to the fact that the king has
only just now acceded to the throne—rather does it serve the purpose
of spreading the rule of righteousness and clemency everywhere and
realizing the salvation of God. Again, behind the king's pity is God's
compassion for the weak and that regard for the life and dignity of the
individual human being (v. 14) which causes the blessing of mercy
and beneficence to redound on the giver (v. 16) and unites the
leader and those he leads in a mutual bond of intercession that is
stronger than all power and violence. **[16–17]** From such deep wells
flows the divine blessing which the people entreat God to send down
and bestow upon their king: the 'grace of kingship' which shall
be manifested in the blessing of the fruits of the earth (cf. Ps. 21.3
ff.),[1] in the prosperity of flourishing cities and in the lasting fame
(name) of the king, will be the visible sign that the promise God has
given to the patriarchs (cf. v. 17b with Gen. 12.2 f.; 22.18) he will
also fulfil upon the king who walks in his ways. **[18–19]** The closing
doxology is almost without exception regarded as a later addition
marking the conclusion of the second book of the Psalter (cf. the
comments on Ps. 41.13). Since, however, this doxology is followed by
the annotation of the compiler of the Psalter, signifying the ending of
the prayers of David (on v. 20 see Intr. 98 f.) and presumably being of
an earlier date than the division of the whole Psalter into five books,
the question deserves serious consideration whether vv. 18 and 19 did
not, after all, form part of the original text of the psalm. If this is the
case, then the praise of God's name and glory, calling to mind the
tradition of the theophany in Isa. 6, would at the end of the psalm

---

[1] An echo of that conception is also to be found in a song belonging to the
document 'The War of the Sons of Light against the Sons of Darkness' which was
discovered at the Dead Sea (see provisionally Hempel, *ZAW* 62, 1950, p. 256, lines
8 ff.).

once more effectively throw into bold relief the theological and cultic background of the prayer for the king, hinted at at the beginning of the psalm, as the setting that simultaneously provides the ultimate meaning of the whole psalm and the limits set to it: the king's reign and its blessing are the reflection of the sovereign rule of God and of his salvation, and his fame is overshadowed by the 'glory' (*kābōd*) of God who alone does wondrous things.

73. AS LONG AS I HAVE THEE

A Psalm. To Asaph[1]

1 Truly God is good to Israel;
   to those who are pure in heart he is the Lord.[2]
2 But as for me, my feet had almost stumbled,
   my steps had well nigh slipped.
3 For I grew hotly indignant at the fools,
   when I saw the prosperity of the wicked.[3]
4 For they suffer[4] no pain,
   their bodies are sound[4] and fat.[5]
5 They are not in trouble as other men are;
   what vexes other men does not vex them.[6]
6 Therefore pride is their necklace;
   violence covers them as a garment.
7 From fatness comes forth their guilt,[4]
   their hearts overflow with their schemes.[7]
8 They scoff and speak with malice;
   arrogantly they speak foolish things.[8]
9 They set their mouths against the heavens,
   and their tongue struts through the earth.
10 Therefore they draw large crowds[4]
   and their words are sipped like water.[9]
11 They say, 'How can God know?
   How could there be knowledge in the Most High?'[10]
12 Behold, this is the way of the wicked;
   always lucky, they increase in riches.[11]
13 All in vain have I kept my heart clean
   and washed my hands in innocence.
14 For all the day long I have been stricken,
   and chastened every morning.
15 If I had thought, I will speak like these,[12]
   I would have betrayed the generation of thy sons.[13]
16 So I thought how to understand this,
   but it was a torment to my eyes,[14]
17 until I went into the sanctuary[4] of God
   and perceived what their end will be.[15]

18 Truly thou dost set them in slippery places;
    thou dost make them fall to ruin.
19 How they are destroyed in a moment,
    vanish and perish in terror![16]
20 They have gone[4] like a dream when one awakes,
    the phantom of which[4] you despise on awakening.[17]
21 When my heart was embittered,
    and I pined away inwardly,[18]
22 I was like a beast without understanding,
    a foolish creature, before thee.[19]
23 Nevertheless I am continually with thee;
    thou dost hold my right hand.
24 Thou dost guide me with thy counsel,
    and afterwards thou wilt receive me to glory.
25 As long as I have thee,
    I wish for nothing else in heaven or on earth.[20]
26 My flesh and my heart may fail,
    but God is my rock[21] and my portion for ever.
27 For lo, those who are far from thee, shall perish;
    thou dost put an end to him who deserts thee.[22]
28 To be near thee,[4] that is my happiness;[23]
    I have made the Lord ' '[4] my refuge,
    that I may tell of all thy works.

[1] See p. 97. (Tr. N.: RSV has 'of Asaph'.)
[2] * RSV has 'to the upright' instead of 'to Israel' and omits 'he is the Lord'.
[3] * In RSV v. 3a is 'For I was envious of the arrogant.'
[4] See BH.
[5] * RSV has 'have no pangs' instead of 'suffer no pains' and 'sleek' instead of
'fat'.
[6] * V. 5b reads in RSV, 'they are not stricken like other men'.
[7] * V. 7 is in RSV:
    Their eyes swell out with fatness,
    their hearts overflow with follies.
[8] See BH. (Tr. N.: In RSV v. 8b reads, 'loftily they threaten oppression'.)
[9] Read: *ūmillēhem k^emayīm yimmāṣū lāmō*. (Tr. N.: RSV renders v. 10:
    Therefore the people turn and praise them;
    and find no fault in them.)
[10] See the comments on Ps. 7.17.
[11] * RSV has 'always at ease' instead of 'always lucky'.
[12] Read *kāhem*.
[13] * In RSV v. 15 is:
    If I had said, 'I will speak thus',
    I would have been untrue to the generation of thy children.
[14] * V. 16 is in RSV:
    But when I thought how to understand this,
    it seemed to me a wearisome task,
[15] * V. 17b reads in RSV, 'then I perceived their end'.
[16] * In RSV v. 19b is 'swept away utterly by terrors!'
[17] * RSV has 'they are like a dream'.

[18] * V. 21b is in RSV 'when I was pricked in heart'.
[19] * In RSV v. 22 is:
I was stupid and ignorant,
I was like a beast towards thee.
[20] Lit.: 'whom have I in heaven (except thee) and I have no pleasure in the earth besides thee'. (Tr. N.: RSV renders v. 25:
Whom have I in heaven but thee?
And there is nothing upon earth that I desire besides thee.)
[21] Read *ṣūrī*. (Tr. N.: RSV has in v. 26b 'the strength of my heart' instead of 'my rock'.)
[22] * RSV reads in v. 27b 'to those who are false to thee' instead of 'to him who deserts thee'.
[23] * V. 28a is in RSV 'But for me it is good to be near God.'

The seventy-third psalm occupies a foremost place among the more mature fruits borne by the struggles through which the Old Testament faith had to pass. It is powerful testimony to a battle fought in a human soul comparable with that in the Book of Job. In the psalm this battle does not indeed attain the gigantic proportions and wide range of background, the artistic greatness and dramatic force of the poem of Job; the structure of the psalm is simpler than that of the Book of Job, but its thoughts are for this reason no less penetrating and profound. Indeed, it is the very simplicity with which the psalmist expresses most profound insights which makes his song in this respect unsurpassed in the Old Testament. It has been contended that as in Psalms 37 and 49 it is for the poet a question of the so-called theodicy-problem, the question, that is, of how the idea of the righteousness of God can be reconciled with the prosperity of the wicked and the suffering of the godly; but in making that contention not everything has been said and not even what is really essential. For what is here at stake is more than merely a theological problem, not simply an intellectual problem—but a matter of life and death: the question of the survival of faith generally. The problem of suffering is really only the occasion and point of departure for religion's comprehensive enquiry into the nature and value of man's communion with God by faith in view of the mysterious reality of human life. To this question the poet brings the utmost seriousness. The psalm is a man's confession whereby he reveals his struggle for a living communion of faith with his God, a struggle which brings him to the verge of despair. It may be assumed that the psalm was recited before the congregation in the sanctuary (v. 28), where the worshipper was granted the insight that released him from his doubts (v. 17). The author is an ordinary member of the community of the godly[1] who is thoroughly tried by suffering (v. 14). Some expositors wanted to conclude from the way in which the problem was formulated and from the contrast between the godly and the wicked, which apparently forms the background of the psalm, as well as from the manner in which the ungodly are characterized as representatives of a demoralizing rationalistic enlightenment, that the psalm has been influenced by Greek thought and was composed in the Hellenistic period of the fourth or third century BC. However, this can as little be proved as the interpretation of the psalm in the sense of a contrast between the proletariat of the Levites and the propertied class of the priests of the house of Zadok (see Intr. 92). The question of the dating of the psalm must be left open.

The construction of the psalm accords with the structure of one's experience in life. A cogent inner thought-sequence is combined with the free moulding of external form. In vv. 1 f. the religious principle which constitutes the problem of the psalm is brought into prominence as the theme, and these verses, together with the conclusion (vv. 27 f.), with its similar orientation, provide a firm framework for the whole psalm. Within that framework the battle in the poet's soul takes place; vv. 3–12 speak of the offence he takes at the prosperity of the wicked; vv. 13–16 deal with his own calamity and doubts; v. 17 presents the turning-point. The poet begins to see everything in a new light, both as regards the wicked (vv. 17–22) and in respect of his own relation to God (vv. 23–26).

[1] At the very beginning the author clearly outlines the foundation to which he clings in defiance of all the doubts that torment him: *truly* God is good to Israel, the people of God, who 'with a pure heart' (without ulterior motives) are unreservedly loyal to God. Here the 'nevertheless' of faith, to which the poet rises in vv. 23 ff., is already slightly hinted at. In the psalmist's opening statement the struggle is still echoed which preceded that confident assurance, and in the answer he gives the question is still perceptible which was the object of his struggle: is there any sense in holding on in this life to the belief in a God who is good?

[2] It was not the fault of God's providential rule, nay, it was the poet's own fault that his 'feet had almost stumbled'. The psalmist

[1] The view held by Würthwein (*Festschrift für Bertholet*, pp. 542 ff.) that the speaker is a king does not seem to me to have been convincingly and sufficiently proved; this is true also of Ringgren's cultic, mythological interpretation of the psalm (*VT* 3, 1953, op. 265 ff.) which also attributes it to a king.

faces with ruthless candour the danger which had reduced him
almost to despair; that he had been on the point of giving up his faith
in God is still discernible in vv. 13 ff. The detailed confession which
now follows shows how it became possible for him to arrive at such a
state of mind.

The wicked (vv. 3–12)

[3–5] The jealousy which the *prosperity of the wicked* aroused in the
poet constituted the occasion for the crisis of his faith. The picture he
portrays of the wicked is seen from the one-sided perspective of a
simple man who enviously perceives only what is denied to him in his
own life: wealth and comfort, good health and vain pleasure. In
doing so, he does not realize that the life of those people, too, by no
means proceeds untouched by sorrow. The severity of this superficial
because eudaemonistic judgment is, however, not simply the manifestation of a sociologically determined contrast between the godly
and the wicked. It is true that, as elsewhere, so also among the people
of Israel, it was above all the wealthy and educated classes who
allowed the spirit of an alien culture and of 'enlightenment' to
pervade their own lives and so gave offence to the devout poet; but
in the contemplation of the prosperity of the wicked there is already
tacitly implied that concern of the poet's faith which is most emphatically his own, the question namely whether the untroubled
existence of the wicked does not, after all, shake the foundations of
belief in God to such a degree that it is bound to be destroyed by the
riddle thus presented.

[6] The poet grows even more hotly indignant at *the behaviour and
the success of the wicked.* They display pride and violence like jewellery
and garments. The riddle which agonizes the poet is the fact that
these people are so entirely unconcerned about the contradiction
between their frame of mind and their outward behaviour and
affairs. [7] With sarcastic words he severely criticizes the accurately
observed connection ('therefore') between their prosperity and their
guilt (v. 7) which, on the other hand, represents a contrast that
offends his feelings very much indeed; he realizes that behind this
contrast there is once more invisibly the question which has yet to be
answered, the question, that is, of whether or not there is a Living
God. [8–9] In vv. 8 f. is explained what in v. 7 is hinted at only in
general: they talk about God and the world in an arrogant and
boastful manner and without being in any way conscious of the

perversity of their behaviour; their slanderous tongue stops at
nothing; the lack of awe, which is the result of human presumption
and is condemned in v. 9 with derision has all along been the typical
accompanying phenomenon of every so-called enlightenment [10]
which causes man to perceive only himself as the centre of everything
that comes to pass, to worship himself and to try to subject all things
to the power of his own reasoning. No wonder these advocates of
enlightenment draw large crowds; all along the masses can be quickly
aroused to enthusiasm whenever it is a matter of something new;
and just as he who is thirsty sips the water, so the crowd eagerly
listens to the fashionable spirit of the 'new age'. [11] The brief
quotation of the question asked by the wicked: 'How can God know?
How could there be knowledge in the Most High?' which is here
probably meant to be understood in the concrete sense that God
does not care for the conduct and welfare of the individual, reveals
the danger of the dissolution of man's personal relationship with God,
entailing the cessation of man's responsibility. [12] In v. 12 the
portrayal of the wicked is concluded with a characterization that is
meant to sum up what has been said before: they are always lucky,
and continually accumulate riches. In this statement the problem
raised by faith is once more touched on: when such things are
allowed to happen, where is God?

The affliction of faith (vv. 13–16)

The *mental distress and inward tension*, through which the poet passes
because of the fate and behaviour of the wicked when he thinks of his
own suffering, is first made wholly understandable in vv. 13–16.
However severe his judgment on the wicked was, he now spares
himself just as little as he once more renders to himself an account of
the doubts which had troubled him. [13] For him it is an inward
necessity to be ruthlessly candid before God; at the same time it is the
means whereby the truth can make him free from himself. [14] He,
too, had searched in vain for a tangible outcome of his striving for
purity in sentiments and actions. [15] And even that is not the whole
story: all day long he had been tormented by an ailment which he
cannot think of in any other way than that it was a punishment
executed by God. But for what purpose? His faith knows no answer
to that, but what is the use of a faith which breaks down in the
decisive moment of crisis? Is not such a faith meaningless and to no
purpose? The poet has not been spared even this last doubt; driven

to thoughts similar to those which he knew were entertained by the wicked, he was on the point of renouncing his personal relationship of faith with the God for whom he was searching with burning eyes. However, there was something which kept him from taking the last step—his loyalty to the community of the faithful. At the very moment when he is no longer able to see his God, he at least perceives the fellowship of the believers. [16] The existence of the cult community becomes for him a signpost pointing the way to God ('thy sons') and with a mysterious power keeps him from betrayal. It is true that the problem which God presents is not solved for the poet by the fact that the support which he received from the religious community did not let him utterly fall into the abyss of despair; the doubt that besets his thoughts continues, and the attempt 'to understand this' ends in perplexity and torment. But in the face of the mysterious nature of actual happenings the doubt about God is of no use either; it does not in the least help the poet to find a solution to his problem; on the contrary, it only reveals the utter inability of man rationally to comprehend how ultimately everything hangs together. The poet is far too seriously minded to rest content with a solution which, after all, is not really a solution. It is not by chance that he first had to reach a stage at which the reflections of his human mind ended in a declaration of failure, before his eyes were opened to a real solution of his inner conflict by looking at it from the perspective of God.

The turning-point (vv. 17–26)

[17] The poet describes the way he attained the renewal of his faith in these words: 'until I went into the sanctuary of God'. This statement probably refers to an experience in the Temple, to an encounter with his God that was brought about by the theophany, assumed to have taken place in the cult of the Covenant Festival (see Intr. 37 ff., 72 f.).[1] The poet has arrived at his new religious insight not by means of his own thinking and laborious meditation (cf. v. 16), but by virtue of God's revelation in his judgment on the wicked and in his salvation for the godly (see Intr. 32 f., 75 f.). First of all, the prosperity of the wicked was then seen in a different light (vv. 17–22). The perception of their end for the first time made clear how their

---

[1] Ringgren (loc. cit.), too, refers to the influence of the 'New Year Festival' on the style of the psalm and on its imagery. It is, however, doubtful whether the portrayal of the wicked is to be understood as following the pattern of gods (powers of chaos).

life had to be judged. Life looks different when viewed against the background of judgment and death; in using the word 'end', the psalmist seems, however, to have had in mind not only death but, as the subsequent verses show, something which is of a 'final' nature, an ultimate inner meaning which first becomes perceptible when death is taken into account. [18] The outward appearance of the life of the wicked, of which the poet had spoken with some exasperation in vv. 3–12, is not the 'final' thing; it is not the decisive factor. Their security in life is not based on a firm foundation. They are set by God in slippery places and are continually exposed to the threat of ruin by God. [19] When God's living power is made manifest by opposing them, the true reality of their existence is revealed in that they break down in a moment; then the demeanour of the wicked 'vanishes' and what in the eyes of men now seems to be an assured happiness collapses, terrified by the reality of God, and is reduced to nothingness. [20] The comparison of their life with the vision of a dream, which on awakening is smiled at, shows the utter boldness of the poet, who dares to declare that what appears to be a fact is actually an illusion. The phrases used by the psalmist allow us to presume that he thinks not only of the transient nature of wealth and of death as the end of every earthly happiness, but of the import of their life altogether, the questionable nature of which he becomes fully conscious of when he takes everything into consideration and contemplates the end. It is a Copernican turn which the poet accomplishes in revaluing the former values; he no longer squeezes God and the interpretation of everything that happens into the narrow compass of his own egocentric trains of thought, but conversely seeks to understand and evaluate the realities of human life in the light of the reality of God which takes hold of him and surrounds him in the experience of God's presence (v. 23). It signifies a radical change in man's attitude of mind when he abandons the ground of visible data as the starting-point of his thinking and relies on the invisible reality of God to such a degree that it becomes by faith the unshakable foundation of his seeing and thinking. [21] Anyone who has struggled with his own self will understand that such a breaking away from the natural ways of human thinking, this being lifted out of and above one's own self, did not come about without creating the most violent spiritual emotions. But because that victory of faith is bought with his heart's blood, it is for that very reason of singular value to the poet. With the new knowledge he has gained, the bitter memory of agonizing hours of doubts and mental distress is interwoven with the feeling of happiness granted to a man who has overcome or, to put it more adequately, who has been overcome by God.

[22] Now he can also clearly see the perversity and foolishness of his doubts. He thinks of himself as a beast which does not 'understand'. That comparison with the beast well characterizes the materialistic and superficial quality of his former attitude when compared with the quite differently conditioned outlook of the attitude of faith which, piercing the outward appearances, discerns how everything hangs together inwardly. However, the phrase used in v. 22, 'a beast before thee' (i.e., in relation to thee), implies at the same time this fundamental difference between human and divine ways of thinking. An entirely new sphere of reality has dawned on him; he sees all things, and above all himself, in a new dimension which previously had escaped his perception. The poet does not spare himself, but frankly speaks of his shame. Genuine faith can only endure in an atmosphere of truthfulness, and ultimate truth becomes manifest only through faith.

But more important than the insight into the life of the wicked with its purely negative results is the positive knowledge of faith which the author gains for his own life from his encounter with God in the sanctuary. [23] The knowledge which he here attains by faith is characterized by the phrase 'nevertheless'. This word comprises a twofold contrast, namely, genuine and firm assurance as opposed to his own doubts and struggles, and further the true happiness of a living communion with God as opposed to the seeming happiness of the wicked. The bold venture of faith to hold on to God against all appearances, even when, nay, precisely when life continues to be wrapped in mystery has found in the psalm a truly classical expression. Here speaks one who does not see and yet believes. In his view to believe means to hold on to a permanent relationship of his life with God in the assurance that God will sustain him when man is no longer able to walk in his own strength. This assurance is not one which is based on his own reasoning and could be proved or shaken by arguments, but is an assurance that is founded on the experience of his own life, with roots reaching down much more deeply. It is characterized not by the possession of visible goods, but by the indestructible energy of a life fed by the invisible resources of communion with God. The poet knows that it is God who 'takes hold of his right hand'. He does not walk in the way of faith by his own

strength, and for that reason the vital energies which are here
granted him are quite different from those provided by the material
pleasures of man's temporal existence. His life is built on a different
foundation; its wealth consists in the inner possession of opportunities
of life granted by God.

[24] A note of childlike and profound humility runs through the
saying 'thou dost guide me with thy counsel'; in a most marked
contrast to the arrogance of the wicked the certitude of being completely sheltered and guided reflects the supreme form of trust:
'Though I may in no wise be able to feel thy power, thou guidest me
nevertheless to my destination, even through the night.'[1] This is not
to be understood in the sense that by this certitude the incomprehensible mystery of life is now elucidated for the poet; there is no
intellectual or theoretical solution of the theodicy; the mystery still
continues to be a mystery to him; but he has the living assurance that
God is also near him in those times when his life is veiled in obscurity,
and will eventually see to it that everything ends well. The knowledge
of *how* he will accomplish this remains God's secret. But the sure
knowledge *that* God will act in this way suffices for him who has
learned to believe in the hidden God. On this fact he bases his hopes
for his whole life in the future, and even beyond death. For in view
of what precedes, it will hardly be possible to interpret the words that
follow, 'and afterwards thou wilt receive me to glory', as meaning
that his sufferings will come to an end during his earthly life; rather
does it seem that in these words is expressed hope in the consummation of his communion with God after death, a thought which
would fit without any difficulty in the context of the ideas developed
in the psalm. The believer knows: life proceeds towards a hidden
glory, and the sufferings of this present time are not worth comparing
with that glory which shall then be revealed. Even death itself does
not set a limit to that hope. Faith overcomes death in the light of the
eternal presence of God. It is God who guarantees the glory, and the
life lived in communion with him is the basis on which this indestructible and victorious assurance of faith can become a living reality.
It is a question not worth asking whether the poet conceived the
overcoming of death as a 'translation' (cf. Enoch, Gen. 5.24) or as
eternal life or as a resurrection after the manner of the hope developed in the mystery cults of his time; here, too, the question of

---

[1] * A literal translation of a quotation from the hymn 'So nimm denn meine
Hände' by Julie von Hausmann (1826–1901).

how this will come to pass has not been asked by the psalmist. He allows the divine mystery to remain a mystery and does not presume irreverently to push open the gates which God still keeps closed. This, too, is an essential mark of his faith.

[25] The ultimate motive of the assurance and blessedness of faith is, however, not hope in a future glory, but joy in the present life of union with God—which is the only good that impregnates the whole of life and is not merely the supreme good among others. In Luther's unsurpassed translation, 'as long as I have thee, I wish for nothing else in heaven or on earth' (*wenn ich nur dich habe, so frage ich nichts nach Himmel und Erde*), this glorious freedom of the child of God rings through, for, delivered from the bondage of earthly possessions, he sees even heavenly delights grow pale when compared with the happiness of his communion with God which means everything to him. Egocentric, eudaemonistic impulses disappear in the face of that communion which gives the poet strength to master even his suffering.

[26] The poet explicitly deals in v. 26 with such conquering of suffering through faith. In doing so his faith soars far above every earthly concern, but this does not at all come about by his being lifted beyond the affliction of the present in a fit of inspired vision; on the contrary, there is not a moment when he loses sight of the terrible reality of suffering. As far as he is concerned, suffering is not abolished; it continues; but it is *endured* thanks to the power of faith. Free from every kind of self-deception, he singles out the worst case— that flesh and heart may fail him—and even in that is able to affirm with joy his trust in the God who is for ever his ultimate support and the indestructible purpose of his life. That life is different: it is lived in the midst of the present earthly life and yet it extends beyond. Here God is exclusively desired and believed in for his own sake. This life lived by faith extends into eternity for God's sake and in its own peculiar way embodies a piece of eternity. Nowhere else in the Old Testament is the power of faith in God to master life so profoundly grasped in such purity and strength, nowhere so forcefully formulated, as in the 'nevertheless', uttered by faith, by which the poet of Psalm 73 commits himself to God.

[27–28] In conclusion the worshipper once more sums everything up. Though the riddles presented by life may remain, nobody can deprive him any longer of the ultimate certitude that has been granted to him in the cultic experience of the presence of God. A life lived in separation from God perishes and leads to destruction, but the nearness of God means life and happiness. The decision of whether the one or the other is going to happen *is* already made; it does not need to be hoped for first; for it is not bound up with man's external life but with his inner life. He who has God, has life; but without God there is only death. Here, too, the poet does not say how he concretely conceives this truth in detail, but in view of vv. 23 ff. the form of his personal testimony to the nearness of God, whereby the thought of v. 1 is again taken up, allows the conclusion that for the poet communion with God leads to the development of a nobler life and that, conversely, the end of the wicked, too, is not only understood in a purely material sense, but as an inward life-lessness and as a spiritual death. The barrier erected by this world is thus broken down and the realization of a new reality made possible which imparts to everything that is real in this world a new and ultimate meaning and value—the reality of God. It is the way from seeing to believing which the poet had had to travel; from this perspective we come to understand his struggle and his doubt as well as his victory and his happiness. In both he discerns the action of God to which he now joyfully and humbly testifies before the congregation by incorporating his own experience of God in the larger context of the whole redemptive work of God ('all thy works'; see Intr. 74 f.). To bear witness with the thanksgiving to these saving deeds of God he simultaneously regards as his duty and his joy.

74. THE DESTRUCTION OF THE TEMPLE

A Maskil.[1]   *To Asaph*[2]

1 O God, why hast thou cast us off for ever?
   Why does thy anger smoke against
   the sheep of thy pasture?
2 Remember thy congregation, which thou hast gotten of old,
   which thou hast redeemed to be the tribe of thy heritage!
   Remember Mount Zion where thou hast dwelt!
3 Direct thy steps to the perpetual ruins;
   the enemy has destroyed everything in the temple!
4 Thy foes have roared in the midst of the place of thy assemblies;
   they set up their own signs ' '[3] . . .

   . . . .

7 They set thy sanctuary on fire;
   to the ground they desecrated the dwelling-place of thy name.
8 They said to themselves, 'We will smash everything to pieces';[4]
   they burned all the meeting-places of God in the land.

9 We did not see our signs;
   there was no longer any prophet;
   and there was none among us who knew which way to turn.[5]
10 How long, O God, is the foe allowed[6] to scoff?
   Is the enemy allowed[6] to revile thy name for ever?
11 Why dost thou draw back thy hand,
   why dost thou hide[7] thy right hand in[7] thy bosom?[8]
12 And yet God is my King from of old,
   working salvation in the midst of the earth.[9]
13 Thou didst frighten away[10] the sea by thy might;
   thou didst break the heads of the dragons on the waters.
14 Thou didst crush the heads of Leviathan,
   thou didst give him ' '[7] as food for the beasts of the wilderness.
15 Thou didst cleave open springs and rivers;
   thou didst dry up ever-flowing streams.
16 Thine is the day, thine also the night;
   thou hast established the stars and the sun.
17 Thou hast fixed all the bounds of the earth;
   thou hast made summer and winter.
18 Remember that the enemy scoffs at the Lord,
   that a foolish people reviles thy name.[11]
19 Do not deliver the soul of thy dove to the wild beasts;
   do not forget the life of thy afflicted for ever!
20 Have regard for thy covenant;
   for the hiding-places of the land are full;
   they are habitations of violence.[12]
21 Let not the downtrodden turn back in disillusion;
   let the poor and needy praise thy name.[13]
22 Arise, O God, plead thy cause;
   remember how the fools scoff at thee all the day!
23 Do not forget the clamour of thy foes,
   the uproar of thy adversaries which goes up continually!

[1] See Ps. 32.
[2] See above, p. 97. (Tr. N.: RSV has 'of Asaph'.)
[3] Delete 'for signs' as dittography. Verses 5 and 6 are corrupt; they continue the description of the work of destruction which seems to be compared with the activities of woodcutters. (Tr. N.: In RSV vv. 4-6 are:
   (4) Thy foes have roared in the midst of thy holy place;
       they set up their own signs for signs.
   (5) At the upper entrance they hacked
       the wooden trellis with axes.
   (6) And then all its carved wood
       they broke down with hatchets and hammers.)
[4] The translation is doubtful. (Tr. N.: RSV has 'We will utterly subdue them.')
[5] * RSV uses throughout the present tense and also has 'who knows how long' instead of 'who knew which way to turn'.
[6] * RSV omits the word 'allow' throughout.
[7] See BH.
[8] * RSV has 'hold back' instead of 'draw back' and 'keep' instead of 'hide'.

9 * V. 12a reads in RSV, 'Yet God my King is from of old.'
10 * RSV has 'divide' instead of 'frighten away'.
11 * V. 18 is rendered in RSV:
     'Remember this, O Lord, how the enemy scoffs,
     and an impious people reviles thy name.'
12 * In RSV v. 20b reads, 'for the dark places of the land are full of the habitations of violence'.
13 * RSV has in v. 21a 'be put to shame' instead of 'turn back in disillusion'.

Though this community lament bewailing the destruction of the Temple exhibits more concrete features than is the case in other laments, it is nevertheless not possible to ascertain for certain whether the object of the lament is the well-known destruction of the Temple of Solomon by the Babylonians in 587 BC or the desecration of the holy place by Antiochus IV in 168 BC; we must also take into account the possibility that behind the psalm is an event that took place during the period from the fifth to the second centuries BC, about which we know almost nothing. [1–3] The psalm is akin to Psalm 79 and to the Lamentations of Jeremiah and, in form, has certain parallels in the Babylonian and Canaanite lament for the temple.[1] The psalm takes as its starting-point the protest of the people against their God, a protest based on their belief in their election. The cult community have grown impatient and tired of waiting 'for ever' for their lot to take the turn for the better for which they hope. This feature speaks in favour (v. 3) of the view that the psalm refers to the catastrophe of 587 BC, whereas in the Syrian religious conflict the Temple could be re-dedicated after only three years. They therefore think they must remind God of his own promises and of his saving deeds (cf. Ex. 19.4; 15.13 ff.) and must draw his attention to the fact that it is *his* dwelling-place which has been destroyed and defiled and that therefore his own cause is here at stake. The devastation of the house of God has become the occasion for a crisis in their belief in God. [3–8] But they do not let him go, though everything points to God's having forsaken his people: the cult community which had formerly been in the habit of celebrating at the time of festival the coming of God to his people in the sanctuary, calls upon God, and that not without experiencing the bitter taste of disappointment, to set out for the—'perpetual ruins'; these had once witnessed his saving presence, but are now a sad memorial

----

[1] Cf. Willesen, *VT* 2, 1952, pp. 289 ff. His conclusion that Pss. 74 and 79 are not to be regarded as community laments, however, is incorrect, since the lament for the dying god found no acceptance by the Yahweh religion.

which calls to mind all the gruesome details of the blasphemous destruction and defilement of what had been sacred and makes the members of the cult community, as they offer their prayers, depressingly conscious of the fact that they have been abandoned by God since that catastrophe. [9–11] There was no sign of the divine presence (we might think of the cultic tradition or of symbols or of the evidence of sacrifices), no comforting word spoken by a prophet, no counsel of a wise man which could have saved the people from their gloomy despair. (We have reason to doubt whether the statement made in v. 9, which is strongly conditioned by the mood which then prevailed, has in mind the extinction of prophecy altogether and, because it says nothing of Jeremiah—the mention of Ezekiel living as an exile in Babylon would here be out of question—is to be interpreted exclusively in the sense of the Prayer of Azariah (v. 15) as pointing to the Syrian religious persecution; as far as Jeremiah was still able to act in public at all, his activities had had an entirely different effect.) And once more they ask the tormenting question 'Why?' and impatiently enquire 'How long?'—questions which show their frustration as God remains hidden in their adversity. [12–17] The unflinching contending for God in prayer, which notwithstanding everything does not let him go, is not denied the blessing which is inherent also in prayer of that kind. In spite of all their memories and impressions crippling, their faith enables them to hold on in a boldly daring resolve ('and yet') to things which comprised the peculiar content of the cult of the covenant and which cannot be destroyed, even though the bridges of the cultic tradition across which the revelation of God and of his salvation was able to advance to penetrate the world of temporal experience are down. It is a much-neglected but striking fact that in the midst of a lament shaking with deep emotion a hymn in honour of God, the King and Creator and Lord of the universe rings out; in it the cult community pictures to itself the reality of his power and of his salvation (see Intr. 44, 62). This fact shows the reserves of energy which were made available to faith in the *Heilsgeschichte* tradition of the cult community, so that its members take up the fight for the hidden God with the help of the God who was revealed to them. But the same fact also shows that a living relationship existed between God and his people which was a spiritual reality and was not always and not everywhere dependent on the agency of public worship in the Temple. Even though there is no longer any Temple, the cult community faces its

Creator, who formed the universe in his struggle with the chaos-
monster (cf. Ps. 89.9 ff.) and who proves himself Lord of the world
by his ordinances. As in Isa. 51.9 and Ezek. 29.3, the traditions of the
creation and salvation histories are here presumably combined with
one another in the comprehensive view of the *Heilsgeschichte* (see
v. 12), so that in vv. 13–15 allusions to the miracles both of the
Exodus and of the entry into the Promised Land (Ex. chs. 14 and 15;
17.5 ff.; Num. 20.8 ff.; Josh. ch. 3) are simultaneously visible through
the garment of the mythical stylization of the creation history (see
Intr. 59 f.).

[18–23] The God, whose power, as it were, has been re-activated
before the congregation in the hymn (cf. Ps. 68.34; see Intr. 55) and
who has thus come once more into close and living contact with them,
is entreated, and now even more urgently than before, to plead his
own cause against his enemies (v. 22), who foolishly imagine that
they can revile the Lord of the world with impunity. This supplication expresses the unshakable belief that God, who has shown
himself in the creation of the universe to be Lord over the chaos, has
now also the power to suppress the revolt of the chaotic powers and
that in view of his covenant promise he will not allow/his downtrodden people to become the defenceless prey (cf. the picture of the
dove in v. 19) of the cruel lust for power of these enemies.

75. IT IS GOD WHO EXECUTES JUDGMENT

To the Conductor. 'Let not be destroyed.'[1] *A Psalm.   To Asaph.*[2]
A Song

1 We have testified to thee, O God; we have testified.
  Near is thy name; they recounted thy wondrous deeds.[3]
2 'When the hour is come which I appointed,[4]
  I will judge with equity.
3 Though the earth may totter and all its inhabitants,
  it is I who firmly established its pillars.[5] *Selah*
4 I said[6] to the boastful: Do not boast!
  And to the wicked: Do not lift up your horn!'
5 Do not lift up your horn on high;
  speak not insolently against the Rock.[7]
6 For (it comes) not from the morning or from the evening,
  not from the wilderness or from[8] the mountains,[9]
7 for it is God who executes judgment,
  bringing one low and exalting another.[10]
8 For in the hand of the Lord there is a cup;
  the wine foams and is full of flavour.

From that cup he pours a draught.
Even[8] down to the dregs they will drain it,
all the wicked of the earth will drink of it.[11]
9 But I will declare for ever,
I will sing praises to the God of Jacob,[12]
10 that he will smash[8] all the horns of the wicked,
but the horns of the righteous shall be exalted.[13]

[1] See Ps. 57.
[2] See above p..97 (Tr. N.: RSV has 'of Asaph'.)
[3] * V. 1 reads in RSV:
We give thanks to thee, O God; we give thanks;
we call on thy name and recount thy wondrous deeds.
[4] Lit.: when I seize the moment. (Tr. N.: RSV renders v. 2a: 'At the set time
which I appoint.')
[5] * RSV has 'When the earth totters. . . .' and 'keep steady' instead of 'firmly
established'.
[6] * RSV has 'I say' instead of 'I said'.
[7] See BH. (Tr. N: In RSV v. 5 continues God's pronouncement begun in v. 4,
second line reads, 'or speak with insolent neck'.)
[8] See BH.
[9] * V. 6 is different in RSV:
For not from the east or from the west
and not from the wilderness comes lifting up;
[10] * RSV opens v. 7 with 'but' instead of 'for' and reads in v. 7b, 'putting
down one and lifting up another'.
[11] * V. 8 in RSV, after the first line:
with foaming wine, well mixed;
and he will pour a draught from it,
and all the wicked of the earth
shall drain it down to the dregs.
[12] * RSV has 'rejoice' instead of 'declare'.
[13] * RSV starts in v. 10 a new sentence the first line of which reads, 'All the
horns of the wicked he will cut off.'

In spite of its similarity with Hannah's psalm of thanksgiving in
I Sam. 2.1 ff., this psalm is not, as most expositors assume, a thanksgiving, but is part of a cultic liturgy which has been preceded by a
testimony by the congregation (v. 1). It treats of God's judgment on
all the presumptuous evildoers, who without and within magnify
themselves against him (vv. 2 f., 6, 8, 10), and evidently turns
against a certain faintheartedness in those who are disappointed
that the mockery of the ungodly has not yet been brought to an end.
[1] In v. 1 we are at once led into the midst of the cultic scene. In a
testimony the congregation briefly recapitulates what has taken
place in the divine service immediately before: God has appeared
and is near to them in the sanctuary (cf. Isa. 30.27; Ps. 68; see
Intr. 29, 39 f.). They have been able to hear the account of his miraculous saving deeds (cf. Ps. 105; see Intr. 42 f.); in hymnic testimony

they have given expression to their being moved by the majesty of
God, and also to their gratitude for his salvation. But the unexpressed
tension between the uplifting theme of the ceremony in the sanctuary
and the hard facts of the world outside, where human malice is
seemingly allowed insolently to rebel with impunity against heaven
and against the Lord and Rock of Israel (v. 5; cf. Ps. 73.9; Isa.
30.29; Hab. 1.12), weighs heavily upon them. [2–4] At any rate, the
Word of God, which subsequently is made known to the congregation and was probably uttered by a prophet or priest, turns against
the impatient anxiety of those who want to forestall God because he
has not yet brought to a standstill the activities of the blasphemers.
God is really the Lord; the order of the world, which he as its
Creator has established on firm foundations, has not escaped from
his hands, though the whole world may be convulsed. This is why
there is also no reason for doubting his judgment. For creation and
judgment cannot be separated from each other. As the Creator of
the world God alone has the power and the right to sit in judgment
on the world; and, conversely, by his judgment God continues to
work out the realization of his order, the foundation of which he has
laid in his creation. He allows no one to forestall him or to interfere
in what is his exclusive concern; he has reserved to himself alone the
right to determine the hour of his judgment and the manner in
which he will execute it. And it is precisely in doing so that he proves
himself to possess absolute sovereignty. There is just as little reason
for doubting the justice of the divine order when man impertinently
defies God, like a bull who senses his strength and raises his horns.
The evildoers are warned against behaving so arrogantly. The
barriers that separate man from God are firmly established, even
though it may sometimes look as if they are pulled down. [5–7] In
reality God like a towering rock stands unshakable above the
commotion of world events. In his pronouncement God once
more exhibited his true character to the doubting congregation, so
that they could see him in his true light; and the speaker follows up
this divine utterance by adding a kind of interpretation (cf. the
comments on Ps. 50.7 ff.), taking up, in doing so, the Word of God
in v. 5: if it is God who alone executes judgment, then it is pointless
to watch the east or the west, the wilderness in the south or the
mountains in the north to see whether a silver lining will appear
somewhere on the horizon; on the contrary, what now matters is to
be in earnest about God by leaving it entirely to him to carry out the

plan by which he has resolved to produce order and not to waver in one's trust in his righteousness whenever he follows a course different from the one suggested by man's own rash way of thinking. God's judgment is beyond the scope of the short-view calculation of human ideas of 'tit for tat'. Nobody is able to check precisely why God exalts one man and brings another low. It is true also of his judgment that as the heavens are higher than the earth, so are his ways and thoughts higher than those of men; they are and continue to be his eternal secret. **[8]** This truth is probably meant to be expressed in the image of the cup from which God makes men to drink the foaming spiced wine; this image, which the psalmist has conceived as in a vision, is also employed elsewhere to illustrate God's judgment (cf. Ps. 60.3; Jer. 25.15 ff.; Isa. 51.17 ff.; Ezek. 23. 31 ff., etc.). It is perhaps borrowed from the custom of an ordeal (cf. Num. 5.11 ff.; see, however, the comments on Ps. 16.5), which, however, as such is no longer of any real practical import in the psalm itself (this point in opposition to Hans Schmidt). Here it is merely used as an illustration of that mystery which surrounds the providential rule of God in his judgment like a thunderstorm; it is also only able and designed to illustrate, not to unveil that mystery. That the spicy drink of life administered by God must be drained down to the dregs, and that it becomes for the ungodly, who in their insatiable greed get intoxicated as they drink from it, a cup which makes them reel and a deadly drink, but for the others a drink that imparts life and salvation (cf. Ps. 116.13) is indeed the mystery of the judgment which God has reserved to himself and which becomes manifest only when it has taken effect—when the cup has been drained to the dregs. **[9–10]** This profound perception likewise forbids all rash impatience with God's judgment; but it also warrants the confident hope that all presumptuous behaviour will be brought to naught and that the community of the righteous will be saved. At the same time it lays upon the latter the obligation of continually proclaiming this judgment of God in the midst of the congregation and singing the praise of God, testifying to him that he is a righteous Judge.

76. GOD IS TERRIBLE AND GLORIOUS

To the Conductor. With stringed instruments. A Psalm. To Asaph.[1]
A Song

1 In Judah God is well known,
  his name is great in Israel.

2 In Salem his tabernacle was established,
    and in Zion his dwelling-place.
3 There he broke the lightnings of the bow,[2]
    the shield, the sword, and the weapons of war. *Selah*
4 Terrible[3] art thou and glorious,
    more majestic than the everlasting[3] mountains.[4]
5 Spoiled were the stout of heart;
    they fell asleep, passing away;
    and every man of war was unable to use his arms.[5]
6 At thy rebuke, O God of Jacob,
    both chariot and horse were stunned.[6]
7 ' '[3] Terrible art thou! Who can stand before thee
    on account of the might[3] of thy anger?[7]
8 From the heavens thou didst utter judgment;
    the earth fears[8] and is[8] still,
9 when God arises[8] to establish judgment
    to save all the sufferers of the earth. *Selah*
10 Surely the wrath of men must testify to thee;
    he who has been spared death[9] must extol[3] thee.[10]
11 Make your vows to the Lord your God, and perform them;
    all you who are around him,
    bring[11] gifts to the terrible God,[12]
12 who subdues the pride of the princes,
    who is a terror to the kings of the earth.[13]

[1] See p.97. (Tr. N.: RSV has 'of Asaph'.)
[2] * RSV renders v. 3a: 'There he broke the flashing arrows.'
[3] See BH.
[4] * In RSV v. 4 reads:
    Glorious art thou, more majestic
    than the everlasting mountains.
[5] * V. 5 in RSV is:
    The stouthearted were stripped of their spoil;
    they sank into sleep;
    all the men of war were unable to use their hands.
[6] * RSV has 'rider' instead of 'chariot'.
[7] * V. 7 opens in RSV with 'But thou, terrible art thou!' and ends with 'when
once thy anger is roused' instead of 'on account of the might of thy anger'.
[8] * RSV uses the imperfect tense in vv. 8b, 9a.
[9] Read *hammāwet*.
[10] * V. 10b reads in RSV, 'the residue of wrath thou wilt gird upon thee'.
[11] Read the imperative mood instead of the imperfect tense.
[12] * RSV has 'to him who is to be feared' instead of 'to the terrible God'.
[13] * V. 12a reads in RSV, 'who cuts off the spirit of princes'.

The psalm is distinguished by the touch of a prophetic spirit. Its
hymnic ardour accords with the greatness of its subject. Both these
factors bring the psalm into a close relationship with Psalms 48 and 46,
to which it is akin in several respects. In expounding the psalm

methods have been used which are similar to those employed in the exegesis of Psalm 47. The following interpretations oppose each other here: firstly, the *historical* interpretation which assumes that the psalm was composed on the occasion of a specific historical event, namely either the siege of Jerusalem by Sennacherib in 701 BC (cf. II Kings ch. 19; Isa. ch. 37) or a victory in the times of the Macca-bees; secondly, the *cultic* interpretation which understands the psalm in the light of the place it occupies according to this view within the context of the festival cult; and, finally, the *eschatological* interpreta-tion which wants all the statements of the psalm to be regarded as prophecies concerning the events that will come to pass at the end of time. Each of these attempts to interpret the psalm contains a grain of truth; but it is this very fact which should warn us against any one-sided alternative. The psalm itself makes quite clear that its first two strophes (vv. 1–3 and vv. 4–6) look back to things of the past, to events which took place at a time when Yahweh had become highly honoured in Judah and his name had become great in Israel, and when his dwelling-place had been 'established' in Jerusalem. Probably this proves true only of the time of David, who, having conquered Jerusalem, made it the national and religious centre of his dual kingdom Judah and Israel; he did this by bringing up the sacred Ark to Jerusalem (cf. II Sam. chs. 5–7). The victorious battle, which the psalm mentions in this connection (vv. 3, 5 f.) could in that case be a reference to David's decisive victory over the Phili-stines at Baal-perazim (II Sam. 5.17 f.), which was gained near Jerusalem. Because of differences in the sources of the Books of Samuel it is unfortunately no longer possible to establish for certain how these events hang together both chronologically and causally which had taken place in the era of the founders. But provided it can be assumed that the psalmist had in mind a specific coherent historical process, then it is probably only the events at the time of David which come into question. It is, however, true to say that the psalm's account does not look as if it were the direct result of the fresh impression produced by these historical events.[1] The psalmist's presentation of that account, cast in the form of a hymn, clearly exhibits features which show that its concrete historical events have

---

[1] Eissfeldt, *TLZ* 82, 1957, cols. 801 ff. (like Graetz), reads in v. 10 the geo-graphical names 'Hamath-Aram' and 'the rest of Hamath', but interprets them as referring to the events reported in II Sam. 8.3–12 and ascribes the psalm to a contemporary of David.

undergone a cultic stylization and generalization. This suggests the view that the historical events are viewed within the larger framework of the *Heilsgeschichte*, the representation and actualization of which were an essential part of the festival cult. The lapse of time involved in the way the psalm reviews things of the past leads us to conclude that the psalm was composed at a later date. In the two strophes of the second part (vv. 7–9 and vv. 10–12) the retrospect is followed by a glance forward to the divine Last Judgment—a cultic and eschatological trend.

First part: retrospect (vv. 1–6)

[1–2] Whereas otherwise in Old Testament reviews of the mighty deeds wrought by God in the past the miracles done at the Exodus from Egypt are mostly discussed, the psalm has in view the decisive events of the era of David. This is to be accounted for by the incorporation of the Davidic tradition into the covenant cult as this was celebrated in the royal sanctuary at Jerusalem (see Intr. 34, 44 f.). It is characteristic that prominence is given not to the historical events as such, but to the divine events and to what God has done. This fact imparts to the whole first part of the psalm the character of a hymn cast in the stylistic form of praise and adoration, so that the 'name' of Yahweh, which is the object of this self-revelation in the cultic theophany (see Intr. 30 f., 41 f., 56 ff.), is proved to be 'great' also on account of the traditional material of the era of David which had been incorporated in the tradition of the *Heilsgeschichte* of the covenant cult. The application to Jerusalem of the poetical name 'Salem', which is reminiscent of the Hebrew term *šālōm* (peace, salvation), is at the same time meant to indicate subtly that the dwelling-place of God is destined to be the city of peace, and that the Temple is appointed to be a place of salvation. In this conception the cultic and eschatological train of thought already shines through to which the psalm will turn in its second part. **[3–6]** The war-like portrayal of the débâcle of the military forces of the enemy at Jerusalem produces an effect which is so much the more powerful as it is set against, and contrasts directly with, this background. The picture seems to be intended as a prelude to the beginning of the divine kingdom of peace. Here, too, historical, cultic and eschatological elements blend inasmuch as the concrete event of the battle against the Philistines is portrayed as being wholly related to God and in such a generalized form (cf. v. 4) that it can at the same time

be understood both as a typical expression of God's way of acting—
this is commemorated in the cult—and as pointing the way to
eschatology. That God destroys the weapons of war is in the Old
Testament also a permanent feature of the prophet's hope for the
future which has its roots in the tradition of the Covenant (cf.
Hos. 2.18; Isa. 9.5; Ps. 46.9). In a poetical metaphor the poet speaks
of arrows as 'lightnings of the bow'; this image probably originated
in a mythological conception according to which the lightnings were
regarded as the arrows of the god who appeared in the storm-clouds.
The interruption of the account by the hymnic refrain praising the
terrible and glorious character of God (v. 4), and the change to the
prayer-form, clearly show how in the cultic actualization of the
Heilsgeschichte historical events serve as background for the manifestation of the nature of God. This also accounts for the fact that the
psalmist, to colour his account, includes in v. 6 features which he has
borrowed from the tradition of the deliverance at the Red Sea
(Ex. ch. 15),[1] so that what happens but once, the historical,
receives its meaning and weight from what is valid for ever (see
Intr. 58, 76). It is part of the peculiar quality of the Old Testament
idea of God that Yahweh is at one and the same time both terrible
and glorious (cf. Ex. 15.11); his glory proves itself in his terrible
power. And when the poet is far more sensitive to this expression of
the power of God in history than to the impressions produced by
Nature ('more majestic than the everlasting mountains'), then the
explanation lies in the dynamic quality of the Old Testament idea of
God; according to this God's nature is revealed in the things that
happen. He is the God who acts and whose sphere of activity is
history. The continuation of the portrayal of war in vv. 5–6 gives
still greater prominence to the supernatural and miraculous character
of God's power in that it illustrates this power by describing the
collapse of *every* human power. Faced by the reality of God, man's
heart fails him; his heroism and his military forces are of no avail;
they fall a victim to plunderers and are doomed to die. God need
only rebuke and they are seized by panic,[2] by a paralysing bewilder-
ment.

[1] Eissfeldt, loc. cit., relates this verse, too, to the battle against the Philistines
(II Sam. 5.17–25).
[2] The idea of the 'terror struck' into the hearts of men 'by God' is an ancient
feature of the sacral tradition; cf. von Rad, *Der Heilige Krieg im alten Israel*, 1951,
p. 12.

Second part: the look ahead (vv. 7–12)

[7] God has proved his terrible and glorious power by demonstrating man's powerlessness. This thought, developed in the first part of the psalm, is the fundamental theme which in the second part leads to the contemplation of the divine judgment; this, too, as an essential part of the revelation of God's glory and the realization of his salvation, was the object of the cultic ceremony (see Intr. 45 f., 64). Nobody is able to hold his own before the power of the divine wrath. The poet here understands the wrath of God in a sense similar to the view of the prophets—as the driving force by which God asserts himself despite all human resistance. This action has nothing whatsoever to do with moody susceptibility that allows itself to be overcome by anger. [8–9] For, if it were otherwise, the psalm could not immediately follow up that statement with the idea of judgment, of God ensuring justice for the oppressed and suffering on earth. This trait of the benevolent love of God, which is peculiar to the Old Testament faith from its earliest beginnings, shines like a sunbeam through the storm-clouds of the impending judgment. Fear and trust are so closely related to each other that, when God arises to sit in judgment, the earth trembles and becomes silent before the God who saves the afflicted! [10] In both these reactions God's surpassing greatness is manifested. And even when men rebel against him, the wrath of men cannot help testifying to God in that, overcome by God, they become involuntary witnesses of his power. And the man whom he exempts from death will thankfully acknowledge to whom alone he owes his deliverance from judgment. So God's judgment ultimately results in God being made known and worshipped not only in Judah and Israel but in the whole world. [11–12] In this perspective people everywhere are called upon to worship by means of vows and gifts the terrible God who is also their God. The conclusion of the psalm sounds like a last warning argument for this; but at the same time it also includes hope for the coming of God's Kingdom of Peace. It once more forcefully strikes the keynote of the psalm, that is, the terrible power of God which is superior to the pride and power of men. God spells the end of wordly despotism. Heroic faith in God—whose path through history is marked by the remains of armies and thrones that have been overthrown, by the fear and trembling of defeated nations and by the songs of praise of those who have been saved by God and praise his help, for his greatness is their sole support and hope—has here found im-

mortal expression in the profound religious experience of great epochs and their tradition. The psalm thus touches upon an aspect of the truth about God and men which usefully supplements the preaching of the Gospel in the New Testament.

77. THOU ART THE GOD WHO WORKEST WONDERS

To the Conductor. According to Jeduthun.[1] To Asaph.[2] A Psalm

1 Aloud (I cry) to God, I will shout
  aloud to God that he will hear me.[3]
2 In the day of my trouble I sought the Lord;[4]
  in the night my hand is stretched out without wearying;
  my soul refuses to be comforted.
3 I think of God—and moan;
  when I meditate, my spirit faints. *Selah*
4 Thou didst hold my eyelids from closing;
  I was so troubled that I could not speak.[5]
5 I considered the days of old,
  I remembered the years long ago.[5]
6 I mused[6] in my heart in the night;
  I meditated, and my spirit enquired:[7]
7 Will the Lord spurn for ever,
  and never again show mercy?[8]
8 Has his grace for ever ceased?
  Has his word become silent from generation to generation?[9]
9 Has God forgotten to be gracious?
  Or has he in anger shut up his compassion? *Selah*
10 Then I said: The illness from which I suffer is this
  that the right hand of the Most High[10] has changed.
11 I will proclaim[11] the deeds of the Lord;
  yea, I will remember thy wonders of old.
12 I will tell of all thy work,
  and recount thy mighty deeds.[12]
13 Thy way, O God, is in the sanctuary;
  who is a God, great as the Lord?[13]
14 Thou art the God who workest wonders;
  thou hast manifested thy might among the peoples.
15 Thou didst with thy arm redeem thy people,
  the sons of Jacob and Joseph. *Selah*
16 The waters saw thee, O God,
  the waters saw thee and trembled;
  yea, even the ancient deep kept shaking.[14]
17 The clouds poured out water;
  the clouds of the sky gave forth thunder;
  thy arrows[15] also flashed on every side.

18 Thy thunder rumbled like[6] wheels;
    thy lightnings lighted up the world;
    the earth trembled and shook.[16]
19 Thy way was through the sea,
    thy path through the great waters;
    yet nobody saw thy footprints.
20 Thou didst lead thy people like a flock
    by the hand of Moses and Aaron.

[1] See BH and Ps. 62.
[2] See above, p. 97. (Tr. N.: RSV has 'of Asaph'.)
[3] * RSV omits 'I will shout'.
[4] * RSV uses the present tense in v. 2a.
[5] * In vv. 4 and 5 RSV uses the present tense.
[6] See BH.
[7] * V. 6 reads in RSV:
    I commune with my heart in the night;
    I meditate and search my spirit:
[8] * RSV has 'be favourable' instead of 'show mercy'.
[9] * V. 8b is in RSV 'Are his promises at an end for all time?'
[10] See the comments on Ps. 7.17. (Tr. N.: In RSV v. 10a reads, 'And I say,
"It is my grief. . . ." ')
[11] * RSV has 'I will call to mind' instead of 'I will proclaim'.
[12] * RSV has 'I will meditate on' instead of 'I will tell of' and 'muse on' instead
of 'recount'.
[13] * V. 13 reads in RSV:
    Thy way, O God, is holy.
    What god is great like our God?
[14] * In RSV v. 16 is:
    When the waters saw thee, O God,
    when the waters saw thee, they were afraid,
    yea, the deep trembled.
[15] = lightnings; cf. Hab. 3.11.
[16] * V. 18a reads in RSV, 'the crash of thy thunder was in the whirlwind'.

The psalm falls into two parts. In vv. 1–9 we are presented with a
lament in the traditional form of individual laments, which differs,
however, inasmuch as here the subject of the lament is not personal
suffering, such as the illness or persecution of the worshipper, but the
affliction of the people that became the occasion for a crisis in the
worshipper's own faith. The second part (vv. 11–20) is a hymn—
dependent on familiar traditions (cf. in particular Ex. 15.1 ff.; Hab.
ch. 3; Ps. 18.7 ff.; see Intr. 42 f., 59, 74 f.)—which glorifies the revelation of God in his miraculous deeds. Verse 10 forms the link between
these two parts, which represent a united whole in spite of the difference in mood and are not to be attributed to two different authors. The
lament of the psalmist, who perhaps takes up a tradition of the
northern kingdom of Israel (v. 15: 'the sons of Jacob and Joseph'),

presupposes conditions in which he thought he had to discern the judgment of God and the end of his grace—but about which we are entirely in the dark. [1-4] The psalmist movingly confesses how he searched in vain for God during sleepless nights (v. 4a); tormented by anxiety, he was unable to find the right word; his brooding over the things of the past and over the things of the present always ended up with the same question: the question of whether God had ceased to be gracious and whether his word had become silent for ever. [5-9] This confession shows to what a large extent the affliction of his time has become for him a tormenting question about God (*Gottesnot*) and with what a great effort he contends for the hidden God that he may become manifest to him, knowing that without God's mercy and grace he will be driven to despair. [10] But his trouble is precisely this—that all his musing and brooding is of no avail. Man cannot force the hidden God to disclose his secret nor can he make him speak when he is wrapped in silence. But v. 10, after all, contains more than merely the bare painful admission that God's way of acting appears to be so entirely different from that of former times, an admission which explains the psalmist's resignation. The poet describes this conflicting impression which God's way of acting has made on him not without good reason as 'the illness from which I suffer', and so indicates that there is something wrong with himself when God appears to him to be the wholly 'Other' and when he is no longer able to find a way out of his present affliction to God. Here the psalmist has gone to the root of the difficult problem which causes many people to suffer shipwreck with their belief in God and with which those very people wrestled who had most sincerely fought for their faith, the problem, namely, that the process of life and the course of history by no means always reveal signs of God's rule, but frequently conceal it so that man loses confidence in God. The root-cause of this problem is to be found not in God's character but in man's shortcomings, his wanting to force God's providential rule to adapt itself to his own standards and to worship him according to the image which man has made for himself. Verse 10 therefore, being the external and internal turning-point of the psalm (see above), is of decisive importance; the form of the verse and its position between lament and hymn also expresses the importance inasmuch as the worshipper here realizes and confesses that the way described in his lament is the wrong way which in the end always leads him only to his own self and to his affliction, but never enables

him to come into contact with God by faith. With that realization
and its admission he has reached the point where his own thoughts no
longer separate him from God like a thick bank of cloud, but where
he can face and worship God and may now both see and praise what
had remained a mystery to him when he meditated in his lament.

[11–15] In the hymn the worshipper begins to recall God's
miraculous deeds of old (v. 11), which are the theme of the second
part of the psalm (cf. Ps. 71.16; notice the characteristic way in which
v. 11 differs from v. 5, a variation which makes clear the inward
change that has taken place in the worshipper's attitude to the
situation behind his lament, and which must not be removed (* as in
RSV) by following the *Q^erē* in preference to the *K^etīb* (cf. LXX, S and
T). This hymn presupposes a cultic situation, and it may be assumed
that the whole psalm was recited in such a context. For the change
in the worshipper's frame of mind, which manifests itself in the fact
that he is now capable of doing what in the time of his affliction he
was no longer able to do (v. 4)—recount God's wondrous acts in a
song of praise—is not to be accounted for only by the newly gained
knowledge that he walked in the wrong way as he doubted God.
That knowledge itself in its turn goes back to something which has its
origin not in the worshipper's own thinking, but in a living encounter
with the God whom he had sought in vain in the darkness of his
affliction, and who has now become manifest to him afresh (v. 14). On
the analogy of the thanksgivings it is this encounter alone which
accounts for the fact that the worshipper feels constrained to bear witness before the congregation to God's miraculous deeds. Verse 13a and
the fact that the worshipper's hymn follows throughout the stylized
form of the theophany tradition (see above and Intr. 37 ff., 56 ff.)—a
procedure to be understood not as the result of literary dependence but
as the necessary consequence of a common cultic tradition—suggest
that this encounter with God is to be looked for in the manifestation of
God and of his saving deeds, the manifestation which had been celebrated in a previous cultic act by the covenant community (cf. also the
comments on Ps. 68.24 ff.), and which is reflected in the hymnic
praise of the worshipper, deeply moved as he was by it. In this
connection attention must be drawn to the significant fact that the
inner change from the lament to the hymn and the poet's personal
considerations underlying that change, the turning from the *deus
absconditus* to the *deus revelatus*, are not brought about by the poet
himself, but are the effect of the self-revelation of God—with which

the worshipper is brought into contact through the sacred tradition at the very moment when, walking in his own ways, he had lost that contact. The newly-granted contact with God is the ground on which he can once more gain a footing; for he, together with his people, may take comfort in the miraculous way God has guided his people and in his redemption—the things he had come to doubt because of his futile brooding over present affliction. **[16–20]** We would not do justice to the significance of the tradition of the *Heilsgeschichte* for the faith of the psalmist if we were to regard his hymn merely as the 'lyrical effusion' of a man fleeing from a bleak present and taking refuge in the recollection of a brighter past; such a view would entail that the liturgical impact of the cultic events to which the hymn refers back is reduced by psychology to a superficial experience. The tradition of the *Heilsgeschichte*, in which as usual the saving deeds wrought by God at the creation (v. 16c), at the deliverance at the Red Sea (v. 19) and in the time of the wilderness (v. 20; cf. also Ps. 114) are combined with his epiphany in an integrated manifestation of his majesty—this has a greater significance than that of preserving the memory of past events. The main emphasis of vv. 17–19 is on God's appearing, in which his majesty and power are revealed. This appearing is the 'way of God in the sanctuary' which the worshipper experiences as an immediate and present reality, so that he bends low in adoration, worshipping (vv. 12–14). God as the good Shepherd had led his people through the chaotic tumult of the elements and through the perils of the wilderness, but there was nobody who 'recognized his footprints'. And this fact becomes for the worshipper the pledge of the comforting assurance that God will not forsake his people in their present distress either, though the eyes of men may not be able to discover the traces of his passage anywhere. In the psalm's peaceful conclusion, where the poet's struggle comes to rest, the note of a new confidence and genuine faith is gently sounded, of a faith, that is, which is able to have complete trust in God even when the traces of his passage through history are veiled in mystery. For faith subsists on the unequivocal revelation of God and not on any ambiguous religious views of history.

78. RIDDLES PRESENTED BY HISTORY

Maskil.[1] *To Asaph*[2]

1 Give ear, O my people, to my teaching;
incline your ears to the words of my mouth!

2 I will open my mouth in wise sayings;
 I will utter riddles from of old.[3]

3 What we have heard and known,
 what our fathers have told us,[4]

4 we will not hide from our children,
 so that they may tell to the coming generation
 the glorious deeds of the Lord, and his might,
 and the wonders which he has wrought.[4]

5 He established a testimony in Jacob,
 and appointed a law in Israel,
 which he commanded our fathers
 to teach to their sons,

6 that the young generation might know them,
 that the sons yet unborn may arise
 and tell them to their children,[5]

7 so that they will put their trust in God,
 and will not forget the works of God,
 but will keep his commandments,[6]

8 and that they will not become[6] like their fathers,
 a stubborn and rebellious generation,
 a generation whose heart was not steadfast,
 whose spirit was not faithful to God.

9 The sons of Ephraim, armed with the bow ' ',[7]
 were forced to turn back on the day of battle.

10 They did not keep God's covenant,
 but refused to walk according to his law.

11 They forgot what he had done,
 and the miracles that he had shown them.

12 In the sight of their fathers he wrought marvels
 in the land of Egypt, in the fields of Zoan.[8]

13 He divided the sea and let them pass through it,
 and made the waters stand like a dam.

14 In the daytime he led them with a cloud,
 and all the night with a fiery light.

15 He cleft rocks in the wilderness,
 and gave them drink abundantly
 of the waters of the primaeval sea.[9]

16 He made streams come out of the rock,
 and caused waters to flow down like broad rivers.[10]

17 Yet they continued to sin against him,
 to provoke the Most High[11] to anger in the desert.

18 They tested God in their heart
 by demanding the food they craved.

19 They spoke against God, saying ' ',[12]
 'Can God spread a table in the wilderness?

20 Behold, he smote the rock so that waters gushed out
 and rivers overflowed.
 But can he also give bread,

or provide meat for his people?'
21 ' '⁷ The Lord heard it and was full of wrath;
and a fire was kindled against Jacob ' '¹³
22 because they had no faith in God,
and did not trust his saving power.
23 Then he commanded the clouds above,
and opened the doors of heaven,
24 let *man*¹⁴ rain down upon them to eat,
and gave them the grain of heaven.
25 Then every man ate of the bread of the angels;
he sent them food in abundance.
26 He caused the east wind to blow in the heavens,
and by his power he led out the south wind;
27 he caused flesh to rain upon them like dust,
and winged birds like the sand of the seas;
28 he let them fall in the midst of their camp,
all around their habitations.
29 They ate thereof and were well filled,
for he gave them what they craved.
30 But they did not cease to be greedy for more.
While they were still eating their food,¹⁵
31 ' '⁷ he slew their noble men,
and laid low the youth of Israel.¹⁵
32 But in spite of all this they sinned again,
and did not believe his wondrous works.¹⁶
33 So he made their days vanish like a breath,
and their years in terror and fear.
34 When he slew them, they sought for him;
they repented and sought God earnestly.
35 They remembered that God is their rock,
and the Most High God¹¹ their redeemer;
36 and they tried to flatter him with their mouths;
to lie to him with their tongue.
37 Their heart was not steadfast toward him;
they did not keep faith with his covenant.
38 Yet he, being compassionate,
forgave their iniquity,
and did not destroy (them);
he restrained his anger often,
and did not give vent to all his wrath.
39 He remembered that they were but flesh,
a breath that passes and comes not again.
40 When they provoked him to anger in the wilderness,
and offended him in the desert,¹⁷
41 they tested God again and again,
and grieved the Holy One of Israel.¹⁷
42 They did not keep in mind his hand,
the day when he redeemed them from the foe;¹⁸

43 when he wrought his signs in Egypt,
   and his miracles in the fields of Zoan.[19]
44 He turned their rivers to blood,
   so that they could not drink of their streams.
45 He sent among them swarms of flies
   which devoured them,
   and frogs which destroyed them.
46 He gave their crops to the rodent,
   and the fruit of their labour to the locust.
47 He destroyed their vines with hail,
   and the figs of their mulberry trees with hailstones.[20]
48 He gave over their cattle to the hail,
   and their flocks to thunderbolts.
49 He let loose on them his fierce anger,
   wrath, indignation, and distress,
   a company of destroying angels.[21]
50 He gave full scope to his anger,
   he kept not their soul from death,
   but gave their lives over to the plague.[22]
51 He smote all the first-born in Egypt,
   the first issue of their strength in the tents of Ham.[23]
52 Then he led forth his people like sheep,
   and guided them in the wilderness like a flock.
53 He led them in safety, so that they were not afraid;
   but the sea overwhelmed their enemies.
54 And he brought them to his holy land,
   to the mountain which his right hand had won.
55 He drove out nations before them;
   he apportioned them by lot for a possession
   and settled the tribes of Israel in their tents.
56 Yet they tested God and provoked him to anger, the Most High,
   and did not observe his testimonies.
57 They acted treacherously and rebelled like their fathers;
   they twisted like a deceitful bow.
58 They provoked him to anger with their high places;
   they provoked him with their images.[24]
59 When God heard, he was full of wrath,
   and he utterly rejected Israel.
60 He destroyed[25] his dwelling at Shiloh,   1 Sam 4
   the tent where he dwelt[7] among men.
61 He delivered his power to captivity,
   his glory to the hand of the foe.[26]
62 He gave his people over to the sword,
   and vented his wrath on his heritage.
63 Fire devoured their young men,
   and their maidens none did praise.[27]
64 Their priests fell by the sword,   1 Sam 22-3
   and their widows were not allowed to weep.[28]

65 Then the Lord awoke as from sleep,
   like a strong man intoxicated with wine.[29]
66 And he put his adversaries to rout;
   he put them to everlasting shame.
67 He rejected the tent of Joseph,
   he did not choose the tribe of Ephraim;
68 but he chose the tribe of Judah,
   Mount Zion, which he loves.
69 He built his sanctuary like the high heavens,[7]
   like the earth, which he has founded for ever.
70 He chose David his servant,
   and took him from the sheepfolds;
71 from the ewes that nursed the young he took him,
   to tend Jacob, his people ' '.[30]
72 And he tended them with a faithful heart,
   with skilful hand he guided them.[31]

---

[1] See Ps. 32.

[2] See above p. 97. (Tr. N.: RSV has 'of Asaph'.)

[3] * RSV has 'in a parable' instead of 'in wise sayings' and 'dark sayings' instead of 'riddles'.

[4] * In RSV v. 3 continues the sentence begun in v. 2b and v. 4 begins a new sentence.

[5] * V. 6 reads in RSV:
   that the next generation might know them,
   the children yet unborn,
   and arise and tell them to their children.

[6] * RSV reads in v. 7a 'should set their hope in God' instead of 'will put their trust in God' and in v. 8a 'should not be' instead of 'will not become'.

[7] See BH.

[8] = Tanis in the eastern section of the delta of the Nile. Cf. Beer, *Exodus*, p. 75, regarding the tracing of the passage through the Red Sea.

[9] * V. 15b reads in RSV, 'and gave them drink abundantly as from the deep'.

[10] See Ex. 17.1 ff.; Num. 20.1 ff.

[11] See the comments on Ps. 7.17. (Tr. N.: V. 17b is in RSV: 'rebelling against the Most High in the desert'.

[12] Delete 'ām'rū.

[13] See BH. (Tr. N.: RSV adds 'his anger mounted against Israel'.)

[14] = manna; see Ex. ch. 16; Num. ch. 11.

[15] * In RSV vv. 30–31 read:
   (30) But before they had sated their craving,
        while the food was still in their mouths,
   (31) the anger of God rose against them,
        and he slew the strongest of them,
        and laid low the picked men of Israel.

[16] * V. 32b reads in RSV, 'despite his wonders they did not believe'.

[17] * In RSV vv. 40 and 41 are differently constructed, reading:
   (40) How often they rebelled against him in the wilderness,
        and grieved him in the desert!

(41) They tested him again and again,
　　　and provoked the Holy One of Israel.

[18] * RSV has 'power' instead of 'hand' and begins v. 42b with 'or'.

[19] See Ex. chs. 7–12.

[20] * V. 47b reads in RSV, 'and their sycamores with frost'.

[21] Cf. Ex. 12.23.

[22] * V. 50a is rendered in RSV: 'He made a path for his anger.'

[23] = Egypt.

[24] * RSV renders v. 58b: 'they moved him to jealousy with their graven images'.

[25] * RSV has 'forsook' instead of 'destroyed'.

[26] See I Sam. chs. 4–6.

[27] * V. 63b reads in RSV, 'and their maidens had no marriage song'.

[28] * RSV has 'made no lamentation' instead of 'were not allowed to weep'.

[29] * V. 65b is in RSV 'like a strong man shouting because of wine'.

[30] See BH. (Tr. N.: In RSV v. 71 reads:
　　from tending the ewes that had young he brought him
　　to be the shepherd of Jacob his people
　　of Israel his inheritance.)

[31] * RSV has 'upright heart' instead of 'faithful heart'.

This psalm deals with the problem of history in a way quite different from the treatment of the same problem in Psalm 77; but its method also differs from that employed in Psalms 105 and 106, and in Deut. ch. 32 with which Psalm 78 is usually connected. It is here not a question of giving an account of the history of early Israel, for instance after the fashion of a chronicle cast in rhymes, comparable with an epic poem. On the contrary, history is here reflected upon in a way which takes for granted that an account of this history has already been given to the cult community—to whom the psalm is addressed (v. 1: 'my people')—and the reflection on it probably follows the recital of the *Heilsgeschichte* in the festival cult (vv. 3, 17; cf. Pss. 44.1; 77; see Intr. 42 f., 59 f.). The psalm does not present a 'recapitulation of history' or of its main data; its intention is neither to give a chronological outline nor to achieve a kind of synopsis of the relevant historical material. **[1–8]** What it wants to portray and impress on the mind is rather 'the riddles from of old' or, as we would say today, the irrational quality of the things that have come to pass, in order that present and coming generations will bear in mind and never forget the revelation of God's nature and will (v. 5: 'testimony and law'), together with the nature of human sin; simultaneously they are admonished to be faithful and obedient (v. 7) and warned against unfaithfulness and fickleness (v. 8), so that this knowledge will be preserved as a living force (vv. 4 f.), as the holy tradition of God's covenant (vv. 10, 37). The psalm, which is probably most

easily understood if we think of it as being uttered by a priest (v. 1:
torah) in connection with the tradition of the Covenant Festival,[1]
is wholly concentrated on this earnest concern—which is emphatically stressed by the leisurely style, that of didactic Wisdom poetry,
used here (cf. Ps. 49.1–4; Deut. 32.1 f.). The meditation on history is
here worked out in detail with an eye on the incomprehensible fact
that the tribe of Joseph (v. 9), the eyewitness of the mighty saving
acts at the time of Moses (v. 11) and the first bearer of the covenant
which God made with the people at Sinai (v. 10), has not remained
faithful to God, believing him and obeying him (vv. 9–33), and that
the descendants of that wilderness generation (cf. vv. 33, 57), of the
leading tribe within the confederacy of the Twelve Tribes, paid no
heed to the memorial of God's mighty and saving deeds and to the
memory of the manifold help he had given at the conquest and
settlement of the Promised Land (what the psalmist has in mind is
probably the neglect of the covenant tradition), but rebelled against
him, turning to the worship of idols and images, so that God gave up
the tribes of Joseph, together with the confederacy's shrine of the Ark
at Shiloh, to enemies (vv. 34–64), and chose the tribe of Judah
and entrusted to David the leadership of the covenant community
and the guardianship of their sacred traditions (vv. 65–72).[2] This
train of thought indicates that the psalm is related to the Temple
at Jerusalem (v. 69). Its affinity with the view of the prophets on
history (cf. Amos 1.9 ff.; 4.6 ff.; Hos. 11.1 f.; Jer. 2.1 ff.) and with the

[1] The liturgy of the feast of the renewal of the covenant of the sect of Qumran,
which obviously made use of ancient traditions, throws some light on the cult of
the Covenant in which such a view of history had its place. In that liturgy the
recapitulation of the divine saving deeds by the priests is followed by the account
by the Levites of the 'sins of Israel', whereupon the congregation 'entering into the
covenant' confesses its own sins and those of its forefathers and thereby affirms its
faith in the righteousness of God, but at the same time also its faith in his grace
and mercy (Burrows, *The Dead Sea Scrolls* II (1951), plate I, 21 ff.). The exhortatory and didactic tendency of the psalm to impress on the people the need for
trust in God's 'testimony and law' and for obedience to them (v. 5), which perhaps
is still indicated in the term *maskil* used in the title (see the comments on Ps. 60),
as well as the peculiar character of its view of history, common to the psalm and to
the liturgy, suggest that the psalm is to be understood as part of the liturgy celebrated in connection with the tradition of the Covenant Festival; and it is from the
ideology of that tradition that this view of history receives its meaning and life.

[2] I am not sure whether the rejection of the tribe of Joseph can be treated as a
parallel to the cursing of the enemies of the covenant in the scrolls of the Qumran
sect (Baumgärtel, *ZAW*, 1953, p. 265). Rather, the reference to the election of the
tribe of Judah and of David (vv. 68 ff.) could suggest a comparison with the testimony of the Qumran community to the mercy of God (Burrows, II, plate II, 1).

ideology and style of Deuteronomy is usually regarded as an argument in favour of a comparatively late date for the psalm. However, we must here consider the question whether and to what extent that affinity is due to a direct literary dependence on the part of the psalmist or whether and to what extent it has its origin in a common cultic tradition (see v. 3; Intr. 59 f., 63), which may belong to a much earlier period than that of its literary record;[1] and this point is to be taken into account above all when the question of the psalm's relation to the sources of the Pentateuch is investigated. In view of the problem which the psalm poses, it can at any rate be regarded as a proof of the pre-exilic date of the psalm that it contains no reference to the destruction of the Temple.

[9–11] At the beginning of his meditation on the history of his people the poet at once mentions as a particularly telling example the fate of the sons of Ephraim which had been brought on by their disobedience to God. The wording and the connection of this reflection with v. 67 at the conclusion of the psalmist's meditation suggest that we should not think of the downfall of the Northern Kingdom, but of the 'day of battle' on the mountains of Gilboa where Saul met his death (I Sam. ch. 31; cf. I Sam. ch. 15); for that battle paved the way for the transition of the kingship, and so of the leadership of the Yahweh community, from Saul to David—that is to say, from the tribes of Rachel, who until now had been the chief bearer of the election of the people of Israel and of its tradition, to the tribe of Judah. The purpose of the historical review that follows is to show how it came about that God's grace turned away from the original bearer of the promise and chose another instrument to carry on the history of his redemptive work; again, it is the purpose of the subsequent historical reflections to exhibit this incomprehensible riddle, that has emerged in the course of the *Heilsgeschichte*, as an example intended to admonish and warn the present bearer of the divine blessings (*Heilsträger*). [12–16] The psalmist's meditation on history takes as its starting-point the fundamental saving deeds at the time of Moses, the deliverance at the Red Sea and the divine

---

[1] Eissfeldt, *Berichte über die Verhandlungen der Sächsischen Akademie der Wissenschaften zu Leipzig, Phil.-hist. Klasse*, vol. 104, no. 5, 1958, pp. 26–43, assigns to the psalm a date in the time before the kingdom was divided (930 BC) and regards it as possible that Asaph, the contemporary of David, was the author. The fact that the historical reflections of the psalm end in the election of David and of Zion is probably connected with the incorporation of the Davidic tradition into the cult of the Temple.

guidance and help in the wilderness, to which alone the people of
God owe their survival. **[17–33]** But the riddle consists in the very
fact that even these tangible proofs of the divine grace did not break
the power of sin (v. 17) in those who had experienced God's power
in their own lives, but that these very same people, overcome by fear
and faintheartedness, rebelled against God or in insatiable greed
categorically demanded stronger and stronger evidence of God's
support and so provoked him to anger. The psalmist sees how these
mysterious depths of the power of human sin create a connection
between the stories of the miraculously produced streams of water
and of the marvellous feeding with manna and quails, a connection
which has the quality of an example; but not less mysterious and
momentous are the associations that exist between these stories when
seen from the perspective of God, showing that notwithstanding
everything God grants men's requests, but causes them to perish in
the midst of the satisfaction of their inordinate desires when his
kindness does not lead to repentance but is followed by even greater
avidity. This makes evident how closely God's grace and his judgment are related to each other. **[34–41]** It is true that God's acts have
by no means always failed to exert an influence on the people; his
judgments have more than once caused the people to return to him
and to remember that he is their Rock and their Redeemer (cf.
Judg. 2.11 ff.). But that penitence did not go deep enough to change
men radically and make them steadfast in their faithfulness and
obedience. It was but a passing mood which quickly disappeared
(cf. Hos. 6.4) or a pious self-deception which spent itself in a superficial lip-service and in the observance of cultic rites (cf. Isa. 29.13)
without involving a change of heart; and that self-deception is the
most dangerous of all human sins since man in his pious delusion lies
not only to himself but to God (v. 36). The figure of the Pharisee
appears as an indictment throughout the history of every religion.
Thus the history of God's saving acts has for all that continued to
remain the scene of the mysterious conflict between the power of God
and the power of sin. Even the mercy of God, who, having compassion on the mortality and weakness of men, suspended his
judgment, forgave sins and in his grace granted to men times of
probation, was frustrated by their ingratitude and their lack of faith
and faithfulness. **[42–64]** Though God's power and his saving will
are impressively attested all along in the holy tradition, from
the first beginnings of the people in Egypt to the conquest and

distribution of the Promised Land among the tribes—the psalm lays particular stress upon the tradition of the plagues in Egypt by means of which God broke the power of Pharaoh (vv. 43-51) in order to pave for his people the way to the Promised Land—they no longer paid attention to these signs (v. 56; cf. v. 42), but slipped back into a cultus which was designed to serve their requirements, and into a worship of God which was in accordance with the image they had made of God for themselves (v. 58). God counters the entirely inexplicable conduct of the people of God in the holy land with a decision which implies a riddle no less difficult to understand: he rejects the bearer of the tradition and of the promise who allowed both of them to sink into oblivion, and even gives up to the enemy the shrine at Shiloh and the sacred Ark, the symbol of his power and glory (v. 61). In the eyes of men God forgoes all his power in order to show that he is the Lord; this is perhaps his providence's most puzzling and most incomprehensible mystery, which found its personal embodiment in Jesus Christ. The end of the ways of men is, however, not the end of the ways of God. **[65–72]** His judgment on the leading tribe whom he had chosen, and on his holy place, is not the last word in the history of God's redemptive work. Just as a strong man, intoxicated by wine, arises from sleep—a very daring picture—so God proceeds to perform new deeds (vv. 65 f.). He carries on the *Heilsgeschichte* by letting it start from a different point in the course of events: as if it were a new creation, a new beginning with the election of Judah, of David and of the sanctuary on Mount Zion (v. 69); and in doing so God pursues his own course contrary to all human expectations and calculations in so far as he entrusts the leadership of his people and the preservation of his legacy to the shepherd boy David—another proof of the inscrutable character of his power, his love and his wisdom. The portrait of history which the psalmist sketches and which he endeavours to grasp in its ultimate depths is not unequivocal, but is burdened with unsolved and unsolvable riddles. It is impossible either to verify or to calculate in advance the continually changing events, no matter whether they are viewed in the light of their human or their divine aspect. The real factors, on which these events are ultimately based, that is to say, the power of God and the power of human sin, are neither of them open to human understanding, either in themselves or in their mutual opposition in history, and cannot be made intelligible by any theological interpretation of the *Heilsgeschichte*, no matter how profound this may be. Even viewed as the history of salvation, history remains a mystery which God has reserved to himself and in which only those participate who submit to him in faith and obedience (vv. 7 f.; cf. Rom. 11.32–36).

79. DESECRATION OF THE SANCTUARY

A Psalm. Of Asaph[1]

1 O God, the heathen have come into thy inheritance;
   they have defiled thy holy temple;
   they have laid Jerusalem in ruins.
2 They have given the bodies of thy servants
   to the birds of the air for food,
   the flesh of thy saints to the beasts of the field.
3 They have poured out their blood like water
   round about Jerusalem,
   and there was none to bury them.
4 We have become a taunt to our neighbours,
   a mockery and disgrace to those round about us.[2]
5 How long, O Lord? Wilt thou be angry for ever?
   Will thy jealous wrath burn like fire?
6 Pour out thy anger on the nations
   that do not know thee,
   and on the kingdoms that do not call on thy name!
7 For they have[3] devoured Jacob,
   and laid waste his habitation.
8 Do not remember against us the iniquities of our forefathers;
   let thy compassion come speedily to meet us,
   for we are very weak.[4]
9 Help us, O God of our salvation,
   for the glory of thy name;
   deliver us, and forgive our sins,
   for thy name's sake!
10 Why should the Gentiles[5] say, 'Where is their God?'
   Let the avenging of the outpoured blood of thy servants
   be known among the Gentiles[5] before our eyes!
11 Let the groans of the prisoners come before thee;
   according to the great power of thy arm
   preserve those doomed to die!
12 Return sevenfold into the bosom of our neighbours
   the taunts with which they have taunted thee, O Lord!
13 But we, thy people, the flock of thy pasture,
   will praise thee for ever;
   from generation to generation we will make known thy glory.[6]

[1] See above, p. 97.

² * V. 4b reads in RSV, 'mocked and derided by those round about us'.
³ See BH.
⁴ * RSV has 'brought very low' instead of 'very weak'.
⁵ * RSV has 'the nations' instead of 'the Gentiles'.
⁶ * RSV opens v. 13 with 'then' instead of 'but' and reads in v. 13b 'we will recount thy praise' instead of 'we will speak of thy glory'.

This passionate lament about the desecration of the Temple and the terrible disaster that had befallen Jerusalem and the Yahweh community was, in late Judaism, used as a prayer, together with Psalm 137; this was done on the anniversaries of the destruction of Jerusalem by the Babylonians (587 BC) and by the Romans (AD 70). In default of concrete allusions it is as little possible as in the kindred psalms, 44 and 74, to ascertain for certain whether the psalm was composed on the occasion of the calamity of the year 587 BC or on the occasion of a catastrophe unknown to us that occurred in the time after Ezra or during the religious persecution under the Seleucids (I Macc. 1.30 ff.; 3.45; II Macc. 8.2 ff.); at any rate, the psalm seems to have served as a prayer of the persecuted cult community in the times of the Maccabees (cf. I Macc. 7.17). In its structure and style the psalm follows entirely the style of the community lament as this was moulded by tradition. This accounts not only for the parallels already mentioned, but also for the fact that various passages are reminiscent of Lam. 5, Psalm 89, and the Book of Jeremiah (e.g. vv. 6 f. = Jer. 10.25).

The lament (vv. 1–4)

[1–4] The lament describes the disaster: the enemy has invaded the country; the Temple is defiled; Jerusalem is laid in ruins; a horrible massacre has been perpetrated amongst the cult community; the ghastly spectacle of corpses lying around unburied meets the eye everywhere; and to this is added the unbearable taunt of neighbours gloating over the misfortunes of the people, and further the distress and anxiety of those who languish in prison and are doomed to die unless help is forthcoming speedily (v. 11). Only he who in a similar affliction has experienced the breakdown of the last safeguards of a secure existence will be able to understand the psalm and so be able to draw comfort from it.

The supplication (vv. 5–12)

[5–12] It is certainly not a small thing that at the very moment when the waves of disaster pitilessly engulf the cult community the way

to God is still open to them at all and that they desperately cling to
him who alone can still support them in such circumstances; that
they can come to him just as they are and confess to him their
impatient anxiety, their bitter indignation and their helpless powerlessness, trusting that he will understand them and will have mercy
upon them and help them. They do not conceal from themselves that
they have to do penance for their own iniquities and for those of their
fathers and are lost without the forgiveness of their sins (vv. 8 f.); but
they are troubled by the question why God in that case did not first
punish also the Gentiles, who offer no prayers to him, before the
people of God fell a victim to their atrocious cruelty (vv. 6 f.). Out
of such pressing affliction, which brooks no delay, the cult community
bids God, as even a Jeremiah has done in the extreme anguish of his
mind, to avenge them and grant restitution. For it is, after all, his
sanctuary that has been defiled, and his people that have been
destroyed; it is, after all, his glory that is mocked by the Gentiles.
And it is indeed this thought which is ultimately at stake also in the
eager prayer that God's glory be restored and his righteousness made
clearly manifest over against all doubts (v. 10). Then those who have
been saved will be able to lift up their eyes to God, the Good Shepherd of his people, trusting him and praising him with an eternal
song of praise that will never end (see Intr. 54 f.), and able to take new
comfort from his glory.

80. LET THY FACE SHINE

To the Conductor. According to 'Lilies'.[1] A testimony. To Asaph.[2]
A Psalm

1 Give ear, O Shepherd of Israel,
   thou who hast led Joseph like a flock!
   Thou who art enthroned upon the cherubim, appear![3]
2 Before Ephraim and Benjamin and Manasseh
   stir up thy might and come to save us![3]
3 Restore us, O God;
   let thy face shine, that we may be saved!
4 O Lord ' '[4] Sabaoth, how long wilt thou
   be angry with thy people's prayers?
5 Thou hast fed them with the bread of tears,
   and given them tears to drink in full measure.[5]
6 Thou didst make us a strife to our neighbours,
   and our enemies mock at us.[6]
7 Restore us, O God Sabaoth;
   let thy face shine, that we may be saved!

P.—S

8 Thou didst bring a vine out of Egypt;
      thou didst drive out the nations and plant it.
9 Thou didst clear the ground for it;
      it took deep root and filled the land.
10 The mountains were covered with its shade,
      the cedars of God[7] with its branches;
11 it sent out its tendrils to the sea,
      and its branches to the river.[8]
12 Why hast thou broken down its walls,
      so that all who pass along the way
      pluck its fruit?
13 The boar from the forest ravages it,
      and the beasts of the field feed on it.
14 Return to us, O God Sabaoth!
      Look down from heaven, and see,
      and visit this vine,[9]
15 the sapling which thy right hand planted,
      and the son whom thou hast reared for thyself![10]
16 It is burned with fire and hacked to pieces;
      they perish at the rebuke of thy countenance.[11]
17 Let thy hand be upon the man of thy right hand,
      the son of man whom thou hast reared for thyself![12]
18 We will not part from thee;
      thou givest us life that we may call on thy name;[13]
19 Restore us, O Lord ' '[14] Sabaoth!
      Let thy face shine, that we may be saved.

[1] See Ps. 45.

[2] See above, p. 97. (Tr. N.: RSV has 'of Asaph'.)

[3] * In RSV the first line of v. 2 continues the sentence begun in v. 1b, and the remainder of v. 2 forms a new sentence.

[4] See BH.

[5] Lit.: the third part of the measure.

[6] See BH. (Tr. N.: V. 6 reads in RSV:
   Thou dost make us the scorn of our neighbours;
      and our enemies laugh among themselves.)

[7] * RSV has 'the mighty cedars' instead of 'the cedars of God'.

[8] = Euphrates.

[9] * RSV reads 'have regard for this vine' instead of 'and visit this vine'.

[10] * RSV has 'the stock' instead of 'the sapling' and omits the second line of v. 15.

[11] * In RSV v. 16, differently worded, conveys a different meaning in that 'they' in v. 16b refers to the enemies and not to the people of Israel:
   (16) they have burned it with fire, they have cut it down;
      may they perish at the rebuke of thy countenance!

[12] * RSV renders v. 17b: 'the son of man whom thou hast made strong for thyself!'

[13] * V. 18 reads in RSV:
   Then we will never turn back from thee;
      give us life, and we will call on thy name!

The psalm is a community lament which presumably was recited at the joint celebration of the cult at the central shrine of the confederacy of the tribes. Since the tribes of Rachel, that is to say, the tribes of Joseph (Ephraim, Manasseh) and of Benjamin are mentioned, probably only the period preceding the downfall of the Northern Kingdom comes into the question of the psalm's dating, and in this connection the superscription given to the psalm in the LXX deserves to be noted, which relates it to the invasion of the Assyrians (cf. II Kings 15.19). Possibly it is a matter of the truncated state of Ephraim at the time of Hoshea, the last king of northern Israel.[1] The territories of the tribes named seem to have been especially afflicted by the enemy invasion. Cities were destroyed and plundered (vv. 12 f., 16); enemies and neighbours quarrel over who should take possession of them (v. 6); the inhabitants fear their threatened ruin (v. 16). In this critical situation the tribes have assembled in the sanctuary to bring before God their lament, their supplications and their intercessions (note the change in the petition from the first to the third person and vice versa). The refrain (vv. 3, 7, 14, 19), which probably was recited as a response by the whole congregation, divides the psalm into several strophes, the construction of which is not entirely symmetrical.

Invocation and petition (vv. 1–3)

[1–2] The fact itself is already noteworthy that the disaster which had befallen some of the tribes is felt to be a common affliction of all which causes all earlier differences to sink into oblivion and unites the covenant people before God. It presupposes that the tribes are conscious of a common responsibility, and this consciousness has its roots in the divine acts of guidance in their history, and in their commonly practised tradition, a tradition which the Old Testament people of God never gave up completely. These facts account for the hymnic predicates ascribed to God in the invocation with which the prayer opens. Their origin lies in the tradition of the *Heilsgeschichte*, which was obviously still practised in joint celebrations of the cult even after the severing of the kingdoms, and they mean for the covenantal cult community the graphic representation and actual confirmation of their salvation. In the light of these facts it is also understandable that the congregation, once more using phrases

---

[1] Cf. in this connection Eissfeldt, *Festschrift für A. Alt.*, 1953, pp. 65 ff.

borrowed from the ancient cultic tradition, calls upon the God of the
sacred Ark, who is enthroned upon the cherubim (I Sam. 4.4; II
Sam. 6.2), to appear in the glory of his radiant light (Ex. 24.10;
Deut. 33.2; Pss. 50.2; 94.1) in the midst of the tribes who are in need
of his guidance and help. It is a strong faith, based on the firm
foundation of tradition, which is here expressed in a manner still reflecting the majesty and power of the Lord of hosts who directs battles.
[3] He only needs to 'stir up' his 'might' (cf. Isa. 9.6) and the people
will be saved. The refrain, too, is based on the same faith which
knows man's whole existence to be in the hand of the mighty God.
The Hebrew text of the first petition (*haŝibēnū*) has a larger meaning
than the translation is able to express. The term comprises simultaneously man's external welfare and what takes place in the human
soul, *metabasis* and *metanoia*: restoration of external circumstances and
the turning of man's soul to God. Both these happenings represent
the 'renewal of the covenant', and both of them are possible only if
God on his part—this is the meaning which the words taken from the
liturgical benediction wish to express—turns again to his people and
brings about that encounter in the theophany from which all the
divine blessings flow. This encounter between God and his people
is the focal point and real theme of the whole psalm.

Lamentation (vv. 4–7)
[4] The affliction of the people of God is fundamentally a trial of
their faith. They suffer from being separated from God, from being
subject to his anger, though they are probably not without a sense of
their own guilt. The prolonged calamity has become a crisis in their
life of prayer. It is not the first time that such prayers ascend to God,
but he keeps silent so that the cult community imagine the anger of
God to be actually directed against their prayers. They face the
incomprehensible problem, which calls into question the meaning of
their whole piety, that the way in which they seek contact with God
leads to their estrangement from him, that they have to realize that
God, upon whom they call as their helper, is their adversary, and that
they have to experience his anger at the very point where they
expected comfort. [5–6] The faithful who have lost confidence in
their God give vent to their bitter disappointment in the suppressed
irony of the statement that the food and drink for which they are
indebted to their God consisted in a full measure of, yes, *tears*, and
that the people of God, to whom the expulsion of their adversaries

and the possession of the land had been promised (cf. vv. 8 f.), have now themselves become a bone of contention and a mockery to their neighbours and enemies. But the greatest trial of their faith lies not in the fact that the guarantees of the *Heilsgeschichte* are called in question, but in that it is God himself who has withdrawn his own promise and plunged his people into misery. **[7]** But in spite of this, nay, precisely for this reason, the cult community in faith dare to pray even to the angry God, because they trust God to do what could not be hoped for on the strength of human analogies. In this bold venture lies the paradox of faith which alone accords with the majesty and incomprehensibility of God. God has chastised; *therefore* he will also heal.

The parable of the vine (vv. 8–14a)

[8] The psalm gives an account of the *Heilsgeschichte* in the traditional form of the allegory of the vine (cf. Gen. 49.22 f.; Hos. 10.1; Jer. 2.21), in which imagery and interpretation intermingle. The vine as a symbol has its origin in Canaan and typifies the Dionysian world of fecundity and growth in the whole realm of nature. The fact that it is used in the Old Testament to symbolize the shaping of the *Heilsgeschichte* according to a definite plan is proof of the blending of the two realms of nature and history, so that from the biblical viewpoint they are regarded as a unity, a unity which has its basis and goal in God's will to save. In the context of the psalm this account of the *Heilsgeschichte* is by no means meant as a sad recollection of the 'good old days' in order that present affliction may become the more impressive against that background; it is, on the contrary, the point where God and his people meet, an encounter, which has not come to pass only once in bygone days, but takes place afresh during the representation of the *Heilsgeschichte* in the cult, and is experienced by those taking part as a present event in which they themselves participate. The past and the present are here inextricably interwoven, because it is God's presence, then and now, which is at stake. This significant fact is indicated by the strange change of tense (hardly possible to copy in the German language) that expresses the simultaneity of events already completed (perfect) and yet still efficacious in the present (imperfect). **[9–11]** During the recapitulation of the saving deeds of God the people know themselves to be near their God, who steadily accomplishes his saving purpose until he has reached his goal; in that recapitulation the Exodus from Egypt, the conquest and settlement of the land of Canaan and the spreading from the Mediterranean to the River Euphrates are thrown into relief by the metaphor of the purposeful activity of the vine-dresser whose work is crowned with planned success (cf. Isa. 5.1 ff.). **[12–13]** The calamity of which the two subsequent verses speak, sounding the note of a lament, contrasts most strongly with that knowledge. Should God want to destroy his redemptive work with his own hand? From this the tormenting question 'Why?' is only too easy to understand and makes clear once more that ultimately it is the problem that God himself presents which troubles the cult community. **[14a]** Having reached this point, they experience their separation from God so intensely that they are only able to offer God, who seems to have turned away from his people, the short fervent prayer 'return to us' in place of the more extensive petitions of the refrain.

The supplication (vv. 14b–19)

[14b–15] At this point the inner reason for the modification of the refrain and for its resumption as transition to the supplication is the same. The petition 'look down from heaven' is resonant, at least to a certain degree, with the feeling of the distance that separates the people from God, a distance which makes them grievously aware of the calamity they have to face and which can be bridged over only by God's intervention. The petition for a visitation from God points in the same direction. The word 'visit' (*heimsuchen*) has a twofold meaning: encounter with God as an affliction and as a deliverance. Forming the content of the petition, this phrase, it is true, is here intended to convey the meaning of a visitation for the people's deliverance, but the petition is addressed to the God whom the people face as the author of their affliction. In the last resort it is meaningful only if both adversity and deliverance are not understood as exclusive antitheses, but as having their ultimate unity in God's character; only if the people have an inkling of the hidden connection of their momentary affliction with the educational purpose of the divine economy of salvation—which they do not dare to doubt even in the face of their misery. The mystery of their present affliction, too, somehow forms a part of the divine redemptive work, though this truth is not yet discernible, and serves that work's purpose with the people of God. It is this belief that underlies the people's description of themselves as the son whom God has reared for *himself*. **[16]** The supplication once more reverts to the note of lament. The cult community envisages once more the utter seriousness of their position. They do not shun the bitter truth that their very existence is imperilled, not only their material position but their innermost being; for he who threatens them is God himself. **[17]** In this situation the faithful thus threatened make one more effort, a last bold venture (cf. v. 7), and in supplication throw themselves into the arms of this God. It is precisely because it is God who threatens them that he is their only help and that their affliction cannot be his final word (if the phrase 'man of thy right hand' is to be interpreted as an allusion to Benjamin, then v. 17 is to be understood as an intercession for that tribe, which was particularly threatened).[1] **[18]** At the point of supreme peril the cult community, because of this faith, do not give themselves up for lost, but reach out the more determinedly for the saving hand of God which despite all appearances to the contrary stretches out towards them from the darkness.

> So doth the shipwrecked mariner at last
> Cling to the rock whereon his vessel struck.

The mystery of the problem which God himself presents with its tormenting question 'Why?' is here not solved by a kind of meditation, but is overcome by a daring *act* of faith, an affirmation of faithfulness, 'We will not part from thee', that is, the peoples resolve to live in communion with God; it is their turning back to the God who has visited his people (see above, pp. 59, 68). In this way a fruitful encounter comes about between God and the cult community, whereby the people of God receive their life from the hand of God in order to consecrate it anew to his service. **[19]** The affliction of their life of prayer, movingly expressed in the lament of v. 4, is thus overcome. Only now, too, the radiant light of the divine presence appears in all its fullness in the refrain's petition, in which the people of God, assured of their salvation, find the way back to God and to themselves.

[1] Eissfeldt (op. cit., pp. 76 ff.) wants to interpret v. 17 as referring to King Hoshea, who is said to have turned to the ancestral cult when he broke with Assyria.

81. GOD DESIRES TO SAVE

To the Conductor. According to the Gittith [tune].[1] To Asaph[2]

1 Sing aloud to God our strength;
  shout for joy to the God of Jacob!

2 Raise a song, and sound the timbrel,
  the sweet cither[3] with the harp!
3 Blow the horn at the new moon,
  at the full moon, on our feast day!
4 For it is a statute for Israel,
  an ordinance of the God of Jacob.
5 He made it a decree in Joseph for a testimony,
  when he went out against the land of Egypt.[4]
  I hear a voice I do not know:
6 I relieved his[5] shoulder of the burden;
  his[5] hands were freed from the basket.
7 In distress you called, and I delivered you;
  I answer you in the secret place of thunder;
  I test you at the waters of Meribah. *Selah*
8 Hear, O my people, and let me testify to you;[6]
  O Israel, if you would but listen to me!
9 There shall be no strange god among you;
  you shall not bow down to a foreign god.
10 I am the Lord your God,
  who brought you up out of the land of Egypt.
  Open your mouth wide, and I will fill it.
11 But my people did not listen to my voice;
  and Israel did not do as I wished.[7]
12 So I let them go because of the stubbornness of their heart,
  and they followed their own counsels.[8]
13 O that my people would listen to me,
  that Israel would walk in my ways!
14 I would soon subdue their enemies,
  and turn my hand against their oppressors.
15 Those who hate the Lord would flatter him,
  and their [life-]span would last for ever.[9]
16 He would feed him with the finest of the wheat,
  and with honey from the rock he would satisfy[10] you.[11]

[1] See Ps. 8.
[2] See above, p. 97. (Tr. N.: RSV has 'of Asaph'.)
[3] * RSV has 'lyre' instead of 'cither'.
[4] * RSV omits 'for a testimony' and reads 'went out over' instead of 'went out against'.
[5] * RSV reads 'your shoulder' and 'your hands'.
[6] * The first line of v. 8 reads in RSV: 'Hear, O my people, while I admonish you!'
[7] * V. 11b is in RSV 'Israel would have none of me.'
[8] * In RSV v. 12 reads:
  So I gave them over to their stubborn hearts,
  to follow their own counsels.
[9] * RSV has 'cringe toward' instead of 'flatter', and 'fate' instead of '[life-]span'.
[10] See BH.
[11] * RSV has 'I would feed you' and 'I would satisfy you'.

The whole tradition of late Judaism, which probably dates back to an earlier custom, relates the psalm to the Feast of Tabernacles. The view that the psalm is to be regarded as a portion of the festival liturgy of the great autumn festival at New Year is suggested by the mention of the ancient custom of blowing the ram's horn at new moon, which according to Lev. 23.24 and Num. 29.1 served as the solemn announcement of the New Year (v. 3), and also by the promise of salvation and of a rich harvest that is made at the end of the psalm; perhaps, too, the superscription 'at the wine-presses' (LXX) may be interpreted in this sense. The mention of Joseph (v. 5) points to the pre-exilic tradition of northern Israel.

[1–5] The psalm falls into two parts: in vv. 1–5b, in hymn-form, the covenant community is called upon to celebrate the feast in a solemn fashion with shouts of joy, songs and music. Indeed, this call must have been made at the beginning of the festival period, which probably lasted fourteen days (vv. 1–3), and it is justified by saying that God himself has decreed this celebration for the covenant people as his holy statute and ordinance in order that it may be a 'testimony' to his redemptive work which began with their deliverance from Egypt (vv. 4–5b). The purpose of the *Heilsgeschichte* and at the same time of the public worship which serves its transmission is fulfilled in the testimony to God. This truth is for the cult community the guiding principle of their celebration; for us it is the key to the true understanding of the psalm. In the present case the cult community seems to be in special need of the call that is made upon it to shout for joy with festal songs, as they obviously suffer from the pressure which the threat of enemies has brought upon them (vv. 14 f.). [6–7] Whilst the members of the covenant community are worried about their deliverance and so are in a state of mind which does not allow them to indulge in an unclouded festal joy, the Word of God rings out, spoken either by a prophet or by a priest (vv. 6 ff.); according to v. 5c, which introduces this Word of God, the speaker claims to be inspired by God himself ('a voice I do not know'). It contains the answer to the questions which, unspoken, harass the cult community and is by no means to be regarded as a mere recollection of the history of bygone days. The fatherly, pastoral touches, as well as the transition from the narrative form to that of direct speech and the little-noticed change of tense (vv. 6 f.), make clear that the cult community are not separated from the past by the interval of history, but have themselves a share in it: they are involved in those events

which they directly experience anew in the ritual of the cult. Before
the presence of God in the sanctuary the barriers of space and time
disappear, and the whole redemptive work of God is concentrated in
a single moment pregnant with immense actuality and directness.
The divine utterance prepares the congregation for this great
moment in the cultic proceedings by a twofold reference to the
manifestation of the nature and will of God which they are going to
experience as the climax of the ceremony. The deliverance from the
Egyptian forced labour is meant to be understood by the congregation as a pledge of the answering of their prayers by the God who
appears in the cloud as in bygone days and, just as he did at the
waters of Meribah, challenges ('tests') the people to make a decision
(v. 7). In the present context this is probably not to be regarded as an
allusion to the aetiological story of Ex. 17.7 (Ps. 95.8 f.), when the
people put God 'to the test', but as a reference to the tradition of the
making of a covenant at Meribath-kadesh (a parallel to the Sinai
tradition), when Yahweh gave the people 'a statute and an ordinance' (cf. Deut. 33.8 f.; 32.51; Ex. 15.25; 16.4; Num. 20.13; 27.14)
and the people decided to side with Yahweh by entering into a
covenant with him. **[8–10]** God will now 'testify' to this covenant
before the people through the imminent act of the solemn renewal of
the Covenant; and as in the ancient traditions (cf. Ex. 19.4 ff.) there
follows the admonition to be faithful to the Covenant, and also the
promise. This explains why the will of God, as this is shown in the
form of the First Commandment, is here quoted before the promise of
grace at the beginning of the Decalogue. The suggestion frequently
made to transpose verses 8 and 9 misjudges the situation. It starts from
the assumption that the psalm intends to quote the whole Decalogue;
but just as a detailed recital of the *Heilsgeschichte* in the cult belongs to
a later stage in the festival's celebration, so does the proclamation of
the text of the Decalogue as a whole. Here we are, however, dealing—
a careful comparison of v. 9 with Ex. 20.2 and Deut. 5.7 shows this,
too—with a free allusion which prepares for that cultic act and is
designed to create the conditions for the renewal of the Covenant.
The most important prerequisite for the renewal is precisely that
faithfulness to God which bars the worship of other gods beside that of
Yahweh (cf. Josh. 24.21 ff., where the cultic rite of the renunciation of
the foreign gods is recorded, which probably may also be assumed to
form the psalm's cultic background; see Intr. 33, 51, 75 ff.). Within the
covenantal relationship the promise of divine salvation is tied up with

loyalty and obedience in religion; for this reason, in contrast with the Ten Commandments, God's affirmation of his faithfulness to his people follows the manifestation of God's will in the present context. That affirmation includes the striking call upon the congregation to open their mouth wide that he may fill it; this also points to the imminence of the theophany and the people's encounter with God, which promise to bring about their salvation, so that, being 'imbued' ('*erfüllt*') with God's Word, they will commit themselves to him. This interpretation of the call (already advocated by the Targum: cf. Jer. 15.16; Ezek. 2.8; Ps. 119.131) is to be preferred to the customary but less pregnant view in which the call has in mind the sating of the people by God's gifts; for it is only at the conclusion of the psalm that the psalmist comes to speak of these gifts. The congregation's testimony to God is likewise ultimately his gift, a present of his grace. Just as in the beginning of history, so also now, God is willing to 'testify' to his people that he is gracious and to let them partake of that grace. **[11–12]** But he knows man's nature—readily prepared to make a profession but just as ready to forget it again. This is why he follows up his offer with an earnest admonition, again having an eye on history which always repeats itself and whose grave consequences affect even the present. When the history of salvation so often ends in disaster in spite of the divine will to save, then this state of affairs is not God's fault, but is brought about by the people's thoughtlessness and disobedience—which caused the *Heilsgeschichte* to become the history of God's judgments. God leaves men to their own devices so that in future they act only in accordance with their own desires and follow their own counsels, with the result that their sin leads to hardness of heart and so to their punishment. Such a view of history frequently occurs in the writings of the prophets (Hos. 11. 1 ff.; Jer. 2.1 ff.; 3.6 ff.; Micah 6.3 ff.), but the passage under discussion can hardly be regarded as the product of a literary dependence on the part of the psalmist; rather should we ask ourselves whether this kind of moralistic view of history has not its roots in the cultus also in so far as the prophets are concerned (cf. Pss. 78; 106). **[13–14]** The fact that the history of salvation manifested itself as the history of God's judgments is, however, by no means to be considered as a sign that God has abandoned his people; on the contrary, behind this history is the same will to save that is behind his promises: the judgment of God is the hand which he stretches out to restore the sinner to himself and lead him in his ways. God does not cease to recall his people to himself; his desire to save and his call-note ring out with an even greater urgency than in v. 8, and he once more confirms that he is willing to help them against their enemies. **[15–16]** Now it depends on the people themselves whether this promise will come true. At the conclusion of the psalm the Word of God is followed by a statement by the speaker himself. It is the Amen that in a stylized form corroborates for the benefit of the congregation God's desire to save and his promise (cf. Pss. 18.44; 66.3; Deut. 32.31) and sets before their eyes the subjugation of enemies, their everlasting existence and the blessing of a rich harvest as the divine blessings which God has in store for them if they keep faith with him and obey his will.

82. THE JUDGMENT OF GOD

A Psalm. To Asaph[1]

1 God stands forth in the assembly of the gods;[2]
  in the midst of the gods he holds judgment:
2 'How long will you judge unjustly
  and show partiality to the wicked? *Selah*
3 Give justice to the weak and the orphans;
  acquit the afflicted and the destitute![3]
4 Deliver the weak and the needy;
  snatch him from the hands of the wicked!'
5 'They have neither knowledge nor understanding,
  they walk about in darkness;
  all the foundations of the earth are shaken.'
6 'I said indeed: you are gods
  and sons of the Most High, all of you!
7 Nevertheless you shall die like men
  and fall like any prince!'
8 Arise, O God, and judge the earth;
  for thou art the Lord to whom all the nations belong![4]

[1] See above, p. 97. (Tr. N.: RSV has 'of Asaph'.)
[2] * V. 1a reads in RSV, 'God has taken his place in the divine council.'
[3] * RSV has 'maintain the right of' instead of 'acquit'.
[4] * V. 8b reads in RSV, 'for to thee belong all the nations'.

The magnificent picture which the psalm unfolds before our eyes is inspired by the lofty flight of fancy of a poet and is sustained by a strong religious and moral power. In colours borrowed from the prophets and from mythology the psalmist depicts a heavenly court scene in which God calls to account the gods who are subordinate to him, because they have not fulfilled their duty of executing justice among men, but have shaken the foundations of the moral order of the universe by their injustice and by showing partiality to the wicked. This conception, which has its roots in mythology, has been embodied in the cultic tradition of the Yahweh religion, having first been divested of its originally polytheistic character (cf. the exegesis of Ps. 58; see Intr. 51). Clothed in the form of a dramatic liturgy in the cult, it here serves to explain the riddle presented by life that violence so often triumphs over what is right, and that the weak and the poor do not come into their own and are exposed to oppression by ungodly rulers. This depressing state of affairs is accounted for by saying that the gods are responsible for the intolerable conditions on earth because of the injustice of their judgments in heaven. The judicial function of the lower deities in heaven has its origin in the root-idea of the celestial archetype or counterpart of the things that happen on earth, an idea that is widespread in the history of religions, and it seems to have penetrated the Old Testament theology of the cultus in order to provide an answer to the question of how the injustice prevailing on earth can be reconciled with belief in the reality of the righteous God (cf. Ps. 58.1 ff.). This could come about the more easily as the idea of dethroned gods, who in the Yahweh religion were regarded as being subject to God and constituted the household of Yahweh, is also otherwise not unfamiliar to the Old Testament (cf., e.g., Pss. 7.7; 89.6 f.; I Kings 22.19; Job 1.6 ff.; 2.1; 15.8; see Intr. 41, 51, 61). In this it is a matter of coming to terms with the deities of the pre-Israelite inhabitants of Canaan and with those of the neighbouring countries of Israel, whose originally polytheistic character was overcome by reducing them to the rank of servants of Yahweh who are subject to his judgment. A special and peculiar function devolves on them in connection with the problem of theodicy that forms the background of the psalm. They contribute by their folly to the ability of the power of evil to hold its own on earth and to triumph again and again. The fact that the attempt to explain the problem thus is made within the scope of the Old Testament is no less strange. For this attempt contains in embryo the dualistic solution of the problem, a solution which, after all, is only an attempt to solve the problem, but is not in itself a proper solution. For the existence of evil is here attributed to the activities of forces hostile to God; but at the same time God's righteousness as such remains untouched by the injustice that exists in the world. A serious concern underlies this outlook, determined as it is by ideas prevailing in contemporary history. Wherever the reality of evil in the world is

felt as a power menacing man's existence, it is considered to be the
result of the activities of a personal power. Both the notion of Satan,
which, springing from other sources, penetrated the Old Testament,
and the figure of the Devil in the Christian faith are but different
figures of speech, expressing the same state of affairs, in which evil
is taken quite seriously as the activity of a real personal being.
However, the psalmist holds the view that the attempt at a dualistic
solution of the problem of theodicy is not the final word in the quest
for God's righteousness. In principle the faith in the One God and in
his righteousness remains unshaken here. With a prophetic assurance
the psalmist recognizes that the real and final solution of the problem is to be found in the ultimate vindication of the righteousness of
God. He speaks of this truth in the traditional form of a court scene
in heaven.

Verse 1 opens the psalm by briefly depicting the situation;
Yahweh's speech as Judge and the verdict he passes on the gods form
the main part of the psalm (vv. 2–7); the poem concludes with an
appeal to God asking him to execute judgment on earth, a
petition which is accounted for by the cultic situation which the
psalm has in view.

Introduction (v. 1)

[1] The psalm opens with a powerful picture. Inspired by a vision,
like Isaiah's account of his call in the Temple of Jerusalem (Isa.
ch. 6) having its origin in the cultic tradition of the theophany, the
psalmist focuses his thoughts on Yahweh and visualizes him as he
stands forth in the midst of the assembly of gods in heaven to deliver
judgment on his celestial subjects. The comprehensive scope of this
picture already indicates that a question of world-wide significance is
at stake here. The gods, hitherto entrusted with the office of judge,
now stand themselves before the judgment-seat of God. This fact
alone already shows how little the psalm is spiritually tied to the
polytheistic root of the conception it here adopts.[1] The psalmist's
portrayal of the situation affords a glimpse of the concentrated
energy with which the moment is charged in which the final verdict
of God is going to be passed. For a time God has watched the

[1] Even if the pre-Israelite idea of the assembly of *El* as the supreme god (v. 6:
ʿelyōn) should still be hidden behind v. 1 (Herbert Schmidt, *ZAW* 67, 1955, pp.
183 f. and Eissfeldt, *El and Yahweh*, *JSS* 1, 1956, pp. 29 f.), the meaning of the
psalm is nevertheless hardly that Yahweh is subordinated to *El*, as can be inferred
from v. 8.

activities of the subordinate divine judges; but now his patience has come to an end.

The speech of the divine judge (vv. 2–7)

[2] God's reproof bursts in upon the assembled gods with a deep solemnity reminiscent of the style of the prophets' rebukes (cf. in this connection especially Isa. 41.21 ff.; 44.7 ff.; 45.20 ff.). He is no longer prepared to tolerate their unjust way of administering justice and the partiality they show to the wicked, which are the real cause of the injustice that prevails on earth. The righteousness of God as the fundamental order, to which everything has to submit, holds good also in heaven. Injustice could persist on earth only because God in his superhuman patience has not already intervened sooner. Hence there is no reason to doubt the justice of the order which his will has decreed. [3–4] The truth of this statement is proved by the directive which God once more explicitly lays down as the principle to which a just verdict has to conform. It includes the same requirements which were continually proclaimed by the prophets, too, as the basis of the covenantal order governing the life of the people. They make clear beyond doubt what the Old Testament means when it speaks of righteousness. It does not think in this connection of something formal and legal: righteousness consists in 'doing justice' to the misery of the poor, the afflicted and the forlorn by helping them effectively. Though elsewhere he who wields power may determine what is right, the thought that the strong has to play an active part in the support of the weak pervades the whole morality of the Old Testament covenant. In this the Old Testament religion has always been superior to the other religions from its first beginnings and right into the time of the Romans enjoyed the respect of the Gentiles precisely because of the high standard of its social ethics. The New Testament, too, established its moral demands on the basis of the lofty moral earnestness which is expressed in the Old Testament's requirement of accepting responsibility for the weak and the oppressed. [5] The divine order aiming at a righteousness of this kind was never annulled for a single moment, but had always been valid; but, of course, how could it operate when the judges to whom its implementation was entrusted possessed neither 'knowledge' nor 'understanding' of the things which truly constitute the divine foundations of the moral order of the universe! God passes this devastating judgment on the gods, as if he had turned away from

them whilst making it in order to answer the religious question of the cult community. A bitter irony is hidden behind his words: they are gods who walk about in darkness, having no understanding! But how could it be otherwise; how should foreign gods know what Yahweh's intentions are! We are probably justified in reading between the lines such a rejection of the polytheistic background, assuming that this reading is in accord with the true meaning of the psalm. No wonder that the foundations of the moral order on earth are shaken when those who had been appointed to act as the heavenly guardians of God's order of the universe themselves do not even know and obey that order! This state of affairs is, however, but a passing phenomenon. **[6–7]** For the prophet has already heard the threatening utterance of God foretelling the end of the gods. In his verdict God makes clear to them with telling force what they have been until now and what they shall be henceforth. It is true that in conjunction with their office he had once granted them divine rank and name (cf. in this connection Deut. 4.19); but now they will share the lot of mortal human beings; deprived of their rank as deities, they shall suffer a sudden downfall such as has already befallen many an earthly ruler. (The comparison made in v. 7 refutes the widespread interpretation of the deities as human judges.) The verdict in God's judgment represents for him the solution of the problem to which the psalm wants to give an answer. It is the final victory of the divine justice in heaven the consequences of which will not fail to make themselves felt in the things which are going to happen on earth. Here ends the heavenly scene.

[8] The cultic, mythological proceedings are followed by the effect which they have in the earthly realm. 'Prayer follows the vanishing vision as the echo follows the shout.'[1] It sounds like man's Amen in response to the divine promise when the appeal is now made to God to appear and take direct charge himself also of the office of Judge of the earth and by virtue of his own authority to enter upon his exclusive Lordship over the nations, which like the possession of an inheritance by the heir is his by right. The religious concern pulsating through the psalm can be directly felt in these concluding words, which similarly reflect the cultic background of the idea of God's judgment on the earth and its nations and of his Lordship over them (see Intr. 32 f., 50). The problem is solved by the trust

---

[1] * 'Dem entschwindenden Gesicht schwingt sich das Gebet nach.' (I have been unable to trace this quotation.)

which the psalmist puts in God's righteousness and which, confident of his faith, he expresses in his petition; and it is solved solely by this trust. Such a faith learns to endure the riddles and afflictions of life; for it knows that these riddles are not God's final word in this matter. It is a question of apprehending this faith in God's righteousness, even though this has to be done through the medium of the psalm's ideas, determined as they are by the spirit of the age, and even though these ideas at first sight may seem rather strange to us. For such a faith has already covered part of the way at the end of which stands the conquest of sin by Jesus Christ.

83. ENEMIES ON ALL SIDES
A Song. A Psalm. To Asaph[1]

1 O God, do not keep silence;
   do not hold thy peace or be still, O God!
2 For lo, thy enemies are in tumult;
   those who hate thee have raised their heads.
3 They lay crafty plans against thy people;
   they consult together against thy protected ones.
4 They say, 'Come, let us wipe them out as a nation;
   let the name of Israel be remembered no more!'
5 Yea, they conspired with one accord;
   and[2] against thee they made a covenant:[3]
6 the tents of Edom and of Moab,[2]
   the Ishmaelites and the Hagrites,
7 Gebal and Ammon and Amalek,
   Philistia with the inhabitants of Tyre;
8 Assyria also has joined them;
   they became the arm of the sons of Lot.[4] Selah
9 Do to them ' '[2] as thou didst to Sisera,
   as to Jabin at the river Kishon,[5]
10 and as to Midian[2] who were destroyed at Endor
   and became like dung in the field.[5]
11 Make[2] their nobles like Oreb,
   and like Zeeb ' '[2] all their princes,[6]
12 who said, 'Let us take possession for ourselves
   of the pastures of God.'
13 O my God, make them like thistles,[7]
   like chaff before the wind!
14 As fire consumes the forest,
   as the flame sets the mountains ablaze,
15 so do thou pursue them with thy tempest
   and terrify them with thy hurricane!
16 Fill their faces with shame,
   that they may seek thy name!

17 Let them be ashamed and dismayed for ever;
    let them perish in disgrace.
18 They will come to know[8] that thou alone,
    whose name is Yahweh,
    art the Most High[9] over all the earth.

[1] See above, p. 97. (Tr. N.: RSV has 'of Asaph'.)
[2] See BH.
[3] * In RSV the present tense is used throughout v. 5.
[4] * V. 8b reads in RSV, 'they are the strong arm of the children of Lot'.
[5] * In RSV vv. 9 and 10 are differently constructed:
    (9) Do to them as thou didst to Midian,
        as to Sisera and Jabin at the river Kishon,
    (10) who were destroyed at Endor,
        who became dung for the ground.
[6] * V. 11 reads in RSV:
    Make their nobles like Oreb and Zeeb,
    all their princes like Zebah and Zalmunna,
[7] * RSV has 'whirling dust' instead of 'thistles'.
[8] * RSV begins v. 18 with 'Let them know that . . .'
[9] See the comments on Ps. 7.17.

The psalm is composed in the style of a community lament.
Though it lists in vv. 6–8 a number of nations, the attempts to explain
the psalm in the light of a specific situation in the history of Israel
differ widely. For we do not know of any warlike situation in which
all the nations named here were united in a coalition formed against
Israel. Again, neither the interpretation which on account of II
Chron. ch. 20 refers the psalm to the ninth century nor that which
because of II Chron. 26.6 ff. relates it to the eighth century are able
to master the consequent difficulties and anachronisms without the
help of questionable re-interpretations; and this is also true, to single
out but these few examples, of the exposition of the psalm on the basis
of I Macc. ch. 5, which is the favourite interpretation of ancient and
modern commentators alike. Since it is more than doubtful whether
the specified nations existed at all at one and the same time, and
since, moreover, neither an actual campaign is discussed nor any
concrete measures of defence are envisaged, but mention is made
only of enemies' plots against God and his people, we shall have to
refrain from any purely historical explanation of the psalm. In place
of that we shall have to give preference to an exposition in the light
of a cultic situation in which the people deliver up to the judgment
of God all their potential and actual enemies, adversaries of the past
and those of the present, and, in doing so, make use of rites which are
appropriate to the occasion (such as, for instance, were observed at

the proscription of hostile kings in ancient Egypt; compare in this connection the oracles of the prophets regarding the foreign nations). It is a well-known fact that such a cursing of the enemies of God—a rite which, after all, is also firmly established in various parts of the *Heilsgeschichte* tradition—and, conversely, the blessings bestowed upon the community of those who were faithful to Yahweh had their place in the cultus (cf., e.g., Ps. 58). The emphasis throughout on the fact that the enemies who are meant to be affected by the judgment are actually the enemies of Yahweh, and the eventual recognition of God by these enemies, which appears in v. 18 as the ultimate aim of that judgment, point to the basic theological idea of the festival cult rather than to a concrete affliction of the people caused by war. For the peculiar character of the psalm consists in the fact that the historical and political events in its foreground are held together and dominated by a theological background which imparts to them the significance of a final decision, or, to put it differently, which invests them with an ultimate—an eschatological—meaning.

[1–2] The appeal with which the psalm opens in v. 1 and its motivation (v. 2), which is reminiscent of Ps. 2.1 f., at once make evident that what is here at stake is not merely an event which takes place on the political level and for which God's help is implored, but God's own cause; and the manner in which that cause will be dealt with is bound to show whether 'his enemies' are allowed to rebel with impunity against him (v. 5), against his people (vv. 3 f.) and against his country (v. 12). [3–5] The fact that at such a critical moment the community as a nation knows its own cause to be at one with that of God and regards the machinations of all its enemies as a coalition ('covenant') unanimously directed against God is the result of faith's simplifying outlook, which levels the differences that mark historical and political conditions and seeks to reduce them to a final common denominator. [6–8] In that method lies the strength of such a way of thinking, but also its danger. Naturally, it was above all the neighbouring nations who pressed into the civilized country from the deserts in the south and in the east and threatened Israel's existence; but in this 'list of denunciations' are named also the Philistines in the south-west and Tyre in the north and, after the small powers, the great empire of Assyria as the most dangerous enemy. In view of the mention of Assyria and the omission of Babylon we shall have to assume that the psalm was composed between the ninth and the seventh centuries. It is beyond our knowledge whether specific political motives are responsible for the fact that Aram (cf. Amos 1.3 ff.) is not included in the list.

[9–15] The second part of the psalm contains imprecations upon enemies; at first these follow the tradition of the Book of Judges (cf. Judg. ch. 4), so that the saving deeds which God wrought in that period for his people are here, as it were, repeated. The form of comparison here is a last echo of magical acts which once accompanied the cursing and originally possessed a miraculous power (e.g. the breaking into pieces of effigies, staffs or vessels; cf. the Egyptian texts of proscription and Ps. 2.9). But there is no room in the Old Testament for any independent magical power exercised by actions or by the spoken word apart from the exclusive power of God; the curses of the past have become petitions and magical analogy is replaced by the actualization of the acts of God, that is to say, by the representation of the acts of deliverance wrought in the *Heilsgeschichte*, which are meant to prove his supremacy over enemies. But the God who has power over history is at the same time also the Lord of the elemental forces of nature; fire, tempest and hurricanes are at his disposal to be used in his judgment on the rebellion of the adversaries; here, too, we seem to be presented with an allusion to the cultic tradition of the theophany (cf. I Kings 19.11 ff.). [16–18] The psalm's conclusion, however, throws a peculiar, significant light upon the cruel and severe imprecations which are uttered by the oppressed people. Here the power and the grace of God have the final say and not human vindictiveness. The ultimate goal of God's terrible judgments, to which both friends and enemies will be subjected, is that his enemies, too, will be made ashamed and will seek him, that they will turn to him in penitence and will come to realize that power and glory upon the whole earth belong alone to God who has revealed his name Yahweh in the epiphany (cf. with regard to this cultic tradition Ex. 33.19 and Intr. 41 f., 74).

84. HOW LOVELY IS THY DWELLING-PLACE, O LORD SABAOTH!

To the Conductor. According to the Gittith [tune].[1]   To the Sons of Korah.[2]
A Psalm

1 How lovely is thy dwelling-place, O Lord Sabaoth!
2 My soul longed, yea, fainted for the forecourts of the Lord;
   now my heart and flesh sing for joy to the living God.[3]

3 Even the sparrow has found a home and the swallow a nest for
   herself
   where she may lay her young,
   at thy altars, O Lord Sabaoth, my King and my God.
4 Blessed are those who dwell in thy house,
   ever singing thy praise! *Selah*
5 Blessed is he whose strength is in thee,
   when he meditates in his heart on pilgrimages.[4]
6 As they pass through the valley of tears,[5]
   they make it a place of springs,
   a place of blessing such as the early rain imparts.[6]
7 They go from strength to strength
   until they[7] appear before God in Zion.[8]
8 O Lord, ' '[9] Sabaoth, hear my prayer;
   give ear, O God of Jacob! *Selah*
9 O God, our shield, behold;[10]
   look upon the face of thine anointed!
10 Yea, *one* day in thy forecourts is better
   than a thousand elsewhere.
   I would rather be at the threshold of the house of God
   than dwell in the tents of wickedness.[11]
11 For the Lord is a battlement and shield ' ';[9]
   he bestows grace and glory;
   no good thing does the Lord[12] withhold
   from those who walk devoutly.[13]
12 O Lord Sabaoth, blessed is the man
   who trusts in thee!

[1] See Ps. 8.
[2] See above, p. 97. (Tr. N.: RSV has 'A Psalm of the Sons of Korah'.)
[3] * In the first line of v. 2 RSV uses the present tense.
[4] See BH. (Tr. N.: V. 5b reads in RSV, 'in whose heart are the highways to
Zion'.)
[5] See BH.
[6] * In RSV v. 6 is:
   As they go through the valley of Baca
   they make it a place of springs;
   the early rain also covers it with pools.
[7] Read plural.
[8] * V. 7b reads in RSV, 'the God of gods will be seen in Zion'.
[9] The word 'God' seems to be a later addition.
[10] * V. 9a is in RSV 'Behold our shield, O God.'
[11] * RSV has 'I would rather be a doorkeeper in the house of my God.'
[12] Transfer 'Yahweh' to the second half-verse.
[13] * RSV has 'sun' instead of 'battlement' and 'favour and honour' instead of
'grace and glory', also 'uprightly' instead of 'devoutly'.

The psalm is a song which seems to have been composed on the
occasion of a pilgrimage to the Temple of Jerusalem; its pattern is

closely followed by the hymn 'Wie lieblich schön, Herr Zebaoth'.[1] Its
style is that of a hymn and in that respect shows an affinity to the
so-called 'Songs of Zion' (see Intr. 45). However, the poet has not
made himself slavishly dependent upon the traditional form; his
striking poetical freedom and talent enable him to find deeply
moving and intimately tender notes to express the things which
arouse festal joy in his heart. The statements which he makes can
without any difficulty be accounted for by the situation in which the
festival pilgrim is placed and also by his frame of mind, so that there
is no need to regard, for instance, vv. 5 and 11 f. as utterances of the
priest and to conceive of the psalm as presenting a piece of liturgy.[2]
Seen in this light, the psalm is a valuable testimony to the mood of
the festival pilgrims and provides us with a graphic illustration of the
Old Testament's devotion to the house of God and the spiritual
aspect of its cultic piety. According to v. 10, the author seems to live
in a pagan (Aramaic) country abroad. Intercession for the 'anointed'
(v. 9) points to the psalm having been composed in pre-exilic days.

[1] The sight of the Temple draws from the pilgrim a cry of deep
joy. The song of rejoicing which he raises to the glory of his God is
resonant not only with the tremendous impression which Solomon's
magnificent building makes upon him, but much more still with his
gratitude and joy that his yearning has been fulfilled. [2] He accepts
the bliss of being able to take part in the worship of the Temple as a
gift from God's hand. It is hardly possible to imagine what the
divine service which as a layman he could attend only in the forecourt of the Temple, may have meant to this man who can say of
himself that he was consumed with such yearning for the forecourts of
Yahweh that he was pining away! To long for God is for him a vital
expression of his own being so deeply and naturally rooted that the
whole man, 'heart and flesh', breaks into a sudden shout of joy as
soon as he becomes fully and almost physically aware that God is
near him in the Temple. The poet feels man, in his uttermost depths,
to be a unity, integrated and unaffected; so here he blends the
material and spatial with the spiritual and emotional. [3] This
direct, elemental trait of piety is expressed in an image that is to the
point and full of tender intimacy. The poet's feelings are like those of
a bird that seeks a place where she can hatch her young and, having
roamed about for a long time, finds at last a shelter where she can

---

[1] * By Matthias Jorissen (1739–1823).
[2] This point in opposition to Baumann, _ZAW_, 1950, pp. 132 ff.

build a nest in which she lays her young. At Yahweh's altars in the house of God the seeking soul of the psalmist has found a home and rest where he knows himself to be safe under God's protection like the bird in the nest. There is a touching trustfulness in the poet's religious need to disclose to his God the sentiments that move his heart as his yearning is satisfied. And yet, by addressing God as 'my King and my God', he makes clear that he is at the same time also conscious of the difference which separates man from God and cannot be obliterated. For in the eyes of faith both these attitudes belong together.

[4] As his whole being is turned to God, the poet is almost inclined to envy the cult officials who have the good fortune of being able to sing the praise of God for ever. To enjoy a perpetual intercourse with God would be for him the supreme bliss. [5] But at the same time he does not ungratefully shut his eyes to what has been granted to him personally, the blessedness, that is, of the devout experience of a pilgrimage. Must not he, too, be called blessed, together with all those who like him were privileged to experience something of the strength which man finds in God when their thoughts turned to the paths of their pilgrimages? [6] The poet at first describes in meta-phorical language what he together with others experienced then; only if understood in this sense is it possible to derive from this verse a meaning that is intelligible. The poet characterizes the fatiguing journey of the pilgrims from the foreign country to Jerusalem with all the strains and dangers it involved as a passing through the valley of tears (cf. Ps. 23.4; Hos. 2.15) which the pilgrims transform into a place of springs; and in doing so he thus alludes to the power of God which works miracles. By virtue of that divine power the believer is able to endure and overcome troubles and dangers so that even the bleak steppe becomes for him a landscape with bubbling fountains and pasture, which the early rain, ardently hoped for after the long spell of summer heat, transforms from a desert into fields richly blessed with fruit. The emphasis of this imagery and its point of comparison lies on the one hand in the unexpected paradoxes and, on the other, in the magnitude of the difference in sentiments which is here overcome. The impossible and the improbable is here made possible and real: affliction is transformed into joy, hardship into rejoicing, weakness into strength. The imagery therefore renders the same service here as the similarly paradoxical saying about the 'faith that removes mountains'. [7] Thus the poet visualizes the power of

God to be at work in the faith of the pilgrims. Without using another
metaphor he now states what is in his mind: 'they go from strength
to strength'; as God is in their heart, their strength increases; where
others would get tired, they are carried along as if they had invisible
wings, so that the way of faith becomes a walking on high mountains
leading from one peak to another. The poet has grasped to their
uttermost depths the paradoxical quality of faith and its inner laws
which distinguish it from other forces; he has experienced something
of what is expressed in the immortal words of Isa. 40.29 ff.:

> He gives power to the faint,
> and to him who has no might he increases strength.
> They who wait for the Lord shall renew their strength,
> they shall mount up with wings like eagles.

The poet is also acquainted with the fact that the divine strength
imparted by faith is something which in nature and effect is entirely
different from any human strength; moreover, it is capable of demonstrating its might precisely when human strength is on the point of
breaking down. His close relationship with God, which has invisibly
guided him on his pilgrimage, finds its external manifestation and
reaches its climax as he appears before God on Zion. Now there is
nothing which can interfere any more with his direct contact with
the 'living' God (see v. 2).

[8–9] This look back, which is full of joy and gratitude, is quite
naturally followed by a prayer in which the poet unites with the
other pilgrims before God in a joint intercession, asking God to hear
the prayer and bestow his gracious favour upon the people and the
king. The fact that the pilgrims pray to God for the king and the
people and not for their personal material well-being hangs together,
of course, with the character of the festival, in which the annual
celebration of the accession of the earthly king to the throne was
connected with that of Yahweh's Enthronement (v. 3; see Intr. 62 f.).
However, it may be permissible to draw attention also to the fact
that those who live abroad in a foreign country have all along shown
a stronger interest in their own people and fatherland than those who
live in their native country. Therefore, what the pilgrims now
experience most intensely is the fact that they are members of the
national and religious community. [10] This accounts for the
petition in v. 9, but at the same time also for the thanksgiving in
v. 10 which is based on the same train of thought. In the eyes of the

worshipper faith and native country belong together; this is why *one*
day in the Temple means more to him than a thousand days spent
elsewhere; he would rather stand like a beggar at the threshold of
the house of God in burning sunshine than dwell in the cool shadow
of the tents with the godless Gentiles! He feels lonely in the foreign
country, a stranger amongst strangers; but here each single step is
taken on native soil which becomes for him the medium enabling
him to have communion with his people, with their faith and with
their God. The poet has an inkling of those mysterious primordial
associations between native soil, nation and religious community
which we cannot dispose of simply by saying that such a view implies
a limitation of religion and its amalgamation with earthly things.
They are the God-willed ground in which the existence of every
human being is rooted and for this reason are also not without
significance for faith.

[11] The pilgrim now briefly sums up what the hours mean to
him which he was able to spend in the sanctuary of his native
country, and what he has gained from them to take with him on his
way home: God is his battlement and shield; in him he is well
sheltered from danger and temptation; with God as his refuge he can
confidently return to the foreign country. He bases his hope on God's
grace, and thus the way home, too, becomes for him a walking in
high places which eventually will bring him to glory. For he carries
with him the assurance of faith that God will not deny his lovingkindness to the man who is wholly devoted to him. (The Hebrew
word is to be understood in this sense and not in the sense of a moral
perfection.) The pilgrim's devotion to God finds full expression
already in the way he expresses his hope. What he hopes for from
God is not the fulfilment of specific individual wishes that spring
from the human heart; he is satisfied with *God*'s grace and *his* glory,
towards which he proceeds; he submits to God; he entrusts himself
to him; and it is on these facts that his assurance is based—it is these
facts which bring about his happiness. The impression produced by
the goodness of God, which he has been privileged to experience in
days of the festival, stays with him on his return to his everyday life
and fills that life, too, with a radiant light. The man who was consumed with his yearning for the Temple has gained fresh courage and
strength. Whoever leaves the house of God in such a spirit, to him it
has become a source of blessing. And anyone who ponders over the
significance which the cultus may have for faith will be able to learn

from this psalm that there fountains can spring up and living forces
be released which will lead to the manifestation of faith's deepest
spirituality.

85. COMFORT AND HOPE

To the Conductor. To the Sons of Korah.[1] *A Psalm*

1 Lord, thou wast favourable to thy land;
  thou didst restore the fortunes of Jacob.
2 Thou didst forgive the iniquity of thy people;
  thou didst cover all their sins. *Selah*
3 Thou didst withdraw all thy wrath;
  thou didst turn from thy hot anger.
4 Restore us again,[2] O God of our salvation,
  and put away thy indignation toward us!
5 Wilt thou be angry with us for ever?
  Wilt thou prolong thy anger to all generations?
6 Wilt thou not revive us again,
  that thy people may rejoice in thee?
7 Show us thy grace,[3] O Lord,
  and grant us thy salvation.
8 I will hearken to what God will say—
  The Lord, yea, he speaks: 'salvation'
  to his people and his godly ones,
  that they do not fall into folly.[4]
9 Surely his salvation is at hand
  for those who fear him,
  that glory may dwell among us,[5]
10 that love and faithfulness may meet,
  and righteousness and peace may kiss each other.[6]
11 Faithfulness will spring up from the earth,
  and righteousness will look down from heaven.
12 The Lord himself will give what is good,
  and our land will yield its increase.
13 Righteousness will go before him
  and salvation[2] on the way of his footsteps.[7]

[1] See above, p. 97. (Tr. N.: RSV has 'a Psalm of the Sons of Korah'.)
[2] See BH.
[3] * RSV has 'steadfast love' instead of 'grace'.
[4] * In RSV v. 8 is:
  Let me hear what God the Lord will speak,
  for he will speak peace to his people,
  to his saints, to those who turn to him in their hearts.
[5] * RSV has 'dwell in our land'.
[6] * RSV makes v. 10 a separate sentence:
  Steadfast love and faithfulness will meet;
  righteousness and peace will kiss each other.
[7] * V. 13b reads in RSV 'and make his footsteps a way'.

The psalm, which has been paraphrased by Paul Gerhardt,[1] shows the distinguishing marks of a liturgy. Verses 1–7 seem to have been sung by the congregation, perhaps antiphonally, whereas in vv. 8 ff. a single voice is heard speaking. The scene is probably that of a service of supplication of the cult community, held within the framework of the festival cult. In a testimony that takes the form of a hymn of praise the thoughts of the members of the congregation first turn to the mighty acts of God in the past when God restored the fortunes of Jacob and forgave the people their trespasses (vv. 1–3). This is followed by a deeply moving supplication which arises out of the affliction of the present (vv. 4–7). From the midst of the praying congregation somebody (probably a prophet) steps forward and listens for what God will say in answer to the prayer. Suddenly he hears the mysterious voice of God speaking. It foretells salvation for the people. Filled with prophetic enthusiasm this seer then reveals to the multitude that listens to him in words full of splendour the promise of divine blessing (vv. 8–13). The dramatic tension which the poet imparts to the psalm in this way arises out of the vivid dramatic character of the cultic experience and accords with the quality of tension peculiar to the real nature of faith to which the psalm gives expression.

Most commentators interpret the psalm in the light of the contemporary situation which the people had to face shortly after their return from the Babylonian exile: the great change in the fortunes of Israel, enthusiastically proclaimed and interpreted by Deutero-Isaiah as the gracious act of God who forgives every sin, belongs to the past. The delight which the people first took in their deliverance from bondage, however, subdued by bitter experiences. In many ways things had turned out quite differently from what people's bold expectations had led them to imagine would happen. The people had not been relieved from the pressure of a foreign rule; they had only exchanged the Babylonians for the Persians. Privations, bad harvests and strife (cf. Hag. 1.10 f.; 2.3 ff.; Zech. 1.12 ff.) were bound to awaken the people to the grievous knowledge that the age of salvation for which they longed had not yet fully appeared, and that God's wrath still continued to press heavily upon them. Under the pressure of their present calamity they sought encouragement and comfort in the mighty acts of divine deliverance wrought in bygone days, which were regarded as an earnest of the future fulfilment of their salvation. To be sure, it is possible to interpret the

[1] 'Herr, der du vormals hast dein Land mit Gnaden angeblicket.'

psalm in this sense, that is to say, in the light of contemporary history, only if we base that interpretation on the by no means certain assumption that v. 1b refers to the deliverance from Exile, which seems to be a later re-interpretation. It is more natural to understand the psalm in the light of the tradition of the festival cult celebrated at the autumn feast (v. 12), when the cult community continually witnessed at first hand (see Intr. 31, 43) the *Heilsgeschichte* as the representation of the gracious acts of God's guidance (deliverance from Egypt, bestowal of the promised land). If the psalm is understood in this sense, we may assume that it was composed in pre-exilic times.

[1–3] In the first part of the psalm the members of the congregation as they pray recall the past, holding it up to themselves and to God. Their eyes do not, however, remain fixed on the external historical events nor do the incidents on the human level seem prominent; but when as they pray they once more picture to themselves God's deeds, their faith takes comfort in the nature and the providential rule of God, who withdrew his wrath and proved his gracious will by forgiving their sins. The search for a firm support here makes itself more strongly felt than the desire to show their gratitude, and it is the recollection of the God who has 'restored' the 'fortunes' of his people and has preferred to show mercy instead of sitting in judgment on them which is able to provide that firm support (see above, p. 46 f.). Thus these verses form the basis of the faith on which the supplication that follows can be founded. The members of the congregation, whose eyes are here firmly focused on God, know who it is to whom they pray and what they can hope for from him in their present affliction. They do not use their calamity in a one-sided manner in order to justify their supplication on spiritual grounds, but they pray on the ground of their encounter with God and his grace. Their prayer thereby gains the support of a faith which is firmly established in the tradition of salvation.

[4–7] The transition from the believing backward look at God's grace to the petition for the putting away of his anger (vv. 4–7) is certainly abrupt, as far as its outward form is concerned, but is spiritually not unheralded. It is true that disappointment at the real state of things, which did not accord with their bold hopes for salvation, is the outward reason for the community's feeling that they are still subject to the wrath of God. But their testimony to the gracious will of God (vv. 1–3) is by no means diminished, let alone invalidated, by that fact. For we are here confronted with the tension which all genuine faith exhibits. If man's eyes are entirely focused on the reality of God, as in vv. 1–3, then he is confronted with the abundant riches of the divine grace on the ground of a faith that possesses that grace (*habender Glaube*); but if his eyes are fixed on the actual state of affairs in the world that surrounds him, then he perceives the distance that separates human reality from divine reality and his faith becomes one that is waiting for God's grace (*harrender Glaube*). The tension between the first two sections of the psalm is therefore to be explained not only 'historically', as arising out of the difference between the past and the present situation, but belongs to the nature of faith itself and is manifest with particular distinctness in the cultic sphere according as the impression made by the divine and by the human reality respectively is emphasized. The New Testament saying (Mark 9.24), 'I believe; help my unbelief!' testifies to the same tension. As they wait for God, the members of the cult community are cast down by the crippling, disillusioning weight of the imperfection of the actual state of affairs on earth, which makes them see the distance that separates them from God and therefore feel his anger. In that frame of mind they pray to God to turn from his anger and grant his grace and salvation to his people, and 'restore' again (cf. the reiteration of the word *šūb*, used in v. 1b) those who in their calamity had believed themselves to be separated from God and lost, so that they can again rejoice in God. In affliction faith is put to the test, and must continually fight for what it holds. The supplication of the cult community likewise turns on the question of the right relationship with God which matters more than the possession of earthly things.

[8] Out of the midst of the worshippers an individual voice can now be heard speaking. He and the congregation with him anxiously listen for what God will say to them in reply. Suddenly he hears something, the sound of a voice. Is it the Lord? Indeed, he speaks. Quite distinctly he hears God speaking one word only—'salvation!' In a masterly fashion the poet knows how to make the excited tension of that moment re-echo in the words which he uses. The people, the community of the faithful, have now received from God the answer which they had longed for. At the moment of the crisis of their faith, as they were in danger of 'falling into folly' and of doubting God's salvation, God himself intervenes to revive and strengthen their

faith by his word. What their prophet had been told in secret serves
to prepare their souls for their encounter with God. **[9]** But the
prophetic seer has even more to foretell: the salvation is imminent
and the glory of God will 'dwell in the land' (cf. Isa. 6.3). The fact
that *God* appears and is present in his 'glory' is the decisive fact of the
new age of salvation which starts with the theophany in the festival
cult as the beginning of a new year of grace. **[10–11]** How completely
that viewpoint here prevails is also shown by the enthusiastic description of the spiritual aspect of salvation (vv. 10 f.). Whereas
elsewhere in the ancient oriental cultic way of thinking it is the
elemental forces of Nature which control the saving events, the
psalmist in a magnificent picture visualizes how the mythologically
personified spiritual powers of divine love and faithfulness (notice
the relation to the renewal of the covenant in the Sinai tradition,
Ex. 34.6; see Intr. 40, 43), of righteousness and peace as God's messengers and servants at his advent are at work to fashion the end of
time. Heaven and earth meet in the proceedings of the cultic ritual;
just as the sun shines down from the sky and draws forth new budding
life from the earth, so the 'righteousness' of God (this term embraces
the saving will of God in all its aspects) evokes the faithfulness and
the faith of men. God bows down from heaven to earth, and the earth
reaches up towards heaven, towards God, a vision whose grandeur
and profundity are equally sublime. **[12]** The hope of salvation
is based solely on God's grace; 'God himself gives what is good'; it is
he who bridges the abyss which man experiences as the wrath of
God. Within the realm of God, the universal unity of which embraces
both the natural and the moral order, the blessing of earthly goods
must not be lacking either. In view of the fact that the idea of a
paradisal fertility is otherwise prominent as the permanent feature
of eschatology (cf. Amos 9.13; Hos. 2.21 f.; Isa. 30.23 ff.; Jer. 31.12),
we are struck here by the extent to which even at the autumn harvest festival the material is treated as secondary to the spiritual.
[13] The conclusion of the psalm, which once more makes the
theophany the centre of the events, leads to the same view. God
appears like a king, suitably escorted, to usher in the age of salvation.
Righteousness precedes him like an outrider and Salvation follows
in his way (cf. in this connection Isa. 40.10; 58.8; 62.11). In the
mystery of the cultic action faith victoriously envisages the future
prepared by God. It waits for the coming of God; it has been tested
and, after struggles and afflictions, has reached through experience a

hope which puts its whole trust in God. And this is the faith that has prevented the religious values of the Old Testament from being utterly defeated by the manifold obstacles raised in the course of history by the actual state of affairs on earth.

86. TEACH ME THY WAY, O LORD

A Prayer. Of David

1 Incline thy ear, O Lord, and answer me,
  for I am poor and needy.
2 Preserve my soul,[1] for I am godly;
  save thy servant ' '[2] who trusts in thee.
3 Thou art my God;[2] be gracious to me, O Lord,
  for to thee do I cry all the day.
4 Gladden the soul of thy servant,
  for to thee, O Lord, do I lift up my soul.
5 For thou, O Lord, art good and forgiving,
  abounding in grace to all who call on thee,
6 Give ear, O Lord, to my prayer;
  hearken to my cry of supplication.
7 In the day of my trouble I call on thee,
  for thou dost answer me.
8 There is none like thee among the gods, O Lord,
  nor are there any works like thine.
9 All the nations thou hast made shall
  come and bow down before thee, O Lord,
  and shall glorify thy name.
10 For thou art great and dost wondrous things,
  thou alone art God.
11 Teach me thy way, O Lord,
  that I may walk in thy truth;
  keep my heart steadfast in this one thing,
  fear of thy name![3]
12 I will testify to thee,[4] O Lord my God, with my whole heart,
  and I will glorify thy name for ever.
13 For great is thy steadfast love toward me;
  thou hast delivered my soul from the nethermost hell.[5]
14 O God, insolent men have risen up against me;
  a band of ruthless men seek my life,
  but their mind is not set on thee.[6]
15 But thou, O Lord, art merciful and gracious,
  slow to anger and abounding in steadfast love
  and faithfulness.
16 Turn to me and be gracious to me,[7]
  give thy strength to thy servant
  and save the son of thy handmaid.

17 Show me a sign of thy favour,
      that those who hate me may see
      how thou hast helped and comforted me,
      and be ashamed.[8]

1 * RSV has 'life' instead of 'soul'.
2 See BH.
3 * RSV takes the last two lines together: 'unite my heart to fear thy name'.
4 * RSV has 'I give thanks' instead of 'I will testify'.
5 * RSV has 'from the depths of Sheol'.
6 * V. 14c reads in RSV, 'and they do not set thee before them'.
7 * RSV has 'take pity on me' instead of 'be gracious to me'.
8 * RSV has after the first line:
      that those who hate me may see
      and be put to shame
      because thou, Lord, hast helped me
      and comforted me.

The psalm is composed in the style of an individual lament.
The numerous borrowings from kindred passages in other psalms
and the lack of a straightforward development of thought lead most
commentators to regard it as a late example of psalmody compiled
from earlier prototypes and showing little importance or originality;
but this view is hardly justified. First of all, the peculiar character of
the individual laments does not lie in the originality of each example,
but in the fact that their form and thoughts are both typical and
generally valid, a fact which is to be accounted for by their association with the cultus. Moreover, we are not justified in regarding the
affinity of the psalm with other songs as the result of borrowing from
other literature in order to mask the author's own incompetence. On
the contrary, we are here dealing with a liturgical style which is
deliberately used to incorporate the personal concern of the worshipper in the larger context of the worship of the cult community and of
the speech-forms and thought-forms proper to it. For that reason
neither the particular affliction of the poet nor the date of the
composition of the psalm can be accurately established. The cultic
setting of which the psalm is a part also accounts for the peculiar
arrangement of the thoughts and themes of the psalm, so that there is
no need to have recourse to the expedient of eliminating (Staerk) or
transposing (H. Schmidt) the hymnic parts (vv. 8–11). These are very
closely related to the prayer of thanksgiving in vv. 12–13 and reflect
the fundamental ideas of the cultic ceremony in the course of which
the psalm seems to have been recited after the prayer of supplication (vv. 1–7) had been answered (see v. 13). The prayer of

supplication (vv. 1–7) is combined with the hymn of praise (vv. 8–11) and with the thanksgiving (vv. 12–14), with the result that they form a unity, and this method is to be explained on the analogy of thanksgiving songs (see Intr. 69 f., 83 f.) in which the customary 'narration' is replaced by the previously offered prayer of supplication. Hence the whole process, starting with the petition and ending with its being granted, is incorporated in the larger context of the worship of the cult community and its significance for salvation as a testimony to the personal saving experience of an individual. It is a special feature of the psalm that this song of thanksgiving is followed in vv. 14–17 by a lament and another petition which has as its subject a new affliction not previously mentioned.

[1–7] The extensive introductory part of the psalm with its petitions for a hearing and for help proceeds in the style of a lament, using the familiar general phrases peculiar to that type of psalm. It is quite natural and psychologically understandable that these petitions at first take the worshipper himself as their starting-point (cf. vv. 1–4: 'for . . . I'), whereas from v. 5 onwards (cf. v. 7) God is recognized as the cause of the answer ('for . . . thou'). This by no means unimportant stylistic form expresses the course which every genuine prayer must take, from lifting up one's soul in search of God to the confidence that comes from having found him. For, as v. 11 proves, the usual interpretation of the grounds of petition here, that the psalmist is boasting of his own piety, is indefensible. The worshipper knows only too well that what he needs in order to be a godly man is precisely God's teaching and help; he is therefore not able to hold up his piety to God as if it were his own merit. Basing his whole confidence on the grace and compassionate goodness of God, he includes at a decisive point in his first as well as in his second petition (vv. 5, 15), and in the form of a hymn, the theme of the fundamental self-revelation of God through the sacral tradition of the *Heilsgeschichte*. These facts allow us to get a glimpse of the cultic background of the psalm (see Intr. 58 f., 74 f.), as does the hymn [8–11], whose fundamental ideas do not originate in the personal circumstances of the worshipper, but are borrowed from the general and much more comprehensive range of ideas associated with the cultic ceremony in which the worshipper participates. God, the Creator and Lord of all the nations and of their history, incomparably superior to all the gods and great on account of his wondrous deeds (cf. Ex. 15.11; see Intr. 52 f., 61), the one to whom alone the name

P.–T

'God' and the adoration of all the nations is due, this is the essential
theme of the festival cult, summed up in the response in the form of
a hymn. What the cultic experience that lies behind this hymn
means to the personal piety of the worshipper, which arises from
that experience and is nourished by it, is precisely this: he faces the
majesty of God as one who, in doing so, becomes thereby for the first
time fully conscious of his own inadequacy and can therefore draw
near to God only in supplication, asking God to teach him the way
which he cannot find by himself, give him the strength to live faithfully and truthfully, and make his distracted heart steadfast in the
fear of God, which is the one thing needful, and the beginning and
the end of all practical wisdom. [12–13] Inspired by the knowledge
that he is wholly dependent on God's help, the worshipper is now
able to pour out before God his feelings of deep gratitude for his
goodness, which has delivered him from suffering that had seemed
to him like the nethermost hell, and which now opens out before him
like heaven itself. Here the thanksgiving has no longer the character
of a payment, whereby an account is settled and disposed of, but is
the living expression of the complete surrender of the worshipper's
heart to God and of his pledge to serve God's glory for ever.

[14–17] There is, however, one more thought which still weighs
heavily upon the poet's soul: the fear of ruthless enemies who seek his
life. He sees clearly enough that he is no match for cruel violence which
always indicates that man has lost sight of God. Trusting in God's
'grace and faithfulness', which he had been privileged to experience,
he therefore prays for strength as well as for some 'sign' of God's favour
which will compel even his adversaries to acknowledge that God has
come to his aid so that they will be put to shame and cease to
threaten him. The worshipper's humble submission to the divine
'Lord' (the term '^{a}dōnāy$ =$ Lord is remarkably frequently used in the
psalm) is reflected not only in the phrases he uses ('thy servant', 'son
of thy handmaid'), but his attitude of mind, too, testifies to the
strength of self-conquest which is granted to one who has entrusted
himself wholly to the guidance of God. For without any feeling of
bitterness or vindictiveness he leaves whatsoever may happen in
future in the hands of his God and contents himself with bringing his
adversaries to a better understanding, so that they will be ashamed
and leave him alone.

87. ALL MY SPRINGS ARE IN THEE

To the Sons of Korah.[1] *A Psalm. A Song*

1 On holy mountains stands the city he founded;
   the Most High[2] himself has established her.[3]
2 The Lord loves the gates of Zion
   more than all the dwelling-places of Jacob.
3 He speaks[4] glorious things of you,
   O city of God. *Selah*
6 The Lord counts the peoples as he registers them
   according to the place in which they were born.[5] *Selah*
4 'Among those who profess me, I reckon Rahab and Babylon;
   and behold, there are Philistia, Tyre and Cush,
   people who were born there.'[6]
5 But of Zion he says,[7] 'Each one was born there.'[8]
7 They sing while they dance, 'All my springs are in thee.'[9]

[1] See above p. 97. (Tr. N.: RSV has 'A Psalm of the Sons of Korah'.)
[2] See the comments on Ps. 7.17.
[3] Through a copyist's error this sentence seems to have been misplaced after
v. 5. (Tr. N.: the RSV follows the traditional order, throughout; it also opens
v. 1 with 'On the holy mount' instead of 'On holy mountains'.
[4] See BH. (Tr. N.: RSV has 'Glorious things are spoken . . .')
[5] Lit.: 'this (this one) was born there.' (Tr. N.: RSV gives v. 6 as:
   The Lord records as he registers the peoples,
   'This one was born there.')
[6] See n. 5. (Tr. N.: RSV gives v. 4 as:
   Among those who know me
   I mention Rahab and Babylon;
   behold, Philistia and Tyre, with Ethiopia—
   'This one was born there,' they say.)
[7] Reading *yŏ'mar*.
[8] * V. 5 is in RSV:
   And of Zion it shall be said,
   'This one and that one were born in her';
   for the Most High himself will establish her.
[9] * RSV begins v. 7 with 'Singers and dancers alike say'.

The text of the psalm seems to have become disarranged in the
course of copying. In order to understand the psalm, we shall therefore not be able to dispense altogether with transpositions of one sort
or another, though we must not make the same mistake which some
expositors have made who transformed the psalm into a very jigsaw
puzzle. But even apart from this problem the psalm presents difficulties of exposition as a result of its peculiar character. The language
of the poet is anything but flowing. He moulds his brief sentences in
such a daring and abrupt manner that only a few characteristic
features are thrown into bold relief while their inner connection is

left in the dark. The thoughts of the psalm, too, match the peculiar character of its language. It is not possible at first glance to see a consistent thought-sequence. It is left to the reader to find out how the thoughts are related to each other. In my opinion the lack of a visible connection of thought and the peculiar stylistic character of the piece have to be explained in the light of the special situation to which the psalm presumably owes its origin. The poet finds himself in the Temple of Jerusalem on the occasion of a great pilgrimage-festival. The festal throng moves along in solemn procession, in step with the rhythm of the hymns. People from all over the world pass by before the eyes of the singer. It is as if the whole world had arranged to meet in this place. They have come from the Nile and the Euphrates, from the lands of the Philistines and of the Phoenicians, and even black figures from distant Ethiopia are not absent from this gathering of nations in the house of God on Mount Zion. However much they may differ from each other in language and appearance, they are all united in *one* faith, believing in the *one* God whom they jointly profess. The hymn which they sing (v. 7) impresses itself deeply on the poet's memory; for all of them the Temple of Jerusalem is their home, though cradled in some remote country. In an imaginative picture of almost visionary power, which at a single stroke embraces things near and far, the poet portrays the thoughts which that vision has awakened in him and around which his song has crystallized, thoughts of the majesty of God, who is worshipped by the whole world, and of Jerusalem's importance as the spiritual centre of the world. It must have been an experience of this kind that led to the composition of the psalm. Such a situation would explain equally well the exultation expressed in the hymn of praise, the prophetic element and the link between the descriptive element and the cult; it also makes understandable why the various thoughts, images and stylistic forms are placed side by side without connection.

It is by no means certain that the psalm presupposes that the Yahweh religion is widespread among the nations and that proselytism exists on a large scale, and whether for that reason the psalm can be attributed only to a later period in the post-exilic era. Proselytes already existed in pre-exilic times (cf. II Kings 5); and it can be assumed that during the great pilgrimage-festival Jerusalem gave shelter within her walls to guests of very varied origin who had come to attend the feast. For all its distinct peculiarities the psalm shows a

certain affinity to the 'Zion Psalms' (Pss. 48; 76; 84; see Intr. 45).
A symmetric construction cannot be expected in view of the directness of the psalmist's impressionistic experience, which in all its
freshness has found graphic expression in the psalm. The following
sections can, however, be distinguished: vv. 1-2 contain a hymn in
praise of Zion, the city of God; vv. 3-6 portray a scene in heaven the
purpose of which is to make known a divine utterance regarding the
relationship of the nations to Yahweh and to Jerusalem; v. 7 briefly
concludes the psalm with an earthly picture of the Temple festival.

The hymn in praise of Zion (vv. 1, 5b, 2)

[1, 5b, 2] The poet stands on the top of Mount Zion absorbed in
thought. What he sees and what he thinks takes shape in his mind
under the impression of the festive mood that surges round about
him everywhere, and becomes a song of praise glorifying Jerusalem,
the holy city of God. His eyes rove over her buildings which lie spread
out before him on the hills. Engrossed in thoughts about God, which
the feast in the Temple had called forth in him, he clothes the scene
upon which he has just gazed in words which have a mysterious
allusive quality: 'On holy mountains stands the city he founded.'
The tradition preserved from ancient times (cf. II Sam. 24; Pss.
78.68 ff.; 102.16; 147.2; cf. also Intr. 34 f., 45), and handed down in
living form right into the days of the singer, now appears before his
mind's eye: the Most High himself has founded the holy place at
Jerusalem (this idea, now standing at the end of v. 5, produces a
fairly tolerable connection of thought only when attached to v. 1).
This is why the love of God is especially directed towards the city of
God in preference to all the other places in the land of Israel; this
view perhaps implies a rejection of the local shrines with their earlier
tradition (cf. Ps. 78.68 ff.). The poet's own sacred experience, momentary and direct, he finds confirmed when he comes to think of the
history and sacred tradition of the city of God. From the foundation of
the Temple of Solomon onwards this holy place was pre-eminent as the
place which Yahweh had chosen and which stood under his special
protection. The deliverance from the armies of Sennacherib (701 BC)
was regarded as a visible proof of the inviolability of the sanctuary,
and even its destruction by the Babylonians was not able later on to
cloud the splendour which had surrounded the sanctuary and which
received a fresh impetus from the reconstruction of the Temple after
the Exile. And when at festivals in the Temple hearts deeply moved

by the singing of the pilgrims were stirred, then it was here above all that they could become assured of the love of God, who does not forsake what he himself has founded. Similar thoughts may also underlie this brief song in praise of Zion.

God's word about Jerusalem and the nations (vv. 3–6)

[3] Whilst the poet ponders over these things, his mood and his thoughts intermingle and produce an imaginative picture, conceived with prophetic power, which he passes on to the city of God, just as a prophet proclaims to the people what God had let him see and hear in a hallowed moment. His eyes have seen a magnificent vision and his ears have heard glorious things (v. 3). Verse 6 is a general narrative introduction to the divine utterance without which the whole psalm is not intelligible; its proper place is therefore after the introduction (v. 3). The poet visualizes the heavenly Lord as he draws up the roll of the nations, classifying them according to their native countries. This image has its origin in the mythological idea of fixing of fates which was common in the ancient Orient and was firmly established in the cult of the New Year festival, according to which the Deity keeps a book in heaven in which the destinies of men during the coming year are determined and recorded. The Old Testament speaks in several passages of the 'book of life' in which Yahweh has recorded the living (Ex. 32.32; Isa. 4.3; Pss. 69.28; 139.16). Here the idea is modified so that the particular nations and human beings who worship Yahweh are recorded in the celestial book like a roll of citizens, classifying them according to their native country. God counts those who profess him. It is an imposing number of people from all over the world. Those who were once the enemies of Israel and so also of Yahweh now belong among his worshippers!

[4] There are Egypt, called by her prophetic-mythological name Rahab, and Babylon, the ancient foe; again there are Philistines as well as Phoenicians from the coast town of Tyre, and even people from distant Ethiopia (Cush) are amongst them. In his statement that these former enemies have now become his friends God almost seems to sound a note of wonder. So far does the divine power extend. So many foreign tongues affirm their faith in the one true God. What the prophets had uttered as an eschatological hope (cf. Isa. 2.2 ff.; 11.10; 18; 19; 20; 23) has become a living reality in the cultic scene which is here portrayed. The divine utterance for the first time

makes clear to the poet the full significance for the comprehensive
range of the Kingdom of God of what he himself sees with his own
eyes when he looks at the proselytes, who have gathered at the
Temple feast from the most diverse countries: the universal Kingdom
of his God and the dawn of the age of salvation linked up with it
have become a living reality!

[5] The faith called forth by God's presence lives in the realm of
realized 'eschatology' (see Intr. 50). But this wider vision which is
granted to the poet is not sufficient to disclose to him the full 'glory'
which he is able to proclaim. He can grasp that glory in all its fullness only after the divine utterance has opened his eyes to Jerusalem's
importance in view of her position as the centre of the Kingdom of
God, which embraces all nations. Of Zion God says, 'Each single
man is born there.' This saying is meaningful only if we understand
it as a metaphor for the spiritual home which everyone has found in
Jerusalem, no matter in which country he may have been born. At
this point, too, the singer recognizes with wonder and joy that a
promise has been fulfilled, a recognition that makes his belief in the
consummation of the Kingdom of God rank with that of the prophetic tradition. There are, for instance, Deutero-Isaiah's promises
to Jerusalem, when the city was subdued and her walls were destroyed during the Exile, that strangers who do not know her will
run to her (Isa. 55.5); and God's word has not returned to him
empty (Isa. 55.11), for the 'barren one' has become the mother of
many sons (Isa. 54.1); she has become the spiritual centre of the
whole world (Isa. 2.2 ff.). The beginnings of that belief, however,
date back to much earlier times (cf. Gen. 12.3; Amos 9.7). It is God
himself who confirms to the poet that his promise has been fulfilled;
for it is God himself who confers upon each one of the 'proselytes'
(literally 'in-comers') the rights of a native of Zion, and thus makes
the city of God the centre of the great people of God which no longer
comprises only Israel but embraces all the nations (cf. Ps. 47.9). Here
the national barriers of religion are overcome, and each individual
believer gains access to God and his sanctuary. Now the way is open
for the true faith in God to go out into all the world and for the
nations to draw near to the one God! The fact that arrogance towards and aloofness from other nations, which constituted the dark
side of the national religion of Israel and a danger to which it was
exposed, could here be overcome in such a large-minded manner is
to be attributed to the influence of the Old Testament faith, which

was exclusively focused on God and by virtue of its theocentric outlook liberated religion from its bondage to national egoism. It is no accident that the profundity and comprehensiveness of the knowledge expressed in the psalm has been gained by keeping God in the centre of the picture.

[7] From the festival dance of the Temple congregation, a song now rises to the poet's ears: 'All my springs are in thee.' It sounds to him like an earthly response to the word of the 'glorious things' which he had heard from God's lips. It shows him that those who have come to the feast confirm by their own testimony the truth of the things which at this great moment fill his own heart with joyous exultation. It is really true that the deepest sources of joy, gratitude, security and trust well up here in the house of God. The invisible forces which link together the lives of the widely scattered people of God, welding them into *one* great family of the divine Father, have their roots in the faith in the God of Mount Zion. It is therefore not unintentionally that the poet brings the psalm to an end in this brief earthly scene taken from the Temple worship. He discerns in the testimony of the pilgrims the congregation's 'Amen' to God's great plan of salvation which finds its visible expression in the history of Jerusalem and its fulfilment in the whole extent of the Kingdom of God.

The peculiar character of the psalm lies in the fact that starting from belief in God it makes manifest the foundation from which Christianity has set out on its way into the world; the psalm shows how the ground was prepared so that the Christian seed could sprout and grow therein. The faith underlying the psalm is in itself a part of the way in the course of which the time was fulfilled; for it testifies to the original divine basis of the mission and of its great religious fellowship which is called to build the Kingdom of God that extends throughout the world.

88. LAMENT

A Song. A Psalm. To the Sons of Korah.[1] *To the Conductor. According to . . .*[2] *Maskîl.*[3] *Of Heman the Ezrahite*[4]

1 O Lord, God of my salvation, I cried by day;
and in the night I am before thee.[5]
2 Let my prayer come before thee,
incline thy ear to my lament!
3 For my soul is sick of suffering,
and my life draws near to the underworld.[6]

4 I am reckoned among those
  who went down to the Pit;
  I am become as a man who has no strength,[7]

5 my bed[8] is among the dead,
  laid into the grave like the slain,
  whom thou dost remember no more,[9]
  for they are cut off from thy hand.

6 Thou hast put me in the nethermost hell,[10]
  in the regions dark and deep.

7 Thy wrath lies heavy upon me,
  and thou hast overwhelmed me with all thy waves. *Selah*

8 Thou hast caused my companions to shun me;
  thou hast made me a thing of horror to them.
  I am shut in so that I cannot escape;

9 my eye grows dim through sorrow.
  Every day I called upon thee, O Lord;
  I spread out my hands to thee.

10 Dost thou work wonders for the dead?
   Or do the shades rise up to profess thee? *Selah*

11 Is thy grace declared in the grave,
   or thy faithfulness in the abode of the dead?[11]

12 Are thy wonders known in the darkness,
   or thy righteousness[12] in the land of forgetfulness?

13 But I, O Lord, I cried to thee;[13]
   in the morning my prayer comes before thee.

14 O Lord, why dost thou cast off my soul?
   Why dost thou hide thy face from me?
   vv. 15–18.

15 Afflicted I pine away from my youth;
   I suffered thy terrors;
   I am at my wit's end.[14]

16 Thy wrath has swept over me like a torrent;
   thy terrors have silenced me.[15]

17 They surrounded me like a flood all day long;
   they enclosed me on all sides.[16]

18 Thou hast caused friends and companions to shun me;
   my acquaintances—darkness![17]

[1] See above p. 97. (Tr. N.: RSV has 'A Psalm of the Sons of Korah'.)

[2] The meaning of this part of the superscription is quite uncertain; it may perhaps be a reference to the tune of a song which begins with the words 'to lament about an illness', or it may mean 'to be sung at the dance' (see BH). (Tr. N.: RSV gives these words as 'according to Mahalath Leannoth'.)

[3] See Ps. 32 n. 1.

[4] See p. 97. (Tr. N.: RSV has 'A Maskil of Heman the Ezrahite'.)

[5] * V. 1 reads in RSV:
O Lord, my God, I call for help by day;
I cry out in the night before thee.

[6] * RSV has 'full of troubles' instead of 'sick of suffering' and 'Sheol' instead of 'the underworld'.

7 * RSV has 'go down' instead of 'went down' and omits 'become as'.
8 The meaning is uncertain; it is perhaps better to read *napši* = my life.
9 * RSV gives these three lines as:
   like one forsaken among the dead,
   like the slain that lie in the grave,
   like those whom thou dost remember no more,
10 * RSV has 'in the depths of the Pit' instead of 'in the nethermost hell'.
11 * RSV has 'Abaddon' instead of 'the abode of the dead'.
12 * RSV reads 'saving help' instead of 'righteousness'.
13 * RSV has 'But I, O Lord, cry to thee.'
14 * V. 15 is in RSV:
   Afflicted and close to death from my youth up,
   I suffer thy terrors; I am helpless.
15 * RSV omits 'like a torrent' and gives v. 16b as 'thy dread assaults destroy me'.
16 * RSV has 'they close in upon me together'.
17 * RSV has 'lover and friend' instead of 'friends and companions' and for v. 18b has 'my companions are in darkness'.

This psalm is the lament, unrelieved by a single ray of comfort or hope, of a man whose life has been marked by suffering from his youth (v. 15). It is a deeply moving testimony to the grievous tempta-tion into which one who believes in God can fall when he feels God's eye gazing menacingly upon him through the mask of an incompre-hensible calamity, and when all his prayers prove unavailing in the face of God's terrible silence. It is not without good reason that such a psalm, so closely akin to the Book of Job, has been included in the Bible side by side with that book. The fact that the lament of this godly man fades away without a single word of comfort and that he cannot even nerve himself to make any more direct requests for God's help is a clear warning against any attempt, however well-intentioned, to gloss over with merely human words of slick easy comfort the tremendous seriousness of the problem presented by a God who is hidden behind such suffering instead of facing it with awe, and even without fear and trembling. Again, the psalmist's repeated references to the prayers he has offered (vv. 1 f., 9, 13), and indeed the psalm itself, are proof that he cannot let God go in spite of the distress experienced in his prayers, which, after all, is the deepest cause of his despair. It would, however, by no means be right to say that his other afflictions press less heavily upon him: chronic bodily ill health (vv. 15, 9), all the terrifying experiences which have made him silent and helpless (vv. 15 f.), the fear of death and hell, which makes him tremble and which he cannot banish from his mind (vv. 3–6, 10–12), the loneliness of one who has been forsaken by his friends and—probably because they abhor his malady—is shunned by them (vv. 8, 18), so that he imagines himself to be like one who lies chained in a prison from which he will never be able to escape (v. 8)—all these overwhelming trials with which he has to struggle become for him according to v. 3a a most grievous temptation. For in *everything* that sweeps over him like a flood, threatening to drown him, he discerns God's incomprehensible wrath directed against him (vv. 7, 14, 16 f.), so that he has not even the chance of confessing his sins and so hoping for God's forgiveness. He can only, by his lament and his questions, cry out in the dark to the hidden God who remains a complete riddle, an inaccessible mystery. His deepest suffering springs from the fact that he needs communion with God and seeks it, but does not find it, and indeed cannot help fearing that he may forfeit it for ever, when according to the popular beliefs of his age, the relationship between God and men which exists during a man's lifetime will be entirely cut off by his approaching death (vv. 10–12). It is true, he is aware, and firmly clings to this thought with trembling hands, that it is the God of his salvation to whom he cries (v. 1a); but that vestige of his former religious experience and former yearning hope vanishes in the darkness of the present dreadful reality of his suffering and of his mortal terror which threatens to engulf him, forsaken as he is, like one who, lonely and unheard, sinks in the frightening expanse of the ocean. As Christians we, too, shall be well advised, when speaking of suffering, to come to terms with the thought that such agonies caused by hopeless loneliness belong to the sphere of the reality of God and are part of man's religious experience. In that case the psalm with its unanswered questions, questions raised by the psalmist as well as by us, can lead us to the one and only place where the ultimate mystery of suffering has been unveiled and the way has been opened to God, to the cross of Christ. It is there alone that the God, who is hidden in the uttermost depths of suffering, has at the same time been revealed; it is there that we find an inexhaustible source of comfort.

89. THE CRISIS OF THE OLD COVENANT

Maskîl.[1] *Of Ethan the Ezrahite.*[2]

1 I will sing of thy[3] mercies, O Lord, for ever;
with my mouth I will proclaim thy faithfulness
to all generations.

2 Thou hast said,[3] 'My grace is built up for ever';
  thy faithfulness thou hast firmly established as[3] the heaven.[4]

3 'I have made a covenant with my chosen one,
  I have sworn to David my servant:

4 I will establish your descendants for ever,
  and build your throne for all generations.' *Selah*

5 The heavens praise thy wonders, O Lord,[5]
  thy faithfulness in the assembly of the holy ones.

6 For who in the skies can be compared to the Lord?
  Who among the sons of gods is like the Lord,

7 a God feared in the council of the holy ones,
  mighty[3] and terrible above all that are round about him?

8 O Lord, God of hosts, who is like thee?
  Thy grace[3] and thy faithfulness are round about thee.[6]

9 Thou dost rule the raging of the sea;
  when its waves rise, thou stillest them.

10 Thou didst crush Rahab like a carcass,
  thou didst scatter thy enemies with thy mighty arm.

11 The heavens are thine, the earth also is thine;
  the earth and all that is in it, thou hast founded them.

12 The north and the south, thou hast created them;
  Tabor and Hermon joyously praise thy name.

13 Thine is the arm and thine is its might;[7]
  strong is thy hand, high is thy right hand.

14 Righteousness and justice are the foundations of thy throne;
  grace and faithfulness go before thee.

15 Blessed are the people who know the festal shout,
  who walk, O Lord, in the light of thy countenance.

16 They exult in thy name all the day,
  they are exalted in thy righteousness.[8]

17 For thou art the glory of their strength;
  by thy favour our horn is exalted.

18 For our shield belongs to the Lord,
  our king to the Holy One of Israel.

19 Of old thou didst speak in a vision
  to thy faithful ones,[9] saying,
  'I have set a young man over the mighty ones,
  I have exalted one chosen over the people.[10]

20 I have found David, my servant;
  with my holy oil I have anointed him,

21 so that my hand shall ever uphold him,
  my arm also shall strengthen him.

22 No enemy shall attack him,
  the wicked shall never oppress him.[11]

23 I will crush his oppressors before him
  and strike down those who hate him.

24 My faithfulness and my grace will be with him,
  in my name will his horn be highly exalted.

25 I will set his hand on the sea
    and his right hand on the rivers.
26 He shall cry to me, "Thou art my Father,
    my God, and the Rock of my salvation."
27 But as for me, I will make him the first-born,
    the highest of the kings of the earth.
28 My grace I will keep for him for ever,
    and my covenant shall[12] stand firm for him.
29 I will establish his line for ever
    and his throne as the days of the heavens.
30 If his children forsake my law
    and do not walk according to my ordinances,
31 if they violate my statutes
    and do not keep my commandments,
32 then I will punish their transgression with the rod,
    and their iniquity with scourges.
33 But I will not remove[3] from him my grace,
    or be false to my faithfulness.
34 I will not violate my covenant,
    or alter the word that went forth from my lips.
35 Once for all I have sworn by my holiness:
    I shall never lie to David.
36 His line shall endure for ever,
    his throne as long as the sun before me,
37 like the moon that is established for ever,
    a faithful witness in the skies.'[13] *Selah*
38 But thou hast cut off and rejected,
    thou hast been full of wrath against thy anointed.[14]
39 Thou hast renounced the covenant with thy servant;
    thou hast defiled his crown in the dust.
40 Thou hast breached all his walls;
    thou hast laid his strongholds in ruin.
41 All that passed by, despoiled him;[15]
    he has become the scorn of his neighbours.
42 Thou hast exalted the right hand of his foes;
    thou hast made all his enemies rejoice.
43 Thou hast caused his sword to turn back from the enemy;[3]
    thou hast not made him stand in battle.[16]
44 Thou hast put an end to his glory,[17]
    and cast his throne to the ground.
45 Thou hast cut short the days of his youth;
    thou hast covered him with shame. *Selah*
46 How long, O Lord?
    Wilt thou hide thyself for ever?
    Shall thy wrath burn like fire?[18]
47 Remember, O Lord,[3] what the measure of life is,
    for what vanity thou hast created all the sons of men!
48 What man can live and never see death?

Who can deliver his soul from the power of the underworld?[19] *Selah*
49 Lord, where are thy mercies of old,
   which by thy faithfulness thou didst swear to David?
50 Remember, O Lord, how thy servants are scorned;
   how I bear in my bosom the insults[3] of the peoples,
51 with which thy enemies taunt, O Lord,
   with which they mock the footsteps of thy anointed![20]

---

[1] See Ps. 32 n. 1.
[2] See above, p. 97.
[3] See BH.
[4] * RSV postpones the words 'Thou hast said' to the beginning of v. 3, and gives v. 2 as:
   For thy steadfast love was established for ever,
   thy faithfulness is firm as the heavens.
[5] * RSV has 'Let the heavens . . . '
[6] * RSV has:
   O Lord, God of hosts,
   who is mighty as thou art, O Lord,
   with thy faithfulness round about thee?
[7] * V. 13a reads in RSV 'Thou hast a mighty arm.'
[8] * RSV gives v. 16b as 'and extol thy righteousness'.
[9] * RSV uses the singular.
[10] Following Albright, *The Archaeology of Palestine* (rev. ed., 1960), p. 234.
[11] * RSV has:
   The enemy shall not outwit him,
   the wicked shall not humble him.
[12] * RSV has 'will'.
[13] * V. 37 is in RSV:
   Like the moon it shall be established for ever;
   it shall stand firm while the skies endure.
[14] * RSV has 'thou art full of wrath . . .'
[15] * RSV uses the present tense.
[16] * V. 43a reads in RSV: 'Yea, thou hast turned back the edge of his sword.'
[17] The meaning is uncertain. (Tr. N.: In RSV v. 44a reads, 'Thou hast removed the sceptre from his hand.')
[18] * In RSV v. 46b reads: 'How long will thy wrath burn like fire?'
[19] * RSV has 'Sheol' instead of 'the underworld'.
[20] Cf. Intr. 21, 100 on the doxology in v. 52:
   Blessed be the Lord for ever!
   Amen and Amen.
(Tr. N.: RSV prints this doxology as v. 52.)

The psalm is clearly divided into three parts: vv. 1–18 contain a hymn in praise of God, who appears—probably at the feast of the Covenant—surrounded by the rejoicing of his celestial attendants (vv. 5 f.) and of his faithful people on earth (vv. 15 f.). The mention of the king (v. 18) and the emphasis laid on the covenant made by God as the theme of the psalm and on the promise made to David

(vv. 3 f.) link up this first part of the psalm with the two other parts that follow, of which vv. 19–37 recapitulate that promise in detail in order to contrast it in the third part with the bitter lament that Yahweh has renounced the covenant and has cast off his anointed. Most commentators seek to identify the catastrophe, which gave rise to this lament, which exposed the country to destruction and looting, and deprived the king of his autonomy, with the downfall of Judah in 587 BC; they therefore regard the psalm as belonging to the exilic or post-exilic period. Since, however, the psalm does not exhibit any concrete feature pointing to that event, such as, for instance, the capture of the king and the deportation of the people, it is presumably a question of an earlier defeat.[1] It seems likely that the psalm, which on the one hand is to be classed with Psalm 18 and, on the other hand, with Psalms 2, 110, and 132, was used in times of a grave national disaster and was recited in the cult when the accession to the throne of both the heavenly King and the earthly king were celebrated together at the Covenant Festival. If we understand the psalm in the light of the tradition of that festival cult, it is unnecessary to derive its several parts from different sources, and, moreover, the relation of the second part of the psalm to the promise made by God to Nathan (II Sam. 7) probably goes back to a common cultic tradition (see Intr. 45, 62 f.).

[1–2] The hymn with which the psalm opens, which is sung by a priest, reminds the cult community of the duty incumbent on them to proclaim in songs of praise God's grace and faithfulness so that this may effectively be preserved from generation to generation as a living tradition. This 'everlasting hymn of praise' has its origin in the eternity of God who has bestowed his 'grace and faithfulness' upon the cult community as the abiding and dependable foundation of salvation (cf. Ex. 34.6; see Intr. 43, 54 f., 58) and sustains it as he does his creation. [3–4] In view of the particular concern discussed in the second and third parts of the psalm the promise of salvation and the covenant made by God with David are singled out, since this is the point at which the promise seems to be called in question by disastrous events. [5–7] This does not mean, however, that confidence in God's power is shaken. The hymn of vv. 5–8 is the jubilant response

[1] Johnson, *Sacral Kingship in Ancient Israel*, pp. 103 f., holds the view that this refers not to an historical event but to the cultic act of the ritual degradation of the king, which can be compared with the degradation of the Babylonian king in the ritual of the New Year Festival.

of the congregation to the revelation of God's character and his
providential rule. The chorus of God's celestial attendants (vv. 5–7;
cf. Isa. 6.1 ff.) is joined by the congregation's hymn **[8–18]**; together
they sing the praise of God's unrivalled perfection (vv. 6, 8);
together they praise the wonders of his 'grace and faithfulness'
(vv. 5, 8, 14) which accompany him like acolytes when he appears
(see Intr. 40). But it is a peculiarity of the revelation of God and of
the faith it calls forth that the terrifying aspect of his power comes
into its own with equal force, and that the rejoicing is just as much
directed at that aspect of his power as at his grace and faithfulness
(v. 7). For with God judgment and grace ultimately belong together
and are only two aspects of his nature (v. 14); from the beginning of
Creation they bear witness to his divine power and majesty. With
echoes of the ancient mythical tradition vv. 9–12 speak of the conquest of the powers of chaos, which are here personified under the
name of Rahab and take the form of the primeval sea rebelling
against God (cf. Pss. 74.13; 93.3 f.; 107.29; Job 9.13; 38.8 ff. and
often; see Intr. 51, 60 f.). By his victory over the powers of darkness
God has created the foundations of the universe and has imposed his
will and his order on the world so that it has become the sphere in
which his power operates and the place of his revelation. The whole
world's rejoicing is the echo of that mighty revelation, so that even
the ancient mountains of the gods in the north, Tabor and Hermon,
hail the Creator with joy (cf. Ps. 68.15 ff.; Job 38.7). And as once
at the Creation, so continually at the Covenant Festival, God
manifests his power before his faithful people who rejoice at his
protection, at the blessing of his nearness (v. 15) and at the vital
energies which flow out from him to the people and their king
(vv. 17, 18).

[19–37] The congregation's hymn is followed in the second part of
the psalm, which represents the king's answer, by the recollection of
the prophetic revelation (*ḥāzōn*) of the great promises made by God
to David and of his covenant with him, on which the historical
institutions of the people of God are based. According to the Old
Testament idea of the divine saving rule, Nature and History,
Creation and Election, are not to be separated from each other. The
eternal reign of God is to be reflected in the sphere of influence of the
earthly ruler whom God has adopted as his son (cf. Ps. 2.7 f.). It is
for this reason and for this reason only that no limits are to be set to
his dominion either in space or time. The gracious will of God, which

is manifested in these promises, stands firm and will not be shaken even if the bearers of these promises cease to walk in the way of responsibility and obedience, which the grace of God implies, so that God has to punish them. Human sin does not put an end to the divine grace, and God's judgment is nothing else than discipline and guidance on the way to salvation. God remains faithful to himself even though men are unfaithful.

[38–51] The sad picture which the lament seeks to present before God (vv. 38–51) contrasts most strongly with the picture created by those promises.[1] Not grace but wrath, not election but rejection seem to be the signs of the time, as the glory of the earthly dominion is dragged through the mire beneath the blows of enemies gloating over their victory. And the affliction of the psalmist's faith consists precisely in this, that he sees God himself at work in all the adversities which have made the king grow old before his time, he sees the hand of God himself, who has renounced the covenant which he himself had made with the king and has taken away from him the very things which he had once solemnly promised him. The psalmist's faith is vexed by the riddle of the inscrutability of God's way of acting in history. Man is not able to resolve by his own thinking the contradiction between the promise and the actual state of affairs; he can only state that contradiction with a bleeding heart; he can only lift his hands to God in prayer and bring his affliction before him and lay before him the problems which his own thinking and reasoning are unable to master. But the strength of such a faith shows itself in the very fact that it does not let go of God at the moment of crisis, but so much the more vigorously recalls both to itself and to God the promise of his grace and faithfulness without which he cannot exist. The riddle of the *Heilsgeschichte* which here comes to light through the rejection of the bearer of the promise has not been solved in the Old Testament. It is true that the promise of God has not become ineffective. It has been fulfilled, not in the person of the king of Israel, but in Christ. And this has been done in a manner which contrary to all human expectations and beyond all human comprehension has revealed the miracle of God's ways and judgments which lead to salvation, a miracle so mysterious that even a man like the Apostle Paul, pondering over these problems, can do nothing else but, deeply stirred, confine himself to the adoration of the unsearchable majesty of God (Rom. 11.33). The early Christians therefore interpreted the

[1] According to Johnson's view (loc. cit.) the speaker is here the humiliated king.

psalm in a Messianic sense as pointing to Christ, and thus have apprehended and believed the wonder and the mystery of the divine way of salvation, from the perspective of its goal.

90. THE ETERNAL GOD

A Prayer. Of Moses, the Man of God

1 Lord, thou hast been our refuge[1] in all generations.
2 Before the mountains were brought forth,
   and the earth and the world were formed in travail,[2]
   thou art God from everlasting to everlasting.[3]
3 Thou turnest men back to the dust,
   and sayest,[2] 'Turn back, O children of men!'
4 For a thousand years in thy sight
   are but as yesterday when it is past,
   or as a watch in the night.
5 Thou dost sweep men away;
   they are like the sleep in the morning,
   like grass that withers away;[4]
6 in the morning it flourishes and grows;
   in the evening it fades and withers.
7 So we are consumed by thy anger;
   by thy wrath we are banished.[5]
8 Thou hast set our iniquities before thee,
   our secret sins in the light of thy countenance.
9 ' '[2] All our days pass away under thy wrath,
   our years pass quickly like a thought.[6]
10 The years of our life are threescore and ten,
   or even by reason of strength fourscore;
   yet their pride is but toil and pain;[7]
   for they are soon gone—we fly away.
11 But who considers the power of thy anger,
   and who is afraid[2] of thy wrath?
12 So teach us to number our days
   that we may get a heart of wisdom!
13 Return, O Lord! How long?
   Have pity on thy servants!
14 Satisfy us in the morning with thy grace,
   that we may rejoice and be glad all our days!
15 Make us glad for as many days as thou hast afflicted us,
   and as many years as we have seen evil.
16 Let thy work appear to thy servants;
   and thy glory to their children.
17 Let the favour of the Lord be upon us;' '[2]
   and establish thou the work of our hands!' '[8]

[1] * RSV has 'dwelling-place' instead of 'refuge'.
[2] See BH.
[3] * V. 2b reads in RSV, 'or ever thou hadst formed the earth and the world'.
[4] * In RSV v. 5 is:
  Thou dost sweep men away; they are like a dream,
  like grass which is renewed in the morning: . . .
[5] * RSV has 'overwhelmed' instead of 'banished'.
[6] * V. 9b reads in RSV, 'our years come to an end like a sigh'.
[7] * V. 10c is in RSV, 'yet their span is but toil and trouble'.
[8] The words that follow, 'upon us, yea, the work of our hands establish thou it' (included in RSV) seem to be a later addition or represent the response of the congregation.

The solemn and earnest spirit with which Psalm 90 is imbued and the nobility and comprehensiveness of its thoughts give it an authority which it is not easy to evade. With a bold and courageous truthfulness the psalmist tackles the problem of the relationship between God and man from the point of view of God's eternal being and man's transient nature, and, taking his faith unflinchingly seriously, pursues this problem to its uttermost depths so that the words of this psalm never fail to appeal irresistibly to men's hearts. Here a man with the mature experience of old age looks back upon human life and against the background of the eternal being of God apprehends its nature and its ultimate coherence. And in so doing he enters upon the way which alone leads from man's denial of life to the true life, that is, to a confident affirmation of life as rooted in God himself. The fact that the superscription, a later addition, ascribes the psalm to Moses, the man of God, still expresses something of the high esteem in which the mighty song of God's eternal being was held and of the reverence that was shown to it, so that one could think of the words of the psalm only as having been spoken by the nation's greatest son. The reason for this ascription may perhaps be found in the fact that the psalm shows reminiscences of the history of creation and of the story of the Fall as well as of the song and blessing of Moses (Deut. 32 and 33). That recapitulation of the Moses tradition as well as the cult community's hope that 'God may appear' to them and that his redemptive work may be made manifest to them (vv. 13 ff.) still reveal the association of the psalm with the tradition of the festival cult (see Intr. 28 ff.).

The structure of the psalm, which is in the form of a 'community lament' (see Intr. 66 ff.), is as lucid and graphic as its words: the keynote of confidence, which echoes throughout the whole psalm, is forcefully sounded in v. 1; vv. 2–6 are grouped round the contrast between God's eternal being and the transient nature of man; vv. 7–12 interpret this antithesis as the opposition of man's will to the divine will, whereupon vv. 13–17 conclude the psalm with a prayer for God's grace and help.

[1] As in Psalm 73 the fundamental idea on which the whole psalm is based is put at the head of the psalm in order to indicate its theme, thus stressing the viewpoint which guides the psalmist as he develops his thoughts in the psalm. His statement 'Lord, thou hast been our refuge from generation to generation' is formally a retrospect which by virtue of the psalmist's trust in God embraces the whole tradition of the past. It is, however, by no means meant to convey the thought that God has now ceased to be the refuge of his people. On the contrary, the backward look upon the past generations, who have continually lifted up their eyes to God as the fixed point in the flux of history and have found their support in him, and the consciousness of standing together with them in the same long living tradition of faith, strengthens the resolve to trust in God, both now and for the future. The worshipper finds his firm support in the faith of his forefathers, which he shares with the other members of the cult community, even though he candidly faces the disturbing truth about the transient nature of life. Without having his feet on the firm ground of that trust in God, he would hardly be able in view of the hopeless position of man, to adopt the course which he follows of asking for God's help (vv. 12 ff.).

God's eternal being and man's mortality (vv. 2–6)

The subsequent statements are almost exclusively related to God. He is both the starting-point and the focal point of the thought of the psalm. This fact at the same time makes clear that the awareness of man's mortality does not arise, as one might think, from the despondent frame of mind of a man whose pessimistic outlook is entirely rooted in this world, but is orientated on the thought of God's eternal being. Here a distinction of fundamental importance is involved. How intensely the poet's mind is occupied by the impression produced by this train of thought is shown by the fact that the same thought-sequence contrasting God and man occurs twice, in vv. 2–3 and 4–6. [2] In the tones of a hymn and in the style of the ancient creation stories the poet gives expression to the wonder and awe which the eternal being of God arouses in his heart. The fact that God exists eternally is forcefully and graphically set off against the majestic background of the primordial events at the creation of the universe which in any case fills man's heart with awe and trembling. The psalmist speaks quite deliberately of the origin of the world in the traditional forms of mythological ideas peculiar to antiquity (see Intr. 60 f.). When he alludes to the 'bringing forth of the ancient mountains' and says that 'the earth was founded in travail', there emerges from this metaphorical language the idea, widespread in antiquity, of 'mother earth' bringing forth plants and animals (Gen. 1.11 f., 24) and from whose womb the sea burst forth (Job 38.8 ff., 28 f.). But of what importance are, after all, those mysterious primordial events, that have come to pass in times immemorial, in comparison with the eternal Being of God, who was *God* before the earth was created, and who will continue to be God, from everlasting to everlasting, when the earth has long ceased to exist. But the divine existence does not comprise only the fullness of time; the statement 'Thou art God' at the same time implies an unlimited abundance of power and a presence that overcomes the barriers of time (see Intr. 43 f., 50). **[3]** Man experiences this fact in his own personal life. It is God who brings him back to dust. He need say but one word and man's life comes to an end. What is man in comparison with the eternal might of God! He is formed of dust and returns to dust according as God's will decrees. Here we catch echoes of the ancient tradition of the story of the Fall; and the poet deliberately chooses phrases which characterize the frailty of human nature. By translating the last words of this verse 'Return, O children of men!'[1] Luther interpreted them in the sense of the rise of new generations through the power of God's Word. But the form of the verse and the connection of thought suggest that it is more natural to interpret the whole verse uniformly as referring to death. As man's eyes are thus focused upon God, he arrives for the first time at a full and true understanding of his own transitoriness; and, conversely, as he reflects upon death and upon the limitations of his own existence, it begins to dawn on him what is actually involved in the eternal being and power of God. **[4]** The subsequent verses 4–6 likewise point in these two directions. Any human attempt to be certain of God's presence and to speak of his eternal being is bound to remain always a mere stammering and necessarily leads once more to the realization of the futility and insignificance of everything that is human. In the sight of God vast spaces of time such as a thousand

---

[1] * 'Kommt wieder, Menschenkinder.'

years, the detailed events of which man cannot even take in at a
glance, are as yesterday when it is past, or as a watch in the night,
which was the smallest unit of time for man in those days. [5] How
man's life shrinks if measured by such standards! Using all the
picturesqueness of oriental speech, the poet endeavours by means of
comparisons to make this thought as clear as possible. Human life is
like the stream by means of which God, as it were, 'sweeps men
away'; or it is like sleep which has no more significance when man
looks back on it in the morning; and, finally, it is like the grass which
quickly 'changes its form'. [6] This last picture, which was both
common and popular, is worked out more in detail: 'all flesh is grass';
it flourishes in the morning and in the evening it withers. What is
here described by the poet is not the product of a gloomy pessimism,
but the result of a simple and sober realism. He sees things as they
really are, though certainly he does not measure them by a standard
that is commonplace and superficial, but sees them from the divine
standpoint. As he looks upon God man's eyes are opened to see the
realities of life as they actually are; and this protects him from self-
deception, because he is thereby encouraged to think soberly and
truthfully. Of course, *sub specie aeternitatis*, things have an appearance
quite different from the one they present to the '*Carpe diem*' philosophy of a life carelessly lived for the present only.

Human sin (vv. 7–12)

The psalmist, however, does not stop at stating facts in order to
accept them, because, things being what they are, he cannot alter
them anyhow; he penetrates to the causes, ulterior as well as immediate, of the contrast that exists between God and man, between the
eternal and the temporal. It is characteristic of the Old Testament
idea of God that it regards the antithesis between God and man as a
moral issue and not only as a matter of fact or as an object for thought.
This attitude already makes itself felt in the stylistic change to 'we'.
Man never faces God as a spectator, who is not concerned with what
is at stake, but as one who is himself directly affected and addressed;
it always somehow involves a decision about his own fate. [7] The way
in which this decision affects him is quite different from the ontological
distinction between the divine and the human; he comes to apprehend it as the antithesis of two volitional powers that oppose one
another, and therefore cannot help discerning in the fact of his own
mortality the will of God in opposition to his own attitude of mind

and the wrath of God directed against him. Here the theological foundations of the Old Testament idea of judgment are to be found, making evident why in the cultic tradition that idea is so closely associated with the theophany, that is, with the revelation of the divine nature and will. On such a basis man's reaction to the reality of God is no longer that of wonder at the infinite nature of God; rather he is 'terrified' by it. It is this attitude of fear, in which he first perceives his own mortality as a dominating feature of his life, that makes it such a fateful burden to him. In this fatal mortality he senses God's negation of his own will to live; for he wants to live for ever in his own strength. And this is why he feels that God is his enemy who opposes him with his own mortality. **[8]** So his rejection of his transitory life is ultimately based on rejection of God and his will, that is, on sin. Where the antithesis between God and man comes to light in this way, there sin is also clearly manifested. It is true that man for the most part hides from himself the shocking fact that by his very nature he is opposed to the will of God; or else he does not always succeed in reaching the point where he is able to apprehend the innermost depths of his nature; however, whatever he may try to hide from himself, God sets it 'in the light of his countenance'. In the presence of God, where his demands are made known, the basic attitude of man who seeks to assert his own will, and not only particular secret faults, is revealed in its true nature as sin, and, as man stands before God, he is in that moment subject to his judgment.

[9] Measured against the will of the inexorable divine Judge, the inward shallowness and futility of human life now becomes obvious, no longer indeed as a mysterious fact, which man seeks in vain to explain, but as the necessary result of a wrong attitude to life and to its divine background, and as having an all too intelligible connection with human guilt and sin. Wherever a pessimistic view may be justified, its cause is to be found not in the course which the world has taken or in the life-span of man in itself, but in human sin, which man, as he meets with the resistance (wrath) of God, comes to recognize in all its perversity as the true cause of the shattering of his confidence in life. **[10]** From this viewpoint and in this mood the psalmist has written the familiar verse which pronounces a completely pessimistic verdict on the brevity and transience of life and does not leave any room for even a mere attempt to take a more positive attitude to life. In this respect the verse is at variance with the tendency to a positive appraisal of human labour which is

occasionally read—in my opinion wrongly—into Luther's translation, 'and if it has been precious, it has been toil and work'.[1] For
the statement 'their pride is but toil and pain' breathes the bitter
irony of a man who is entirely disappointed with life. No wonder that
a man who seeks in life *his* will and *his* pleasure is bound to end in
this disappointment; for all pleasure seeks perpetuity. In death God
has set a limit to such human aspirations. And for that reason the
sense of disappointment, which necessarily leads to pessimism, is
both the result of sin and an indication of the divine judgment which
takes effect in this way (cf. Gen. 3.17 ff.). We would, however, be
mistaken if we were to regard this pessimistic verdict of the psalm as
its author's final word regarding the problem of mortality. From
vv. 12 ff. it follows quite distinctly that the poet is familiar with a
different attitude to life which he deems to be the right one. But if
that is the case why does he first lead his train of thought to this
conclusion, which, after all, does not provide him with the final
answer, and indeed from the standpoint of faith, which is the ultimate
object of his psalm, does not even present the right answer? [11] The
answer to this question can be inferred from the verse that follows.
The poet observes that part of the nature of sin is that men hardly
ever realize the ultimate relationship between mortality and sin,
because they live for the moment and are unconcerned about the
opposition between the divine and the human will. In view of this
widespread failure of the divine reality to produce any impression
upon men, who may not even be aware of God's wrath and on that
account do not show any fear of God, it is the poet's aim to make his
words bring home to men the importance of the fact of God, and to
impress upon their minds how God sees human sin and the pessimistic valuation of life as linked together. By drawing the ultimate conclusion from that attitude of mind and by carrying it so far that it
leads to the complete negation of life, the poet executes with ruthless
honesty the self-judgment which sin entails, and so at the same time
indicates the inner impossibility of such an attitude towards life. But
this is exactly the point to which man must be brought in order to be
made aware of the despair which such an attitude of mind will bring,
and so to pay attention to that other eternal reality which transcends
the evanescent life of man and which alone is able to impart to it
a lasting purpose and value. There is no other way to a genuine
faith than the one which continually compels a man in remorseless

---

[1] * 'Wenn es köstlich gewesen ist, dann ist es Mühe und Arbeit gewesen.'

sincerity to abandon all hope in his own strength and cast himself wholly upon God. The psalmist not only wants to show others this way of renunciation, which leads to true faith; he takes it himself and in no way excludes himself from the radical and realistic valuation of human life as such. For this experience is for him, too, the inner prerequisite to the subsequent petition in which, filled with complete trust in God, he seeks refuge in him alone. Though it cannot be denied that a tension exists between the pessimistic realism of the psalmist and the optimistic background of his petition, it is a tension which has its root-cause in the nature of faith itself and should not be removed by splitting up the psalm in two parts whose different spirit betrays a different origin. [12] It signifies the profundity of the author's knowledge of sin that he is well aware of man's incapability of achieving by his own efforts that other attitude to life which does not end in negation and despair. God himself must give him the ability to see everything in a new light and the strength to lead a new life. This is why the psalmist prays, 'Teach us to number our days.' In view of what has gone before this petition can surely only mean that he is aiming at a new positive valuation and utilization of his life-span which differs from the pessimistic attitude in so far as in it God's will will in future be respected and valued. The wisdom of which the verse under discussion speaks is, in the context, divine wisdom, which comes from God in the form of knowledge of the finite nature of human life, but in content it signifies the overcoming of that negative attitude to life by an affirmation that is a gift from God and springs from faith and trust. At this point the thoughts of the poet once more take up the theme of trust in God which is indicated in v. 1 as the keynote of the whole psalm. For this reason it would be a mistake, though one that has often been made, to say that the psalm is permeated with the spirit of utter hopelessness. Though the poet does not at all indicate how he conceives of that hope in practice, the confidence with which he directs his petition to God in face of the futility of human affairs nevertheless tacitly implies that in view of the transitoriness of life he seeks and finds permanent support in God. Thus it is precisely death as ordained by God and the transitoriness of life which become the point at which the poet realizes that God shows him the way to the true and ultimate meaning of life. In the same direction points also

The prayer of supplication (vv. 13–17)

[13] Its subject-matter is very closely bound up with the psalm's

train of thought; in outward form, too, the poet links up by means of an intercession with those whom he included in the confession of sins (vv. 7 ff.). The appeal to the grace and mercy of God is here made on the basis of the same attitude of faith as in v. 12, that is, that man cannot transform his life by his own efforts, but needs God's help and grace to achieve this end. It is true that the psalmist does not directly speak of the forgiveness of sins, but the words 'have pity' essentially express the same thought that God may disregard men's sins and may once more deal graciously with them. The sense of urgency expressed in the prayer 'How long?' shows the seriousness of the psalmist's perception that he is wholly dependent on God. [**14**] Just as man is in need of food, so he is in need of God's grace if he is to achieve a joyful affirmation of life; the petition 'Satisfy us in the morning with thy grace' is meant to convey the thought that each day is to be started afresh with that need in mind. God's grace is the stay and substance of man's life. It presents the standard by which man is to number his days (v. 12). We must not overlook the fact that the psalmist does not pray for particular earthly blessings such as wealth, health and happiness. The poet's aspirations are quite generally focused on God's grace; his concern is to experience God himself; and that experience means to him joy in life and happiness in abundance. [**15**] For that reason, too, the petition 'Make us glad for as many days as thou hast afflicted us, and as many years as we have seen evil' is not to be interpreted in the obvious sense of a recompense, only aiming at the formal settling of accounts, as if the poet at the decline of his life would still expect to be compensated for the years of suffering by an equal number of years of happiness. The point of the thought here is not God's justice and recompense, nor his compensation, for which there would be no justifiable claim, but only and solely his *grace*. And that grace consists in the very fact that the hand which inflicted the wounds is alone able to heal them (cf. Hos. 6.1) or, to speak without using metaphorical language, that the days and years during which man has been groaning under God's judgment on his guilt and sin will be transformed by God's grace into light and joy, and that his life, as it were, will now be bestowed upon him once more by means of the knowledge that the opposition between God and man, expressed in God's judgment, is overcome by his grace and transformed into a union on a higher level. At the very point at which man is cast down by God, God raises him up again; judgment and grace go together. [**16**] The work which God

accomplishes for the benefit of his servants and for the manifestation
of which the poet prays is precisely that in the very judgment of God
his gracious will may be made manifest and effectual, and so that
his inconceivable glory may be revealed in the life of generations
present and to come. It is this divine work which imparts to man's
life, so wretched in itself, an ultimate and imperishable meaning
and fills it with the splendour of eternity. Here is the place where
God's gracious nature and rule appear in all their glory and where
his redemptive work is realized. [17] The poet expresses this thought
quite clearly in v. 17 in the form of a final wish and, as he rightly
recognizes that without God's blessing man's actions are bound to
prove futile, he adds the petition, 'And establish thou the work of our
hands.' This is how the reality of human life appears when seen from
the other side, that is, the Godward side: it is God's grace alone which
gives purpose to life and durability to the work of man.

The same man who in view of man's sinfulness has described life
as being toil and pain can now face this life with a heart full of hope
and joyous confidence; in the light of God's grace his eternity, too,
is reflected in man's life and work. Seen in the light of God what is
evanescent becomes durable, what is miserable becomes glorious, and
what is meaningless becomes meaningful, because everything is
bathed in the light of eternity. It is only when we have walked the
whole way together with the poet, who does not disregard the actual
facts under the influence of a fanciful illusion but, with the courage
to be ruthlessly honest about both life and himself, recognizes the
hopelessness of man's position and his sense of terror before God, that
we are able to grasp against this background the true significance of
faith, which is able to reach out for the eternity of God in the midst
of man's passing life and like a star from another world shines upon
the psalm in the words, 'O Lord, our God, thou art our refuge for
ever and ever.'[1]

[1] * Weiser here quotes Luther's translation of Ps. 90.1.

91. UNDER GOD'S PROTECTION

1 In the shelter of the Most High shall he dwell[1]
  and in the shadow of the Almighty shall he abide,
2 who says[2] to the Lord, 'My refuge and my fortress;
  my God in whom I trust.'[3]
3 For it is he who will deliver you from the snare of the fowler
  and from the deadly pit.[4]

4 He will cover you with his pinions,[2]
   and under his wings you will find refuge.
   His faithfulness is a shield and weapon.[5]

5 You will not fear the terror of the night,
   nor the arrow that flies by day,

6 nor the pestilence that stalks in darkness,
   nor the epidemic that rages at noonday.[6]

7 A thousand may fall at your side,
   ten thousand at your right hand;
   but it will not come near you.

8 You will see it with your eyes[7]
   and behold the recompense of the wicked.

9 For, as for you—the Lord is your[2] refuge;
   you have made the Most High your shelter.[8]

10 No evil shall befall you,
   no scourge come near your tent.

11 For he will give his angels charge of you
   to guard you in all your ways,

12 so that they will bear you upon their hands,[9]
   lest you dash your foot against a stone.

13 You will tread on lions and adders,
   the lions and dragons you will trample under foot!

14 'Because he cleaves to me in love, I will deliver him;
   I will protect him, because he knows my name.

15 When he calls me, I will answer him;
   I will be with him in times of trouble,
   I will rescue him and honour him.

16 With long life I will satisfy him,
   and show him my salvation!'

[1] Read *yēšēb*.
[2] See BH.
[3] * RSV translates vv. 1 and 2 not as a promise but as a factual statement:
   He who dwells in the shelter of the Most High,
   who abides in the shadow of the Almighty,
   will say to the Lord . . .
[4] In the transmitted text 'the pestilence of destruction'; see BH. (Tr. N.: RSV has 'deadly pestilence'.)
[5] The Hebrew term is not known to us; its meaning must be inferred from the context. (Tr. N.: RSV has 'buckler' instead of 'weapon'.)
[6] * RSV has 'nor the destruction that wastes at noonday'.
[7] * RSV has 'You will only look with your eyes'.
[8] Lit.: habitation. (Tr. N.: RSV has:
   Because you have made the Lord your refuge,
   the Most High your habitation,
and this sentence is continued in v. 10, 'no evil . . .')
[9] * In RSV v. 12 starts a new sentence, 'On their hands they will bear you up.'

Together with Psalm 46, Psalm 91 is the most impressive testimony in the Psalter to the strength that springs from trust in God.

Though there is an inward affinity between these two psalms, there is something which imparts to each of them its specific character. In Psalm 46 it is the cult community's trust in God, set against the whole wide background of the *Heilsgeschichte* and of eschatology. In the psalm under discussion, springing from the same cultic source, it is the wholly personal and intimate relationship of trust in God portrayed within the narrow scope of the personal circumstances of an individual. The psalm has been included in the treasury of Christian hymns in the form of two paraphrases, the one by Paul Gerhardt[1] and the other by Heyden.[2]

The fact that even as early as the Targum the text was assigned to different voices points to the liturgical usage of the hymn. The psalm was probably associated with the cultus from the beginning, and is to be understood as the promise and the assurance of salvation which was pronounced by the priest and brings home to the worshipper in the Temple in powerful and solemn language and with an almost inexhaustible wealth of illustrations, the blessing and strength that flow from placing one's trust in God. The psalm strongly impresses on our mind how much courage and heroism, how much mental activity and strength to overcome through trust in God, could be inspired by the hours of worship spent in the house of God.

The author of the psalm deserves our special attention on account of his poetical gifts, too. The strength of his faith is matched by the forcefulness of his language. Bold and tender illustrations are set over against each other in striking contrast (see the comments on vv. 4, 11 f., 13); again, the poet continually changes the object on which his thoughts dwell, speaking now of God (vv. 3, 11 f.), now of man (vv. 5 f., 7 f., 13)—one object sometimes directly merges into another (vv. 4, 9 f.). And all this imparts to the whole psalm a lively inner rhythm and gives an inkling of the active interest which the poet himself takes in what he has got to say about trust in God.

It is impossible to assign a date to the psalm. In form it clearly falls into two sections: in vv. 1–13 divine protection and human steadfastness in every danger are promised to the man who seeks his refuge in God and places his trust in him; in vv. 14–16 this promise is confirmed and reinforced by a divine assurance.

[1–2] The general promise in liturgical style with which the psalm opens strikes the keynote of the whole psalm. It assures the man who

---

1 * 'Wer unterm Schirm des Höchsten sitzt.'
2 * 'Wer unterm Schutz des Höchsten ist', by Sebald Heyden (1494–1561).

takes shelter in the house of God, having professed his trust in him (see Intr. 58 f., 91), of God's protection. True confidence in God will never be in vain. Whosoever adopts a personal attitude of trust in God which enables him to say to him, 'My refuge, my fortress, my God in whom I trust', thereby, in fact, already dwells in the shelter of the Most High and is already safe in the shadow of Almighty God. The fundamental idea of these two verses is typical of the Old Testament, where faith is actively and vitally interested both in the realization of the divine help, in which man places his trust, and also in the manifestation of the reality of God in the form of an actual event. The true aim of the whole psalm, which stands out prominently right from the beginning, is to demonstrate that this living relationship with God has the quality of actuality which the man who trusts in God will be able to experience in his own person in all the afflictions and perils of life as the saving, protecting, strengthening power of God. The two figurative phrases which speak of the 'dwelling in the hiding-place (shelter) of the Most High' and of the 'staying overnight (abiding) in the shadow of the Almighty', and have in view primarily the sojourn in the Temple, are intended to depict the peace and security of having found refuge in God's shelter. But further than that, dwelling in the hiding-place of God is meant to express the safety and peace of mind that come from a sense of protection against persecution, whereas staying overnight in the shadow of the Almighty is meant to express that feeling of being out of danger which springs from the knowledge that someone else keeps guard. This latter picture is derived from the custom of the right to hospitality according to which the wanderer, sojourning in the shadow of the roof of the hospitable house, is entrusted to the protection of his host. In this connection the poet deliberately uses ancient divine names (translated above 'Most High' and 'Almighty'; cf. the comments on Ps. 68.14) which, originating in the pre-Israelite phase of religion and conferred upon Yahweh in the Old Testament, are meant to impress by their venerable sound and to represent the transcendent power of the Old Testament God in its true light. For it is quite impossible to compare the protection which this God is able to grant with what others may look for in other patron gods or in any other place of refuge. The singular comprehensiveness and depth of the trust placed in the Old Testament God is based on the miraculous fact that the supreme God, whose name men dare utter only with awe and trembling, is precisely the One whom the individual may call 'my God',[1] as if he existed only for his sake. Thus the God-fearing man feels himself to be lifted out of his environment by his personal confession of trust in God, so that his life is placed in a new relationship which imparts to his whole existence a special character. The main part of the psalm now works out this thought in detail.

[3] The change of style to direct address is significant. Though the subsequent verses formally represent the basis of the general promise made in vv. 1–2, the more urgent note sounded in them brings out the point here, which, as far as trust in God is concerned, is the individual cause of the person addressed. With outstretched finger the psalmist first points to God: 'It is he who will deliver you.' It is only because God is *God* that absolute trust in him is at all possible and meaningful. The two images used to illustrate the danger are borrowed from hunting. The snare of the fowler (cf. Ps. 124.7) as well as the pit designed to trap wild animals (occasionally also used as a metaphor for the underworld, Ps. 18.5) allude to deceitful plots in order to show how anxiety growing uneasy through lack of confidence is overcome by trust in God. And these illustrations point also into another direction. The greatness of the divine power to help can be judged only by the magnitude of the affliction. Even if man is helplessly exposed to destruction like the animal caught in a snare or in a pit, he who himself is greater than any kind of affliction is able to help.

[4] A popular and even more powerful illustration, which refers to the God who is present above the wings of the cherubim upon the sacred Ark (see Intr. 40 f., 72 f.), emphasizes the same thought. Just as the mother-bird protects her young brood by spreading her wings over them (cf. Deut. 32.11; Matt. 23.37), so God covers the godly in every kind of danger, and they find in him a shelter in which to hide. The divine and the human aspect of the relationship based on trust are here placed side by side in a way that shows how closely they are related to each other, and impart to the whole a note which is both strong and intimately tender: on the one hand the will and the power of God to help and, on the other hand, the trustfulness of the man who knows himself to be safe in that divine will. The last line of v. 4 employs illustrations taken from war and, producing an impressive effect by contrast, brings out the militant strength of the faith which has the courage to defy any kind of danger on account of its trust in

---

[1] Cf. Eissfeldt, *ZAW* 61, 1945/48, pp. 3 ff., on the various religious meanings of this phrase in the Old Testament.

God. God's 'faithfulness' is the defensive weapon in the hand of the
godly. Though man-made weapons may break to pieces, God's
faithfulness will not fail. The valour of faith is, however, not to be
identified with man's courage or strength, but rests on God's un-
changing character; it is his strength, continually granted anew to
his people as long as they trust in him, which lifts them above all
anxieties and spiritual dangers. The subsequent verses deal with this
thought.

[5–6] The difference between belief and unbelief could not be
expressed more clearly than in the simple, positive and firm statement 'you will not fear', made in the face of the sinister and gruesome forces that existed in popular belief and are now reviewed by
the poet in turn. With a double alternation he speaks in each verse
of a danger that threatens by night and of another that threatens
in the daytime. At first he only employs obscure allusions which
accord with the weird atmosphere created by these evil forces. The
'terror of the night' probably refers to those powers of a superhuman
kind who exist in popular belief at all times and strike fear and terror
during the night hours. The arrow that flies by day is no human
weapon, but the dreaded missile of a demonic power, and on the
analogy of v. 6 is most easily interpreted as referring to sunstroke
(cf. Ps. 121.6). Just as in Greek mythology Apollo causes diseases by
his arrows, so is Yahweh occasionally thought of in the Old Testament as being himself the divine archer (Ps. 38.2; Lam. 3.13; Job
6.4) who causes illness by his arrows. It is, however, doubtful whether
prominence is here given to this latter conception, which has its
origin in the idea of the exclusive power of Yahweh, rather than to
the familiar view, held by popular belief, according to which other
demonic powers are held to be the cause of the epidemics. The same
is true of v. 6. Just as it is said in Babylonia of the pest-god Nergal
that he goes about at night and invades the homes of people through
locked doors, so the Old Testament tells of Yahweh sending his
plague-angel at night to afflict the army of the Assyrians (Isa.
37.36; cf. II Sam. 24.16) and himself slaying the first-born of the
Egyptians on the Passover night (Ex. 11.4 f.; cf. 12.23). The psalmist
does not use this latter belief but the popular one when he perti-
nently characterizes the grim impression produced by the danger of
epidemics by graphically personifying the latter as demons. Among
many peoples noonday is thought of as the hour of evil spirits just as
midnight is; to the terror at night there is added the danger in broad

daylight when the burning sunbeams hatch out diseases, so that it is impossible to say which of these two evils is more to be feared. It is the knowledge of the existence of a constant threat to human life which is manifested in the subjective form of that widespread superstition (cf. John 16.33). But it is precisely that background of man's fear of the uncanny powers who surround him that sets off the more forcefully the fearlessness of the man who is sustained by the strength of his trust in God. The greater the danger, the more powerfully faith reaches out towards heaven in the absolute certainty, 'You will not fear', and overcomes anxiety and superstition by the feeling of being safe in God's protection.

[7–8] Faith rises to even greater heights in the familiar and often quoted saying, 'A thousand may fall at your side, ten thousand at your right hand, but it will not come near you.' Admittedly, one cannot quite clearly see whether this daring view refers to the previous illustrations of the epidemics and the pestilence, or whether we are here presented with a new illustration; the structure of the psalm as a whole with its vivid change of illustrations makes the latter interpretation seem to me to be the more probable. In that case we shall have to think of a war-time scene. The essential idea, however, becomes clear even without the help of such an interpretation. Though the victims may fall right and left in murderous destruction, he who trusts in God alone remains upright when round about him the harvest is gathered in by the pitiless reaper Death! Here faith reaches its ultimate soaring height, leaving behind in its bold flight every doubt which a sober and realistic valuation of the situation might raise. What, humanly speaking, is quite improbable and indeed almost impossible, is within the reach of faith; this is the divine miracle. Such a faith sees only the God who saves; all else sinks into oblivion beside him. And its greatness, one-sided though it is, and its strength that can remove mountains, lie precisely in this undoubting concentration on God. There is no room for a human 'Why?' when once God's miracle and the bold venture in alliance with him are accepted. This truth will be understood by anyone who, perhaps in a war, has faced a similar situation and, after an incomprehensible deliverance from a deadly peril, has asked the unanswered and indeed unanswerable question: Why did it not happen to me? It is not possible either to evoke or to justify such trust by reasoning. It is the realization of what appears to be a miracle which alone furnishes the proof that such trust is justified and

P.–U

reveals its strength. This is why the psalmist points out: 'You will see it with your own eyes.' This statement shows not only the this-worldliness of the Old Testament faith, but also its interest in the manifestation of 'reality', that is, in man being enabled to encounter the God in whom he believes as actually existing and active. From that angle we shall also have to understand the last line of v. 8, which speaks of the requital of the wicked. That text seems to me to be misinterpreted when some expositors seek to identify the wicked with the author's fellow countrymen who fall at his side in their thousands and ten thousands; for the text itself does not provide any conclusive reference to that effect, and such a strange, uncomprehending, self-willed, severe and unjust verdict against the others can, moreover, by no means be accounted for by the situation depicted in the psalm itself, not even if we made allowance for a blunder on the part of the author. On the other hand, it does make sense if we understand the term 'wicked', as is so often the case in the Psalter, quite generally to cover the ungodly as a whole without making the further assumption that thereby those who had been mortally wounded are referred to. The clause in question therefore provides a sort of supplement to what has gone before in so far as it adds to the picture of the trustworthiness of God, which on the one hand is illustrated by the deliverance of the godly, another frequent feature, that the reality of God will assert itself in the judgment on the ungodly in such a way that the godly will be able to see it, too. Understood in this sense, v. 8b fits easily into the train of thought expressed immediately beforehand, and follows from the cultic tradition in which the judgment has its firm place (see Intr. 32 f., 47). Here, too, the religious interest in the power and reality of God, rather than any malicious gloating over the misfortunes of others or passing of hard-hearted judgments on others, occupies a prominent place. But it is true to say that however much we may understand the religious concern to which that train of thought gives expression, we cannot overlook the fact that in this passage, too, the idea of retribution represents a limitation and narrowing of the religious beliefs of the Old Testament.

[9–10] Having reached the climax of his enthusiastic and daring faith—notice in this connection the abrupt and disconnected style—the poet reverts to the words used at the beginning of the psalm, but with the difference that what was then expressed in a general and hypothetical way, and thought of as a mere wish and as a call upon

those who were addressed, is now given the form of a positive assertion and a firm statement: 'You have made the Most High your
shelter'; this statement, too, presupposes a cultic situation. So the
promise in v. 10 that no evil and no scourge will befall him also
issues from the same certitude born of trust.

[11–12] The last thought is further developed in a delightful and
cheerful picture. Miraculous help is promised to the friend of God.
God charges his angels, divine beings whose power is superior to that
of man, to guard this man and protect him in danger. The idea of
guardian-angels, which has been preserved from the earliest Babylonian times to the present day, the Old Testament (Gen. 24.7; Dan.
3.28) and the New Testament (Matt. 4.6 f.) included, as an expression of the almost motherly solicitude of God, is here depicted in
particularly delicate colours. They will carry him like a child, carefully and protectively, so that not even once will he dash his foot
against a stone, an accident which otherwise frequently happens on
the stony roads of Palestine. Thus the believer knows himself to be
cared for and to be safe in God's keeping and proceeds on his way
unconcerned about the dangers that threaten him. The fact that
Jesus in the Temptation narrative rejects this saying, which threatens
to become a danger to him, when spoken by the devil, saying, 'You
shall not tempt the Lord your God', clearly shows the limits set to the
trust in God. Man's trust in God is not just something of which he
can dispose independently and at his own discretion; rather is it
given to him by God in and with the affliction for which it has value
applied, and it cannot be dissociated from the exigencies of the given
circumstances, which are in the hand of God and not of man.

[13] The next illustration, which gives an example of the manly
courage to which the trust in God is able to rise, forms a marked and
effective contrast with the previous portrait of childlike security and
protective care. This more active trend towards a heroic attitude
deserves our special attention in view of the rather passive character
of the trust placed in God which is elsewhere prominent in the psalm
and shows itself in the enduring of afflictions and tensions. The hero
of faith strides with bold steps over every kind of danger. The phrase
'lions and adders' is probably used in a metaphorical sense to describe dangers in general; for the second part of v. 13, 'You will
trample lions and dragons underfoot', clearly shows that the psalmist
is not thinking of dangerous and terrifying journeys through the
jungle in the course of which a lion suddenly jumps up from the reed

or the wanderer treads on a serpent (cf. in this connection Jer. 12.5), but rather has in mind the idea, widespread in the ancient Orient and handed down in the cultic myth (see Intr. 51, 60 f.), of the god killing a dragon and as a sign of his victory over the monster putting his foot on its neck. And whereas the popular belief in Egypt led to the manufacturing of amulets with the picture of a god treading on a lion, and by its magic power giving protection against wild animals, in the Old Testament it is faith itself which supplies man with super-human, divine strength to overcome every kind of danger. What is humanly impossible is possible to faith.

From a formal point of view the second part of the psalm is dis-tinctly marked off from the first part as a word of promise and assurance from God; in content it provides God's own verification and corroboration of the statements made so far by man, and in its form as a divine assurance of salvation it still lets us see clearly the cultic background of the psalm (see Intr. 79).

[14] Man's faithfulness in worshipping God and his intimate communion with God are described as 'cleaving to God in love' and as 'knowing the name of God'. The knowing of the name, which presupposes the revelation of the name of the Deity in the cult as well as the believers' testimony to it (cf. Ps. 138.2; see Intr. 41 f., 58, 74), does not, however, only serve the purpose of being able to call upon the Godhead. According to the views held in antiquity the name includes the nature of the person in question, and 'to know' signifies in Hebrew more than merely 'being informed' about some-thing; it comprises at the same time 'to be on terms of intimacy' with someone and to be inwardly devoted to someone. Only the man who lives in such intimate communion with God may be assured of his help: as he assumes the attitude of faithful trust, he sees God's love and care directed towards him.

[15] This communion is a communion in prayer and is sustained by the certitude that the prayer will be heard. As God is with him, the believer does not walk alone in times of trouble, and he will be able to thank God for the freedom and honour which he will bestow upon him.

[16] The promise that God's blessings will be abundantly granted embraces the whole of reality, material and spiritual, earthly and heavenly, the satisfaction of a long life and the privilege of beholding the divine salvation. It is the promise of the salvation of God, realized in the ritual act which in the very midst of dangers lifts the

godly above purely temporal affairs and effectively concludes the psalm.

The hymn is a sturdy comrade; its boldness and unbroken courageous testimony to God has already enabled many a man to overcome all sorts of temptations. By virtue of the soaring energy of its trust in God it leaves behind every earthly fear, every human doubt and all inhibiting considerations, and lifts man up above the depressing realities of life to the hopeful certitude of a faith which is able to endure life and to master it. True, the Christian's trust in God requires a further readiness to submit to God's will, even when he has resolved to deal with us in ways other than those we expected the venture of faith to take.

92. IT IS GOOD TO MAKE CONFESSION BEFORE THE LORD

A Psalm. A Song. For the Sabbath

1 It is a precious thing to make confession before the Lord,[1]
   to sing praises to thy name, O Most High;[2]
2 to declare thy grace in the morning,
   and thy faithfulness by night,
3 to the music of the psaltery[3] and the harp,
   to the string music of the cither.[4]
4 For thou hast made me glad by thy work;
   at the work of thy hands I sing for joy.
5 How great are thy works, O Lord,
   how deep are thy thoughts![5]
6 He is an animal who knows this not;
   a fool who does not understand it![6]
7 When the wicked sprouted like grass,
   and the evildoers all flourished,
   it was only that they should be destroyed for ever.[6]
8 But thou remainest the Most High[7,2] for ever.[8]
9 For, lo, thy enemies, O Lord,
   for, lo, thy enemies will perish;
   all evildoers will be scattered.
10 But thou hast exalted my horn like that of the wild ox;
   and hast anointed[7] me with fresh oil.[9]
11 My eyes gloat over my enemies,[7]
   my ears rejoice when they hear the fate of the wicked.[10]
12 The righteous will flourish like the palm tree;
   he will grow like the cedar in Lebanon.[11]
13 Planted in the house of the Lord
   they flourish in the courts of our God;
14 they still bring forth fruit in old age;
   they will be full of sap and green,[12]

15 to declare that the Lord, my rock, is righteous,
   and that there is no unrighteousness in him.[13]

[1] * In RSV, 'It is good to give thanks to the Lord.'
[2] See Ps. 7.17.
[3] Lit.: ten-stringed (instrument); cf. Ps. 33.2. (Tr. N.: RSV has 'lute' instead
of 'psaltery'.)
   [4] * RSV has 'to the melody of the lyre'.
   [5] * RSV has 'Thy thoughts are very deep!'
   [6] * Here v. 6 refers back to v. 5; RSV links vv. 6 and 7, reading:
       The dull man cannot know,
       the stupid cannot understand this:
       that, though the wicked sprout like grass
       and all evildoers flourish,
       they are doomed to destruction for ever.
   [7] See BH.
   [8] * RSV reads 'but thou, O Lord, art on high for ever'.
   [9] * The RSV has 'thou hast poured over me' instead of 'and hast anointed me
with'.
      [10] * In RSV v. 11 is:
       My eyes have seen the downfall of my enemies,
       my ears have heard the doom of my evil assailants.
   [11] * RSV uses the present tense.
   [12] * V. 14b reads in RSV, 'they are ever full of sap and green'.
   [13] * In RSV v. 15 is:
       to show that the Lord is upright;
       he is my rock and there is no unrighteousness in him.

The psalm, which according to its superscription was used in
later Judaism in public worship on the Sabbath, itself originated in
the public worship of the cult community, where it was recited to
music as a hymn and thanksgiving song (v. 3). When v. 2 speaks of
the confession which is uttered in the morning and by night, the
thought which most easily comes to our mind in this connection is
that the poet must have stayed at the sanctuary for several days
during the festival season (cf. Pss. 55.17; 134.1), possibly during the
New Year Festival, at which according to tradition a cultic ceremony took place during the festival night. This setting would also
explain the subject-matter of the psalm (see Intr. 31 ff., 45 ff., 55 ff.,
74 ff.), which is as follows: commemoration of the saving deeds of God
(vv. 2, 4 ff.), judgment on the wicked (vv. 7–9, 11), and thanksgiving
for God's help and salvation which the worshipper experienced in his
own life, and which he hopes will be granted to the whole community of the righteous also in the future (vv. 10, 12 ff.).

[1–4] The hymnic introduction reflects the solemn joy of the festival mood which fills the worshipper's heart at the moment when, in
response to God's 'grace and faithfulness' (cf. Ex. 34.6, which is the
basic text of the cultic tradition; see Intr. 42 f., 74 f.), he is able to de-

clare and praise them in the form of a hymn in the midst of the congregation. Through the revelation of God's redemptive work and the recital of the *Heilsgeschichte* (cf. Pss. 28.5; 30.9; 105.5; 106.2; 111.2 ff.), these have become to him a cultic experience, and therefore a directly present reality, and he feels that they have become his personal possession by faith. The term *ṭōb*, translated by Luther 'a precious thing', means both 'beautiful' and 'good';[1] this shows to what a high degree the aesthetic and artistic and the ethical and religious aspects of the worshipping life are here comprehended as a unity by those who are subject to the vivid impression produced by the glory of God. The sustaining foundation of true piety is the joy in God that is awakened in the worshipper by God himself. **[5–6]** The encounter with God, however, finds its expression not only in the poet's mood of exaltation; it also makes demands on his thinking and stimulates him to ponder over the greatness of the divine revelation and the profundity of its significance, and to testify joyfully to these in a hymn. To man alone is reserved the knowledge of God; and that knowledge is the precious gift which is offered to him at the festival. Whosoever unmindfully ignores it is like an animal to which such an insight into the nature of God remains a mystery (cf. Ps. 73.22). Only through the relationship with God is man enabled to recognize ultimate truth and reality; without that relationship he lapses into a deceptive illusion. For the measure of all knowledge and wisdom is God and not man. **[9–11]** This is proved true when we look at the prosperity of the wicked to which the poet—like the authors of Pss. 37; 49; 73—has given serious thought.[2] He no longer lets himself be troubled by the impression of seeming injustice which the success of the wicked might at first sight be able to produce. The eye of faith, focused on God, penetrates the deceptive illusion and recognizes the ultimate divine purpose to which the wicked, too, are subject: to demonstrate the power and the glory of God. Their happiness and prosperity serve to provide the background of the transitoriness of all purely human affairs ('like grass'; cf. Ps. 90.6) against which the eternal being of God, that is, the final character of his absolute sovereignty, is made manifest when his judgment is executed on all his enemies (cf. Judg. 5.31). To the ritual of the festival cult belong both the judgment

[1] The verse is in the style of a Wisdom saying; cf. Lam. 3.26.
[2] Here, too, the influence of the way of thinking developed in the Wisdom literature can be established (see Intr. 88 f.).

on the wicked (v. 11) and the salvation of the community of
the godly, in which the worshipper may thankfully confess that
he shares (see Intr. 39 f.). When the worshipper declares that he
rejoices to hear the fate of his wicked enemies, we must understand
this in the light of these cultic connections. This is an expression not
of gloating over his adversaries' well-deserved fate, but of joy in the
manifestation of God's power which signifies judgment for his
enemies, but salvation for the godly (cf. 'thy enemies'). The enemies
of God perish; they are scattered; they have no further share in the
vital energy and festal joy—this is what the two illustrations in v. 10
purport to express—which in the worshipper's mind are included in
the divine revelation and dispensation of salvation that takes place
in the cult. (On the exaltation of the horn as a symbol of vitality cf.
I Sam. 2.1, 10; Pss. 89.24; 132.17; on anointing with oil in public
worship cf. Ps. 23.5.) **[12–15]** A new vitality and hope, which underlie the promise which concludes the psalm, spring for the whole
community of the 'righteous' from the saving experience of the
celebration of the feast. In this connection the image of the flourishing growth of the palm tree and cedar, which in contrast to the
picture of the grass in v. 7 is the symbol of longevity and fertility,
attains a greater spiritual depth: amazing energies, which do not let
the godly man grow feeble or weak even in old age, are continually
imparted to him afresh by his living communion with God, which
is ever renewed and constantly maintained in the house of God and
in its worship (this last statement is the meaning of the image used
in v. 13; cf. Pss. 52.8; 23.6); again, it is the proper native soil for
faith in which every life has its root. In this connection it is worth
noting what the poet means by 'bringing forth fruit' so that in his
view the meaning of life is thereby fulfilled: clearly recalling the
beginning of the psalm (v. 2) and consciously overcoming the
temptation, which assails faith (vv. 7 f.), to doubt God's justice in
view of the prosperity of the wicked, the poet comes to realize that
the proclamation of the righteousness of God and the profession and
testimony that there is no unrighteousness in him represent the
ultimate purpose and true meaning of a life which finds its security
in placing its trust in God (see Intr. 65) and which thereby itself
becomes a genuine 'service rendered to God'.[1]

---

[1] * *'Gottesdienst'* can mean either 'divine service' or a 'service rendered to God'.
Here it is used in the latter sense, but with overtones of the former which it is
hardly possible to reproduce in English.

93. THE MAJESTY OF GOD

1 The Lord is become King, robed in majesty;
  the Lord is robed in strength and girded with might.
  He establishes[1] the world that it cannot be shaken.[2]
2 Thy throne is established from of old;
  thou art God[1] from everlasting.
3 The floods once rose up, O Lord,[3]
  the floods lifted up their voice,
  the floods lift up their roaring.
4 Mightier than the thunders of many waters,
  more glorious than the raging of the sea
  is the glory of the Lord on high.[4]
5 Thy testimonies are true and faithful;
  holiness befit thy house
  O Lord, for evermore![5]

[1] See BH.
[2] * In RSV v. 1 is:
  The Lord reigns; he is robed in majesty;
  the Lord is robed, he is girded with strength.
  Yea, the world is established; it shall never be moved.
[3] * V. 3a reads in RSV, 'The floods have lifted up, O Lord . . .'
[4] * V. 4bc reads in RSV:
  mightier than the waves of the sea,
  the Lord on high is mighty!
[5] * RSV gives v. 5a as: 'Thy decrees are very sure' and uses the indicative in v. 5b.

The psalm is a song in praise of Yahweh's kingship. This is made clear by the so-called 'acclamation' of the king (*Königsruf*), with which the psalm opens, pronouncing that 'Yahweh is become King', which in its turn points to the acclamation on the occasion of the enthronement of the earthly king (cf. II Sam. 15.10; II Kings 9.13). In this respect the hymn is closely related to Psalms 47, 97 and 99. The enthronement of Yahweh presumably constituted one of the rites of the Covenant Festival which was celebrated in autumn at New Year and lasted several days (see Intr. 33 f., 62 f.). The ritual of the enthronement ceremony has its origin not in Israel but in Mesopotamia. The mention of the Creation in this connection can probably likewise be traced back to the Babylonian source of the Enthronement Festival, where the celebration of the world's new year included the enthronement of the god Marduk as a victory over the powers of chaos at the creation of the world. We can still see, from the affinity of the psalm with documents from Ugarit, how the ideas that furnish the material for the psalm had reached Canaan

and Israel at a comparatively early date.[1] Taking everything into
consideration, however, the psalm with its hymnic style exhibits
those typical features which are the hall-mark of the Old Testament
faith. The hope of the Kingdom of God, the coming of which is linked
up with the Enthronement of Yahweh, and the emphatic linking
of creation and eschatology within the idea of the eternal reign of
God, have sprung from Old Testament soil and are the ripe fruit of its
belief in God.

Using terse and powerful language, the hymn rushes along like
the roaring water of which it speaks. The subdued reminiscences of
mythical ideas and images are outshone by the poet's powerful
exultation over the majesty of God, to which all his thoughts are
subordinated to form a forceful unity. On the other hand the alternation between the hymnic testimony to God (vv. 1, 4) and the style
of prayer (vv. 2, 5), which depends on the reference of the psalm to
the cultic proceedings, produces a vivid dynamic form, which
effectively contrasts with the consistency of the thought-sequence
(see Intr. 55 f.).

[1] At the very beginning of the psalm the peculiar character of
the Old Testament way of thinking in terms of the cultus and of the
Heilsgeschichte is thrown into relief by means of the acclamation
'Yahweh is become King'. With fervent emotion God's assumption
of his kingship, accomplished in the cultic act, is celebrated as a
present event (cf. vv. 2 f.). What follows shows that this kingship of
God both embraces the whole past, however remote, and includes
the consummation of the Kingdom of God at the end of time.[2] He is
the God who was, who is and who is to come, and before whose
reality the barriers of time disappear so that what happened long
ago and what will come to pass in the future both simultaneously
call for a decision at the present moment. The eye of faith, focused
on the reality of God, is opened to a living understanding of reality
by means of which pre-history and the end of time, creation and
eschatology, acquire an actuality that is charged with energy and is
concentrated on the present by the very fact that God shows himself
at work in it. In the light of that dynamic quality of the revelation
of God in the sacral act we can also understand that on the analogy
of the portrayal of the glory of the earthly king the glory of God is
praised not in the form of a description of his divine being, but in the

[1] Cf. Jefferson, *JBL* 71 (1952), pp. 155 f.
[2] See also the comments on Ps. 47.8.

form of an account of the way in which God *acts*: 'He has robed himself in majesty and girded himself with might.' In the image of the royal mantle and adornment of the divine Ruler poetic inspiration and reverent awe unite; the poet can only speak of the majestic garment of God, but not of his person; this is forbidden by awe and the limit set to human perception. In this he is in accord with the way in which Isaiah (ch. 6) speaks of the appearance of God at his call. At that point of the hymn at which as a rule on the occasion of the enthronement of the earthly king the expansion and durability of his reign is portrayed, Yahweh is glorified as the King and Ruler not only of Israel but of the whole world. Yahweh's kingship is based on the idea of creation; because he has 'established' the world so that it cannot be shaken (cf. in this connection Ps. 104.5), the world is subject to him; it is *God* who has endowed it with durability. Whereas elsewhere there is praise of the manifestations of Yahweh's might in the history of the people of Israel (Judg. 5. 11; Ps. 47.3 f.; cf. the exegesis of the latter), here a more far-reaching perspective is achieved by means of a vision of God which embraces the beginning and the end and simply cannot be surpassed by anything else. The note of confidence intermingles with the expressions of wonder and awe and imparts to the hymn, which is resonant with joyful exultation, a ring of its own.

[2] Passing on to the style of prayer, which reveals that a stronger personal bond based on faith exists between the psalmist and God, the psalm now draws the conclusion from the idea of creation. God's dominion does not begin with his enthronement at the end of time, nor with the annually repeated ceremony of his enthronement, at which his reign is palpably manifested; nay, it is established from eternity; again, it is based on his creation and is justified by the fact that he is 'God from everlasting' (cf. the comments on v. 1). Its durability and trustworthiness are guaranteed by the fact that it is God who holds in his hands the reins of government. The eternal being of God warrants that his dominion will last for ever. The statement made in v. 2 expresses man's trust in that divine rule and his feeling of being safe under it. And this throws into relief the superiority of the Old Testament idea of God over the Oriental idea of the cycle of the cosmic years which is somehow related to fatalism. The sphinx of destiny is unmasked and her dark power is broken by the belief in the meaningful rule of a personal God and, accordingly, it has become possible for man to adopt a personal attitude of faith and trust.

[3] Changing once more from the form of address to that of description, the poet uses a tremendous word-picture to praise the glorious majesty of God. The scene of the rising up of the roaring floods is borrowed from the mythological idea of the combat of the gods against the powers of chaos in primordial times, as it had been handed down in the Babylonian myth of the victory of the god Marduk over the primeval flood Tiamat, which was celebrated at the New Year Festival; in the form of Yahweh's victory this still finds echoes in the Old Testament, e.g. in Pss. 89.9 f.; 104.7. The Old Testament poet speaks of that battle of Yahweh only in allusions which are considerably softened down, thus deliberately avoiding the impression that the myth still retained its original significance for him. He sets the primeval rebellion of the floods over against their rebellion at the end of time; the beginning and the end are drawn together so that they represent a threat to the world concentrated at that very moment when the sacral proceedings are taking place. The verse nevertheless does not sound a note of fear, ensuing from that threat, but rather rings with joy at the roaring of the seas (cf. Ps. 46.2 ff.); for behind them towers the mighty God, whose power gloriously proves itself in the taming of the raging elements (see Intr. 60 f.).

[4–5] The triumph of God rises above the raging of the seas and the roaring of the floods, and the majestic power of God shines forth the more gloriously on high above the tumult of the elements. The hope of an eschatological victory at the end of time is implied in the belief in creation, thought of as of God's victory over the powers of chaos. The tremendous cosmic background, all the mythological features of which now serve in the poet's view the sole and primary purpose of representing the glory and the greatness of God in their true light, give this belief a tremendous impact that springs from an inspired enthusiasm and from a theocentric attitude. These far-flung dimensions of a lofty vision of God also form the background of the poet's subsequent thoughts, as he now turns from the Ruler of the universe to the God who has manifested himself in the history of the people of Israel. By the 'testimony' of God is probably meant the tradition of the *Heilsgeschichte* which was recited in the covenant cult. The linking up of creation and history in the psalm therefore has its origin in the cultic and festival tradition (see Intr. 34, 60 f.). God's testimonies have proved themselves to faith as true and trustworthy. Man can entrust himself to this God, to his power and to his Word, without being disappointed. In the sovereignty of God's might, which embraces the whole world and its seasons, the believer finds the guarantee of the reliability of the revelation of God in history, where indeed the poet perceives the same glory of God attested, though he does not make a direct statement to that effect. And thus in imagination he transfers that holy sublimity of God to the place where his Word is proclaimed and his testimonies are heard by the believers, that is, to the Temple, which is the visible pledge of the divine presence, and calls for holy awe. His wish of blessing for the house of God is perhaps occasioned by the danger of defilement of the Temple, in opposition to which its permanent inviolability is emphasized. But even without such an explanation the wish of blessing for the holy place is to be accounted for by the fundamental idea of the festival cult as the place where God's salvation is realized. Here, too, we once more find an expression of awe at God's majesty, which inspires the poet to exultant praise of the greatness and glory of God and makes him rise boldly above himself and his everyday life in whole-hearted surrender to joy in God's majesty and complete absorption in it.

94. JUSTICE WILL RETURN TO THE RIGHTEOUS

1 O Lord, thou God of vengeance,
    thou God of vengeance, appear![1]
2 Rise up, O judge of the earth;
    render to the proud their deserts!
3 O Lord, how long shall the evildoers,
    how long shall the wicked exult?
4 They foam with rage; they speak arrogantly;[2]
    they boast, all the evildoers.
5 They crush thy people, O Lord,
    and afflict thy heritage.
6 They slay the widow and the stranger,
    and murder the orphans;
7 and they say, 'The Lord does not see;
    the God of Jacob does not perceive.'
8 Understand, O dullest of the people!
    O you fools, when will you be wise?
9 He who planted the ear, does he not hear?
    He who formed the eye, does he not see?
10 He who chastens the nations, does he not chastise,
    he who teaches men knowledge?[3]
11 The Lord, he knows the thoughts of men
    that they are but a breath.

12 Blessed is the man whom thou dost chasten, O Lord,
    and whom thou dost teach out of thy law,
13 to give him respite from days of trouble,
    until a pit is dug for the wicked.
14 For the Lord will not forsake his people;
    he will not abandon his heritage.
15 For justice will return to the righteous,[4]
    and all the upright in heart will follow it.
16 Who rises up for me against the wicked?
    Who stands up for me against the evildoers?
17 If the Lord had not been my help,
    my soul would dwell in the land of silence.[5]
18 Whenever I thought, 'My foot slips',
    thy grace, O Lord, helped me up.
19 When the cares of my heart are many,
    thy consolations cheer my soul.
20 Can the throne of destruction be allied with thee,
    which frames mischief on the basis of statutes?[6]
21 They band together against the life of the godly,
    and condemn the innocent to death.
22 Then the Lord became my stronghold,
    and my God the rock of my refuge;
23 he brought back on them their iniquity
    and wipes them out for their wickedness.
    The Lord, our God, will wipe them out.[7]

[1] * RSV has 'shine forth' instead of 'appear'.
[2] * V. 4a reads in RSV, 'They pour out their arrogant words.'
[3] * In the RSV vv. 10b and 11 form one sentence, reading:
    (10b) He who teaches men knowledge,
    (11)   the Lord, knows . . .
[4] Lit.: the judgment turns to righteousness (= salvation).
[5] * RSV has 'would soon have dwelt'.
[6] The verse has in mind the throne of a judge (Ps. 122.5) who under the form of
the law perverts justice. (Tr. N.: In RSV v. 20 is:
    Can wicked rulers be allied with thee,
    who frame mischief by statutes?)
[7] * RSV uses the future tense throughout.

This 'psalm of vengeance' falls into two parts which clearly differ
from each other. Verses 1–11 contain a prayer that God may execute
vengeance on the 'evildoers'; vv. 1–3 in particular utter a rebuke and
a warning in view of the way in which the latter think and act
without caring for God and their fellow men. The second part of the
psalm (vv. 12–23) is a psalm of thanksgiving in which the poet
praises God for the help and comfort which he received from him
whilst he was persecuted and tempted by the evildoers. The psalm of
thanksgiving opens with a general 'beatitude' of the man who lets

himself be chastised by God and with an affirmation of the poet's confidence that God will do justice to the community of the godly (vv. 12–15). This last both in form and content forms the transition from the first to the second part, so that a splitting up of the psalm in two independent hymns is not advisable. The expectation that God will appear to sit in judgment (vv. 1 f.), the reference to the people of God (vv. 5 f., 14 f.), and the turning from personal prayer to the collective testimony in v. 23 point to the festival cult of the covenant community in the sanctuary as the place where the poet hopes for the execution of God's judgment on the evildoers, and where he has experienced the answering of his prayer and the help of his God, to which he now testifies in his psalm in the midst of the community of the godly and during the service of thanksgiving (see Intr. 38 ff., 45 ff, 69 f.).

[1–3] By calling upon God, the 'Judge of the earth', to rise up and appear to execute vengeance, the poet gives vent to his righteous indignation so long repressed; for he is no longer able to watch helplessly the arrogant behaviour of ungodly evildoers. The poet's faith in God's righteousness is shaken to its very foundations, and he cannot think of any other remedy than to urge on God the execution of vengeance at the moment when with the congregation he waits in the sanctuary for the theophany which will convey to them the revelation of the divine judgment and salvation and the renewed realization of God's sovereign authority. The psalmist's passionate outburst of righteous anger is here interwoven with an understandable anxiety resulting from the temptation of his faith in God's righteousness. We must first try to understand this important background before we can pass judgment on the 'Old Testament limitation' which such a prayer for vengeance represents when viewed in the light of the New Testament teaching on prayer. [4–7] Like the prophets, the psalmist castigates the *hubris* of the boastful arrogance with which the evildoers ignore the divine statutes decreed for the people, oppressing and cruelly persecuting innocent widows and orphans and imagining in their foolishness that God turns a blind eye to their wickedness. [8–11] In fact, they themselves are the blind 'fools', because they do not take God seriously and are unwilling to grasp the fact that the Creator is more and is more powerful than his creature (v. 9; cf. Ex. 4.11; Prov. 20.12), and that God as the Ruler of the nations and the Teacher of men has the right and the power to call them to account. That warning reproof, which uses the stylistic forms of the Wisdom literature, is linked up with the manifestation of God in creation and in history, which represents the essential theme of the cultic ceremony. In the presence of such a God all men boasting of their own strength are silenced; in his sight all human thoughts are but a 'nothingness'. From that truth the wicked cannot help gathering the judgment which is in store for them (see Intr. 32 f., 45 ff.).

[12–13] Quite otherwise, however, is the man who is devoted to God, and who submits to be taught and chastised by him. For him the promise of salvation is intended so that he knows himself to be protected in adversity and can calmly and confidently wait for the wicked to perish. [14–15] Since he is a member of the community of the godly, for whom God's judgment means salvation just as it means disaster for the wicked, he is justified in assuming—and there can be little doubt that the psalmist here speaks from his own experience— that the certitude that God will not reject his people but will stand up for them by executing righteous judgment applies to himself.

[16–23] The worshipper sets the testimony to his personal saving experience within this context of the cult community's general assurance of salvation by combining the theme of his former lament and doubts with the thanksgiving for the comfort and support which he has now been able to find in God. The prayer is uttered after it has been granted (vv. 18, 22 f.), so that the whole way, along which the poet's soul travelled in its inward struggles until he had found refuge and help in God, now appears as the way to salvation in which he was led by God till his grace was revealed before the eyes of the cult community in the judgment on the evildoers who are expelled from the midst of the community and wiped out (see Intr. 47, 78 f.). In this way the testimony to the spiritual struggles and experiences of the individual worshipper also serves the purpose of strengthening the faith of the cult community by contributing to the increase of the glory of God.

95. THE ENCOUNTER WITH GOD

1 O come, let us sing to the Lord;
   let us make a joyful noise to the rock of our salvation!
2 Let us come before his face and bear witness to him;[1]
   let us make a joyful noise to him with songs of praise!
3 For the Lord is a great God,
   and a great King above all gods.

4 In his hand are the depths of the earth;
  the heights of the mountains are his also.
5 The sea is his, for he made it,
  and the dry land, for his hands formed it.[2]
6 O come, let us fall down at his feet;
  let us bow down and kneel before the Lord, our Maker![3]
7 For he is our God,
  and we are his people, the sheep of his pasture.[4]
  O that today you would hearken to his voice!
8 Harden not your hearts, as at Meribah,
  as on the day at Massah in the wilderness,
9 when your fathers tested me,
  and put me to the proof,
  though they saw my work.[5]
10 For forty years I loathed that generation
   and said, 'They are a people who err in heart,
   and they have not known my ways.'[6]
11 Therefore I swore in my anger
   that they should not enter my rest.

[1] * V. 2a reads in RSV, 'Let us come into his presence with thanksgiving.'
[2] * In RSV v. 5b is, 'for his hands formed the dry land'.
[3] * V. 6 reads in RSV as follows:
    O come, let us worship and bow down,
    let us kneel before the Lord, our Maker!
[4] See BH. (Tr. N.: V. 7a is in RSV after the first line:
    and we are the people of his pasture,
    and the sheep of his hand.)
[5] * RSV has 'though they had seen my work'.
[6] * The last line of v. 10 reads in RSV, 'and they do not regard my ways'.

The Mishnah regarded the psalm as a New Year psalm; that view probably originated in an ancient tradition. The song is that portion of a liturgy of the autumn festival in which Yahweh is revealed as the Creator and Lord of the universe (vv. 4 f.), enters upon his reign as King (v. 3) and renews the covenant he made with his people by pledging them anew to keep the commandments he ordained in that covenant (vv. 7 f.). In this respect the psalm is most closely related to Psalm 81. We shall have to think of the psalm as having been recited before the festival congregation entered the sanctuary (vv. 2, 6). In its first part (vv. 1-7a) it contains a hymn preparing the congregation for their impending encounter with God, the Creator and Lord of the covenant; the second part (vv. 7b-11) comprises a warning from God, calling upon them to obey him and ending in a grave, almost threatening prospect (see Intr. 46, 55, 60).

[1-2] The first part again falls into two subsections each of which

opens with a liturgical call. The call that is made upon the congregation in the hymn to 'come before the face of God' with a testimony and songs of praise reflects the mood of joyful surrender to God which is meant to be offered to him when he appears in the sanctuary to bring salvation to his people. The great cultic event which the festival pilgrims are going to experience fills the scene with its radiant light before it actually takes place: **[3–5]** God proves the infinite greatness of his might and the pre-eminence of his kingship even over the gods in that he is the Creator of the whole universe. It is not without good reason that beside the sea and the dry land the depths of the earth and the tops of the mountains are specially mentioned as belonging to the sphere of God's influence; for popular belief regarded the underworld as the realm of other powers (Amos 9.2; Pss. 6.5; 30.9; 88.10 f.; 115.17) and the high mountains as the abode of the gods (Pss. 68.15 f.; 89.12). The psalm deliberately destroys this belief: God's power knows of no limitations—this is the unshakable foundation of his salvation **[6]**, and for that reason the praise and the thanksgiving of every creature is his due **[7a]**, as is also at the same time the humble submission of the congregation who pay homage to him. They worship him not only as their Maker but as the Lord who has made a covenant with them—v. 7a takes up the 'covenantal formula', 'Yahweh the God of Israel and Israel the people of God'—and who has 'chosen' them and has deigned to guide them by his grace throughout their history. The profound meaning of the liturgical festival as an encounter between God and his people finds its fulfilment in the fact that the ancient tradition of the *Heilsgeschichte* regarding creation, election and the making of the covenant at Sinai is here renewed as a present sacral event (cf. the 'today' in v. 7b), and that God's power and saving grace are here revealed before the eyes of his people, who in their turn humble themselves in his presence, offering him their humility and adoration, their gratitude and trust, their submission and obedience (see Intr. 42 ff., 59 f.).

[7b] Old Testament cultic piety is characterized by profound concern for inner truthfulness—this is proved by the fact that all the sentiments of solemn and joyful emotion aroused by the hallowed character of the encounter with God are regarded as legitimate only if they are accompanied by readiness to obey God's voice and keep his commandments. This matter is dealt with by the divine utterance[1] in the second part of the psalm with its admonition

---

[1] Probably spoken by a priest or by a prophet officiating at the cult.

and warning, the purpose of which is to prepare the cult community for the proclamation of God's commandments as the order of his covenant (cf. Ps. 81.5 ff.; Ex. 19.5; 34.10 ff.; see Intr. 31 f., 42 f.). **[8–11]** With renewal of the *Heilsgeschichte* and the covenant the cult community face anew the decision they are called upon to make 'today' before God—whether they want to follow the way of faithful obedience that leads to their promised salvation or whether they prefer to enter upon the way of hardness of heart and disobedience, as once their fathers did at Massah and at Meribah in the wilderness (cf. Ex. 17.1–7; Num. 20.1–13; Ps. 81.7). Though the latter saw the saving deeds wrought by God, they rebelled against him or tried in short-sighted lack of faith to make him serve their own ends, with the result that he withheld from them the rest he had promised they would enjoy in the Promised Land and made them wander about in the wilderness for forty long years. This divine judgment is set up as a warning reminder in the midst of the exultation of festal joy; the decision has to be made afresh whether the encounter with God shall lead to the fulfilment of the promise of his peace, which has not yet been brought about, or whether it shall lead to judgment. The former will come to pass in the consummation of salvation when the cult community will come to realize by faith the things which make for peace, whereas the latter will be such that God will leave the people to the restlessness and strife of their erring hearts—which can be far off from him even though glad confession be made with the lips that God has drawn near.

96. GOD COMES TO JUDGE

1 O sing to the Lord a new song;
  sing to the Lord, all the earth!
2 Sing to the Lord, praise his name;
  tell of his salvation from day to day!
3 Declare his majestic power[1] among the peoples,
  his marvellous works among all the nations!
4 For great is the Lord, and greatly to be praised;
  terrible is he beyond all gods.[2]
5 For all the gods of the peoples are idols;
  but the Lord made the heavens.
6 Majesty and brightness are before him;
  power and splendour are in his sanctuary.[3]
7 Ascribe to the Lord glory, O you families of the peoples,
  ascribe to the Lord glory and strength.

8 Ascribe to the Lord the glory due to his name;
  bring an offering, and come into his forecourts!
9 Fall down at the feet of the Lord in holy array;
  all the earth tremble before his face![4]
10 Say among the nations, 'The Lord is become King!
  He has established[5] the earth that it cannot be shaken.
  He will judge the peoples with equity.'[6]
11 Let the heavens be glad, and let the earth rejoice;
  let the sea roar, and all that fills it;
12 let the field exult, and everything that grows in it!
  Yea, all the trees of the wood shall sing for joy[7]
13 before the Lord, that he has come;
  for he has come to judge the earth.
  He judges the earth with righteousness,
  and the peoples with his truth.[8]

[1] * RSV has 'glory' instead of 'majestic power'.
[2] * V. 4b reads in RSV 'he is to be feared above all gods'.
[3] * RSV has 'Honour and majesty' instead of 'Majesty and brightness', and 'strength and beauty' instead of 'power and splendour'.
[4] * In RSV v. 9 is:
  Worship the Lord in holy array;
  tremble before him, all the earth!
[5] See BH.
[6] * V. 10 begins in RSV,
  Say among the nations, 'The Lord reigns!
  Yea, the world is established, it shall never be moved . . .'
[7] * V. 12b is in RSV 'Then shall all the trees of the wood sing for joy.'
[8] * RSV differs in the tenses used:
  before the Lord, for he comes,
  for he comes to judge the earth.
  He will judge the world. . . .

The psalm is a cultic liturgy appointed for the celebration of the Enthronement of Yahweh (v. 10) and related to Psalms 47, 93 and 97 ff. In I Chron. 16.23 ff. a somewhat abridged form has been linked with the first part of Psalm 105 and associated with the bringing up of the sacred Ark to Jerusalem by David. It contains reminiscences of Psalms 29 and 33 and of Deutero-Isaiah, but they are probably not to be explained by any literary dependence on the part of the psalmist but by their relationship to the festival cult which they have in common. The main theme of the cultic ceremony, which extended over several days (v. 2), is the proclamation and realization of salvation (vv. 2 f.) when God appears at the New Year Festival (v. 13) and once more enters upon his reign over the world.[1] Exultant shouts of joy from the celebrating cult community, who

[1] See the comments on Ps. 47.8.

have gathered in the sanctuary from the most diverse places, and who are inspired and welded together by their common saving experience, resound continually. The keynote of the festival, and so of the psalm, is joy in God, who has come into the sanctuary (v. 13) to reveal his greatness and his glory in his creation (vv. 5, 10 ff.), and in the righteousness of his judgment (vv. 10, 13). The outward and inner order of the world is the guarantee of God's Kingship and the foundation of his salvation (see Intr. 62).

[1] At the New Year Festival, when the new salvation brought about by the renewal of the Covenant takes effect as fresh saving energies pervading outward and inner life, the cult community respond by singing a new song, echoing their common saving experience (cf. Pss. 33.3; 40.3; 98.1; 144.9; 149.1). The congregation, who have listened to the history of creation read out in the cult and have experienced it at first hand, personify in this solemn moment, as the members face God, 'all the earth'. [2–3] They are called upon to pass on the knowledge of the miraculous saving deeds of God to 'all the nations', so that his majestic power may be praised. The thought which suggests itself most easily in this connection is that here the representatives of the various nations are referred to who are present at the festival; there can, I presume, hardly be any question here of missionary activity in the strict sense. [4–5] In the explanation which follows, in form a hymn, the fundamental idea of the tradition of salvation, the superiority of God over the gods, is taken up again and attributed to the fact that God created heaven. In this train of thought we can still detect a vestige of the ancient mythological conception of the combat of the gods against the powers of chaos; this preceded Creation and ended in the dethronement of the gods by the creator-god. In the Old Testament this thought serves to throw the exclusive power of Yahweh the more strongly into relief against such a background (cf. Ps. 47. 2; see Intr. 60 f.). Here the ultimate conclusion is not yet drawn, that is, the denial of the existence of gods which we find in Deutreo-Isaiah. [6] In v. 6 the hymn passes on to a description of the theophany in the sanctuary (see Intr. 29 f., 38 ff., 57); it is a remarkable feature, showing the spiritualization of the psalmist's outlook, that in this account the bright light and the majesty, the power and the glory of God appear as his escort at his solemn entry into the Temple. [7] The hymn which the festival congregation sing is now meant to let the revelation of God which they have received shine back upon God, thereby

establishing a living relationship with God; for they now 'ascribe' to God in their turn 'glory and strength' and, **[8–9]** offering up their gifts in humble adoration and with fear, pay homage to him with the 'acclamation of the king' (*Königsruf*), joyfully saluting the Ruler of the universe as he enters upon his reign. **[10]** The experience of God's presence entails that fear and trembling and rapturous joy are here interwoven, indicating the peculiar character of the mood and attitude of a man who is deeply stirred by the greatness of God. The proclamation of the Kingship of God is linked up with the declaration of the two foundation-pillars of the realization of his salvation—creation and judgment—so that the idea of judgment here appears as the sequel to the idea of the universe. The order of Nature in creation and the order of History in judgment are planned by God in such a way that they are tuned to each other and supplement each other, both being directed towards their common goal, and that goal is the realization of the 'righteousness of God' in his plan of salvation. **[11–13]** This tremendous vision, based on faith and embracing every sphere of life, also makes silent Nature join in the roaring shouts of joy which resound in the ears of the divine King when he appears to judge 'the earth'. For God's judgment does not, after all, consist only in calling his opponents to account; it serves to restore his order in the world. This order manifests itself as much in the realm of Nature as in that of History; as much in the blessing of the fertility of the earth as in the blessings bestowed upon the nations. In both these manifestations is revealed God's 'truth', i.e. the realization of his 'faithfulness'.

97. THE LORD AND JUDGE OF THE WORLD

1 The Lord is become King; let the earth rejoice;
　 let the multitude of the isles be glad![1]
2 Clouds and thick darkness are round about him;
　 righteousness and justice are the foundation of his throne.
3 Fire goes before him,
　 and burns up his enemies round about.
4 His lightnings lighten the world;
　 the earth saw it and trembled.[2]
5 The mountains melted like wax ' '[3]
　 before the face of the Lord of all the earth.[4]
6 The heavens proclaimed his righteousness;
　 and all the peoples beheld his glory.[5]
7 All worshippers of images are put to shame,

who make their boast in idols;
all gods bowed down before him.

8 Zion heard this and is full of joy.
The daughters of Judah rejoice
because of thy judgments, O Lord.[6]

9 For thou ' '[3] art the Most High over all the earth;
thou art exalted far above all gods.[7]

10 You who love the Lord, hate evil![8]
He preserves the souls of his saints;
he delivers them from the hand of the wicked.

11 Light dawns[9] for the righteous,
and joy for the upright in heart.

12 Rejoice in the Lord, O you righteous,
and testify to his holy memory![10]

[1] * RSV has 'The Lord reigns' instead of 'The Lord is become King' and 'the many coastlands' instead of 'the multitude of the isles'.

[2] * RSV uses the present tense in v. 4b.

[3] See BH.

[4] * RSV uses the present tense in v. 5 and adds 'before the Lord' at the end of the first line.

[5] * Throughout v. 6 RSV uses the present tense.

[6] * Whereas here the first line of v. 8 refers to v. 7, and what follows forms a new sentence with a new thought of its own, v. 8 contains in RSV only one sentence expressing one thought only:
Zion hears and is glad,
and the daughters of Judah rejoice,
because of thy judgments, O God.

[7] * V. 9a reads in RSV, 'For thou, O Lord, art most high over all the earth.'

[8] * RSV's v. 10a reads, 'The Lord loves those who hate evil.'

[9] Lit.: is sown.

[10] * V. 12b reads in RSV, 'and give thanks to his holy name'.

The psalm originated in the liturgy of the Enthronement of Yahweh in use at the Covenant Festival and is to be classed with Psalms 47, 93, 96 and 98 f. (see Intr. 62). From the mention of Zion and the daughters (provincial cities) of Judah (v. 8) the Temple at Jerusalem is to be assumed as the place at which the festival was celebrated. The stereotyped forms of liturgy and a certain conservative tendency peculiar to every cultic tradition account for the fact that in a comparatively great number of places the psalm accords with other psalms and prophetic passages or exhibits reminiscences of them; in part it is even verbally identical with them. To regard this fact as an indication of the inferior value of the psalm would be tantamount to applying the wrong standard. Compared with other 'enthronement' psalms, the psalm has a character of its own in spite of its language and ideas being tied to stereotyped forms; and this

special character allows an insight into the depth and comprehensiveness of the Old Testament idea of the Kingdom of God. The
psalm falls into two parts: vv. 1–6 deal with the appearance of God,
vv. 7–12 with the effect which that appearance has on the Gentiles
and on the cult community of Yahweh.

[1] The hymn which opens the psalm begins with the 'acclamation
of the king' (cf. the comments on Ps. 93.1); this presupposes that the
cultic act of enthronement has previously taken place and, being
itself a hymnic response by the congregation, ends in the call to the
whole world to join in the exultation in the King. The multitude of
the 'isles' is, as in Isa. 42.10 ff., etc., in the first place a reference to
the isles of the Aegean Sea; but it is also meant to refer quite generally
to the remotest coastlands of the whole earth. The rejoicing of the
whole world demonstrates the world-wide significance of the glad
tidings of the beginning of the Kingdom of God.

First of all, the appearance of God is depicted—this had its fixed
place in the cultic tradition[1]—and this is done in archaic forms cast
into a rigid mould which are derived from the account of the Sinai
theophany and, as regards their mythological colouring, in part
reach back to pre-Israelite times (cf. Judg. 5.4 f.; Micah 1.3 ff.;
Hab. 3.3 ff.; Deut. 4.11; 5.4; see Intr. 28 ff., 38 ff., 57 f.). The verbal
forms refer back to the theophany as an event that has already taken
place in the course of the cultic ceremony. This account is in more than
one respect worthy of note. [2] God appears as one who is veiled.
Whereas in other religions the unveiling of the image of a god, the *epop-
teia* (the vision of the god), represented the solemn climax of the cultic
ceremony, the Old Testament idea of God as one who is surrounded by
the impenetrable darkness of clouds reverently maintains the
mystery of his nature and impressively indicates the threateningly
serious character of his appearing. In another word-picture the
psalm illustrates the true nature of God: the foundations of God's
rule are righteousness and justice; God is the Ruler of the world and
the Judge of the world. [3] This is the essential theme of the psalm; it
glorifies God's power and righteousness. In v. 3 the psalmist passes
on from the portrait of God's appearance to a description of what
actually happens; this method accords with the peculiar character
of the Old Testament idea of God. The nature of God cannot be

---

[1] Westermann (*Das Loben Gottes in den Psalmen*, p. 109) contends that this account
of the epiphany is secondary. However, though he does so with every confidence,
he neither proves nor explains this hypothesis.

graphically portrayed in static terms as something which is objective and static in essence, but must be experienced in a personal encounter as a power that has a dynamic effect. This is why also the account of the theophany does not confine itself to the realm of Nature (cf. Ps. 50.3), but at once proceeds to that of History: the annihilation of all the enemies is the proof of the power of God who is also the Lord of history. [4] The traditional idea that lightnings and earthquakes show that God is drawing near (cf. Pss. 77.16 ff.; 68.8) serves to illustrate the greatness and comprehensiveness of the divine power, whereas [5] the melting of the mountains like wax before the face of God (cf. Micah 1.4), a feature similarly borrowed from tradition and raised to the level of a miracle, emphasizes the intensity of God's momentous power that is charged with energy; elsewhere in the Old Testament that power of God is often described as his 'zeal'. All the individual features from the realm of natural phenomena in the traditional account of the theophany are used by the poet merely as a means of throwing into bold relief the nature of the power of the 'Lord of all the earth'. That Yahweh's proper function is to be seen in natural phenomena, with the result that he is meant to make his arrival obvious in the realm of natural religion, can, however, here as little be assumed as in the vision of Elijah (I Kings ch. 19), where the view that Yahweh could be found 'in' the natural phenomena is explicitly rejected. The fundamental idea of the psalm is much more profound: Nature serves to reveal the divine glory to all the nations (cf. Ps. 19.1 ff.); [6] the heavens as God's heralds have proclaimed to all the world wherein that 'glory of God', his majesty and his 'honour' consist—in his 'righteousness'. The Hebrew term ṣedeq has a wider meaning than the translation: it comprises God's entire plan of salvation, its order and its contents, and could, in fact, be translated here directly by the word 'salvation'. Thus the glad tidings whereby the heavens announce in the psalm the advent of God (cf. Ps. 50.6) are much more closely related to the song of praise of the multitude of the heavenly host in the Christmas story than might at first appear. The feast of the epiphany of Yahweh, that was celebrated in the Old Covenant, is the cradle of the Advent belief in the coming of God, in the beginning of his reign, and in the realization of his salvation for the whole world, a belief which embraces the *Heilsgeschichte* from its first beginnings to its consummation at the end of time. The solemn proclamation at the end of the theophany of the divine righteousness as the universal principle of salvation at the same time gives the theme of the psalm's second part in which the psalmist turns his thoughts more particularly to the future and envisages the effects that follow on God's appearing.

[7] In v. 7 the theme is used which is known also to non-biblical religions, but is here deepened and spiritualized, the theme namely that the enthronement of God is preceded by combat against the other gods and by his victory over them. The mythological concept of the theomachy is replaced by the idea of the conquest of the gods by spiritual means. Within the cultic context of the testimony borne in the hymn this verse at the same time contains the renunciation of foreign gods and the powers of evil (see Intr. 47 ff., 61). The mere appearance of God suffices to compel the latter to acknowledge in a magnificent act of homage the majesty of God and so their own powerlessness and their subjection to him. The result of this proof of God's power is that all the worshippers of images lose confidence in their 'idols', as the psalmist emphasizes with deliberate contempt, and are similarly compelled to acknowledge that they are defeated by God's exclusive majesty. The effect which the 'righteousness' of God has on them is that it becomes for them his judgment. This term, too, is used by the psalm to signify a larger sphere of reality than we would associate with it. What follows makes clear that it comprises the whole divine plan of salvation, that is to say, it comprises both its negative *and* its positive aspects (see Intr. 64). [8–9] In contrast to its negative aspect, but also in contrast to the effect of God's appearing mentioned in v. 4 (cf. v.4: 'saw it and trembled' with v. 8: 'heard this and is full of joy'), the message of God's judgment, which the congregation in the Temple had been able to hear in the course of the cultic ceremony, is for them glad tidings, so that they feel constrained to sing jubilant songs of praise in honour of their God,[1] who triumphs over the whole world and over all gods—and to do so with devotion and enthusiasm. For them God's judgment means the realization of their salvation. [10] After the note of joy sounded by the hymn the warning addressed to the cult community to fight against evil strikes us as strange, but that does not justify the altering of the text by substituting the popular reading 'Yahweh loves those who hate evil.' This warning, on the contrary, stresses the obligatory

---

[1] It is in this form that the designation of God as ʿelyōn, which originally belonged to the realm of polytheistic thinking, and the whole body of tradition associated with it has been incorporated in the Yahweh tradition; for further details cf. the comments on Ps. 7.17.

character of the revelation of God. Since the Sinai theophany this moral aspect of the manifestation of the divine will is indissolubly connected with God's nature, and in the teaching of Jesus, too, belongs to the fundamentals of the order of salvation of the Kingdom of God. The description of the cult community as those who love God indicates that it is in the love of God that we find on the one hand the motive power that leads to moral obedience to his commandments and, on the other, the decisive mark of belonging to the cult community; this idea represents a spiritualization of the notion of the religious community in Old Testament thought which should not be overlooked! This, too, is part of the great saving event of the reign of God which is about to begin that his power is manifested in the hearts of the godly as a power for good. To them is promised the protection of God and deliverance from the violence of the wicked. The outcome is indeed certain, but the struggle in which the cult community is engaged still continues, and they still live in a world in which wickedness and oppression prevail. [11] The God who has appeared is at the same time the God who will come; therefore the cult community in the midst of exultation over the Advent is at the same time also the cult community which still hopes, waiting in the darkness for that light which, as the psalmist says in a beautiful and profound word-picture that embraces the past and the future, 'is sown'[1] for the righteous so that those who are pure in heart may hope for a new harvest of joy. We cannot read this promise of God's Advent without being reminded of the similar tones and word-pictures with which the Christmas Gospels in Luke and John report the fulfilment of that promise. With the call to the congregation to join in the world's rejoicing the psalmist reverts to the beginning of his psalm and so rounds off the whole to form a hymnic circle; but he does not do so without once more urging the cult community at the end of the psalm to be mindful of the purpose of this solemn hour, the purpose namely of cultivating by witness and confession and as a sacred tradition[2] the remembrance of God's Kingship. To that sacred tradition we owe the handing down of these festival hymns in the Psalter.

[1] * Cf. v. 11 and note 9 to the Psalm.
[2] The view that the call at the end of the psalm to sing songs of praise is 'a sure indication that the psalm has been composed at a late date' (Westermann, op. cit., p. 109) is based on a one-sided overestimation of external forms and on a misunderstanding of the psalm's cultic background. Such a formalistic method does not help the exposition of other psalms either (e.g. Ps. 99).

98. SING TO THE LORD A NEW SONG!

A Psalm

1 O sing to the Lord a new song,
for he has done marvellous things!
His right hand and his holy arm
have gotten him victory.

2 The Lord has made known his salvation;
he has revealed his righteousness in the sight of the nations.[1]

3 He has remembered his grace and faithfulness
to the house of Israel.
All the ends of the earth have seen
the salvation of our God.[2]

4 Make a joyful noise to the Lord, all the earth;
rejoice, shout for joy and sing praises![3]

5 Sing praises to the Lord with the cither,
with the cither and the sound of melody![4]

6 With the sound of trumpets and of the horn
make a joyful noise before the face of the King ' '[5]!

7 Let the sea roar, and all that fills it;
the world and those who dwell in it!

8 Let the streams clap their hands,
and let the mountains shout for joy together

9 before the Lord that he has come;
for he has come[6] to judge the earth.
He judges the earth with righteousness,
and the peoples with equity.[7]

[1] * RSV has 'victory' instead of 'salvation' and 'vindication' instead of 'righteousness'.
[2] * RSV has 'victory' instead of 'salvation'.
[3] * V. 4b reads in RSV, 'break forth into joyous song and sing praises'.
[4] * RSV has 'lyre' instead of 'cither'.
[5] See BH. (Tr. N.: RSV has 'before the King, the Lord' instead of 'before the face of the King'.)
[6] See BH.
[7] * In RSV v. 9 is:
before the Lord, for he comes to rule the earth.
He will judge the world. . . .

The psalm has been included in the treasury of Christian songs through Jorissen's hymn 'Singt, singt Jehova neue Lieder'.[1] In structure and thought, and often even in wording it is so closely related to Psalm 96 that some expositors have thought it necessary to attribute both songs to the same author. This affinity can, however, most naturally be accounted for by the fact that both compositions

[1] * Matthias Jorissen (1739–1823).

have their origin in the same cultic situation and so draw on the same stereotyped liturgical forms associated therewith; there is therefore no need to assume that one of these hymns is the paraphrase of the other. Here, too, we are dealing with a fragment of the liturgy of the Enthronement of Yahweh (see Intr. 62). This fact determines the psalm's essential link in the cult with the *Heilsgeschichte* and eschatology. The saving events of past and future are concentrated in the festival cult's 'representation' (vv. 1–3, 9) in such a way that they form a single liturgical saving act which produces a powerful effect in the present and is vividly reflected in the hymn sung by the congregation. The cultic hymn, which is divided into three strophes, speaks in vv. 1–3 of Yahweh's marvellous deeds and calls in vv. 4–6 upon the world and in vv. 7–9 upon Nature to pay homage to God at his Advent with shouts of joy.

[1] The psalm opens with the hymnic formula: 'O sing to Yahweh a new song.' The old songs no longer suffice in view of the large-scale process of renewal that sets in with the Advent of God; the renewal of God's covenant for the new year (see pp. 28 f., 61 f.) must be matched by a new song. The power of faith that presses onwards and is focused on the future thus creates for itself a palpable form of expression. The miracle which God himself has wrought occupies the forefront of the events continually coming to pass afresh at the cultic festival before the congregation, and is at the centre of these events. The cult community's hope is based not on the power of men but solely on what God himself has done in the past and is doing now. This fundamental idea is thrown into relief in a striking fashion: 'his right hand and his holy arm have gotten him victory' (cf. Ex. 15.6; Pss. 20.6; 21.8, etc.). This means: God does his work by virtue of his own strength; he needs no help, either from a world power or from Israel. For this reason only Yahweh's arm is exalted (holy), and no human power shares in his honour. The psalmist, in order to give all the praise to God alone, here boldly disregards all historical possibilities and intensifies the character of the miraculous by concentrating his thoughts on God. [2] Following up the idea of the exclusive efficacy of God, the psalmist's faith draws the ultimate—and theoretical—conclusion of his theocentric, monotheistic way of thinking; and in doing so he moves away from the realm of the things which are tangible and real and forgoes any attempt to understand rationally God's way of acting. And yet it is precisely the psalmist's concentration of his thoughts on God which leads him back to a new and deeper

understanding of reality as it is in actual fact in that it makes him
view these events as ultimately divine, and so decisive—which
imparts to that reality an eschatological goal. This goal is the manifestation of the divine salvation and God's 'righteousness' to the
whole world.

[3] God's activity. is aimed at the whole world of nations. The
meaning of the divine advent celebrated at the festival is the revelation of the innermost nature of God, that is to say, the revelation of
his righteousness. What was manifested in the history of Israel is thus
consummated in the world. 'He remembers his grace and faithfulness
to the house of Israel.' God 'remembers' his own love and promise
with which he had set Israel's history in motion (cf. Hos. 11.1 ff.;
Jer. 2.2 f.); that is to say, he once more reminds the people of them
and carries them into effect, ensuring that they are recognized.

He had once freely resolved to grant his salvation to this people,
and he has remained faithful to them both in his judgments and in
his grace, even though they have often enough been unfaithful to
him (see Intr. 35 f., 43). But now the ends of the earth will recognize
this will of God to save and will bow down before him with reverent
joy. This is a magnificent historical vision in which the profound
meaning of the Old Testament's religious concept of history finds its
fulfilment, the meaning, that is, of seeing in history God's *Heilsgeschichte*, whose purpose is that his salvation and righteousness may be
revealed there before the whole world. In God's plan of salvation the
election of Israel has its appointed place. Israel stands out among the
nations not as a people who are distinguished from other nations by
special superior qualities, and whose election could therefore be
regarded as a kind of reward for these superior qualities, but as the
people in whose history the divine will to save is continually made
manifest afresh both in promise and in threat, in grace and in judgment as the meaning of history in general. The meaning of their
election is therefore that a duty is laid upon them, that they are
meant to serve God's plan of salvation. The psalmist sees in the
propagation of the Kingdom of God throughout the world the divine
mission which has been entrusted to his people. The history of his
people as the *Heilsgeschichte* of God reaches its ultimate universal
goal with God's recognition by the world, with the coming of the
Kingdom of God on earth.

[4–6] From this vision of the salvation of the world, which God
will bring about when his Kingdom has come, the psalm proceeds to

call upon the whole world to perform a great act of homage before God as the Ruler of his Kingdom. Just as the earthly Ruler is acclaimed when on his enthronement he has assumed the rule of his kingdom, so shall the world salute God with shouts of joy when he now enters upon his world-dominion as King (v. 6) that will last for all times. The rhythm and tone of these verses let us feel the strength of the psalmist's enthusiasm who in faith experiences God's position as Ruler of the world as something which is already a present reality and, having already an inkling of the coming of God's Kingdom, anticipates it. Before the 'face' of God, that is to say, in his presence (v. 6), the whole past is also revived at the same time and together with the future is viewed as a unity; and all this is experienced in the cultic ceremony of the Enthronement of Yahweh as a present reality. It is only in this way that the call to break forth into jubilant songs of praise, to be sung in the procession of homage accompanied by cithers, trumpets and trombones, evokes a ready inner response.

[7–8] But the strength flowing from that vision of God opens up still wider vistas. As in Pss. 96.11 ff.; 103.22; Isa. 42.10 f.; 44.23; 49.13, inanimate Nature, too, is made to join the chorus of rejoicing. In a magnificent and poetical personification of Nature the psalmist discerns in the roaring of the sea and the earth and in the streams' 'clapping of hands' (cf. Isa. 55.12) manifestations of the homage which Nature pays to the King of the universe (cf. II Kings 11.12). It is not the idea of the animation of Nature that inspires the poet to use this picture, but reminiscence of the ancient cultic tradition of the creation of the world—and the concentrated power of his faith in God. Consequently, he visualizes all Nature as set in motion by the glory of God, and everything seems to him to be harmonized in the exultant chorus of the whole world singing praises to the glory of God.

[9] We are told only at the conclusion of the psalm that it is intended for the God who has appeared to judge the world. That God's judgment is awaited with joy and not with fear shows how greatly this hope is sustained by the faithful's devotion to God and by trust in God's will to save. The yearning for God and the absolute certitude of God's gracious will prove themselves to be too strong to be overshadowed by fear. This advent faith prepared the ground within the scope of the Old Testament piety for the fulfilment of salvation through Christ.

99. THE HOLY GOD

1 The Lord is become King—this makes the peoples tremble;
  he sat down upon the cherubim—
  this makes[1] the earth shake.[2]
2 The Lord is great in Zion;
  he is exalted over all the peoples.
3 Let them praise thy name; great and terrible,
  yea,[3] *holy is thy name.*[4]

4 And a mighty one is become King[1] who loves justice.
  Thou hast established equity;
  thou hast executed justice and righteousness in Jacob.[5]
5 *Extol the Lord our God;*
  worship at his footstool!
  yea,[3] *holy is he.*[6]

6 Moses and Aaron are among his priests,
  and Samuel is among those who call on his name;
  they cried to the Lord, and he answered them;
7 he spoke to them in the pillar of cloud.

  They kept his testimonies, and the statutes that he gave them.[7]
8 O Lord, our God, thou didst answer them;
  thou wast a forgiving God to them,
  but didst justice also to their sin.[8]
9 *Extol the Lord, our God,*
  and worship at his holy mountain!
  Yea, holy is the Lord, our God![9]

[1] See BH.
  * V. 1 is in RSV:
    The Lord reigns; let the peoples tremble!
    He sits enthroned upon the cherubim;
    let the earth quake!
[3] This is to be supplemented in accordance with v. 9.
[4] * V. 3 reads in RSV:
    Let them praise thy great and terrible name!
    Holy is he!
[5] * The first line of v. 4 reads in RSV, 'Mighty King, lover of justice'.
[6] * RSV omits 'yea' at the beginning of the last line.
[7] * Here the first line of v. 7 continues the sentence begun in v. 6; RSV begins a new sentence in v. 7 and treats the whole verse as an independent thought-unit.
[8] Lit.: 'an avenger of their wrongdoings'. (Tr. N.: The last line of v. 8 reads in RSV, 'but an avenger of their wrongdoings'.)
[9] * The last line of v. 9 is in RSV 'for the Lord our God is holy!'

An artistic composition, the hymn is occasioned by the Enthronement of Yahweh (see Pss. 47 and 93–98; Intr. 62). Beyond that the psalm is, however, remarkable for the distinct peculiarity of its formal construction as well as of its religious thoughts. A short refrain concludes each of the three 'strophes', which, it is true, are not symmetrically constructed; this tunes the whole hymn to a uniform keynote to which the various thoughts continually return, and that keynote is the holiness of God (vv. 3, 5, 9; cf. Isa. 6.3). The refrain was probably sung by the choir as a response to the call made upon them to sing a hymn; it thus indicates the cultic character of the song as an echo of the divine epiphany and revelation that has taken place at the Covenant Festival. In the individual strophes light is thrown on various aspects of the theme of the holiness of God. In the first strophe (vv. 1–3) God's holiness is praised as it is expressed in the sublimity of his world-dominion; the second strophe (vv. 4–5) praises God's holiness as it is manifested in the establishment of righteousness, and the third strophe (vv. 6–9) praises the holiness of God revealed in Israel's history through his acts of grace and through the severity of his judgments. The song, sustained as it is by lofty earnestness and respectful joy, testifies to fundamental traits of the Old Testament revelation of God. The allusions to the sacred Ark (vv. 1, 5, 7) indicate that the psalm originated in the pre-exilic era of the kings.

God's enthronement and world-dominion (vv. 1–3)

[1–3] The psalm opens with the acclamation of the king: 'Yahweh is become King' (cf. II Sam. 15.10), which is a rite with which we are familiar from the enthronement of the earthly king. The beginning of the second half-verse, 'he sat down upon the cherubim', likewise runs parallel to this statement. For both are statements which have in mind the advent of God at the cultic festival to enter upon his Kingship (see Intr. 33 f., 39 ff., 62).[1] The portrayal of the divine epiphany exhibits the traditional features of the Sinai theophany. When God appears in his majestic power a tremor runs through the whole world; the nations tremble and the earth quakes—an involuntary indication of the terrible and sublime power of the God of Mount Zion over the whole world. The poet discerns the holiness of his God in this pre-eminent and comprehensive power which causes everything that is created to tremble. And the involuntary witness which the trembling nations and the quaking earth bear in the presence of the holy God constrains the poet, too, to call upon all men to praise the holy name of God, the revelation of which had

[1] See the comments on Ps. 47.8.

taken place in the course of the theophany (cf. Ex. 33.19 and Intr.
41 f., 58) and which is therefore present in the poet's mind in all its
greatness and terrifying power. Fear and trembling and respectful
joy here jointly represent the spiritual atmosphere which is created in
the congregation by the advent of God.

The righteousness of God (vv. 4–5)

[4–5] The opening phrase of the second strophe runs parallel to
the acclamation of the king in the first strophe; it first takes up again
the thoughts which had been developed there and then throws light
on another aspect of God's holiness. God's holiness shows itself not
only in his sovereign power but also in his righteousness. In this his
innermost nature is revealed: God *loves* justice. It is he who has
established the rule of law that governs the life of the people of
Israel, and who in the history of that people has not only ordained
justice as the divine principle determining their life, but has seen to
it that justice was done. Through and in this history God's will for
the way the people of Israel should live their lives was continually
revealed—but at the same time also the fact that God has the will
and the power ('a mighty one') to carry this his order into effect.
Thus to the eyes of faith Israel's history is a living testimony to the
reality of the divine justice as the principle governing History's life
in general. It illustrates this fundamental truth of national life:
'Righteousness exalts a nation but sin is a reproach to any people'
(Prov. 14.34). This part of the hymn expressed reverential earnestness, but also grateful joy, a sense of responsibility in the face of this
absolutely trustworthy divine order and also the feeling of being safe
in such a divine order. The intimate character of this section receives
special emphasis from the fact that the hymn now turns to the
prayer style of dialogue with God. The attitude of mind thus created
quite naturally leads to the adoration and praise of God, and the
poet now calls upon the congregation to do this. In view of v. 1 and
of I Chron. 28.2; Ps. 132.7 we may perhaps presume that the phrase
'worship at (lit. fall down before) his footstool' is meant to refer to
gesture in worship before the Ark of the Covenant above which God
is thought to sit invisibly enthroned on his sublime mercy-seat; for
in that case the Ark stands 'at his feet' like a footstool (see Intr.
33 f., 40 f., 45). Elsewhere the phrase is understood in a wider sense as
referring to the Mount of Zion (Isa. 60.13; Ezek. 43.7) or to the
whole earth (Isa. 66.1; Matt. 5.35). The worshipping congregation

bow down before the God whose holiness is manifested in his
righteousness (cf. Isa. 5.16); they do so with awe and thanksgiving
and in the joyous hope of the coming of the righteous rule of their
God over the whole world.

God's grace and judgment in history (vv. 6–9)

[6] In the third strophe the poet pursues his subject on an even
deeper level and comes to speak of the innermost core of God's
holiness. The greatest statement he is able to make with regard to
God's nature is neither that God's universal might has a power that
can shake the whole world nor that God has established the rule of
law that governs every life, but that he has shown himself to be the
God of *grace*, which has transformed the history of Israel into a
Heilsgeschichte. That the poet envisages the past as *Heilsgeschichte* is
proved by his naming as the great figures of Israel's history not
politicians but religious heroes such as Moses, Aaron, and Samuel.
He regards them as men whom God has given to his people as
priests, mediators and intercessors that they might establish and
cultivate the relation between God and the people and his communion with them. In holding this view the author of the psalm
takes his stand on the Old Testament tradition of the *Heilsgeschichte*
which was preserved in the cultic festival and to which he in part
refers (cf. Ex. 17.11 f.; 32.11 ff., 30 ff.; Num. 12.13; 14.13 ff.; 16.22;
21.7; I Sam. 7.5, 8 f.; 12.6 ff.). The tenses used in this connection
show that that tradition is experienced and believed as a living action
of God which is extended into the present.[1] The activities of these
figures who acted as mediators and intercessors demonstrate on the
one hand the inaccessible majesty of God whom the people did not
dare to meet face to face, but on the other hand, too, his gracious
will to enter into a mutual relationship with the people and to live
in communion with them. [7] Thus the inaccessible God has spoken
to Moses and Aaron out of the pillar of cloud, which hid him from
the presumptuous glances of men but was nevertheless also the sign
of his presence (Ex. 33.9; Num. 12.5). The tradition of the pillar of
cloud and the idea of the cherubim upon the Ark, symbolizing
the cloud on which Yahweh appears, can presumably be traced back
to the same root (see Intr. 29); the poet therefore also understood

---

[1] It cannot be inferred from the text of the psalm that the intercession is to be
understood in an eschatological sense, as Hesse, *Die Fürbitte im Alten Testament*,
1952, pp. 73 f., assumes.

God's speaking to Samuel from above the sacred Ark (I Sam. 3.3 ff.) as a speaking out of the pillar of cloud. Yahweh used the mediation of these great men of God to give the people his testimonies and statutes that they might keep them in a sacred cultic tradition; this divine means of salvation became a fountain from which faith was continually able to draw new strength for the present and hope for the future. **[8]** In such events of bygone days as the Old Testament tradition has preserved and at any given time represented in the cultic ceremonies as a present reality, the faithful experience the grace of God, that for ever remains true to itself, and feel it to be intended for themselves even when the story told is of the answered prayers of their great forefathers. This is hinted at in the psalm by the change to the invocation of God in prayer ('O Lord, our God'); it is clearly expressed in the attitude of the congregation that is presupposed in v. 9. Even in his grace God remains a holy God. And that holiness manifests itself in the fact that the utter seriousness of the righteousness by which he punishes the sins of men invariably continues to hold its own side by side with the seriousness of the love by which he forgives sins. It is this co-existence of God's judgment and grace, so incomprehensible to the human mind, this insight into the real nature of a God who takes sin just as seriously as the forgiveness of sins, which is the innermost core of God's holiness before which the congregation falls down and worships. The peculiarity and strength of the biblical belief in God lies in this twofold perception of the divine nature and of the consequences resulting therefrom. The thought of the God who forgives imbues the faithful, whose faith is shaken by sin, with fresh courage and with a new impetus; the thought of the severity of God's judgments, on the other hand, guards the man who relies on God's grace against the danger of unscrupulously evading his responsibility. It is in this light that the psalmist visualizes the 'holy' God since the times of Moses (on God's 'righteousness' cf., for instance, Num. 20.10 ff.; 27.13 f.; Deut. 3.23 ff.); it is in this light that the poet visualizes God in the present —and on this God he sets his hope, the hope with which he looks forward to the coming of the Kingdom of God. **[9]** Having reached this culminating point, the hymn quite naturally ends in the call to the congregation to praise God, to worship and adore him. The hymn concludes with the congregation's testimony. In almost the same words as at the end of the second strophe, it expresses simultaneously their difference from God and their bond with him, their awe and terror and their joyful confidence. It is the joint effect of both these which alone is able to produce the true note of biblical faith.

100. MAKE A JOYFUL NOISE TO THE LORD, ALL THE LANDS!

A Psalm. For the thank-offering

1 Make a joyful noise to the Lord, all the lands!
2 Serve the Lord with gladness!
  Come into his presence with shouts of joy!
3 Know this: the Lord, he is God!
  It is he that made us, and we are his;[1]
  we are *his* people, the sheep of his pasture.
4 Enter his gates with praise,
  and his courts with psalms![2]
  Testify to him and praise his name![3]
5 For the Lord is good; his grace endures for ever,
  and his faithfulness from generation to generation.[4]

[1] See BH.
[2] Lit.: song of praise (hymn). (Tr. N.: RSV has 'with praise' instead of 'with psalms'.)
[3] * RSV has 'with thanksgiving' instead of 'with praise' in the first line of v. 4 and renders the last line: 'Give thanks to him, bless his name!'
[4] * RSV has 'steadfast love' instead of 'grace' and 'to all generations' instead of 'from generation to generation'.

It is evident from the psalm itself that it was sung at the entry into the Temple (v. 4), perhaps antiphonally by the choir as a hymn, and that it has probably been part of the liturgy of the divine service (v. 2) at which God's 'name' and his 'grace and faithfulness' were made known to the congregation who now extol them in a hymn (vv. 4–5). These facts point to the festival cult of the covenant community (see Intr. 30 f., 41 ff., 56 f.). In this as well as in the wording of several passages the psalm is akin to Psalm 95. It observes the customary forms of the hymn, which are couched in such general terms that it is impossible to determine the date of the psalm accurately. The psalm falls into two analogically constructed parts each of which opens with a call (vv. 1 f. and 4) that leads on to the actual praise of God (vv. 3 and 5). The very fact that this short composition confines itself to the usual forms and ideas allows us a valuable insight into the principal concerns of the piety of the cultic hymn. The keynote of the psalm is the joy in God which is the motive power of faith and lifts up the hearts of men. The service is

here the place where that joy finds expression and at the same time
draws fresh strength from new sources.

[1] The psalm opens with a hymnic call to sing the praise of God
with shouts of joy. The echo of the exultant joy in God shall resound
not only in the midst of the festal congregation in the Temple; it
shall be heard in 'all the lands'. In the presence of God the members
of the worshipping congregation feel themselves united with all his
worshippers in *one* great communion of faith. [2] The call to worship
which follows in v. 2 is addressed to the congregation assembled in
the Temple. It expresses the motive and the aim and at the same
time the spirit of the 'service' rendered to God in worship, that is,
enthusiastic joy in the presence of God. This note of a joy that is
utterly devoted to God and leaves behind it every earthly sorrow
that may burden the heart is not only reflected in the opening verses
but resounds through the whole psalm. (In the immortal setting by
Max Reger its basic mood has been made the subject of a noble
artistic interpretation.) [3] It passes on to the hymn proper with the
words: 'Know this: the Lord, he is God', with which the true nature
of the hymn becomes clear. It serves the purpose of representing
God as a living reality and of imparting the knowledge of God
associated therewith. The congregation is to appear before God (see
Intr. 58 f.) praising him and glorifying his deeds, and is to draw
near to him by turning to him in spirit. In this way the hymn becomes
not only an expression of the spirit that moves in the hearts of men
but also the point where man meets his God and wholly surrenders
to joy in him. The statement which is the most important one from
the standpoint of the Old Testament faith comes first: Yahweh
alone is God. By this the reality which the word 'God' implies is
brought before the mind's eye of the believer in all its fullness. And
that reality of God awakens in man the sense of creaturehood.
Human self-assurance and man's independent value vanish in the
sight of God. What man is, he is not by virtue of his own efforts;
what he has, is not owned by him. 'It is *he* that made us, and we are
his': this is the way in which the creature speaks of his Maker and
Lord on whom he depends in everything and to whom alone he can
turn for help. And with the idea of creation is here closely linked
that of history and election which is the second characteristic mark
of the Old Testament belief in God. It is by this linking up that history
as God's history and the people as God's people obtain their specific
significance, while on the other hand everything that is human in

Nature and in History is put in its place by awe of the Creator. For this reason the profession of loyalty, 'We are his people, and the sheep of his pasture', simultaneously expresses pride and humility, awe and trust (see Intr. 58 f.). The co-existence of these two basic sentiments is accounted for by the fact that God's love and care are always at the same time felt to be an expression of his power.

[4] The opening words of the second part of the psalm were probably sung by the choir of priests, before the festival congregation passed through the gates of the Temple and entered its forecourts. As in the first part of the psalm, they begin with a call to enter the sanctuary with songs of praise in order to testify there to God and to praise his name. [5] In the second part the actual hymn consists in a liturgical formula (cf. Pss. 106.1; 107.1; 118.1; 136), which is well known elsewhere and was presumably to be repeated by the congregation as a response. The theme is now the goodness of God and his everlasting 'grace and faithfulness' as the unshakable foundation on which the cult community's experience of God and the hope of its faith are based from of old (see Intr. 58 f.). Goodness is of the very essence of God's nature, and his acts of grace are not the product of a momentary friendly whim or manifestations of the arbitrary mood of a divine despot. That the cult community is capable of 'believing' in God and of 'trusting' in him finds its justification in the constancy and, consequently, in the reliability of God's gracious purposes within the covenant relationship (this is what the term 'faithfulness' means in the context). The knowledge of God's grace and faithfulness is the true source from which the joy and the enthusiasm of the psalm spring, and from which it is not easy to escape. The joy expressed in the psalm is simultaneously joy derived from God and joy in God; it emanates from him and returns to him, and in that process lies the deepest meaning of the Old Testament worship. The hymn 'Nun jauchzt dem Herren, alle Welt'[1] shows that the Christian Church, too, lives by this fountain of piety.

[1] * By David Denicke (1603–1680), based on a hymn by Cornelius Becker (1561–1604).

101. THE IDEAL PRINCE

Of David. A Psalm

1 I will exercise[1] love and justice;
   I will hearken[2] unto the[2] Lord.[3]

2 I will give heed to the way that is blameless;
   truth[1] shall abide with me.[4]
   I will walk with integrity of heart within my house.
3 I will not set before my eyes anything that is base.
   I hate to do evil; it shall not cleave to me.[5]
4 A perverted heart shall depart from me;
   I will not know the wicked.[6]
5 Him who slanders the neighbour secretly
   I will reduce to silence;
   the man of haughty looks and arrogant heart
   I will not suffer.[7]
6 My eyes shall be on the faithful in the land,
   and they may dwell with me;
   he who walks in the way that is blameless
   shall minister to me.[8]
7 No man who practises deceit
   shall dwell in my house;
   no man who utters lies
   shall continue in my presence.
8 Morning by morning I will destroy
   all the wicked in the land,
   to cut off all the evildoers
   from the city of the Lord.[9]

[1] See BH.
[2] *ešmā ʿā*, and *le* instead of *lekā*.
[3] * In RSV v. 1 is:
   I will sing of loyalty and of justice;
   to thee, O Lord, I will sing.
[6] * This line in RSV reads, 'Oh when wilt thou come to me?'
[5] * RSV has 'I hate the work of those who fall away' instead of 'I hate to do evil'.
[6] * V. 4 reads in RSV:
   Perverseness of heart shall be far from me;
   I will know nothing of evil.
[7] * RSV has 'destroy' instead of 'reduce to silence'.
[8] * RSV has 'I will look with favour' instead of 'My eyes shall be . . .'
[9] * RSV has 'cutting off' instead of 'to cut off'.

Already at a very early date it was believed that it is a reigning
prince who speaks in this psalm, and that with good reason. For the
one whose utterance the psalm records has a large house at his
disposal (vv. 2, 7), which offers a home to many people (v. 7); it is
an honour to be able to serve him (v. 6); he possesses far-reaching
power (vv. 5, 6), and he has the judicial authority to expel the
evildoers from the city of Yahweh (v. 8). All these facts make clear
beyond doubt that the speaker is a prince of Judah in Jerusalem.
The psalm is probably a proclamation issued by the King at his
enthronement festival. He does not render an account of the actual

state of affairs, but makes a declaration in which he expresses the lofty ideal principles whereby the conduct of a ruler shall be guided.[1] The true prince shows himself in that he first applies to himself the demands implicit in these principles (vv. 1–3) before he issues directions for the conduct of others (vv. 4–8). The bond that unites leader and led consists in the fact that they are equally accountable to a higher authority.

[1] The king subjects his own person and his office to the demands which God makes upon men. He, too, is one who obeys; he is not a despot. The right behaviour towards God entails the right behaviour towards men. The terms 'love' and 'justice' imply both these aspects, that is to say, they imply his behaviour towards God in the sense of 'piety' and 'obedience' to the demands made upon him by the divine law, but at the same time also the love and justice that he exercises with regard to men. In the Bible moral and religious conduct are inseparable. [2] It is not certain particular precepts which engage the ruler's mind at this great moment of his life; he is more concerned with the situation as a whole and with fundamental principles: no evil *can* possibly result from a basic attitude of mind that is devout and truthful and from a heart that is pure. If the whole man is good, then his deeds are good as well. This perception, which lies behind his words, matches the depth of New Testament ethics (cf. Matt. 7.17 ff.). If such a spirit is the dominant force in the house of the reigning prince, then he has not only the right but also the strength to exercise true leadership. [3] But an attitude of mind based on morality is also an effective safeguard against any temptation to do evil; anything that is vile fails to produce an effect on a pure heart; for the latter harbours a natural hatred towards any kind of sin. [4–7] Just as this prince himself does not allow any evil thoughts to enter his mind, so treacherous and wicked men have no access to him (v. 4). His own principle of loyalty to his faith and of veracity entitles him to oppose slander, deceit and lies among his subjects (vv. 5, 7) and, on the other hand, to bestow his special care upon the trustworthy and upon those who are faithful to Yahweh and upright in heart and to summon them to service in his house (v. 6). That he does not suffer the proud and the arrogant to keep company with him (v. 5b) does

---

[1] At the root of this is, perhaps, the influence which the Egyptian 'royal proclamation' (i.e. at the king's accession) exerted on the form of the Judaic royal ritual. Cf. Herrmann, *Wissenschaftliche Zeitschrift der Karl-Marx-Universität Leipzig, Gesellschafts- und Sprachwissenschaftliche Reihe*, 3, 1953/54, p. 37.

credit to this king who knows himself to be in the service of a higher Being. **[8]** He greatly exaggerates when he proclaims as the aim of his daily administration of justice (cf. II Sam. 15.2; Jer. 21.12) the cleansing of Jerusalem, the city of God, from all evildoers; that hyperbole would in some measure be understandable in view of the mood that prevails in that great hour, but perhaps we should rather think of that proclamation as a reference to the ritual act of the self-purgation of the covenant community from the wicked and evildoers amongst them, which was done day by day during the festival, a ritual act for the execution of which the king knows himself to be responsible (see Intr. 64); in the latter case the assumption of a hyperbole would be groundless.[1] All in all, a devout king amidst a devout people! This is an ideal of which surely no king need to be ashamed!

The psalm is imbued with the intense moral earnestness of Old Testament religion. The otherwise customary vows, endowments and sacrifices to the Deity are not so much as mentioned here; again, the king does not make any promises out of weakness in order to meet half-way any kind of wishes that might be uttered from amidst his people. What unites him with his people is their common subjection to the will of God, which shows both him and them the way that leads clearly to a régime ordered by God. It is this consistent and firm religious and moral attitude that gives its greatness and ageless value to the psalm, which is still able to serve even in our day as a model of true leadership.

---

[1] Possibly it is a question of the jurisdiction of the king, which he has reserved to himself in the city-state of Jerusalem, which belonged to the dynasty (cf. Begrich, *ZAW* 58, 1940/41, p. 26); this was included in the royal ritual of the Temple.

102. PRAYER OF LAMENT AND HYMN

A Prayer of one afflicted, when he is faint and pours out his complaint before Yahweh

1 Hear my prayer, O Lord;
   let my cry come to thee!
2 Do not hide thy face from me
   in the day of my distress!
   Incline thy ear to me when I call,
   answer me speedily![1]
3 For my days pass away like[2] smoke,
   and my bones burn like a furnace.

4 My heart is smitten and withered like grass
  so that I forgot to eat my bread.[3]

5 Because of my constant groaning
  my bones cleave to my flesh.[4]

6 I became like a pelican in the wilderness,
  like an owl in ruined places.[5]

7 I lie awake,
  I have become like a lonely bird on the house-top.

8 My enemies reviled me day by day,
  those who rave against me, cursed me.[6]

9 For I ate ashes like bread,
  and mingled tears with my drink,[7]

10 because of thy indignation and anger;
  for thou hast taken me up and struck me down.[8]

11 My days are like an evening shadow;
  and as for me, I wither away like grass.

12 But thou, O Lord, art enthroned for ever;
  and thy memorial endures from generation to generation.[9]

13 Thou wilt arise and have pity on Zion;
  for it is time to be gracious to her;
  the hour has come.[10]

14 For thy servants hold her stones dear,
  and they love her dust.[11]

15 And the nations fear thy[2] name,
  and all the kings of the earth thy majesty.[12]

16 For the Lord did build up Zion;
  he has appeared in his glory.[13]

17 He regarded the prayer of the destitute
  and did not despise his supplication.[14]

18 Let this be recorded for a generation to come,
  so that a people that has been reborn may praise the Lord![15]

19 For he looked down from his holy height,
  from heaven the Lord looked at the earth,[16]

20 to hear the groans of the prisoners,
  to set free those who were doomed to die,

21 to declare the name of the Lord in Zion
  and his glory in Jerusalem,[17]

22 when peoples gather together,
  and kingdoms, to serve the Lord.

23 He has broken my strength in mid-course;
  he has shortened my days.

24 I said,[2] 'O my God, take me not hence
  in the midst of my days;
  thy years endure from generation to generation.[18]

25 Of old thou didst lay the foundation of the earth,
  and the heavens are the work of thy hands.

26 They will perish, but thou dost endure;
  they will all wear out like a garment.

Thou layest them off like raiment—
they change and then pass away;[19]

27 but thou art the same,
and thy years have no end.

28 The children of thy servants shall continue;
their posterity shall be established before thee.'[20]

[1] * The word-order of the third and fourth lines is different in RSV:
Incline thy ear to me;
answer me speedily in the day when I call!

[2] See BH.

[3] * RSV renders the first line 'My heart is smitten like grass, and withered'
and has 'forget' instead of 'forgot' in the second line.

[4] * RSV has 'loud' instead of 'constant'.

[5] * The first line reads in RSV, 'I am like a vulture of the wilderness' and has
in the second line 'of the waste places' instead of 'in ruined places'.

[6] * In RSV v. 8 is:
All the day my enemies taunt me,
those who deride me use my name for a curse.

[7] * RSV uses the present tense.

[8] * RSV has 'thrown me away' instead of 'struck me down'.

[9] * RSV has 'name' instead of 'memorial'.

[10] * V. 13 reads in RSV after the first line:
it is the time to favour her;
the appointed time has come.

[11] * RSV has 'have pity on her dust' instead of 'love her dust'.

[12] * RSV renders the first line of v. 15, 'The nations will fear the name of the
Lord' and has in the second line 'glory' instead of 'majesty'.

[13] * RSV uses throughout the future tense.

[14] * Here, too, RSV uses throughout the future tense and moreover has 'their'
instead of 'his' supplication.

[15] * RSV has 'a people yet unborn' instead of 'a people that has been reborn'.

[16] * RSV regards vv. 19–22 as a continuation of v. 18, beginning v. 19: 'that
he looked down . . .'

[17] * V. 21 is in RSV:
that men may declare in Zion the name of the Lord,
and in Jerusalem his praise,

[18] * The second half of v. 24 reads in RSV:
thou whose years endure
throughout all generations!

[19] * V. 26 is rendered in RSV after the second line:
Thou changest them like raiment,
and they pass away;

[20] * The RSV has 'shall dwell secure' instead of 'shall continue'.

According to its superscription the psalm served as a kind of
pattern, which was used in public worship (cf. v. 18; see Intr.95) for
the prayers of lament of an individual. It is the fifth of the penitential psalms of the Ancient Church. Though lament and supplication
are the dominant feature in that part of the psalm which concerns
the individual (vv. 1–11, 23 f.), the theme of penitence here receding

into the background, it is nevertheless the worshipper's humble submission to God's judgment—in addition to the statements he makes in vv. 9 and 23—which gives him strength and imparts to his psalm the fundamental character of the utterance of a contrite heart. The exposition of the psalm faces the difficult problem how the part which is a hymn (vv. 12–22) fits into the framework of the prayer of lament. The great majority of commentators have tried to solve this problem by splitting the piece up into two different psalms or by assuming that the lament of an individual had been reinterpreted at a later date as a community lament. It seems to me, however, that this exegetical problem has to be solved in the light of the setting and content of the cultic ceremony in the course of which the psalm was recited (cf. I Sam. 1.9 ff.); the latter makes sufficiently clear why the concern of an individual is woven into that of the whole cult community and imparts to the psalm a certain paradigmatic character. The essential theme of the cultic ceremony, the appearance of God before the cult community (v. 16), at which his dominion and his salvation are revealed and realized afresh, is for the worshipper, too, the point at which he becomes assured that his supplications have been granted (vv. 17, 20); this is a saving event to which he not only testifies in the midst of the congregation by word of mouth, reciting the words of the psalm, but which he also wishes to be recorded in writing so that God may be glorified (v. 18). Here we gain an interesting insight into the ultimate religious motives that gave rise to the composition of certain psalms as 'literature'. Whether we are forced in view of vv. 14, 20 to regard the exilic or post-exilic period as the time in which the psalm was composed, as most commentators assume, seems to me to be open to question. Verse 14 does not necessarily presuppose the destruction of Jerusalem (cf. in this connection v. 16); and our knowledge of the historical details is so scanty that the mention of prisoners and of those doomed to die by no means compels us to assume that it can be only a reference to the Babylonian captivity. At any rate, we shall have to reckon with the possibility of a pre-exilic origin of the psalm.

The psalm first begins with the supplication and lament; they, too, are part of the saving event to which the psalmist wishes to bear witness in his song. For it is only against this background that the blessing which the worshipper may hope for is made manifest in all its magnitude. **[1–2]** The invocation and the petition for the answering of the prayer observe the traditional forms and are followed by

the lament; which is elaborated in detail and is presented in an
extraordinary way. **[3–11]** The worshipper is emaciated as a result
of the burning fever of his illness (vv. 3, 5) and sees his life wither
away like grass (vv. 4, 11); he is tormented in the innermost recesses
of his heart (v. 4a) by the frightening realization of the transient
nature of his life, which 'passes away like smoke' (v. 3), reminding
him of the lengthening evening shadows though he has only reached
the middle of his life (v. 24). Reviled by his enemies, who treat him
as a typical example of one who is accursed (v. 8), he becomes aware
of his loneliness (vv. 6 f.) as he lies awake fasting (vv. 4b, 9a) and
groaning (vv. 7, 5a, 9b); and the sting of that loneliness lies in the
fact that he cannot help discerning in his suffering the truth that he
is not only forsaken by God but is punished by him (v. 10). **[12–13]**
Against the dark background of his lament, and both outwardly and
inwardly in strong contrast with it, the prayer (vv. 12–22) arises in
the form of a hymn. It is an echo of what the worshipper has experienced in the midst of and together with the congregation during the
service: the long-desired encounter with God (*mō'ēd*), when he
'arises' to 'appear in his glory' (v. 16) before the cult community
in a festive 'hour' (v. 13) and assures them of the presence of his grace
(v. 13). God's eternal rule is revealed in the face of the transient
nature of everything human, and is celebrated by means of the
'memorial' of a continuous cultic tradition (v. 12). **[14]** No wonder
that the pilgrims attending the feast look upon the buildings of the
city of God and upon their sacred ground with joy and love (cf. Ps.
84.10), **[15–16]** remembering that it was, after all, God himself who
'built up' Zion, that is to say, made it his habitation, the place where
he appears in his glorious majesty so that the whole world bows
down before him in awe (cf. Pss. 87.1 f.; 78.69; 147.2; see Intr. 33 ff.,
45). **[17–18]** Being a member of the cult community, for whom the
salvation which has been revealed in the theophany is intended, the
poet knows that God has spoken to him in his personal affliction, too,
and has answered his prayer. God's grace has been granted anew to
him, too (cf. v. 10). God no longer hides his face from him (cf. v. 2).
The psalmist wants not only to bear witness to that grace by means of
his psalm at this very hour of public worship, but also to record his
testimony in writing for the benefit of future generations, when as the
ever newly-created people of God they sing their hymns to his glory
at the feast of the renewal of the Covenant. For it is God's glory that
is concerned; to glorify him is the purpose and task of the worshipping

community. That truth is expressed in an unmistakable manner in vv. 18 ff. **[19–22]** The public worship for which the various tribes and nations assemble every year at Jerusalem is the place where God appears, reveals his 'name' and manifests his saving rule (v. 21; from the grammatical point of view the same subject is to be assumed in v. 21 as in v. 20; cf. in this connection Ex. 33.19; see Intr. 41 ff.); and that saving rule is the theme of the hymns sung by the congregation to the glory of God (cf. v. 18), but for one who uses this psalm in prayer it is the memorial of God's compassion, which has continually saved from perdition the prisoners and those who were doomed to die. The granting of the poet's personal petition and his deliverance are but a link in the long chain of divine saving acts, whose permanent commemoration, according to v. 12, is entrusted to the cult community as a sacred tradition. **[23–28]** It is in this sense that we must understand the fact that the psalmist at this point once more reverts to his own affliction and prayer of lament and, conscious of the transient nature of his own being, humbles himself under the eternal Being of God to whom as the Creator of heaven and earth belongs the power over life and death. In that he humbly submits to the Creator and Judge of the world—both these aspects belong to the constitutive basic ideas of the festival cult (see Intr. 44 ff.)—he reaps the finest fruit which his penitence yields in his encounter with God, namely, the inward comfort of knowing that he now may praise God's eternal rule with joy in his heart and in the sure knowledge that his enemies will perish (v. 26; the usual interpretation of this verse as referring to the transient nature of heaven and earth is refuted by the word 'all'), whereas he knows himself to be at one with the community of the people of God whose fellowship he shares and whose continuity is guaranteed by the presence of God. In the sharing with them of the same faith personal loneliness and affliction are here overcome by humble submission to the presence of the eternal God.

103. BLESS THE LORD, O MY SOUL

Of David

1 Bless the Lord, O my soul;
   and all that is within me, bless his holy name!
2 Bless the Lord, O my soul,
   and forget not all his benefits,
3 who forgives all your iniquity,
   who heals all your diseases,

 4 who delivers your life from perdition,[1]
   who crowns you with grace and mercy,
 5 who satisfies your longing[2] with goodness
   so that your youth is renewed like the eagle's.
 6 The Lord works righteous acts[3]
   and justice for all who are oppressed.
 7 He made known his ways to Moses,
   and his deeds to the people of Israel.
 8 The Lord is merciful and gracious,
   slow to anger and abounding in lovingkindness.
 9 He will not always chide,
   nor will he keep his anger for ever.
10 He does not deal with us according to our sins,
   nor requite us according to our iniquities.
11 For as high as the heavens are above the earth,
   so high[4] is his grace over those who fear him;[5]
12 as far as the morning is from the evening,
   so far does he remove our transgressions from us.[6]
13 As a father has compassion on his children,
   so the Lord has compassion on those who fear him.[7]
14 For he knows our frame;
   he remembers that we are but dust.
15 As for man, his days are like grass;
   he flourishes like a flower of the field;
16 when the wind passes over it, it is gone,
   and its place knows it no more.
17 But the grace of the Lord is from everlasting to everlasting ' ',[4]
   and his salvation is to children's children,[8]
18 to those who keep his covenant
   and remember to do his commandments.
19 The Lord, his throne is[9] in heaven,
   and his kingdom rules over the universe.[10]
20 Bless the Lord, O you his angels,
   you mighty ones, who fulfil his command ' '![11]
21 Bless the Lord, all his hosts,
   you servants that do his will![12]
22 Bless the Lord, all his works,
   in all places of his dominion.
   Bless the Lord, O my soul!

[1] * V. 4a reads in RSV, 'who redeems your life from the Pit'.
[2] Following LXX read ʿorgēk = your desire. (Tr. N.: RSV renders v. 5b, 'who satisfies you with good as long as you live'.)
[3] * RSV has 'vindication' instead of 'righteous acts'.
[4] See BH.
[5] * V. 11 reads in RSV:
    For as the heavens are high above the earth,
    so great is his steadfast love toward
    those who fear him.

⁶ * The first line of v. 12 is in RSV:
'as far as the east is from the west'.
⁷ * RSV has 'pities' instead of 'has compassion on'.
⁸ * RSV adds in the first line 'upon those who fear him' and in the second line
has 'righteousness' instead of 'salvation'.
⁹ Following Staerk delete *hēkīn*.
¹⁰ * RSV renders the first line of v. 19, 'The Lord has established his throne in
the heavens' and in the second line has 'over all' instead of 'over the universe'.
¹¹ See BH. (Tr. N.: RSV renders v. 20 after the first line:
you mighty ones who do his word,
hearkening to the voice of his word!)
¹² * In RSV the second line reads, 'his ministers that do his will'.

This psalm is one of the finest blossoms on the tree of biblical
faith. Its roots reach deep down to where the most powerful springs of
biblical piety flow, and by the noble and serene tones in which it
praises the grace of God it has enriched both poetry and life in the
course of the centuries. The man who speaks in this psalm is able to
talk from personal experience which has led him through adversity
and suffering caused by sin till he was able to enjoy the full sunlight
of the grace of his God. His own life has taught him to apprehend
what the greatest among the men of the Bible had been able to assert
of God's nature and of his truth and, combining therewith ideas
which had been preserved in the festival cult by means of the sacred
tradition, he sums up all these experiences and ideas in an impressive
song of praise, glorifying the gracious rule of the inconceivably great
and omnipotent God. The marked dependence on words and
concepts of the biblical tradition which the psalm shows is to be
accounted for by this relation to the cultic tradition. We would not
do justice to the poet if on account of that dependence we were to
dispute his originality and regard the psalm as a compilation of
quotations taken from other sources. The special distinctiveness of
the psalm lies precisely in the inner connection between the poet's
personal experience of God and the understanding of the faith worked
out in the biblical testimonies of the Fathers, which are woven into
an organic whole; and in that respect the psalm can still serve also
today as a guide to the right interpretation of Holy Scripture. On
account of his jubilant song in praise of God's fatherly love the poet
is to be included in the great line of witnesses to God's Kingdom of
grace that leads from Moses and the prophets to Christ. In the
hymn 'My soul, now praise thy Maker'¹ the psalm has found an
impressive Christian echo.

¹ * Catherine Winkworth's translation of 'Nun lob, mein Seel, den Herren' by
Johann Gramann (1487–1541).

As far as its form is concerned the psalm is a mixture of a hymn
and a song of thanksgiving and as such was probably recited in the
cult of the covenant community to whose traditions it more than
once refers (see the comments on vv. 8 ff.). Its outward structure
reflects the natural and unconstrained thought-sequence which flows
from the personal experience of the poet combined with his devout
meditation on the cultic tradition (v. 7). Far from being an artificial
and clumsy piece of work, such as the hymnic form could easily
have led him to produce, even its outward form appeals to us by its
natural and simple style such as only an inward truthfulness is able
to fashion in an impressive manner. The opening song (vv. 1–2)
begins with a hymnic call to bless the Lord, which the psalmist
directs to himself; then follow his reflections on his own personal
experience of the divine grace (vv. 3–5) just as freely and easily as
the extension of his meditation on the evidence of God's acts of grace
which are to be found in history and tradition (vv. 6–13). The
contrasting of the transient nature of man with the eternal Being of
God (vv. 14–18) likewise has its roots in the personal attitude of the
poet and leads on with a powerful and elevating effect to the hymn
which, embracing the universe, glorifies the Kingship of God
Almighty (vv. 19–22) and concludes the psalm with full chords.

The opening song (vv. 1–2)

[1–2] Unlike other hymnic openings, in which the choir or the
worshipping congregation are called upon to sing the praise of God,
the poet addresses his call to himself, creating a solemn atmosphere
by means of the repeated use of the same opening phrase. At the root
of that stylistic form is the will to hearken to God's voice, to meet him
face to face, and to open the soul to the impact of his living presence.
It follows from the nature of the hymn as a response to the revelation
of God that man is not satisfied with the fulfilment of his duty to
give thanks to the Deity in a particular case, but desires more than
that: he wants to see God, as it were, once more face to face and
enjoy his living presence; again, he wants to be able to encounter him
and to hold on to him; all this is part of the original impulses
involved in the attitude of prayer which causes the *whole* man ('all
that is within me') to turn to God. In fact, this attitude is imbued
with a twofold feeling matched by two different aspects of the reality
of God. The singer faces God's *holiness* with *respectful awe* and yet at
the same time *gives himself up to the love of God* as revealed to him in

God's saving deeds. Out of the interaction of both these sentiments the marvellous melody is woven which combines in the psalm the notes of sublimity and of intimacy. The poet is simultaneously aware of the *God who is far removed* and before whose majestic sternness man sinks down in the consciousness of his sinfulness, and of the *God who is near* and takes loving care of man. The true theme of the psalm is, however, not the juxtaposition of these aspects of the reality of God, which the human mind can conceive only as antitheses, but their interaction. To the eye of faith the God who is far off and the God who is near do not imply an antithesis, but are one and the same reality. Faith grasps the connection which remains hidden from reason. The sublimity of God, far removed from any human way of thinking and comprehension, shows itself in the very fact of his gracious condescension even to the man who sinks into nothingness before him. This is the ultimately 'divine' in God that, where man sees only the chasm, God in his compassion bridges it. None of these things stands alone: it is only in his love *for the sinner* that the sublime holiness of God fully manifests itself, and that love draws its surpassing strength and its redeeming power from the fact that it is the love of the *holy God*. Here we meet the same profound knowledge of God which Hosea (11.8 f.) describes in these words:

My heart recoils within me,
my compassion grows warm and tender.
I will not execute my fierce anger,
I will not again destroy Ephraim;
for I am God and not man,
the Holy One in your midst.

This keynote which is clearly struck in the first two verses rings throughout the psalm to its very end. And the psalmist's exhortation to himself, not to forget the benefits which God has bestowed upon him, not only contains a warning against the common danger of accepting life as a matter of course without letting oneself be impressed by it, but arouses man's soul to the consciousness of what it means to be encompassed by the compassionate love of the holy God (v. 1).

The personal experience of the grace of God (vv. 3–5)

[3–5] As the soul of the psalmist has thus become responsive to God, there flood into it in overwhelming abundance thoughts of the greatness of God, which has manifested itself in his loving care for the singer. As he thinks of all the things for which he is indebted to God, his life appears to him to be pervaded by the light of God's grace, which shines most clearly in those very circumstances in which man's eyes see only darkness, that is, sin, illness, death. The whole of life thus takes on a different complexion and acquires a fresh impulse and new strength. It is characteristic of the utter seriousness of the poet's religious reflection on himself that his first thought is of the forgiveness of his sins. He knows that no life can prosper as long as it is separated from God through sin, and so he regards as the most important foundation of his faith the certitude that God himself removes the most serious obstacle by forgiving all his transgressions and thereby provides his life with a new basis. In the face of illness and death that threaten man's life the poet knows himself to be safe in the hand of God who has graciously delivered him from illness and from the danger of death. What imparts to these verses the note of joyful confidence is not only the psalmist's gratitude for the help he has experienced but also his conviction that he will be encompassed by God's love in the future, too. His suffering, which once distressed him because he saw in it God's punishment, is now the means whereby God's lovingkindness is revealed to him. He sees this realization as the crown of his life and the fulfilment of his desires, and there springs from it, like the eagle's pinions, the strength that comes from a new vitality. The poet realizes that the opportunities which life offers lie before him just as they did in the sunny days of his youth; he is able to infer from his own experience that it always means a new beginning when God enters into a man's life. This is the Old Testament understanding of what the New Testament describes as 'being born again'.

The gracious God in history and tradition (vv. 6–13)

The poet's experience in his own life now becomes for him the means of comprehending God's nature and rule outside his own personal sphere. The very fact that he does not confine his meditation to his own person proves that God is at the centre of his thoughts: it is God who is here the subject throughout, not only in so far as the poet is directly indebted to him for something or other, but more than that, in that God is praised for his own sake. This way of thinking originates in the cultic conception of the covenant community (cf. 'us' in vv. 10 ff.; 18). The tradition of God's saving deeds, which is actualized in the cult, is both the point of departure and the vast setting in the light of which the poet sees his own experience; and at the same time his personal experience of God becomes for him the key to the true understanding of God in the tradition of the *Heilsgeschichte*; for it is the same reality of God which on both levels appeals to the heart of man. And, conversely, the tradition confirms his own religious experience because both lead to and are recognized in the same attitude to life. **[6]** The poet begins his retrospect with a statement which reduces all that has happened in the past to the common denominator of God's righteousness. It is a magnificent attempt to understand history as a divine order in which man can put his trust. It is this general religious idea, and not only its formal legal element, that is first of all meant by the words 'righteous acts' and 'justice'. As far as its substance is concerned, the righteousness of God represents itself to the psalmist as the steadfastness of his love and graciousness which expresses itself in the help given to the oppressed. **[7]** It is from this perspective that we must understand the reference to Ex. 33.13. In disclosing his intentions and his will to Moses and in granting to the Israelites by his deeds an insight into his way of acting, God has shown his 'righteousness' to be a succession of gracious acts which run right through the whole history of Israel. **[8]** The history of his people is a proof to the poet of God's grace. As he focuses his gaze on God, the psalmist, with the eye of faith which had first been opened by his personal experience, sees the past as a living present reality; and the profound meaning of the fundamental truth of God's self-revelation, 'Yahweh is a God merciful and gracious, slow to anger, and abounding in grace and faithfulness' (Ex. 34.6), flashes upon him anew. **[9-10]** How narrow in comparison with this true nature of God the idea of retribution which seeks to squeeze God's inconceivable majesty into an arithmetical scheme devised by man's thinking! How faint-hearted man's fear born of sin that God might keep his anger for ever (cf. in this connection Jer. 3.5, 12; Isa. 57.16)! It would not be true to say that the poet uses the idea of God's grace to attenuate the seriousness of the consciousness of sin, which cannot help admitting that the wrath of God is fully deserved. As long as man has not plumbed the depths of the knowledge of sin he does not really know what grace means. It is precisely because sin is the most shattering experience in his life that the poet is able to recognize the truth that God's grace is greater than man's sin and that his love is stronger than his anger. **[11-13]** In word-pictures that thrill us because of their exquisite beauty and

remind us of the classic saying in Isa. 55.8 f. (cf. Ps. 36.5), the poet
seeks to illustrate the overwhelming greatness of the divine grace, an
effort which is bound to end up in demonstrating man's incapability
to produce anything on his side that could bear comparison with
God's incomparable grace. Even the largest dimensions such as the
distance between heaven and earth or the interval between sunrise
and sunset do not suffice to make clear the difference between the
world of human sin and the reality of the divine grace into which
God allows the sinner to enter. This is why the poet has recourse to
another word-picture which he takes from another 'dimension' in
order to be able to penetrate to the uttermost depths of the nature of
grace. He chooses a simile from the sphere of man's personal life
which Hosea (11.1–4) has portrayed in the most beautiful colours,
that is, the picture of God's fatherly love. Just as true fatherly love
never deserts the child but guides him with a strong hand and does
so even when the child does wrong, and just as his compassion
proves itself to be greatest in precisely this latter case, so is God's love
for the man who fears him. In spite of all the intimacy of his thoughts
the poet does not forget even now, as his hymn reaches its culminating
point, that man sets the majesty of the divine grace over against the
basic attitude of the fear of God and that on this account the grace of
God is for him a matter of immense seriousness which makes the
nothingness of man in the sight of God all the more evident.

[14–16] The psalmist dwells on these thoughts in familiar phrases
and word-pictures, which call to mind Gen. 2.7; 3.17 ff.; Isa.
40.6 ff.; Ps. 90.5 f.; Job 7.7 ff., and perhaps can be traced back to
the tradition of the covenant community (v. 18). God knows that
man is a creature born of dust, ephemeral as grass and quickly
withering like the splendour of the flowers, and unable to live without
his compassion. But the miracle of his grace consists in the very fact
that the Creator shows mercy to his creature; and only the man who
is aware of and grieves over the wretchedness of his creaturely life
has any inkling of this, because, like the narrator of Genesis and the
singer of Psalm 90, he discerns that behind the burden of mortality
is man's aspiration to be himself eternal in opposition to the eternal
God, in other words, as a sin, which can see God only as man's
enemy. [17–18] Against this background the inscrutable majesty of
God is seen the more clearly, for man's transitoriness serves to show
up the eternal power of God's grace and 'righteousness' in its true
light. So the poet comes to realize the true meaning of history: God

has granted to mortal man a share in his eternal grace, if he will 'keep God's covenant', seek to enter upon a life-long relationship with him and submit to him in obedience to his commandments.

The closing song (vv. 19–22)

[19] In the realization that the transience of the human race serves to reveal the glory of the divine grace, the poet's religious vision has reached a comprehensiveness and profundity which enables him, with a final stepping-up of outlook and action which takes him beyond the scope of history, to divine and praise God's omnipotence in the universe. The barriers of space and time disappear in the presence of God on which the eye of faith is focused. Like Isaiah (Isa. 6.1 ff.), the psalmist, having just witnessed the theophany in the cult, sees God, the royal Ruler of the universe, sitting upon an exalted heavenly throne. [20–22] The singer's praise does not in itself suffice to render to such a God the honour which is due to him. In a solemn refrain he therefore calls upon the choir of the heavenly voices to join in the response which alone is worthy of the revelation of the divine glory. The angels and the mighty ones, God's heavenly hosts and his servants, the whole celestial household of the Ruler of the universe shall unite with the whole creation on earth in singing in a powerful crescendo the chorale which proclaims the glory of God in all the places of his eternal Kingdom (see Intr. 41). The poet now expounds some of the most profound ideas of the biblical tradition such as we also find in First Isaiah and in Deutero-Isaiah, in the history of creation as well as in Ps. 19.1 ff. His eyes and ears are now wide open to the first and last theme of all that comes to pass in the world, the theme which Isaiah had heard the seraphim sing: 'Holy, holy, holy is the Lord of hosts; the whole earth is full of his glory.' At this point the psalmist reverts to the beginning of his psalm and calls upon his soul to join in this world-wide chorale sung to the praise of God. But now his song re-echoes with all the notes which he has struck in the psalm. He has been granted an insight into the heart of the majesty of God, and what he has found there is grace.

104. GOD'S CREATION

1 Bless the Lord, O my soul! ' '1
   My God, thou art very great!
   Thou art clothed with honour and majesty,

2 who coverest thyself with light as with a garment,
  who hast stretched out[1] the heavens like a tent,
3 who hast laid the beams of thy balcony[2] on the waters,
  who makest the clouds thy chariot,
  who ridest on the wings of the wind,
4 who makest the winds thy messengers,
  fire and flame thy ministers,
5 who[1] didst set the earth on its foundations,
  so that it should never be shaken.
6 The deep covered it as with a garment,[3]
  the waters stood above the mountains.
7 At thy rebuke they fled;
  at the sound of thy thunder they took to flight.
8 Then the mountains rose, the valleys sank down
  to the place which thou didst appoint for them.
9 Thou didst set a bound which they should not pass,
  so that they might not again cover the earth.
10 Thou makest springs gush forth in[1] streams;
  they flow between the mountains,[4]
11 they give drink to every beast of the field;
  the wild asses quench their thirst.
12 By them the birds of the air have their habitation;
  they sing their songs among the branches.
13 From thy lofty abode thou waterest the mountains;
  the earth is satisfied with the gift of thy heaven.[5]
14 Thou dost cause the grass to grow for the cattle,
  and seed for man to cultivate,
  that he may bring forth bread from the earth.[6]
15 And let wine gladden the heart of man,
  so that oil may make his face shine[7]
  and bread may refresh his[1] heart.[8]
16 The trees of the Lord are sated,
  the cedars of Lebanon which he planted.[9]
17 In them the birds build their nests;
  the stork has her home in their tops.[1]
18 The high mountains are the preserve of the wild goats,
  the rocks are a refuge for the badgers.
19 He made the moon to mark the seasons,
  and the sun that knows its time for setting.[10]
20 Thou makest darkness, and it is night,
  when all the beasts of the forest creep forth.
21 The young lions roar for their prey,
  seeking their food from God.
22 When the sun rises, they return
  and lie down in their dens.[11]
23 Then man goes forth to his work
  and to his labour until the evening.
24 O Lord, how manifold are thy works!

In wisdom hast thou made them all;
the earth is full of thy blessings.[12]

25 There is the sea, so great and so wide,
which teems with things innumerable,
beasts both small and great.

26 Sea-monsters[1] swim therein,
Leviathan which thou didst form for thyself as a plaything.[13]

27 These all look to thee,
that thou givest them their food in due season.

28 When thou givest to them, they gather it up;
when thou openest thy hand, they are sated ' '.[14]

29 When thou hidest thy face, they are dismayed;
when thou takest away their breath,
they die and return to their dust.

30 When thou sendest forth thy breath, they are created;
thus thou renewest the face of the earth.[15]

31 May the glory of the Lord endure for ever,
may the Lord rejoice in his works!

32 When he looks on the earth with anger, it trembles;
when he touches the mountains, they belch forth smoke.[16]

33 I will sing to the Lord as long as I live;
I will make melody to my God while I have being.[17]

34 May my meditation be pleasing to him,
for I rejoice in the Lord.

35 Let sinners be consumed from the earth,
and let the wicked be no more!
Bless the Lord, O my soul![18]

[1] See BH.

[2] * RSV has 'chambers' instead of 'balcony'.

[3] * V. 6a reads in RSV, 'Thou didst cover it with the deep as with a garment.'

[4] * RSV has 'in the valleys' instead of 'in streams' and 'hills' instead of 'mountains'.

[5] Read *šāmekā*. (Tr. N.: V. 13b is in RSV 'the earth is satisfied with the fruit of thy work'.)

[6] * RSV has 'plants' instead of 'seed' and 'food' instead of 'bread'.

[7] As a symbol of festal joy; cf. Ps. 23.5 and Luke 7.46.

[8] * V. 15 is in RSV:
and wine to gladden the heart of man,
oil to make his face shine,
and bread to strengthen man's heart.

[9] * RSV has 'are watered abundantly' instead of 'are sated'.

[10] * V. 19 in RSV begins the first line with 'thou hast made the moon . . .' and the second with 'the sun knows . . .'

[11] * The first line of v. 22 is in RSV: 'When the sun rises, they get them away.'

[12] * RSV has 'full of thy creatures' instead of 'full of thy blessings'.

[13] * RSV reads:
There go the ships,
and Leviathan which thou didst form to sport in it.

[14] See BH. (Tr. N.: RSV reads, 'they are filled with good things' instead of 'they are sated'.)

¹⁵ * RSV has 'thy Spirit' instead of 'thy breath' and the second line of v. 30 reads, 'and thou renewest the face of the ground'.
¹⁶ * V. 32 is in RSV:
who looks on the earth and it trembles,
who touches the mountains and they smoke!
¹⁷ * RSV has 'I will sing praise' instead of 'I will make melody'.
¹⁸ * RSV adds 'Praise the Lord!' after 'Bless the Lord, O my soul!'

As far as poetic value is concerned, Psalm 104 is certainly one of the most beautiful in the Psalter. The relation of this nature-hymn to the story of creation in the first chapters of Genesis is like that of a coloured picture to the clear lines of a woodcut. This impression is perhaps to be accounted for by the fact that both have their origin in a common cultic tradition (cf. the comments on vv. 2–4, 32 f.). The psalmist is a man who combines the capacity for profound religious thought with the gift of reflecting on nature with an affectionate intimacy; moreover, he possesses the talent of giving immortal expression to sentiments which are sublime and powerful as well as sweet and tender. The way in which he sees beauty and purpose in the world extolling the glory and wisdom of its Creator, however, also shows his independence of tradition. The picture of the world which is in his mind bears the imprint of the spirit of his age and, in composing it, the psalmist has made use of the most varied features of the contemporary world-view to which we can find numerous parallels in Babylonian, Egyptian, Greek and Nordic mythology; it is, however, hardly possible to assume that the psalmist has directly drawn on these parallels (cf. in this connection Gunkel's more detailed discussion; see Intr. 34, 59 f.). The most striking of these features is the affinity of the psalm to the well-known hymn to the Sun composed by the Egyptian king Ikhnaton[1] at the beginning of the fourteenth century BC.

The theme (v. 1)
[1] A brief summons to himself to sing the praise of God, to which the poet reverts at the end of the psalm, is followed by a devout exclamation of wonder at the greatness and glory of God. That utterance powerfully sums up the occasion for the whole psalm, its spirit and its fundamental ideas: here a man sees himself standing before God, to whom he confesses in a hymnic prayer the thoughts which fill his soul. What he perceives in nature and what he knows

[1] * Pharaoh Amenophis IV, who reigned from 1375–1358 BC.

about the origin of the world and its life, again, what he thinks about
the question of what it is that at bottom keeps the world in being,
all these things in their own way tell him of the *one* mighty God and
exemplify to him his majesty and wisdom.

The heavens (vv. 2–4)

[2–4] The poet's eye and thought first linger on the theophany
of God from heaven. It tells him of the omnipotence of God, the
heavenly King. The brilliance of the heavenly light in which he
appears is his glorious royal robe; he has miraculously built his
royal palace—on firm pillars in the rolling waters of the celestial sea,
above the canopy of heaven; he uses the clouds as his chariot (cf.
Ps. 18.10 f.; see Intr. 29); the wind is his winged horse; the elemental
forces of nature such as storm and lightning are the servants of the
'Lord of the heavenly hosts' who attend his epiphany. The poet has
taken his colours from the palette of the ancient nature-mythology,
which has been preserved longest in the language of the cultus, and
has painted with them this picture which, subduing everything that
is of a mythical and pagan nature, serves the representation of one
religious idea only: the idea that God has created that celestial
world *for his own sake* so that it may serve his will, bear witness to his
power and wisdom, and reveal his glory; a thought which states for
all ages to come the ultimate meaning of all study of nature (cf.
Rom. 11.36).

The earth (vv. 5–9)

[5–9] The poet with equal awe and wonder reflects on the origin
of the earth: God has driven away the primeval flood which once
covered the mountains (v. 6) by the voice of his thunder—a reminiscence of the ancient myth of the combat of the gods against the powers
of chaos—(v. 7; cf. the comments on vv. 24–26; see Intr. 60 f.) and has
set an impassable bound to the water (v. 9; cf. Job 38.10 f.). Thus the
earth, shaped like a circular disk, now floats on the ocean and is yet
firmly established on invisible foundations (v. 5); like the celestial
palace it is a wonderful miracle wrought by God! It is the first step
from chaos to cosmos! Though our ideas of the world and of its
origin may be different from those of antiquity, the impulses of faith
which lie at the root of these ideas, *awe* at the creative power of God
that subdues the elements and *trust* in his omnipotent will as revealed
to us in the fixed orbits of the ordered universe, are equally essential

elements of a belief in creation even in the relation to a modern view of nature.

The living things on earth (vv. 10–18)

[10–18] The portrayal of the origin of life on earth directly continues the thoughts which have been developed so far. Not content with laying the foundation of the universe by subduing the waters of the primeval flood and by appointing a fixed place for them as the celestial and subterranean oceans (vv. 3, 7 ff.), God did something even more miraculous in using these waters in the service of his creation in order, with their help, to establish life on earth. From the subterranean ocean rise the springs and flow the streams on whose banks the beasts lead a pleasant life (vv. 10–12); from the celestial ocean flows the 'heavenly gift' of rain (v. 13; on this conception cf. Gen. 7.11; 8.2) and accomplishes the miracle of clothing the parched brown earth with welcome verdure, so that it affords a habitation and food for man and beast (vv. 14–18). With consummate poetic skill in miniature the poet intersperses this train of thought with charming scenes which afford a glimpse of mountains and valleys, forests and fields, gardens and vineyards; they are individual word-pictures which are among the most beautiful which Old Testament lyric poetry has to offer. However, the poet's enthusiasm for nature derives ultimately not from his joy in discovering the variegated wealth of its several beauties but from the grandeur of his total religious view of the whole of nature as a single all-embracing organism based on a divine and meaningful world-order. From the perspective of God, the mighty Creator and Lord of the earth, he is able to understand the individual scene on which his mind's eye lovingly dwells; and for this reason the smallest details, even those things which do not serve any human purpose (vv. 11, 16–18), fill him with a deep sense of devotion, because they vividly reveal to him the glory and the wisdom of the Creator.

Moon and Sun (vv. 19–23)

[19–23] The thought of the vast living organism of the divine cosmos leads the singer's gaze back to the heavens. The ordering of small things corresponds with that of the great ones. How could life be possible unless in addition to *space* (vv. 2–18) *time*, too, is subject to a wise control! For this purpose God in his wisdom created the sun and the moon to serve as the world's great time-pieces. From their position and shape man, living close to nature and not yet knowing mechanical clocks and printed calendars, directly gathers the chronological order as willed and 'taught' by God (v. 19; cf. Gen. 1.14). The poet once more illustrates with the help of a particular scene, in which he combines with eminent and unsurpassed skill an excellent power of observation and a striking poetic vividness, the fundamental religious idea of God's order of creation. God's wisdom is proved by the fact that he has reserved the night to the wild beasts of the forest, but the day to man for his work; thus neither of them interferes with the life of the other (vv. 20–23). Here we see the full depth of the psalmist's theocentric attitude of faith which makes him to think only of God and not of himself and enables him to sense even in the grim nightly prowling of the beasts of prey the loving care and wisdom of God's provision and to interpret the horrid roaring of the lions as their prayer to God for food (cf. Job 38.41).

The sea (vv. 24–26)

[24–26] The profundity of this knowledge based on faith draws from the poet an exclamation of wonder at the abundance of the divine wisdom and works (v. 24). Then he lets his mind's eye rove more widely over the vast and almost unending expanse of the sea which teems with innumerable animals. The infinitely great and the infinitely little—and all of them are God's handiwork and belong to him. Even the sea-monsters of which man can think only with terror —it is possible that behind the term 'Leviathan' lurks the ancient mythological idea of the chaos-monster as the embodiment of the primeval flood—are created by God for his own sake 'as playthings'. This last word strangely combines sublime power of the poet's religious vision and the childlike directness of its profundity. It was the strength of the monotheistic belief in God that it transformed the primeval world-dragon, of whom the story was told that he was once defeated in his combat against the creator-god, into a pliant creature of God—in Gen. 1.2 there is, strange to say, no mention of God's creation of the 'primeval flood' ('the deep'). And it betrays a moving naïveté and the profound insight of the purest piety, that the poet here finds the religious meaning of creation in God's joy in his creature ('to play with him'), a joy that is entirely detached from any thought of human calculation or expediency (cf. Job 40.29).

God the Preserver of Life (vv. 27–30)

[27–30] Just as God brought every living thing into existence, so through him its life is preserved. Here we get a charming picture: the whole creation is waiting for God that, like a benevolent lord of the manor, he may open his hand and scatter food so that everybody may have enough (vv. 27 f.; cf. Ps. 145.15 f.). But the serious aspects of life, death and passing likewise speak to the poet of God's power. Life is the breath of God: when he holds his breath, then what is alive becomes dust (v. 29); on the other hand, when he breathes out, then new life comes into being. This is a magnificent and deeply religious interpretation of the coming into being and passing away of everything in Nature (v. 30)! Because the psalmist envisages the world in the light of God's affirmation of it, he does not stop at the tragic aspect of dying, but discerns in the coming into being and passing away of living things the conquest of death by means of the continual process of re-creation by the ever-active, ever-living God. That this is not a frivolous optimism which deliberately shuts its eyes to the dark side of life is demonstrated by the *serious thoughts with which the poet brings his hymn to a close.* **[31–35]** It is his most ardent desire that the 'glory' of God, to which his whole psalm is devoted, may endure for ever and that God's joy in the work of his hands, the reflection of which in the heart of the poet shines throughout the psalm, may never be clouded (v. 31). But he is also aware of the fact that God's answer can be a negative one; he is aware of the awesome majesty of one who stalks the world in huge catastrophes, in earthquakes and in fires (probably an allusion to the Sinai theophany) and destroys what seeks to oppose him (v. 32). Hence the striking petition that the sinners and the wicked may be consumed from the earth (v. 35). The idea of the elimination and annihilation of the wicked originates in the cult (see Intr. 32 f., 46 ff.). It is the wicked who by their rejection of and rebellion against God stifle the thanksgiving which is due to him and thus dim the glory of the divine creation. The poet longs for the time when God's joy in his creature and the creature's joy in his Maker (v. 34) will unite in perfect harmony, but he does so not from hatred of the sinners but because of the purity of his joy in God and in his creation. The cultic tradition and the psalmist's joyous affirmation of God are the source both of this longing and of the vow, in which the poet once more unreservedly opens his heart to God, that his whole life shall be a song of praise to the glory of God (v. 33; the votive formula in v. 34a indicates the connection of the psalm with the cult; see Intr. 69 f., 79 f., 85 f.). Thus not only nature as this poet was able to see it but the poet's whole life is radiant with God's sunshine. Who would not gladly let himself be guided by such a child of God's light when he calls to us, 'Go out, my heart, and search for joy!'?[1]

[1] * This is the opening line of Paul Gerhardt's hymn 'Geh aus, mein Herz, und suche Freud.'

105. THE DIVINE COVENANT

1 O testify to the Lord,[1] call on his name,
  make known his deeds among the peoples!
2 Sing and make melody to him,[2]
  tell of all his wonderful works!
3 Glory in his holy name;
  let the hearts of those who seek the Lord rejoice!
4 Seek the Lord and his strength,
  seek his face continually!
5 Remember the wonderful works that he has done,
  his miracles, and the judgments he uttered.
6 O you offspring of Abraham his servant,
  sons of Jacob, his chosen one![3]
7 He, the Lord, he is our God;
  his judgments are in all the earth.[4]
8 He is mindful of his covenant for ever,
  of the word that he commanded for a thousand generations,
9 the covenant which he made with Abraham,
  and his sworn promise to Isaac.
10 He confirmed it to Jacob as a statute,
  to Israel as an everlasting covenant ' ',[5]
11 saying, 'To you I will give the land of Canaan
  as your portion for an inheritance.'
12 When they were few in number,
  of little account, and sojourners in it,
13 they wandered from nation to nation,
  from one kingdom to another people.
14 But he allowed no one to oppress them;
  he rebuked kings on their account,
15 saying, 'Touch not my anointed ones,
  do my prophets no harm!'
16 Then he summoned a famine on the land,
  and broke every staff of bread.[6]
17 He sent a man ahead of them,
  Joseph, who was sold as a slave.[6]
18 His feet[5] were put in the stocks,
  he came to lie in[5] fetters of iron;[7]

19 until what he had said came to pass,
    the word of the Lord tested him.
20 The king sent and released him,
    the ruler of the peoples set him free;
21 he made him lord of his house,
    and ruler of all his possessions,
22 to punish[8] his princes at his pleasure,
    and to teach his elders wisdom.
23 Then Israel came to Egypt;
    Jacob sojourned in the land of Ham.
24 But he made his people very fruitful,[9]
    and made them stronger than their oppressors.
25 He turned their hearts to hate his people,
    to deal craftily with his servants.
26 Then he sent Moses his servant,
    and Aaron whom he had chosen.
27 He wrought[5] his signs among them,
    and miracles in the land of Ham.
28 He sent darkness, and made the land dark;
    but they did not give heed[5] to his words.[10]
29 He turned their waters into blood,
    and caused their fish to die.
30 Their land swarmed with frogs,
    they came into the chambers of the king.[11]
31 He spoke, and there came swarms of flies,
    and gnats throughout their country.
32 He gave them hail for rain,
    and flaming fire in their land.[12]
33 He smote their vines and figtrees,
    and shattered the trees of their country.
34 He spoke, and the locusts came,
    and young locusts without number.
35 They devoured all the vegetation in their land,
    and ate up the fruit of their ground.
36 He smote all the first-born in their land,
    the first issue of all their strength.
37 Then he led them forth with silver and gold,
    and there was none among their tribes who stumbled.[13]
38 Egypt was glad when they departed,
    for dread of them had fallen upon it.
39 He spread a cloud for a covering,
    and fire to give light by night.
40 They asked,[5] and he brought quails;
    he satisfied them with bread from heaven.[14]
41 He opened the rock, and water gushed forth;
    it flowed through the desert like a river.
42 For he remembered his holy promise
    to Abraham, his servant.[15]

43 So he led forth his people with joy,
   his chosen ones with singing.
44 And he gave them the lands of the Gentiles;
   and they took possession of the fruit of the peoples' toil,
45 to the end that they should keep his statutes,
   and observe his laws. Hallelujah.[16]

[1] * V. 1 opens in RSV, 'O give thanks to the Lord'.
[2] * The first line of v. 2 reads in RSV: 'Sing to him, sing praises to him.'
[3] See BH. (Tr. N.: RSV has 'his chosen ones'.)
[4] * V. 7a reads in RSV: 'He is the Lord our God.'
[5] See BH.
[6] * In RSV vv. 16 and 17 form one sentence, reading as follows:
     (16) When he summoned a famine on the land,
          and broke every staff of bread,
     (17) he had sent a man ahead of them,
          Joseph, who was sold as a slave.
[7] * V. 18 is in RSV:
     His feet were hurt with fetters,
     his neck was put in a collar of iron.
[8] * RSV has 'instruct' instead of 'punish'.
[9] * RSV reads 'And the Lord made' instead of 'But he made'.
[10] * V. 28b reads in RSV, 'they rebelled against his words'.
[11] See BH. (Tr. N.: V. 30b is in RSV 'even in the chambers of their kings'.)
[12] * RSV renders v. 32b: 'and lightning that flashed through their land'.
[13] * RSV has 'led forth Israel' instead of 'led them forth'.
[14] * In RSV v. 40b is 'and gave them bread from heaven in abundance'.
[15] * RSV has 'and Abraham his servant'.
[16] See Intr. 22. (Tr. N.: RSV has 'Praise the Lord' instead of 'Hallelujah'.)

The fact that in I Chron. 16.8–22 Ps. 105.1–15 is quoted as a
festal hymn, together with the Enthronement Psalm 96 and Ps.
106.47 f., in connection with the narration of David's solemn
bringing up of the Ark of the Covenant to Mount Zion, serves to
remind us that the psalm was originally used in the festival cult of
the Yahweh community. For the opening verses 1–6 make it
abundantly clear that the psalm is not to be regarded as a didactic
poem but as a cultic hymn of the covenant community. The 'offspring
of Abraham', the 'sons of Jacob', are addressed as the bearers of the
covenant tradition (cf. v. 10). They have appeared as festival
pilgrims at the covenant shrine (vv. 3 f.; 'to seek God' or 'to seek his
face' is a technical term for the pilgrimage to the holy place; cf.
Amos 5.4) to rejoice in the presence of their God with loud shouts of
joy, to remember his saving deeds, and to make them known among
the peoples in songs of praise so that God may be glorified. The
'hymn' proper, which begins in v. 7, follows the sacred tradition of

P.–Y

the divine saving deeds; it takes them for granted and is to be understood as the response of the cult community to the revelation of God, his name (vv. 1–3) and his might (v. 4) which had just taken place at the cultic ceremony by means of the representation and actualization of the sacred story, and which was followed by the solemn renewal of the covenant between God and his people (see Intr. 28 ff., 41 f., 56 ff.). accounts, on the one hand, for the psalm's affinity to the Pentateuchal tradition of the *Heilsgeschichte*, which in its turn is to be understood as the literary record of the cultic representation of the *Heilsgeschichte*, and, on the other hand, for the variations in details which make a direct literary dependence of the psalm on the Pentateuch or on one of its sources appear improbable. **[1–6]** The hymnic introduction (vv. 1–6), whose beginning is comparable to that of Pss. 106.1; 107.1; 118.1; 136.1, is addressed to the covenant community, and calls upon them to participate in the cultic ceremony through prayers, hymns and the hymnic praise of God. They are assembled in the sanctuary, not only in their obvious rôle as descendants of Abraham and Jacob, but also as the bearers of the promises of blessing made to the Patriarchs, in order to celebrate the presence of their God as in other years (this is the meaning of vv. 3b and 4b), with songs and stringed instruments (v. 2a), through testimonies and prayers (v. 1a), and through the ritual proclamation of God's wonderful saving deeds (vv. 1, 2, 5) and of his judgments. In this manner the psalm provides an insight into an essential constituent part of the Old Testament cult of the Covenant Festival.[1]

[7–11] The theme of the hymn which follows is briefly sketched in the cult community's testimony, introduced by the 'covenant formula', to the God who established his covenant with their forefathers and promised them the land for an inheritance, and whose law and order are binding on every age and every part of the earth, so that his judgment embraces the whole world. That theme is the fulfilment of the promises made to the forefathers, to which the account given in vv. 12–41 is devoted. This makes clear how the people of God interpreted their historical traditions as God's *Heilsgeschichte*, as his miraculous acts that continually led men to

[1] In the liturgy of the feast of the renewal of the covenant at Qumran the praise of God (cf. vv. 1–6) is the duty of the priests and Levites; the proclamation of the saving deeds of Yahweh (cf. vv. 12–41) is the duty of the priests. Accordingly it may be assumed that from the standpoint of the history of tradition the main substance of the psalm is to be regarded as a kind of prototype for this last-mentioned portion of a festival liturgy.

salvation, and how they continually experienced them in the cult as a living present reality related to their own lives. In these statements God is almost always the subject of the action (vv. 14, 16 f., 24 ff., 39); the story serves to prove his 'faithfulness and grace' (see Intr. 43). As in the Decalogue, so here, too, God is first the Giver before he makes demands (v. 45).

[12-15] The first section (vv. 12-15), alluding to the wanderings of the Patriarchs, stresses the thought that from the smallest beginnings and through their seemingly aimless wanderings to and fro God carries out his plan of salvation in spite of all the dangers that imperil his promise (vv. 14 f. have in view the story of the danger which threatened Sarah; cf. Gen. 12.10 ff.; 20.6). [16-23] Under the aspect of the same fundamental religious idea that God accomplishes his purposes contrary to every human calculation and expectation, Joseph's rise in Egypt is briefly referred to in vv. 16-23, in a form which indicates their independence of the account given in Genesis (see above). [24-38] The story of the Exodus from Egypt is mentioned in even greater detail, but here, too, in a form which presupposes a proper narrative account of the events, which are here only briefly referred to, and only intended to recall this account but not to replace it. At the same time it accords with the peculiar character of the faith expressed in the hymn that again all the miraculous events are traced back to God as the subject of the action, while the men who had a share in them either recede into the background or sink in complete insignificance. This *Heilsgeschichte* treatment of events has developed a style of its own which clearly differs from that of pure historical narrative and is to be accounted for by the fact that religious thought is directly related to God. Joy in the power of God, which triumphs over every obstacle and in a wonderful way achieves its objects, is the active response which the actualization of the *Heilsgeschichte* evokes in the congregation. [39-41] The miracles that occurred during the wilderness wanderings are dealt with more briefly: the psalm mentions the pillars of cloud and of fire, the miraculous feeding with manna and quails (cf. Ex. 16.3 ff.; Num. 11.4 ff., 31 ff.) and the water from the rock (Ex. 17.6 f.; Num. 20.11 ff.). The conception of the pillar of cloud as a covering 'spread' like a canopy has no parallel in the Pentateuch. It must be related to the idea of the cloud as the chariot of the Deity, which belongs to the tradition of the theophany and in its turn has found its cultic representation in the winged cherubim upon the sacred Ark (cf. Ex. 33.9 ff.; 18 ff.; see Intr. 28 ff.).

[42–45] The conclusion reverts to the beginning (cf. vv. 7 ff.) and once more throws into bold relief the fundamental idea of the fulfilment of the covenant promises. God constantly keeps in mind his pledge to the fathers; his promises are valid for ever. The rejoicing of the people at the Exodus (this is probably a reference to the hymn in Ex. ch. 15) has once testified to this truth, and it is confirmed again for their own day by the triumphant song with which the members of the cult community once more celebrate the saving deeds of their God (cf. vv. 1 ff.). The grace of God, who first gives before he makes demands, is followed at the end of the psalm by a very brief reference to the covenantal duty of obedience in response to the manifestation of the divine will, which has had its place in the liturgy of the festival cult in exactly the same way as the revelation of God's nature (cf. Ex. 19.5 ff.; 20.1 ff.; see Intr. 31 f.). We are probably not mistaken in assuming that in this context the Decalogue, which exhibits the same basic structure of an inner link between God's grace and his statutes, had its place in the annual festival cult as the second prerequisite of the renewal of the Covenant which was executed by means of a ritual act. This would explain the parenetic note of the *Heilsgeschichte* which is sounded throughout the psalm (cf. also the exposition of Psalm 106).[1]

[1] This parenetic note, which aims at the renewal of the Covenant, also dominates the liturgy of the feast of the Covenant at Qumran and is particularly emphasized in its introductory portions.

106. THE GRACE OF GOD AND THE SIN OF THE PEOPLE

1 Hallelujah!
   O testify to the Lord, for he is good;
   for his steadfast love endures for ever![1]
2 Who can utter the mighty doings of the Lord,
   and show forth all his praise?
3 Blessed are they who observe justice,
   who do[2] righteousness at all times!
4 Remember us,[2] O Lord, by showing favour to thy people;
   visit us[2] with thy salvation;[3]
5 that we may see the prosperity of thy chosen ones,
   that we may rejoice in the gladness of thy people,
   that we may sing praises with thy heritage.[4]
6 Both we and our fathers have sinned;
   we have committed iniquity and[2] have done wickedly.
7 Our fathers, when they were in Egypt,
   did not consider thy wonderful works;

they did not remember the abundance of thy grace,
but rebelled against the Most High[2] at the Red Sea.
8 Yet he saved them for his name's sake,
that he might make known his mighty power.
9 He rebuked the Red Sea, and it became dry;
and he let them march through the deep as through pasture-land.[5]
10 So he saved them from the hand of the hater,[6]
and delivered them from the power of the enemy.
11 And the waters covered their oppressors;
not one of them survived.
12 Then they believed his words;
they sang his praise.
13 But they soon forgot his works
and[2] did not wait for his counsel.
14 They had a wanton craving in the wilderness,
and put God to the test in the desert.
15 Then he gave them what they asked,
but sent a wasting disease among them.
16 They inveighed against Moses in the camp,
against Aaron, the holy one of the Lord.[7]
17 The earth opened and swallowed up Dathan,
and covered the band of Abiram.[7]
18 Fire also broke out in their company;
the flame burned up the wicked.
19 They made a calf in Horeb
and then worshipped the molten image.[8]
20 They exchanged their glory
for the image of an ox that eats grass.[9]
21 They forgot God, their Saviour,
who had done great things in Egypt,
22 wondrous works in the land of Ham,
and terrible things by the Red Sea.
23 Therefore he meant to destroy them—
had not Moses, his chosen one,
stood in the breach before him,
to turn away his wrath from destroying them.
24 Then they despised the pleasant land,
having no faith in his promise.
25 They murmured in their tents,
and did not obey the voice of the Lord.
26 Therefore he raised his hand against them
to make them fall in the wilderness,[10]
27 to disperse[2] their seed among the Gentiles,
scattering them over the lands.[10]
28 They attached themselves to the Baal of Peor,
and ate sacrifices offered for the dead;[11]
29 they provoked the Lord to anger with their doings,
and a plague broke out among them.

30 Then Phineas stood up and gave judgment,[12]
  and the plague was stayed.
31 That has been reckoned to him as righteousness
  from generation to generation for ever.
32 They angered him at the waters of contention,[13]
  and it went ill with Moses on their account;
33 for they made his spirit bitter,
  and he spoke words that were rash.
. 34 They did not destroy the peoples
  as the Lord commanded them,
35 but they mingled with the Gentiles
  and learned to do as they did.
36 They served their idols,
  which became a snare to them.
37 They sacrificed their sons
  and their daughters to the idols;[14]
38 they shed innocent blood ' ',[15]
  so that the land was polluted through blood-guilt.
39 Thus they became unclean by their acts,
  and were unfaithful[16] in their doings.
40 Then the anger of the Lord was kindled against his people,
  and he abhorred his heritage;
41 he gave them into the hand of the Gentiles,
  so that those who hated them ruled over them.
42 And their enemies oppressed them;
  they were brought into subjection to their power.
43 Many times he delivered them,
  but they opposed his[2] counsel ' '.[17]
44 Nevertheless he regarded their distress,
  when he heard their cry.
45 He remembered for their sake his covenant,
  and relented according to the abundance of his steadfast love.
46 He caused them to be pitied
  by all those who held them captive.
47 Save us, O Lord our God,
  and gather us from among the Gentiles,
  that we may testify to thy holy name
  and glory in thy praise!
48 Blessed be the Lord, the God of Israel,
  from everlasting to everlasting!
  And let all the people say, 'Amen!'
  Hallelujah!

[1] * RSV opens with 'Praise the Lord' instead of 'Hallelujah', and then continues 'O give thanks to the Lord, for he is good. . . .'
[2] See BH.
[3] * In RSV v. 4 is:
  Remember me, O Lord, when thou showest favour to thy people;
  help me when thou deliverest them;

4 * RSV has 'I' instead of 'we' throughout, and 'glory' instead of 'sing praises'.
5 * V. 9b reads in RSV, 'and he led them through the deep as through a desert'.
6 * RSV has 'foe' instead of 'hater'.
7 * In RSV vv. 16 and 17 form a single sentence reading:
> (16) When men in the camp were jealous of Moses
>   and Aaron, the holy one of the Lord,
> (17) the earth opened and swallowed up Dathan,
>   and covered the company of Abiram.

8 * V. 19b is in RSV 'and worshipped a molten image'.
9 * RSV has 'the glory of God' instead of 'their glory'.
10 * In RSV vv. 26 and 27 are:
> (26) Therefore he raised his hand and swore to them
>   that he would make them fall in the wilderness,
> (27) and would disperse their descendants among the nations,
>   scattering them over the lands.

11 * RSV has 'sacrifices offered to the dead'.
12 * RSV reads 'and interposed' instead of 'and gave judgment'.
13 * RSV has 'the waters of Meribah' (which means 'the waters of contention').
14 * RSV has 'demons' instead of 'idols'.
15 The sentence 'the blood of their sons and daughters whom they sacrificed to the idols of Canaan' is an explanatory gloss in prose. (Tr. N.: RSV includes this sentence in v. 38 after the first line.)
16 Lit.: they played the harlot. (Tr. N.: In RSV v. 39b reads, 'and played the harlot in their doings'.)
17 See BH. (Tr. N.: V. 43 reads in RSV after the first line:
> but they were rebellious in their purposes,
> and were brought low through their iniquity.)

This psalm, too, like Psalm 105, seems to be connected with the autumn festival and its tradition of the *Heilsgeschichte*. This is suggested not only by the way in which vv. 1, 47 f. are used in I Chron. 16.34 ff. (see the exposition of Psalm 105), but also by the opening verses 1–5, which are to be understood as a preparation for the experiencing and praising of the saving deeds of Yahweh in the right spirit (vv. 2 f.), and which according to v. 4 seem to have had a place in the cultic ceremony preceding the actual revelation of God's salvation. It is improbable that the psalm was originally united with Psalm 105 in a single composition; for despite the similarity of structure of the two psalms, no doubt occasioned by the liturgical tradition, their fundamental tendency is too different. In Psalm 105 the thanksgiving for the saving acts of God in history and therefore the obedience owed to him are central; in Psalm 106, on the other hand, the ingratitude and disobedience of the people are at the centre, so that it is more closely related to Psalm 78 and in its basic mood is to be compared rather with a national penitential lament. In my view it is possible to explain the different outlook of Psalms 105 and 106, which is striking in view of the similarity of the outline

of the *Heilsgeschichte* underlying both these psalms, in the light of the
liturgy of the Qumran *Manual of Discipline*.

The liturgy of the annual feast of the renewal of the Covenant
includes amongst other items:

1 The praise of God in a hymn sung by the priests and Levites and the
   congregation's response, 'Amen. Amen.'
2 The recital by the priests of the divine saving deeds (*ṣidᵉqōt 'el*).
3 The recital by the Levites of the 'sins of the Israelites'.
4 The confession of sins of those who 'enter into the Covenant', made in
   recognition of God's righteousness and mercy.[1]

Whereas the tendency and main content of Psalm 105 invite
comparison with the narrative of God's saving deeds spoken by the
priests (see 2 above), we may look in Psalm 106 for the Old Testament prototype in the history of tradition of the recital by the
Levites of the sins of the Israelites (3). The *Heilsgeschichte* as the basis
common to both these psalms as well as the dissimilarity of their
points of view (the righteousness and grace of God on the one hand
and the sins of his people on the other), which fundamentally belong
together from the theological point of view, are most easily accounted
for if these two modes of reflecting upon the *Heilsgeschichte* have once
been constituent parts of one and the same covenantal liturgy. This
is perhaps also the reason why the Psalter has handed down the two
psalms side by side. The date of the psalm cannot be determined with
any degree of certainty; vv. 46 f. do not necessarily presuppose the
Babylonian exile, as is almost universally held; nor do they compel
us to assume that the psalm was composed or recited by the exiles.

[1] The opening verses 1–5, which some expositors—to my mind
wrongly—want to link with Psalm 105, begin like that psalm with a
call to the community to testify to the everlasting goodness of God of
which they are once more made aware in the cult by the abundance
of his saving deeds, which are the main content of the manifestation
of his character. [2] Human speech is neither able nor worthy to
proclaim to the congregation to the glory of God his mighty acts—
we have probably to think of these words as having been uttered by
the priest, whereas v. 1b was recited as a response either by the
congregation or by a chorus (cf. Pss. 118.2–4; 136). The guilty
conscience of the community already casts on these opening verses a
shadow which lies on the whole psalm. [3] Against such a background
the petition for blessing in v. 3 sounds like an exhortation to obey

[1] Burrows, *The Dead Sea Scrolls* II, pl. I, 18—II, 1.

the divine commandments which are likewise made known to the covenant community within the framework of the ritual. **[4–5]** The supplication in vv. 4 f., that God may think favourably of his people, probably refers to the promises of salvation and to the saving acts whose renewed realization in the course of the festival worship is awaited by the community and is to end in the jubilant hymn of the chosen covenant people.[1]

But for this to happen the guilt that separates the people from their God must first be removed. The main part of the psalm (vv. 6–46) serves this purpose by means of its singular way of looking at the tradition of the *Heilsgeschichte*, that is by reflecting upon the acts of grace which God in his mercy has continually wrought for the sake of his people in spite of their frequent ingratitude and disobedience (vv. 44 f.). This confession of guilt based on their history and applied also to the present is the way of repentance in which God's goodness guides his people so that they are once more able to lift up their hands and hearts to him in supplication for his blessings (v. 47; cf. I Kings 8.46 ff.; Neh. 9.33; Dan. 9.5 ff.). **[6]** The confession of guilt including both past and present and uniting the members of the congregation with their forefathers before God[2] makes evident and impressive the weight of the responsibility of all history to God if that responsibility is related to the present. **[7–12]** To begin with, the tradition of the Exodus from Egypt is considered from the point of view of the unbelief of the people who negligently pass by the wonderful works of God and rebel against his will; the variations from the tradition of the Pentateuch (cf. v. 7 with Ex. 14.10 ff.; v. 9 with Ex. 14.15 f.; v. 12 with Ex. 14.31) show that there can be no question of a direct literary dependence by the psalm on the Pentateuch; both of them seem to originate in a common cultic, liturgical tradition. As in Psalm 105, so here history serves to demonstrate the power of God and to reveal his salvation in spite of the opposition of the people; it is—this, too, is to be understood in the light of the cultus—*Heilsgeschichte*, that is to say, evidence of the presence of God in everything that has come to pass (cf. Isa. 63.10 ff.); this is also shown in the cultic hymn in Ex. ch. 15, to which v. 12 seems to allude. **[13–15]** Compared with the account of Num.

---

[1] Cf. in this context the 'confession' of the members of the Covenant, mentioned above under no. 4 in connection with the liturgy of the *Manual of Discipline*.

[2] Cf. the similar text of the confession of sins in the *Manual* which unfortunately is preserved only in part.

11.4 ff., the interpretation of the story of the quails and of the graves
of the people who had the craving has its own emphasis, while it is
noticeable that, in the reference to the rebellion of Dathan and
Abiram **[16–18]** (cf. Num. 16; 26.9 ff.), the company of Korah is
not named as well. **[19–23]** In view of the purpose of enumerating
the sins committed in the course of the nation's history, the mention
of the story of the golden calf (Ex. 32; Deut. 9.8 ff.), the refusal of
the people to believe the spies **[24–27]** (cf. Num. 13; 14), the people's
defection to the idolatrous Moabite worship of the Baal of Peor
[28–31] (notice the variation from Num. 25), and the story of the
waters of contention **[32–33]** (cf. Num. 20.2 ff.) are only what one
would expect. **[34–46]** The next section has in view the events of the
conquest and settlement of the land of Canaan, as reported in the
Book of Judges (cf. Judg. 1.21, 27, 29; 2.1 ff.). The people's inability
to conquer the inhabitants of the land is explained by their disobedience to God's command (cf. Ex. 23.32 f.; 34.11 f.). The fact
that the people are specifically charged with mingling with the
Gentiles, human sacrifices and idolatry, which are characterized as
uncleanness and harlotry, still shows the cultic origins of that way of
thinking, which stems from the morality of the covenant with
Yahweh. From this point of view the wars and defeats of the covenant
people at the beginning of their time in Canaan are likewise interpreted as Yahweh's punishment of the people. Verses 43 ff. give a
religious interpretation of that early history similar to that in the
Book of Judges: it is ever again the gracious God who, remembering
his covenant, shows mercy to his people in their distress and gives
ear to their prayers. **[47]** And this, too, is the basis of the community's
hope that in response to its confession of guilt God will not deny his
help, but will bring together the members of the Covenant scattered
amongst the nations, so that thanksgiving for his help and praise of
his holy lovingkindness in the mouth of the congregation may
resound in his ears.[1] It cannot conclusively be proved that here the
whole people is thought to be in exile; the verse can just as well be
understood to refer to a calamity that has come upon the people, for
instance after the destruction of the Northern Kingdom. **[48]** Verse
48 is usually interpreted as a doxology added at a later date and
concluding the Fourth Book of the Psalter. This hypothesis cannot
claim to be definitely proved. Here, too, we shall have to reckon

---

[1] Cf. the same linking up of the people's guilt with God's judgment and mercy
in the liturgy of the *Manual of Discipline*.

with the possibility that the verse is designed to conclude the psalm and then represents the congregational hymn which v. 47 envisages. In that case the compiler would have placed the psalm at the end of the Fourth Book of the Psalter just because it ends with this hymn.

107. THE REDEEMED OF THE LORD

1 O testify to the Lord,[1] for he is good;
   for his grace endureth for ever!
2 Let the redeemed of the Lord say so,
   whom he has redeemed from trouble
3 and gathered in from the lands,
   from the east and from the west,
   from the north and from the south.[2]
4 They were lost in the desert,[3]
   in the steppe where there is no way,
   finding no way to a city to dwell in.
5 Hungry and thirsty,
   their soul fainted within them.
6 Then they cried to the Lord in their troubles,
   and he delivered them from their distress;
7 he led them upon the right way,
   till they reached a city to dwell in.
8 Let them confess to the Lord his grace,
   and his wonderful works to the sons of men,[4]
9 that he has satisfied him who was parched with thirst,
   and has filled the hungry with good things.[4]
10 Such as sat in darkness and in gloom,
   prisoners in affliction and in irons,[5]
11 because they had rebelled against the words of God
   and spurned the counsel of the Most High,[6]
12 whose hearts were bowed down[2] with hard labour,
   they fell down with none to help.
13 Then they cried to the Lord in their trouble,
   and he delivered them from their distress;
14 he brought them out of darkness and gloom,
   and broke their bonds asunder.
15 Let them testify to the Lord that he has been gracious,
   and his wonderful works to the sons of men,[7]
16 that he has shattered the doors of bronze,
   and has cut in two the bars of iron.[7]
17 Such as were sick[2] through their sinful ways,
   and because of their iniquities suffered affliction,[8]
18 who loathed any kind of food
   so that they drew near to the gates of death,
19 they cried to the Lord in their trouble,
   and he delivered them from their distress;

20 he sent forth his word, and healed them,
and saved their lives[2] from the Pit.[9]
21 Let them testify to the Lord that he has been gracious,
and his wonderful works to the sons of men.[10]
22 Let them offer sacrifices of thanksgiving,
and tell of his deeds with shouts of joy.[11]
23 Such as went down to the sea in ships,
doing business on the great waters,
24 they saw the deeds of the Lord,
and his wondrous works in the deep.
25 He commanded, and raised a stormy wind,
which lifted up the waves of the sea.
26 They mounted up to heaven,
they went down to the depths;
their courage melted away in their evil plight;
27 they reeled and staggered like drunken men,
and were at their wits' end.
28 Then they cried to the Lord in their trouble,
and he delivered them from their distress;
29 he made the storm be still;
then the waves of the sea[2] were hushed.
30 But they were glad because they had quiet,
and he brought them to their desired haven.
31 Let them testify to the Lord that he has been gracious,
and his wonderful works to the sons of men.[10]
32 Let them extol him in the congregation of the people,
and praise him in the assembly of the elders:
33 He turns rivers into a desert,
springs of water into thirsty ground,
34 a fruitful land into a salty waste,
because of the wickedness of its inhabitants.
35 He turns a desert into pools of water,
a parched land into springs of water.
36 There he let the hungry dwell;
they established a city to dwell in;[12]
37 they sowed fields, and planted vineyards,
and got a fruitful yield.[12]
38 By his blessing they multiplied greatly;
and he suffered them not to be in want of many things.[13]
39 Yet they were diminished and brought low
through oppression, adversity and sorrow.[14]
40 He poured contempt upon princes
and made them wander in trackless wastes.
41 He raised up the needy out of affliction,
and made families like flocks.
42 The godly see it and are glad;
and all wickedness stops its mouth.
43 Who is wise? Let him remember these things;

let him give heed[2] to the gracious deeds of the Lord.[15]

[1] * In RSV v. 1 opens with 'O give thanks to the Lord'.
[2] See BH.
[3] * V. 4a reads in RSV, 'Some wandered in desert wastes.'
[4] * Vv. 8 and 9 read in RSV:
    (8) Let them thank the Lord for his steadfast love,
        for his wonderful works to the sons of men!
    (9) For he satisfies him who is thirsty,
        and the hungry he fills with good things.
[5] * RSV divides vv. 10–12 into two sentences, beginning v. 10 with 'Some sat in darkness . . .' and v. 12 with 'Their hearts were bowed down . . .'
[6] See the comments on Ps. 7.17.
[7] * Vv. 15 and 16 read in RSV:
    (15) Let them thank the Lord for his steadfast love,
        for his wonderful works to the sons of men!
    (16) For he shatters the doors of bronze,
        and cuts in two the bars of iron.
[8] * RSV divides vv. 17–19 into two sentences, beginning v. 17 with 'Some were sick . . .' and v. 19 with 'Then they cried . . .' (cf. note 5 above).
[9] * V. 20b reads in RSV, 'and delivered them from destruction'.
[10] * RSV renders this refrain in vv. 21 and 31 as in vv. 8 and 15 (see notes 4 and 7 above).
[11] * RSV has 'in songs of joy' instead of 'with shouts of joy'.
[12] * RSV uses the present tense throughout.
[13] * RSV uses the present tense throughout and renders v. 38b: 'and he does not let their cattle decrease'.
[14] * RSV links vv. 39–41 in a single sentence, thus:
    (39) When they are diminished and brought low
        through oppression, trouble and sorrow,
    (40) he pours contempt upon princes
        and makes them wander in trackless wastes;
    (41) but he raises up the needy out of affliction,
        and makes their families like flocks.
[15] * V. 43 reads in RSV:
    Whoever is wise, let him give heed to these things;
    let men consider the steadfast love of the Lord.

According to v. 22 this community thanksgiving was probably recited before the offering of the sacrifice of thanksgiving in the festival cult of the Yahweh community (v. 32), for which festival pilgrims from every part of the world had gathered in the sanctuary (v. 3). In the first part of the psalm (vv. 1–32), in which four strophes of unequal lengths, marked by a twofold refrain (vv. 6, 8; 13, 15; 19, 21; 28, 31), stand out, it is still possible clearly to recognize the liturgical, responsorial character of the hymn, with the priests' call for a prayer of thanksgiving (vv. 1 f., 8, 15, 21 f., 31 f.) and the responses (vv. 1b, 9, 16). The second part of the psalm (vv. 33–41), in form a hymn, is probably the general testimony of the whole cult community to the God whose saving rule for the blessing of his people (v. 38) they praise as the revelation of his grace, in which they themselves joyfully share (vv. 42 f.). That the psalm dates from the late post-exilic period can be inferred neither from the mention of seafaring (vv. 23 ff.; cf. in this connection Judg. 5.17: 'Dan went to foreign countries on ships'[1] and Solomon's sea-borne trade in I Kings 9.27 f.) nor from certain echoes of Deutero-Isaiah, since we have to reckon with the possibility, if not with the probability, that that prophet made use of ancient cultic traditions.

[1–3] Verses 1–3 serve as an introduction to the whole psalm. The way in which this general introduction was recited by the priests and the congregation antiphonally (cf. Ps. 106.1) is illustrated in Pss. 118.2–4 and 136 and is based on v. 2. The members of the community, who have come together in the house of God to give thanks and testify to him, know themselves to be the fellowship of the 'redeemed', who have seen the hand of God at work not only in their deliverance from affliction but also in the fact that they have been able to gather together from many different countries for joint worship in the sanctuary—the same God who has manifested himself through his 'goodness and grace' as in the early period of Israel's becoming a nation. This is the inner bond that links the congregation together. [4–9] The subsequent sections, which formally have the same function as the 'narrative' has in individual thanksgivings, enter into the deliverance from affliction in more detail (see Intr. 83 f.). From the grammatical point of view vv. 4–9 directly continue the thought developed in the general introduction and are therefore to be understood of the whole community's experience of salvation and not only, as most commentators assume, of a particular group of those taking part in the festival (for instance, merchants or leaders of caravans). The personal experiences of the pilgrims are woven into the recollection of the afflictions of the people of God and the times they went astray during the wilderness wanderings, when God had led them in a wonderful way to their destination in the Promised Land; and, to become an undivided experience of the wonderful providence of God which has found its long-promised and long-awaited culmination at the festival in the city of God. In the cultic experience of the encounter with the God who lives in the *Heilsgeschichte* the cult community sees itself made partaker of that divine history which, beginning with God's revelation in the time of the Patriarchs, culminates in God's actual presence

[1] * In RSV this passage is rendered: 'Dan, why did he abide with the ships?'

in the ritual act that vouchsafes to the community the abundance of
his grace and salvation. They are now bound to give grateful
testimony in response to what has once again become for them a
certainty of faith. [10–32] The grammatical form of the three
following strophes intimates that now particular groups of the
community are called upon in turn to give thanks for their deliverance from their several afflictions. In vv. 10–16 they are captives
who have regained their freedom, in vv. 17–22 sick people who have
recovered from their illness, in vv. 23 ff.[1] seafarers who had the good
fortune to escape the perils of the sea. The accounts of their deliver-
ances are meant to unite them in a many-voiced choir who with
shouts of joy and thankfulness testify to God's wonderful saving grace
and so increase his glory in the assembled congregation that he will
appear in all his greatness and majesty as the deliverer from all
afflictions (v. 32). The innermost meaning of the community's
thanksgiving service, which outwardly closes with the sacrifice of
thanksgiving (v. 22), finds its fulfilment in the realization of the
presence of God, whereby the religious experience of the individual
becomes the concern of the whole congregation (see Intr. 75).

[33–41] The second part of the psalm is probably to be regarded
as the general cultic hymn which the whole congregation now begins
to sing in response to the call of the priest. This interpretation
accounts for its general character and for the way in which it differs
from the first part in both form and subject-matter; it is therefore
not necessary to attribute the second part to a different author and
to a different situation. The hymn glorifies the sovereign power of the
divine saving rule which, starting from the basic events of the
Heilsgeschichte, that is, the deliverance of the Red Sea, the entry into
the land and the settlement in Canaan, continually manifests itself
in the baffling ups and downs of life, in its fluctuations between
wealth and poverty, adversity and deliverance, wickedness and faith
(notice how the imperfect and narrative tenses interchange in order
to express the actualization of past events in the cult in the present),
and in the divine blessing which becomes obvious to the present
generation in the fertility of the land and the nation's prosperity.
[42–43] The conclusion of the psalm once more sums up the effect
produced by the revelation of the divine saving rule before the eyes
of the congregation: the godly ones, who 'see' it, that is, who experience it at first hand in and through the ritual act as a present event

---

[1] V. 20 seems to have in view a priestly oracle foretelling future salvation.

that concerns them directly, are filled with joy in God, but every criticism and wickedness directed against God is struck dumb before the power of his revelation. For that reason prudence demands that the gracious acts of God be heeded and remembered, so that they become a lasting possession of faith (see Intr. 31, 41 ff.). This parenetic warning, which is customary especially in the thanksgiving and makes use of the style of the 'Wisdom' literature, emphasizes the educational aspect of the appropriation of salvation that remains efficacious also after the cultic ceremony has come to an end (see Intr. 86).

108

Psalm 108 was probably compiled for liturgical purposes from ancient cultic traditions also used in Ps. 57.7–11 and in Ps. 60.5–12 (cf. the exposition of Pss. 57 and 60, especially that of Ps. 60.6–8).

109. AGAINST CURSING

To the Conductor. Of David. A Psalm

1 O God, who art my glory,
   be not silent![1]
2 For they opened their wicked[2] and deceitful mouth against me,
   they spoke to me with a lying tongue.[3]
3 They beset me with words of hate,
   and attacked me without cause.
4 In return for my love they accuse me,
   but I pray for them.[4]
5 They rewarded[2] me evil for good,
   and hatred for my love:
6 'Appoint a wicked man against him;
   and let an accuser stand at his right hand![5]
7 When he is tried, let him come forth guilty;
   let his prayer be counted as sin!
8 May his days be few;
   and his office let another take![6]
9 May his children be fatherless,
   and his wife a widow!
10 May his children wander about and beg;
   may they be driven out of the ruins they inhabit!
11 May the usurer seize all that he has;
   may strangers plunder the fruits of his toil!
12 Let there be none to extend kindness to him,
   nor any to pity his fatherless children!
13 May his posterity be cut off;
   may his name be blotted out
   in the second generation!

14 May the iniquity of his fathers
   be remembered before the Lord,
   and let not the sin of his mother
   be blotted out!
15 Let them be before the Lord continually;
   and may he cut off their memory from the earth!
16 For he did not remember to show kindness,
   but pursued the wretched poor,
   the brokenhearted, to kill him.[7]
17 He loved to curse; let curses come on him!
   He did not like blessing; may it be far from him!
18 He clothed himself with cursing as his coat,
   may it soak into his body like water,
   like oil into his bones!
19 May it be like a garment which he wraps round him,
   like a belt with which he daily girds himself!'
20 May this be the reward of my accusers ' ',[2]
   of those who plan to cause mischief to me.[8]
21 But thou, O Lord ' ',[9] deal on my behalf for thy name's sake,
   for thy grace is good; deliver me![10]
22 For I am afflicted and poor,
   and my heart is stricken within me.
23 Like a shadow when it lengthens I go hence;
   I am swept away like locusts.[11]
24 My knees are weak through fasting;
   my body visibly grows lean.[12]
25 I am become an object of scorn to them;
   when they see me, they wag their heads.
26 Help me, O Lord my God!
   Save me according to thy steadfast love!
27 That they may know that this is thy hand,
   that thou, O Lord, hast done it.[13]
28 Let them curse, but thou dost bless.
   My assailants will be put to shame,[2]
   but thy servant will be glad.[14]
29 My enemies clothe themselves with dishonour;
   they wrap themselves in their own shame
   as in a mantle.[15]
30 With a loud voice I will testify to the Lord,
   I will praise him in the midst of the throng,[16]
31 that he stands at the right hand of the poor,
   to save him from those who condemn him.[17]

[1] * V. 1 reads in RSV, 'Be not silent, O God of my praise!'
[2] See BH.
[3] * RSV renders v. 2:
   For wicked and deceitful mouths
   are opened against me,
   speaking against me with lying tongues.

4 See BH. (Tr. N.: V. 4b reads in RSV, 'even as I make prayer for them'.)
5 * RSV has 'bring him to trial' instead of 'stand at his right hand'.
6 * V. 8b is in RSV 'may another seize his goods'.
7 * RSV's v. 16 after the first line:
  but pursued the poor and needy
  and the brokenhearted to their death.
8 * RSV adds 'from the Lord' in the first line and renders the second line 'of those who speak evil against my life'.
9 'adōnāy is probably a later addition. (Tr. N.: RSV reads, 'But thou, O God my Lord.')
10 * V. 21b is in RSV 'because thy steadfast love is good, deliver me!'
11 * In RSV v. 23 reads:
  I am gone, like a shadow at evening;
  I am shaken off like a locust.
12 * V. 24b is in RSV 'my body has become gaunt'.
13 * V. 27 reads in RSV:
  Let them know that this is thy hand;
  thou, O Lord, hast done it!
14 * RSV has 'but do thou bless' instead of 'but thou dost bless' and reads after the first line:
  Let my assailants be put to shame;
  may thy servant be glad!
15 * RSV uses the imperative mood throughout instead of the indicative.
16 * V. 30a reads in RSV, 'With my mouth I will give great thanks to the Lord.'
17 * RSV opens v. 31a with: 'For he stands . . .' and adds in v. 31b 'to death'.

This psalm is an individual lament, prayed by a man who, if we understand the psalm aright, is accused of being guilty of the death of a poor man (v. 16), presumably by means of magically effective curses (vv. 17 ff.). It can be assumed that the accusation brought by his adversaries at the trial by ordeal, which we can infer from their words preserved in vv. 6–19, was one of sorcery, which was forbidden in the Yahweh religion and liable to punishment (cf. Ex. 20.7). The psalmist feels guiltless and helpless in the face of such an accusation. Only one remedy is left to him in this situation and that is prayer. He confides to his God his lament and his integrity (vv. 1–5); he repeats before him the terrible imprecations which his accusers have uttered against him (vv. 6–19), and he turns to him in prayer imploring him to deliver him from the impending penalty of death and disclosing to him all the misery that afflicts his body and his soul (vv. 20–27); and at the end of the psalm he rises in the presence of the assembled congregation to bear testimony to his trust and hope and to make a vow of thanksgiving (vv. 28–31; see Intr. 74 f.).

[1–5] The lament breathes the deep indignation which the futile struggle against the lies and hatred of his enemies arouses in the worshipper's soul; for he knows himself to be innocent and sees his love, which had once manifested itself in intercessions for his present adversaries, rewarded with malicious denunciation. This attitude of mind is not only understandable from the human point of view but does credit to the worshipper because of his love of truth and because of the utter candour of his prayer to God. In his struggle for the truth and for his own integrity, the fact that he can open his wounded heart to God is a relief to him and meets his innermost needs. **[6–19]** This is why he once more unfolds before God the unjust and cruel imprecations which his adversaries have uttered against him and against which he has no other power at his side than the God whose help he invokes. (The change from the plural in vv. 1–5 and 20 ff. to the singular in vv. 6–19 is satisfactorily accounted for only if vv. 6–19 are interpreted as a quotation of the imprecations directed against the psalmist.)[1] The complete unscrupulousness of the enemies is revealed in their desire that the trial may end with the conviction of the accused, again, that even his prayers may be counted as sin, and that within a short time he may be brought from life to death. And even this is not the whole story. The copious detail in which the dire consequences of his death as a criminal are described betrays the cruel and ardent hatred of his adversaries and gives us an inkling of the utter misery of defenceless powerlessness which makes the worshipper tremble under the impact of his enemies' curses, which are already permeating his body like poison and water that brings the curse (v. 18; cf. Num. 5.22).

[20–27] Encompassed by this atmosphere of cursing as by a garment, the worshipper seeks to break out of the constricting circle of curses by returning them upon his adversaries (v. 20) and invoking God's grace to deliver him (v. 21). God is the only power capable of breaking the curses of men. The moving lament rings out once more; this time it portrays the worshipper's pitiable state, in which he feels his physical and spiritual energies failing on account of the agitation of his mind and the sorrows that consume him. There is only one thing that can still save him: God himself must intervene and make his enemies realize that it was he, God himself, who caused the sudden death of that poor man, and not dark, magic machinations which are laid to the charge of the worshipper (v. 27). **[28–31]** In his frank dialogue with God the poet has wrestled in prayer till he has

---

[1] Hence there is no need to alter the text and interpret vv. 6–19 as describing the common fate of the wicked, as in the Book of Job (this point in opposition to Kissane, *The Irish Theological Quarterly* 18 (1951), pp. 1 ff.).

attained the certitude of faithful trust that leaves behind it all fears and doubts and wholeheartedly throws itself wholly upon God, who will break the power of the adversaries and their curses, but will bestow his blessing upon him, so that he will be able to testify before the whole congregation with gratitude and joy that God is the Helper of the innocent and oppressed against the unjust judgment of men. It is only when God takes the affairs of men into his own hands that the net woven by human lies and hatred is torn to pieces, and cursing is turned into blessing and fear of man into joy in God, who ensures the ultimate triumph of truth and justice.

110. THE PRIEST-KING

Of David.   A Psalm

1 Thus said Yahweh to my lord:
  'Sit at my right hand,
  till I make your enemies your footstool!'
2 The Lord stretches forth from Zion the sceptre of your power—[1]
  rule in the midst of your foes!
3 Your people will offer themselves freely
  on the day you lead your host[2];
  in holy array, at the dawn of the morning,
  your youth will come to you like dew.[3]
4 The Lord has sworn, he will not repent:[4]
  'You are a priest for ever after the order of Melchizedek.'
5 The Lord protects you;[5]
  he will shatter kings on the day of his wrath.
6 He will execute judgment among the nations,
  surrounded by corpses;[6]
  he will shatter the chiefs over the wide earth.
7 He will drink from the brook by the way;
  therefore he will lift up his head.

[1] * V. 2a reads in RSV 'The Lord sends forth from Zion your mighty sceptre.'
[2] * RSV reads here 'upon the holy mountains' and renders the rest of the verse:
    From the womb of the morning
    like dew your youth will come to you.
[3] Read *ketal* (haplography).
[4] * RSV has 'and will not change his mind' instead of 'he will not repent'.
[5] * The first line of v. 5 reads in RSV, 'The Lord is at your right hand.'
[6] * RSV has 'filling them with corpses' instead of 'surrounded by corpses'.

The superscription attributes the psalm to David, and thereby makes clear that later Judaism interpreted the psalm as referring to the Messiah whom it recognized as the 'lord' addressed by David (v. 1). Even Jesus himself makes use of that contemporary inter-

pretation when according to Matt. 22.41 ff. he seeks, by referring to
v. 1, where David calls the Messiah his lord, to prove to the Pharisees
that the Messiah must be something more than merely 'the son of
David', a designation which was usually applied to him. Again, in
Matt. 26.64 Jesus interprets the sitting at the right hand of God
(v. 1) in connection with Dan. 7.13 as referring to his divine status
and authority. It is in the light of these facts that we have to understand why the psalm was interpreted in a number of New Testament
sayings in a Messianic sense and as referring to Jesus, and also why
that special significance was ascribed to it which the psalm, thus
understood, has gained in the exposition of the Christian Church
(cf. I Cor. 15.25 ff.; Eph. 1.20; Col. 3.1; I Peter 3.22; Heb. 1.13;
8.1; 10.12 f.; 5.6; 7.17 ff.). That reinterpretation was made easier
by the fact that it is precisely the fundamental religious ideas of the
psalm themselves with their theocentric tendency and their universal
outlook (vv. 5 f.) which carry with them the possibility of turning
man's thoughts beyond purely earthly and historical events to the
things that will come to pass at the end of history. For the psalm
regards the priestly kingship of the earthly ruler as the representation
of God on earth who is the Lord of history. And it is precisely the
religious factor which was of such importance for the Old Testament
kingship which thus continued to be effective and live on, and was
finally lifted by Jesus out of the sphere of politics and nationalism,
and consummated in the breadth and depth of God's sovereign rule.

The psalm was originally a royal song, composed at a time when
under the kings of Judah national enthusiasm was still a living and
unbroken force. As regards form and subject-matter and very
probably also in respect of the occasion to which it owes its origin,
the psalm is very closely related to Psalm 2. Two divine oracles
(vv. 1 and 4), which are made known to the king at Jerusalem,
probably by one of his court prophets, form the nucleus of the psalm.
The solemn tone and exalted language of the oracles are thus most
easily accounted for. On account of the content of the two divine
oracles it is the most natural thing, as in Psalm 2, to think of the
festival of the king's enthronement as the occasion on which the
psalm was used (see Intr. 62); for these divine oracles speak of
the investiture of the king as the viceregent of God (v. 1) and of the
conferring of the office of priesthood on the ruler (v. 4). As has
already been shown in detail in the exegesis of Psalm 2, so here, too,
the poet who composed Psalm 110 makes use of the 'court style' that

was customary on such occasions in every part of the ancient Orient. This accounts for the affinity of particular phrases and word-pictures of the psalm to numerous ancient oriental parallels.

The power of the ruler (vv. 1–3)

[1] Using the form of the prophetic oracle the poet makes known what God has 'whispered' in his ear as his command and promise to the king, his 'lord'. God calls upon the king to occupy the place of honour at his right hand.[1] By this his kingship is authorized by God; the earthly ruler is shown to be the viceregent of God, and his office is proved to function in virtue of the divine will. In this religious establishment of the kingship as an institution willed and ordained by God lay its dignity and strength, but also its obligation and responsibility to its divine Lord, as we can gather from the struggles of the prophets against the secularization of the kingship and against its degradation by the autocratic conduct of the kings. At the same time God promises the king that he will be victorious over his enemies. Yahweh himself is the supreme commander; he will conquer the hostile nations and will force them to acknowledge the king. They will prostrate themselves before his throne and, in accordance with an ancient and widespread custom, he will put his foot on their necks as a symbol of his power (cf. Josh. 10.24). [2] Passing from the form of the divine oracle to the style of a prophetic utterance, the psalmist expresses the same thought in another bold word-picture. Yahweh himself holds in his hand the sceptre of the king, the 'rod of his power', and stretches it forth from Zion far over the land, giving this command to the king: 'Rule in the midst of your foes.'[2] We can grasp the full extent of the power of these words only if we bear in mind that the symbolic act of God as well as his utterance are conceived to be operative forces really capable of accomplishing what they convey. The king is therefore backed up by the effective power of God, and this fact imparts to the prophetic promise the significance of a deed that will make history and carries with it the assurance

[1] On account of II Kings 11.14 (II Chron. 23.13), II Kings 23.3 (II Chron. 34.31) and parallels in the coronation ceremony in Egypt (cf. Herrmann, Die Königsnovelle in Ägypten und Israel, *Wissenschaftliche Zeitschrift der Karl-Marx-Universität Leipzig*, Gesellschafts- und Sprachwissenschaftliche Reihe, 3.Jahrgang 1953/54, p. 37) we may think of a special 'place of the lord' (king) 'by the pillar' in the Temple.
[2] This saying was perhaps confirmed by the ritual and symbolic act of the investiture of the king with the sceptre.

of its accomplishment though the nation may be threatened by enemies on all sides. [3] The further promise that the people will readily serve the king in times of war (v. 3), a promise which probably presupposes the presence of the hosts at the ceremony of the reception of 'power' by the king, is likewise founded on that unbroken faith which forms its background. From of old it was regarded as a sacred religious duty (cf. Judg. 5.23) to obey the call upon the covenantal armies to wage the 'wars of Yahweh'. In the magnificent word-picture, borrowed from myth, of the dew that abundantly flows from the womb of the dawn and refreshes Nature in the early morning, the psalm speaks of the young men in the army who in holy warlike array are at once at the disposal of the king, ready in their vigorous and youthful strength and numerically as abundant as the drops of dew in the morning. The fact that Yahweh's will governs the king and his people gives this national enthusiasm its particular strength.

The priestly office (v. 4)

[4] The second divine oracle, probably uttered in the same context, is characterized as such by an especially solemn introduction composed in the prophetic style. God confirms his word, installing the king in the office of priest by means of an oath which he will not retract (cf. Amos 4.2; 6.8; 1.3 ff.). This utterance is perhaps directed against the aspirations towards autonomy of a priesthood which was prompted by hierarchical desires and striving for the separation of the ecclesiastical power from the secular one. The psalm, on the other hand, very forcefully emphasizes—the solemn way in which the divine oracle is introduced cannot be without significance here— that the priesthood will for ever remain vested in the king after the order of Melchizedek, that Canaanite priest-prince of Jerusalem in ancient times (cf. Gen. 14.18) who likewise combined both these offices in his person; when David took over the Jebusite kingship of the city of Jerusalem these two offices were conferred on him and, as the psalm shows, continued to be held by the Davidic dynasty. The link between throne and altar or, to put it differently, the incorpora- tion of the royal tradition in the cult of the Covenant, which is here supported by an ancient Jerusalem tradition also embodied in the Pentateuch, does not seem to have been accomplished without difficulty (cf. the exposition of Ps. 132 and Intr. 33, 44, 62). In that union of throne and altar the poet discerns God's will for his people.

The Day of Yahweh (vv. 5–6)

[5–6] From v. 5 onwards the psalm takes a strange turn. Passing on from the form of the divine oracle to the style of a prophetic utterance, in exactly the same way as was done in v. 2, the speaker promises the king God's protection; Yahweh will be at his 'right hand'. (This phrase which is here used in a metaphorical sense[1] is not necessarily at variance with v. 1.) Thereafter, however, the psalmist proceeds to portray the day of the divine wrath on which Yahweh will give judgment on the nations and their kings, striding across corpses like a terrible and mighty warrior and dashing to the ground whoever gets in his way. The hope of the 'Day of Yahweh', which was perhaps especially popular in nationalistic circles of court prophets, formed already at a comparatively early date a constituent part of the Israelite tradition and probably belonged to the range of ideas associated with the Covenant Festival of Yahweh at which the enthronement of the king was celebrated. The people awaited with trembling joy the day when Yahweh would rise to the final and decisive battle against Israel's enemies in order to overcome them and grant victory and salvation to his people. And in their imagination the particular events of the catastrophe that would then overwhelm the nations assumed strong colours which were a mixture of cruel realism and ardent hope (cf. Joel 3.1 ff.; Nahum 1.8 ff.; Zeph. 3.6 ff.). The words of the psalm, too, draw a similar picture which does not fall short of the other pictures as far as its realistic colours are concerned. We must, however, bear in mind in this respect that what is expressed in such features is not so much human cruelty gloating over other people's misfortunes and giving vent to its feelings, but rather the vivid impression produced by the terrifying power of the divine might revealed at the celebration of the 'Day of the Lord'. Here this seems to prove true all the more as in the words about God's judgment the person of the king and his enthronement are lost behind the exclusive activity of God, and as the psalmist's gaze is focused entirely on God. It was this perspective that also suggested the possibility of a purely eschatological interpretation of the whole hymn on the lines of God's judgment on the whole world being the Last Judgment and the person of the king being reinterpreted as that of the Messiah.

[1] * Whereas RSV renders the first line of v. 5 as indicated in note 5 to the psalm (above), Weiser's translation reads 'The Lord protects you', though his exposition actually presupposes the text rendered in RSV.

[7] The conclusion of the psalm does not seem to have been preserved in its entirety. The passage 'He drinks from the brook by the way; therefore he lifts up his head' is hardly possible, as it stands if understood as a statement about God. But it also raises difficulties if we regard this account as a direct reference to the king who is still addressed in v. 5. Perhaps the verse is to be understood as a cultic instruction (or description) issued within the framework of the festival ritual, according to which, on the analogy of one of the Ras Shamra texts, the king drinks from the sacred fountain[1] in order to get new strength by means of the 'partaking of the sacrament' for the war against the nations which he has to wage as Yahweh's chosen one.

The psalm is a testimony to the national religion of Israel. It shows us that the belief in God was a source of energy that gave a tremendous impetus to the actions of the nation; and it is an example of the close relationship between faith and history in the Old Testament cultus. On the other hand, however, the psalm cannot conceal the dangers which are inherent in a close link between religion and politics in which the political will makes faith serve its own ends. The fact that, for instance, Amos (5.18 ff.) destroys that national religious hope in the Day of Yahweh because he realizes that God is thereby degraded to a partisan of national arrogance and that human will tries to get control of God, makes it clear that in the Old Testament itself these dangers are recognized and opposed from the standpoint of an attitude of faith which is careful to render to God the things which are God's.

---

[1] Reminiscences of such a ritual could be contained in I Kings 1.9, 45.

III. HE HAS CAUSED HIS WONDERFUL WORKS TO BE REMEMBERED

1 Hallelujah[1]
 I will testify to the Lord with my whole heart,
 in the assembly of the godly, in the congregation.[2]
2 Great are the works of the Lord,
 they who have pleasure in them come to know them.[3]
3 Full of honour and majesty is his work
 and his righteousness endures for ever.
4 He has caused his wonderful works to be remembered;
 the Lord is gracious and merciful.
5 He provides food for those who fear him;
 he is ever mindful of his covenant.

6 He has shown his people the power of his works,
  took away the heritage from the Gentiles and gave it to the people.[4]
7 The works of his hands are without deceit and just;
  all his precepts are thoroughly trustworthy;
8 they are a source of strength for ever and ever;
  they are performed with uprightness[5] and faithfulness.[6]
9 He sent redemption to his people;
  he has commanded them to keep his covenant for ever.
  Unapproachable and terrible is his name![7]
10 The fear of the Lord is the beginning of wisdom;
  a good understanding have all those who practise it.
  His praise endures for ever!

[1] The introductory liturgical 'Hallelujah' stands outside the alphabetical order and must therefore be a later cultic addition (see Intr. 22). (Tr. N.: RSV reads 'Praise the Lord' instead of 'Hallelujah'.)

[2] * RSV has 'I will give thanks to the Lord' instead of 'I will testify to the Lord'.

[3] * V. 2b reads in RSV, 'studied by all who have pleasure in them'.

[4] * V. 6b is in RSV 'in giving them the heritage of the nations'.

[5] See BH.

[6] * RSV renders v. 8:
  they are established for ever and ever,
  to be performed with faithfulness and uprightness.

[7] * RSV has 'holy' instead of 'unapproachable'.

Paul Gerhardt has paraphrased this psalm in his hymn, 'Ich will mit Dank kommen.' It is the testimony of an individual, in form a hymn, which according to vv. 1, 5, 9 seems to have been composed for the purpose of its recital at the festival cult of the covenant community. In the Hebrew the half-lines begin with the successive letters of the Hebrew alphabet.[1] This artificial conceit imposes an outward form which is certainly not conducive to a consistent thought-sequence. The several hymnic statements about what God means to the worshipper and the cult community are loosely placed side by side, like a string of unmatched pearls, in the form of general propositions, and without any very systematic arrangement. They provide us, however, in this very form with a true picture of the faith held by the members of the cult community and also show to what high degree God's rule in Nature and in History was continually able at their festival to arouse them to grateful adoration and deep emotion. The date of the composition of the psalm cannot be established for certain; it cannot be taken for granted that the inclusion of a theme of the Wisdom literature (v. 10) points to a late origin (see Intr. 88 f., 91).

[1] * The translation in the German edition preserved this feature.

[1] The hymnic introduction with which the worshipper begins his song indicates its cultic background, that is, a festival of the covenant community. It praises the great redemptive work of God, whereby his might and greatness, his righteousness and grace have been made known to the people, in such a way that the worshipper, too, knows himself to be directly affected by it and involved in it and so testifies to this God in and with the congregation in a hymn of praise 'with his whole heart'. The psalm then reverts to what had been the theme of the cultic ceremony: it is the congregation's reaction, expressed by an individual member, to the revelation of God's salvation and its actualization for his people, a reaction that reflects the fundamental ideas of the festival cult and clearly shows how completely God and his acts are the focus of religious experience. **[2–3]** The greatness of God is known in his works. In the Old Testament God is always the God who acts. This feature imparts to the Old Testament notion of God its peculiar dynamic quality, a vitality far removed from any abstract intellectual speculation and from the sultry atmosphere of mystical absorption, but so much the more closely related to the reality of life itself. The poet expresses a profound truth when he says precisely in this context that the works of God come to be known (literally 'explored') by those who have pleasure in them. Only the man whom God has seized in the innermost recesses of his soul is able to apprehend God; only he who sees all things with the eye of faith and with the joyous acceptance of one who has given himself up to God, is capable of finding God's footprints in his works. This is the fundamental prerequisite of the biblical understanding of God. Thus the worshipper 'sees' the splendour and glory of God manifested in his works, and discerns that God's righteousness and salvation are the divine meaning and the governing principle of every event. **[4]** The poet contemplates God's acts from the perspective of the Old Testament cultic tradition. The latter is referred to by the statement 'He has caused his wonderful works to be remembered' (cf. Ps. 78.3 f.). The cultic transmission of the *Heilsgeschichte* is willed and instituted by God (Ex. 12.14), so that the 'memorial' of God's rule in history is for ever kept alive in the life of the people. It cannot be proved that the poet has in mind here the Feast of the Passover as the occasion when the tradition of the deliverance from Egypt, to which the subsequent verses allude, was particularly commemorated, or that the psalm itself is a 'Passover hymn'; rather shall we have to think of the autumn Covenant Festival at which the renewal of the Covenant was celebrated within the framework of the realization of salvation. For the nation the age of Moses had been precisely that period in their history which was the manifestation *par excellence* of God's grace and mercy, and for all time to come. **[5]** In this context the saying concerning the feeding of the godly is best understood as referring to the story of the miraculous feeding in the wilderness as handed down in the tradition of the *Heilsgeschichte*. We are led to this conclusion also by the reference to God's everlasting covenant, in which at Sinai he has expressed his will to deal graciously with his people. The early Church interpreted the verse as referring to the Lord's Supper; so in the tradition of the Church the psalm is regarded as eucharistic. **[6]** The next verse likewise has in view the events of the early period of the nation's history. The psalmist recalls with pride and gratitude the conquest of Canaan, once the possession of pagan nations, with whose soil Israel's national history continued to be linked up. The people of Israel were proudly conscious of their own character, and we shall not be able to blame them for the fact that they did not judge the events that led to the establishment of their historical existence from the perspective of the forum of an international court of justice, but encompassed the nation and their homeland in their belief in God. The psalm shows that, taking everything into consideration, they did not, in doing so, succumb to the danger of glorifying themselves and of making God serve their own national interests. On the contrary, the history of the nation serves the will of God 'to show his people the power of his works' (this in accordance with the text of v. 6). The deepest meaning of the study of history is not hero-worship but the worship of God.

[7–8] The intensity with which the *Heilsgeschichte* is here experienced as God's own presence is shown by the statements on the essential nature of the works of God; here the poet's personal joyous interest finds even stronger expression. The works of God manifest his 'faithfulness' and 'justice'. It is God himself who thus makes possible man's trust in and reliance on him; his rule has never yet been found wanting. And the manifestation of his will in his precepts has unshakable validity as the basis of the order that rules the life and conduct of the nation. Their promises and threats are to be taken equally seriously, and constitute the firm and permanent foundation, 'established for ever and ever', on which the order willed by God rests as the order of the Covenant. Man knows himself to be sheltered in that order and to be safely guided by it through the dangers with which life is beset. No wonder that from this point of view the divine law was bound to appear to the godly of the Old Testament not as a burden but as a help. But God does even more. He has also provided for the carrying out of his precepts. He accomplishes his will in the same truthful and upright spirit in which he once declared it. 'The history of the world is the judgment on the world'; the promises of God carry with them the Yea and the Amen of their fulfilment. **[9]** Verse 9 once more sums up the thoughts of the hymn. The poet reflects on the deliverance which God has brought to his people—probably not only their release from bondage in Egypt but also their continually recurring deliverance from the oppression of their enemies—and on the everlasting covenant which God has commanded (!) his people to keep. And in so doing he recognizes the gift of the divine grace and the obligatory nature of the demand made by his holy will as the two inseparable aspects of the God who is at once unapproachable and near. That the psalmist is able and indeed feels constrained to speak in one breath of deliverance and of the terrible nature of the 'name' of God is in itself evidence of the inscrutable greatness of the God whose praise he wishes to proclaim. **[10]** Continuing the thought just expressed in v. 9, the poet now draws the practical conclusion and gives his song a didactic ending (see Intr. 86) by adding to the hymn a familiar maxim from the Wisdom literature (cf. Prov. 1.7; 9.10; Job 28.28) which describes the fear of God as the 'foundation' of all practical wisdom and fits in well with his own thoughts. The personal comment added by the poet in explanation characterizes the depth of the experience he has gained in his own life. 'A good understanding have all those who practise (this wisdom).' The most valuable perceptions gained in life are not to be found in the sphere of intellectual thought, but in that of a knowledge that is true to life and becomes a certainty through action; practical wisdom is a knowledge experimentally obtained and thereby becomes an unforgettable personal experience. This thought supplements what the poet has to say in v. 2 about joy in God's works as a means of 'coming to know' them. Ultimate perceptions claim man's whole being. The psalm concludes by turning to God. The poet visualizes his own song of praise set in the widest possible context. The praise of God will endure for ever, and yet another link in that endless chain of the divine glory which was maintained in an unbroken

cultic tradition (see Intr. 36 f.) is formed by this psalm, which its
author dedicates with inspired emotion to him who, according to
his own and his people's faith, is the basis of all existence.

112. THE BLESSEDNESS OF FEARING GOD

1 Hallelujah[1]
  Blessed is the man who fears the Lord,
  who greatly delights in his commandments!
2 His descendants will be mighty in the land;
  the generation of the godly will be blessed.
3 Wealth and riches are in his house;
  and his righteousness endures for ever.
4 To those who fear God he is like a light that shines in darkness;
  he is merciful, gracious and righteous.[2]
5 It is well with the man who is merciful and lends;
  he conducts his affairs with justice,[3]
6 for he will never be moved;
  the righteous will be remembered for ever.[3]
7 He is not afraid of evil rumours;[4]
  his heart is firm, trusting in the Lord.
8 His heart is confident,
  he is afraid of nothing,
  so that he can (calmly) watch his enemies.[5]
9 He has given generously to the poor;[6]
  his righteousness is established for ever;
  his horn is exalted in honour.
10 The wicked man sees it and is angry;
  he is dismayed and gnashes his teeth;
  the desire of the wicked comes to nought.[7]

[1] See above, p. 22. (Tr. N.: RSV has 'Praise the Lord'.)
[2] * V. 4 reads in RSV:
  Light rises in the darkness for the upright;
  the Lord is gracious, merciful and righteous.
[3] * Here vv. 5 and 6 form a single sentence, but they are differently rendered in
RSV:
  (5) It is well with the man who deals generously and lends,
    who conducts his affairs with justice.
  (6) For the righteous will never be moved;
    he will be remembered for ever.
[4] * RSV has 'evil tidings' instead of 'evil rumours'.
[5] * V. 8 reads in RSV:
  His heart is steady, he will not be afraid,
  until he sees his desire on his adversaries.
[6] * RSV renders the first line of v. 9, 'He has distributed freely, he has given to
the poor.'
[7] * In RSV the second line of v. 10 reads, 'he gnashes his teeth and melts
away'.

The praise of God in Psalm 111 is followed in Psalm 112 by praise of the blessedness of the godly, which seems to be an intentional counterpart to Psalm 111. The formal affinities between the two psalms, such as the fact that the half-lines begin with the successive letters of the Hebrew alphabet as well as a number of parallel phrases, likewise suggest the view that both psalms are from the same author. The psalm, which has found its way into Protestant hymn-books in Paul Gerhardt's version,[1] has a certain resemblance in subject-matter to Psalm 1, though Psalm 112 lays a stronger emphasis on the praise of godliness and gives less prominence to the wicked. In view of the general nature of its subject-matter it is impossible to assign a definite date to the psalm. As in Psalm 1 so also in Psalm 112 we shall have to consider whether the promise of salvation for the godly man may not be connected with the bestowal of blessing which had its place in the cultic ritual, the more so as the relations of 'Wisdom' to the cultus need to be more closely investigated by scholars, who would have to explain the remarkable connection between the forms of the hymns and their parenetic tendency (see Intr. 86, 88 f., 92 f.).

[1] This psalm, too, regards the fear of God as the beginning of wisdom. It is the source of obedience to his commandments and fearless trust in him (vv. 7 f.). One of the characteristics of the biblical belief in God is that it carries with it the tension between fear and joy and further that it resolves this by means of trust in God; for that belief springs from and is nourished by the vivid impression produced by God's power and love. [2–3] From this flows every blessing manifested in the life of the family and its descendants, and in material prosperity as well as the blessing manifested in 'righteousness', which is here not understood in the sense of a moral quality but as God's gift of happiness in man's inward and outward life. The fact that words similar to what has been asserted of God in Psalm 111.3 are said of the godly man in v. 3 indicates that his blessedness in the last analysis means that he partakes of the nature of God. [4–6] He who is blessed by God becomes in his turn a blessing to others who fear him. Like a light in the darkness he shines as an example to these other people; he becomes himself a living testimony to and an indication of God's mercy, grace, and righteousness (v. 4). The godlike character of a moral life is here clearly recognized and expressed. This fact is overlooked by those who contrary to the

[1] 'Wohl dem, der den Herrn scheuet.'

stylistic form used here (notice the plural 'those who fear God', whereas otherwise the singular is used throughout the psalm) seek to interpret the statement made in v. 4 as referring to God. The compassion of the godly man proves itself in his liberality to the poor; his righteousness proves itself in the manner in which he conducts his affairs (or lawsuit) so that he lives on in the memory of his fellow men as an example that cannot be shaken. **[7–8]** It is true that the godly man is not immune from evil rumours and from the accusations of malicious adversaries; but his trust in God gives him a firm and confident heart, so that he has no need to be afraid. That fearless assurance, too, is a gift from God (notice the passive voice!) and has nothing in common with light-hearted self-assurance. **[9–10]** By way of a summary the godly man's compassion towards the poor and righteousness (see vv. 5 f.) are once more praised as the meaning of a life that is blessed by God, honoured by men, and lived in the fullness of strength (this is the meaning conveyed by the metaphor of the horn). The strength flowing from blessedness stands out so much the more clearly as it is contrasted with the helpless anger of the envious wicked, whose desires are doomed to frustration (see Intr. 47 ff., 75 f., 93).

113. GOD'S SOVEREIGNTY AND COMPASSION

1 Hallelujah[1]
  Praise, O you servants of the Lord,
  praise the name of the Lord!
2 Blessed be the name of the Lord
  from this time forth and for evermore!
3 From the rising of the sun to its setting
  the name of the Lord is to be praised!
4 The Lord is high above all nations,
  and his sovereignty above all the heavens![2]
5 Who is like the Lord, our God,
  who is enthroned on high
6 and looks down
  upon the heavens and the earth?
7 He raises the lowly from the dust,
  he exalts the poor from the dung.[3]
8 He makes him[4] sit with princes,
  with the princes of his people.[5]
9 He gives the barren woman authority in the house,
  gives her joy[4] as the mother of her children.[6]
  Hallelujah[1]

[1] See above, p. 22. (Tr. N.: RSV reads 'Praise the Lord!')
[2] * RSV has 'glory' instead of 'sovereignty'.
[3] * RSV has 'poor' instead of 'lowly' in v. 7a, and renders v. 7b 'and lifts the needy from the ash heap'.
[4] See BH.
[5] * V. 8 reads in RSV:
    to make them sit with princes,
    with the princes of his people.
[6] * RSV renders v. 9 as:
    He gives the barren woman a home,
    making her the joyous mother of children.
    Praise the Lord!

With Psalm 113 begins the small collection of the so-called Hallel-psalms (113–118) which were used in Jewish worship and had their place in the liturgy for the feasts of pilgrimage, Passover, Weeks, and Tabernacles, as well as at the New Moon and at the Feast of the Dedication of the Temple. At the family Passover celebration Psalms 113 and 114 were sung before the meal and Psalms 115–118 afterwards (cf. Matt. 26.26, 30; Mark 14.22, 26). The psalm is a hymn sung in praise of Yahweh and from the outset seems to have been composed for liturgical use by the congregation. This is suggested by the fact that the 'worshippers' of Yahweh are addressed in v. 1 and that the psalm quite deliberately employs archaic and solemn language such as at any time can be observed in use in the cultus. Thus the psalm provides a valuable insight into the fundamentals of the Old Testament worship of the cult community. It is above all the realization of God's presence which the worshipping congregation in reciting the hymn experiences with a continually renewed vividness as the source of strength that sustains its fellowship. The marked use of customary forms and traditional ideas which imparts to the psalm a Mosaic character reveals on the one hand the significance which the tradition of the Old Testament had for the cultus, and, on the other hand, the important part which the cultic liturgy played in respect of the transmission and preservation of the religious treasure of the Old Testament. Two fundamental ideas form the nucleus of the psalm, both concerned with the nature of God, namely the incomparable majesty of God and his no less wonderful compassion on those who are despised among men. The psalm is divided into three parts; vv. 1–3 speak of the endless continuance and limitless sway of the 'name' and glory of God; vv. 4–6 deal with his sublime nature and vv. 7–9 with his compassion.

[1–3] The whole first section takes the form of an accumulation of introductory hymns. This form and the fact that the word 'praise' is repeated three times allow us to presume that the opening of the psalm is intended to be some sort of extension of the liturgical shout 'Hallelujah', no matter whether the Hallelujah ('Praise the Lord'), with which the psalm opens, belongs to the original text of the psalm or was prefixed to it only subsequently. The members of the cult community, who are called upon to sing the praise of God, are addressed as 'servants', that is, worshippers, of Yahweh. This designation, which is borrowed from the service rendered at the court of a prince, equally expresses their privilege and their duty, and comprises deeply rooted characteristics of the Old Testament religion, the unconditional obligation in face of God's commandments and the joy of being allowed to live in a permanent relationship with him. The subject-matter of these verses can be traced back to the revelation of the name of God which was a constituent part of the tradition of the festival cult (Ex. 33.19) and was echoed in the 'everlasting hymn' of the congregation (see Intr. 30 f., 54 f.). The thoughts expressed in v. 2, modifying the usual forms of a hymnic introduction, reach beyond the present moment and want to see the praise of God boundlessly extended in both time and space, as accords with God's nature and his limitless power (cf. in this connection Mal. 1.11; Ps. 48.10). These three verses are inspired not by the idea of the spreading of the worshippers of Yahweh over the whole world but by the theocentric thought of the magnitude and comprehensiveness of the divine revelation. Faith takes comfort from the greatness of God which it praises. In the uniform concentration on God of the worshipping congregation, in their attitude of faith, conscious of the universal sweep of the setting in which they are placed, they form a united front of those who in their joint praise of God are borne as on invisible wings by the power of him for whom it is intended. This is the invisible foundation on which the words of the psalm are based.

[4-6] To provide the spiritual basis of this call to praise, the second section of the psalm glorifies the sovereignty of God over History and Nature. Yahweh is exalted over the whole world of nations (Pss. 99.2; 46.10); he is even placed far above the heavens, above the sphere of the whole creation (cf. Pss. 8.1; 57.5, 11; I Kings 8.27). His being coincides neither with Nature nor with the history of the nations. As faith lifts up its eyes to him who himself 'looks down upon the heavens and the earth' (v. 6), it finds a stay that lifts it

above the insecurity of all temporal existence. The words describing
the sublime nature of God at the same time imply the knowledge
that he is 'the wholly Other' and that there is nothing in this world
which could be put on a level with God. The question 'Who is like
Yahweh, our God?' (cf. Ex. 15.11; see Intr. 61) is in line with this
trend of thought. The very form of the rhetorical question, which
is a feature of the hymnic style, shows how strongly the reflective
mood of faith here comes into the foreground. At the root of it is
the deliberate refraining from any attempt to seek to comprehend
the nature of God by way of reasoning and comparison, an attempt
that is always bound to end in the incomparability of God and
the admission of his sublimity, not only relative but absolute, and
of the unbridgeable chasm between him and the world. The saying
that God looks down upon the heavens and the earth (cf. Pss. 33.13;
138.6), which probably alludes to the theophany, emphasizes this
idea of the infinite and absolute superiority of God over the world.
A note of happiness, however, accompanies this wonder at the
divine glory; though man's mind may in vain endeavour to get to
the root of the nature of God, the worshipping congregation may
nevertheless call this God 'their God' who does not let them out
of his sight. The bridge which man himself cannot throw across
to reach the remote, transcendent God nevertheless exists; it is
built by God himself so that in spite of all the disparity between
God and man a communion exists between them which enables
man to believe that the God who is far off is also the God of the
here and now. What remains a mystery to the mind of man is revealed to the eyes of faith: that the exalted God not only looks
down upon men but inclines graciously to them. The final section
of the psalm deals with this greatest of miracles, which can be
apprehended only by faith.

[7-9] The psalmist grasps the greatness of God in all its fullness
only as he comes to realize that it is precisely the afflicted, those
whom men despise and reject, for whom God cares. In that the
psalmist speaks of raising the poor and lowly from dust and dung
(literally 'ash'), he probably has in mind the sick who, expelled
from the human community, are compelled to eke out a lamentable
existence on a rubbish heap outside the city (cf. Job 2.8). What is
made impossible by human custom is made possible by God; he
lifts the lowly from the dust (cf. I Sam. 2.8; I Kings 16.2; Job 5.11)
and gives them a place of honour among the princes of the nation

(cf. Job 36.7). The idea expressed in v. 9 and modelled on I Sam.
2.5 is in line with this train of thought. Childlessness was regarded
in the ancient Orient as a disgrace and could result in the expulsion
of the barren woman from the household or in the diminishing of
her privileges. The mother of children, on the other hand, was
protected against her dismissal by the law; the Code of Hammurabi
(§§ 135 ff.) already contained a rule to that effect. The fact that
God takes care of the childless woman, who is outside the pale of
the law, bestows upon her domestic authority and grants her the
blessing of children, shows that God's grace is superior to the human
law; and that he causes the barren woman to become the mother
of children simultaneously reveals his miraculous power. At the root
of the joyous submission to the sovereignty of God and of the
comforting certitude of his grace is a strong, simple faith, willing
and able to endure affliction, oppression, humiliation and injustice
without being defeated thereby. The fact that God's greatness is
manifested precisely in his compassion upon those primal miseries
of human life points beyond the limitations of the Old Testament
to the Cross as the sacred place where the ultimate depths of
God's nature were revealed.

114. THE EXODUS

1 When Israel went forth from Egypt,
the house of Jacob from a people of strange language,
2 Judah became his sanctuary,
and Israel became[1] his dominion.
3 The sea saw (him) and fled,[2]
the Jordan turned back.
4 The mountains skipped like rams,
the hills like young lambs.
5 What ails you, O sea, that you flee?
Why do you turn back, O Jordan?
6 Why do you skip like rams, O you mountains,
like young lambs, O you hills?[3]
7 Tremble, O earth, at the presence of the Lord,
tremble at the presence of the God of Jacob,
8 who turns the rock into a pool of water,
the flint into a flowing fountain![4]

[1] See BH.
[2] * RSV reads 'looked' instead of 'saw him'.
[3] * In RSV vv. 5 and 6 virtually form a single sentence:
　　(5) What ails you, O sea, that you flee?
　　　　O Jordan, that you turn back?

(6) O mountains, that you skip like rams?
O hills, like lambs?
⁴ * RSV has 'into a spring of water' instead of 'into a flowing fountain'.

According to the tradition of later Judaism the psalm was regarded as a Passover hymn which was sung in the liturgy appointed for the eighth day of that festival, but it is impossible to say how far back this practice goes, or whether the psalm was specially composed for the Feast of Passover. The reference to the Kingship of God and to his epiphany (vv. 2, 7) points rather to the Covenant Festival of Yahweh as the place where the psalm was originally used. It may be assumed that its transfer to the Feast of Passover took place in the late pre-exilic or in the post-exilic period. The psalm is a hymn in praise of the God who in the events of the time of Moses chose the people 'as his sanctuary', a decision that represents the fundamental saving fact of the cult of the Covenant Festival. In form and subject-matter the hymn is distinguished by its original and independent character. Leaving the beaten track of poetry of this kind, it proceeds with a terse and gripping brevity and a startling vividness that still clearly portrays the dramatic character of the cultic proceedings. The events of the time of Moses, which brought the people and the religion of the Old Testament into existence, are not regarded by this people as a story which has no longer any meaning for them, but as an activity of God which possesses the quality of an actual and present event, and which was continually experienced afresh and 'represented' in the traditions of the annual festival rites. It is in the light of this attitude of mind that the peculiar character of the psalm first becomes fully understandable. Since the two kingdoms of Judah and Israel are mentioned side by side (v. 2) and so are probably thought of as being still in existence, the psalm seems to date back to the time before the downfall of the northern kingdom (721 BC). It consists of four symmetrically constructed strophes. Verses 1 and 2 speak of the Exodus and of the election of the people, vv. 3 and 4 of the miracles that accompanied the Exodus; vv. 5 and 6 contain the question of the poet, asked in amazement and ironically, as to the cause of these miracles; in vv. 7 and 8 he answers the question himself by referring to the epiphany of the mighty God.

First Strophe: The Exodus and the birth of the nation (vv. 1–2)
The psalm begins with the account of the election of the people of Israel at the Exodus from Egypt. According to the earliest

traditions, which have preserved a true record of the historical facts as
they were still remembered, the history of the people begins with
their deliverance from Egypt. The psalm, however, conforms to the
Old Testament tradition not only as regards the preservation of
historical reminiscences but also in the fact that at the emergence of
the people as a nation history and *Heilsgeschichte* synchronize. God
stands in love and power at the cradle of the nation. To the psalmist
the Exodus from Egypt is essentially the saving act of the God who
helped his people and had compassion on their affliction. This is
made clear in v. 1, where the poet speaks of the Egyptians as of
'barbarians'. The reason why he regards deliverance from their rule
as a specific act of grace is that the burden of foreign rule was felt
so much the more strongly as the oppressor spoke a language that
was unintelligible to the Israelites. At the same time v. 1 expresses
also the pride of a people who are conscious of their own character
and have gained their freedom. Following the example of Ex. 19.6
the psalm singles out the tradition of the election of the people as the
beginning of the *Heilsgeschichte*: 'Judah became his sanctuary and
Israel his dominion.' Parallelism forbids us to look for an essential
difference between the terms which are here used or to try to
understand the term 'sanctuary' as a reference to the Temple,
showing preference for Judah above Israel. The author wants to
emphasize that the rule of God holds sway in both these states, and
therefore, more particularly, that the spiritual unity of the two
brother kingdoms is both given and demanded. This represents the
tradition of 'Greater Israel' and the theology of the cult of the
Covenant, both of which are reflected in the psalm. The singular
character of the history of Israel as God's *Heilsgeschichte* lies in the
fact that the people of Israel as a whole are a people holy to Yahweh.
To serve the *Heilsgeschichte* is the special task for which Yahweh has
chosen this people. The psalmist deliberately avoids speaking openly
of Yahweh here; he refers to him only by hints; in this way he
maintains the tension until he reaches the conclusion of v. 7 and
also reinforces the weird impression which the subsequent verses
produce.

Second Strophe: The miracles accompanying the Exodus (vv. 3–4)
    The poet knows no better way of representing the significance of
the events of the Exodus and the greatness of the God to whom the
nation owes her existence than that of describing the Nature miracles

which accompanied those historical events. It demonstrates the wide scope of the idea of God in the Old Testament, and the comprehensive way in which its faith sees everything as a unity, that themes of the Creation tradition are intermingled with those of the Exodus from Egypt and entry into Canaan; again, that Nature and History are viewed as a unity and are understood as pointing to the sovereign power of the *One* God who is the Lord of both. The majesty and power of the Lord of history is thrown into bold relief by means of the effects of his presence upon Nature which the psalm describes. It is the dread of the terrible majesty of God which causes the sea to flee from him, the Jordan to turn back and the mountains to tremble. The fact that the poet does not give a full and connected account of the historical events, but only picks out particular features of the most striking events that took place at different times, and views them as in a single act, imparts to the whole a concentrated power which originates in the cultic representation of the theophany and of the *Heilsgeschichte*, where everything points to one and the same ultimate reality. This is why incidents which took place at different times fuse into a single event that is full of meaning. The effect of that foreshortened perspective of faith is still further heightened by the fact that the poet, in his enthusiasm for God's greatness, goes beyond the known traditions of the Exodus period by intensifying the miraculous element. Thus the receding of the sea on the occasion of the deliverance at the Red Sea (Ex. 14.21 f.) becomes for the poet a flight from God as he draws near, and he changes the tradition of Josh. 3.14 ff. that the Jordan 'stood still' into a turning back of the river; again, he depicts the quaking of the mountain at the revelation of God at Sinai (Ex. 19.16 ff.), as in Ps. 29.6, with the grotesque word-picture of rams and lambs skipping on the pasture (see also the comments on v. 8). The same vitality of faith is expressed in the fact that the psalmist does not follow the ancient traditions by letting Nature be conquered, but discerns in the miracles the response of Nature, which reacts independently to the power of the divine majesty by showing its terror and fear, and in this way becomes a visible witness to and interpreter of the divine epiphany.

Third Strophe: The intervention of the poet (vv. 5–6)

The poet himself intervenes in the events which he has reported with a question that expresses ironical astonishment, asking the sea, the River Jordan and the mountains why they behave so strangely.

This original stylistic form is not only the fruit of an exuberantly flourishing poetical imagination; at the root of it is rather the peculiar character of the Old Testament religious interpretation of history which has arisen out of ideas associated with the cultus. Whole centuries of history are skipped, events long past are experienced in the representation of the *Heilsgeschichte* in the ritual as having an immediate actual significance. To the eye of faith history is not something dead but something alive and dynamic. For in *everything* that comes to pass in history faith encounters the God who is working in it and through it. The quality of the *Heilsgeschichte* as history that is related to the present, and is brought near by the reading in the cult of the historical traditions contained in Scripture, rests in the Old Testament on the practical and dynamic character of belief in God. This enables us to see why the poet with unprecedented dramatic power intervenes in events that happened centuries ago as if they had taken place just now, repeating in interrogative form what he has just narrated: 'What ails you, O sea, that you flee . . .?' (cf. Ps. 68.16). The purpose of his questions is not only to indicate participation in the past as if it were present, but also to allow time for further reflection, so that the miraculous character of the effects on Nature of God's appearing is thereby rendered still more prominent and the impression of awe and terror produced by the theophany is emphasized. At the same time these questions exhibit a real touch of humour and irony, expressing the freedom and spiritual superiority of a man who by virtue of his faith unreservedly gives himself up to joy in God's sublime nature and sides with him in his bold dealings with Nature. This striking mixture of reverent and trembling awe and of utterly devoted joy in the world-shaking majesty of God is a characteristic feature of Old Testament piety.

Fourth Strophe: The answer (vv. 7–8)

After what has been said so far, it is not surprising that the author of the psalm once more reverts to the solemn note of awe that is sounded in his narrative (vv. 3–4) as he now answers his own questions in the form of a call addressed to the earth and clothed in an original and dramatized form. Only now does he lift the veil which had hitherto lain over his hints at the epiphany of God, and openly states: 'Tremble, O earth, at the presence of Yahweh.' Thus he gives his answer: Nature will surely have good reason to be terrified at the appearing of him who is the Lord. For it is the glory of God which is exalted in this way by his creation at his epiphany. This aspect of the presence of God broadens the psalmist's viewpoint into a comprehensive cosmic vision. He calls upon the *whole* earth to tremble at the presence of the Lord and to give to the God of Jacob the honour that is his due. Once more the psalmist's triumphant joy rings out at the fact that he may call this mighty God the God of his own people and see him at work in the history of the nation as a merciful Deliverer. The closing verse deals with this theme in the style of a hymn and reverts to that note of faith and gratitude which the poet had already touched on at the beginning of the psalm. The same enthusiasm as before prompts him also to embellish the reminiscence of the ancient tradition of the miracle of the spring at Kadesh (Num. 20.8 ff.; cf. Ex. 17.5 f.); he speaks not merely of the water which flowed from the rock to quench the thirst of the people, but of the rock which became 'a pool of water' and of the solid 'flint' which was 'turned into a flowing fountain'. The greatness of the miracle is a measure of the greatness not only of the transcendent majesty of the divine Lord, but also of his incomprehensible grace.

115. NOT TO US, O LORD, BUT TO THY NAME SHOW HONOUR!

1 Not to us, O Lord, not to us,
but to thy name show honour[1]
for the sake of thy grace and thy faithfulness!
2 Why should the Gentiles[2] say,
'Where is then their God?'
3 Our God is in the heavens;
he created whatever he pleased.[3]
4 Their idols are silver and gold,
the work of men's hands.
5 They have mouths, but cannot speak;
they have eyes, but cannot see.
6 They have ears, but cannot hear;
they have noses, but cannot smell.
7 Their hands—they do not feel with them;
their feet—they do not walk with them.[4]
They do not make a sound in their throat.
8 Those who make them are like them;
so are all who trust in them.
9 O Israel, trust in the Lord!
He is their help and their shield.

10 O house of Aaron, put your trust in the Lord!
 He is their help and their shield.
11 You who fear God, trust in the Lord!
 He is their help and their shield.
12 The Lord has been mindful of us;
 he will bless us;
 he will bless the house of Israel;
 he will bless the house of Aaron.
13 He will bless those who fear the Lord,
 both small and great.
14 May the Lord give you increase,
 you and also your children!
15 You are the blessed of the Lord,[5]
 who made heaven and earth.
16 The heavens are the Lord's heavens,
 but the earth he has given to the sons of men.
17 The dead do not praise the Lord,
 nor do any who went down into silence.
18 But we will praise the Lord
 from this time forth and for evermore.
 Hallelujah[6]

[1] * RSV reads 'give glory' instead of 'show honour'.
[2] * RSV has 'the nations' in place of 'the Gentiles'.
[3] * V. 3b is rendered in RSV, 'he does whatever he pleases'.
[4] * The first two lines of v. 7 read in RSV:
 They have hands, but do not feel;
 feet, but do not walk;
[5] * V. 15a is in RSV 'May you be blessed by the Lord.'
[6] See above, p. 22. (Tr. N.: V. 18 ends in RSV: 'Praise the Lord!')

It has long been recognized that Psalm 115 is a cultic liturgy. According to vv. 9–13 the 'house of Israel', the house of Aaron and those who fear God, both adults and children, are assembled in the sanctuary, so that probably one of the great pilgrimage festivals of the covenant cult was the occasion on which the psalm was recited antiphonally (compare the changing into the vocative in vv. 9 ff. with the statements in vv. 1 ff., 12, 18, made in the first person plural). The main theme of the cultic ceremony as well as of the psalm is the revelation of the name and of the 'honour' of God (cf. Isa. 6.1 ff.; see Intr. 30 f., 41 f.), which results in the blessing bestowed upon the cult community and in their songs of praise to the glory of God and in recognition of 'the honour of his name'. It is probable, too, that the arguments used against the Gentiles and their gods, which in vv. 2–8 form the background of the manifestation of the majesty of God, had their place in the cult of the Covenant from

ancient times (cf. the renunciation of the foreign gods in Josh.
24.14 ff., 23 ff.; Gen. 35.2 and Intr. 32 f., 51, 60 f.), and must therefore
not be separated from the psalm as a foreign body. Because the
house of Aaron is mentioned as well as those who fear God, by whom
commentators have understood proselytes of the period of later
Judaism, the psalm has been thought to be relatively late. But that
hypothesis cannot conclusively be proved, since the phrase 'those
who fear God' can just as well mean either the whole Yahweh
community or worshippers of Yahweh of non-Israelite origin, who
already existed in pre-exilic times (cf. I Kings 8.41; Ex. 18.9 ff.;
II Kings 5.17 and the exposition of Psalm 118; also Intr. 37);
moreover, the tradition of the Aaronite priesthood dates from an
earlier period than that of the priestly writings of the Pentateuch.
For these reasons a pre-exilic origin for the liturgy is not excluded,
even though the lack of particular references makes the exact dating
of the psalm impossible.

[1–2] In the opening vv. 1 and 2 the congregation in the style of
the community lament utters a petition for the manifestation of the
power, majesty and glory of God (this is the actual and more far-
reaching meaning of the phrase which has been rendered above by
the term 'honour'). These verses contain the fundamental theme of
the psalm and indicate the main purpose of the cultic ceremony: not
the honour of the congregation but the honour of God! Their chief
concern is that his name and fame be magnified (Ex. 33.19) and that
his 'grace and faithfulness' as the fundamental aspects of the revelation of his nature (Ex. 34.6) be shown to be efficacious (see Intr. 43,
58 f.). In humility they bow down before God knowing only too well
that they themselves cannot claim any honour in comparison with
him and that for their part they are also not able to show God the
honour that is his due unless he himself takes his cause into his own
hands and restores his honour when human failure gives occasion to
the Gentiles to doubt the reality of his power and to blaspheme his
name. The petition of the congregation, which thus expresses their
concern for the honour of God and for the realization of his power
and majesty, implies the profound recognition of their own weakness
and inadequacy which is bound to arise whenever man is faced by
the vivid impression of the greatness and 'glory' of God (cf. Isa.
6.1 ff.): the encounter with the glory of God takes place exactly in
and through the perception of man's own wretchedness. [3] It is
only by focusing their thoughts upon God that the members of the

congregation have the right to compare themselves with the Gentiles; seen through human eyes they do not differ from them. In fact, it is the thought of God the Creator and of his omnipotence, as revealed to all the world in his creation, which refers back to the Creation tradition of the biblical *Heilsgeschichte* (cf. Ps. 135), which provides the answer to the question of the pagan scoffers: 'Where is then their God?' The statement in v. 3a, 'Our God is in the heavens', does not only answer, as has been assumed, the question of God's dwelling-place—even the question asked in v. 2b has much wider scope—but emphasizes the infinite difference between the being of the Creator-God, who is superior to everything else, and the whole created world which he has ordered according to his own personal will, each—heaven, earth, underworld; see v. 16—in its own sphere. **[4–8]** This belief in the almighty Creator-God who is active in everything is the basis of and the criterion for the verdict on the Gentiles and their graven images which forms a counterpart to the hymn in v. 3 and so effectively throws into bolder relief the omnipotence of God. The powerlessness of the images of the gods and of their worshippers is portrayed by using traditional trains of thought and phrases indicating that they belong to the type of firmly stylized forms probably stamped by liturgical tradition (cf. Deut. 4.28; I Sam. 12.21; Hab. 2.18 f.; Jer. 10.3 ff.; 16.19 f.; Isa. 40.19 f.; 44.9 f.; Pss. 96.5; 135.15 ff.). Though the psalmist's criticism of the worship of images may not do full justice to the essence of the ideas that are at the root of it, he nevertheless has clearly grasped the cardinal truth that thereby the barriers between Creator and creature are pulled down, the distinction between God and man obliterated. As man is, so are his gods; indeed, man is actually their master, since he manufactures the inanimate images of his gods, and yet he is at the same time also a fool because he worships the work of his own hands and puts his trust in these images as if they possessed a 'power' of their own. With this the essence of the utter perversion of all belief in gods is grasped and aptly characterized.

[9–11] As an antithesis to the false and foolish trust in the inanimate gods there follows now the exhortation to show genuine trust in the Living God. The words of mockery and the renunciation of the foreign gods are followed, with deliberate liturgical solemnity, by the priest's threefold call upon the covenant community 'Israel', upon the Aaronite priesthood and upon those who fear God (see above); each call is answered by the group who is addressed with the same hymnic affirmation of trust in God. The impersonal form of the response—we would rather expect the response to read 'He is *our* help and *our* shield'—is perhaps intended to emphasize in contrast to the idols the objective fact of God's living power over the followers of the gods, a power that is discernible in history. The fact that their own persons are pushed into the background may perhaps also express their humble sense of the vast difference between themselves and God (thus H. Schmidt). In more recent times the attempt has rightly been abandoned to interpret the refrain as referring to a concrete war situation; rather is it the congregation's affirmation of their trust in the God to whom the people owe their protection and their salvation from of old, an affirmation that was commonly used in the cult (cf. Ps. 33.20). The Old Testament people of God gain their trust in God from the religious experiences of their forefathers which are continually actualized in the sacral tradition. **[12–15]** It is to such a trust alone that the blessing of God, which the priest now proclaims to the congregation (vv. 12–15), will prove fruitful. The words of v. 12, 'The Lord has been mindful of us; he will bless us', presuppose a cultic act—perhaps the theophany with its assurance of salvation guaranteed by the presence of God—by means of which the priest is authorized solemnly to pronounce the divine blessing upon the individual groups of those who take part in the cult. Unbroken blessing upon a numerous posterity, which here, as in the priestly tradition of the Pentateuch, is associated with the Creation tradition, is the saving gift which is constantly bestowed afresh upon the members of the congregation and confirmed to them by the priest (v. 15). They continually receive anew, as a blessing from the hand of the Creator, their strength for and confidence in life. **[16–18]** Having received this blessing, they now in their turn give honour to God (cf. vv. 1, 3) as their heavenly Lord who has assigned to men the earth as their sphere of life and activity where his blessing takes effect. Though they are aware of the limits set to their life on earth and know that the dead cannot praise God, they nevertheless have a share in the everlasting praise of God and this also lifts them above the barriers of death. These two trains of thought are placed side by side without being harmonized with each other, and no attempt is made to resolve intellectually the tension that exists between them. And yet the conclusion of the psalm indicates the perspective from which alone it is possible to overcome the power of death, that is, the eternal Being of God and the

community's permanent living relationship as the people of God
with their almighty Creator, who is also the Lord of the *Heilsgeschichte*.
The consummation of that, however, and the final personal victory
over the power of death lie beyond the scope of the Old Testament,
in the divine mystery of the death and resurrection of Christ.

116. A PSALM OF THANKSGIVING

1 I love the Lord, because he hears my fervent supplications;[1]
2 because he inclined his ear to me, when [2] I cried to him.[3]
3 The snares of death encompassed me;
  torments of hell laid hold on me;
  I suffered distress and anguish.[4]
4 Then I called on the name of the Lord:
  'O Lord, I beseech thee, save my soul!'[5]
5 Gracious is the Lord, and righteous;
  our God is merciful.
6 The Lord preserves the simple;
  I was brought low, but he helps me.[6]
7 Return, O my soul, to your rest;
  for the Lord has dealt bountifully with me.
8 Yea, thou hast delivered me from death,
  my eyes from tears, my feet from stumbling;
9 I may walk before the Lord
  in the land of the living.[7]
10 I kept my faith, even when I said,
  'I am greatly afflicted';
11 I said in my distress,
  'All men are liars.'[8]
12 What shall I render to the Lord
  for all his bounty to me?
13 I will lift up the cup of salvation
  and call on the name of the Lord,
14 I will pay my vows to the Lord
  in the very presence of all his people!
15 It is too hard in the eyes of the Lord
  when his godly ones die and are no more.[9]
16 O Lord, I am indeed thy servant;
  I am thy servant, the son of thy handmaid;
  thou hast loosed my bonds.
17 I will offer to thee the sacrifice of thanksgiving
  and call on the name of the Lord.
18 I will pay my vows to the Lord
  in the very presence of all his people,
19 in the courts of the house of the Lord,

in your midst, O Jerusalem!
Hallelujah[10]

[1] See BH. (Tr. N.: RSV reads 'he has heard' instead of 'he hears' and 'my voice and my supplications' instead of 'my fervent supplications'.)

[2] See BH.

[3] * In RSV v. 2 is a new sentence with a different meaning:
Because he inclined his ear to me,
therefore I will call on him as long as I live.

[4] * The second line of v. 3 reads in RSV, 'the pangs of Sheol laid hold on me'.

[5] * RSV has 'save my life'.

[6] * V. 6b reads in RSV, 'when I was brought low, he saved me'.

[7] * RSV has in the first line 'I walk before the Lord.'

[8] * V. 11 is in RSV:
I said in my consternation,
'Men are all a vain hope.'

[9] * RSV renders v. 15:
Precious in the sight of the Lord
is the death of his saints.

[10] See above, p. 22. (Tr. N.: In RSV the psalm ends: 'Praise the Lord!')

The psalm, which inspired Paul Gerhardt to compose the hymn 'Das ist mir lieb, dass Gott mein hört', is a thanksgiving which the poet recites in public worship in the presence of the congregation (vv. 5, 14, 18) after his prayer has been granted (vv. 6 f., 16) and before he pays his vow (v. 18) and offers the sacrifice of thanksgiving (v. 17). He owes God thanks for delivering him from a danger that threatened his life (vv. 3, 8, 16). It cannot be established for certain whether sickness or persecution (v. 11) was the cause of his affliction. If we take v. 16 literally, then God's verdict (see v. 13) has set him free from prison bonds. Making free use of the stylistic form of the thanksgiving, the psalm gives rein to the diverse sentiments and moods of its poet, who has struggled through mortal terror and deep anguish, in bitterness and despair against all mankind (vv. 10 f.), until he has reached the quiet happiness of a heart sheltered in the love of God and wholly surrendered to the bliss of being able to give him thanks.

[1–2] The psalm opens with a confession of love for God which sums up its essence: the worshipper's intimate communion with God, which fills his heart with a feeling of blissful happiness, rests on the fact that God has answered his prayers. Man's love for God has its cause and lasting support (notice the use of the imperfect tense in v. 1, expressing the worshipper's continuing certitude) in God's favour, which in the first instance evokes man's love in response to God's love for man, so that man's love and gratitude melt into one

another. **[3-4]** The 'narration' of the personal affliction of the worshipper, which takes the form of a lament (vv. 3-4; see Intr. 69 f., 83 f.
immediately changes once more into a general testimony **[5-6]** to
God's grace, righteousness and mercy, of which the poet is convinced
as a living present reality (notice here, too, the use of the same tenses
as in v. 1) and which constrains him to bear witness to the things
that fill his heart with bliss, as representing a valid truth. **[7]** The
monologue of his soul, which may now 'return home' to God and
finds its rest in him, has a particularly intimate ring. Here the image
fuses with the thing it describes: for the worshipper the house of
God has become the place where he is as safe as in his own home, and
the intimate nearness of God the source of his peace of mind. **[8]**
Thus he feels impelled to pray in order to confess to God once more
in a direct dialogue and quite personally what he owes to him. **[9]**
His life, which God has snatched away from the abyss of death, has
been granted to him anew, he is allowed to walk before the face of
God, that is, in communion with him and in his sight, but at the same
time bound by an obligation to do the will of the divine Giver.

[10-11] The psalmist once more recalls the time when he was
depressed and lamented his past affliction; but now he looks at those
bygone days with different eyes. Though men may have caused him
grief that filled his heart with anguish and bitterness, yet behind and
beneath his lament was his faith in God, which he did not let go.
[12] And that faith was not put to shame; overwhelmed by God's
favour the poet rises, full of the joy of thanksgiving. **[13-19]** He lifts
up the 'cup of salvation' (we may perhaps think in this context of an
ordeal where the effect of a drink [cf. Num. 5.11 ff.] determined the
guilt or innocence of the accused[1]) to invoke God and offer to him his
votive-offering in the presence of the assembled congregation, and
to testify to the love and faithfulness of him to whom the life of his
godly ones is too precious for him to abandon them. The words used
in v. 16 express his faithful devotion, prompted by his love for God,
and at the same time his humble submission to the obligation laid
upon him by God's gracious will. With these words he enlists anew
in God's service as his 'bond-servant' and thereby joyously testifies
to the fact that his thanksgiving means more to him than the fulfilling of a cultic duty or a fleeting emotion. It is the surrender of the
innermost being of the whole man to God, evoked and sustained by

---

[1] Compare, however, also the possibility of the interpretation discussed on Ps.
16.5 above.

the love for one who himself has bestowed his own love upon him.

117. THE PRAISE OF GOD

1 Praise the Lord, all peoples!
  Extol him, all nations!
2 For mighty is his grace over us,
  and the truth of the Lord endures for ever.[1]
  Hallelujah[2]

1 * V. 2 reads in the RSV:
  For great is his steadfast love toward us;
  and the faithfulness of the Lord endures for ever.
  Praise the Lord.
2 See above, p. 22.

It is hardly possible that this shortest of all the psalms was originally an independent composition. The view, already suggested by
Hebrew manuscripts and held by several expositors, that it once
formed the conclusion of Psalm 116 is, however, refuted by the
different character of the latter, which is complete in itself and does
not require a continuation of this kind. Other Hebrew manuscripts
treat Psalm 117 as an introduction to Psalm 118, where, however, it
would be in conflict with the liturgical introduction of the latter
(Ps. 118.1–4). Psalm 117 is a call at the opening of the service
addressed by the priest to the whole festival congregation (v. 1), to
sing a hymn to God.[1] This call is justified by briefly recapitulating
the basic facts on which the divine salvation rests and which have
been made known in the theophany (v. 2). On the connection between the divine 'grace' and 'truth'[2] and the self-revelation of God
compare the basic text in Ex. 34.6 (see Intr. 43, 58 f.). So Psalm 117
is to be understood as a liturgical formula to introduce the festival
hymn which follows the theophany and is sung by the whole congregation of pilgrims who have gathered in the sanctuary for the celebration of the feast from different 'peoples' and 'nations' (cf. Pss. 87;
96.1 ff., 7 ff.), and who are called upon to give expression to the
experience of God's salvation which will never cease to be granted
anew. The meaning and purpose of life, for nations as well as
individuals, finds its fulfilment in praising God. In the presence of
God the political and national barriers disappear, and across the
frontiers of countries and states men are linked together in a bond

1 The same characteristic is exhibited by the paraphrase, 'Lobt Gott, den
Herrn, ihr Heiden all'. (Tr. N.: A hymn by Joachim Sartorius, 1552–1600.)
2 * Weiser uses the term 'Wahrheit' (truth) and not 'Treue' (faithfulness), as
one might expect in view of his reference to Ex. 34.6 and to Intr. 43, 58 f.

which unites them in God in fellowship with one another. It is the revelation of the divine grace and truth[1] in which they all share, which alone imparts to the life of the nations its ultimate and deepest meaning and sets every concrete historical situation in a living relationship to something final which in the midst of history endows it with eschatological significance (cf. Rom. 15.11, where the psalm is quoted) and grants it a share in God's everlastingness.

[1] * See previous note.

118. A LITURGY OF THANKSGIVING

1 Testify to the Lord, for he is good;[1]
   for his grace endures for ever!
2 Let Israel say,
   'For his grace endures for ever.'
3 Let the house of Aaron say,
   'For his grace endures for ever.'
4 Let those who fear the Lord say,
   'For his grace endures for ever.'
5 Out of my distress I called on the Lord;
   he answered me and set me free.
6 The Lord is on my side, I do not fear.
   What can men do to me?
7 The Lord is on my side, he helps me;
   I look (without fear) on my enemies.[2]
8 It is better to trust in the Lord[3]
   than to rely on men!
9 It is better to trust in the Lord[3]
   than to rely on princes!
10 All nations surrounded me;
   in the name of the Lord—I destroyed them.[4]
11 They surrounded me on every side;
   in the name of the Lord—I destroyed them.[4]
12 They surrounded me like bees the honeycomb;[5]
   in the name of the Lord—I destroyed them;[5]
   they blazed[6] like a fire of thorns;
   in the name of the Lord—I destroyed them.[4]
13 I was pushed hard that I might fall,
   but the Lord helped me.[7]
14 The Lord is my strength and my song;
   he has become my salvation.
15 The tents of the righteous resound
   with the cry of triumph and victory:
   'The right hand of the Lord gives us victory;[8]
16 the Lord has raised his right hand,
   the right hand of the Lord gives us victory!'[9]

17 I shall not die, but I shall live,
   and recount the deeds of the Lord.
18 The Lord has chastened me sorely,
   but he has not given me over to death.
19 Open to me the gates of righteousness,
   that I may enter through them
   and testify to the Lord![10]
20 This is the gate of the Lord;
   the righteous shall enter through it.
21 I testify to thee that thou hast answered me
   and hast become my salvation.[11]
22 The stone which the builders rejected
   has become the chief cornerstone.
23 This is the Lord's doing;
   it is marvellous in our eyes.
24 This is the day which the Lord has made;
   let us rejoice and be glad in it.
25 Save us, we beseech thee, O Lord!
   O Lord, we beseech thee, give us success!
26 Blessed be he who comes in the name of the Lord!
   We bless you from the house of the Lord.
27 The Lord is God, he has given us light.
   Bind the festal procession with branches,
   up to the horns of the altar!
28 Thou art my God, I will praise thee;[12]
   my God, I will extol thee!
29 Testify to the Lord, for he is good;[1]
   for his grace endures for ever!

[1] * RSV opens with 'O give thanks to the Lord'.
[2] * V. 7b reads in RSV, 'I shall look in triumph on those who hate me.'
[3] * RSV has in vv. 8 and 9 'to take refuge in the Lord' instead of 'to trust in the Lord'.
[4] * In vv. 10, 11 and 12 d RSV reads each time 'I cut them off' instead of 'I destroyed them'.
[5] See BH. (Tr. N.: RSV omits 'the honeycomb' and also the following line.)
[6] See BH.
[7] * V. 13a is in RSV 'I was pushed hard, so that I was falling.'
[8] Lit.: strength.
[9] * In RSV vv. 15 and 16 are:
   (15) Hark, glad songs of victory
        in the tents of the righteous:
        'The right hand of the Lord does valiantly,
   (16) the right hand of the Lord is exalted,
        the right hand of the Lord does valiantly!'
[10] * RSV reads in the last line, 'and give thanks to the Lord'.
[11] * V. 21 opens in RSV, 'I thank thee that thou hast . . .'
[12] * RSV reads 'and I will give thanks to thee' instead of 'I will praise thee'.

This psalm was Luther's favourite psalm. He said of it: 'This is my psalm which I love—for truly it has deserved well of me many a time and has delivered me from many a sore affliction when neither the Emperor nor kings nor the wise nor the cunning nor the saints were able or willing to help me.' This is easily understood, for the psalm is a powerful testimony to the strength of faith that flows from the direct experience of the help of God and in gratitude and joyful surrender to him is able to overcome all human afflictions and fears. With such a character, it is well able to be a help to others in adversity, comforting them by the uplifting power of the strength of its faith, when depressing thoughts weigh heavily upon them, and leading them to trust for help in the living force of God's loving kindness.

It is a fact, already known to the Targum (the ancient Aramaic translation of the books of the Old Testament) and the Talmud, that the psalm was appointed to be antiphonally recited in the liturgy; there are several indications of this in the psalm itself. The ceremony in which the psalm was used took place on a particular day, during the feast (v. 24); it was enacted before the gates of the Temple as well as inside the Temple (vv. 19–20) and seems to have reached its outward climax in a cultic dance round the altar (v. 27). Among those who took part in the ceremony the Israelite participants in the feast, the priests and 'those who fear God', that is, proselytes, are distinguished in vv. 1–4 and are called upon to sing the choral songs alternately. This introductory part is followed (vv. 5–21) by the thanksgiving of an individual—according to vv. 10 ff., 22 presumably that of the king—praising God as man's help in distress. In vv. 22–25 the choir of pilgrims attending the feast joins in the praise of God. Thereafter the blessing pronounced by the priests greets (vv. 26–27) at the gate of the Temple those who enter through it, and the priests call upon the festival congregation to dance round the altar. This is followed by a personal word of thanks addressed to God (v. 28)— probably uttered by the king who is the speaker in vv. 5–21—and the choral refrain sung by the congregation rounds off and concludes the liturgy with the same words that are used in the beginning of the psalm. The feast for which the psalm is appointed is not mentioned. Some expositors, who also assign the verses of the psalm to the several speakers in a different way, think it was the Feast of the Dedication of the Temple, be it in the time of Ezra (Ezra 6.15 f.) or Nehemiah (Neh. 8) or in the Maccabean period (I Macc. 4.54 ff.; II Macc. 10.1 ff.). The absence of any concrete allusions and the general character of the liturgy, however, rather point to the autumn festival of Yahweh, as does the Jewish tradition relating the psalm to the Feast of Tabernacles. The argument that the mention of proselytes points to a late date of the psalm cannot be maintained; for proselytes of the Yahweh religion existed from an early date (I Kings 8.41 ff.; II Kings 5.17; Ex. 18.9 ff.; see Intr. 37).

Introduction (vv. 1–4)

The liturgy is introduced by a chorus of testimony, sung antiphonally by the whole festival congregation. It is understandable that the congregation join in the testimony since what happened to the king affected also their own destiny and their faith. **[1]** The first verse— probably spoken by the precentor—renders the traditional liturgical testimony-formula (cf. Jer. 33.11; Pss. 106.1; 107.1; 136), which provides the framework of the liturgy. Its content, testimony to the abiding goodness and grace of God is the theme of the psalm; in this theme the congregation and the king unite. **[2–4]** The different groups of those who take part in the offering of thanksgiving are called upon in turn to join in singing the refrain attached to the testimony: first of all 'Israel', the people of the Covenant, then 'the house of Aaron', that is, the priesthood, and finally 'those who fear God', that is, the proselytes of non-Israelite origin (similarly Pss. 115.9–11; 135.19–21). By their testimony they set themselves without distinction under the everlasting grace of God of which they have once more been able to gain assurance in the celebration of the festival (see Intr. 42 f.).

The individual thanksgiving (vv. 5–21)

The choral introduction is followed by the king's thanksgiving, which forms the main part of the psalm; the use of the first person singular throughout enables it to be recognized as a complete unit. **[5]** In the opening verse, which contains a brief summary, the king anticipates the account of the events which have called forth his testimony (cf. Ps. 40.1 ff.). His afflictions and his supplications, God's granting of his prayers and deliverance, are all vividly in his mind; and his faith constrains him to bear witness before the congregation to what God has done for him. **[6–7]** He begins by speaking of the feeling of fearlessness and of trust in God that sustains him (cf. Ps. 27.1). If God is for him, who can be against him? With God as his Helper, he knows no fear of men; for what can men do to him when

God appears to help him! Then man is no longer confronted by man,
but by God himself. The fear of men diminishes in proportion to
consciousness of the greatness of God; but so does trust in men and in
human help. **[8–9]** In the form of a general principle of practical
wisdom the psalm expresses, and so makes fruitful for the whole
congregation, a truth based on personal experience. There is only
one place where we can take our stand without ever being shaken
and that is at God's side. This truth is universally valid because it
quite soberly reckons with the ultimate reality and takes this with
that utmost seriousness which it demands. Genuine faith can grow
only where man has completely ceased to trust in men and hanker
after earthly powers and temporal means of power, only where
every human support has broken down and trust in God has become
the only living force. This is the spiritual atmosphere in which the
courage and the clarity of such an attitude of faith can be gained and
preserved.

It is only at this point that the psalm, having defined the fundamental position from which it proceeds, changes into the full and
detailed account of the 'narration' (vv. 10–18; see Intr. 83 f.). This is
dictated by the immediate impression produced by events, as is
shown by the fact that they are not recounted in their chronological
order; on the contrary, the magnitude of the danger and the mighty
power of God's help, the threat issuing from men and the deliverance
wrought by God are set against each other with a descriptive power of
almost eruptive force (vv. 10–14). The account ends in the exultation
over God's victory (vv. 15–16) and in the new hope of life of the one
who has been saved (vv. 17–18). **[10–12]** In powerful rhythms,
strengthened by the antithetic form of these sentences and by the
hammer-blows of the four times repeated refrain, the king describes
his engagement with the adversary. He still trembles at the burden
of those hours in which life and death hung in the balance. This
accounts perhaps for the use of exaggerated word-pictures which on
the one hand describe the threat from which there was, humanly
speaking, no escape, but on the other hand bring into prominence
against this very background the greatness of the divine deliverance.
Thus he tells how he was encircled by 'all the nations' as by a swarm
of bees or a blazing fire of thorns, but destroyed the enemies in the
name of Yahweh. It is, however, also possible that language,
influenced by the original cultic and mythological idea of the combat
of the deity against the hostile primeval powers and of his victory

over them, has here been historicized, that is, applied to the present enemies of Israel whom the king as God's representative defeats 'in his name', thereby securing God's salvation for his people (vv. 13 f.). This battle was 'commemorated' in the cultic festival in that it was 'represented' as a saving act accomplished by the king and once more lived through by the congregation (see vv. 13 f.).[1] It is characteristic of the king's position that in spite of the flush of victory he does not speak with presumptuous pride, but in humility bows down before him who helped him to gain the victory (cf. in this connection vv. 15 f.). **[13–14]** This attitude of the king, who, though conscious of his victory, remains humble and grateful, can be clearly heard in vv. 13 f. The fact that the human plot of the enemies who sought his life has been thwarted by means of God's help has made him realize that human power can do nothing. It is *God* who is 'his strength' and 'his song', a confession which shows the humility and the joyous gratitude of a man who knows that he owes everything to God. **[15–16]** The triumphant shouts now burst forth like victory trumpets upon the fluctuations of battle; a victory-hymn resounds 'in the tents of the righteous', that is, among the festival pilgrims: 'The right hand of the Lord gives us victory, the Lord has raised his right hand, the right hand of the Lord gives us victory.' Here God is envisaged as a mighty hero who stretches out the arm that gives victory and raises it high to do a mighty deed (cf. Isa. 5.25). Such a powerful vision is granted only to the faith which feels itself caught up by the vividness of its impression of the greatness of the ever-present God. **[17–18]** And not only so; the king who has looked death in the face is so strongly dominated by his experience of God that he can comprehend his future life and even the affliction that lies behind him only in the light of the God whom he has encountered. His life has been granted to him anew and filled with a new meaning. He will live henceforth according to God's will and for God, that he may testify to God's power and majesty. The deed done by God is not completed with the king's deliverance, but points to the future; the Helper-God is also the God who demands. The God who gives life claims it for his service. In the light of this truth the singer is even able to penetrate the darkness that had lain over his struggle. He now realizes that God has dealt graciously with him even during the time of suffering brought about by his enemies. God has indeed

---

[1] Johnson, *Sacral Kingship in Ancient Israel*, pp. 116 ff., interprets the psalm in a similar sense.

chastened him, but not in order to give him over to death, but with the intention of guiding him to the point where his life would take on new meaning. Now the straight course pursued by God, which cuts right across the fluctuations in his life, has become quite clear to him: by means of God's guiding discipline he was to be brought to the stage where he would be able to bear witness both in word and deed to 'the deeds of the Lord', his power and his greatness.

[19] The thanksgiving of the man who has been saved seems to have been recited in front of the gate of the Temple. At any rate, in v. 19 he stands near to the entrance to the sanctuary and calls to the gate-keepers to open the locked 'gate of righteousness'—in Babylon, too, the several gates of the Temple have their special names—that he may enter to give thanks to Yahweh. [20] This verse is best understood as the response of the gate-keepers, who invite him to enter the sanctuary. Certain conditions are however attached to this invitation, as Psalms 15 and 24 make quite clear. Only the 'righteous' may enter the house of God. In the holy place of the Temple the worshipper is encompassed by the devout and solemn atmosphere of the festive hour. [21] He falls down in prayer to confess before his God with thanksgiving that he 'has answered him and has become his salvation'.

The testimony of the congregation (vv. 22–25)

The change of the subject (we) in the subsequent verses, which speak of the king in the third person, indicates that it is now the turn of the congregation to speak. [22] They express what has happened to the king, in the now famous parable of the stone which, rejected by the builders, has become the chief cornerstone. The chief cornerstone, an ashlar that has been squared, has to be selected with special care, as it has to carry the weight of the building pressing on it from two directions, and only good and strong material can be used for such a purpose. The parable illustrates the change that has taken place in the fortunes of the saved man: he was rejected, despised and persecuted by men, but was saved and honoured by God and was entrusted by him with a particularly important task. The interpretation of this saying in late Judaism as referring to David and to the Messiah, which also led to its application to Christ in the New Testament (Matt. 21.42; Acts 4.11; I Peter 2.7), is presumably based on the correct recollection that the king appeared in the cult in the rôle of David (cf. Ps. 18; see Intr. 96), and that the royal cult entailed that at any given time the tradition of his ancestor was revived in the person of the actual representative of the Davidic dynasty. [23] The members of the congregation, too, regard what has happened to the one who has been saved as the work not of men but of God. Their words, expressing awe and wonder at the miracle wrought by God, are the firstfruit of that testimony of the king recounting God's saving deed. Any testimony borne by faith kindles new faith and creates a fellowship of faith. [24] Their collective joy in God's victory means that for them the joyful festival becomes the 'Day of the Lord' which God himself has instituted (cf. Ps. 111.4). [25] The thanksgiving naturally passes into the petition that in the future, too, God may grant his salvation and give them success.

[26] Having reached the interior of the sanctuary those who enter therein are greeted by the blessing pronounced by the priests. We have to think of them as the speakers in v. 26 and perhaps also in v. 27. The first part of the blessing, which has also been used in the account of the entry of Jesus into Jerusalem (Matt. 21.9), is addressed to the king, the second part to the festival congregation. [27] The blessing comes 'from the house of the Lord', where God is present. With the words 'The Lord is God, he has given us light', which are modelled on the Aaronite benediction (Num. 6.24 ff.) and point to the theophany (see Intr. 38 ff.), the priests, too, now join in testifying to God, and so include themselves with the one who has been saved and with the testifying congregation, united by their joint declaration of faith. The second part of the verse contains the call to a festal dance around the altar; this call is most easily understood as being uttered by the priests. The phrase 'Bind the festal procession with branches, up to the horns of the altar' probably means that as the festal bouquets and branches of palms or willows touch each other, as well as the horns of the altar, its quality of holiness will be imparted to the dancers; other commentators translate 'ropes' instead of 'branches' and see in this the widespread custom of using ropes to mark the congregation off as a holy people, thus separating them from what was regarded as profane.

[28–29] The thanksgiving of the king (v. 28) and of the choir (v. 29) concludes the psalm; it was probably sung as a hymn accompanying the dance. Thus all feelings unite in a hymn testifying with deep gratitude to God, whose goodness has once more been brought vividly before them all, on which they can rely and from which they can draw comfort in every adversity. The closing words, which hark back to the beginning of the psalm, are resonant with the inward happiness that springs from faith, a happiness granted to the congregation, who are able to bear witness to God's everlasting salvation and grace.

119. THE WORD AND THE STATUTES OF GOD

1 Blessed are those whose way is blameless,
who walk in the law of the Lord!
2 Blessed are those who keep his testimonies,
who seek him with their whole heart!
3 They have done no wrong,
they have walked in his ways.[1]
4 Thou hast thyself given thy precepts,
that they may be kept diligently.[2]
5 O that my ways may be steadfast in keeping thy statutes!
6 Then I shall not be put to shame,
having my eyes fixed on all thy commandments.
7 I shall testify to thee with an upright heart,
when I learn the ordinances of thy salvation.[3]
8 I will observe thy statutes;
O forsake me not utterly!

9 How can a young man keep his way pure?
By giving heed to thy words.[4,5]
10 With my whole heart have I sought[6] thee;
let me not wander from thy commandments!
11 I have laid up thy word in my heart,
that I might not sin against thee.
12 Blessed be thou, O Lord;
teach me thy statutes!
13 With my lips I declared[7] all the ordinances of thy mouth.
14 In the way of thy testimonies I delight
as much as in all riches.
15 I will meditate on thy precepts,
and fix my eyes on thy ways.
16 I will delight in thy precepts;
I will not forget thy word.

17 Deal bountifully with thy servant,
that I may live and give heed to thy word!
18 Open my eyes, that I may behold
wondrous things out of thy law!
19 I am a sojourner on earth;
hide not thy commandments from me!
20 My soul is consumed with longing for thy ordinances at all times.
21 Thou hast rebuked the insolent.

Let him be accursed who wanders from thy commandments![8]

22 Take away from me disgrace and contempt,
for I have kept thy testimonies.[9]

23 Even though princes sit plotting against me,
thy servant will meditate on thy statutes.

24 Yea, thy testimonies are my delight,
thy statutes[10] are my counsellors.

25 My soul cleaves to the dust;
revive me according to thy word!

26 When I told of my ways, thou didst answer me;
teach me thy statutes!

27 Make me understand the way of thy precepts,
and I will meditate on thy wondrous works.

28 My soul weeps for grief;
O strengthen me according to thy word!

29 The way of lying put far from me;
and graciously teach me thy law![11]

30 I have chosen the way of truthfulness,[12]
I set thy ordinances before me.

31 I cleave to thy testimonies, O Lord;
let me not be put to shame!

32 I run in the way of thy commandments,
for thou enlargest my heart.[13]

33 Teach me, O Lord, the way of thy statutes;
and I will keep it as a reward.[14]

34 Give me understanding, that I may keep thy law
and observe it with my whole heart!

35 Let me walk in the paths of thy commandments,
for I delight in it.[15]

36 Incline my heart to thy testimonies,
and not to gain!

37 Turn my eyes from looking at vanities;
revive me by thy word.[16]

38 Confirm to thy servant thy promise,
which is for those who fear thee!

39 Turn away the reproach which I dread;
for thy judgments are good![17]

40 Behold, I long for thy precepts;
in thy righteousness give me life!

41 Let thy mercies come to me, O Lord,
thy salvation according to thy word,

42 that I shall have an answer for him who reviles me;
for I trust in thy word.

43 Take not the word of truth out of my mouth ' ',[5]
for my hope is in thy judgments![18]

44 I will keep thy law continually, for ever and ever,
45 that I may walk in freedom;
   for I have sought thy precepts.[19]
46 I will speak of thy testimonies before kings,
   and am not ashamed of them.[20]
47 For I find my delight in thy precepts, which I love.
48 I lift up my hands to thy commandments ' '[5]
   and meditate on thy statutes.[21]

49 Remember thy word to thy servant,
   in which thou hast made me hope!
50 This is my comfort in my affliction
   that thy word gives me life.
51 Insolent men utterly derided me;
   but I did not turn away from thy law.[22]
52 I thought of thy judgments from of old,
   O Lord, and take comfort.[23]
53 Hot indignation seized me because of the wicked,
   who forsake thy law.
54 Thy statutes have become[24] my songs
   in the house of my pilgrimage.
55 I remembered thy name in the night, O Lord,[7]
   and give heed to thy law.
56 This blessing has fallen to me,
   that I keep thy commandments.[25]

57 The Lord is my portion;
   I promise to keep thy words.
58 I cried to thee[26] with all my heart:
   be gracious to me according to thy word!
59 I considered my ways,
   and turn my feet to thy testimonies.[27]
60 I hastened and did not delay to keep thy precepts.[1]
61 Though the cords of the wicked ensnared me,
   I did not forget thy law.[7]
62 At midnight I rise to praise thee
   because of thy righteous judgments.[17]
63 I am a friend of all who fear thee,
   of those who keep thy commandments.
64 The earth, O Lord, is full of thy grace;
   teach me thy statutes!

65 Thou hast dealt well with thy servant,
   O Lord, according to thy word.
66 ' '[5] Teach me good judgment and knowledge,
   for I believe in thy precepts!
67 Before I was brought low, I went astray;
   but now I give heed to thy word.[28]

68 Thou art good and kindhearted;
  teach me thy statutes!
69 The insolent men besmear me with lies,
  but with my whole heart I keep thy commandments.
70 Their heart is gross like fat,
  but I delight in thy law.
71 It is good for me to be brought low,
  that I may learn thy statutes.[28]
72 I take a greater delight in the law of thy mouth
  than in a thousand gold and silver pieces.[29]

73 Thy hands have made and fashioned me;
  give me understanding that I may learn thy commandments!
74 Those who fear thee rejoice when they see me,
  because I wait for thy word.[30]
75 I know, O Lord, that thy judgments are righteous,
  and that in faithfulness thou hast brought me low.[28]
76 Let thy grace be ready to comfort me
  according to thy promise to thy servant.
77 Let thy mercy come to me, that I may live;
  for thy law is my delight.
78 The insolent men will be put to shame,
  because they have oppressed me with deceit;
  as for me, I will meditate on thy ordinances.[31]
79 Those who fear thee turn to me,
  and so do those who know thy testimonies.[32]
80 May my heart be blameless in thy statutes,
  that I may not be put to shame!

81 My soul languishes for thy salvation;
  I hope for thy word.
82 My eyes pine for thy word;
  when wilt thou comfort me?[33]
83 For I have become like a wineskin in the smoke;
  yet I have not forgotten thy statutes.
84 How long must thy servant endure?
  When wilt thou judge those who persecute me?
85 Insolent men have dug pitfalls for me,
  men who do not conform to thy law.
86 All thy commandments are truth;[34]
  they persecute me with falsehood; help me!
87 They have almost made an end of me on earth;
  but I have not forsaken thy commandments.
88 In thy grace quicken me
  that I may observe the testimonies of thy mouth![35]

89 For ever, O Lord, thy word is firmly fixed in the heavens.
90 Thy faithfulness endures to all generations;

thou hast established the earth, and it stood fast.

91 By thy appointment it stands to this day;
   for the universe is thy servant.[36]
92 If thy law had not been my delight,
   I should have perished in my affliction.
93 I will never forget thy precepts;
   for by them thou hast given me life.
94 I am thine, save me; for I have sought thy commandments.
95 The wicked lie in wait to destroy me;
   but I give heed to thy testimonies.
96 I have seen a limit to all things;[37]
   but thy commandment is exceedingly broad.

97 Oh, how I love thy law!
   It is my meditation all the day.
98 Thy commandment makes me wiser than my enemies,
   for it is ever with me.
99 I have more understanding than all my teachers,
   for thy testimonies are my meditation.
100 I have more discernment than the aged,
    for I have kept thy precepts.
101 I held back my feet from every evil way,[7]
    in order to keep thy word.
102 I did not turn aside from thy ordinances,[7]
    for thou hast taught me.
103 How sweet are thy words[5] to my taste,
    sweeter than honey to my mouth!
104 Through thy precepts I got understanding;[7]
    therefore I hate every false way.

105 Thy word is a lamp to my feet and a light to my path.
106 I have sworn on oath and kept it,
    to observe thy righteous ordinances.
107 I am sorely afflicted;
    quicken me, O Lord, according to thy word!
108 Accept the freewill offerings of my mouth;
    teach me thy ordinances, O Lord![38]
109 I hold my life in my hand continually,
    and I did not forget thy law.[39]
110 The wicked have laid a snare for me,
    but I did not stray from thy ordinances.[7]
111 Thy testimonies are my heritage[5] for ever,
    for they are the joy of my heart.
112 I incline my heart to perform thy statutes,
    for the reward is for ever.[40]

113 I hate double-minded men,
    but I love thy law.

114 Thou art my hiding-place and my shield;
   I hope for thy word.
115 Depart from me, you evildoers;
   I will keep the commandments of my God.[41]
116 Uphold me according to thy promise,
   that I may live and not be put to shame in my hope!
117 Hold me up, and I shall be safe,
   and delight in thy statutes.[42]
118 Thou dost spurn all who go astray from thy statutes;
   for falsehood is their deceit.[43]
119 All the wicked of the earth thou dost count[5] as dross;
   therefore I love thy testimonies.
120 My flesh trembles for fear of thee,
   and I am afraid of thy judgment.

121 I have done what is just and right;
   do not leave me to my oppressors.
122 Be surety for thy servant for good,
   that the insolent men do not oppress me!
123 My eyes pine for thy salvation,
   and for the word of thy righteousness.[44]
124 Deal with thy servant according to thy grace,
   and teach me thy statutes!
125 I am thy servant; give me understanding,
   that I may know thy testimonies!
126 It is time for the Lord to act,
   for they have broken thy law.
127 Therefore I love thy commandments
   above gold, above fine gold.
128 Therefore I walk[5] rightly according to all thy instructions;[45]
   I hate every false way.

129 Thy testimonies are wonderful;
   therefore my soul keeps them.
130 The gate[5] of thy words shines;[46]
   it imparts understanding to the simple.
131 I open my mouth and pant,
   because I long for thy commandments.
132 Turn to me and be gracious to me,
   as is due to those who love thy name.[47]
133 Keep steady my steps by thy word.[48]
   let no iniquity get dominion over me.
134 Redeem me from men's oppression;
   I will keep thy precepts!
135 Make thy face shine upon thy servant,
   and teach me thy statutes!
136 My eyes shed streams of tears,
   because men did not keep thy law.[7]

137 Righteous art thou, O Lord,
    and right are[5] thy judgments.
138 Thou hast appointed thy testimonies
    in righteousness and in all faithfulness.
139 My zeal consumes me,
    because my foes forgot thy words.[7]
140 Thy word is wholly pure,
    and thy servant loves it.[49]
141 I am small and despised,
    yet I did not forget thy statutes.[7]
142 Thy righteousness is in the right for ever,
    and thy law is truth.
143 Trouble and anguish have come upon me,
    but thy commandments are my delight.
144 Thy testimonies are righteous for ever;
    give me understanding that I may live!

145 With my whole heart I cry; answer me, O Lord!
    I will keep thy statutes.
146 I cry to thee; save me,
    that I may observe thy testimonies.
147 I rise before dawn and cry[50];
    I hope for thy words.
148 My eyes are awake before the watches of the night,
    that I may meditate upon thy word.[51]
149 Hear my voice, O Lord, in thy grace;
    quicken me according to thy justice![52]
150 They draw near who persecute me[5] with evil purpose,
    they are far from thy law.
151 But thou art near, O Lord,
    and all thy precepts are truth.
152 Long have I known from thy testimonies
    that thou hast founded them for ever.

153 Look on my affliction and deliver me,
    for I did not forget thy law.[7]
154 Plead my cause and redeem me;
    give me life according to thy promise!
155 Salvation is far from the wicked,
    for they do not seek thy statutes.
156 Great is thy mercy, O Lord;
    give me life according to thy justice.[5]
157 Many are my persecutors and my adversaries,
    but I did not swerve from thy testimonies.[7]
158 When I see the faithless, I am disgusted,
    because they do not give heed to thy word.[53]
159 Consider how I love thy ordinances!
    O Lord, give me life according to thy grace![54]

160 The sum of thy words[5] is truth;
and everyone of thy righteous ordinances endures for ever.

161 Princes persecute me without cause,
but my heart stands in awe of thy word.

162 I rejoice at thy word
like one who finds great spoil.

163 I hate and abhor falsehood,
but I love thy law.

164 Seven times a day I praise thee
for thy righteous ordinances.

165 Great peace have those who love thy law;
nothing can make them stumble.

166 I hope for thy salvation, O Lord,
thy commandments alone have I done.[55]

167 My soul has kept thy testimonies
and loves them exceedingly.

168 I have kept thy ordinances and testimonies,
for all my ways are before thee.

169 Let my cry come before thee O Lord;
give me understanding according to thy word!

170 Let my prayer come before thee, O Lord;
deliver me according to thy word!

171 My lips shall pour forth praise,
for thou teachest me thy statutes.[56]

172 My tongue shall sing of thy word,
for all thy statutes are righteous.[56]

173 Let thy hand be ready to help me,
for I have chosen thy precepts.

174 I long for thy salvation, O Lord,
and thy law is my delight.

175 Let my soul live that I may praise thee,
and let thy ordinances help me.

176 I have gone astray; seek thy servant like a lost sheep,
for I did not forget thy statutes.[57]

1 * V. 3 reads in RSV:
who also do no wrong,
but walk in his ways!
2 * RSV renders v. 4:
Thou hast commanded thy precepts
to be kept diligently.
3 * RSV reads 'thy righteous ordinances' instead of 'the ordinances of thy
salvation'.
4 * V. 9b is in RSV, 'By guarding it according to thy word.'
5 See BH.
6 * In RSV v. 10a reads, 'With my whole heart I seek thee.'
7 * RSV uses the present tense.

8 * V. 21 reads in RSV:
    Thou dost rebuke the insolent, accursed ones,
    who wander from thy commandments.
9 * RSV, relating v. 22 to v. 21, renders v. 22a, 'take away from me their
scorn and contempt'.
10 See BH. (Tr. N.: RSV reads in v. 24b 'they' instead of 'thy statutes'.)
11 * In RSV v. 29a is 'Put false ways far from me.'
12 * RSV has 'the way of faithfulness' instead of 'the way of truthfulness'.
13 * RSV reads 'I will run' instead of 'I run' and renders v. 32b, 'when thou
enlargest my understanding'.
14 * In v. 33b RSV reads 'to the end' instead of 'as a reward'.
15 * RSV has 'lead me in the path . . .'
16 See BH. (Tr. N.: 37b is in RSV 'and give me life in thy ways'.)
17 * RSV has 'ordinances' instead of 'judgments'.
18 * RSV adds 'utterly' after 'the word of truth' and has 'ordinances' instead
of 'judgments'.
19 * V. 45a reads in RSV, 'and I shall walk at liberty'.
20 * In RSV v. 46b is 'and shall not be put to shame'.
21 * V. 48 reads in RSV:
    I revere thy commandments, which I love,
    and I will meditate on thy statutes.
22 * RSV has 'godless men' instead of 'the insolent men' and uses throughout
the present tense.
23 * V. 52 is in RSV:
    When I think of thy ordinances from of old,
    I take comfort, O Lord.
24 * RSV has 'have been' instead of 'have become'.
25 * RSV has 'that I have kept' instead of 'that I keep'.
26 Lit.: I have smoothed (caressed) thy face. (Tr. N.: RSV renders v. 58a, 'I
entreat thy favour with all my heart.')
27 * RSV reads, 'When I think of thy ways, I turn . . .'
28 * RSV has 'afflicted' instead of 'brought low'.
29 * In RSV v. 72 reads, 'The law of thy mouth is better to me than thousands
of . . .'
30 * V. 74 is in RSV:
    Those who fear thee shall see me and rejoice,
    because I have hoped in thy word.
31 * In RSV the first two lines of v. 78 are:
    Let the godless be put to shame,
    because they have subverted me with guile;
32 * V. 79 reads in RSV:
    Let those who fear thee turn to me,
    that they may know thy testimonies.
33 * In RSV v. 82 is:
    My eyes fail with watching for thy promise;
    I ask, 'When wilt thou comfort me?'
34 * RSV has 'are sure' instead of 'are truth'.
35 * RSV reads 'spare my life' instead of 'quicken me'.
36 * RSV has 'they stand this day' instead of 'it stands to this day' and renders
v. 91b, 'for all things are thy servants'.
37 See BH. (Tr. N.: V. 96a is in RSV 'I have seen a limit to all prefection.')
38 * In RSV v. 108 reads:
    Accept my offerings of praise, O Lord,
    and teach me thy ordinances.

[39] * V. 109b begins in RSV, 'but I do not forget . . .'
[40] * V. 112b is in RSV 'for ever, to the end'.
[41] * RSV has in v. 115b 'that I may keep' instead of 'I will keep'.
[42] * In RSV v. 117 is:
Hold me up, that I may be safe
and have regard for thy statutes continually!
[43] * V. 118b is in RSV 'yea, their cunning is in vain'.
[44] * In RSV v. 123 is:
My eyes fail with watching for thy salvation,
and for the fulfilment of thy righteous promise.
[45] See BH. (Tr. N.: V. 128a reads in RSV, 'Therefore I direct my steps by all thy
precepts.')
[46] * RSV renders v. 130a, 'The unfolding of thy words gives light.'
[47] * RSV reads 'as is thy wont toward those' instead of 'as is due to those'.
[48] * RSV has 'according to thy promise' instead of 'by thy word'.
[50] * RSV adds 'for help'.
[51] * RSV has 'upon thy promise' instead of 'upon thy word'.
[52] * The second line of v. 149 reads in RSV, 'O Lord, in thy justice preserve
my life.'
[53] * V. 158 is rendered in RSV:
I look at the faithless with disgust,
because they do not keep thy commands.
[54] * V. 159b reads in RSV, 'Preserve my life according to thy steadfast love.'
[55] * V. 166b is in RSV 'and I do thy commandments'.
[56] * In RSV vv. 171 and 172 have 'will' instead of 'shall'.
[57] * RSV rearranges and punctuates v. 176a to read: 'I have gone astray like
a lost sheep; seek thy servant,' and also reads the present tense in v. 176b.

This psalm, the most comprehensive of all the psalms, is a
particularly artificial product of religious poetry. It shares with
Psalms 9, 10, 111 and others the formal feature of the alphabetic
acrostic, with the difference, however, that here the initial letter
remains the same for each of the eight lines of a section. In accordance
with the number of the letters of the Hebrew alphabet twenty-two
such 'poems' are joined together; these, however, neither show a
consistent thought-sequence one with another nor represent units
complete in themselves. This formal external character of the psalm
stifles its subject-matter. The psalm is a many-coloured mosaic of
thoughts which are often repeated in a wearisome fashion; in the
hymn 'Wohl denen, die da wandeln vor Gott in Heiligkeit'[1] they are
condensed with welcome brevity. The types of poetry, too, change
without any recognizable order and reinforce the impression of
restlessness produced by the whole psalm. Sayings concerning
blessedness (vv. 1–3) and cursing (v. 21), hymns (vv. 13 f., 54, 71 f.,
89 ff., 105, 172) and thanksgivings (v. 7), confessions (vv. 31 ff.) and

[1] * Composed by Heinrich Schütz (1585–1672) after a text by Cornelius
Becker (1561–1604).

assertions of the psalmist's own righteousness (vv. 11, 98 ff., 111, 121, 162 ff.), themes borrowed from laments and supplications (vv. 8, 107, 153 ff.), affirmations of trust (v. 42) and Wisdom sayings (vv. 9, 99) frequently follow each other without any real connecting link, so that it is not possible to discover their *Sitz im Leben*; the psalm is a purely literary product. For all that, it has a dominating focal point round which the thoughts of its author revolve: the word of God and the law of God as the decisive factor in every sphere of life. There is hardly a verse which does not contain a reference to God's word and law. Even though different terms are used to describe them, such as 'ordinances', 'testimonies', 'precepts', and 'statutes', they are nevertheless always meant to express the same thing. It cannot be proved that the poet borrowed these terms from Psalm 19 nor that he has employed eight different synonyms in each individual strophe, as indeed we must not fall into the error of letting the artificial form of the psalm make us overlook the personal religious experiences as well as the religious life of the poet, which form the background of the psalm, and of regarding the psalm as a 'general pattern' as regards subject-matter, too (this point in opposition to Kittel; see Intr. 64 f.). The statements concerning persecution and oppression (vv. 61, 78, 84 ff., 110, etc.) are to be taken quite seriously; and it is only if we understand them as being at the root of the poet's utterances that we can apprehend the strength and the comfort which God's word and his law impart to the life of the poet. They mean so much to him that he who has been brought low through suffering and has been enlightened by the law (vv. 67, 71, 75) regards the latter as his most precious treasure (vv. 72, 127), as the source of his joy and delight (vv. 16, 24, 47, 70 and often), as the goal of his knowledge and the standard of his conduct in life (vv. 12, 26, 64, 68), and as the object of his love (v. 47). It is possible to deduce from the psalm a full-fledged 'theology' of the law, in both its theoretical and its practical aspects. The simple form of the diction makes it unnecessary to expound the psalm in detail. It only remains to point out that the kind of piety, based on the law, such as is presented to us in the psalm does not yet exhibit that degeneration and hardening into a legalistic form of religion to which it succumbed in late Judaism and which provoked Jesus' rebuke. On the other hand, however, one cannot fail to realize that a piety such as is expressed in the psalm, according to which God's word and law take the place of God himself and his wondrous works (v. 13), are even worshipped (v. 48) and become the source of that comfort which as a rule is bestowed upon man by the divine saving grace (vv. 50, 92), carries with it the germs of a development which was bound to end in the self-righteousness of the Pharisees and scribes.

120. STRIVING FOR PEACE

A Pilgrim Song[1]

1 In my distress I cried to the Lord,
  and he answered me:[2]
2 'Save my life, O Lord,
  from lying lips,
  from a deceitful tongue.'[3]
3 What will he give you,
  what more will he do to you,
  you deceitful tongue?[4]
4 A warrior's arrows, sharpened—
  and glowing coals of the broom tree as well!
5 Woe is me, that I sojourned in Meshech,
  that I dwelt among the tents of Kedar![5]
6 Too long has my soul already dwelt
  with him who hates peace.[6]
7 I love peace; but when I speak,
  they seek to quarrel with me.[7]

[1] See above, p. 100. (Tr. N.: RSV translates 'A Song of Ascents'.)
[2] * RSV, using the present tense, reads:
  In my distress I cry to the Lord,
  that he may answer me.
[3] * RSV has 'deliver me' instead of 'save my life'.
[4] * The first two lines of v. 3 are rendered in RSV:
  What shall be given to you?
  And what more shall be done to you,
[5] * RSV uses the present tense throughout.
[6] * V. 6 is rendered in RSV:
  Too long have I had my dwelling
  among those who hate peace.
[7] * RSV reads 'I am for peace' instead of 'I love peace' and 'they are for war' instead of 'they seek to quarrel with me'.

It is not evident from the psalm itself why this psalm, with which the Book of Pilgrim Songs (Pss. 120–134) opens, has been included in this special collection. It may be that the literal interpretation of the statements made in v. 5, in which the poet speaks of his 'dwelling' among alien nations, has led to the view, which was also held by later expositors, that the psalm was composed by a Jew living in the Diaspora who had made a pilgrimage to the sanctuary to attend a

festival. Since, however, the references to places in v. 5 are probably
to be understood in a figurative sense (see below), we shall have to
forgo that explanation, just as we shall have to refrain from discussing
in greater detail the external historical situation to which the psalm
owes its origin. As far as that situation is concerned, we are here as
much in the dark as in many other psalms.

[1] In form the psalm is a testimony uttered after the prayer has
been granted (v. 1). It is unnecessary and hardly legitimate, though
fashionable nowadays, to translate the perfect tenses by the present
tense, thus marking the whole psalm as a prayer of lament. [2] As in
Psalm 41 and often, it is rather a question of the testimony (thanksgiving) of a worshipper, in the course of which he repeats his previous
lament in order to throw once more into bold relief before God and
the congregation all the blessings bestowed upon him as a result of
the answering of his prayers. Hence v. 2 by no means introduces a
new petition, as some commentators assume, but recapitulates the
supplication which has now been granted—probably in connection
with the occasion when the psalm was recited, that is to say, during the
cultic ceremony (see Intr. 69 f., 82 f.). The worshipper—according to
v. 7 a peace-loving man—had been afflicted by the mendacious and
deceitful machinations of other people, with whom he perhaps had
lived (vv. 5 f.); he had been persecuted by them, and they had probably
indicted him so that his case had to be decided by an ordeal. [3]
We are led to this view by v. 3, which obviously contains an allusion
to the oath which his adversary had to swear on such an occasion, and
which also makes use of the wording of the oath formula, 'May God
do this or that to me and more also . . .' (cf. I Sam. 3.17; 14.44;
20.13 and often), in asking the adversary what God will give him, the
man with a deceitful tongue, in answer to his oath (see Intr. 76 ff.).
This interpretation of the verse under discussion deserves preference
to the other explanation which regards the question as being
addressed to God meaning: 'After all, is there a great deal which a
deceitful tongue can give thee?'; for against the latter interpretation
objections must be raised which are based on the grammar of v. 3
as well as on its content and context. The worshipper takes God and
the oath which has to be sworn before him so seriously that he takes
his enemy at his word and is convinced that God will bring to pass
in a terrible way upon the man who takes an oath lightly the
cursing of his own person, which every oath formula contains. [4]
This thought is directly continued in v. 4, which contains the answer

to the question asked in v. 3 (on its stylistic form cf. Hos. 9.14). The two metaphors which the poet uses, of the sharpened arrows of the warrior and of the glowing coals of the broom tree, are as much as to say 'murder and fire', that is, death and destruction. By these the poet has been able to express a singularly fine thought: since the tongue is frequently compared with the arrow (cf. Pss. 7.13; 11.2; 57.4; 64.3) and coal made from the hard wood of the broom tree is regarded as particularly effective for heating power, these metaphors intimate that the false word uttered in the oath redounds upon the perjurer, just as the treacherous arrow hits the archer himself and the lie destroys the liar by its consuming fire. The poet discerns in this self-destruction of the wicked, which he proclaims to the adversary, the effect which the ordeal has on the man who does not deal truthfully before God and men. The form of the (rhetorical) question and the way in which the psalmist expresses that truth in his answer prove that for him the divine righteousness is not a problem but a certitude. **[5–6]** The lament in v. 5 shows the depth of the worshipper's own earnest conviction that he can be sure of God's righteousness. The literal interpretation of the verse, according to which the parallel statements regarding the sojourning at Meshech and the dwelling among the tents of Kedar point to the Diaspora as the worshipper's place of residence, is refuted by the fact that Meshech, which according to Gen. 10.2 (cf. Ezek. 27.13; 32.26) is to be looked for somewhere between the Black Sea and the Caspian Sea, and Kedar, a tribe of Bedouins in the Syrian-Arabian desert (cf. Gen. 25.13; Isa. 42.11), are too far removed from each other to come into question as purely geographical designations intended to describe the author's domicile. We shall therefore have to understand these statements as metaphors by means of which the poet wants to express his feeling of regret that for such a long time he has had house-fellowship with his quarrelsome adversaries, who now appear to him to be like 'Turks and infidels'; the Bedouins of Kedar were after all regarded as savage and pugnacious people who were entirely worthy of their ancestor Ishmael (cf. Gen. 16.12). This view is confirmed by v. 6 which, without using metaphor, gives expression to the same thought which is expressed in v. 5 with that picturesque vividness typical of the oriental manner of speech.

[7] Against this background the poet therefore emphasizes so much the more strongly his own peaceful intentions, which accord with his whole character, when in a striking phrase he says literally: 'I am peace.' But he had to undergo the bitter experience: 'Even the most devout man will not be left in peace if it does not please his wicked neighbour.'[1] As soon as he speaks of peace, his adversaries seek to quarrel with him; and this is the incomprehensible disharmony in his life from which he has suffered, and which once more is thrown into relief as trenchantly as possible. For only so does it become manifest what God's granting of his prayer in response to his lament means to him. Thus his former lament is now presented as a sign of the experience of answered prayer, and this makes the psalm a testimony to the greatness of the divine help and righteousness, which is able to accomplish what is impossible with men and grants to a man's soul that peace of which he had been robbed by men and which the world cannot give.

[1] * In the German original,
    Es kann der Frömmste nicht im Frieden bleiben,
    Wenn es dem bösen Nachbarn nicht gefällt,
a quotation from Schiller's *Wilhelm Tell* (Act IV, Scene 3).

121. I LIFT UP MY EYES TO THE HILLS

A Pilgrim Song[1]

1 I lift up my eyes to the hills.
   From whence does my help come?
2 Help[2] comes from the Lord,
   who made heaven and earth.
3 May he not suffer your foot to slip,
   may he who keeps you not slumber![3]
4 Behold, he who keeps Israel
   does neither slumber nor sleep.[4]
5 The Lord is your keeper and ' '[5] shade;
   he defends your right.[6]
6 The sun shall not smite you by day,
   nor the moon by night.
7 The Lord will keep you from all evil;
   he will keep your soul.[7]
8 ' '[8] He will keep your going out
   and your coming in
   from this time forth and for evermore.[9]

[1] See above, p. 100. (Tr. N.: RSV reads 'A Song of Ascents'.)
[2] Delete the suffix 'my' which through the mistake of a copyist seems to have been added in adaptation to the preceding passage. (Tr. N.: In RSV v. 2 begins: 'My help comes . . .')
[3] * V. 3 reads in RSV:
    He will not let your foot be moved,
    he who keeps you will not slumber.

4 * RSV uses the future tense.
5 Read w^e instead of *yahweh*.
6 * RSV renders v. 5:
     The Lord is your keeper;
     the Lord is your shade
     on your right hand.
7 * RSV has 'life' instead of 'soul'.
8 See BH.
9 * RSV begins v. 8: 'The Lord will keep . . .'

This psalm produces by the simplicity of its language and piety a deep impression that continues until this day.[1] It does not show us the bold soaring of a man's faith to the high places where the storms rage; it does not portray man's struggles and inner tensions—but with the calm and comforting assurance of an unshaken trust it takes its course in a peaceful and straightforward manner. In this inward stability lies its strength, which communicates itself to the reader. And yet we cannot fail to recognize, even within this simplicity and directness of its thought, a certain dynamic quality, which is reflected, first of all, in the tension between the anxious question asked in v. 1 and the confident utterances which follow (vv. 2–8), and has also found formal expression in the confrontation of two different persons who act as speakers. At the same time an intensification takes place between vv. 2 and 5 in so far as a distinct increase and growth can be observed in the strength and assurance of the trust here expressed.

According to its superscription the psalm is a pilgrim song and seems to have been used by pilgrims on their way to Jerusalem, as is also suggested by its inclusion in the Book of Pilgrim Songs (Pss. 120–134). It is, indeed, another question whether it was originally composed for that purpose. This remains, to say the least, an open question, since conclusive evidence of a pilgrimage to Jerusalem cannot be found in the psalm itself. The problem of the precise circumstances that led to the composition of the psalm and of its original purpose is most closely related to the proper understanding of its form. The fact of a change of speaker in v. 3 has been differently interpreted within the compass of that problem. Some commentators hold the view that the dialogue is merely a poetical device to depict the poet's communing with his own soul and point out that he himself supplies his own answer to his question concerning help, and acts, so to speak, as his own priest. A comparison with the form

1 Cf. the hymn, 'Ich heb mein Augen sehnlich auf', by Cornelius Becker (*1561–1604).

of analogous monologues (e.g. in Pss. 42, 43), however, dissuades us from accepting this interpretation. The assumption that there are two different speakers is undoubtedly the more obvious and natural explanation. An attempt on those lines, however, to comprehend the psalm as a cultic liturgy, in which vv. 1–4 are said to represent the question and supplication of the congregation and vv. 5–8 the response of the priestly choir, is doomed to failure in view of the personal character of the piece, which does not admit of a collective, cultic interpretation; the most plausible one is that which assumes that the two voices are those of individuals. We can think either of a conversation between a father and his son or of the comfort, intercession, promise and blessing for his journey which a priest gives in response to the question of a man who asks for his help; this latter view is supported by a certain liturgical and solemn ring about the answer. The reference to the wealth of ideas associated with the cultic tradition of creation and of history (vv. 2–4) would thus be sufficiently accounted for, and the particular phrases used in the psalm could in that case quite naturally be interpreted as referring to a perilous enterprise such as a long journey. Then v. 1 would have to be understood as the question asked by a man who sets forth on a journey and vv. 2–8 as the utterance of the one who stays behind, speeding the other on his way. The later use of the psalm during pilgrimages, which were likewise not without danger, is no obstacle to this interpretation. **[1]** The speaker in v. 1 stands ready to take his departure; he looks up towards the mountains and asks the anxious question: 'From whence does my help come?' Since the mountains round about Jerusalem can hardly be referred to in default of any more direct specification, we shall perhaps have to think of mountains over which his way will lead him, and it may be the very thought of the perils of a journey through a mountain-range, with its steep paths, ravines and gorges, the hiding-places of wild beasts and robbers, which makes it hard for him to bid farewell, so that he anxiously looks out for help. Other commentators think of the high places on the mountains which served as shrines, to which the speaker looks up for help. Luther's translation of the second sentence in v. 1 by a relative clause 'from which my help comes' does not accord with Hebrew linguistic usage; the sentence is rather a question in which the man who sets out on a journey gives full vent to his anxiety and to his feeling of insecurity: 'From whence does my help come?' **[2]** The answer given to this question most strongly contrasts with that mood and behaviour and for this very reason, if not for any other, cannot be spoken by the same person who asks the question. (The original text seems to have been altered merely as a result of the carelessness of a copyist who, as at the end of v. 1, wrote 'my help' instead of 'help'.) The second speaker in stating the fundamental truth: 'Help comes from Yahweh', sounds a categorical note and speaks with a precision of thought from which nobody is able to escape. If there is anyone who can help at all, then it is God. This knowledge removes every doubt and provides firm ground for the hesitant. Trust in God is the unassailable basis and presupposition of the comfort with which the speaker sets the traveller on his way. It is worth noting that this trust in God's help is based on the idea of his creative power; this follows a firmly established cultic tradition in which creation and salvation (blessing) belong together (cf. Pss. 124.8; 134.3). The speaker's train of thought at once begins with the widest possible perspective. Because all things are God's handiwork, he has the power to help whatever may happen; for even now all things are still in his hand. The distinctive character of the Old Testament concept of creation comes out clearly here. It ministers not to a theoretical explanation of the universe but to the mastering of a concrete situation in life in a practical way. It represents not a piece of knowledge but a decision to submit oneself to God's creative will and power. It is the same faith which we encounter in Paul Gerhardt's hymn:[1]

> Who points the clouds their course,
> Whom winds and seas obey,
> He shall direct thy wandering feet,
> He shall prepare thy way.

This belief that man as God's creature is in his hand is the source of the firm confidence on which are based all the subsequent statements of the psalm.

The speaker derives from the concept of creation both the right and the strength to offer this prayer of intercession: 'May he not suffer your foot to slip.' [3] These words are most easily understood as a reference to the perilous way which the imminent journey entails. The popular Old Testament figure of the shepherd, which was originally used to describe Yahweh's relationship to his people

---

[1] * Quotation from the first verse of Paul Gerhardt's hymn, 'Commit thou all thy griefs' ('Befiehl du deine Weg'), translated into English by John Wesley.

and so betrayed its cultic origin (see v. 4 and the exposition of Ps.
23), is here related to an individual in the same way as in Psalm 23
and thereby gains even more in intimacy. It throws a singular light
on the biblical concept of creation that the intercessor is able to pray
in this context, 'May he who keeps you not slumber.' For from this
it appears that the concept of creation is not limited to the thought
of the creation of the universe as an act of God that happened but once.
The activity of the Creator extends beyond the creation of the world;
the Creator-God is not dormant, but continues to act; he is for ever the
living God. Thus creation in the biblical sense is comprehended as the
living power of God which continues to operate and is constantly
creative. The fact that the biblical idea of creation is related to life
in a practical manner and possesses a vitality of its own is based on
the permanent activity of the never-resting God, it entails that
creation and history, the past and the present, are welded into a
unity, and it imparts to the latter the significance of an actual event
which affects the life of the individual. [4] This verse testifies to this
truth. The fact that here the same thought is taken up once more
already points to the inner connection between the intercession and
the reflection on the history of Israel from which the speaker gains a
still broader and more obvious foundation for his confidence. The
reference ('behold') to the tradition of the history of his people is
taken as proof that God is at work and is always the living God.
History is not something past and complete in itself; it is an activity
of God which in a significant way extends into the present. This is
why the individual, too, as a member of his people has a share in its
history and in the God who is at work in it. Hence the national
tradition of the *Heilsgeschichte* becomes for him a source of personal
trust in the God who is present in it. The character of the history of
his people as *Heilsgeschichte* makes him to realize that the saving will
of the Creator-God is also directed to him personally, and thus he
comes to trust in his care in all circumstances.

[5] It is only at this point, after the offering of the prayer of
intercession and after the harmonization of the ideas of creation and
of history, that the full assurance and feeling of absolute security is
attained which in the wanderer's mind takes the shape of an enduring
comfort and a genuine promise. The calm assurance of faith which
almost sounds as if it were a matter of course, though it is in fact
anything but that, is reflected in specific statements about God and
in simple and unpretentious figures of speech. It represents itself as

the unbroken and joyous trust of a child of God, which does not first require an attempt to justify it in order to be sure of itself, and by this very fact is able to inspire trust also in others. What previously was still clothed in the form of desire and supplication is now pronounced as a firm assurance and promise: 'Yahweh *is* your keeper and shade.' The latter figure has probably been chosen in view of the dangers involved in the wandering in the blaze of the sun and thus forms a transition to the next verse. It expresses here the same thought of providing protection as in the subsequent phrase 'he is on your right hand', that is to say, he is on that side on which the counsel and protector would stand (Pss. 16.8; 109.31). **[6–8]** Being under God's protection, the wanderer has therefore no need to fear either the danger of sunstroke or that of the moon, which in antiquity was regarded as the cause of diseases, a belief which is still popularly held in Palestine today. Reaching still further the promise then goes on to say that in every kind of danger God will keep him from evil and will guard his life. His 'going out and coming in' enjoys God's protection; may he walk with God and, guided by him, safely return home again! The solemn liturgical closing words 'from this time forth and for evermore' once more open up the widest possible vista. Where God is the helper, there constant help is given; he is the keeper everywhere, now and for ever. Out of the grandeur of the vision of God which is presented in this psalm and embraces creation, history and eternity has grown that unshakable strength springing from trust in God which has caused this song to become a source of comfort that even today does not cease to flow.

122. PRAY FOR THE SALVATION OF JERUSALEM

A Pilgrim Song.[1]   Of David

1 I was glad when they said to me,
  'Let us go to the house of the Lord!'
2 Our feet have been standing
  within your gates, O Jerusalem!
3 You are built on high, O Jerusalem, as a city
  where the assembly of the people meets,[2]
4 to which the tribes went up, the tribes of the Lord;
  for it is decreed for Israel
  to testify to the name of the Lord.[3]
5 For there the thrones for judgment are[4] set,
  the thrones of the house of David.

6 Pray for the salvation of Jerusalem!
   May they live in peace who love you![5]
7 Salvation be within your walls,
   and peace within your towers![6]
8 For my brethren and companions' sake
   I will say, 'Salvation be within you!'[7]
9 For the sake of the house of the Lord, our God,
   I will seek your good.

[1] See above, p. 100. (Tr. N.: The RSV reads 'A Song of Ascents'.)
[2] With LXX, Symm. and Jer., read *šeḥebrā lā*, as this fits more easily into the context. Some commentators have attempted to interpret the version of the MT, 'which is bound together', as referring to the rebuilding of the city walls completed by Nehemiah. (Tr. N.: In RSV v. 3 reads:
   Jerusalem, built as a city
   which is bound firmly together.)
[3] * RSV has 'go up' instead of 'went up' and after 'the tribes of the Lord' continues 'as was decreed for Israel, to give thanks to the name of the Lord'.
[4] * RSV uses the imperfect tense.
[5] * RSV reads 'peace' instead of 'salvation' and 'prosper' instead of 'live in peace'.
[6] * RSV reads 'peace' instead of 'salvation' and 'security' instead of 'peace'.
[7] * RSV has 'peace' instead of 'salvation'.

The psalm is a simple pilgrim song which was probably sung by the pilgrims at the time of their departure from Jerusalem, the city of 'peace' (see below) and of festal joy. The mention of the tribes, who went up on their pilgrimage to the covenant sanctuary of the city of God, and of the throne of the royal house of David as the most striking features of the poet's memories of the festival point to the composition of the psalm in pre-exilic times. It cannot be proved that v. 3 presupposes the reconstruction of Jerusalem and of her walls in the time of Nehemiah, though that view is often maintained. In view of I Kings 12.27 f. it is not even possible to infer from v. 4 that the psalm originated in the post-deuteronomic era (this point in opposition to Mowinckel and Gunkel).

[1–2] The poet recalls in his song all the joyful events of the festival which now lie behind him. He remembers first of all the pleasure of anticipation at home during the planning and preparation of the pilgrimage to Jerusalem, and then the fulfilment of the expectations which his sojourn in the city of God had brought and which he once more pictures to himself before he sets out on his homeward journey. [3–5] His feet had been able to tread the sacred ground of the towering holy city where the community of the people of God, grouped together according to the tribes to which they belonged, had assembled for the celebration of the festival in order to

'appear before God's face' (cf. Ex. 23.17; 34.23) and to 'testify to the name of their God' according to ancient sacred custom; he had been able to walk on the sacred ground of the holy city where the rule of God, the heavenly King, and of his earthly representative is continually established anew on the basis of the order of law and is realized within the framework of the festival cult by means of the divine judgment and salvation (see Intr. 28 ff., 37 ff., 57 ff.). The poet firmly impresses all these facts on his memory in his hymnic dialogue with Jerusalem in order to take these memories with him to his native country as the precious of gift the time spent at the festival.
[6–9] The hymn is followed by a prayer for God's blessing upon the holy city and for her salvation which includes all those who like the poet have affectionately taken her to their hearts. In that prayer the terms 'peace' and 'salvation' (*šālōm*), as used in the original language, reflect the second element of the name of Jerusalem, a device which to man in antiquity signifies more than a mere ingenious play upon words. *Nomen est omen:* the city of God and the house of God within her as the places where peace reigns and as the springs of salvation— this is the deepest meaning of the blissful experience which unites the poet with his brethren, pervades the whole psalm and in a condensed form culminates in the prayer for salvation and in the desire that peace may reign from this time forth and for evermore.

123. LOOKING UPWARDS TO GOD
A Pilgrim Song[1]

1 To thee I lift up my eyes,
  O thou who art enthroned in the heavens!
2 Behold, as the eyes of the servants
  look to the hand of their master,
  as the eyes of a maid
  to the hand of her mistress,
  so our eyes look to the Lord, our God,
  till he look graciously upon us.[2]
3 Be gracious to us, O Lord, be gracious,[3]
  for ' '[4] we have had more than enough of contempt!
4 Too long our soul has been sated
  ' '[5] with the contempt of the proud.

1 See above p. 100. (Tr. N.: RSV reads 'A Song of Ascents'.)
2 * The last line of v. 2 is in RSV, 'till he have mercy upon us'.
3 * RSV has 'Have mercy upon us, O Lord, have mercy upon us.'
4 See BH.
5 'With the scorn of those who are at ease' seems to be a later addition (Kittel).
(Tr. N.: RSV includes this addition as the second line of v. 4.)

This brief and unpretentious prayer is grouped round a single word-picture imbued with moving tenderness. It springs from a disposition of heartfelt and profound piety. Here an individual takes the affliction of his people so greatly to his heart that he makes it the object of his prayer; even from a purely stylistic point of view this has been expressed by the transition from the style of personal prayer (v. 1) to that of community prayer (vv. 2–4). The prayer seems therefore to have been recited in corporate public worship. The background of the psalm can be inferred from vv. 3 f. The nation has long been exposed to the contempt and scorn of arrogant adversaries. Most commentators explain this fact by referring to the pressure that weighed heavily upon the people in post-exilic times under the overlordship of Persia; it is, however, also possible that their affliction has been due to conflicts within the nation itself.

[1] The words which the worshipper uses in his opening prayer make clear how he conceives of his own position in relation to God. In the midst of the distress caused by his depressing situation he has lifted up his eyes to him who sits enthroned in heaven. In doing so he is aware of the immense difference between his human powerlessness and the greatness of the power of the heavenly King, on which alone he depends. His words express humble submission, but at the same time also firm trust. The worshipper knows to whom he prays. God is the only one who can help him.

[2] His consciousness of the attitude that is fitting before God is expressed even more distinctly in the peculiar line he takes in his meditation in v. 2. He no longer visualizes himself as being alone face to face with God—after all, it is not a private concern which he presents in his prayer—but unites in a fellowship of prayer with his fellow believers, who with yearning await their encounter with God (v. 2c). The poet expresses in a simple and impressive simile what links the members of the congregation together before God in their common affliction. Like the eyes of the servants to the hand of their master and the eyes of the maids to the hand of their mistress, so their eyes look to God, their Lord. The comparison is couched in such general terms that in interpreting it we must not restrict ourselves to one particular point of comparison and single out *one* feature only, such as the moment of fearful dread of being punished by the stern master and the timid waiting for a sign of mercy or, as in Ps. 104.27, the idea of the kind father of a family who serves out food while all eyes are fixed on the hand that conveys the gift. It may well be that

in the psalmist's moving picture both these thoughts are implied and probably even more. It expresses *reverential* awe, submission and humility, which are the result of the awareness of being utterly dependent on the sovereign will and power of God, as on the Lord with whom nobody can interfere; but it also expresses at the same time devoted love and trustful hope in the fatherly care that God, as the Lord, will give his own. It is only when both these sentiments combine that the genuine attitude of prayer is achieved. Reverential awe restrains the worshipper from encroaching upon the majesty of God through importunate petition, while trusting love alone makes it possible for him to pray with confidence and to confide his affliction to God in prayer. Thus at the end of the verse the waiting for the moment when God will appear and 'look graciously upon' his people (see Intr. 38 ff., 72 f.) is not to be understood in the sense that the members of the congregation want to press their human desires on God, but rather that in spite of the utter urgency of their concern they are yet satisfied to wait patiently upon the Lord, to whom they show the honour due to him by their whole-hearted surrender to his mercy. There is therefore no need to assume that the prayer for Yahweh's grace presupposes that he has hitherto been angry with his people; for seen in the light of the idea of God as the Lord, which underlies the simile, the hoped-for granting of man's supplications is always grace, since there can be no question of an obligation on God's part to man, not even within the sphere of the cultus. The simile of slave and master likewise excludes such a view. This has nothing whatsoever to do with a cowardly 'slave mentality'; on the contrary, only by humbly submitting to God is man set free from any kind of cringing submission to the power of men, so that he is able to resist any attempt to bring him low through human pressure.

[3–4] The humble trust with which the worshipper lifts his eyes to God provides the background for his petition, 'Be gracious to us, O Lord.' The poet is a man of few words. His attitude expresses the spirit of prayer more effectively than an abundance of fine words could do. It is not till he adds a reason to his petition that the tenderness of his trust and the purity and restraint of his surrender to God appear in their true light; for it makes us realize how grievously the worshipper and his people suffer from the contempt of the proud oppressors, so that the lifting up of his eyes to God is the only light that shines in that darkness. And when he candidly confesses before him that humanly speaking all patience to endure such scorn is at an end, even these words of bitter complaint still reflect that heartfelt trustfulness which makes the whole psalm one of the finest examples of piety, expressed in prayer—simple, truthful, natural and sincere.

124. THANKSGIVING OF THOSE WHO HAVE BEEN DELIVERED

A Pilgrim Song.[1] *Of David*

1 If it had not been the Lord who was on our side,
   let Israel now say—
2 if it had not been the Lord who was on our side,
   when men rose up against us,
3 then they would have swallowed us up alive,
   when their anger was kindled against us;
4 then the flood would have swept us away,
   the torrent would have gone over us;
5 then over us would have gone
   the raging waters.
6 Blessed be the Lord,
   who has not given us
   as prey to their teeth!
7 We have escaped as a bird
   from the snare of the fowlers;
   the snare is broken,
   and we are free![2]
8 Our help is in the name of the Lord,
   who made heaven and earth.

[1] See above, p. 100. (Tr. N.: RSV reads 'A Song of Ascents'.)
[2] * V. 7d reads in RSV, 'and we have escaped'.

According to v. 1 the psalm is intended for liturgical use as a community thanksgiving, though this does not prove that it was recited antiphonally. It has been paraphrased in hymns by Luther[1] and Walther.[2] The psalm has a moving effect on account of the directness with which it vividly grasps and portrays in striking images the magnitude of both the danger and the deliverance wrought by God. It cannot be established with any degree of certainty what particular national danger is referred to; it is equally possible to think of a concrete particular event, which admittedly cannot be defined in precise terms, or, on the other hand, to interpret the psalm, on account of the quite general character of its allusions, as referring to God's manifold acts of deliverance, which have

[1] * 'Wär' Gott nicht mit uns diese Zeit'.
[2] * 'Wo Gott der Herr nicht bei uns hält', by JohannWalther (1496–1570).

repeatedly taken place in the course of the history of Israel. For the same reason it is hopeless to try to fix the date of the psalm accurately. The construction of the psalm is simple: vv. 1–5 give the psalmist's reflections on the danger in question, vv. 6–7 envisage the deliverance wrought by God, and v. 8 concludes the psalm with a testimony to his help.

[1–5] Without any kind of introduction the thanksgiving begins with a passionate recognition of the greatness of the God who has granted his help, and it does so in the graphic form of a reflection on what would have happened without God's help 'when men rose up against the nation'. The general character of this phrase suggests that we might think in this context of diverse dangers that threatened Israel in the course of her eventful history. Two striking images describe the irremediable disaster to which the nation would have been exposed without God; they are perhaps an echo of the tradition of the combat against the powers of chaos and of the primeval flood which had their place in the sacral tradition of the *Heilsgeschichte* (see Intr. 51, 60 f.). In v. 3 the poet compares the adversaries with powerful sea-monsters (cf. Jer. 51.34) who, driven by ferocious greed, wanted to swallow up the people alive; in vv. 4 f. he compares them with the overflowing waters of a mountain stream whose torrential floods expose the wanderer even today to the danger of being swept away after a heavy rainfall. The thought of what would have become of them without God makes the people realize fully for the first time the value of God's help. In their own powerlessness they come to see clearly the power of God and its decisive significance for their deliverance. In this way the psalm attains the right view of the true standards that govern the relationship between God and man.

[6–7] Out of the direct experience of the magnitude of the divine help, there arises a voice of praise[1] and thanksgiving to the God who has not forsaken his own or given them up to their enemies 'as prey to their teeth'. Here we get another image comparing the other nations with wild beasts of prey. How vividly the people feel that the saving acts of their God are miracles is shown by the last picture, in which they draw a comparison between themselves and birds which, though already captured in the snare of the fowler, regain their liberty when the wooden frame of the net breaks in pieces. Having barely escaped from disaster the people exult in glad and thankful enjoyment of their freedom. Well they know to whom alone

[1] For the formula 'Blessed be Yahweh' compare Intr. 56.

they owe it. **[8]** This is shown in the humble and yet firm affirmation
of trust in God with which the psalm closes, and which has found a
place in the Christian liturgy and retained it until this day. As in
Ps. 121.2, trust in God is based on his power as Creator; this still
gives a hint of the connection, firmly established in the cultic
tradition, between creation, revelation of God's name and salvation.
God's help can be relied on unconditionally, because as Creator he
possesses all power in heaven and on earth. But it is precisely this fact
which becomes an impenetrable miracle as soon as one experiences
the divine power in one's own life or imagines the grief of being
without it. The psalmist has begun his song by focusing his thoughts
on this mighty God, and he concludes it by turning his thoughts once
more to him. It is out of the knowledge of man's own helplessness
that there grows the strength of a faith which relies wholly on him
who alone is equal to every kind of danger. That faith has been
granted to the people of the Old Testament through their experience
of the miraculous help of God. From the thanksgiving for their
deliverance there springs the strength of fresh confidence, so that at
the end of the psalm they can hopefully face whatever may happen
in the future. For genuine thanksgiving is more than a mere
retrospect, and this is true also of the people whose history could
provoke the exclamation:

> Praise to the Lord, who o'er all things so wondrously reigneth,
> Shelters thee under his wings, yea so gently sustaineth.[1]

[1] * 'Praise to the Lord, the almighty', by Catherine Winkworth (1829–1878),
is a rather free translation of 'Lobe den Herren', by Joachim Neander (1650–
1680). The line quoted here, 'In wievel Not hat nicht der gnädige Gott über dir
Flügel gebreitet?', means literally, 'In how many dangers has not God graciously
spread his wings over you?'

125. THE PROTECTOR OF HIS PEOPLE

A Pilgrim Song[1]

1 Those who trust in the Lord are like Mount Zion,
  which cannot be moved, but abides for ever.
2 As the mountains are round about Jerusalem,
  so the Lord is round about his people
  from this time forth and for evermore.
3 For the sceptre of wickedness will not remain[2]
  on the land allotted to the righteous,
  lest the righteous put forth their hands to do wrong.

4 Do good, O Lord, to those who are good, and to those who are
 upright in their hearts!
5 But those who turn aside upon their crooked ways may the Lord
 abandon together with the evildoers![3]
 Peace be in Israel!

[1] See above, p. 100. (Tr. N.: RSV reads 'A Song of Ascents'.)
[2] * RSV has 'shall not rest upon' instead of 'will not remain on'.
[3] * RSV reads 'the Lord will lead away with evildoers'.

The psalm is an affirmation of trust followed by a supplication
(vv. 4 f.). Through the inward strength of its trust in God there
sounds a silent warning to maintain this trust and establish it afresh
wherever it is on the decline or in danger. It is not the faith of an
individual but of the whole people that is here at stake, in view of the
danger that the members of the Yahweh community might themselves 'turn aside' from the way of righteousness under the pressure
of wicked powers. The psalm does not give any precise indication of
the particular situation which it presupposes (see the comments on
v. 3). In vv. 1–3 the psalmist, using words of comfort and exhortation,
speaks of trusting in God's protection; in vv. 4 and 5 he changes over
to an intercession for 'those who are good' and to the petition to
eliminate the evildoers. The psalm ends in a prayer for the salvation
of the covenant community of Israel (see Intr. 32 f., 45 ff.).

[1–2] By means of two images the author seeks to encourage his
people to trust in God and to rekindle their declining hopes. In
doing so he gives a fine testimony to his own trust in God. First he
compares those who trust in God with Mount Zion as the symbol of
divine protection which cannot be moved and abides for ever. This
simile contains two points of comparison. Mount Zion stands unshakably firm, since according to an ancient belief it is deeply rooted
in the womb of the earth. Such unshakable stability is one of the
marks of trusting in God. But more than that, according to the Old
Testament belief (cf. Isa. 28.16) on Mount Zion rests the promise of
God; it is, as it were, the visible guarantor of Israel's salvation and
eternal hope. Hence trust in God and hope in eternity are not to be
separated from each other. The second image portrays the situation
of the city of Jerusalem which, surrounded on all sides by mountains,
is walled in, like a fortress, by protecting ramparts. That scene, upon
which the poet may often have looked with pensive eye, now becomes
for him a symbol of the 'situation' of his people as they pass through
evil days. God's protecting presence walls his people in; he is their

safe stronghold 'from this time forth and for evermore'. His will to
protect and preserve his people is the real ground of their trust in
him. So the second image provides the basis for the first. **[3]** Verse 3
gives an explanation of the general statement about trust in God,
and applies it to the concrete case of the people's present affliction.
It is a postulate of faith that the sceptre of wickedness (perhaps the
symbol of foreign overlordship; cf. Gen. 49.10) cannot remain for
ever on the lot of the righteous, that is, on the land of Canaan, which
as Yahweh's 'inheritance' had been 'drawn' by God 'by lot' to serve
as a dwelling-place for his holy people (Josh. 14 ff.). If God is truly
God—so the poet argues in the light of his faith—then for his own
sake he cannot tolerate any wickedness which arrogates to itself
rights that belong to God alone. But neither for the sake of his
people will God permit such wickedness. He will also guard his
people against that inward assault upon their faith which is expressed
in the words 'lest the righteous put forth their hands to do wrong',[1]
that is, abandon their faith because they are in danger of losing their
trust in God under the pressure of the evildoers. These words of the
psalmist are likewise dictated by his fear that his fellow believers
might lose their trust in God. In the eyes of the psalmist betrayal of
one's people is betrayal of God. The people are therefore divided into
those who, like the author of the psalm, have remained loyal to the
faith and tradition of their ancestors and into those who have proved
faithless (see Intr. 32 f., 45 ff.).

[4] The supplication in vv. 4 f. becomes understandable in the
light of this assumption. It is sustained by the same concern for the
preservation of the traditional faith as are the statements about trust
in God, made in vv. 1–3. The psalmist seeks for the faithful—he calls
them here 'those who are good'—who unflinchingly adhere to their
faith, God's goodness and protection and help so that they may be
preserved from the danger of abandoning their faith and from
oppression (see v. 3). The worshipper's own trust in God is by no
means dependent on a prior confirmation supplied by the actual
arrival of help in a visible form; rather does it already previously
exist, as vv. 1 ff. show, and his intercession is a prayer of genuine
trust, springing from a faith which is already active before it is
supported by visible signs. **[5]** The imprecation upon his unfaithful

---

[1] To speak in concrete terms, one could think in this connection of the influence
of the cults of foreign nations, the adoption of which was forced upon the kings
of tributary states as the symbol of their subservience to the foreign overlordship.

fellow countrymen, 'who turn aside upon their crooked ways' and consort with the strangers, is based on the same assurance of faith as his intercession for the godly. The man who has abandoned his fellowship with God has forfeited his help and has no longer any share in the religious community. The man whom God on his part 'abandons' is doomed to perish like other evildoers and common criminals who by their own deeds have excluded themselves from fellowship with God and his people. Drawing from these religious reflections the inevitable conclusions, the poet cannot help apprehending the true meaning of the self-purification and cleansing of the covenant community brought about by the divine judgment; he now knows that only those will endure who by virtue of their faith in God are able to find comfort in communion with him. The psalmist concludes his song with a prayer for the salvation of his people (cf. Ps. 128.6). This prayer naturally fits in with the cultic tradition and with the thought-sequence of the psalm, which is sustained by concern for the people of God, and so is not to be regarded as a later addition. It expresses within the scope of the psalm the perception, representing a valid truth, that the peace and the existence of a people are ultimately guaranteed only if loyalty to the nation is firmly established in faithfulness and responsibility to God.

126. THOSE WHO SOW IN TEARS WILL REAP WITH SHOUTS OF JOY

A Pilgrim Song[1]

1 When the Lord restores the fortunes[2] of Zion,
   then we are like those who dream.[3]
2 Then our mouth is[3] filled with laughter,
   and our tongue with shouts of joy;
   then they say[3] among the Gentiles,
   'The Lord has done great things for them.'
3 The Lord has done great things for us;
   we are glad.
4 O Lord, restore our fortunes
   like rivers in the southern country![4]
5 Those who sow in tears will reap with shouts of joy.[5]
6 They go along weeping
   and sow their seed;
   they come home with shouts of joy,
   and bring their sheaves with them.[6]

[1] See above, p. 100. (Tr. N.: RSV reads 'A Song of Ascents'.)
[2] See BH.

³ * RSV uses the past tense.
⁴ * V. 4b reads in RSV, 'like the water-courses in the Negeb'.
⁵ * In RSV v. 5 reads:
    May those who sow in tears
    reap with shouts of joy!
⁶ * V. 6 reads in the RSV:
    He that goes forth weeping,
    bearing the seed for sowing,
    shall come home with shouts of joy,
    bringing his sheaves with him.

Homely and yet profound piety is here combined with noble simplicity of artistic form in a wonderful harmony which imparts to this widely known psalm its singular value. The psalm is like a precious stone in a simple and yet worthy setting. The gentle spirit of a heartfelt and trusting hope based on faith pervades the whole psalm; and from this very trustfulness springs the strength of that hope which is a living fountain of true piety. It proves equally true of the pure childlike delight in the hoped-for happiness and blessing (vv. 1–2), of awed and wondering praise of the majesty and grace of God (v. 3), of the intimacy and assurance with which the psalmist prays (v. 4), and also of the powerful comfort which that hope imparts on the way through darkness to light (vv. 5–6). The psalm speaks of the cult community's expectation of salvation in times of adversity and is probably to be interpreted in the light of the religious ideas associated with the autumnal feast (vv. 1, 5 f.).

[1–2a] At the very beginning of the psalm the faith of the cult community spreads the wings of its thoughts in a bold flight into the future, and looks into the smiling fields of blissful hope as through a widely opened gate. They do not dare to push open with their own hands the gate which separates the dismal present from the bright future, knowing by faith that the decisive transformation of their present circumstances lies in the hand of God alone. This is why their entire hope is founded on God, to whom they owe the restoration of the fortunes of Zion. The tense used in v. 1b suggests the view that at the root of the community's hope are reminiscences of previous experiences of the divine restoration of the fortunes of Zion which are part of the cultic tradition and which give support to their prayer. The past and the present meet in the presence of God; and the cult community's testimony to God's former saving activities serves as the starting-point of their liturgy of intercession. The original text uses a phrase which literally means 'to turn a turning', and is used as a formula for the cultic-eschatological realization of salvation; in it is implied also the thought that man has to account to God for the sin he has committed, and that for that reason only God himself can deliver him from his guilt by a new act of his grace. The miracle of the divine redemption becomes apparent in all its fullness only in the light of the knowledge that man is in bondage to sin and that it is impossible for him to free himself by his own efforts. The people in whose lives that divine miracle becomes true are 'like those who dream'. It is wonder at the miraculous power of God which turns the tears of those who mourn into happy laughter; and it is the exultant joy of being able to experience the greatness of the divine grace in their own lives which is expressed in these two verses. In such an attitude of mind, open to God's revelation, the congregation awaits the realization of salvation.

[2b–3] The revelation of salvation to Israel, however, entails also the revelation of God to the other nations. The Gentiles, too, will have to stand silent before this mighty God and will have no other choice than to acknowledge the great things he has done. This is the deepest meaning and the purest form of the Old Testament belief in Israel's election, and, if understood in this sense, it does not give any offence whatsoever. What is involved here is not the glory of Israel, before which the other nations would have to bow down, but simply and solely the glory of God which is made manifest to the other nations through Israel's *Heilsgeschichte*. How little one can speak here of self-glorification is shown by the simple and devout way in which Israel herself joyfully joins in the testimony of the Gentiles and, herself overwhelmed by the overflowing goodness of God, already expresses childlike rejoicing over the future which God holds in his hand. In the realm of cultic thought the past and the future are themselves already part of the living present by virtue of the presence of God. Joy in God casts its light on the future, and such an assurance of faith conquers grief.

[4] It is precisely against the background of this assurance that the religious profundity of the supplication to God, asking him to bring about a radical change in their fortunes, first becomes fully understandable. Without that absolute trust in God's miraculous power, by which the prayer is sustained, it would be wicked presumptuousness to make such a request to him. For, as the addition of the simile 'like rivers in the southern country' shows, the congregation expect from their God nothing less than the absolute miracle—rivers in the sun-scorched desert in the south, an impossible thought indeed! But

it is just this impossibility that faith trusts God to perform; he is capable of transforming the steppe, on which according to popular belief his curse rested, into watered fertile land, a deed which is worthy of him and which he alone is able to do (cf. Hos. 2.15). So may God now, in the same way, in gracious forgiveness take his curse from the people and lead them towards a new spring! In their humble recognition of that divine power and confident reliance on that mighty God (vv. 1, 3) lies the strength of faith which alone gives the community the spiritual authority to utter such a petition and so makes this prayer profoundly devout and humble.

[5–6] The community's supplication (v. 4) is followed by the answer (vv. 5–6), which was probably uttered by the priest or a prophet. The promise is clothed in the proverbial image of the sowing in tears and reaping with shouts of joy. The motive for the choice of this is to be found in the festival cult, which among other things served the purpose of securing the blessing of fertility for the new year at a time when the Yahweh religion was taking over Canaanite agriculture and the cults connected with it. In order to understand this image, which does not simply speak of the periodical succession of sowing and reaping in the sense, for instance, of the proverbial phrase 'The calm after the storm',[1] we must study it in the light of its contemporary background. It is a very common ancient idea, which is reflected in various customs of the nations,[2] that the time of sowing was to be considered as a time of mourning. We know from Egyptian examples that sowing was accompanied by funeral hymns as a symbol of the burial of the god Osiris. At the root of this ceremony was the interpretation of the natural process as the dying and rising again of living things, a view which, as discoveries at Ras Shamra have confirmed, was also shared by the Canaanite cultic myth, and which has also found expression in the German proverb, 'Do not laugh when you sow; otherwise you must weep when you reap'; it also underlies the biblical parable of the grain of wheat which must die in order to bear much fruit (John 12.24; I Cor. 15.36). It is only from this point of view that the phrases used in the psalm, 'those who sow in tears' and 'they go along weeping', become intelligible. The poet shows his artistic power in keeping to

---

[1] * Lit., 'Rain is followed by sunshine.'

[2] Cf., e.g., for the archaic period in Greece Nilsson, *Geschichte der griechischen Religion* I (1951), p. 639.

the metaphor of sowing and reaping and not adding an explanation. Of course he intends a reference to their present calamities; in present suffering and death he discerns not only the *allusion* to the future glory of a new life but, as in the case of the seedcorn planted in the earth, he sees already at work the mysterious power of God which creates new life out of death (cf. Ezek. 37). In the last analysis here, too, it is faith in the miraculous life-giving power of God which transfigures the sufferings of the present time and shows them to be the way willed by God which alone is able to lead men out of darkness into light. To that faith is revealed a hidden divine law: sowing in tears and reaping in joy are inseparable. To the eye of faith temporal suffering is a necessary stage on the way to joy in God's glory. Suffering and death, too, are part of God's work of redemption. They are a divine seed which sprouts in secret and ripens for God's blessed harvest.

127. EVERYTHING DEPENDS ON GOD'S BLESSING

A Pilgrim Song.[1]   *Of Solomon*

1 Unless the Lord builds the house,
   those who build it, labour in vain.
   Unless the Lord watches over the city,
   the watchmen stay awake in vain.
2 It is in vain that you rise up early
   and go late to rest;
   you eat the bread of anxious toil all the same;
   for he gives to his own[2] in sleep what is proper.[3]
3 Behold, sons are a heritage from the Lord,
   the fruit of the womb a reward.
4 Like arrows in the hand of a warrior,
   so are the sons of one's youth.
5 Happy is the man who has
   filled with them his quiver!
   He will[4] not be put to shame
   when the enemies quarrel with him[4] in the gate.[5]

[1] See above, p. 100. (Tr. N.: RSV reads 'A Song of Ascents'.)
[2] Lit.: to his beloved.
[3] * In RSV the last two lines of v. 2 are:
     eating the bread of anxious toil;
     for he gives to his beloved in sleep.
[4] See BH.
[5] * The last line of v. 5 reads in RSV, 'when he speaks with his enemies in the gate'.

The psalm clearly falls into two parts which are quite unrelated
as far as subject-matter is concerned.[1] Verses 1 and 2 emphatically
point out the significance of divine providence in human life; vv. 3–5,
on the other hand, praise the blessing of God as exhibited by a
goodly number of children. Both parts are in the form of an enlarged
'Wisdom saying' and for that reason have probably here been
combined in a single 'psalm' (see Intr. 88 f.). The content of the first
part accords with the proverb 'The blessing of Yahweh makes rich,
and man's own toil can add nothing to it' which has been preserved in
Prov. 10.22.[2] But there is also an inscription on a Babylonian building
which says of the god Marduk: 'There is no house whose foundation
is laid without thee . . . ; who can do anything without thee?' The
title ascribes the psalm to Solomon, probably because he was
regarded as the author of the Old Testament Wisdom sayings. In
the rabbinical tradition the view was held that the opening words
regarding the building of a house (v. 1) referred to the building of
the Temple of Solomon; but there is no justification for this. Since
the psalm is couched in general terms it is not possible to assign it to
any particular historical situation; it belongs to the timeless world
of the proverb.

[1–2] It accords with the didactic character of the Wisdom sayings,
that, like our own proverbs, they illustrate a general truth by the use
of particular examples. It is therefore entirely in line with the
intentions of the author to take the statements about building the
house and watching over the city as referring quite generally to
human toil and care. Furthermore, the pedagogic zeal with which
any particular point is expressed explains a certain one-sidedness in
the train of thought from which we must not draw too far-reaching
conclusions. That one particular point which the author wants to
throw into relief in order to produce a lasting impression is the
decisive significance of God's actions in man's everyday life. The
poet's eyes are so firmly focused on this one thought that everything
else seems to him to recede into the background beside it, and he
describes as futile all human labours and cares which leave God out
of account. In the face of that radical turning to God the significance

---

[1] The Christian paraphrase, 'Wo Gott zum Haus nicht gibt sein Gunst (*by
Johann Kolrose, 1487–1558), has not been able to harmozine these two different
parts either.

[2] * In RSV this saying is:
   The blessing of the Lord makes rich,
   and he adds no sorrow with it.

of everything human shrinks into nothingness. The verdict 'in vain', which is passed three times on man's literally 'God-less' activities sounds quite sinister and shattering. This radical formulation has been chosen in order to effect the radical renunciation of an attitude of mind which is so absorbed in work and worries that it loses sight of God's providence and his effect on life. We should therefore be mistaken if we were to take the words of the psalm as meaning that work as such is unnecessary. Of course, the author knows that no building can take place without the labour of man's hands, and he is surely not of the opinion that the watchmen of the city could neglect their duties without inflicting any harm. He does not speak of these things, because it is not a question here of work in general but of an attitude to work which leads man to believe that he can leave God out. Only work of this kind is in vain, because it is done in the delusion that man is able to achieve by his own efforts what is reserved to God. It does not spring from faith and so stands condemned by God. The view that man can and must accomplish everything by his own efforts results from man's mistrust of God and from a wrong confidence in his own power. The psalm, on the other hand, endeavours to pave the way to a right attitude to God by leading man to the renunciation of his own importance and to the recognition of human weakness. Only when he has realized how trivial and insignificant are his own cares and achievements, only when he sees how apart from God he wastes away in the treadmill of work, and eats 'the bread of anxious toil', gaining only the depressing knowledge that man works to eat and eats to work, will he apprehend in his own experience that verdict 'in vain' upon all human toil and care of which the psalm speaks. Without God, work becomes hardship and care becomes anxious worry, but this is a state of mind which has no ultimate meaning and to which God has set a limit (cf. Gen. 3.17 ff.). In view of this fact no other choice is left open than that of confident trust in God, and it is this thought which is expressed in the last sentence of v. 2. In saying that 'He gives to his beloved in sleep what is proper', the author certainly does not mean to say that God will grant to man without his co-operation all that he desires but cannot achieve by his own labours. Not what man himself desires, but 'what is proper'—in the eyes of a God who cares—is what he will give him. This is the true attitude of faith, which really casts all anxieties on God and gratefully leaves it to him to grant what he himself thinks needful. And behind that attitude there may be the insight that man himself is by no means always able to judge what the proper thing for him is. The blessing of God often lies hidden in some quite different place from where man seeks it in the first instance. This providence of God which is concealed from man is suggested by the phrase 'in sleep', which, of course, also emphasizes the contrast with human toil and worry. In this way the psalm forms the Old Testament counterpart to Jesus' saying about being anxious (Matt. 6.25 ff.; Luke 12.22 ff.). Both spring from the same basic attitude of faith which, through confident surrender to God, attains that inward freedom from the world and in relation to the world, because it is linked with a higher Power and knows itself to be sustained by his care, which is the only guarantee of lasting blessedness and success.

[3-5] The second Wisdom saying (vv. 3-5) is of a different character. Springing from a wholesome delight in life and a conviction that the source of strength of a nation lies in the family, it praises children as a gift entrusted by God. The phrase 'heritage from Yahweh', used figuratively, reflects the Old Testament conception of family and nation, which is deeply rooted in religion. Just as the Promised Land, from which the phrase 'heritage from Yahweh' is borrowed, is regarded as a treasure entrusted by God which inwardly binds the nation to him, so the psalmist recognizes in the family, too, that peculiar relationship in which are manifested both God's grace and his claim. The further elaboration of the proverb in v. 4 admittedly pursues the thought of the image only in one direction and proudly praises the blessing and the wealth which a large number of sons entail. The sons are compared with arrows in the hand of a warrior. Born to the father in his youth, they will be able to protect and defend him like a weapon when he is getting old and is in need of support. Though envious adversaries may rise up against him in the gate, the place of the administration of justice, the band of gallant sons will not forsake the father, but will help him to gain vindication in the face of every sort of lie. Such unqualified joy in a child as a gift bestowed by God's gracious will is in itself a part of the divine blessing, even though, or perhaps just because, that joy has to be bought with care, toil and suffering. For in the last analysis it is joy in the abundance of life which comes from God and which he bestows upon a healthy nation.

128. DOMESTIC BLESSINGS

A Pilgrim Song[1]

1 Blessed is everyone who fears the Lord,
 who walks in his ways!
2 You can enjoy the fruit of the labour of your hands;
 happy are you, and it is well with you.[2]
3 Your wife is like a fruitful vine
 within your house;
 your children are like shoots of olive-trees
 around your table.[3]
4 Behold, thus the man is blessed
 who fears the Lord.[3]
5 The Lord bless you from Zion,
 that you may see[4] the prosperity of Jerusalem
 all the days of your life,
6 and that you may see[4] your children's children—
 salvation be upon Israel![5]

[1] See above, p. 100. (Tr. N.: RSV reads 'A Song of Ascents'.)
[2] * RSV has 'you shall eat' instead of 'you can enjoy' and gives v. 2b as 'you shall be happy, and it shall be well with you'.
[3] * RSV uses the future tense in vv. 3 and 4a.
[4] * RSV begins a new sentence, 'May you see . . .'
[5] * RSV reads 'peace' instead of 'salvation'.

The psalm, to which one of Luther's hymns[1] owes its origin, begins with a 'beatitude' on the godly (v. 1,) praises his good fortune (vv. 2–4) and concludes with a benediction (vv. 5–6). The beginning and end of the psalm indicate that it was used in community worship. Judging by its form, the psalm has been developed out of the act of pronouncing blessing which was customary in the cult (vv. 5 f.) as a parenetic exegesis of some sort. The description of the blessing (vv. 2–4) which precedes this is distinguished by its didactic character being intended to exhort the people to fear God and to glorify the labour of man and domestic happiness, so that the blessing of God may be recognized therein.

[1] The point of the psalm is made at the very beginning. In the 'beatitude' the poet sets forth, as a principle binding on the community of the godly, the foundation of right conduct and of true happiness, that is, the fear of God and walking in God's ways. In the fear of God man's basic attitude of humility is manifested as he realizes and acknowledges that God is the Lord of his life. In the Bible God always confronts man as a powerful Will that makes

[1] * 'Wohl dem, der in Gotts Furchte steht.'

demands upon him, so that the attitude of obedience to God and his commandments and of walking in his ways and according to his ordinances cannot be separated from the recognition of him as Lord. If God is the Lord of life, then his power operates as blessing precisely in those cases in which his ordinances for man's life are obeyed. The inner logic of the psalm is based on this thought, which is orientated upon God. The examples which the poet uses to praise the blessing which the God-fearing man finds bound up with these ordinances are to be understood in the same way. **[2]** With the change to the second person, in the attractive description of the blessing and its application to the individual, the psalmist draws the attention of his hearers to the things which man is so easily in danger of taking thanklessly for granted, because he prefers to seek his happiness somewhere else and takes no notice of the blessings which are bestowed upon him day by day. The singular happiness which falls to the lot of the God-fearing man becomes evident in the very fact that he is able to enjoy the fruit of his labours, without groaning or breaking down under the burden of them and to experience God's goodness in the knowledge that 'it is well with him'. For man's grateful enjoyment of the fruit of his labour links him spiritually with God's care for him, and this link brings with it a blessing and a joy which do not belong to work as such and are denied to it if it is done without God's help. It is therefore by no means necessary to regard these thoughts as an indication that they arose at a time when the people were under oppression and so they lowered their expectations to an absolute minimum. On the contrary, the statement made in v. 2 represents a universal truth that holds good in every age and perhaps was rather directed against expectations that were pitched much too high. **[3–4]** The delight in the domestic happiness of the family, which the poet has portrayed in two charming images, should be understood in the same sense. He compares the wife, who as the mother of children rules within the house, with a fruitful vine, and the happy company of children, gathered round the table, with the flourishing shoots of an olive-tree. The refreshing spirit of a healthy, simple, and unspoilt joy in life and vitality emanate from these words. However, it is not these sentiments alone to which the poet wants to give expression by his choice of these images. The vine and the olive-tree are regarded in the Holy Land as blessings bestowed upon man by God. The deeper meaning which the psalmist associates with both these similes and wants to bring out is that a man's delight in wife and children is experienced as joy in God, and that the happiness of the family is thankfully recognized and experienced as God's blessing. It is this attitude which first transforms happiness into 'blessing'; for without religion the very element which makes these things a blessing is missing, and the way to such deep spiritual happiness is open only to the man who is responsive to God and surrendered to him. Again, it is a universally valid truth that true blessing dwells only in a house in which the fear of God reigns and provides the inner strength and unity of the members. Verse 4 once more emphasizes this fundamental idea of the psalm by way of a closing summary. This verse has found a Christian echo in Spitta's deeply-felt hymn, 'O happy home where thou art loved the dearest'.[1] It is the pedagogic intention of the psalmist to lead man to that stage where he learns with God's help to be satisfied with what he has, to see the importance of homely things, and to find in them his riches and dignity. In view of this exhortation to devout contentment and the endeavour to open man's eyes to the gifts of God bestowed upon the God-fearing man in the little happinesses of everyday life, it would be wrong to assume that these things are regarded by the psalmist as his highest ideal or to seek to construct from them an Old Testament standard of values. The psalm deliberately confines itself to a strictly limited field of devout conduct in everyday life and should be understood within those limits.

[5–6] In the liturgical blessing spoken by the priest with which the psalm ends the psalmist goes beyond these thoughts and places the blessing on the individual in a wider cultic and national context; for he now prays that Yahweh may let the godly man see the prosperity of Jerusalem all the days of his life and experience the happiness of having grandchildren of his own. Here too, however, an inward connection exists with what precedes: the happiness of the nation depends on blessing on its work and on the happiness of the family. Justice upholds a nation. Where the fear of God constitutes the foundation of domestic peace, there the peace of the whole nation is firmly warranted. So the closing supplication for the salvation of 'Israel' fits into the psalm as a whole not only from the point of view of the external form of the covenant cult (cf. the comments on Ps. 125.5) but also with regard to its spirit. The pedagogic tendency of the psalm means that its author does not envisage, any more than in Psalm 1, those cases in which the

---

[1] * 'O selig Haus, wo man dich aufgenommen', by Carl Johann Philipp Spitta (1801–1859), translated by Sarah Laurie Findlater (1823–1907).

visible sign of a happy earthly life is denied to the godly man. He would render a bad service to the people whom he has to instruct if he were to burden and paralyse their power of decision right from the beginning by making them face the problematic nature of the mysteries of life. But even the fact that many godly people have to struggle with sorrow does not nevertheless invalidate the other truth that wherever happiness enters a home it is gratefully and humbly enjoyed as a gift from God. And the general fundamental idea of the psalm, that God by granting his blessing acknowledges the ordinances which he has laid down for man's life if man in obedient faith submits to them, does not lose its fundamental significance or its practical value even in face of the problem of suffering.

129. SO FAR AND NO FARTHER

A Pilgrim Song[1]

1　'Sorely have they afflicted me from my youth,'
　　let Israel now say—
2　'Sorely have they afflicted me from my youth,
　　yet they have not prevailed against me.
3　The ploughers ploughed upon my back;
　　they made long their furrows.'[2]
4　The Lord is righteous;
　　he has cut the cords of the wicked.
5　May all who hate Zion
　　be put to shame and turned backward!
6　Let them be like the grass on the house-tops,
　　which the east wind withers,[3]
7　with which the reaper does not fill his hand
　　or the binder of sheaves the pad of his garment,[4]
8　to whom those who pass by do not say,
　　'The blessing of the Lord be upon you!'[5]
　　'We bless you in the name of the Lord.'

[1] See above, p. 100. (Tr. N.: RSV reads 'A Song of Ascents'.)
[2] See BH.
[3] See BH. (Tr. N.: V. 6b is in RSV, 'which withers before it grows up'.)
[4] * RSV has 'his bosom' instead of 'the pad of his garment'.
[5] * In RSV v. 8 begins, 'while those who pass by . . .', and the last two lines are put in the mouth of a single speaker.

The psalm is intended as a liturgical formulary of the Israelite covenant community (v. 1b; cf. Pss. 118.2 ff.; 124.1), to be used in a cultic ceremony that ends in the cursing of those 'who hate Zion' and a benediction upon the congregation (v. 8; see Intr. 32 f., 47). In form

and subject-matter the psalm is akin to Psalm 125, except that in
Psalm 129 the two parts, that is, the affirmation of trust associated
with themes of thanksgiving (vv. 1–4) and the curse and blessing
(vv. 5–8), are worked out more distinctly and are more clearly
marked off from each other. The psalmist looks back upon the
history of Israel, so often crushed beneath the oppressor's rule; but
this does not justify us in assigning the psalm to the late post-exilic
period. **[1–4]** The historical retrospect of the numerous afflictions
which Israel had to endure from her 'youth', that is, the Exodus from
Egypt (cf. Hos. 11.1; Jer. 2.2 and often), though without ever
experiencing complete national annihilation, seems to have arisen
not out of a concrete historical situation, which brought about the
deliverance of the people from foreign bondage, but rather in the
cultic rite of the representation of history as the history of salvation,
in which the festival congregation was able to rejoice in their God
and become assured of his salvation. It is therefore not worth while
to look for the specific event to which the psalm owes its origin. The
encounter with the God who is at work in history simultaneously
makes present and real to the Old Testament cult community the
history both of disaster and of salvation (cf. Pss. 78; 106). The
judgments of God, which have manifested themselves in threats to
the people and their oppression by the violence of the enemies, who
like the ploughman's coulter have left behind long-drawn-out furrows
and indelible traces, are to be taken just as seriously as his 'righteousness' (v. 4), that is, his faithfulness to his covenant, on account of
which he has made his promises of salvation to come true in the midst
of disaster and has broken to pieces the chains of slavery. The
Heilsgeschichte which the cult community experiences is the repeated
emergence of the people from oppression into freedom, from fear
and trembling into triumphant joy. And the psalm itself takes the
same road from mournful lament to the affirmation of trust and of
certainty that God sets a limit to every affliction which he sends, a
limit which will not be exceeded.

[5–8] This assurance of salvation, which derives its strength from
the actualization of the divine *Heilsgeschichte*, accounts for the attitude
of opposition to those 'who hate Zion' which the psalm adopts in its
second part. These can hardly be the hostile authorities of whom the
first part speaks, but rather members of the covenant of Yahweh—
perhaps Israelites from the Northern Kingdom?—who are opposed
to the Jerusalem cult; for one would expect a different description

for Gentiles, and v. 8, too, would sound strangely harmless if applied to a foreign foe. These members of the covenant of Yahweh are excluded from the cult community—this, too, is to be thought of as a sacral cultic act—by means of the imprecations in vv. 5–7 and the withholding of the blessing with which the festival closes (cf. Ps. 125.5). It may be assumed that the concluding verse of the liturgy was spoken by the priest. He pronounces upon the covenant community, called 'Israel', the blessing with which the congregation is dismissed from the sanctuary.

130. OUT OF THE DEPTHS
A Pilgrim Song[1]

1 Out of the depths I cried[2] to thee, O Lord:
2 'Lord, hear my voice!
  Graciously incline thy ear[3]
  to the voice of my supplications!
3 If thou, O Lord, should mark iniquities,
  ' '[4] who could stand?[5]
4 But there is forgiveness with thee,
  that thou mayest be feared.'
5 I waited for the Lord,
  my soul hoped for his word.[6]
6 My soul waited[2] for the Lord
  more than watchmen for the morning ' '.[7]
7 ' '[8] Yea, with the Lord there is grace,
  and with him is plenteous redemption.
8 And it is he who will redeem Israel
  from all his sins.[9]

[1] See above, p. 100. (Tr. N.: RSV reads 'A Song of Ascents'.)
[2] * RSV uses the present tense.
[3] * RSV has 'Let thy ears be attentive' instead of 'Graciously incline thy ear'.
[4] See BH.
[5] * V. 3b reads in RSV 'Lord, who could stand?'
[6] Following LXX. (Tr. N.: RSV translates:
  I wait for the Lord, my soul waits,
  and in his word I hope.)
[7] See BH. (Tr. N.: In RSV the line 'more than watchmen for the morning' is repeated.)
[8] According to the Greek manuscripts the sentence 'O Israel, wait for the Lord' seems to be a later addition, cf. Ps. 131.3. (Tr. N.: In RSV v. 7a reads, 'O Israel, hope in the Lord!')
[9] * In RSV v. 8 begins: 'And he will redeem . . .'

This favourite psalm of Luther, which served as a model for his famous penitential hymn, 'Out of the depths I cry to thee',[1] is the

[1] * 'Aus tiefer Not schrei ich zu dir', translated into English by Catherine Winkworth (1829–1878).

sixth of the penitential psalms of the ancient Church. It combines tender sentiments, simple and sincere language, and a most profound understanding of the nature of sin and grace. With sure religious feeling Luther has grasped the affinity of the psalm with the spirit of New Testament devotion and has classed the psalm with the 'Pauline' psalms (Pss. 32, 51, 130 and 143) as the best psalms of the Psalter. The psalm is the confession of a God-fearing man who was able to rise from the uttermost depth of anguish engendered by sin to the assurance of the divine grace and forgiveness. According to v. 8, it can be assumed that the psalm was recited by the poet in the community's worship. The worshipper sees his personal assurance of forgiveness in connection with the presence of God (v. 4) and the general assurance of forgiveness given to his people (vv. 7 f.). In vv. 1–4 he reiterates before God the prayer of repentance which he had offered to God when he was afflicted by sin, and then in vv. 5–8 gratefully testifies before the congregation how his yearning and waiting for God's gracious forgiveness had found their fulfilment. The intimate connection between these two parts, which calls to mind the style of the laments and thanksgivings, proves that man's assurance of forgiveness cannot be separated from the affliction caused by the consciousness of his sinfulness and from the knowledge of God's judgment. It is only as a result of the cumulative effect of both these that the process takes place which the Bible calls repentance.

[1–2] The soul of the worshipper reaches up to God from abysmal agony (on the use of the term 'depths' as a metaphor for mental and physical affliction cf. Pss. 69.2, 14; 18.4 f., 16; 32.6; 40.2). The single word 'depths' expresses in all its fullness the poet's grievous anguish as he becomes conscious of being separated from God. It is not so much physical suffering and the fear of death which torments him, but rather the feeling of being separated from God by the unbridgeable chasm of sin. Without God man is lost, and only God can throw across the gulf the bridge which man has broken off by his own guilt. So from the depths the worshipper stretches out his hands to God and pleads that he may graciously stoop down to him. [3] 'Like a chastised child who avoids looking his father in the face', he does not dare to plead directly for the forgiveness of his sins; he feels too strongly that his situation scarcely justifies such a request. Whether or not God will forgive depends solely on his own free decision. In his own helplessness, of which he becomes fully conscious only as he prays to God, he also begins to plumb the depths of consciousness of sin: no man *can* abide before the holy God, because no living person is righteous in his sight. At the root of the question which the psalmist asks, 'If thou, O Lord, should mark iniquities, who could stand?' is the shattering perception of the tremendous power of sin and of the paralysing powerlessness of man in his bondage to it. Man is unconditionally delivered up to God, from whom man's true condition cannot be concealed. But—and this is what is so wonderful—the realization of the true nature of sin at the same time opens his eyes to the greatness of the divine grace. **[4]** In forgiving sin, God proves himself to be more powerful than sin itself, and, because he alone has the power of overcoming sin by his forgiveness, he is to be feared just because he is also the God who forgives. In the simple words 'There is forgiveness with thee, that thou mayest be feared' the psalmist expresses what has thus begun to dawn on him as the ultimate truth about God and man as he wrestled in prayer. Since it is God that he is primarily concerned with, the forgiveness of sins does not have the effect of soothing and lulling his religious perceptions, but on the contrary of revealing the humanly incomprehensible greatness of God (the idea of the God who is present in the theophany [see Intr. 28 ff.,] lies behind this). This greatness exceedingly alarms man just because it becomes manifest to him only against the background of the perception of his own sinfulness and of God's judgment on sin. The belief in the forgiveness of sins is an entirely serious matter; the grace of God cancels sin, but not its seriousness. Indeed, the claim of the holy God upon man's obedience, far from being reduced by his grace, only becomes weightier than ever. And in this the poet sees God's true intentions:

> And so must all men fear thee,
> And by thy grace must live.[1]

This thought of the psalmist, that forgiveness leads to the fear of God, reaches the height of the New Testament realization of the kindness of God which leads man to repentance (Rom. 2.4; cf. Luke 5.8). It expresses the paradoxical tension inherent in the fact that man simultaneously believes in the mercy of God, on which he utterly depends, and in the holiness of God, to which he is wholly subject.

---

[1] * This is a literal rendering of two lines from the second strophe of Luther's hymn already mentioned (see p. 772). The English translation is too free to be useful here.

[5-6] From v. 5 onwards the prayer form is abandoned; here the poet makes a confession before the congregation, recalling how he waited with yearning for the moment when he could come into the presence of God and hear the promise of forgiveness. It is only at this point that he realizes the ultimate relatedness to other things of true repentance; for he now visualizes at one and the same time both his anxious waiting and hoping and the fulfilment which has been granted to him by God. The true attitude of repentance, which differs from a merely transient mood of penitence, is a state of being according to which the believer lives in a constant inward tension (the element of tension is particularly emphasized in the Hebrew word used for 'hoping') between hoping and possessing, because he is simultaneously conscious of the kindness and the severity of God. This is the point of the simile in v. 6b. With even greater longing than the watchmen, who in the darkness of the night look out for the first dawn of day, the poet continually waits in prayerful hope (this is expressed in the tense of the verbs as well as in the repetitions), for God and for his word of forgiveness, though he can be as sure of these as the watchmen are of the coming of the day. [7] Thus he is able to exclaim once more as if he had made a new discovery, 'Yea, with the Lord there is grace' (cf. v. 4); and though he has again and again to pass through nights of anguish caused by sin, his life guided by God's hand is nevertheless a way from redemption to redemption, so that he can testify on his own account: 'With him is plenteous redemption.' [8] The psalm concludes with a far-reaching prospect. The poet envisages the redemption from sin which he himself has experienced in the context of the general assurance of redemption for the people of God, to whom he is conscious of belonging as he worships with them in the sanctuary. Thus the closing affirmation of the psalm echoes the promise of salvation for the whole cult community from which the worshipper derives the assurance of his own redemption; at the same time it is a testimony born of his own personal experience which he wants to make fruitful for the congregation. And it is the mark not only of the Old Testament faith but of all genuine religious insight that it does not stop at the individual, but points out a road for the fellowship of all believers. Like all great champions of faith this psalmist, too, has had on his mind the concerns of his fellow men as well as his own, and has prayed for them whilst he was engaged in his personal struggle for the assurance of redemption from sin; and thereby he has gained—for the benefit of his

people and beyond them for anyone who finds himself brought face to face with this God—the knowledge that God is a God who redeems men from *all* their sins.

131. HUMILITY

A Pilgrim Song.[1] *Of David*

1 O Lord, my heart is not haughty,
 my eyes are not raised too high;
 I do not occupy myself with ambitious desires
 nor with things which are too marvellous for me.[2]
2 Yea, I have calmed and quieted my soul.
 As a weaned child rests quietly at his mother's breast,
 so is my soul quieted within me.[3]
3 O Israel, wait for the Lord[4]
 from this time forth and for evermore.

[1] See above, p. 100. (Tr. N.: RSV reads 'A Song of Ascents'.)
[2] * RSV has 'lifted up' instead of 'haughty' and translates v. 1bc:
 I do not occupy myself with things
 too great and too marvellous for me.
[3] * V. 2bc reads in RSV:
 like a child quieted at its mother's breast;
 like a child that is quieted is my soul.
[4] * RSV has 'hope in the Lord' instead of 'wait for the Lord'.

This psalm of trust in God, which unfortunately is too little known, is a wonderfully tender and intimate little song. It is the outpouring of a mature faith and deserves to be classed with the most beautiful psalms of the Psalter. The delicate tones of humble trust sound like the peaceful chime of bells at eventide in a quiet valley which the last rays of the setting sun fill with their soft light. This prayer, unassuming yet full of moving childlike warmth, rises to God from the soul of a man who, after the lofty aspirations of youth and its emotions, and after the hard battles he has fought during the stormy days of his past life, has now found peace in communion with God. [1] The worshipper lays his heart open to the eyes of God with childlike candour and lets him feel the pulse of his inner life. It is a kind of confession which in comparison with other protestations of innocence, which are often self-satisfied, produces by its simple candour the effect of greatness. The fact that the poet feels constrained to make this frank confession before God reveals what is important to him and what is not. He does not harbour in his heart aspirations for things which are too marvellous for him nor ambitious desires; there is one thing only which he values, and that is to be united with his God in a relationship of sincere trust. As usually in life, so here, too, humility is the prerequisite of genuine trust. The poet humbly confesses that he has learned to forgo his own lofty projects and proud thoughts; not as if he wanted acquiescently to abandon his claims upon living a full life, but he has found the balance of mind that enables him to be satisfied with what has been granted to him. And this balance of mind arises from the fact that his soul is at peace with God. This is all the happiness he needs. **[2]** Of course, he did not achieve this end without any struggle and mental affliction. The poet briefly and simply indicates this fact: 'I have calmed and quieted my soul.' We can but surmise how many struggles against his own arrogance and sinfulness and against striving for honour, wealth, and recognition, how many renunciations of the beautiful dreams of youth and the headstrong ambitions of manhood are concealed behind that statement, till at last he holds in his hands the prize of victory: the peace which passes all understanding. Now that he is firmly upheld by the peace of God, he is able to speak with sublime equanimity of that struggle, which once filled his heart with turbulent emotions. His words reflect the firmness and self-control of a man who has wholly mastered himself. The poet characterizes his present state of peace of mind by an attractive image: his soul rests on God's heart and finds its happiness in intimate communion with him, not like an infant crying loudly for his mother's breast, but like a weaned child that quietly rests by his mother's side, happy in being with her. Here his heart has found rest; he knows himself to be safe with God and to be sheltered in the love of his heavenly Father. No desire now comes between him and his God; for he is sure that God knows what he needs before he asks him. And just as the child gradually breaks off the habit of regarding his mother only as a means of satisfying his own desires and learns to love her for her own sake, so the worshipper after a struggle has reached an attitude of mind in which he desires God for himself and not as a means of fulfilment of his own wishes. His life's centre of gravity has shifted. He now rests no longer in himself but in God. This gives him his balance of mind, and it also gives him sufficient strength to subordinate his own wishes to the will of God.

[3] The psalm concludes with a call upon the cult community 'Israel' to hope confidently in God; this is couched in a stylized liturgical form and shows that such personal confessions of an individual also had had their place in the covenant cult. The fact that a confession springing from such profound piety and bearing witness to a wholly personal and intimate relationship with God was uttered in the worship of the cult community and was spiritually assimilated by the community indicates the way in which the ground was prepared in which the seed of the Gospel was able to grow.

132. DEDICATION OF THE TEMPLE

A Pilgrim Song[1]

1 Remember, O Lord, in David's favour,
   all the hardships he endured;
2 how he swore to the Lord
   and vowed to the Mighty One of Jacob,
3 'I will not enter the tent in which I dwell
   or ascend the bed on which I rest;[2]
4 I will not give sleep to my eyes
   or slumber to my eyelids,
5 until I find a place for the Lord,
   a dwelling-place for the Mighty One of Jacob.'
6 'Lo, we heard of it in Ephrathah,
   we found it in the fields of Jaar.
7 Let us go to his dwelling-place;
   let us worship at his footstool!'
8 'Arise, O Lord, and go to thy resting-place,
   thou and the ark of thy might!'
9 Thy priests get clothed with salvation
   and thy saints shout for joy.[3]
10 For thy servant David's sake
   do not reject thy anointed one![4]
11 The Lord swore to David a sure oath
   which he will not retract:[5]
   'A king[6] from your offspring
   I will set on your throne.
12 If your sons keep my covenant
   and my testimonies which I shall teach them,
   their sons also for ever
   shall sit upon your throne!'
13 For the Lord has chosen Zion;
   he has desired it for his habitation:
14 'This is my resting-place for ever;
   here I will dwell, for I have desired it.
15 I will abundantly bless her provisions;
   I will satisfy her poor with bread.
16 Her priests I will clothe with salvation,
   and her saints shall[7] shout for joy!
17 There I will make a horn to sprout for David;
   I have prepared a lamp for my anointed.

18 His enemies I will clothe with shame,
   but as for him his crown shall flourish!'[8]

[1] See above, p. 100. (Tr. N.: RSV reads 'A Song of Ascents'.)
[2] * RSV has '. . . enter my house
     or get into my bed'.
[3] * RSV has:
     Let thy priests be clothed with righteousness,
     and let thy saints shout for joy.
[4] * RSV has 'do not turn away the face of thy anointed one'.
[5] Lit.: 'he does not turn away from it.' (Tr. N.: RSV has 'from which he will
not turn back'.)
[6] Supply *melek*, see BH. (Tr. N.: In RSV v. 11cd reads:
     'One of the sons of your body
     I will set on your throne.')
[7] * RSV has 'will' instead of 'shall'.
[8] * RSV has 'but upon himself his crown will shed its lustre'.

This strange psalm represents part of the festal liturgy of the feast
of the dedication of the Jerusalem Temple. Since the sacred Ark is
mentioned in vv. 7 f. and since the intercession in v. 10 and the
promise in vv. 17 f. are intended for the king, the psalm must
originate in the pre-exilic period. From the last-named fact as well
as from vv. 12 and 15 it can be inferred that the dedication of the
Temple together with the festival of the enthronement of the king
was a constituent part of the Covenant Festival of Yahweh which was
celebrated in autumn, and whose first beginnings can be traced back
to the time of the sacral confederacy of the Twelve Tribes when
Israel was not yet a state; it was adopted by David together with the
central shrine of this confederacy and was localized by him at the
royal sanctuary in Jerusalem, probably not without encountering
some difficulties, as is also indicated by the psalm. The connection
of the psalm with the dedication of the Temple is also evident from
II Chron. 6.41 f., where Ps. 132.8–10 forms the conclusion of the
prayer offered on the occasion of the dedication of the Temple and
put into the mouth of Solomon, a custom which probably dates back
to an ancient tradition (cf. I Kings 8.2 as regards the celebration of
the feast in autumn). Though a liturgy of such a kind as the psalm
represents is timeless, there is nevertheless nothing which prevents us
from assuming that the basic elements of the form in which it has
been handed down date from the era of Solomon. It is possible that
details of its present wording may have suffered modifications in
the course of history (see Intr. 28, 40 f., 45).

The psalm falls into two parts: the first part (vv. 1–10) sounds the
note of supplication; in the second part (vv. 11–18) the divine

promise prevails. The two fundamental ideas of the psalm, the promise made to the house of David and the problem of the election of Zion as God's dwelling-place, are linked together in II Sam. 7 and in Ps. 78.68 ff. also. There is therefore no reason for dividing up the psalm into two different poems; for in all these passages we seem to be dealing with a firmly fixed tradition.

[1–5] The liturgy begins with a supplication (of the congregation?) addressed to God, asking him to remember all the hardships which David had to endure till he found a dwelling-place for Yahweh. It takes for granted familiarity with the events reported in II Samuel 6, 7 and 24, probably in a more detailed account than those biblical records give us. The explicit mention of Yahweh by the name 'Mighty One of Jacob' points to a merging of this tradition of the God of the patriarchs, which was originally the native tradition of the tribes of the future Northern Kingdom (cf. Gen. 49.24), with the Yahweh cult of the Ark of the Covenant at Jerusalem, a merger which it will hardly have been possible to accomplish without friction. It may be assumed that the overcoming of the rivalry of the tribes and of their traditions, which not only had repercussions in the political field but, as we can infer from I Kings 12.26 ff., exercised its influence on account of the competition of the several sanctuaries in the cultic sphere also (cf. also Ps. 78.67), is to be numbered among the 'hardships' as a result of which David has deserved well of Yahweh. These hardships are now to be remembered by God, just as they are present in the minds of the members of the festival congregation as a result of the account which they have just heard in the course of the cultic ceremony. [6] Such a recital in the presence of the congregation of the changing fortunes of the Ark of the Covenant is alluded to in v. 6, which summarily speaks of its earlier abode in Ephraim ('Ephrathah' is probably to be understood in this sense according to I Sam. 1.1), that is to say, in Shiloh, and of its latest sojourn in the fields of Jaar, that is to say, in Kiriath-jearim (I Sam. 7.1 ff.; II Sam. 6.2 ff.), whence the sacred shrine was brought up by David to Jerusalem. This cultic re-enactment of past events makes such a vivid impression on the members of the congregation that they imagine themselves seeing and hearing and experiencing at first hand the events of the past as things which actually happen in their presence. This is one of the essential marks of the Old Testament understanding of history, which is rooted in the cultus and, in that it overcomes the time-factor that separates the historical events from each other, fundamentally differs from the modern understanding of history which has its roots in the scientific way of thinking. [7] The recital of the history of the establishment of the sanctuary, the *hieros logos* of the dedication of the Temple, is followed by the congregation's summons to itself to worship before the sacred Ark in the Temple, above which Yahweh would appear to the congregation, so that it is termed 'the stool of his feet' (cf. I Chron. 28.2; II Sam. 6.2). [8] The appeal to Yahweh (spoken by the priest?), which in its stylized form follows the example of the ancient liturgical formulae associated with the Ark in Num. 10.35 f., begins the theophany, the climax of the cultic ceremony. There is no question here, as many commentators have assumed, of carrying the Ark in procession; according to v. 7 it is, after all, already in the Temple; rather is it a question of the appearing of God from Sinai or from heaven, as in Num. 10.35 ff.; Judg. 5.4 f.; Isa. 6.1 ff.; Pss. 18.9 ff.; 68.17, 24, and especially in I Kings 8.10 f. (see Intr. 29 f., 38 ff.), and therefore of his advent at his resting-place above the wings of the cherubim upon the Ark, which personify the clouds, the chariot of the Godhead, and so also the presence of God. In that solemn moment the members of the congregation throw themselves to the ground before God, who invisibly is present above the Ark, and worship him in awe and adoration. [9] The priests receive God's 'salvation' (cf. v. 16) to pass it on to the congregation by means of the blessing they pronounce. The multitude burst out into rapturous shouts of joy at the revelation of the divine salvation. [10] The special intercession for the king who is present (Ps. 84.9) which links up with the beginning of the psalm, concludes this cultic scene which forms the background of the first part of the psalm with dramatic force and tension (see Intr. 45).

The tension is resolved by the subsequent revelation of the divine utterance which as God's answer to the prayer follows in the second part of the psalm, being spoken by the priest or by a prophet officiating at the cult. [11–12] God confirms anew his sworn promise to David (cf. II Sam. 7). He will adhere to his covenant if the king on his part will keep 'covenant and testimonies',[1] that is to say, if he will prove his faithfulness by bearing testimony to God and by his

---

[1] Von Rad, 'Das judäische Königsritual,' *TLZ* 72 (1947), col. 214 = *Gesammelte Studien zum Alten Testament* (1958), p. 210, interprets *'ēdūt* as referring to the royal protocol which was presented to the king by the priest on the occasion of his enthronement as a document whose content was in the form of a promise. This view is, however, refuted by the context in which this term is used in the psalm; see also Johnson, *Sacral Kingship in Ancient Israel*, pp. 21 f. n. 5.

obedience to his will. It can be assumed that it was actually a question
of the ritual act of the renewal of the covenant, which was accompanied by the acknowledgment of the revelation of the nature and
will of God and the obligations this carried, as they had been laid
down in the tradition of the covenant made at Sinai and also
were at the root of the 'covenant made with David' (see Intr. 30 ff.).
God's promise holds good—and this is true even for the royal
house—only if man submits to him and obeys him. This condition
continues throughout the Old Testament to be the foundation of the
history of the people of Israel and the criterion by which the kingship, too, is judged (cf. Ps. 89.30 ff.). **[13–14]** The ultimate ground
on which this divine covenant rests is, however, not the faithfulness
and the obedience of men, but the election which God has decreed
and which has its cause in his incomprehensible grace. It is this
election alone which imparts to the tradition its legitimacy and
which puts the divine seal on the measures taken by David in
pursuance of his policy in the cultic sphere, whose object was the
transfer of the Ark, the central shrine of the confederacy of the
tribes, and the removal of the covenant cult to Jerusalem. And this
prevents a musunderstanding, to which not only man in the ancient
world is liable, the idea that God's presence and the worship of
God are inevitably bound up with the sanctuary in which the cult
is celebrated. God alone decides where he wants to appear and
reveal his salvation, and it is his free and gracious will which alone
continually transforms the sanctuary into a place where he is
personally present. **[15–18]** Thus it is not possible to achieve a
'guarantee of salvation' merely by means of a cultic technique or a
sacral tradition. Only the promise which God himself makes of
his own accord provides the assurance of salvation and guarantees
the fertility of the earth (v. 15) and the inward happiness of the
community of the saints (v. 16). In the same way the power and the
stability of the kingship—this is the meaning of the two images in
v. 17—the king's victory over his enemies and the expansion and the
flourishing state of his rule, are a gift from God which the earthly
ruler receives from the hand of the heavenly King.

133. THE UNITY OF THE FAMILY

A Pilgrim Song.[1]   *Of David*

1 Behold how good and pleasant it is
    when brothers dwell together (in unity)!

2 It is like the precious oil upon the head,
   running down upon the beard,
   like the beard of Aaron,
   running down on the hem of his garment![2]
3 It is like the dew of Hermon,
   which falls on the mountains of Zion!
   For there the Lord has commanded
   blessing and life for evermore.[3]

[1] See above p. 100. (Tr. N.: RSV reads 'A Song of Ascents'.)
[2] * In RSV v. 2cd reads:
   upon the beard of Aaron,
   running down on the collar of his robes.
[3] * In RSV v. 3cd reads:
   For there the Lord has commanded the blessing,
   life for evermore.

The form of the opening words of the psalm, which has its parallels also in the corresponding Egyptian literature, as well as its subject-matter show that we are here dealing with a 'Wisdom saying' which, as in Ps. 127.3 ff., has taken a feature from family life and has made it the subject of its teaching on the practical conduct of life (see Intr. 88 f.). The aim of the Wisdom saying is presumably to preserve a good ancient custom at a time when it was in the process of declining. It is a question of the 'dwelling together of brothers' within the family circle, a custom which in antiquity was a form of life that was widespread amongst many nations. The Old Testament, too, is familiar with this custom and regards it as an ideal state of family life in that it represents the parting of Abraham and Lot (Gen. 13.6 ff.) and of Jacob and Esau (Gen. 27.41 ff.; 36.7) as the exception and as the regrettable result of family strife. The dwelling together of brothers is also presupposed by the law concerning levirate marriage (Deut. 25.5). At the root of this custom is probably the desire to keep the hereditary possession undivided by means of joint management, coupled with a strong sense of the unity of the family as the firm bond and the fundamental order from which the nation as a community derives its strength. As regards the date to be assigned to the psalm, we can start from the assumption that the custom of dwelling together within the family circle was probably commonly observed in the time of Saul (cf. I Sam. 10.14) and was still in existence in the seventh century at the time of Deuteronomy (Deut. 25.5), but was then no longer the general rule which suffered no exception, so that the psalm seems to have been composed about the time when that custom was in danger of declining.

[1] The poet at once tackles his main theme and seeks to awaken the attention and the interest of his hearers by means of a spirited exclamation in which he throws into relief the dwelling together of brothers as a most beautiful and delightful example. He is not mistaken in doing so; for his mind's eye is fixed on the lofty ideal of a family in which a proper family sense, a common concern for the whole family, and a conciliatory spirit animating the members of the family in their mutual relationships constitute the inner bond and the source of energy which sustains the family and makes itself felt in the fact that the members of the family continue to dwell together. The poet is aware of the spiritual value of the good ancient custom which he enthusiastically advocates in his Wisdom saying. It is therefore entirely in line with the intentions of the author to think like Luther of the dwelling together as taking place 'in unity', though this interpretation goes beyond the actual wording of the Hebrew original. [2-3] The same tendency as in v. 1 is shown in the colourful images by means of which the poet first illustrates the harmonious beauty and charm of the ideal in order to get his hearers interested in it and to win them over for it. The parables are to be understood in the light of oriental taste. The deliciously scented oil which slowly drips down from the head upon the beard is regarded as something especially beautiful and refined not only by the Israelites, but also by the Egyptians and the ancient Greeks. Again, to the oriental a long flowing beard is—even today—a mark of manly beauty and dignity. The beard of Aaron, which according to the priestly law (Lev. 21.5) must not be cut so that it reaches down to the edge of the collar of the garment, is apparently for the poet the sacred model for such an adornment of man. The third word-picture is chosen from the realm of Nature. The poet has probably in mind a summer morning when the region of the mountains of Zion, intensely hot in the daytime under the blazing heat of the sun, has been refreshed in the night by the ample fall of dew and now in the radiant freshness and splendour of its colours presents a picture of rejuvenated beauty and joy in life. The term 'dew of Hermon' seems to be used in a proverbial sense as an image within an image because of the exceptionally ample quantity of dew which used to fall on Mount Hermon. It is therefore unnecessary to ask how the dew on the mountain-range in the north of Palestine could possibly fall on the mountains at Jerusalem. The trait common to these three different word-pictures is the illustration of *beauty* and

charm; they serve therefore, first of all, the purpose of illustrating the statement made in v. 1 regarding the dwelling together of brothers. It must, however, not be overlooked that the poet deliberately uses the same term (*yōrēd* = coming *down*) in all three word-pictures. In this fact lies a second point of comparison which in my opinion does not allude to the mutual relations existing between the brothers, for instance in the sense that, as some expositors assume, the wealthy party shares its plenty with the poorer party and, in doing so, somehow stoops *down* to them; rather is it used with a view to the concluding statement of the psalm in order to indicate the *descent* of the divine blessing upon the family community whose members live together. In their total content the three word-pictures also fit in very well with the divine blessing. They therefore look both ways: the mention of beauty looks back to the beginning, the coming down to the end of the psalm, which by means of this twofold movement of the parables is welded at its centre into an artistic unity. And it is only in this way that the conjunction 'for' in the concluding sentence of the psalm, which refers back to the similes, can be explained in its immediate context. This concluding sentence leads the 'interpretation' of the three parables in the other direction. The outward link between these two series of thoughts is established by the mention of Zion, where God at the feast of the renewal of the covenant has 'commanded' blessing and life for his people and, inasmuch as the people comply with the order he has decreed, renews that salvation for their benefit in a regularly reiterated ritual act. At this point the connection of the covenant tradition and of the covenantal order with the festival cult, as well as the connection of the 'Wisdom' movement with the cultus, become evident. The psalmist recognizes that the family is an institution willed by God and established by him as the inescapable condition for the perpetuation of life and for the bestowal of blessing upon the covenant people (cf. Ex. 20.12); and it is for this very reason that he so vigorously advocates the preservation of a custom in which he discerns many possible ways of developing the innermost and strongest forces of family life. In spite of its archaic character the psalm has the appearance of being a modern composition in view of its realization of the true basis of national life, a realization which is both healthy and deeply rooted in religion; for the psalmist perceives that the strength and the peace of a family that lives in unity are the fruit of God's blessing and the fulfilment of his promise. The psalm points to an ancient truth which is yet continually new because it is part of the divine ordinances that govern man's life.

134. CONCERNING BLESSING

A Pilgrim Song[1]

1 Come, bless the Lord,
  all you servants of the Lord,
  who stand by night in the house of the Lord!
2 Lift up your hands to the holy place,
  and bless the Lord!
3 May the Lord bless you from Zion,
  he who made heaven and earth!

[1] See above, p. 100. (Tr. N.: RSV reads 'A Song of Ascents'.)

This short liturgy,[1] which concludes the Book of Pilgrim Songs, is mostly regarded, because of v. 1b, as being related to a vigil service in the Jerusalem Temple, either during a festal night at the autumnal feast (cf. Isa. 30.29) or as part of the regular nightly duties of the Temple personnel (I Chron. 9.33). It is not possible to infer directly from the psalm that it was itself recited during such a vigil service. It is equally possible that vv. 1 and 2 were addressed by the pilgrims to the Temple officials who would spend the night there. In that case v. 3 would represent the blessing which is pronounced on the pilgrims as they depart from Zion and is meant to accompany them on their journey, a view which at the same time would also make it clear why this psalm has been placed at the end of the Pilgrim Songs.

[1–2] In any case vv. 1 and 2 contain a call, addressed to the priests or Levites in a fixed and stylized form (this point in opposition to Gunkel; cf. Ps. 135.2), to 'bless' Yahweh by singing songs of praise, lifting up their hands to the holy place. At the root of this call is the profound conception of the significance of the hymn. Whereas the hymn as such is man's response to the revelation of God, the effect, as it were, of the power of blessing that emanates from God, it on its part reflects back that power of blessing to God in order that he may be praised more and more and his 'might' be magnified and so once more be imparted to the congregation in the form of God's blessing and salvation (cf. Ps. 71.14). The members of the congregation join in this continuous unbroken circle of divine blessing by calling upon the priests to 'bless' Yahweh and are now

[1] It was the model for the hymn 'Lobt Gott, den Herrn der Herrlichkeit', by Matthias Jorissen (1739–1823).

[3] able to receive for their part the blessing of God which the priests, acting as God's mediators, impart to them. In this connection the ancient liturgical form of the Aaronite benediction (Num. 6.24) is used which, though the form of address is in the singular, yet is at one and the same time addressed to the congregation as a whole and to its individual members. The form which is here used for the blessing is enlarged by the theme of the idea of creation, which is peculiar to the hymn, and it may be assumed that this feature has its origin in the revelation of God as the Creator, which is firmly established in the festival cult and here, as in Pss. 121.2; 124.8, is meant to make the hearers aware of the greatness of the power of God and of all that his blessing means and effects.

135. CREATION AND ELECTION

1 Hallelujah[1]
  Praise the name of the Lord,
  give praise, O you servants of the Lord,
2 you that stand in the house of the Lord,
  in the courts of the house of our God!
3 Praise the Lord, for the Lord is good;
  sing to his name, for it is sweet![2]
4 For the Lord has chosen Jacob for himself,
  Israel as his own possession.
5 For I know that the Lord is great,
  and that our Lord is above all gods.
6 Whatever the Lord pleased he did,[3]
  in heaven and on earth,
  in the seas and all deeps.
7 He it is who makes the clouds rise at the end of the earth,
  who changes lightnings into rain[4]
  and brings forth the wind from his storehouses.
8 He it was who smote the first-born of Egypt,
  both of man and of beast;
9 who sent signs and wonders ' '[5]
  against Pharaoh and all his servants;
10 who smote many nations
   and slew mighty kings,
11 Sihon, king of the Amorites,
   and Og, king of Bashan,
   and all the kingdoms of Canaan,
12 and gave their land as a heritage,
   a heritage to his people Israel.
13 Thy name, O Lord, endures for ever,
   thy memory, O Lord, from generation to generation.[6]

14 For the Lord vindicates his people,
   and has compassion on his servants.[7]
15 The idols of the nations are silver and gold,
   the poor work of men's hands.
16 They have mouths, but cannot speak,
   they have eyes, but cannot see,
17 they have ears, but cannot hear,
   nor is there any breath in their mouths.
18 Like them be those who made them—
   yea, every one who trusts in them!
19 O house of Israel, praise the Lord!
   O house of Aaron, praise the Lord!
20 O house of Levi, praise the Lord!
   You that fear God, praise the Lord!
21 Blessed be the Lord from Zion,
   he who dwells in Jerusalem!
   Hallelujah![1]

[1] See above p. 22. (Tr. N.: RSV reads 'Praise the Lord'.)
[2] * RSV has 'sing to his name, for he is gracious'.
[3] * RSV uses the present tense.
[4] * RSV has 'who makes lightnings for the rain'.
[5] See BH. (Tr. N.: RSV begins v. 9 'who in thy midst, O Egypt'.)
[6] * V. 13b reads in RSV, 'thy renown, O Lord, throughout all ages'.
[7] * RSV uses the future tense.

Because of various points of contact with other psalms and other Old Testament passages this psalm is mostly regarded as a mosaic, reiterating thoughts borrowed from other literary sources without presenting them in a consistent thought-sequence with its own independent significance. For this reason and because of the mention of those 'that fear God' (v. 20), who are understood to be proselytes of later Judaism, the psalm is held to belong to the latest portions of the Psalter. However, just as in the case of Pss. 150.11 and 118.4 (see *ad loc.*), so here, too, it is doubtful whether the psalm under discussion has in mind the proselytes of this later time when it speaks of those who fear God. It is equally possible to interpret the phrase 'you that fear God', which is used in v. 20, as a summary description of the various groups of the Israelite cult community who have previously been addressed in the psalm. There is no need to have recourse to the idea of literary dependence on the part of the psalmist as copying other literary sources because he was incapable of composing an original poem of his own, in order to account for the fact that various parallels can be found to particular verses of the psalm, an idea which, after all, is strange and misleading when we come to consider how the psalms have come into being. This fact is rather to be accounted for by the psalmist's deliberate adherence to the fixed and stylized forms of the tradition which had their place in the cultus. For we can clearly see that Psalm 135 is in all its parts a liturgical hymn which was appointed to be recited antiphonally at the festival cult of the Israelite covenant community; this view also explains why the structure of its individual components exhibits a well-thought-out unity. Just as in the case of Psalm 115 so here the possibility of pre-exilic origin has to be seriously considered. The hymn reflects the essential features of the festival cult: the revelation of the name of Yahweh (vv. 1, 3, 13) and of the transcendent majesty of his nature as manifested in creation (vv. 5–7), in the election of Israel (v. 4), in history (vv. 8–12), in God's goodness (v. 3) and in his judgment (vv. 3, 14); finally the renunciation of the pagan gods and the cursing of their worshippers (vv. 15–18; see Intr. 28 ff., 32f.). The concluding call (vv. 19–21) upon the Israelite covenant community and upon the priests and the Levites to sing the praise of God reverts to the beginning of the psalm. How tenaciously the framework and the individual elements of the festal liturgy have been preserved can now be gathered from the liturgy of the Qumran sect, which in the ritual of the feast of the renewal of the covenant still seems to be familiar with the essential ingredients of the tradition that are exhibited in the psalm.

[1–4] In contrast with Ps. 134.1 the call to glorify God in a hymn of praise is addressed not only to the cult officials, who are in the sanctuary, but also to the members of the congregation gathered in the forecourt of the Temple to attend the feast. The hymn praises the name of God which in connection with the theophany is proclaimed at the festival cult (Ex. 33.18 f.; see Intr. 41 f.). This name, so to speak, is the compressed manifestation of the divine nature and will and within the context of the praise expressed in the hymn also represents at the same time the congregation's testimony to their divine Lord and to his goodness. The joy in God which pervades the whole psalm is based on his grace which is manifested in the incomprehensible miracle of the election of Israel as the people of God (cf. Ex. 19.5 f.). During the celebration of the feast, the main themes of which the subsequent verses take up again in a concise hymnic form, the congregation is once more made conscious of the happiness which that grace imparts. [5–7] A solo voice (v. 5), which probably speaks on behalf of the cult community as a whole, sums up the knowledge which has been granted afresh to the congregation in the praise of the greatness of God who is above all gods, a greatness which has been revealed in creation and in his Lordship over Nature. The allusion to clouds, lightnings and rain probably ensues from the connection with the autumn festival which has in view the end of the harvest and the beginning of the rainy season and therewith the fertility of the new year. **[8–12]** The recapitulation of the tradition of creation is followed, once more in a concise hymnic form, by mention of the traditions of the Exodus and the conquest of the land, which likewise had their firmly established place in the Old Testament cult of the Covenant. Creation and redemption are the two pivots of the Old Testament teaching on God; God is the Lord of both Nature and history; and it is only by means of the mutual relatedness of creation and election that God's acts assume the character of a *Heilsgeschichte* in which the members of the cult community know themselves to be involved by God whenever they hear the recital of the tradition of that *Heilsgeschichte* in the course of the celebration of the cultic festival. **[13–14]** The festival congregation summarize the whole cultic experience of their encounter with the God who is present in the *Heilsgeschichte* in a prayer in the form of a hymn which, leading back once more to the beginning of the psalm, emphasizes that perpetual presence of the divine name in the service of commemoration, which is duly performed from generation to generation (v. 13), and glorifies God as the righteous Judge and as one who, because he is gracious, has compassion on his worshippers (see Intr. 28 ff., 36, 41 ff.).

[15–18] What the cult community owe to their God brings with it the obligation of unconditional faithfulness to their divine Lord. That faithfulness manifests itself in the renunciation of the foreign gods which had its place in the cultus as a reverse effect, as it were, of the impression produced by the greatness of God (cf. Josh. 24.14, 23 and Intr. 33, 51, 61); as in Ps. 115.4 ff. that renunciation in stylized form derisively throws into relief the powerlessness of the idols and ends with a curse on their worshippers. True faith in God requires at this point a clear separation and decision.

[19–21] Against such a background the greatness of God is so much the more radiantly set off in the final chord of the hymn, in which the different voices of the priests and Levites and of the members of the whole congregation unite in order to pass on in powerfully ringing tones to those outside the blessing in which the Temple congregation has shared.

136. THE PERPETUAL GRACE OF GOD IN
CREATION AND HISTORY

1 O testify[1] to the Lord, for he is good,
    for his grace[2] endures for ever!
2 O testify[1] to the God of gods,
    for his grace endures for ever!
3 O testify[1] to the Lord of lords,
    for his grace endures for ever;
4 to him who alone does great wonders,
    for his grace endures for ever;
5 to him who made the heavens with wisdom,[3]
    for his grace endures for ever;
6 to him who spread out the earth upon the waters,
    for his grace endures for ever;
7 to him who made the great lights,
    for his grace endures for ever;
8 the sun to rule over the day,
    for his grace endures for ever;
9 the moon and stars to rule over the night,
    for his grace endures for ever;
10 to him who smote the first-born of Egypt,
    for his grace endures for ever;
11 and brought Israel out from among them,
    for his grace endures for ever;
12 with a strong hand and an outstretched arm,
    for his grace endures for ever;
13 to him who divided the Red Sea in sunder,
    for his grace endures for ever;
14 and made Israel pass through the midst of it,
    for his grace endures for ever;
15 but cast Pharaoh and his host into the Red Sea,
    for his grace endures for ever;
16 to him who led his people through the wilderness,
    for his grace endures for ever;
17 to him who smote great kings,
    for his grace endures for ever;
18 and slew famous kings,
    for his grace endures for ever;
19 Sihon, king of the Amorites,
    for his grace endures for ever;
20 and Og, king of Bashan,
    for his grace endures for ever;
21 and gave their land as a heritage,
    for his grace endures for ever;
22 a heritage to Israel his servant,
    for his grace endures for ever;

23 to him who remembered us in our misery,[4]
   for his grace endures for ever;
24 and rescued us from our oppressors,[5]
   for his grace endures for ever;
25 to him who gives food to all flesh,[6]
   for his grace endures for ever;
26 O testify[1] to the God of heaven,
   for his grace endures for ever.

[1] * RSV has 'give thanks' instead of 'testify'.
[2] * RSV uses the term 'steadfast love' instead of 'grace' throughout.
[3] * RSV has 'to him who by understanding made the heavens'.
[4] * RSV has 'It is he who remembered us in our low estate.'
[5] * RSV has 'foes' instead of 'oppressors'.
[6] * RSV has 'he who gives food to all flesh'.

This psalm, which in the tradition of late Judaism was also called the 'Great Hallel', is preserved in the form in which it was recited in the cult, and has its parallel in Christian worship in the litany (cf. *Kyrie eleison*). The first half of each verse of this liturgy in the form of a hymn is to be thought of as having been sung by the priest (priestly choir), and the congregation responded to it by singing each time the identical antiphony 'for his grace endures for ever' (on this antiphony cf. Pss. 106.1; 107.1; 118.1; Ezra 3.11; and also II Chron. 7.3, where it appears in the form of homage paid by the festal congregation at the theophany that took place on the occasion of the dedication of Solomon's Temple). In structure and subject-matter the psalm is strikingly similar to Psalm 135 (vv. 17–22 accord with the latter almost word for word), so that some commentators want to attribute both psalms to the same author. It is, however, hardly possible to prove the correctness of this view of a hymn which exhibits such a strong liturgical character and follows the traditional ways. Again, the various reminiscences of other Old Testament traditions, in particular of those fashioned by the Deuteronomists and by the priestly writings (with vv. 2 f. cf. Deut. 10.17; with v. 12 cf. Deut. 4.34; with vv. 7–9 cf. Gen. 1.16), are likewise to be accounted for, as in the case of Psalm 135, by regarding them not so much as borrowings from other literary sources but rather as the result of a dependence on common traditions which, as smaller modifications of details indicate, were preserved in an oral cultic tradition. For this reason, too, the comparatively late linguistic form in which the psalm is preserved cannot directly be regarded as proving the late origin of the psalm as a comparison with Psalm 135 shows (this point in opposition to Gunkel and others). From v. 25

we can infer that the psalm, like Psalm 135 (cf. Ps. 135.7), belonged to the liturgy of the harvest festival, which was celebrated in autumn, and likewise reflects the fundamental elements of the tradition of that feast, that is, the revelation of God's salvation in creation (vv. 5–9) and in history (vv. 10–24); the psalm ends in a thanksgiving to God for the blessing of the harvest.

Though from an artistic point of view the antiphonal testimony of the congregation may appear to be wearisome, it constitutes the focal point which sustains the whole psalm and to which all the hymnic praises in the first half of each verse are meant to be related, and in the light of which the statements they make are intended to be understood. God's eternal grace is the motive power of the wondrous work of his creation and ordering of the universe, as well as of the saving deeds he has wrought for the benefit of the people of Israel, and both these are the visible proof of the transcendent power and wisdom which exalt him above all the gods and make him the 'Lord of lords'. The members of the congregation know themselves to be upheld by that eternal grace as they listen to the cultic recital which represents God's rule in Nature and in history as well as in creation and in redemption, and so come to experience God's grace as something that is present with them (that 'endures for ever'), and, further, are enabled to become once more assured of it by the fact of the bestowal and possession of the Holy Land (vv. 21 f.) and through their enjoyment of the blessing of harvest (v. 25). In the light of that grace the people are conscious of their own human wretchedness (v. 23) and so also know what it means for the Creator and Lord of the universe to stoop down to them in his goodness and for them to give thanks to the 'God of heaven' and testify to him as their Lord (v. 26). This remarkable range of thought gives the psalm its peculiar character and its religious profundity.

137. BY THE WATERS OF BABYLON

1 By the waters of Babylon
  we sat down and wept,
  when we remembered Zion.
2 On the willows there
  we hung up our harps,[1]
3 For there our captors
  required of us songs,
  and our tormentors[2] mirth, saying,
  'Sing us one of the songs of Zion!'

4 How shall we sing the Lord's song
  in a foreign land?
5 If I forget you, O Jerusalem,
  let my right hand wither![2]
6 Let my tongue cleave to the roof of my mouth,
  if I do not remember you,
  if I do not set Jerusalem
  above my highest joy!
7 Remember, O Lord, against the sons of Edom
  the day of Jerusalem,
  how they cried, 'Rase it, rase it!
  Down to its foundations!'
8 O daughter of Babylon, you devastator![3]
  Blessed[4] shall he be who requites you
  with what you have done to us!
9 Blessed[4] shall he be who takes your little ones
  and dashes them against the rock!

[1] * RSV has 'lyres' instead of 'harps'.
[2] See BH.
[3] Following ancient translations; the MT reads 'you who are doomed to die'.
[4] * RSV has 'happy' instead of 'blessed'.

This psalm, the model for a well-known hymn by Dachstein,[1] shows great poetical power and forcefulness. It reveals the sufferings and sentiments of people who perhaps experienced at first hand the grievous days of the conquest and destruction of Jerusalem in the year 587 BC, who shared the burden of the Babylonian captivity and after their return to their homeland now, at the sight of the city still lying in ruins, give vent with passionate intensity to the feelings lying dormant in their hearts.

The poet begins with the melancholy recollection of the time of mourning in Babylon. He once more experiences the indignation he had then felt in all its fullness as he recalls how the Babylonian rulers had hurt his most sacred religious and patriotic feelings and those of his fellow countrymen by their arrogant mockery. And, finally, he gives full rein to the wrath against his enemies which he has restrained for so long, and works himself up to a blind hate and a rage which he is no longer able to master.

[1] The statements made in the first two verses do not merely present us with imagery with whose help the poet's imagination tries to depict in colourful language but quite generally the silent mourning of the exiles in the land of Babylon. On the contrary, they describe the precise features of an actual experience which the poet

1 * 'An Wasserflüssen Babylons', by Wolfgang Dachstein (1487–1553).

now recalls. His mind goes back to the agonizing hours when together with his compatriots he sat sadly far from his homeland, and when, with tearful eyes and homesick hearts, they began to accompany their songs of lament with the melancholy music of their harps. It may not have been only the suffering of homesickness with which their souls were eaten up; what probably pressed upon them even more heavily than their physical separation from their homeland was the feeling of separation from God, since they were deprived of the opportunity of becoming assured of his presence, as they had once been at the feasts celebrated at the Temple (cf. Ps. 42.2 ff.). Moreover, they were tormented by the uncertainty whether they had been rejected by God for ever or whether they still had access to him. What the prophets of Israel had continually foretold had now come true; they felt that the hand of the living God was upon them in punishment.

[2–3] But they are not allowed to keep even their mourning exclusively to themselves. Their lament falls silent and they hang up their harps on the willows; for they hear their tormentors walking towards them. To make the prisoners aware of their power, the latter call upon them with cruel mockery to sing for them a merry song (cf. Judg. 16.25), one of the songs of Zion—we might think, for instance, of Psalms 46, 48, 84 and 122—for the entertainment of the Gentiles! [4] With holy indignation the men from Israel refuse to obey this demand, which they regard as monstrous. What they are able to say in reply does credit to their way of thinking and allows a deep insight into their attitude. The mockery affects not only themselves but even more the honour of their God. Not every place and hour, not every inward frame of mind and not every human environment, is suitable for sounding forth God's praise. There are situations in which it would be wicked to praise God. Here men quite clearly perceive the inward falsehood and hypocrisy of which they would be guilty if they were to force their anguished hearts to sing a hymn to the glory of Yahweh, and, consequently, rebel against such a violation of their soul. But they do not simply feel that the sacred character of their grief is profaned; for more is involved here than personal humiliation. The holiness of God is affected when the Lord's song is degraded to a means of entertainment for a heathen audience. The thought of the holy God lifts the souls of these prisoners to that pinnacle of reverent pride reminiscent of the saying of Jesus in the Sermon on the Mount (Matt. 7.6): 'Do not give dogs

what is holy; and do not throw your pearls before swine'; and they
courageously take their stand as champions of God's holiness.

[5–6] How strongly that violation of his innermost feelings still
leaves the poet's soul quivering with emotion we can gather not only
from the passionate note he sounds in his self-imprecation but also
from the fact that he changes over to the entirely personal style of
speaking with 'I'. Sooner shall his hand wither than touch the
strings; sooner shall his tongue cleave to the roof of his mouth as if he
were dying of thirst than a song of Zion pass his lips, of Zion whose
grievous fate he will never be able to forget (v. 5); to see her rebuilt
will be the greatest of all his joys (v. 6). It would mean the betrayal
of his people and of his fatherland if he were to expose his homeland
to the mockery of the enemies. But it would just as much mean
forgetting God if he were to turn away his thoughts from Jerusalem,
seeing that the power of the living God is revealed in the fate of
Jerusalem, in her fall *and* in her rebuilding for which the poet longs.

[7–9] It is these thoughts which prompt the psalmist to turn to
God—but not to ask him to avenge him for the humiliation he has
personally suffered; it is faith in the power of God which is here at
stake. The reason why the psalmist calls down God's punishment on
the enemy is in order to show with whom the final decision rests,
whether with men who blaspheme in their arrogant mockery or with
God who is not mocked. For his own sake Yahweh cannot tolerate
infringement of his own majesty by the enemy's mockery. This is the
ultimate concern of the psalmist which we must not fail to see, even
though it is obscured and suppressed by his subsequent words of
blind hate and vulgar rage. Deeply moved by the recollection of the
dreadful day of Jerusalem's destruction, the psalmist prays to
Yahweh to requite the Edomites for what they did on the 'day of
Jerusalem', when they gave unrestrained expression to their hatred
(cf. Obad. vv. 11 ff.; Ezek. 25.12 ff.; 35.5 ff.; Lam. 4.21); moreover,
they were one of the most dangerous adversaries of the Israelites
after the return from Exile. And the thought of all that his people
have had to suffer from Babylon, the 'devastator', now causes the
passion which the psalmist has struggled hard to repress to break out
openly; he has no longer either the strength or the will-power to curb
his mounting rage. In a frightfully cruel outcry he wishes for the
complete extermination of Babylon (v. 9). Apparently he does not
rest content with the lenient treatment which was Babylon's lot
when she was conquered by the Persian king Cyrus in 539 BC.

We shall not be able to contemplate here, without being ourselves deeply affected, how the poet plunges into the abyss of human passion. We must, however, neither generalize this humanly understandable outburst of hate, with which we are also confronted in Isa. 13.16, and regard it as the Old Testament's exclusive attitude towards Babylon (cf. Jer. 29.7), nor must we forget because of it how earnestly and bravely the poet has previously striven for the assurance of his continued relationship with God and for God's honour before he was overcome by human passion.

138. THE ANSWERING OF PRAYER

Of David

1 I will praise thee, O Lord,[1]
  with my whole heart;
  I will sing thy praise before God;[2]
2 I will worship toward thy holy temple
  and praise thy name because of thy grace and faithfulness;
  for thou hast magnified thy word above thy name.[3]
3 On the day I called, thou didst answer me;
  thou givest new strength to my soul.[4]
4 All the kings of the earth praise[5] thee, O Lord,
  for they have heard the words of thy mouth;
5 and they sing[5] of the ways of the Lord,
  for great is the glory of the Lord.
6 For though the Lord is exalted, he regards the lowly;
  but the haughty he knows from afar.
7 And though I walk in the midst of great trouble,
  thou preservest me against the wrath of my enemies;
  thou dost stretch out thy hand,[6]
  and thy right hand saves me.
8 The Lord will accomplish it for me;[7]
  thy grace, O Lord, endures for ever.
  Do not forsake the work of thy hands.

[1] See BH.
[2] The translation 'before the gods' is also possible. (Tr. N.: RSV gives v. 1 as:
  I give thee thanks, O Lord,
  with my whole heart;
  before the gods I sing thy praise.)
[3] * RSV has 'I bow down' instead of 'I will worship' and 'give thanks' instead of 'praise'; it gives the last line as 'for thou hast exalted above everything thy name and thy word'.
[4] * RSV has 'my strength of soul thou didst increase'.
[5] * RSV uses the future tense.
[6] * In RSV the phrase 'against the wrath of my enemies' follows 'thou dost stretch out thy hand'.
[7] * RSV has 'The Lord will fulfil his purpose for me.'

This psalm of thanksgiving, which the Septuagint ascribes to Zechariah, was recited by the worshipper within the precincts of the sanctuary, whilst he gazed at the Temple buildings (v. 2). It contains besides the thanksgiving for the answering of his prayer (v. 3) the ringing notes of a hymn in which the poet gives expression to his enthusiasm (vv. 4–6) and which are to be understood as an echo of the cultic experience which gave him the assurance that his prayer had been heard and a share in God's dispensation of his salvation. This accounts for the fact that he envisages and interprets his own encounter with and experience of God in the widest possible context. That the poet has been a leader of the nation or even the king himself cannot be inferred from the psalm; v. 6 rather suggests that he was a simple member of the cult community. For this reason any attempt to fix the date of the psalm proves unavailing, because of the complete absence of any other concrete clues.

[1–2] The opening verses 1 and 2 sketch both the outward and the inward situation which prompts the psalmist to testify to God in order to express his gratitude to him. He stands in the forecourt of the Temple and his face is turned towards the sanctuary where he wants to worship 'before God' and 'praise his name', that is to say, where he wants to give expression to his faithfulness to God. 'Worship' and 'bearing testimony to God' belong to the fundamental and essential constituent parts of divine worship. (The other possible translation, 'before the gods', would allow us to think of the appearance of God with his celestial court [cf. Pss. 82.1, 6; 58.1], a conception according to which the gods of polytheism are reduced to the rank of servants of Yahweh and which can still be detected in Isa. 6 also.) It is obviously presupposed that God has 'appeared' in his holy place and has made known his 'name' and his 'grace' and 'faithfulness' (cf. the basic text in Ex. 33.18 ff.; 34.5 ff. and Intr. 29 ff., 38 ff.). It is the cultic act of the theophany in which the worshipper has taken part, together with the congregation in the Temple, through God's presence receiving assurance that his prayer is heard (v. 3) and of salvation (v. 7). By that personal experience of the answered prayer and assurance of salvation, which goes beyond the general promises of salvation, something special has been granted to him, beyond his fellow worshippers, so that he is able to say of that experience: 'thou hast magnified thy word above thy name.' [3] God gives more than he is asked for; he not only answers the prayer of the poet in preserving his life against the wrath of his enemies

(v. 7), but he grants him salvation and imparts to his soul new strength such as he had not known before. **[4–6]** In the view of some commentators the subsequent statement that all the kings of the earth praise God because they have heard his Word is either to be interpreted in an eschatological and Messianic sense or is to be regarded as an extravagant expression of the poet's inspiration, which sweeps all before it. These verses, however, probably refer to the event of the revelation of the 'honour' (*kābōd* = glory) of God in his words and deeds as well as in the manifestation of his nature and will, a revelation which took place within the framework of the cultic ceremony and is of significance not only for Israel's salvation but for the whole world, since to the cultic way of thinking the presence of God in the ritual act guarantees that the whole history is also present as a living reality (cf., e.g., Isa. 6.3; Pss. 68.32; 96.7 ff.; 98.3; 99.2 f.; see Intr. 42 ff., 50 f.). **[7]** In the world-wide context of the revelation of the divine salvation the worshipper first becomes conscious of what it means for the God to whom all the kings of the earth pay homage to stoop down to him in his lowliness and deliver him from his affliction and preserve his life; and so he comes to understand that his own salvation forms a part of the salvation of the whole world, part of the revelation of God's glory. **[8]** The worshipper's confidence that God will accomplish his redemptive work is likewise based on this knowledge. He knows himself to be safe in God's everlasting grace. God's cause has become his own to such a degree that he prays to God not to forsake his work; for God's work is, after all, his own salvation, too; and God's saving activities go on for ever.

139. WHITHER SHALL I GO FROM THY SPIRIT?

To the Conductor.[1] *Of David. A Psalm*

1   O Lord, thou hast searched me
    and known me!
2   Thou knowest when I sit down
    and when I rise up;
    thou discernest my thoughts from afar.
3   Thou searchest out my path and my lying down,
    and art acquainted with all my ways.
4   Even before a word is on my tongue,
    lo, O Lord, thou knowest it altogether.
5   Thou dost encompass me on all sides[2]
    and hast laid thy hand upon me.

 6 Such knowledge is too wonderful for me;
  it is too high, I cannot attain it.
 7 Whither shall I go from thy spirit?
  Or whither shall I flee from thy presence?
 8 If I ascend to heaven, thou art there!
  If I make my bed in hell,[3] thou art there too!
 9 If I took the wings of the dawn
  and dwelt in the uttermost parts of the sea,[4]
10 even there thy hand would seize[5] me,
  and thy right hand would take hold of me.[6]
11 If I said, 'If only darkness would cover[5] me,
  and the light about me be night,'
12 even the darkness would not be dark to thee,
  the night would be light to thee as the day ' '.[7]
13 Yea, thou didst form my inward parts,
  thou didst knit me together in my mother's womb.
14 To thee I testify, for thou art to be feared;[5]
  as miracles didst thou create[8] thy works;
  my soul knowest it right well.[9]
15 My frame was not hidden from thee,
  when I was being made in secret,
  intricately wrought in the depths of the earth.
16 Thy eyes beheld my days;[5]
  in thy book they are inscribed, everyone of them;
  they were written before[5] they were formed,
  when as yet there was none of them.[10]
17 How inscrutable to me are thy thoughts!
  How vast, O Lord, is the sum of them.[11]
18 If I would count them,
  they are more than the sand;
  were I to come to the end,[5]
  I would still be with thee.[12]
19 O that thou wouldst slay the wicked, O God,
  that the men of blood would depart[5] from me,[13]
20 men who speak[5] of thee deceitfully,
  and abuse thy name[5] shamefully.[14]
21 Shall I not hate them that hate thee ' '?[5]
  And shall I not loathe them that oppose[5] thee?[15]
22 I hate them with perfect hatred;
  I count them my enemies.
23 Search me, O God, and know my heart!
  Try me and know my thoughts!
24 See whether I walk in the way that leads to evil,[16]
  and lead me in the way everlasting!

[1] * RSV has 'to the choirmaster'.
[2] Lit.: thou hast [*RSV, dost] beset me behind and before.
[3] * RSV has 'Sheol' instead of 'hell'.
[4] * RSV uses the present indicative.

⁵ See BH.
⁶ * RSV has 'shall lead me' instead of 'would seize me' and 'shall hold me' instead of 'would take hold of me'.
⁷ See BH. (Tr. N.: RSV has:
    even the darkness is not dark to thee,
    the night is bright as the day;
    for darkness is as light with thee.)
⁸ Read the second person of *Hiph'il* [*i.e. the causative].
⁹ * RSV gives v. 14 as:
    I praise thee, for thou art fearful and wonderful.
    Wonderful are thy works!
    Thou knowest me right well.
¹⁰ Following Kittel and others. (Tr. N.: V. 16 of RSV reads:
    Thy eyes beheld my unformed substance;
    in thy book were written, every one of them,
    the days that were formed for me,
    when as yet there was none of them.)
¹¹ * RSV has 'precious' instead of 'inscrutable'.
¹² * V. 18b is in RSV 'When I awake, I am still with thee.'
¹³ * RSV has 'and that men of blood' instead of 'that the men of blood'.
¹⁴ * RSV has:
    men who maliciously defy thee,
    who lift themselves up against thee for evil!
¹⁵ * RSV has 'Do I not' instead of 'Shall I not' in both lines.
¹⁶ * RSV has 'And see if there be any wicked way in me'.

It is not without good reason that this psalm has been abundantly echoed in many poetical compositions of different kinds which have used it as a model and have become a part of the treasure of Christian hymns. Even today its words are still felt to be a classical testimony to what the theologians intend to convey by such concepts as the omnipresence, omniscience, and omnificence of God, and this is because one of the problems which mankind has to face, which has continually been raised by men and which they have continually attempted to solve whenever the relationship between God and man occupied the thought of those who believe in him, is here discussed in the widest possible setting. It is therefore not surprising, especially in view of the general form in which the problem has been raised, that we light upon similar thoughts also outside the Old Testament, above all in India (*Atharva Veda* IV, 16) but also among the Canaanites and Greeks and in Islam; an external dependence of the psalm on other literary documents, however, cannot be conclusively proved. In contrast to these parallels the psalm shows its peculiar character, a character typical of the Old Testament, above all in the fact that the poet does not shape his thoughts impersonally in abstract theological definitions, but develops them in the sphere of his personal experience of the reality of God in which he sees his

P.—CC

whole life to be embedded. It has not come about by chance that he
clothes his thoughts in the unusual mixed form of a hymn and of
prayer and speaks of God by addressing him on the basis of a
personal I-Thou relationship and not by making objective statements *about* God to others. Even in those passages in which intellectual reflections go beyond the limits of a hymn the poet does not
slip back into the ways of abstract philosophical thinking, but
ponders over his theme in the light of his existence as determined by
God. This method imparts to his words those fresh, lively tones
which even today still directly touch the heart of the reader. It is
not possible to assign a definite date for the composition of the
psalm. Verses 23 f. (cf. vv. 19 ff.) and parallels outside Israel suggest
the view that the psalm served as a preparation for the judgment
which God was going to pass and so originally had its place within
the sphere of public worship (cf. Intr. 76 f.).[1]

Starting from his personal experience of God the psalmist develops
his thoughts in stages which are determined by a certain thought-
sequence and stand in an inward relationship to each other, but are
not arranged in strophes. Verses 1–6 speak of God's omniscience;
vv. 7–12 of his omnipresence; vv. 13–16 of his omnificence. The
psalmist's meditation on God's nature is concluded in vv. 17 and 18
by his confession of man's inability to comprehend God's greatness.
This is followed by a petition (vv. 19–22) for the destruction of the
wicked which is not unrelated to the general problem, and the psalm
ends in a personal petition (vv. 23–24) for a divine test and for God's
guidance.

God's omniscience (vv. 1–6)

[1–4] The outward form of the *hymnic prayer* already reveals the
poet's attitude of mind, out of which he composed the psalm. It
shows the simultaneous interaction of awe and wonder at the inconceivable greatness of God and of devoted and trustful submission
to him. As the poet looks back over his life, he sees it beneath the
searching eye of God, which has always rested and still rests upon
him. No matter where he may look or whether he stands still or
walks, sits or lies down, everywhere he meets God's eye testing him
and watching him continually; indeed, God even knows what he is
going to say before he has uttered a word and even discerns his

[1] Cf. in this connection also the detailed references in Würthwein's article
'Erwägungen zu Psalm 139', *VT* 7 (1957), pp. 165 ff.

thoughts from afar. These verses express the astonishment of a man who discovers that in all his ways he is involved in relations which remain hidden from the natural eye; that he no longer belongs entirely to himself or lives his life exclusively for his own sake, because it points everywhere to those invisible bonds which unite him to the reality of God. This feeling affects even his style, which continually brings God into prominence as the subject. The human 'I' is merely the object of God's knowledge and reality. [5] This is a perception which at first is not so much cheering as depressing. The knowledge that he is 'encompassed' by God on all sides and that he will always feel God's arresting hand upon him has a rather paralysing than liberating effect; it has something uncanny about it. [6] In the face of this disturbing character of the supremacy of God's knowledge and of his constant presence nothing else is left to the psalmist but to express his wonder and confess man's inability to grasp the miracle of God's reality, which is so entirely different from that of man, and accept the contrast between God and man whereby man is entirely known by God, but on his side is not able to grasp God's nature. True faith is possible only on such a basis when man encounters God in every situation of his life and is continually attentive to him. For faith is an attitude to life which takes hold of the whole man only if he recognizes every situation in life as related to another, to an ultimate reality.

God's omnipresence (vv. 7–12)

[7] Starting from the experience of the divine presence which encompasses him on all sides, the poet ponders over the omnipresence of God in a series of hypothetical statements. The intellectual possibility on which the poet here reflects is one which he can only pursue in a form which, though wholly focused on God, is yet quite concretely related to his own existence (see above): 'Whither shall *I* go from *thy* spirit?' The mere fact that the question is formulated in this way already shows how much his thinking is influenced by his own experience of God; it also shows that the uncanny and over-whelming impression which the divine presence produces on him afflicts him so much (see the comments on v. 5) that he seeks to flee from God. It is not at all the bad conscience of a sinner, in whose position the poet places himself, which is expressed in these words, but the innate reaction of a man who trembles at the greatness of God. The possibilities which come to the author's mind make it

clear to him that it is impossible to escape from the reality of God. God is Spirit (v. 7) and for that reason he is not tied to space. **[8–10]** Everywhere, in the topmost height of heaven as well as in the nether-most depths of the underworld, in the remotest east, where the dawn rises, as well as in the distant west, where the sun sinks into the sea, even if he were to flee across the sky with the speed of the dawn (which in antiquity was thought to be winged), God would 'seize' him and take hold of him. Man is not able to protect himself against God. One can see this truth particularly clearly if one contemplates the particular religious thought-world which forms the background of these ideas. Heaven and the underworld were originally regarded as the abodes of different deities, so that in the realm of the one god one could feel safe from the other; again, the ancient idea of magical flight seems to be at the root of the poetical image of the wings of the dawn. The poet, however, rejects both these conceptions. His conception of God (cf. Amos 9.2) is so sublime and so comprehensive that the idea of a place outside the sphere of God's power is unthink-able; in his view no attitude or mode of action is at man's disposal which would enable him to escape from the sphere in which the reality of God reigns. It is in accord with the trend of this last thought that the poet considers the possibility of a magical hiding from God. **[11–12]** But even if he could call upon the darkness to envelop him like a magic cloak that makes its wearer invisible, there is no darkness through which God's eyes could not pierce. In the face of his all-penetrating reality all human possibilities are bound to fail, and what is impossible with men sets no limit to the divine reality. At the root of this sequence of hypothetical statements there is the same living experience of God as has been expressed in vv. 1–6. And the same conclusion is reached: even the boldest flight of man's imagina-tion does not succeed in reaching the limits of God's power or in fathoming his nature.

God's omnificence (vv. 13–16)

[13] After the failure of the attempt to escape from God, albeit only in thought, the poet now adopts the opposite course of turning to God in a quite personal way, the way that leads from negation to affirmation, through the idea of creation. He applies this to his own person, and so it becomes for him a means of expression by which man achieves a positive relation to the all-embracing reality of the omniscient God and to his presence. For the Old Testament idea of creation makes quite clear both that man's whole existence belongs not to himself but totally to God and has no meaning without him, and also that God is actively involved in it right from the beginning, not only as knowing about it but as controlling and moulding it and effecting the whole thing. God's nature becomes understandable only to those who focus their attention upon his activity as directed towards man. The problem which God himself presents is therefore for the God-fearing man of the Old Testament not a problem of the being of God, which he would attempt to approach theoretically by way of abstract thinking, but a question that is concerned with *actuality* in the strict sense of the word, an actuality which becomes manifest in the real facts of practical everyday living. The key to the understanding of God's omnipresence and omniscience lies for the poet in the omnificence of the Creator. It is because God has created everything that he knows everything. This does not mean at all that the nature of God could thereby be 'explained' or the mystery and wonder of his Being 'revealed'. Even to the man who has experienced in his own person the truth of the doctrine of creation, God is always manifest only as the hidden one, and the mystery of God remains a mystery which is not even revealed to the eye of faith. But in seeing himself included in the mystery of God, as he expresses in the magnificent image, 'Thou didst knit me together in my mother's womb', the poet thereby attains a different inward attitude to God and to the mystery of his life. [14] This change of attitude finds expression in a hymn which interrupts the psalmist's train of thought and takes the form of a 'testimony' (v. 14) expressing both awe and trust. Just because he is a creature of God, the poet senses the infinite difference between himself and his Maker; he knows that he does not possess an independent being of his own making which he could set over against the divine reality. He can do nothing else but testify to God, praising him for his wondrous works and trembling with awe at the sublime mystery of God. The disparity between himself and God is, however, not the only thing which he perceives. The knowledge that his own existence is woven into the divine miracle of creation prompts him at the same time to approach God directly; he is the God who holds his life in his hands and with whom he has known himself to be safe since the first days of his childhood. [15–16] That note of trust in God now gets the better of the fear that prevailed in the poet's soul at the beginning of the psalm (especially in vv. 7–12). But this trust, too, is directed to the *hidden* God. God was present when man was being made in secret and 'was intricately wrought in the depths of the earth'. The poet apparently uses here the ancient mythological idea of the earth, the mother of all living things, as a poetical image to illustrate the divine mystery which in his eyes surrounds his birth. But it is not only the beginning of his life which is exposed to the clear light of God's knowledge; the total sum of the days he is permitted to live is also recorded by God in the 'book of the living' (cf. Pss. 56.8; 69.28; Ex. 32.32 f.) and is therefore fore-ordained by the divine will even before these days actually come to pass. At the root of the idea of the book of the living, which bears analogy to the tablets of destiny known from Babylonia, is the original conception of the efficacious power of the written word. In accord with this trend of thought the idea of predestination is here used by the poet for the same purpose as in Jer. 1.5, that is, to make clear to himself the overwhelming impression which God has made upon him throughout his life by investigating God's omnificence even before it began. Such a method of thinking by faith admittedly does not enable him to explain the divine mystery of God's providential rule; but it provides his life with an altogether different kind of support and substance in that it enables him to envisage the reality of life in its entirety under the aspect of 'God' and so expresses a sense of security. The believer cannot and does not wish to penetrate the mystery of God; he submits to it in awe and trust; he also accepts the hidden God because he recognizes in him the power to which he owes his existence and which alone decides about his life. **[17–18]** This is why the poet once more stands still in reverential wonder at the greatness and at the vast sum of God's inscrutable thoughts. Even if he wanted to count them till his strength failed him. he would not reach the end, but would still be dealing with God.

Petition for the destruction of the wicked (vv. 19–22)

[19–22] To our way of feeling the petition for the destruction of the wicked and the utterance of hatred towards them follows rather abruptly. But this indicates that the idea of judgment is rooted in the cultic tradition (cf. Ps. 104.35). And there is also an inner connection between this new turn of thought and the poet's previous reflections. In view of the idea of the omnificence of God the existence of the wicked presents the psalmist with a new and difficult riddle which, at least so it seems to him, is not actually solved until the wicked are destroyed. In the context of the psalm the worshipper's petition, which in spite of everything strikes us as strange, and his remaining aloof from these evildoers (vv. 20 f.), a kind of renunciation or protestation of innocence, are to be understood as a supplement to v. 14 if we consider them in the light of the presuppositions which have previously been discussed and also on the basis of the cultic observance of the self-purification of the covenant community from wicked elements (v. 20: 'who speak of thee deceitfully and abuse thy name shamefully'; see Intr. 46 ff.); they are therefore not to be understood as expressing merely human hatred and vindictiveness. It is *for the sake of God* that he hates the 'men of blood' who speak of God deceitfully and shamefully abuse his holy name (cf. Ex. 20.7). This is the point of the poet's question, whether his hatred is justified. It is because they are God's enemies that they are also his enemies. Though we can fully understand such motives of hatred which do not spring from the lower sphere of sentiments that are far too human, we must, however, not overlook the fact that the poet here actually stops at the limits set by Old Testament tradition. It would be more in keeping with the awe due to God if he realized that the enigma of the divine inscrutability also includes the existence of the wicked and would pause before it and rest satisfied with the knowledge, 'my thoughts are not your thoughts', or if the fact that God allows his enemies to remain alive gave him an inkling of the forbearance and compassion of God, whose goodness transcends all human standards just as much as his greatness does. Since the psalmist is under the influence of the cultic ideology of his time, he is, however, unable to follow this course which in the end leads to the divine compassion that Jesus showed on the cross.

The petition for guidance (vv. 23–24)

[23–24] It looks as if the poet himself is aware of the limitations and of the vulnerability of his position; the petition he utters at the conclusion of the psalm is evidence of this. He suffers from a feeling of inadequacy. The fact that he by no means fancies himself to be faultless, but is vividly aware of how completely he is at the mercy of God's testing and guidance, imparts to his song a conciliatory parting note. The psalmist has found in God's omniscience the basis for complete trust in him. God, who sees into his heart, knows whether he walks in the way that leads to 'torment' (this is the literal meaning of v. 24a) or in the way that leads to life. And the one who is the Creator of all is the only one who can guide man in the way everlasting. As in Psalm 1 and in the Sermon on the Mount (Matt. 7.13 f.), we find used here the image of the two ways, one of which leads to destruction, the other to true life which as a life lived before God lasts for ever. By his confident petition that God may try him the poet draws the practical conclusion from his basic attitude to God which he has expressed throughout the psalm: man's life is so wholly embedded in God's knowledge and activity, that he is not able to present any achievement of his own of which he could boast before God or on which he himself could rely. And because the decision exclusively rests with God, faith and trust comprise the only possible attitude which man can adopt in his relation to the God who is omniscient, omnipresent and omnific.

140. AGAINST SLANDERERS

To the Conductor. A Psalm. Of David

1 Deliver me, O Lord, from evil men;
   preserve me from violent men,
2 who plan evil things in their heart,
   and stir up[1] quarrels continually.[2]
3 They make their tongue sharp as a serpent's,
   and under their lips is the poison of vipers. *Selah*
4 Guard me, O Lord, from the hands of the wicked;
   preserve me from violent men,
   who have planned to trip up my feet!
5 Arrogant men have hidden a snare and cords[1] for me;
   they have spread a net in my way
   and have set a trap for me.[3] *Selah*
6 I said to the Lord, Thou art my God;
   give ear ' '[1] to my fervent supplication.[4]
7 O Lord, who art my strong help,
   thou hast protected my head in the day of strife.[5]
8 Grant not, O Lord, the desires of the wicked;
   do not further his evil plot![6]
9 ' '[1] If those who surround me lift up their head,
   then may the mischief of their lips come upon[1] them.[7]
10 May burning coals fall upon them;[8]
   may he cast them into the fire, into pits,
   that they never rise up again![9]
11 A man of (evil) tongue will not be established in the land;
   calamity will pursue the violent man blow upon blow.[10]
12 I know that the Lord maintains the cause of the afflicted
   and executes justice for the needy.
13 Surely the righteous will testify to thy name;
   the godly will dwell in thy presence.[11]

[1] See BH.

[2] * RSV has 'wars' instead of 'quarrels'.

[3] * In RSV v. 5 is:
Arrogant men have hidden a trap for me,
and with cords they have spread a net,
by the wayside they have set snares for me.

[4] * V. 6b reads in RSV, 'give ear to the voice of my supplications, O Lord!'

[5] * RSV has:
O Lord, my Lord, my strong deliverer,
thou hast covered my head in the day of battle.

[6] * RSV adds 'Selah' at the end of v. 8.

[7] * RSV has:
Those who surround me lift up their head,
let the mischief of their lips overwhelm them!

[8] Translation doubtful.

[9] * V. 10bc reads in RSV:
Let them be cast into pits,
no more to rise!

[10] * RSV has:
Let not the slanderer be established in the land;
let evil hunt down the violent man speedily!

[11] * RSV has 'shall' instead of 'will' in both lines, and 'give thanks' instead of 'testify'.

This psalm is a lament of a man who is tormented by insidious slander and asks for God's protection and help against his enemies. In some respects the psalm bears analogy to Psalm 64, but in many passages it follows its own course with regard to both form and subject-matter. To assign a date is not possible, because of the absence of any concrete features; it cannot be proved that controversies between the religious parties of later Judaism form the background of the psalm. The opposition between the godly and the wicked is not confined to the later period of Israel's history, but was already at an early date one of the burning problems of the cultic and religious life of Israel. The worshipper twice turns to God in prayer and asks for his help (vv. 1, 4); each time he follows up his petition by a lament in which he describes the conduct of his adversaries. Using the images of war (vv. 2, 7) and of hunting (cf. Pss. 7.12 ff.; 9.15; 57.6 and often), he portrays the quarrelsome and insidious way in which they behave. In asking for God's protection the worshipper relies on his previous experience of God's help (v. 7). He is therefore able to pray in faith and confidence; and this imparts to his prayer its particular force. The imprecations levelled against his adversaries (vv. 8 ff.), which follow the petition for God's help, also spring from the sure knowledge that God will not tolerate arrogance and violence for ever. The curses of his adversaries will redound upon themselves; the judgment of God will come upon them like the catastrophe of Sodom and the destruction of the company of Korah (v. 10). The concluding thought (v. 11) that the slanderer will not 'be established in the land' probably expresses a general principle of the ritual law (cf. Ex. 20.12) which throws an interesting light on the connection of the psalm with the cultic tradition. For the psalmist probably alludes here to the rite of divine judgment executed by the elimination of the wicked from the cult community, as a result of which the latter lose the right to own property in the Holy Land. The divine judgment spells disaster for the wicked, but on the other hand it executes justice for the 'righteous' and for the 'godly', that is, for the faithful members of the Yahweh community, and grants them salvation, which is shown by the fact that the godly are able to 'dwell in the presence of God', to rejoice in his presence at the cultic ceremony, and to share in the testimony and praise of the cult community (vv. 12 f.). As if it were a truth which he had just discovered, the worshipper has once more become conscious and personally assured ('I know') of that truth in his encounter with the God who graciously stoops down to the afflicted and sees to it that justice is done to the needy and defenceless. The feeling of gratitude for being able to sing the praise of God in the midst of the cult community, and the peace of mind which unites the members of the cult community among themselves and with God, in the end dominate the character of the psalm as a whole and enable it to conclude on a hopeful and liberating note. (See Intr. 44, 48, 69, 72, 76 for the fact that the psalm is firmly rooted in the festival cult.)

141. TEMPTATION

A Psalm.　Of David

1　I called[1] upon thee, O Lord;
　　make haste to help me!
　　O hear my voice, when I call to thee!
2　Let my prayer be counted as incense before thee,
　　and the lifting up of my hands
　　as an evening sacrifice!
3　Set a guard[2] over my mouth, O Lord,
　　keep watch[2] over the door of my lips!
4　Let not my heart be inclined to any evil,
　　to busy myself with wicked deeds
　　in company with men who work iniquity;
　　I will not eat of their dainties![3]

5 If a righteous man strikes me in kindness
   and chastises me,
   my head shall not refuse to be anointed with oil.[4]

6-7 . . . .[5]

8 For my eyes are toward thee, O Lord, ' '[2]
   in thee I find refuge;
   pour not out my soul![6]

9 Keep me from the trap which they have laid for me,
   and from the snares of the evildoers!

10 Let the wicked fall into their own nets,
   while I at the same time pass by![7]

[1] * RSV uses the present tense.
[2] See BH.
[3] * RSV begins v. 4 with 'Incline not my heart . . .' and ends it 'and let me not eat of their dainties'.
[4] * RSV has:
   Let a good man strike or rebuke me in kindness,
   but let the oil of the wicked never anoint my head;
   for my prayer is continually against their wicked deeds.
[5] The meaning is obscure; lit.: '(5c) for continually and my prayer during their wicked deeds. (6) Their judges were cast down into the hands of the rock, and they have heard my words, for they are pleasant. (7) Like one who ploughs and rends the earth, our bones are strewn at the mouth of Sheol.'
   (Tr. N.: RSV has:
   (6) When they are given over to those who shall condemn them,
       then they shall learn that the word of the Lord is true.
   (7) As a rock which one cleaves and shatters on the land,
       so shall their bones be strewn at the mouth of Sheol.)
[6] * RSV has:
   But my eyes are toward thee, O Lord God;
   in thee I seek refuge; leave me not defenceless!
[7] * RSV adds 'together' after 'the wicked' and gives the second line as 'while I escape'.

The psalm, which in the ancient Church was regarded as the appropriate evening hymn (v. 2), is an individual prayer of lament. On account of the corruption of the text in the middle of the psalm, which cannot be eliminated, the connection between the first and the second parts of the psalm is no longer clearly discernible.

[1-2] The elaborate introduction derives its importance from the fact that in v. 2 prayer is counted before God as incense and as an evening sacrifice and, consequently, is meant to take the place of the sacrifice. This fact indicates a spiritualization and a deepening of the idea of God and of man's intercourse with him which puts the psalm in the same class with Psalms 40, 50, 51, 69 and 71 (see Intr. 71). The comparison with the daily morning and evening sacrifices is presumably intended to point to the prayer which the poet daily

offers to God. **[3–5]** The theme of his prayers is the petition that he may be kept from being seduced to do evil both in words and deeds, by men whose luxurious life threatens to become an allurement and a temptation for the worshipper. We might perhaps think of temptations which are similar to those of which the poet of Psalm 73 speaks. **[8–10]** Through communion with God in prayer the psalmist hopes to master the temptation which he feels it will not be possible for him to overcome by his own efforts, though he clearly perceives the danger and is anxious to be subjected to the discipline of the 'righteous' and with it to know himself to be sustained (cf. Prov. 27.6) by the love of the godly community (or of his teacher) rather than to respond to the tempting invitations of the wicked who ask him to share in their opulent banquets. In the closing portion of the psalm the psalmist asks for preservation from death, that is, that God may not 'pour out' his soul as one would shed blood, and for protection against the insidious persecutions of his adversaries (for the image cf. the comments on Ps. 140.5; in this connection it is doubtful whether these adversaries belong to those circles whose seduction the worshipper fears in the first part of the psalm). It is possible that the worshipper is awaiting a judicial sentence passed by God; for v. 8a indicates that the worshipper is in the Temple and that God is present at the cultic ceremony. At any rate, the psalmist knows for certain that the wicked will be caught in their own snares, whereas he will survive the judgment in safety (see Intr. 74 ff.).

142. FORSAKEN BY MEN

Maskil.[1] *Of David when he was in the cave.*[2] *A Prayer*

1 I cry with my voice to the Lord,
  with my voice I make supplication to the Lord.
2 I pour out my complaint before him,
  and tell my trouble before him.
3 When my spirit within me languishes,
  it is thou who knowest my way![3]
  In the path where I walk
  they have hidden a trap for me.
4 If I look to the right and watch,[4]
  there is none who takes notice of me.
  No refuge remained to me,
  and no man cares for me.
5 I cried to thee, O Lord;
  I said, Thou art my refuge,
  my portion in the land of the living.[5]

6 O give heed to my supplications,
   for I am quite exhausted![6]
   Deliver me from my persecutors;
   for they are too strong for me!
7 Bring me out of prison,
   that I may testify to thy name!
   The righteous will surround me,
   when thou wilt deal bountifully with me.[7]

[1] See Ps. 32, n. 1.
[2] Cf. I Sam. 22.1.
[3] * RSV has:
   When my spirit is faint,
   thou knowest my way!
[4] See BH.
[5] * RSV uses the present tense in vv. 4b and 5.
[6] * RSV has 'for I am brought very low'.
[7] * RSV has 'give thanks' for 'testify' and in the last line 'for' instead of 'when'.

This simple psalm is a deeply felt prayer of lament of a man who has been forsaken. Persecuted by people who are mightier than he (v. 6) and brought to the verge of despair by their malicious plots, he offers a fervent and moving lament which arises out of most intense physical and mental suffering, to the God who is the only refuge left to him after even his friends have turned their back on him or, what can no longer be clearly recognized, were prevented from caring for him by the violent measures taken by his persecutors (v. 4). The latter would be the case if the petition (v. 7) to be set free from prison could be interpreted literally. In that case the worshipper would have been put into prison as a result of the insidious machinations of his adversaries (v. 3) and without being guilty would probably be languishing in custody, where, separated from his friends and without any hope of human help, he would have to face trial by ordeal. The psalm would then have been uttered during Temple worship (v. 2: 'before his face'), a fact to which the presence of the cult community (v. 7: 'the righteous') also points (see Intr. 78). No matter how we may picture to ourselves the external circumstances of the psalmist, it is his affliction of soul and his attitude of mind which give the psalm its distinctive character, and these features can fairly clearly be recognized. In the midst of his isolation the worshipper reaches with trembling hands and with a heart full of childlike trust for the one last support left to him and which he has never lost sight of during the whole of his suffering, and that support is God. It is not the first time that he turns to God in supplication. Already on previous occasions (v. 5) he has confessed to him in prayer that he is his only refuge. At the very moment when he is in danger of losing all power of resistance (v. 3) he strains every nerve in a last effort and, uttering the moving words of the psalm, once more clings to God, who is the only one who understands as the psalmist now pours out his heart before him in his lament and through his petition for deliverance hopes to become assured of God's help.

The composition of the prayer of lament, which is on the lines of the customary structure of the lament, is as plain and simple as its character. The introduction (vv. 1–3a) contains the invocation which ends in v. 3 on the theme of trust in God; this is followed in vv. 3b–5 by the 'lament' which takes the form of a description of the worshipper's physical and spiritual distress; the petition in vv. 6 and 7 for deliverance followed by a vow and a prospect of the future forms the conclusion of the psalm. The later tradition established in the superscription of the psalm attributed the prayer to David 'when he was in the cave' (cf. the superscription of Psalm 57), and in doing so probably had in mind his persecution by Saul (I Sam. 22.1). This dating and interpretation can, however, as little be proved as the other one according to which the psalm is said to refer to the people of Israel during the Babylonian exile. Neither of these interpretations is at all plausible in view of the fact that the lament is couched in general terms and is for an individual.

[1–2] A loud outcry to God breaks forth from the anguished soul of the persecuted psalmist. The affliction caused by his persecution, the uncertainty of his fate and the loneliness which leaves him to his own resources press so heavily upon this troubled human being that the outcry breaks forth from him with elemental force. He must have someone to whom he can complain of his suffering. This is why he 'pours out' his lament 'before the face of God' (see Intr. 39 f., 72ff.). Forsaken by all men, the mere fact that he knows of one who will hear him and with whom he can converse already brings about a certain relief from the almost unbearable pressure. The fact that he may confide his complaint to the God to whom he knows himself to be bound, and may tell him his trouble as a child does to his mother, already brings him a little of the comfort which in his loneliness he so sorely misses. [3] What God means to the worshipper at the very moment when his own power of resistance threatens to fail him, he expresses in movingly simple and humbly intimate words: 'It is *thou* who knowest my way!' In devout and childlike trust he places his whole destiny in the hands of God and knows that it will be safe with him. Though the poet keeps before his mind's eye the fact that his affliction is not hidden from the omniscient God, he yet feels constrained to speak to him about that affliction. This shows clearly how already the mere possibility of being able to pour out his heart before God like a child and be in living contact with him provide an opportunity for the worshipper to allay his fear and are a source of strength for his dwindling energies. The phrase 'my way', however, does not only refer to what has happened to the worshipper in the past, but includes also the destiny which the future holds in store for him. As he fixes his eyes on the future the worshipper realizes that he will be safe with God even then. He not only knows that God understands him, but he also knows that God sustains him. That sure knowledge, which is based on trust, imparts to his praying its inner dignity and, despite all its passionate fervency, its quality of believing self-control, and provides it with an inward pivot for his communion with God, whom he knows to be near him at the festival in the holy place. His praying is not an uncontrolled petitioning aimed only at extorting from God the external fulfilment of his desire for deliverance. It is in the light of that trust in God which forms the basis of his prayer that the poet is also able to judge his whole position.

In his 'lament' he first recounts how he came to be in the position in which he now finds himself. Just as the spring-trap (cf. Pss. 69.22; 124.7) is laid where the game haunts so that it may be caught in it, so his adversaries have lain in wait for him with insidious and malicious plots and, though he is innocent, have so misrepresented his position that it has perhaps become the subject of their slanderous accusations before a court of justice. [4] Continuing his lament, he then contemplates his present circumstances, which are no less desperate. When he looks to the right, which is the place where his counsel and helper would normally stand (cf. Pss. 16.8; 110.5; 121.5), he sees that he is solitary and forsaken. He has none who takes care of him. He has lost all hope of human help. Even his friends no longer care for him. This fact is possibly connected with his imprisonment, which restrained his friends from visiting him. [5] This verse is still a part of the 'lament'. Already in the past God had been the psalmist's only refuge when he was just as much forsaken by men as he is now. More than once had he testified in prayer to the God who was his sole sure possession in his desperate situation. After all, it is only God and his promises that can still fall to his 'lot' after all men have forsaken him. This seems to be the

meaning of the image of the 'portion in the land of the living' which
has its origin in the distribution of the land in the festival cult
(see Intr. 44), and here forms the transition to the subsequent
petition.

[6] This petition begins in v. 6. The worshipper clings to God with
a last effort of his dwindling energies and by his reference to his
weakness seeks to evoke the pity of God, who he believes is the only
one who will still sympathize with him. Here, too, we encounter the
same intimacy in his dialogue with God as we find in vv. 1 f. The
psalmist is not able to defend himself against his powerful enemies
in his own strength. On account of their influential position they
have other means and methods at their disposal than their helpless
victim has. But greater than the power of men is the power of God,
upon which the psalmist confidently calls for deliverance. [7] On the
analogy of Ps. 88.8 and Lam. 3.7 the petition to be brought 'out of
prison' could be understood in a figurative sense, meaning that he
asks to be delivered from a grievous calamity; if, on the other hand,
it is understood literally, then the poet's position as a prisoner would
stand out more distinctly and would help to make some features of
the psalm more comprehensible. In his petition the poet looks
beyond his deliverance, and after the manner of a vow (cf. Ps. 22.22)
adds as motive and aim the thought that he will 'testify' to the name
of God as his Deliverer (see Intr. 58 f., 74). His deliverance and the
personal experience of the living power of God acting on his own
behalf are here closely intertwined. For the worshipper it is a question
of whether or not his trust in God is to any purpose; according to his
faith this will be decided by the destiny which the future holds in store
for him. But at the same time his thoughts reach even further. It is
not only he himself but also the 'righteous' (= the community of
the godly) who are interested in his destiny. If God will deal bountifully with him, then they will surround him to praise God together
with him (cf. Ps. 22.23). At this point it becomes clear how closely
the individual and the cult community belong together in virtue of
their faith. What happens to the faith of an individual member of the
cult community is the concern of the cult community as a whole; for
thereby the faith of all its members is decisively influenced because
it is God and the testimony that is borne to him that are the ultimate
purpose of worship. In that the individual is united with God in
spirit, his destiny is set free from its former isolation and is drawn
into the corporate life of the religious community, which is based on a

common faith mutually enriching the religious life of its members. Isolation in loneliness and fellowship grounded in a common faith are the two poles around which the thoughts of the psalmist revolve as he wrestles in prayer. In holding fast to his trust in God the worshipper enters upon the way which leads to the resolution of the tension resulting from that polarity. In this lies the strength of this intimate prayer which appeals to us so much because of its simplicity and humility.

143. LAMENT AND PENITENCE

A Psalm. Of David

1 Hear my prayer, O Lord;
  give ear to my supplications!
  In thy faithfulness answer me,
  in thy righteousness!
2 Enter not into judgment with thy servant;
  for no man living is righteous before thee.
3 For the enemy sought to kill me;
  he has knocked me down to the ground;
  he has made me sit in darkness
  like those who are dead for ever.[1]
4 Therefore my spirit languished within me;
  my heart within me grows stiff.[2]
5 I remembered the days of old,
  I meditated on all that thou hast done;
  I mused on what thy hands have wrought.
6 I stretched out my hands to thee;[3]
  my soul thirsts for thee like a parched land. *Selah*
7 Make haste to answer me, O Lord! My spirit fails!
  Hide not thy face from me,
  lest I be like those who go down to the Pit.
8 Let me hear in the morning of thy grace,
  for in thee I put my trust!
  Teach me the way I should go,
  for to thee I lift up my soul!
9 Deliver me, O Lord, from my enemies;
  in thee I seek refuge.[4]
10 Teach me to do thy will,
  for thou art my God!
  Let thy good spirit lead me on a level path![4]
11 For thy name's sake, O Lord, preserve my life!
  For the sake of thy righteousness[5] brings me out of trouble!
12 In thy grace wipe out[6] my enemies,
  and destroy all that oppress me,
  for I am thy servant!

¹ * The first two lines of v. 3 read in RSV:
For the enemy has pursued me;
he has crushed my life to the ground;
and in the last line RSV has 'long dead' instead of 'who are dead for ever'.
² * The RSV has 'faints' instead of 'languished' and 'is appalled' instead of 'grows stiff'.
³ * RSV has the present tense throughout vv. 5 f.
⁴ See BH.
⁵ * RSV has 'in thy righteousness' instead of 'for the sake of thy righteousness'.
⁶ * RSV has 'cut off' instead of 'wipe out'.

The psalm is regarded as the last of the seven penitential psalms of the Church. Though it cannot really be classed with the type of the penitential songs, but rather represents the song of lament of a man who is oppressed by enemies (vv. 3, 9, 12) and in a state of outward and inward helplessness prays God to preserve his endangered life, the tradition of the ancient Church was nevertheless not far wrong in supposing that the psalmist's attitude of penitence imparts to the psalm its peculiar character. For in face of his calamity the poet becomes conscious of the grave and universal character of human sin, and so also of his own sinfulness in the presence of God (v. 2), so that he sees himself to be thrown upon God's grace only and puts his whole trust in that grace (v. 8). He clearly recognizes his own powerlessness and therefore prays God to teach him the right way and lead him in it (vv. 8, 10); and the earnest character and the sincerity of his longing for God (v. 6) cannot be doubted. Even though his prayer descends in some passages from the high level of such thoughts to the lower level of utterances of fear for his own life, which are humanly speaking quite comprehensible (vv. 9, 12), those loftier perceptions and aspirations which tend towards repentance nevertheless remain the spiritual and religious pivots of the prayer which impart to it its distinctive character and its value.

The private character of the composition, which is far removed from the sphere of great historical events, and the general style of the forms peculiar to the song of lament do not allow us to assign a definite date to the psalm. The construction of the psalm is transparently simple: vv. 1 and 2 contain the invocation, vv. 3 and 4 the lament with its portrayal of the psalmist's physical and mental afflictions; vv. 5 and 6 present his reasons for putting his trust in God which serve as a preparation for the petition that extends from v. 7 to the end of the psalm. In a twice-repeated thought-sequence (vv. 7–9 and vv. 10–12) the poet beseeches God to save his life, to teach and guide him, and to protect him against his enemies.

The invocation (vv. 1–2)

[1] Trusting in God's faithfulness and righteousness the worshipper, tormented by suffering, turns to God with a plea to hear his
prayer. As he reveals in the next verse his awareness that no man
living is righteous before God, he cannot mean here that God's
righteousness signifies a will to retaliate which matches man's own
behaviour and is rooted in a sort of legalistic righteousness meting
out reward and punishment, but rather that on the analogy of God's
faithfulness his righteousness is that divine voluntary action which
aims at man's salvation, entering into the specific circumstances of
the worshipper and doing 'justice' to them by taking seriously man's
will for communion with God and coming to meet it on his part.
[2] Under the impression of his desperate situation—only so does
the conjunction 'for' at the beginning of v. 3 become intelligible—
the conscience of the worshipper is roused. As he faces God in prayer
his sinfulness dawns on him; at the same time he comes to realize
that God would be quite justified in 'entering into judgment with
him'. He visualizes his sinfulness within the larger context of the
universal sinfulness of mankind and so recognizes its ultimate
seriousness as a failure before God that is inherent in man's nature
and therefore cannot be overcome by his own efforts (cf. Ps. 130.3;
Job 4.17 ff.; 14.4). And when he bases his petition that God may
not enter into judgment with him on the argument that no man
living is righteous before him, then this statement is not meant as an
excuse which by pointing to the others who are subject to the same
condemnation seeks to reduce his own guilt and responsibility. On
the contrary, he discerns in the fact that all men are in bondage to
sin and are unable to free themselves from it by their own efforts
(cf. vv. 8, 10) the utter seriousness and power of sin; he realizes that
this is his own personal situation in which but *one* way is left open to
him: to give himself wholly up to the grace of God. This is why he
does not even make the slightest attempt, which we frequently
encounter elsewhere, to protest his innocence and look for a legal
claim that might justify his petition. As he utters his petition, which
includes the confession of sin, he comes before God as a suppliant,
not as one who makes demands on him.

The lament (vv. 3–4)

[3–4] It is only after the poet has achieved this true attitude of
prayer that he dares to complain to God of his affliction. Persecuted

by enemies and threatened with death, he sees himself encompassed by hopeless darkness, like the dead, for whom according to popular belief there is no further hope. External afflictions and an inward sense of helplessness have robbed him of all energy to go on living, so that he imagines himself to be like one who languishes and already feels his body growing stiff in death.

The retrospect (vv. 5–6)

[5–6] On the verge of despair, the worshipper's thoughts reach out for a last support whilst he looks round for help. Though the poet's present situation is shrouded in complete darkness, he still sees a single light to lighten him as he recalls the days of old when the tradition of the *Heilsgeschichte* had been brought home to him anew in the holy place and he had continually become absorbed in it as he worshipped (v. 6). Like the worshipper of Ps. 22.3–5 (cf. Ps. 77.5, 11), he draws strength and comfort from this recollection and gains from it initiative and confidence to cope with his present personal predicament. In fact, it is not what is done by men in history, it is not great deeds of ideal historical figures that makes history important and valuable to him; his eyes are fixed on the works of God, on his deeds and actions within the events and great men of history. In this way the poet takes his stand not only on the ground of the Old Testament historical tradition in general, but at the same time embarks on a course which leads the individual to a personal relationship with history of a practical kind, in which his concern is not to know the events that have taken place in history but to discern in them the signs that bear witness to the activity of the Living God. For in the cultic tradition history becomes *Heilsgeschichte*, that is, it becomes God's presence in historical events, and past events extend into and affect man's personal life as pointers to God's nature, to his power and to his ways with men. The divine reality which is behind the manifold events of the days of old and of the present is always the same. In that the poet ponders over the days of old, he is led to face that reality of the divine presence. The longer he muses, the stronger becomes his soul's yearning for God. From such reflections hidden springs well up. That yearning for God has been aroused in him like an irresistible necessity of life, and he finds for it the beautiful and profound simile of the parched land that longs for the refreshing rain. Here the prayer of the psalmist rises to the heights of Christian piety as he longs for God, not in order to make use of him for the achievement of some purpose or other but in order to have him for his own sake as the sole fountain of life.

The petition (vv. 7–12)

[7] It is understandable that in view of that lofty yearning the urgent petition breaks forth from the lips of the worshipper that God may answer his prayer and may not hide his face from him, indeed, that he may be near him at this very moment, since otherwise he will be overcome by imminent death. The fact that the popular belief of his time is tied up with man's temporal existence and that the barriers erected by that limitation are only rarely consistently overcome in the Old Testament means that the poet fears by his death to lose again his communion with God at the very moment when it has appeared before his mind's eye as the supreme goal and as the sole source of happiness. This accounts for his inner agitation and for the impatience with which he clings to the preservation of his life as the only means of establishing a relationship with God. [8] He is, of course, at the same time aware of his own human powerlessness. If God's grace is not daily bestowed upon him afresh, if God does not himself teach him the way he should go, then the way back to life remains closed to him. He is not able to walk in that way by himself. This is why he puts his whole trust in God's gracious guidance. [9] Again, it is God alone who can save him from his enemies.

[10] The second thought-sequence of the petition proceeds on similar lines (vv. 10–12). How firmly the will for repentance and for a life well pleasing to God is fixed in the foreground of the worshipper's mind follows from the fact that he puts the petition for guidance by God's good spirit before everything else. The poet is also conscious of the fact that the way from knowing the good to doing it, the way from willingness to achievement, is a long one which cannot be travelled without God's help. He knows the human weaknesses and inhibitions which assail man on that way and can be overcome only if God's good spirit constantly stands at man's side and smooths the way so that he may not trip up because of his own faults. (See on Ps. 51.11 f. with regard to this conception of the bestowal of the Spirit, which within the Old Testament is noteworthy.) [11] In view of this prerequisite the petition for deliverance and for the preservation of his life is based on something more profound than a mere natural vital instinct of self-preservation. What matters to the worshipper, even in respect of the preservation of his

life, is God. May God save him for the sake of *his* name and for the sake of *his* righteousness; in other words, the question whether God even now continues to be a reality for the worshipper to which he will be able to testify or whether he will remain excluded from that reality (cf. v. 7) will be decided, as far as the poet is concerned, by his own future destiny, by the question whether or not he will be saved. It must, however, be admitted that notwithstanding the strength of the religious attitude which becomes evident here the faith of the worshipper remains tied not only to man's temporal existence but also to his own person. The poet does not envisage the fact that for God's gracious rule other possibilities exist beside those conceivable by man. The ultimate conquest of self by seeing himself from God's point of view is denied to this worshipper. It is this fact that sets a limit upon this psalm. [12] That limitation of the religious knowledge and attitude of the worshipper stands out even more clearly in his petition for the annihilation of his enemies. Though the idea of the destruction of enemies by means of the divine judgment is firmly established in the Old Testament tradition of the cult of the Covenant (see Intr. 32 f., 45 ff., 75 ff.), this is not the last word that has been said in respect of man's attitude to the enemy even in the Old Testament, and the worshipper's request must not make us forget the traces of genuine penitence and perception of the truth to which the rest of the psalm bears impressive witness.

144. SALVATION
Of David

1 Blessed be the Lord, my rock,
   who trains my hands for battle
   and my fists for war;
2 my grace and my fortress,
   my stronghold and my deliverer,
   my shield and he in whom I take refuge,
   who subdued my people under me.[1]
3 O Lord, what is man that thou dost regard him,
   or the son of man that thou dost think of him!
4 Man is like a breath,
   his days are like a passing shadow.
5 Bow thy heavens, O Lord, and come down!
   Touch the mountains that they smoke!
6 Flash forth lightnings and scatter them,
   shoot out thy arrows and strike terror into them![2]
7 Stretch forth thy hand from on high,

redeem me and deliver me from the many waters,
from the hand of strangers,
8 whose mouths speak lies,
and whose right hand is a right hand of falsehood.
9 I will sing a new song to thee, O God;
upon a ten-stringed harp I will play to thee,
10 who givest victory to the kings,
who hast rescued David, thy servant.[3]
11 . . . .[4]
12 Blessed[5] our sons who in their youth
are like plants that grow well;
blessed[5] our daughters who are like pillars
carved for the structure of a palace![6]
13 Our garners are full, providing all manner of store;
our sheep bring forth thousands and ten thousands
in our fields;[7]
14 our cattle are heavy with young,
suffering no mischance or failure in bearing;
there is no cry of distress in our streets.[7]
15 Blessed the people to whom this happens!
Blessed the people whose God is the Lord![8]

[1] * RSV reads in v. 2a 'my rock' instead of 'my grace' and in v. 2d 'who subdues the peoples under him'.
[2] * RSV has 'rout them' instead of 'strike terror into them'.
[3] * RSV has 'rescuest' instead of 'hast rescued'.
[4] Vv. 10c and 11: 'Rescue me from the evil sword, and deliver me from the violence of the strangers whose mouths speak lies, whose right hand is a right hand of falsehood', are a misplaced textual variant of vv. 7b and 8.
(Tr. N.: In RSV vv. 10c (Hebrew) and 11 form one verse, beginning:
Rescue me from the cruel sword,
and deliver me from the hand of aliens,
and continuing as v. 8.)
[5] See BH.
[6] * In RSV v. 12 is:
May our sons in their youth
be like plants full grown,
our daughters like corner pillars
cut for the structure of a palace.
[7] * In RSV vv. 13 and 14 are in the optative mood throughout, each sentence beginning with 'may'.
[8] * RSV gives v. 15a as 'Happy the people to whom such blessings fall!' and repeats 'happy' instead of 'blessed' in v. 15b.

This psalm, which the Septuagint and the Targum link with David's fight with Goliath, is to be understood like Psalm 18 as a cultic liturgy intended for the royal feast. The various close affinities with this and other psalms as well as with other passages of the Old Testament are to be accounted for by a common and fixed liturgical

tradition, and not, as most commentators assume, as borrowings from
other literary sources; hence the very common view, on the assumption of borrowings from other literary sources, of a late date for the
psalm is untenable. Though the psalm is secondary in comparison
with Psalm 18, the roots of this royal thanksgiving song (it is not only an
imitation of this, as Gunkel thinks) can nevertheless be traced back
to the period of the kings of Judah. The late linguistic forms, above
all in the last part of the psalm, merely indicate that the psalm—
perhaps as a result of re-interpretation in a Messianic sense—was
still in use at a late date in the history of Israel. Any understanding
of the psalm must therefore start from the elements of the royal
feast which are reflected in the psalm (see Intr. 45, 63).

[1–2] The two opening verses contain an invocation in the form
of a hymn, inspired by the theme of trust in God, to whom the king
owes his rule over his people, and also of thankfulness for God's
protection and help. The set phrases used here follow the Davidic
style (cf. Ps. 18.46, 34, 47), and express the view that the new king
partakes of the 'mercies of David' (cf. Ps. 89.3, 49; Isa. 55.3); in
other words, that the Davidic 'grace of kingship' is realized afresh in
the person of the new member of the Davidic house at his enthronement feast (see on v. 10). The royal worshipper simultaneously recalls
the past and looks into the future; his words express both pride and
humility: by the grace of God I am what I am. [3–4] As a preparation for the encounter with God (vv. 5 f.) there follows the confession,
also in a fixed stylized form, which puts an end to any kind of pride,
the confession that every dignity that man possesses—even that of
the king—is in itself of no significance in the sight of God (cf. Isa.
6.5), but consists only in the fact that man is the object of God's
thoughts and care. [5–6] It is only this attitude of humility before
God (cf. Pss. 8.4; 39.5) which guards the psalmist's bold petition
that God may bow the heavens and appear in a powerful theophany,
as once at Sinai (see on Ps. 18.9 ff.), against the danger of a blasphemous trespass beyond the acknowledged limits that are set to
man's conduct by God. [7–8] The king's prayer of supplication for
redemption and deliverance from the depths of his affliction (cf.
Ps. 18.16), caused by foreign adversaries, as well as by covenant-
breakers and oath-breakers, is offered to God, who appears when the
celebration of the feast has reached its climax. [9–10] The king's
prayer ends in a vow to sing a song of praise which shall follow the
victory for which he has prayed and will be dedicated to God, to

whom all his predecessors on the throne of David, including David himself, owe their victories and their deliverance.

[12–15] Most commentators fail to recognize the connection of the psalm with the festival cult, and consequently regard the concluding part as a detached fragment of another psalm. This concluding part is, however, a testimony to the general salvation of the people which, fitted into a framework of 'beatitudes' (vv. 12, 15), takes the form of a hymnic account put into the mouth of the whole cult community. In the festival cult the 'grace of kingship' and the blessings bestowed upon the people are mostly closely related to each other; in fact, they are almost identical. The earthly wealth of a healthy rising generation, endowed with vital energy, the blessing of a rich harvest, fecundity of the flocks and peace both in country and in town are the visible signs of the blessings imparted by the divine grace (cf. Ps. 72.16). And joy in God and in communion with him is the root-cause and the deepest meaning of the bliss that unites the king and his people before God, in the sure knowledge of his salvation, to extol him in a song of praise.

145. THE EYES OF ALL WAIT UPON THEE

A Song of Praise. Of David

1 I will extol thee, my God;
   thou art the King,[1]
   and I will praise thy name for ever and ever.
2 Every day I will praise thee,
   and laud thy name for ever and ever.
3 Great is the Lord, and greatly to be praised,
   and his greatness is unsearchable.
4 One generation lauds thy works to another,
   and they declare thy mighty acts.[2]
5 They speak[3] of the splendour of thy majesty and glory,
   they tell[3] of thy wondrous deeds.[4]
6 They proclaim the power of thy terrible acts,
   and they declare thy mighty deeds.[5]
7 They pour forth the memorial of thy abundant goodness,
   they shout for joy because of thy righteousness.[6]
8 The Lord is gracious and merciful,
   slow to anger and abounding in lovingkindness.
9 The Lord is good to all,
   and his compassion is over all that he has made.
10 All thy works shall testify[7] to thee, O Lord,
   and thy saints shall praise thee!

11 They shall speak of the glory of thy kingdom,
    and tell of thy power,
12 to make known to the sons of men thy[3] mighty deeds,
    and the glory and splendour of thy[3] kingdom.
13 Thy kingdom is an everlasting kingdom,
    and thy dominion endures throughout all generations.
    The Lord is faithful in all his words,
    and gracious in all his deeds.[3]
14 The Lord upholds all who are falling,
    and raises up all who are bowed down.
15 The eyes of all wait upon thee,
    and thou givest them their food in due season.[8]
16 Thou openest thy hand
    and satisfiest every living thing with thy favour.[9]
17 The Lord is just in all his ways,
    and gracious in all his doings.
18 The Lord is near to all who call upon him,
    to all who call upon him in truth.
19 He fulfils the desire of all who fear him;
    he hears their cry and helps them.
20 The Lord protects all who love him;
    but all the wicked he will destroy.
21 My mouth will speak the praise of the Lord,
    and let all flesh praise his holy name!
    We praise the Lord from this time forth and for evermore. Hallelujah[10]

[1] * RSV reads 'my God and King' instead of 'my God; thou art the King'.
[2] * RSV uses the future tense throughout.
[3] See BH.
[4] * V. 5 is in RSV:
    Of the glorious splendour of thy majesty,
    and of thy wondrous works, I will meditate.
[5] * In RSV v. 6 reads:
    Men shall proclaim the might of thy terrible acts,
    and I will declare thy greatness.
[6] * RSV has:
    They shall pour forth the fame of thy abundant goodness,
    and shall sing aloud of thy righteousness.
[7] * RSV has 'give thanks' instead of 'testify'.
[8] * RSV has 'look to thee' instead of 'wait upon thee'.
[9] * V. 16b reads in RSV, 'thou satisfiest the desire of every living thing'.
[10] See BH. (Tr. N.: In RSV v. 21bc forms one line, 'and let all flesh bless his holy name for ever and ever'.)

On account of v. 15 this psalm was sung in the ancient Church as a psalm at the time of the midday meal. In spite of the personal style of its beginning and of its end (see, however, on v. 21c) it is a liturgical hymn of the cult community which, in familiar and current ideas (this explains the points of affinity with other psalms),

gives expression to the religious beliefs held by the cult community.
The strong emphasis laid on the kingship of God (vv. 1, 11 ff.), as
well as the praise for the blessing of a rich harvest (vv. 15 f.) and for
the mighty acts wrought by God in the *Heilsgeschichte* (vv. 5 f.),
suggest the view that the song was recited at the feast of the covenant,
which was celebrated in autumn, and is modelled on the fundamental
ideas of that feast at which the idea of the kingship of Yahweh played
an important part (see Intr. 33 f., 62). As in Psalms 111; 119, etc, the
opening words of each verse are arranged according to the Hebrew
alphabet; the strophe beginning with the letter *Nun* is admittedly
missing in the Massoretic text, but is to be supplemented from the
Septuagint, the Vulgate and the Syriac. In spite of this outward
bondage to an acrostic form, we must recognize that the thought is
not without a certain order and depth.

[1–3] The introduction (vv. 1–3), in which, in contrast with Pss.
5.2; 84.3, God is addressed in the style in which one would address
the reigning monarch, at once throws into relief the fundamental
idea which pervades the whole psalm, that is, the everlasting praise
of the 'name' (nature) of God, who has revealed himself in all his
majesty and unsearchable sublimity (see Intr. 30 ff., 54 ff.). [4–7] The
God-fearing man of the Old Testament recognizes the perpetual
presence of the divine salvation in the fact that the festal hymn and
the festal shouts of joy ring out ever anew year by year when the
sacred tradition of the miraculous mighty acts of God, the 'memorial'
of the *Heilsgeschichte*, which is passed on from one generation to
another, is made known in the cultic ceremony. The cult community
responds with its unbroken hymnic tradition to that perpetual
presence of the divine salvation, and the poet wants his song of
praise to be incorporated in this, too. 8–9 are perhaps to be understood as a hymn of praise of the cult community which, summarizing
the ancient cultic tradition (cf. Ex. 34.6), extols as the main feature
of the revelation of God's nature the lovingkindness and mercy
which he shows to all his creatures. Though the mighty wondrous
deeds of God and the 'terrible acts' of his judgment (v. 6) manifest
the sovereignty of his power, the true greatness of God lies in the
tenderness and intimacy of the compassion with which the divine
Father loves his creatures (cf. Hos. 11.1 ff.).

[10–13a] This is the keynote of the whole psalm and the presupposition of the prayer of thanksgiving which the whole creation
and in particular the community of the godly are called upon to

offer to God; they are asked to acknowledge on their part the glory of God which as his kingship is manifested ever anew before their eyes and in their hearing. **[13b–17]** At the beginning and end of the first section stands as theme and summary a general form of testimony (vv. 13b, 17). The words and the deeds of God which are made known to the cult community are the living expression of his 'grace and faithfulness', and the testimony to his righteousness (see Intr. 58 f.). There is particular praise for the fatherly care of God, and for the help and comfort which those who have gone astray and those who are bowed down find in God (v. 14). God gives to all who hunger their food in due season and, more than that, he also satisfies all spiritual hunger with his favour and with grateful joy in the divine Giver. **[18–19]** For the nearness and the presence of the God who gives help in abundance and grants his blessing is the precious gift which he holds in readiness for those who seek him with the utter sincerity of a humble and God-fearing man and call upon him with a 'single' heart, and who will be able to experience the fact of their prayers being heard. **[20]** To fear God (v. 19) and to love him, this is the attitude which the members of the community of the godly adopt, and whose roots reach deep down into the ultimate irrational depth of their religious life; and in which they know themselves safe in God's protection. For with God is life; to be without him means death. The exultation expressed in the psalm is set off against the stern background of the divine judgment (cf. vv. 17 ff.) and of the righteousness (v. 7) executed in it in a twofold way: for the wicked it spells disaster, but to the community of his faithful people it means salvation. This idea of judgment, too, is an echo of the cultic ceremony for which the psalm is intended and in whose light it is to be understood (see Intr. 46 f.). **[21]** In the assurance of salvation the psalmist goes back to the beginning by calling upon the cult community to sing a hymn in praise of the holy name of God. Uniting his personal testimony with that of the whole body of 'all flesh', he sums it up by stating the ultimate purpose which all creatures serve, the praise of God. In this, according to the evidence of some manuscripts, the congregation joins with a hymnic response (cf. Ps. 115.18).

146. PRAISE THE LORD, O MY SOUL

1 Hallelujah[1]
  Praise the Lord, O my soul!

2 I will praise the Lord as long as I live;
  I will sing praises to my God
  while I have being.

3 Put not your trust in princes,
  in a son of man, in whom there is no help!
4 When his breath departs, he returns to the dust;
  on that very day his plans perish.

5 Happy is he whose help[2] is the God of Jacob
  whose hope is in the Lord his God,
6 who made heaven and earth,
  the sea and all that is in them.

Who keeps faith for ever;
7 who executes justice for the oppressed;
  who gives food to the hungry.

The Lord sets the prisoners free.
8 The Lord opens the eyes of the blind.
The Lord lifts up those who are bowed down.
The Lord loves the righteous.

9 The Lord watches over the strangers.
He upholds the widow and the orphans,
but he perverts the way of the wicked.[3]

10 The Lord is King for ever,
  thy God, O Zion, to all generations!
  Hallelujah[1]

[1] See above, p. 22. (Tr. N.: the RSV has 'Praise the Lord!')
[2] See BH.
[3] * V. 9b reads in RSV, 'but the way of the wicked he brings to ruin'.

This psalm is a simple hymn expressing trust in God. It is its very simplicity which creates a strong impression. It served as a model for a hymn by Paul Gerhardt[1] as well as for a familiar and powerful one by Herrnschmidt.[2] The poet draws the strength of his trust in God from the ageless treasure of the Old Testament cultic tradition and religious beliefs, and in a testimony, which has a strong touch of the hymn of praise (vv. 1–2, 6–9) and serves an exhortatory purpose, expresses the former in a most original fashion. In this way the testimony has an active emphasis which throws a significant light on

[1] * 'Du, meine Seele singe, wohlauf und singe schön.'
[2] * 'Lobe den Herren, o meine Seele', by Johann Daniel Herrnschmidt (1675–1723).

the binding character of the religious beliefs held by the cult community, reflecting the revelation of the nature and of the will of
God which was at the centre of the feast for which the psalm was
originally composed. According to v. 10, the psalm leads up to the
celebration of the eternal kingship of God (see Intr. 33 f., 62). In later
Judaism the psalm was used as part of daily morning prayer. The
psalm opens (vv. 1–2) with a hymnic introduction; its middle portion
contains a warning against false trust in the power of men (vv. 3–4)
and an exhortation, in the form of a benediction, to right trust in
God (vv. 5–6); this is supported by the subsequent statements (vv.
7–9) in the form of a hymn about God as the gracious Helper of the
weak; these produce a powerful effect on account of their symmetrical
structure. At the conclusion of the psalm the poet has again recourse
to a theme taken from the hymn and sums up the whole in reflections
on Yahweh's eternal kingship (v. 10).

[1–2] The poet opens the psalm with a hymn calling upon himself
to sing God's praise (cf. Pss. 103.1, 22; 104.1, 35). That call expresses
the emotion and exaltation that have taken possession of his soul as
well as his joy in the fact that by singing the praise of God he is able
to be near him. The greatness and lovingkindness of God which the
poet extols in his song catch him up out of himself and give him such
a lift of soul that he desires to dwell on these heights as long as he
lives, looking up to God in faith and singing his praise. The psalmist's
most precious possession resulting from his faith is an immense,
selfless and wholehearted devotion to God. But such a faith carries
obligations. [3–4] The Old Testament faith does not consist in being
addicted to the enjoyment of material things or indulgence in
moods. In the midst of the happiness which trust in God creates
the psalmist is aware of man's responsibility for his fellow men and
this gives his hymn that striking feature which turns it into a piece of
admonition and advice (for the form used cf. I Sam. 2.3 and Intr. 86).
This is first given in the form of a warning against false trust in the
power of men. The advice not to rely on princes likewise appears to
be meant merely as an illustration of human power in general in
view of the context; the second part of the verse speaks quite generally
of man as such and of his powerlessness; for the same reason it may
be assumed that none of the rulers who played a part in the history of
Israel is particularly in mind. The warning against false trust in man
is based on the knowledge of his transitoriness and powerlessness.
As man reflects on God and faces the prospect of death he becomes

conscious of the limits set to his own importance. This is by no means
the result of the inferiority complex of a man who is at the end of his
tether. The boldness with which any suggestion of either hankering
after human power or bowing down before human rulers is here
excluded should surely warn us against passing such a judgment.
Rather is it the outlook of a man who has the courage to be truthful
which is here expressed; he looks at life as it really is with complete
ruthlessness about himself and does not shrink from even the harshest
truths of life as he faces the reality of God and becomes aware of his
own helplessness. The point where man is no longer master of himself,
in the face of death, that is, shows up with inescapable clarity who it
is who alone possesses power and of how little importance in the last
analysis human power and human planning really are. How should
a man be able to base his trust on other men and their plans, which,
after all, turn to dust and perish in a moment!

[5–6] It is not without good reason that the negative statement,
the warning against false trust in men, precedes the praise of the
blessedness of right trust in God. It is only when man has come to
realize the fragility of the human supports of life, only when he has
learned to forgo them completely, that he finds himself in a position
in which alone the right trust in God becomes possible. For trust in
God means unreserved confidence in him, not holding in reserve the
prospect of some other sort of help beside his. There is only one who
can really help; but in turning to him one must risk everything, one
must set one's entire hope exclusively on him. It is only by adopting
such an attitude that man is entirely freed from every kind of
oppression by temporal afflictions and fears and becomes entirely
happy in leaving his cause and his troubles to God. Not only the
'beatitude' in v. 5 but also the entire justification for it presented in
hymnic form (vv. 6–9) owe their peculiar and striking quality to that
feeling of unrestrained happiness which springs from the poet's
genuine trust in God. The God in whom he trusts is the 'God of
Jacob' and at the same time 'his God'. In this way the God-fearing
man is united with his forefathers and with the members of the cult
community in the same great tradition of faith in the God of history
(cf. Ps. 22.4). That reflection on history gives as much support to
man's trust in God as does the lifting up of his eyes to the Creator of
the universe. Men can truly trust only in him to whom all power
belongs; he who has created all things is alone the Lord of all. This
provides the strongest motive for trust. Here, too, we can clearly see

that the Old Testament beliefs about creation and history do not satisfy an inquisitive thirst for knowledge about matters of fact as they actually exist; as a belief in the saving activities of God they are most intimately bound up with the actual state of affairs and with the vital decisions required by the practical necessities of everyday life, again, they do not answer a question that seeks information; they decide a question that affects the whole of existence.

[7–9] The subsequent statements about God, which because of their symmetrical structure produce a solemn effect, follow throughout the style of the hymn and provide the inner justification of the exhortation to trust in God. As an affirmation of genuine trust in God they are intended to evoke trust in their turn. They provide an eloquent picture of how the Old Testament believer thinks of his God and perceives the wealth of the divine lovingkindness and strength on which he can base his life. Prominence is here given to God's everlasting faithfulness which consists in the absolute reliability of his intentions, and in the stability of his rule, on which the God-fearing man can count. The particular statements (vv. 7–9) deal with the question of the nature of these divine intentions. All of them have one thing in common; they show that the power and the loving-kindness of God prove their efficacy in the very cases in which the power of man fails. The oppressed and bowed down, the prisoners, the hungry, the sick, and the defenceless, as well as strangers, orphans and widows—all these people find help and deliverance in God. This is a typical feature of Old Testament religion, which has its origin in God's self-revelation of his nature and will. With the exultation proper to a hymn the psalmist praises the fact that God's power is made perfect in weakness; this is what is divine about it. And so God can be wholly trusted by the man who recognizes in his own person the powerlessness of all that is human, and who at the same time can be assured that in adversity God will not be far away from him; that is just when he will be near. The godly man knows that he is safe in God's love; nor need he fear the plans of the wicked; for God 'perverts' their 'way'; he takes care that what they have in mind does not succeed. This view of the wicked, which is in line with the idea of judgment associated with the cult of the Covenant, is also a part of the bold assurance of a trust based on faith that overcomes all human fear. [10] The hymn concludes on a note of joy and pride as the psalmist reflects on God's eternal kingship which is the culmination of the tradition of the *Heilsgeschichte* as transmitted in the Old Testament covenant cult. The trust in God the Lord which links past and future generations in a homogeneous community of faith leads the eye up to the level of eternity. It is a straight path from this trust in God to the New Testament faith which the Apostle Paul has expressed in the immortal words: 'as unknown, and yet well known; as dying and behold we live; as punished, and yet not killed; as sorrowful, yet always rejoicing; as poor, yet making many rich; as having nothing, and yet possessing everything' (II Cor. 6.9 f.).

147. THE GRACIOUS AND MIGHTY GOD

1 Praise the Lord!
  For it is good to make melody to our God;
  yea, it is pleasing, and a song of praise is seemly.[1]
2 The Lord built Jerusalem;
  he gathered the outcasts of Israel.[2]
3 He heals the brokenhearted,
  and binds up their wounds.
4 He determines the number of the stars,
  he calls all of them by name.[3]
5 Great is our Lord, and abundant in power;
  of his wisdom there is no end.[4]
6 The Lord lifts up the downtrodden,
  he casts the wicked to the ground.
7 Answer the Lord with a testimony,
  make melody to our God upon the cither![5]
8 He covers the heavens with clouds,
  he prepares rain for the earth,
  he makes grass grow upon the mountains
  for the service of man.[6]
9 He gives to the beasts their food,
  and to the young ravens which cry.
10 His delight is not in the strength of the horse,
  nor his pleasure in the thighs of a man;
11 but he takes pleasure in those who fear him,
  in those who hope in his grace.
12 Praise the Lord, O Jerusalem;
  praise your God, O Zion!
13 For he strengthened the bars of your gates;
  he blessed your sons within you![7]
14 He bestows salvation upon your country,[8]
  he fills you with the finest of the wheat.
15 He sends forth his command to the earth,
  and his word runs swiftly.
16 He gives snow like wool,
  and scatters hoar frost like ashes.

17 He casts forth his ice like morsels;
 who can withstand his cold?
18 He sends forth his word, and melts them;
 he makes his winds blow, and the waters flow.
19 He declares his word[9] to Jacob,
 his statutes and ordinances to Israel.
20 He has not dealt thus with any other nation;
 the law, they do not know it. Hallelujah[10]

[1] * RSV has 'for he is gracious' instead of 'yea, it is pleasing'.
[2] * RSV uses the present tense throughout.
[3] * V. 4b reads in RSV, 'he gives to all of them their names'.
[4] * V. 5b reads in RSV, 'his understanding is beyond measure'.
[5] * RSV has in v. 7a 'Sing to the Lord with thanksgiving' and in v. 7b 'lyre' instead of 'cither'.
[6] See BH. (Tr. N.: RSV omits 'for the service of man'.)
[7] * RSV uses the present tense throughout.
[8] * RSV has: 'He makes peace in your borders.'
[9] See BH.
[10] See above, p. 22. (Tr. N.: In RSV v. 20b reads, 'they do not know his ordinances. Praise the Lord!')

This liturgical hymn, to which the Nuremberg hymn, 'Lobet den Herren, denn er ist sehr freundlich',[1] which ends on a Christian note, owes its origin, is in form clearly divided into three parts, each of which opens with a call to praise God. The thoughts are less strictly arranged, not, as has frequently been assumed, because the psalm is a compilation of quotations taken from earlier literary sources, but because the thoughts revolve round two basic themes and continually revert to them, so that they constitute the sustaining melody of the song of praise; they are the power of God and his compassionate grace as manifested in creation and election. The point of this psalm is the fundamental theme which forms the essence of the Old Testament tradition of worship; and the points of affinity with other Old Testament traditions do not go beyond what has to be regarded as the common treasure of the religious beliefs of the cult community of the Old Covenant. It is by no means beyond doubt whether vv. 2 and 13 (the building of Jerusalem and the gathering of the outcasts of Israel) are to be interpreted as referring to the Exile or to the rebuilding of the walls of Jerusalem by Nehemiah; it is therefore not possible to assign a more precise date to this psalm. The form and content of v. 13 point to an event that has already taken place; it is presumably a matter of a tradition, maintained and continually actualized in the Temple worship so that it became a present experi-

[1] * Composed about 1560.

ence, as in Pss. 78.68 ff.; 87.1; 102.16, which regarded Yahweh as the founder of Jerusalem and of his sanctuary there (see Intr. 45). The 'gathering of the outcasts' could perhaps be a reference to a festival assembly in which citizens of the northern kingdom also took part (after 721 BC) as members of the covenant.

[1–6] The first part strikes a note of comfort and obviously pre-supposes the existence of a calamity. Praise is directed to God, who is the Saviour of the afflicted among his people. This is why the members of his cult community call themselves the 'downtrodden' (v. 6) in contrast to the 'wicked'. Behind these terms lies the expectation of the divine judgment, in which God executes his righteousness, which means help and salvation for his faithful people but doom for the wicked. The comforting trust in God's mercy is justified in vv. 4 and 5 by reference to his power and wisdom as the Creator and Lord of the whole universe. He who summons the stars to appear, addressing them by their names, has sufficient strength and understanding to rise above all obstacles and effect his purpose of abundant grace and help (see Intr. 45 ff., 59 f., 91 f.).

[7–11] The second part is more attuned to thanksgiving. Behind it lies the expectation of the blessing and fertility of the coming year, such as found its cultic expression in the autumnal feast (cf. Ps. 135.7). But as in Psalm 104, the poet, remembering the loving care of God, does not linger on selfish thoughts, as man is prone to do; but with selfless and abandoned joy in God, and with the fine understanding characteristic of a poet and a religious man, he also includes in v. 9 in his grateful praise of God his care for the young ravens. With what tenderness and purity of thought the psalmist experiences the intimate security which God's care imparts can be gathered from the rejection of all false self-confidence that relies on external power and on human skill (v. 10; cf. Ps. 146.3), and also from the positive way in which the testimony is formulated that God on his part takes pleasure only in those who fear him and in hope entrust themselves utterly to his grace.

[12–15] In the third part (vv. 12–20) the psalmist turns to the city of God, the place where God's Word and will are manifested for the benefit of his worshippers in a special way as both election and demand. The peace which the city enjoys under God's protection, the vitality of the nation and the yield of the earth are for the members of the cult community the visible proofs of the grace and power of their God (see Intr. 44).

[16–18] The hymn in praise of the fundamental creative significance of the Word of God (see Intr. 41 ff.), in which the psalm at its conclusion reaches its climax, is impressively illustrated in vv. 16–18 by the fact that God's Word suffices to turn snow, hoar-frost and ice into water, an incident which happened rarely enough to make a particularly powerful impression on the mind of the oriental. The Word of God shapes Nature and History. **[19–20]** For the people of God that history culminates in their election and in the proclamation of the divine will; this, too, reflects the proceedings that take place during the celebration of the cultic feast. Here lies the special meaning of the historical existence of the people of Israel whereby they are distinguished from the other nations: the fact that the statutes and ordinances of God are given to them as the order that is meant to govern their lives. Election implies increased duties and responsibilities before God (cf. Amos 3.2): 'Everyone to whom much is given, of him will much be required.'[1]

[1] * Luke 12.48.

148. LET THE WHOLE WORLD PRAISE THE LORD!

1 Hallelujah[1]
Praise the Lord from the heavens,
praise him in the heights!
2 Praise him, all his angels,
praise him, all his host!
3 Praise him, sun and moon,
praise him, all you shining stars!
4 Praise him, you highest heavens,
and you waters above the heavens!
5 Let them praise the name of the Lord,
for he commanded and they were created.
6 He established them for ever and ever;
a statute he ordained, which they[2] do not transgress.[3]
7 Praise the Lord from the earth,
you dragons and all deeps,
8 fire and hail, snow and clouds,
stormy wind fulfilling his command!
9 You mountains and all you hills,
fruit trees and all cedars!
10 You beasts and cattle,
creeping things and all flying birds!
11 You kings of the earth and all nations,
you princes and all judges of the earth![4]

12 You young men and also you maidens,
   you old men and all children!
13 Let them praise the name of the Lord,
   for his name alone is exalted,
   its majesty above heaven and earth.[5]
14 He has exalted the horn of his people,
   a praise for all his saints,
   for the sons of Israel, the people that is near to him![6] Hallelujah[1]

[1] See above, p. 22. (Tr. N.: RSV reads 'Praise the Lord!')
[2] See BH.
[3] * V. 6b reads in RSV, 'he fixed their bounds which cannot be passed'.
[4] * RSV has 'rulers' instead of 'judges'.
[5] * V. 13c is in RSV, 'his glory is above earth and heaven'.
[6] * In RSV v. 14 reads:
He has raised up a horn for his people,
praise for all his saints,
for the people of Israel who are near to him.
Praise the Lord!

Psalm 148 has been copied in the song of praise of the three men in the burning fiery furnace (added in the Septuagint to Dan. 3).[1] In form it is an extended hymnic introduction, which we may think of as sung by the priest (choir) at a cultic ceremony, which according to v. 14 was based on the establishment of salvation for the Israelite cult community. The revelation of the divine 'name' (see Intr. 30 f., 41 f. and its majesty and of the presence of God in the midst of his people are the theme of the song of praise which the whole world is called upon to sing. The glorification of the Creator and Preserver of the world fulfils the ultimate depth of meaning which unites the inanimate created things and the living creatures in a mutual relationship; to praise the sole majesty of God is the final goal which unites the whole universe in a communion of God's service. This tremendous vision of God and of the world has found expression in the magnificent architectural structure of the psalm: starting with the heaven (vv. 1–6), the call to praise God descends to the earth (vv. 7–10), then turns to mankind (vv. 11–13) and ends (vv. 13, 14) with the community of God's people, in whose midst the divine salvation which is the cause and the theme of the hymn became visible and actual. The hymn follows as it were, the course of the epiphany which God and the revelation of his salvation take as he comes down from heaven to appear before his people.

[1] * Included in the Apocrypha (vv. 28–68) as The Song of the Three Holy Children (the Benedicite).

[1–6] The song of praise sung by the heavens opens in the heights the grand symphony which the world created by God sings to the praise of its Maker. The celestial hosts, angels and principalities, sun, moon and shining stars, even the celestial ocean; in short, all the things which have been called into existence by God's command and are maintained by his decrees are messengers of God called to proclaim his creative power and glory (cf. Ps. 19.1). **[7–10]** This is the service which the celestial world owes to its divine Lord. The *vox coelestis* is joined by the voices of the earthly choirs: land and sea (the mention of the dragons in this context is striking and shows that the creation story with its tradition of the combat of the gods against the powers of chaos forms the background of the psalm), the natural elements which traditionally precede the theophany as God's attendants (cf. the Sinai theophany and especially I Kings 19.11 ff.), fire, hail, snow and 'smoke', and the wind that executes the divine command, mountains and plants and all kinds of animals (cf. Gen. 1)[1] are engaged in the same service, that of glorifying their Maker.

[11–14] In the third section (vv. 11–14), where the call to sing the praise of God forms the conclusion, the psalmist turns to mankind, in particular to the rulers of the world of nations (v. 11) and to the whole cult community, comprising all ages (v. 12). Verses 13 and 14 contain both the justification for and the theme of the song of praise: to the cult community are revealed both the name of God and his exclusive supremacy and majesty over heaven and earth; his nearness and presence convey to the people of God both assurance of salvation and new vitality (this the meaning of the image of the 'exalting of the horn'; cf. Pss. 89.1 132.17). That belief in salvation is the culmination of the whole psalm and is of crucial importance to the whole world. For it points at the same time beyond itself to the consummation of salvation which the angel host proclaimed from heaven to all the world at the first Christmas as the Good News of the birth of a Saviour.

[1] Von Rad, *VT* Suppl. III (1955), p. 293 = *Gesammelte Studien zum Alten Testament* (1958), pp. 262 ff., has pointed out the form-critical connections with the 'Science of catalogue-making' known to us from Egypt.

149. THE JUDGMENT ON THE GENTILES

1 Hallelujah[1]
 Sing to the Lord a new song,
  his praise in the assembly of the godly!
2 Let Israel be glad in his Maker,
  the sons of Zion rejoice in their King.[2]

3 Let them praise his name with dancing,
    making melody to him with drum and cither![3]
4 For the Lord shows favour to his people;
    he adorns the humble with salvation.[4]
5 The godly exult in glory,
    they shout with joy on their couches.[5]
6 High praises of God in their mouths,[6]
    and two-edged swords in their hands,
7 to wreak vengeance on the Gentiles[7]
    and chastisement on the peoples,
8 to bind their kings with chains,
    and their nobles with fetters of iron,
9 to execute on them the judgment written,
    this is the glory for all his godly ones.[8]
    Hallelujah[1]

[1] See above, p. 22. (Tr. N.: RSV reads 'Praise the Lord!')
[2] * V. 2b reads in RSV, 'let the sons of Zion rejoice in their King'.
[3] * RSV has 'timbrel and lyre' instead of 'drum and cither'.
[4] * RSV has 'victory' instead of 'salvation'.
[5] * RSV uses the imperative mood ('let . . .') throughout vv. 5 and 6.
[6] * RSV has 'Let the high praises of God be in their throats'.
[7] * RSV has 'nations' instead of 'Gentiles'.
[8] * RSV takes v. 9b as a separate sentence, and has 'faithful ones' instead of 'godly ones'.

From the fifth century AD up to the present day the psalm has constantly been interpreted as referring to Maccabean times, though the composition itself does not go beyond very general allusions which fit into every age. During the Thirty Years War the psalm was used as a battle-cry on behalf of the Roman Catholic princes and was also misused by Thomas Münzer to sanction his lust for vengeance. We cannot even be certain that the psalm was composed for a victory celebration. All that we can infer from it is that it is a hymn sung to celebrate the kingship of Yahweh (v. 2) during the worship of the community of the 'godly ones' (v. 1), who, dancing the festal dance to the accompaniment of musical instruments, praise the 'name' of God as their Maker (v. 3), rejoice in the salvation granted to the people of God, and discern in the execution of the judgment on the Gentiles and their rulers the task which according to the written tradition (v. 9) God has allotted to them. All these features can equally well be accounted for by the festival cult of the pre-exilic period, and even v. 6, which some commentators want to be understood in the light of II Macc. 15.27 or Neh. 4.16, can without any difficulty be interpreted as a reference to the presence of the covenantal armies at the cultic feast (see Intr. 37).

[1-3] Like Pss. 33.3 and 96.1 the psalm opens with a call to the festival congregation resting (v. 5) in the grounds of the Temple at Jerusalem (v. 2) to sing the praise of God, who as their Maker and King has revealed his 'name' and has once more entered upon his reign at his feast (hence a 'new song'; see Intr. 61). **[4-6]** In v. 4 the reasons for this call are given: God's gracious good pleasure rests upon the members of the cult community and this fact inspires them with awe and humility, so that the worshippers are here called 'the humble'. But the members of the festal congregation are at the same time lifted up by the salvation whereby God glorifies himself in them so that they reflect that 'glory' back to the divine Giver in their song of praise. This is the proper duty of the cult community celebrating the feast and the true meaning of their worship, of which vv. 5 and 6 are an inspired description. **[7-9]** The opposite aspect of salvation is the judgment on the ungodly Gentiles; this, too, serves the glorification of God's rule and had its traditional place in the cultic ceremony (see Intr. 32 f., 45 ff.).[1] The fact that it is described as the 'judgment' on them, that is 'written', allows us to presume here an allusion to a tradition fixed in writing, perhaps the destruction of the pagan nations of Canaan, the accomplishment of which had continually been made the religious duty of the people of Israel (cf. Deut. 7.1 ff.; 20.13) and which was described in the earlier historical tradition (e.g. in the Book of Joshua). In listening to those ancient traditions the members of the Israelite community of Yahweh have obviously experienced the manifestation of the terrible severity of the divine power as an actual present event, just as vivid as the miraculous help which they themselves were able to receive from God; and the concluding statement that by means of the execution of the judgment on the pagan nations the glory of the people of God is also made manifest is to be understood exclusively on the assumption that it is the glory of God which is the real subject throughout.

[1] Cf. Johnson, *Sacral Kingship in Ancient Israel*, p. 83, who sees in this passage an allusion to a subsequent ritual act.

150. THE GREAT HALLELUJAH

1 Hallelujah[1]
Praise God in his temple;
praise him in his mighty firmament!
2 Praise him for his mighty deeds;
praise him according to the abundance
of his power![2]

3 Praise him with trumpet sound;
  praise him with harp and cither![3]
4 Praise him with drum and dance;
  praise him with strings and flute![4]
5 Praise him with resounding cymbals;
  praise him with loud clashing cymbals!
6 Let everything that breathes praise the Lord!
  Hallelujah![1]

[1] See above, p. 22. (Tr. N.: RSV reads 'Praise the Lord!')
[2] * RSV has 'according to his exceeding greatness' instead of 'according to the abundance of his power'.
[3] * RSV has 'lute and harp' instead of 'harp and cither'.
[4] * RSV has 'timbrel' instead of 'drum' and 'pipe' instead of 'flute'.

The keynote of all the last hymns of the Psalter has been that of a song of praise, and at the very end the great Hallelujah (= praise the Lord!), now swells into a mighty final chord. The last psalm is simply and solely a call to sing the praise of God, in which all the voices on earth and in heaven unite to the accompaniment of the triumphant strains of the entire orchestra of the Temple-music (v. 1a). The account of the particular musical instruments shows that we are here dealing with a piece of the festival liturgy of the Temple worship which the redactor of the Psalter has deliberately included as the keystone of his collection, so that from this position it may shed light on the whole Psalter. In praising God the meaning of the world is fulfilled. To praise the abundance of his power is the purpose which links together the most diverse voices in heaven and on earth in a tremendous symphonic hymn of praise. In that praise the members of the cult community join; for to them it is given in a special way to bear witness to God's mighty deeds, which entail the realization of salvation, their salvation, which at the same time implies the salvation of the whole world. It accords with this train of thought that in conclusion 'everything that breathes' is called upon to join in the praise of God, who as the Lord of the world has revealed himself in his power.